INFANT TEACHER'S HANDBC

Mary Rose Selman

Oliver & Boyd

Oliver & Boyd
Longman House
Burnt Mill
Harlow
Essex CM20 2JE
An Imprint of Longman Group UK Ltd

ISBN 0 05 004357 9

First published in 1989
Third impression 1992

Set in Times Roman 10 on 12 pt Linotron 202
Produced By Longman Singapore Publishers Pte Ltd
Printed in Singapore

The publisher's policy is to use paper manufactured from sustainable forests.

INTRODUCTION

This book is written for supply teachers and permanent teachers who are always on the lookout for ideas for enthusiastic classes of infant children.

The twelve chapters follow through the year and are divided into two topic sections. The first is appropriate to the month, the other to the time of year. All the work is based on ideas that have been successfully taught in schools.

As the book was written with supply teachers primarily in mind, I have tried to include in the text all the poems and songs mentioned; there is a list of basic equipment needed (none of it too difficult to acquire), and where possible suggested readings for 'Storytime' with the whole class. The Mastercopies are free of copyright so that enough quantities can be reproduced for the children to use. I preferred to work independently of class books, as it allowed more freedom and a surprise topic did not look out of place when the class teacher returns.

The topics are divided into work for younger and older children. As those who have worked with infants know, the range of ability can be enormous (especially where Reception Class means 4+). So younger means 4–6, and older, means 6–8. Grouped under basic headings (Written and Language Work, Number, Artwork, Bodywork, Music) all the work for each topic is linked by the theme. I have not included obvious instructions (e.g. warm-ups for PE, putting out Art equipment) as most teachers have their preferred methods for these.

It is a book of suggestions, not directions; some of them will be familiar, others not. It is impossible to include all the information and ideas that surround each topic – they can all be expanded, and the children will let you know which are their favourites soon enough. Infants have their own ideas, and these often enrich, amuse and educate too!

There is a companion volume *Primary Teacher's Handbook* by Mary Rose Selman and Mary Baird
ISBN 0 05 003985 7

EQUIPMENT

These are probably things that you already have; if you haven't, they are simple enough to acquire, and always useful to have ready:

A large picture calendar
Magazines
Cardboard inner tubes
Old toothbrushes and sponges
Plastic pots and containers
Wool
Straws
White paper doilies
White paper plates
Lolly sticks
Cocktail sticks
Silver foil
Silver and gold spray paint
Self-adhesive stars
Vegetables suitable for printing
Pasta shapes
Dried pulses
Dice
Playing cards
Clear plastic folders
A heavy-duty stapler
Tape recorder
Tapes with pre-recorded music

CONTENTS

1 JANUARY

NEW YEAR

The New Year starts in January and so it is a time of change. In January there is a new month, a new year and perhaps even a new decade to learn about. The children know that they are going to be a year older. They may have heard about New Year's resolutions, always an amusing and sometimes surprising topic with the young.

At the beginning of term it is a time of getting back to normal after the excitement of Christmas. A time to swap news of the holidays and compare notes on favourite presents and treats from the Christmas break. With older children it can be fun to do a review of last year in school, or list the things that they found important in the previous year, or the things they would most like to forget!

Save old calendars, invest in a current one as well. They are always useful not only for obvious reasons but for counting, story-telling ideas, art work and in the end a good source of material for cutting up for collage work!

Suggested Reading

The Tale of Mucky Mabel
by J. Willis and M. Chamberlain (Beaver/Sparrow)

YOUNGER CHILDREN

Written Work and Language

Materials A large calendar

Method

1. Recite the rhyme below

Thirty days hath September,
April, June and November;
All the rest have thirty-one
Excepting February alone,
Which hath twenty-eight days clear,
And twenty-nine in each leap year.

Traditional

2. Repeat the rhyme and see if the children can join in.
3. Do they know it is a new year? Using the calendar show the year, month and look at the days and dates, remembering the rhyme.
4. Find out in which month their birthdays fall and how old they will be.
5. They can write the sentence and draw the picture, e.g. 'In April I will be 5.'

Extension

Material The story below

The Pig Brother

There was once a child who was untidy. He left his books on the floor, and his muddy shoes on the table; he put his fingers in jam pots, and spilled paint on his best clothes; there was no end to his untidiness.

One day the Tidy Angel came to his house. The Angel was shocked to see the mess and told the child to go out and play with his brother while she tidied. The child said that he had not got a brother, but the Angel said he had and that even if the child did not recognise his brother, his brother would recognise him. The child did not really understand, but he went into the garden to wait.

Presently a squirrel came along, whisking his tail. The child asked if he were his brother. The squirrel looked him over carefully and said, 'Well, I should hope not! My fur is neat and smooth, my nest is handsomely made and in perfect order, and my young ones are properly brought up. Why do you insult me by asking such a question?' He whisked off, and the child waited.

A wren came hopping by, and the child asked if he were his brother. 'No indeed!' said the wren. 'You will find no tidier person than I in the whole garden. Not a feather out of place, and my eggs are the wonder of all for their smoothness and beauty. Brother indeed!' She hopped off ruffling her feathers, and the child waited.

By and by a large cat came along, and the child asked him the same question. 'Go and look at yourself in the mirror,' the cat said haughtily, 'and you will have your answer. I have been washing myself in the sun all morning, while it is clear that no water has come near you in a very long time. There are no such creatures as you in my family, I am thankful to say.' He walked on waving his tail, and the child waited.

Just then a pig came trotting along. The child did not want to ask if the pig were his brother, but the pig did not wait to be asked. 'Hello brother!' he grunted. 'I'm not your brother,' exclaimed the child. 'Oh yes you are,' said the pig. 'I confess I'm not proud of you, but there is no mistaking the members of our family. Come along and have a good roll in the farmyard.

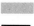

There is some lovely black mud there!'

'I don't like mud,' said the child.

'Tell that to the hens!' said the Pig Brother. 'Look at your hands and your shoes and your clothes! Come along I say and have some of the pig-swill for supper.'

'I don't want to eat pig-swill,' said the child and he began to cry.

Just then the Tidy Angel came out. She said that she had tidied up and that now the child must decide whether to go with his Pig Brother or return with her and be a tidy child. The child did not hesitate and took the Tidy Angel's hand. The Pig Brother grunted. 'Small loss,' he said, 'there will be more pig-swill for me!' and he trotted off.

S. Bryant (adapted)

1. The New Year is a good time for all those resolutions. Did the story give the class any ideas?
2. This can be a good story to act out instantly in the classroom.

Number

Materials Large print calendar

Method
1. Remind the class of the rhyme (Written Work and Language). Check with them, using the calendar to see if it is correct. Check to see if they know what year it is. Explain the value, in years, of each digit.
2. Orally count the days in January. Usually calendars are divided into weeks. Count how many days in a week. How many full weeks in a month? Is each month the same?

Extension

Materials As above or Mastercopy 1.1

Method
1. Have a quiz. Choose a child to help to point to the numbers. Ask for date, then see if they can count on 1, 2, 3, 4, 5 from that number. If the child gives the correct answer they can help with the pointing. Repeat with counting back as well.

Artwork

Materials Picture calendars, paint grouped in seasonal colours (see below)

Method
1. Look at the different sorts of pictures the artists have chosen to illustrate each month. Have they a favourite? Most calendars have appropriate seasonal pictures for each month. Go through the seasons and see if there are any colour associations, e.g.:
   Spring – (pastels) green, yellow, blue, pink
   Summer – (bright) yellow, red, blue
   Autumn – orange, brown, red, yellow
   Winter – white, black, brown, blue
2. Ask the children to paint a picture using the colours appropriate to the chosen season. Keep the season a secret until it is finished and then let the others guess which season or month it is.

Extension

Materials The poem below

In January falls the snow,
February cold winds blow.
In March peep out the early flowers.
And April comes with sunny showers.
In May the roses bloom so gay,
In June the farmers mow their hay,
In July brightly shines the sun,
In August harvest is begun.
September turns the green leaves brown,
October winds then shake them down.
November filled with bleak and drear,
December comes and ends the year.

Traditional

Method
1. A good poem to illustrate if you are left with a large wall space to cover!

Bodywork

Method
1. Play 'Tag' with these rules.
2. One person is 'it'. He must tag the other children one at a time. The first person he catches is January, second February, third March, and so on.
3. When a child is tagged he must 'freeze' until all the other months are used up in the correct order.
4. 'December' person becomes the next catcher.

Music

Materials Song below

Method

As you have learned the rhyme 'Thirty days hath September' in Written Work and Language, now put it to music.

Music: Martin Shaw

OLDER CHILDREN

Written Work and Language

Materials Small pieces of paper to write on. Make a book of stapled sugar paper for the class

Method

1. Talk about New Year's resolutions. Find out what they are not very good at, e.g.:

Keeping bedrooms tidy	Eating with good table manners
Brushing teeth regularly	Sharing their toys

2. Now is a good time to try and change those things – a new year, a new beginning! Ask everyone to write down their resolutions. Exchange ideas, then they can stick them in the class New Year Book.

Extension

Materials Mastercopy 1.2

Method

1. Look at the Mastercopy and ask the children to complete the picture for the New Year.
2. Underneath they can can write opposite adjectives:

bad	good	broken	complete
untidy	tidy	sad	happy
dirty	clean		

Extension

Materials The poem below

Between Birthdays

My birthdays take so long to start,
They come along a year apart,
It's worse than waiting for a bus;
I fear I used to fret and fuss,
But now, when by impatience vexed
Between one birthday and the next,
I think of all that I have seen
That keeps on happening in between.
The songs I've heard, the things I've done
Makes my un-birthdays not so un-.

Ogden Nash

Method

1. The New Year means that everyone is going to be a year older. What things have the class done for the first time since their last birthday? e.g.:
   Learned a new skill
   Joined a Club (Brownies/Cubs)
   Started music lessons
2. What are they looking forward to doing when their next birthday comes round?

Number

Materials Mastercopy 1.1, calendar, coloured pencils

Method

1. Show the calendar to check the children know the months. Notice how many days are in each month. Repeat the rhyme 'Thirty days hath September' (Younger Children/Written Work and Language).
2. Draw their attention to how each month is divided into weeks and each week date matches a day of the week. Give each a copy of Mastercopy 1.1 and let them answer the following questions:
   a. Which month of the year could it be?
   b. What dates are the Tuesdays?
   c. What dates are the Fridays?
   d. How many Sundays are there?
   e. What date is the fourth Thursday?
   f. On which day of the week will the next month start?
   g. What date is the third Saturday?
   h. Is the 19th a Saturday?

Extension

Materials Paper, pencils

Method

1. Write the correct date. Go through it with the class to make sure they know it and can all write it correctly.
2. Check the children know the difference between ordinal and cardinal numbers and how to write them.
3. Sometimes the date is written in numbers only. Do they have any suggestions as to why this happens? Can they write their birth date in numbers only?

Artwork

Materials Templates cut from card (old cereal packets do just as well) for the letters J, F, M, A, S, O, N, D, old coat hangers (metal variety), paper, crayons

Method

1. Make a Mobile. Using the templates draw round and cut out one letter for each month of the year.
2. Letters can be coloured in with the appropriate colours (see Younger Children/Artwork).

Extension

Materials Templates as above

Method

1. As you have made the templates, let the children experiment with making patterns using the letters.

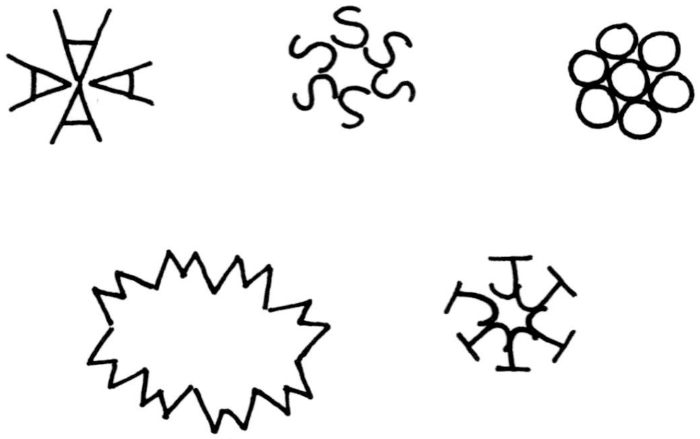

Bodywork

Materials Poem as below, tape and tape recorder

A apple pie,
B bit it,
C cut it,
D dealt it,
E eat(ate) it,
F fought for it,
G got it,
H had it,
I inked it,
J joined it,
K kept it,
L longed for it,
M mourned for it,
N nodded at it,
O opened it,
P peeped in it,
Q quartered it,
R ran for it,
S stole it,
T took it,
V viewed it,
W wanted it,
X,Y, Z, and ampersand
All wished for a piece in hand.

Margaret Tarrant

Method

1. Say the poem onto a tape. Let the class listen to it, see how much they can pick up.
2. Explain all the words (e.g., ampersand).
3. Group children in a circle and use the tape to mime with.
4. End the mime with an alphabet song (see Older Children/ 'Bonfire Night' Music).

Music

Materials Old plastic pots (empty baby-wipe ones are excellent as they have snap tops), waterproof markers, rice, beans, paper clips, newspapers, tape, kitchen scrubbers if necessary

Method

1. Scrub the patterns or print off the pots. Choose which 'filling' sounds best for each size pot. Seal pots, then decorate with markers.
2. To make soft shakers: roll up the newspaper (a double sheet will do) and slice down the sides of one end; extend the roll slightly. Shaken these make a good, soft sound compared with the beans and rice.
3. Use the shakers to accompany favourite nursery rhymes or learn the January, February poem (see Younger Children/Artwork).

SNOW

The first fall of snow always brings great excitement – will it settle, or melt straight away? Will it be good enough for snowballs and snowmen? Maybe there will even be enough to dust off the sledge . . . or even stop us getting to school! Snow can be great fun to play in if you are dressed for it, but it can be miserable if you get too wet as the snowballs melt inside your wellies and gloves.

Most children like snow, some adults like snow, people who go on winter sports holidays love snow; but a lot of people do not really like it very much. The farmers worry about their animals, drivers find the roads difficult and old people are afraid to go out in case they fall in the slippery conditions.

We do not get a lot of snow in this country, but when it does come it always brings a lot of fuss and confusion!

YOUNGER CHILDREN

Written Work and Language

Materials Mastercopy 1.3, crayons

Method

1. When it is snowing we need to wear special clothes and footwear. What are the types of things we need?
2. Do the children have favourite warm and waterproof clothes? Let them draw them on the Mastercopy.
3. Practise the 'S' shapes in the corners to check they can form them correctly.

Extension

Materials Paper, pencils

Method

1. Make a list of compound words. Let the children see how many they can think of:

snowman	snowplough
snowflake	snowslide
snowdrift	snowdrop
snowball	snowstorm

Number

Materials Mastercopy 1.4

Method

1. Self-explanatory; use as to each child's capabilities, whether it be simple colour and count or adding sets to ten.

Extension

Materials Ten snowmen

Method

1. Use the snowmen to help the children with practical work, joining sets to make ten.

Artwork

Materials Paper doilies (the smaller the better), white wool, large-eyed needles

Method

1. To make a snowstorm. If the doilies are small, use as they are. If the doilies are large let the children tear them carefully to make smaller pieces.
2. Thread the wool through the doilies (see diagram).
3. Use the snowmen at the bottom to anchor the snowflakes.

Extension

Materials Mastercopy 6.4, coloured crayons

Method
1. With the crayons make curvy 'S' shapes down the page. Ensure that each curve starts from the correct side. The children can make the 'SSSS' sound as they draw.

Music

Materials Paper, pencils, crayons

Method
1. Let the children help you as much as they are able! Make ten snowmen (see diagram above).
2. Choose ten children to hold a snowman each.
3. Sing an old song with new words (10 Green Bottles tune)
   10 white snowmen standing in the snow, (repeat)
   1 white snowman melted right away,
   9 white snowmen standing in the snow!
4. I think the miming should be obvious!

Bodywork

Materials Pieces of paper

Method
1. Think of all the 'ing' words that are linked with snow, e.g.:

snowing	skating	building
freezing	skiing	running
throwing	sledging	slipping
rolling	sliding	

2. Practise all the movements in mime.
3. Make a mime story (teacher as narrator) to include the words. How about something like this:

It was freezing and then it started snowing. The children came outside after school. Some of them were slipping and sliding, others started rolling snowballs straight away and then began throwing them at each other. A few children had started building a snowman. All around, their friends were pretending to be skating, skiing, or just rolling in the snow for fun.

4. As a calming down activity after all that action:

Walking

Walk fast in snow, in frost go slow,
And still as you go tread on your toe;
When frost and snow are both together,
Sit by the fire and spare shoe leather.
Traditional

OLDER CHILDREN

Written Work and Language

Materials Poem (see below)

Winter Morning

Winter is the king of showmen,
Turning tree stumps into snowmen
And houses into birthday cakes
And spreading sugar over lakes.
Smooth and clean and frosty white,
The world looks good enough to bite.
That's the season to be young,
Catching snowflakes on your tongue.
Snow is snowy when it's snowing
I'm sorry it's slushy when it's going.
Ogden Nash

Method
1. Use the poem as a starting point to ask what is good and bad about snow.
2. Make a good/bad list.
3. Think of the people who like/dislike snow.

Extension

Materials Mastercopy 1.3

Method
1. What do people need to wear in snowy weather? Add the appropriate clothing to the figure on the Mastercopy.

Number

Materials Paper, scissors

Method

1. Snow is made up of flakes and each flake has six points. No two snowflakes are exactly the same.
2. Fold and make a snowflake (see diagram). This is also an opportunity for talking about symmetry.

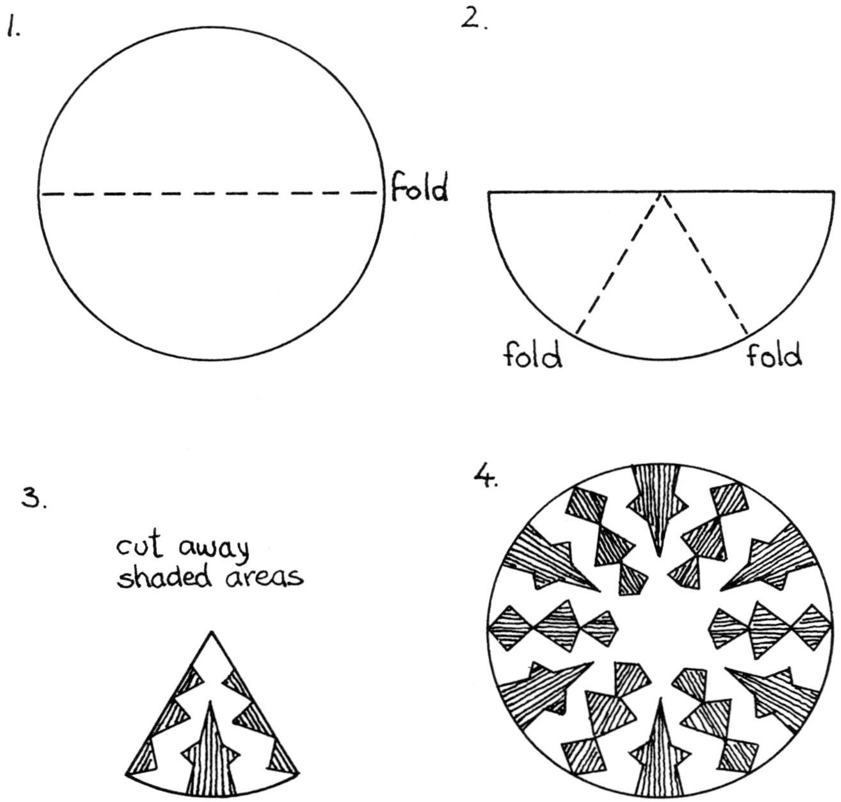

3. Make a giant snowflake using their snowflakes, noting:
   a. How many it takes to make the snowflake all together;
   b. How many have to be divided into six piles (keep remainder safe);
   c. As you make it, point out the symmetry again.

Extension

Materials Jar, snow, clock

Method

1. This can only be done if it is snowing of course! Not only does a snowflake have six points, it takes up six times as much room as water.
2. Fill the jar with snow, measure the side, check time, let the snow melt and measure again.
3. Time the melting process out of interest.

Artwork

Materials Mastercopy 1.3, poem below

Let's put on our caps
And our snug snow suits,

And our fuzzy mittens
And big warm boots,

Let's open the door
And run outside . . .

'Cause the yard's all icy
And we can slide.

Kathryn Jackson

Method

1. Using the poem and the Mastercopy make a class picture of everyone playing in the snow, or compile a winter fashion book. These days there are far more fashion ideas about the clothes we wear in the cold; what about leg-warmers, ear-muffs, padded anoraks?

Music

Materials Chime bars, triangles, tambourines

Method

Practise with the instruments and find out all the different sounds that can be made. Group the children so that they can provide an accompaniment to the story in Bodywork.

Bodywork

Materials The story (see below), any snowflakes that may have been left from Number activity, musical instruments (as above)

The Snowman

It started snowing one night just before Christmas. At first the large soft flakes drifted down, settling on the ground. Then gradually more snowflakes fell, swirling and twirling, drifting and tumbling around the garden until everything was covered in a blanket of white.

When the children woke up in the morning they could hardly believe their eyes. Everything in the garden was white, not a blade of grass in sight. Even the little fir tree was sprinkled with snowflakes. It looked just like a Christmas card. They wanted to rush out straightaway but their mother made them dress up warmly before they went out to play. She was quite glad, as she had so much to do before Christmas Day.

The children made footprints in the snow. They made snowballs and threw them at each other and shook the snow off the little fir tree. Then they decided to make a snowman. They gathered handfuls of snow and patting it firmly together slowly the snowman's shape appeared. He needed eyes and a hat and a scarf. When he was finished the children stood back and admired him. They went off to collect their mother to show her the snowman. What the children hadn't noticed was that the sun was beginning to shine on the garden, and as the sun shone so the snowman began to melt away. By the time the children came back with their mother all that was left was a small heap of snow, the hat and the scarf. 'Never mind,' said Mother, 'tomorrow it's Christmas and you never know, it may snow again tonight.'

Method

1. Although this is written for the Christmas period, it can quite easily be changed to suit the time of year. Divide the class into groups so that one group are the musicians, one group are the snowflakes, three children can play the characters, three children play the tree.
2. Let the musicians decide their accompaniment (e.g. start with chime bars for the first fall of snow, increasing to triangles and adding tambourines for the 'drifting and tumbling').
3. Concentrating on the action words, ask the rest of the class to practise these movements. Plan where the garden is, the fir tree, the house.
4. If there are snowflakes, attach them to the chosen children's hands.
5. The difficult part is building the snowman! It takes roughly five children, but see if the class have any ideas. The little fir tree can be made by three children, two kneeling holding round waists with one arm extended, and the third standing behind with both arms extended.

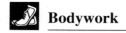

NEW YEAR

Mon.	Tues.	Wed.	Thurs.	Fri.	Sat.	Sun.
				1	2	3
4	5	6	7	8	9	10
11	12	13	14	15	16	17
18	19	20	21	22	23	24
25	26	27	28	29	30	31

OLD YEAR
NEW YEAR

SNOW

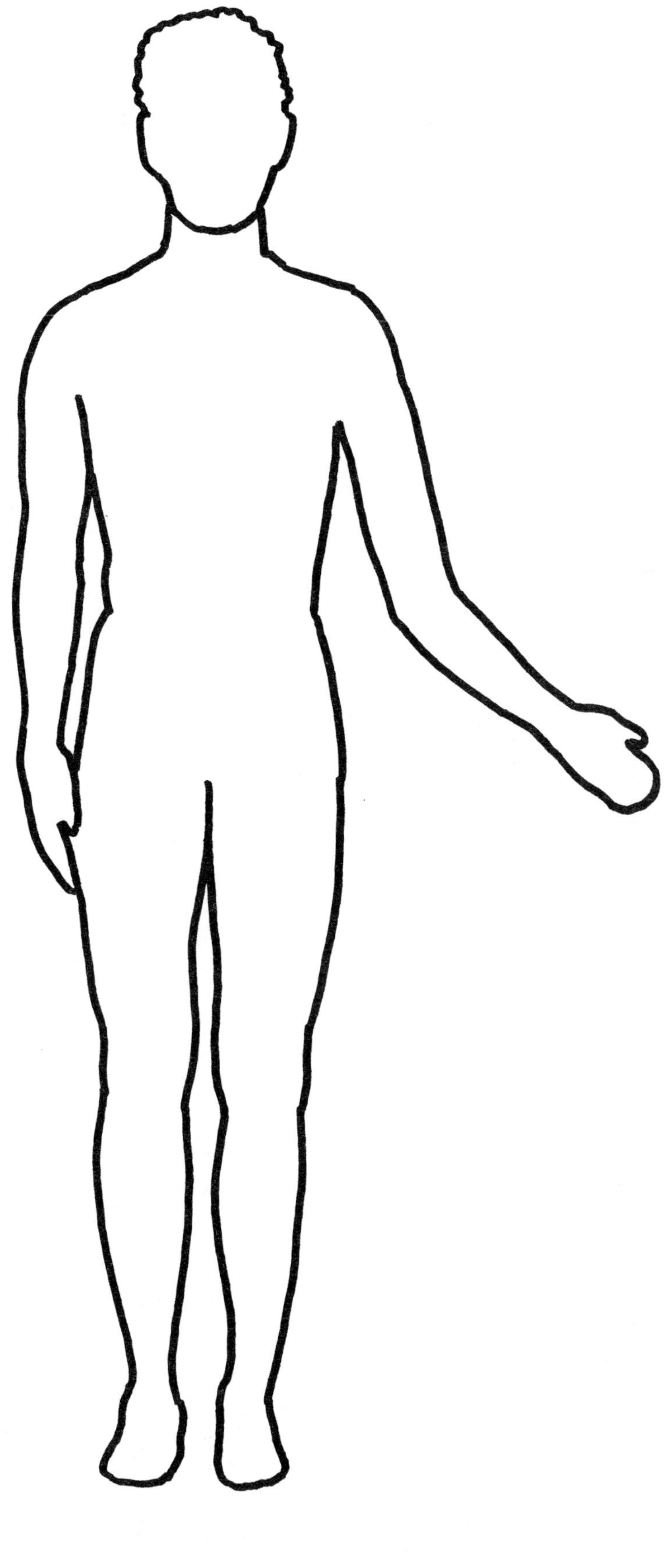

Mastercopy 1:4 **SNOW**

How many in each set?

Draw a line to link sets with the same 'snow' things.

How many altogether for matched sets?

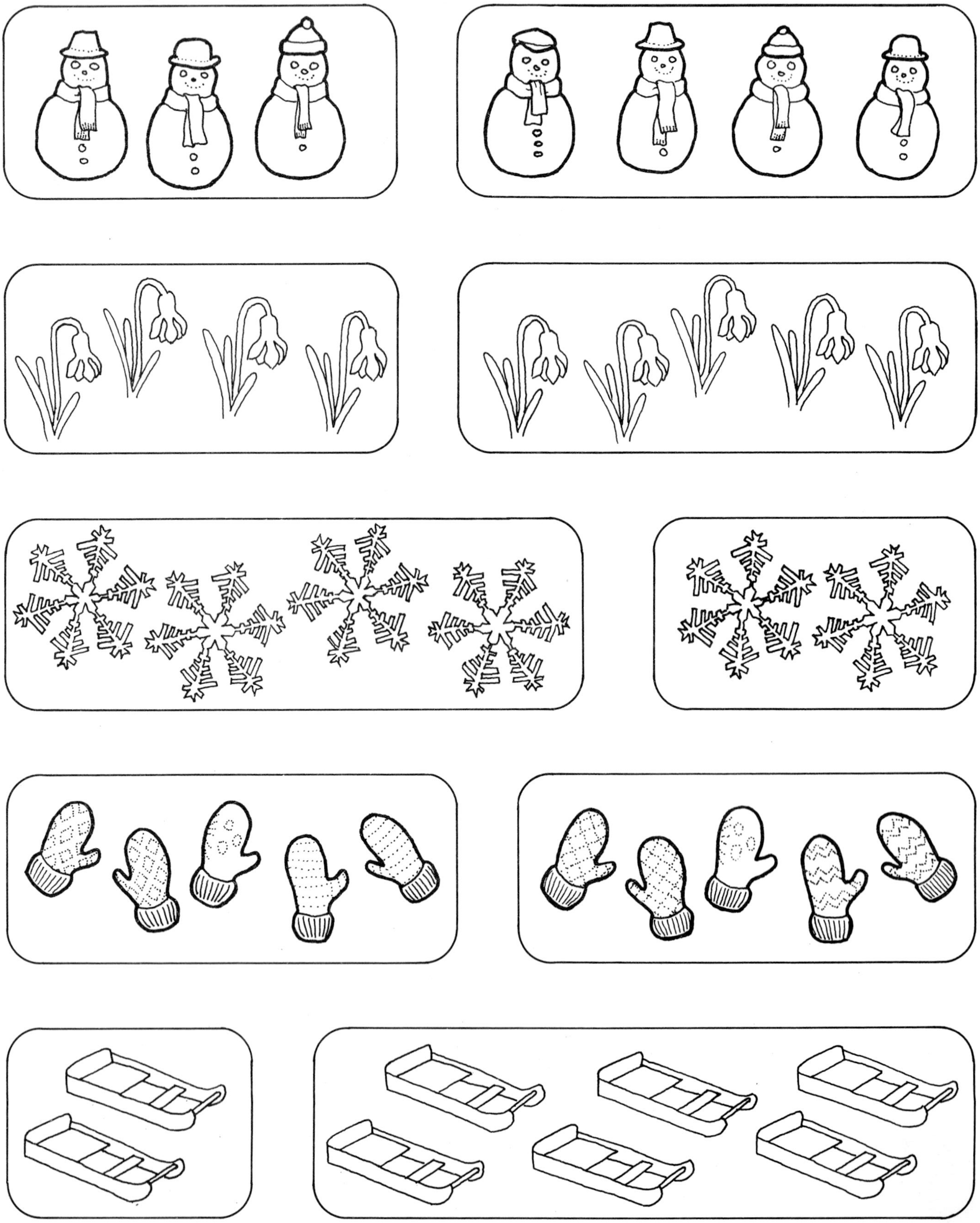

2 FEBRUARY

VALENTINE'S DAY

Valentine's Day provides the opportunity for making a card or present for someone special. It can be for anyone that the children recognise as kind and loving. I'm sure St Valentine would be amazed at the industry that has grown up around his story. Hearts and flowers abound in every stationer's window; but the basic message is still the same – to show that you care about someone.

YOUNGER CHILDREN

Written Work and Language

Materials Paper, crayons, scissors

Method

1. St Valentine was a Christian priest sentenced to death by Emperor Claudius II. He got to know his jailor's daughter who was blind. It is said that he was able to make her see again and that the night before he died he sent her a message signed 'from your Valentine'.
2. Who are the people who are kind and loving to us?

Parents	Aunts and Uncles
Grandparents	Friends in school

3. Valentine's Day is a time when we can show them that we appreciate them. Draw a picture of one of the people on the list, cut it out and put it on a heart shaped display.

Extension

Materials Mastercopy 6.4

Method

1. Valentine begins with a V, a good pattern to practise. Use the Mastercopy to help with the pattern making, working left to right, joining the dots with a different colour for each row.

Number

Materials Pre-cut heart, diamond, crescent, zigzag and star, Mastercopy 2.1

Method

1. These may be shapes the class is familiar with, but may not have worked with before. Name each shape and get the children to describe them. Ask what each one reminds the children of:
   Heart – Valentine's Day symbol
   Diamond – maybe a kite
   Crescent – moon shape
   Zigzag – lightning
   Star – a sign of good work
2. Using the Mastercopy, match up the name to the shape.
3. Cut out one shape, colour it and make a picture around it. (The Valentine's Heart could always be given to someone special.)

Artwork

Materials White card, white doilies, red pre-cut heart shape, stapler, crayons

Method

1. Colour the doilies on newspaper. Mount on the white card and staple.
2. Cover the staple with a red heart to finish off the card.

Bodywork

Materials Valentine's hearts (or beanbags!)

Method

1. Form two teams each with a heart for a relay race.
2. Divide each team in half. Two halves, one at each end of the hall.
3. The first child in each team holding the heart runs and gives it to the opposite child on his/her team at the other end of the hall. That child returns back down the hall, while the first child sits down. The winning team is the first to be completely seated.

Extension

Materials A heart (another beanbag) and a lot of practice!

Method

1. Along the lines of 'I sent a letter to my love and on the way I dropped it.' Seat all the children in a circle except one who stands outside the circle with the heart.
2. The circle chant 'I sent a Valentine to my love and on the way I dropped it

. . . etc.', while the one on the outside skips round the circle. When the word 'dropped' is said the Valentine heart is dropped behind a child.
3. The first child continues skipping in the same direction, the seated child gets up and runs round the circle in the opposite direction.
4. The first person to sit in the space left stays sitting, the one standing starts off again.

Music

Materials The song below

Magic Penny

Chorus: Love is something if you give it away,
give it away, give it away.
Love is something if you give it away,
You end up having more.

1 It's just like a magic penny;
Hold it tight and you won't have any;
Lend it, spend it, and you'll have so many,
They'll roll all over the floor, for
Chorus: Love is something if you give it away . . .
. . .
2 So let's go dancing till the break of day,
And if there's a piper, we can pay.
For love is something if you give it away,
You end up having more.
Chorus: Love is something if you give it away

Words and melody: Malvina Reynolds

OLDER CHILDREN

Written Work and Language

Materials The poem below, paper, scissors, crayons

The Owl and the Pussycat

The Owl and the Pussycat went to sea
  In a beautiful pea-green boat,
They took some honey, and plenty of money,
  Wrapped up in a five-pound note.
The Owl looked up to the stars above,
  And sang to a small guitar,
'O lovely Pussy! O Pussy, my love,
  What a beautiful Pussy you are
    You are,
    You are!
What a beautiful Pussy you are!'

Pussy said to the Owl, 'You elegant fowl!
  How charmingly sweet you sing!
O let us be married! too long we have tarried:
  But what shall we do for a ring?'
They sailed away for a year and a day,
  To the land where the Bong-tree grows,
And there in a wood a Piggy-wig stood,
  With a ring at the end of his nose,
    His nose,
    His nose,
With a ring at the end of his nose.

'Dear Pig, are you willing to sell for one shilling
  Your ring?' Said the Piggy, 'I will,'
So they took it away and were married next day
  By the Turkey who lives on the hill.
They dined on mince and slices of quince,
  Which they ate with a runcible spoon;
And hand in hand, on the edge of the sand,
  They danced by the light of the moon,
    The moon,
    The moon,
They danced by the light of the moon.

Edward Lear

Method

1. Now here are two great Valentines! To help learn the poem make a large version for the wall.
2. Choose which words could be replaced with a simple picture, e.g.:
   owl
   cat
   boat
   honey
   money
   ring
   year & a day
   Bong-tree
   nose
3. Teacher writes the words, leaving space for the children's illustrations of the words chosen.
4. As each child finishes drawing they could colour and cut out a heart to decorate the edge of the poem.

Number

Materials Mastercopy 2.2, pack of playing cards, rulers.

Method

1. The heart is the Valentine symbol. If folded in half it is symmetrical; show and explain.
2. Look at the Mastercopy. If there shapes were folded in half would they be symmetrical?
3. Ask the class where they have seen the shapes before. Show them the pack of cards, explain the suits. See if there are any symmetrical patterns on the cards.

Extension

Materials Mastercopy 6.4

Method

1. Fold the Mastercopy in half. On one half draw a pattern using the dots to help.
2. Open out the paper and make an identical pattern using the fold as the line of symmetry.

Artwork

Materials White doilies, white card, crayons, coloured wool, stapler

Method

1. Colour the doilies on newspaper.
2. Thread wool round the outer edge and leave enough to tie a bow.
3. Attach the doily to the card and finish off with a heart.

Bodywork

Materials Knowledge of the poem 'The Owl and the Pussycat'

Method

1. Hopefully having learned the poem, it is an ideal story to dramatise. Let the children play all the parts, including the boat and the island!

Music

Materials The song (see below)

If You Were The Only Girl In The World

If you were the only girl in the world,
And I were the only boy,
Nothing else would matter in the world today,
We would go on loving in the same old way.
A garden of Eden, just made for two,
With nothing to mar our joy;
I would say such wonderful things to you,
There would be such wonderful things to do,
If you were the only girl in the world,
And I were the only boy.

HEALTH

To stay healthy we need to do several things: eat well and sensibly, exercise, get enough sleep and fresh air. It is better to feel good and healthy, than miserable and ill. We cannot stop certain 'childhood' illnesses, but we can aim to keep coughs and sneezes at bay. Being healthy means having the energy to do things and for children it means growing properly.

Children can look after some aspects of health care themselves: brushing their teeth, combing their hair. As adults we can help them to understand why we want them to do other things, like going to bed at a reasonable hour during school-term time, or doing something more energetic than constantly watching television.

We should encourage them in healthy eating and exercise habits from an early age.

Suggested Reading

Willisk's Tooth
by Andrew Martyr (Hamish Hamilton)

YOUNGER CHILDREN

Written Work and Language

Materials Paper plates, hole punch

Method

1. It's much nicer to feel healthy rather than ill. Make a comparison chart with the children. Good for opposites!

Healthy	**Ill**
happy	sad
strong	weak
energetic	lazy

2. When they have completed the list, they can make a healthy face/ill face using either side of the paper plate.

Extension

Materials The poems below

Sneezing

Sneeze on Monday, sneeze for danger
Sneeze on Tuesday, kiss a stranger
Sneeze on Wednesday, get a letter
Sneeze on Thursday, something better
Sneeze on Friday, sneeze for sorrow
Sneeze on Saturday, see your sweetheart tomorrow.

Traditional

Sneezles

Christopher Robin
Had wheezles
And sneezles,
They bundled him
Into
His bed.
They gave him what goes
With a cold in the nose
And some more for a cold
In the head.
They wondered
If wheezles
Could turn
Into measles,
If sneezles
Would turn
Into mumps;
They examined his chest
For a rash,
And the rest
Of his body for swellings and lumps.
They sent for some doctors
In sneezles
And wheezles
To tell them what ought to be done.
All sorts of conditions
Of famous physicians
Came hurrying round
At a run.
They all made a note
Of the state of his throat,
They asked if he suffered from thirst;
They asked if the sneezles
Came AFTER the wheezles,
Or if the sneezle
Came first.
They said 'If you teazle
A sneezle
Or wheezle,
A measle
May easily grow.
But humour or pleasle
The wheezle
Or sneezle,
The measle
Will certainly go.'
They expounded the reasles
For sneezles
And wheezles,
The manner of measles
When new.
They said 'If he freezles
In draughts and in breezles,
The PHTHEEZLES
May even ensue.'

****

Christopher Robin
Got up in the morning,
The sneezles had vanished away.
And the look in his eye
Seemed to say to the sky,
'Now how to amuse them to-day?'

A. A. Milne

Method

1. Two of the most noticeably unhealthy things in school are coughs and sneezes. The two poems give the opportunity to learn one and read and enjoy the other.

Number

Materials Mastercopy 2.3

Method

1. Talk about the care of teeth: why we brush them, how often, what happens if we don't. (For list of good/bad snacks see Older Children/Number.) The British Dental Association now suggests that one good three-minute brush every 24 hours, is more effective than quick brush-overs twice a day.
2. The Mastercopy is really self-explanatory.

Artwork

Materials Fresh foods to print with, paints

Method

1. An old established activity, but it can reinforce discussion that has gone on before. Try and choose fruits and vegetables that the class will recognise as 'healthy' foods.

Bodywork

Materials Open space!

Method

1. Exercise is good for you, it helps you take care of your body. Exercise should stretch your muscles and make your heart beat a little bit faster. Get the children to feel their chests and see if they can feel their hearts beating. Let them feel their chests after they have done a few exercises!
2. Do these exercises (a good way of seeing which basic skills they have mastered) for one minute with a rest time in between:
   running on the spot
   jumping 2:2
   skipping
   hopping (on one leg only!)
3. Sit them down to do stretching exercises in the same way:
   touching toes
   sit-ups
   sit with knees bent, soles of feet together and bounce for eight counts
   sit straight-legged, reach fingers beyond toes nine times
4. See if they can sit cross-legged on the floor and then get up without putting their hands on the floor. Try it yourself first, as they are bound to ask if you can do it!

Music

Materials Good voices

Method

1. There are lots of songs that have a healthy message:
   'Heads and Shoulders' – for exercise
   'Here we go round the Mulberry Bush' – verses to include:
   brush our teeth
   brush our hair
   stand up straight
   eat our food
2. Then there's the one for poor 'John Brown's Baby' (see Older Children/Music).

OLDER CHILDREN

Written Work and Language

Materials The poem (see below)

Bedtime

Go to bed early – wake up with joy
Go to bed late! cross girl or boy.
Go to bed early – ready for play,
Go to bed late – moping all day.
Go to bed early – no pain or ills,
Go to bed late – doctors and pills.
Go to bed early – grow very tall,
Go to bed late – stay very small.

Traditional

Method

1. A good starting point for talking about the benefits of sleep and its particular importance when we are young.
2. To help learn the poem, divide the class: girls to say 'earlies', boys to say 'lates'.
3. Have fun with the dramatic emphasis.

Extension

Materials Paper and crayons

Method
1. Explain why we need to have fresh air and sunshine.
2. Divide the paper in half so that they can draw a healthy picture (outside in the sunshine!) with an unhealthy picture (inside glued to the TV).

Number

Materials Paper and pencils

Method
1. Tooth decay: explain that it is not just sweet things that damage teeth, but how long sweet food stays in your mouth and whether the food causes your mouth to become acid, which erodes the teeth. Also whether the food you are eating will cause a build up of plaque. Ask them what they think are good and bad foods for healthy teeth and gums.
2. Here is an interesting list. Give each child one item to write down or draw:
   a. sugarless gum
   b. peanuts
   c. bread and butter
   d. potato crisps
   e. ice lolly
   f. chocolate-covered peanuts
   g. chocolate caramel bar
   h. apple
   i. cream filled biscuit
   j. ice cream
   k. sweet chocolate
   l. sugared chewing gum
   m. plain sweet biscuit
   n. sweetened orange drink
   o. toffee
   p. boiled sweet

Dr M Edgar. Newcastle Dental School

3. Categorise the list simply:
   Bad = very sweet, eat slowly, sticky
   Good = not sweet, eat quickly, not sticky
4. Ask the children to stand at random and show their drawing or word. Group the children into good/bad foods according to the categories decided above. If a food gets two out of three points in each category, that decides whether it is good or bad.
5. Read the list to the children again in order; see if they are surprised at what is worst for your teeth.

Extension

Materials Mastercopy 2.4

Method
1. A quick 'fill-in' activity for fast finishers.

Artwork

Materials Old magazines or catalogues, scissors, glue

Method
1. Glueing and sticking for collage work is a favourite! Limit them to finding pictures of foodstuffs. They can work in small groups, which makes the picture appear faster and choose their title:
   Food We Like
   Food We Don't Like
   Healthy Food
   Unhealthy Food

Bodywork

Materials Open space

Method
1. Experiment with a comparison of movement effort.
   Healthy and strong movements:
   stamping, marching, pushing, pulling, moving fast
   Ill and weak:
   creeping, crawling, sliding, moving slowly
2. As a change, work in pairs and sing and act 'Row, Row, Row Your Boat'.

Music

Materials The song below

John Brown's Baby

1 John Brown's baby had a cold upon his chest,
John Brown's baby had a cold upon his chest,
John Brown's baby had a cold upon his chest,
And they rubbed it with camphorated oil.
2 Omit word 'baby' throughout and do motion
3 Omit 'baby' and 'cold' and do motions
4 Omit 'baby,' 'cold,' and 'chest' . . .
5 Omit 'baby,' 'cold,' 'chest', and 'rubbed' . . .
6 Omit 'baby,' 'cold,' 'chest,' 'rubbed,' and 'camphorated oil' . . .

Motions: (not done on verse 1)
baby – rock baby in arms
cold – sneeze
chest – slap chest
rubbed – rub chest
camphorated oil – hold nose and make a face

Mastercopy 2:1

VALENTINE'S DAY

star, zigzag, crescent, heart, diamond

VALENTINE'S DAY

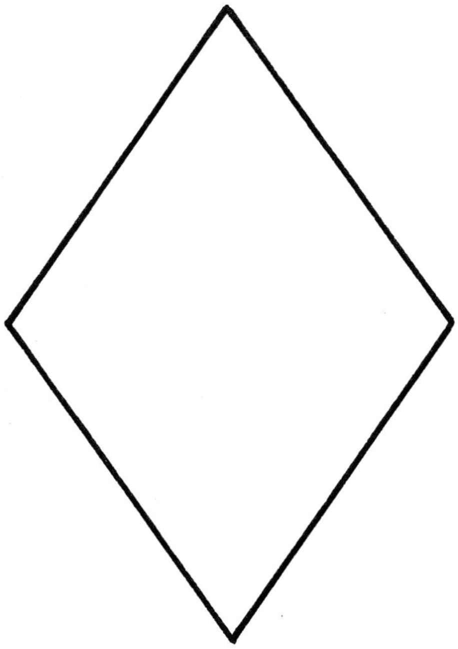

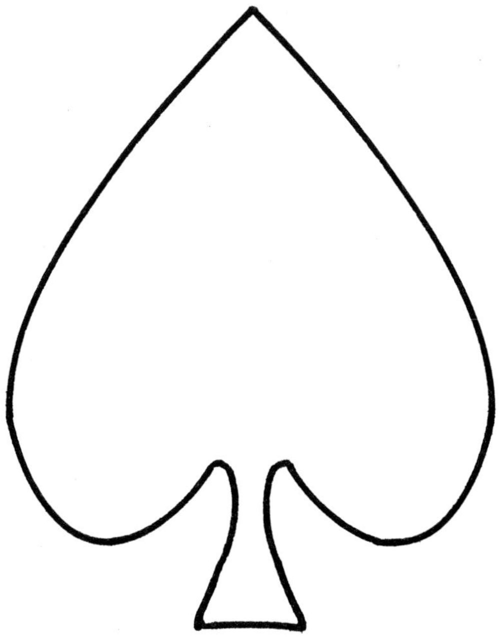

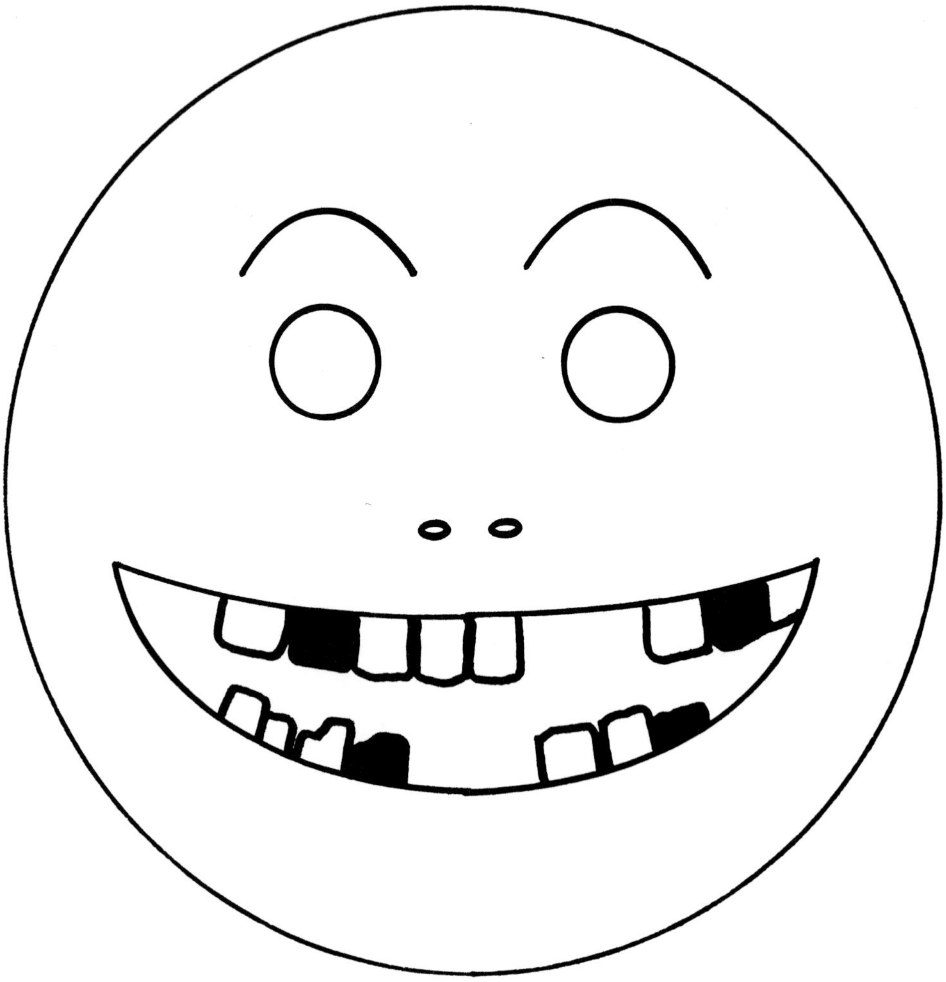

1. How many teeth are there altogether?
2. How many good teeth are there?
3. How many bad teeth are there?
4. How many teeth are missing?
5. How many times do you brush your teeth each day?
6. How many times do you think you should brush your teeth each day?

HEALTH

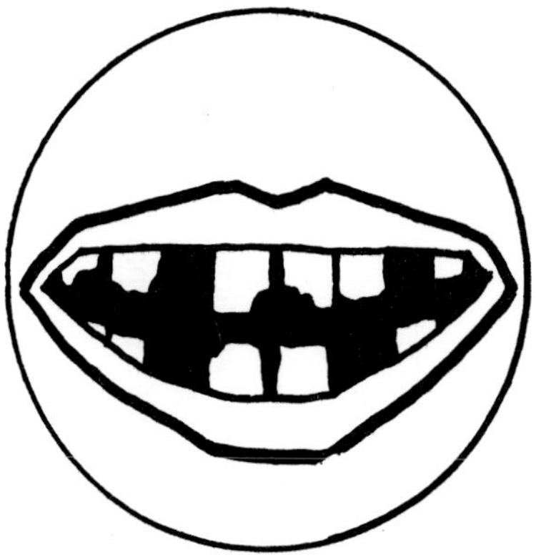

Give a ✓ for healthy.

Give a ✗ for unhealthy.

3 MARCH

MOTHER'S DAY

Mother's Day is a very old festival and since everyone has a mother it is a good day to celebrate. Mother can encompass grandmothers if the situation arises or if you have time.

Children like to surprise mothers and treat them to things they have made. I know the things I value are the lopsided cards and stuck-together presents that come home as a surprise.

Pancake Day has been included in this section as Shrove Tuesday mainly seems to fall at this time of year.

Suggested Reading

Just Like That
by Meri Fox and Kilmary Niland (Hodder & Stoughton Ltd)
The Trouble with Mum
by Babette Cole (Fontana/Picture Lions)

YOUNGER CHILDREN

Written Work and Language

Materials Mastercopy 3.1, Plasticine, crayons, clear plastic folders, one for each child

Method

1. All mothers are special. Ask the children how mothers take care of us:
   feed us — read us stories
   dress us — take and collect us from school
   hug us — play with us
   teach us to talk
   Don't forget that mothers get cross with us too!
2. As she is so special, what would we like to give her if we could give her anything we liked, for Mother's Day?
   A crown fit for a queen — A bunch of flowers
   New warm slippers — New earrings and a necklace
3. Use the Mastercopy. Colour in with the correct features for each Mum (hair colour, glasses, etc.). Then slip each picture in a plastic folder and add the 'present', by making it out of Plasticine.
4. Those capable can always write why they chose that present afterwards.

Number

Materials Paper, crayons

Method

1. Ask the children to draw a Mother's Day bouquet, but it must have these flowers in it:
   5 Red Roses
   4 Yellow Daffodils
   3 Orange Lilies
   2 Pink Daisies
   1 Bluebell
   how many flowers are there in Mother's bouquet?

Artwork

Materials Pink toilet paper, cotton, safety pins (white paper can be coloured)

Method

1. Take two sheets of paper and loosely roll/gather them up.
2. Wind cotton round the centre section tightly.*
3. Open out individual layers of paper.
4. Hold between finger and thumb and arrange so that all layers face the same way.*
5. Pinch firmly at base and then attach a safety pin. This makes a pretty flower brooch or buttonhole.

* These operations need a lot of supervision, if not complete adult help!

Bodywork

Materials The poem below, beanbags

Stir a Pancake

Mix a pancake, stir a pancake
Pop it in a pan
Fry the pancake, toss the pancake
Catch it if you can.

Christina Rossetti

Method

1. Mothers make pancakes on Shrove Tuesday. Sometimes we eat them with sugar and lemon juice, sometimes with syrup. Whichever way, this is a lovely rhyme to learn and mime.
2. Divide the class into teams, with four or five in each. Stand them in lines with a small space between each child in the line. Give each team a 'pancake' (beanbag).
3. A pancake race. The leader of each team tosses the 'pancake' backwards over her head to the next child, who tosses it backwards, and so on, until the 'pancake' reaches the last person in the line, then the whole line sits down.

Music

Materials The song below

Knees up, Mother Brown

Knees up, Mother Brown! Well!
Knees up, Mother Brown!
Under the table you must go,
Ee-i-ee-i-ee-i-oh!
If I catch you bending,
I'll saw your leg right off.
So, knees up, knees up!
Don't get the breeze up,
Knees up, Mother Brown! Ooh!

Knees up, Mother Brown! Well!
Knees up, Mother Brown!
Come along, dearie, let it go,
Ee-i-ee-i-ee-i-oh!
It's yer blooming birthday,
Let's wake up all the town!
So, knees up, knees up!
Don't get the breeze up,
Knees up, Mother Brown! Ooh!

Words and music:
Harris Weston and Bert Lee

OLDER CHILDREN

Written Work and Language

Materials Paper, pencils

Method

1. Mother is one name for a Mum, she could have lots of others. See if the class can make a list, e.g.:
   Mother
   Grandmother
   Aunty
   Mrs
   Miss
   Lady
   Woman
   Sister
2. See if they know the opposites of all these titles.

Extension

Materials Paper, pencils

Method

1. Ask the children to make a list of all the things they can do to help their mothers on Mother's Day. (They can have help from the rest of the family too.) Perhaps:
   Tea in bed
   Breakfast made for her
   Tidy the living-room
   Give a special present
   They can take the list home to act as a reminder!

Number

Materials Mastercopy 3.2

Method

1. Look at the Mastercopy, explain the difference between a.m. and p.m.
2. Let the class pretend that this is the nearest Saturday to Mother's Day when they are going to put into action all the things they talked about in Written Work and Language. Fill out the timetable with all their good ideas! I suggest that the timetable could start: 7 a.m. I wake up and stay quietly in my bedroom so that Mum gets a lie-in!

Artwork

Materials Mastercopy 3.1, crayons.

Method

1. Let everyone give their Mum a new outfit for Mother's Day. Use the Mastercopy to help.

Extension

Materials See Younger Children/Artwork.

Method

1. Make your Mother a Carnation Brooch. If you use felt-tip pens to colour the edges of the paper it makes a very pretty effect.

Bodywork

Materials The song in Music Section

Method

1. Learn the song first.
2. Practise skipping and galloping before starting work on bringing the song to life!
3. The cast list should read something like this:
   2 children to act as window
   2 children to act as washing line
   7 girls to do washing tasks
   7 boys to do the beholding!
   If each boy matches up with a girl at the end, so much the better.

Music

Materials The song below

Dashing Away With The Smoothing Iron

1 'Twas on a Monday morning,
When I beheld my darling;
She looked so neat and charming
In every high degree;
She looked so neat and nimble, O,
A-washing of her linen, O,
Dashing away with the smoothing iron,
Dashing away with the smoothing iron,
She stole my heart away.

2 'Twas on a Tuesday morning, etc.
A-hanging out her linen, O, etc.

3 'Twas on a Wednesday morning, etc.
A-starching of her linen, O, etc.

4 'Twas on a Thursday morning, etc.
A-ironing of her linen, O, etc.

5 'Twas on a Friday morning, etc.
A-folding of her linen, O, etc.

6 'Twas on a Saturday morning, etc.
A-airing of her linen, O, etc.

7 'Twas on a Sunday morning, etc.
A-wearing of her linen, O, etc.

(The lines in italics are repeated in every verse)

Arranged by Cecil J. Sharp

WIND

There are all sorts of sayings about the wind: 'If March comes in like a lion it goes out like a lamb'; 'March winds and April showers, Bring forth May flowers'.

Wind is moving air; when it moves slowly it is a breeze, when it moves very fast it is a gale. When the wind blows gently it can be useful for flying kites and hot-air balloons, or drying the washing, or sailing a boat. If it blows strongly it is not as much fun for going about in, or playing outdoor ball games and at sea it can cause storms with frightening waves.

There are lots of things you can do that are to do with the wind. Here are a few suggestions.

Suggested Reading

The Wind Blew
by Pat Hutchins (Bodley Head)

YOUNGER CHILDREN

Written Work and Language

Materials The poem below, Mastercopy 3.3, pencils and crayons, scissors, wool or string

Wind on the Hill

No one can tell me,
Nobody knows
Where the wind comes from,
Where the wind goes.

It's flying from somewhere
As fast as it can
I couldn't keep up with it
Not if I ran.

But if I stopped holding
The string of my kite
It would blow with the wind
For a day and a night.

And then if I found it,
Wherever it blew,
I should know that the wind
Had been going there too.

So then I could tell them
Where the wind goes . . .
But where the wind comes from
Nobody knows.

A. A. Milne

Method

1. Ask the children if they have any ideas where the wind comes from, after you have read the poem. It can come from different directions: north, south, east, west. Suggest they watch the weather forecast when they get home and see if they can pick up which direction the forecaster says the wind is blowing.
2. When the wind is blowing we can use it for flying kites; adults use it for hot-air ballooning. Get the class to think of 'windy' words that could describe a kite flying in the air (N.B. -'ing' ending to words).
   whirling blowing
   whipping puffing
   whooshing fluttering
   whisking dancing
   soaring
3. Use the Mastercopy to colour, then cut out the kite. Attach wool or string and then get the children to choose the words they think are best and write them in the small boxes at the corner of the page. These can be stuck on to the string as decoration.

Extension

Materials Mastercopy 6.4

Method

1. Use the dots to practise writing W W W's, large and small, left to right.

Number

Materials Mastercopy 3.4, pencils

Method

1. All the things on the Mastercopy need the wind, they also have four of

something. Can the children correctly name each picture and can they find the four?
4 sails on the windmill
4 points on the weather vane
4 corners on the sail
4 sides to the kite
2. Finish off by writing four correctly at the bottom of the page.

Extension

Materials Coloured and cut-out kites from Written Work and Language if possible.

Method
1. Each kite should have five tags on its tail. If each child holds their kite it provides a practical way of counting in fives.

Artwork

Materials Mastercopy 3.3

Method
1. This can always be used simply as artwork.

Extension

Materials Pre-cut, hot-air balloon shapes and small squares, cotton

Method
1. Decorate the balloon shapes on both sides with a WWWWWWWW pattern. Let them write their names on the square piece of paper and attach each square to the underneath of the balloon as the basket. Hang balloons from the ceiling.

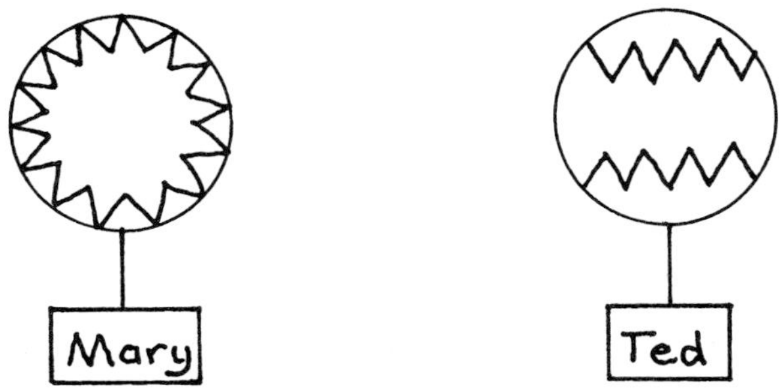

Bodywork

Materials The story below

The North Wind and the Sun

The North Wind and the Sun were arguing as to which of them would first have the cloak off the traveller's shoulders. The wind began and blew for all he was worth, thinking to strip the wearer by force. But the traveller would not let go; he grasped his cloak more firmly and wrapped it closer round his body as he headed into the blast. Then the sun came out: his welcome rays dispersed the bitter cold; the traveller felt the genial warmth, and as the sun shone brighter and brighter he sat down, exhausted with the heat, and took off his cloak.
MORAL: Persuasion is better than force.

Aesop's Fables (Translated by J. Warrington)

Method
1. A good story to mime.

Music

Materials The song below

The Wind Blow East

1 Oh, the wind blow east,
The wind blow west,
The wind blow the *Sunshine*
Right down in town.

Chorus: Oh, the wind blow the *Sunshine*
Right down in town,
Oh, the wind blow the *Sunshine*
Right down in town.

2 Oh, the wind blow east,
The wind blow west,
The wind blow the *Setting Star*
Right down in town.

Chorus: Oh, the wind blow the *Setting Star*
Right down in town,
Oh, the wind blow the *Setting Star*
Right down in town.

Words and music: from Nassau, Bahamas

Sunshine and *Setting Star* are the names of two ships. They were blown right down in town by a hurricane in the Bahamas.

Children will enjoy suggesting other things which may be blown down in town by the wind, e.g. autumn leaves.

Written Work and Language

Materials The story below

Tom's Kite

One day Tom set out to fly his kite in the park.

The kite was very pretty, with red and blue stripes, and ribbons on the string. It was so windy in the park that Tom soon had the kite flying. He held tight on to the string, letting it out more and more until the kite was far away in the sky.

Suddenly the wind changed, and the kite flew out of Tom's hand. It sailed over the lake and out of sight. Tom ran round the lake, trying to see where his kite had gone. It was not in the water, nor on the path, nor even on the grass. Tom sat down with a bump on the park bench.

'I've lost it now,' he cried. 'Oh, bother!'

'Pardon,' said a voice. It was the park-keeper, picking up paper with his pointed stick. 'What's all this, then?'

'I've lost my kite, park-keeper.'

'Is it red and blue with ribbons?' asked the park-keeper.

'Yes,' said Tom, 'How did you know?'

'Well it came whizzing over here and gave me a fearful surprise, and now it's up there.' The park-keeper pointed to a tall tree, and there was the kite.

'Oh,' Tom cried, 'but how can we get it down?' The park-keeper tried to reach the string of the kite with his paper picking up stick, but it was no good. The park-keeper said he was very sorry, but Tom would have to wait until next week, when the tree cutters came with their ladders.

'That's no good,' thought Tom, as the park-keeper walked off. He sat down again. 'Oh, fish and chips!' he shouted. He always shouted that when he was angry.

'Do you mind?' said a voice. It was a fisherman from the edge of the lake. 'You're scaring all the fish away, shouting fish and chips like that.'

Tom said he was sorry, and explained about his kite being caught in the tree.

'Well,' said the fisherman, 'as you've scared all the fish away with your crying, I'll get my fishing rod and fish for your kite.'

The fisherman brought his fishing rod from the lake and tried to poke the kite out of the tree, but it was just too high.

So he let out his line a little and flicked the rod; and down came Tom's kite. 'It's battered a little and torn,' the man said, 'and you'll need some more string for it.'

'That's all right,' Tom laughed; 'next time I fly it I'll tie the end of the string round my middle.'

'If it's as windy as today, I expect you will fly off with it,' laughed the fisherman, 'and I couldn't fish you out of a tree, could I?'

Tom thanked the kind man who had saved his kite, and whenever he went to the park after that he walked round the lake to say 'hello' to the fisherman. But he said it very quietly, in case he scared away the fish.

Malcolm Carrick

Method

1. Read the story to the class and then ask them to answer the following questions:
    1. What was the little boy's name?
    2. Can you describe Tom's kite?
    3. Where did the kite go, when it blew away?
    4. What did Tom say when he couldn't find his kite?
    5. Who told Tom where his kite had got stuck?
    6. Who would Tom have to wait for to help him?
    7. What did Tom shout when he was very angry?
    8. What happened next?
    9. Where was Tom going to tie the string of his kite to stop it flying away again?
    10. Why did Tom always speak quietly to the fisherman after that day?

Extension

Materials Mastercopy 3.4

Method

1. Ask the children to name the pictures. Can they think of anything else that needs wind power? e.g.:
   A wind sock at air-fields
   Hot-air balloons
   Windsurf boards

Number

Materials The Beaufort Scale see below:

The Beaufort Scale

Force 0: less than 1 m.p.h. – Calm
1: 1–3 m.p.h. – Light
2: 4–7 m.p.h. – Light
3: 8–12 m.p.h. – Light
4: 13–18 m.p.h. – Moderate
5: 19–24 m.p.h. – Fresh
6: 25–31 m.p.h. – Strong
7: 32–38 m.p.h. – Strong
8: 39–46 m.p.h. – Gale
9: 47–54 m.p.h. – Strong Gale
10: 55–63 m.p.h. – Strong Gale
11: 64–75 m.p.h. – Strong Gale
12: above 75 m.p.h. – Strong Gale
Strong Gale can also be called Storm
Winds averaging over 75 m.p.h. can be called Hurricanes.

Method

1. Lots of numbers and abbreviations to play with! You may not need them all, but if copied large enough they can be interesting check points during class work.
2. Ask the children if they can guess what actually happens at different points on the Beaufort Scale. A drawing of a house with chimney is a good way to illustrate the different forces. Children love the higher numbers where structural damage can occur!
3. Ask the children to listen to the weather forecast, and see if the weatherman mentions the wind (direction and speed). If they are watching TV suggest they note down the symbol for wind.

Artwork

Materials Strong card/paper, sticks, paper squares, paper fasteners, long pins, beads

Method

1. Make a windmill (see diagram below).
2. You will need two pieces of paper of different colours. Draw and cut out a square 20 cm × 20 cm from each piece of paper and stick them together.
3. Draw lines from corner to corner. Cut along the lines, leaving about 3 cm at the centre uncut.

4. Turn the right-hand corner of each piece over into the centre and push a long pin through from the front.
5. Now thread a large bead on to the pin before pushing its point into the end of a stick.

Extension

Materials Mastercopy 3.3, scissors, crayons

Method

1. Cut out the kite shape and either duplicate it several times, or as a class activity, make patterns using the shape.

Bodywork

Materials The poem (see below)

Miller, miller meet the farmer
When the weather has turned warmer.
Buy his wheat and stack it till
You shall take it to the mill
Windmill, windmill, turn around,
Never stop till the wheat is ground.
Baker, baker, hurry and go
To the bakehouse and bake your dough!
Oven, oven, cook the bread
Or else the children cannot be fed.
Oven, oven, see that you bake
An icy, spicy, sugary cake.
A sugary cake and a loaf of bread,
And so, the children will be fed.

Method

1. Lots of opportunity for miming work actions and making a story to go with the poem.

2. Cast List could read:
   Miller – 1
   Farmer – 1
   Mill workers – 2 to carry sacks to the mill
   2 to carry flour to the baker
   Windmill – 8 children standing in cross shape
   Bakers – 2
   Oven – 5
   Children – as many as you have left!

Music

Materials The song below

Wonderful Weather

1 In windy weather
When we're out together,
We can shout 'Hip, hip, hurray!'
As our kite soars high
In the blue, blue sky,
It's such fun to run about and play.
And if it's snowing
To the hills we're going
To see winter's white display.
As we sledge and slide,
With our friends we ride,
We're as merry as the month of May.

2 And if it's raining,
Then we're not complaining,
We can still feel bright and gay,
As we jump and splash,
Through the rain we dash,
With our friends, we're singing all the way.
And if it's sunny,
Then we don't need money,
To enjoy the world around.
If we look with care,
There's so much to share,
And true happiness with friends is found.

Words and music: from the Scunthorpe & District Teacher's Centre Book, 'Foundations and Music 5–7: Religious Education'

MOTHER'S DAY

MOTHER'S DAY

7.00 a.m.	
8.00 a.m.	
9.00 a.m.	
10.00 a.m.	
11.00 a.m.	
12.00 a.m.	
1.00 p.m.	
2.00 p.m.	
3.00 p.m.	
4.00 p.m.	
5.00 p.m.	
6.00 p.m.	

WIND

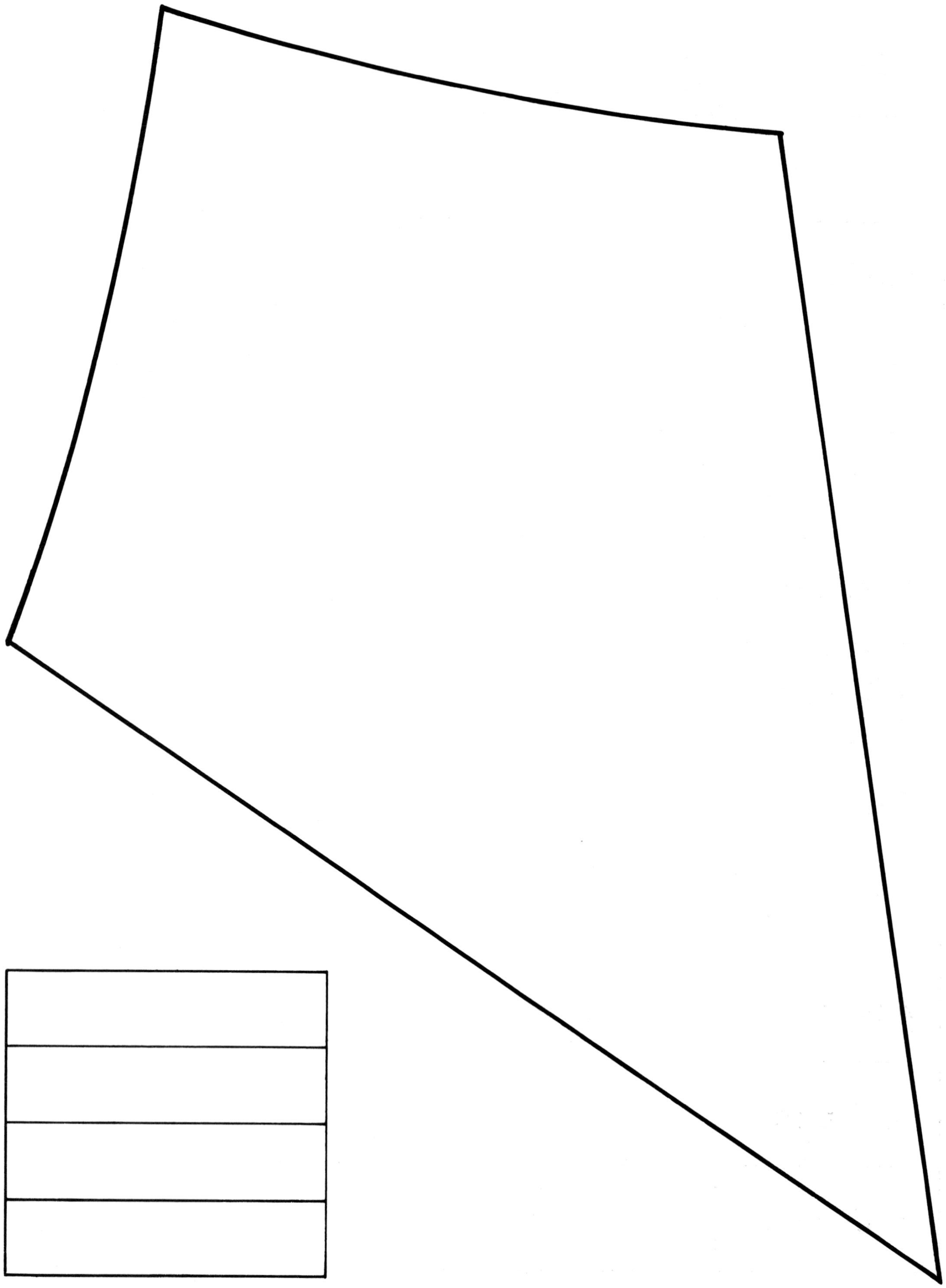

WIND

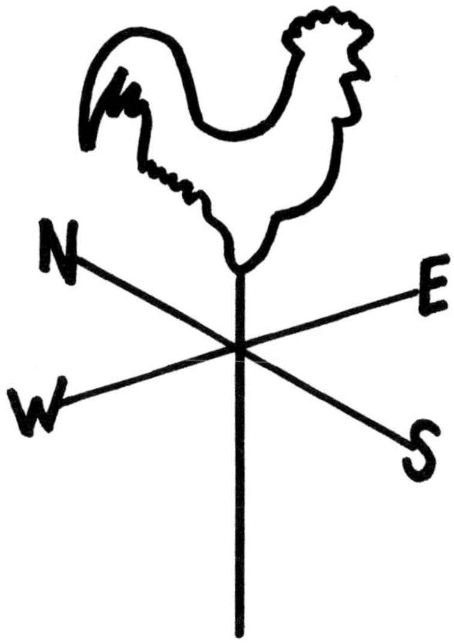

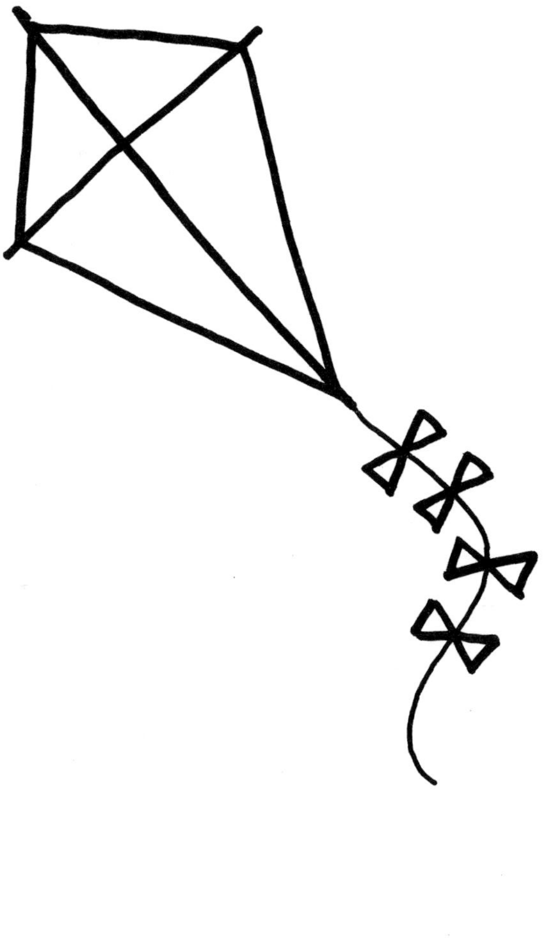

4 APRIL

FESTIVALS

There are festivals throughout the year, many of which have religious 'roots'. Whatever the festival or religion there are many common points: people are happy to celebrate by wearing special clothes, eating special food, exchanging gifts and cards, and generally sharing together in some way.

Easter, the Christian festival, celebrates the Resurrection of Jesus Christ from the dead. It is a difficult festival to explain to children, but they are more than happy to accept Easter Eggs.

Hanukkah is the Jewish festival of Light, which is celebrated over eight days. The story dates back many years B.C. As with the Easter festival there is special food to eat, and cards and gifts are exchanged.

The Hindu festival for the new year is called Divali, which means 'row of lights'. Every home is decorated with little lamps, and patterns made with sand or coloured rice decorate the doorsteps to welcome Lakshi, the goddess of wealth.

The Muslims celebrate Id al Fitr at the end of the month of Ramadan (a time of fasting). It is a day when everyone gets up, bathes and puts on new clothes. They go to the Mosque to pray and afterwards there is a celebration meal and the children receive gifts and sweets.

There may be children in the class of other religions, or who come from a part of the world that has a special festival time. Use their ideas to supplement the ones in this section.

Suggested Reading

Feasts and Festivals
by J. Rhodes and C. Storr (Patrick Hardy Books)

YOUNGER CHILDREN

Written Work and Language

Materials Card, scissors, crayons, pencils

Method

1. For Christians, Easter is a very important time. Following the death of Jesus on Good Friday comes the celebration of Easter Sunday, when he came alive again. Everyone is happy and churches are decorated with flowers to celebrate. Easter Eggs are given as a symbol of this new life.
2. To make a card to send to someone at Easter, use the symbol of the egg. It is an easy shape for the children to draw and can be decorated simply. Remind the class that eggs were not always chocolate; in years gone by children would decorate the hard boiled variety.
3. Write an appropriate greeting on the inside.

Number

Materials Mastercopy 4.1

Method

1. Use the Mastercopy for counting and colouring. Tell the class a little about each festival as they are working.
2. The bottom part of the page is for them to think of other things that they associate with festivals, e.g.:
   Christmas trees
   fireworks
   pancakes

Artwork

Materials Mastercopy 4.2, crayons

Method

1. Here is a pattern similar to the ones that Hindu women make out of coloured rice or sand. In this country the weather is not always good enough to allow them to make the patterns on the doorstep so they can be made inside.

Bodywork

Materials A large space, percussion instruments if possible

Method

1. A festival is a time to celebrate. We do it with our friends and families and it is a time when we sing favourite songs and dance.
2. Here are some songs and dances to do with the class; see what they can come up with too. As long as they are happy songs they don't necessarily need to be associated with any particular festival.

'Girls and Boys Come Out to play' – skipping leader chooses another to join him and then another, etc., so forming a dancing line.
'Hokey Cokey' – always popular if you are feeling energetic and don't mind the noise!
'Here We Go Round the Mulberry Bush' – an easy circle dance that can have the verse words changed to make them fit in.

Music

Materials Drums and shakers, tambourines

Method

1. Practise these rhythms: skipping, walking, lilting.
2. If they can move and play let them do so, if not take turns by dividing the class, so that they can see the difference in rhythms.
3. Make up an excuse for a class festival:
   the end of term?
   a birthday?
   1st day of the month?
   and have a celebratory procession. Start off working on a 'Follow My Leader' principle.
4. Do the rhythms remind the children of any songs they know? e.g.
   If You're Happy', *Apusskidu* (A & C. Black)
   'Stand up, clap hands, shout thank you Lord', *Someone's Singing Lord* (A & C. Black)

OLDER CHILDREN

Written Work and Language

Materials Paper and pencils

Method

1. The story of Hanukkah goes back to a time when the Seleucid Greeks ruled over Palestine and tried to make the Jews worship their gods. The Jews fought the Greeks, but found that their temple had been defiled. They had to repurify it but then discovered that the Eternal Lamp was about to go out for the lack of the right oil. There was only enough to last for one day and the journey to get more would take eight days in total. By a miracle the Eternal Lamp kept burning until the oil was brought eight days later. This is where the tradition of lighting candles on each of the eight days of Hanukkah comes from. Nowadays, there are parties on each day with specially prepared food to eat. There are Potato Latkes, which are little fried cakes, Nut Crescent Biscuits and Cheese Blintzes, which are small pancakes.
2. There are other times when we celebrate with special food, from your own birthday, to weddings, or Christmas, Divali and Id al Fitr. Can the class think of any more and describe the food that goes with them?
3. Which festival food would they like to eat most? Is it a festival they know or is it one that they have heard about?

Number

Materials Mastercopy 4.1. crayons

Method

1. Colour in the Mastercopy.
2. Use the Mastercopy orally as a class activity for subtraction skills. The teacher gives the number to be subtracted each time.
3. A variation on this is to divide the class into teams and see which team can get the most correct answers out of a given number of questions.

Artwork

Materials Eggs, cold water dye in red and blue. Scraps of cotton material, string, onion skin

Method

1. To make Marbled Eggs. Pierce the tops of the dye tins and sprinkle a little of each colour at either end. Wrap a piece of onion skin around the egg and then make it into a parcel with the cotton.
2. Tie up the parcel with the string.
3. Place the eggs in boiling water for 10–15 minutes.
4. Cool, unwrap and admire your handiwork! The marbled effect is most attractive and can be improved by rubbing with a little cooking oil.

Extension

Materials Mastercopy 4.1 (use as for Younger Children)

Bodywork

Materials As for Younger Children

Method

1. Remind the children of the parades that happen at Mardi Gras in New Orleans where everyone turns out in masks and fancy dress to celebrate before the fast of Lent begins.
2. If no musical instruments are available, use the song on p. 83, 'The People Band', to help with the festival atmosphere.

Music

Materials See if the class can learn this song for Hanukkah.

Hanukkah

Hanukkah, Hanukkah,
Festival of light.
Candles burn, tops spin round,
Time of great delight.
Hanukkah, Hanukkah,
Let us dance and sing.
Candles burn, guests come in,
Presents they will bring.
Words and music: Jewish folk song

ANIMALS

Some children will have pet animals at home, some schools will have animals that are cared for by the children. Springtime is when we think of young animals which always appeal to young children. There seems to be an instant appreciation of their size and newness.

There is a wealth of nursery rhymes and songs about every animal under the sun, be they real or imaginary. This topic could last for weeks!

Suggested Reading

There's no such thing as a Dragon by Jack Kent (Abelard-Schuman Ltd)

The Enormous Crocodile by Roald Dahl (Puffin)

A.B.C. by Brian Wildsmith (Oxford University Press)

YOUNGER CHILDREN

Written Work and Language

Materials Mastercopy 4.3, as many nursery rhymes and songs as you can remember

Method

1. Animals can live mainly on land, mainly in water, or mainly in the air. Look at the Mastercopy and let the class name each animal and categorise them.
2. Find the nursery rhymes that are associated with the animals:

LAND	WATER	AIR
Three Blind Mice	Five Little Speckled Frogs	Sing a Song of Sixpence
Hey Diddle Diddle	Five Little Ducks (went swimming)	Ladybird, Ladybird
I love Little Pussy	Crocodile Song (see Mastercopy 4.4)	
Baa Baa Black Sheep		
Little Miss Muffet		

3. A poem to learn quickly!

The Octopus

Tell me, O Octopus I begs
Is those arms, or is they legs?
I marvel at thee, Octopus;
If I were thou, I'd call me
Us.

Ogden Nash

Extension

Materials Mastercopy 4.3 each

Method

Play Twenty Questions and see if they can correctly identify each animal.

1. This animal is very small, has whiskers, a long tail and can be a pet.
2. This animal lives in water and has a speckled skin and webbed feet.
3. This animal has two legs, two wings and a yellow beak.
4. This animal has fur, whiskers, a long tail and purrs.
5. This animal has four short legs, is long and low and has a big snappy mouth.
6. This animal is tiny, has wings and black spots.
7. This animal has four legs, chews grass and gives us milk.
8. This animal has no legs, but it does have a tail, two eyes and scales.
9. This animal has two feet with claws, two bright eyes, a big beak and lots of colour.
10. This animal has a tail that can wag, legs that like walking and a cold nose.
11. This animal has a useful coat, four legs, a short tail and lives outside.
12. This animal is huge, has flapping ears and a very funny nose.
13. This animal loves the water and has eight legs, or are they arms?
14. This animal is small, but can sometimes talk as it sits on its perch.
15. This animal has hands and feet and a tail that can be used as either, when it comes to hanging on.
16. This animal has two wings and two webbed feet and likes to live near water.
17. This animal has wings, too, and loves the water, in fact it has a watery name.
18. This animal has four large paws, a big lumbering body and growls.
19. This animal hops along at great speed and uses its tail to balance.
20. This animal has lots of legs and can spin a trap to catch its tea.

Number

Materials Mastercopy 4.3 cut out, and hoops to put on the floor

Method

1. Cut out the animals and get the children to group them into sets:
   Land
   Sea
   Water
   Air
   Some may be part of two sets!

Extension

Materials Mastercopy 4.3

Method

1. Play 'How many legs?'
2. How many have 2 legs
   4 legs
   6 legs
   8 legs?
3. Practise counting ×2, ×4.

Artwork

Materials Paints and paper

Method

1. Not all animals need be real. Can they paint an imaginary animal? How many heads should it have, or arms, or legs, etc?

Bodywork

Materials A large space

Method

1. Think how different animals move:
   Rabbit – bunny jumps, low and crouched
   Elephant – side to side, heavy and swinging
   Sheep – small steps hither and thither
   Kangaroo – big bounding jumps
   Snake – sinuous gliding and sliding

Music

Materials Mastercopy 4.4, the 'Crocodile' song to learn with activities

Extension

Method

1. Animal noises. Ask the children to imitate the following animal noises. Then let them decide whether they are high/low, or loud/soft. Which noises do they like/dislike?
   moo
   miaou
   twitter
   buzz
   growl
   splash
   purr
2. The song 'Old MacDonald' could end the session.

OLDER CHILDREN

Written Work and Language

Materials Mastercopy 4.3, dictionaries if possible

Method

1. Name the animals and then put them into alphabetical order.
2. Some animals have special names for their young. See if the children know, or can find out the correct names for the ones on the Mastercopy.

Extension

Materials Pencils, paper, crayons, scissors, glue

Method

1. Some animals make good pets, others are unsuitable. Ask if any of the children have pets at home. Let them tell the class how they have to be cared for (food, grooming, exercise).
2. What would happen if you took an unusual pet home? Choose an unlikely animal from the Mastercopy, cut it out and then write what your family said when you got it home.
3. If the activity is a success, it could always be the start point for some impromptu drama work.

Number

Materials Mastercopy 4.3, either one large piece of paper marked out (see diagram), or children could rule out their own

Method

1. Practise categorising skills.

Land	Air	Water

Extension

Materials Mastercopy 4.3, scissors, pencils

Method

1. Count the number of legs of the animals. Cut them out and group accordingly (2, 4, 6, 8,).
2. Use for multiplication:

Long form	4 + 4 + 4 + 4
Short form	4 lots of 2
Sign	2 × 2

Artwork

Materials Cardboard boxes, paint, paper, scissors, a sheet or some sort of drape

Method

1. Dragons. This month sees St George's Day. Do the children know the story of St George and the Dragon? They might know about Welsh Dragons or the Chinese Dragons that are made to celebrate the Chinese New Year. Whichever, let them create their own type from the amassed collection of boxes.
2. When the head is made, the body can be created by a chain of children covered with the sheet.
3. The Dragon can be the centre of the Bodywork production.

Bodywork

Materials The story below, a large space

The Dragon

A long time ago, in a land far away, a strange adventure took place.

It was a happy land, with mountains and trees, sunshine and flowers. The people worked hard to earn a living from the land to feed their families. They had a good King. He had a beautiful daughter. The King loved and looked after his people, and they in their turn loved him.

There was only one thing to spoil all this. High on the mountain, in a big dark cave there lived a Dragon. A hungry Dragon!

The people were terrified of the Dragon. The only thing that kept him away from the village was to feed him.

This was all right until all the sheep had been eaten up. Then the people became sad. They didn't want to work. The children didn't dance. They were all miserable. Only the Dragon was happy. And still hungry!

The people wanted to know what to feed the Dragon, so they went to the King. The only thing left to do was to choose one of themselves to be offered to the Dragon to eat. The King said they should all draw lots. To the King's horror, when the lots were drawn it was his daughter who was chosen to be the Dragon's next meal. The King was sad, but he let the guards take the Princess up the mountainside.

As she sat there, terrified, a young man rode up. When he found out why she was there he said that he would save her!

George called to the Dragon. The Dragon came out of his cave. He was hungry. Immediately George challenged him to a fight. The fight was terrible, but in the end George triumphed. He took the Princess home and the King shook him by the hand and declared a Holiday for everyone.

Method

1. A suggested cast list:

King	6 children to be playing
Princess	4 ladies to be wives and mothers
George	6 inside the Dragon!
3 guards	1 narrator
4 men to work in the fields	musicians

2. Use the song in the Music section to break up the story into parts. It is not necessary to sing it verse by verse. The chorus can be used every time the Dragon makes an appearance.

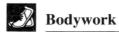

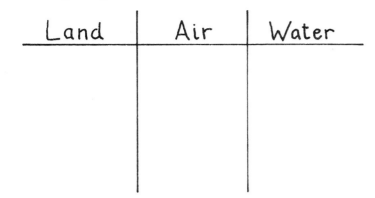

3. The children can make up their own words to add to the basic script.
4. If the class really enjoy acting and you end up short of musicians, see if any other class can join in and help with the accompaniment.

Music

Materials The song (see below), percussion instruments, chime bars, rattles

Method

1. Having read the story (Bodywork), make up a musical accompaniment.
2. Learn the song!

Maggon, the bad-tempered dragon

1 Once there was a dragon,
A bad-tempered dragon,
Maggon the Dragon
Was his name.
Lived inside a cavern
On top of a mountain;
People could see
His smoke and flames.

Chorus: Maggon the Dragon,
The bad-tempered dragon,
Liked eating cows
And bulls and sheep,
And all through the
daytime,
He had such a gay time,
But when night-time came
Couldn't sleep.

2. Spiky back and long tail,
A body of green scales,
Maggon had such
An appetite.
And when he felt hungry
He roared down the valley,
Swallowed the cattle
With one bite.

Words and music: Peter Canwell

Mastercopy 4:1

FESTIVALS

How many lights are to be lit for Divali?

This is a special candle holder for Hanukkah.
How many candles are lit?
The extra light is the serving candle.

How many Easter Eggs are there?

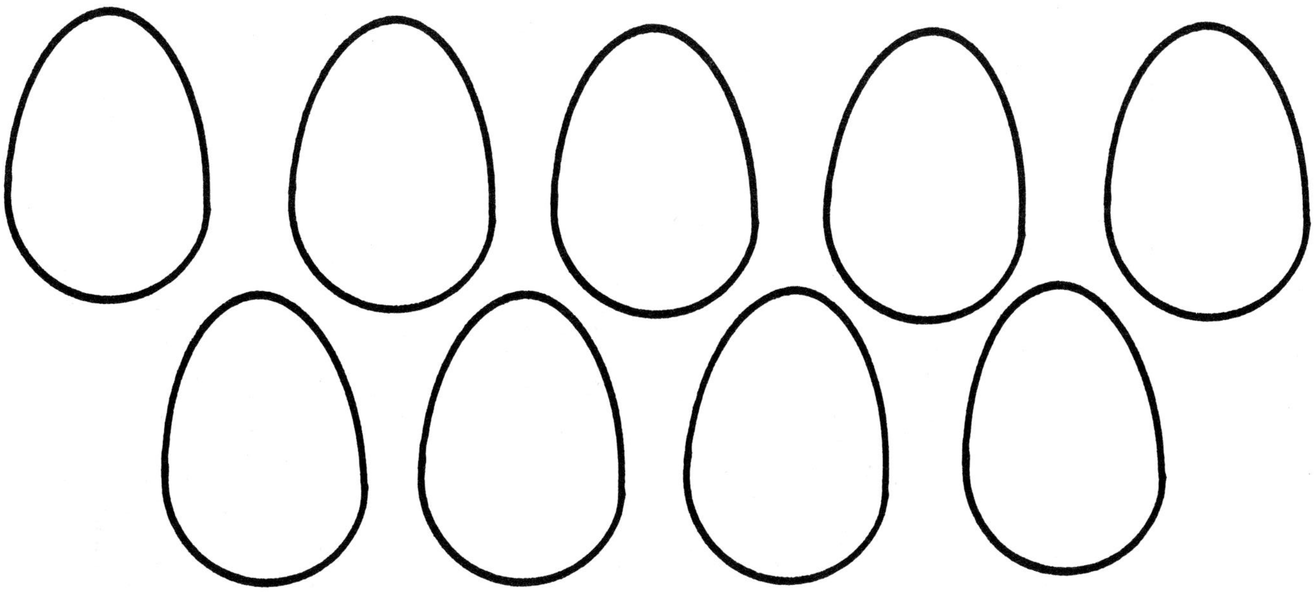

Decorate the Easter Eggs for your friends.

ANIMALS

ANIMALS

Motions:

She sailed away . . . crocodile – palm on back of other hand, thumbs extended and moving with a rowing motion
"You see," said she – point and shake finger
"He's as tame as tame can be" – pet back of hand
"I'll ride him down the Nile" – same as line 1
The croc winked his eye – point to eye and wink
Bade them all good-bye – wave
Wearing a happy smile – fingers to mouth, push up corners
End of the ride – same as line 1
Lady was inside – pat tummy
Smile was on the crocodile – fingers to mouth, push up corners

5 MAY

MAY DAY

May Day is traditionally celebrated with dances around the Maypole, choosing a May Queen, and celebrating with a holiday whilst looking forward to the summer.

Some May Day traditions are very ancient, and people are not sure of their origins. It is said that May Day Eve is the time when the doors between the land of Fairies and of Mortals are open!

In Britain on May Day morning, Morris Dancers put on displays of dancing. They often have a 'hobby horse' dancing with them, and they wear special clothes with bells and ribbons attached. It doesn't matter that we do not really know all the histories behind the customs, it is all part of the festival.

YOUNGER CHILDREN

Written Work and Language

Materials The story below, Mastercopy 5.1

Method.

1. Read the story to the class.

Queen of the May

'The First of May is May Day,' said wise old Daddy-long-legs. 'On that day we insects choose the prettiest of us all to be our May Queen.'

'I don't suppose I shall be chosen, do you?' asked Katie. She was a very plain green caterpillar – not even one of those fine furry ones with orange stripes.

'No, I'm afraid not,' said Daddy-long-legs, kindly. 'Never mind, you will be able to watch the May Queen being crowned. Everyone will be there to throw petals at her as she passes by.'

Katie was very sad as she went to bed that night. 'How lucky some creatures are to be born beautiful,' she thought, as she tucked herself up in her cosy cocoon and went to sleep. Katie did not know how long she had slept, but when she awoke, the warm sun was shining on her cocoon. She nibbled her way through and struggled out into the sunshine.

As she sat sunning herself on a flower, she felt different. She wriggled her shoulders and discovered that she had grown wings – beautiful green and blue wings!

'Why, how did I get these?' she asked herself. But she did not have time to find out because, just then, she heard chattering and laughter. Suddenly Katie was surrounded by a crowd of excited insects shouting: 'Here is the most beautiful of us all! Let us crown her Queen of the May!'

Someone put a crown of petals on her head and lifted her off her feet. Katie was flying! And all around her petals were falling. It was the most exciting day of her life.

Later that day, tired but happy, Katie remembered that her mother had told her she would turn into a butterfly one day.

'So some creatures are not born beautiful, but they GROW beautiful instead!' she sighed as she went off to sleep.

K. Jackson

2. Help the children to tell the story using the three-part Mastercopy to help.

Number

Materials Mastercopy 5.2, pencils, crayons.

Method

1. Look carefully at the Mastercopy and then answer the questions.
2. Look at the children; how many ribbons will they need to dance with?
3. Colour the girls' ribbons yellow and the boys' ribbons blue.
4. How many does each group have? (girls/boys)

Extension

Materials Coloured wool, scissors

Method

1. Help the children learn how to plait. In pairs give each pair a length of wool. First, they must divide the wool into three equal lengths.
2. With one child holding the three pieces, show the others how to plait. If there is time let them swap over half way through. It can help to knot one end – this is best done by the teacher!

Artwork

Materials Strips of card, pasta shapes (bows and twizzles are best), gold/silver spray, P.V.A. adhesive

Method

1. Cut the strips to fit round each child's head. They are going to make their own May Crown. Glue or secure the card, then put it on newspaper.
2. This part is messy, but is worth it! Let them make a pattern with the pasta shapes, glueing the shapes on to the card. Do not dilute the glue. As the glue dries clear it doesn't matter if it looks a little untidy.
3. When the glue has dried, spray the crown with gold or silver.

Bodywork

Materials A large space, cheerful music or songs

Method

1. Practise skipping and galloping.
2. Divide the class into partners. Line them up so that the partners face each other in two lines about two metres apart.
3. Dance pattern: All do 4 skips towards partner, 4 skips back. Pair at one end skip together, hold hands, gallop up the centre aisle. At the other end they separate and gallop outside the children back to their places. Next pair set off in the same way, but must go the full length of the outside line and return to their places up the middle of the aisle.

Music

Materials Songs that you may remember!

Method

1. What do the children think would be appropriate songs to sing to the Queen of the May. How about 'Lavender's Blue Dilly Dilly' for a start?
2. 'Girls and Boys Come Out to Play', would be a good song to sing as you dance around the maypole.

OLDER CHILDREN

Written Work and Language

Materials The 'Queen of the May' (see Younger Children), Mastercopy 5.1, pencils and crayons

Method

1. Read the class the story and talk about it in general. Then see if they can retell the story. Start with one child and then pass the storyline on.
2. As with Younger Children, let them illustrate the story using the Mastercopy.

Extension

Materials Mastercopy 5.2, enough clear plastic folders for one each.

Method

1. Place a copy of the Mastercopy in a plastic folder and allow the children to add the ribbons using Plasticine. They can plait or twist the ribbons, to show the dance in progress.

Number

Materials Mastercopy 5.2, pencils, four coloured crayons

Method

1. How many children are there?
2. Draw each child a partner.
3. How many ribbons will the children need?
4. Give each child four colours. Divide the ribbons so that there is the same number for each colour.
5. How many pairs of legs are there dancing round the maypole?

Artwork

Materials Paper, scissors, coloured wools, glue, old magazines, plastic pots

Method

1. When children dance around the maypole the ribbons make a pattern. This is really like weaving on a grand scale! Using the coloured wools see how many children can plait.

2. If they can plait a good length, it can be used to decorate an old plastic pot by glueing and winding the plaited strip around the outside of the pot.
3. Take a piece of paper and cut vertical slits in it about 4 cm apart. Cut coloured strips of the same width from the old magazines and use these to weave a pattern. By changing the vertical lines to diagonal lines a different effect can be achieved.

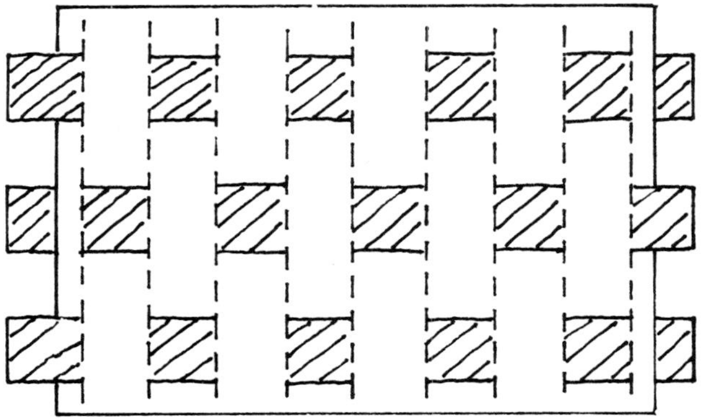

Bodywork

Materials An open space and quite a lot of patience to begin with. Music that you can skip to (country dancing type music is perfect)

Method

1. Practise simple skipping.
2. Teach the children how to do a Grand Chain. Every child has a partner, and stands in one large circle facing that partner. Try the next part walking.
3. Hold *right* hands, then move past your partner towards the next person holding out your *left* hand, this will naturally turn you a little. Keep moving forwards, leaving your original partner behind. Go on moving round the circle, changing hands alternately until you meet your first partner.
4. When you think they have got the hang of it, try the whole thing skipping.
5. Then try a variation. Skip the chain for eight counts. Stay with the eighth partner and with cross-held hands skip them round for another count of eight. Repeat the pattern.

Extension

Method

1. If they can learn a Grand Chain try teaching them the Gay Gordons!

Music

Materials The song below

May morning

1 Join us on this happy day,
Out in the fields we can play,
Make this a good holiday,
First of the year.

Chorus: Come with a song and a shout,
We shall dance round and about,
Weaving our steps in and out,
On this May morning.

2 Come show us how you can sing.
Join hands and dance in a ring.
We say hello to the spring,
First of the year.

Chorus: Come with a song . . .

Words and music: traditional

SHAPES AND SIZES

Shapes and sizes interest small children. It is always important to know who is 'the biggest', and they like to find things that are smaller than themselves. Tall buildings must seem even taller from their point of view, large lorries appear giantlike. In contrast they will watch ants crawling around for ages, fascinated by their movements as well as their size.

This is a poem I particularly like as it combines size and shape in natural forms and introduces the mathematical ideas at the same time.

Shapes

Everything comes in different shapes
People and noses and bunches of grapes
Bugs and machinery, mountains and tyres
Vegetables, trees and smoke from fires.

Hexagons, triangles, rhombuses and rings
Rectangles and spirals make interesting things
Shapes that are square and shapes that are round
Shadows make shapes upon the ground.

Shapes that are long and shapes that are thin
Water's the shape of the thing that it's in
Shapes all around us up high and down low
Shapes that go fast and shapes that go slow.

Shapes on their own and shapes fitted together
Shapes that are made by people and weather,
Shapes all around us so many to see
But the best shape of all are my family and me.

Evelyn Davidson

Suggested Reading

Jenny's Baby Brother
by Peter Smith (Fontana Picture Lions)

YOUNGER CHILDREN

Written Work and Language

Materials Paper, pencils, crayons

Method

1. Read the poem as it gives a good starting point. Move the discussion to their shape. Compare the differences between the children in the class so that they become aware of height, length of hair, limbs, size of tummies, noses, eye colour, etc.
2. Ask several children to describe the people in their family group. Remember not all will have two parents, so suggest Grans and Grandads too. Who is the tallest in their family? Who is the fattest? etc.
3. Ask them to draw a picture of another child in the class. Make sure they draw what they have talked about!

Extension

1. Look at the pictures, see if they can recognise each other. Ask them how they think they will change in size and shape as they grow up. Will they be as tall as their Mummy? Do they think they will have bigger feet than their sister? etc.
2. Draw a comparison picture: 'How I will look when I am grown up'.

Number

Materials Paper, pencils, scissors, crayons, glue

Method

1. Read the poem 'Shapes' again and help the children find the plane shapes in the word pictures: e.g.:
   circles = grapes, tyres
   square = machinery
   triangle = mountains, noses
   rectangle = tree trunks
   Be ready to help with sketches and imagination!
2. Help the children to reproduce one or two of the shape things. Cut them out and regroup together in the appropriate set.

Extension

Materials Precut shapes for hexagon, rhombus, drawn spiral in a circle, cut rectangular strips

Method

1. Look at the shapes the children might not know. Explain by showing what you have prepared. Notice the curved and straight edges. How do they compare to the shapes that are easily recognised?
2. Divide the children into groups with each group having a different shape(s) and task:
   a. Hexagons and rhombus shapes to be coloured and made into patterns.
   b. Spirals lightly coloured, cut out and hung (or kept for artwork – see below).
   c. Colour rectangles and then turn them into rings!

Artwork

Materials
Black paper, pencils, scissors, Mastercopy 5.3

Method

1. Talk about shadows; if possible find shadows in the classroom or take them outside to see their own.
2. Show the shadow shapes on Mastercopy 5.3. Identify each shape.
3. Let the children cut out the shadow shapes, then draw the real things to match. Stick the shadow on to the picture in the right place.

Extension

1. Use the spirals made in Number Work. Cut out the cat from the Mastercopy and add the curly tail. Then hang from the ceiling.

Bodywork

Method

1. Remember the rhyme:
   Tall as a house
   Small as a mouse
   Thin as a pin
   Wide as a gate
   Children love to learn and chant this while doing the appropriate movements.
2. To practise simple skills, use individual lines of the poem to punctuate, e.g. walking normally, then stop with thin as a pin, continue with another activity, jumping, then stop with small as a mouse, change activity to hopping, etc.

Extension

Materials Tapes with popular music the children might know

Method

1. Take the lines from the poem:
   Shapes all around us up high and down low
   Shapes that go fast and shapes that go slow
   Practise the movements literally in a sequence. Do this as a class activity 'Follow the Leader', with you as leader. Music always helps this sort of thing!
2. Once the children are confident about the sequence let them work in small groups or pairs alternating who is the leader. Let them watch each other – half the class doing the motions, the other half watching.
3. Choose two or three pairs and get the rest to copy their shape movements.

Music

Materials Any of these that are available: drums, tambourines, triangles, blocks, beaters, bells; crayons and paper

Method

1. Start by asking the class to listen carefully to the sound each instrument makes. Is it a loud or soft sound? Is it a long or short sound?
2. Once sounds have been satisfactorily described let some children play while you and the others experiment with the sort of shapes that come to mind when each sound is made. Use crayons!
   e.g.

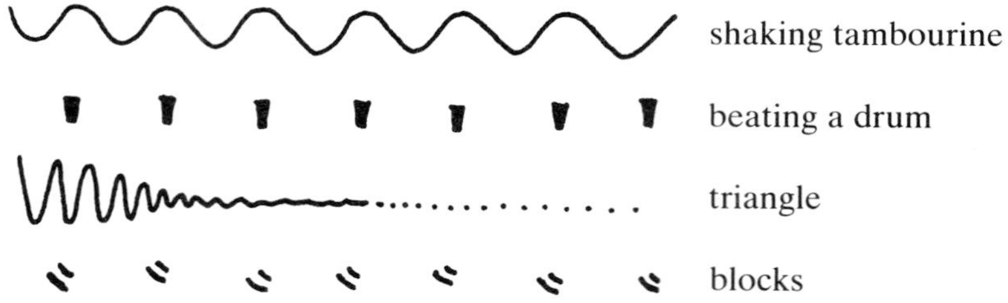

3. Change players and see if the instruments can make different sounds.

Extension

Materials As above

Method

1. After practising making sounds and agreeing which ones are the most

preferred, choose nursery rhymes that are simple to sing and work out the accompaniment, e.g.:

Three Blind Mice

Three blind mice, Three blind mice,
See how they run, See how they run.
They all ran after the farmer's wife,
Who cut off their tails with a carving knife.
Did you ever see such a thing in your life,
As three blind mice?

2. See if the children can write it down.

OLDER CHILDREN

Written Work and Language

Materials Paper, pencils

Method

1. Read the shapes poem on p. 59 with the children. Has the author chosen shapes that interest her, or shapes that she likes, or both? Can they picture the shapes in the poem? What does she mean 'shapes that go fast and shapes that go slow'?

   Once the children are thinking about what the poem is describing, ask them if they can think of things that have a special shape. Do they have a special mug or glass at home that they really like to use? Is there a doll or a toy they like to look at or hold? Have they got a cuddly soft toy – is it the same shape as when it was new? Some things become special because of their shape. See if they can draw that special shaped thing and comment on it.

Extension

Materials Mastercopy 5.3, black paper, scissors

Method

1. Show them the shapes on the Mastercopy. These are really shadow shapes. Some shadows are frightening. Are any of those shown frightening? Could they become frightening? (The witch's cat, the haunted house?)
2. The shapes of some insects and animals terrify some people and it is not always their size that matters – those long-legged hairy spiders spring to mind! Make a collage of drawn and cut-out nasty shapes.

Number

Materials Mastercopy 5.4

Method

1. A and B are self explanatory. Use C then let the children find something the same size, larger (but portable!) and smaller than their hand. Get them to notice the shape of their hand compared to the chosen object.
2. Cut out their hand shape and make a graph to show who has the largest and smallest. This is interesting as it is not always the one you expect with the largest hands.

Extension

Materials Mastercopy 6.4

Method

1. Use the Mastercopy to practise making shapes. Decide which ones are possible. This means a discussion of straight and curved edges beforehand.

Extension

Materials Mastercopy 6.4

Method

1. Play the Square Game. In pairs let them take turns to draw a straight line that only joins at two points. They must be horizontal or vertical. Every time a player completes a square he can put his initial in it. The winner is the player with the most squares.

Artwork

Materials Plasticine, size and shape words written on pieces of paper to help with spelling

Method

1. Words have shapes. The shape is made of letters. Let the children experiment with making letters and words out of Plasticine.

2. Demonstrate how the word shape can sometimes be made to look like the meaning.
3. If you are feeling adventurous, paint can be applied to the Plasticine words and used to print with. Press clean paper on top – the word is reversed, another topic of conversation!

Bodywork

Materials See the poem below

Jack-in-a-Box

Jack-in-a-box
Is a funny old man
He hides in his box
As small as he can.

He hides in his box
As small as he can
Then suddenly out
he jumps.
Up! Down! Up! Down!
Funny Jack-in-a-box.

Method

1. Use this as a base for work. Take a simple storyline which the children will be familiar with and can work towards, e.g. A Party.

The Birthday Party

a. Guests arrive for party
b. Lots of presents to unwrap
c. One last mystery present (shape)
d. Unwrapping the parcel
e. Surprise!
f. Who sent the present?

2. The story can be mimed, spoken or a combination of speech and movement. Practise individual movements:
   a. Skipping and galloping in a circle = party guests
   b. Crouching down and springing up = Jack
   c. Stretching up and reaching out and over = box and wrapping paper
3. Build up the story, letting the children play all the parts. Include shapes in the activity. The guests can skip and sing in circles and spirals, make the box a square shape, etc.

Music

Method

1. Songs can have shapes too. 'Here we go round the Mulberry Bush', sung and skipped in a circle. Change the words to fit in with the theme:
   This is the way we crouch down small . . .
   This is the way we stand up straight . . .
   This is the way we twist around . . .
2. Other songs are called rounds. How about trying:
   'London's Burning'
   'Frère Jacques' or even . . .
   Pink Parasol
   'I left my pink parasol on the upper deck of a Hammersmith bus
   Oh bother! Oh bother!'

MAY DAY

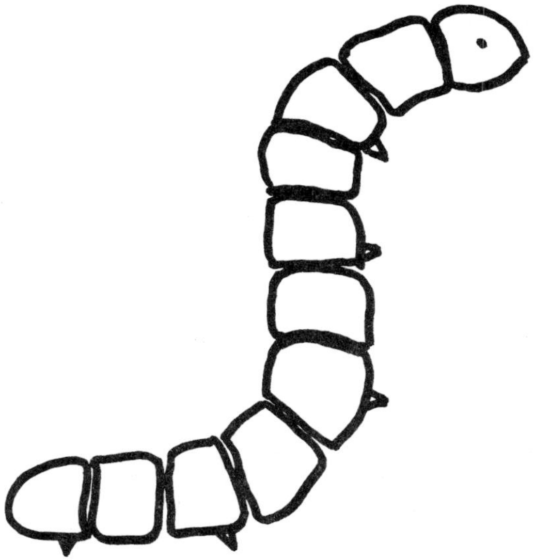

YOU MAY PHOTOCOPY THIS PAGE

MAY DAY

SIZES & SHAPES

Mastercopy 5:4

SIZES & SHAPES

Ⓐ

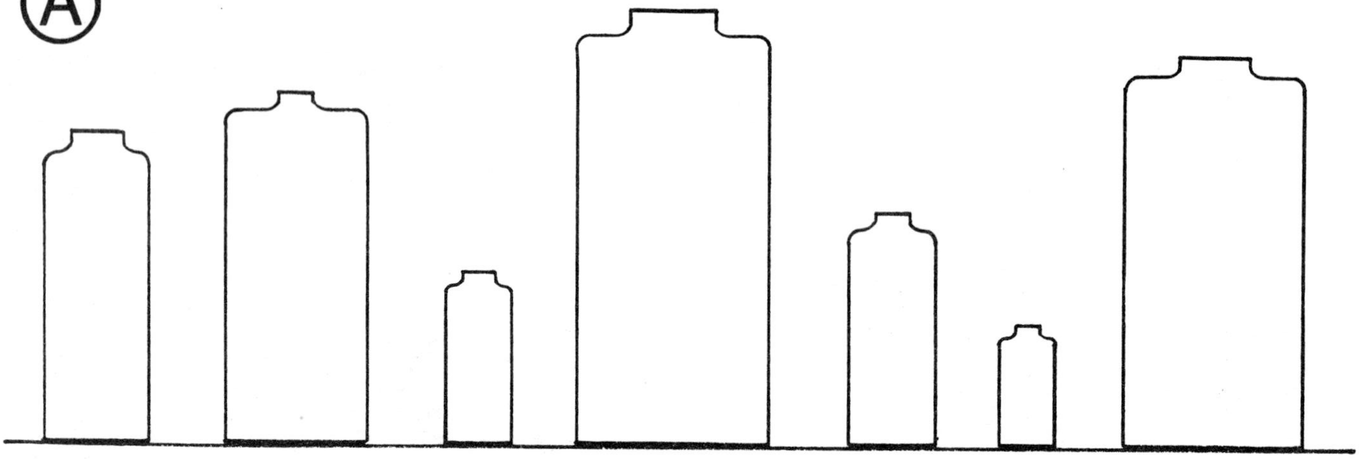

Are all the jars the same shape?
Number the jars in order of size.
Number 1 should be the largest.

Ⓑ

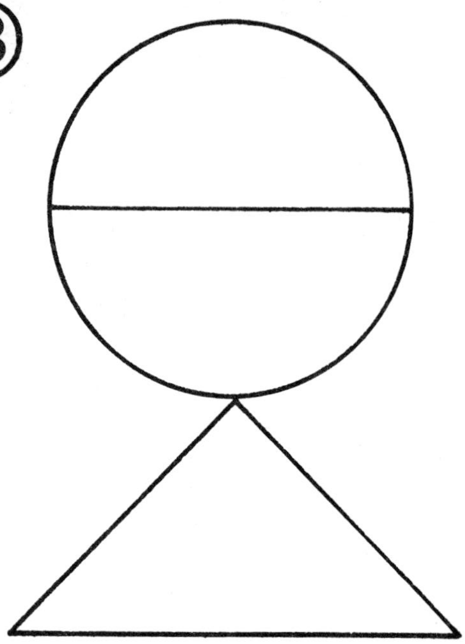

How many shapes are there?
Name the shapes with curved edges.
Name the shapes with straight edges.
What else can you make using these shapes?

Ⓒ Draw round your hand.

6 JUNE

BIRTHDAYS

Everybody has a birthday, and for children they are very important milestones. There are many ways of celebrating birthdays, but the basics remain the same, with cards, presents and a special cake. Sometimes if children's birthdays fall in school time there are greetings and a song in the class.

A birthday party is always an exciting event, whether it is celebrated within the family or by asking friends to join in the fun. Nowadays, children decide to do other things on their birthdays – a trip somewhere, a visit to a cinema or theatre, a meal in a favourite restaurant or snack bar. One thing is for sure, children love that one special day that is *their* birthday.

YOUNGER CHILDREN

Written Work and Language

Materials The poem below, strips of paper with a day of the week written on each, crayons, glue

Method

Monday's Child

Monday's child is fair of face
Tuesday's child is full of grace
Wednesday's child is full of woe
Thursday's child has far to go
Friday's child is loving and giving
Saturday's child works hard for a living
But the child that is born on the Sabbath day
Is bonny and blythe and good and gay.

Traditional

1. First check to see if they know the date and month of their birthday (class register to check). See if they can find out on which day they were born.
2. Recite the poem with the children and explain any of the words that they do not understand.
3. Talk about what sort of people, or type of skills people might have if that rhyme were true.
4. Let the children choose a piece of paper (unseen) and see which day they have picked. They can stick that to the top of their page, and draw the appropriate child, and write the correct line from the rhyme underneath.

Number

Materials Mastercopy 6.1, pencils

Method
1. Self-explanatory

Extension

Materials Large squared paper

Method
1. A birthday block graph is always quick to make and the children enjoy the results

Extension

Materials Children who are five!

Method
1. As most children are five years old on entering their school or during the first year, gather them together to practise counting in fives.

Artwork

Materials Mastercopy 6.2 as plan, card is best for making up

Method
1. Instead of making a birthday card for someone make them a birthday box.

Bodywork

Materials Taped dancing music

Method

1. Think of all the birthday party games you can and have an instant party.
   Musical Statues (set shape in advance)
   Musical Bumps
   Pass the Parcel (execute a basic skill, instead of unwrapping something)
   'Simon Says'

Music

Materials The song below

For He's A Jolly Good Fellow
For he's a jolly good fellow,
For he's a jolly good fellow,
For he's a jolly good fellow,
And so say all of us!
And so say all of us!
And so say all of us!
For he's a jolly good fellow,
For he's a jolly good fellow,
For he's a jolly good fellow,
And so say all of us!

Method

1. Teach them the song. See if they have a special school song to sing on birthdays. It might be this one:

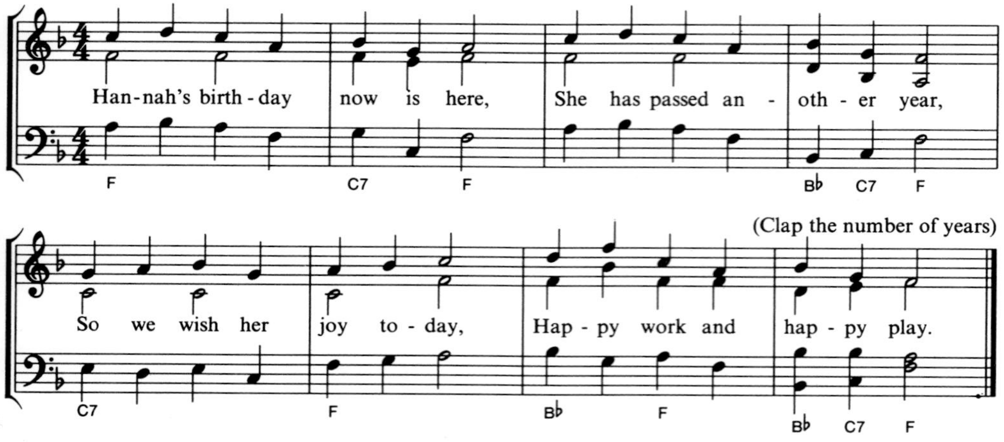

Written Work and Language

Materials The poem below

The End

When I was One,
I had just begun.

When I was Two,
I was nearly new.

When I was Three,
I was hardly Me.

When I was Four
I was not much more.

When I was Five,
I was just alive.

But now that I'm Six, I'm as clever as clever.
So I think I'll stay Six now for ever and ever.
A. A. Milne

Method
1. This is a much enjoyed poem and I've never met a child who didn't like to learn it. It is also a good starting point for work.
2. At each of the ages mentioned in the poem children achieve different skills. Ask the class what they think they could have done at each age.
   One – clap hands, stand up, say a few words?
   Two – walk a little, feed themselves, say family names?
   Three – walk and run, not need nappies! go to a playgroup?
   Four – walk, run and skip, try to write and read?
   Five – go to school, ride a bike?
   Six – well, the sky's the limit!
3. Ask if any of them have brothers or sisters that they can tell the class about.

Number

Materials Mastercopy 6.1, pencils

Method
1. As Younger Children p. 67.
2. Note that the cake is divided into ten sections. Use for 'sharing' questions – colour the slices. They could even be cut out as a practical activity, e.g.:
   a. If I have six friends to my party and each has a slice of cake, how many slices are left.
   b. How many slices does Mummy need to cut for me. Daddy, my brother and Granny?

Extension

Materials Mastercopy 6.2, glue, crayons

Method
1. Using the Mastercopy make a cube shape.
2. Explore the shape so that these questions can be answered:
   a. How many corners are there?
   b. How many edges?
   c. How many faces?

Artwork

Materials Ladybird and MacDonald books on gem stones if you can get them, paper, pencil, colours

Method
1. Here is a list of Birthday Stones. Use the information to make a colour wheel. The children will be interested to know which stone is their 'birth' stone. They can always find out about their stone and do a drawing of it from any reference books that are available.
   I have given a rough idea of the colour of each stone, it is not definitive!
   January – Garnet – Red
   February – Amethyst – Purple
   March – Aquamarine – Blue/Green
   April – Diamond – White
   May – Emerald – Green
   June – Pearl – White/Pink
   July – Ruby – Red
   August – Sardonyx – Reddish/Brown and White
   September – Sapphire – Blue
   October – Opal – White with Blue/Green flecks
   November – Topaz – Yellow
   December – Turquoise – Sky Blue

Bodywork

Materials An open space!

Method

1. On your birthday you are given three wishes. One can be for something physical (beauty, strength, stature, etc.), the second can be to help someone else, the third can be to give yourself a very special present.
2. Divide the class up into small groups (four or five at most). Give them the outline of the wishes. They may use all of them or only one, but let them work out a short story. Talk about some of the possibilities as a class first.

Music

Materials The song below

Method

1. Everyone has a birthday. It is their own and makes them extra special for that day. Here is a song that can help us to feel special.

I Love the Sun

1 I love the sun,
It shines on me,
God made the sun,
And God made me.

2 I love the stars,
They twinkle on me,
God made the stars,
And God made me.

3 I love the rain,
It splashes on me,
God made the rain,
And God made me.

4. I love the wind,
It blows round me,
God made the wind,
And God made me.

5. I love the birds,
They sing to me,
God made the birds,
And God made me.

Words and music: Gwen F. Smith

TIME

Time can be separated into two parts: the passage of time through years, months, weeks and days; and the telling of time using clocks.

The growing awareness of time passing comes slowly to children; next week could be next year, and a term at school seems an age. It's always good to notice seasonal changes so that the idea of a year passing can be recognised. Christmas, the long Summer holiday, Bonfire Night, and Easter help to anchor certain times within those seasons. Once they go to school children quickly learn the difference between weekdays and weekends!

Telling the time is another matter. Nowadays, children have digital watches as often as regular watches; and with the increase in video recorders attached to televisions, travel timetables and foreign travel, many of them will have become aware of a twenty-four-hour clock in action.

YOUNGER CHILDREN

Written Work and Language

Materials The poems below

Method

1. Learning poetry can often help with learning the order of things.

January falls the snow,
February cold winds blow,
In March peep out the early flowers
And April comes with sunny showers.
In May the roses bloom so gay,
In June the farmers mow their hay,
In July brightly shines the sun,
In August harvest is begun.
September turns the leaves to brown,
October winds then shake them down,
November fills with bleak and smear,
December comes and ends the year.
Traditional

2. What are the seasons? Which months are included in each season? In which season does their birthday fall?

3.

Solomon Grundy
Born on Monday
Christened on Tuesday
Married on Wednesday
Took ill on Thursday
Worse on Friday
Died on Saturday
Buried on Sunday
This is the end
Of Solomon Grundy.
Traditional

Extension

Materials Pre-cut circles, colours, pencils

Method

1. There are four seasons, so help the children to divide the circles into four by folding. A good opportunity to notice 1/2, 1/4, 3/4.
2. Each quarter can be used to illustrate a season, and the appropriate name can be written on the outer edge of the quarter.

Number

Materials Mastercopy 3.2, digital clock, working regular clock

Method

1. Start by getting everyone to remember and recite a well-known rhyme ('Hickory, Dickory, Dock').
2. O'Clock is what we call every hour. As the hands of a clock, or the numbers of a digital clock move, we can see minutes (and sometimes seconds) move. Check the present time on clocks.
3. Use the Mastercopy to see what happens at every o'clock during the school day. Write in the activity for them, noticing a.m. and p.m.

Extension

Materials Mastercopy 6.3, 2 dice

Method

1. Let each child cut out the hands and set them to 12 o'clock.
2. Each child throws the dice and depending on the total number can draw in that o'clock on their own clock face.

3. When they have decided whether it is a.m. or p.m., they can decorate the page with what generally happens at that hour.

Artwork

Materials Poem on the months in Written Work and Language, paint or crayons

Method

1. This is a nice poem to use as an inspiration.

Extension

Materials Paper and paints

Method

1. Remind the children of all the times that time has played an important part in a story or nursery rhyme and let them choose to illustrate one. Tell them to keep it a secret until they have finished it, then everyone can guess the title.

Bodywork

Materials An open space

Method

1. 'What's the Time Mr Wolf?' is a good noisy game. Can you remember the rules?
   a. The wolf stands facing away from the children.
   b. The rest of the class stand at the other end of the hall and chant: 'What's the time Mr Wolf?' The wolf can reply any o'clock time.
   c. The children must move that many steps towards the wolf. The object being to 'tag' the wolf.
   d. However, if the wolf decides to say 'Dinner Time', instead of o'clock, he may turn and run and chase the children. Any that he catches, he can take back with him to his lair.

Music

Materials The song below

Method

1. This is a very simple song to learn, if the children don't know it already. It lends itself to lots of interpretations. The song can be sung in small groups, individual children can sing one day. Several different percussion instruments can be used for counting the days of the week.

Each day different

Chorus: Sunday, Monday, Tuesday, Wednesday;
Thursday, Friday, Saturday, too.
One, two, three, four, five, six, seven days:
Each day diff'rent and ev'ry day new.

1 Wet days, dry days, bright days, cloudy days,
Hot days, cold days, windy days, too.
One, two, three, four, five, six, seven days:
Each day diff'rent and ev'ry day new.
Sunday, Monday, Tuesday, Wednesday . . .

2 High days, low days, sad days, happy days,
Good days, bad days, other days, too.
One, two, three, four, five, six, seven days:
Each day diff'rent and ev'ry day new.
Sunday, Monday, Tuesday, Wednesday . . .

3 Work days, rest days, wash-days, shopping-days,
Birthdays, sports-days, holidays, too.
One, two, three, four, five, six, seven days:
Each day diff'rent and ev'ry day new.
Sunday, Monday, Tuesday, Wednesday . . .

Words and music: Peter Lewis

Chorus and verse
Sun - day, Mon - day, Tues - day, Wed-nes-day,
D A7 D A
Thurs - day, Fri - day, Sat - ur - day, too.
D A7 D A7
One, two, three, four, five, six, sev - en days:
D A7 D A7
Each day diff - 'rent and ev - 'ry day new.
D G A7 D

OLDER CHILDREN

Written Work and Language

Materials The poems below, a globe if possible

Method

1.

In winter I get up at night
And dress by yellow candlelight.
In summer quite the other way,
I have to go to bed by day.

R. L. Stevenson

It's nice to know, when I'm in bed,
That across the world
It's day instead –

And children are having fun,
While it's their turn
To have the sun.

365 Stories

2. Explain simply the rotation of earth and sun (one rotation = one day, 365 = the year). This helps explain the poems. Look and see which countries are the ones to be opposite to us in time.

Extension

Materials General knowledge books, encyclopaedias

Method

1. In the story of the 'Sleeping Beauty', the Princess sleeps for one hundred years before she is awakened by the Prince. Ask the children if they can imagine all the changes that have happened in the last hundred years. Wouldn't the Princess be amazed if she woke up today after sleeping for a hundred years?
2. Make a list of all the obvious things that would be different:
   clothes
   travel
   electrical equipment (TV, video)
   Children can check in resource books to see what people looked like one hundred years ago.
3. If they have thought of inventions, let them check dates in their resource books too. Sometimes it is surprising to see the date.

4. What do you think the Princess would think when she woke up? Would she like the look of her Prince?!

Number

Materials Mastercopy 6.4

Method

1. Numbers on digital clocks and watches look very different from the way children are first taught to write numbers. Show the class how seven-segment display works and let them experiment by making the numbers (four and nine seem to be the trickiest).

Extension

Materials Mastercopy 6.3, pre-cut circle and part circle shapes ($\frac{1}{2}$, $\frac{1}{4}$, $\frac{3}{4}$), 2 dice

Method

1. Go over $\frac{1}{2}$ hour = 30 minutes
   $\frac{1}{4}$ hour = 15 minutes
   $\frac{3}{4}$ hour = 45 minutes
2. Go over $\frac{1}{2}$ past
   $\frac{1}{4}$ past
   $\frac{3}{4}$ past = $\frac{1}{4}$ to
   using the semi-circle and part circle shapes.
3. Teacher chooses the pre-cut shape, children roll the dice to determine the hour, relate to digital time display:
   e.g.

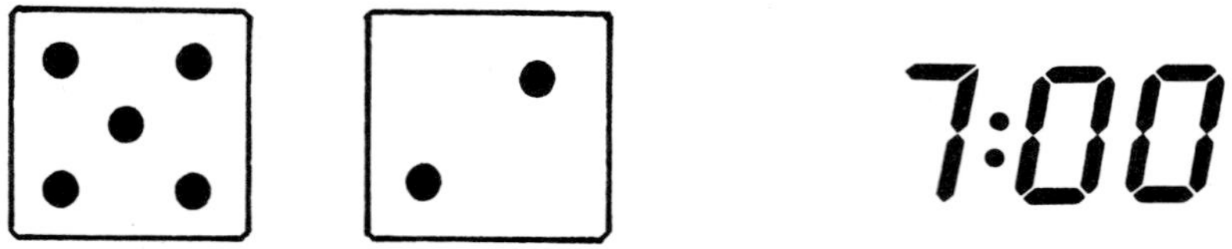

4. If the children are able they can write down the answer after the dice have been rolled before you agree the correct answer.
5. If a standard teaching clock face is available get one of the class to move the hands to the correct time.

Artwork

Materials Mastercopy 6.3, crayons or felt-tip pens

Method

1. Use the clock face to make a picture. Choose the time of day and the time of year. They could choose from a category:
   Seasonal clock – spring, summer, autumn, winter
   Festive clock – Christmas, Easter, Birthday
   or simply remind them of 'Hickory Dickory Dock'.

Bodywork

Materials Taped music in $\frac{2}{4}$, $\frac{3}{4}$, $\frac{4}{4}$, time

Method

1. When we dance, the 'time' of the music leads us to dance and move in different ways. Explore simple rhythms with the class, by clapping. Relate them to songs they know: 'My Grandfather's Clock' (see Music), 'Grand Old Duke Of York' is good for $\frac{2}{2}$, 'Let's Go Fly A Kite' (also see Wind/Music p. 39). Let them sing, clap and walk in those rhythms.
2. Play the music you have on tape (it's fun to have pop music as well) and see if the children can tell in which time it is written.
3. Use the taped music for dancing, either on their own or with a partner. Tell, or if you can, show them the more formal ways of dancing (waltz, quickstep, rock and roll!).

Music

Materials The song below

My Grandfather's Clock

1 My grandfather's clock was too large for the shelf,
So it stood ninety years on the floor;
It was taller by half than the old man himself,
Though it weighed not a penny weight more.
It was bought on the morn of the day that he was born,
And was always his treasure and pride;
But it stopped short, never to go again,
When the old man died.

Chorus: Ninety years without slumbering, tick, tock, tick, tock
His life seconds numbering, tick, tock, tick, tock
It stopped short never to go again,
When the old man died.

2 My grandfather said that of those he could hire,
Not a servant so faithful he found;
For it wasted no time and had but one desire,
At the close of each day to be wound.
And it kept in its place, not a frown upon its face,
And its hands never hung by its side;
But it stopped short, never to go again,
When the old man died.

Chorus: Ninety years without slumbering . . .

H. C. Work

Mastercopy 6:1

BIRTHDAYS

How old are you? 1

Circle the right number.

How many candles will you need for your next birthday cake? 2

Draw the right number in the box.

3

Write your birthday date in the box.

4

Draw the right number of candles on your cake. 5

6

7

8

9

10

BIRTHDAYS

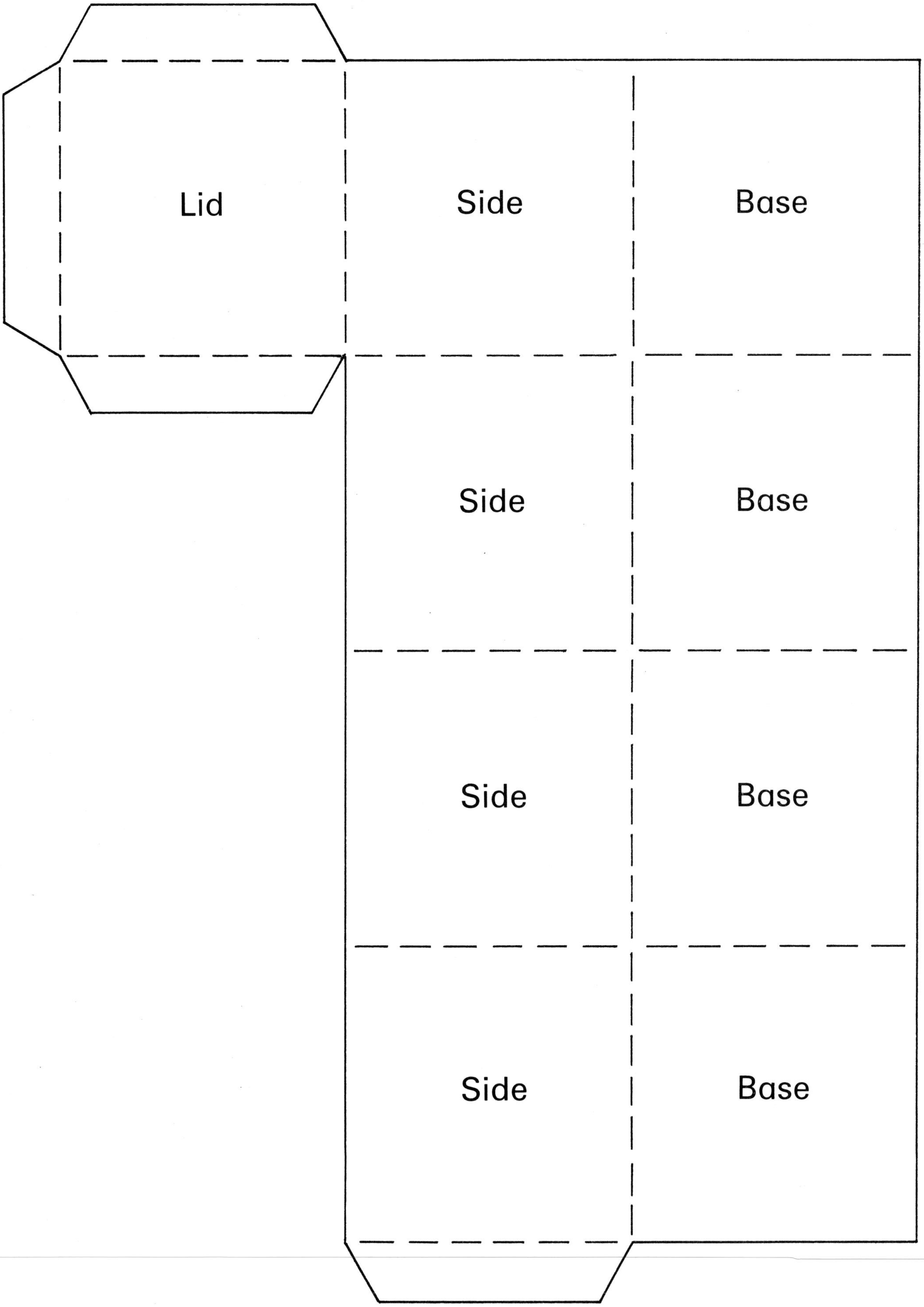
Lid
Side
Base
Side
Base
Side
Base
Side
Base

Mastercopy 6:3 **TIME**

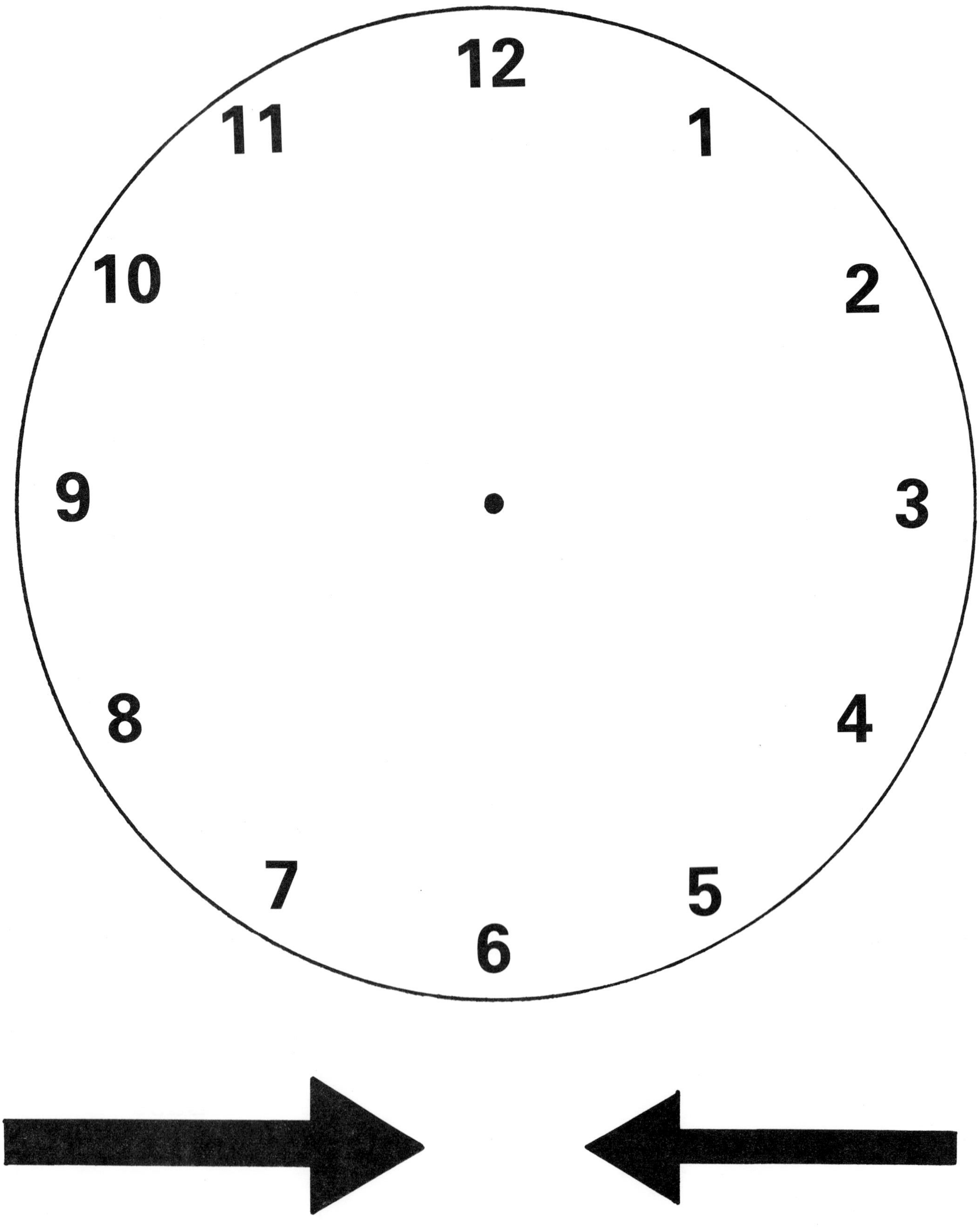

7 JULY

FETES

Whether it is called a Fete or a Gala, most schools aim to put on one event in the summer term to have fun, raise funds for school-related projects and, perhaps, include displays by school groups and teams.

There is always a fever of activity behind the scenes to provide all the things necessary and have enough stalls and 'rides' to entertain everyone. Refreshments are needed and perhaps a star event with a professional display team needs to be organised.

Finally, the day arrives and all that is left is to pray that the weather stays fine!

YOUNGER CHILDREN

Written Work and Language

Materials The story below, slips of paper, wool, scissors, glue, crayons

The Fete

It was a lovely sunny day for the School Fete. The children waited excitedly at the gate of the field next to the school. The Fete was to start at 2.30 p.m. and through the bars of the gate they could see the stalls.

There were tables round the outside of the field, with guessing games and a Treasure Map. There was a skittle alley set up, and two of the Dads were having a practice shot! Mr Bluck had brought his tractor and small trailer to give Bumpy Rides, and Mrs Kinchin had brought her pony, Snowy, to give another sort of bumpy ride. There were tables set out for teas and cakes, a Tombola stall, and a big space roped off in the middle of the field where the Brass Band would play. But the most exciting thing of all for the children was the huge yellow Bouncy Castle that had been inflated in one corner of the field. All the children loved that and had made sure they had saved their pocket money to have lots of turns bouncing from side to side. Everywhere was decorated with coloured bunting and flags. The mums and the teachers were all busily putting the finishing touches to their stalls.

At last it was 2.30 p.m. and the gate was opened. Over the loudspeaker the headteacher welcomed everyone to the Summer Fete and hoped they would enjoy themselves.

Method

1. Read the class the story. Ask them if they have been to a fete. What did they see? What were their favourite things? Had they had to help with the preparations in any way?
2. Make a class picture of the fete. Decide beforehand what stalls and rides. Use the story as a base but add any of the children's suggestions.
3. As they finish their drawing they can cut it out and stick it on the field. Then they can help decorate the edge.
4. Those able to write, can put the names of the rides on the slips of paper. Stick these round the outer edge and match to the correct ride with the wool strands.

Number

Materials Pencils, crayons, Mastercopy 7.1

Method

1. Revise coin value with the class.
2. Explain the Mastercopy. They must link the child to its purse and then see which ride the child can afford.

Extension

Materials Ten empty cardboard tubes numbered 1–10, Mastercopy 7.1

Method

1. Play indoor skittles. Colour and number rolls and set up (see Mastercopy). Scrunch up a piece of paper to act as a ball.
2. Children have one turn and must add up their own score.
3. Make a chart with each child's name, so that they can keep a note of their score.

Artwork

Materials Cardboard boxes, paint, scissors, paper

Method

1. Make a Wishing-Well Game. Cut the edges away from one face of the box.

Paint the outside to resemble a wishing well. Scrunch up pieces of paper to make 'stones' to throw in the well.
2. Don't forget to make a sign for the stall.

Extension

Materials Cardboard tubes, felt-tip pens, paper

Method
1. If you didn't make the skittles in Number, do so now. Remember the sign for the stall.

Extension

Materials Cleaned egg shells as whole as possible, paints, egg boxes or sand

Method
1. Make a guessing game. Decorate the egg shells and leave them to dry.
2. When they are dry, put a mark in some of the shells, place the shells in the boxes, or in the sand so that only the decorated parts show.
3. Let the others guess which shells are the marked ones. Did they make a sign for the stall?

Extension

Materials Paper and paints

Method
1. We cannot make all the stalls and rides in school, so let them design a sign for those not mentioned: Pony rides, Bouncy Castle, teas, etc.

Bodywork

Materials Artwork (see above), or small apparatus (stools, hoops, beanbags)

Method
1. Practise rolling, under arm throwing and catching skills.
2. Set up stalls around the room. If no skittles have been made, use hoops placed on the floor with number value for each one and throw beanbags instead of rolling balls.
3. Wishing Well: mark distance from which the 'stones' must be thrown. Three 'stones' thrown into the well and you can choose another stall.
4. Other stalls can be invented on the spot. How about: standing jumps; balancing along a beam with a beanbag on your head; a short obstacle course that makes the children go under, round, through and over benches and stools?

Music

Materials 'Macnamara's Band' (see below and p. 82) and a little imagination!

Method
1. Every fete has music of some sort. Perhaps it could be 'Macnamara's Band'. Even if you don't use the tune the words may give you a good idea.
2. Make up a class band. Combine instruments if you have them, or use the childrens' voices; they can be very inventive about being flutes and horns and cymbals!
3. When they are ready they could practise a few songs to play at the fete.

Macnamara's Band

1 My name is Macnamara, I'm the Leader of the Band,
And though we're small in number we're the best in all the land.
Oh! I am the Conductor, and we often have to play
With all the best musicianers you hear about to-day.

Chorus: When the drums go bang, the cymbals clang, the horns will blaze away,
MacCarthy puffs the old bassoon while Doyle the pipes will play;
Oh! Hennessy Tennessy tootles the flute, my word! 'tis something grand,
Oh! a credit to Ould Ireland, boys, is Macnamara's band!

2 We play at wakes and weddings, and at every county ball,
And at any great man's funeral we play 'Dead march in Saul.'
When the Prince of Wales to Ireland came, he shook me by the hand,
And said he'd never heard the like of 'Macnamara's band.'

Chorus: When the drums go bang . . . *etc.*

Shamus O'Connor

OLDER CHILDREN

Written Work and Language

Materials Paper, pencils, crayons, scissors, glue, backing paper

Method

1. Read the class the story (see Younger Children/Written Work). Talk about fetes and galas, use their experiences. Suggest that you build up a picture of a summer fete using themselves as the characters in the story.
2. Decide as a class which stalls there would be at the fete. Jot down a list.
3. Let each child draw himself/herself and perhaps one other person, preferably an adult. Cut them out.
4. Assemble all the characters on the backing paper. Now decide what the characters would be saying if they were at the fete. Would they be asking for their turn? Would they be buying an ice cream? Would they be talking about the weather? Would they be discussing something totally unrelated to the fete?

5. Each child must decide what their characters are saying, and then they can write these phrases down on balloons of paper and attach them to their drawings.
6. The finished picture should give the impression of the day and each small part could tell a story. The picture need not be tidy or all the same size, what is important is to try and get the feel of the day and the movement of people and conversation.

Number

Materials Mastercopy 7.2, pencils

Method
1. Top part is self-explanatory.
2. Use the skittles for subtraction activities:
   e.g. Thomas knocks down 3 skittles, how many are left?
   Pippa knocks down 5 skittles, how many are left?
   Lorna knocks down 1 skittle, how many are left?

Artwork

Materials Mastercopy 6.4, crayons, pencils

Method
1. Make a grid from the Mastercopy.
2. Tell the children to turn the paper over and then they can draw a Treasure Island on the reverse. Each one can choose where they hide their treasure and mark it on the grid side with a pencil cross.
3. They can guess where they have hidden other children's treasure, or their maps can be displayed and another class asked to guess.
4. Another way of doing this is to draw the Treasure Island on the grid side, with the grid marked off. When other children guess where the treasure lies, they have to give the coordinates.

Bodywork

Materials Small apparatus: benches, mats, beanbags, hoops

Method
1. Continuing the theme of buried treasure, create an obstacle course for the children with the 'treasure' at the end.
2. When they have completed the course they must collect the 'treasure' (beanbag?) and they must transport it without using their hands back to the start of the course.

Extension

Materials See Younger Children/Bodywork

Method
1. Let the children make up their own activities for a Fete.
2. You could also run some alternative races: crawling on all fours, running backwards, hopping (one leg only), slow motion.

Music

Materials The song below, instruments if possible

People Band

We are the People Band,
When we play it's really grand,
Hear us as we clap our hands,
Clap, clap, clap, clap, clap our hands.

Music with Mr Plinkerton
– Compiled and arranged by
Eleanor Gamper

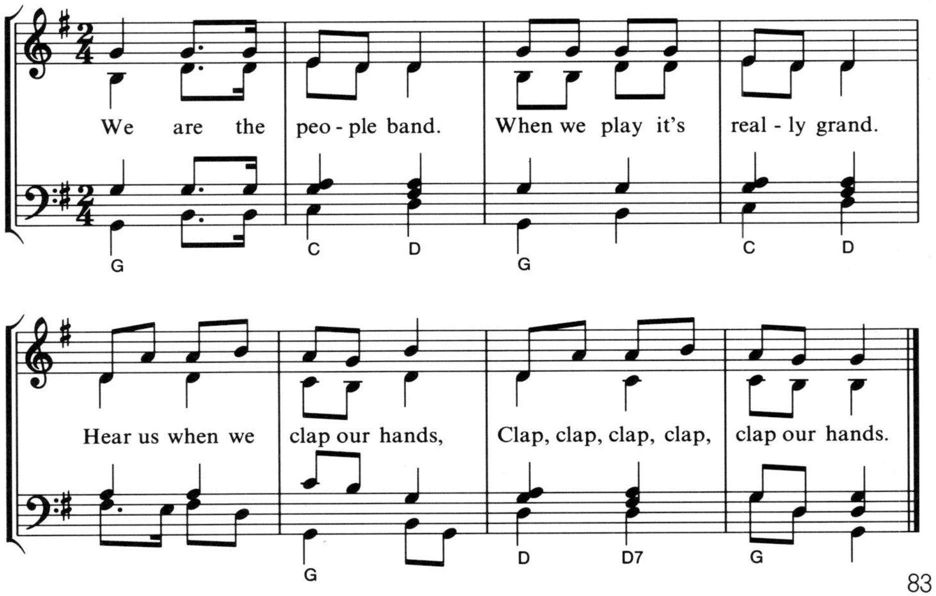

TRAVEL

Children these days are far more likely to have travelled by sea and air as well as by land. They are aware of space travel, both in reality and in the glamour of cartoon film and science fiction.

Sometimes the travelling can be more exciting than the arriving. Sometimes the travelling is only part of the adventure. Children travel to school by different means: foot, car, bus, taxi, train or a combination of them.

On the other hand, travelling can be tedious and tiring. Ask any child who has been strapped into the back seat of a car in a holiday traffic jam. Most adults are familiar with the question 'Are we nearly there yet?' If you have your own answer to the question, then incorporate it here! If not, then here are some rhymes old and new and a few more ideas on the topic of travel.

Suggested Reading

Our Train
by Beatrice Phillpotts (MacDonald)

YOUNGER CHILDREN

Written Work and Language

Materials The rhymes below and any more you can remember

Method

1. Travelling provides the perfect time for singing songs and saying rhymes. Do the class know these ones?

I saw a ship a-sailing,
A-sailing on the sea;
And, oh! it was laden
With pretty things for thee!

There were comfits in the cabin,
And apples in the hold;
The sails were all of silk,
And the masts were made of gold.

Ride a cock-horse to Banbury Cross,
To see a fine lady upon a white horse;
With rings on her fingers and bells on her toes
She shall have music wherever she goes.

As I was going to St Ives,
I met a man with seven wives,
Every wife had seven sacks,
Every sack had seven cats,
Every cat had seven kits:
Kits, cats, sacks, wives,
How many were going to St Ives?

There was an old woman tossed up in a basket,
Ninety times as high as the moon;
Where she was going, I couldn't but ask it,
For in her hand she carried a broom.

'Old woman, old woman, old woman,' quoth I,
'Oh whither, oh whither, oh whither so high?'
'To brush the cobwebs off the sky!'
'Shall I go with thee?'
'Ay, by and by.'

2. After you have enjoyed saying or learning these rhymes there is the opportunity to choose one and make a picture of it. The third rhyme is best done as a group effort!
3. Starting with how they all come to school, help them make a list of all the different ways they have travelled.
4. Ask if any of them have a favourite story about travelling, or a television programme that features a special way of travelling that they could tell the rest of the class about.
5. Do any of the class have a hobby that involves travel? It could be model making, or model trains, or train spotting.

Number

Materials Mastercopy 7.3, crayons, dice

Method

1. The Mastercopy shows a rocket that can be used for practice in counting backwards and forwards. It can also be used as a number line for quiz games.
2. Use the dice as one way of practising addition. Let the children work in small groups or pairs (it depends on how many dice you have) rolling the dice. If they can roll the correct number, starting at ten and working backwards, they can colour in that band on the rocket.
3. When all the rockets are coloured in, they can be cut out and displayed orbiting the classroom.

Artwork

Materials Boxes, tubes, pots (junk); glue and paint

Method

1. There always has to be a time when the children can just explore using their own imagination, and making a spacecraft is a good topic. No one can actually say you have done it incorrectly if it is unique!

Bodywork

Materials An open space

Method

1. We travel when we move. If you ask the class to walk I am sure they will automatically walk round the hall in a circle! Watch them do it.
2. There are of course other pathways they can use: straight, curved and zig-zag are three to start off with.
3. Get the children to move in these ways and then add extra instructions. See if they can move with one particular part of their body leading: try elbow, side of the body, one foot.
4. Play 'Follow My Leader', teacher to take the lead and get them started moving as practised. Pass the lead on to another child after a while. This can also be done in pairs, though not with the very young.
5. Agree on a signal for each way of moving (curved, straight and zig-zag). When the teacher makes that signal see how quickly everyone can change their movement pathway. Watch out for those who don't watch out!

Music

Materials The songs below

1. 'The Wheels of the Bus', *Okki-Tokki-Unga* (A & C Black)
2. 'Morningtown Ride'

Morningtown Ride

1 Train whistle blowin',
Makes a sleepy noise;
Underneath their blankets
Go all the girls and boys.

Chorus:
Rockin', rollin', ridin',
Out along the bay,
All bound for Morningtown,
Many miles away.

2 Driver at the engine,
Fireman rings the bell;
Sandman swings the lantern
To say that all is well.

3 Maybe it is raining
Where our train will ride;
All the little travellers
Are warm and snug inside.

4 Somewhere there is sunshine,
Somewhere there is day;
Somewhere there is Morningtown,
Many miles away.

Words and music: Malvina Reynolds

OLDER CHILDREN

Written Work and Language

Materials Mastercopy 7.4, pencils, crayons

Method

1. All ways of travelling, concentrating on the -'ing' words. They can talk about, colour and fill in the correct answer.
2. Following on from travelling to school, how would they like to arrive at the school gates? Would it be in a chauffeur-driven car, hovercraft, coach and horses, or perhaps on a motor-bike!

Extension

Materials The poem below

A Good Play

We built a ship upon the stairs
All made of the back bedroom chairs,
And filled it full of sofa pillows
To go a-sailing on the billows.

We took a saw and several nails,
And water in the nursery pails:
And Tom said, 'Let us also take
An apple and a slice of cake';
Which was enough for Tom and Me
To go a-sailing on, till tea.

We sailed along for days and days,
And had the very best of plays;
But Tom fell out and hurt his knee,
So there was no one left but me.

R. L. Stevenson

Method

1. Has anyone in the class built a special vehicle? Did it really travel or was it one similar to the one in the poem?
2. If they could travel anywhere this very day, where would they go, and how would they travel? They might like to take a friend with them too.

Number

Materials A large piece of paper (see diagram), pencils

Method

1. Taking London as the starting point, let the children complete the table.

How is it possible to travel from London to the following places?

	On Foot	Bicycle	Car	Train	Aeroplane	Boat
Edinburgh						
Paris						
New York						
Birmingham						
Sydney						
Hong Kong						
Manchester						

2. As they finish ask them to link each type of transport with its terminal, e.g.:
   Train – station
   Aeroplane – airport, etc.

Artwork

Materials Sticky backed paper cut into a variety of shapes, backing paper

Method

1. Look at the diagram for inspiration. Let the children create some sort of vehicle using the shapes. Point out that it is better to plan the shape of the vehicle before they lick the sticky back. It also saves a lot of wastage!

Bodywork

Materials An open space

Method

1. Play 'Silent Relays'. Divide the class into four teams, and then divide each team so that one half is at either end of the hall. Name a team leader for each team.

2. Using the words that were on Mastercopy 7.4 tell the class that the relay is going to be run thus. At the given signal the first member of each team travels to the other end of the hall, in the manner announced, e.g. flying. The second member of the team must return down the hall, travelling as announced, e.g. sailing. The method of travelling can be changed every 'leg', or left to the teacher to decide.
3. Decide as a class what movement characteristic each method of travelling will have, e.g.:
   Flying – arms outstretched and running on toes
   Sailing – moving backwards with hands doing a rowing motion
   Orbiting – spinning slowly down the room

Music

Materials The song below, open space if possible

Method

1. Learn the song and improvise the movements when the words and tune are secure.

I'm going up to London

I'm going up to London,
Can't you see,
I'm riding on my bicycle,
To buy a cup of tea.

I'm going up to London,
Can't you see,
I'm sailing in my boat.
To buy a cup of tea.

I'm going up to London,
Can't you see,
I'm riding on my motor-bike,
To buy a cup of tea.

I'm going up to London,
Can't you see,
I'm riding on my tractor,
To buy a cup of tea.

I'm going up to London,
Can't you see,
I'm riding in a bus,
To buy a cup of tea.

I'm going up to London,
Can't you see,
I'm driving in my motor car,
To buy a cup of tea.

I'm going up to London,
Can't you see,
I'm flying in my aeroplane,
To buy a cup of tea

FETES

Castle
(10) (10) (10)
Treasure Hunt
(20) (5)
Ice cream
(20)
Skittles
(10) (5)
Pony Rides
(2) (2) (2) (2) (2)
Guess the number of SWEETS IN A JAR
(1) (1) (1) (1) (1)

The Bumpy Ride

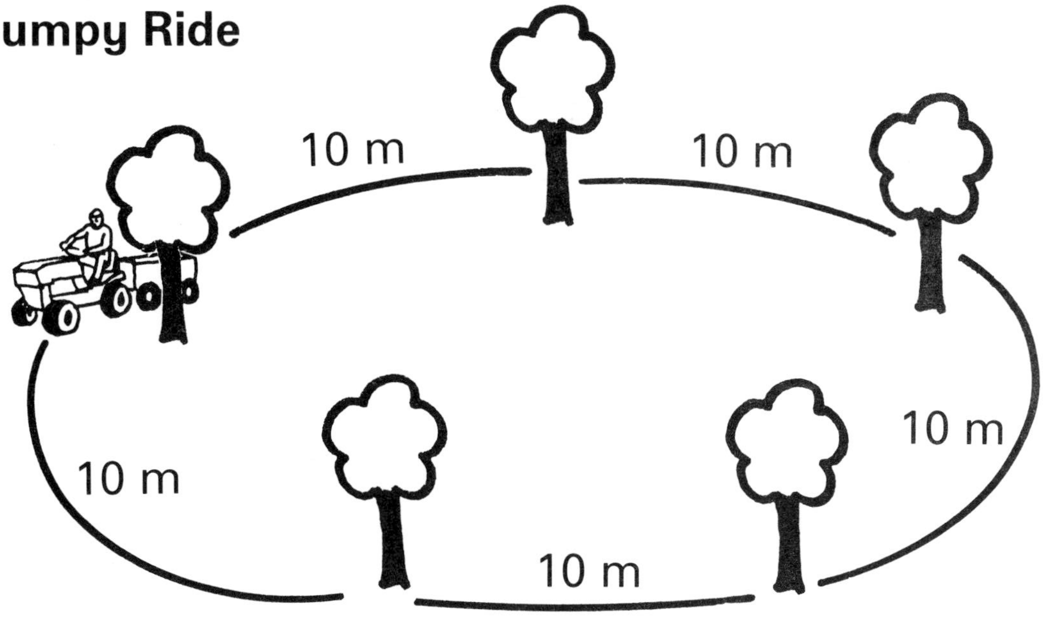

How many metres in one circuit?
1 circuit costs 20p.
How far, in metres, after two circuits?
How much does it cost for two circuits?

Skittles

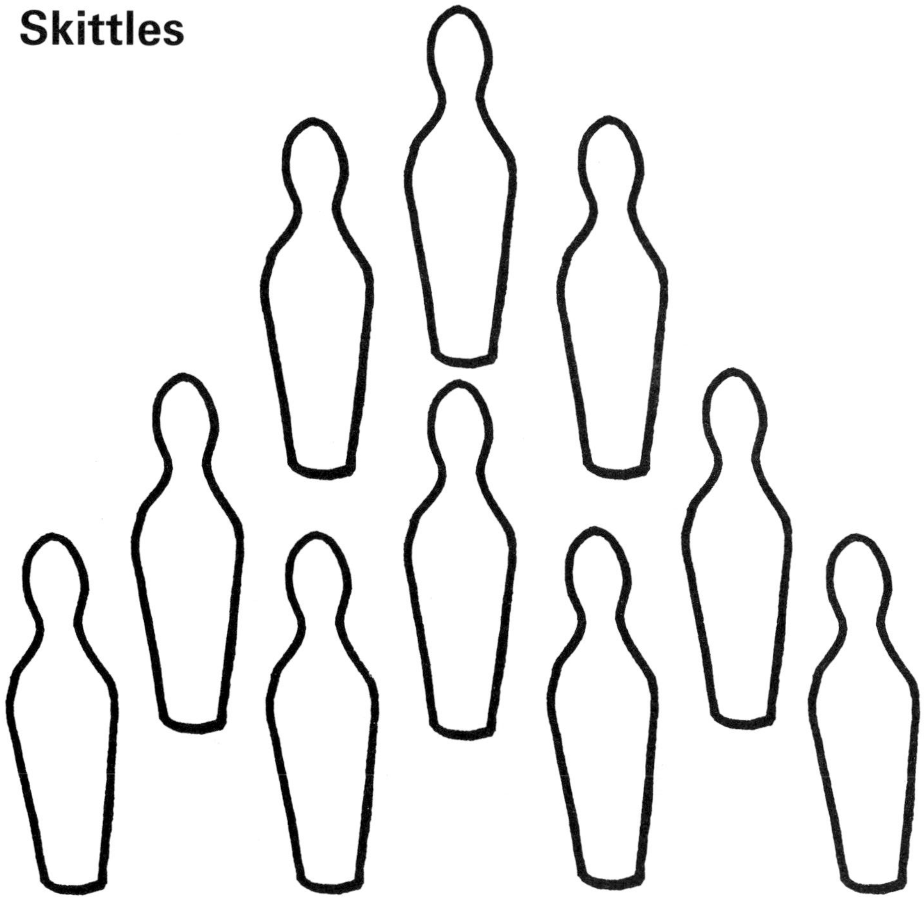

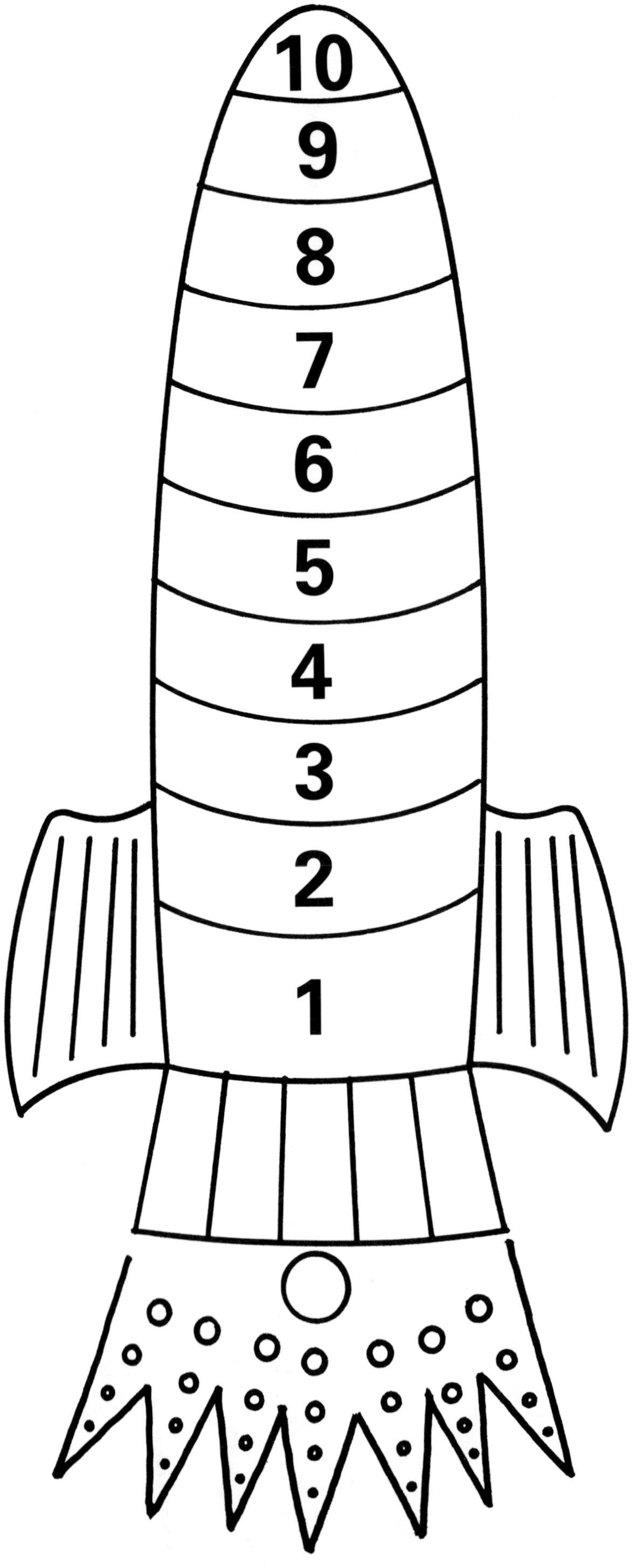
10
9
8
7
6
5
4
3
2
1

TRAVEL

Look at the 'ing' words. Link them to the right picture.

The ship is _____ on the sea.

The car is _____ along the street.

The aeroplane is _____ in the sky.

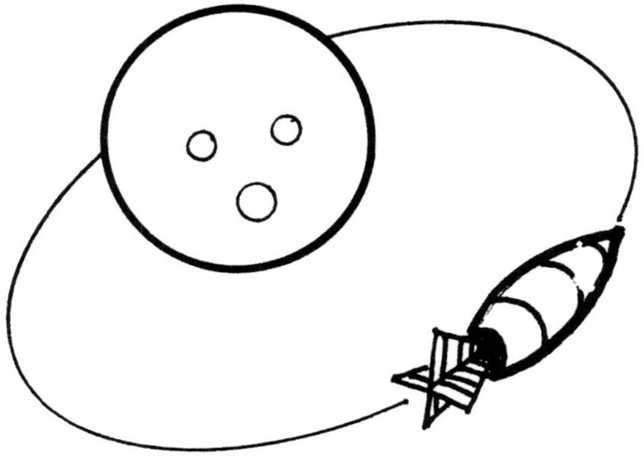

The rocket is _____ the moon.

The train is _____ on the tracks.

Alice is _____ to school.

sailing	orbiting	driving	travelling	flying	walking

8 AUGUST

HOLIDAYS

Everyone likes to go away on holiday. Nowadays, the type of holiday can vary from the traditional seaside summer holiday to summer camps designed specially for children, to winter sports holidays. People travel further on their holidays, some of the children may have already travelled abroad by boat or plane. The variety is enormous, but all linked by the same excitement and anticipation that starts with deciding where to go and when.

I have chosen to stick with the summer seaside holiday, but it is only a start point. Remember that going to Granny's might be a holiday for some, especially if she lives a long way away. When children start school they have very little idea of terms and holiday times. My daughter got very confused when she reached half-term! But the 'big' holiday always sticks in their minds.

Suggested Reading

Topsy and Tim Go On Holiday
by Jean and Gareth Anderson (Blackie & Son)

YOUNGER CHILDREN

Written Work and Language

Materials Pre-cut strips of paper in an 'S' shape, photographs of your holidays

Method

1. Ask the class if they can remember going on holiday. Collect the different types of holiday: seaside, inland, canal, holiday camp, skiing, visiting relations.
2. Why do we go on holiday? Is it because we need a change? To get some sunshine and seaside air? To travel to somewhere we have never been before? Get the children to say where they have been and who went with them. Did they enjoy themselves?
3. Once enough has been found out, show the children your holiday photographs. Suggest that they might like to bring a picture to school.
4. Most people go on holiday in the summer and try to see the sea. What do we find at the seaside? Lots of 's' sound words. Make a Sunshine Seaside Holiday Picture.

Extension

Materials Plastic envelopes, Mastercopy 8.1, Plasticine, crayons

Method

1. Show the children the Mastercopy picture. What could they add to make the picture more interesting (see 's' words)? How about putting themselves in the picture too?
2. Let some children draw on their pictures and others put the picture inside the plastic envelope. Then they can use Plasticine to make three dimensional pictures.

Number

Materials Pencils, Mastercopy 8.1, crayons

Method

1. Use the Mastercopy and give oral instructions for the children to follow.
   a. Put four shells in the sand.
   b. Draw two birds in the sky.
   c. Make one sandcastle.
   d. Colour five waves in the sea.
   e. Draw three boats on the water.

Extension

Materials Pencils, crayons, scissors or sticky paper squares

Method

1. Make a graph of holidays. Use the types discussed in Written Work and Language.
2. Depending on the capability of the children, ask them to draw a picture of themselves and put it in the correct category. Or they could write their name on a piece of sticky paper which can be stuck in the correct place.

Artwork

Materials Paint, sponges, brushes

Method

Waves

There are big waves and little waves
Green waves and blue
Waves you can jump over
Waves you dive through
Waves that rise up
Like a great water wall
Waves that swell softly
And don't break at all
Waves that can whisper
Waves that can roar
Tiny waves that run at you
Running on the shore

Eleanor Farjeon

1. Practise making wave shapes on scrap paper, so the children get the idea.
2. Make a colour wash for background.
3. Add to the picture by choosing wave colour:
   calm – blue, pale green, white, curves;
   stormy – dark blue, grey, dark green, white, peaks and troughs.

Bodywork

Materials Mastercopy 8.2

Method

1. Teach the children to sing the song on the Mastercopy.
2. Number the lines 1–11.
3. Now make a musical story with simple movements: in pairs skipping (lines 1–2), walking hand in hand (lines 3–4). Mime the brass band on their own (choose an instrument and give it a movement pattern). Gallop into a large circle (lines 6–7). The girls step into the circle, face outwards and curtsey (lines 8–9). If possible join hands with a boy and gallop in a circle (lines 10–11); if not possible ask the boys to bow!

Music

Materials Mastercopy 8.2

Method

1. The same as for Bodywork.

OLDER CHILDREN

Written Work and Language

Materials Children

Method

1. A 'Circle Game' for the class to play. Seated in a circle one child says that they are going on holiday and they would like some help packing their suitcase. The child starts off by saying 'I packed my suitcase and in it I put . . .' she chooses something and the game passes to the next person who has to repeat the start phrase and first item and then add something else. The game continues and the list grows longer!
2. As children forget, or the game slows, change the type of holiday.

Extension

Method

1. A variation on 'Desert Island Discs.' Ask the class to think of three things they really couldn't do without if they were stranded on a desert island (that might need explaining, too).
2. Let them draw the three things and, if able, write the reason for taking them. Be available to write for the children whose explanations exceed their ability to write.

Number

Materials Paper and pencils

Method

1. Discuss with the children what it takes to organise a holiday. See if they think about things like cancelling the milk or sending the dog to kennels.
2. Let them organise these details into a logical order.

e.g.		
	pack case	travel
	cancel milk	decide where to go
	choose dates	lock house
	animal care	book holiday

Extension

Materials Atlas, road maps, O/S maps if coastal area

Method

1. Group work on finding out which is the nearest seaside to the school.
2. Find the fastest way to get there. Is it by:
   motorway
   dual carriageway
   A roads
   B roads
3. See if they can find these famous seaside resorts:
   Blackpool
   Rhyll
   Brighton
   Scarborough

Artwork

Materials Paint brushes, glue, heavy paper, sand or ground rice or semolina, old toothbrushes or combs, cottonwool, pieces of sponge

Method

1. Create a seaside picture working in pairs with the above.

Bodywork

Materials Baskets, bins to represent buckets, small beanbags and balls to represent sand

Method

1. The object is to make as many 'sandcastles' as possible.
2. Two teams either end of the hall each with a number and some 'sand'. Their 'buckets' are at the opposite end.
3. The 'sand' has to be transported to 'buckets' without using hands. Set the number of 'grains of sand' to each bucket, which can be turned over to make the sandcastle. Make one or two children responsible for checking their teams and sandcastles.
4. When certain numbers are called they must transport sand to the 'bucket' without it falling or themselves being tagged by a member of the opposite team. If anything happens they must return to base and start again.
5. The winning team has the most sandcastles.

Music

Materials Song on Mastercopy 8.2

SUN

When the days are short and wintry, we all look forward to the long summer days of sunshine. The sun gives us daylight and warmth and makes us feel happy.

The sun with its blinding light and power has always been a source of myths and legends, and has inspired worship. The people of South America, the Mayas, Aztecs and Incas, were known as the Sun People because of their worship of the sun.

The sun helped people to tell the time and thus make calendars. It has helped to create fire and was often used to make signals, by reflecting the sun's rays.

It is an inspiration for songs and nursery rhymes, for paintings and decoration.

YOUNGER CHILDREN

Written Work and Language

Materials Mastercopy 8.3, paper, lots of yellow crayons, scissors, tape

Method

1. Talk about the words associated with the sun:

sunshine	sunburn
sunbeams	sundial
sunglasses	sunflower, etc.
sunbonnet	

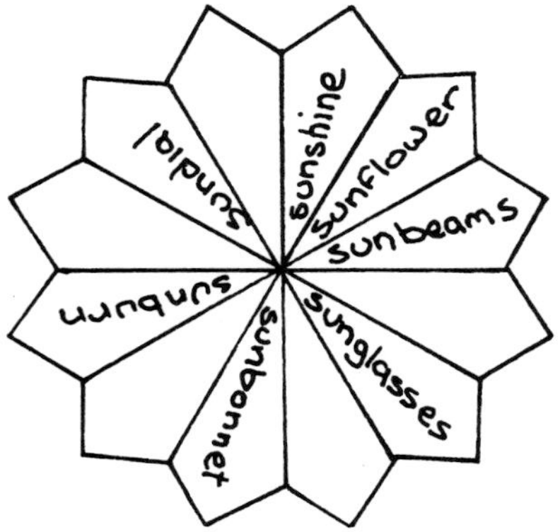

2. Show them a 'sunburst' shape, and explain that they can make one to hang in the classroom. If they write a 'sun' word inside the kite shape and make the shape look 'sunny', then they can cut out the shape.
3. When the shapes are cut out they can be assembled to make a sunburst.
4. As they finish their sun word they can make their own 'sunshine' picture. It need not tell a story, but could be all the things they have talked about earlier.

Number

Materials Mastercopy 8.3, crayons

Method
1. Self-explanatory.

Extension

Materials Mastercopy 8.4

Method
1. The children can use the Mastercopy designed for the Older Children. They can colour it in and spot the differences.

Artwork

Materials Potatoes, paint, paper

Method
1. The Maya People worshipped the sun. They thought that it must be a god. They were called the Sun People and they used to decorate their clothes and buildings and even their bodies with designs and patterns that celebrated the sun. Potato prints can help us make patterns like the Mayas.

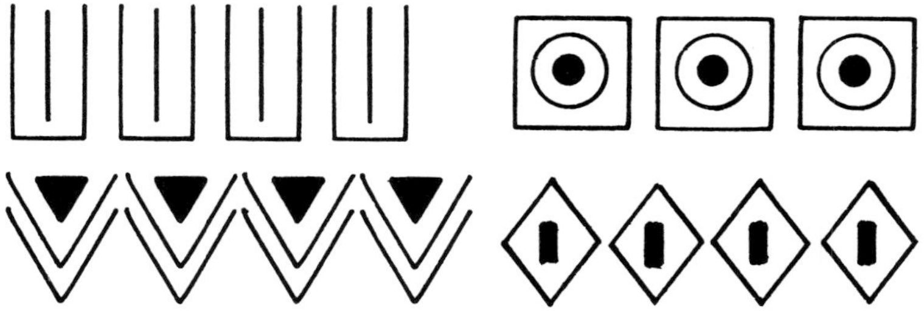

2. If you cannot manage potatoes instantly, use Mastercopy 6.4 to help organise the pattern making!

Extension

Materials The rhyme below

Incy Wincy Spider

Incy Wincy Spider climbed up the spout,
Down came the rain and washed poor spider out.
Out came the sunshine, and dried up all the rain,
So, Incy Wincy Spider went up the spout again!

Method
1. The sunshine helped Incy Wincy Spider. Say the rhyme, do the actions; inspiration for a painting!

Bodywork

Materials An open space

Method
1. Thinking of sunrise and sunset brings to mind movement patterns. Growing and stretching and rising, shrinking and closing and sinking.
2. It gives ideas of working at different levels, from low down, to high and wide, just as the sun moves through the sky.
3. Sunshine can make us happy and bright, ready to skip and run, or it can make us lethargic, moving lazily and slowly, enjoying its warmth.
4. When you have explored all these possibilities, put together a movement sequence with the children. It can have a simple story, or just be a celebration of the sun.

Music

Materials Two cheerful sunny songs that I'm sure you remember!

The Sun has got his Hat on

The sun has got his hat on
Hip, hip, hip, hooray.
The sun has got his hat on
And he's coming out to play.
Everyone is happy, everyone is gay,
The sun has got his hat on and he's coming out to play.

You Are My Sunshine

Chorus: You are my sunshine,
My only sunshine,
You make me happy
When skies are grey.
You'll never know, dear,
How much I love you;
Please don't take my sunshine away.

OLDER CHILDREN

Written Work and Language

Materials The story below, pencils and paper

Daedulus and Icarus

A long time ago on an island called Crete there lived a man called Daedulus. Daedulus was a clever man, and he was fascinated by the way in which birds could fly. He watched them closely, how their wings moved and how the feathers of their wings overlapped and how they varied in size.

He spent his time gathering feathers that had fallen from the birds and thought that he could make wings to fly. He decided to fasten the feathers together with wax, overlapping them as he had observed. He made the wings in a curved shape and fitted them to his arms. Daedulus at last put on his wings and practised moving them like a bird until he could fly.

Now Daedulus had a son called Icarus, who persuaded his father to make him some wings. Daedulus warned Icarus that he must be careful when he flew. He must never fly close to the sun, or the wax holding the feathers together would melt. Icarus listened to his father, but when he started to fly he soon forgot the words of warning.

Icarus loved to swoop and soar like the birds. He flew over the land and far out to sea. He flew higher and higher, nearer and nearer to the sun, until he felt like a god. But just as he thought this, he felt the warmth of the sun and realised that the wax in his wings was beginning to melt in the heat. Too late he remembered the words that his father had said; his feathers were falling away, and Icarus fell with them into the sea below and drowned.

Method

1. Read all but the end of the story and see if the children can guess the end.
2. Ask them to think what Daedulus would have said to Icarus when he warned him. An opportunity to work in pairs on dialogue.
3. This is a good story to retell in parts:
   a. Daedulus watches the birds and wants to fly
   b. Daedulus makes the wings with Icarus watching
   c. Daedulus and Icarus fly
   d. Icarus flies too near the sun
   Fold paper into four and mark each section a, b, c, d to correspond with the suggested headings above.

Extension

Materials Paper and pencils

Method

1. Make up some tongue twisters and let the class see how fast they can say them accurately, e.g.:
   Slowly sinks the summer sun at sunset

Number

Materials Mastercopy 8.4

Method

1. Use as a simple exercise in 'spot the difference'.
2. Add the following questions to the exercise. Use the top picture.
   a. How many sunbeams are there?
   b. Which is the tallest sunflower?
   c. Which sunflower has the most leaves?
   d. How many fence posts are there?

e. If Amy is facing north, which way is the sun moving?
f. If the snail takes five minutes to travel half a metre, and the sunflower is two and a half metres tall, how many minutes until it reaches the top of the flower?
g. Which glass has more liquid in it?
h. How many things beginning with 'sun' can you see in the picture?

Artwork

Materials Diagrams for inspiration, felt-tip pens or crayons, paper

Method
1. Try to make overlapping patterns like the ones that Daedulus observed on the wings of birds. Another example of this sort of pattern is on brickwork.

Extension

Materials Pre-cut card circles, safety pins, felt-tip pens, clear sticky plastic if available or tape

Method
1. Sunshine tends to make us smile. Perhaps if we wore sunshine badges it would make other people feel happy too. Let the class make themselves a Sunshine Smile Badge.

Bodywork

Materials The story of 'Daedulus and Icarus' (see Written Work and Language)

Method
1. Enlarge on Point 2 of Written Work and Language. Give the children some help with the conversation. Be prepared to act as one of the characters.
   a. How did Daedulus warn Icarus?
   b. Did Icarus listen or was he rather rude and offhand and think his father silly?
   c. What did Icarus' mother think of all this flying around?
   d. If you looked out of the window now, and saw Icarus flying past, what would you say to your teacher? Do you think she would believe you?

Music

Materials Musical instruments if possible

Method

1. See if the children can compose an accompaniment to 'sunny' or 'summery' songs. Try the ones that are in Younger Children/Music.
2. Another fun thing to do is to sing and accompany 'rounds'. How about

   'Summer is a-comin' in'

3. Ask them which songs they associate with the sun and summer. There is always one particular pop song that is on everyone's tongue in the summer.
4. The song below.

I Have Seen the Golden Sunshine

1 I have seen the golden sunshine,
I have watched the flowers grow,
I have listened to the song birds
And there's one thing now I know,
They were all put there for us to share
By someone so divine,
And if you're a friend of Jesus,
CLAP CLAP CLAP CLAP
You're a friend of mine.

I've seen the light, I've seen the light,
And that's why my heart sings.
I've known the joy, I've known the joy
That loving Jesus brings.

2 I have seen the morning sunshine,
I have heard the oceans roar,
I have seen the flowers of springtime,
And there's one thing I am sure,
They were all put there for us to share
By someone so divine,
And if you're a friend of Jesus,
CLAP CLAP CLAP CLAP
You're a friend of mine.

Words and music:
Charlie Chester and Benny Litchfield
Title: Friend of Jesus, friend of mine

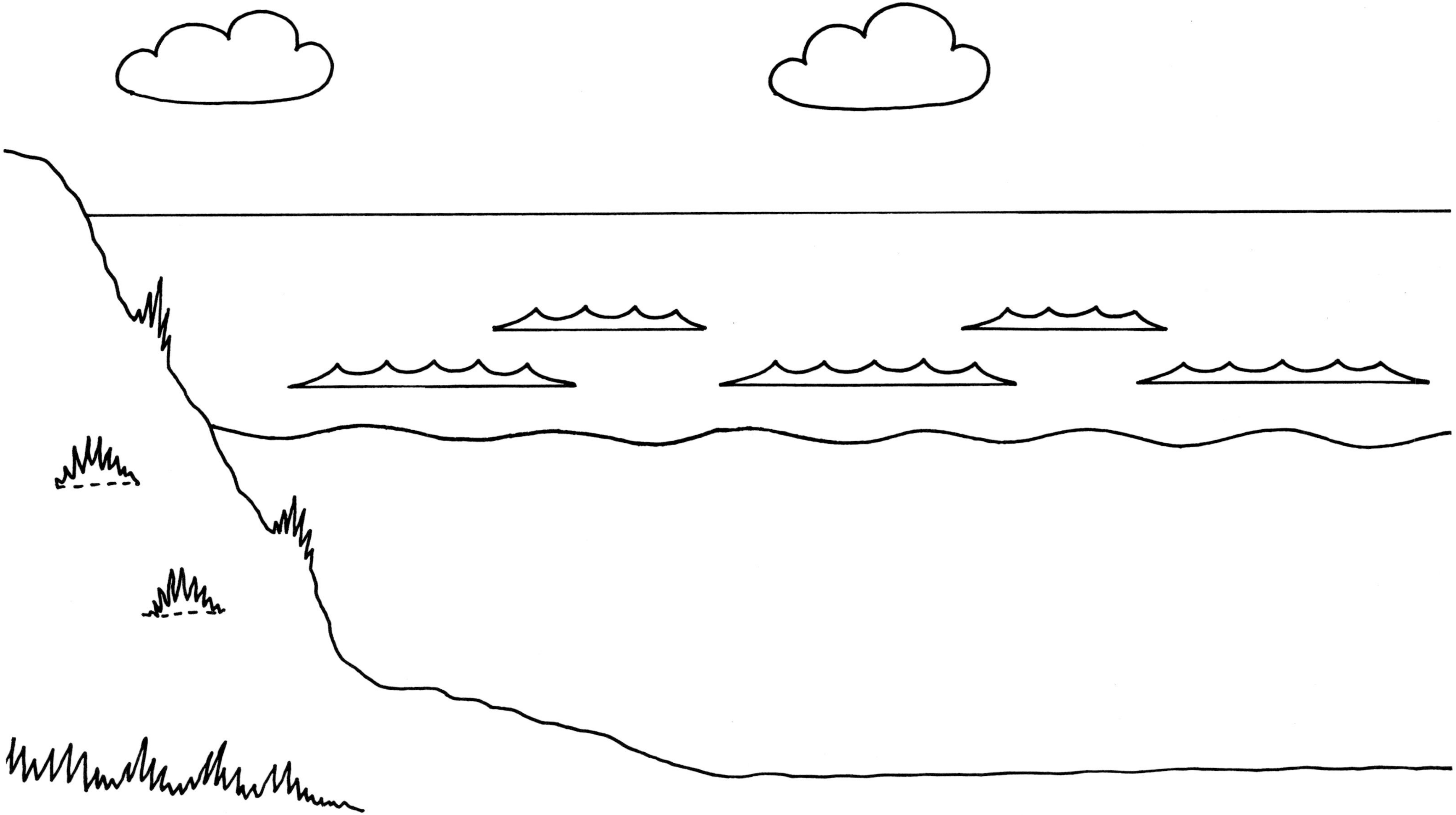

Beside the Sea

Oh I do like to be beside the seaside,
I do like to be beside the sea.
I do like to stroll along the Prom, Prom, Prom
Where the brass bands play,
Tiddley-om-pom-pom!
So just let me be beside the seaside,
I'll be beside myself with glee.
And there's lots of girls besides
That I'd like to be beside,
Beside the seaside,
Beside the sea.

YOU MAY PHOTOCOPY THIS PAGE

SUN

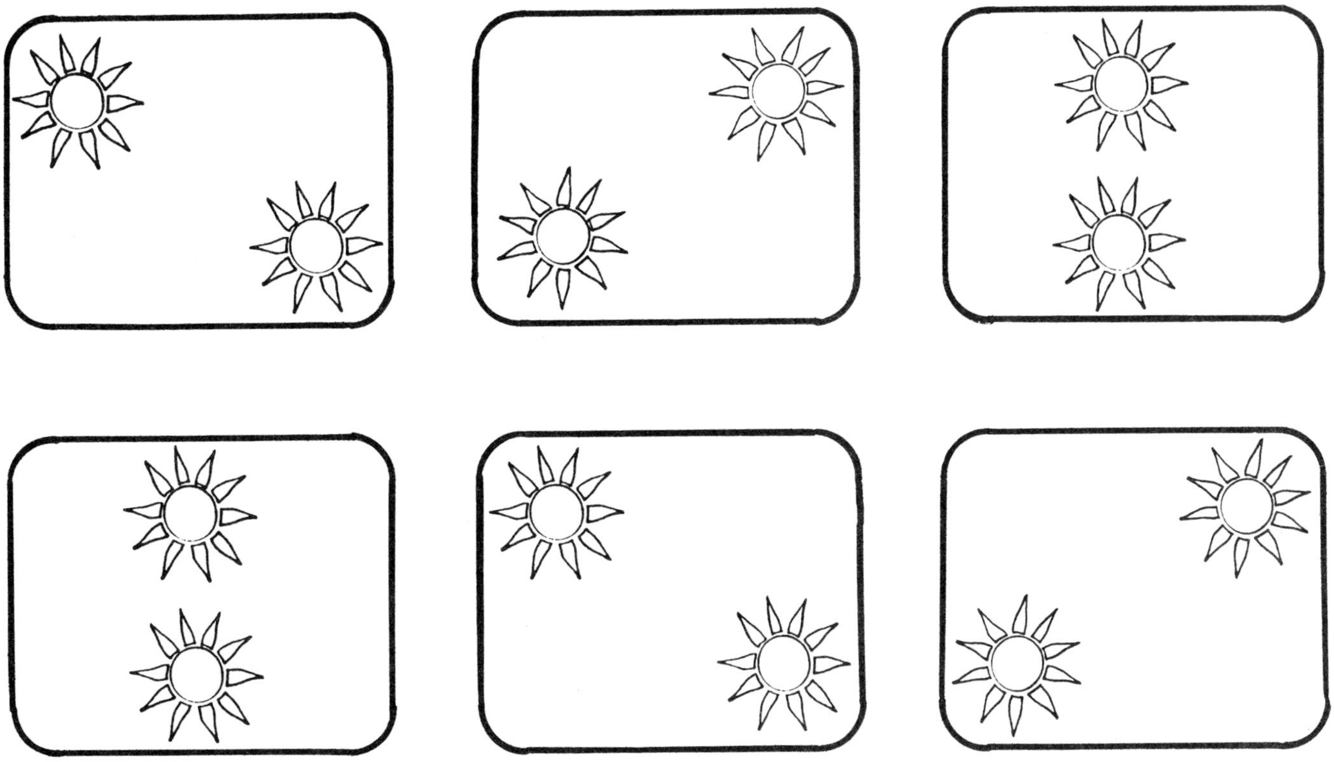

Match the sets that are exactly the same.

How many sunbeams?
How many sunflowers?
Which is the largest sunflower?
Which sunflower has the most leaves?

SUN

9 SEPTEMBER

HARVEST

Harvest time is celebrated by the gathering of fruit and vegetables, and even of canned foods. They are displayed in churches and in schools and a special service is conducted to give thanks for all the blessings that have brought about a good harvest. The food is then distributed to the needy or the elderly in the local community.

We know that the traditions of harvest go back a long time, but do the children realise this? They are used to seeing machines do all the hard work and perhaps do not know about the times when a horse and cart did the heavy work. As well as being a time of thanksgiving, the harvest is also a sign of autumn approaching.

The 'season of mists and mellow fruitfulness' follows on quickly after the harvest and with it comes a wealth of ideas. It is a time of changing colours and a dying down of all the summer flowers. A time to collect the seeds for next year. It is also the start of the school year, when some children start school and others move on to new classes and to new teachers.

Suggested Reading

Animal Stories (Usborne Books)

YOUNGER CHILDREN

Written Work and Language

Materials Master copy 9.1, paper, crayons, scissors.

Method

1. Check that they know the meaning of the word harvest.
2. Nowadays we have combine-harvesters and big machines to help bring in the harvest; but in the olden days the farmer relied on his horse and cart. The grain and the hay had to be stored in the barn, ready for the grain to be turned into flour for bread, and the hay kept to feed the animals when they could not graze outside. The last sheaf of corn to be cut was twisted into a 'Corn Dolly' (see Mastercopy) and brought home atop the cart. The dolly was kept all through the winter until the next year, for the farmer thought it would mean a good harvest the next year. The Dolly also embodied the 'spirit of the corn' and would bring new life into the new seeds. Colour and cut out the Corn Dolly.
3. Let the children think of all the things that can be harvested now: apples, pears, plums, potatoes, carrots, cauliflowers, marrows. They can draw something from the list, cut it out and add it to a class Harvest Picture with their Corn Dollies.

Extension

Materials Mastercopy 9.2, pencils, colours

Method

1. Tell the story of the 'Ant and the Grasshopper', and let the children write simple sentences underneath the pictures so that they tell the story, e.g.:

a. The Grasshopper was dancing in the sun
b. The Ant was busy working
c. The Grasshopper laughed at the Ant
d. The Ants stored their food
e. The winter came and the Grasshopper was hungry
f. The Ants had lots to eat
g. Young children love to be righteous so they will enjoy the moral of the tale!

Number

Materials Paper, pencils

Method

1. Give the class some simple problems to work out. They can draw the sums as they go along to help them work out the answers. Suggest how they draw the items.
2. Start by drawing the farmer a big square barn.
3. The farmer stores the hay in the barn. He has 6 cows, and each cow needs 6 bales of hay for the winter. Draw the right number of bales in the barn.
4. The farmer also has 12 chickens, and he needs 1 sack of corn for each 6 chickens. Draw the number of sacks that he needs.
5. The farmer has 10 sheep, he needs 2 bales of straw for each sheep to make a pen for them in the winter. How many bales does he need to stack next to the barn?
6. How many bales of hay does the farmer have?
7. How many bales of hay and straw does the farmer have altogether?
8. If each chicken lays 2 eggs, how many eggs will the farmer's wife have?

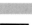

Artwork

Materials As many acorns as you can find, used match sticks, felt-tip pens

Method

1. Read the poem of 'Acorn Bill'. Children love to have a go at making their own little man.

Acorn Bill

I made a little acorn man
And inked his smiling face,
I stuck four pins for arms and legs,
Each firmly in its place.

I found a tiny acorn cup
To put upon his head,
And then I showed him to my friends;
'Meet Acorn Bill', I said.

Ruth Ainsworth

Bodywork

Materials Balls and a large stool for each team

Method

1. Divide the class up into two teams and stand them in lines with a reasonable space between each child.
2. Have an upended stool at the end of each team line.
3. The teams are going to make a 'haystack' using the balls as bales.
4. The balls are to be kept at the other end to the stool. When the start word is given the child nearest the balls collects one and then passes it along the line to the next child and so on until the child nearest the 'haystack' has it. They must get the 'bale' into the stack before the team can start to pass the next bale along.
5. You can stipulate the way in which the bales are passed to practise various ball skills, e.g.: rolling, throwing, bouncing.

Music

Materials The song below

See, here are red apples

1 See, here are red apples for you and me,
We eat them to make us grow strong.
So now we are glad and say 'Thank You' to God,
And sing Him our Harvest song.

2 See here are bananas. . .
3 See here are green marrows. . .
4 See here are big turnips. . .
5 See oranges golden. . .
6 See grapes white and purple. . .
7 See loaves big and crusty. . .

Words: H. E. Barnard
Music: E. G. Barnard

OLDER CHILDREN

Written Work and Language

Materials Atlas, paper, pencils

Method

1. There are harvest festivals all over the world to give thanks for a variety of crops that provide us with food to eat. Use the atlas to find out where these countries are:

Italy Spain France	grape harvest to make wine
North Eastern USA	fish
Barbados	sugar cane
Canada	autumn festival for hunters and trappers
Germany	hop harvest to make beer

2. Remember in the USA they have a special Thanksgiving Day, a national holiday. This is when they give thanks not only for the safe arrival of the early settlers, but also for the successful raising and harvesting of crops by those settlers. See what the children can find out about Thanksgiving Day.

Extension

Materials Mastercopy 9.2, pencils, crayons

Method

1. Tell the story of the 'Ant and the Grasshopper'. Let the class listen and then, as a class, divide the story into parts, to match the Mastercopy.
2. When they are happy that they have got that story the right way round, suggest that they retell the tale, using words and pictures on the Mastercopy.
3. This is a simple story to act out in the classroom.

Number

Materials As many seeds as you can find; don't forget all the ones in the kitchen

Method

1. Do this before Artwork! Jumble up all the seeds. Divide the class into groups and give each group a handful or more of seeds.
2. The first task is to sort the seeds into sets of the same type of seed.
3. Get the children to identify and write down how many there are in each set. Ask them to further sort the seeds in each set into groups of ten. Again, write down how many groups of ten for each set of seeds.
4. As a class activity they can then total the number of each type of seed in the classroom, and how many seeds there are all together. The gathered information can be used to make graphs.
6. Use the seeds for size comparison.
7. Estimate the size of plant that grows from each seed.

Artwork

Materials The seeds after you have used them in Number work. Glue, paintbrushes, paper

Method

1. Make pictures using the seeds. A simple idea is to make a face from the seeds. Flower shapes are also effective.

Extension

Materials Thickish yellow/orange wool cut into strands, cotton

Method

1. Make your own Corn Dolly using the wool. It's a bit fiddly and they will need help. If they can use something to stuff the head with so much the better (cotton wool will do).

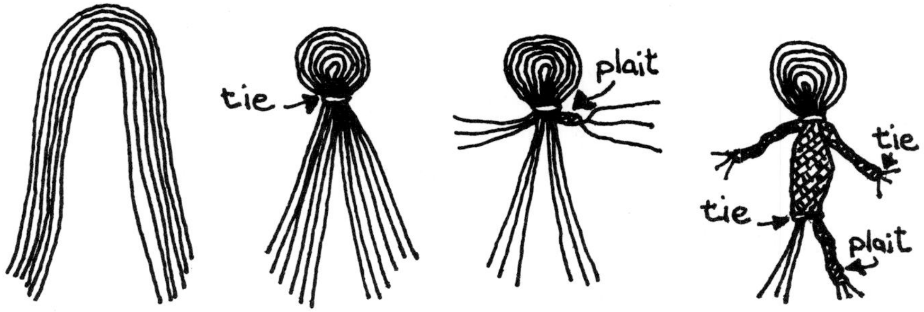

Bodywork

Materials An open space, musical instruments if you wish

Method

1. Talk about the way in which the harvest was gathered-in manually and transported by horse and cart.

2. Work actions can be practised: reaping, stacking, loading the corn, the procession home (remember repetition and rhythm).
3. Use a song that the class can make up the words for and that has a simple rhythm to help with the action, e.g.:
   This is the way we cut the corn, cut the corn, cut the corn,
   This is the way we cut the corn, for the harvest time is with us.
   (To the tune of 'Here We Go Round the Mulberry Bush'.)

Music

Materials The songs below

Method

1. They will probably know both songs, so just sing and enjoy them.

Oats and Beans and Barley Grow

1 Oats and beans and barley grow,
Oats and beans and barley grow,
But neither you, nor I, nor anyone knows,
How oats and beans and barley grow.

2 First the Farmer sows his seed,
Then he stands and takes his ease,
Stamps his feet and claps his hands
And turns him round to view the land.

(Sometimes spoken)
3 Waiting for a partner,
Waiting for a partner,
Open the ring and take one in
And kiss her in the centre.

4 Now you're married you must obey,
You must be true to all you say,
You must be kind, you must be good
And help your wife to chop the wood.

Dance the first verse, then do suitable actions for the other verses and end by repeating the first verse.

2. Don't forget this old faithful:
   'All Things Bright and Beautiful'

SCHOOL

Starting school is a milestone for children and parents! For children, even if they have been to some sort of organised pre-school activity, it is the first time they are away from home all day. There are so many things to learn: names, routines and rules. Before they actually start there has been a round of new clothes and shoes and probably a hair cut.

Once the novelty has worn off, September usually brings a class move, and with it a new teacher to get to know. They become aware of the progression through the school, of even being a junior! The playground isn't quite so busy and daunting and a little more confidence is acquired.

Left at home are the parents. They wonder how the day progresses, whether the children are happy, will they eat their school dinner? After the initial worries wear off, there is more interest in what the children are doing; there is the excitement of the first reading book and the immortal phrase 'Well, Miss says so'!

Suggested Reading

My School
by Sumiko (Heinemann)
Lucy & Tom Go To School by Shirley Hughes (Carousel)

YOUNGER CHILDREN

Written Work and Language

Materials Paper and pencils

Method

1. Names are very important. Make sure the children know yours and explain who you are. Can they write their own full name, too?
2. If they have just started school, play a quiz game to see if they know the names of:
   the Headteacher
   classroom helper
   dinner ladies
   school secretary
   caretaker/cleaner
   Write the names for the children.
3. All these people are important to the running of the school. Let the children draw (and label if possible) these helpful people.

Extension

Materials Paper, pencils and crayons

Method

1. Ask the class to remember what it felt like when they first came to school. Did they have new clothes? Did they make new friends? Did they find the day very long?
2. Break the day up into parts:
   arriving at school
   before playtime
   after playtime
   dinnertime

   playtime
   afternoon
   going home
   Talk about each stage. Do they write in the mornings and paint after dinner? Do they eat in the school hall? When do they do PE?
   Divide the class into groups and get each group to illustrate a part of the day. Get them to decide beforehand what the activity will be.

Number

Materials Mastercopy 9.3, pencils

Method

1. Five is a very important number. It is the age when you start school. Look at the Mastercopy, it shows some other important fives.
2. Identify and practise writing number five.
3. Practise counting × 5.
4. Count forwards and backwards to five.
5. Use the Mastercopy to help you count on from five.

Artwork

Materials Paint and paper

Method

1. When you start school there are times when you can paint without Mummy saying that it's too messy or inconvenient! Children like to paint, so ask them to do a painting of themselves busy in the classroom.

2. If the teacher is absent for a long time, get them to do pictures of the teacher to send to her. Check the physical details before they start work!

Bodywork

Materials Apparatus that the class can get out

Method

1. It's always a good idea to teach the children how to lift and move apparatus before and after a lesson. Make sure they lift and carry correctly and enough children move each piece of apparatus. Simple instructions like using the handles on mats, facing the same direction as you walk carrying a bench, always walking when you put out any equipment. These are just as important as the lesson itself. It ensures everything gets put out safely and that the equipment itself is used correctly and lasts longer.
2. If you get out apparatus, let the children explore, but set tasks so that at a given signal they all must move around the apparatus, or over or through.
3. Make sure that every child has a turn on several pieces during the lesson. Give a changeover activity, e.g.: rolling between pieces, hopping or walking on tiptoe.

Music

Materials The songs below

Method

1. Having talked about five during number time, start by singing '1,2,3,4,5, once I caught a fish alive'.
2. To count even further:

One, two, buckle my shoe;
Three, four, knock on the door;
Five, six, pick up sticks,
Singing this silly old song.

Seven, eight, lay them straight;
Nine, ten, a good fat hen;
Eleven, twelve, dig and delve,
Singing this silly old song.

Thirteen, fourteen, maids are courting;
Fifteen, sixteen, maids in the kitchen,
Seventeen, eighteen, maids are waiting,
Nineteen, twenty, my plate's empty –
Singing this silly old song.

3. For a change, do you remember how to sing the A,B,C,?
4. The song below

At half past three we go home to tea

1 At half past three we go home to tea,
Or maybe at quarter to four;
And ten pairs of feet go running up the street
And in at their own front door:
And it's rough and tumble, rattle and noise,
Mothers and fathers, girls and boys;
Baby in the carry-cot, cat by the stove;
A little bit of quarrelling,
A lot of love.

2 Lord Jesus taught that his children ought
To forgive one another each day,
And to give and take for his dear sake;
So help us, Lord, we pray:
For it's rough and tumble, rattle and noise,
Mothers and fathers, girls and boys;
Baby in the carry-cot, cat by the stove;
A little bit of quarrelling,
But much more love.

Words: Margaret Rose
Music: M. R. Cook

mp
1. At half past three we go home to tea, Or may-be at quar-ter to four; And
C F G7 C G C
ten pairs of feet go run-ning up the street And in at their own front door: And it's
G7 C G7 C G D7 G
rough and tum-ble, rat-tle and noise, Mo-thers and fa-thers, girls and boys;
C G F C F Em F G
Ba-by in the car-ry-cot, cat by the stove; A lit-tle bit of quar-rel-ling, A lot of love.
C F G C G C G F G C

OLDER CHILDREN

Written Work and Language

Materials The poem below and pencils and crayons

Method

1. How many of the class had to have new shoes for the beginning of term?

New Shoes

Buying new shoes
takes so long
When the colour is right
the size is wrong.

The lady asks
How does it fit?
I say to Mum
Pinches a bit.

But that's not true
It's just because
I don't want brown
I prefer blue.

The lady goes inside
brings another size
this time the blue
Not too big. Not too tight

As you guessed
Just right, just right.
Mum says, 'The blue will do'
And I agree. Don't you?

John Agard

Ask them what else they had to buy new for the school term. Did they get what they wanted, or did they have to have what their parents decided?

2. Ask them to think of all the things they would like to wear to school. When they have written down, or drawn, their ideas, talk about why schools insist on a certain type of dress.

Extension

Materials A quiz-type idea that needs paper and pencils, or a blackboard

Method
1. There are lots of words that we come across in school all the time. See if they can sort out the following jumbled up words. Add the headteacher's name and that of their class teacher, too.

LALH	REDNIN
BLEL	YRLBIAR
SCALS	STNFIAN
GORUDPAYLN	OLOCHS

Number

Materials Paper, pencils

Method
1. If possible try to take the class on a tour of the school. When you return to the classroom, make a simple plan of the school. Notice the shapes of rooms and where the largest spaces are.
2. The same exercise can be done for the outside of the school, noticing where access roads are, playgrounds, sports fields, school gates, staff car park.

Extension

Materials Mastercopy 9.3

Method
1. Use in the same way as the Younger Children/Number, concentrate on the × 5 table.

Artwork

Materials Mastercopy 9.4, felt-tip pens, crayons

Method
1. Use the mastercopy to help with 'Doodle Patterns'. The pattern continues until the page is full.

Extension

Materials Paper and crayons, or charcoal if available

Method
1. Returning to what they were doing in Number, take them outside to draw a picture of the school.

Music

Materials The song below

I went to school one morning

(Dance about freely in the room, miming the actions of walking, hopping, splashing, galloping, hobbling, standing and running.)

1 I went to school one morning,
And I walked like this,
Walked like this, walked like this.
I went to school one morning,
And I walked like this,
All on my way to school.

2 I saw a little robin,
And he hopped like this,
Hopped like this, hopped like this.
I saw a little robin,
And he hopped like this,
All on my way to school.

3 I saw a shiny river,
And I splashed like this,
Splashed like this, splashed like this.
I saw a shiny river,
And I splashed like this,
All on my way to school.

4 I saw a little pony,
And he galloped like this,
Galloped like this, galloped like this.
I saw a little pony,
And he galloped like this,
All on my way to school.

5 I saw a poor old lady,
And she hobbled like this,
Hobbled like this, hobbled like this.
I saw a poor old lady,
And she hobbled like this,
All on my way to school.

6 I saw a tall policeman,
And he stood like this,
Stood like this, stood like this.
I saw a tall policeman,
And he stood like this,
All on my way to school.

7 I heard the schoolbell ringing,
And I ran like this,
Ran like this, ran like this.
I heard the schoolbell ringing,
And I ran like this,
All on my way to school.

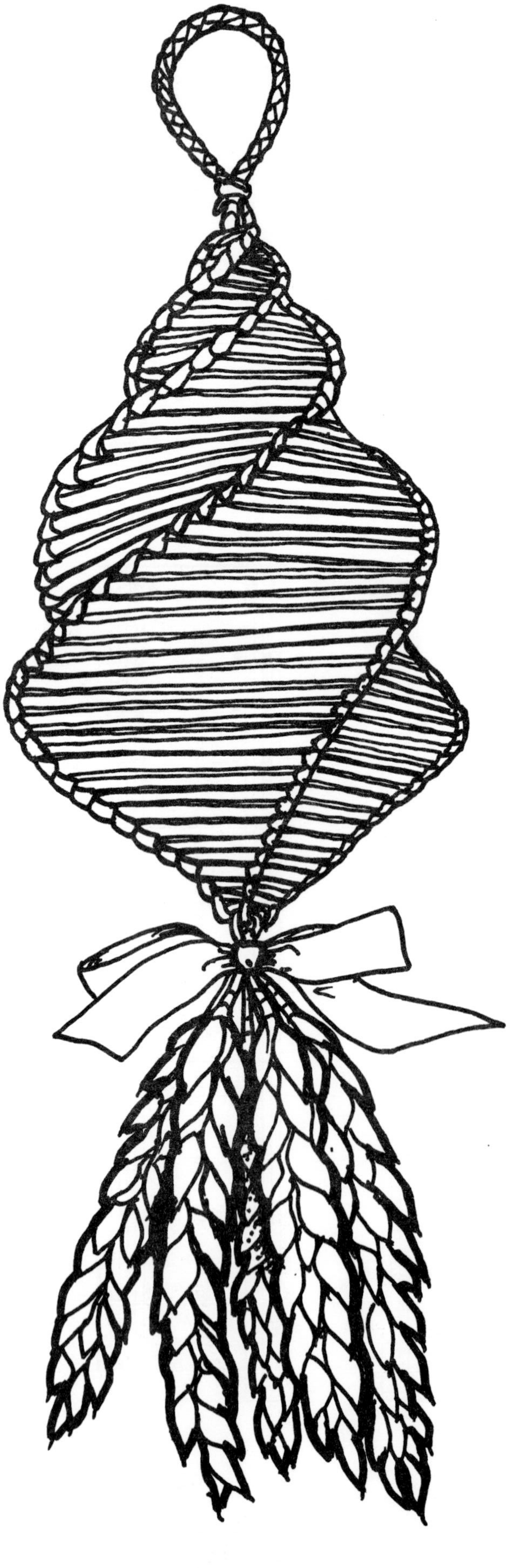

The Ant and the Grasshopper

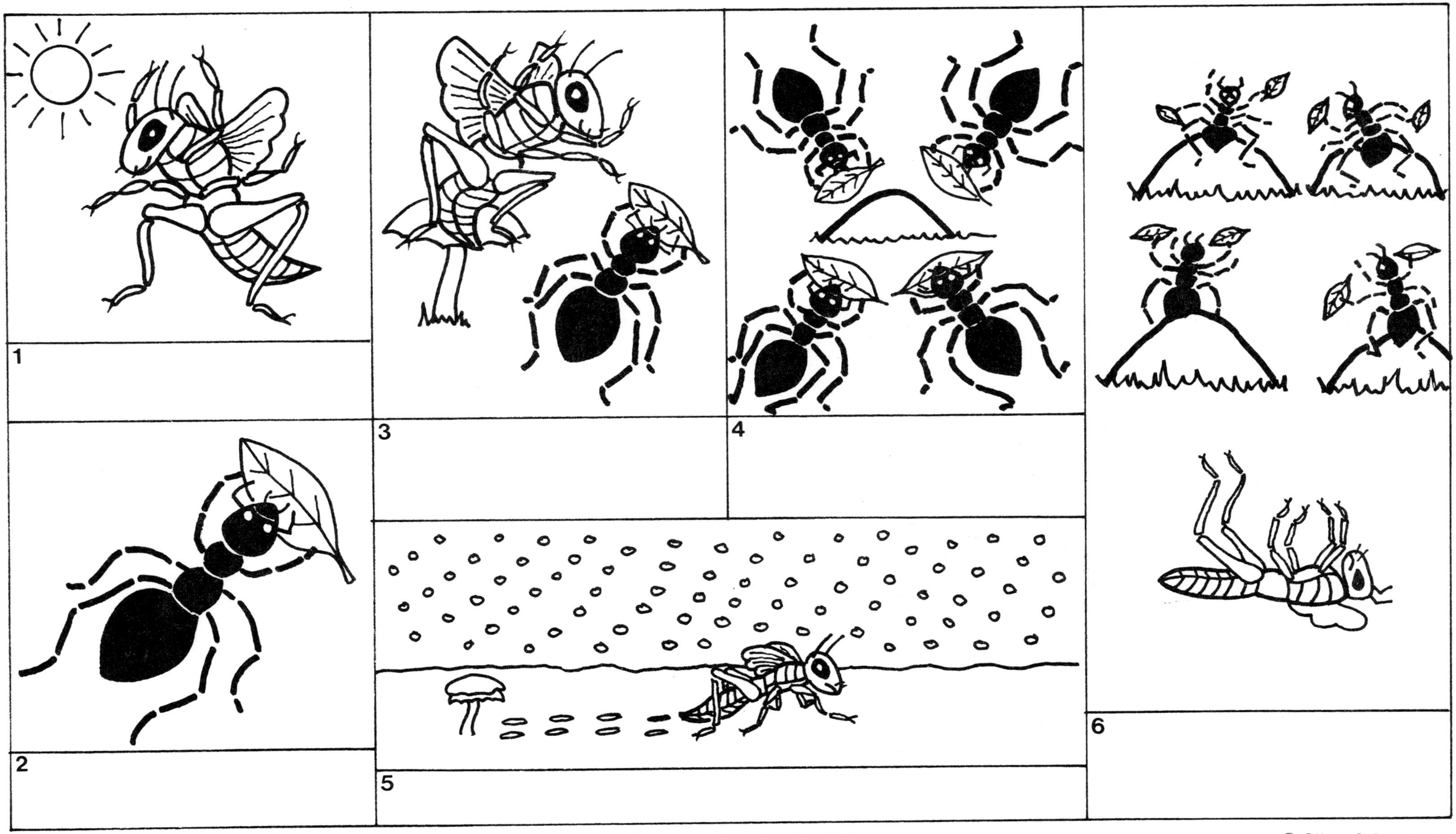

SCHOOL

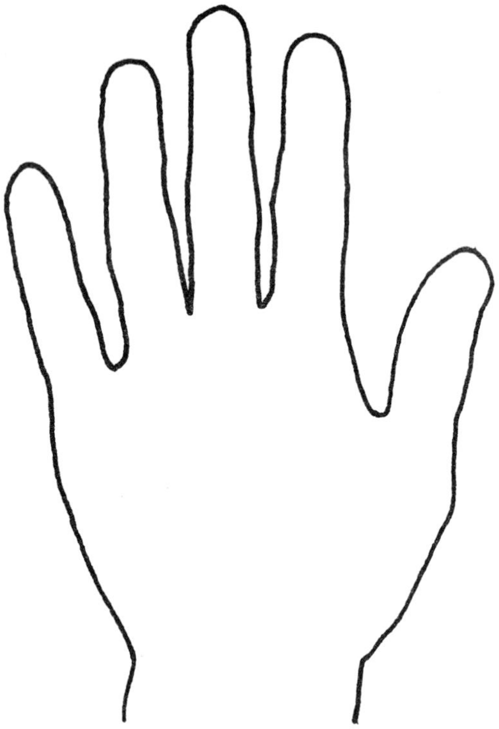

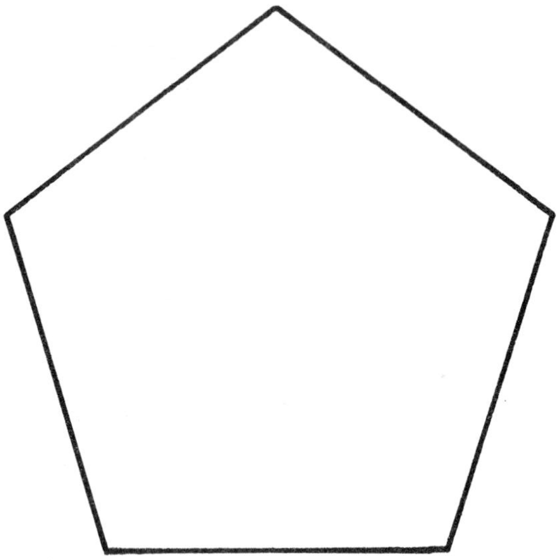

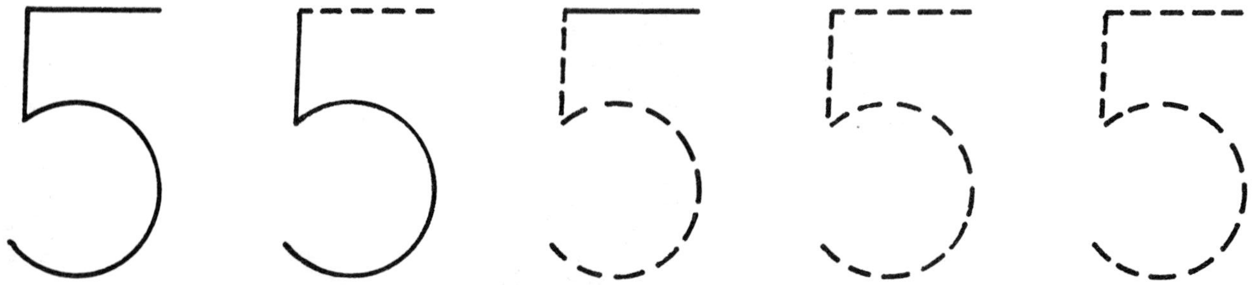

SCHOOL

10 OCTOBER

HALLOWEEN

Young children love Halloween, with the witches and spookiness and spells attached to it. They like making 'witchy faces', chanting strange words for spells, in fact doing everything in a 'witchy way'. It is always a favourite for display work which can cause problems in the black sugar-paper supply! Here are a few more ideas.

Suggested Reading

The Witch and the Mischievous 7
by Ali Mitgutsch (J. M. Dent)
Any of the *Meg and Mog* series
by Nicol Pienkowski
Funny Bones
by Janet & Allan Ahlberg (Picture Lion)

YOUNGER CHILDREN

Written Work and Language

Materials A large black-paper cauldron, smaller pieces of paper (black if possible)

Method

1. Talk about Halloween and find out what they know. Taking the witch as central, discuss and write down what else is associated with them:

broomstick	witch
cat	cloak
toad	cauldron
hat	spells

Words that describe the witch:

ugly	spooky	mean	spikey
crooked	magic	miserable	

2. Get the class to repeat the words as you write them. Let the more able have a go at writing their own, the others can help by sticking the 'witchy words' round the cauldron.

Extension

Materials Same written words as above

Method

1. Using the teacher's words see if the children can make some sentences. Be ready to write more words. This work can be done on the floor if table-top space is difficult.
   e.g. The ugly witch flew her magic broomstick
   The spooky witch had a magic hat for making spells.
2. Get the children to read the sentences back to you in 'witchy voices'.

Number

Materials Paper, crayons

Method

1. Discuss spells, they are rather like recipes. Remind them of:
   'Sugar and spice and all things nice'
   'Half a pound of tuppeny rice' (did it really make a weasel?)
2. To make a spell you have got to get the right ingredients. Ask them for suggestions. You have also got to get the right amount of ingredients. Decide how you are going to measure: in cups, or bowls, or jugs? Think of the other measuring words: full, half full, light, heavy.
3. Make a class spell to change something into something else (*Meg and Mog* stories are invaluable). Remind everyone they have to decide how much or how many of each ingredient they need (volume/weight).

Artwork

Materials Black paper, straws, wool, paint, glue

Method

1. Simple witches' faces can be made with black-paper triangles, painted on faces, wool for hair. Hang from the ceiling.

Extension

Materials Mastercopy 10.1, pre-cut circles, cocktail sticks

Method
1. Use the Mastercopy to make the black witch's cat with the circle cut into a spiral for the tail. Stick cocktail sticks for whiskers.

Bodywork

Materials Taped music ('Danse Macabre' is a good one)

Method 1. Think of witch shapes; they will be:
spikey sharp
twisted pointed
Explore these shapes with the whole body, emphasising elbows, knees, toes and fingers.
2. How does a witch move:
stealthily, quickly/slowly,
creepily, with tiny/large steps?
3. Try chanting the spell you made up in Number Work while they move around an imaginary cauldron making a spell.
4. Or how about:

Round and round the cauldron
Like a spooky witch,
Black cloak, black hat.
And a black broomstick!

Music

Materials 'There Was An Old Witch' in *Apusskidu* (A & C Black)

Method
1. You really cannot beat this song!

OLDER CHILDREN

Written Work and Language

Materials Mastercopy 10.1 cut up, paper, pencils, glue

Method
1. Halloween is a spooky, slightly frightening time. Show the class all the pictures on the Mastercopy. Discuss why these can be scary when linked to Halloween.
2. Invent a class spooky story. It could begin with the line:
'It was a dark and misty night when we crept up to the old house. . .' Who were the 'we'? Why were they there? What did they find/hear? How did it turn out in the end?
3. Use the pictures to help order the story.

Extension

Materials Read the verses from *Macbeth* below

Round about the cauldron go;
Double, double toil and trouble;
Fire burn; and cauldron bubble.

Fillet of a fenny snake,
In the cauldron boil and bake;
Eye of newt, and toe of frog,
Wool of bat, and tongue of dog,
Adder's fork, and blind-worm's sting,
Lizard's leg, and howlet's wing,
For a charm of powerful trouble,
Like a hell-broth boil and bubble.
Act IV Scene 1

Method
1. Help the children make up spells of their own.

Number

Materials Counting aids 0–20

Method
1. The Halloween Party. The witch can only have 20 to her Halloween

celebrations in the haunted house. How many of her friends can she invite? Make the numbers correct.
witch = 1
spiders = ?
wizards = 2
cats = ?
toads = 6
bats = ?

total = 20

2. Then she remembers she has forgotten the two ghosts who live in the haunted house. How does she alter the numbers?
witch = 1
ghosts = 2
wizards = ?
cats = 4
toads = ?
bats = 3
spiders = ?

total = 20

Artwork

Materials Mastercopy 10.2, straws, thin elastic thread, white paint, black paper

Method

1. Make some hanging bats by using the Mastercopy as a guide, on black folded paper. Paint in bat features with white paint.
2. Make witch cards using the Mastercopy. Again, decorate with white paint. Use a straw poked through the paper for a broomstick and shredded paper for the brush part.

Bodywork

Materials Balls, large box (cauldron)

Method

1. Team Game 'Frogs In The Cauldron'.
2. The teacher can be the good fairy! The children are the witches, the balls are the frogs. The good fairy gets the frogs out of the cauldron to release them before they are boiled. The witches have to get them back in. (Remember bouncing, rolling, throwing.) If the good fairy touches a witch he or she is are frozen until the end of the game. The end of the game can be when all frogs are boiled or all witches frozen or exhausted!

Extension

Materials Beanbags

Method

1. 'Where's My Cat?' Make the children form a circle standing very close together. Two children (witches) go in the middle. Two more children on opposite sides of the circle have a beanbag (cat) each. On a given signal cats are passed behind backs, on a second signal stop passing and the children in the centre have to guess which child has the cat. If they are correct they change over, if not they stay inside the circle.

Music

Materials Song below

Method

Halloween's coming

Halloween's coming, Halloween's coming,
Skeletons will be after you;
Witches, cats, and big black bats,
Ghosts and goblins, too!
Flap, flap, flap, go the big black bats,
Oooooooooooooooooooooo!
'Meow, meow, meow,' say the ugly cats.
Oooooooooooooooooooooo! BOO!

Words and music: Children of a Third Grade class, U.S.A.
(Teacher: Esther Alkire Getts)

Mysteriously
Hal-lo-ween's com-ing, Hal-lo-ween's com-ing, Skel-e-tons will be af - ter you;
Em B7 Em B7 Em
Wit-ches, cats, and big black bats, Ghosts and gob-lins, too!
B7 Em
Flap, flap, flap, go the big black bats, Oooooooooooooooo ooooooooooooooo!
B7
'Meow, meow, meow', say the ug - ly cats, Oooooooooooooooo ooo! BOO!
Em B7 Em

RAIN

We seem to have a lot of rain in the British Isles. It is hard to remind yourself of all the benefits, when the constant downpours keep the children cooped up inside during playtimes.

It is a good idea to travel with a lot of instant ideas for wet playtimes, or work that can be left for the children to complete on their own during playtimes.

Here are a couple of poems that I rather like for those rainy days. The first must have been written for us on this island!

The South wind blows and brings wet weather;
The North wind gives wet and cold together;
The West wind comes brimful of rain;
The East wind drives it back again.
Then if the sun in red should set;
We know the morrow must be wet;
And if the eve is clad in grey
The next is sure a rainy day!

The rain it raineth on the just
And also on the unjust fella.
But chiefly on the just, because
The unjust steals the just's umbrella.
Baron Charles Bowen

Suggested Reading

Postman Pat's Rainy Day
by J. Cunliffe (Scholastic Publishers)
Noah's Ark, retold
by L. T. Lorimer (Random House)

YOUNGER CHILDREN

Written Work and Language

Materials The nursery rhyme on page 120. Paper, pencils, crayons

Method
1. Say the rhyme with them:

Doctor Foster

Doctor Foster went to Gloster
In a shower of rain
He fell in a puddle, right up to his middle,
And never went there again.

Ask the class if they have ever fallen in a puddle? How do they think Dr Foster must have felt? What sort of words would they use to describe being all drippy wet after such an accident?

2. Try a three-part picture:

Maybe the rainbow would have cheered up Dr Foster.

Extension

Materials Paper plates, string, pre-cut raindrop shapes, pencils

Method
1. Rain comes in tiny droplets from heavy grey clouds. Using the 'rainy words' that the children can think of let them make their own rain clouds to hang in the classroom.

Number

Materials Mastercopy 10.3, pencils and crayons

Method
1. Link the correct words and sets.
2. Colour and count the sets.

Artwork

Materials Large piece of paper and crayons. The poem below

Happiness

John had Great Big Waterproof Boots on
John had a Great Big Waterproof Hat on
John had a Great Big Waterproof Mackintosh –
And that (said John)
Is that. *A. A. Milne*

Method
1. Draw round one/two children and add the same clothes as John!

Extension

Materials Mastercopy 10.4 cut out and mounted on card to use as a template. Pencils and crayons

Method
1. An umbrella is extremely useful when it's raining. It also makes a good shape to use for drawing round and making patterns.
2. Decorate the edge of the page with a 'UUUUUUUUUUUUU' shape.

Bodywork

Materials Imagination. The music to 'Singin' in the Rain', if you have it

Method
1. Lead the children through getting ready to go out in the rain. Putting on a waterproof coat, finding a hat, putting on your wellington boots and collecting the umbrella. Remember not to open the brolly inside, that's bad luck.
2. As you are walking down the street a big lorry drives past and splashes muddy water all over you. What can you do? I bet you are cross with the driver, but he's already gone.

3. The rain is really pouring down now and the wind is blowing and tugging at your umbrella. Suddenly a strong gust blows your umbrella inside out, and nearly wrenches it out of your hands. You are pulled along the street.
4. Because you are not looking where you are going you bump into a tree and end up in a heap in a muddy puddle. Don't you wish you had never gone out?

Extension

Materials Balls

Method

1. Play a variation on 'Wounded Soldier'. Tell the children to stand in a circle. Ask them to remember the 'rainy' words they used during Written Work and Language. You stand in the centre of the circle, holding the ball.
2. You say which rainy word and as you throw the ball to a child they must spell the word, one letter at a time to match with each throw of the ball. Keep the words short!
3. If they spell the word and catch the ball they can change places with you and they get to choose the word.
4. The activity need not be throwing and catching, but can include any ball skills that you feel are appropriate.

Music

Materials The songs suggested below

Method

1. Sing the well-known 'I Hear Thunder' with actions.
2. The children love 'Sing a Rainbow'.

Sing a rainbow

1 Red and yellow and pink and green,
Purple and orange and blue,
I can sing a rainbow,
Sing a rainbow,
Sing a rainbow, too.
Listen with your eyes,
Listen with your eyes
And sing everything you see.
You can sing a rainbow,
Sing a rainbow,
Sing along with me.

2 Red and yellow and pink and green,
Purple and orange and blue.
Now we can sing a rainbow,
Sing a rainbow,
Sing a rainbow, too.

Words and music: Arthur Hamilton

OLDER CHILDREN

Written Work and Language

Materials Book made from ten pages. Story of Noah's Ark (Genesis 6–10, for reference), Mastercopy 10.4

Method

1. Tell the story of Noah and his ark, and tell the class that they are going to make their own story book.
2. Give each a book, break down the story as a class activity:
   a. Front cover – title
   b. Building the ark
   c. Animals being loaded
   d. The rain starts
   e. The flood
   f. The dove
   g. Mount Ararat
   h. Unloading the ark
   i. The rainbow
3. As the ark features quite largely, there is one on the Mastercopy to start them off.

Extension

Materials Pictures of the British countryside, deserts, jungles

Method

1. Explain the rain cycle to children, so that they know rain comes in tiny droplets from certain types of cloud.

2. In the British Isles we get quite a lot of rain as the winds blow in clouds over the sea. This gives us green grass and trees, rivers, lakes, etc. (a new word – 'temperate').
3. There are many parts of the world that do not have any rain. Explain that these are called deserts; show any pictures you have. Some parts of the world suffer drought. Remind them of Ethiopia. A drought can make a country look like a desert.
4. Other parts of the world have a lot more rain than us. These areas have very dense trees and undergrowth – jungle.
5. Talk about the different needs of people living in these areas. Food, clothing, travelling. Though it might be interesting to visit a desert or a jungle, would the children really like to live there?

Number

Materials A line of children two by two helps!

Method

1. The animals, it is said, entered the ark two by two. Do the children know their × 2 table?

Extension

Materials Mastercopy 10.3

Method

1. Complete as for Younger Children/Number.
2. Use to help with addition.

Artwork

Materials Paint and paper, plenty of newspaper, toothbrushes

Method

1. Do some rainy/watery paintings:
   a. Drip some spots of paint at the top of the page. Lift the top edge gently and see what happens.
   b. Use toothbrushes to execute 'splatter paintings'.
   c. Try blot and fold 'butterfly' pictures.

Extension

Materials Paint and paper

Method

1. Make a class painting of Noah's ark. Take it in turns to paint. Different parts of the picture could be done in different ways: sponge printing for the sea rising, sticky paper raindrops cut out, the ark and the rainbow painted separately and assembled later.

Bodywork

Materials Drums and shakers

Method

1. Practise skipping and hopping.
2. Practise moving in lines, weaving and circling, moving in a spiral.
3. The North American Indians used to do a dance to bring on the rains. Let the children have a go at making a rain dance for themselves.

Music

Materials The songs below

Method

1. 'Who Built the Ark?' is a good one.

Who Build the Ark?

Who built the ark?
Noah, Noah,
Who built the ark?
Brother Noah built the ark.

1 Now in come the animals two by two,
Hippopotamus and kangaroo.

2 Now in come the animals four by four,
Two through the window and two
through the door.

3 Now in come the animals six by six,
Elephant laughed at the monkey's tricks.

4 Now in come the animals eight by eight,
Some were on time and the others were late.

5 Now in come the animals ten by ten,
Five black roosters and five black hens.

6 Now Noah says, go shut that door,
The rain's started dropping
and we can't take more.

Words and melody: J. Rosamund Johnson
Piano accompaniment: G. C. Westcott

2. How about:

When You're Smiling

When you're smiling, when you're smiling,
The whole world smiles with you;
When you're laughing, when you're laughing,
The sun comes shining through;
But when you're crying, you bring on the rain,
So stop you're sighing, be happy again;
Keep on smiling, 'cause when you're smiling,
The whole world smiles with you.

M. Fisher, J. Goodwin, L. Shay

HALLOWEEN

HALLOWEEN

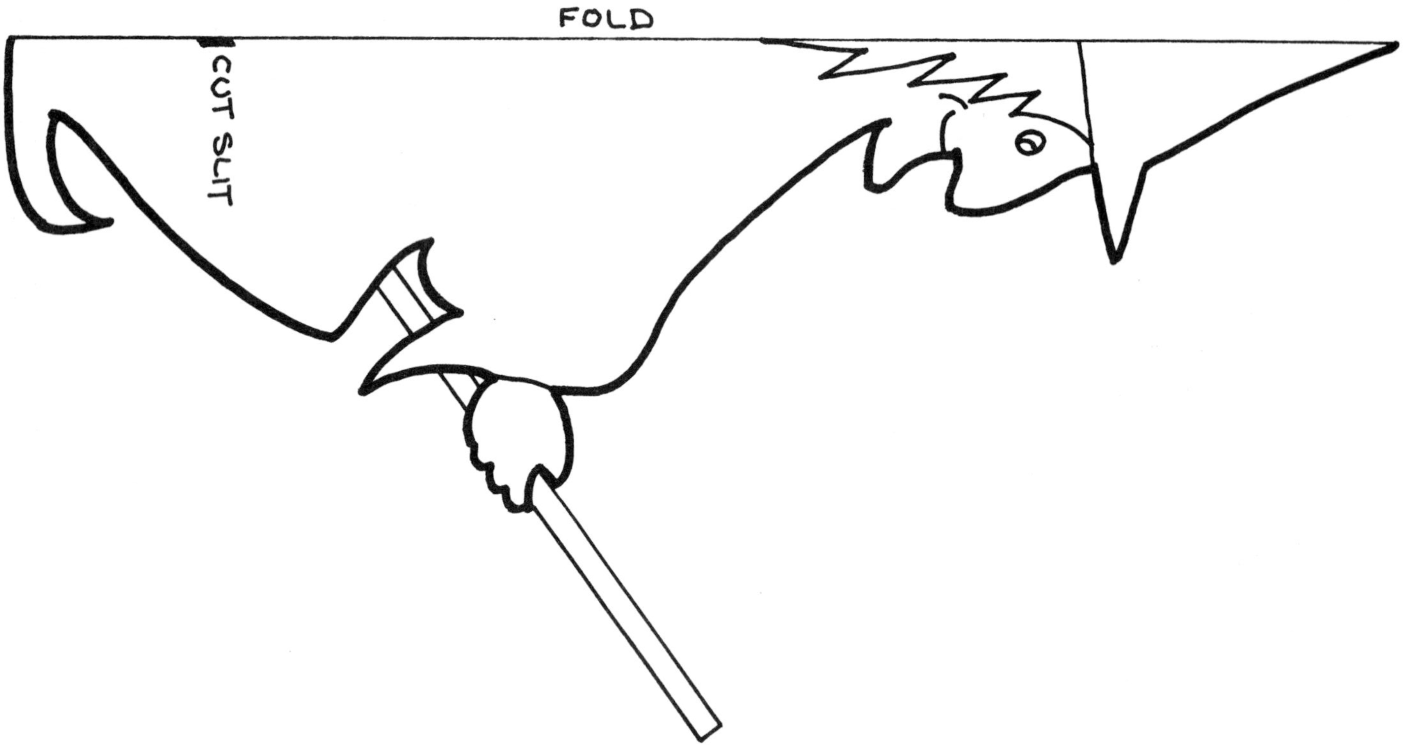

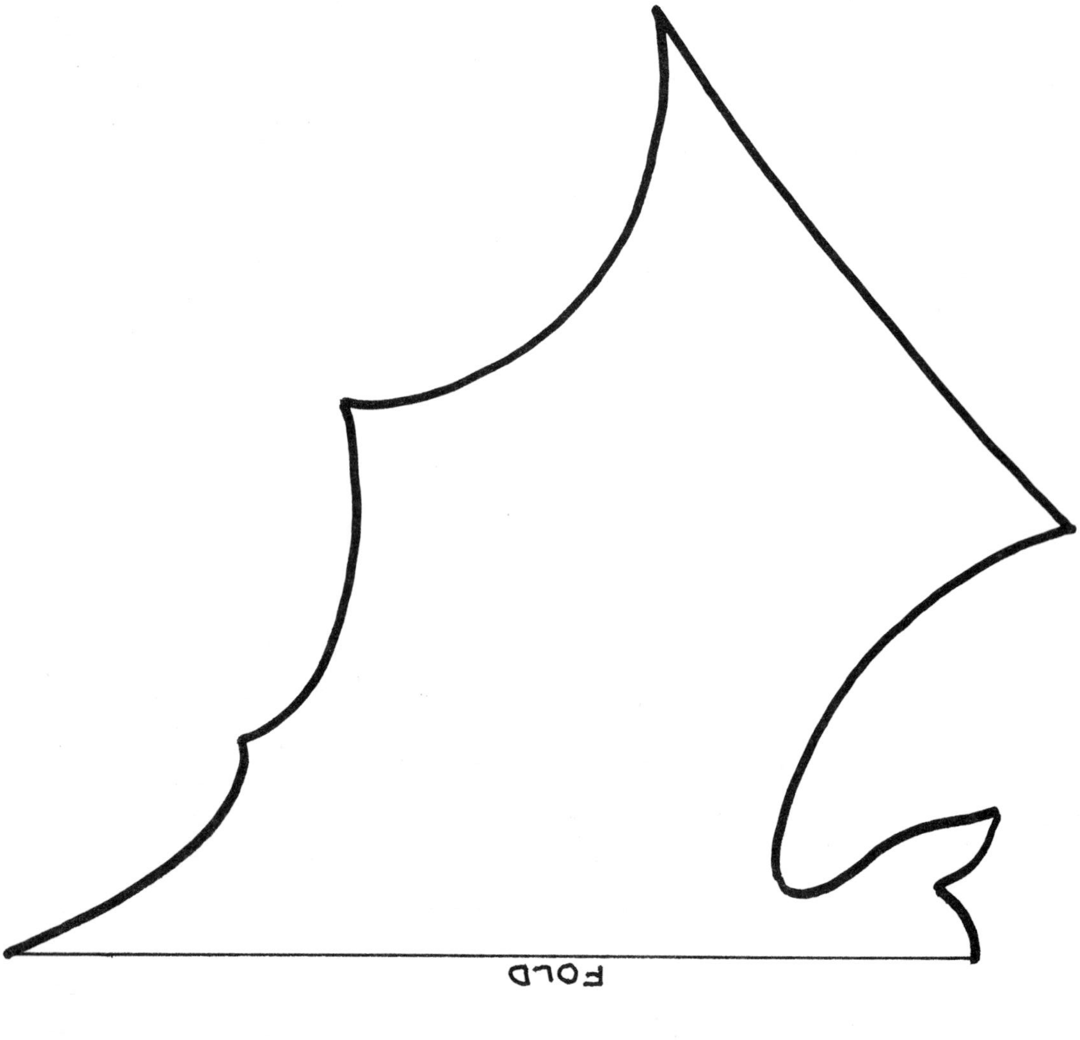

raindrops rainbow rainclouds raincoats rainhats

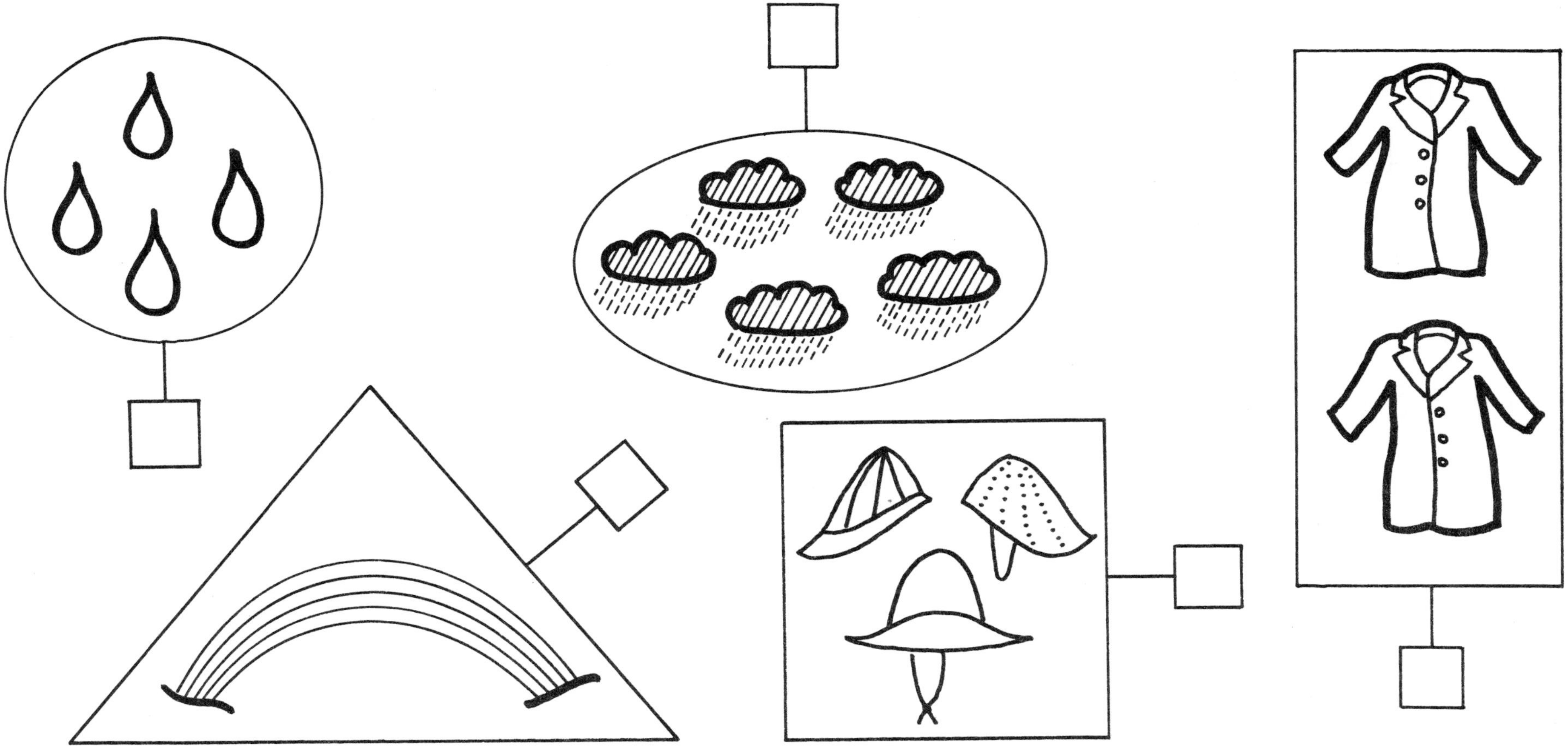

1 2 3 4 5

11 NOVEMBER

BONFIRE NIGHT

Bonfire Night is still celebrated, but not perhaps with the historical significance so much in mind, more as an entertainment that can be enjoyed by all the family. Small children love the excitement, from being up and outside in the dark to the thrill and magic of fireworks.

These sections contain work based on the theme. The younger children may need help remembering what fireworks look like and with their names. The older ones could certainly go over the Firework Code.

Suggested Reading

The Owl Who Was Afraid of the Dark
by Jill Tomlinson (Penguin)

YOUNGER CHILDREN

Written Work and Language

Materials Action words written on pieces of paper, paper, glue, pencils, 2 × A4 pieces of paper folded and stapled to make a small booklet

Method

1. Show the children the booklet and tell them that the front page is going to read 'I like fireworks because they. . .' They can fill up the rest of the book with the fireworks they like best.
2. To help imagine the fireworks, show them the pieces of paper with the written words: zoom, whoosh, bang, whizz. Discuss what sort of fireworks those sounds represent.
3. Give each child a booklet with the starter sentence written on it. Let them illustrate the front page as they wish and then choose a different firework for each of the following pages.
4. Those who are able can write the word after they have drawn the picture. Those who cannot, may use one of the small pieces of paper with the correct word already written and glue it on the page.

Number

Materials Mastercopy 11.1

Method

1. Different uses:
   Colour all rockets blue.
   Colour all bangers red.
   Colour all catherine wheels yellow.
   Colour all waterfalls green.
2. Put the fireworks into sets. How many in each set?
3. If you add 1/2/3/more to each set how many fireworks do you have?

Extension

Materials Numbers 0–20 written large on pieces of paper

Method

1. For explanation see Older Children/Number. Another use would be to draw each section of a Guy as a number is recognised.

Artwork

Materials Cardboard rolls, crepe paper, silver foil, paint, glue, wooden lolly sticks/barbecue skewers

Method

1. Paint rolls, stick on silver foil shapes, attach wooden sticks.
2. Stick crepe paper streamers to the inside of the tube to finish off the rocket.

Bodywork

Materials Wooden blocks or xylophone, tambourine, triangle, shakers

Method

1. Choose a musical instrument to match a firework:
   rocket = tambourine
   bangers = wooden blocks
   catherine wheel = triangle
   waterfall = shakers
   (add to the list if you want)

2. Ask children if they can imagine the sort of movement that might match the sound:
   rocket = starting small, shooting up
   bangers = quick crouching jumps all around
   catherine wheel = spinning
   waterfalls = shooting up and spiralling as they fall
3. Divide the class, some to make sounds, others to try out firework movements. Which is their favourite movement? Remember to change the groups around.
4. The musical children could always sit in the middle of the space (the bonfire!). Can they make a firework display?

Music

Materials Various! Include triangles, tambourines, shakers, cymbals then whatever comes to hand

Method

1. After reading the following story, make a sound accompaniment. Here are a few suggestions:
   people noises = voices
   bonfire = scrunching brown paper or rubbing sand paper
   smoke = voices
   rockets = tambourines and shakers
   catherine wheels = triangles
   bangers = clapping hands quickly
   waterfalls = shakers (paperclips in a tin will do)
   volcanoes = cymbals
   The song at the end can be a class favourite or '99 Bottles of Pop' or 'If You're Happy and You Know it. . .'.

The School Bonfire

It was the night of the school Bonfire Party. There were lots of children, Mums, Dads, Grans and Grandads and even teachers (   ) round the fire. The headteacher lit the bonfire (   ) and all the people cheered (   ). We watched as the flames licked around the wood (   ) and saw the poor old Guy disappear in the smoke (   ). Suddenly there was a sound (   ) and a rocket zoomed into the air, bursting into hundreds of silver stars (   ). Then came another and another; the display had started. Everyone gasped (   ) at every new explosion! As the fire continued to burn (   ), more fireworks were let off, catherine wheels (   ), waterfalls (   ) and even a few bangers (   ), not too many as no one wanted to frighten the small children or any animals that might be about. Some of the Mums had made hot chocolate with marshmallows floating on the top, which the children loved drinking (   ). There were crisps to eat (   ) and it was good to see everyone feeling warm and happy as they stood around the bonfire (   ). There were more fireworks to come with roman candles (   ), and volcanoes that erupted twinkling lights (   ) and at the end of the display came the biggest rockets (   ). The fire had begun to die down when they had finished (   ) and the headteacher suggested that we all sing a song round the fire. Can you guess which song we all sang?

OLDER CHILDREN

Written Work and Language

Materials Paper, crayons, felt-tip pens, glue, scissors

Method

1. Discuss with the children the different sorts of fireworks (sparklers, Roman candles, bangers, rockets, waterfalls) and what happens to them after they are lit.
2. Choose one type and draw it on a piece of paper. When coloured, cut it out.
3. Explain that this is the start of their story. Can they draw a story and then stick the firework in it. For example, a rocket:
   a. He thought he was the biggest and best firework of all, but was he?
   b. The rocket flew up into the sky, as high as the moon.
   c. The rocket went 'bang' over the bonfire and burst into a shower of stars.

Number

Materials Mastercopy 11.2, a large piece of paper, crayons or blackboard and chalk

Method

1. Explain that you are going to make a Guy to go on the bonfire. Show the example of the Guy on the Mastercopy.
2. Discuss how he is made and how his body is divided into sections.
3. To draw each section and make the Guy the children must get a sum correct. The child who completes the picture can choose the next type of sum if the game moves fast enough.

4. Activities could then include:
   number bonds 0–10, orally;
   counting on from a given number, orally;
   writing numbers 10–20.

Artwork

Materials Mastercopy 11.2, scissors, glue, paint or crayons

Please To Remember

Here am I
A poor old Guy.
Legs in a bonfire,
Head in the sky,

Shoeless my toes,
Wild stars behind,
Smoke in my nose,
And my eye-peeps blind,

Old hat, old straw –
In this disgrace;
While the wildfire gleams
On a mask for a face

Ay, all I am made of
Only trash is,
And soon – soon,
Will be dust and ashes.

Walter de la Mare

Method

1. Read the poem and discuss. Use the Mastercopy to colour and cut out.
2. Either make individual pictures and stick the Guy on top, or make a class picture by dividing up the tasks:
   One group – black sky and ground
   One group – bonfire
   One group – fireworks
   One group – people
   Assemble group work and top with the Guys.

Bodywork

Materials Netballs

Method

1. 'Firework Relay'. Divide the children into teams, then each team in half, one half at either end of the hall facing each other. Give each team a netball.
2. Line the children up and give each a firework name: rocket, banger, catherine wheel.
3. Explain the relay must be raced with each letter having a different movement:
   all Rs must run to pass the ball;
   all Bs must hop to pass the ball;
   all C.W.s must spin to pass the ball.
4. The children must sit after they have run their part of the relay. The winning team being that which has all members sitting first.

Music

Materials Piano if possible!

Method

1. Songs for round and bonfire. Start by learning to sing the Alphabet to the tune below.
2. When they have learned it, it becomes the chorus. Then try singing a nursery rhyme as a verse to the same tune. Here are some that work:
   'Jack and Jill'
   'Mary Mary Quite Contrary'
   'Jack Sprat'
   'Pussy-cat, Pussy-cat'
   'Hey diddle, diddle, the Cat and the Fiddle'

SAFETY

This topic is divided into four areas: safety at home, safety at school, water safety and road safety. These are covered in school during normal classroom activities, and the relevant services (Police, Fire) are excellent at teaching and informing the children about safety.

We cannot prevent all accidents, but we can constantly remind children of Safety Rules. It is a topic that is 'neat' for the supply teacher, as it can be completed or extended depending on the amount of time you have with the class.

Suggested Reading

Topsy and Tim Take No Risks
by J. & G. Anderson (Blackie)

YOUNGER CHILDREN

Written Work and Language

Materials A piece of paper for each child (to make a book), pencils, crayons

Method

1. **Danger** is a good word for the children to learn. Explain that this is a warning word and should be obeyed.
2. Talk about the places where they might see this word: road works, scaffolding, poisonous fluids, packets of cigarettes. Then go on to think of all the times the word would be used: playing with matches, crossing the road carelessly, playing too near water, fooling around at the top of stairs (the list is endless).
3. Let them choose one example and draw a picture of it. At the bottom of the page they can write 'Danger'. Put all the pages together in a book.

Extension

Materials Copy of school rules if there are any

Method

1. In school we have rules. They are there to protect us and make school-time pleasant for everyone. If there is a school rule book, read it to the class. If not, suggest some of the things that would make good rules, to ensure everyone's safety.
2. We care about each other, so we should not slam doors.
   We care about each other, so we shouldn't run along corridors carelessly.
   We care about each other, so we should be careful on apparatus.
   We care about each other, so we shouldn't leave things lying around for people to trip over, etc.

Number

Materials Mastercopy 11.3

Method

1. Talk about and identify the signs and discuss where we might find them.
2. There are six road signs to learn and some warnings to watch out for.
3. There are also six points to the Green Cross Code. Use fingers to help learn the six points.
   a. Find a safe place to cross, then stop.
   b. Stand on the pavement near the kerb.
   c. Look all around the traffic and listen.
   d. If traffic is coming let it pass. Look all round again.
   e. When there is no traffic near, walk straight across the road.
   f. Keep looking and listening for traffic as you cross.

Extension

Materials Paper and pencils

Method

1. Think of all the important numbers to learn and have in your memory, e.g.:
   Your telephone number
   999 Emergency number

Extension

Materials Mastercopy 11.4

Method

1. Children may like to play the game as the Older Children/Number p. 133, but in teams or as a class activity.

Artwork

Materials Paper plates and paint or felt-tip pens

Method

1. Using Mastercopy 11.3 as inspiration and a guide make some warning signs.

Try making some special ones for the classroom following the 'We Care About Each Other' work. Remember to make some traffic light colours as well.

Bodywork

Materials Traffic-light plates from Artwork, benches and mats

Method
1. Set up the benches and mats as you wish, the children can move round the apparatus, but they must obey the signals. Give the signals without speaking, so the class must look and be alert.
2. Decide on the meaning of the signal:
   Red – stop moving
   Amber – change direction
   Green – move on the apparatus
3. Set what must be done on each piece of apparatus:
   Mats – rolling, somersaults
   Benches – balancing, sliding, jumping over

Music

Materials Nursery rhymes

Method
1. Remember all the people in these nursery rhymes who might not have ended up in the way they did if they had been a little more careful!
2. 'Humpty Dumpty'
   'Ladybird, Ladybird'
   'Jack and Jill'
   'Hush-a-bye, Baby'
   'Ring-a-ring of roses.'

OLDER CHILDREN

Written Work and Language

Materials Road signs

Method
1. As thousands of children are injured annually outside schools, this is a good place to start. Organise the children to go to the school gates and observe:
   a. Gates to the outside (to stop children running onto the road)
   b. Signs outside the school (to slow the traffic down)
   c. Road markings (to prevent parking where children might cross)
   d. Traffic passing the school (cars should drive slowly)
   e. Provision for crossing the road (Zebra, Pelican, Lollipop Lady)
2. Return to the classroom and discuss what has been seen. Ask the children how they arrive and are collected from school. Go through the Green Cross Code (see Younger Children/Number).
3. Do the children have a Lollipop Lady? What is on her sign? What other safe ways are there of crossing the road?
4. Look at Mastercopy 11.3. Can the class identify these signs? Add any that might be outside the school.

Number

Materials Mastercopy 11.4, dice, crayons

Method
1. In pairs they can play this road safety game. If they land on a square they must identify it; if they can't then they miss a turn. Some squares must be coloured in before the start, to be used as traffic lights:
   Red = go back one square
   Amber = miss one throw
   Green = one more throw

Artwork

Materials Paint, paper, scissors, glue

Method
1. Make some posters to bring Water Safety to people's attention.
2. Print some signs and let them be painted red (see diagram). Cut them out.

3. Children love to play with water, but don't realise how dangerous it can be. Tiny children should never be left unsupervised near water, and the sooner they learn how to swim the better. Ask the class to think of all the places where water can be dangerous: canals and ponds (especially if frozen), the seaside, even in the bath if small children are left unattended.
4. Let them choose a water scene that could be dangerous for children. Get them to paint a large picture of the scene and then they can stick their cut out 'Danger' sign across one corner.
5. The posters can be displayed in the classroom or somewhere more noticeable for the rest of the school.

Bodywork

Materials An open space

Method

1. Play a variation on 'Grandmother's Footsteps' and call it 'Traffic Lights'.
2. Teacher (Controller) stands with his/her back to the class, who are at the other end of the hall.
3. Controller calls Green, class may hop towards him. If the Controller calls Amber, the class must crawl carefully along. If the Controller calls Red, and turns around quickly, the class must freeze. The Controller turns back again for Amber and stays that way for Green.
4. Always follow the traffic light sequence.
5. Anyone who disobeys the signal, or moves on Red, is out.
6. The first person to reach the Controller takes over as the new Controller.

Music

Materials The song below

Crossing Over

1 'Now here's a rule,' said little Jane
'For safely crossing over:
Look right, look left, look right again –
All children should remember!'

2 She always used a crossing place,
Or took great care without one;
She never ran and never raced,
But walked when she was certain.

3 So Jane did just as she had learned,
With care and thought, not hasty;
To right and left, then right she turned –
And crossed the roads with safety!
BUT. . .

4 'Now what's the rule,' said little Len,
'For safely crossing over?
Look right, look left, look right again –
That's it, I do remember!'

5 But rules require some care and thought,
The crossing code like many;
Else we might be as badly caught,
And copy little Lenny.

6 For Len did just as he had learned
(His end must make us shiver),
To right, and left, then right he turned –
And tried to cross a river!

Lyrics: R. Blythe
Music: S. Maw

Now here's a rule said li - tle Jane, for safe - ly cross-ing
F C Gm7 C7
ne - ver ran and nev - er raced, but walked when she was
B♭ F B♭ F C
o - ver look right, look left, look right a - gain, all
F B♭ F B♭ F
cer - tain. So Jane did just as she had learned, with
F Dm A
chil - dren should re - mem - ber. She al - ways used a
G G7 C F
care and thought not has - ty to right and left, then
Dm Gm A F B♭ F
cross - ing place, or took great care with - out one, she
C Gm7 C7 F
right she turned, and crossed the roads with safe - ty.
B♭ F C F

BONFIRE NIGHT

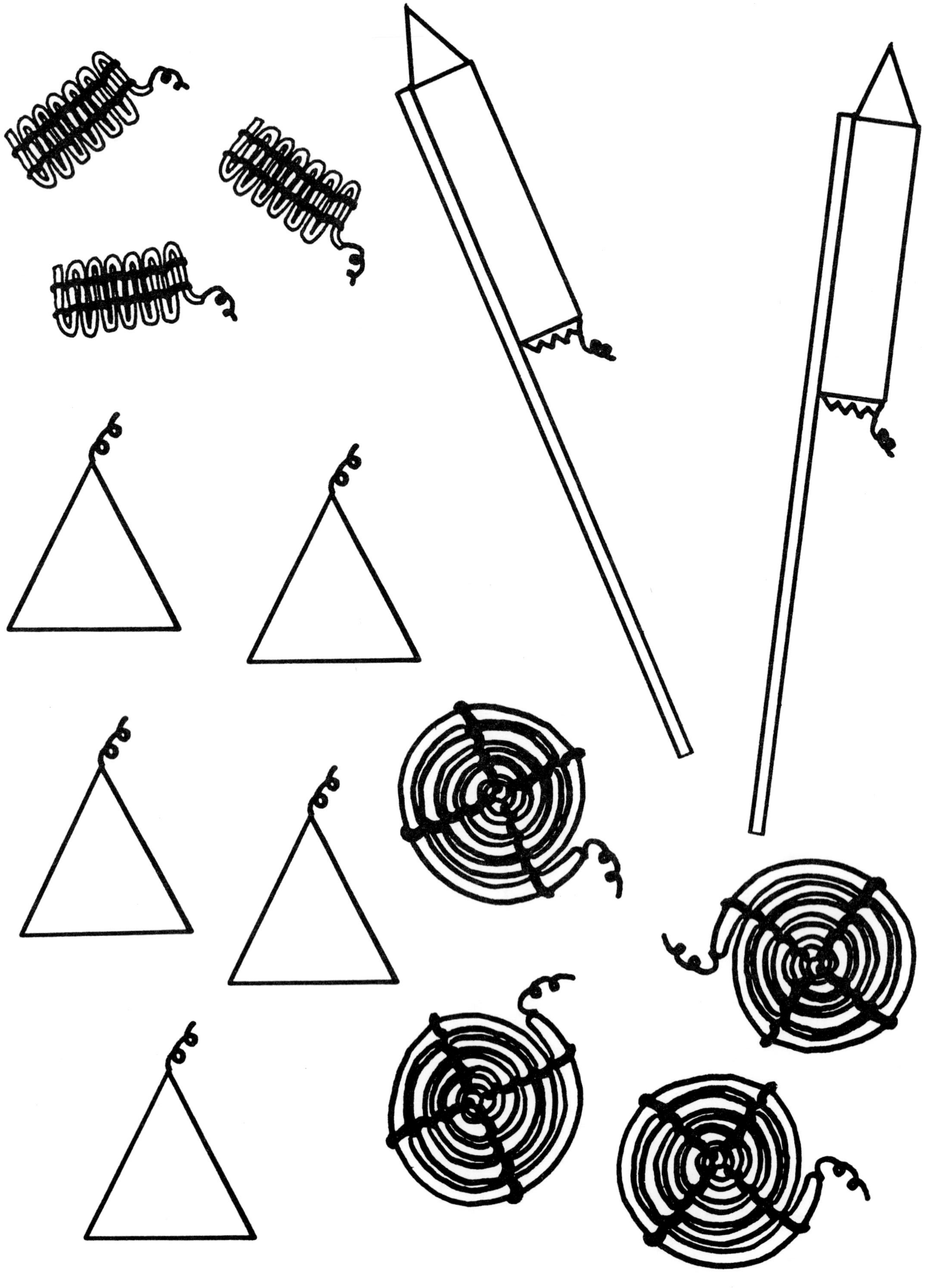

BONFIRE NIGHT

SAFETY

Look for these signs and words on toys and games. The warning words are to help you stay safe and healthy.

APPROVED TO BRITISH STANDARD

UNSUITABLE FOR CHILDREN UNDER 3

CAUTION

DANGER

POISON

SAFETY

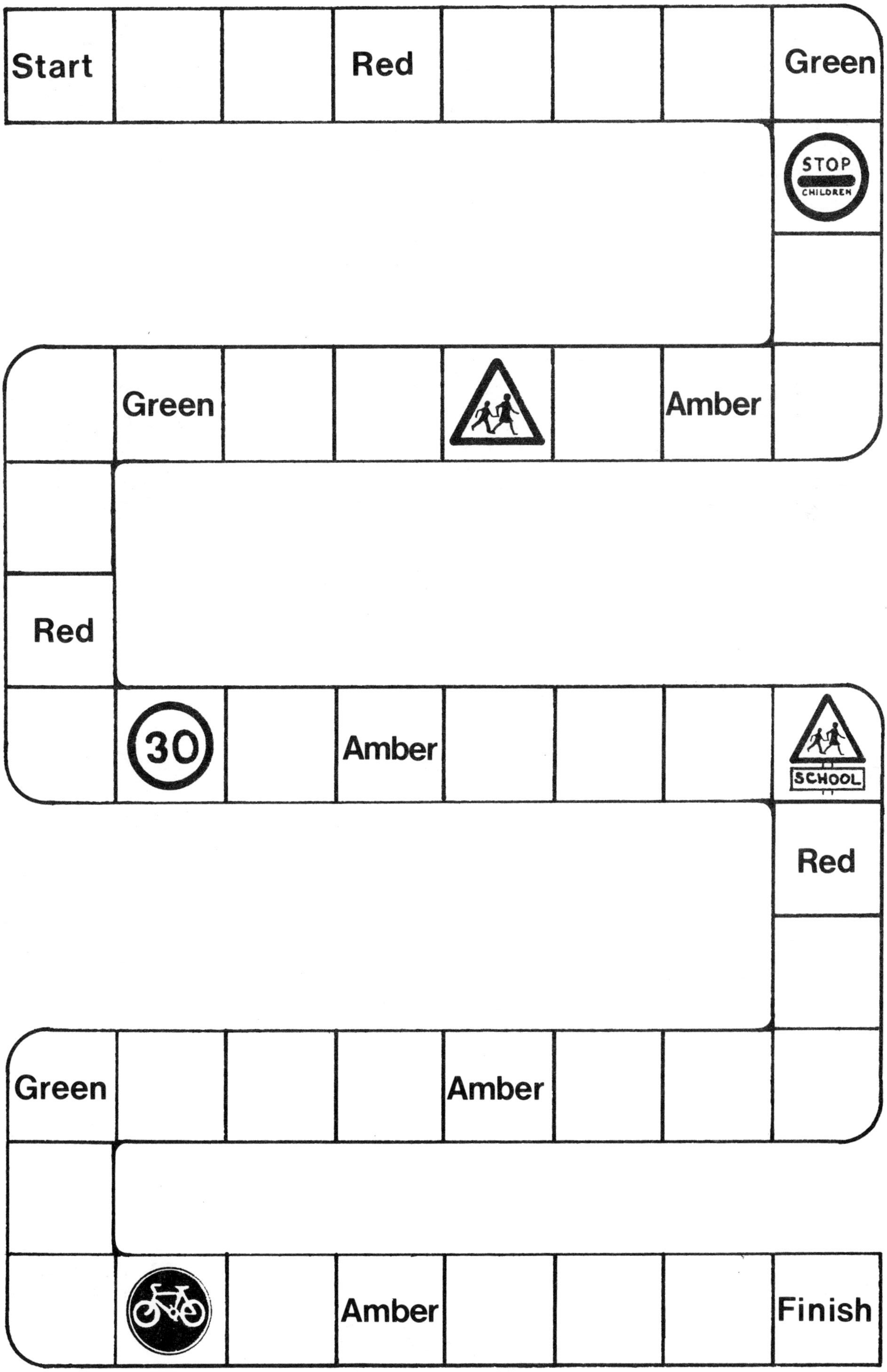
Start
Red
Green
STOP
CHILDREN
Amber
Green
Red
30
Amber
SCHOOL
Red
Amber
Green
Amber
Finish

12 DECEMBER

CHRISTMAS

Christmas comes early in school! Classrooms and hall have to be decorated by the first week of December and seemingly hours of time given to the Christmas Play. So, this section is filled with material to use during the frequently interrupted days around this time.

The Mastercopies are designed to spark off work and remind you of old favourites. More of the work is aimed at display, or things to decorate with and then take home.

In our multi-cultural society it may be inappropriate to overstate the Christian message; however the feelings of love, the generosity of giving, the pleasure and excitement of the birthday of Jesus can be enjoyed by all.

Suggested Reading

Three Ways To Tell The Christmas Story
by M. K. Richardson (Mayhew MacCrimmon)

YOUNGER CHILDREN

Written Work and Language

Materials Mastercopy 12.1, crayons, Plasticine, glitter, plastic envelopes

Method

1. Read the story below:

The Little Fir Tree

Once upon a time there was a little fir tree that stood in the middle of a great forest among the big fir trees. The little fir tree was very unhappy because no one noticed him; even the birds flew to the big trees to make their nests because they thought him too small.

When the wind came blowing through the forest it played with the big trees, bending and rocking them. The little fir tree called, 'Oh please, dear Wind, come and play with me!' but the Wind always said, 'Oh no, you are too small'.

In the winter, when the snow fell gently and covered all the great trees, giving them wonderful white coats and hats, the little fir tree undercover of the others would call, 'Oh please, dear Snow, give me a hat too!' but the Snow always said, 'Oh no, you are too little, too little!'

The little fir tree grew sad. The other trees were cut down by men with axes and sledges. They were taken away to become the masts of mighty ships, or parts of great houses – but always the little fir tree was left behind; he was too small and the men passed him by. How he wished to be chosen to be something useful.

Then one winter's morning the men came and the little fir tree heard them say: 'There are none little enough.' The little fir tree stood straight with his needles all shiny and green. 'Oh there is one,' said a voice and a hand touched the little fir tree. He was so excited, he had been chosen, he wondered what would happen next as they carried him away.

The men took him to the town and put him in a little tub, and stood him on the pavement. The little fir tree saw all the people and cars and lights. He didn't know what was going to happen next. Then two small children came, looked at him and said, 'This is perfect, we'll take him please.' He was carried away even more puzzled. He couldn't become the mast of a ship if he was being taken by children.

He was taken to a building and put in a little room. Two ladies in blue dresses with white aprons and hats came in with the children. They carried a brown box. The children emptied the box and the little fir tree couldn't believe it. They played with him and dressed him and decorated him, just as he had wanted the wind and snow to do. But this was much better, for when they finished playing, he was a glittering, shining tree covered with coloured bells and strands of shimmering tinsel. Little lights had been put in his branches and best of all a beautiful white angel sat on his topmost branch. The little fir tree could hardly believe how wonderful it all was. What was it that he was now? Why was all this glory for him?

The children and the pretty ladies left. It began to get dark, and the little fir tree began to get lonely. Sometimes he thought he heard a child crying and he wondered what it was all about.

Then suddenly the pretty ladies came back and lifted the little fir tree onto a trolley. They pushed him out of the little room, down a corridor and into a long room. The little fir tree saw that there were lots of beds in the long room. There were more children, some propped up on pillows, some sitting in chairs, others in wheel-chairs. He wondered why they looked so pale and white. He didn't know that he was in a Hospital, but before he could wonder any more his breath was quite taken away by the shout those little children gave. 'Oh! How beautiful!' they called. 'How pretty! How magical! Isn't it wonderful!' He knew they must mean him, and he stood as straight and tall as he could. Then one small voice called out, 'It's the nicest Christmas tree I ever saw!' And at last the little fir tree knew what he was. He was a Christmas tree! And then he felt so happy and glad from his top to his feet, because he was just little enough to be the nicest kind of tree in the world.

S. C. Bryant (adapted)

2. Think of all the things needed to decorate the Christmas tree. Then find an adjective to match each one:
   tinsel
   baubles
   bells
   lights
   balls
   snowmen
   angels
   stars, etc.
3. Use the Mastercopy inside a plastic envelope with different coloured Plasticine to create the little fir tree's transformation.

Extension

Materials Paper, crayons or paints

Method

1. This is a good story on which to base a wall display. Break the story into parts and let the class illustrate the story. It can be a class activity.
   a. Small tree in a big forest.
   b. Small tree standing outside a shop.
   c. Small tree being decorated.
   d. Small, beautiful Christmas tree in a hospital ward.

Number

Materials Pre-decorated Mastercopy, silver and gold and coloured stars

Method

1. Use as a class activity. Decorate the tree with the stars and use for counting skills to 20.
   a. How many silver stars?
   b. How many gold stars?
   c. How many coloured stars?
   d. Add different colour combinations.

Extension

Materials As above

Method

1. Reverse the activity and ask the children to decorate their Christmas trees with a set number of stars.

Artwork

Materials Mastercopy 12.2

Method

1. The Mastercopy gives drawn examples of the finished product and the things you need to make them. Most are self-explanatory. They all look better with the addition of a little spray glitter!

Bodywork

Materials An open space

Method

1. The little fir tree story could be an alternative to the more usual Christmas plays. It can have quite a large cast and is easy to dress.
2. Suggested cast list:
   Little Fir Tree – 1
   Big trees – 8 standing on chairs
   Wind – 4
   Snow – 8 (1 for each large tree)
   Men – 4
   Children – 2
   Nurses – 2
   Children – as many as you have left!

Extension

Materials Satsumas (or netballs)

Method

1. Divide the class into two teams and get them to sit down with their legs straight touching the feet of the opposite team. One satsuma per team.
2. The satsuma is passed along the line of legs on ankles, when it reaches the last person, they pick it up and race to the other end of the line. They sit down and the race starts again.

3. The winners are the team that returns to the start position first.

Music

Materials Amid all the carols, how about singing this?

Method

1. The tune is the same as 'Sing a song of Sixpence'

Sing a song of mincemeat
Currants, raisins, spice.
Apples, sugar, nutmeg;
Everything that's nice.
Stir it with a ladle
Wish a lovely wish –
Drop it in the middle
Of your well-filled dish.
Stir again for good luck,
Pack it all away,
Tied in little jars and pots
Until Christmas Day!

OLDER CHILDREN

Written Work and Language

Materials The poem below

The Stable Cat

I'm the Stable Cat, a working cat,
I clear the place of vermin.
The cat at the Inn
Is never thin
But I am never fat.

But I don't complain of that.
I'm lithe and sleek and clever.
The mice I chase
About the place
For I'm the Stable Cat.

But tonight, well, things are different.
I make the small mice welcome.
I ask them all
To pay a call
And keep my claws in velvet.

Sparrows out of the weather,
The mild, roo-cooing pigeons,
These flying bands
Are all my friends,
We're happy together.

All live things under this roof,
All birds, beasts, and insects,
We look with joy
At Mary's Boy,
Are safe in His love.

Leslie Norris

Method

1. Discuss the poem and talk about the creatures that could have been in the stable that night:

ox	ass	cat	mice
pigeons	dogs (shepherds)	spiders	sheep

2. Did the animals know it was a special night? What did they think about this special baby in their midst?
3. Use the poem as a start point for drawing and writing of how unusual it was that all the animals, birds and insects should be friends on this one night.

Extension

Materials General knowledge books

Method

1. See if the class know or can work out or find out a little bit of the history of Christmas traditions.
   a. Christmas tree
   b. Yule log
   c. Father Christmas
   d. Christmas pudding (and the charms that you put in it)

Number

Materials Mastercopy 6.4, scissors, crayons, paper, glue

Method
1. Advent starts at the end of the term. It is a time of preparation in the Christian religion. We use it as a count down to Christmas Day.
2. Use the Mastercopy 6.4 to help you space the doors of an Advent Calendar. Start with the large square in the centre for number 24.
3. The calendar can be done in two ways, using the things that remind us of Christmas (decorations, etc.), or by simply telling the story of the Nativity.

Extension

Materials Mastercopy 1.1

Method
1. Check that the days are correctly aligned for the month of December.
2. Class activity to answer the questions:
   a. How many days until Christmas?
   b. How many Sundays until Christmas?
   c. How many shopping days until Christmas?
   d. What day is Boxing Day?
   e. How many school days until the Christmas holidays?

Artwork

Materials Mastercopy 12.2

Method
1. The diagrams will give a good idea of what the finished product should look like and the materials needed to complete it.

Extension

Materials Mastercopy 12.1, crayons, glue, glitter

Method
1. Use as a guideline and then decorate

Extension

Materials A square of paper, ruler, scissors, scrap of tinsel

Method
1. See diagram for finished star.
2. It is necessary to be accurate for this to work.

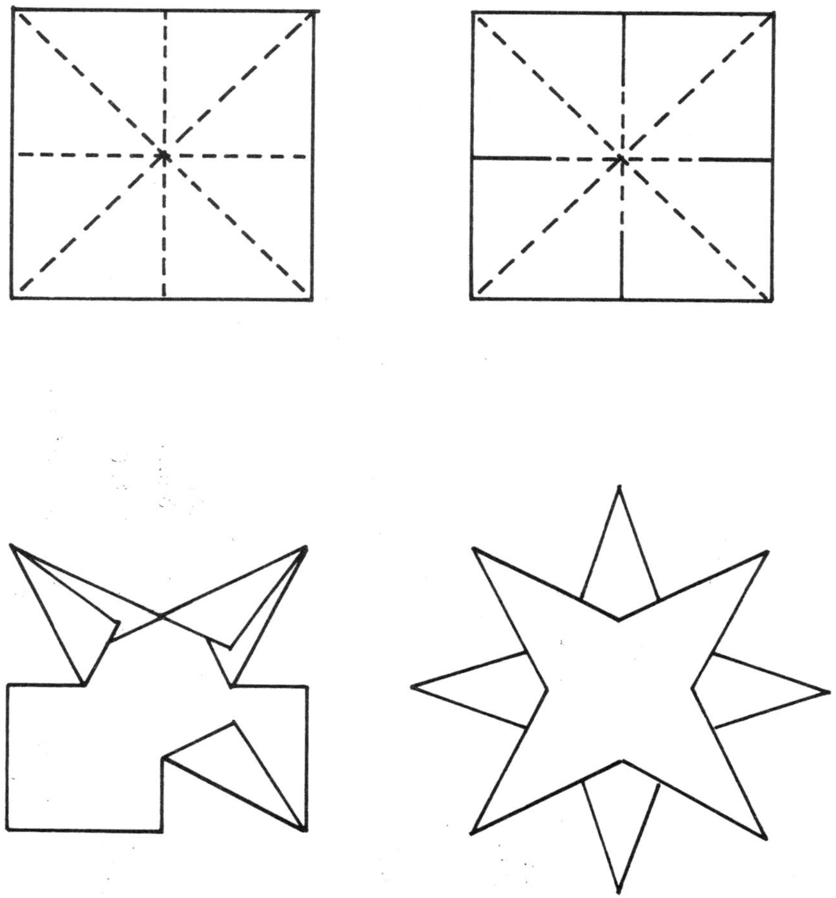

Bodywork

Materials 'The Stable Cat', a poem to act for Christmas, as part of the Nativity

Method
1. The poem can be a part of the play, if the children learn it to allow some movement. Include all the other animals that the class discussed might be in the stable that night. This gives a lot of scope for practising all the characteristic movements of those animals.

Music

Materials The song below

Pray God Bless all friends here.
A merry, merry Christmas and a Happy New Year.

FOOD

There has been a growing concern about children's eating habits. The benefits of processed and preserved foods can be abused, so it is important that the children know what is good for them. They can then distinguish what is good for them to eat at any time, what is good for them in small quantities, and those foods that should be eaten sparingly.

The variety of food is enormous with better communications, foreign travel, and food technology being able to provide most foodstuffs all year round, regardless of season. It is hard for children when there is so much choice. Getting a balanced diet is not their responsibility, but they can be made aware of those foods that give them energy, help them grow healthy teeth and bones, and those that may be fun but do little to aid development.

Children all have favourite foods, and at Christmas time there always seems to be a surfeit. Food plays an important role in the festivities, which is why this section appears at this end of the book! After Christmas, a good many adults think seriously about their diet, usually because of the extra inches acquired in the few weeks previous. It is a good time for new resolutions. While we train ourselves to eat a healthy balanced diet, we are also helping our children.

Suggested Reading

The Magic Stone (Ladybird Books)
The Very Hungry Caterpillar
by E. Carle (Picture Puffins)
Avocado Baby
by J. Burningham (Jonathan Cape)

YOUNGER CHILDREN

Written Work and Language

Materials Mastercopy 12.3

Method

1. Ask the children to write the correct start letter next to each item of food. Can they see they have an alphabet of food? In this case U = ugli fruit, V = vermicelli, Z = zucchini.
2. See if they can group the food into sets (cutting out if they like) of fruit, vegetables, animal, store cupboard (to cover things like jelly!).

Extension

Materials Mastercopy 12.3, pencils

Method

1. Have the children heard of the words: protein, vitamin? Explain that they are some of the things food is made of and that the best food to eat while we are growing contains lots of protein and vitamins.
2. We know we eat when we are hungry, but we also need to eat to grow, to give us energy and to keep us healthy. Foods fall into these categories too:
   To grow – meat, cheese, fish, eggs
   For energy – sweet things, starchy things, fats
   For health – vegetables, fruit, nuts, pulses
   We really need to eat food from each group to give us a 'balanced diet'.
3. With the help of the Mastercopy, see if you can make a balanced diet for a day's meals as a class. Divide the meals into:
   Breakfast
   Dinner
   Tea
   Snacks

Extension

Materials Nursery rhymes

Method

1. Think of all the food rhymes that the children might know:

   'Five Currant Buns'
   'Five Fat Sausages'
   'Pease Pudding Hot'
   'Jack Sprat'
   'Sing a song of Sixpence'
   'Little Jack Horner'
   'Peter, Peter, Pumpkin Eater'
   'If All the World was Apple pie'

2. And this nonsense rhyme

   I eat my peas with honey
   I've done it all my life
   It makes the peas taste funny
   But it keeps them on my knife.

Number

Materials Jars or bags of beans (approx. 50)

Method

1. Help the children to estimate the number of beans. Tell them it is more than 20.
2. Write down the numbers they guess.
3. Ask a child to help you count. Group the beans in tens.
4. When you have the answer and have found who has the nearest estimate, you can use the grouped beans for × 10 table, place value and sharing skills.
5. With the last activity (sharing), choose one child to share the beans between ten children making sure that each child receives ten beans.

Artwork

Materials The greedy story below

The Cat and the Parrot

Once there was a cat and a parrot. And they had agreed to ask each other to dinner, turn and turn about: first the cat should ask the parrot, then the parrot should invite the cat, and so on. It was the cat's turn first.

Now the cat was very mean. He provided nothing at all for dinner except a pint of milk, a little slice of fish, and a biscuit. The parrot was too polite to complain but he did not have a very good time.

When it was his turn to invite the cat, he cooked a fine dinner. He had a roast of meat, a pot of tea, a basket of fruit, and, best of all, he had baked a whole clothes basket full of little cakes – little brown, crispy, spicy cakes! Oh, I should say as many as five hundred. And he put four hundred and ninety-eight cakes before the cat, keeping only two for himself.

Well, when the cat came to dinner he ate everything, including the cakes, all of them! Then he turned to the parrot and said, 'I'm hungry, haven't you got anything else to eat?' The parrot was surprised but offered the two cakes he had kept back. The cat ate those and rudely asked for more. The parrot said there was nothing left except for himself. The cat looked at the parrot, licked his lips and before you could say Slip, Slop, Gobble, down his throat went the parrot.

An old lady who was passing saw what had happened and scolded the cat. 'How dreadful of you to eat your friend,' she said. 'What's a parrot to me,' said the cat, 'I've a good mind to eat you too.' And before you could say Slip, Slop, Gobble, down went the old woman.

The cat strutted off down the street, and soon he met an old man driving his donkey. 'Get out of my way cat,' he shouted, 'my donkey might tread on you.' The cat just looked at him and said, 'Donkey indeed! I have eaten five hundred cakes, my friend the parrot, and an old woman. What's to stop me eating a miserable man and his donkey?' And Slip, Slop, Gobble, down went the pair of them!

The cat swaggered on down the road until he met a procession. It was the King and his new bride, and behind him were all his soldiers, and behind them were some elephants walking two by two. The King was feeling very kind, because it was his wedding day, so he spoke gently. 'Get out of our way, pussy, my elephants might hurt you.'

'Hurt me!' said the cat, shaking his fat sides. 'Ho, ho, I've eaten five hundred cakes, my friend the parrot, an old woman, a man and his donkey; what's to stop me eating all of you?' And Slip, Slop, Gobble, down went the King and the entire procession!

The cat had to walk more slowly now, but a little farther on he met a pair of land-crabs, scuttling along in the dust. 'Get out of our way, Pussy,' they squeaked. 'Ho, ho, ho!' cried the cat in a terrible voice. 'I've eaten five hundred cakes, my friend the parrot, an old woman, a man and his donkey, the King and all his procession; and now I'm going to eat you too.' And with that Slip, Slop, Gobble, down went the land-crabs.

Now it was very dark inside the cat's tummy and when the land-crabs arrived they could just see all the people the cat had eaten. Even the elephants who were treading on each other's toes, and in one corner the parrot with his feathers all drooping holding on to the two cakes, the ones he had saved for himself. 'Let's get to work,' said the land-crabs, and snip, snap, snip, snap, they began to make a little hole in the cat's side with their sharp claws. The cat didn't notice, because he had fallen asleep after eating so much.

When the hole was big enough out came all the people: the King and Queen and the soldiers. Out came the elephants, two by two; the man and his donkey, the old woman and last of all the parrot. When the cat woke up, he had to spend the rest of the day sewing up the big hole in his side, and it was sore for a very long time afterwards.

S. C. Bryant (adapted)

2. This story provides endless inspiration for artwork, e.g. the teacher outlines a large cat and then the class fills it with all the characters mentioned.
3. Retelling the story in pictures, makes a very good wall frieze.

Bodywork

Materials Any of the rhymes that they can sing about food

Method

1. Make it a fun session, with the children acting the part of the food as well as singing the songs. Divide the class into groups and let each group show the others their song.
2. Practise how you think sausages would sizzle in a pan, what a fat sugary currant bun would look like. Add to the list: 'Polly put the kettle on', 'Pat-a-cake, pat-a-cake, baker's man' and 'Hot cross buns'.
3. Another way to do this is to go through all the rhymes first. Then divide up the class, and secretly give each group one rhyme to mime for the others. If the class can guess the rhyme, they must sing it and then it is their turn.

Music

Materials Tapes or records that include songs about food

Method

1. As there seems to have been a lot of singing already, have a change. Play the children the music you have collected and see if they can spot all the references to food, e.g.:
   'Food Glorious Food' – soundtrack of the film *Oliver*
   'The Candy Man' – soundtrack of the film *Charlie and the Chocolate Factory*
   'Toot Sweet' – soundtrack of the film *Chitty, Chitty, Bang, Bang*

OLDER CHILDREN

Written Work and Language

Materials Mastercopy 12.3, pencils, crayons (see also p. 144)

Method

1. Tell the class that the Mastercopy is an alphabet of food and they must sort it out.
2. When they have done that, go over with them the composition of food. Explain that food is made up of three basic properties: proteins, fats and

carbohydrates. These all include vitamins to help us grow and develop normally. When we are growing up it is really important that we eat the right sorts of foods, and those are the ones that contain these properties. We need to eat a variety of foods because then we know that we are getting all those things that help us grow strong and healthy.

3. More simply, we need food for three reasons:
   a. Food for growth – meat, cheese, fish, eggs
   b. Food for energy – sugar, starch, fats
   c. Food for health – vegetables, fruit, nuts, pulses and fibre

   Look at the alphabet of food and see if the class can decide which foods fall into which categories.

Extension

Materials Mastercopy 12.4, pencils

Method
1. A quick idea is to ask the children to decide and group the alphabet of food into sweet or savoury things.

Extension

Materials General knowledge books, atlas

Method
1. A lot of the food we eat originates from another country. See if they know where these foods come from originally:

Spaghetti	Sweet and Sour Pork
Curry	Chop Suey
Haggis	Hamburgers
Kebabs	Paella

Number

Materials Mastercopy 12.4, pencils

Method
1. Let the children fill in the bottom line for themselves.
2. See if they can find the answers to the questions.
   a. Who likes sausages?
   b. Who likes apple juice?
   c. Who likes ice cream?
   d. Who likes chocolate?
   e. Who likes pizza?

Artwork

Materials Paint, onions, potatoes, carrots, empty cans and jars, boxes

Method
1. Food comes in cans and boxes which you can use to print with. The vegetables, sliced, also make good printing materials.
2. It is as well to have a supply of the boxes and vegetables. Enthusiasm tends to mean these things perish rather quickly during use.

Extension

Materials The story below, paints, paper

Method
1. After 'The Cat and the Parrot', remember Aesop's Fable of 'The Dog and the Meat.' A bone could be used instead of the meat for artistic purposes!

The Dog and The Meat

A dog was crossing a river with a piece of meat he had stolen from the butcher's shop. Catching sight of his reflection in the stream, he mistook it for another dog with another piece of meat, and determined to get hold of that, too. But in trying to do so he dropped what he had, and thus lost both the substance and the shadow.

Aesop's Fables
(Translated by J. Warrington)

Bodywork

Materials Balls, baskets

Method
1. Play 'Apple Pie'. Divide the class into teams of approximately ten, each with a ball.
2. Each team has to get their ball in a basket (roll/throw). If it goes in they can start to spell the word apple pie. One ball in scores one letter.
3. When the person throwing the ball scores a hit and says the correct letter, they must collect the ball and give it to the next team member. A misspelling means the person must throw again.

Music

Materials Mastercopy 12.4

Method

1. Use the already written words to clap the rhythm of the word.
2. Explain that this is one way in which music is organised.
3. Try clapping different rhythms $\frac{1}{2}$, $\frac{3}{4}$, $\frac{4}{4}$ and counting the beats.
4. Do any of the foods fit in with those rhythms?
   (apple-pie $\frac{3}{4}$
   pizza $\frac{2}{2}$
   banana $\frac{3}{4}$
   apple crumble $\frac{4}{4}$)

Extension

Materials The song below

Method

1. And as a final piece of nonsense:

Nobody Likes Me

1 Nobody likes me,
Evr'ybody hates me,
Guess I'll go eat worms,
Long, thin, slimy ones,
Short, fat, juicy ones,
Itsy, bitsy, fuzzy wuzzy worms.

2 Down goes the first one,
Down goes the second one,
Oh, how they wiggle and squirm,
Long, thin, slimy ones,
Short, fat, juicy ones,
Itsy, bitsy, fuzzy wuzzy worms.

3 Up comes the first one,
Up comes the second one,
Oh, how they wiggle and squirm,
Long, thin, slimy ones,
Short, fat, juicy ones,
Itsy, bitsy, fuzzy wuzzy worms.

CHRISTMAS

CHRISTMAS

Cards

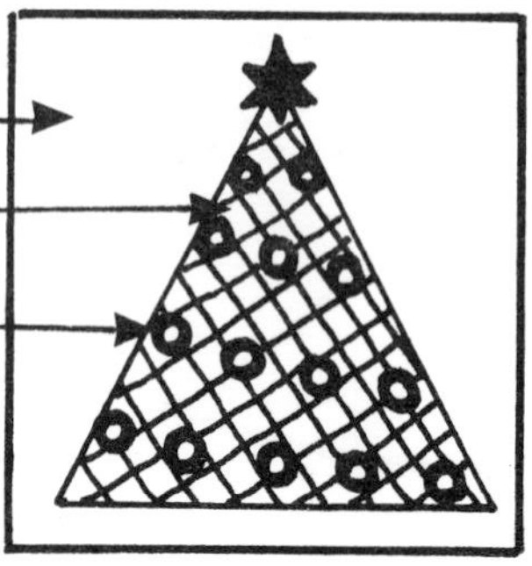

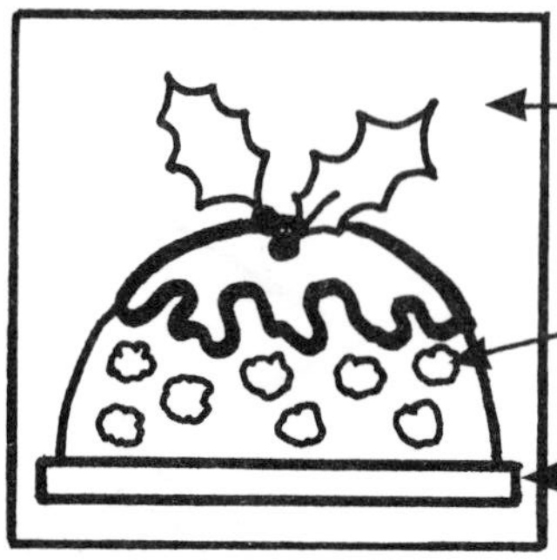

Decorations

Tree

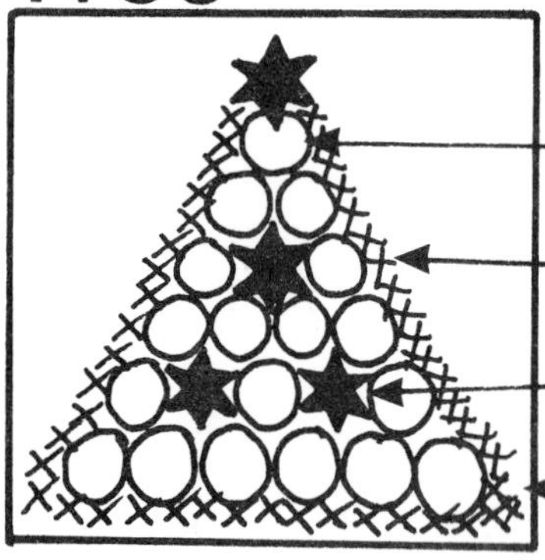

Tree

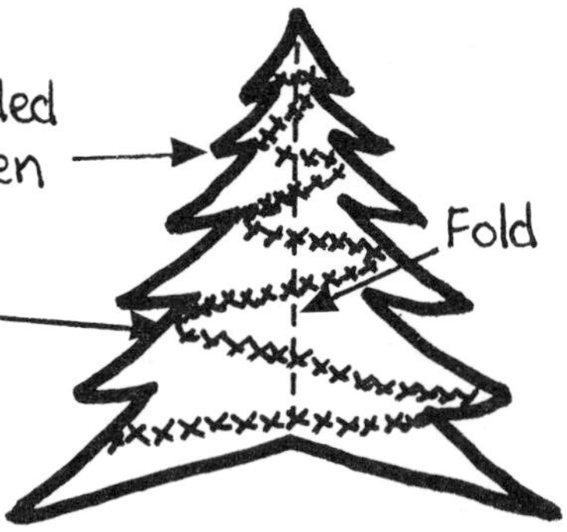

Tree

Card pre-cut into tree shape
2 per tree

Cover with wrapping paper

Slot shapes together to make tree

Anchor in plasticene to ensure they stand

Angels

Thin card

Gold spray

Fan of paper with cut outs

Glue

Tissue paper (glued to the reverse side making a "stained glass" effect)

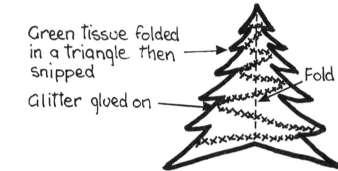

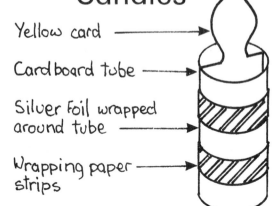

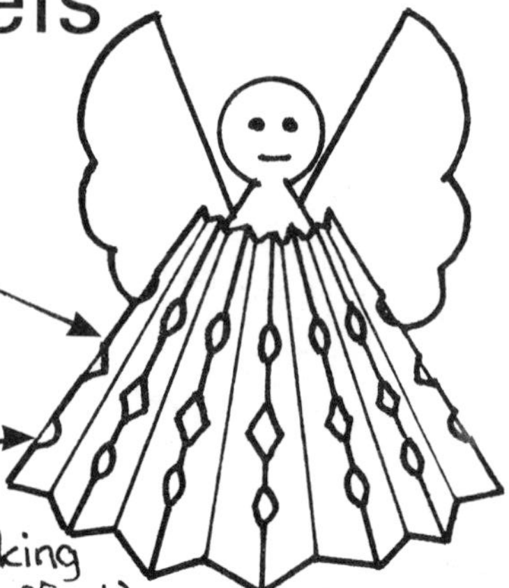

Candles

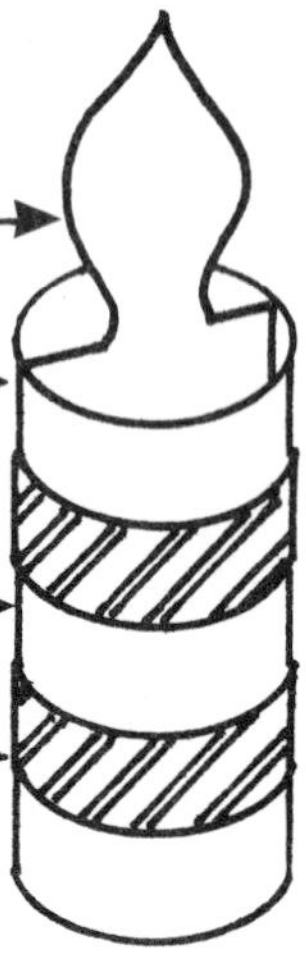

Pretty Dish for Presents

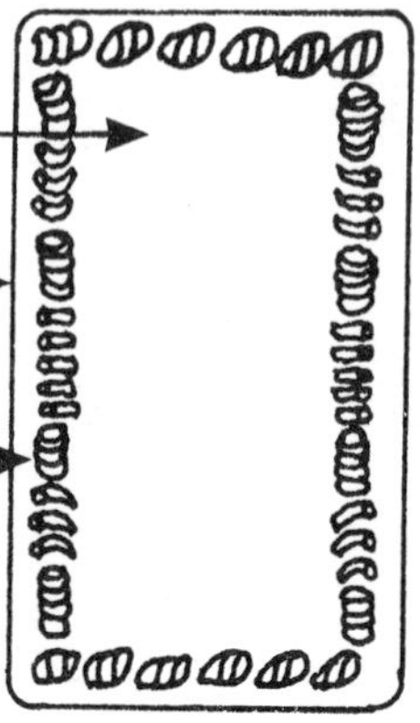

Fill with home-made sweets.

Bubble-bath balls.

Coloured cotton-wool

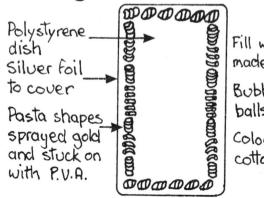

FOOD

	Favourite sweet food	Favourite savoury food	Favourite drink	Favourite snack
Lucy	ice cream	pizza	coke	bar of chocolate
Trevor	apple crumble	sausages	orange juice	baked beans
Robin	chocolate cake	hamburgers	lemonade	crisps
Mary	strawberries and cream	fish fingers	apple juice	banana
Your name				

The *quilter's stitch* Bible

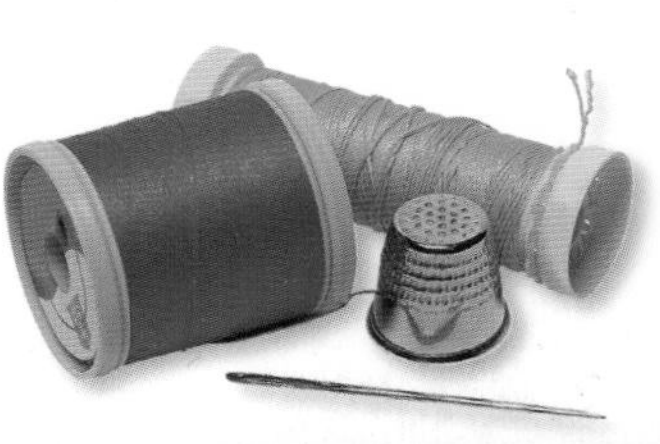

The *quilter's stitch* Bible

The essential illustrated reference to over 200 stitches with easy-to-follow diagrams

NIKKI TINKLER

CHARTWELL BOOKS, INC.

A QUARTO BOOK

Published in 2013 by
Chartwell Books, Inc.
A division of Book Sales, Inc.
276 Fifth Avenue, Suite 206
New York, New York 10001
USA

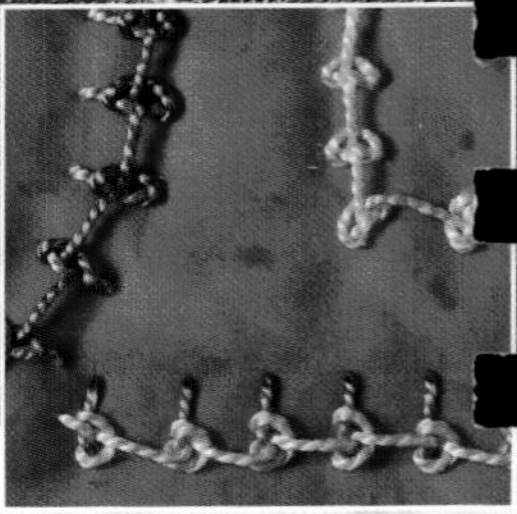

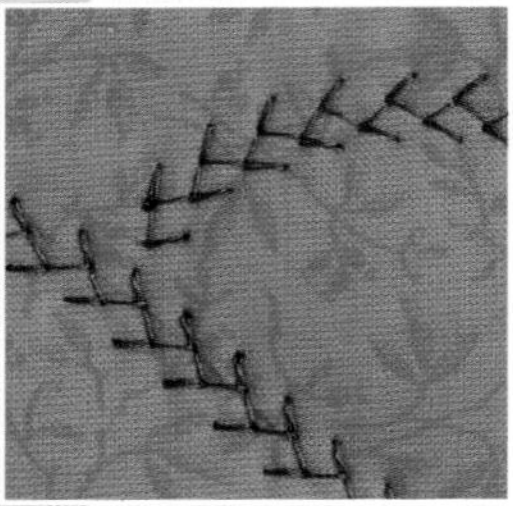

ISBN 978-0-7858-3105-1

QUAR.QSB

Conceived, designed and produced by
Quarto Publishing plc
The Old Brewery
6 Blundell Street
London N7 9BH

Project editor Liz Pasfield
Senior art editor Penny Cobb
Designer Karin Skånberg
Copy editor Fiona Corbridge
Illustrators Coral Mula, Carol and John Woodcock, Kuo Kang Chen
Photographers Paul Forrester, Martin Norris

Art director Moira Clinch
Publisher Paul Carslake

Color separation by Universal Graphics Pte Ltd, Singapore
Printed by Midas printing International Limited, China

10 9 8 7 6 5 4 3 2 1

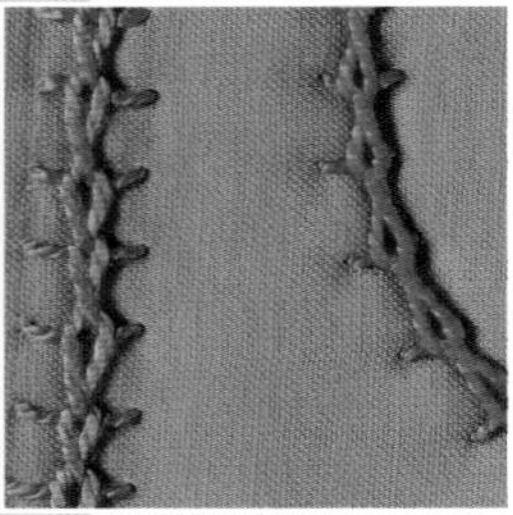

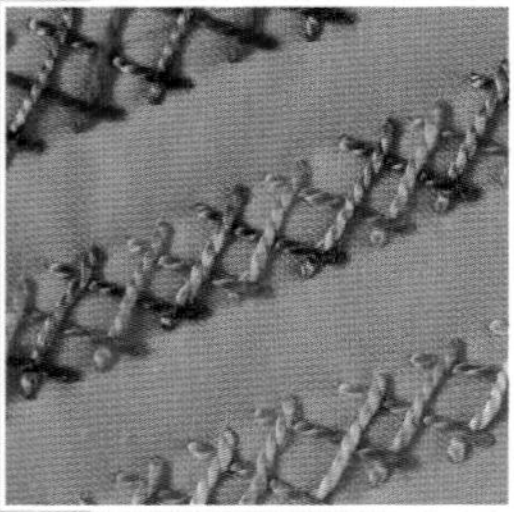

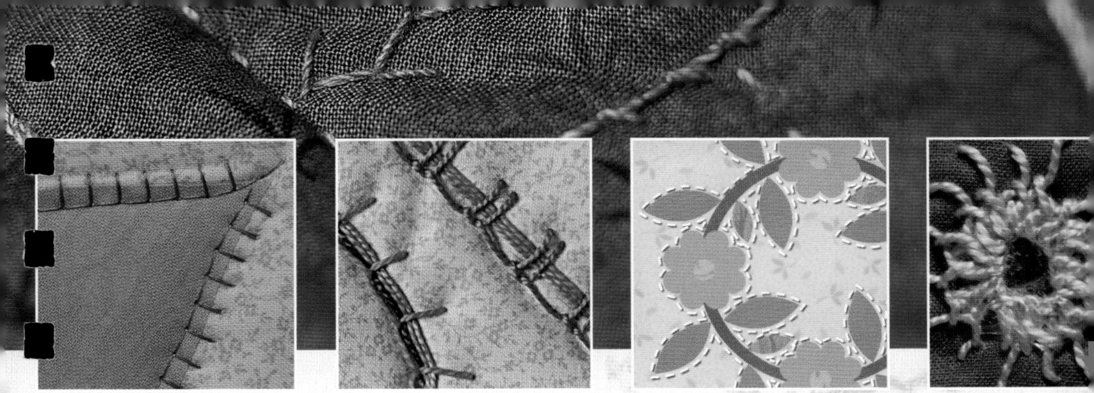

Contents

Introduction

Quilt-making and embroidery are two distinctly different disciplines. I am most definitely a quilter and quilt-maker, rather than an embroiderer. It is intriguing that works of embroidery are regularly exhibited within quilt exhibitions, yet we rarely see quilts and quilted work exhibited in embroidery exhibitions. I have a perennially inquisitive nature so I knew, shortly after I began quilt-making, that it wouldn't be long before I began experimenting with more exotic and textured threads, and what I now refer to as "alternative quilting stitches." It was the start of a fascinating journey.

I hope that this book opens up a whole new world of quilting for you. You may be a beginner, an embroiderer looking for a new challenge or an experienced quilter looking to expand your vocabulary of stitches; *The Quilter's Stitch Bible* aims to provide inspiration and practical reference in equal measure. The keyword for this book is "experiment." So often,

ALTERNATIVE STITCHES
Hand-sewn alternative stitches can sometimes add more textural interest to quilt work than traditional stitches.

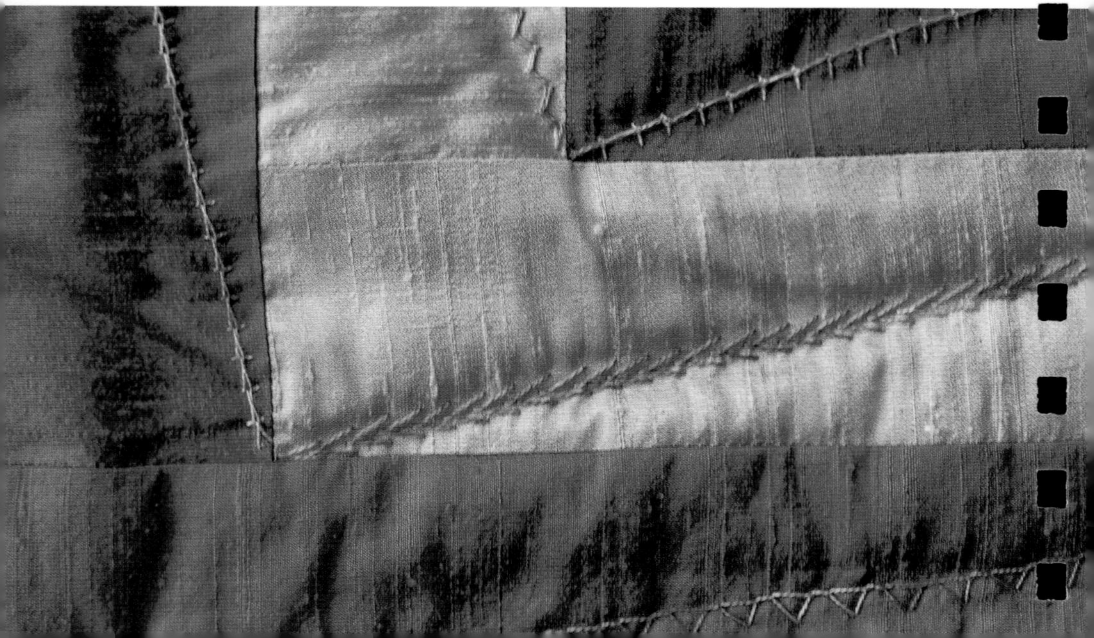

PATCHWORK AND QUILTING

Simple patchwork designs are complemented by hand-sewn, textural stitches.

when we reach the quilting stage of our all-important quilt projects, we don't allow ourselves the time or the freedom to experiment—and we've all got skeins of thread that we've acquired, like magpies, and never touched because we have no idea what to do with them. So, get ready to extend your creative horizons.

PATCHWORK

Originally, the joining of scraps of fabric to make a patterned quilt was an attempt to make new, yet economical, bed coverings from what had gone before. Nothing was wasted; the padding or batting would often be from another quilt or blanket, which had become worn with age and use. For students of textile history, the fabrics and prints used in quilts

ENHANCING PATCHWORK

Using fancy threads on traditional quilting designs can add an extra dynamic to basic patchwork.

over the years are testament to the changes and constraints brought about by economic revolutions. The modern revival of interest in quilt-making has seen the practical quilt of history develop into something more sophisticated in its use of color, fabric and design. Traditional patchwork designs are still popular, but now stunning contemporary quilts and textile art, which bring a fresh approach to the old craft, are displayed alongside them.

QUILTING

In Europe, the practice of quilting can be traced back to Roman times, when it was used extensively for both clothing and furnishings. Early British settlers took traditional quilt-making techniques to America, where they developed into American folk art, and the quilting groups and guilds that now meet nationwide.

While there are countless forms of quilting in different countries and cultures, the basic purpose of quilting and the "quilting stitch" remain the same—to hold two or more layers of fabric together while providing some form of decoration. This can be as complicated or as simple as the quilt-maker chooses, and is open to hand-stitchers and machine-stitchers alike for exploration and experimentation.

Our ancestors, piecing patchwork quilts from old clothing and worn-out quilts, would hardly recognize a piece of contemporary textile work as a quilt, but would recognize the universal and unwavering need that quilters worldwide have to put a needle into fabric and to create patterns.

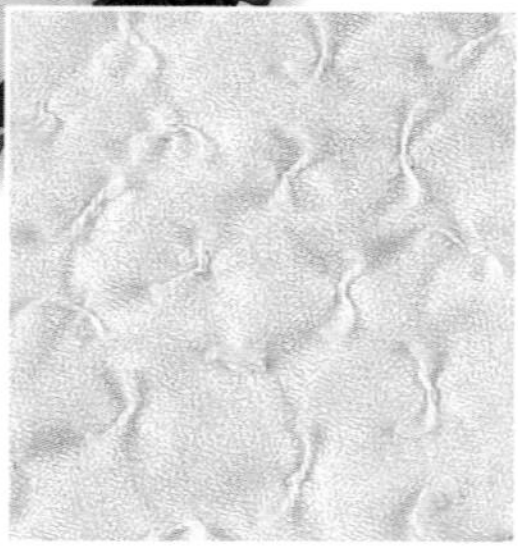

MIXING UP STITCHES

Contemporary quilts may contain a mixture of both machine and hand quilting. These work well together and complement the design of the patchwork.

STITCHES FOR QUILTING

Most people will be familiar with the traditional "quilting stitch"—that is based on the basic running stitch—but there is a lot more to quilting than just sewing a running stitch. A quilting stitch is basically a stitch that secures and holds two or more layers of fabric together; so in reality there is an enormous number of "alternative" stitches that can be used for this purpose. If a stitch is doing the job of quilting, then it can feasibly be referred to as a "quilting stitch," irrespective of its shape and size.

All the stitches in this book are based on traditional quilting and embroidery stitches. Some embroidery stitches are unsuitable for quilting because they need to be worked and remain stretched on a frame; others are not appropriate for items such as bed quilts because they are untidy on the back of the work. But many, many others can be used for quilting.

CHOOSING STITCHES

The busier stitches offered within this book lend themselves very well to "wholecloth quilting," that is sewing a quilt that has a single piece of fabric for the quilt top, and no patchwork. Straightforward patchwork and appliquéd patterns can sometimes benefit from a little more textural interest, which can be provided by the more involved stitches. Busier patchwork and appliqué designs, however, may require the use of some of the simpler stitches. Don't forget, when quilting your designs, mix the simpler stitches, such as running stitch, chain stitch and blanket stitch, with the busier, wider and more decorative stitches, such as wheatear stitch and single-feather stitch. This will help you achieve a good visual balance within your work.

Some of the stitches will require a little more patience to perfect than others; so, perhaps if you don't like a particular stitch to begin with, at your first attempt, don't ignore it completely—have another go at a later date. You could try sewing it smaller, larger, narrower, wider, on a curve, or with different thread—it may become a stitch that you come to enjoy using. All of the stitches may be sewn with finer or thicker threads than standard.

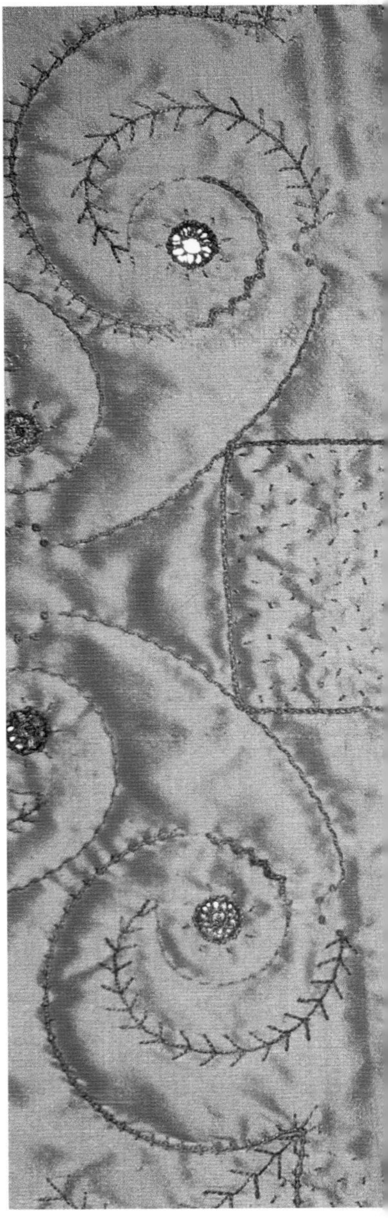

SHOWING TEXTURE

Textural quilting stitches are shown to their best effect on "wholecloth" quilts.

Quilting Essentials

Over the next few pages, you'll find suggestions for various tools and equipment that are all designed to help you make the most of your quilting and patchwork. Some of these items will already be found in your toolbox at home. Other tools and gadgets should be viewed as an investment toward your future quilt-making.

Tools and Equipment

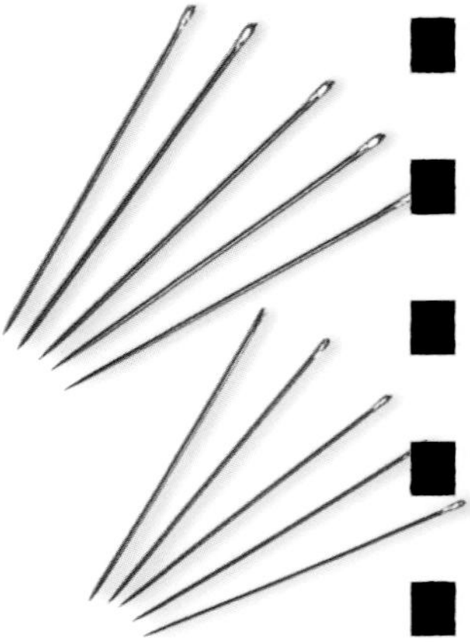

Sharps (top) and betweens (bottom)

Specialist tools and equipment enable us to quilt to a good standard. You will already have some of the listed items; purchasing additional equipment may increase your enjoyment of quilt-making and make it less problematic.

Needles, pins and scissors are all essential; so are thimbles, a sewing machine and good lighting, depending on the techniques you prefer to use. Costs for these essentials vary enormously, but it is worth spending just that little bit more on good-quality items.

HAND-SEWING NEEDLES

A quilting needle (known as a "between") has a short, rigid shank and a sharp point. Embroidery needles and mixed household needles can be used for the more elaborate alternative stitches and thick threads—the shank of these needles is less rigid, but the longer length is more comfortable to hold. Keep a selection of needles for the different stages of quilt construction, including basting, hand-sewing, quilting, appliqué and beading.

SEWING MACHINE NEEDLES

The width of a needle shank and the type of point it has (sharp or ballpoint) is designed to suit a particular weight and type of fabric. Fine needles are designed for use on delicate fabrics such as silk, voile and lawn, whereas thick needles are generally designed for fabrics of a heavier weight, such as furnishing fabrics and denim. There are special needles for jersey fabrics and leathers, and twin needles for creating a double line of stitching.

Quilter's checklist

Hand-sewing needles

- Embroidery needles
- Bodkin needles
- Easy-thread needles
- Beading needles
- Mixed household needles
- Betweens

Sewing machine needles

- Machine needles (different sizes for different weights of fabric)
- Twin needles
- Ballpoint needles
- Needles for stretch fabrics
- Jeans needles
- Quilting needles

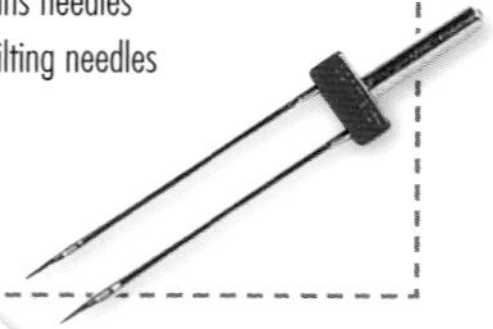

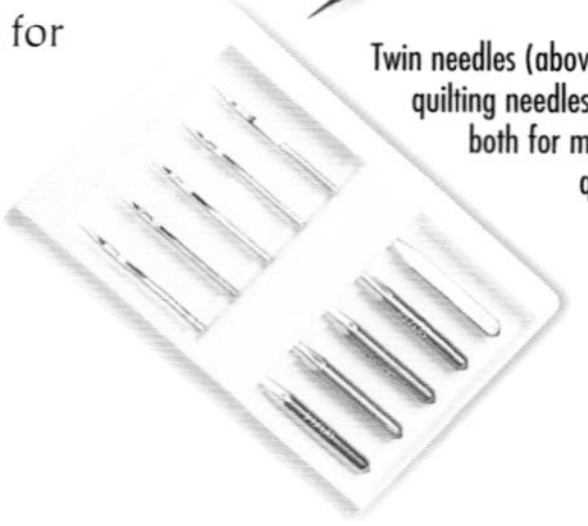

Twin needles (above) and quilting needles (left), both for machine quilting

Quilter's checklist

Pins
- Bobble-headed pins
- Lace pins
- Dressmaking pins
- Safety pins
- Quilter's safety pins
- Appliqué pins
- Flathead pins

Scissors
- Dressmaking shears
- Serrated-edge patchwork scissors
- Craft scissors
- Embroidery scissors
- Pinking shears
- Appliqué scissors
- Spring-loaded scissors
- Soft-handled scissors
- Scissor sharpeners

Flathead pins

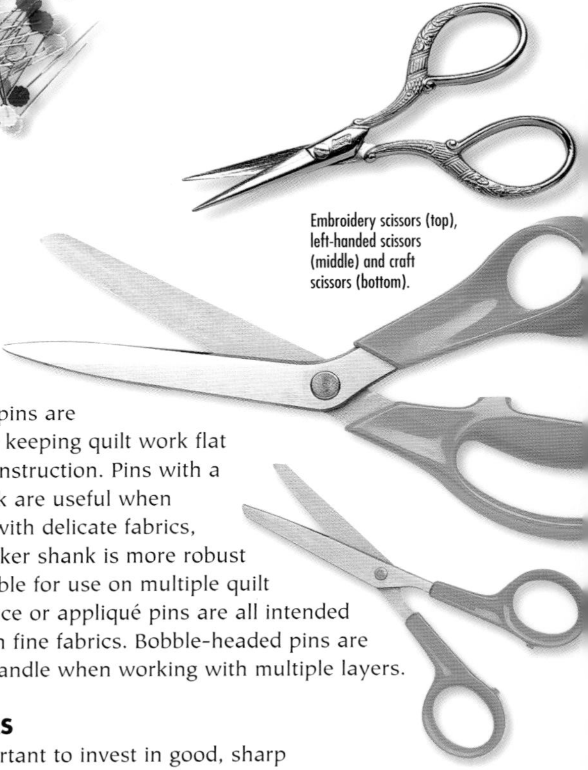

Embroidery scissors (top), left-handed scissors (middle) and craft scissors (bottom).

PINS

Flathead pins are useful for keeping quilt work flat during construction. Pins with a fine shank are useful when working with delicate fabrics, but a thicker shank is more robust and suitable for use on multiple quilt layers. Lace or appliqué pins are all intended for use on fine fabrics. Bobble-headed pins are easy to handle when working with multiple layers.

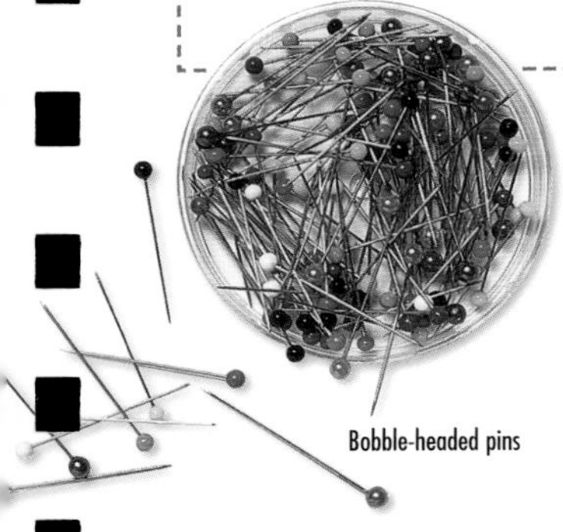

Bobble-headed pins

SCISSORS

It is important to invest in good, sharp dressmaking shears or serrated-edge patchwork scissors. Dressmaking shears have long blades to make it easy to cut large areas of fabric. You also need smaller scissors, such as embroidery scissors, for thread-snipping. Keep scissors for thread and fabric separate from those for paper and card. This is in order to make sure that the fabric scissors remain sharp and cut fabric cleanly without pulling at the fibers of the fabric or thread—paper and card will blunt a blade.

If you are left-handed, you may wish to purchase special left-handed scissors. The blades (and often the handle) are set differently from other scissors and consequently are more comfortable to use.

MISCELLANEOUS NOTIONS

Rotary cutters should be handled with care, and always used in partnership with safety rulers and safety cutting mats.

Quilting frames and hoops come in a range of shapes, sizes and materials. Quilts can be clipped into lightweight plastic frames easily and quickly. Wooden floor-standing quilt frames vary from a simple round frame on a single stand to large frames designed to accommodate bed-sized quilts. For machine quilters there are quilting hoops, machine-quilting clips and "easy-grip" gloves. Seam rippers make short work of unpicking unsatisfactory stitching.

FABRIC-MARKING TOOLS

There are countless fabric-marking tools and gadgets on the market for quilt-makers to use. However, there is no single marker that is suitable for marking every fabric, so it is well to build up a collection of different markers.

Tools for marking fabrics range from Hera markers, which leave an indentation on the fabric, to a variety of pens and pencils. All fabric markers should be tested

Quilter's checklist

Additional notions available to quilters

- Basting gun and basting tacks
- Rotary cutting equipment (safety cutting mat, safety ruler, cutters of various sizes)
- Thimbles: Metal, leather, plastic
- Bobbin boxes
- Needle-threaders
- Layout sheets
- Seam rippers
- Quilting frames/hoops (for hand and machine quilting)
- Hera markers
- Fabric glues
- Stencils and templates
- Cutting and pressing boards
- Tape measures
- Quilter's quarter rods and wheels
- Quilting gloves and quilting clips
- Lightbox
- Color wheel
- Magnifying glass

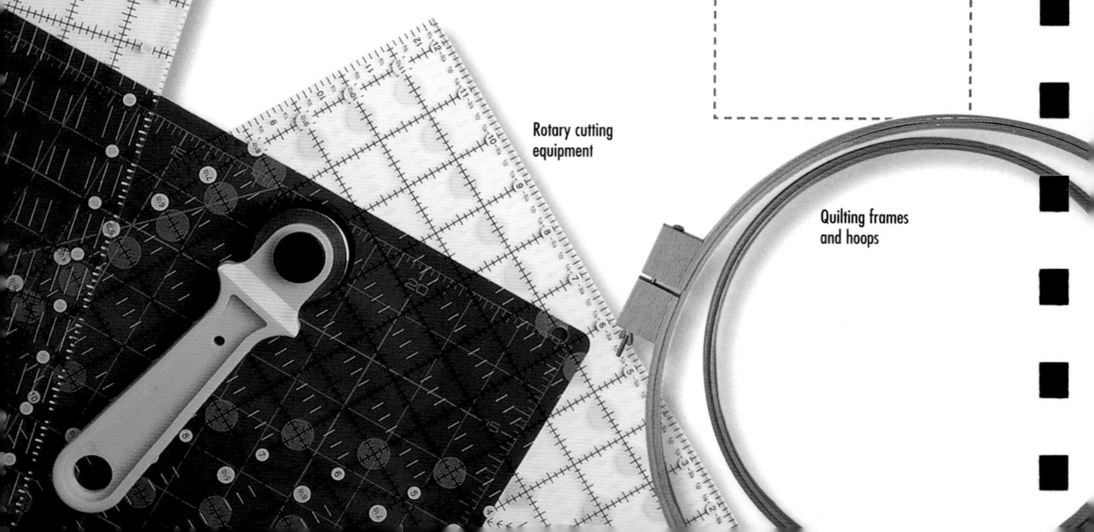

Rotary cutting equipment

Quilting frames and hoops

Quilter's checklist

- Fabric-marking pencils for pale fabrics
- Fabric-marking pencils for dark or heavily patterned fabrics
- Fabric-marking pens for pale fabrics
- Fabric-marking pens for dark or heavily patterned fabrics
- Quilter's non-smudge lead pencil
- Fabric eraser
- Extra-long ruler
- Quilter's quarter-inch masking tape
- Chalk wheels
- Tailor's chalk
- Large bodkin needle or Hera marker
- Air-soluble pen (vanishing pen)
- Water-soluble pen
- Dressmaker's carbon paper
- Colored fabric-marking pens and pencils

Fabric-marking pens, pencils and eraser

Tailor's chalk

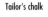

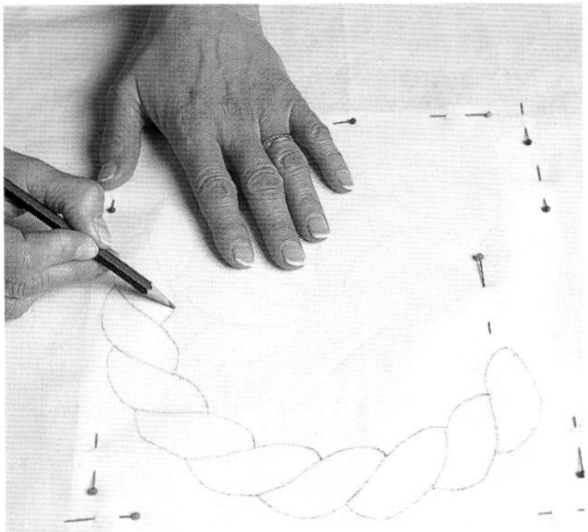

TRACING DESIGNS

Quilting designs can be traced onto the quilt top before layering, while the quilt is still a single layer of fabric.

before use to see how they react with the fabric, how well they show up and how difficult (or otherwise) they are to remove.

The list above is a good, basic selection of markers and other equipment to keep in your quilt-making toolbox.

QUILTING STENCILS

You may like to begin collecting specialist quilting stencils. These are available from patchwork materials suppliers and by mail order. Stencils can be used for marking designs on a quilt, either before layering, when it is a single piece of fabric, or after layering. Some stencils are described as "continuous line designs," and these allow the pattern to be stitched continuously without a lot of stop and start points, which you may prefer if you are machine quilting. Some continuous line designs are supplied as a long strip of rolled paper, which you pin or tape on the quilt top and stitch the design through the paper itself.

You may like to add quilting patterns from magazines and books to your collection. Trace the design onto the quilt top before the quilt has been layered, either by using a lightbox or by taping the design and fabric to a window (in daylight) so that the design shows through. Alternatively, trace the pattern onto a sheet of template plastic and then cut your own stencil from this.

Another way to transfer a design from a book is to trace or photocopy the design, then make holes at regular intervals along the lines of the design (either by prodding the paper by hand with a large, thick needle, or by machine-stitching along the lines without thread in the machine (using an old, blunt needle). Once the paper has been perforated, you can transfer the design onto the quilt fabric by "pouncing"—filling a wad of cloth (an old sock or similar) with chalk and shaking it through the holes.

The tools, gadgets and techniques you choose to employ for marking a design on fabric will vary with each quilt, depending on the colors, prints and textures of the fabric used within it and whether or not the quilt has been layered. Do remember that chalks and air-soluble pens (vanishing pens) are all very temporary and useful only for short, straight lines or very small areas of quilting. If you have an elaborate design that is going to cover a large area, choose a method of marking that is easy to see and that will stay in place until the quilting has been completed.

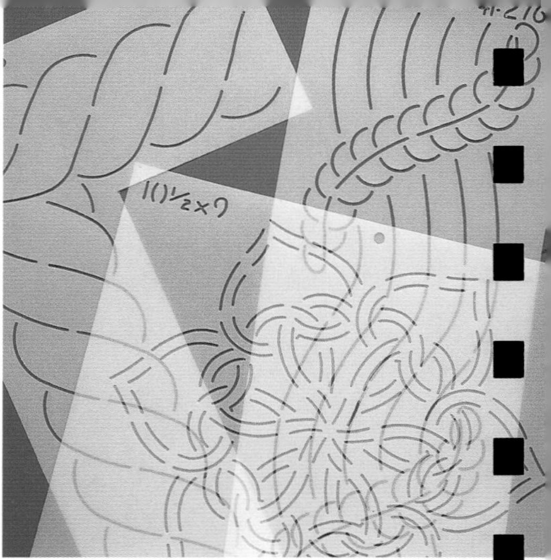

A selection of stencils

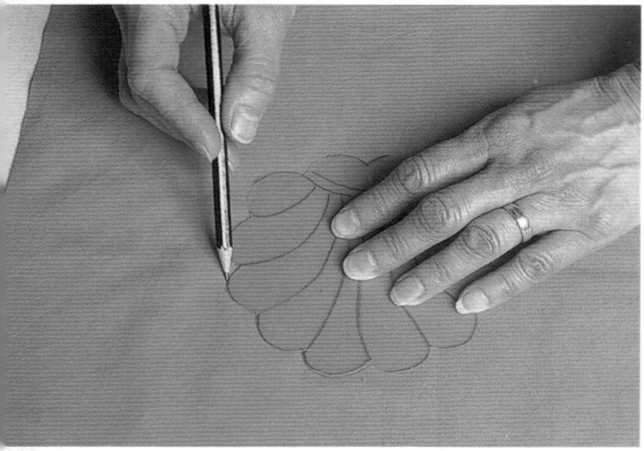

SPECIALIST STENCILS

Specialist quilting stencils can be used before, or after, all the quilt layers have been put together.

Hand-sewing Techniques

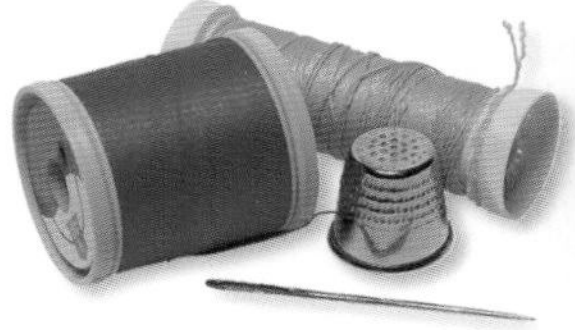

Many quilt-makers prefer to sew their work completely by hand, because they love the process of putting a needle into fabric.

Perhaps we like to get back to basics and work like our predecessors did, with a minimum of tools, equipment and expense. Whichever way you choose to sew, do remember that the making of a quilt should be viewed as a marathon and not a sprint. If you prefer hand-sewing and have the time to devote to it, don't be put off by those around you who appear to be producing machine-sewn quilts at a rate of knots. Take the time to enjoy every minute of your own work.

PATCHWORK PIECING

When joining patches of fabric together, a small, neat running stitch with a single thread is all that is required. Mark this line with a pencil first.

At the beginning of the sewing line, use either a knot or take two or three same size stitches into the same spot ("overstitches"), so that they sit on top of each other. Begin stitching forward along the sewing line, taking several small, neat stitches onto the needle at one time before pulling the thread through. Each time the thread is pulled through, make a small backstitch to continue the next group of running stitches; this will help to strengthen hand-sewn piecing.

Finish with several overstitches to secure the thread. Press the seams to one side, usually to the darker or busier of the two fabrics, to help to strengthen the seam and prevent any batting "bearding" through between stitches.

LEFT-HANDED QUILTERS

All the diagrams in this book are aimed at right-handed quilters. If you are left-handed, most of the stitches can easily be worked as a mirror image. Stitches that are worked vertically and horizontally by right-handed quilters are also worked vertically and horizontally if you are left-handed.

When following step-by-step instructions and diagrams, try imagining that you are looking in a mirror rather than copying them exactly. Some of the diagrams will be easy to follow if they are turned upside down. When following instructions for whipped or threaded stitches, take the working thread in the opposite direction to that shown. When reading instructions, read "right" for "left" and vice versa.

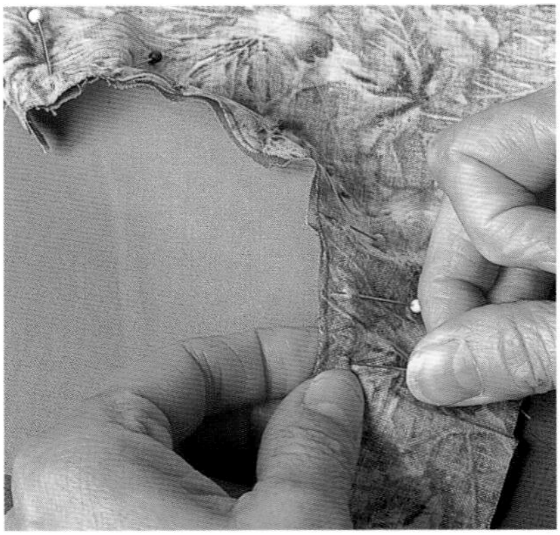

PATCHWORK ON A CURVE

The piecing of curved seam patchwork requires careful pinning and sewing. Clip the seams gently to release any tension in the fabric.

STITCHES FOR APPLIQUÉ

When preparing to stitch appliquéd motifs on a background fabric, it is best to pin the appliqué in position and then use basting thread and stitches to secure it, removing the pins as you progress.

Once the motif has been securely basted to the fabric, there are several different stitches that can be used around the edge of it. To start the stitching, make a small, neat knot in the thread (this can be hidden inside the seam allowance of the turned-over edge of the appliqué, or even left on the reverse side of the background fabric, as this will be hidden eventually).

Slipstitch Use a small slipstitch to catch up a small piece of backing fabric and a small piece of the appliqué in one go, and pull the thread through. Continue in this way around the motif.

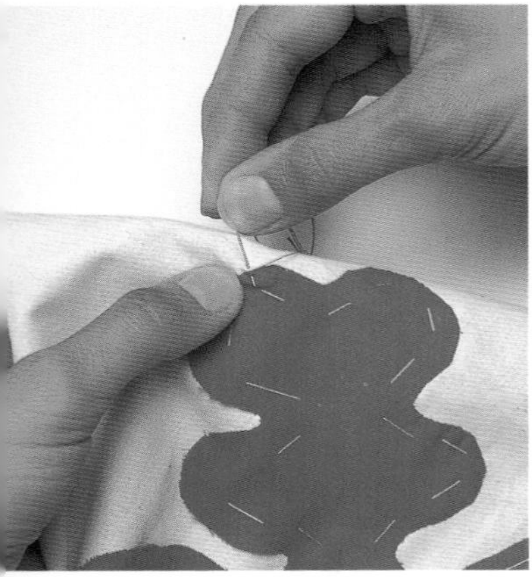

APPLIQUÉ SHAPES

Baste your appliquéd motif to your fabric before you begin to stitch.

Ladder stitch Work a ladder stitch by catching up a small section of the background fabric with the needle, then pull the thread through and take a small section of the appliqué, directly on the folded edge, and pull the thread through once more. Make four or five ladder stitches before gently pulling the group of stitches tight.

Blanket stitch Work blanket stitch around the edge of the appliqué. It can be used to secure either a folded edge, or a raw edge (if bonding web has been grafted onto the back of the appliqué).

Running stitch Make a small, neat row of running stitches just inside the edge of the appliqué.

MAKING UP A QUILT

There are various stages in quilt construction: Making the quilt top, layering the fabrics that make up the quilt (quilt top, batting and backing fabric), basting the layers together, quilting and binding.

Basting Use cheap thread and a fairly long needle for speedy basting. Thread the needle with a generous length of thread. Knot the end, or work several large but fairly loose "overstitches" on the same spot.

Make large even basting stitches, approximately 1 in. (2.5 cm) long, ensuring that all the layers of the quilt are caught up. Work several stitches in a group before pulling the thread through. Finish the line of basting with several overstitches to secure the thread.

Quilting with a traditional quilting stitch
Traditionally, a quilter's needle called a "between" would be used, along with a specialist quilting thread.

Cut a length of thread 12-18 in. (30-45 cm) long. Thread the needle by using the thread in the same direction as it comes off of the reel, to help to prevent knots and tangles. Make a neat knot in the end of the thread. Take the needle into the quilt top fabric and batting only, and bring the needle up at the starting point for the quilting design.

Pull the thread through and "pop" the knot into the batting to secure it.

Holding the needle almost perpendicular to the

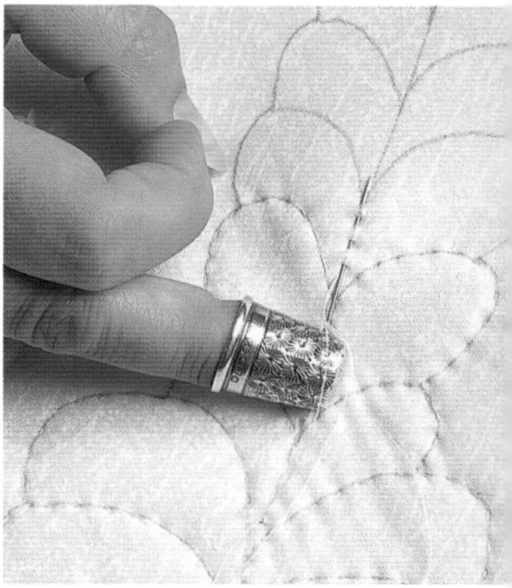

TRADITIONAL QUILTING
Use a quilter's between needle and specialist quilting thread for traditional hand quilting.

TRIMMING THE LAYERS
Once the quilt layers have been basted, trim the surplus fabrics away for easier handling.

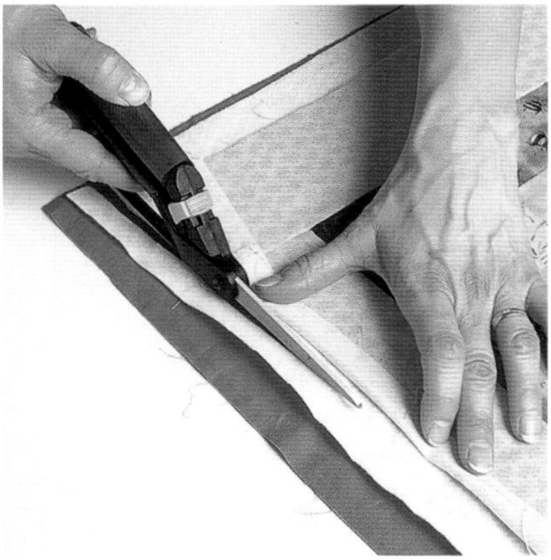

REVERSE OF WORK

If you are sewing by hand, the appearance of the stitches on the reverse of your work will not remain absolutely consistent (they are liable to vary more than on the surface of your work). Remember: These stitches are being sewn by hand. Make allowances for altering stitches, changing the position of your hands, and stopping and starting to renew threads.

fabric, take the needle down and then up again in one movement, making sure that all of the layers are caught up. Take several stitches like this on the needle at a time before pulling the thread through, just tight enough for the thread to be lying on the surface of the fabric.

Continue stitching the quilting design until you have approximately 4 in. (10 cm) of thread left, or until you have reached the end of the design. Make a neat knot in the remaining thread, close to the surface of the fabric.

If you have room for one more stitch, take the needle into the top fabric and batting only, bringing the needle out of the fabric approximately a needle's length away from the finishing point, and pop the knot into the batting to secure it. If there is no room for an extra stitch, make a backstitch before popping the knot.

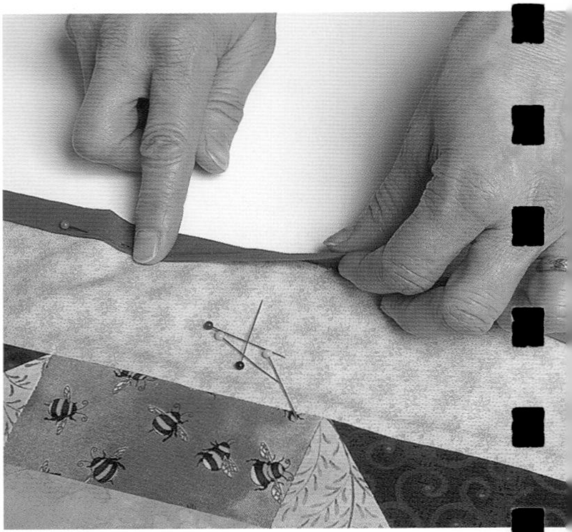

ATTACHING BINDING
Slipstitch the folded edge of binding fabric neatly to the back of your quilt.

Threaded or whipped stitches Thread or whip the base stitch in one direction with one color of thread, and then thread or whip the stitches a second time, in the opposite direction, using the same color for a denser effect, or a second color for more visual impact. A dramatic effect can be achieved by whipping or threading the base stitch with interesting yarns. The loops that are created can be left fairly loose in a decorative project such as a wallhanging or a framed work. However, if you are working on a quilt that will be laundered and handled excessively, pull them a little tighter so that they do not catch and snag.

Working stitches in from different angles Move the needle to a different angle, rather than trying to turn your whole hand and wrist joint at an awkward angle.

Wide stitches When marking out a design in preparation for quilting a project, do not draw parallel tramlines for sewing the wider stitches. Overall evenness will come naturally.

Binding When hand-sewing a binding fabric to a quilt, first use a backstitch so that all the layers and bulk at the edge of the quilt are strengthened.

When the binding is folded to the back of the quilt, a neat slipstitch is all that is needed to secure the fabric and cover the existing row of backstitching.

Machine-sewing Techniques

We live in a wonderfully advanced world of technology. Most of the sewing tasks that our predecessors spent hours and days carrying out can now be whizzed through in a matter of minutes with a machine.

There is an enormous array of sewing machines to choose from. If you plan to buy a good, basic sewing machine, it should be light enough to lift easily, provide basic stitches such as straight stitch and zigzag stitch and have no drawbacks such as temperamental tension problems. For more experimental work such as free-form quilting or machine embroidery, you ought to have a machine that also has the facility to lower the feed dogs.

PATCHWORK PIECING

When joining pieces of fabric by sewing machine, cut the patches of fabric to include a seam allowance of ¼ in. (6 mm), then align the raw edges alongside the ¼ in. (6 mm) foot on the sewing machine, or put a ¼ in. (6 mm) mark on the machine as a guide. Alternatively, mark the sewing line with a pencil.

Set the machine to use straight stitch. Test both the tension and the stitch

MACHINING PATCHWORK

Several pieces of patchwork can be passed through the sewing machine, one after the other, to speed the piecing process.

length on a folded scrap of fabric before starting. Place a small, folded piece of scrap fabric in front of the first patch, and start your line of stitches on the scrap. Most sewing machines perform better if stitching is started in the center of a piece of fabric rather than close to a raw edge. Stitch to the edge of the scrap fabric and then continue directly onto the edges of the patches to be joined. Continue stitching and when you reach the end, stitch directly across the seam allowance and off the raw edges of the fabric to finish. If you need to continue with more piecing, bring the line of sewing onto either another small, folded scrap of fabric, or onto the next two patches to be sewn together.

Press the seams to one side, as with hand-sewn pieced patchwork, or press them open for a flatter appearance.

STITCHES FOR APPLIQUÉ

When preparing to stitch appliquéd motifs on a background fabric, pin the shapes in place, then secure with basting thread and stitches, and remove the pins as you go. Pins can get in the way of the needle. Once secure there are several basic sewing machine stitches that can be used to sew around the edges or the motifs.

Zigzag stitch This is usually available on the most basic sewing machines. The width and length can be altered to suit the fabrics and threads used, the size and shape of the motifs and your required end result. Use on raw-edge or folded-edge appliquéd shapes.

Satin stitch Satin stitch is a closed-up variation on zigzag stitch and will give a heavier, denser end result. Care needs to be taken to achieve a neat finish. Particularly suitable for use on raw-edge appliqué.

Blanket stitch Blanket stitch can be used where a more decorative, yet open,

MACHINE-SEWN APPLIQUÉ

A variety of sewing machine stitches can be used to secure appliqué motifs in place. The stitch you choose will depend on how complicated your motif is and whether or not you have a raw edge of fabric to be covered.

stitch is needed. The "spikes" of blanket stitch can either radiate outward from the appliqué or inward. The length and width of the stitch can be experimented with. Use on raw-edge or folded-edge appliquéd shapes.

Straight stitch A simple row of straight stitch can be sewn just inside the edge of the appliqué motif. Straight stitch can also be used when free-form sewing, to secure motifs. Particularly suitable for use on raw-edge appliqué.

Overlocking stitch This stitch can be found on more expensive sewing machines and, where a less noticeable stitch is preferred, it can be used with an invisible thread to provide a good substitute for hand-sewn appliqué. Particularly suitable for use on folded-edge appliqué.

BASTING

Virtually every part of a quilt can be sewn on a sewing machine, including the basting. Set the machine to use straight stitch, and set the stitch length facility to the longest available setting. (Alternatively, if your machine has it, use the basting stitch facility.)

Machine-sewn basting stitches will have a tighter tension than hand-sewn basting, so make allowances so that the backing fabric is not pulled too tight by this added tension.

MACHINE QUILTING

If you enjoy using your sewing machine, you'll probably enjoy experimenting and pushing the boundaries of machine quilting. In comparison to a hand-quilted project, machine quilting will produce a

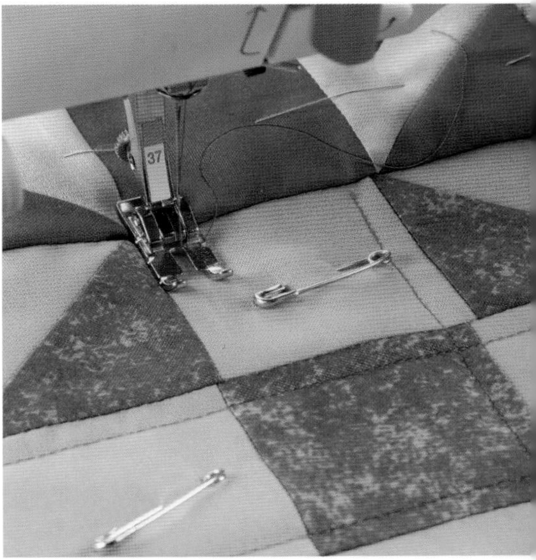

USING MACHINE QUILTING

Machine quilting, an essential part of the construction of a quilt, which secures the three layers together, should not be confused with machine embroidery, which is used primarily for embellishment.

slightly more rigid quilt, which is also flatter in appearance. There are two distinctly different techniques used for machine quilting: Straight stitching and free-form stitching.

Straight stitch technique Use a straight stitch, with the feed dogs in the normal position, to:

- Quilt in the ditch (literally, to sew in the valley of the patchwork seam).
- Contour-quilt around fabric patches.
- Echo quilting.
- Sew continuous line quilting designs.

On a folded scrap of fabric, test both

the tension and the stitch setting before starting. If you have an even-feed foot (dual-feed or walking foot), fit this in place so that all layers of the quilt will pass through the machine evenly. Or place pins at right angles to the seam at regular intervals, removing them as the needle approaches.

Start sewing with the needle in the "down" position at the starting point of the design. Use the stitch-locking facility if you have this on your machine. Alternatively, lock the threads by reducing the stitch length to 0.5 and making one stitch forward, one back, one forward and one back. Stitch along the patchwork lines or marked quilting design, and finish the line of machine-sewn quilting in the same manner as you began.

Free-form technique For free-form quilting (also known as random, stipple and free-motion quilting):

- Lower the feed dogs.
- Fit a machine embroidery foot (free-form quilting foot).

Set the stitch length and stitch width settings to zero. Fit the machine with a large needle (size 100). You may also find you need to adjust the tension on your machine—work on a practice piece first to establish what is needed.

Place your quilt work within a machine-quilting frame, or use machine-quilting gloves or gripping brackets to keep a secure hold on your work. Slide the work under the needle and bring both the top thread and the bobbin thread to the surface of the work; hold these firmly away from you while you lower the presser foot.

Make two or three stitches on the same spot to lock the threads. Begin moving the work underneath the needle as you press down on the foot pedal, and start stitching your design.

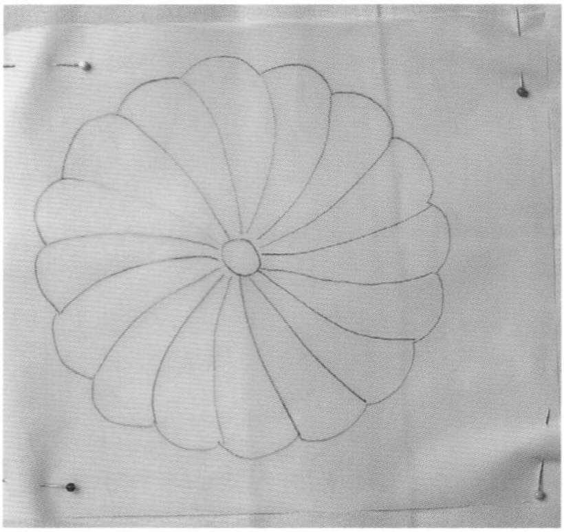

CHOOSING DESIGNS

Look for designs with a continuous line when machine quilting. These have less "start and stop" junctions.

This technique requires some practice. Remember, you are moving the fabric yourself, instead of the machine moving it with the feed dogs. Finish by making two or three stitches on the same spot to lock the threads before snipping them to neaten.

BINDING

When adding binding fabrics to a quilt, a straight stitch is all that is needed to begin with. This will ensure that all the layers of the quilt and binding are caught together in a strong seam.

Once the binding has been folded to the back of the quilt, a slipstitch sewn by hand can be used to cover the line of machine-sewn stitching.

Fabrics

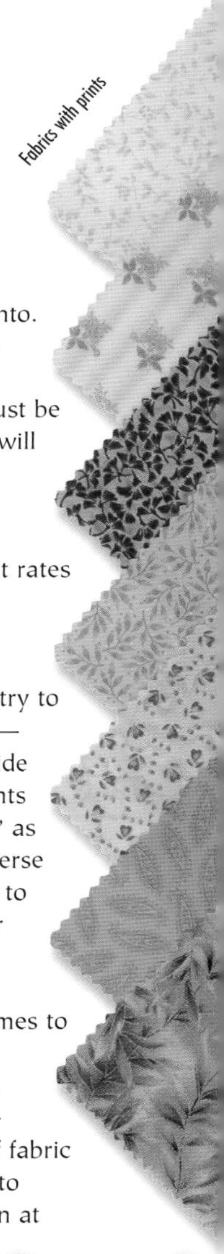

When choosing fabrics for patchwork, try to eliminate those that are difficult to handle, or have a very open weave and are liable to fray excessively.

Two fabrics are ideal for beginners: 100 percent cotton and "Dupion silk" (make sure they are craft or dress weight and avoid using furnishing fabrics at this stage). When starting out, you will benefit from using the same weight of fabric throughout your quilt. Once you become more confident, you can diversify and introduce more interesting or exotic fabrics. Slippery, lightweight or open-weave fabrics can always be backed with an iron-on interfacing to make them more stable, but do remember that this added layer may make the fabrics more difficult to quilt by hand.

WASHING

Make sure that fabrics are both washable and colorfast: Many patchworkers prefer to prewash all their fabrics before using them in a quilt, just to be on the safe side, but we all know how wonderful new fabric feels. If you choose to prewash fabrics before cutting into them, you can get that "new" feel back by using a spray starch at the ironing stage—this will help give some stability back to the washed fabric and make it easier to handle and cut into.

It is possible to use old clothes and other fabrics if they have a sentimental value for you. You must be aware, though, that these fabrics will have been worn, handled and laundered far more than a new fabric and, therefore, may wear through far sooner and at different rates to new fabric.

FABRIC COLLECTION

When building a stash of fabrics, try to achieve a good selection of prints—large, medium and small—alongside a selection of plain fabrics (or prints that are so subtle that they "read" as plain from a distance). Keep a diverse selection of colors. You may stick to navy, beige and white within your wardrobe, but a restricted color palette in a fabric collection may restrict your creativity when it comes to patchwork. Most specialist patchwork and quilting shops sell bundles of fabric known as stash-builders; these are small pieces of fabric specifically cut and sold together to enable you to build your collection at

minimum cost. However, if you do prefer a restricted and more subtle fabric palette, don't forget to inject that all-important tiny piece of strong color very gently, here and there, to add interest.

COLOR AND TONE

Tonal values are important for adding definition to patchwork patterns—you need a range of tones in each color, from dark tones, through medium tones to light tones. A lot of people find it difficult to see the tonal values of fabrics, but here are a couple of tips. First, cut swatches of fabric in a particular color, such as red, and lay them in a tonal strip, ranging from dark to light. Glue these to a sheet of paper and photocopy it on a black and white photocopier. Second, if you have a digital camera, set it to black and white photography mode and take a picture of the fabrics. Both methods will help you to see the tonal values more clearly than looking at the actual fabric color itself.

Another thing to bear in mind is that the tone of one fabric may alter, depending on the fabric that is placed next to it.

THE BACK OF A QUILT

If you choose a plain fabric for the back of a quilt, remember that the stitches will show up more clearly than if you choose a patterned fabric. If you are happy with the appearance of the stitches on the back of your quilt, it does not matter whether the backing fabric is plain or print. However, when stitching appears to be very busy or uneven on the back of your work (perhaps you have had to stitch through thick and bulky patchwork seams and junctions, for instance), a backing fabric printed with a pattern may be preferable. This is not an excuse for sloppy work, but it may just take some pressure off you at the quilting stage of a project.

Threads

Many different types of thread are available for use in both quilted and embroidered projects. It's a good idea to consider the fabrics that you've used throughout a quilt before choosing the thread for the construction stages and quilting stages.

For instance, if a project is predominantly made from silk, you may prefer to carry the theme through and use a silk thread, especially where fine, hand-stitched appliqué is concerned.

If the quilt has been constructed from fairly robust 100 percent cotton, it makes sense to continue with the natural fiber theme by using 100 percent cotton thread for both construction and quilting.

HAND-QUILTING THREADS

For traditional hand quilting, quilting thread is available in a whole host of colors, both as mercerized cotton and polyester fiber. There is no need to run the quilting thread through a block of beeswax before using it, as early quilters did. However, if you tend to twist the needle and thread while you are sewing, beeswax may certainly go a little way toward preventing the thread from tangling and knotting.

HAND-QUILTING THREADS

1 HAND-QUILTING THREAD: 100% cotton

2 HAND-QUILTING THREAD: 100% cotton, extra strong

3 HAND-QUILTING THREAD: cotton-covered polyester, extra strong

4 SILK THREAD: 100% silk, very fine

5 COTTON PERLE: 100% *coton à broder*—available in different weights

6 COTTON PERLE: 100% cotton crochet yarn—available in different weights

7 METALLIC THREAD: 100% polyester yarn—not very strong, but useful for embellishment

VARIEGATED/SPACE-DYED THREADS

8 PEARL COTTON: 100% cotton, twisted, glossy thread—available in different weights

9 PERLE THREAD: 100% cotton, hand-dyed

10 SASHIKO THREAD: 100% cotton, specialist thread for Sashiko quilting

Some machine-quilting threads such as 100% mercerized cotton and 100% long-staple cotton are also suitable for hand-sewing.

MACHINE-QUILTING THREADS

1 COTTON: 100% cotton all-purpose thread, suitable for hand-sewing and machine work

2 POLYESTER: 100% polyester all-purpose thread, suitable for hand-sewing and machining

3 SILKY: 100% viscose glossy embroidery thread

4 SILKY: 100% acrylic glossy embroidery thread

5 METALLIC: 60% polyester, 40% polyester high-gloss thread

6 METALLIC: 70% polyamide, 30% polyester fibrous thread

7 METALLIC: 100% polyester high-gloss, hologram-effect thread

8 INVISIBLE THREAD: man-made fiber for "invisible" machine quilting

VARIEGATED/SPACE-DYED THREADS

9 MACHINE QUILTING: 100% mercerized cotton

10 MACHINE QUILTING: 100% long-staple cotton, suitable for heavier quilting or topstitching

When choosing fabrics and threads for a quilt project, especially for some of the more decorative stitches, remember that it is always possible to work a large stitch with fine thread on thick and heavy fabric. It is virtually impossible to work a tiny stitch with thick thread through a fine fabric.

MACHINE-QUILTING THREADS

When it comes to choosing machine-quilting threads, there is an enormous choice of threads designed for both machine quilting and machine embroidery.

Give some thought to the fibers that are in the materials that you've used for the quilt, and to which machine-quilting technique you will use

Using machine-quilting thread Before beginning to machine-stitch have a trial run on some scrap fabric layered with a length of batting.

Test both the upper and lower tensions on the machine: One or the other may need to be adjusted, especially if you have loaded the bobbin with a thread in a different weight to that on the top of the machine. Using metallic thread often requires a slight adjustment to the tensions, as does free-form machine quilting or machine embroidery with the feed dogs lowered.

Check the stitch length, width and setting (if using a preset stitch). Finally, choose a selection of threads and try them out on your practice piece first. That way, you'll be more relaxed and confident when it comes to using the machine on your precious quilt.

Construction Materials

The final appearance of a quilt and the ease with which it is quilted will depend very much on the "filling in your sandwich," i.e. the batting and stabilizer fabrics.

BATTING

The choice is wide and varied—there are battings that are specifically designed for hand quilting, battings that are manufactured to support machine quilting, and some that are suitable for either. There are several things to consider when choosing the batting for a quilt project:

- The quilting technique and threads you will be using.
- The final appearance you would like your quilt to have.
- The sort of wear and tear that the quilt will be subjected to.
- Your budget.

Techniques and threads Some battings designed for machine quilting are very difficult to work through if quilting by hand. If you plan to mix the two techniques within one quilt, opt for a batting that is suitable for both hand and machine quilting, so that you get the best of both worlds.

Final appearance A batting made of 100 percent polyester will give a lot of loft (plumpness) to the puffs and pillows of a quilting design. However, it will flatten if you try to iron the quilt at a later date. Many of the battings made from natural fibers or mixed fibers have a more compressed appearance and, therefore, the quilt will have a flatter appearance, too. This is fine for a wall-hanging, but you might prefer a plumper appearance for a bed quilt, in which case it would be better to use a higher loft batting.

Wear and tear If you are making a quilt for a child, or an elderly person who is living in a retirement home, it may experience a great deal more laundering than might otherwise be expected. Choose a batting that will live up to the extremes of laundering in a washing machine at a fairly high temperature. Some battings are preshrunk, others will have to be preshrunk by the quilter before being used. Some quilters prefer to purposely "antiquate" their quilts after they are made by using a batting that will specifically shrink and make the quilt look older than it is.

Budget Battings containing man-made fibers are generally cheaper than those made from natural fibers. However, if your quilt is meant to be an heirloom piece, or is destined for exhibition, you may prefer to spend a little more at this stage on an extra-special batting that you've had your eye on or have been meaning to experiment with.

STABILIZERS

Stabilizing fabrics are commonly used in needlework for dressmaking and soft furnishings. Their uses in quilt-making are less well known, but when dealing with materials of different weights, different structures, and varying durability (such as silks of different quality, or open-weave fabrics such as cheesecloth, Indian cottons or Osnaburg), they are invaluable.

SOME OF THE BATTINGS AVAILABLE

1 POLYESTER (FLUFFY):
High loft, easy to launder.

2 POLYESTER (COMPRESSED):
Thermal qualities.

3 POLYESTER (GRAY/BLACK):
For use with dark fabrics.

4 100% COTTON:
Flatter appearance, very stretchy, may need prewashing to shrink.

5 100% COTTON WITH SCRIM:
Designed for machine quilting; may need prewashing.

6 COTTON/POLYESTER MIX:
Has the feel of natural fibers with less stretch than 100% cotton. May provide some controlled shrinkage for effect.

7 100% WOOL:
Quite expensive; extra care needs to be taken with storage and cleaning.

8 100% LAMBSWOOL:
Very dense and fluffy; expensive.

9 WOOL/POLYESTER MIX:
Less stretchy, same considerations needed for storage and cleaning as 100% wool.

10 SILK:
Very expensive, more difficult to use, a little unstable.

STABILIZERS FOR QUILT-MAKING

1 IRON-ON INTERFACING:
Available in different weights. Sew-in interfacing.

2 QUICKSCREEN INTERFACING:
Useful as a permanent foundation fabric.

3 BONDING WEB:
Used for bonding fabrics when doing raw-edge appliqué. Available in different weights. Use baking parchment to protect your iron and ironing board cover.

4 FREEZER PAPER:
Used as a support for appliquéd motifs.

Other commonly used stabilizers are: Tear-away stabilizer (useful for foundation pieced patchwork), water-soluble interfacing (for machine quilting/embroidery; it dissolves when immersed in water and is available for use in hot or cold water), heat-soluble interfacing (it disintegrates when heat is applied), heavyweight interfacing (used to mold three-dimensional shapes) and sheer gauze (for capturing decorative threads).

Utility materials All of these can provide a stabilizing effect within quilted work used for items such as placemats, purses and millinery, as well as quilts.

- Muslin. Available in different weights.
- Buckram.
- Canvas.
- Calico or cheesecloth.
- Insulating fabrics with thermal properties.

FOUNDATION MATERIALS

5 TEMPORARY:
Tear-away stabilizer, brown paper, waxed paper,photocopy/typing paper.

6 PERMANENT:
Calico, muslin, quickscreen interfacing, fabric.

Fabric Preparation

Fabrics must be prepared before you can begin work.

PREWASHING FABRICS

- Prewash if you are unsure about the stability of a fabric (whether it has been preshrunk or not) and if you have any doubts about its colorfastness.
- If the quilt is to be laundered regularly, it is wise to prewash the fabrics to see how they behave in a washing machine at different temperatures. Once a fabric has been washed, it may need stretching back into shape.
- If you've prewashed fabrics and they feel flimsy, give them a new lease of life by adding spray starch when you press them. They'll feel good as new and be easier to handle.

REASONS NOT TO PREWASH FABRICS

- There's nothing as nice as the feel of brand new fabrics; they usually contain a dressing or starch, which makes them more resistant to creasing.
- Lack of opportunity. Short, one-day workshops held within a store usually involve using fabric straight off the shelf. In this situation, try to choose colors that won't be so prone to dye loss, and opt for good-quality printed and closely woven fabrics.
- If you're using exotic fabrics such as metallics and silks, you may choose not to prewash those.
- Hand-dyed fabrics have usually been washed so many times in the dyeing process that they have no shrinkage left in them by the time they are used within a quilt. Be wary, though, of dyes that are notoriously difficult to set, such as reds and purples. Use a dye-catcher cloth in the washing machine and a cool temperature setting.

GRAIN

- Check the grain on a fabric before cutting into it. The lengthwise grain is known as the "warp" and runs down the length of the fabric; the crosswise grain is known as the "weft" and runs across the width of the fabric between the two selvedges.
- The warp and weft are the straight grain. Where stability is needed, items should always be cut on the straight grain, especially within patchwork.
- Grain that runs diagonally across the width of the fabric (at an angle of approximately 45°) is known as the "bias." Bias-cut fabric is very stretchy: Once stretched, it won't spring back into place, so be careful where you use bias-cut edges. It is ideal for strips or patches of fabric that need to be manipulated around a curve.

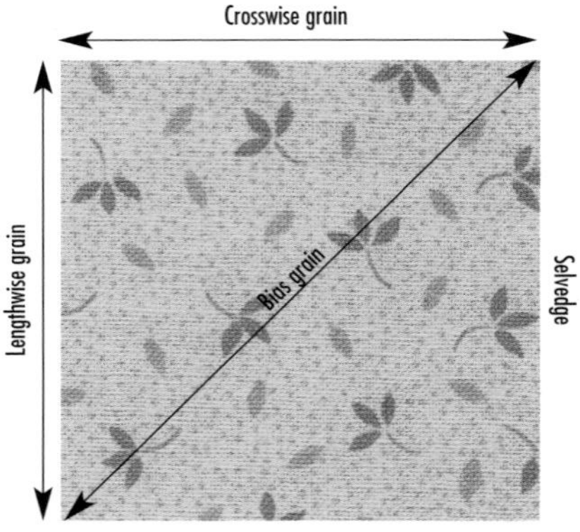

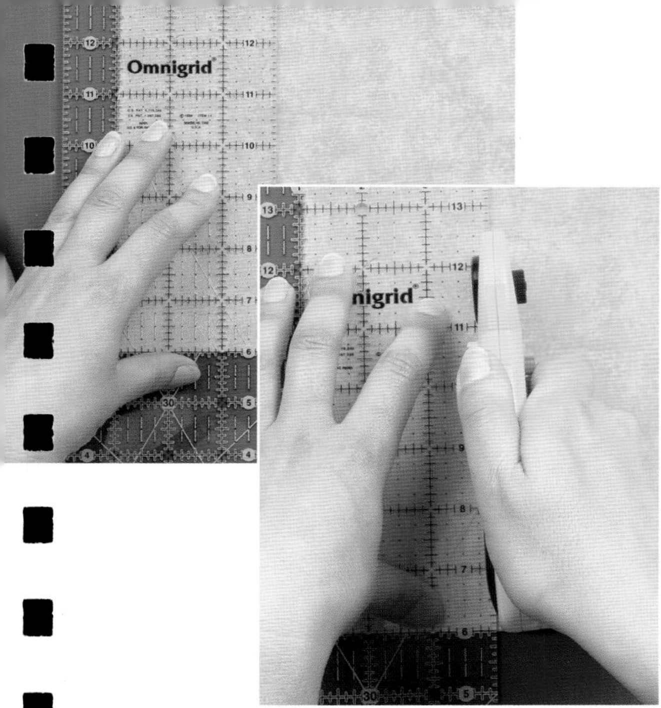

ROTARY CUTTING

When using a rotary cutter to cut fabric always use a specialist cutting mat, safety ruler and a sharp blade. It is safer to "bridge" the hand that is holding the ruler. Always cut away from yourself rather than toward yourself.

SAVING TIME

Using spring-loaded scissors with long blades can make short work of cutting fabrics by hand.

CUTTING INTO FABRIC

- Before cutting into a length of fabric, remove the tightly woven selvedges so that they don't distort the main body of the material. Iron out any creases.
- If using rotary cutting equipment, large lengths of fabric can be folded to fit the cutting board. Up to eight layers of fabric can be cut into easily, but make sure you're using a sharp blade.

MIXING FIBERS

If you're using fabrics of various fiber types within a quilt project, take the time to stabilize the weaker ones with an iron-on interfacing or calico. This will ensure that all the fabrics are easy to handle and have more or less the same weight when it comes to the quilting process. It also makes the aftercare of the quilt easier.

Quilt Construction

Quilt construction begins with the making of the quilt top. You may have chosen to piece this in patchwork, you may have preferred stitching appliqué, perhaps you've mixed the two, or perhaps you've made a wholecloth quilt, with no piecing or embellishment at all.

Whichever methods you chose for the quilt top, once you're ready to work on the next stage—the layering—give the top a good press.

HOW TO BEGIN

Choose, prepare and press the backing fabric. This needs to measure approximately 2–4 in. (5–10 cm) larger all around than the quilt top, to allow for any reduction in size caused at the quilting stage. Remove the selvedges to reduce any tension at the sides of the fabric.

If the quilt is large and you've chosen standard-width fabric, the backing fabric may need to be cut and joined. (It is possible to buy extra-wide fabric, which is sold specifically for backing quilts.) Press the seams open to flatten them. (If you've hand-sewn them, press the seams to one side to strengthen them.)

BACKING FABRIC

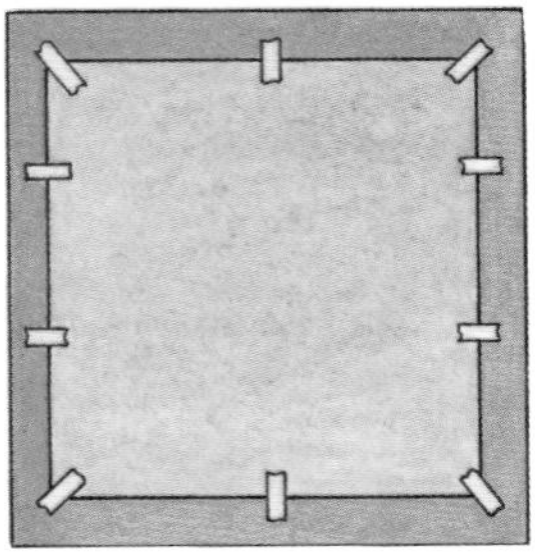

Choose an area that is large enough for you to lay out the complete quilt; this could be a generous-sized tabletop or the floor. Lay out the backing fabric, right side down, square it up and smooth it out. Using low-tack masking tape, tape down the four corners of the fabric and, in the case of larger quilts, the halfway point on each side. This will keep the fabric flat and taut while you add the next layers.

BATTING

If the batting has been prepacked, unwrap it and spread it out on a bed or similar area to allow it to breathe, preferably overnight.

If the batting is narrower than the quilt, you may have to join sections of batting together: Place two edges alongside each other, butting together neatly without overlapping, and then stitch them together with a large whip stitch or cross stitch, a neutral thread and a big needle. Make sure that the join in the batting is not too near to the edges of the quilt.

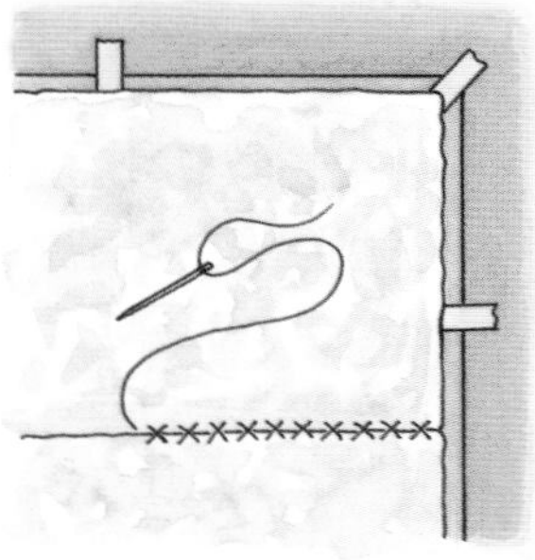

Again, the batting needs to measure approximately 2–4 in. (5–10 cm) larger than the quilt top: Make it the same size as the backing fabric if you can. When you're ready, lay the batting on top of the backing fabric and gently tape the four corners (and the halfway points if you're working on a large quilt). Make sure any lumps have been smoothed out.

QUILT TOP

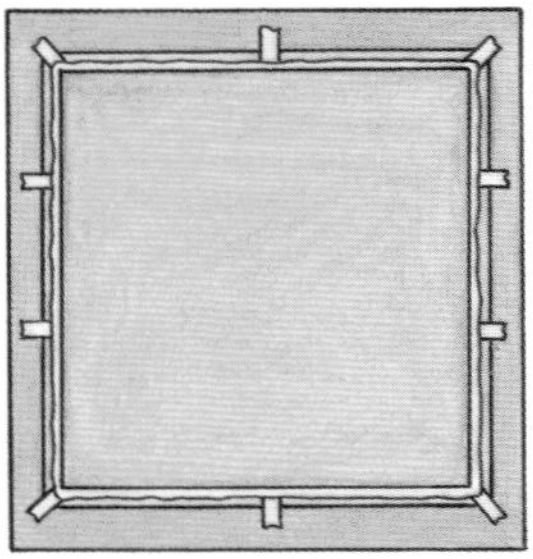

Now lay the quilt top, right side up, on top of the batting. Ensure that the edges are parallel with the edges of the backing fabric and batting, smooth out any ripples in the fabric and tape it in the same way. If you prefer, you can add a few pins to stop the layers from traveling while you work on them.

BASTING

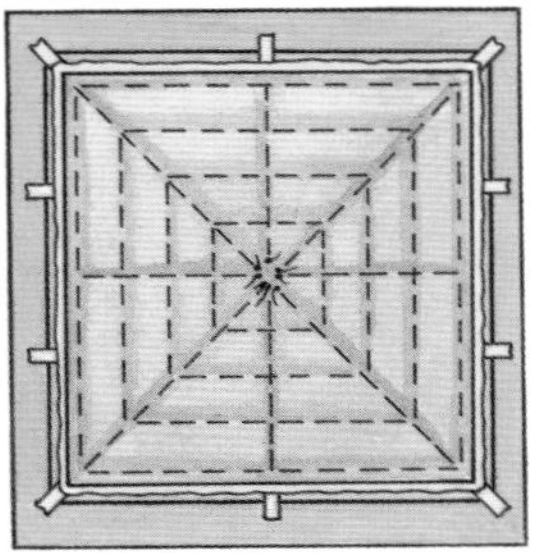

The basting stage needs to be worked from the center outward: Begin by tacking the cross-grid (the vertical and horizontal lines that pass through the center) and the full diagonals. Start each line of basting in the center and work outward. Follow this by working a grid all over the quilt in each direction. This can be worked from side to side, or on one quarter of the quilt at a time. Aim to work a grid of approximately 2–3 in. (5–7.5 cm) wide—this will stop the layers of the quilt from traveling when you reach the quilting stage.

TIP

There are alternatives to basting in the traditional fashion: You may prefer to hold the layers together with safety pins, or use a basting gun and clips. These are a good option if you need to work in a hurry, or you are restricted for space in which to do the basting, or if you prefer machine quilting (sometimes a basting thread can get caught up in machine quilting).

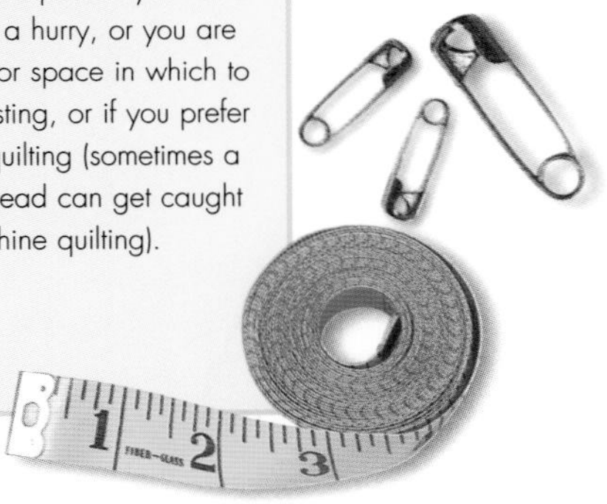

Marking and Quilting

LIGHTBOX

If you have a design that is on paper (a photocopy or in a book) and you'd like to transfer it to a quilt, without going to the trouble of making a template, the easiest thing to do is to trace it on a lightbox.

HOMEMADE STENCIL

Another option is to trace the design onto template plastic and make your own stencil. Use a craft knife or a special stencil-cutting hot knife to cut out the design. If the design is linear only, make a photocopy of it, glue it to some card and cut around the outer edge of the design to make a template.

MARKING A QUILT BEFORE LAYERING

There are various ways to carry out marking of a quilt before layering.

Window In daylight, tape the design to a window, tape the fabric over this and trace the pattern. This technique is only suitable for pale fabrics. See photographs opposite for other methods.

MARKING A QUILT AFTER LAYERING

This is by far the easiest stage at which to mark a quilting design, because the quilt top fabric has been stabilized by adding further layers.

All of the fabric-marking options suggested under Fabric-marking Tools (see page 14) are available to you at this stage (except for tracing a design). If you choose to stitch your quilt in a frame or a hoop, any designs for a section will need to be marked before the work is set into the frame.

Marking a design Mark up the design over the entire quilt top before you start, or mark each section as you go. This may have a bearing on which marking tool or gadget you use and how long the marks have to stay put while the quilt is being handled. A powdery chalk, for instance, will soon disappear as you begin to quilt. A chemical-based pen, such as a water-soluble pen, will stay in the fabric for longer, but the marks may need to be removed as the quilting progresses if you are worried about permanent setting.

Stencils Use stencils and templates to add further interest. Choose designs and patterns that complement the quilt itself. Blocks of patchwork can have parts of templates/stencils stitched within patches of fabrics.

QUILTING STITCHING METHODS

CONTOUR-QUILTING

Contour-quilting involves quilting around each part of a design to outline it. Quilt around individual pieces of patchwork or appliquéd motifs.

ECHO QUILTING

This method of quilting allows you to create exciting patterns by quilting around a patch or motif and then echoing the shape of this stitching by stitching further lines that run parallel to it.

QUILTING IN THE DITCH

Quilting in the ditch is a method of adding puffiness to a quilt with unobtrusive stitching that does not detract from the design. To do it, work a straight stitch in the dead center of the seamline.

INFILL STITCHING

Once appliqué motifs have been contour quilted, areas of background fabric can be quilted with infill stitching designs.

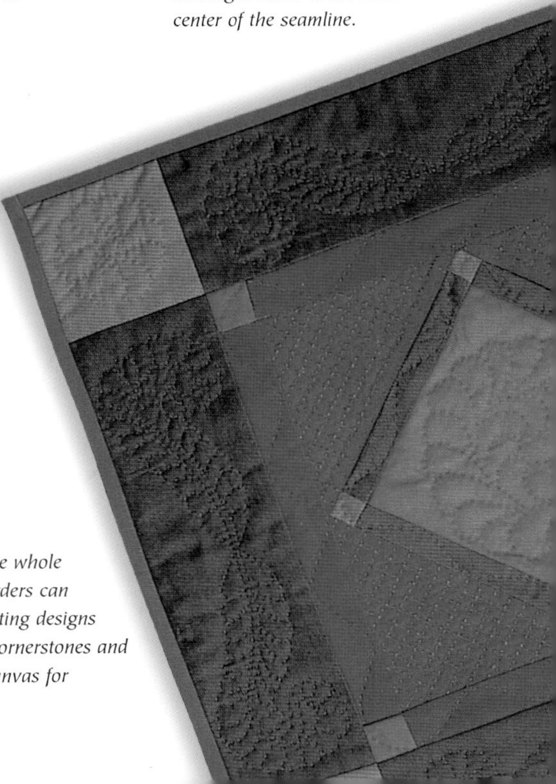

BORDERS AND CORNERSTONES

The quilting of borders can be incorporated into the whole design, or they can be quilted separately. Long borders can provide an opportunity to use a long run of interesting designs such as cable, cable and feather, plaits or vines. Cornerstones and setting squares within quilts can provide a good canvas for interesting square patterns.

Types of Quilting

Quilting and quilt-making are universally popular. It is fascinating to see how different countries have approached needlework in this form and how cultural influences have determined a recognizable type of quilting from each corner of the world.

Sashiko Quilting

This form of quilting comes from ancient Japan. The most identifiable work is stitched with a thick, white perle thread and a simple running stitch through two layers of indigo-dyed cotton fabric, with no batting between the layers. Sashiko was originally used as utility stitching on garments and later became a form of decorative "embroidery." It is simple to adapt Sashiko "embroidery" to do the job of quilting and a variety of brightly colored Sashiko threads, preprinted stencils and patterns are available.

TIPS

Sashiko designs are based on a grid, so you need squared paper when designing your own patterns. You may also like to use paper printed with an isometric grid for triangles, hexagons or diamonds, etc. Several designs may be used within a project.

PREPRINTED DESIGNS

Some stores stock pads of paper printed with designs that could easily be interpreted in Sashiko quilting.

DESIGNS

Regular curvilinear and geometric designs such as these are all suitable for Sashiko quilting.

MARKING THE FABRIC

Mark your chosen design on the fabric. It could consist of a single all-over pattern, or of several sections, each filled with a different pattern.

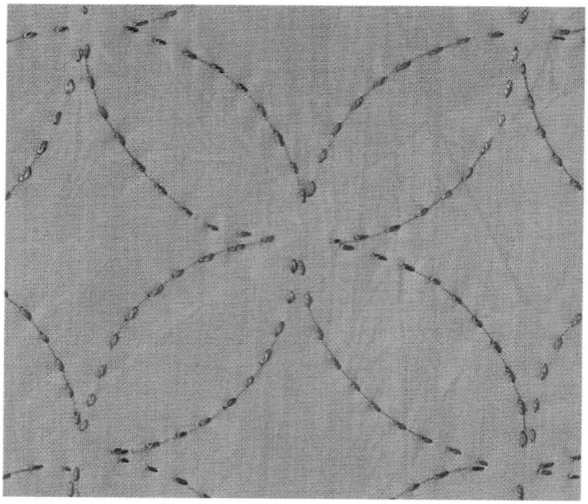

STARTING TO STITCH

Tie a neat knot in the thread: This can be "popped" through the top fabric and into the batting, as with traditional quilting.

STITCH LENGTH

In Sashiko quilting, longer stitches are traditionally sewn. Stitch your design using approximately 3–5 running stitches per 1 in. (2.5 cm).

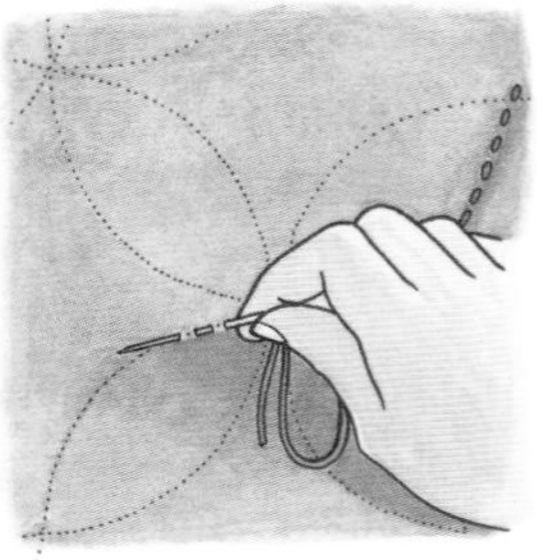

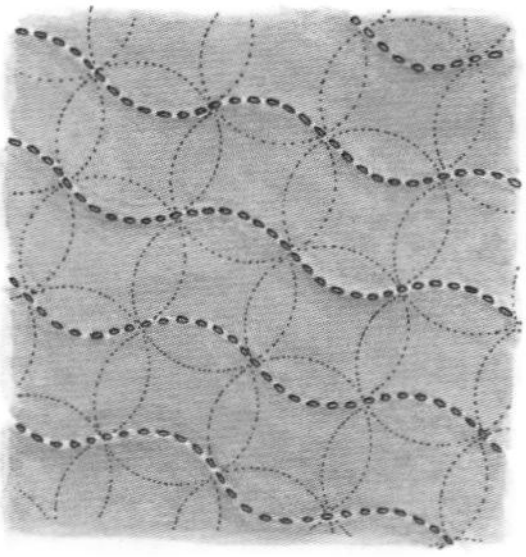

CONTINUOUS STITCHING

Work continuous lines of stitching from one side of a project to the other. Study the design and work out how to sew as many lines as possible continuously, in order to have the fewest breaks in the thread.

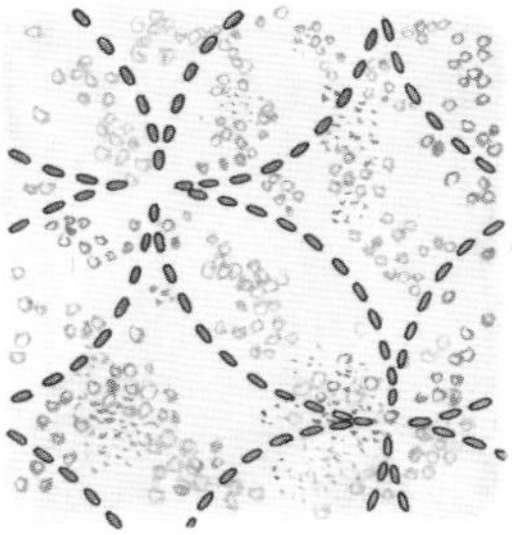

JUNCTIONS

When several lines of a design meet at a junction, leave a space between the stitches (or at that particular junction) rather than having the stitches overlap or run into each other.

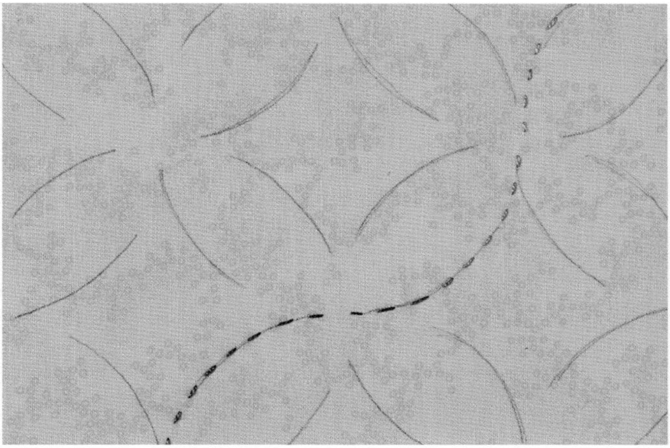

FINISHING

Complete each line of the design by "popping" the knotted thread through the top fabric once again, into the batting layer, and snipping the tail of thread to finish neatly.

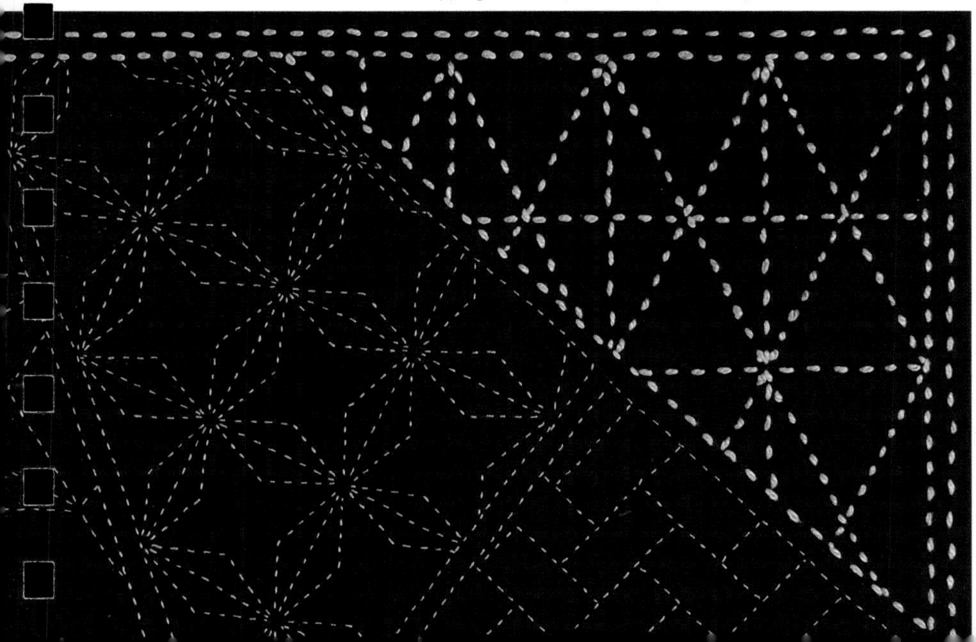

Italian Quilting

Italian quilting has been popular throughout Europe and the Middle East for centuries, both for embellishing garments and on bed quilts. Batting is not used. It consists of corded channels, which give an attractive three-dimensional effect. These are produced with traditional quilting wool and a large-eyed blunt needle. This technique is used mainly on wholecloth quilts. The French equivalent is called *Boutis*, and uses very fine cord to produce a more intricate design.

DESIGN SECTION

KNOTS

Knot design with suitable areas for cording.

HEARTS

Heart design with suitable channels for Italian quilting.

TIP

Choose a design that incorporates, or can be interpreted, with "tramlines" (double parallel lines). These will be the channels and should be of a size to comfortably accommodate the cording thread or wool you are using. Mark the design on the fabric.

MATERIALS SECTION

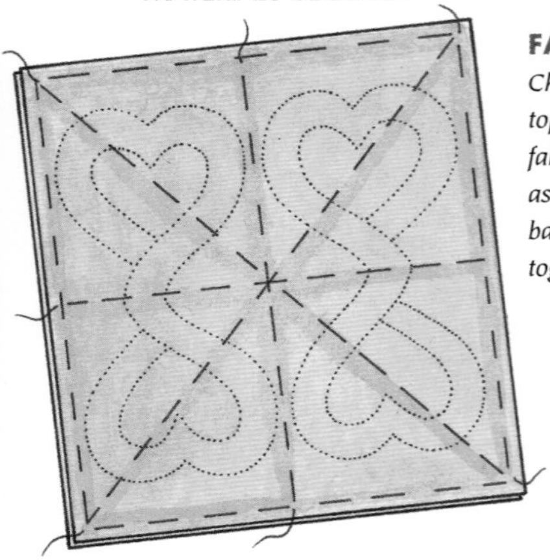

FABRICS

Choose a fine cotton for the top layer. You will also need a fabric with a loose weave, such as calico or cheesecloth, to back this. Baste the two layers together.

TIPS

- Make sure the yarn that you choose for cording has been prewashed to prevent shrinkage at a later date.
- For additional interest, use colored wools such as knitting yarns, under a top layer of fabric that is almost transparent.

CHANNELS SECTION

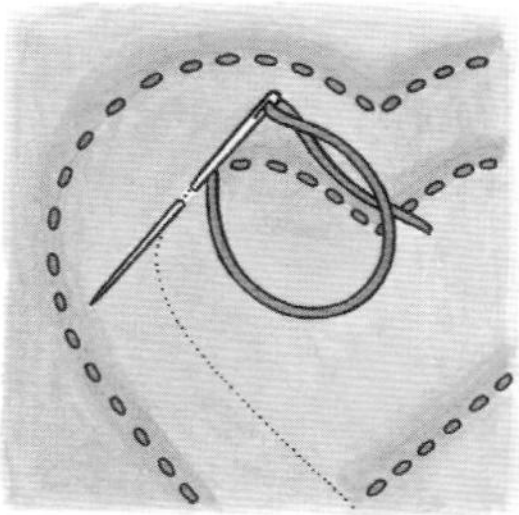

HAND-SEWN CHANNELS

Channels may be stitched by hand using running stitch, backstitch, or chain stitch.

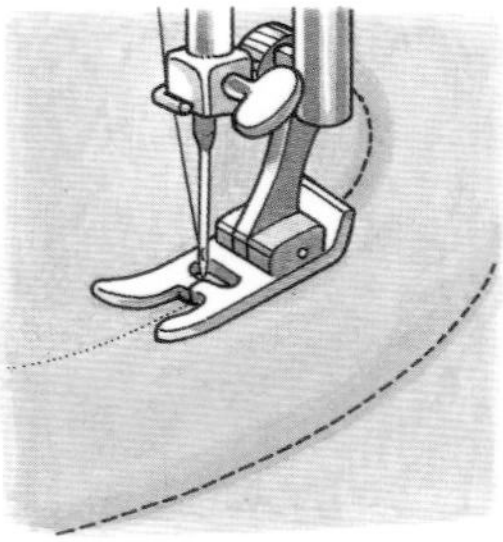

MACHINED CHANNELS

Channels sewn by machine require a medium-length stitch.

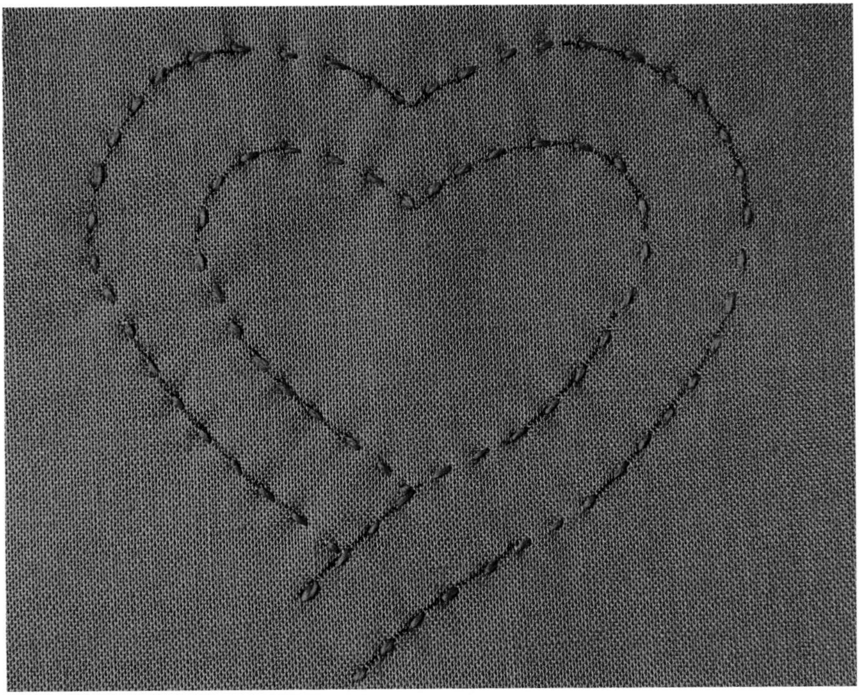

STITCHING THE BASIC DESIGN

Stitch the channels of the design prior to cording.

CORDING SECTION

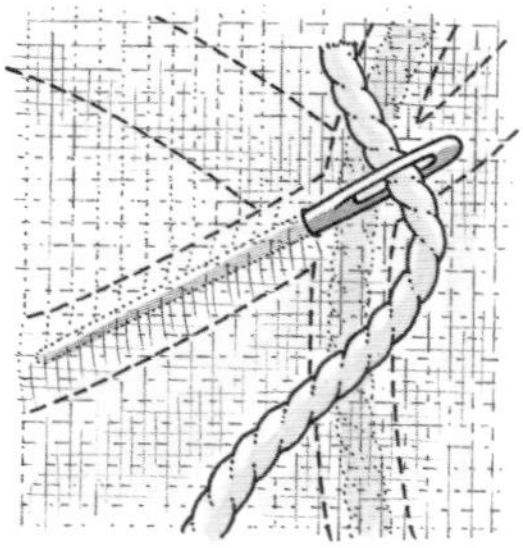

NEEDLE

Use a blunt tapestry needle or bodkin to run the yarn through the channels in the design. Insert it through a small slit made in the calico backing.

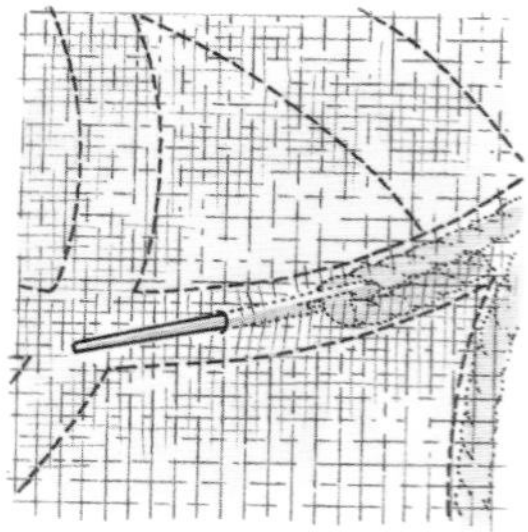

PULLING THE CORD THROUGH

Bring the needle out of the calico backing at regular intervals.

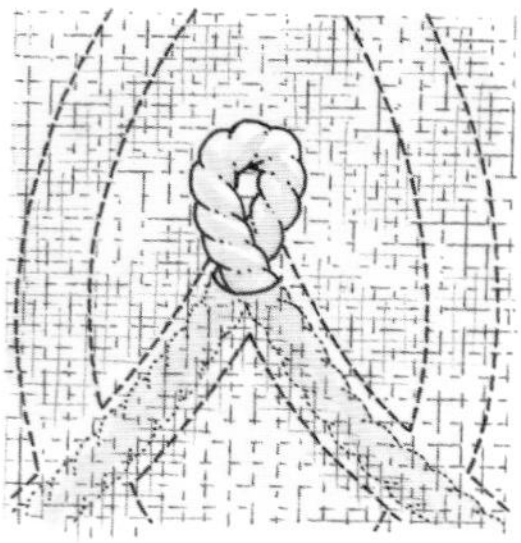

TENSION LOOPS

Leave small loops of cord on sharp curves or corners.

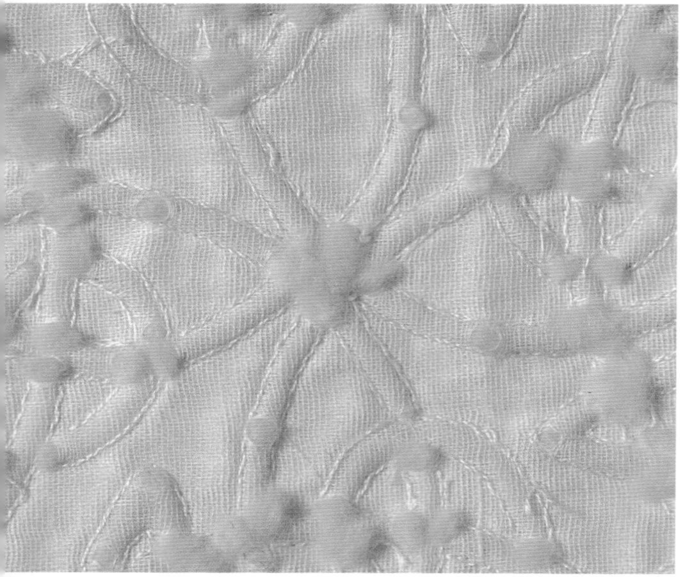

TENSION LOOPS THROUGHOUT A DESIGN

Loops of wool or yarn are left outside the calico on curves and corners to prevent the quilting being pulled too tight.

TIPS

- Tension loops will settle into place as the work is handled and will prevent the fabrics from being distorted by overly tight cording.
- Stop and start a new length of yarn when turning a sharp corner or at junctions in the design. Leave "stop" and "start" tails of yarn outside the calico.

QUILTING SECTION

A piece of Italian quilting may also be further quilted to help throw the corded design into relief. Once the entire design has been padded with yarn, layer the work with a backing fabric, or a backing fabric plus a thin, compressed batting (so that the batting does not detract from the corded areas).

Quilt around the entire design, making quilting stitches directly next to the original outline stitching.

CORDING AND QUILTING

A design that has been corded with Italian quilting, and then hand quilted afterward for added effect.

Trapunto

Trapunto adds a dimensional effect to quilt work by the insertion of stuffing into areas of the design. It is traditionally used on wholecloth quilts (without patchwork or appliqué). Trapunto has a long history and has been used for clothing, soft furnishings, and bed quilts. Although highly decorative, it is also quite time-consuming to produce. Designs are marked as for traditional quilting. A layer of calico is then placed behind the top fabric to hold the stuffing in place.

CHOOSING THE STUFFING

The stuffing needs to have a loose consistency. Use specialist toy stuffing or pull apart scraps of polyester batting. You will find it easier to manipulate the stuffing if you use a pair of tweezers, especially for the smaller areas.

MARKING THE DESIGN

Begin by marking the design on the fabric. Choose a design with "enclosed" areas that are ideal for being padded, such as this flower and feather.

APPLYING CALICO

Add a layer of fine calico (or cheesecloth) to the reverse side of the fabric and baste the two layers together.

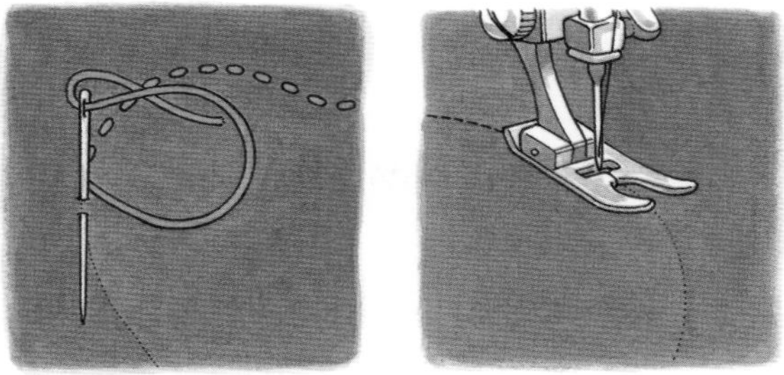

STITCHING THE DESIGN

Using a self-colored thread and a small, neat stitch (hand-sewing or machining), stitch along all the lines of the design. Any thread knots can be left at the back of the work as they will eventually be hidden by further layers.

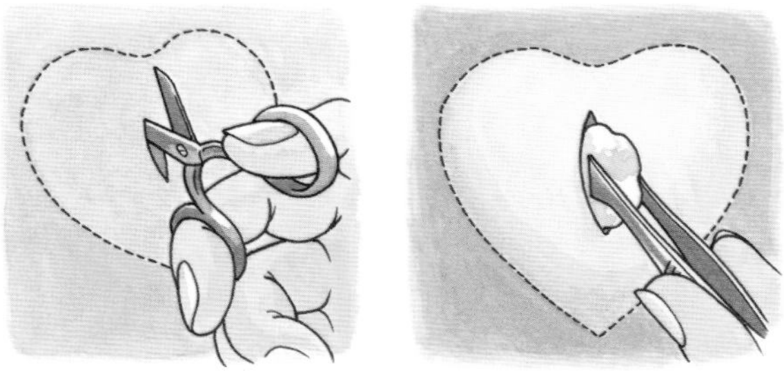

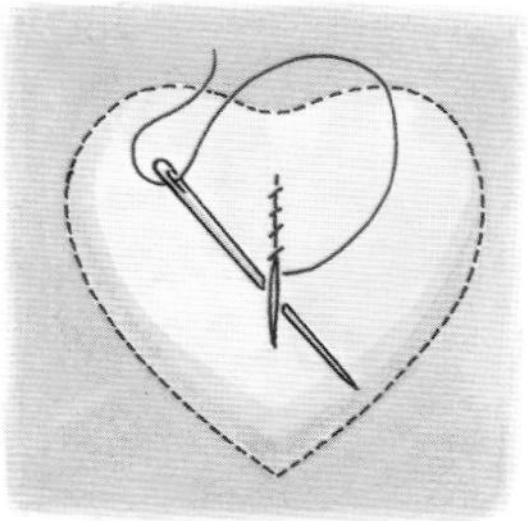

PADDING THE DESIGN

Determine the first area to be padded. Make a small, neat cut in the calico covering this area, not too close to the stitching lines. Using a pair of tweezers, push small scraps of stuffing behind the calico. Don't overstuff the area, as this will distort the surface fabric.

CLOSING THE CALICO

Gently whipstitch the calico to close the gap and hold the stuffing securely.

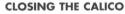

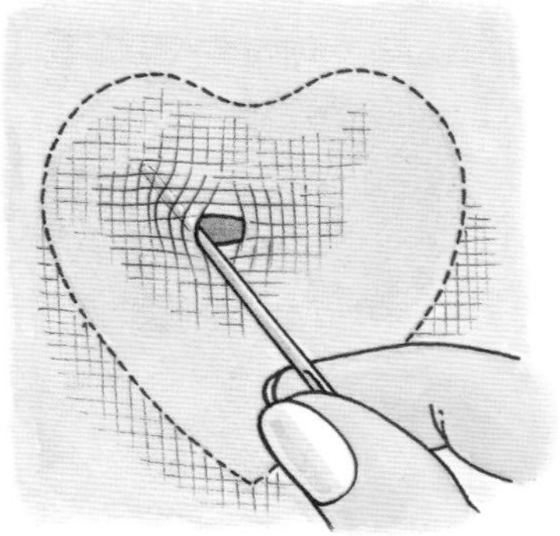

ALTERNATIVE METHOD

Alternatively, prise the fibers of the calico apart to form a hole large enough for the stuffing to be pushed through, and then gently manipulate them back into position to close the gap.

COMPLETING THE PADDING

Repeat this process to pad all the relevant areas of the design.

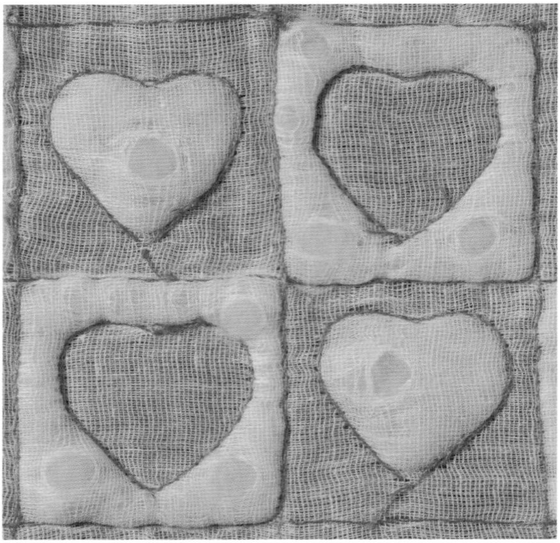

ADDING A BACKING

Layer the work, either with a backing fabric and no batting, or a backing fabric and a light, compressed batting (so that the stuffed areas do not become confused with unstuffed areas).

QUILTING THE DESIGN

Quilt around the design, making the quilting stitches directly next to the original outline stitches of the design. Quilting the background areas will make the padded design stand out even more.

Kantha

Kantha quilting originated in Bangladesh, where it was often stitched on sari fabric. A small, neat running stitch is employed throughout. Colored threads are used to sew a decorative border and to outline a central design. The design is then infilled with various colors and shapes. The colored threads can be chosen to add areas of shading to the design. Traditionally, several layers of fine cotton material were basted together without batting. However, this technique can easily be adapted for use on padded quiltwork.

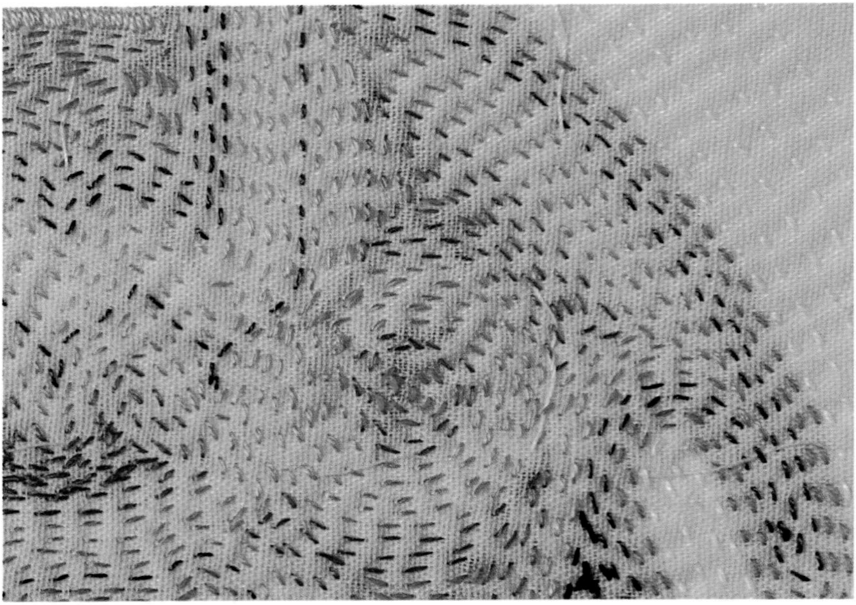

THE BACKGROUND

The background area around the design is filled with stitching, beginning with contour lines and echo lines around the central design itself and working outward to fill the entire space. The background area is sewn with a thread that matches the color of the fabric.

DESIGNS

Motifs and designs suitable for Kantha quilting.

STARTING OFF

Make a template for the outline design and use it to mark the design on the fabric.

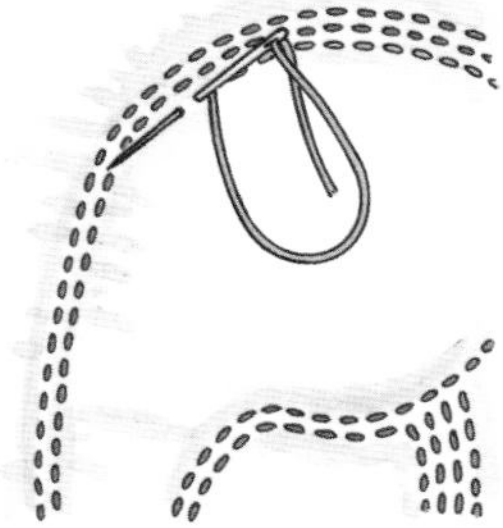

THE STITCHING PROCESS

Begin by stitching the central design itself, using small, neat running stitches. Stitch around the outline and then fill the whole design with continuous running stitches.

TIPS

- Taking several stitches onto the needle at once will help with evenness, although this will be more difficult to do on tight curves.
- Use different shades of thread color to add shadow and light to the design in a painterly way.

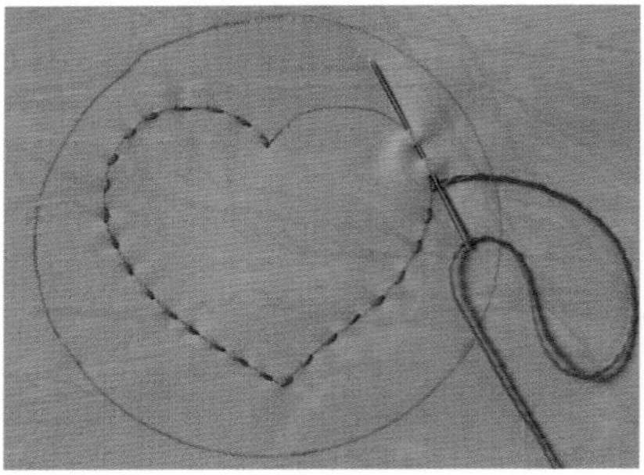

STARTING AND FINISHING
Start your thread with a knot. "Pop" the knot through the top fabric and into the batting or between the fabric layers to secure it.

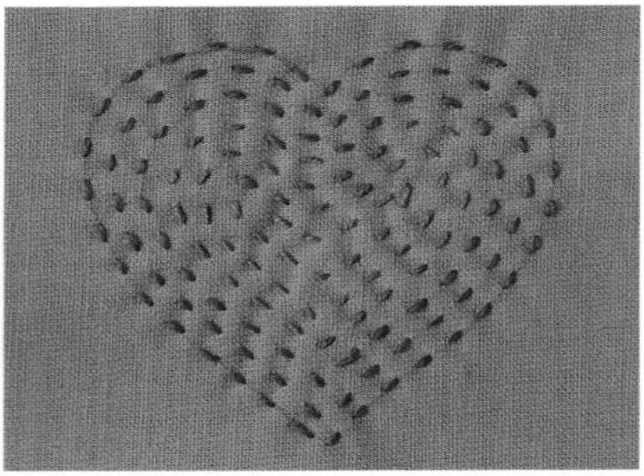

CENTRAL AND BORDER DESIGNS
Once the entire central design has been sewn, decide on a border design and sew this.

QUILTING THE BACKGROUND
Take a self-colored thread and begin contour quilting, and then echo quilting, around the central design. Continue in this way until the entire background has been filled with stitching. Finish each length of thread by "popping" the knotted thread through the top fabric and into the batting, snipping the tail of thread to finish neatly.

Hand and machine quilting

KNOTTING AND TUFTING

This traditionally utilitarian form of quilting can add textural interest to a modern quilt. Thread is used to make individual knots at regular intervals through all the layers of a quilt. The tufts of thread can be sewn into the quilt layers for a neat finish, or left on the surface of the quilt top or backing fabric for effect. Buttons, charms, scraps of fabric, or decorative threads can also be included.

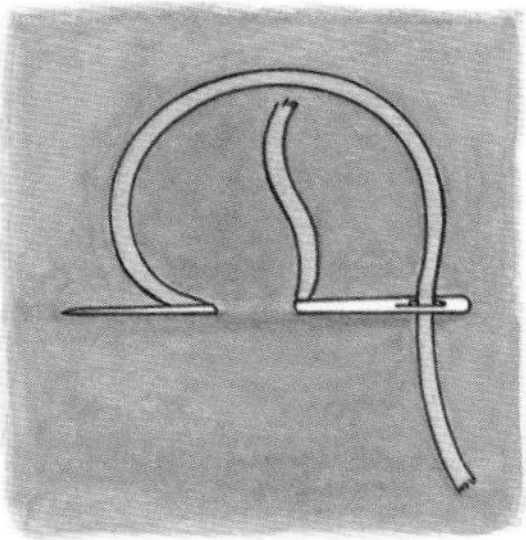

TYING A KNOT

Take the thread or yarn into the fabric layers and up again. Repeat on the same spot.

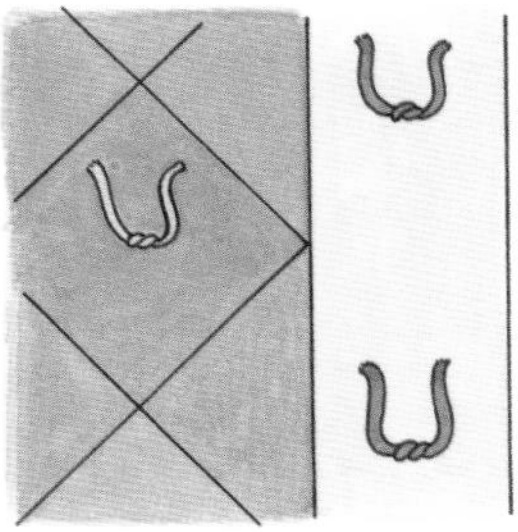

TUFTING

Leave tufts of thread on the surface of the quilt for a decorative effect.

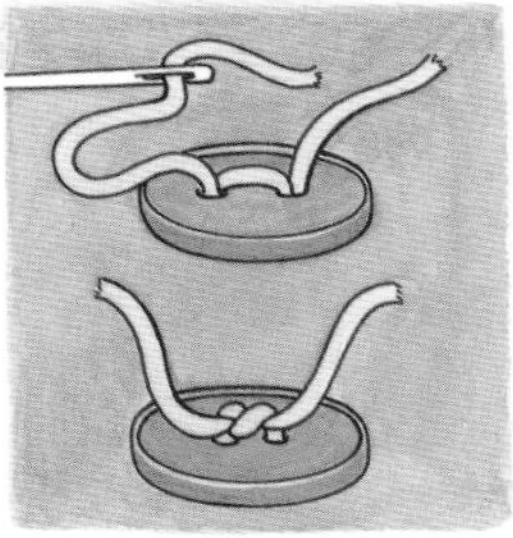

EMBELLISHMENT

Add buttons, charms, or other items as a focus of interest.

WHOLECLOTH QUILTING

The quilt top is made from one large piece of cloth and marked with a quilting design that covers the entire area. Patchwork and appliqué are not involved. Some designs are traditional in certain geographical locations, so it is often possible to determine where an antique quilt was made and, in some cases, help to date it.

MARKING OUT A WHOLECLOTH DESIGN

Mark the quilt with a traditional quilting design that covers the whole area of the quilt top fabric, or draw a freehand and contemporary design of your choice.

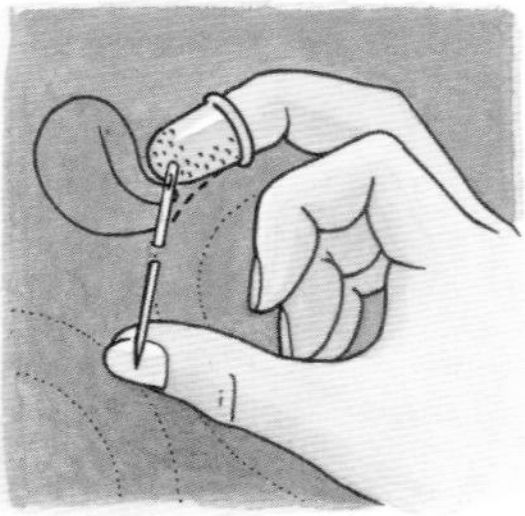

WHOLECLOTH QUILTING BY HAND

For hand quilting, use running stitch, backstitch, or chain stitch.

PREPARING TO QUILT BY MACHINE

Baste the quilt and then roll it in preparation for quilting by machine.

WHOLECLOTH QUILTING BY MACHINE

Quilt from the center outward, working on the most difficult to reach area first and ensuring that all the quilt layers travel outward evenly.

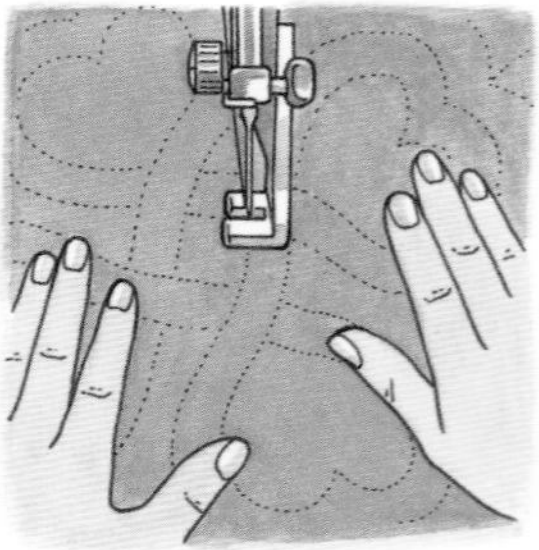

MACHINING THE DESIGN

Try to find continuous line designs to machine, so that you don't have too many "stop and start" junctions in your work.

HAND-SEWN WHOLECLOTH DESIGN

A central motif can be thrown into relief by the use of infill quilting designs in the background, such as squares, diamonds and circles.

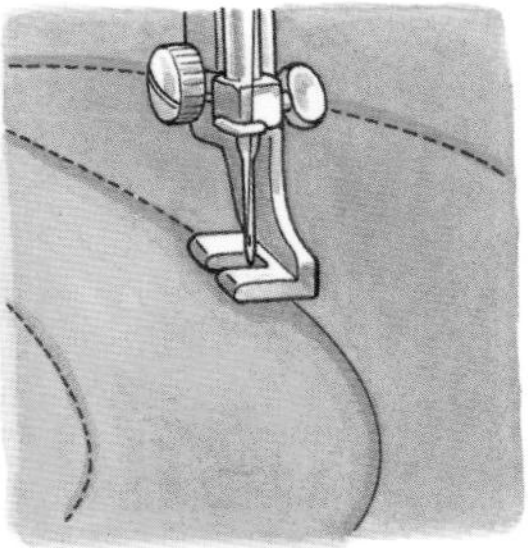

QUILTING IN THE DITCH

This technique is used in projects where you want pieced patchwork fabrics to be more prominent than the quilting. The quilting stitches are sewn in the ditch or valley of the seam, where two pieces of patchwork have been joined together. Use an unobtrusive thread that will blend with the fabrics.

CONTOUR- AND ECHO QUILTING

Contour-quilting can be used to emphasize areas on printed panels, printed fabrics, pieced patchwork and appliqué. Quilting stitches are sewn just to the side of the seam (or around the relevant line of the printed design).

Echo quilting is used to add definition to previous quilting and to highlight a pattern further. You can use a single echo line or several, depending on the pattern and how much of the background area you wish to fill.

INFILL QUILTING

Infill quilting is used to add interest to an area surrounding a design that has already been quilted, and to quilt areas of background that are too large to leave unquilted. This can consist of one pattern or a combination of patterns, geometric or curvilinear, which are often designed on a grid. An infill pattern should complement the main quilted design and not detract from it.

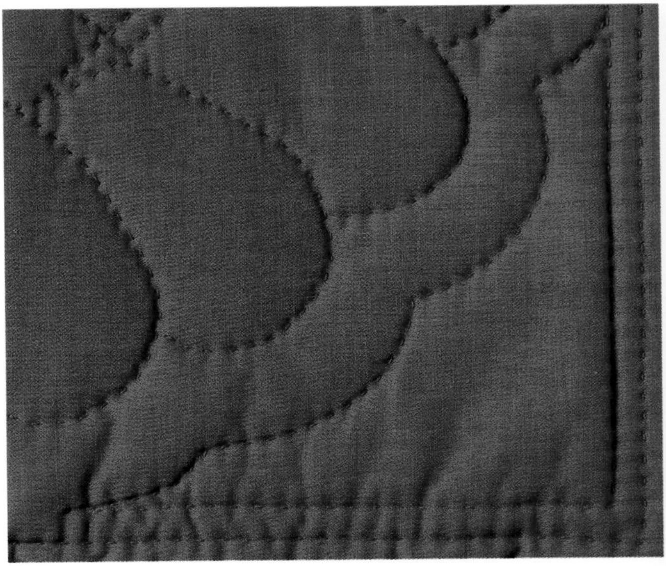

RANDOM QUILTING

Random designs are usually continuous and can be used to complement patchwork and appliqué, or to fill large areas such as backgrounds and borders. Although the work is not meant to follow a set design, specific patterns can be achieved, such as stipple or vermicelli patterns, geometric grids, curved lines, motifs and even lettering. All are usually sewn without premarked designs to guide the quilter. If you are unsure about this, you may prefer to draw a design to follow.

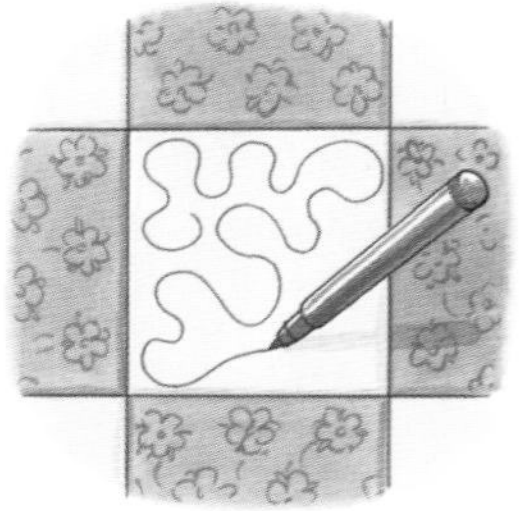

DESIGNS

Designs may be premarked or stitched completely randomly.

HAND-STITCHED RANDOM QUILTING

Using a running stitch, take several stitches onto the needle at one time if the design allows. If your quilting pattern begins to look uniform, turn your work and head off in another direction to achieve a "random" appearance throughout the design.

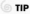

RANDOM QUILTING BY MACHINE

Fit a quilting foot to your machine and reduce the stitch length and width to "nil." Bring both threads to the surface of the work before you begin—you may also need to adjust your machine tension. Lower or cover the feed dogs. Your hands will be guiding and moving the fabric instead, and you'll be "drawing" with the needle.

TIP

When random quilting by machine, try using a faster stitch speed (using the foot pedal) together with a slower movement of the fabric (with your hands.)

TEXTURE AND PERSPECTIVE

Metallic and colored threads intermingle in this randomly quilted design. The design is stitched into sheer organza and layered over scraps of fabrics in differing greens to produce an illusion of perspective and landscape.

The Stitch Collection

The stitches in the following collection have been chosen for their suitability for quilting, as well as for their added textural interest.

The diagrams are crucial to the position at which you need to sew these stitches. For instance, if the step-by-step sequence shows a stitch being worked horizontally, that is because it is the easiest way to work that particular stitch. If you are tempted to turn your work and sew the stitch in another direction (for comfort, ease or preference), do turn the diagram so that it matches the way you are working and prevents confusion.

Stitch Selector

STITCHES FOR HAND QUILTING PAGE 66

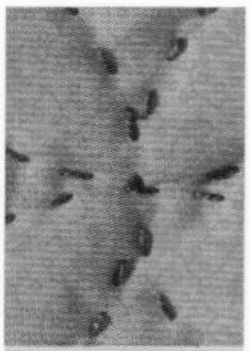
PAGE 67

On the next few pages you'll find all of the quilting stitches included in the book. Use this selector to choose the stitch you want, then turn to the correct page for step-by-step instructions.

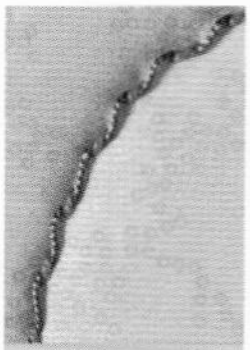
PAGE 68

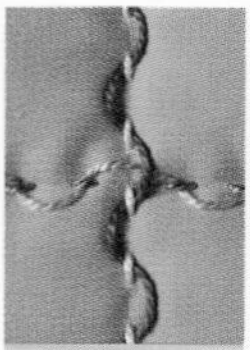
PAGE 69

PAGE 70

PAGE 71

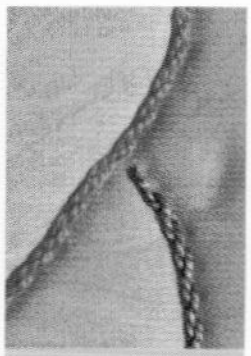
PAGE 72

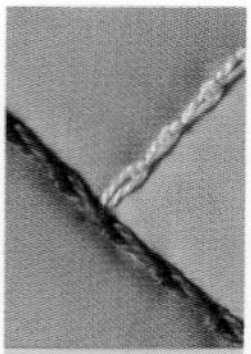
PAGE 73

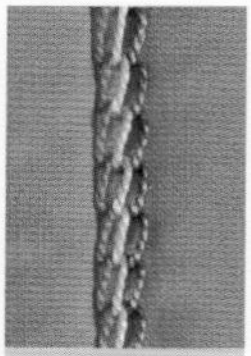
PAGE 74

PAGE 75

PAGE 76

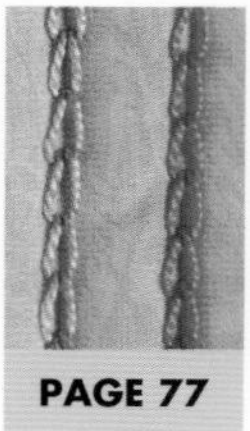
PAGE 77

PAGE 78

PAGE 79

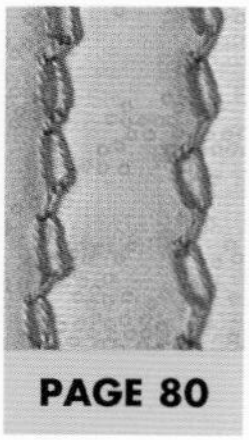
PAGE 80

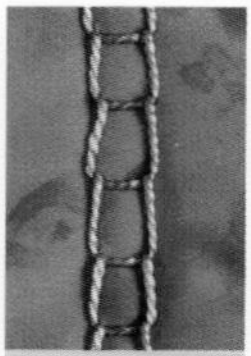
PAGE 81

PAGE 82

PAGE 83

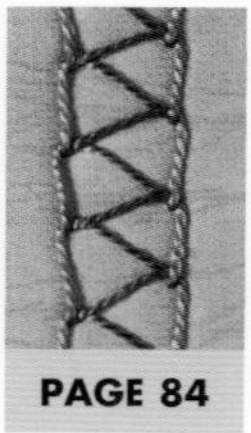
PAGE 84

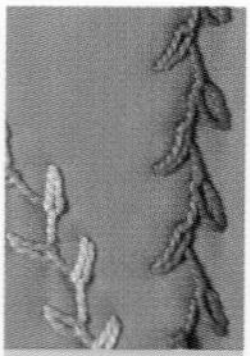
PAGE 85

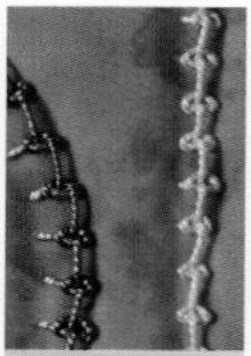
PAGE 86

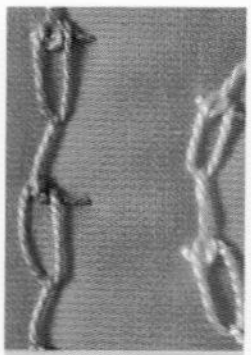
PAGE 87

PAGE 88

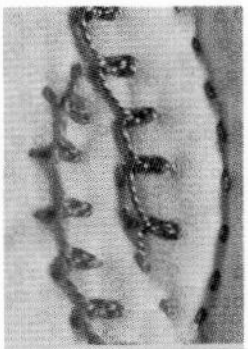
PAGE 89

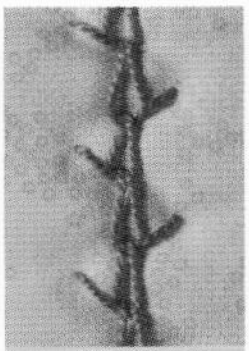
PAGE 90

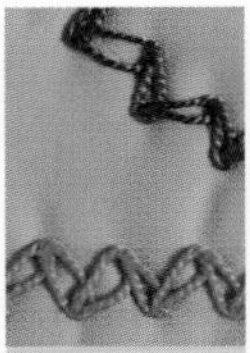
PAGE 91

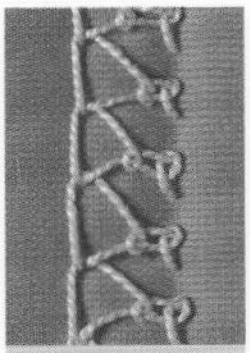
PAGE 92

PAGE 93

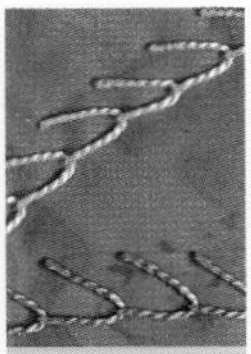
PAGE 94

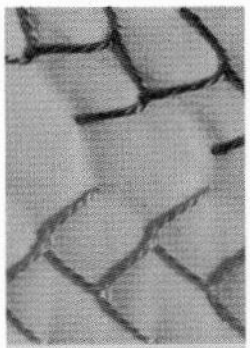
PAGE 95

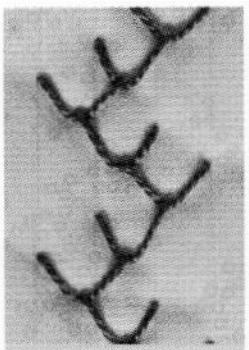
PAGE 96

PAGE 97

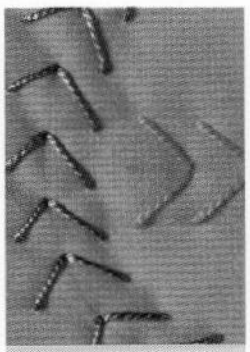
PAGE 98

PAGE 99

PAGE 100

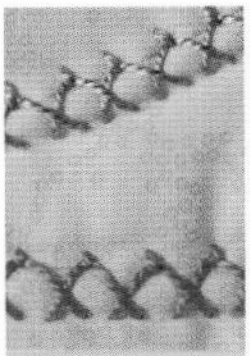
PAGE 101

PAGE 102

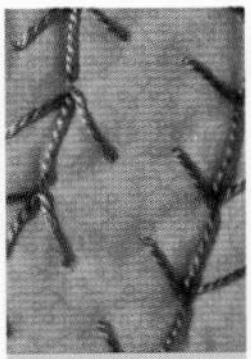
PAGE 103

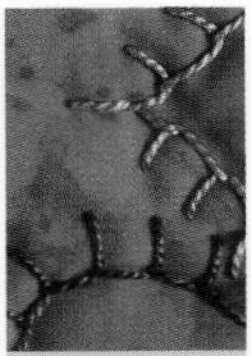
PAGE 104

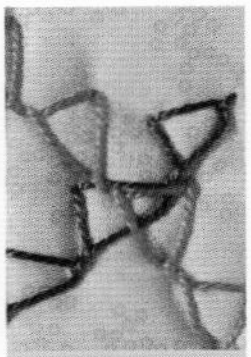
PAGE 105

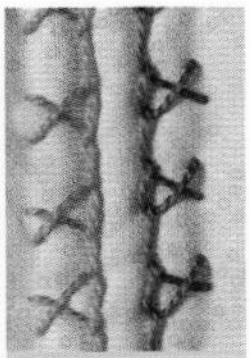
PAGE 106

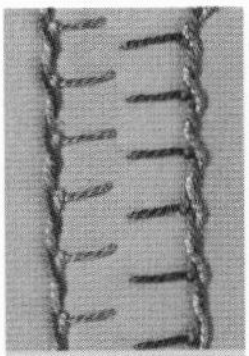
PAGE 107

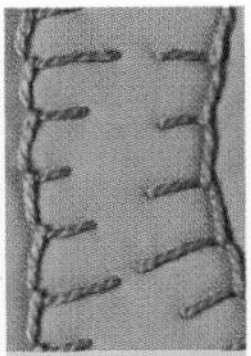
PAGE 108

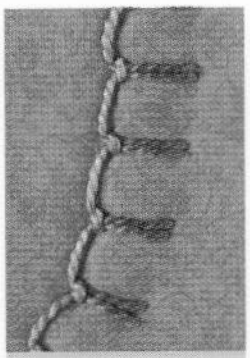
PAGE 109

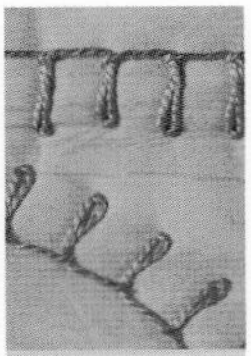
PAGE 110

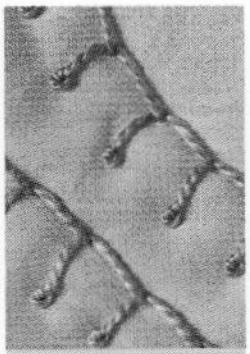
PAGE 111

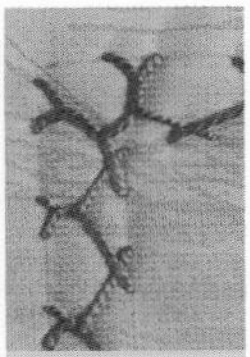
PAGE 112

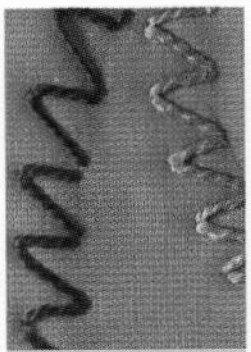
PAGE 113

PAGE 114

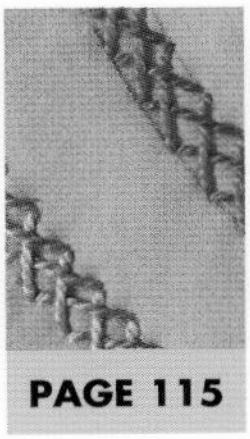
PAGE 115

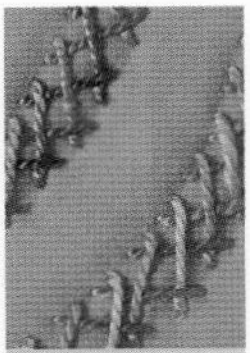
PAGE 116

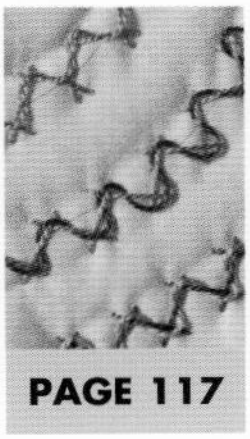
PAGE 117

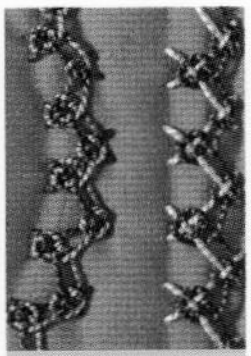
PAGE 118

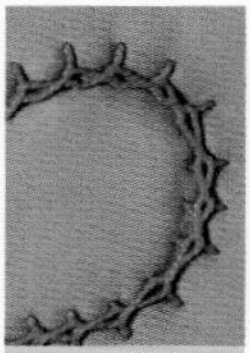
PAGE 119

PAGE 120

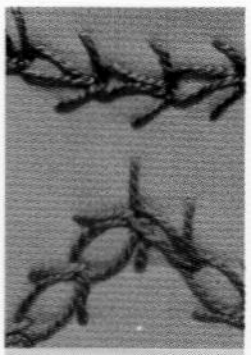
PAGE 121

PAGE 122

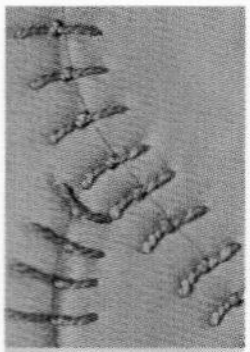
PAGE 123

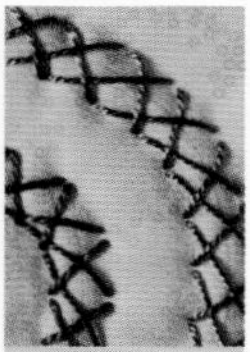
PAGE 124

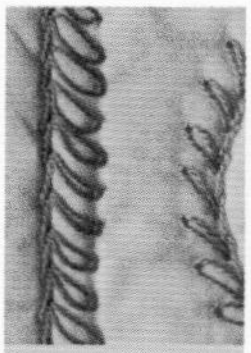
PAGE 125

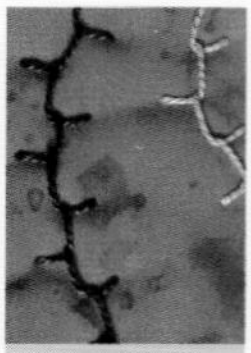
PAGE 126

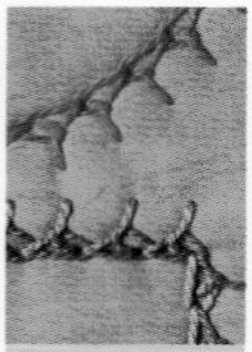
PAGE 127

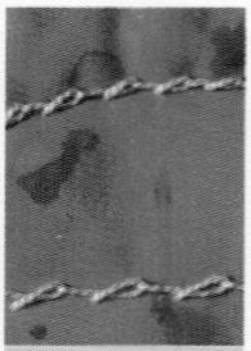
PAGE 128

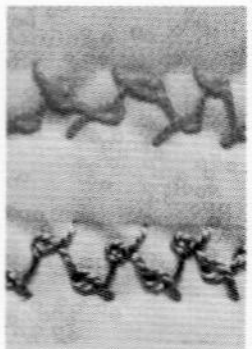
PAGE 129

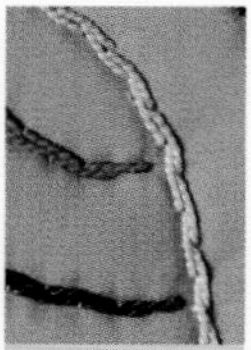
PAGE 130

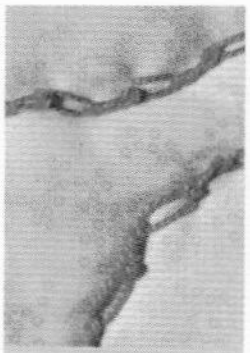
PAGE 131

PAGE 132

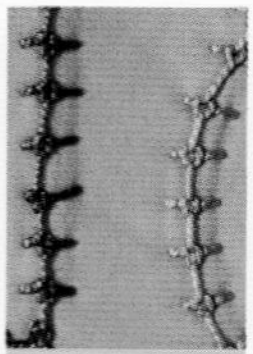
PAGE 133

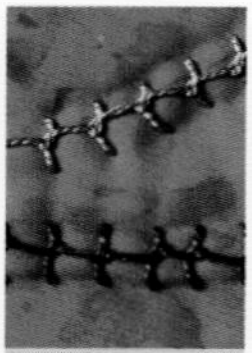
PAGE 134

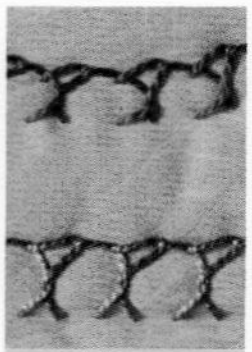
PAGE 135

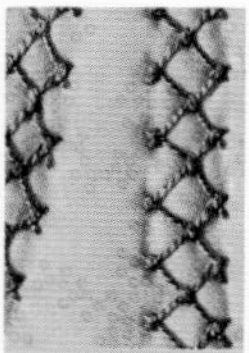
PAGE 136

HAND-QUILTING FILLING STITCHES PAGE 137

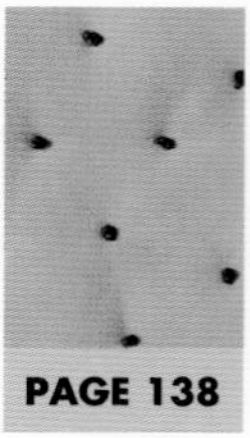
PAGE 138

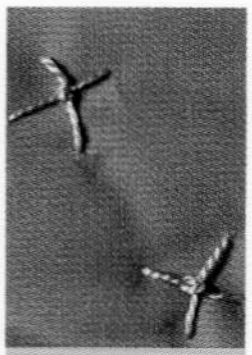
PAGE 139

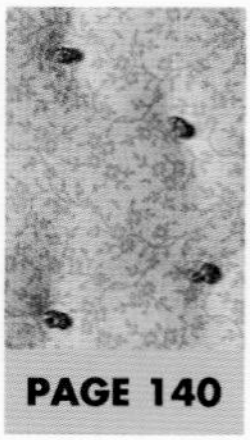
PAGE 140

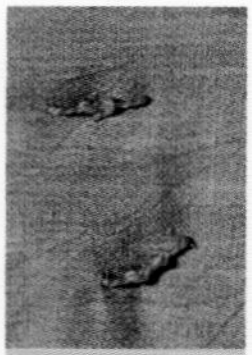
PAGE 141

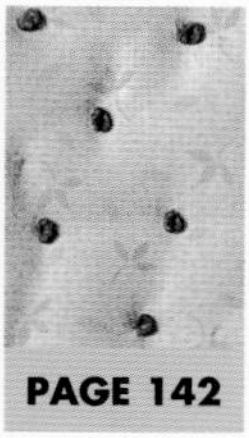
PAGE 142

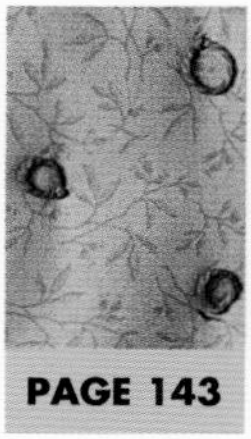
PAGE 143

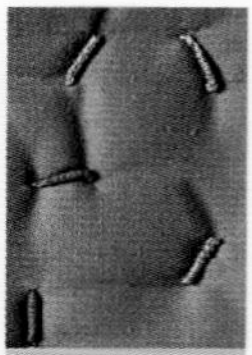
PAGE 144

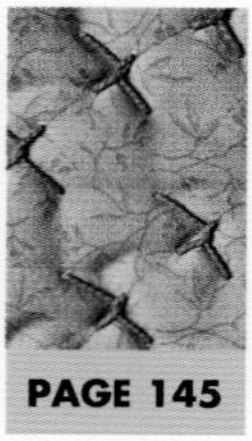
PAGE 145

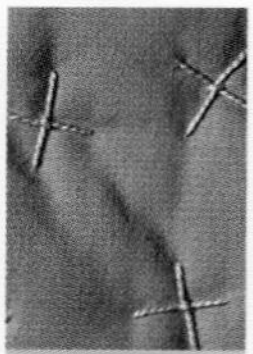
PAGE 146

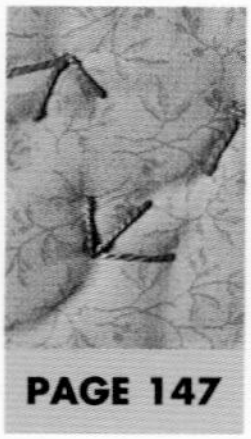
PAGE 147

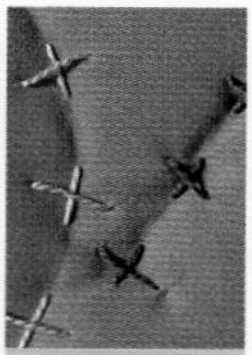
PAGE 148

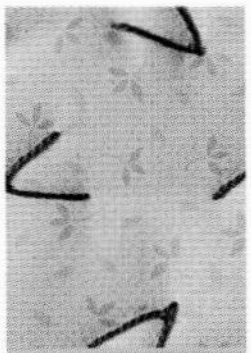
PAGE 149

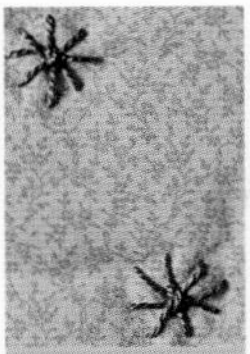
PAGE 150

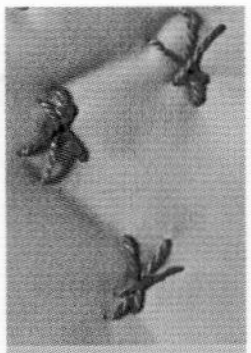
PAGE 151

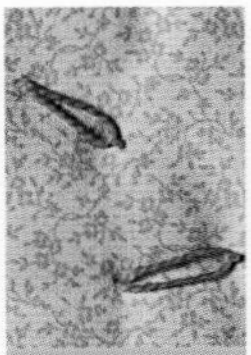
PAGE 152

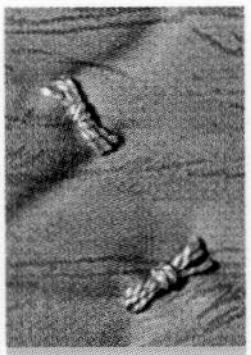
PAGE 153

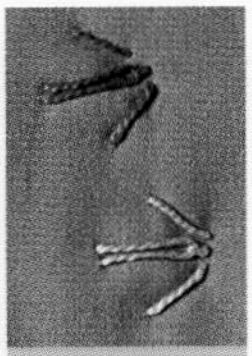
PAGE 154

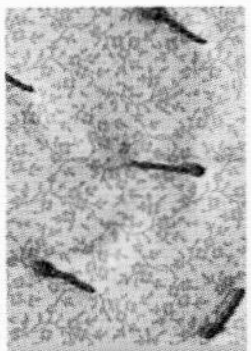
PAGE 155

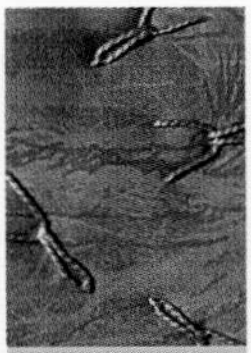
PAGE 156

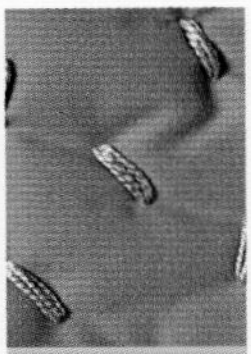
PAGE 157

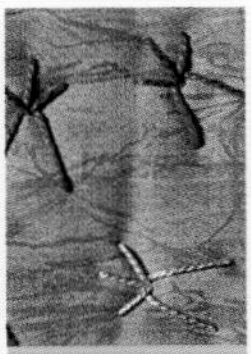
PAGE 158

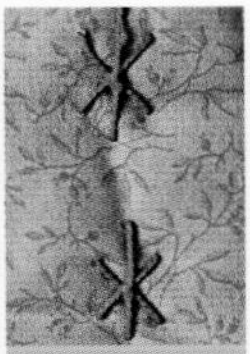
PAGE 159

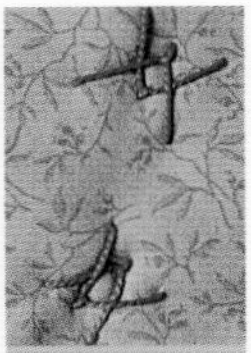
PAGE 160

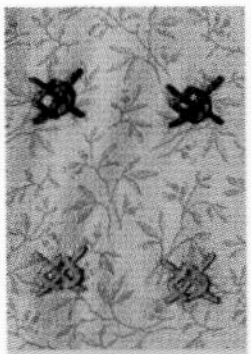
PAGE 161

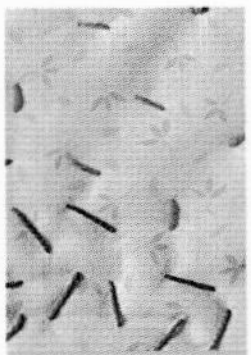
PAGE 162

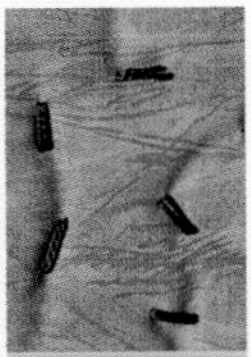
PAGE 163

HAND-SEWN SURFACE EMBELLISHMENT PAGE 164

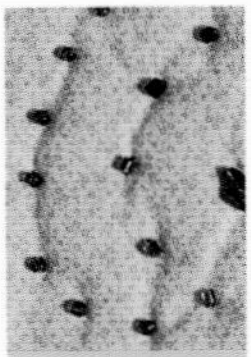
PAGE 165

PAGE 167

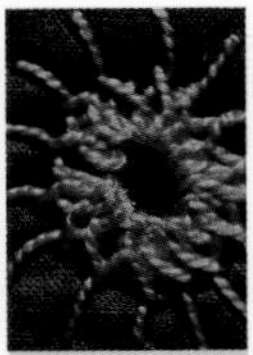
PAGE 168

PAGE 171

HAND-SEWN INSERTION STITCHES PAGE 179

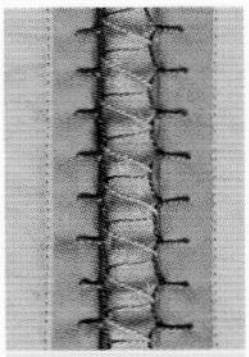
PAGE 180

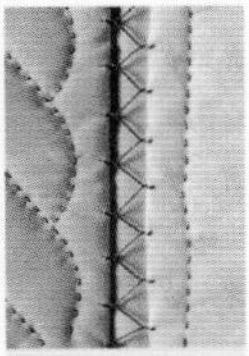
PAGE 181

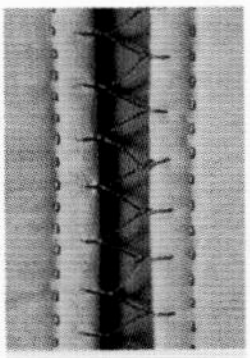
PAGE 182

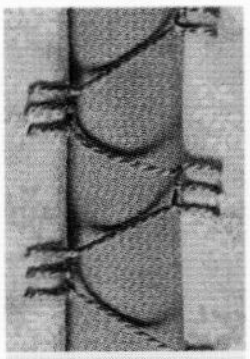
PAGE 183

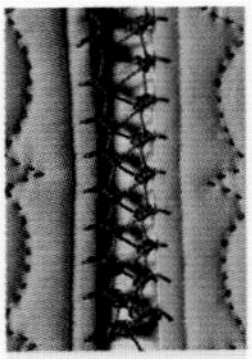
PAGE 184

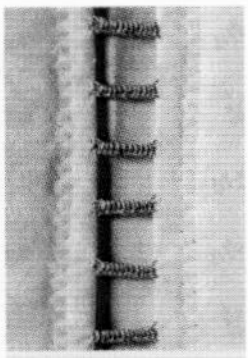
PAGE 185

STITCHES FOR MACHINE QUILTING PAGE 186

PAGE 187

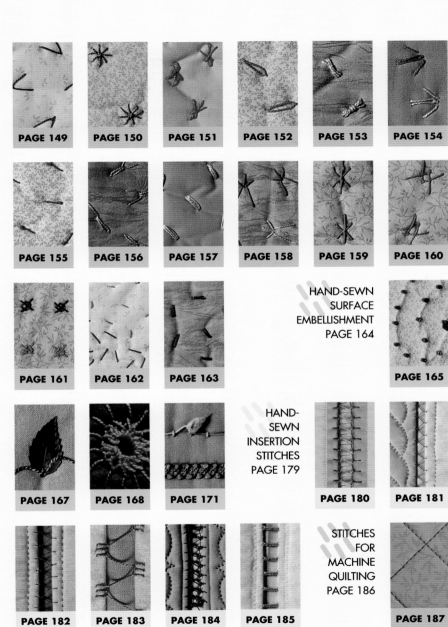

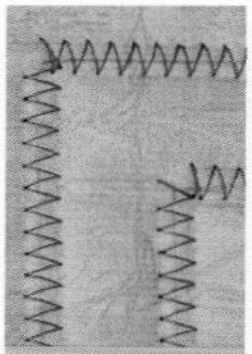
PAGE 188

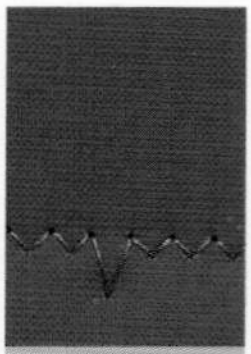
PAGE 189

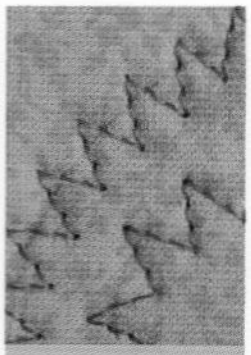
PAGE 190

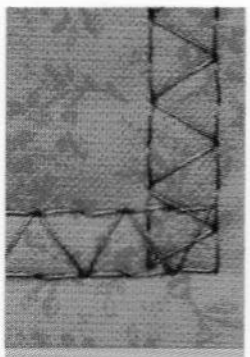
PAGE 191

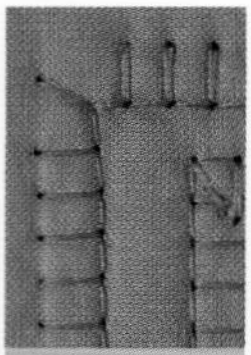
PAGE 192

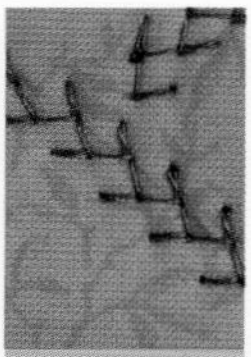
PAGE 193

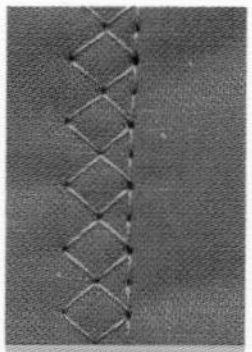
PAGE 194

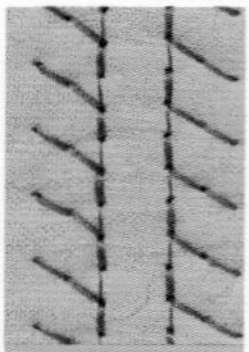
PAGE 195

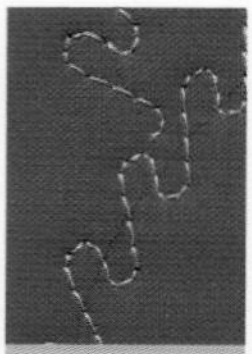
PAGE 196

PAGE 197

PAGE 198

PAGE 199

PAGE 200

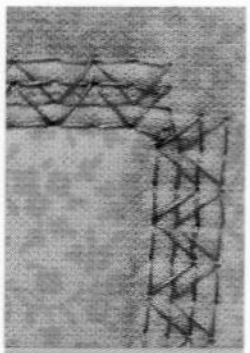
PAGE 201

MACHINE-SEWN SURFACE EMBELLISHMENT
PAGE 202

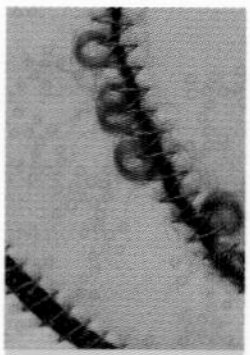
PAGE 203

PAGE 204

PAGE 205

MACHINE-SEWN CONSTRUCTION AND INSERTION STITCHES
PAGE 206

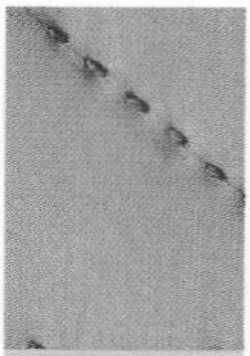
PAGE 207

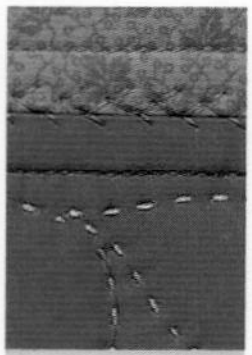
PAGE 208

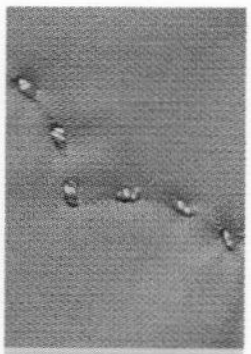
PAGE 209

QUILTING YOUR PATCHWORK
PAGE 210

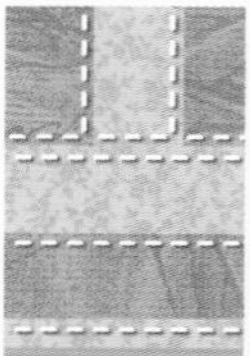
PAGE 211

PAGE 212

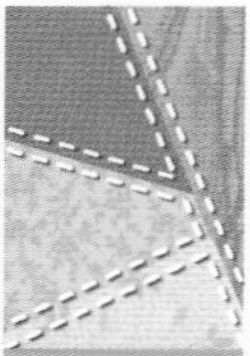
PAGE 213

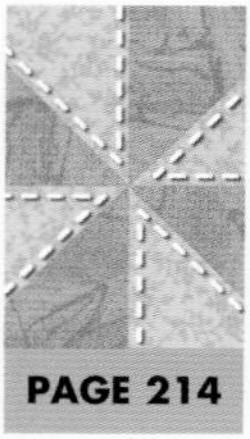
PAGE 214

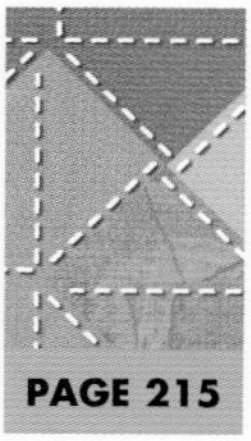
PAGE 215

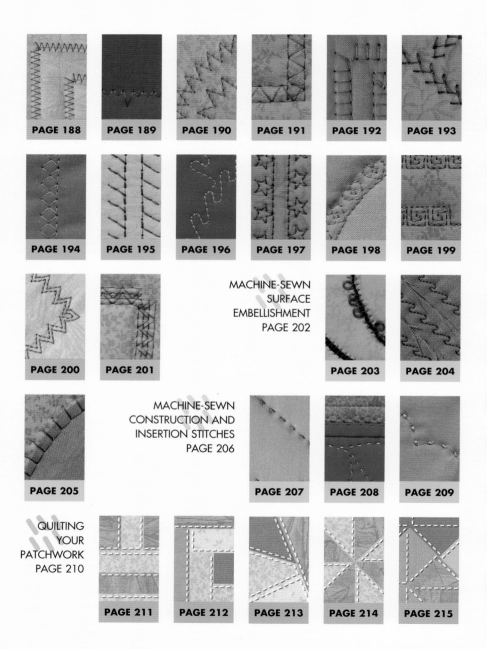

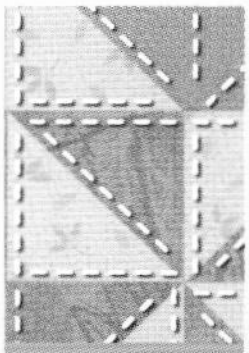
PAGE 216

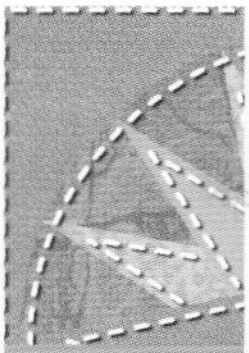
PAGE 217

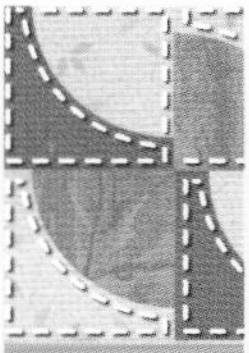
PAGE 218

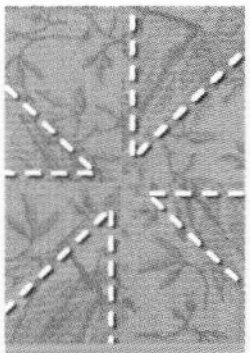
PAGE 219

PAGE 220

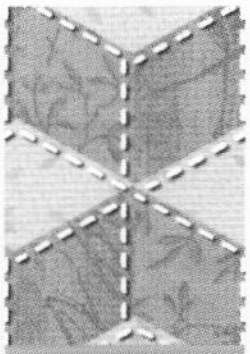
PAGE 221

PAGE 222

PAGE 223

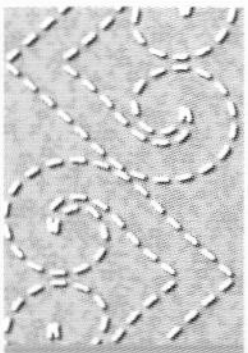
PAGE 224

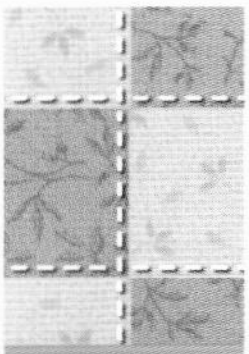
PAGE 225

QUILTING YOUR APPLIQUÉ
PAGE 226

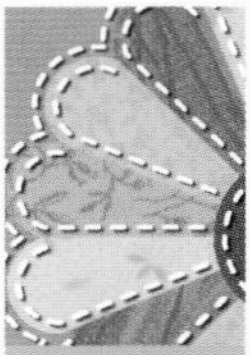
PAGE 227

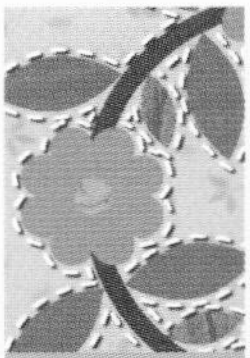
PAGE 228

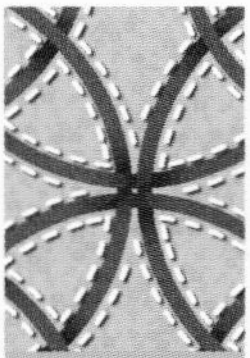
PAGE 229

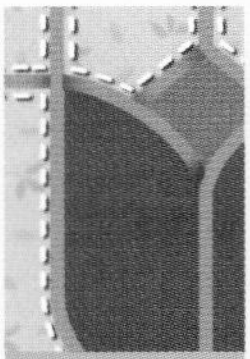
PAGE 230

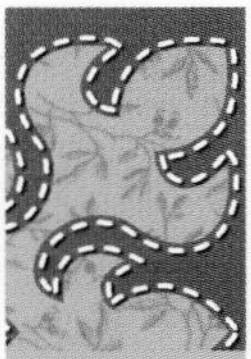
PAGE 231

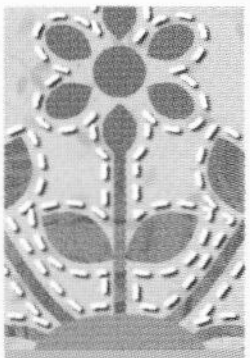
PAGE 232

PAGE 233

QUILT EDGE FINISHINGS
PAGE 234

PAGE 235

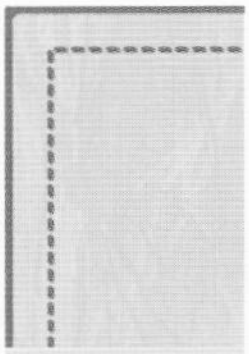
PAGE 236

PAGE 237

PAGE 238

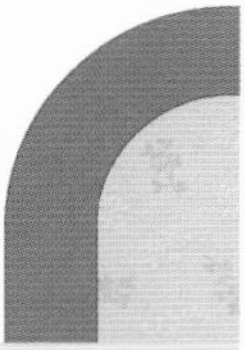
PAGE 239

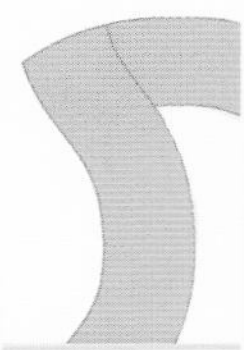
PAGE 240

PAGE 241

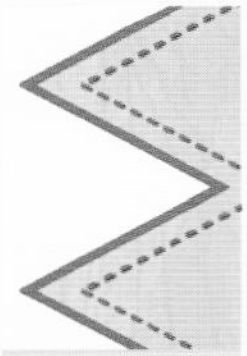
PAGE 242

PAGE 243

PAGE 244

PAGE 245

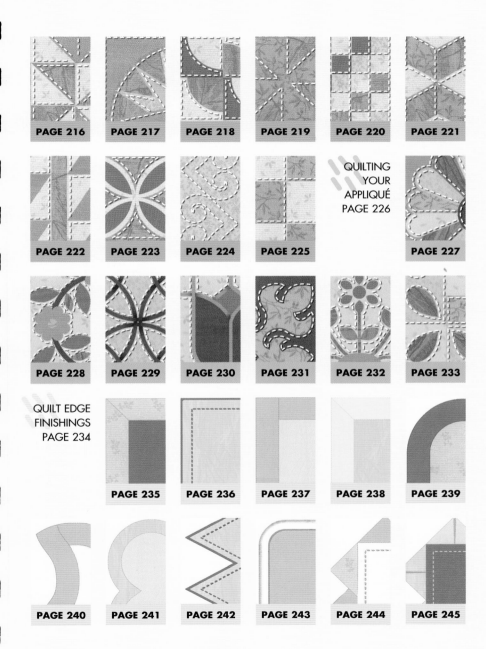

Stitches for Hand Quilting

All quilters will be familiar with the traditional quilting stitch based on a running stitch. You can use the more interesting stitches shown here to add textural interest to your work.

All of these “alternative” quilting stitches can be sewn along a single quilting mark without the need to draw parallel tramlines. Any loops created by “threading” and “whipping” yarns can be left looser on decorative projects, or pulled tighter if used for a bed quilt.

If you sew with your left-hand, many of the stitch diagrams will need to be worked in mirror-image.

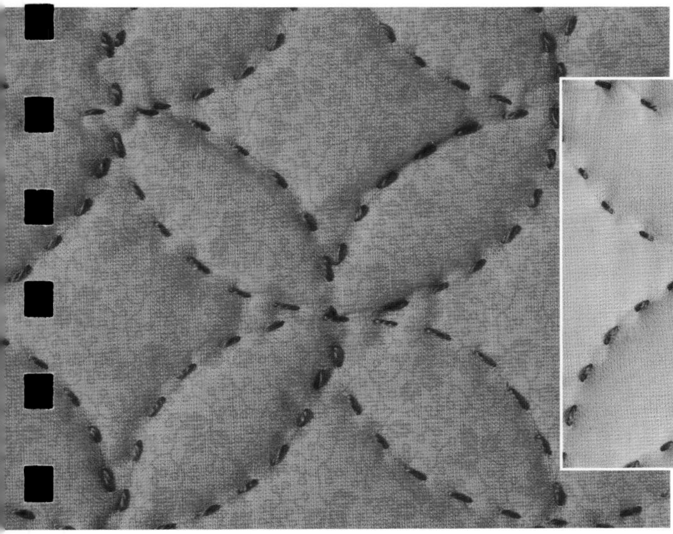

REVERSE OF WORK

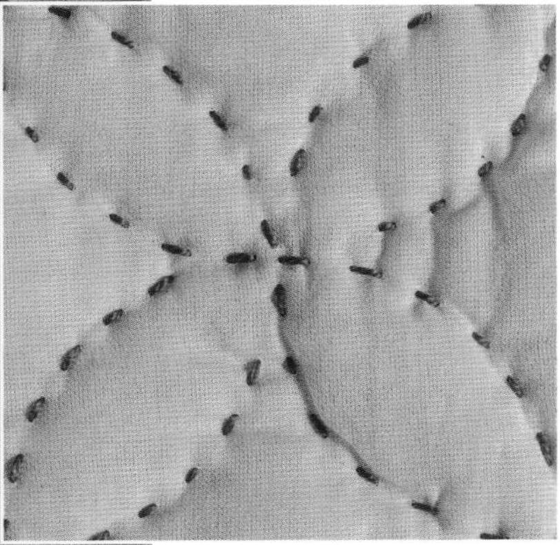

Running stitch

Use this versatile stitch for hand-quilting traditional designs and contour-quilting (outlining) motif patterns. Space stitches regularly, whether on straight or curved lines.

STEP 1

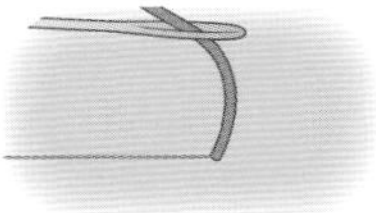

Begin by bringing the needle to the surface of the work.

STEP 2

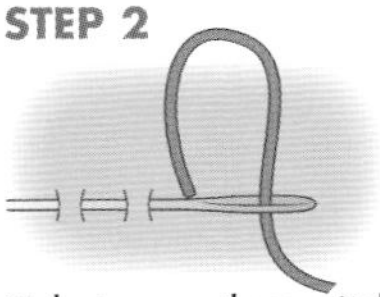

Take two or three stitches forward along the line, ensuring that the needle passes through all three layers of fabric with each stitch.

STEP 3

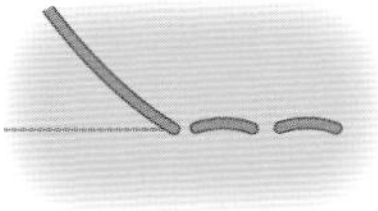

Pull the thread through until it lies on top of the fabric, without being too loose or too tight.

TIPS

- Hold the needle almost perpendicular to the fabric to help you to take up all three layers.
- Take several stitches on the needle at one time to help produce even stitching (more difficult to do on a tight curve).

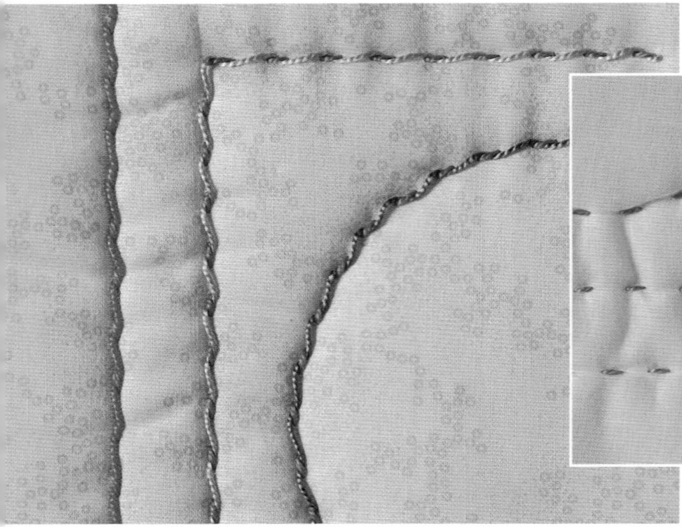

REVERSE OF WORK

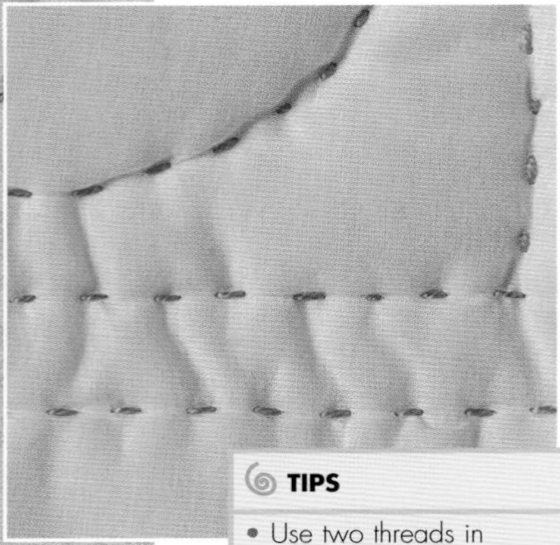

Whipped running

This stitch has a slightly raised appearance and can be effective when a little definition is needed for quilting and/or outlining motif patterns.

TIPS

- Use two threads in different colors for an interesting effect.
- Work the basic running stitches slightly longer than normal to make it easier to pass the whipping thread underneath them.
- Use the eye of the needle for whipping, or change to a blunt tapestry needle.

STEP 1

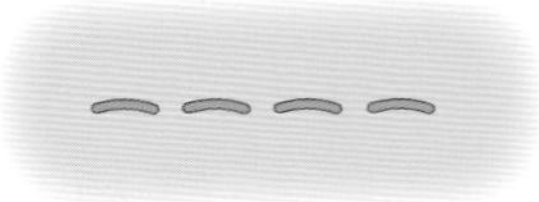

Bring the needle to the surface of the work and sew a line of running stitch.

STEP 2

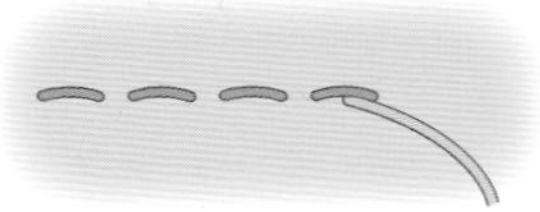

Bring the whipping thread to the surface of the work, just below the center of the first running stitch.

STEP 3

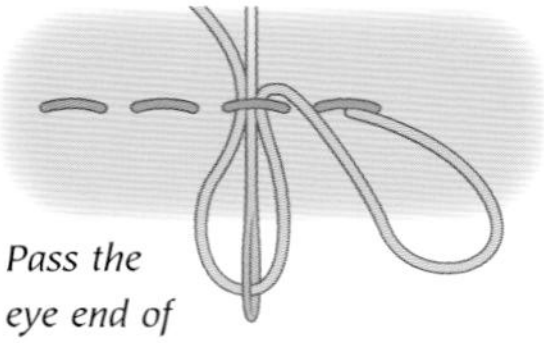

Pass the eye end of the needle behind each individual running stitch in turn, working in the same direction each time.

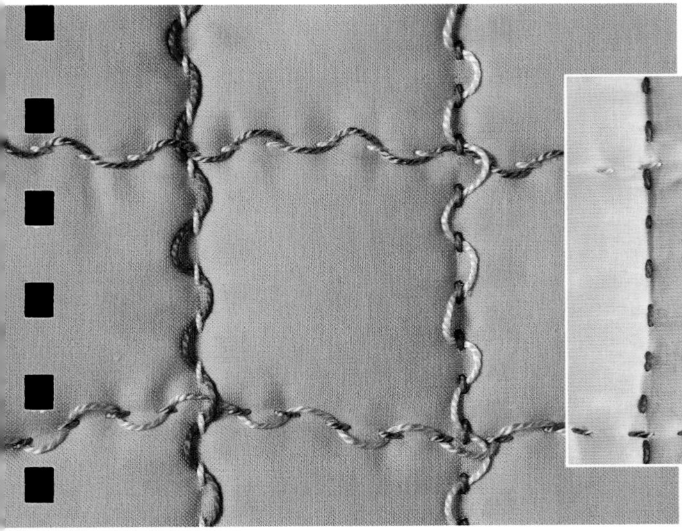

REVERSE OF WORK

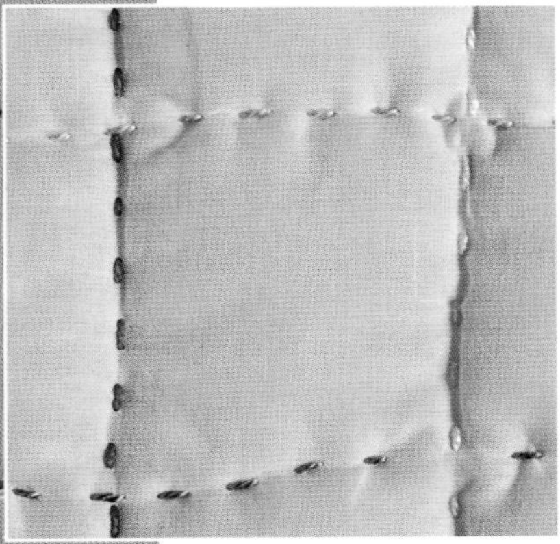

Threaded running

A second thread snakes in and out of the running stitches, forming small loops: Keep these tight if you are quilting a bed quilt, as they might snag and pull.

TIP

Use two threads in different colors for an interesting effect.

STEP 1

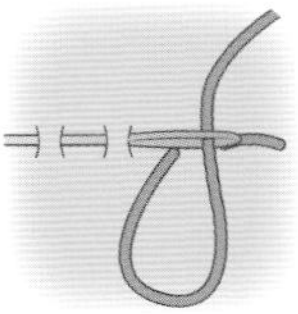

Bring the needle to the surface of the work and sew a line of running stitch.

STEP 2

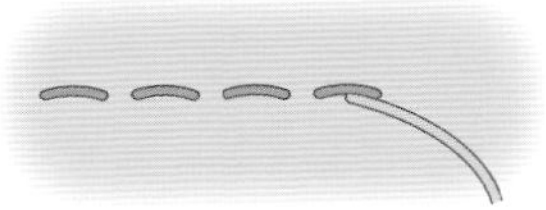

Bring the second thread to the surface of the work, close to the front of (or below the center of) the first running stitch.

STEP 3

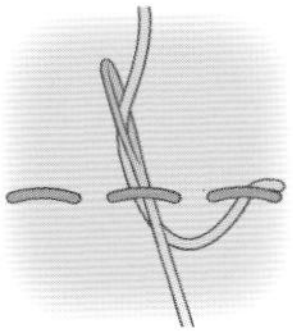

Pass the eye end of the needle down behind the first running stitch and then up behind the second running stitch.

STEP 4

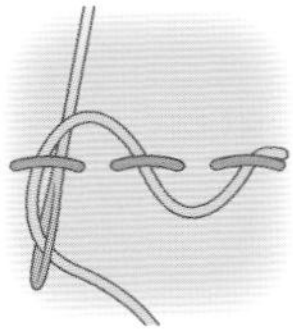

Continue in this way along the row, alternating the direction of the needle with each stitch in turn.

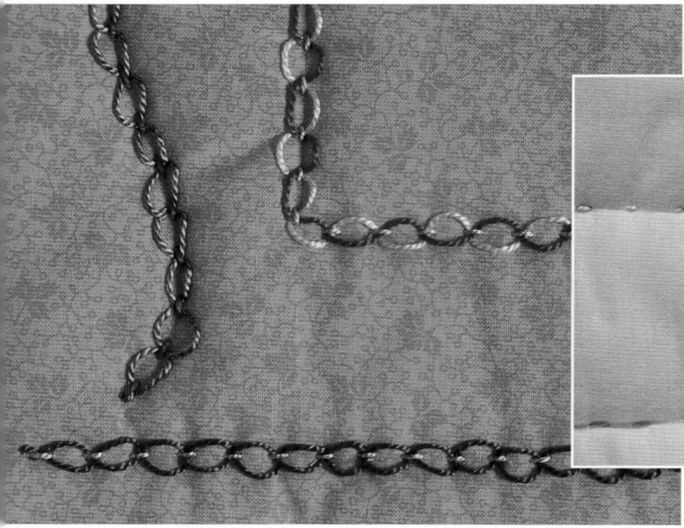

REVERSE OF WORK

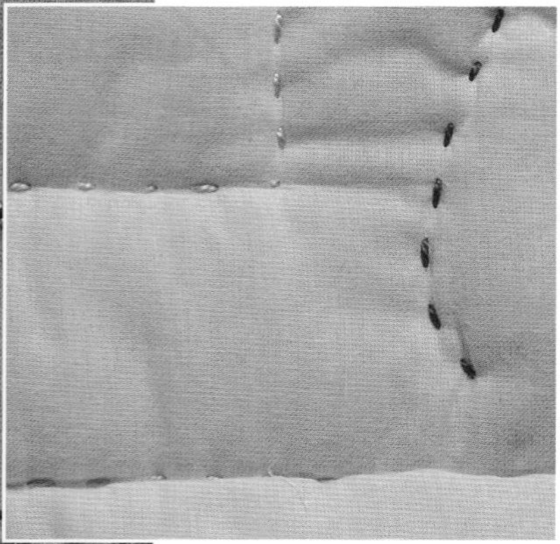

Double threaded running

This is very decorative in multiple colors. Support the previous stitches and loops with your other hand as you work. For a more dramatic effect, leave the loops slightly loose.

STEP 1

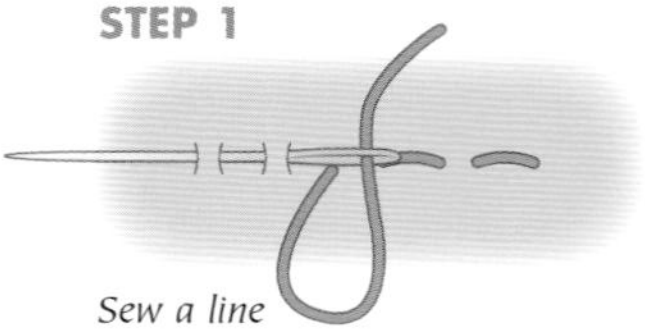

Sew a line of running stitch.

STEP 2

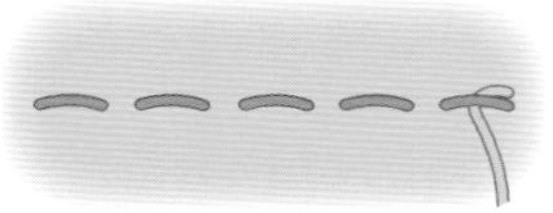

Bring the second thread to the surface of the work at the beginning of the first stitch (or underneath at the center point).

STEP 3

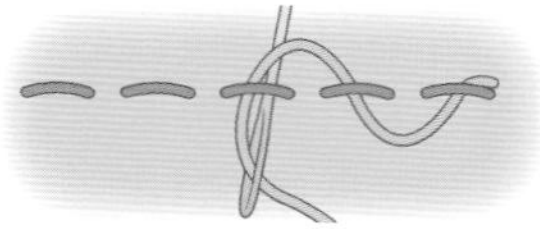

Pass the needle down behind the first stitch and up behind the second stitch; continue to the end of the row of stitches.

STEP 4

Bring the third thread up at the beginning of the work and weave behind each running stitch in the opposite direction.

REVERSE OF WORK

Backstitch

A good outlining and contouring stitch, which resembles a machined stitch. It is quite dense in appearance and so will give a solid feel and end result to your quilting.

STEP 1

Bring the thread to the surface of the work, at the beginning of the quilting line.

STEP 2

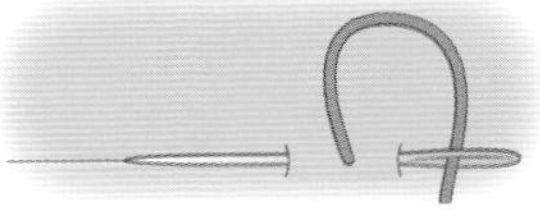

Move a stitch length backward along the line, take the needle down into the fabric and bring it back up to the surface approximately two stitch lengths further along the line.

STEP 3

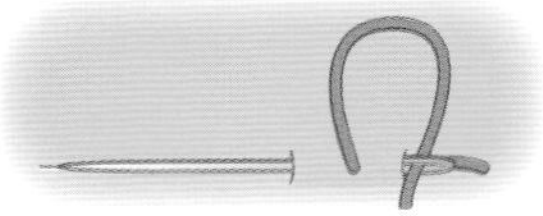

Move back along the line and take the needle down into the same hole as the previous thread; bring it up approximately two stitch lengths further along the line. Continue to the end of the line.

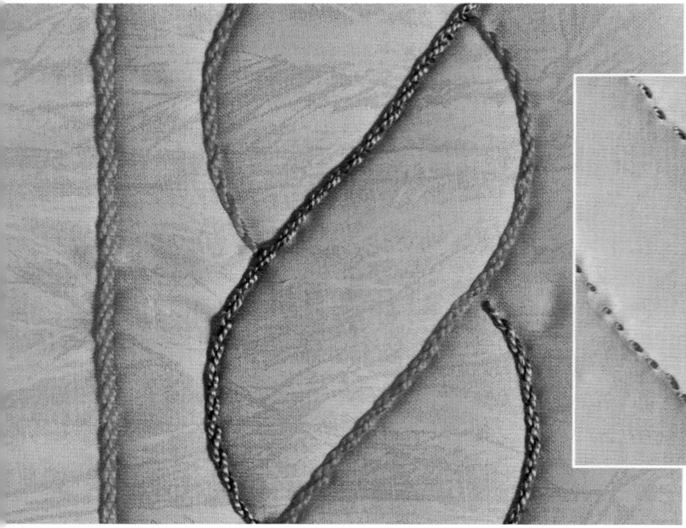

REVERSE OF WORK

Stem stitch

Stem stitch is a popular outlining stitch and one of the thicker stitches that can be successfully used for quilting.

TIP

For a broader stitch, work it at a slight diagonal (take the needle in below the line and bring it to the surface above the line).

STEP 1

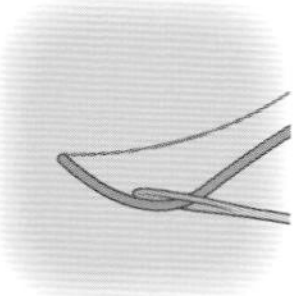

Bring the thread to the surface of the work, at the beginning of the quilting line.

STEP 2

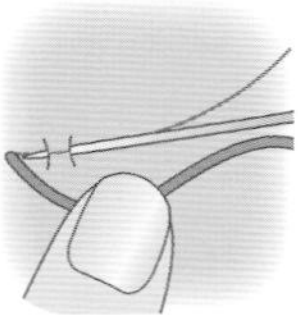

Holding the thread below the line with the thumb of your non-sewing hand, take a small stitch backward (i.e. facing toward the starting point of the line).

STEP 3

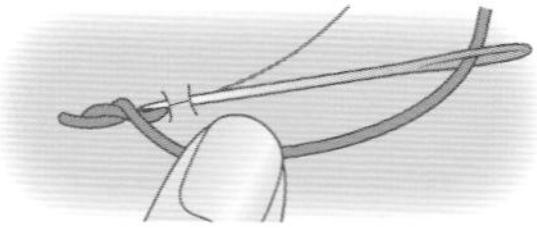

Repeat the stitch along the line, ensuring that the needle is brought up at the point at which the thread of the previous stitch entered the fabric. Don't forget to hold the thread below the line with each stitch.

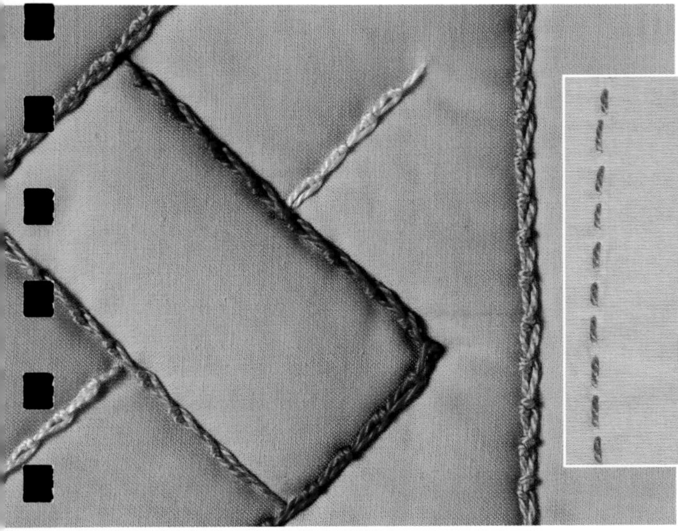

REVERSE OF WORK

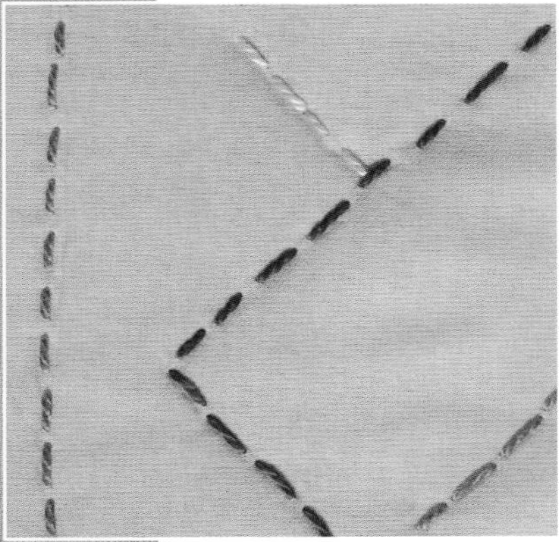

Portuguese knotted stem

This ideal outlining stitch has added textural interest. The knots are constructed from two whipping stitches on the surface of the work.

STEP 1

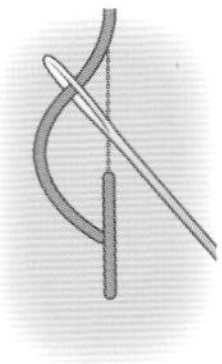

Bring the needle to the surface of the work and, working upward and away from you, take it in on the line and then back toward you, bringing it up at the halfway point and on the left of the stitch you have just made.

STEP 2

With the thread above the needle, slide the needle (or eye of the needle) from right to left under the large stitch and pull the thread through to make the first wrap.

STEP 3

With the thread above the needle again, slide the needle under the first stitch a second time, pulling the thread through and ensuring that the second wrap is beneath the first one. This forms a knot.

STEP 4

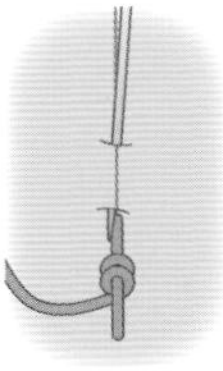

To begin the second stitch, move along the line and take the stitch back toward yourself, bringing it up halfway and to the left of the large stitch, ready to start the two-stage wrapping sequence again.

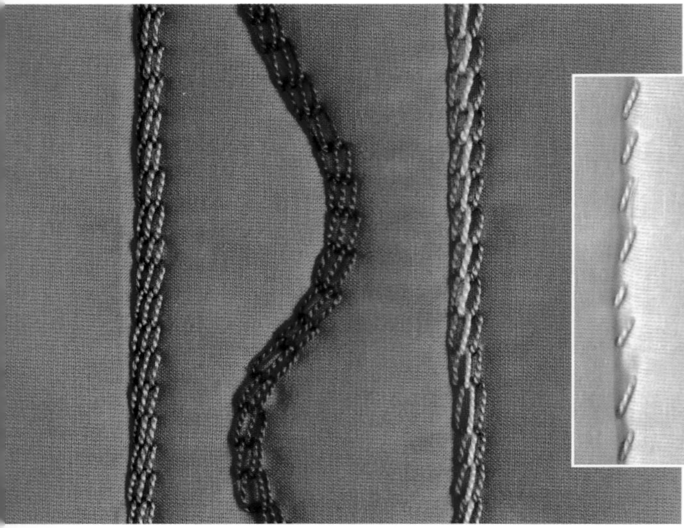

REVERSE OF WORK

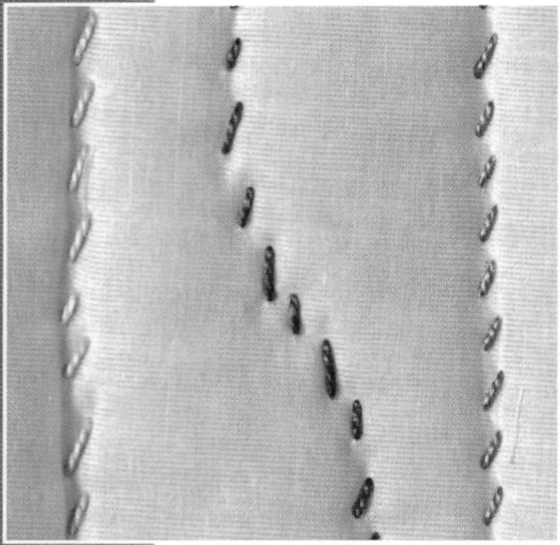

Raised stem

A ladder of base stitches is covered with stem stitch to give a raised appearance, entirely covered by working more rows.

STEP 1

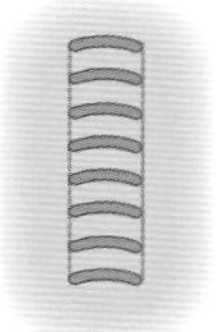

Bring the thread to the surface of the work and stitch a row of base stitches to make a ladder—work from one side of the quilting line to the other, either horizontally or vertically (whichever you find easiest).

STEP 2

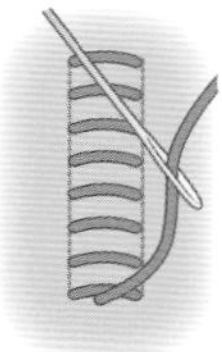

Start the stem stitch: Bring the wrapping thread to the surface of the work at the center of the first ladder stitch. The stem stitch is worked on the surface of the work only.

STEP 3

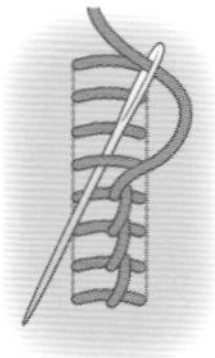

Hold the fabric so you are working "up" the ladder and take the needle down behind the first ladder. Pull the thread through and take the needle down behind the second ladder. Continue in this way.

STEP 4

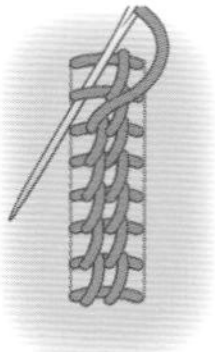

When you have reached the end of the row of base stitches, go back to the beginning and work another row of stem stitch. Continue working rows of stem stitch over the ladder of base stitches until you have achieved the desired result. Use the same color of thread or change the colors for each row.

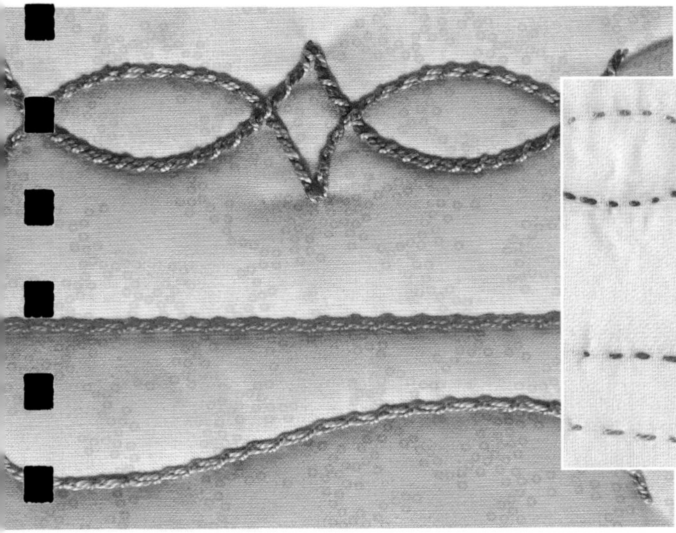

REVERSE OF WORK

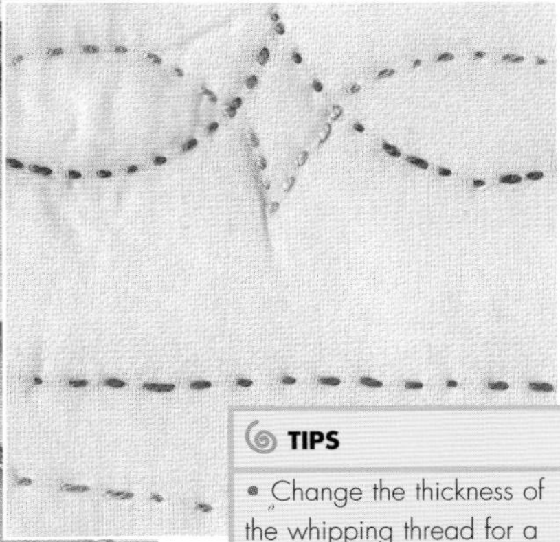

TIPS

- Change the thickness of the whipping thread for a different result.
- This stitch is useful where a heavily defined row of quilting is required.
- Pass the eye of the needle through first, or use a blunt tapestry needle, to prevent catching fibers of fabric or thread.

Whipped stem

A foundation row of stem stitch is whipped over with a second thread—this can be the same color as the first thread or a different one for a more dramatic finished result.

STEP 1

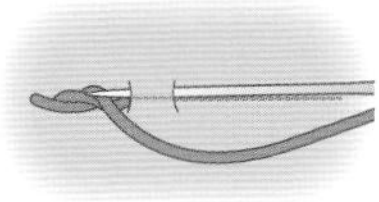

Bring the thread to the surface of the work and sew a base line of stem stitch.

STEP 2

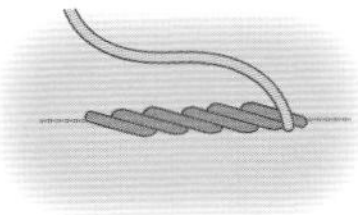

Thread the needle with the whipping thread and bring this to the surface of the work at one end of the base row of stem stitch.

STEP 3

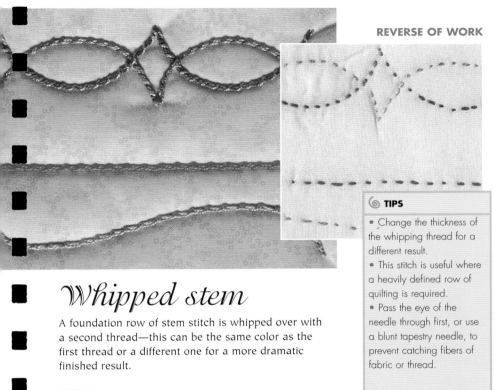

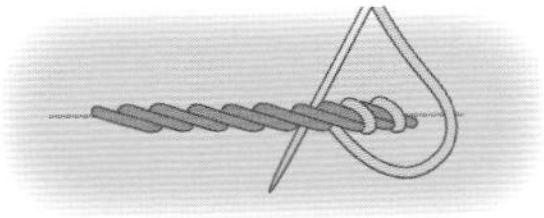

Pass the needle down behind each stem stitch in turn, working in the same direction each time and avoiding catching up any fabric. Whip each stitch individually, pulling the thread through fully after each stitch.

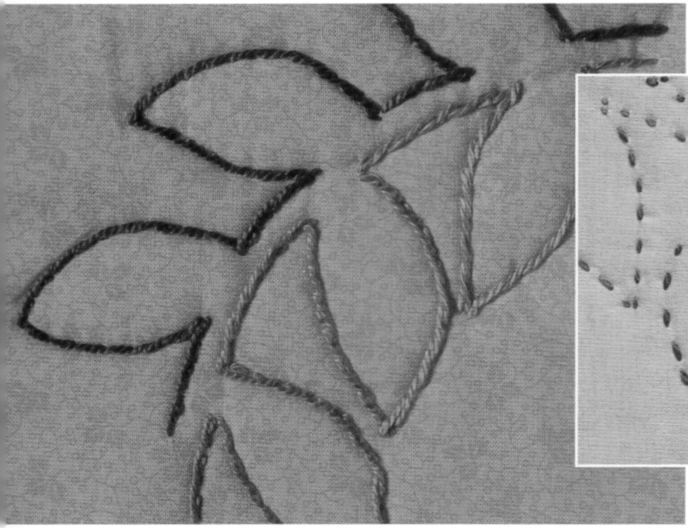

REVERSE OF WORK

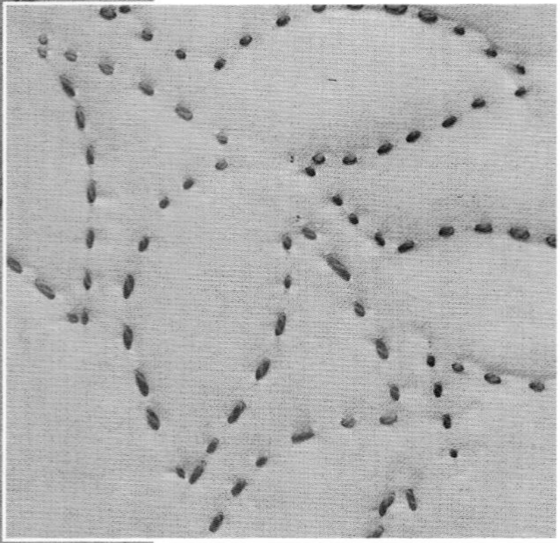

Outline stitch

Outline stitch is very versatile and useful for contour-quilting motifs as well as continuous line quilting designs, because it makes a neat twisted line.

STEP 1

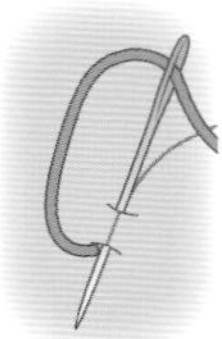

Bring the thread to the surface of the work, at the beginning of the quilting line. Holding the thread above the line, take a stitch back along the line toward your starting point.

STEP 2

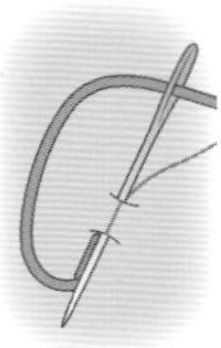

Pull the thread through and make the next stitch: Move further along the line, stitch back (ensuring that the needle comes up where the thread for the last stitch entered the fabric), and pull through.

STEP 3

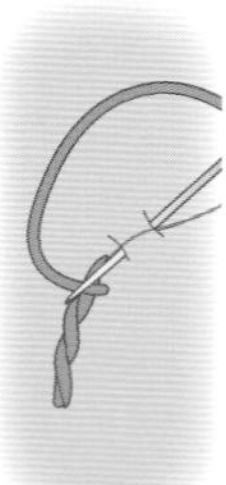

Continue in this way along the line. The stitches will twist in the opposite direction to those of stem stitch.

TIPS

- Use various thicknesses of thread for differing results.
- Always hold the thread above the needle—make use of the thumb on your non-sewing hand.

(This stitch is very similar to stem stitch, where the thread is always held below the needle.)

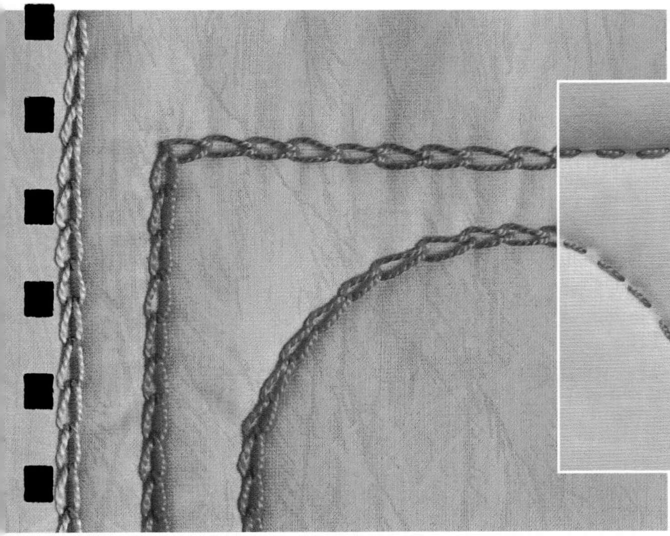

REVERSE OF WORK

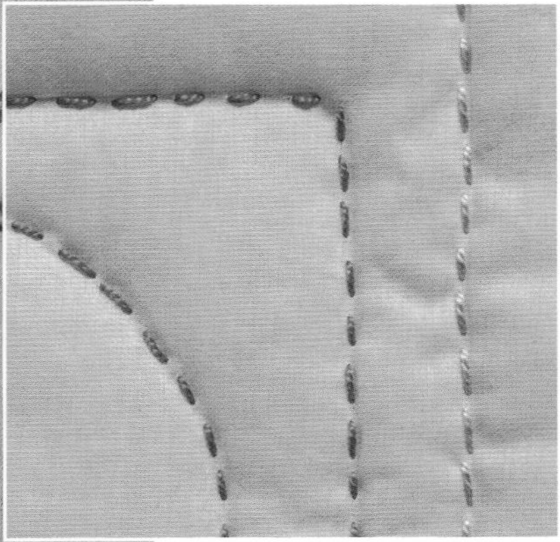

Chain stitch

This decorative stitch is equally effective worked in fine or thick thread. It is useful for continuous line designs as well as contour-quilting (outlining) motifs.

STEP 1

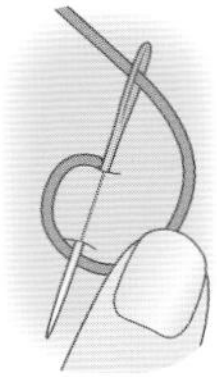

Bring the thread to the surface of the work, at the beginning of the quilting line. Using the thumb of your non-sewing hand, hold the thread forward along the line to form a loop. Take the needle back into the hole where the thread was initially brought out; at the same time, take a stitch forward along the line.

STEP 2

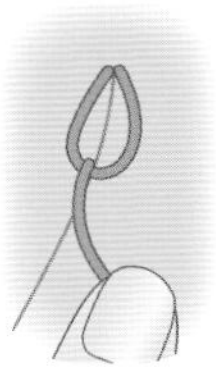

Bring the needle up inside the waiting loop of thread, pull the thread through, and hold the thread along the line to form a loop ready for the next stitch.

STEP 3

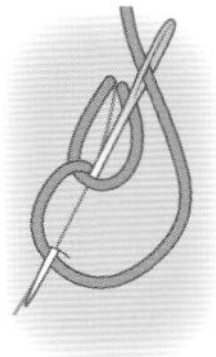

Take the needle down into the hole (or very slightly to one side of it) where the thread last came out—this will be inside the previous chain sewn.

STEP 4

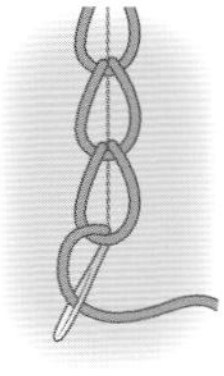

Take a stitch forward and bring the needle up into the waiting loop of thread. Continue in this way, securing the final chain with a small stitch outside the last chain that you sew.

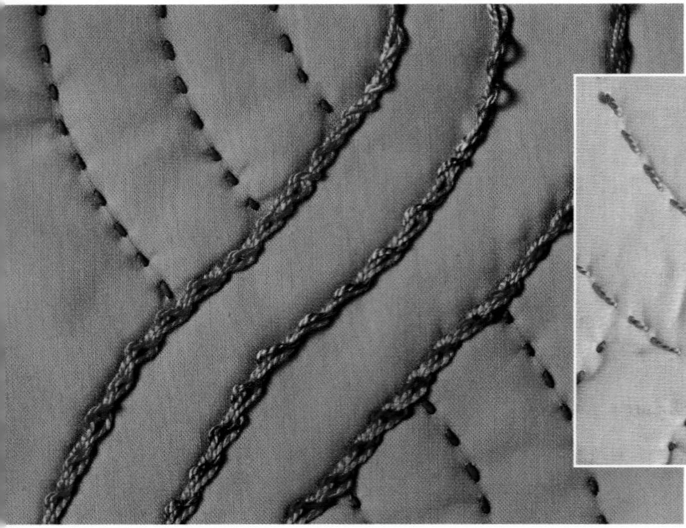

REVERSE OF WORK

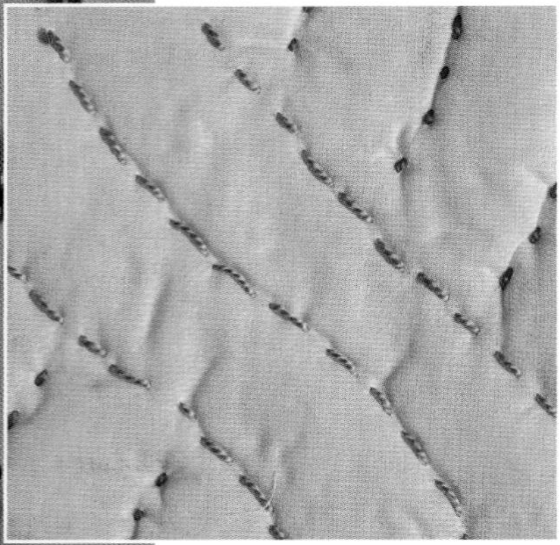

Whipped chain stitch

Whipping a row of chain stitch will change the original stitches quite dramatically. The end result will resemble a decorative braid sitting on the surface of the work.

STEP 1

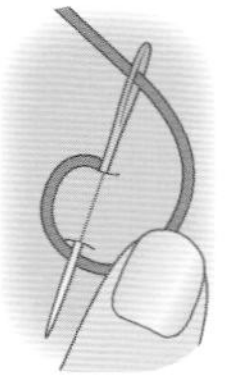

Bring the thread to the surface of the work, at the beginning of the quilting line, and sew a base line of chain stitch (see page 77).

STEP 2

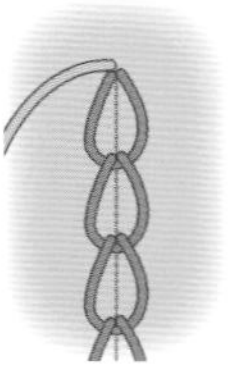

Bring the whipping thread to the surface of the work at the beginning of the first chain stitch.

STEP 3

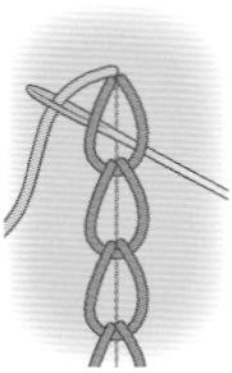

Pass the needle under each full chain stitch in turn, working in the same direction each time and being careful not to pull the whipping thread too tight.

STEP 4

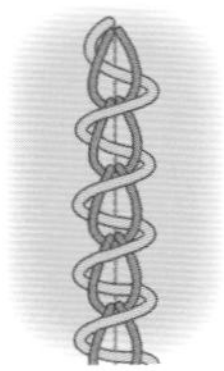

Carry on in this way along the row of chain stitch. Use a finer thread if you want the chain stitch to show through more, and a thicker thread if you want the resulting "braid" to look heavier.

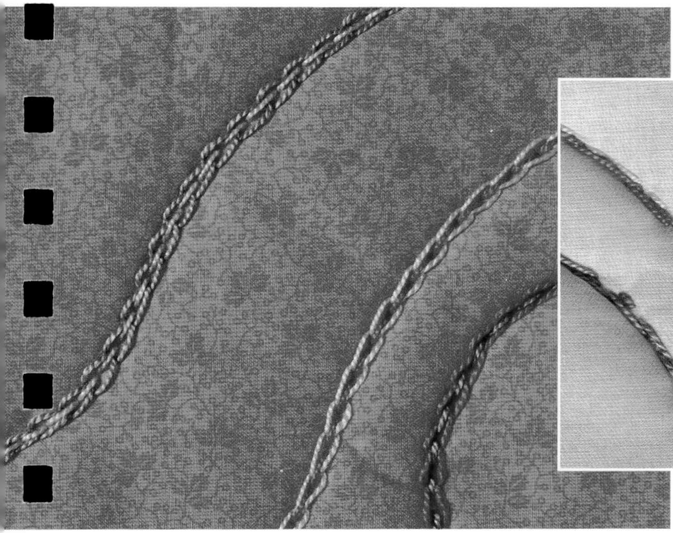

REVERSE OF WORK

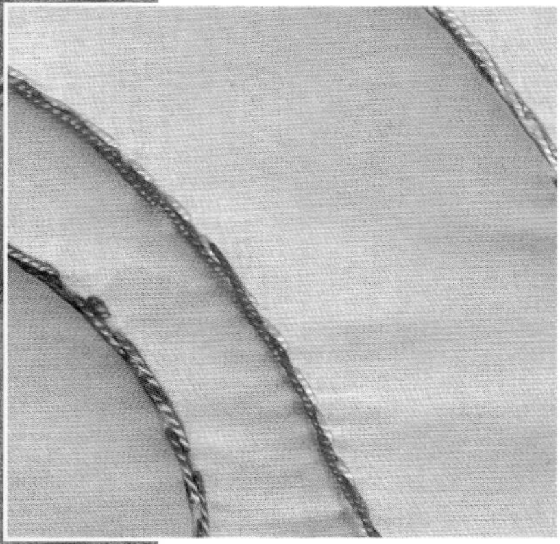

Backstitched chain

The chain links are oversewn with backstitch worked in the same color and thickness of thread, or a contrasting color and/or thickness for a more decorative effect.

STEP 1

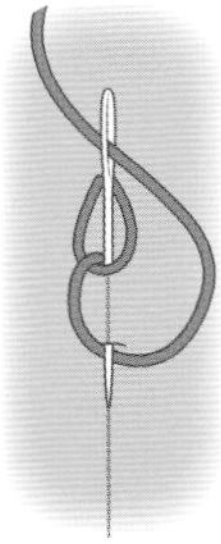

Work a foundation row of chain stitch (see page 77). Bring the thread to the surface of the work, at the beginning of the quilting line. Hold the thread forward and take a quilting stitch through all layers, forward along the line, bringing the needle up into the waiting loop of thread. Repeat along the line, taking the needle into each previous chain in turn, with each stitch.

STEP 2

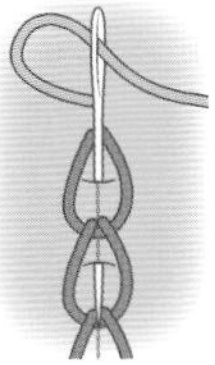

Now work the backstitch (see page 71) row. Bring the second/contrast thread to the surface of the work at the beginning of the chain stitch row. Take the needle into the first link of the chain and stitch forward, bringing the needle up in the second link.

STEP 3

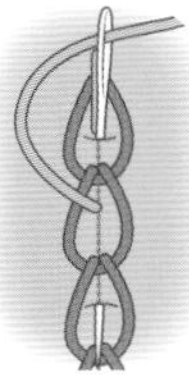

Take the needle down in the first link again, and stitch forward two links to come up inside the third link. Progress along the line in this way, securing the second/contrast thread outside one of the chain stitch links.

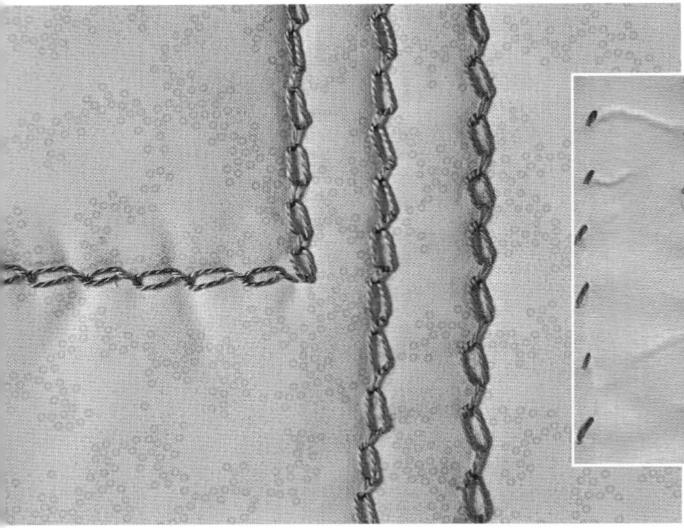

REVERSE OF WORK

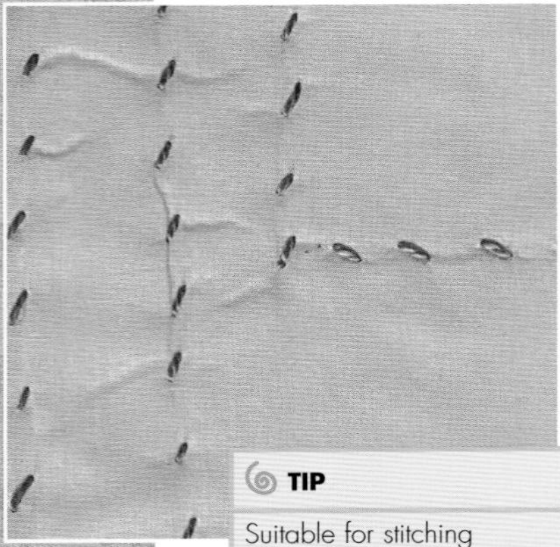

TIP

Suitable for stitching continuous line quilting designs and for outlining or contouring motif patterns.

Knotted chain

A stitch formed by making a knot between each link of a line of chain stitch, produced by twisting the thread in a certain way. This stitch has a slightly zigzag finished appearance.

STEP 1

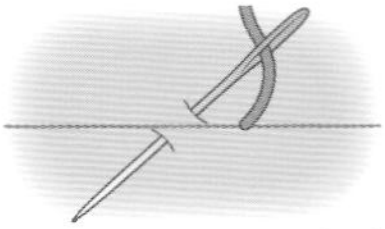

Bring the thread out at the beginning of the quilting line. Take a diagonal stitch forward, in above the line and out below.

STEP 2

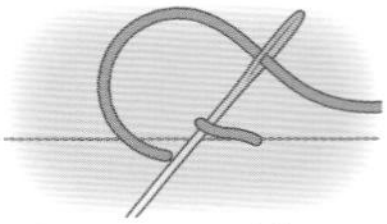

Hold the thread forward and pass the needle behind the diagonal stitch, without taking up any fabric. Pull the thread through and adjust the loop as necessary.

STEP 3

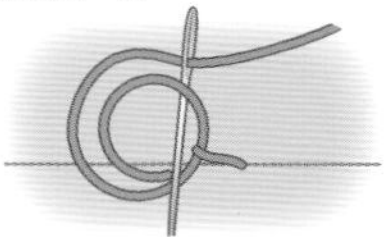

Hold the thread forward and pass the needle through the loop of thread without taking up any fabric.

STEP 4

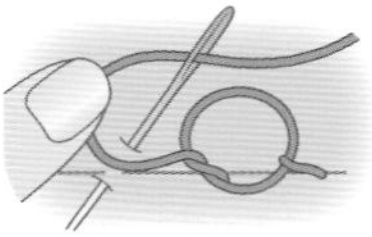

Support the loop with your free thumb while taking the next diagonal stitch.

Repeat steps 1, 2 and 3 to continue along the quilting line.

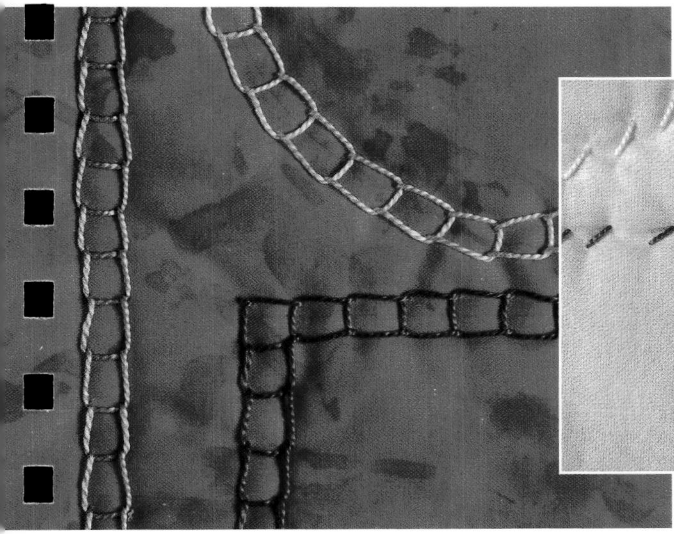

REVERSE OF WORK

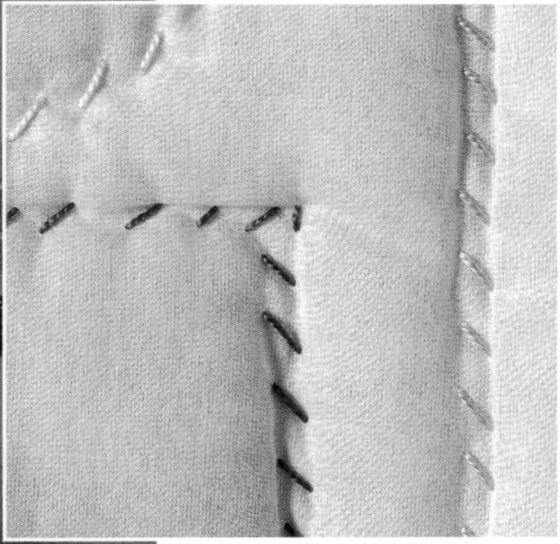

Open chain

This variation on chain stitch gives an open, ladder-like result. Work the stitches down toward you to help to get the stitches even.

TIP

Always use the thumb on your non-sewing hand to hold the thread so the complete stitch does not collapse sideways.

STEP 1

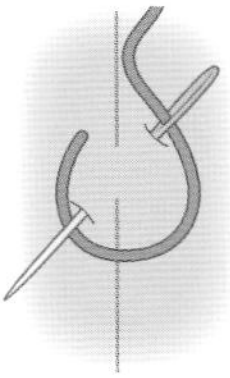

Bring the thread out to the left of the quilting line. Hold it forward so it forms a loop. Take the needle in on the right of the line (level with the left-hand thread) and take a diagonal stitch forward, bringing the needle out on the left of the line again and into the waiting loop of thread.

STEP 2

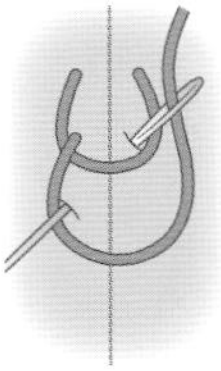

Hold the thread forward to form the next loop. Use the needle to stretch the previous chain sideways, take the needle inside the last (stretched) chain and take a diagonal stitch forward again, bringing the needle up on the left of the line and into the waiting loop of thread.

STEP 3

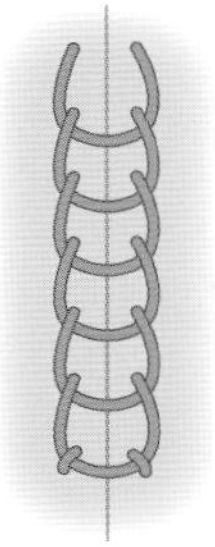

Continue in this way. Secure the very last open chain with two tiny securing stitches, so you finish with a square stitch or "box."

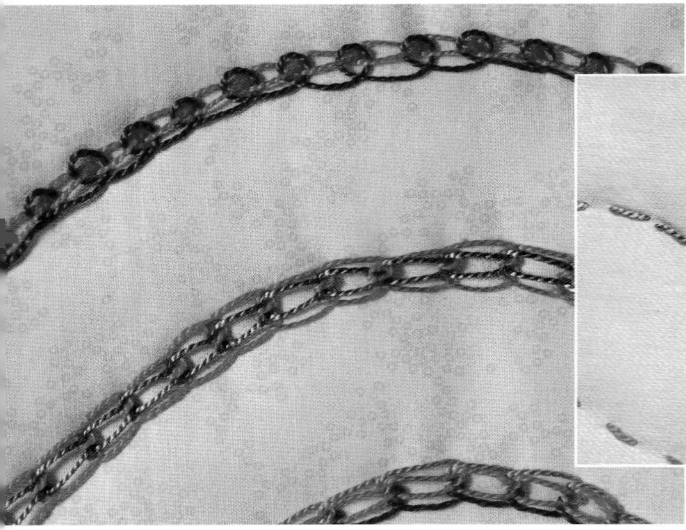

REVERSE OF WORK

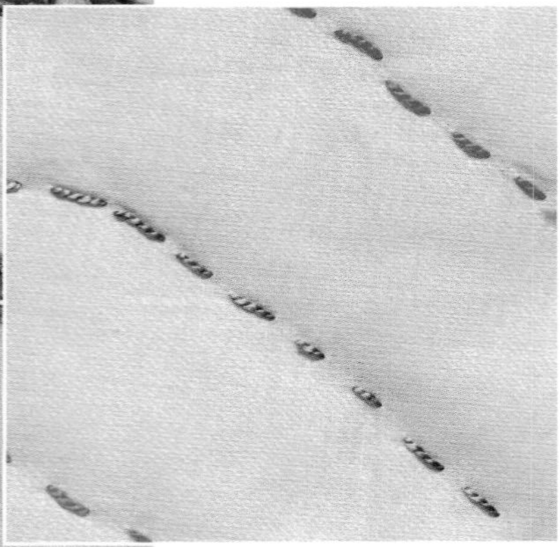

Interlaced chain

Work one row of interlacing to one side of the chain, or a row on both sides to give a more symmetrical result. The interlacing does not go through the fabric.

STEP 1

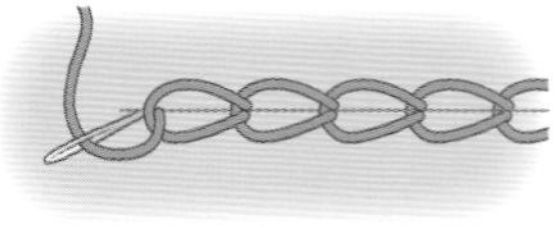

Bring the thread out at the beginning of the quilting line and stitch a foundation row of plain chain stitch (see page 77).

STEP 2

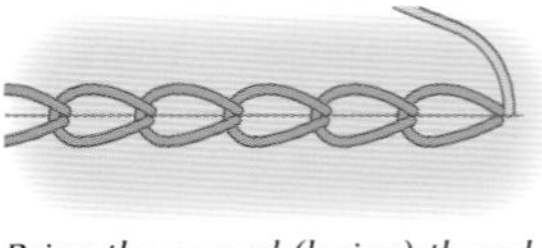

Bring the second (lacing) thread to the surface of the work at the beginning of the first chain stitch.

STEP 3

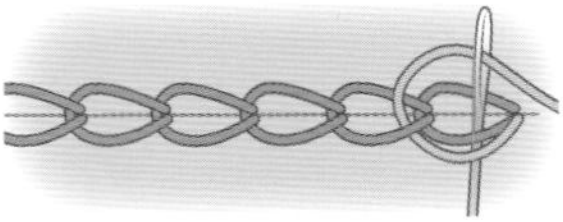

Take the needle up and under the bottom part of the second chain stitch in line, then come down behind the bottom part (and the lacing thread) of the first chain stitch.

STEP 4

Take the needle up and under the bottom part of the third chain stitch, then come down behind the bottom part (and the lacing thread) of the second chain stitch. Continue in this manner—two chains forward and one back.

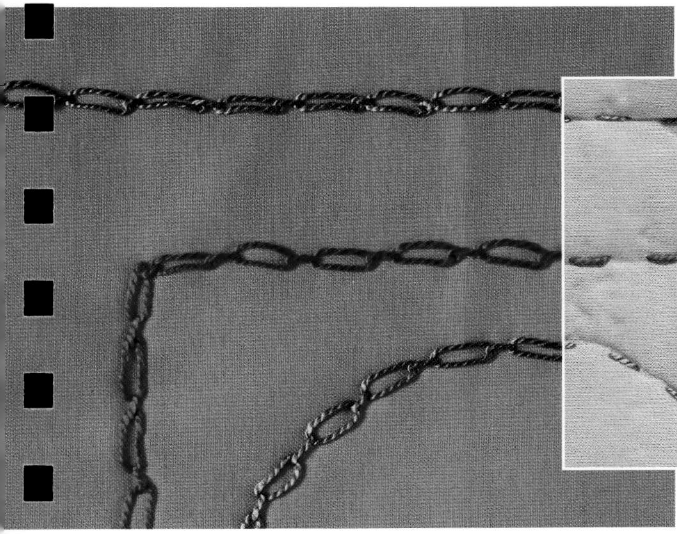

REVERSE OF WORK

Cable chain

This stitch has a small linking stitch between the loops of the chain which can be made a feature of by elongating it or shortening the link.

STEP 1

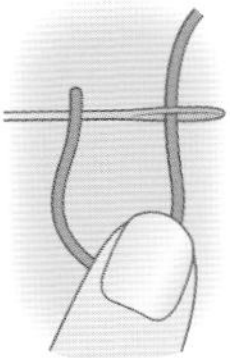

Work this stitch down toward you. Bring the thread out at the start of the quilting line. Hold it forward along the line and pass the needle behind it.

STEP 2

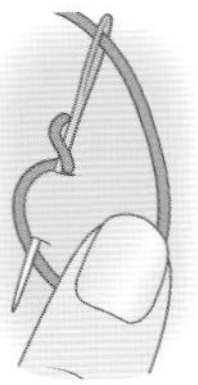

Hold the thread on the surface of the fabric with your non-sewing thumb, and with a twist, bring the needle forward over the thread again and into the fabric, take a quilting stitch (through all layers) forward along the line, and bring the needle back up into the waiting loop of thread.

TIPS

- If you are making a bed quilt don't elongate the linking stitch too much in case the thread snags.
- It is easy to work this stitch on corners and curves. Try to balance the stitches on the approach to a corner so the chains are even.

STEP 3

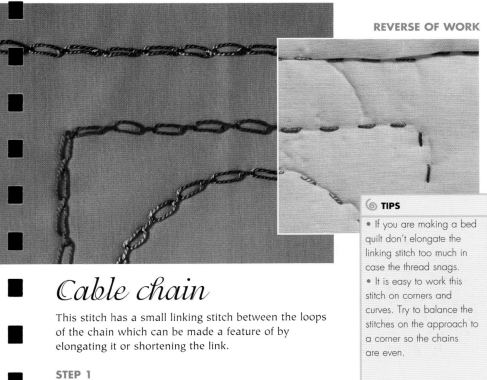

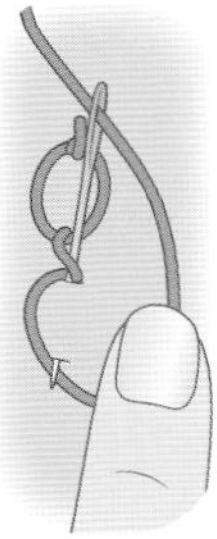

Continue in this way along the quilting line. Finish with a small securing stitch outside the last chain.

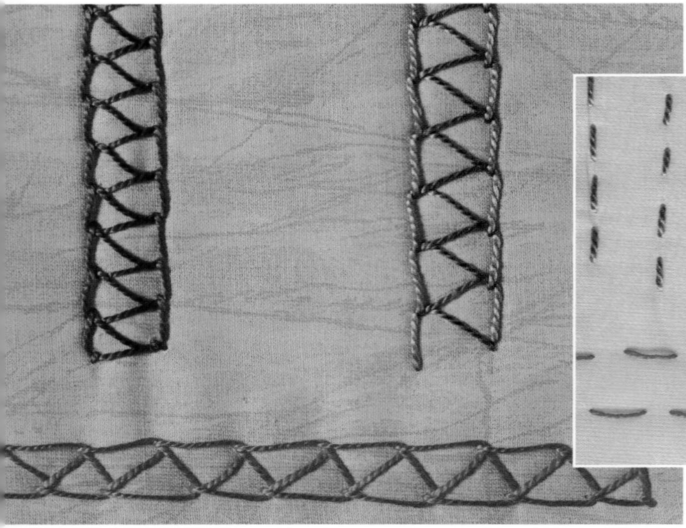

REVERSE OF WORK

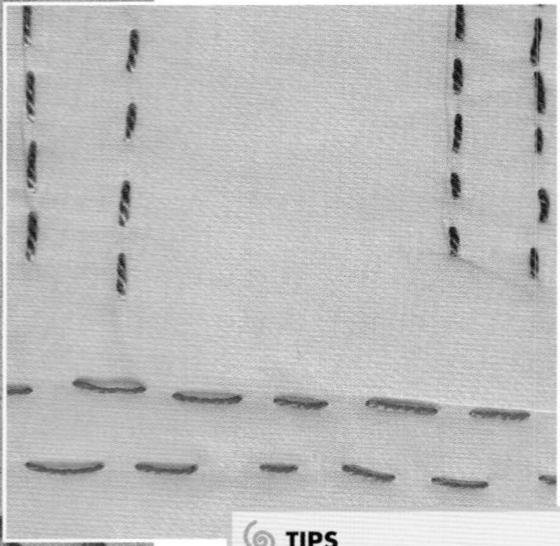

Double chain

This wide stitch should be used in areas of a design where there is plenty of space. Don't be tempted to work it too wide, as it would then distort the fabric.

TIPS

This stitch is easiest to sew when it is worked vertically, down toward you.

STEP 1

Bring the thread to the surface of the work, on the left of the quilting line. Hold the thread forward (in the direction in which the needle will be traveling) and over to the right, and take a vertical quilting stitch (through all layers) toward you and on the right of the line, bringing the needle into the waiting loop of thread.

STEP 2

Hold the thread forward and over to the left, take a vertical quilting stitch, taking the needle in at the same point that the thread started, and stitching forward and toward you, passing the level of the right-hand thread point.

STEP 3

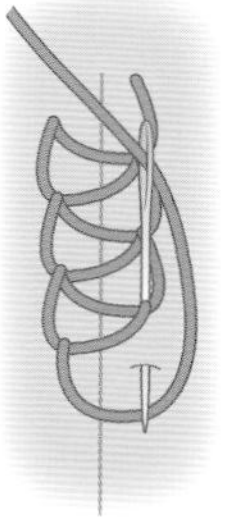

Hold the thread forward and over to the right, take the needle into the fabric behind the last stitch sewn and stitch forward and toward you into the waiting loop of thread. Continue in this way, finishing with a small securing stitch to hold the final triangle open.

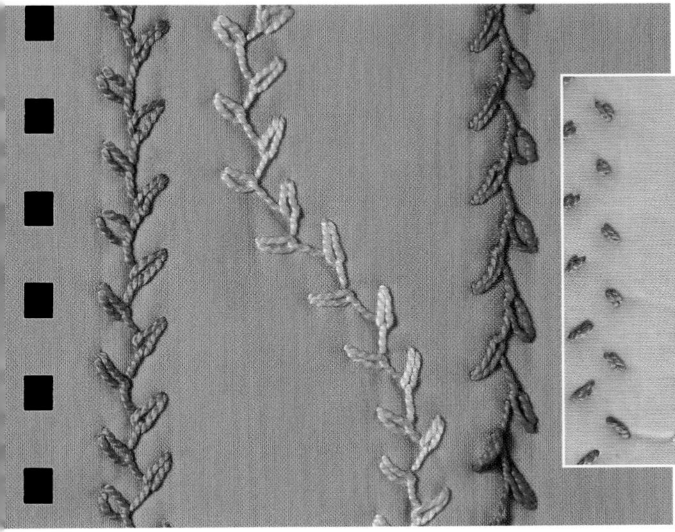

REVERSE OF WORK

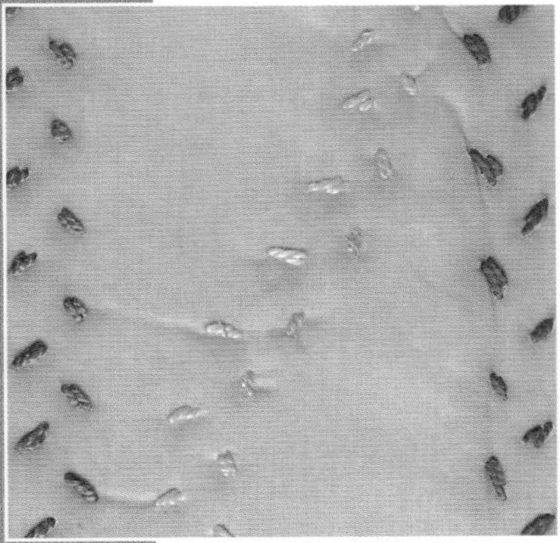

Feathered chain

This decorative stitch consists of little diagonal chains that resemble leaves on a trellis. The feathering can be worked narrow or wide.

STEP 1

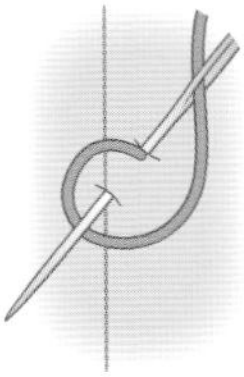

Bring the thread to the surface of the work and on the right-hand side of the quilting line. Hold the thread forward and round to the right, insert the needle in the same place it came out, and take a small chain stitch forward, bringing the needle up into the waiting loop of thread to form a chain.

STEP 2

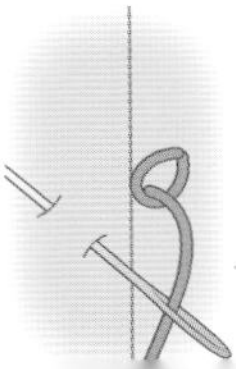

Take the needle in on the left of the quilting line and stitch diagonally backward and up to the left.

STEP 3

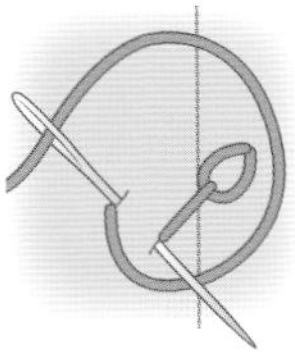

Insert the needle into the same place it came out and, holding the thread forward and round to the right, take a small chain stitch forward, bringing the needle up at the same place the previous thread went in, and into the waiting loop of thread to form a chain.

STEP 4

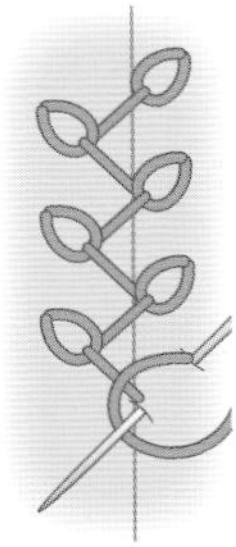

Take a backward, diagonal stitch to the right and repeat stages 1, 2, and 3. Continue working along the line and finish with a small securing stitch outside the last chain stitch.

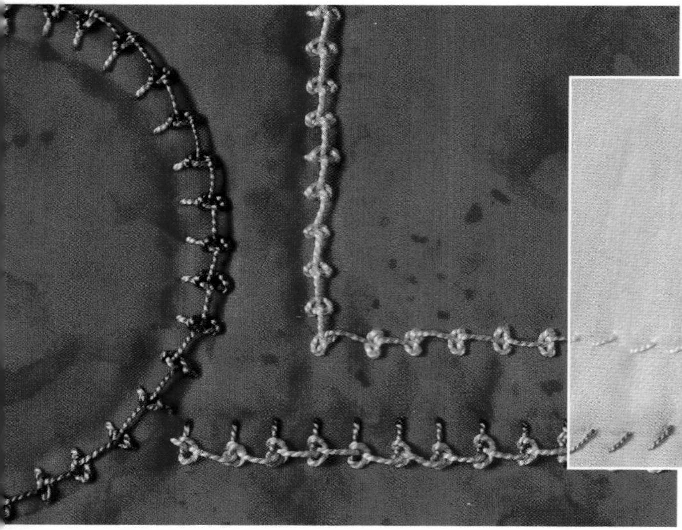

REVERSE OF WORK

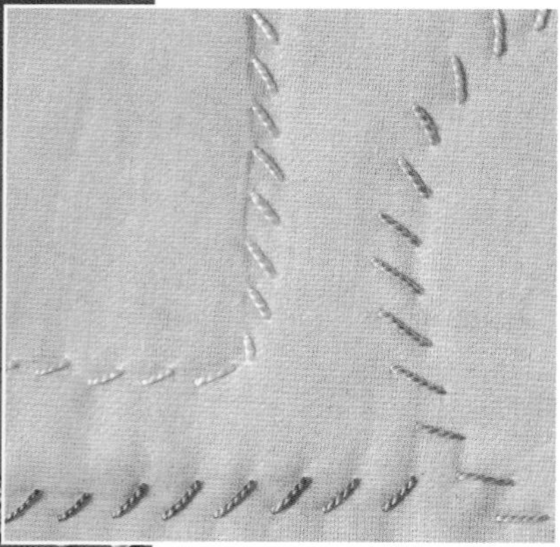

Raised chain

There are two stages to this stitch: Making a ladder, then wrapping or knotting it—these stitches can be worked in the same thread or contrasting colors.

STEP 1

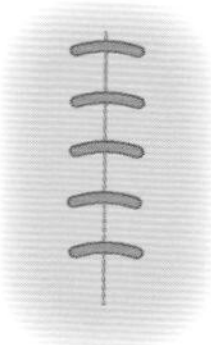

Bring the thread to the surface of the fabric, and stitch a row of horizontal quilting stitches (passing through all layers).

STEP 2

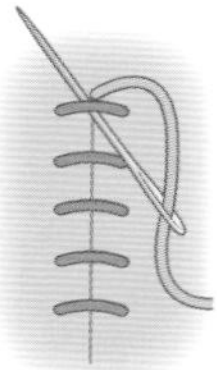

Bring the second (wrapping) thread to the surface, on the quilting line and central to the ladder of horizontal stitches. Pass the needle up and under the first stitch on the ladder (do not catch the fabric).

STEP 3

Holding the thread down and around to the right to form a loop, take the needle down behind the first stitch on the ladder and into the waiting loop of thread.

STEP 4

Repeat stages 2 and 3 as you progress along the ladder.

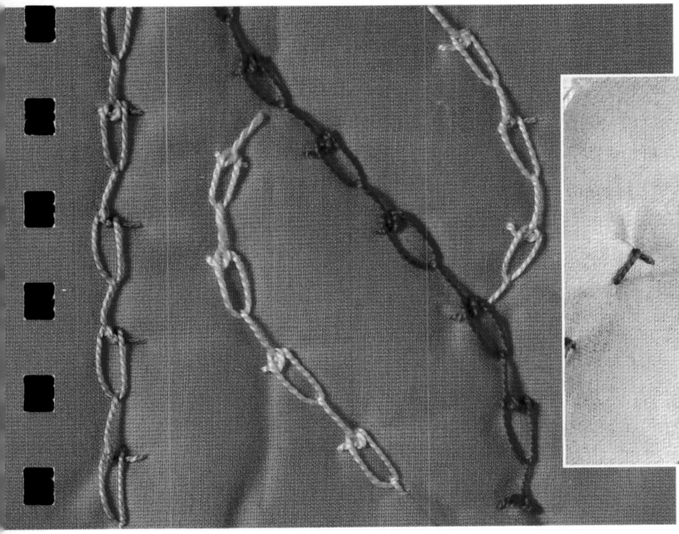

REVERSE OF WORK

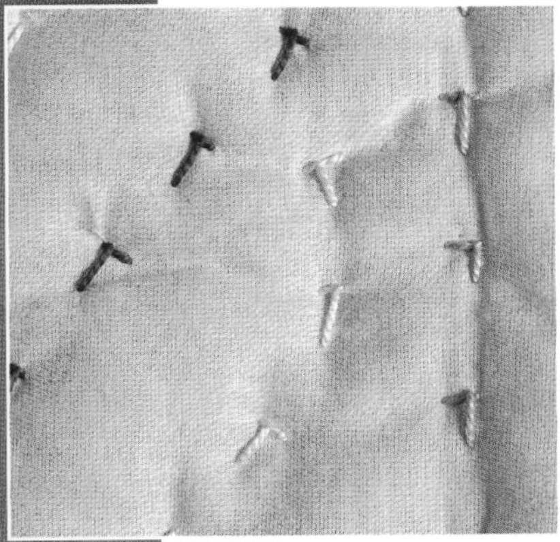

Knotted cable

This stitch is based on coral stitch and chain stitch, with an intriguing and ornate raised knot between each link in the chain. It has a slightly zigzag finished appearance.

STEP 1

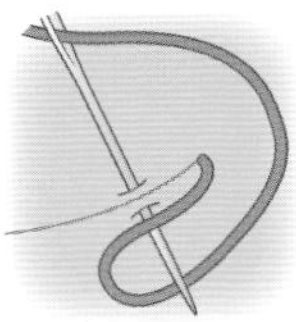

Bring the thread to the surface of the work, at the beginning of the quilting line. You will be working horizontally and from right to left. Hold the thread forward along the line and looped down and backward. Take a small vertical quilting stitch downward through all layers, bringing the needle out below the line. Pull the thread through.

STEP 2

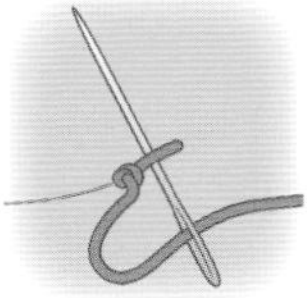

Pass the needle under the existing stitch without catching up any of the fabric.

STEP 3

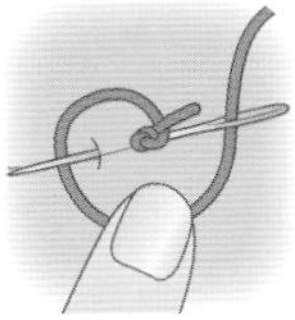

Hold the thread forward and downward and take a small horizontal stitch forward above the line.

STEP 4

Repeat steps 1, 2, and 3 to progress along the quilting line. Finish the thread outside a knot or a chain stitch to secure the work.

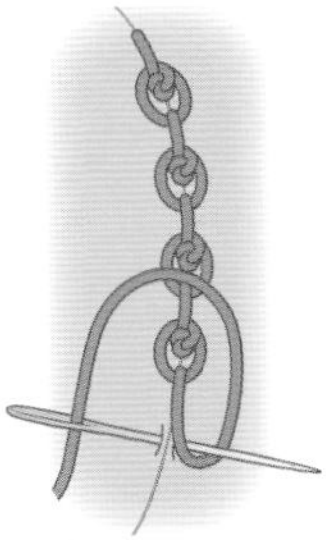

REVERSE OF WORK

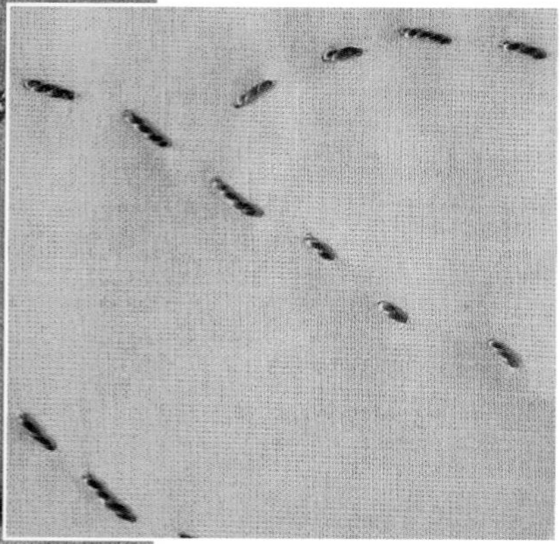

Twisted chain

This is a more textured variation of basic chain stitch. It is quite narrow, so useful for continuous line designs and outlining or contour-quilting around motifs.

STEP 1

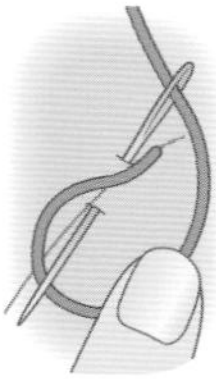

Bring the thread to the surface of the fabric, at the beginning of the quilting line. Hold the thread forward along the line, and take the needle in above the thread and to the left of the line. Bring the needle out below the thread, to the right of the line and into the waiting loop. The chain will twist automatically.

STEP 2

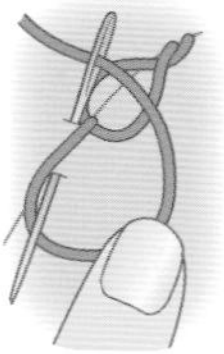

Hold the thread forward along the line and repeat for the next stitch. Continue along the line and finish with a small securing stitch outside the final chain.

TIPS

- Don't be tempted to make the loops of the chain too long, or they will become quite narrow and lose the effect of a linked chain.
- As with all chain stitch variations, make use of the thumb on your non-sewing hand to place the thread to form a loop, ready for the next stitch.

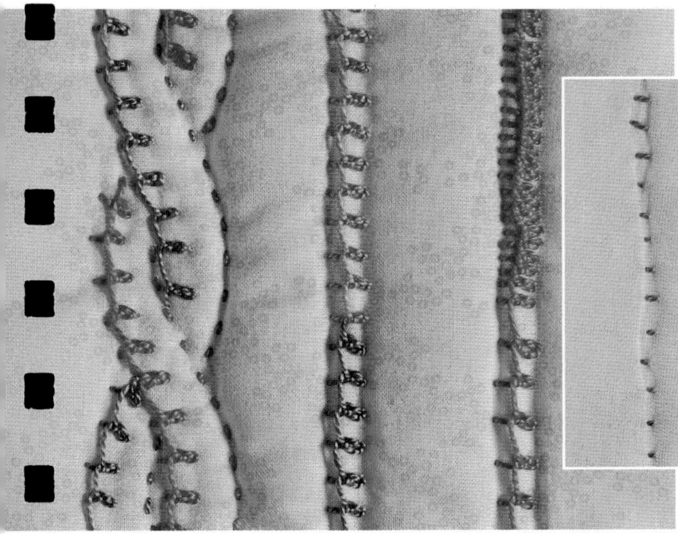

REVERSE OF WORK

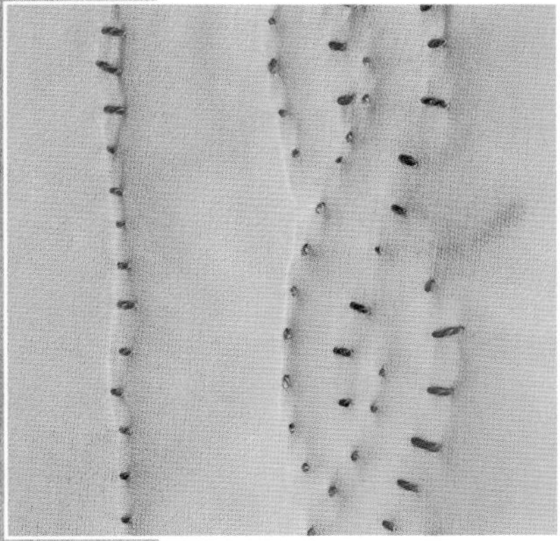

Rosette chain

This wide stitch produces a decorative result similar to a braid. Don't make the stitch too wide—it will become too unstable for use in quilting.

STEP 1

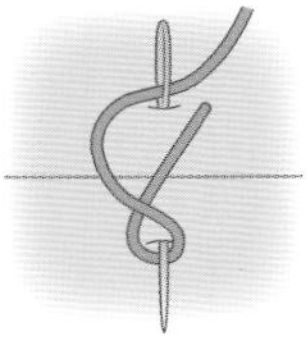

Working horizontally, bring the thread to the surface of the work, above the quilting line. Take a vertical stitch (in above the line and out below the line) and hold the thread so it wraps forward and around and under the needle. Pull the thread through and hold the stitch with the thumb of your non-sewing hand while you continue.

STEP 2

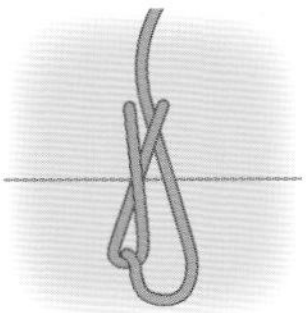

Take the needle upward, underneath the starting thread, without catching the fabric.

STEP 3

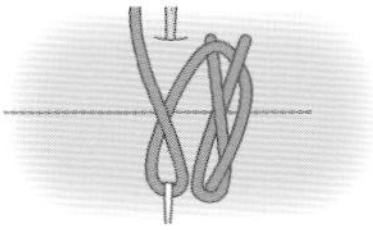

Make the next vertical stitch, in above the line and out below the line, wrapping the thread forward and around and under the needle.

STEP 4

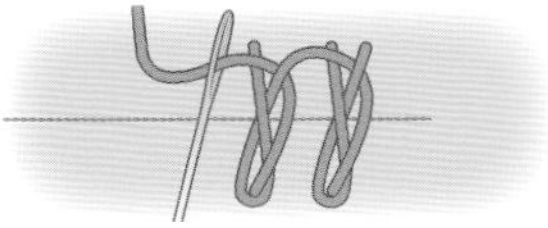

Continue as before, this time passing the needle upward under the existing bar of thread that is sitting between the two looped chains. Finish with a small securing stitch outside the final chain loop.

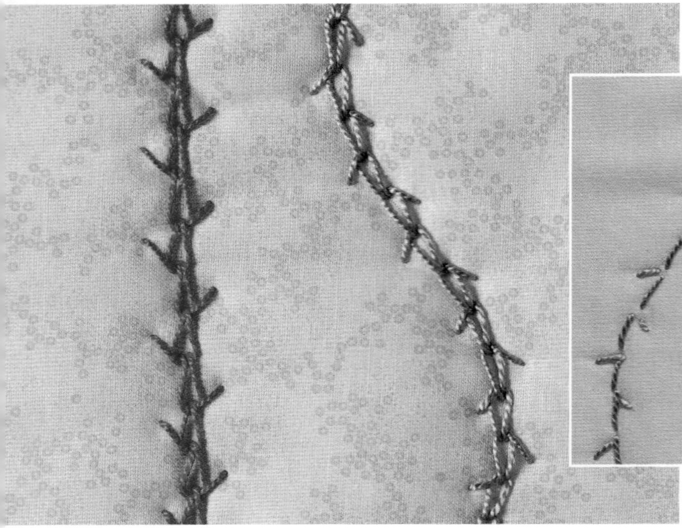

REVERSE OF WORK

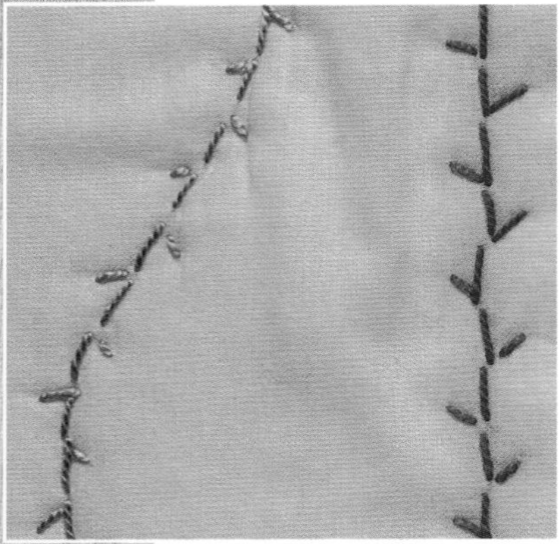

Spine chain

Once you have practiced chain stitch (see page 77), it is easy to make the extra, intermittent diagonal stitches to add more movement to your work.

STEP 1

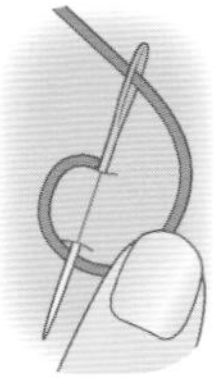

Bring the thread to the surface of the work, at the beginning of the quilting line. Holding the thread forward and looped around, take the needle into the same place as the thread emerged. Make a quilting stitch forward along the line through all layers, bringing the needle up on the line and into the waiting loop of thread.

STEP 2

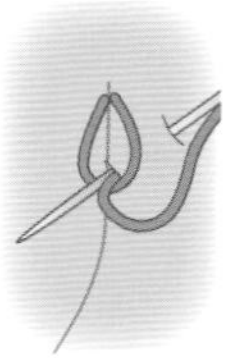

Now take the needle into the fabric on the right-hand side of the line, slightly further back. Stitch diagonally down and inward, toward the line, bringing the needle up inside the first chain that you have sewn (do not loop the thread at this stage).

STEP 3

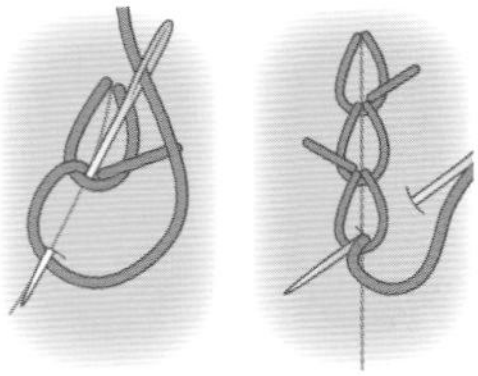

Holding the thread forward along the line and looped around, take the needle inside the previous chain and stitch forward along the line, bringing the needle up inside the waiting loop of thread. Now make a diagonal stitch on the left-hand side, bringing the needle up inside the previous chain. Continue in this way along the quilting line, finishing with a chain stitch or a diagonal stitch. Secure the thread outside the last chain.

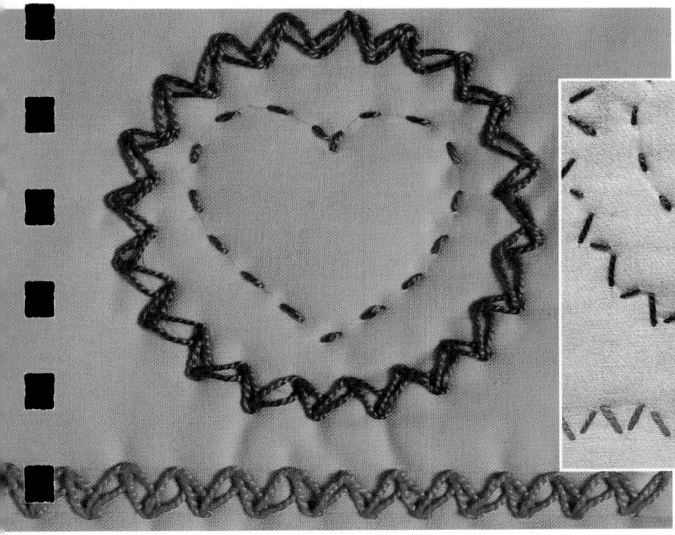

REVERSE OF WORK

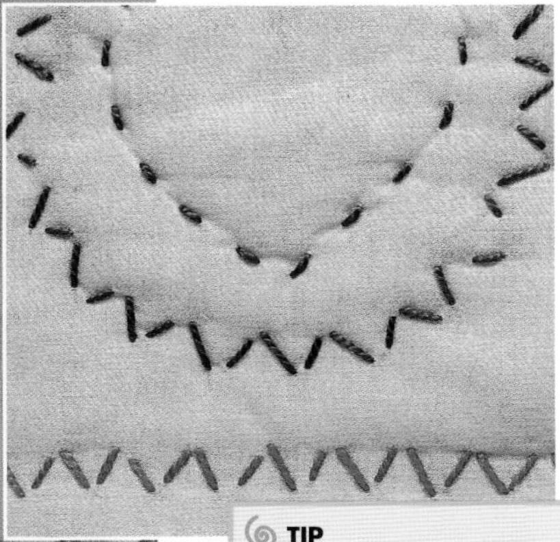

TIP

Keep the diagonal stitches upright and at a fairly acute diagonal to the quilting line.

Zigzag chain

This stitch can be found on very old embroideries. When worked very small, it will resemble a decorative braid laid on the fabric, rather than an obvious chain stitch.

STEP 1

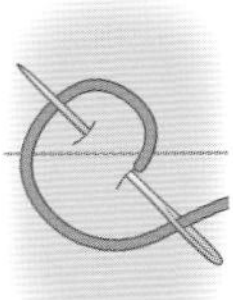

Bring the thread to the surface of the work, just below the quilting line. Working horizontally, hold the thread forward and around in front of the needle, to form a loop. Insert the needle at the same spot (or slightly to one side of) the thread originally came out of and make a quilting stitch diagonally upward (through all layers), bringing the needle out above the quilting line and up into the waiting loop of thread.

STEP 2

Hold the thread forward to form a loop again. This time, pierce the thread of the previous chain and stitch diagonally downward, bringing the needle out below the line and into the waiting loop of thread.

STEP 3

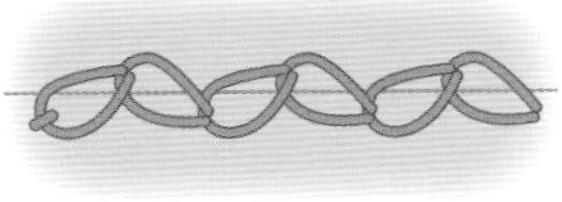

Continue working either side of the line, alternating one stitch upward with one stitch downward. Secure the last chain with a small stitch outside the chain loop.

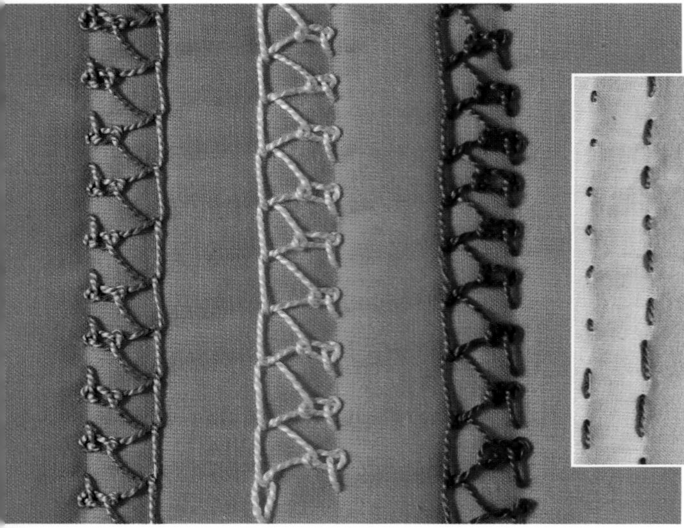

REVERSE OF WORK

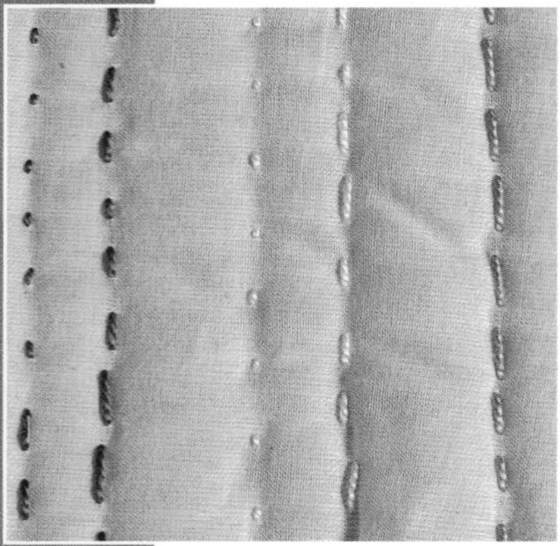

Crested chain

This combination of chain and coral stitches can be worked horizontally (as shown below) or vertically. Leave space between stitches to achieve a lacy effect.

STEP 1

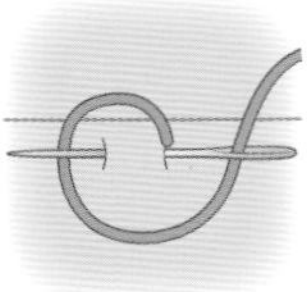

Bring the thread to the surface of the work. Form a loop and take the needle into the same place that the thread came out of the fabric. Make a horizontal quilting stitch forward bringing the needle out into the waiting loop of thread.

STEP 2

Hold the thread above the work and loop it forward and down. Make a quilting stitch forward into the waiting loop of thread.

STEP 3

Pass the thread forward and behind the central bar of thread that is sitting between the top and bottom stitches (do not catch any fabric).

STEP 4

Hold the thread forward and looped down and around. Take the needle into the previous chain sewn and make a quilting stitch forward, into the waiting loop of thread. Repeat stages 2, 3, and 4 and continue along the quilting line. Finish with a small securing stitch outside the last chain.

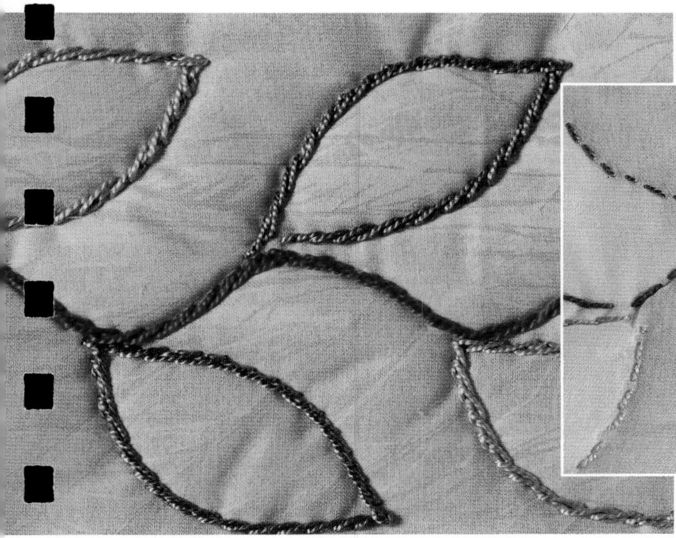

REVERSE OF WORK

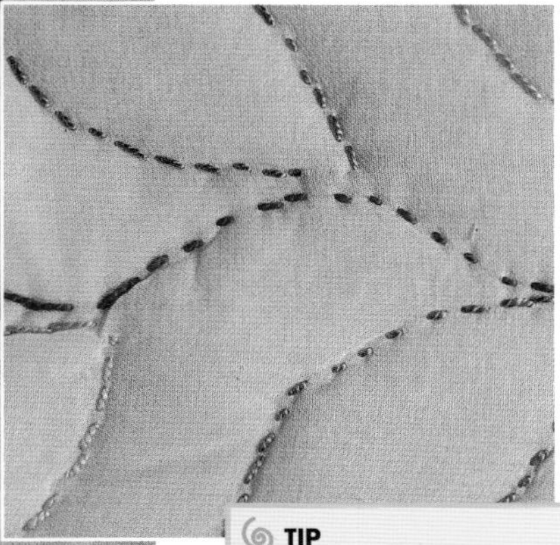

TIP

The illustrations show the stitch sewn vertically, but it is equally easy to work it horizontally.

Rope stitch

Rope stitch is a narrow, solid stitch with a slightly raised effect and a rope-like formation, ideal for continuous line designs and contour-quilting motifs.

STEP 1

Bring the thread to the surface of the work, on the quilting line. Hold it forward and around so it loops to the right. Take the needle in to the left of the thread emerging from the fabric and make a quilting stitch forward (through all layers), bringing the needle up again further along the line and into the waiting loop of thread.

STEP 2

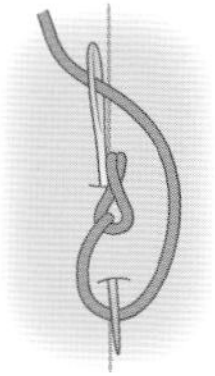

Hold the thread forward and around to the right. This time, take the needle slightly to the left of the line and also halfway back along the previous stitch. Tuck it in snugly alongside the previous stitch. Take a very slight diagonal stitch this time, bringing the needle out on the line again and into the waiting loop of thread.

STEP 3

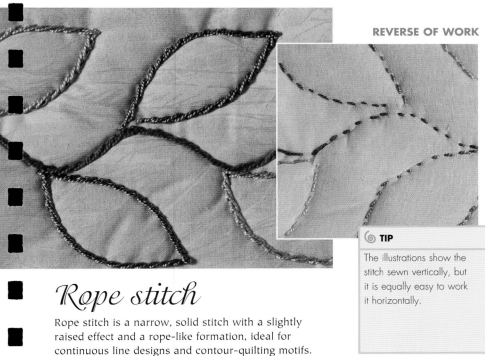

Carry on along the quilting line and secure the last knot or loop with a small securing stitch.

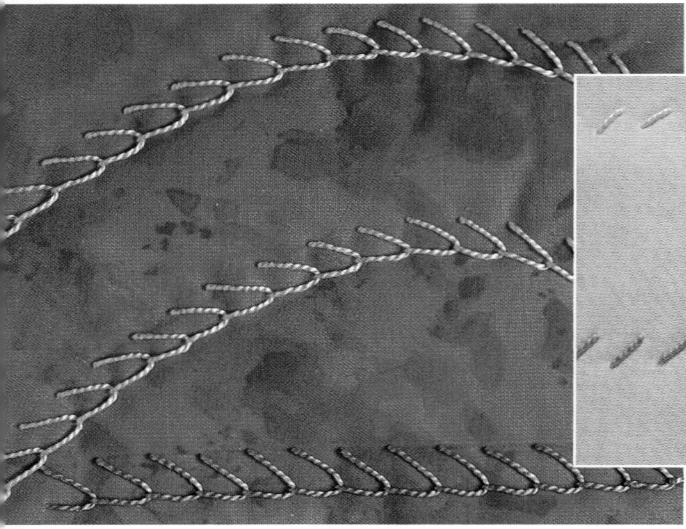

REVERSE OF WORK

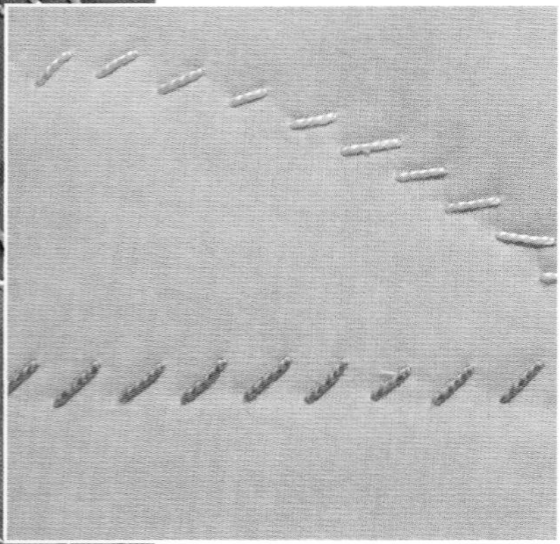

TIP

Keep the needle at quite an acute angle, to emphasize the angle of the stitches and ensure that they stay at a diagonal.

Half feather

Incredibly easy to sew, half feather stitch can add a lot of movement to a quilting design while being sewn speedily and fluidly.

STEP 1

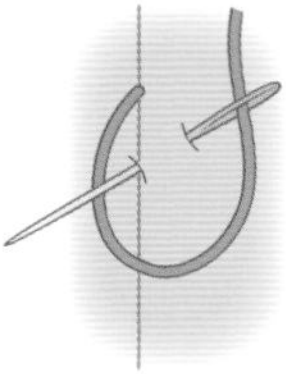

Bring the thread to the surface of the work, at the beginning of the quilting line. Hold the thread down on the line and, working toward you, take the needle into the fabric on the right of the line. Make a quilting stitch diagonally forward and bring the needle up on the line, into the waiting loop of thread.

STEP 2

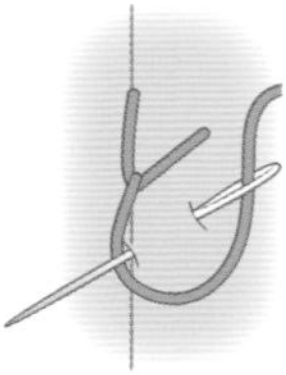

Again, hold the thread down on the line with the thumb of your non-sewing hand and make the next quilting stitch, sewing diagonally forward and bringing the needle up on the line inside the waiting loop of thread.

STEP 3

Continue in this way until you have reached the end of the design or thread. Finish the work with a small securing stitch outside the last stitch to be sewn.

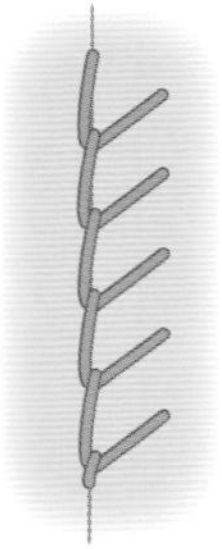

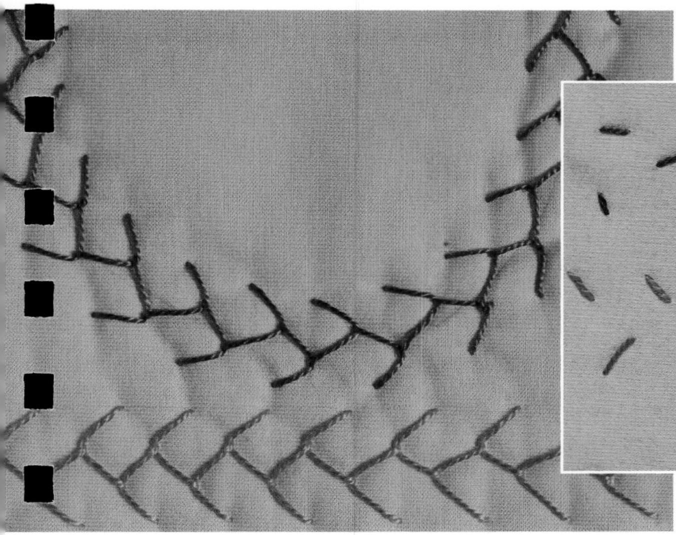

REVERSE OF WORK

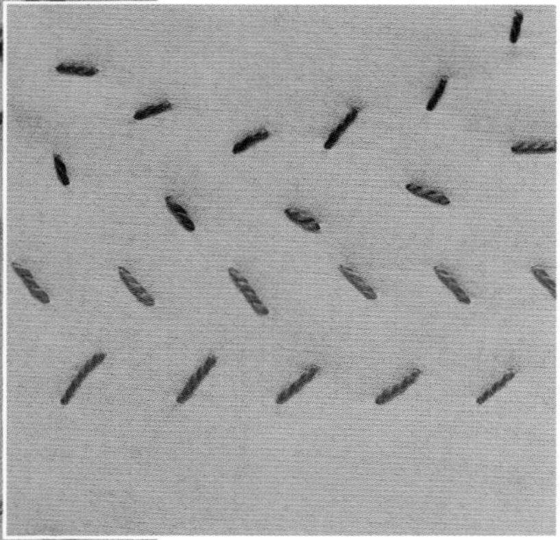

Single feather

The delicate and attractive appearance of this stitch can be further enhanced by varying the angle of the needle and the length and spacing of the stitches.

STEP 1

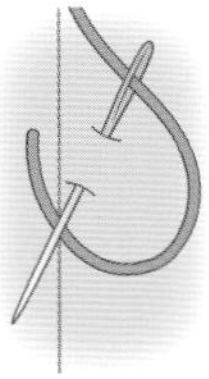

Bring the thread to the surface of the work, at the beginning of the quilting line. Working down toward you, hold the thread down on the line and looped around to the right. Make a quilting stitch (through all layers) on the right of the line, stitching diagonally downward and inward toward the line, but not actually touching it, and bringing the needle up into the waiting loop of thread.

STEP 2

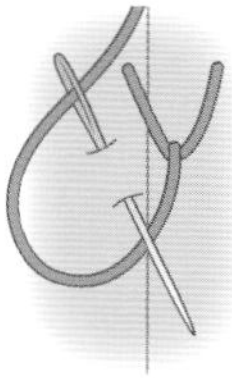

Hold the thread down on the line and now loop it around to the left. Make a quilting stitch on the left of the line, taking the needle into the fabric level with where the thread last came out on the right. Stitch diagonally down and inward toward the line, without actually touching it, and bring the needle up into the waiting loop of thread.

STEP 3

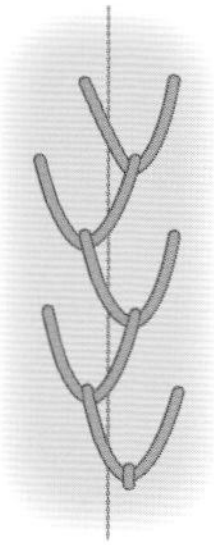

Carry on in this way, working either side of the line, but not actually touching it. This will help you to achieve the little pattern that resembles bird's footprints. Finish with a small securing stitch outside the last V-shaped stitch.

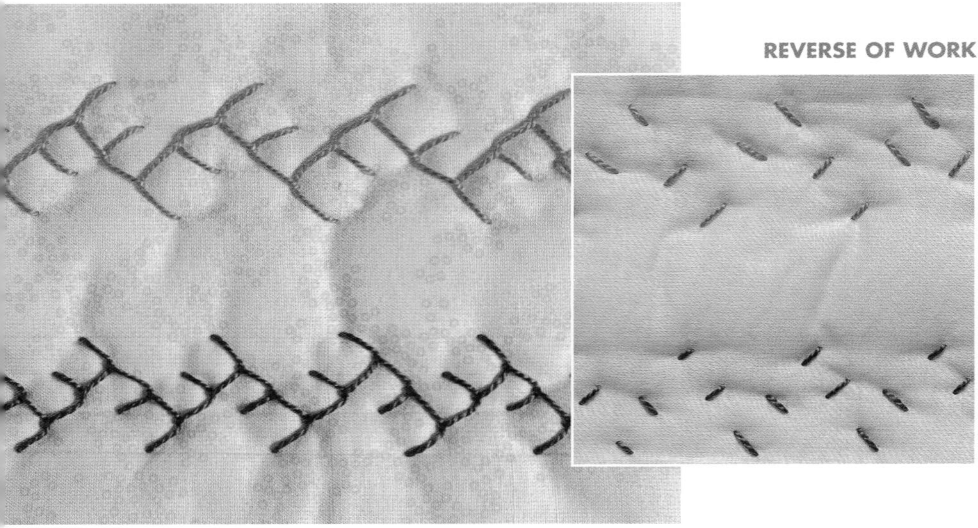

Double feather

This is a wider variation of single feather stitch. The result is a decorative, feathery line that is more ornate than the narrower, "bird tracks" appearance of single feather stitch.

STEP 1

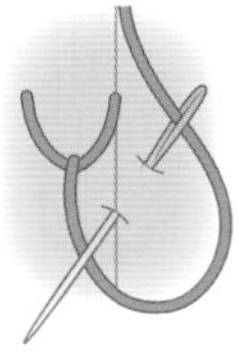

Bring the thread to the surface of the work and to the left of the quilting line. Hold the thread down toward you and looped around to the right. Make a quilting stitch (through all layers), stitching diagonally downward and inward from right to left, and bringing the needle up into the waiting loop of thread. Repeat to make a second stitch, working diagonally inward from right to left.

STEP 2

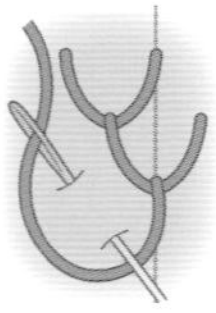

Hold the thread down toward you and now loop it around to the left. Make a quilting stitch to the left of the previous stitches, taking the needle into the fabric level—where the thread last came out on the right. Stitch diagonally down and inward, bringing the needle up into the waiting loop of thread. Hold the thread down and around to the left and make another stitch, working diagonally inward from left to right.

STEP 3

Carry on in this way, working two feather stitches on the right and two on the left.

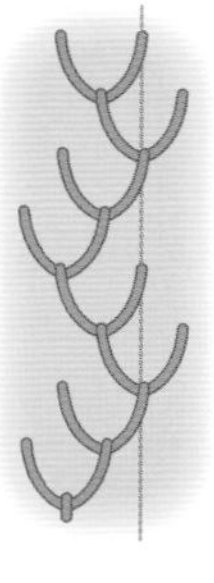

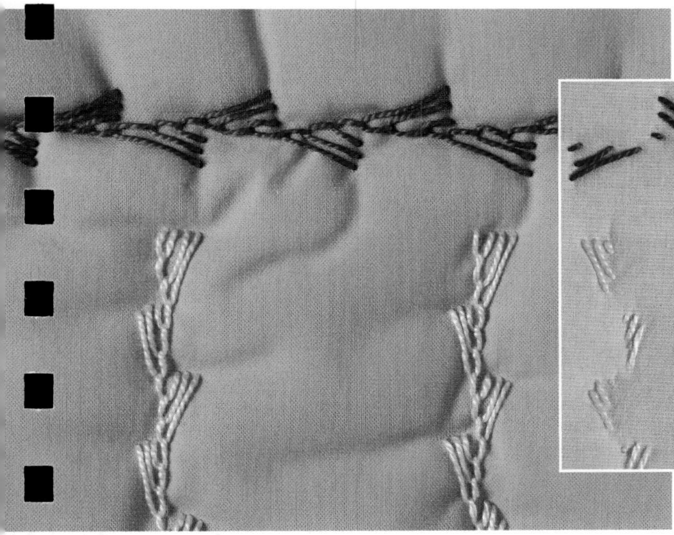

REVERSE OF WORK

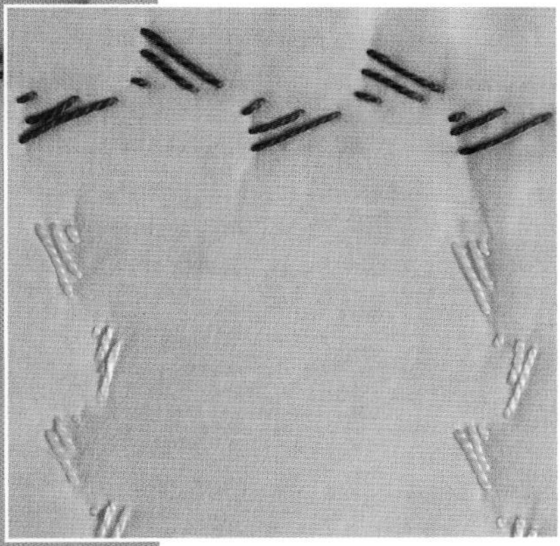

Maidenhair

A decorative variation of basic single feather stitch, which is concentrated on a single central line. Keep the longest, outer branches tucked well in against their neighbors.

STEP 1

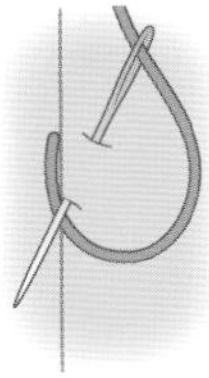

Bring the thread to the surface of the work, at the beginning of the quilting line. Working vertically, down toward you, hold the thread down on the line and around to the right with your non-sewing thumb. Make a diagonal quilting stitch through all layers, working in from the right of the line, stitching down and inward toward the line, bringing the needle up on the line and into the waiting loop of thread.

STEP 2

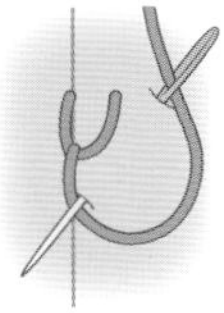

Hold the thread in the same way and do a second diagonal stitch. Keep the top of the stitch level with the branch of the first one and bring the needle out on the line into the waiting loop of thread.

STEP 3

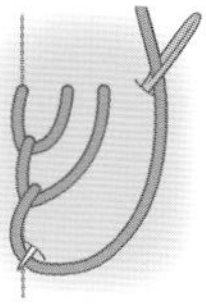

Make a third stitch in the same way, tucking the needle in close to the previous stitches on the line.

STEP 4

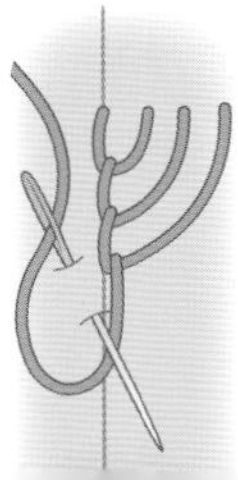

Now hold the thread down and to the left. Repeat sequence of stitches, work in from the left. Continue working three stitches either side of the line.

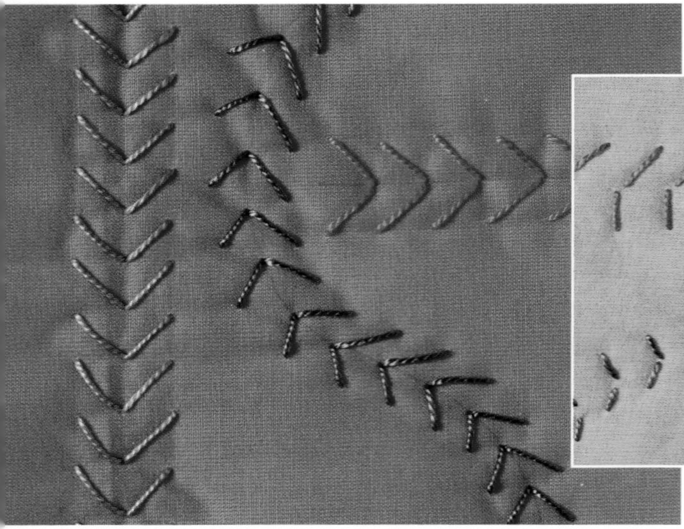

REVERSE OF WORK

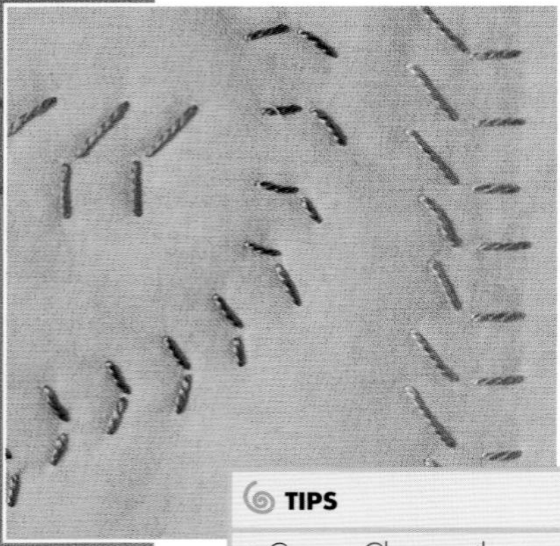

TIPS

- Curves: Close up the gaps between the stitches on the inside edge of the curve; space them slightly further apart on the outside edge of the curve.
- Spacing: Ideally, have the top points of each V-shape level with the bottom point of the previous V-shape. If a more densely stitched effect is required, sew closer together.

Arrowhead

A versatile and speedy quilting stitch, which is simple to sew on a straight line and even easier to sew on a gently curving line. It bears a slight resemblance to fly stitch (see page 99).

STEP 1

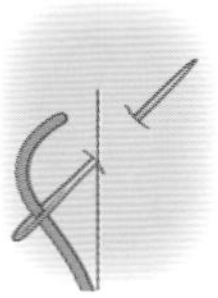

Bring the thread to the surface of the work, on the left of the quilting line. Take the needle in on the line, a little further down than your starting point, and make a diagonal stitch upward and out to the right of the line.

STEP 2

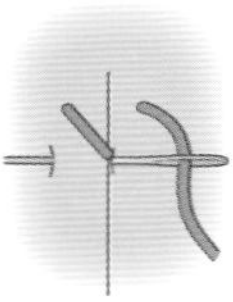

Pull the thread through. Take the needle into where the thread previously went in and stitch horizontally, out to the left of the line.

STEP 3

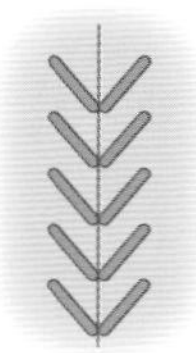

Pull the thread through and repeat the first two stages, progressing along the line. Finish with a complete V-shaped stitch.

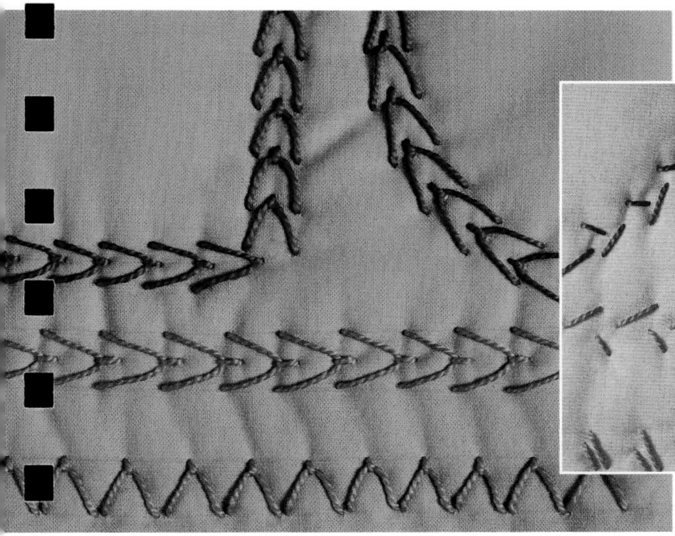

REVERSE OF WORK

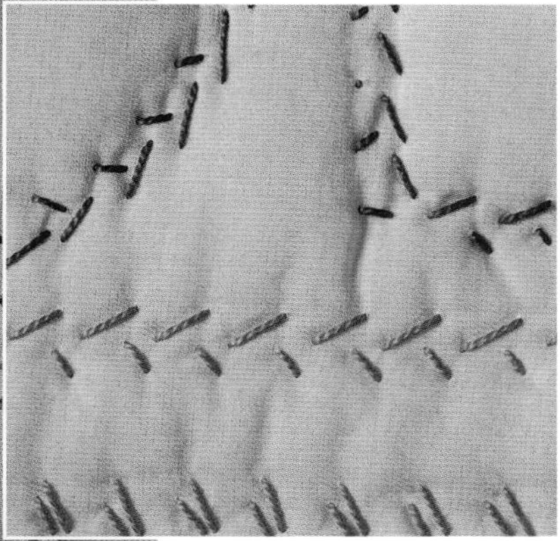

Fly stitch

This stitch can be sewn horizontally or vertically; it can also be used as a filling stitch. It can form a "Y" (longer securing stitch) or a "V" shape (shorter securing stitch).

STEP 1

Bring the thread to the surface of the work, on the left of the quilting line. Hold the thread downward and looped around to the right. Take the needle in on the right-hand side of the line (level with where the thread started on the left) and make a quilting stitch through all layers, at a downward diagonal, bringing the needle up on the line and into the waiting loop of thread.

STEP 2

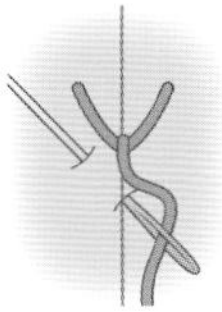

Take the needle back into the layers, on the line and underneath the V-shaped stitch that you have just sewn. Bring the needle up on the left-hand side of the line.

STEP 3

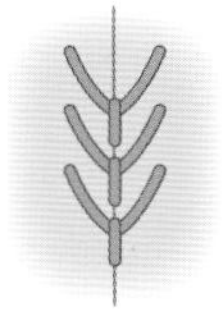

Repeat these two stages. Ensure that the thread is held down and looped around. Carry on along the quilting line and secure the last V-shaped stitch when you finish off.

STEP 4

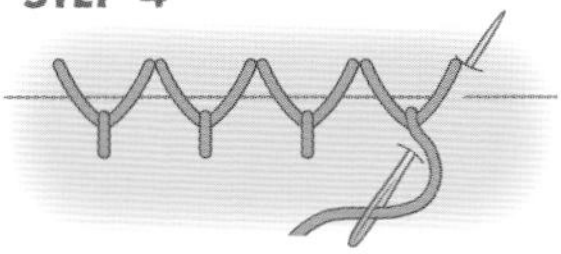

When working along a horizontal line, work above and below the quilting line.

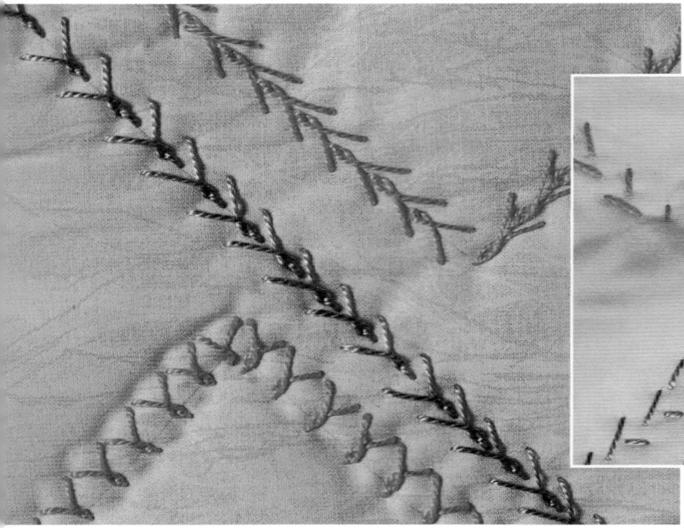

REVERSE OF WORK

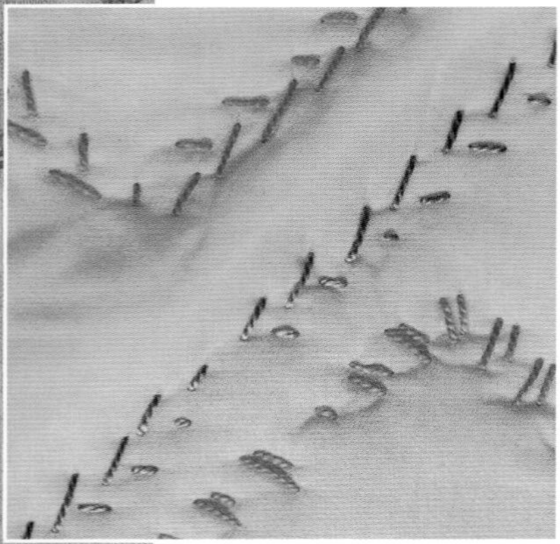

Twisted fly

This has a decorative twist in the thread below each fly stitch, which provides added textural interest. For a denser effect, work the stitches closer together.

STEP 1

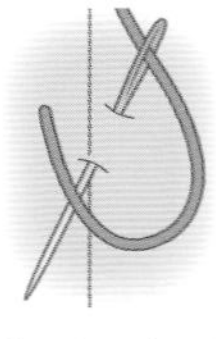

Bring the thread to the surface of the work, on the left of the quilting line. Hold it downward and looped around to the right. Take the needle in on the right-hand side of the line (level with where the thread started on the left) and make a quilting stitch through all layers, at a downward diagonal, bringing the needle up on the line and underneath the waiting thread loop.

STEP 2

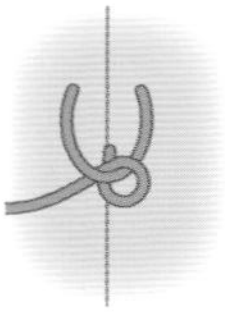

Keep the loop of thread in place and pass the needle over the top of it and behind it.

STEP 3

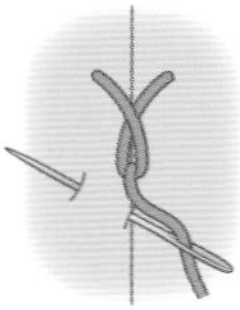

Take the needle into the fabric on the quilting line and make a quilting stitch out to the left of the line to start again. Carry on along the line and finish with a central securing stitch.

ALTERNATIVE

This stitch can also be worked horizontally. Instead of working either side of the line, work above and below it in the same manner as horizontal fly stitch (see page 99).

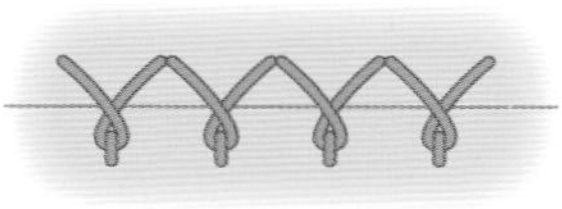

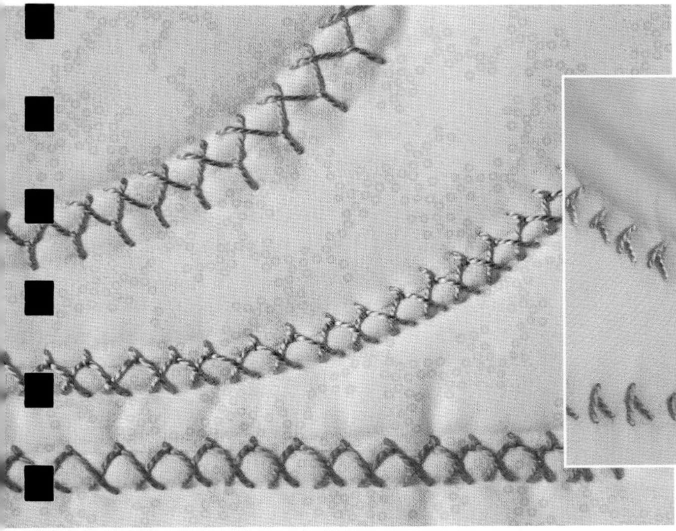

REVERSE OF WORK

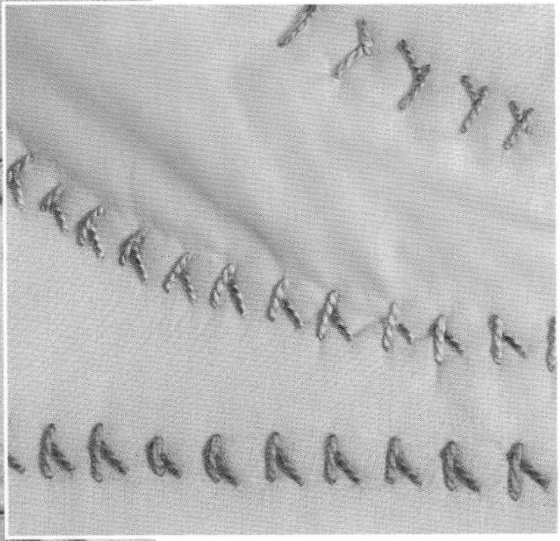

Plaited fly

Plaited fly stitch needs to be sewn horizontally along the quilting line so the branches of the individual stitches overlap. It is very easy to keep this stitch even.

STEP 1

Work horizontally, from left to right. Bring the thread to the surface of the work, above the quilting line. Hold it downward and around to the right. Take the needle in above the quilting line, slightly further along the work and level with the starting point. Make a quilting stitch at a diagonal, downward and inward, bringing the needle up on the line and into the waiting loop of thread.

STEP 2

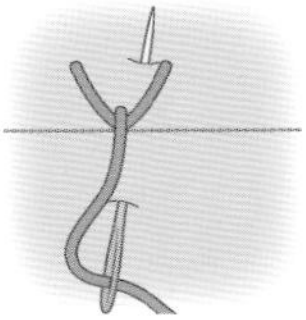

Take the needle into the fabric under the line and centrally under the V shape. Make a vertical quilting stitch upward, bringing the needle out above the line level with the two branches of the "V".

TIP

It is possible to elongate or shorten the securing stitch in the center of each V shape; however, there is not a lot of scope for altering the spacing between the stitches.

STEP 3

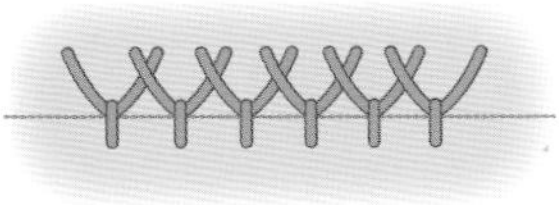

Make a second fly stitch and progress along the work, overlapping the branches of the fly stitches as you go. Secure the work with the thread outside and below the last V-shaped fly stitch.

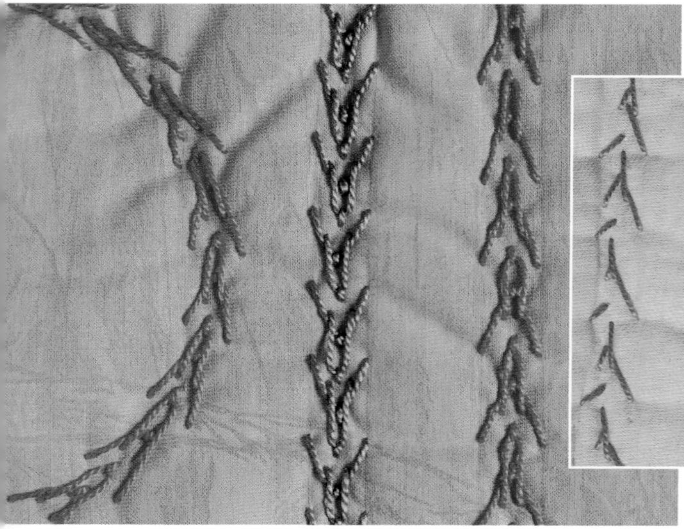

REVERSE OF WORK

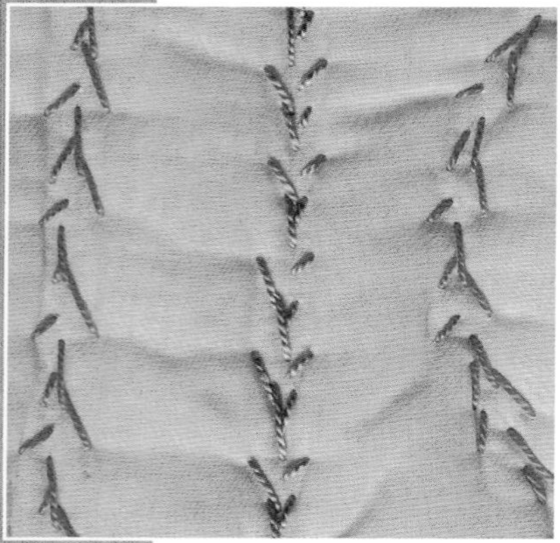

Double fly

The basic fly stitch has to be stitched at quite an exaggerated length to enable a second, narrower fly stitch to sit inside and overlap the first.

STEP 1

Bring the thread to the surface of the work and to the left-hand side of the quilting line. Working horizontally and down toward you, hold the thread so it loops down and around to the right. Take the needle in on the right of the line and make a quilting stitch through all layers, diagonally downward and inward toward the line, bringing the needle up on the line and into the waiting loop of thread.

STEP 2

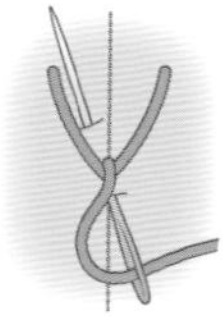

Take the needle in on the line, beneath the V-shaped stitch that you have produced, and bring it out inside the previous fly stitch.

STEP 3

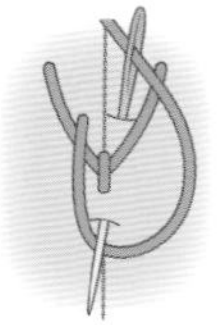

Hold thread down and to the right. Take the needle in on the right and stitch diagonally, bringing the needle up on the line, below the previous stitch and into a loop of thread.

STEP 4

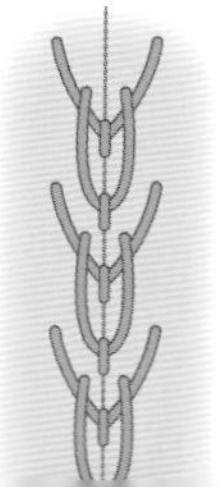

Repeat these combined stitches, working along the quilting line. Finish with a complete double fly stitch and secure the thread outside the last V-shaped stitch.

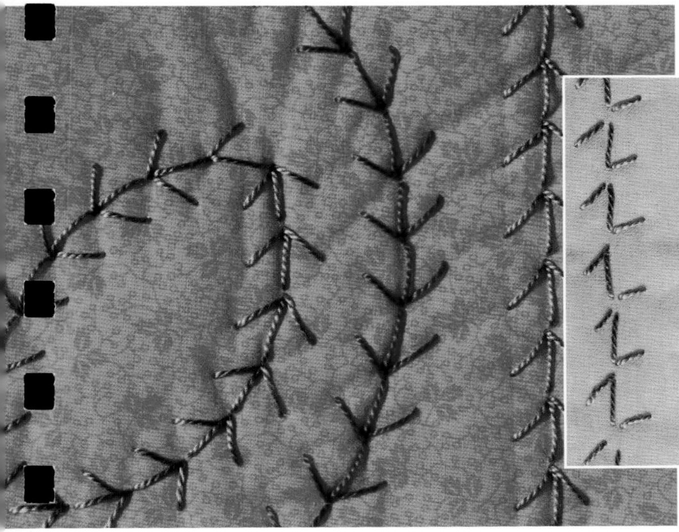

REVERSE OF WORK

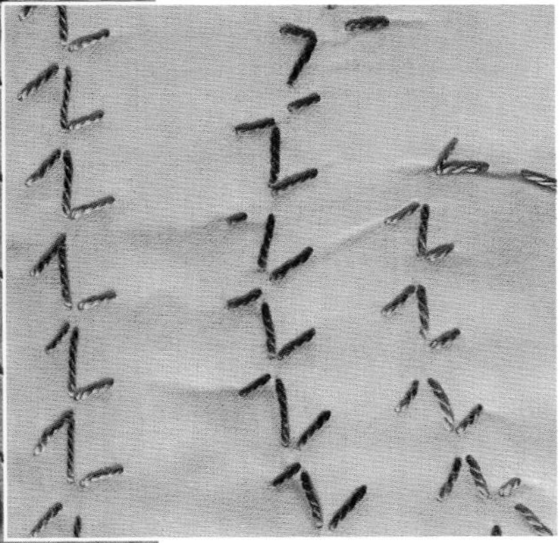

Fern stitch

This pretty line can be worked with all three points of the "fern" level with each other, or with the central point of the "fern" higher and the two outside stitches lower.

STEP 1

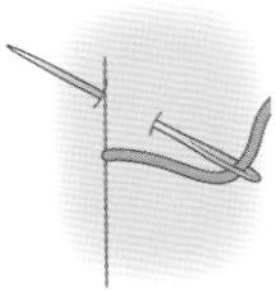

Bring the thread to the surface of the work, on the quilting line. Take the needle out further up and to the right of the line. Make a quilting stitch through all layers, diagonally upward (or horizontally for a level "fern"—see step 4 picture) and pull the thread through.

STEP 2

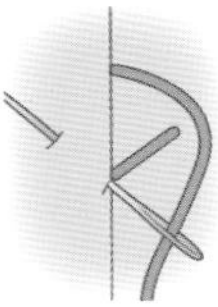

Take the needle in at the starting point again and stitch diagonally upward and out to the left.

STEP 3

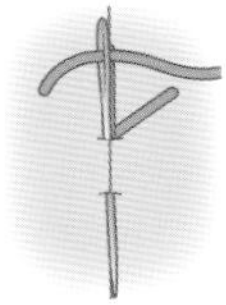

Take the needle in at the starting point once more and stitch down toward you, coming out on the line again, ready to start the next complete stitch.

STEP 4

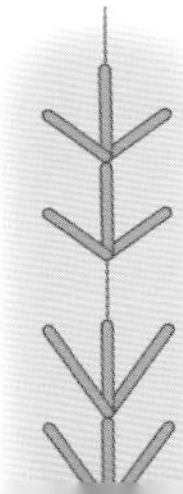

To make the tops of the stitches level, make a horizontal stitch at step 1, and a sharper diagonal stitch at step 2.

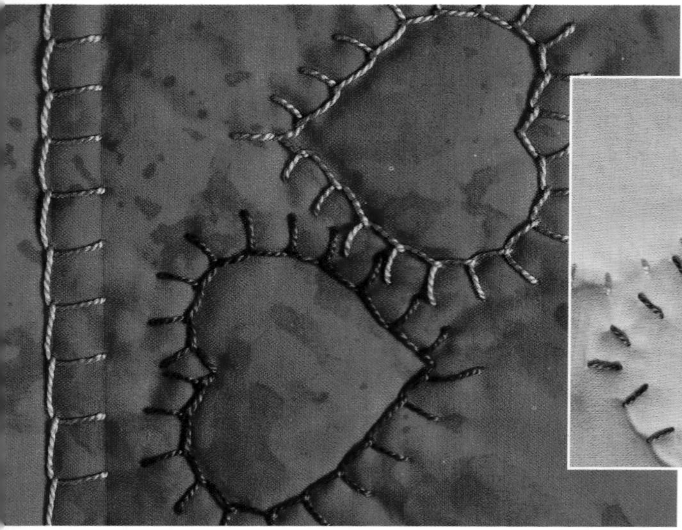

REVERSE OF WORK

Blanket stitch

This fast, simple stitch is often used for edging fabric and for overstitching raw edges of appliqué. It can add quite a lot of movement to a project.

STEP 1

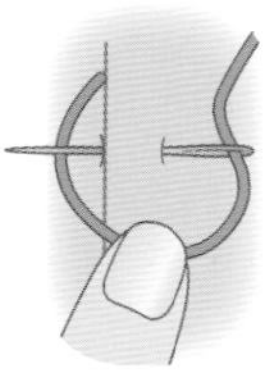

Bring the thread to the surface of the work at the start of the quilting line and on the line itself. Hold the thread down on the line and, working toward you, make a quilting stitch through all layers from right to left, bringing the needle back up on the line and into the waiting loop of thread.

STEP 2

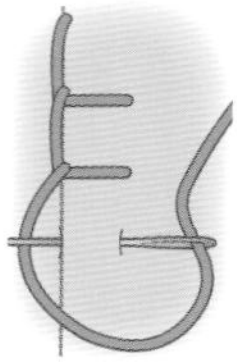

Hold the thread down on the line and stitch from right to left again.

STEP 3

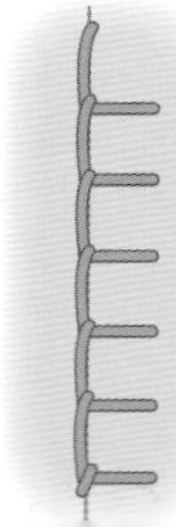

Work along the line in this way, spacing the stitches evenly. Finish the row of stitches with a small securing stitch outside the last blanket stitch, to hold the shape.

TIPS

- Don't make the stitch too wide as it will distort the fabric.
- If the stitches are too close together, they will resemble buttonhole stitch, which may be too dense.
- Curves and circles: Different effects can be achieved, depending on whether the "spikes" are on the outside or inside of the curve.

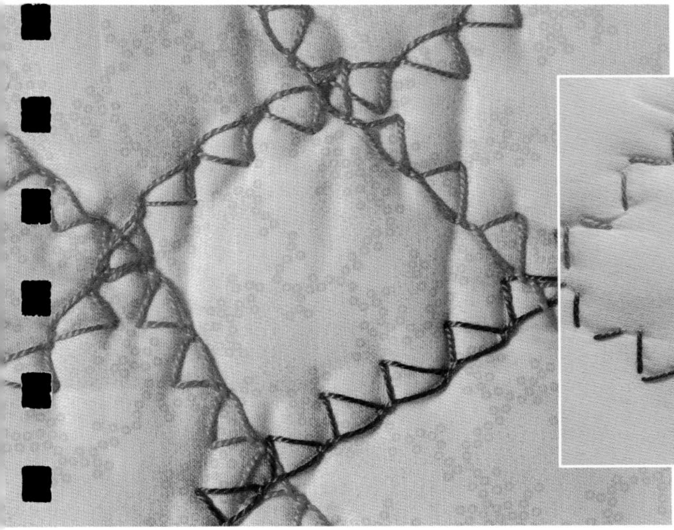

REVERSE OF WORK

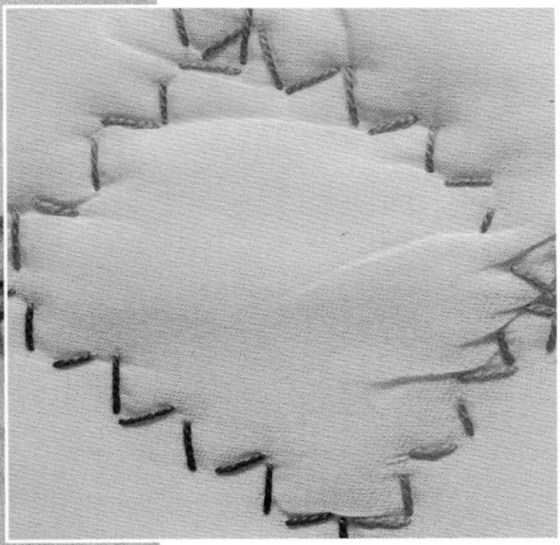

Closed blanket

It is easiest to work this stitch vertically down toward you, because of the angles required to form it. Vary the spaces within the triangles by making the diagonal stitches deeper or shallower.

STEP 1

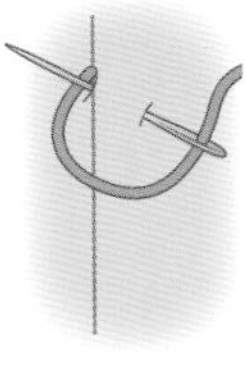

Bring the thread to the surface of the work at the start of the quilting line and on the line itself. Hold the thread down on the line and take the needle in to the right of the line, making a quilting stitch through all layers upward and diagonally in toward the line, bringing the needle out on the line again and into the waiting loop of thread. Pull the thread through.

STEP 2

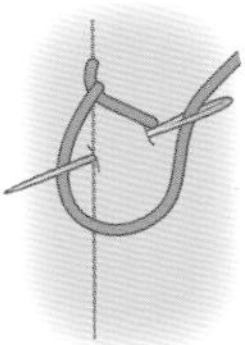

Hold the thread down on the line and take the needle in at the same place. Make a diagonal stitch downward and in toward the line, bringing the needle out on the line and into the waiting loop of thread. Pull the thread through.

STEP 3

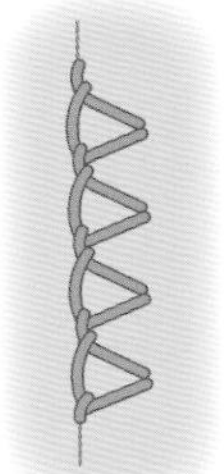

Hold the thread down on the line, take the needle in on the right of the line and stitch diagonally upward and in toward the line, bringing the needle into the waiting loop of thread but outside the previously formed triangle. Pull the thread through. Repeat step 2 to complete this second stitch. Continue working along the line and finish with a securing stitch outside the last triangle.

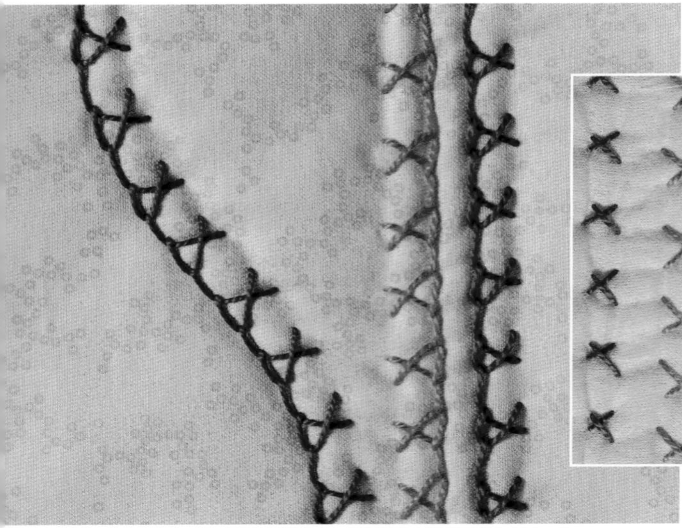

REVERSE OF WORK

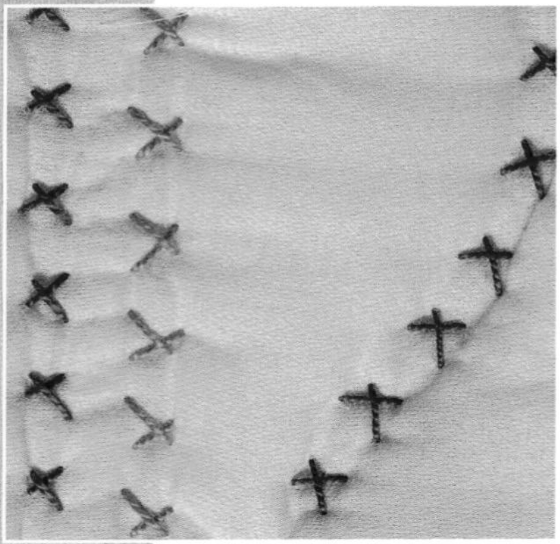

Crossed blanket

The two branches of each stitch overlap to create a cross on the surface of the work, separated by a bar stitch that can be elongated or reduced as desired.

STEP 1

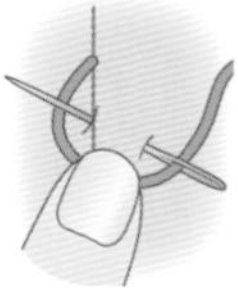

Bring the thread to the surface of the work, at the beginning of the quilting line. Working vertically and down toward you, hold the thread down on the line and looped around to the right. Make a quilting stitch through all layers, taking the needle in to the right of the line and stitching diagonally upward/backward along the line, bringing the needle out on the line and into the waiting loop of thread.

STEP 2

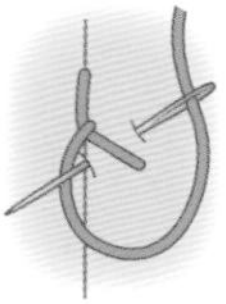

Holding the thread down on the line and looped around to the right again, take the needle back in on the right and about a stitch length above/away from the previous stitch. Make a diagonal quilting stitch downward/forward, bringing the needle up on the line and into the waiting loop of thread.

STEP 3

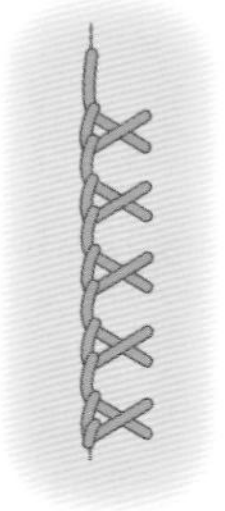

Repeat steps 1 and 2 to progress along the quilting line, spacing the individual stitches evenly. Finish the thread outside the "second" part of a stitch to secure the work.

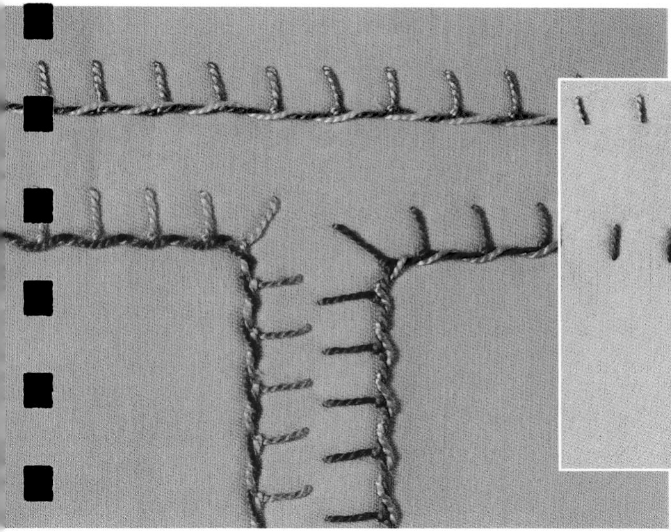

REVERSE OF WORK

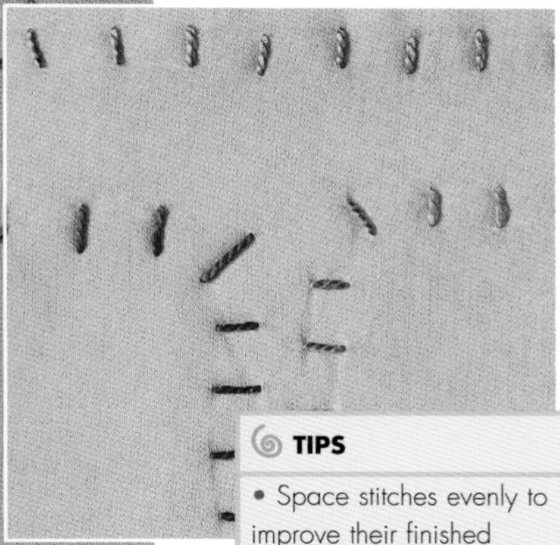

Whipped blanket

Whipping a row of blanket stitch adds a slightly raised effect to the lower edge of the stitch; you can make a feature of this by using a contrasting thread.

STEP 1

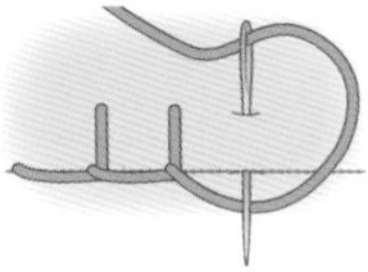

Bring the thread to the surface of the work, at the start of the quilting line and on the line itself. Work a row of blanket stitch (see page 104).

STEP 2

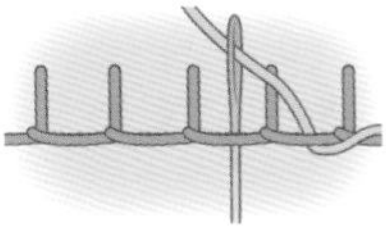

Bring the second or contrasting thread to the surface of the work at the beginning of the row of blanket stitch and at the same starting point. Pass the needle under each straight bar stitch in turn, in the same direction each time.

STEP 3

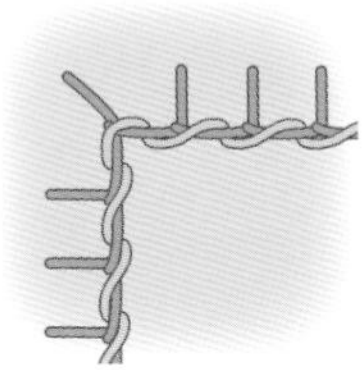

For corners, carry on in the same way—the whipping thread and stitches will fall into place.

TIPS

- Space stitches evenly to improve their finished appearance. The spaces between the stitches can be altered, as can the length of the "spikes."
- "Spikes" can be stitched on the inside or outside edge of a curve, circle, or corner.
- Pass the eye of the needle through first when whipping, or use a blunt tapestry needle.

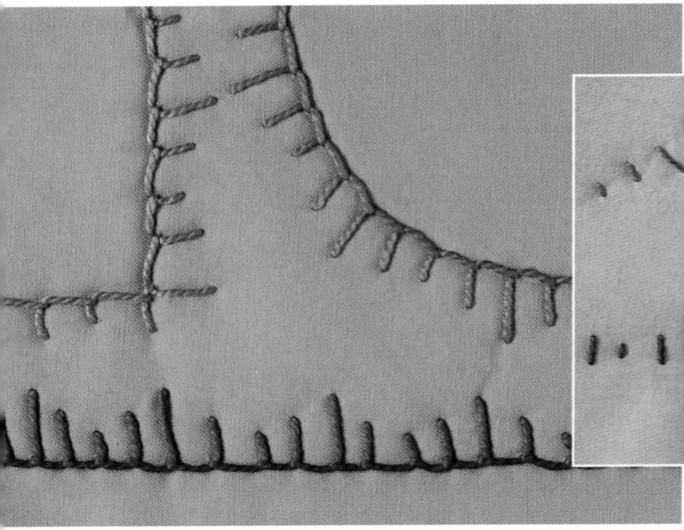

REVERSE OF WORK

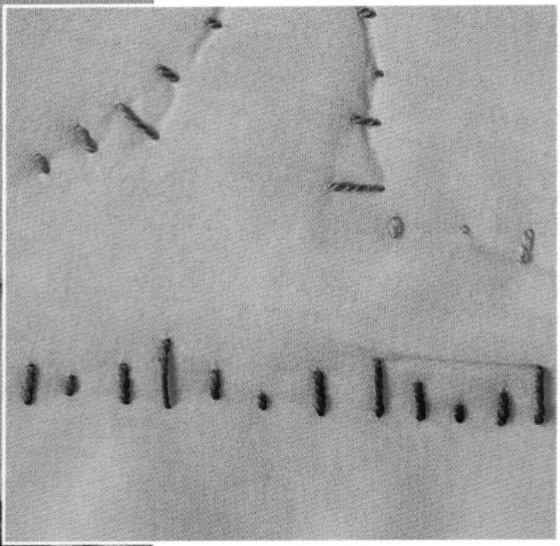

TIP

Don't make the longer stitches too wide because this will distort the fabric.

Long and short blanket

You can have a lot of fun with plain blanket stitch (see page 104) simply by altering the length and width of the stitches, or clustering the stitches together more closely.

STEP 1

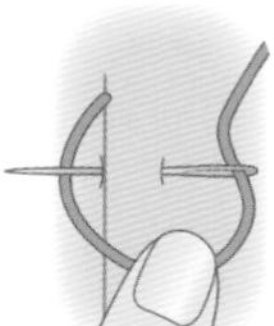

Bring the thread to the surface of the work, at the start of the quilting line and on the line itself. Hold the thread down on the line and take the needle into the fabric on the right of the quilting line. Make a stitch in toward the line and bring the needle up on the line into the waiting loop of thread. Pull the thread through.

STEP 2

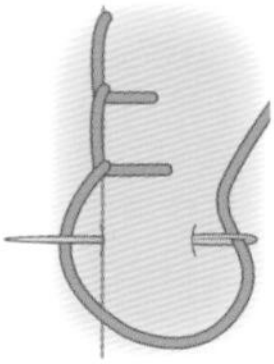

Repeat the stitch as above, but make the next stitch slightly wider, or shorter, according to how you would like your work to look.

STEP 3

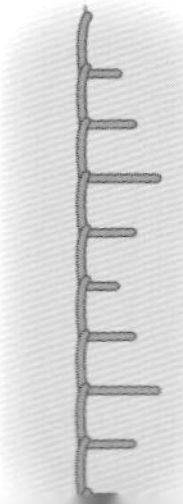

Carry on along the quilting line and finish with a small securing stitch outside the last blanket stitch to be sewn.

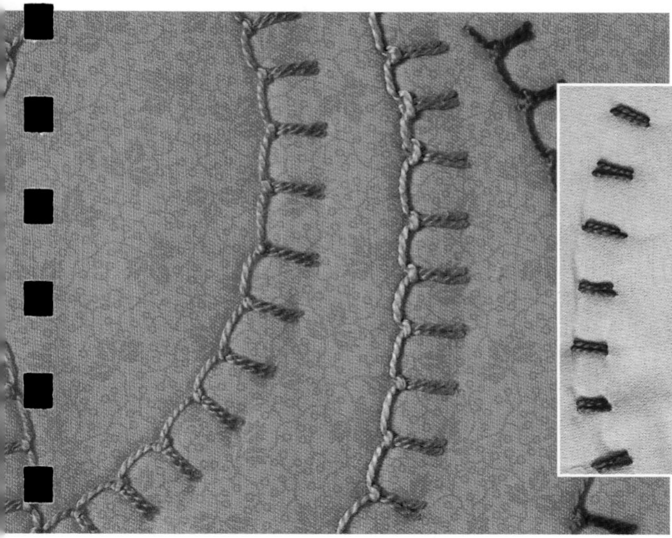

REVERSE OF WORK

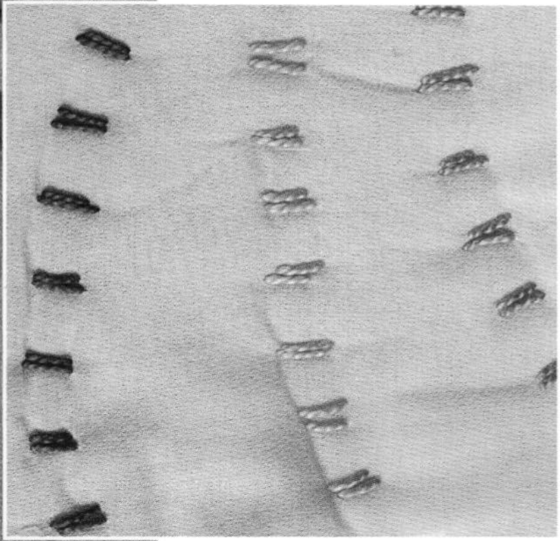

Up and down blanket

This has a heavier finished appearance than basic blanket stitch (see page 104). Two stitches sit close to each other and give a more raised effect at the stitch base.

STEP 1

Bring the thread to the surface of the work, at the start of your quilting line and on the line itself. Hold the thread so it is looped down and around to the right. Take the needle into the fabric above the line, make a quilting stitch downward, and bring the needle up on the line and into the waiting loop of thread. Pull the thread through.

STEP 2

Now hold thread upward and to the right. Take the needle in on the line, directly next to the point at which the thread last came out of the fabric. Make a quilting stitch upward, bringing the needle out level with the last stitch, directly alongside it and into the waiting loop of thread.

TIPS

- Ensure that the two stitches sit as close together as possible without using the same fabric entry point.
- It may take a little while to get used to turning the needle from one direction to the other, but a little practice will make perfect.

STEP 3

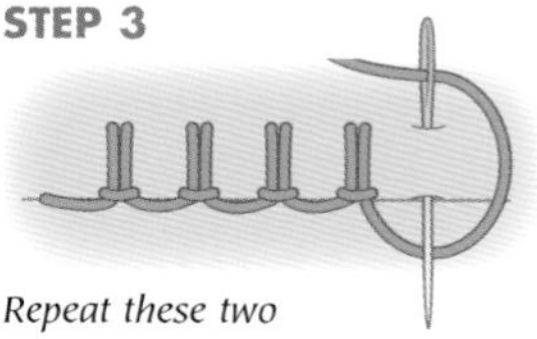

Repeat these two stages to work along the line. Finish with an upward stitch and a small securing stitch outside the last stitch.

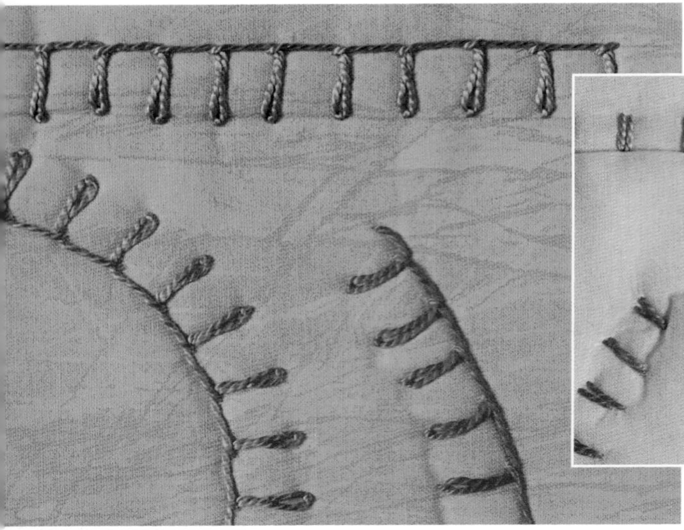

REVERSE OF WORK

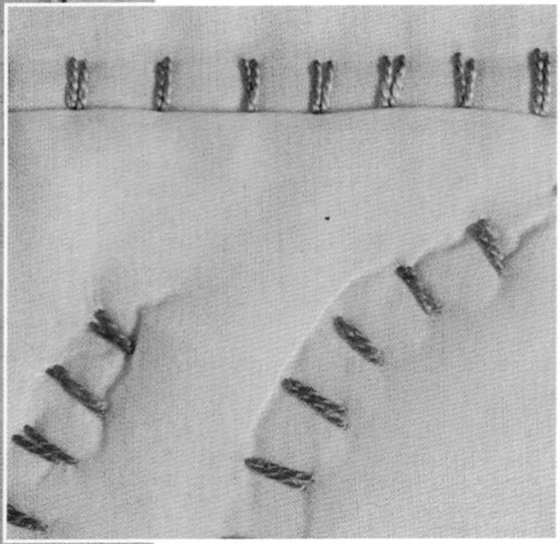

Basque stitch

One of the more unusual stitches used for quilting, originating in Spain, where it was traditionally worked with red thread on green fabric, or white thread on blue-green fabric.

STEP 1

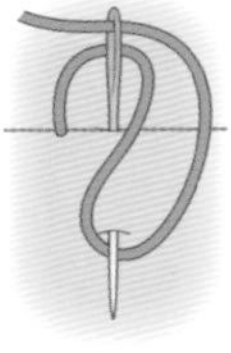

Bring the thread to the surface of the work, at the beginning of the quilting line. Working horizontally and from left to right, make a deep, vertical quilting stitch through all layers. Take the needle in on the line and bring it out below the line but, before the needle is pulled through, wrap the thread behind the eye of the needle from left to right, across the front of the needle from right to left, and around behind the pointed end of the needle from left to right. Hold this firmly while the needle and thread are both pulled through.

STEP 2

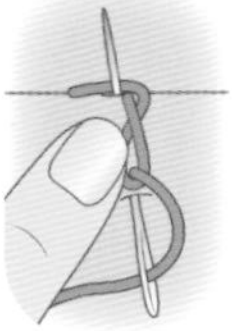

Keep your non-sewing thumb on this loop of thread while you make a second quilting stitch, vertically upward, taking the needle in below the stitched loop to secure it and back up to the quilting line, bringing the needle in to the left of the loop and below the bar of thread at the top.

STEP 3

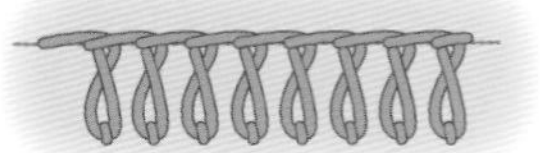

Repeat steps 1 and 2 to progress along the quilting line, finishing the thread after an upward vertical stitch and outside the last loop.

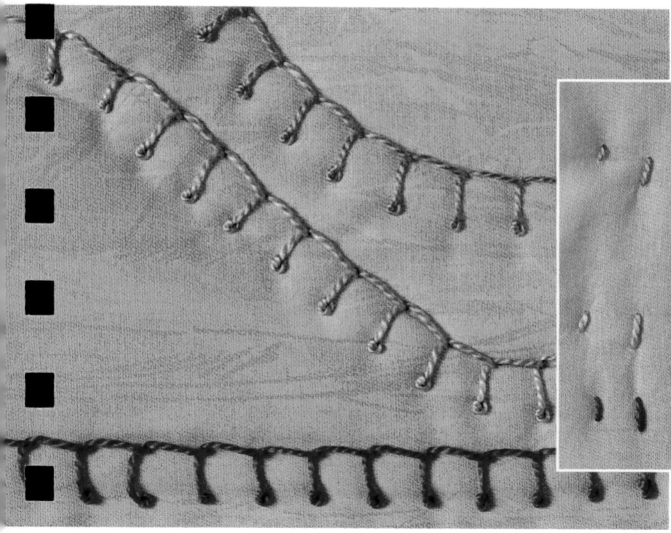

REVERSE OF WORK

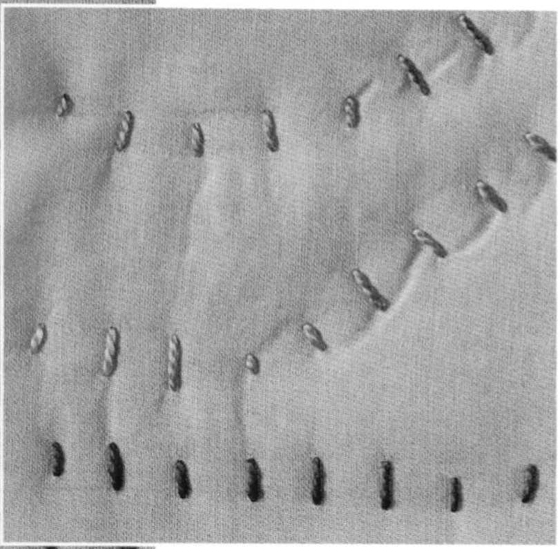

Knotted blanket

An extra twist is added to the thread to form a small, decorative and tactile knot, that sits on the surface of the work at the top of the "spikes" of the blanket stitch.

STEP 1

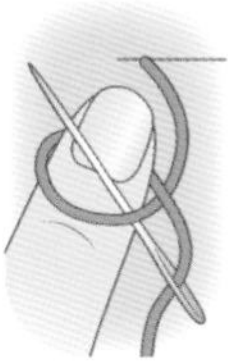

Bring the thread to the surface of the work, at the beginning of and above the quilting line. Wrap the thread around your non-sewing thumb (the one that is not holding the needle): Bring the thread around the right-hand side of the thumb, across the front to the left, around the back to the right and let it cross over itself. At this stage, take the needle upward and behind the thread passing over the front of your thumb.

STEP 2

In one movement, gently slip the twisted thread off your thumb and take the needle into the fabric above the line. Make a quilting stitch down toward the line, and bring the needle up on the line and into the waiting loop of thread. The twisted thread will form a knot at the top of the "spike."

STEP 3

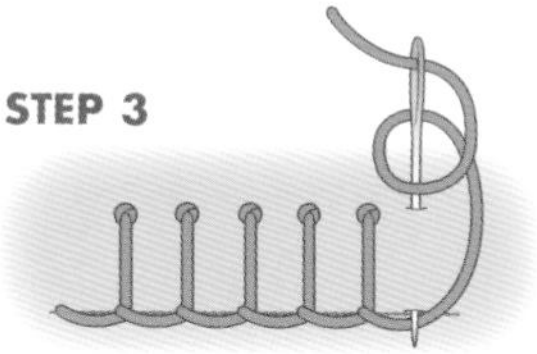

Repeat this along the quilting line; finish with a small securing stitch outside the last stitch on the quilting line.

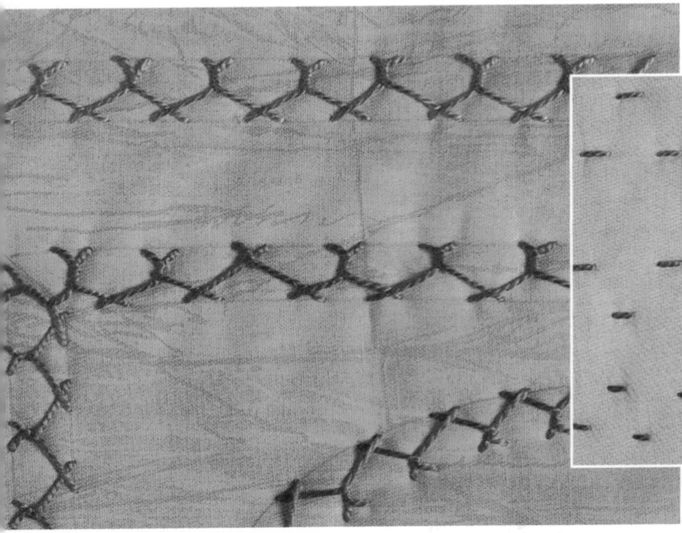

REVERSE OF WORK

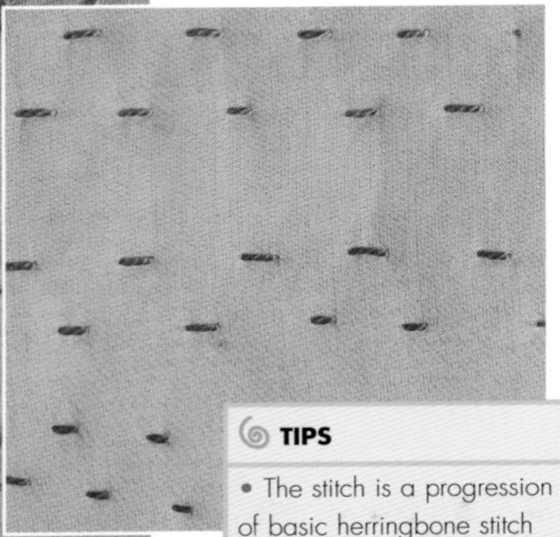

TIPS

- The stitch is a progression of basic herringbone stitch (see page 114), and you might like to practice this first.
- Different results can be achieved by elongating the thread and altering the spacing between stitches.

Breton stitch

This unusually twisted stitch gets its name from embroideries found in Brittany. It was characteristically sewn using a blue thread on white fabric, or white thread on blue fabric.

STEP 1

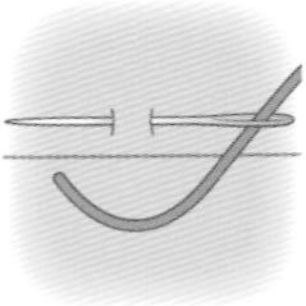

Bring the thread out below the quilting line (you will be working horizontally, from left to right). Make a horizontal quilting stitch through all layers, above the quilting line and working from right to left.

STEP 2

Pass the needle under the diagonal stitch you have created, from right to left and without catching up the fabric.

STEP 3

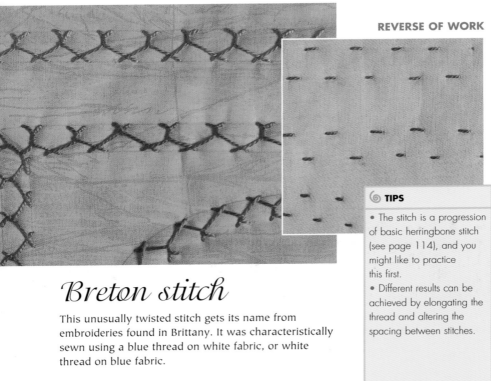

Make a horizontal quilting stitch below the line, working from right to left. Progress in this way, finishing the thread by taking it into the fabric where it would naturally go for the next stitch.

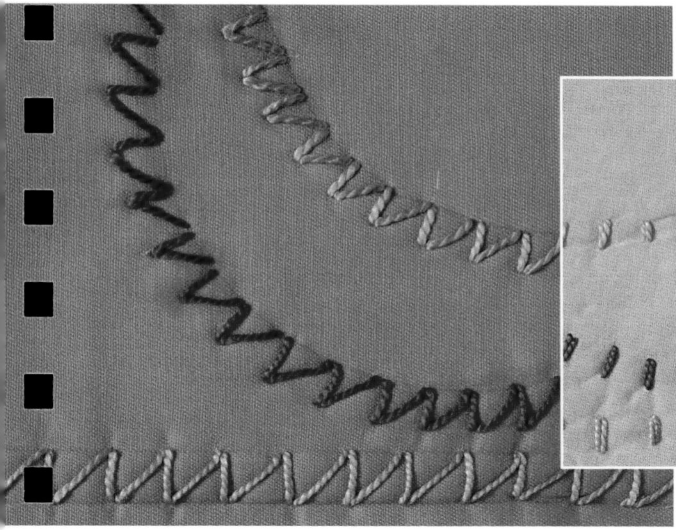

REVERSE OF WORK

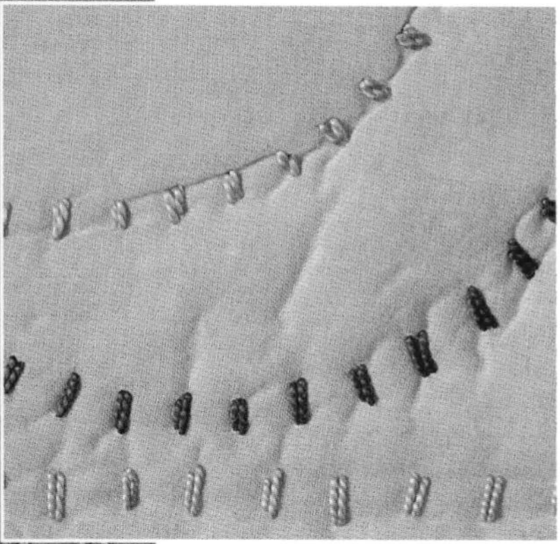

Glove stitch

Traditionally, this stitch was used in the making of fine leather gloves. Two stitches are taken into the same place with each repeat, so the back of the work looks heavier than some.

STEP 1

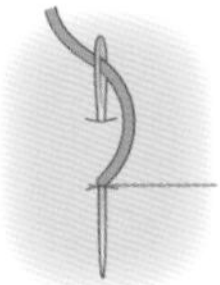

Bring the thread to the surface of the work, on the quilting line. Working horizontally, take the needle in above the line and make a vertical quilting stitch down toward you, bringing the needle out on the line at the original starting point.

STEP 2

Move along the line and take the needle in above the quilting line once more, stitching vertically and down toward you, bringing the needle up on the line.

STEP 3

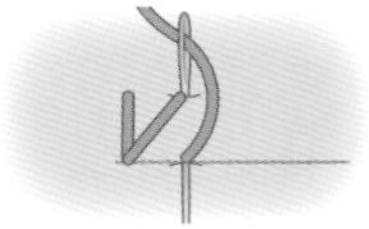

Take the needle in above the line at the same point that it went into previously. Make a vertical quilting stitch down toward you, bringing the needle out on the line at the same point used previously.

STEP 4

Move along the line and make the next vertical quilting stitch. Continue in this way along the quilting line.

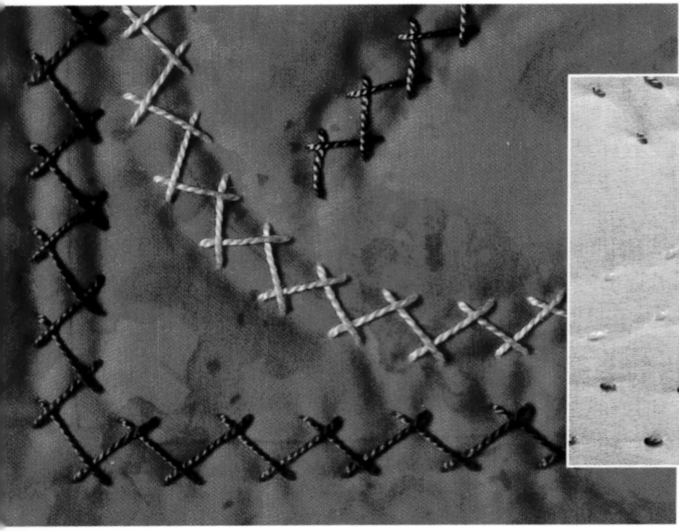

REVERSE OF WORK

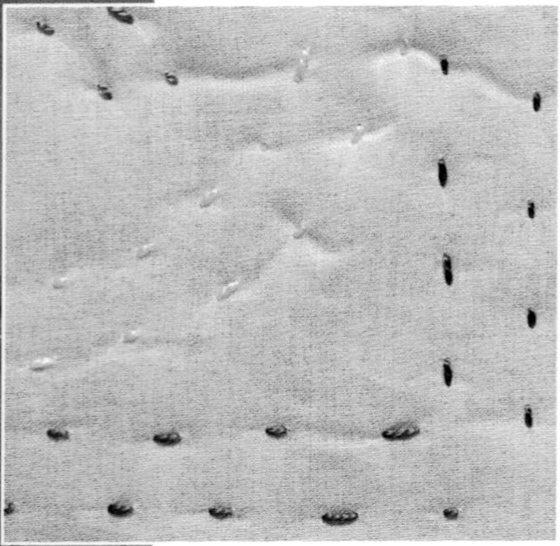

Herringbone stitch

You can have fun altering the appearance of this stitch by either widening the stitch above and below the line, or elongating or shortening it along the line.

STEP 1

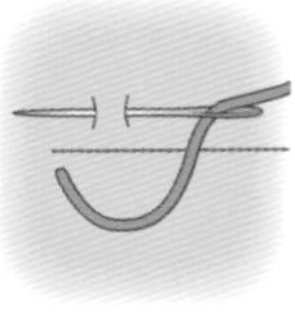

Bring the thread to the surface of the work, below the quilting line. Move forward along the quilting line in the direction you want the sewing to go. Take a small, horizontal quilting stitch through all layers, above the line, working backward.

STEP 2

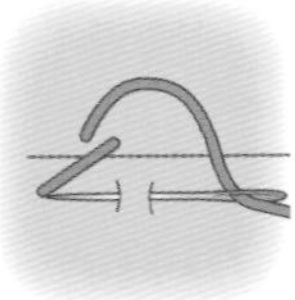

Move forward along the line again. Take a small, horizontal quilting stitch under the line, working backward.

STEP 3

Repeat steps 1 and 2 to complete the row.

STEP 4

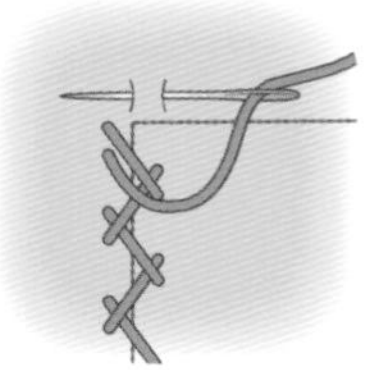

To take the herringbone neatly around a corner, make two stitches outside the corner of the quilting line and then carry on as before.

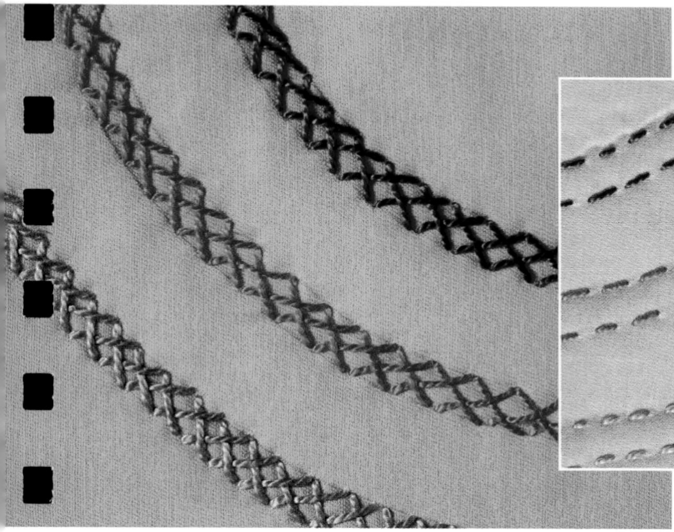

REVERSE OF WORK

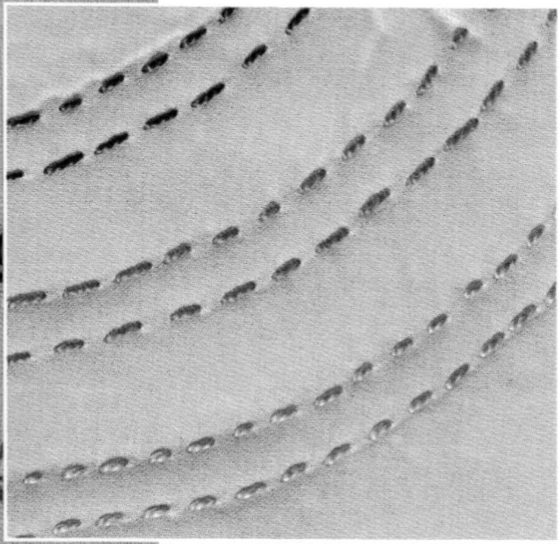

Closed herringbone

Closed herringbone stitch is useful when a definite, fairly heavy line of stitching is required for added emphasis.

STEP 1

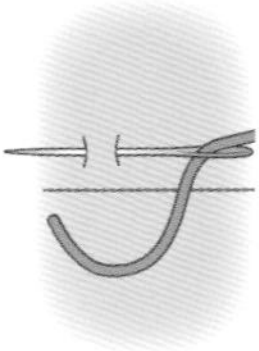

Bring the thread to the surface of the work, above the quilting line. Move forward in the direction you want the sewing to go. Take a small, horizontal quilting stitch through all layers, above the line, working backward.

STEP 2

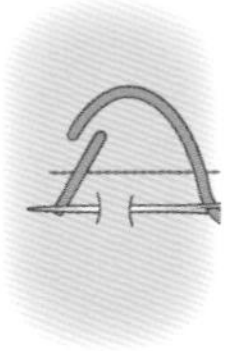

Move forward along the line again. Take a small, horizontal quilting stitch under the line, working backward.

STEP 3

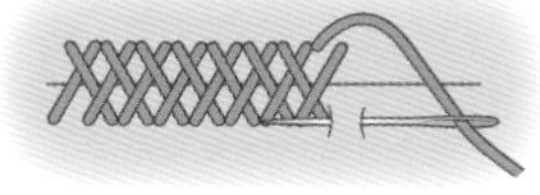

Repeat steps 1 and 2, making sure that each stitch touches the previous stitch, both above the line and below it.

TIPS

- This stitch can be worked wider, but if taken too wide it will distort the fabric.
- The spacing of the stitch will depend on the length of the quilting stitch that is taken above and below the quilting line.

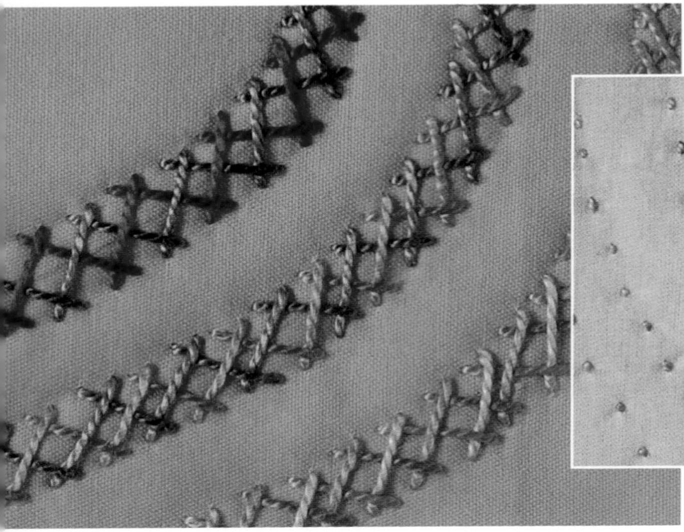

REVERSE OF WORK

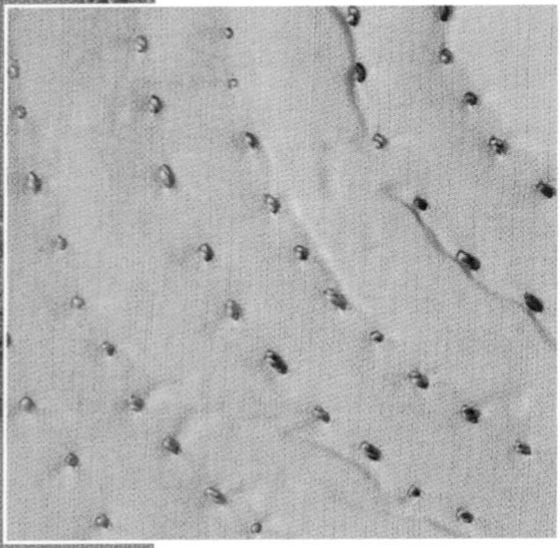

Double herringbone

Work a row of double herringbone stitch in areas where more definition is required. The spacing can be varied, as can the depth and width of the stitches.

STEP 1

Bring the thread to the surface of the work, below the quilting line, and work a row of basic herringbone stitch (see page 114).

STEP 2

Bring the second or contrasting thread out at the beginning of the quilting line, but this time start above the quilting line.

STEP 3

Move along the row and make a quilting stitch in a backward direction in the first space provided by the previously sewn herringbone stitches.

STEP 4

Pass the needle under the next sloping thread (do not catch the fabric) before taking the next quilting stitch above the line, working backward and between the next two base herringbone stitches. Carry on in this way, working in the spaces provided by the row of herringbone stitch and only passing the needle under a thread on its way upward (the needle does not go through the fabric).

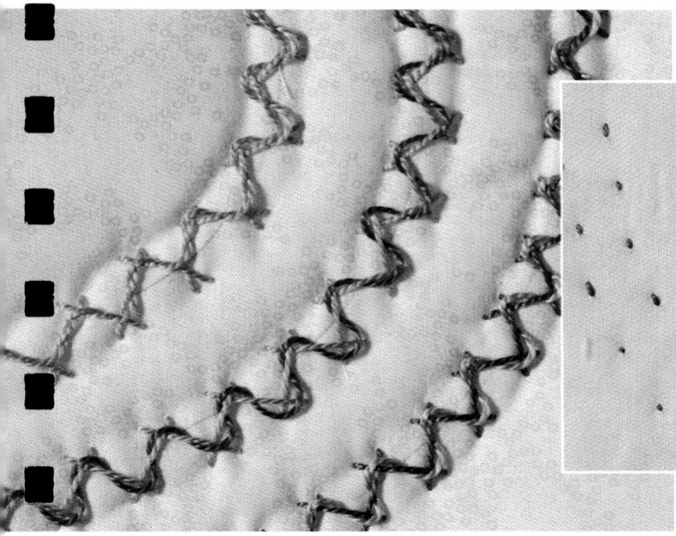

REVERSE OF WORK

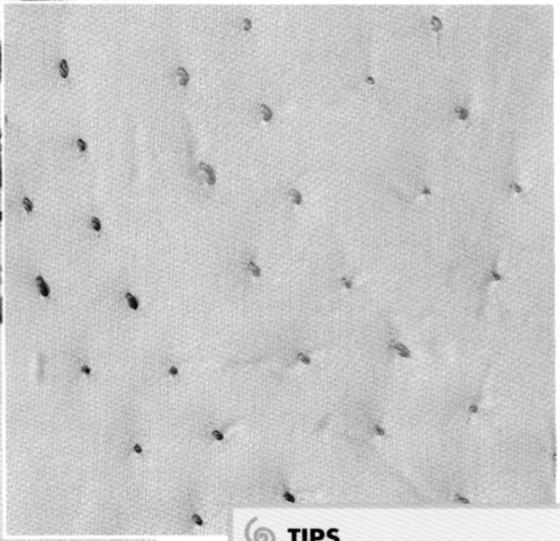

TIPS

- Don't pull the second thread too tightly or it will distort the line of herringbone stitch.
- Pass the eye of the needle through first when threading, or use a blunt tapestry needle.

Threaded herringbone

When the basic herringbone stitch needs a little more texture and interest, it can be threaded through with a contrasting thread for added emphasis.

STEP 1

Bring the thread to the surface of the work, below the quilting line, and work a row of basic herringbone stitch (see page 114).

STEP 2

Bring the second or contrasting thread out at the beginning of the quilting line, at the same point that the original herringbone stitch thread began. Pass the needle under the first sloping stitch, from right to left.

STEP 3

Pass the needle under the next sloping stitch, from right to left. Continue in this way, working along the base row of herringbone stitch. Finish the second or contrasting thread in the same place that you finished the thread of the herringbone stitch.

REVERSE OF WORK

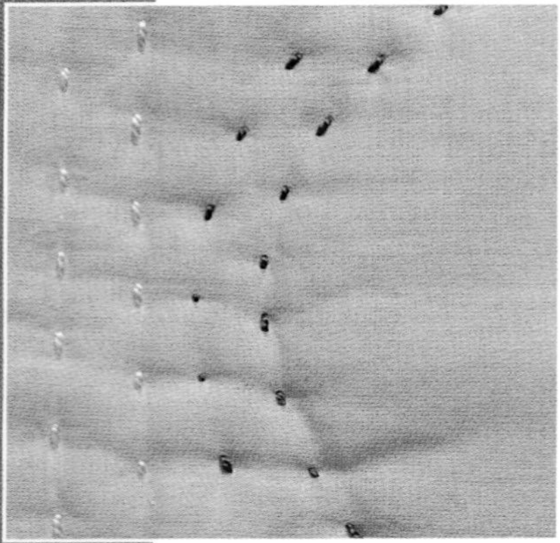

Laced herringbone

An extremely decorative stitch. The tight loops are less likely to snag than other types of lacing, so it's suitable for items frequently handled, such as a bed quilt.

STEP 1

Work a row of herringbone stitch (see page 114) and turn upside down. Bring out the second thread at the beginning of the herringbone row. Starting below the line, work in a counterclockwise direction around the crisscross part of the base thread: Pass the needle from left to right under the first part of the base thread, continue over and under the base thread.

STEP 2

Now take the needle over the next base thread and back under the second thread; over the next sloping thread base thread; under the next base threads. Then move along to the next crisscross of base thread above the line.

STEP 3

Work in a counterclockwise way around this. Go under, over, under, and over the base threads; under the contrast thread, as shown; over, under, over, and under the base threads; over the contrast thread and back down to the next crisscross section below the line.

STEP 4

Go back down to the next crisscross section below the line, and repeat, as shown.

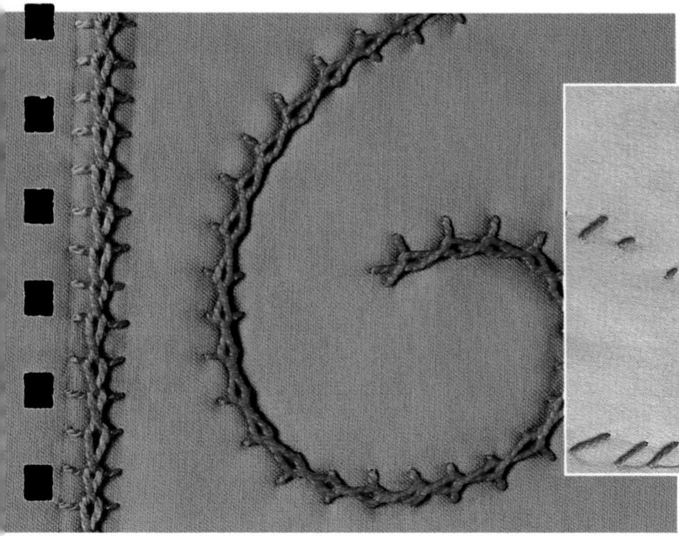

REVERSE OF WORK

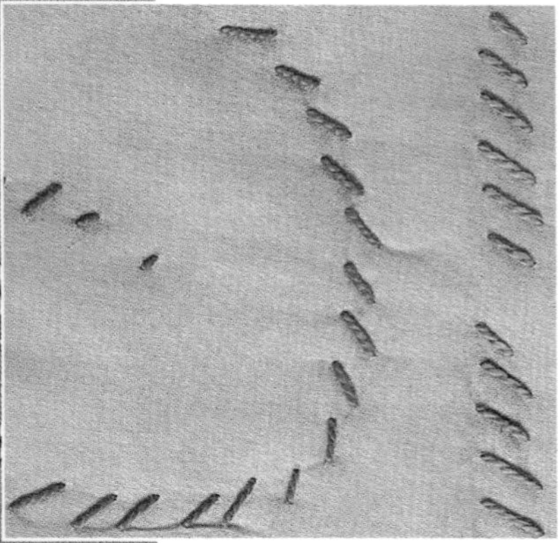

Vandyke stitch

Vandyke stitch is attractive and deceptively simple. It has a raised, central chain effect and this will be more pronounced if a thicker thread is used.

STEP 1

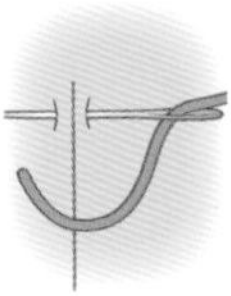

Bring the thread out on the left of the quilting line and a little way down from your starting point. Take the needle back up to the beginning of the quilting line and make a small, horizontal quilting stitch.

STEP 2

Take the needle in on the right of the line, level with where the thread came out on the left of the line, and make a quilting stitch through all layers, downward and diagonally across the line, back to the left-hand side.

STEP 3

Pass the needle behind the two crossed threads that have appeared and pull the thread through.

STEP 4

Repeat steps 2 and 3, finishing with a step 2 stitch.

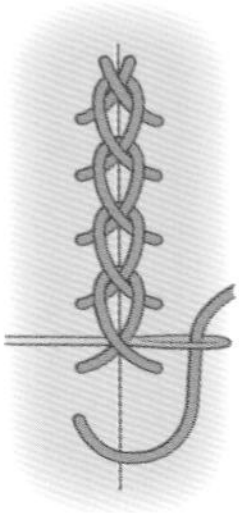

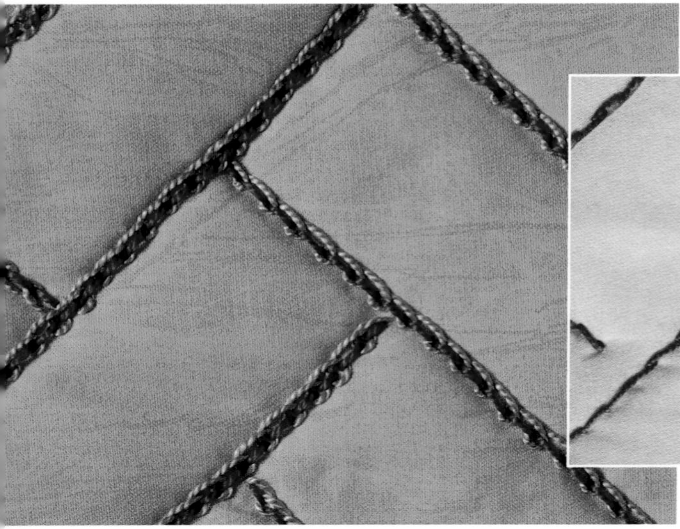

REVERSE OF WORK

Pekinese stitch

An attractive and ornamental stitch with a slightly raised appearance, Pekinese stitch gives the impression of a decorative braid sitting on the surface of the work.

STEP 1

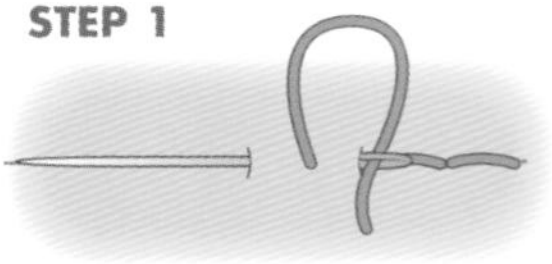

Bring the thread to the surface of the work, at the beginning of the quilting line. Work a foundation row of basic backstitch (see page 71).

STEP 2

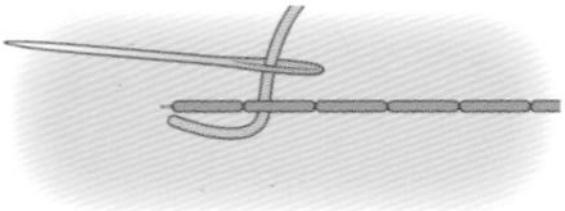

Bring the second or contrasting thread up at one end of the quilting line, but this time slightly below the line itself. Pass the needle upward and underneath the second stitch along in the foundation row.

STEP 3

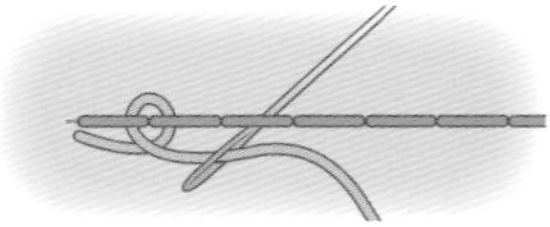

Return along the foundation row and pass the needle down behind the first stitch of the foundation row, bringing the needle in front of the contrast thread sitting below it.

STEP 4

Move along two stitches on the foundation row and repeat steps 2 and 3. You are moving two foundation stitches forward followed by one foundation stitch back each time.

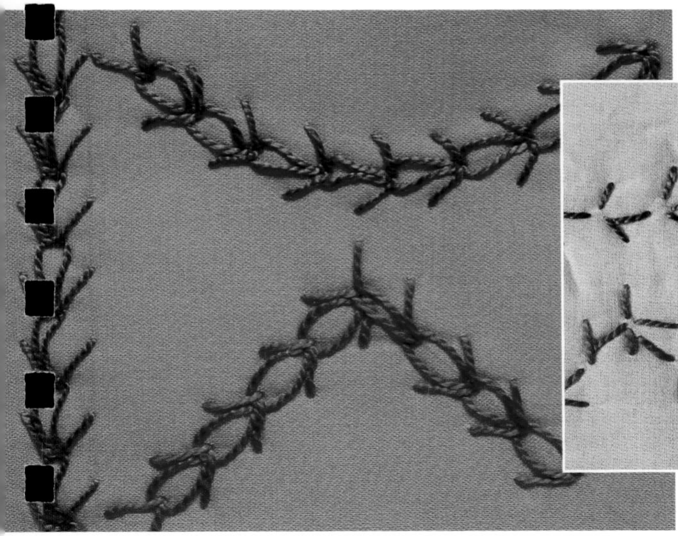

REVERSE OF WORK

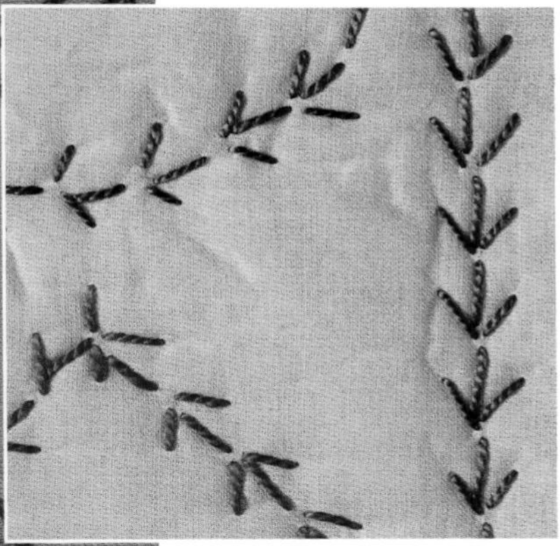

Wheatear stitch

This stitch looks similar to an ear of corn. It is constructed from a mixture of quilting stitches and looping stitches.

STEP 1

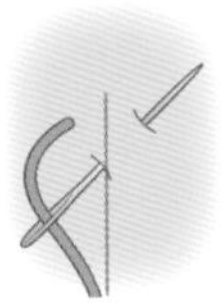

Bring the thread to the surface of the work, on the left of the quilting line. Take the needle into the fabric slightly further down the line and on the line itself. Make a quilting stitch through all the layers, diagonally to the right and upward.

STEP 2

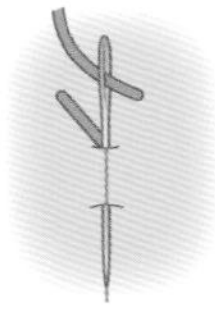

Take the needle back into the fabric, at the same point where the thread last went in, and make a quilting stitch down toward you, bringing the needle out on the line.

STEP 3

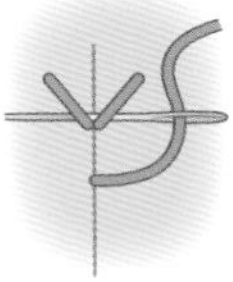

Pass the needle from right to left behind the two stitches of thread that have now appeared.

STEP 4

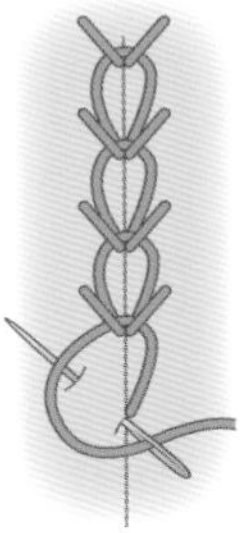

Take the needle back in on the line, at the same point where the thread last came out, and make a quilting stitch diagonally upward and out to the left to start again. For subsequent stitches, when you pass the needle behind the two outer "legs" of the previous stitch, bring the needle in front of the central loop at the same time—this will help the stitch to lie flat on the surface of the fabric.

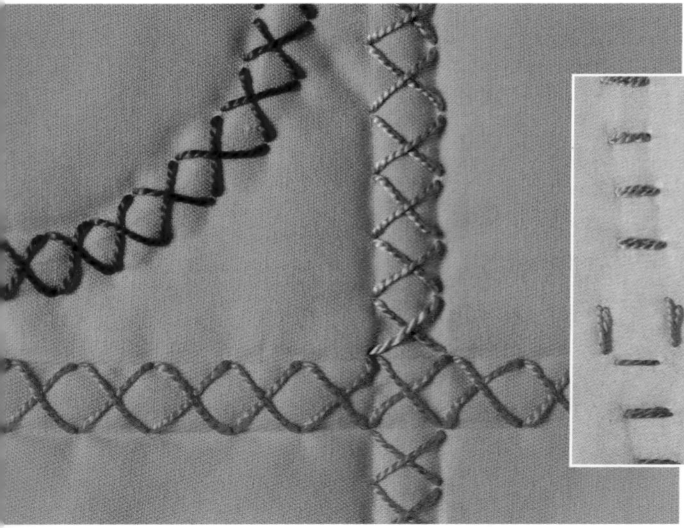

REVERSE OF WORK

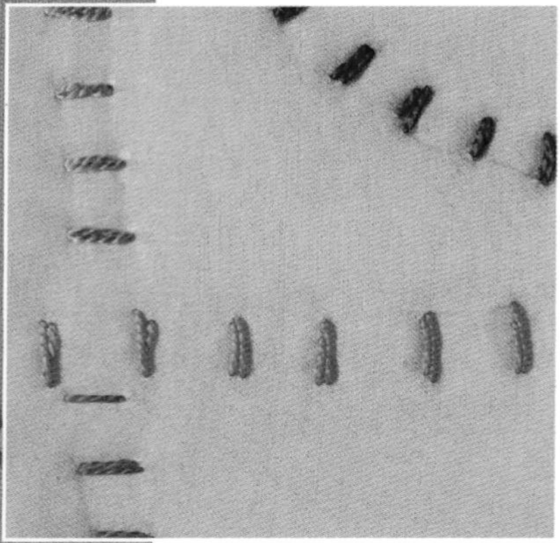

Cross stitch

Cross stitch is probably one of the oldest and most recognizable of embroidery stitches, and one not readily associated with quilting. There are many alternative ways to stitch it.

STEP 1

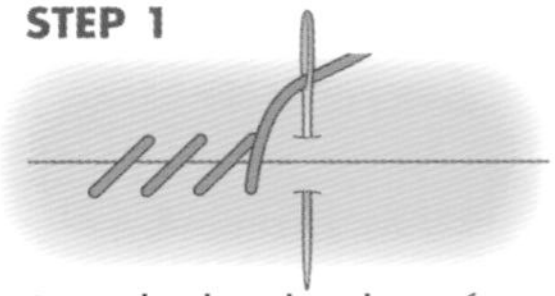

Bring the thread to the surface of the work, just below the quilting line. Moving forward along the line, take the needle in above the line, make a vertical quilting stitch through all the layers, and bring the needle out below the line.

STEP 2

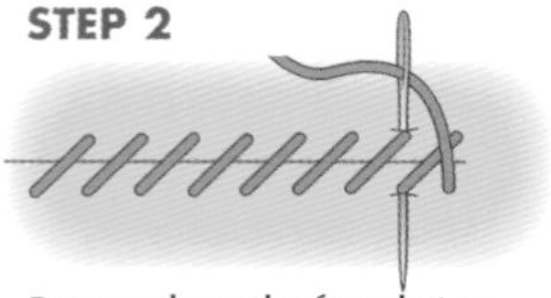

Return along the foundation row of diagonal stitches to complete the crosses, working in the opposite direction, but still taking a vertical quilting stitch, using the previous exit and entry points for the thread as a guideline.

TIPS

- This method maintains a neat appearance on the back of the project.
- It is a good method for closely woven fabric, where you do not have the benefit of an open weave to guide the length and width of the stitches.

STEP 3

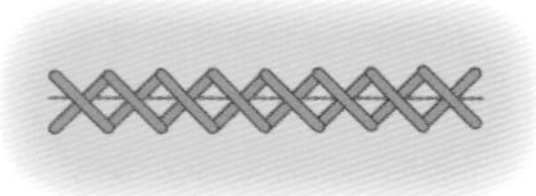

Continue working along the row until you have covered all the foundation row and changed the diagonal stitches to cross stitches.

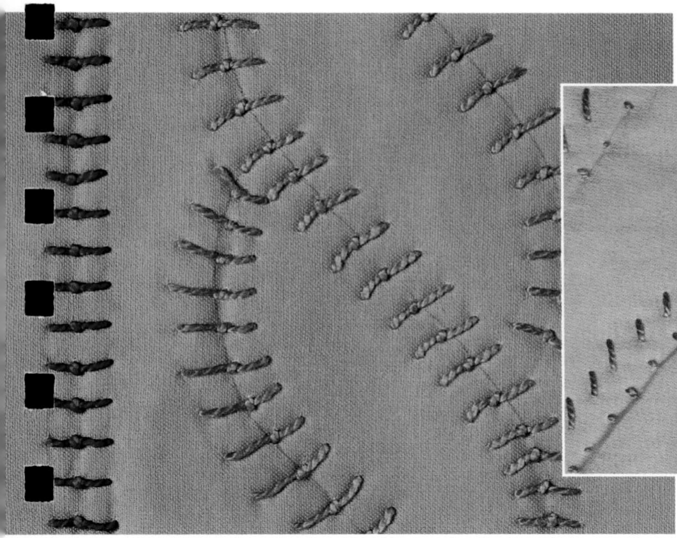

REVERSE OF WORK

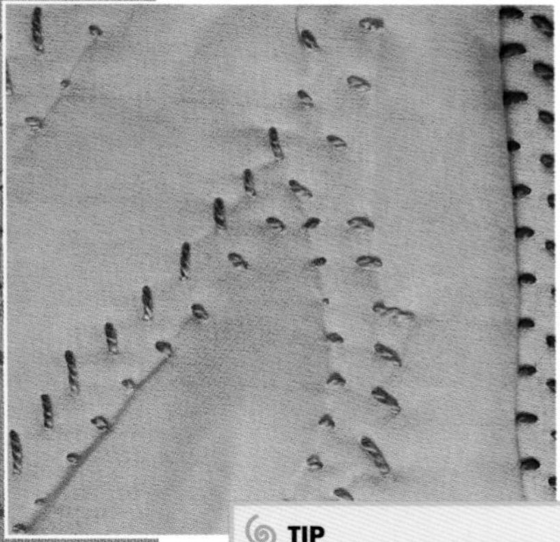

Romanian stitch

Traditionally, this stitch is worked very closely, providing a dense appearance. Here it is worked evenly spaced to make it more suitable for quilting projects.

TIP

You may find it easier to sew this stitch if you have previously practiced fly stitch (see page 99).

STEP 1

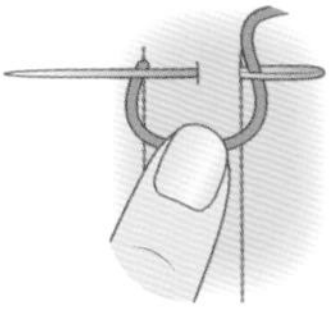

Bring the thread to the surface of the work, to the left of the quilting line. Holding the thread down and around to the right, take the needle into the fabric on the right-hand side of the quilting line, level with where the thread began on the left, and make a quilting stitch horizontally, bringing the needle up in the center and above the waiting thread.

STEP 2

Now take the needle in, below the waiting thread, to secure it. Make a diagonal stitch downward and out to the left, bringing the needle up level with your original starting point.

STEP 3

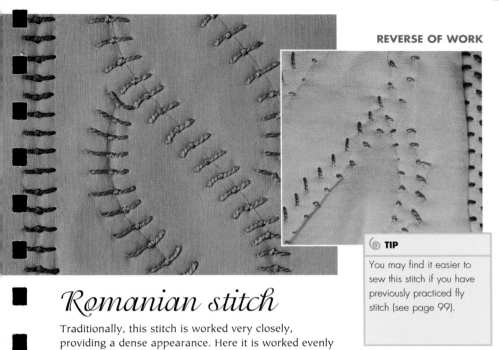

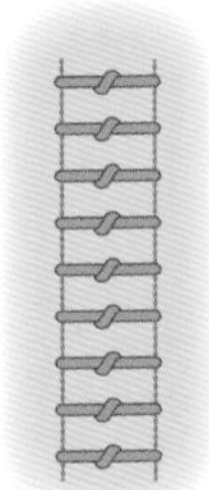

Hold the thread down and around to the right, take the needle in on the right-hand side and bring it up in the center again, above the waiting thread. Repeat this and step 2 to progress along the quilting line. Finish with a small securing stitch in the center.

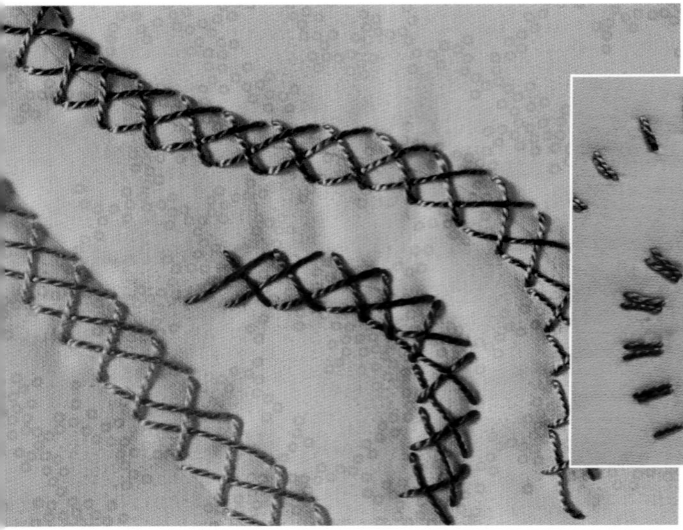

REVERSE OF WORK

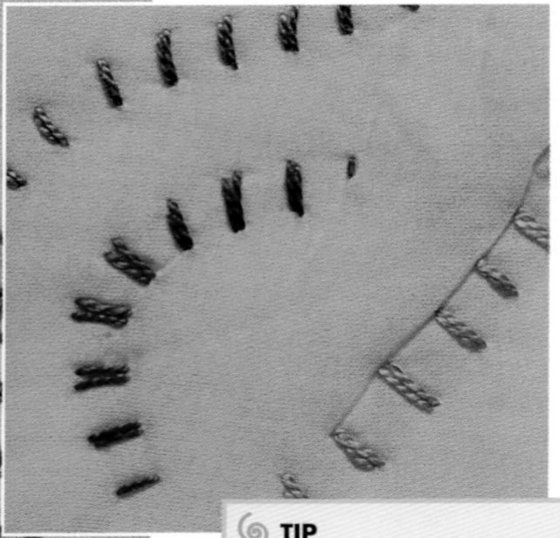

TIP

Don't overemphasize the longer stitch—if you are making a bed quilt, an overlong stitch may snag and pull.

Long-arm cross

Often to be found on counted thread work, this stitch is equally useful and easy to sew on closely woven fabric for a quilting pattern.

STEP 1

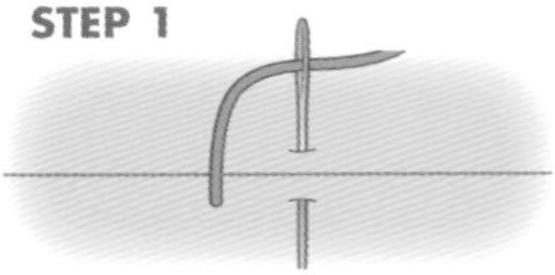

Bring the thread to the surface of the work, below the quilting line. Move forward along the line (approximately twice the length of the required shorter stitch). Take the needle into the fabric above the line, and make a vertical quilting stitch down toward you through all the layers, bringing the needle out below the line.

STEP 2

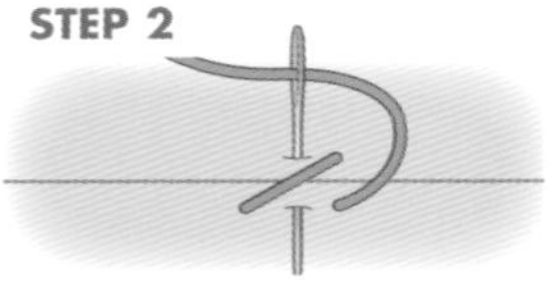

Bring the needle halfway back along this first stitch, take it in above the line (level with the top of the previous stitch) and, making a vertical quilting stitch, bring the needle out below the line (level with the bottom of the previous stitch).

STEP 3

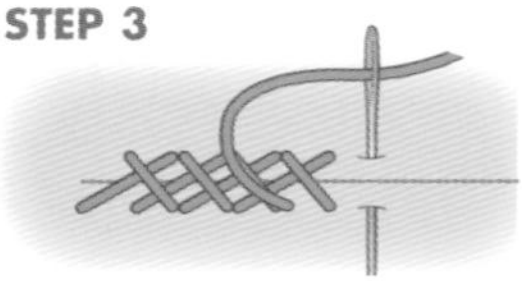

Move forward along the line, twice the length of the shorter stitch, and make a vertical stitch down toward you again. Repeat steps 2, and 3 and continue working along the quilting line, balancing the spacing of the stitches as evenly as possible. (You will need to adjust the spacing when working this stitch on a curve.)

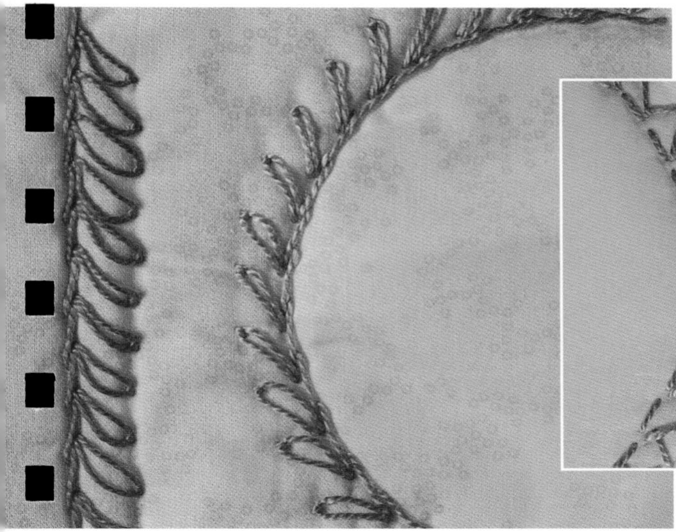

REVERSE OF WORK

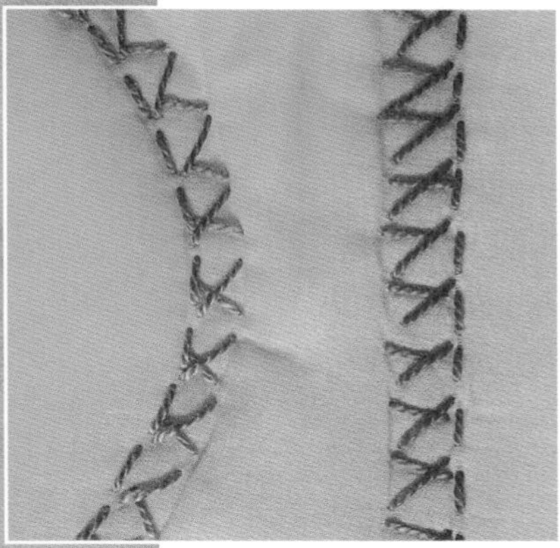

Petal stitch

The diagonal loops of this stitch give the impression of flower petals blowing in the breeze. It is most effective when used on the outer edge of a curved design.

STEP 1

Bring the thread to the surface of the work, a little way forward along the quilting line. Hold the thread above the work, take the needle back to the beginning of the quilting line and make a short quilting stitch through all the layers, following the line and bringing the needle out underneath the waiting thread.

STEP 2

Hold the thread around to the left to form a loop. Take the needle in on the line, underneath the stitch and at the point where the thread last came out of the fabric. Make a quilting stitch diagonally over to the left, bringing the needle out into the waiting loop of thread.

STEP 3

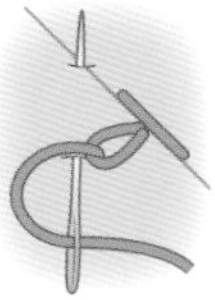

Take the needle in under the loop of thread and stitch diagonally upward and to the left, bringing the needle out on the line and at a length of two stitches away from the previous stitch.

STEP 4

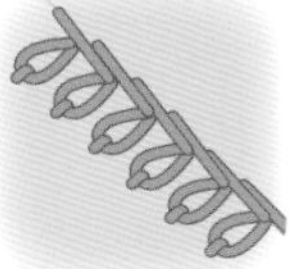

Repeat step 1, taking the needle in at the top of the last loop and below the bar stitch sitting on the line.

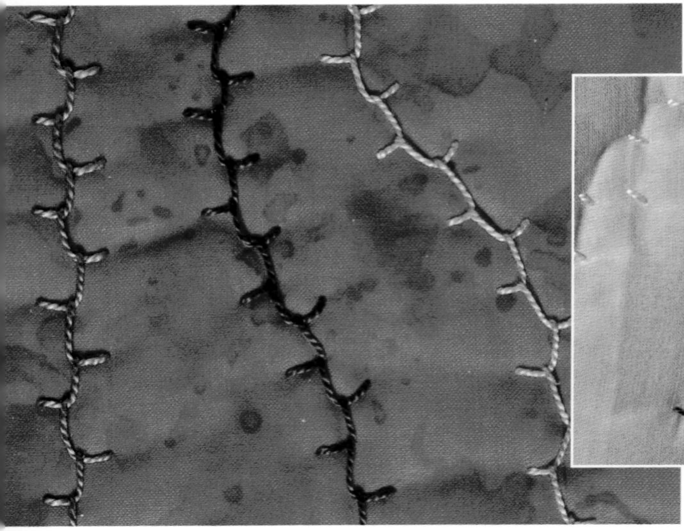

REVERSE OF WORK

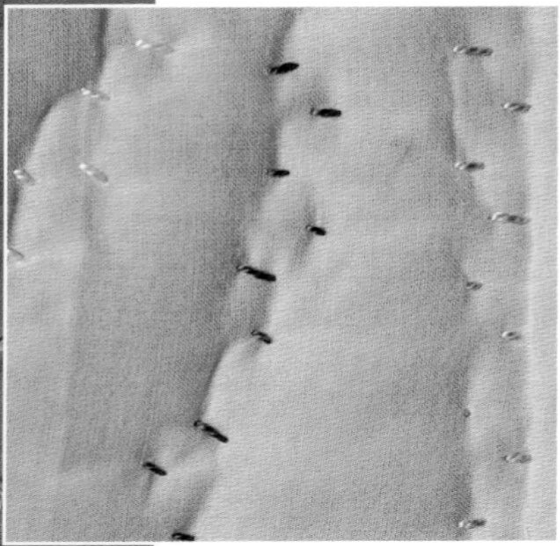

Open Cretan

Open Cretan stitch is not usually associated with work on closely woven fabric, but it makes an interesting quilting stitch—a slight variation on herringbone stitch (see page 114).

TIPS

- Because of the two angles (upward and downward) required for the needle, and the need to loop the thread, this stitch is better worked horizontally.
- Use the thumb of your non-sewing hand to place the thread ready for the next stitch.

STEP 1

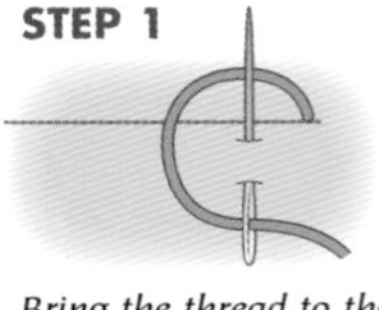

Bring the thread to the surface of the work, at the beginning of the quilting line. Hold the thread over to the left and downward. Make a small, upwardly vertical quilting stitch through all layers, below the quilting line and into the waiting loop of thread.

STEP 2

Hold the thread to the left and upward. Make a small, downwardly vertical quilting stitch, above the quilting line and into the waiting loop of thread.

STEP 3

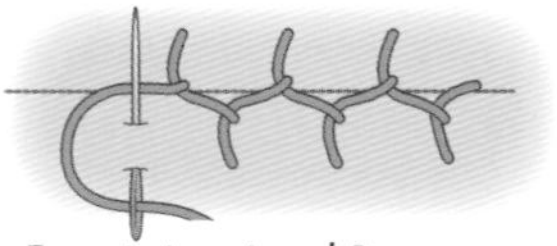

Repeat steps 1 and 2 as you progress along the quilting line from right to left.

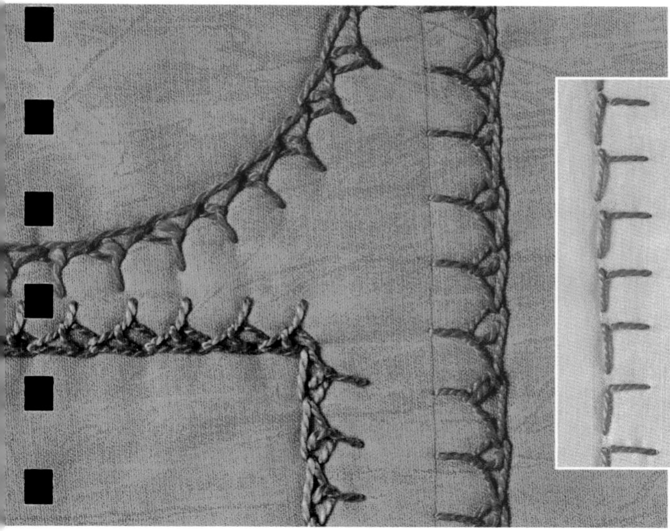

REVERSE OF WORK

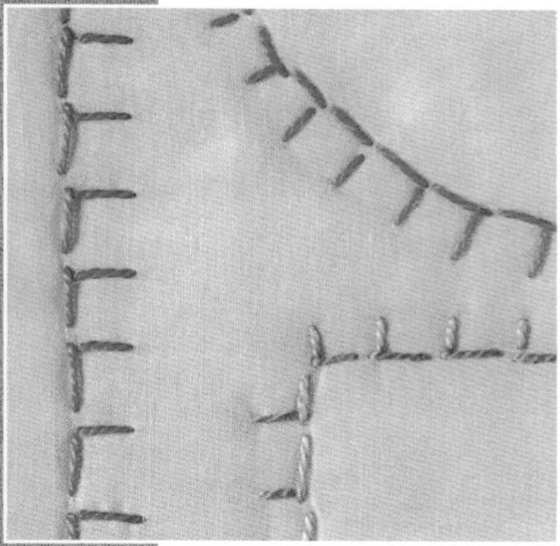

Mountmellick

Mountmellick stitch was originally to be found on whitework embroidery stitched in Ireland. This unusual and complex stitch is amazingly easy to sew.

STEP 1

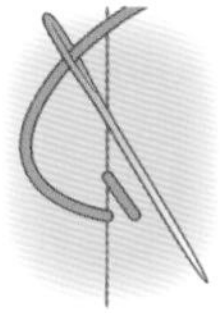

Bring the thread to the surface of the work, at the beginning of the quilting line. Move a little way down the quilting line and make a horizontal quilting stitch through all layers, working from right to left and bringing the needle up on the quilting line.

STEP 2

Pass the needle under the existing stitch (not through the fabric) from right to left.

STEP 3

Loop the thread to the left and upward, and take the needle in at the original starting point. Make a quilting stitch forward along the line, bringing the needle up to meet the last stitch and into the waiting loop of thread.

STEP 4

Repeat steps 1, 2, and 3, making sure at step 3 that the needle is taken into the chain of the previous thread. Progress along the quilting line and finish with a small securing stitch outside the last complete Mountmellick stitch.

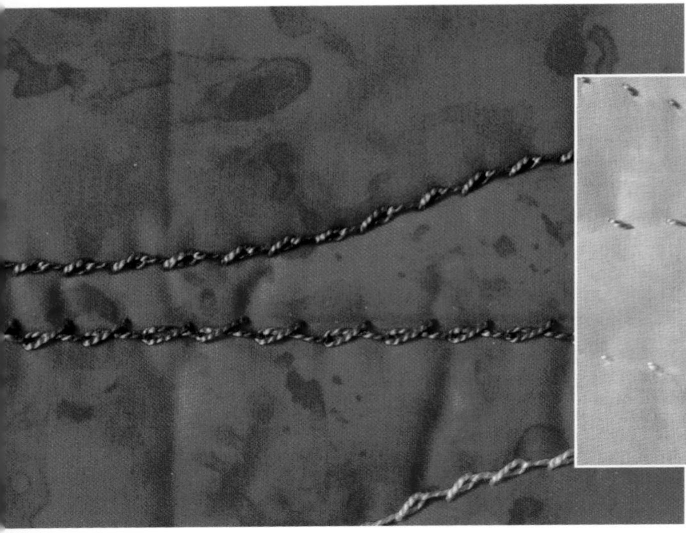

REVERSE OF WORK

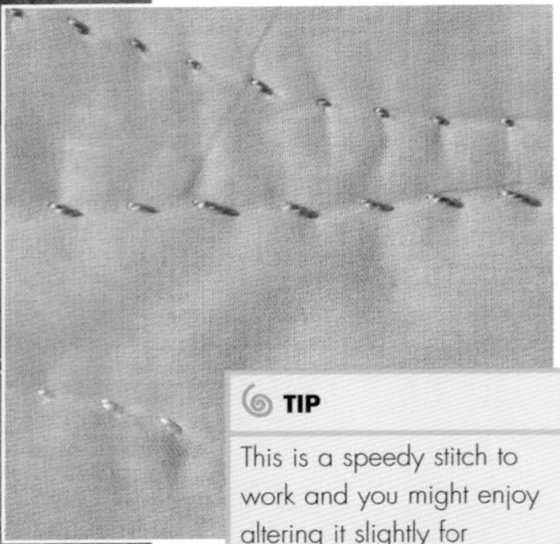

TIP

This is a speedy stitch to work and you might enjoy altering it slightly for different effects. The knot will be more defined if thicker thread is used.

Coral stitch

The final appearance of a row of coral stitch depends on the spacing of the stitches, and the sharpness and length of the diagonal stitch that is taken through all the layers.

STEP 1

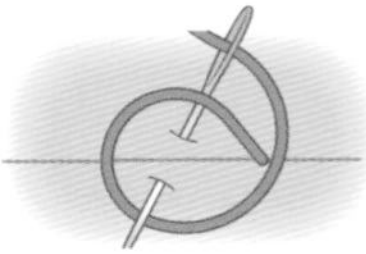

Work horizontally and from right to left. Bring the thread to the surface of the work, at the beginning of the quilting line. Hold the thread ahead of the work, along the line and looped down and around to the right. Make a shallow, diagonal quilting stitch through all layers, in above the waiting thread and the quilting line, bringing the needle out below the waiting thread, below the quilting line and into the waiting loop of thread.

STEP 2

Hold the thread forward along the line again. Make a second quilting stitch, in above the thread and the line, and out below the thread and the line, into the waiting loop of thread.

STEP 3

Continue in this way, finishing the thread outside a knot or loop.

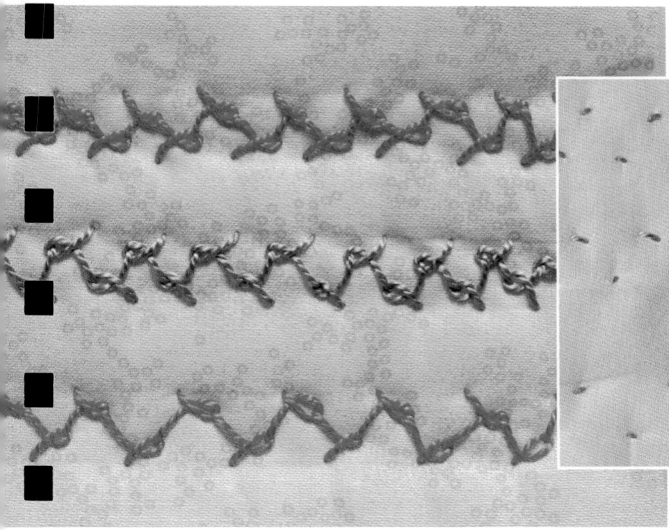

REVERSE OF WORK

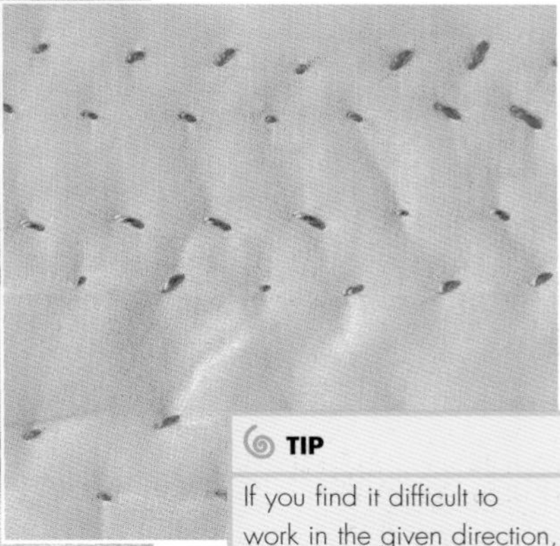

TIP

If you find it difficult to work in the given direction, try sewing horizontally, or vertically.

Zigzag coral

This is a wide stitch, good for areas of a design that need more of a "space-filling" stitch. It can take a little while to get used to the different angles required for the needle.

STEP 1

Bring the thread to the surface of the work, above the quilting line. Working from right to left, hold the thread forward along the line and down and around. Make a diagonal quilting stitch through all layers, in above the thread, forward and down toward the line, bringing the needle out below the thread and into the waiting loop of thread.

STEP 2

Hold the thread forward and upward this time. Make a diagonal quilting stitch, taking the needle in to the right of the thread, stitching forward and up toward the line, bringing the needle out on the left of the thread and into the waiting loop of thread.

STEP 3

Continue in this way, finishing with the thread outside either the top or bottom coral stitch to secure it.

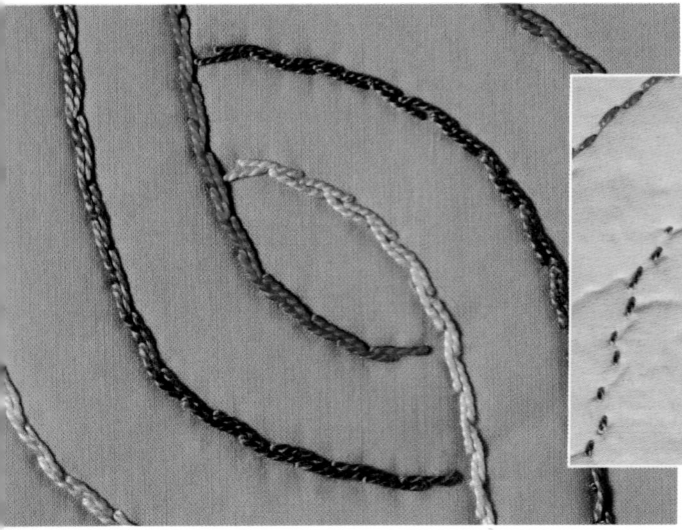

REVERSE OF WORK

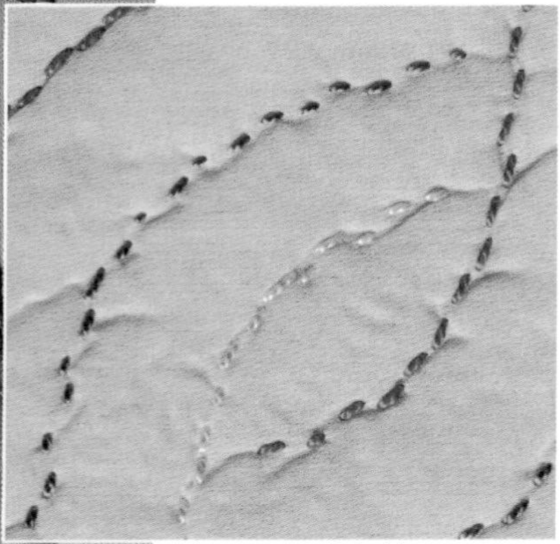

Cable stitch

This narrow, solidly defined stitch is very versatile and ideal for stitching continuous line quilting designs and for contour-quilting (outlining) motif patterns.

TIPS

- Make sure the stitches are fitted snugly together and worked very close to the quilting line, if not directly on it.
- Alter the appearance of the stitch by shortening or lengthening the individual quilting stitches taken.

STEP 1

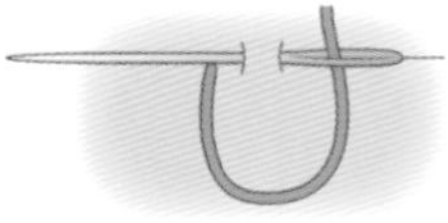

Bring the thread to the surface of the work, at the beginning of the quilting line. Working horizontally, hold the thread below the line and move forward along the line—make a small horizontal quilting stitch backward, either on the line or just below it.

STEP 2

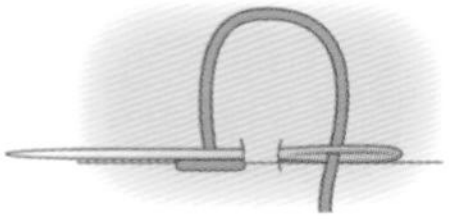

Hold the thread above the work now and, moving along the line, make a small horizontal stitch backward, either on the line or just above it, making sure that it touches the previous stitch.

STEP 3

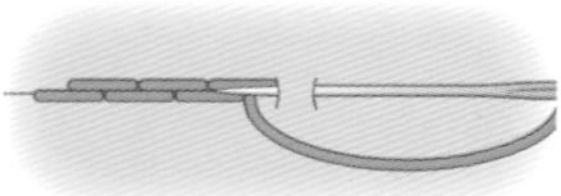

Repeat steps 1 and 2 to progress along the quilting line.

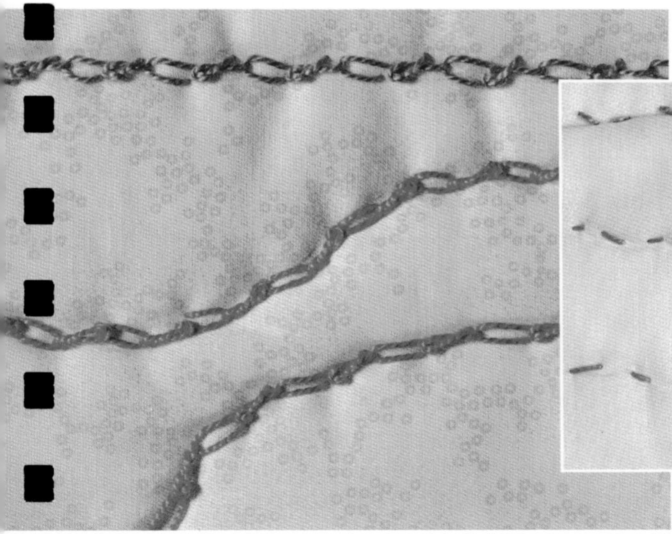

REVERSE OF WORK

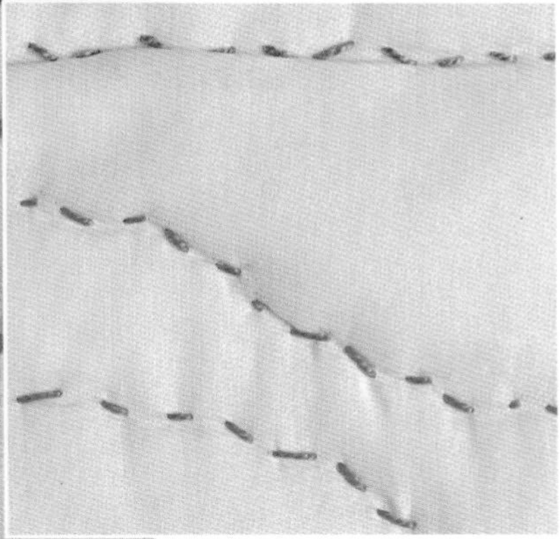

Knotted cable chain

This combination of chain stitch and coral stitch includes a knot worked within each chain loop. It is quite simple to sew—the little knots hold the links of the chain in place.

STEP 1

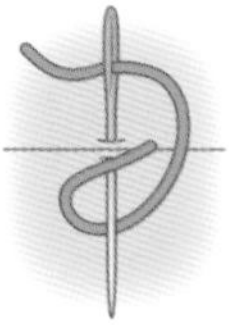

Bring the thread out to the surface of the work, at the beginning of the quilting line. Working horizontally, take a small, vertical quilting stitch, in above the line and out below the line, wrapping the thread forward, around, and under the needle. Pull the thread through.

STEP 2

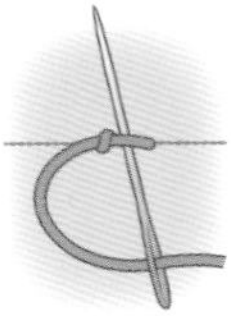

Pass the needle upward and under the previous stitch that has been sewn (not passing through the fabric).

STEP 3

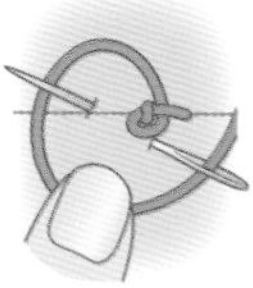

Use the thumb of your non-sewing hand to hold the thread forward to form a loop. Take the needle in under the knot and forward along the line, through all layers, to sew a chain stitch.

STEP 4

Make the next vertical quilting stitch, wrapping the thread forward, around, and under the needle and repeating steps 2 and 3.

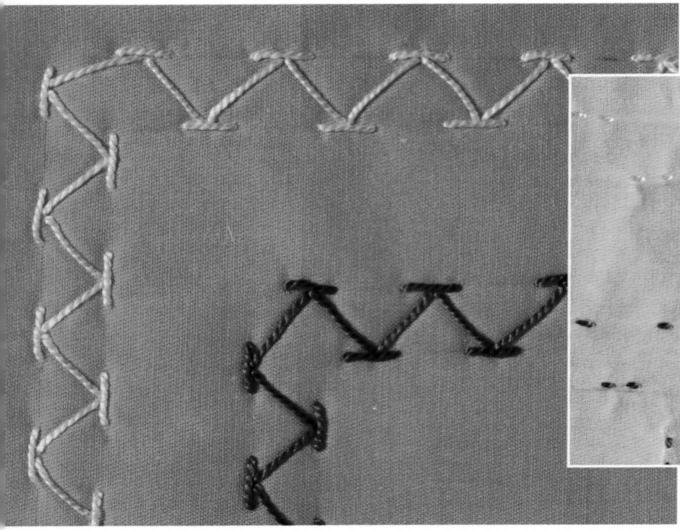

REVERSE OF WORK

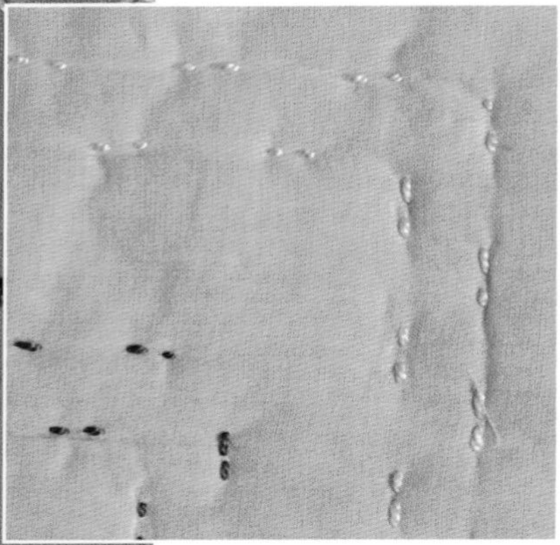

Chevron stitch

This stitch can be elongated or shortened, widened, or narrowed to suit the desired finished result. It works well on gentle curves and corners.

STEP 1

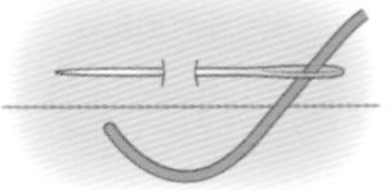

Bring the thread to the surface of the work, below the quilting line. Move forward along the line and make a horizontal quilting stitch through all layers, working backward.

STEP 2

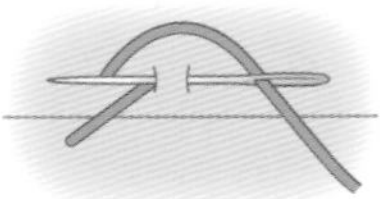

Hold the thread above the work and make another backward quilting stitch in front of the previous horizontal stitch. These two stitches form one horizontal bar above the line.

STEP 3

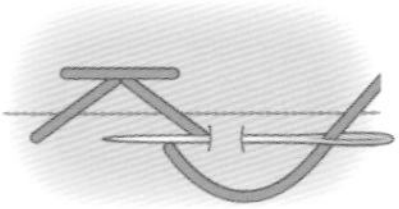

Move forward along the line and make a horizontal stitch backward below the line. Hold the thread below the work and make another horizontal stitch backward below the line, in front of the previous horizontal quilting stitch. These two stitches form one horizontal bar below the line.

STEP 4

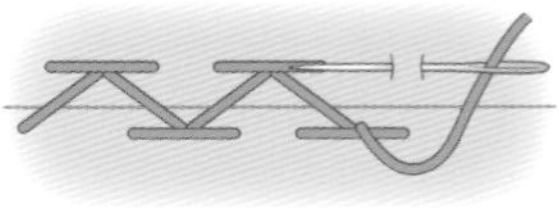

Repeat steps 1, 2, and 3 to continue along the line. Finish the thread after completing one full bar either above or below the line.

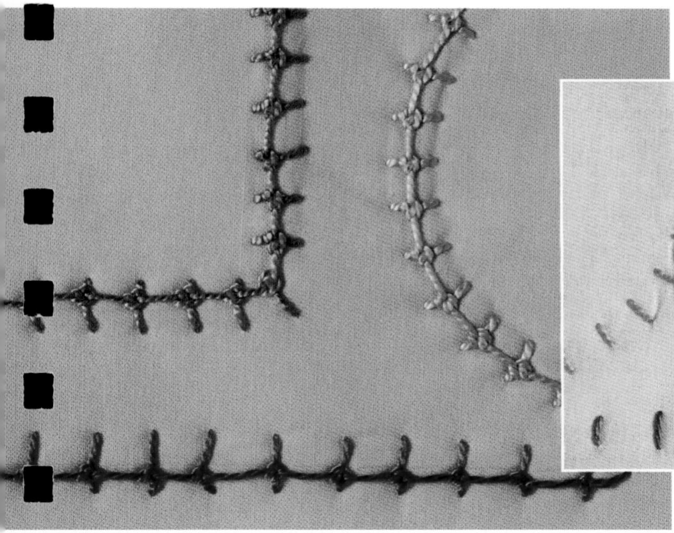

REVERSE OF WORK

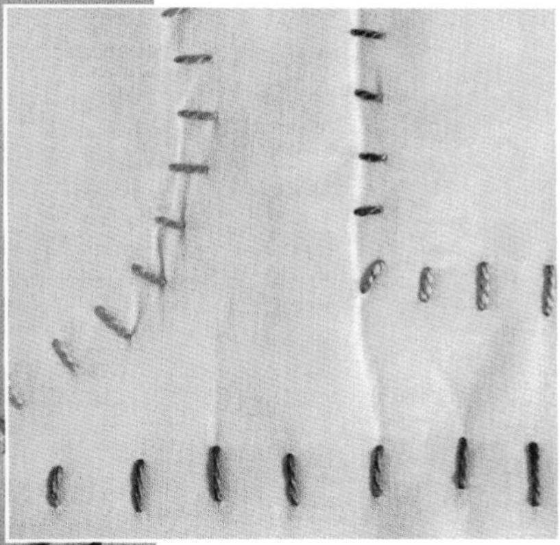

Double knot

A narrow stitch, ideal for continuous line quilting designs and for contour-quilting motif patterns. It has a slightly raised effect with intermittent knots.

STEP 1

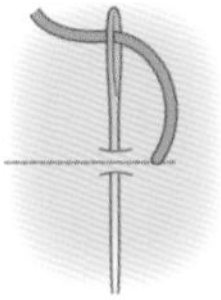

Bring the thread to the surface of the work, at the beginning of the quilting line. Move forward along the line and make a vertical quilting stitch through all layers, taking the needle in above the line and bringing it out below the line. Pull the thread through.

STEP 2

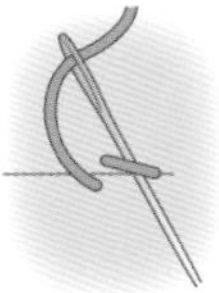

Hold the thread forward and above the work and pass the needle under the previous stitch made (not through the fabric). Pull the thread through.

STEP 3

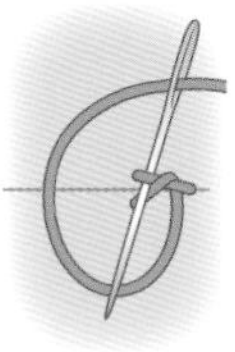

Use the thumb of your non-sewing hand to hold the thread forward and above the work. Pass the needle under the top bar of the previous stitch, bringing the needle over the lower bar and into the waiting loop of thread. Pull the thread through to form the double knot.

STEP 4

Move along the quilting line to make the next quilting stitch and repeat steps 1, 2, and 3 to form a row of double knot stitch. Finish the thread outside the last double knot sewn.

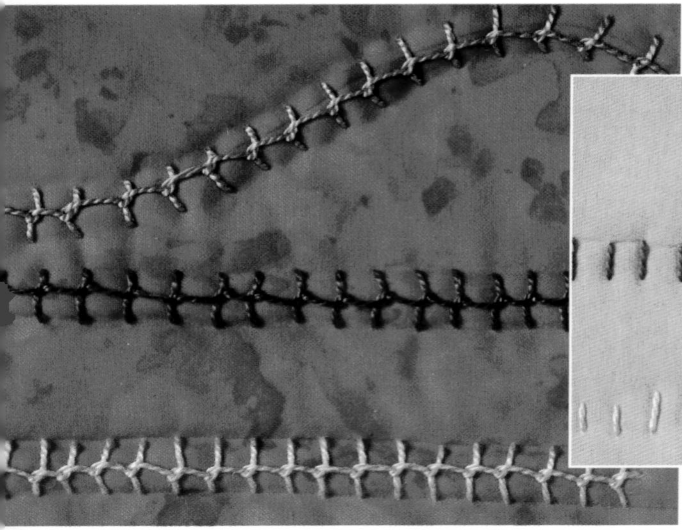

REVERSE OF WORK

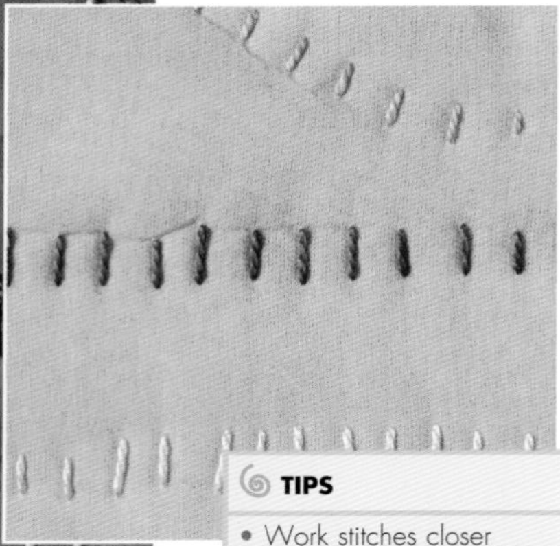

Loop stitch

Loop stitch is a wide stitch made up from one quilting stitch and one looping stitch, with a slightly raised center. It is an easy stitch to sew fluidly and speedily.

TIPS

- Work stitches closer together for a more dense appearance, or further apart as required.
- Pass the eye of the needle under the previous stitches, rather than the point, to avoid catching unwanted fibers or thread.

STEP 1

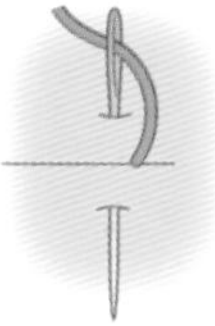

Bring the thread to the surface of the work, at the beginning of the quilting line. Move forward along the quilting line and make a vertical quilting stitch through all layers, taking the needle in above the line and bringing it out below the line. Pull the thread through.

STEP 2

Use the thumb of your non-sewing hand to hold the thread forward and pass the needle under the previous stitch made and over the waiting thread in front of it (it does not pass through the fabric). Pull the thread through.

STEP 3

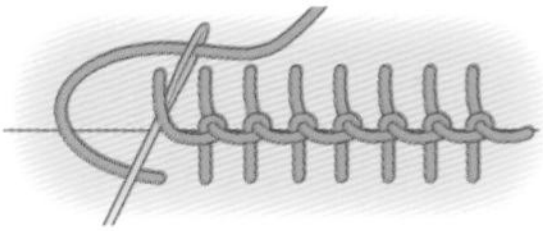

Move along the quilting line and make the next vertical quilting stitch, repeating steps 1 and 2 to create a row of loop stitches. Finish the thread after a looping stage.

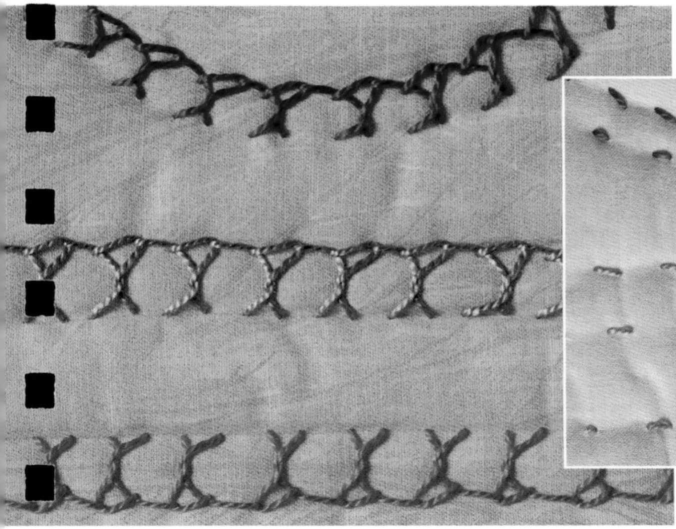

REVERSE OF WORK

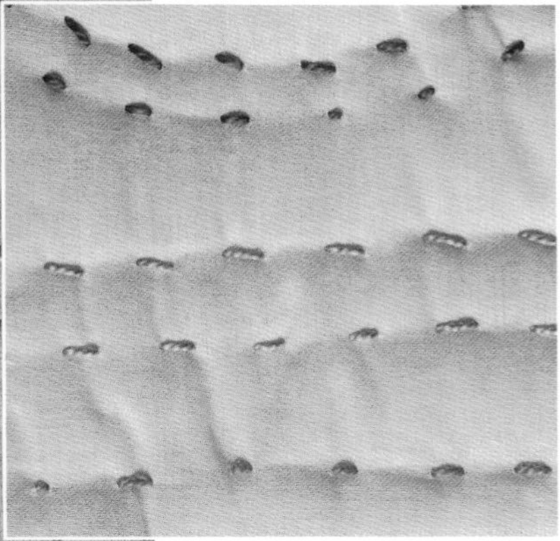

Bonnet stitch

Bonnet stitch is a wide stitch with a complex twisted appearance on the surface of the work, but with neat, parallel rows of running stitch on the back.

TIPS

Alter the final appearance of the stitch by changing the spacing between each stitch and also the width at which it is sewn.

STEP 1

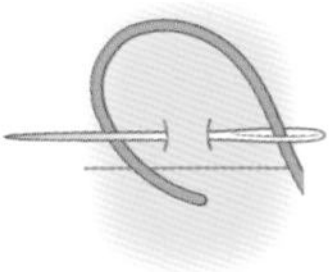

Bring the thread to the surface of the work, below the quilting line. Working from right to left, hold the thread forward along the line, upward and around to form a loop. Make a small, horizontal quilting stitch above the line through all the layers, bringing the needle into the waiting loop of thread.

STEP 2

Now hold the thread forward and downward. Make a small, diagonal quilting stitch below the line and downward, taking the needle in front of the previous thread and into the waiting loop of thread. The center of the stitch will twist during this process.

STEP 3

Hold the thread forward and above the line again and, moving forward along the line, make the next horizontal quilting stitch above the line. Repeat steps 2 and 3 to progress along the quilting line, securing the thread after a diagonal stitch below the line.

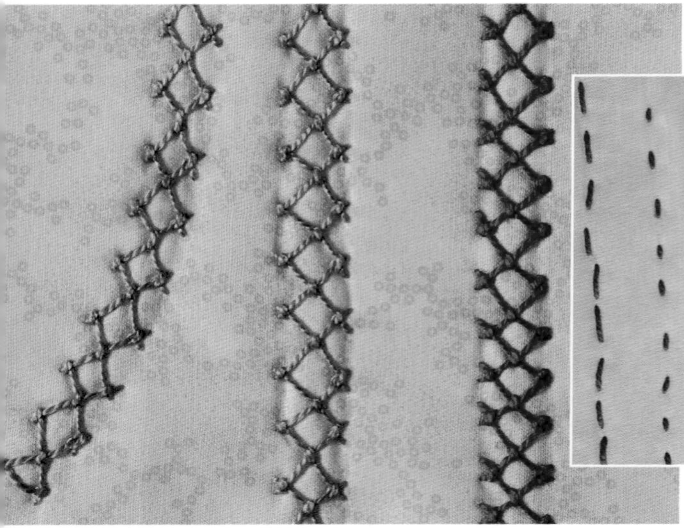

REVERSE OF WORK

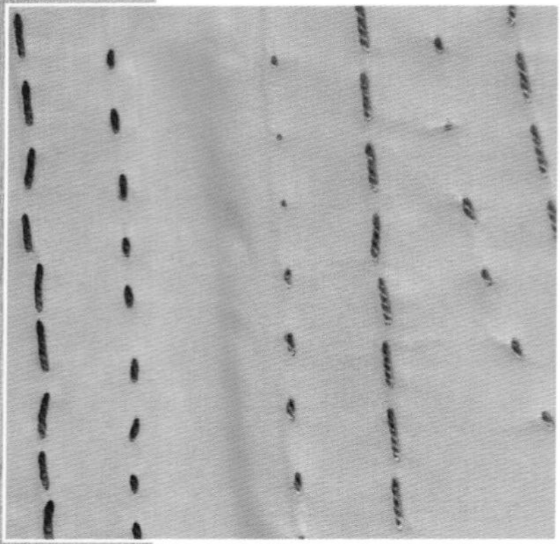

Diamond stitch

This is one of the wider stitches available for quilting.

STEP 1

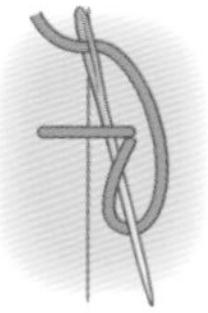

Bring the thread out on the left of the quilting line. Make a short, vertical quilting stitch to the right of the quilting line. Pass the needle behind the stitch that you have just created and hold the thread over the needle to the left and then under the needle to the right before pulling the thread through to form a knot.

STEP 2

Take the needle to the left-hand side of the quilting line. Pass the needle behind the previous stitch and hold the thread over the needle to the left and under the needle to the right before pulling through to form a knot.

STEP 3

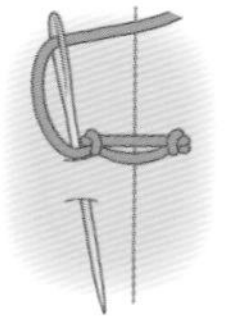

Take the needle into the fabric directly underneath the left-hand knot and make a longer, vertical quilting stitch downward.

STEP 4

Take the needle behind the horizontal thread lying across the quilting line and wrap the thread over the needle to the right and under the needle to the left. Pull through to form a knot.

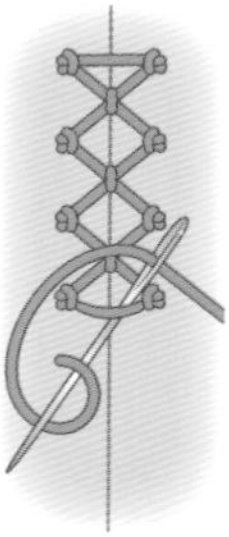

Hand-quilting Filling Stitches

Filling stitches can be used to add textural interest to areas of quilting designs that would otherwise remain unquilted and may also look uninteresting.

These stitches can also be used to replace formal quilting designs—entire areas of a quilt can be covered with filling stitches worked in a stylistic and freehand way.

If the appearance of the quilt stitches on the back of your quilt is important for your project, try using a printed fabric rather than a plain fabric for the backing. This will help you relax your stitching.

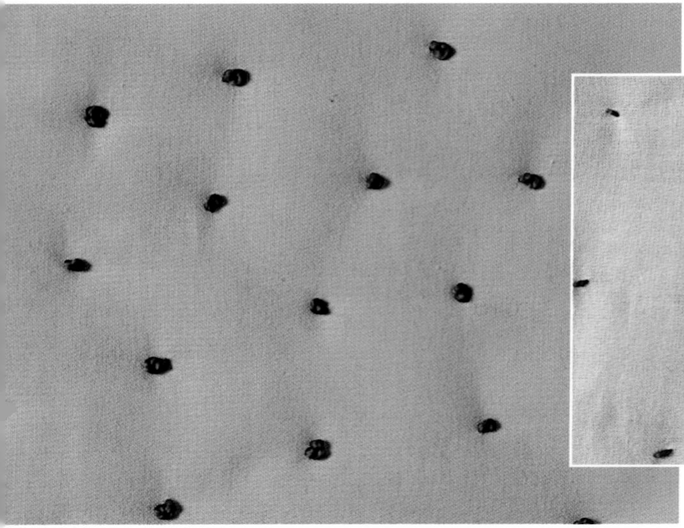

REVERSE OF WORK

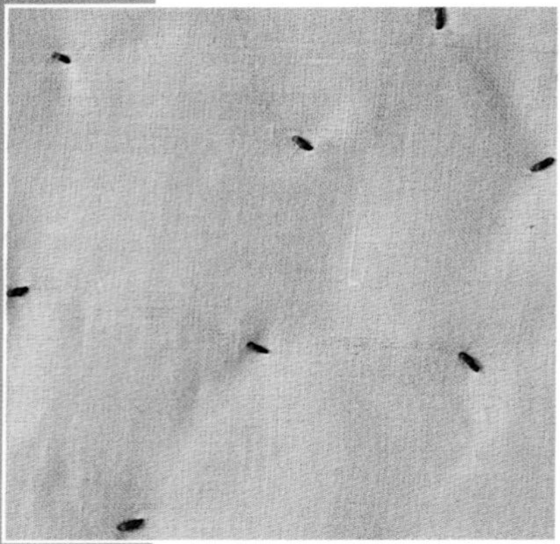

Colonial knot

The colonial knot is also known as a candlewicking knot. It is very similar in appearance to the French knot (see page 140), but is slightly larger and sits higher.

TIP

These knots are commonly stitched close together to form a continuous line, but also make a versatile alternative knot for a hand-quilting filling stitch.

STEP 1

Bring the thread to the surface of the work. Hold the thread over the needle to the right and under the needle to the left; and back over the needle point to the right and under the needle point to the left.

STEP 2

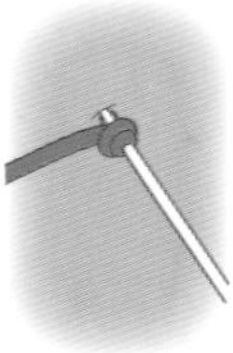

Pull the thread taut to stabilize the knot while you take the needle into the fabric through all layers, just to one side of where the thread initially came out.

STEP 3

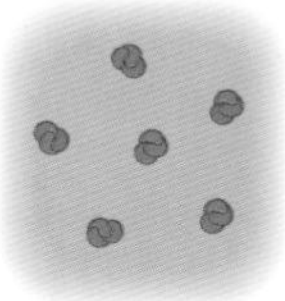

If you are working several knots within a short space of each other, use the stitch to quilt through all the layers of the project. Make a small quilting stitch on the back of the work, then take the point of the needle into the batting and travel through the batting to the area for the next knot.

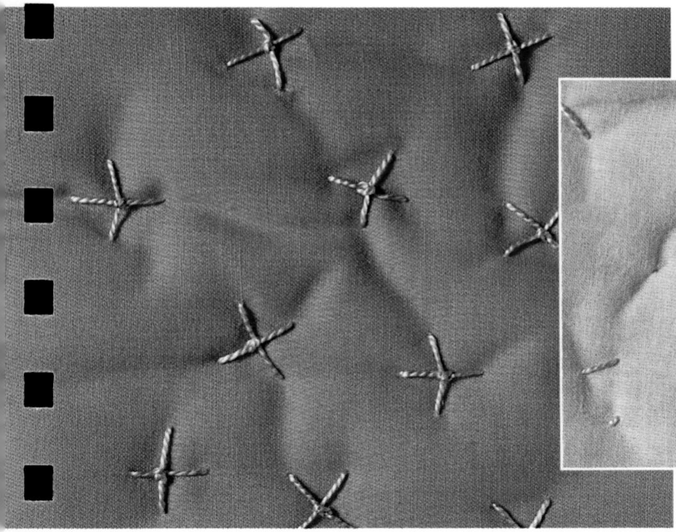

REVERSE OF WORK

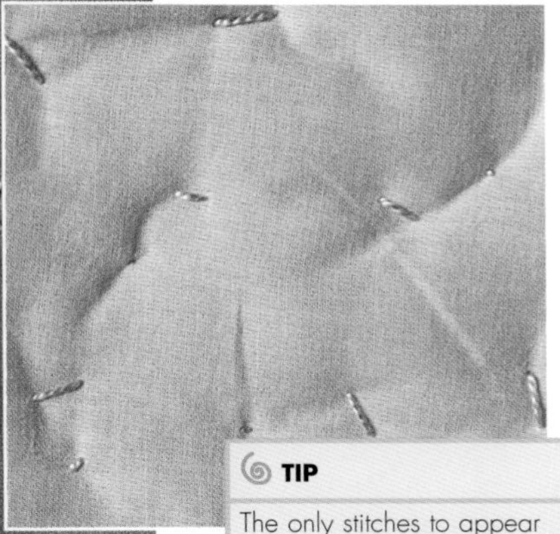

Four-legged knot

The four-legged knot is an attractive knot, which resembles an upright cross stitch with a textural knot in the center.

STEP 1

Bring the thread to the surface of the work. Hold the thread down vertically and make a diagonal stitch upward and out to the right.

STEP 2

Hold the thread across the vertical stitch and loop it downward. Pass the needle behind both of these crossed threads, at a diagonal downward and into the waiting loop of thread. Pull through to form a central knot.

STEP 3

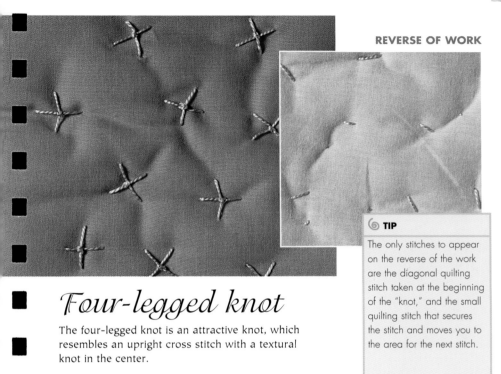

Take the needle out to the left of the four-legged knot to complete it. If working several knots within a short space of each other, use this last stitch to quilt through the layers of the project. Make a small quilting stitch through to the back of the work, then take the point of the needle into the batting and travel through the batting to the area for the next knot.

TIP

The only stitches to appear on the reverse of the work are the diagonal quilting stitch taken at the beginning of the "knot," and the small quilting stitch that secures the stitch and moves you to the area for the next stitch.

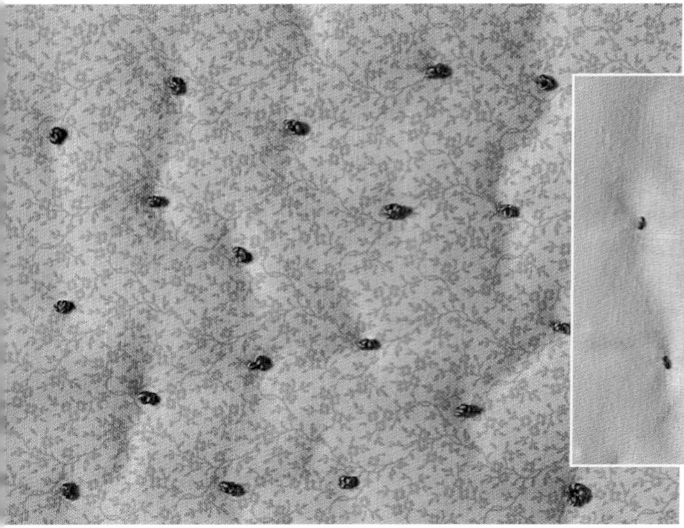

REVERSE OF WORK

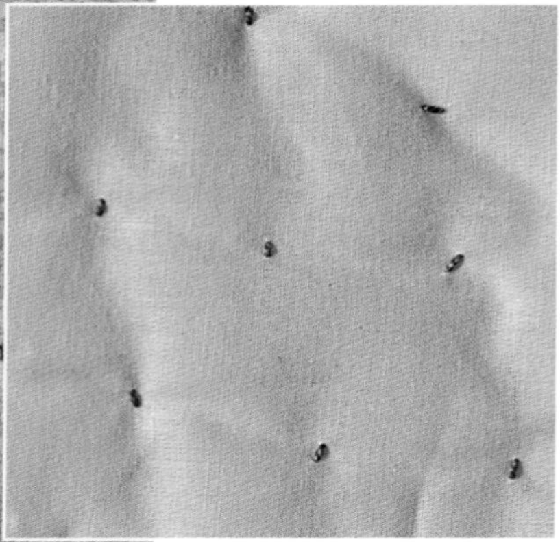

TIP

For a chunkier knot, use a thicker thread to give more definition to the end result.

French knot

When making the French knot, the thread is wrapped around the needle before it enters the fabric. Make one or two wraps of the needle, according to the preferred size of knot.

STEP 1

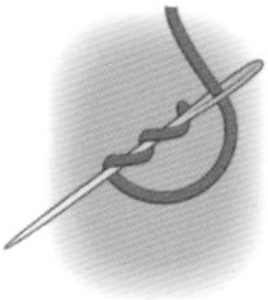

Bring the thread to the surface of the work. Hold the needle in your sewing hand and wrap the thread forward over the needle and back toward you under the needle (for a chunkier knot, repeat once more).

STEP 2

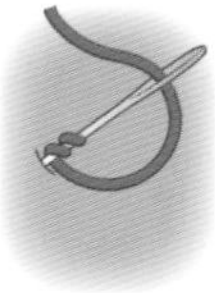

Hold the thread taut so the wrapped thread stays firm while you take the needle back into the fabric close to where the thread initially emerged.

STEP 3

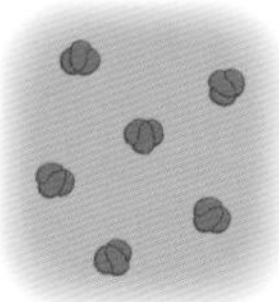

If working several knots within a short space of each other, use this last stitch to quilt through the layers of your project. Make a small quilting stitch through to the back of the work, then take the point of the needle into the batting and travel through the batting to the area for the next knot.

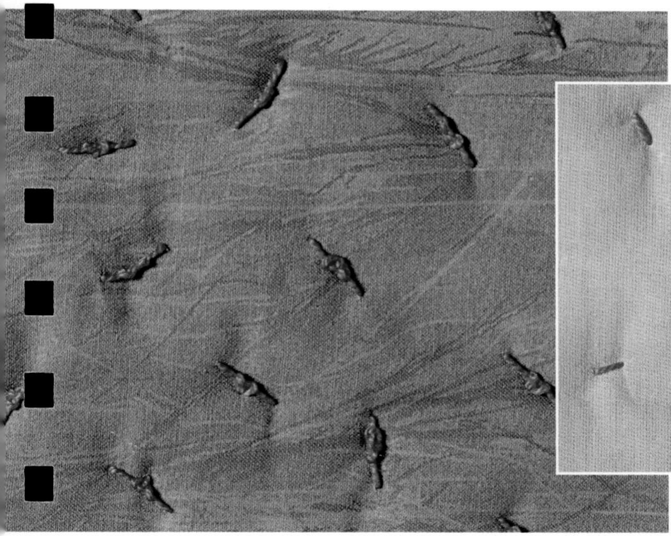

REVERSE OF WORK

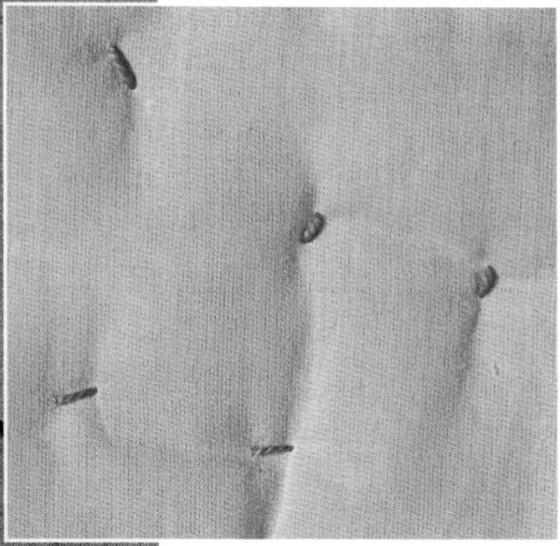

Danish knot

This stitch looks like a chunky knot on a long bar. The knot is formed by wrapping the thread under the existing bar stitch without catching the fabric.

STEP 1

Bring the thread to the surface of the work. Take the needle in any direction and make a quilting stitch back to the center of the previous stitch, bringing the needle up to the left-hand side of the thread.

STEP 2

Hold the thread down and around to the right, and pass the needle under the long bar stitch without catching up any fabric. Pull the thread through.

STEP 3

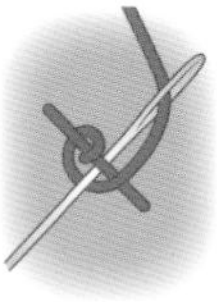

Hold the thread down and around to the right again. Pass the needle under the long bar stitch, below the previous wrap and bring the needle into the waiting loop of thread. Pull the thread through to form a knot.

STEP 4

Take the thread into the fabric close to the knot to secure it. If working several knots within a short space of each other, use this last stitch to quilt through the layers of the project. Make a small quilting stitch through to the back of the work, then take the point of the needle into the batting and travel through the batting to the area for the next knot.

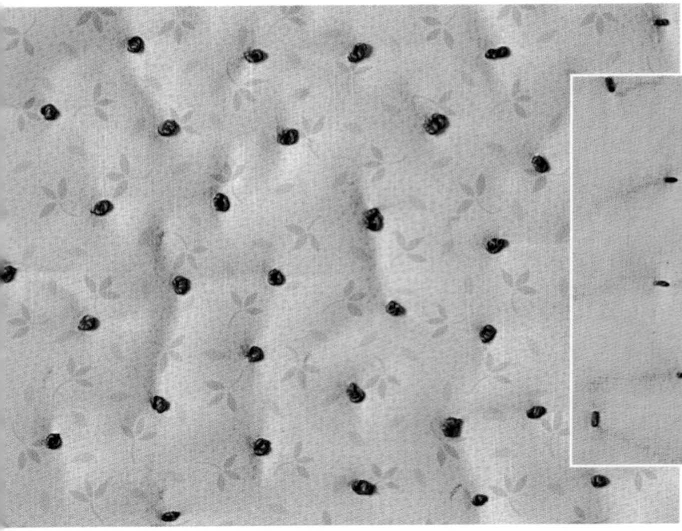

REVERSE OF WORK

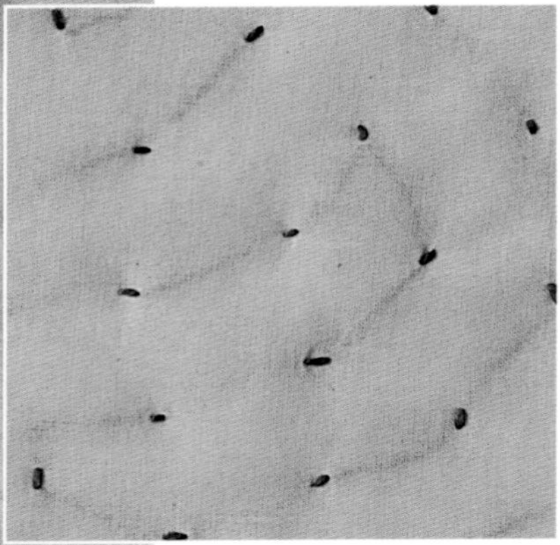

Chinese knot

Chinese knots are also known as Pekin knots or forbidden knots. They can be found in antique embroideries throughout China.

TIP

Similar in appearance to a French knot, but with a slightly different shape. It also tends to sit flatter on the surface of the fabric.

STEP 1

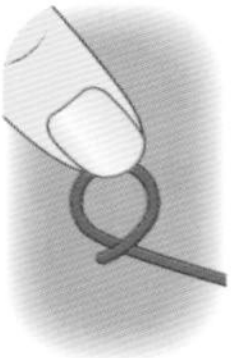

Bring the thread to the surface of the work. Loop the thread down and around to the left to form a clockwise circle. Using your non-sewing hand, lift this loop up and over on itself so that it forms a circle traveling counterclockwise.

STEP 2

Support the loop of thread with your non-sewing thumb, take the needle into the fabric inside the loop and make a stitch to secure it.

STEP 3

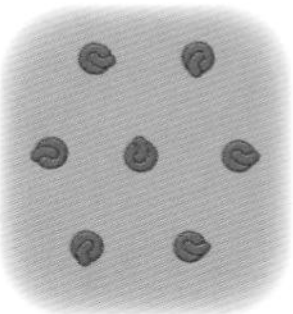

If working several knots within a short space of each other, use this last stitch to quilt through the layers of the project. Make a small quilting stitch through to the back of the work, then take the point of the needle into the batting and travel through the batting to the area for the next knot.

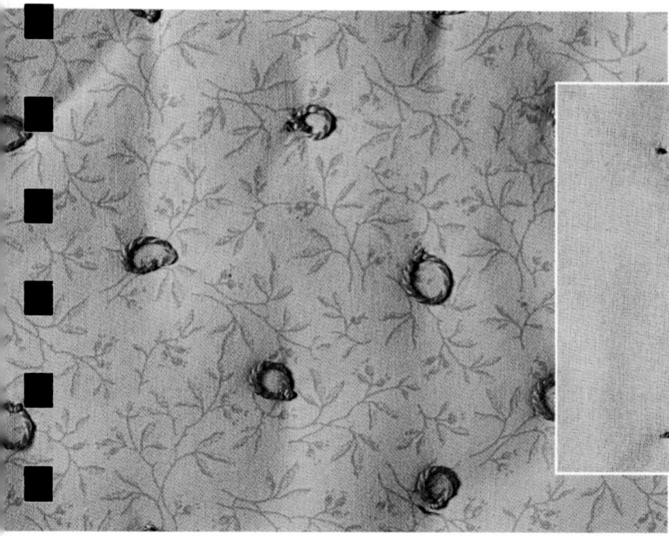

REVERSE OF WORK

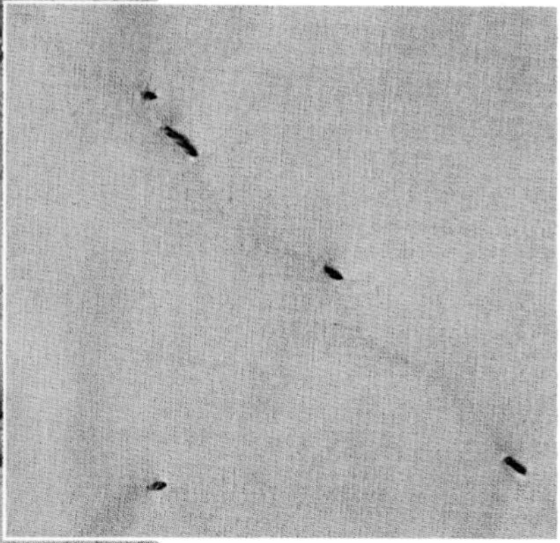

Looped Chinese knot

Practice the Chinese knot (see page 142) before trying this variation, which features an additional decorative loop. Make the loop as small or as large as you prefer.

STEP 1

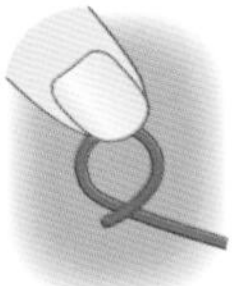

Bring the thread to the surface of the work. Loop the thread down and around to the left to form a clockwise circle. Using your non-sewing hand, lift this loop up and over on itself so that it forms a circle traveling counterclockwise.

STEP 2

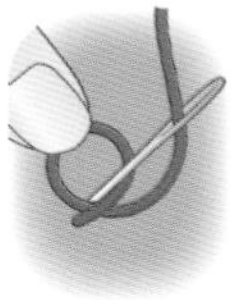

Support the loop of thread with your non-sewing thumb, while taking the needle into the fabric inside the loop.

STEP 3

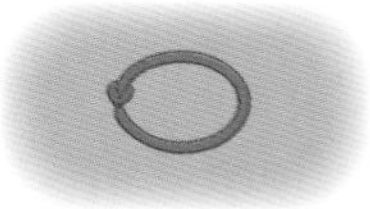

Keep hold of the loop so it doesn't disappear as the needle is taken into the fabric. Once the thread and the knot are pulled taut, the loop will sit on the surface of the work.

STEP 4

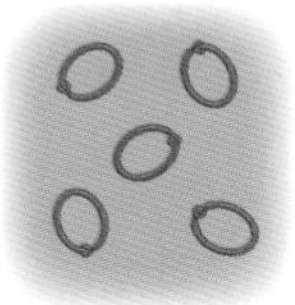

If working several knots within a short space of each other, use this last stitch to quilt through the layers of the project. Make a small quilting stitch through to the back of the work, then take the point of the needle into the batting and travel through the batting to the area for the next knot.

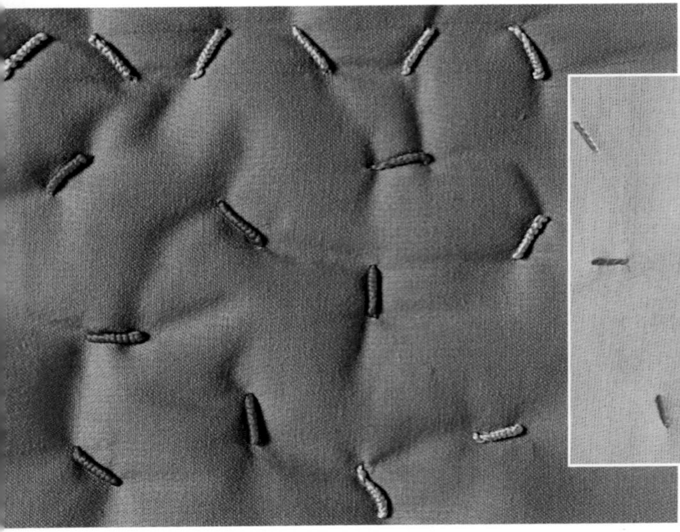

REVERSE OF WORK

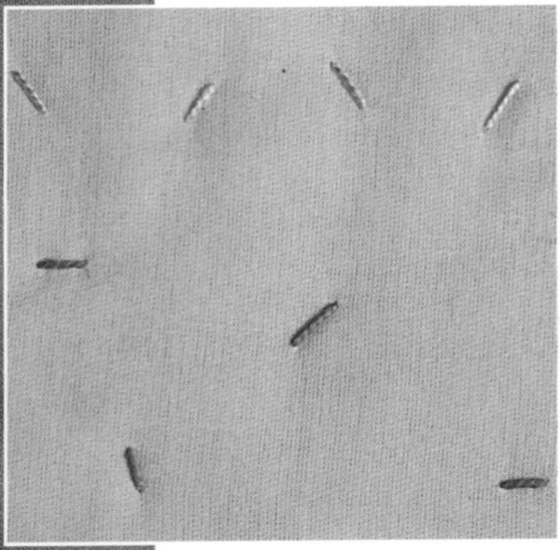

Bullion knot

The thread is wrapped several times around the core thread to form each stitch. Bullion knot can be worked to whatever length you prefer.

STEP 1

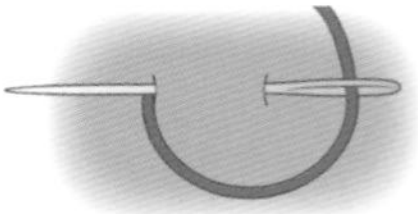

Bring the thread to the surface of the work. Take the needle into the fabric and make a quilting stitch through all layers, working toward your starting point. Bring the needle up through the fabric close to where it first emerged, but do not pull it through at this point.

STEP 2

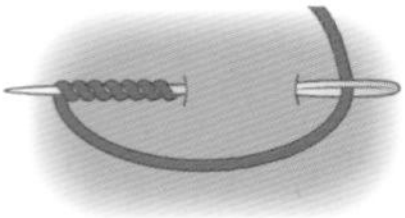

Hold the needle and, using your other hand, firmly wrap the thread around the shank of the needle several times—as many times as required to fill the length of the stitch.

STEP 3

Hold the wrapping threads very securely while you pull the needle through.

STEP 4

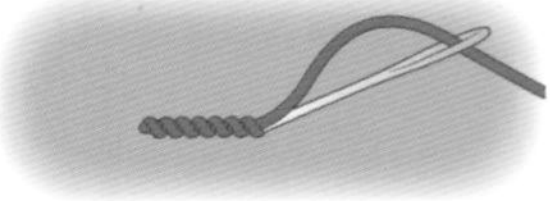

To secure the knot, take the needle back into the same place as used for making the first stitch. If working several knots within a short space of each other, use this last stitch to bridge through the batting to the next area.

REVERSE OF WORK

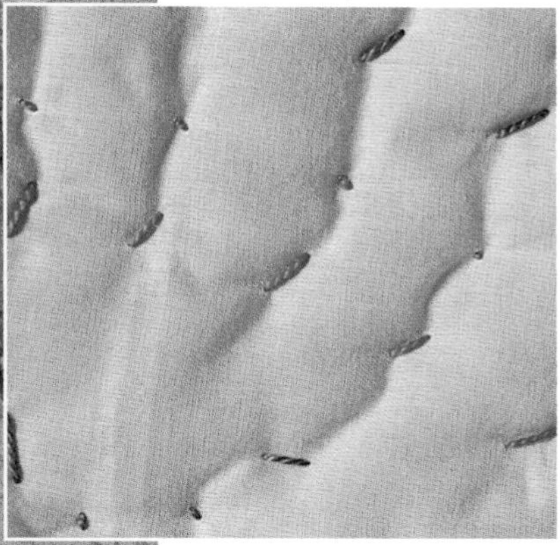

Sword-edge stitch

This stitch can be sewn in a line for continuous line quilting designs, or used as a filling stitch, scattered across your work. The length and width can be varied.

STEP 1

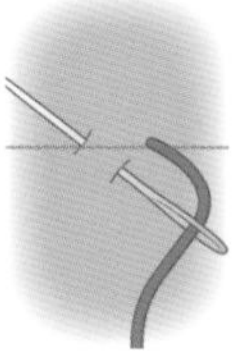

Bring the thread to the surface of the work. Take the needle in below and slightly to the left of the starting point. Make a quilting stitch diagonally up and to the left, through all layers and pull the thread through.

STEP 2

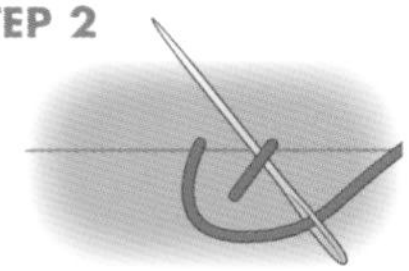

Pass the needle upward, or from right to left, under the existing diagonal stitch.

STEP 3

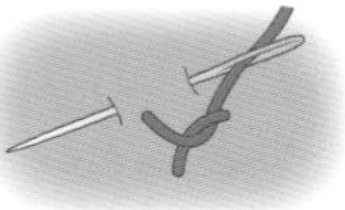

Take the needle in directly above the lower leg of the sword-edge stitch to secure it.

STEP 4

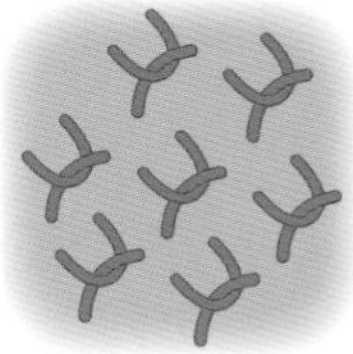

If working several scattered stitches within a short space of each other, use this last stitch to quilt through the layers of the project. Make a small quilting stitch through to the back of the work, then take the point of the needle into the batting and travel through the batting to the area for the next knot.

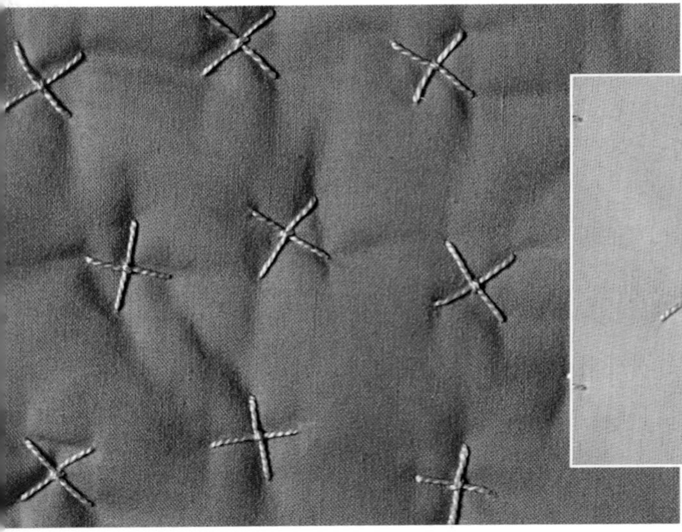

REVERSE OF WORK

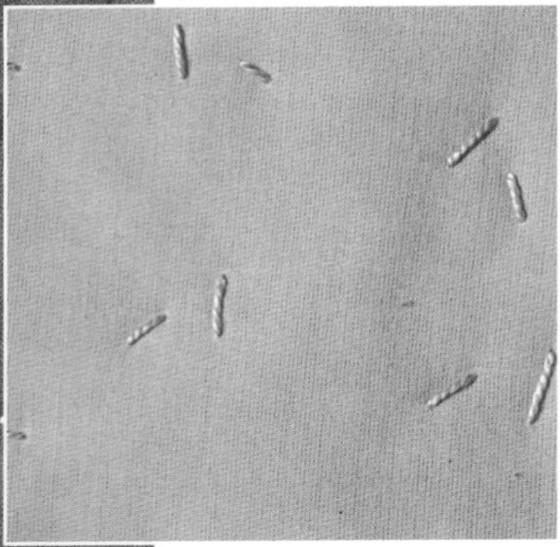

Tied cross

This makes an interesting filling stitch when scattered over a quilt project. It is possible to vary the size of the cross stitch legs, but they should remain even.

STEP 1

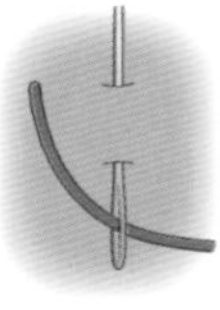

Take the needle into the fabric a short distance away. Make a quilting stitch through all the layers, vertically and upward, bringing the needle out level with where the thread first emerged.

STEP 2

Carry the thread across the existing stitch just produced. Take the needle into the fabric level with the upper leg of the stitch, working diagonally toward the center of the cross, bringing the needle up to one side of it.

STEP 3

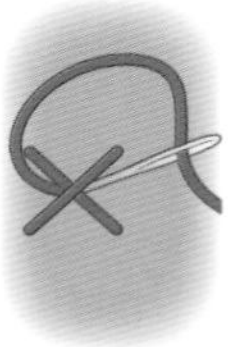

Take the needle down on the opposite side of the cross, close to the existing threads, to secure it.

STEP 4

If working several scattered stitches within a short space of each other, use this last stitch to quilt through the layers of the project. Make a small quilting stitch through to the back of the work, then take the point of the needle into the batting and travel through the batting to the area for the next stitch.

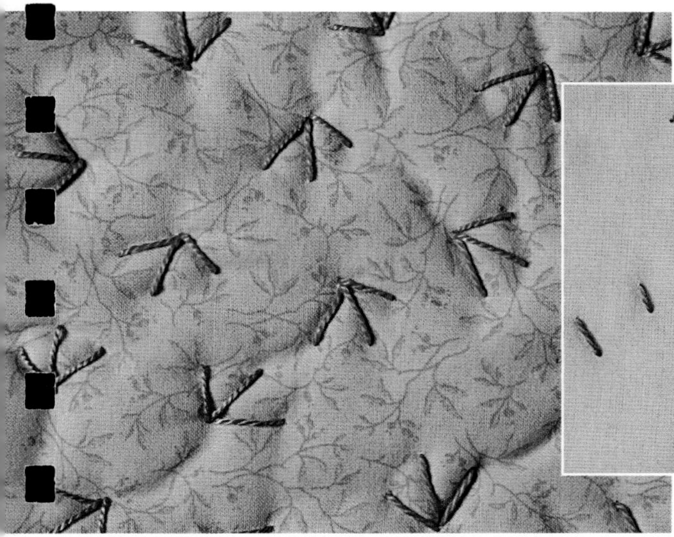

REVERSE OF WORK

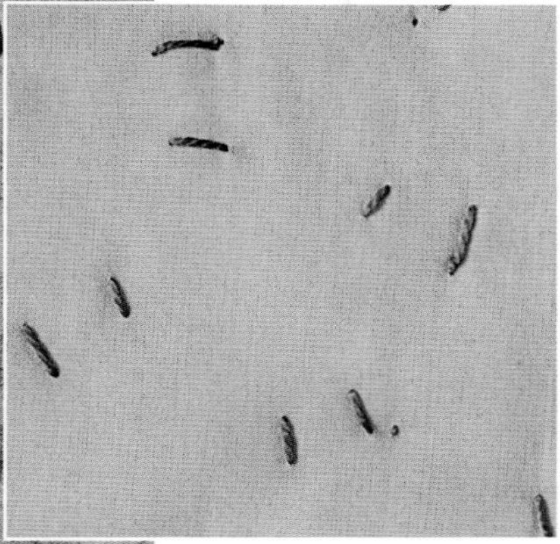

Detached fern

Detached fern stitches can be scattered at random and positioned in different directions across a quilt project, providing a pretty foliage effect.

STEP 1

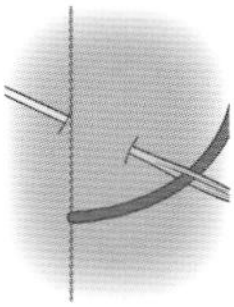

Bring the thread to the surface of the work. Take the needle out to the right and make a quilting stitch through all layers, stitching diagonally to the left and slightly upward. Pull the thread through.

STEP 2

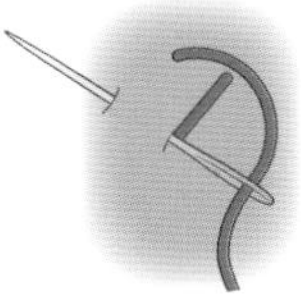

Take the needle in at the place where the thread first emerged and make a quilting stitch diagonally to the left and slightly upward.

STEP 3

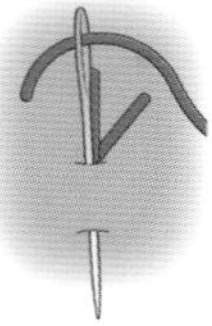

Take the needle back into the fabric at your initial starting point to secure the stitch.

STEP 4

If working several scattered stitches within a short space of each other, use this last stitch to quilt through the layers of the project. Make a small quilting stitch through to the back of the work, then take the point of the needle into the batting and travel through the batting to the area for the next stitch.

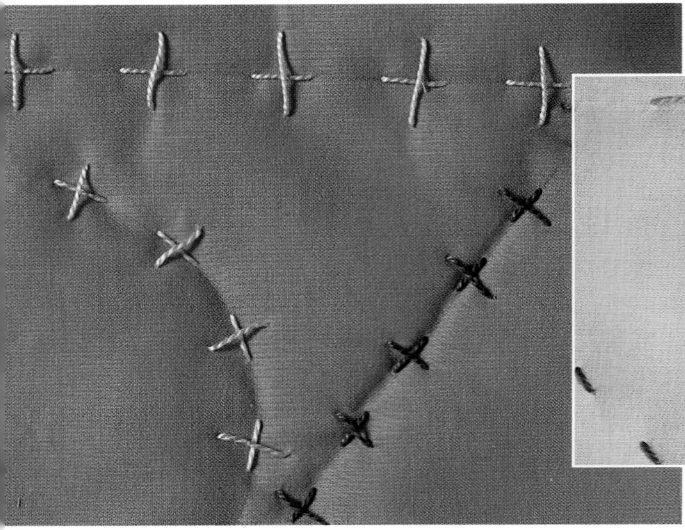

REVERSE OF WORK

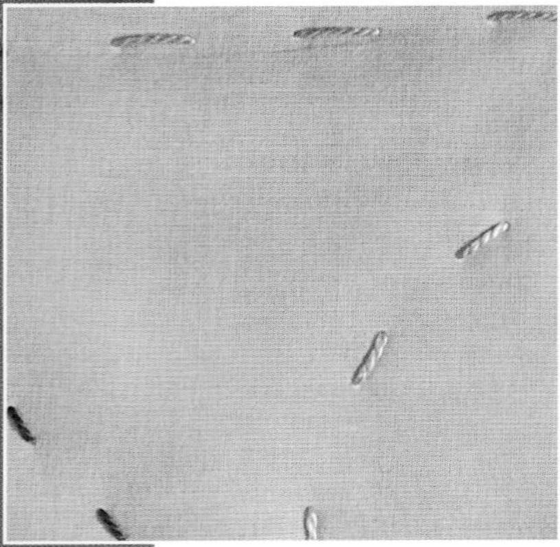

Upright cross

Upright cross stitch is a variation of basic cross stitch (see page 122) and a looser variation of tied cross stitch (see page 146). The two stitches are not linked or looped together.

STEP 1

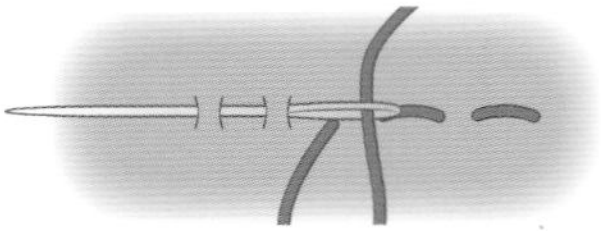

Bring the thread to the surface of the work and work a line of basic running stitch (see page 67).

STEP 2

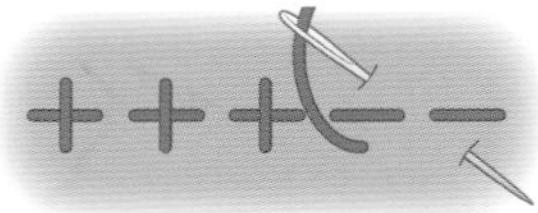

Turn your work and, starting at the beginning of the row, take the needle in above each horizontal stitch, centrally, and out below the next horizontal stitch, centrally. Do not work these stitches through all layers—pass the needle through the top fabric and the batting only.

STEP 3

If working several scattered stitches within a short space of each other, sew one horizontal bar stitch and then cross it over with a second stitch running at right angles to the first stitch. Use the last stitch to quilt through the layers of the project. Make a small quilting stitch through to the back of the work, taking the point of the needle into the batting and traveling through the batting to the area for the next stitch.

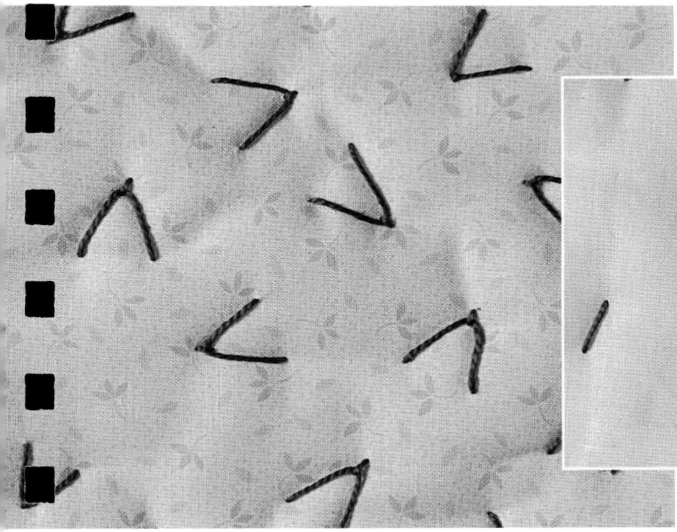

REVERSE OF WORK

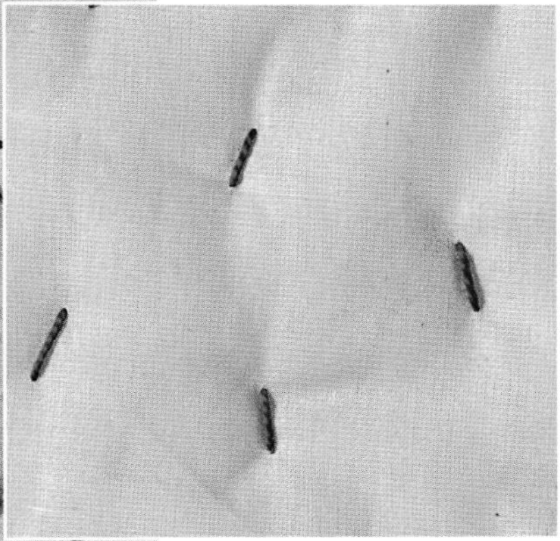

TIPS

- While sewing the V-shape, one quilting stitch is taken through all the layers of the work.
- The securing stitch at the bottom point of the "V" can be run into the top fabric and the batting only.

Detached fly

Detached fly stitch makes a wonderfully quick and simple filling stitch, adding movement to your quilt work.

STEP 1

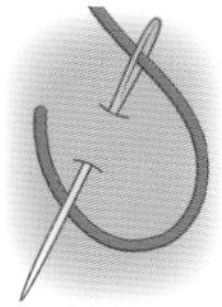

Bring the thread to the surface of the work. Hold the thread downward and around to the right. Make a quilting stitch through all layers, working diagonally downward and slightly to the left, bringing the needle into the waiting loop of thread.

STEP 2

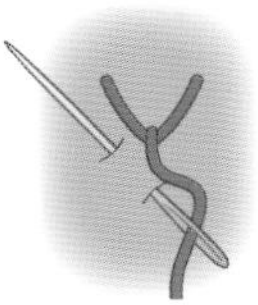

Make a quilting stitch to secure the detached fly stitch.

STEP 3

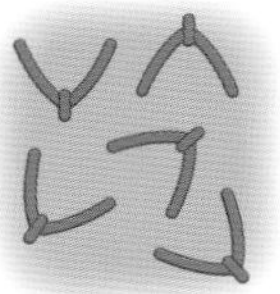

If working several scattered stitches within a short space of each other, use the last stitch to quilt through the layers of the project. Make a small quilting stitch through to the back of the work, taking the point of the needle into the batting and traveling through the batting to the area for the next stitch.

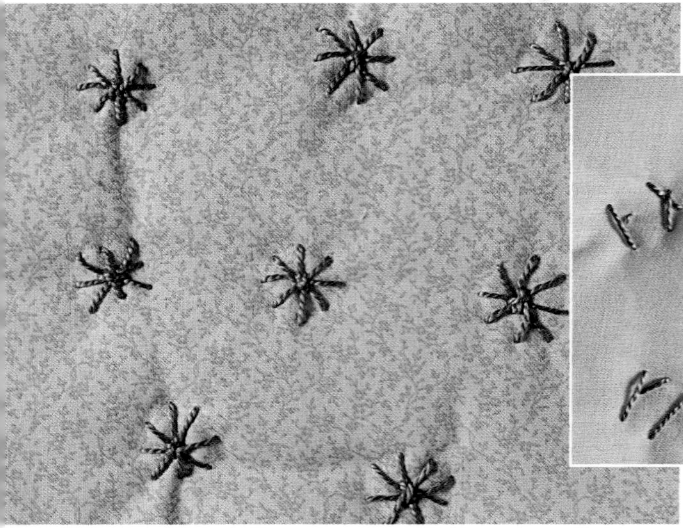

REVERSE OF WORK

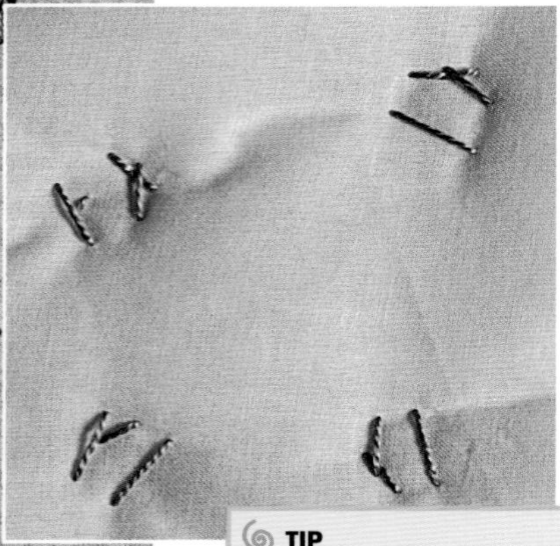

TIP

The stitches pass through all layers of the work, so try to keep to the same formation with each individual star stitch.

Star stitch

Star stitch is a decorative filling stitch, adding both texture and interest to quilt work. The cross stitches may be worked in different colors.

STEP 1

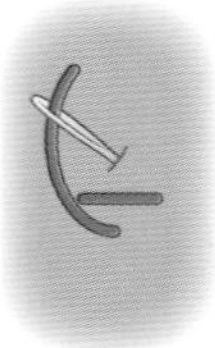

Bring the thread to the surface of the work and, working through all layers, work a large and upright cross stitch by placing two diagonal stitches, one on top of the other.

STEP 2

Work an equal-sized diagonal cross stitch on top of the previous upright cross stitch, ensuring that the legs of the second cross stitch sit evenly between those of the first stitch.

STEP 3

Finish by working a tiny cross stitch centrally over all the previous stitches, in order to secure them. If working several scattered stitches within a short space of each other, use the last stitch to quilt through the layers of the project. Make a small quilting stitch through to the back of the work, taking the point of the needle into the batting and traveling through the batting to the area for the next stitch.

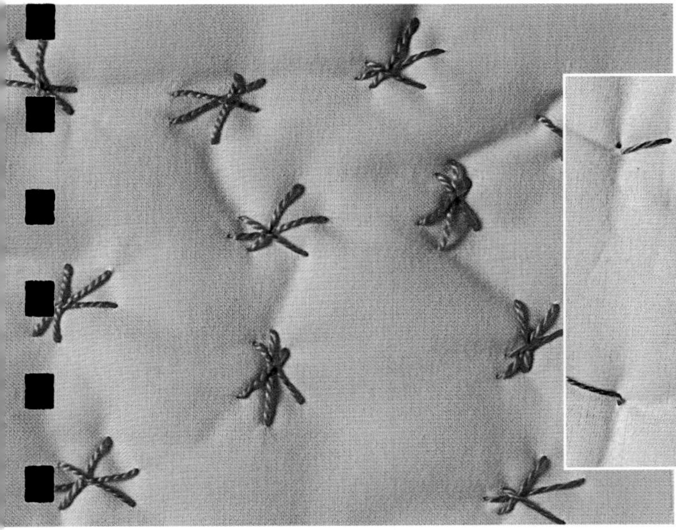

REVERSE OF WORK

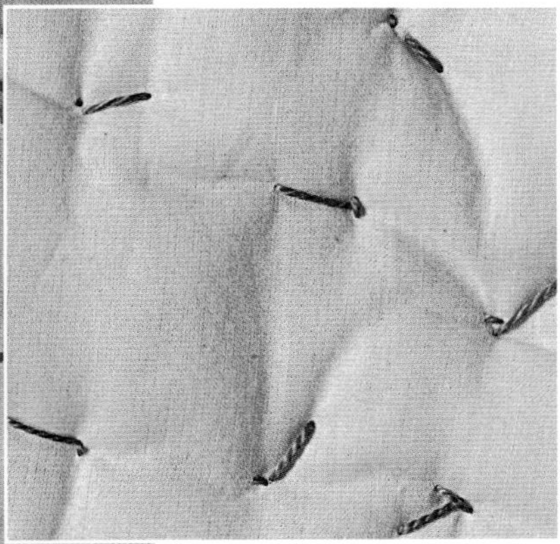

Ermine stitch

Ermine stitch is a very versatile stitch, which can be worked in formal rows and lines, as well as used for filling areas to give added texture and interest.

STEP 1

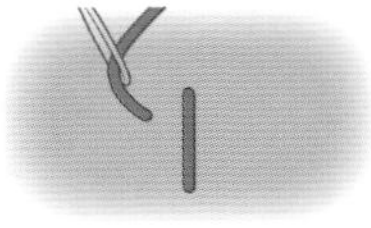

Bring the thread to the surface of the work. Take the needle into the fabric vertically beneath your starting point, and make a quilting stitch through all layers diagonally upward and to the left of the previous stitch. Pull the thread through.

STEP 2

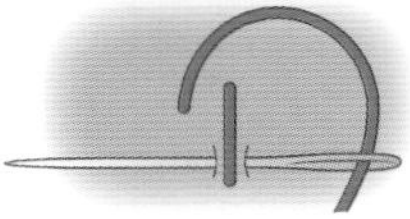

Take the needle in to the right of the first vertical stitch and just a short way up from the bottom of this stitch. Make a short, horizontal quilting stitch, bringing the needle up to the left of the first vertical stitch.

STEP 3

Carrying the thread across the previous two stitches, take the needle in on the right of the first vertical stitch, level with the left-hand branch, to secure this stitch. If working several scattered stitches within a short space of each other, use the last stitch to quilt through the layers of the project. Make a small quilting stitch through to the back of the work, taking the point of the needle into the batting and traveling through the batting to the area for the next stitch.

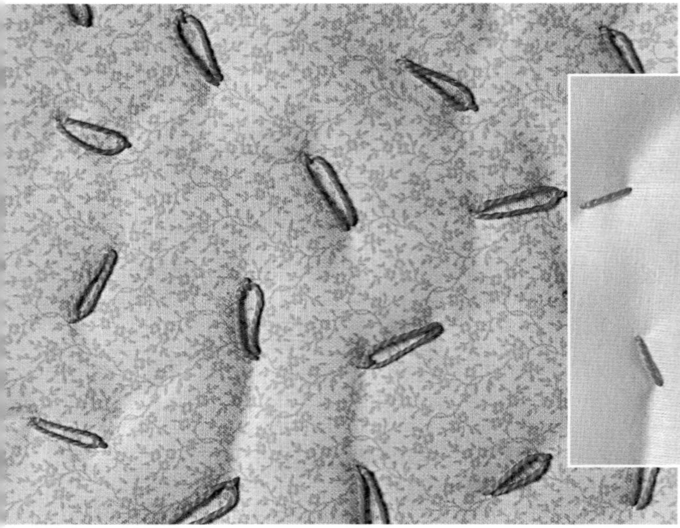

REVERSE OF WORK

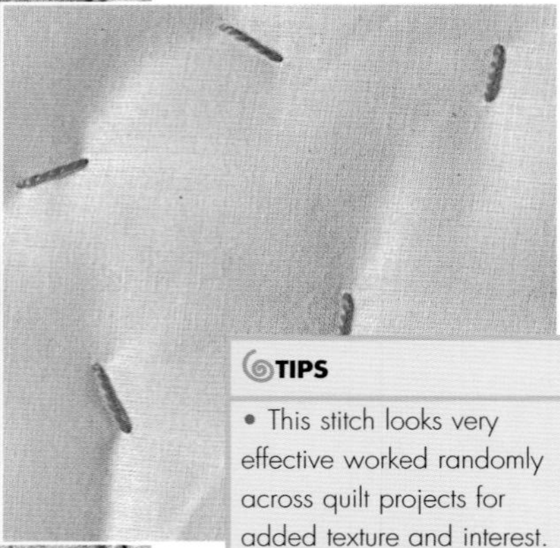

TIPS

- This stitch looks very effective worked randomly across quilt projects for added texture and interest.
- The length of the looped stitch can be varied to suit your preferred end result.

Detached chain

One of the most popular of the filling stitches, detached chain stitch is also commonly known as lazy daisy stitch. It is often used to sew flowers and leaves.

STEP 1

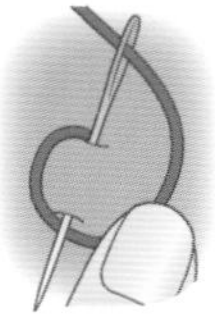

Bring the thread to the surface of the work. Hold the thread forward, ahead of your work and looped around. Take the needle back into the fabric where the thread first emerged (or very close to it) and make a quilting stitch forward through all layers, bringing the needle up into the waiting loop of thread. Pull the thread through.

STEP 2

Make a quilting stitch to secure the looped stitch.

STEP 3

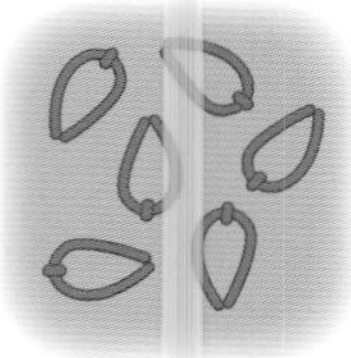

If working several scattered stitches within a short space of each other, use the last stitch to quilt through the layers of the project. Make a small quilting stitch through to the back of the work, taking the point of the needle into the batting and traveling through the batting to the area for the next stitch.

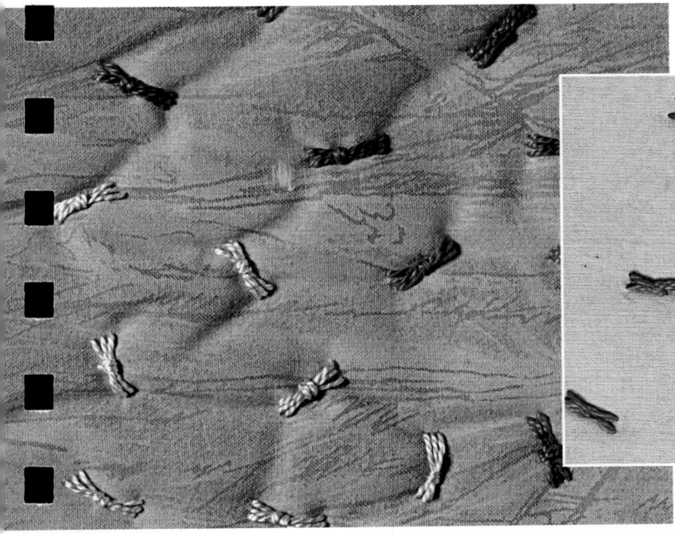

REVERSE OF WORK

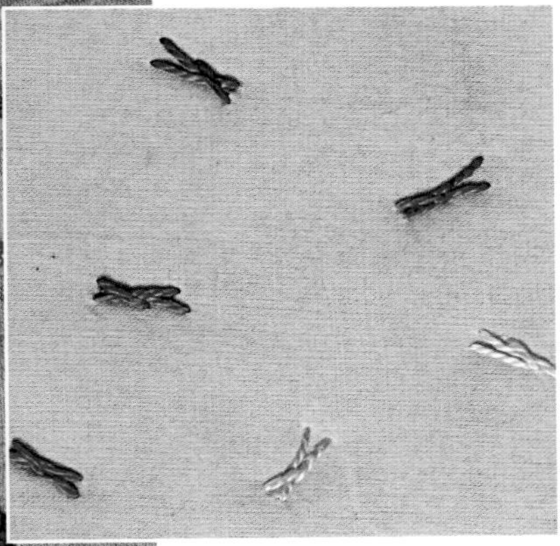

Sheaf stitch

Sheaf stitch is a combination of three parallel stitches that are then tied in the center with a loop of thread and bear a resemblance to a sheaf of wheat.

STEP 1

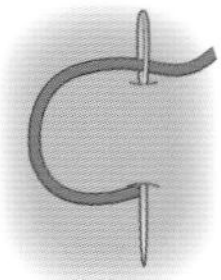

Bring the thread to the surface of the work and work a vertical quilting stitch through all layers. Bring the needle back out close to your original starting point and just to the right of it.

STEP 2

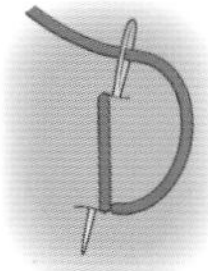

Work a second vertical stitch, bringing the needle up alongside your original starting point, but this time on the opposite side.

STEP 3

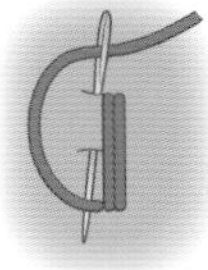

Take the needle into the fabric to complete the three vertical stitches and bring it out to the left, halfway up the three stitches.

STEP 4

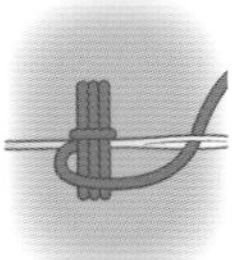

Pass the needle twice around the three stitches without catching up any fabric, pulling the thread in firmly to clinch them in their center. Make a quilting stitch to secure this complete sheaf stitch. If working several scattered stitches within a short space of each other, use the last stitch to quilt through the layers of the project. Make a small quilting stitch through to the back of the work, taking the point of the needle into the batting and traveling through the batting to the area for the next stitch.

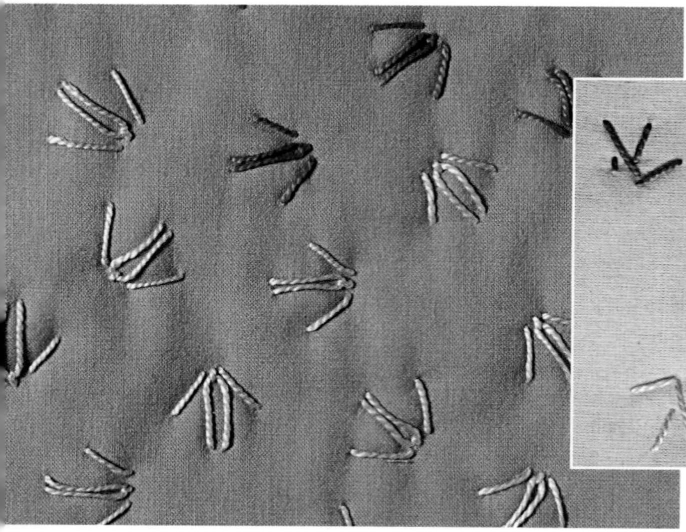

REVERSE OF WORK

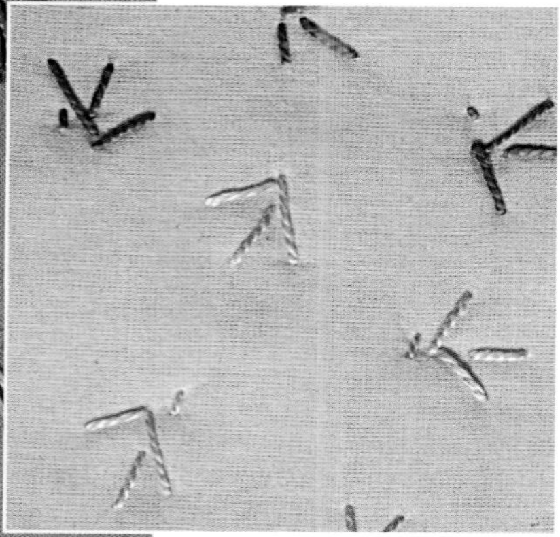

Tête de boeuf

Tête de boeuf stitch produces a very attractive filling stitch. The name means "bull's head"—you can see the "bull's horns" on either side of the "head."

STEP 1

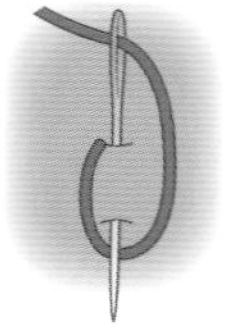

Holding the thread forward and round and taking the needle into the fabric close to the starting point, make a quilting stitch. Bring the needle up a short distance away and into the waiting loop of thread.

STEP 2

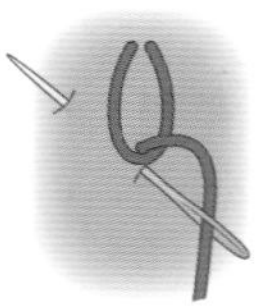

Take the needle into the fabric underneath the loop that you have made and make a diagonal quilting stitch, upward and out to the left of the loop.

STEP 3

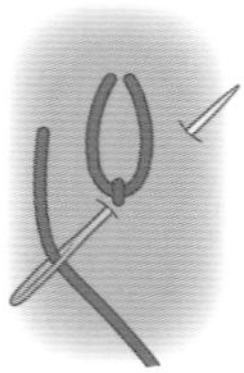

Take the needle into the fabric just below and to the left of the center of the loop stitch. Stitch diagonally upward and out to the right of the loop stitch.

STEP 4

Take the thread back into the fabric, to the bottom right of the central loop, to secure it. If working several scattered stitches within a short space of each other, use the last stitch to quilt through the layers of the project. Make a small quilting stitch through to the back of the work, taking the point of the needle into the batting and traveling through the batting to the area for the next stitch.

REVERSE OF WORK

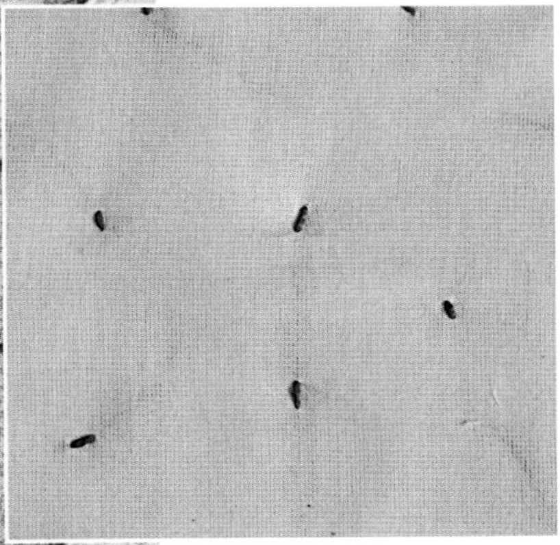

Pistil stitch

Pistil stitch is a very narrow and delicate filling stitch, comprised of a long bar stitch with a French knot sewn at the end for added textural interest.

STEP 1

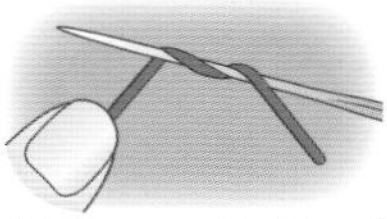

Bring the thread to the surface of the work. Holding the thread firmly with your non-sewing hand and keeping the needle a short distance away from the fabric, wrap the thread over the top of the needle to the right and under the point of the needle to the left. Repeat at least twice, but make more wraps if you want a larger knot.

STEP 2

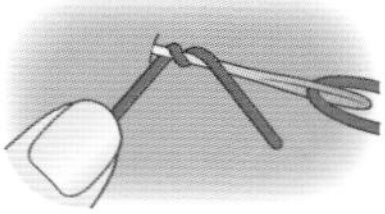

Still holding the thread taut, turn the point of the needle into the fabric, through all the layers. Push the wrapped threads down the needle and onto the surface of the fabric.

STEP 3

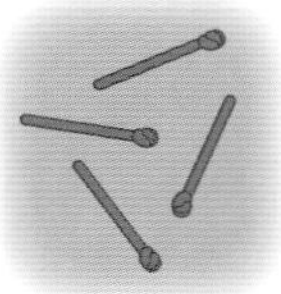

Hold the threads firmly with your non-sewing thumb while you take the needle through the fabric to make a quilting stitch. If working several scattered stitches within a short space of each other, after making the small quilting stitch through to the back of the work, take the point of the needle into the batting and travel through the batting to the area for the next stitch.

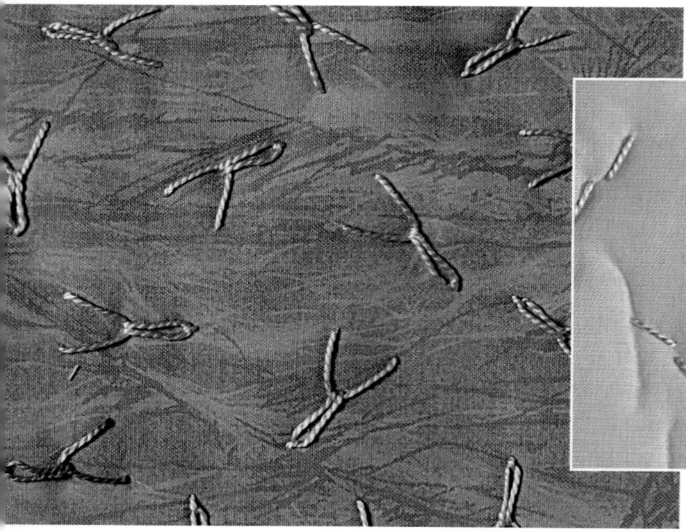

REVERSE OF WORK

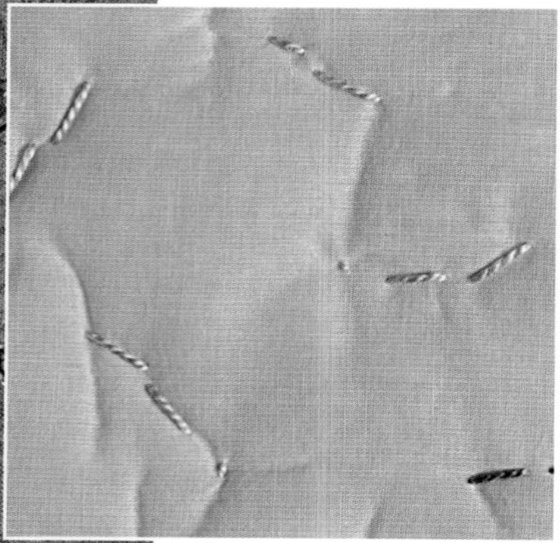

Detached wheatear

This stitch is constructed from two looped and secured stitches only. It makes a decorative filling stitch, scattered randomly for added texture and interest.

STEP 1

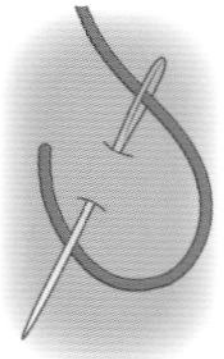

Hold the thread forward and downward and take the needle in on the right of your starting point, level with where the thread originally emerged. Make a quilting stitch through all layers, diagonally downward and over to the left, bringing the needle up into the waiting loop of thread and at a central point between the two upper parts of the stitch.

STEP 2

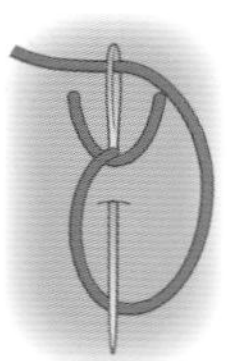

Hold the thread down and around to the right, take the needle back into the previous V-shaped stitch, close to where the thread came out of the fabric and make a vertical stitch downward, bringing the needle into the waiting loop of thread.

STEP 3

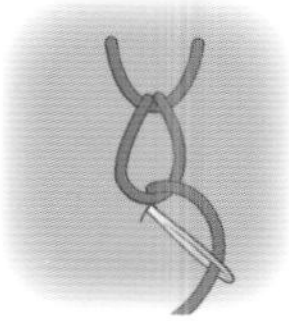

Make a quilting stitch outside the last loop to secure it. If working several scattered stitches within a short space of each other, use the last stitch to quilt through the layers of the project. Make a small quilting stitch through to the back of the work, taking the point of the needle into the batting and traveling through the batting to the area for the next stitch.

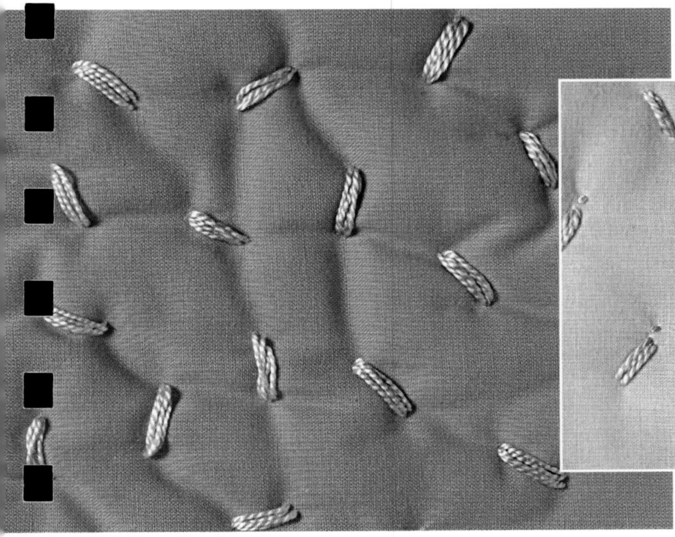

REVERSE OF WORK

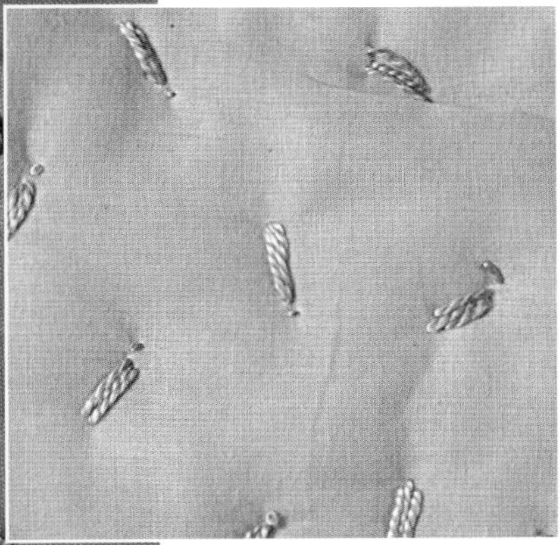

Granitos stitch

Each granitos stitch is worked through only two holes in the fabric, which helps to plump up the stitch for a textural result.

STEP 1

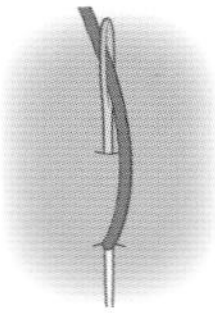

Taking the needle in a workable distance above your starting point, make a vertical quilting stitch down and toward you, bringing the needle out into the same hole that the thread first came out of. Pull through.

STEP 2

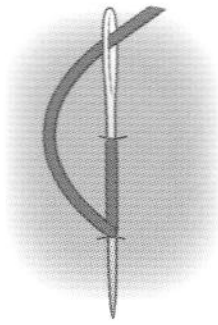

Holding the thread over to the left of the first stitch, make a second quilting stitch, working vertically down toward you and using the same two holes as before.

STEP 3

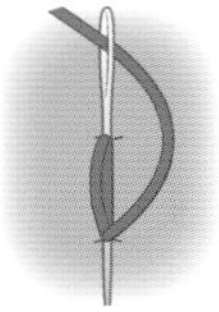

Hold the thread over to the right of the previous stitches and make a third vertical quilting stitch, using the same two holes to work through. Ensure that the thread sits to the right of the previous stitches.

STEP 4

Work a fourth stitch to the left of the previous stitches. Make a quilting stitch to secure the completed granitos stitch. If working several scattered stitches within a short space of each other, use the last stitch to bridge through the batting to the next area.

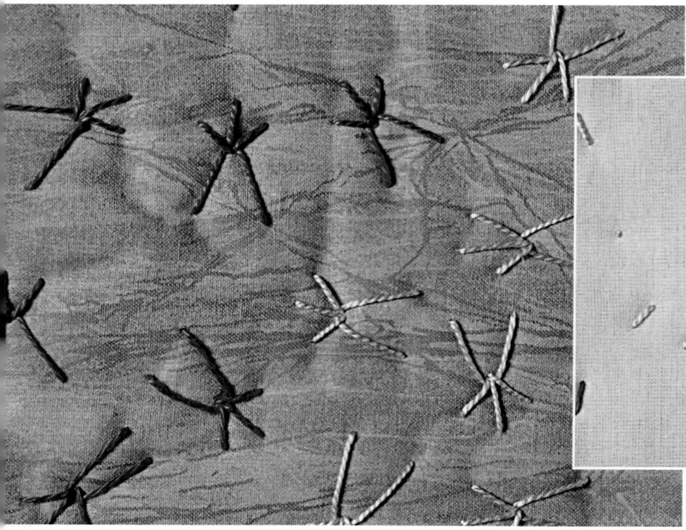

REVERSE OF WORK

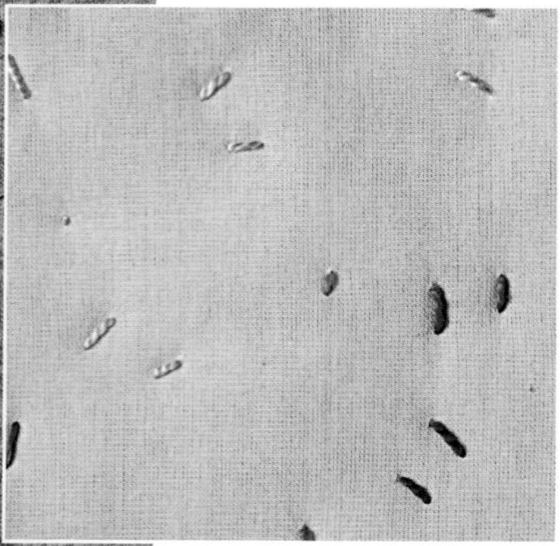

Crown stitch

When used as a randomly placed filling stitch, it is not important which way up crown stitch is sitting—the diagrams show the easiest way to sew this stitch.

STEP 1

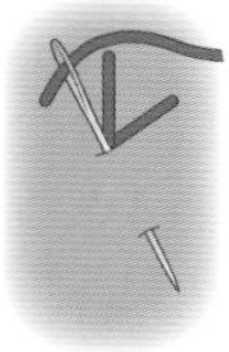

Bring the thread to the surface of the work and work a basic fern stitch (see page 103) through all layers, ensuring that the two side branches of the fern are slightly lower or shorter than the central one. End the completed fern stitch by taking the needle in at the same point as the previous threads, and bringing it out diagonally downward and to the right-hand side of the work.

STEP 2

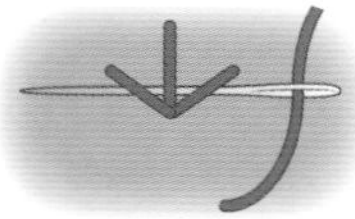

Pass the needle behind all three stitches, making sure that you do not catch up any fabric, and take the needle into the fabric on the left-hand side of the work, level with the right-hand stitch. Use a quilting stitch at this point to secure the completed crown stitch.

STEP 3

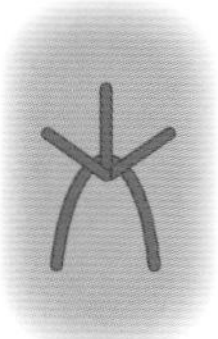

If working several scattered stitches within a short space of each other, use the last stitch as a small quilting stitch carried through to the back of the work. Take the point of the needle into the batting and travel through the batting to the area for the next crown stitch. This helps to keep the reverse of the work as neat as possible.

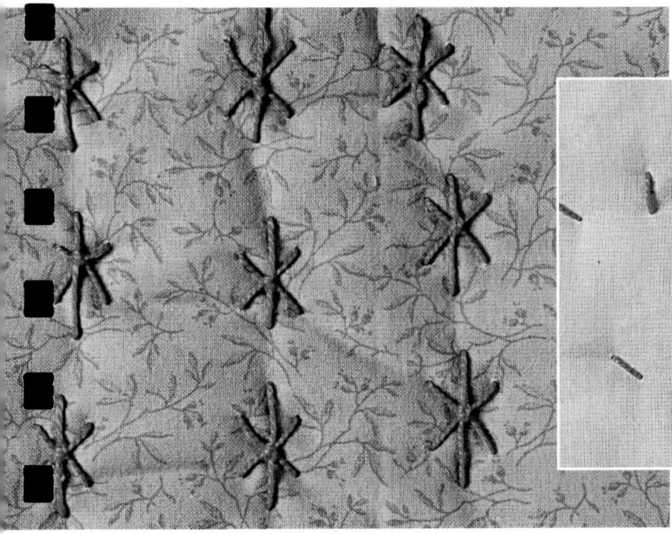

REVERSE OF WORK

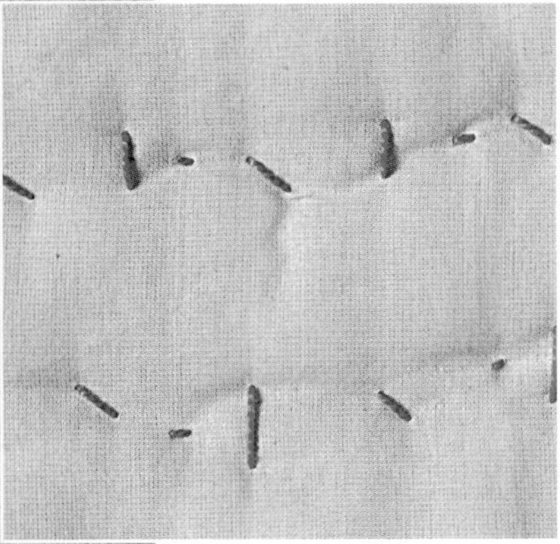

Cross and twist

Cross and twist stitch is a wide stitch with a star-like appearance. A looped thread is knotted around the center, raising the stitch and adding textural interest.

STEP 1

Work a basic cross stitch (see page 122) through all layers. End this stitch by taking the needle upward and bring it out centrally above the top of the cross stitch.

STEP 2

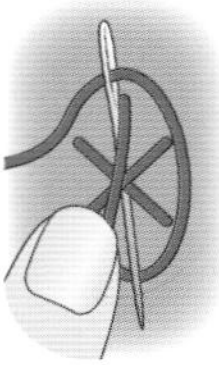

Hold the thread down the center of the cross stitch with your non-sewing thumb. Take the needle in from the left of this thread, behind the cross stitch legs (without catching up any fabric) and out to the right of the waiting thread. Make sure that the waiting thread wraps itself behind the point of the needle from left to right.

STEP 3

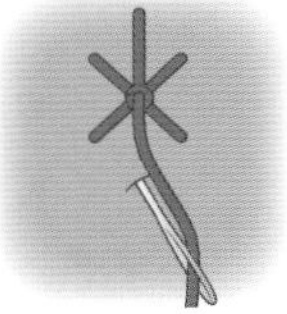

Secure the completed cross and twist stitch by making a quilting stitch centrally below (and further down from) the lower legs of the base cross stitch.

STEP 4

If working several scattered stitches within a short space of each other, use the last stitch to bridge through the batting to the next area.

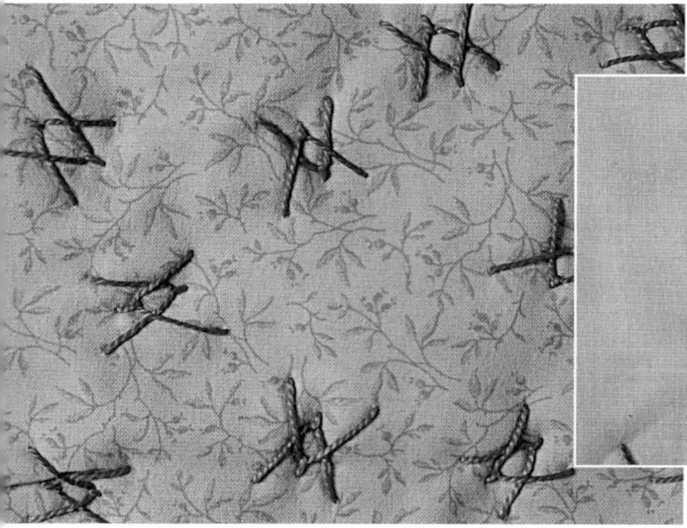

REVERSE OF WORK

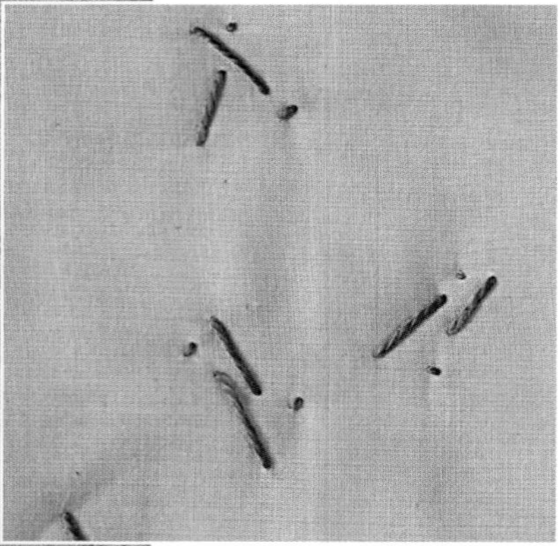

Reversed fly

This intriguing combination of two fly stitches is simple to work. One fly stitch is sewn first, and then a second one is placed on top and upside down.

TIP

Try to ensure the two overlapping fly stitches are of the same length and width as each other.

STEP 1

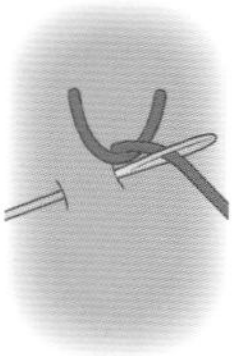

Sew a basic fly stitch (see page 99) through all layers. End this first fly stitch by bringing the needle out to the bottom left-hand side, slightly lower than the level of the fly stitch.

STEP 2

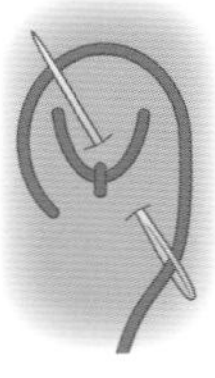

Hold the thread forward and to the right. Take the needle in on the right of the fly stitch and make a quilting stitch upward at an inward diagonal, emerging centrally within the fly stitch and bringing the needle into the waiting loop of thread. Secure this inverted V-shape with a quilting stitch above it.

STEP 3

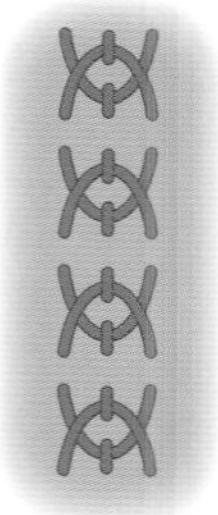

If working several scattered stitches within a short space of each other, use the last stitch as a small quilting stitch carried through to the back of the work.

REVERSE OF WORK

Square boss

Square boss stitch is a little more formal than some of the available filling stitches. You might like to make a feature of the geometric shape by aligning the stitches in rows.

TIP

If working in rows, achieve extra movement by working stitches randomly and at different angles.

STEP 1

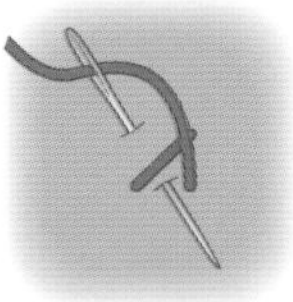

Work a basic cross stitch (see page 122) through all layers. Make a quilting stitch bringing the needle out at the bottom of the cross stitch, a little higher up than the two lower branches.

STEP 2

Take the needle in on the right of the stitch and between the two right-hand branches, bringing it out on the left and between the left-hand branches.

STEP 3

Take the needle back in at the bottom and stitch vertically upward to exit between the top branches. Follow this with a stitch from right to left, and then finish with a stitch in at the top again to secure the complete square boss stitch. If working several scattered stitches within a short space of each other, use the last stitch as a small quilting stitch carried through to the back of the work. Take the point of the needle into the batting and travel through the batting to the area for the next square boss stitch, thereby helping to keep the reverse of the work as neat as possible.

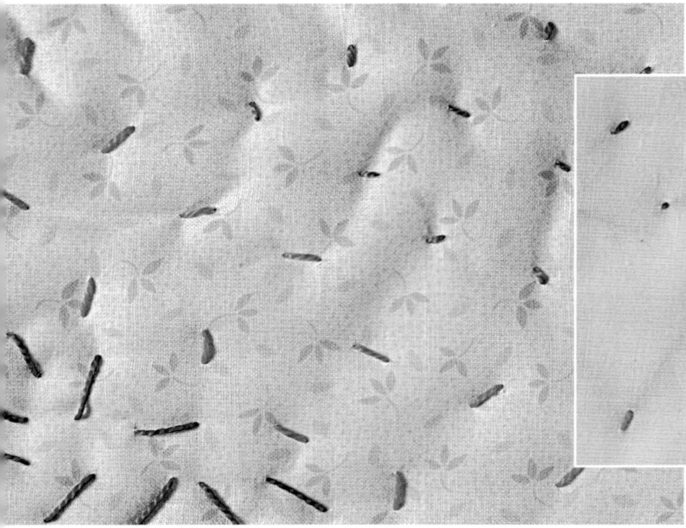

REVERSE OF WORK

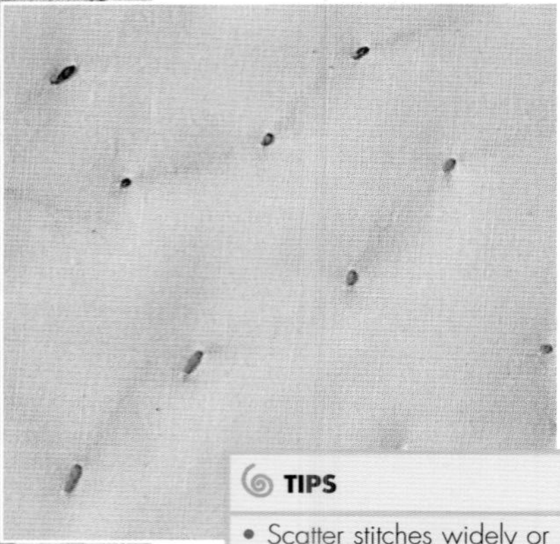

Seed stitch

Also known as utility quilting stitch, seed stitch is a fast and versatile filling stitch. It can be worked to any length you prefer.

TIPS

- Scatter stitches widely or work them closer together for dense, more compact quilted areas.
- Work stitches in even lengths across your quilt project, or vary them for greater effect and dimension.

STEP 1

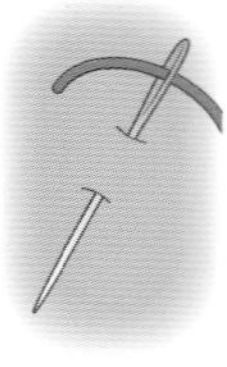

Make a quilting stitch through all layers, at any angle and in any direction you like—the distance from the starting point to where the needle enters the fabric will determine the length of the seed stitch.

STEP 2

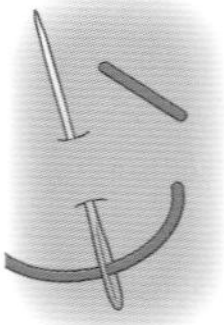

Make a second quilting stitch at a different angle to the first. Seed stitches are meant to be placed randomly. If your stitches begin to look uniform, try turning your work.

STEP 3

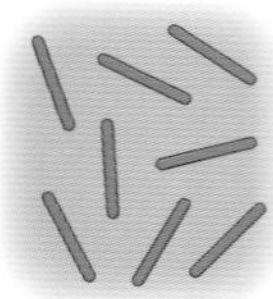

If working several scattered stitches within a short space of each other, use the last stitch as a small quilting stitch carried through to the back of the work. Take the point of the needle into the batting and travel through the batting to the area for the next stitch. This also means that you will end up with only small seed stitches on the back of the work.

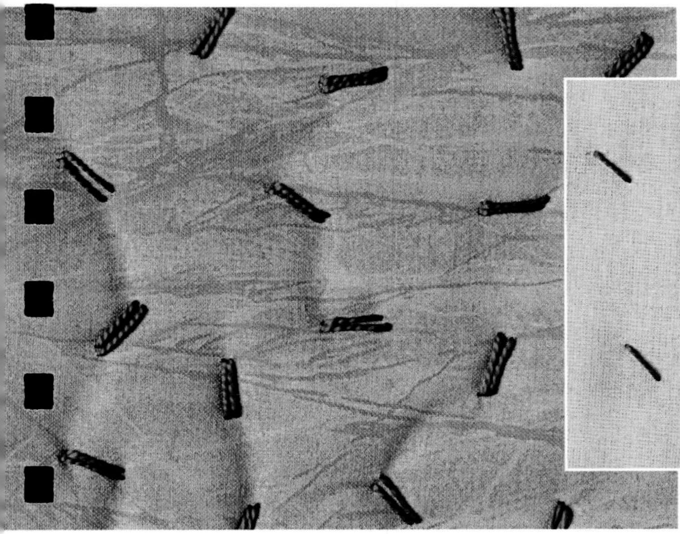

REVERSE OF WORK

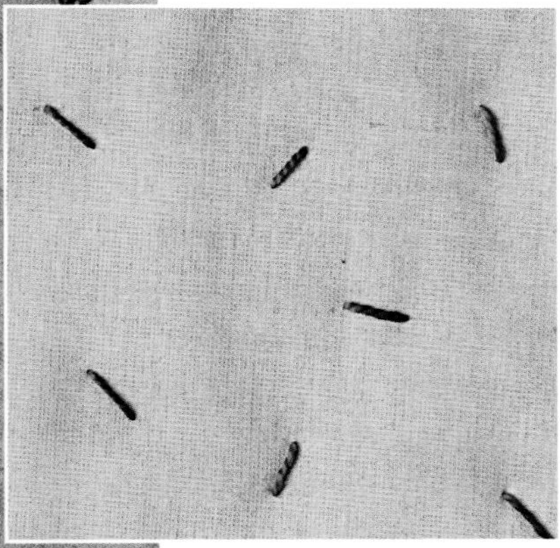

Double seed

These double stitches can be worked to any length, and scattered widely or worked close together. For variation, change the length of individual pairs.

STEP 1

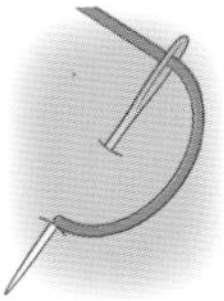

Make a quilting stitch through all layers, at any angle and in any direction you like—the distance from the starting point to where the needle enters the fabric will determine the length of the seed stitch.

STEP 2

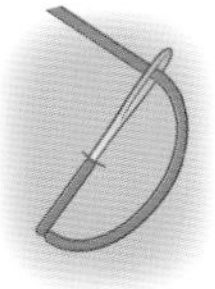

Make a second quilting stitch alongside the first one, ensuring that they sit snugly next to each other.

STEP 3

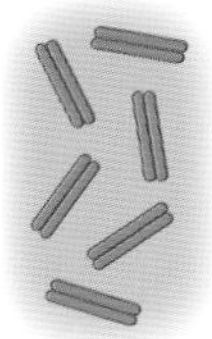

Make a second set of two stitches, at a different angle to the first pair. Continue in this manner, and try to position the pairs of stitches randomly. Turning your work regularly can help you to head off in another direction.

STEP 4

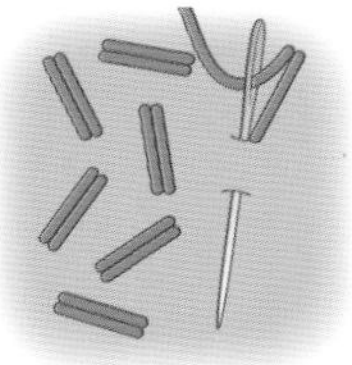

If working several scattered double seed stitches within a short space of each other, use the last stitch as a small quilting stitch carried through to the back of the work. Take the point of the needle into the batting and travel through the batting to the area for the next pair of stitches. In this way, you will end up with only small seed stitches on the back of the work.

Hand-sewn Surface Embellishment

The embellishment techniques and suggestions shown here are additional to your quilted work. They can be valuable decorations to quilt projects such as wallhangings, when further surface interest is required.

Please note that it is inadvisable to add detachable surface embellishments to quilts that will be handled by babies and children.

Buttons, charms and beads

A great variety of buttons, charms and beads are available, and they can make fun and unusual additions to quilt work. Dot individual items around or cluster them together in groups.

BUTTONS AND CHARMS

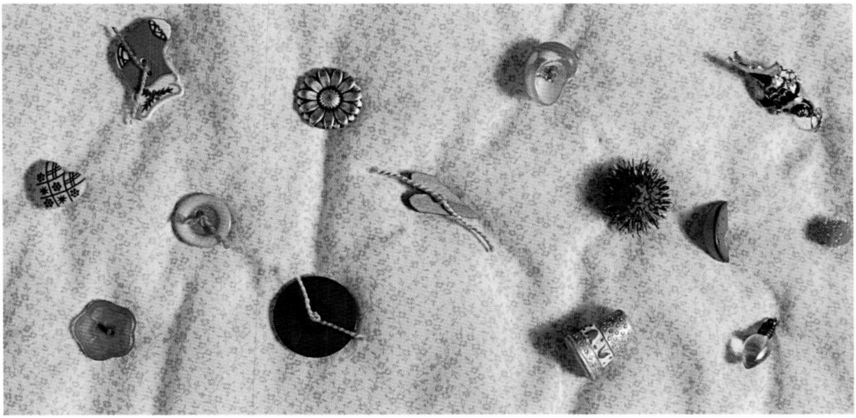

STEP 1

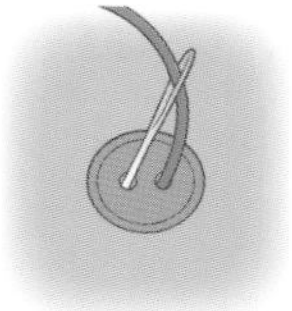

Bring the thread to the surface of the work, and take the needle through the button or charm. Now either take the needle back into the fabric through a second hole in the item, or loop the thread over the edge of the item and back into the fabric. Decorative thread can be tied through the holes and knotted on the surface of the work for additional texture and interest.

TIPS

- Threads for securing buttons and charms should preferably be taken through all layers of a quilt project to secure the items tightly.
- Be aware of what is happening on the back of the work and, where it is necessary to have a stitch appear on the reverse side of your quilt project, ensure that it is short and tidy.

STEP 2

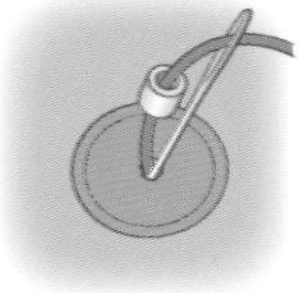

Alternatively, pass the thread through a bead before taking the needle back through the same hole—the bead will secure the thread on top of the button or charm.

STEP 3

Make a stitch through all layers of the quilt work to secure the item. Finish the stitch with a quilting stitch, or tie and leave the thread as a decorative feature on the surface of your work. Textured or metallic threads are particularly effective used in this way.

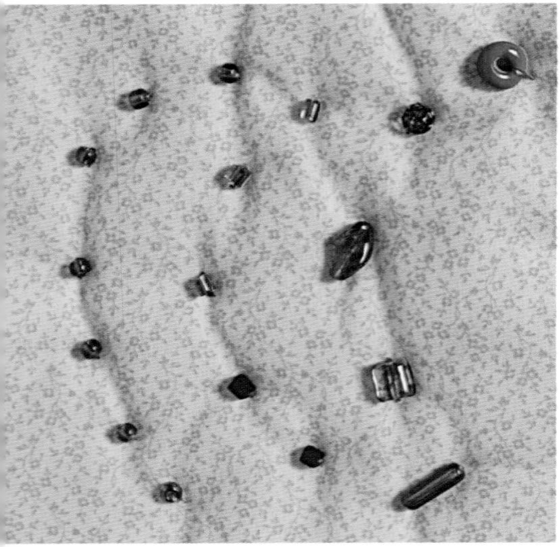

BEADS

STEP 1

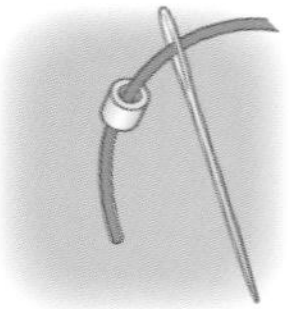

Choose a needle that will fit through the hole in the bead. Bring the thread to the surface of the work. Pass the needle through the hole in the bead.

STEP 2

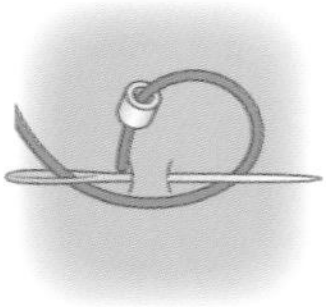

Take the needle back into the fabric close to the spot where the thread initially emerged. Make a short quilting stitch through all layers, forward, but before pulling the needle through, loop the thread forward and around the point of the needle. Pull the thread taut before pulling the needle through the fabric. Secure with a quilting stitch. Push the needle through the batting to the area for the next bead, thereby maintaining a neat appearance on the reverse of the work.

Sequins

Sequins come in all shapes, sizes and colors. They can provide individual highlights or be clustered together in groups for massed shimmer and sparkle.

STEP 1

Bring the thread to the surface of the work. Pass the needle through the hole in the sequin. Loop the thread over the edge of the sequin and take the needle back into the fabric.

STEP 2

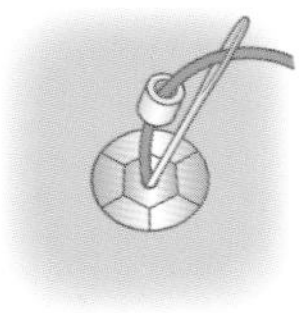

Alternatively, pass the needle through a bead before taking it through the same hole in the sequin—the bead will secure the thread on top of the sequin.

STEP 3

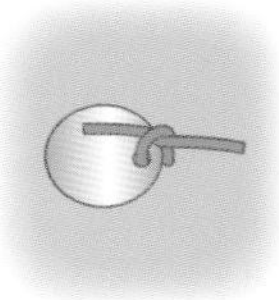

Make a stitch through all layers of the quilt work to secure the sequin. Finish the stitch with a quilting stitch, or tie and leave the thread as a decorative feature on the surface of your work. Textured or metallic threads are particularly effective used in this way.

Shisha

The word "shisha" means "little mirror." Shisha embroidery is a traditional Indian technique used on clothing and furnishings, in which tiny mirrors are inserted into the design and embroidered to hold them in place. These little mirrors can add a lovely twinkle to your quilt work. Traditionally, shisha are made from cut glass, but you could use a large sequin if you prefer. Do not worry if the edges of the shisha are uneven, because the stitches will cover them.

First of all, a base grid is sewn to hold the mirror in place. The thread needs to be kept taut at all stages during this process. Keep the stitches of the base grid parallel (in both directions), as close to the center of the mirror as is possible. (Later, when additional embroidery stitches are worked into the base grid, the grid will be pulled outwards a little to uncover the mirror.) If the base grid is too loose or too near the edge of the mirror, it will slip off and fail to keep the mirror in place.

Now additional embroidery stitches can be added for decorative effect. These can be worked very closely together, providing a heavy and dense look. Alternatively, they can be spaced farther apart, to make a filigree-like trellis, through which more areas of the mirror will shine.

CLOSED SHISHA

STEP 1

Hold the mirror in place on the surface of the fabric with your non-sewing thumb (or use fabric glue or double-sided sticky tape if you prefer). Bring the thread to the surface of the work alongside the mirror's edge. Work two horizontal and parallel stitches across the mirror, as close to the center as you can, making a small stitch on the opposite side of the mirror before returning to the side that you started on.

Take the needle into the fabric and bring it out by one of the remaining sides of the mirror. Work two vertical and parallel stitches at right angles to the first pair. Work upward and away from you, take the needle down behind each of the first stitches in turn and at the edge of the mirror, make a small stitch sideways. This completes the base grid.

STEP 2

Now take the needle into the fabric and bring it up somewhere alongside the edge of the mirror. Hold the thread forward and upward and, working in a clockwise direction, make a blanket stitch down behind the base grid.

Closed shisha

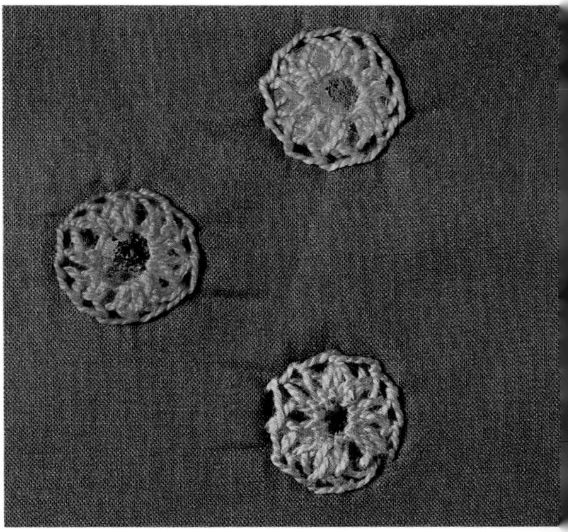

STEP 3

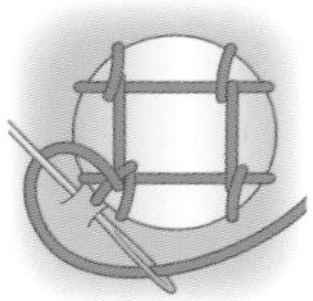

Hold the thread forward and downward and make a chain stitch alongside the edge of the mirror. Repeat steps 3 and 4 until you have worked all the way around the mirror. Secure the last chain by taking the thread into the fabric outside the last chain.

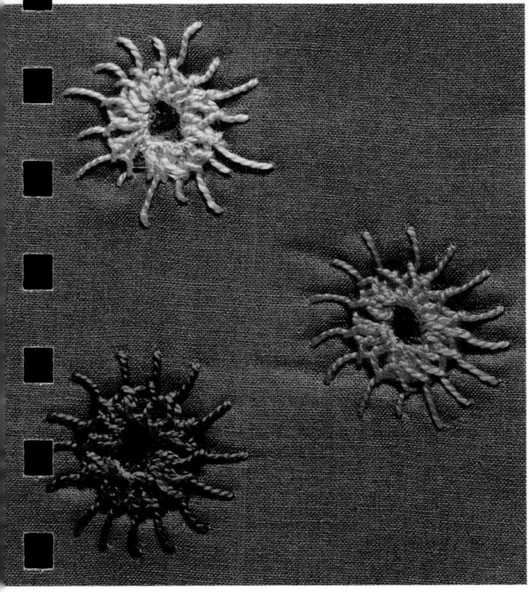

Open shisha

OPEN SHISHA

STEP 1

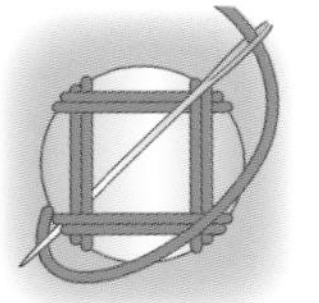

Hold the mirror in position. Bring the thread to the surface alongside the mirror's edge and work a set of double parallel lines across the center of the mirror. Take the needle into the fabric, come up on one of the remaining sides of the mirror and work a second set of double parallel lines at right angles to the first, weaving the thread over and under the previous set of parallel stitches. This completes the base grid.

Take the needle into the fabric and bring it out somewhere alongside the edge of the mirror. Working in a counterclockwise direction, hold the thread down and around to the right. Make a blanket stitch into the base grid and pull the thread through.

STEP 2

Hold the thread down and around to the right. Make a blanket stitch into the fabric, bringing the needle into the waiting loop of thread. As the needle is pulled through, hold the thread across the center of the mirror and the blanket stitch will sit snugly against the side of the mirror.

Continue around the mirror, repeating steps 1 and 2. Secure the last blanket stitch with a quilting stitch outside it.

TIP

The extra embroidery stitches surrounding the shisha are based on basic chain stitch (see page 77) and basic blanket stitch (see page 104).

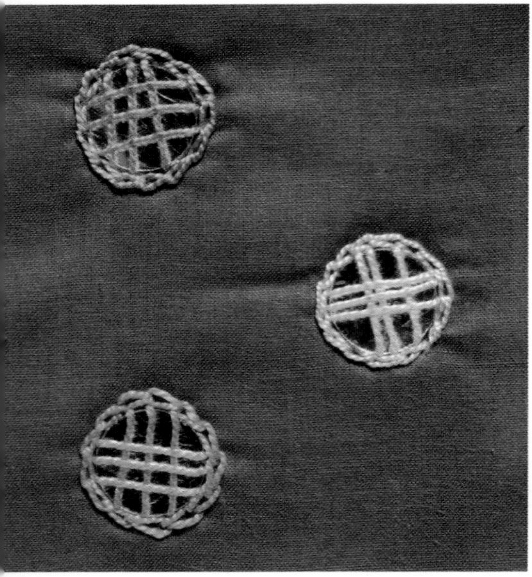

Contemporary shisha

CONTEMPORARY SHISHA

STEP 1

Hold the mirror in position and secure it with a set of three rows of thread, evenly spaced, across the center of the mirror. Take the needle into the fabric, come up on an unused side of the mirror and stitch a second set of three rows of thread at right angles to the first. This completes the base grid.

STEP 2

Hold the thread forward and down and, beginning at the top of the mirror and working in a counterclockwise direction, sew a series of chain stitches alongside the edge of the mirror. Secure the final chain stitch with a stitch outside the last link.

Couching

The word "couching" is derived from the French word "coucher," which means "to lay something down horizontally." Some threads are too thick, too textured or too weak to be used for the quilting process, which demands that they are constantly passed through layers of fabric and batting. However, these threads can still be used for embellishment, by placing them on the surface of the work and attaching them to the fabric with a couching stitch. Couching is done using a secondary thread (or several threads) in the same color as the main thread, or in a strong or subtle contrast. Couched threads can add a great deal of raised texture and decorative interest to the surface of quilt work.

COUCHED THREAD

Couched threads can be worked in single lines, which are suitable for following quilting designs or for contour-quilting (outlining) motif patterns. You can couch around geometric shapes, curves and circles. The actual thread to be couched can consist of chunky and textured threads, multiple fibers, several strands of thread, fancy ribbons, yarns and so on.

You have two options for starting and finishing the ends of the thread(s) to be couched. If the thread can be accommodated in a needle, it can be brought to the surface of the fabric at the beginning of the line and taken back down through it at the end of the work. You might even find that you can use the traditional quilter's knot to start and finish. A large-eyed, bodkin-style needle is useful at this stage.

If this approach is not possible, there are other solutions. You can hide the raw edges of the thread under a cluster of securing stitches, or knot the end of the thread and leave it on the surface of the work as a textural feature. Alternatively, you can catch the raw ends of the thread into the seams of the quilt pieces as they are sewn—this needs forward planning into the design and may not be the easiest option.

COUCHING STITCHES

The stitches used for the actual job of couching— holding down the main thread, which then becomes the couched thread—can be worked singly or in clusters, using straight stitches or diagonal stitches. You can also make use of more decorative, wider stitches. Couching stitches require some space between them to allow the couched thread to remain visible.

You might like to do the job of quilting at the same time as couching. To do this, the couching stitches need to pass through all layers of the quilt work. This is where some of the wider stitches will be useful.

TIP

When working long lengths of couched thread, it is advisable to place pins across the thread at regular intervals to hold it in position.

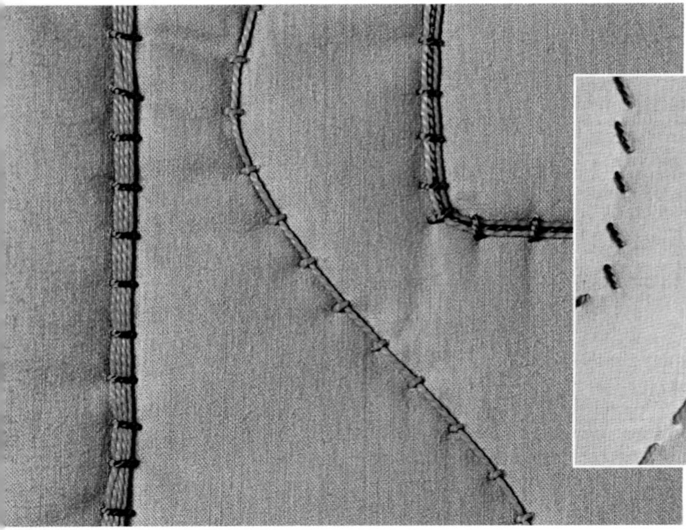

REVERSE OF WORK

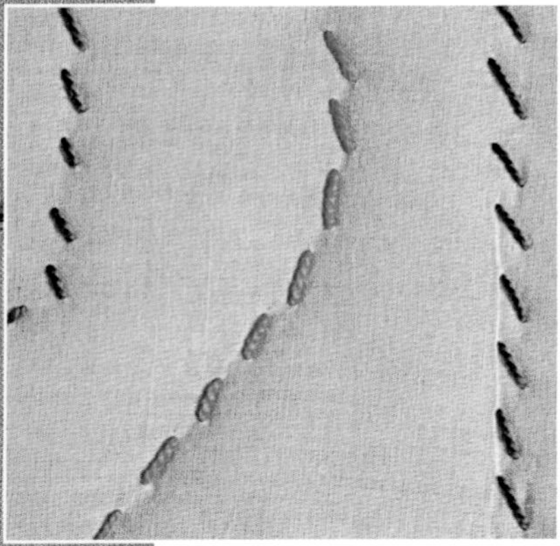

SINGLE STITCHES *Couching with single straight stitches over single thread and multiple threads.*

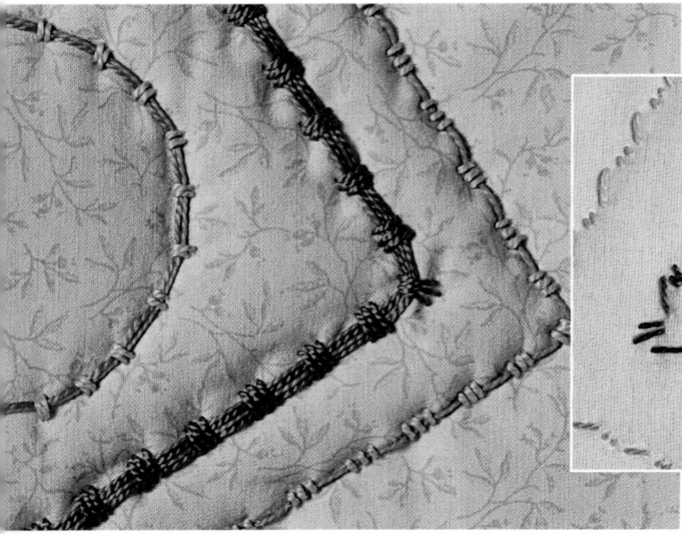

REVERSE OF WORK

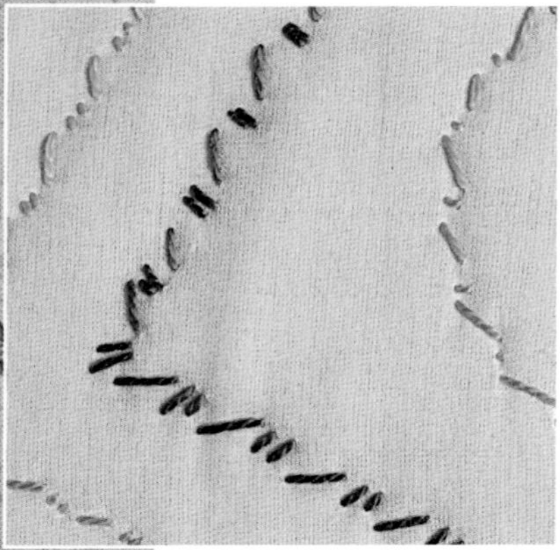

CLUSTERED STITCHES *Couching with clustered straight stitches over single thread and multiple threads.*

REVERSE OF WORK

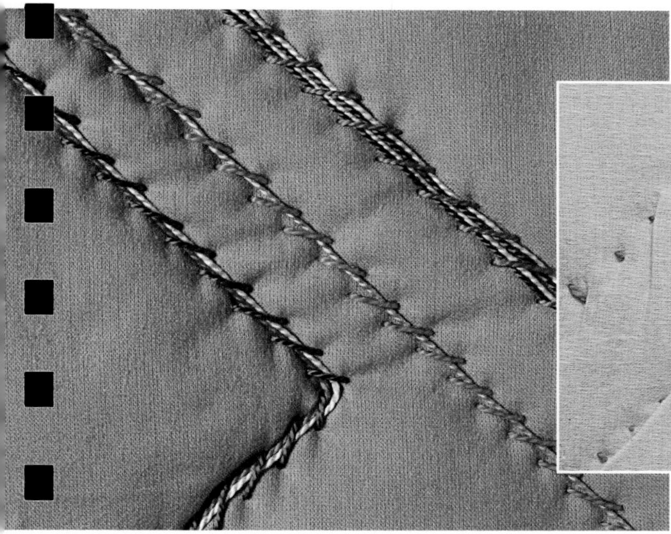

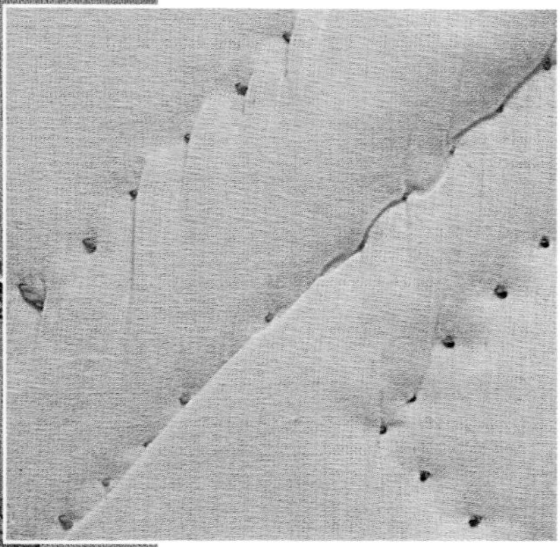

SINGLE DIAGONAL STITCHES *Couching with single diagonal stitches over single thread and multiple threads.*

REVERSE OF WORK

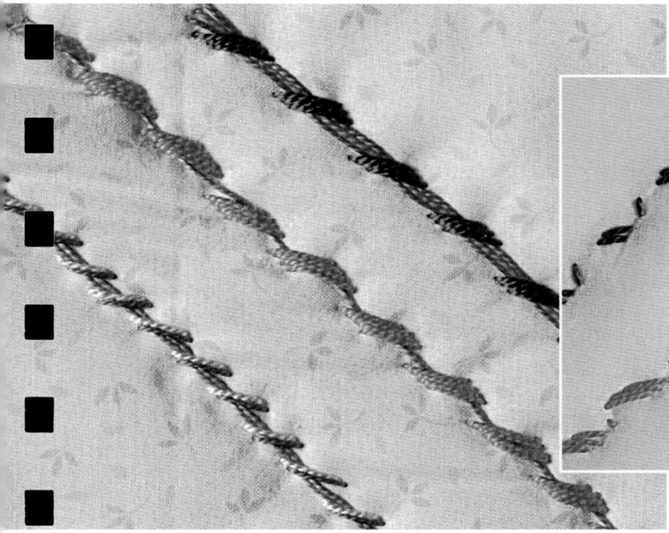

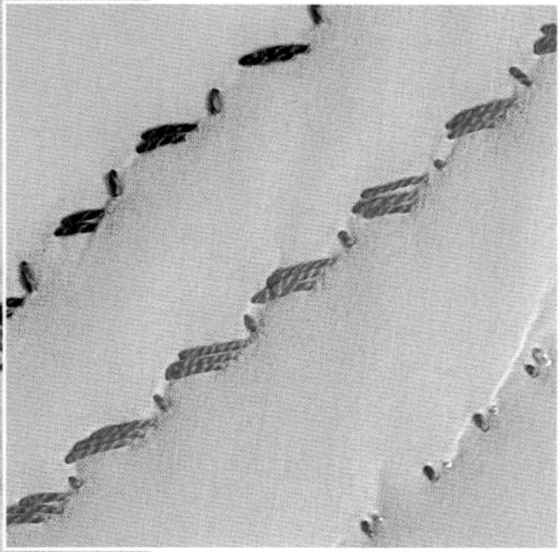

CLUSTERED DIAGONAL STITCHES *Couching with clustered diagonal stitches over single thread and multiple threads.*

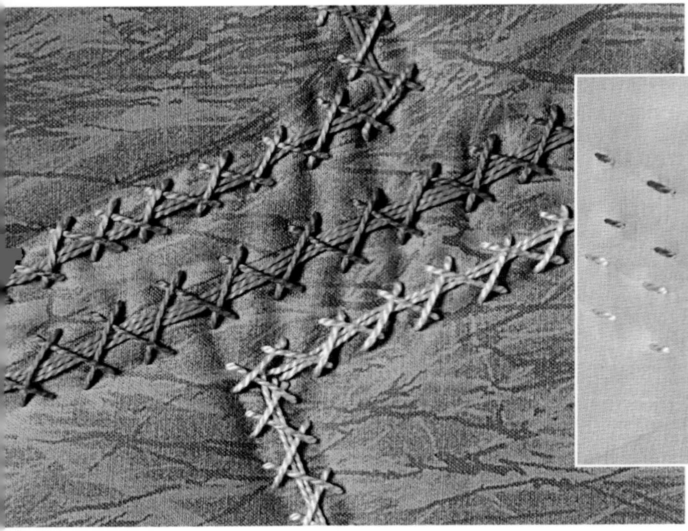

REVERSE OF WORK

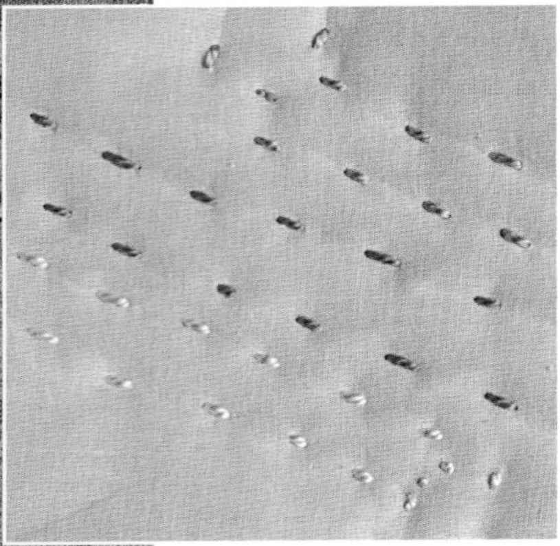

HERRINGBONE STITCH *Couching with basic herringbone stitch (see page 114) over multiple threads.*

REVERSE OF WORK

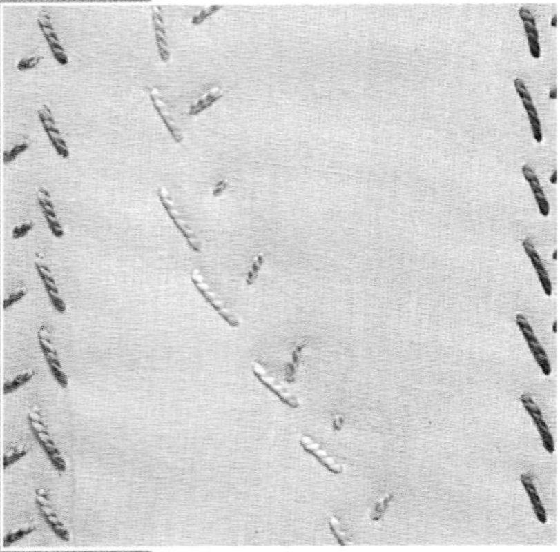

FLY STITCH *Couching with basic fly stitch (see page 99) over multiple threads.*

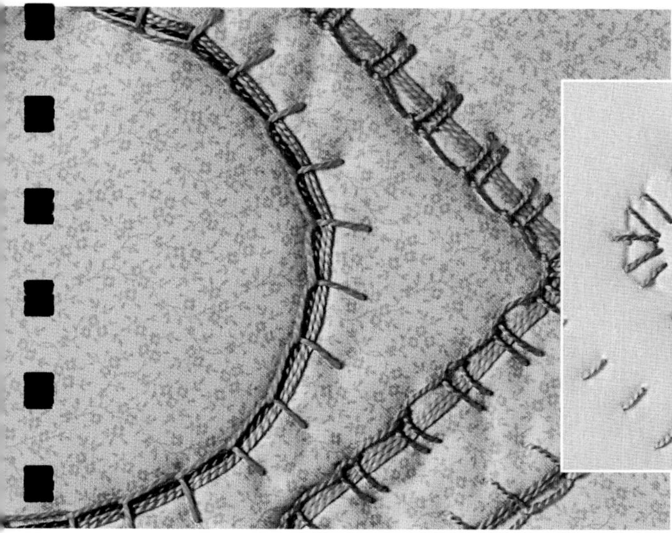

REVERSE OF WORK

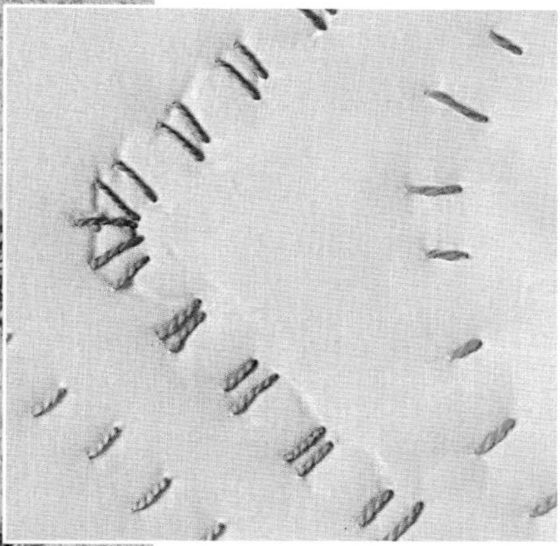

BLANKET STITCH *Couching with single and clustered basic blanket stitch (see page 104) over multiple threads.*

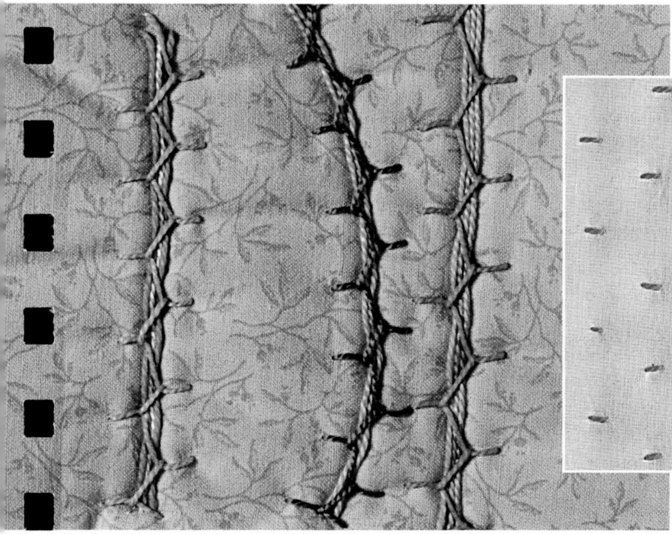

REVERSE OF WORK

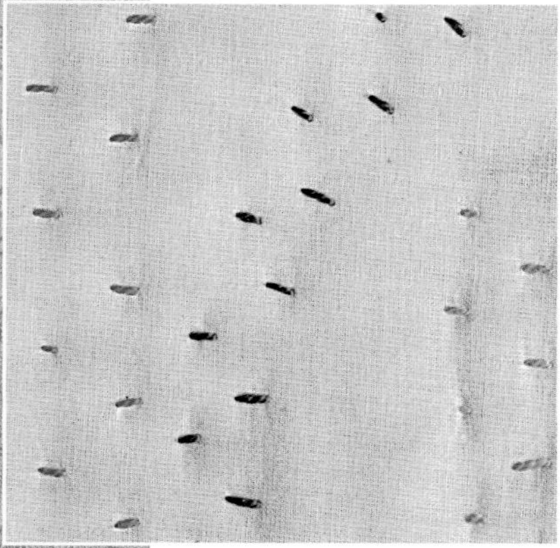

CRETAN STITCH *Couching with basic Cretan stitch (see page 126) over multiple threads.*

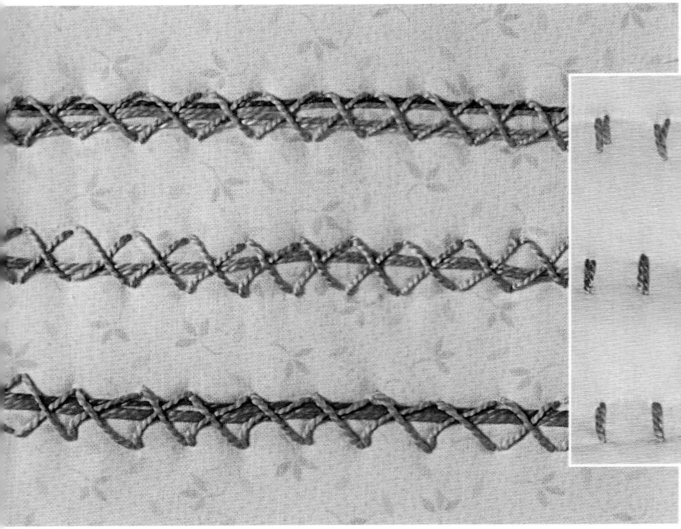

CROSS STITCH *Couching with basic cross stitch (see page 122) over multiple threads.*

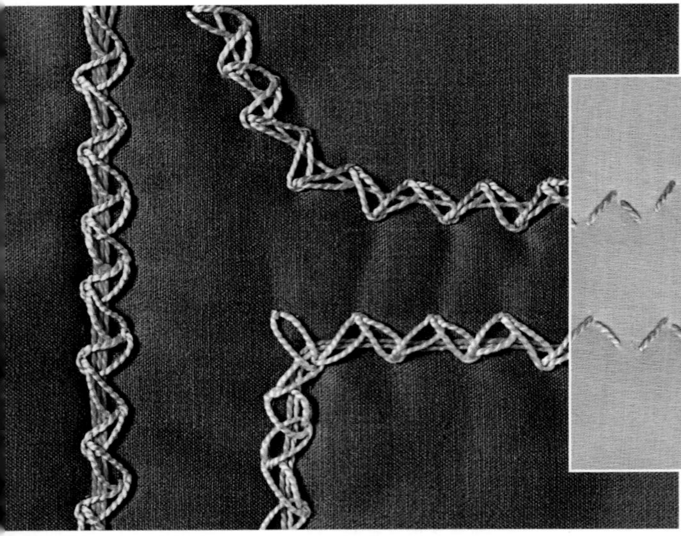

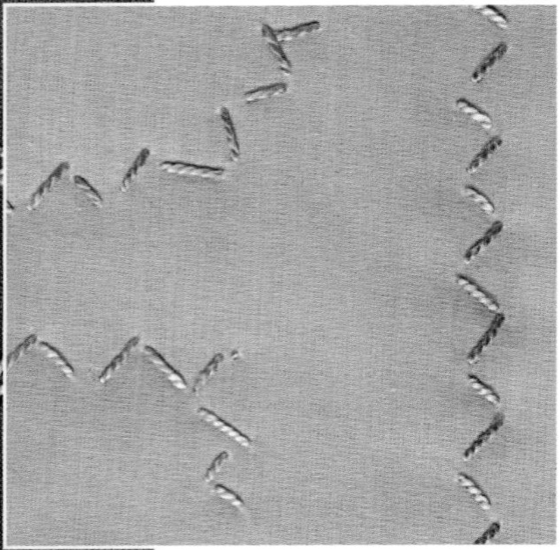

ZIGZAG CHAIN *Couching with basic zigzag chain stitch (see page 91) over single thread and multiple threads.*

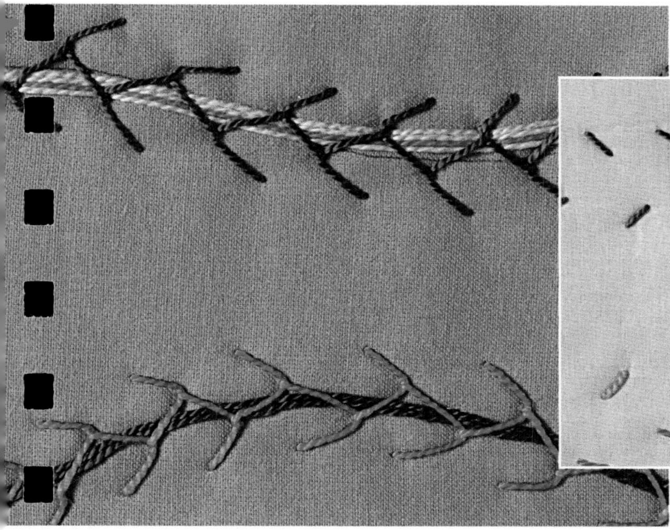

REVERSE OF WORK

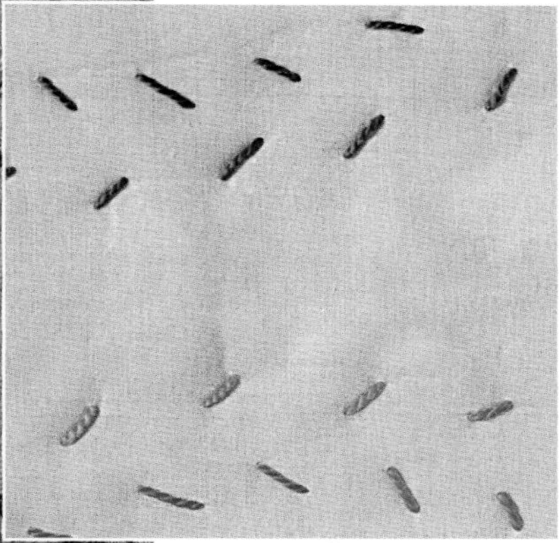

FEATHER STITCH *Couching with basic single feather stitch (see page 95) over multiple threads.*

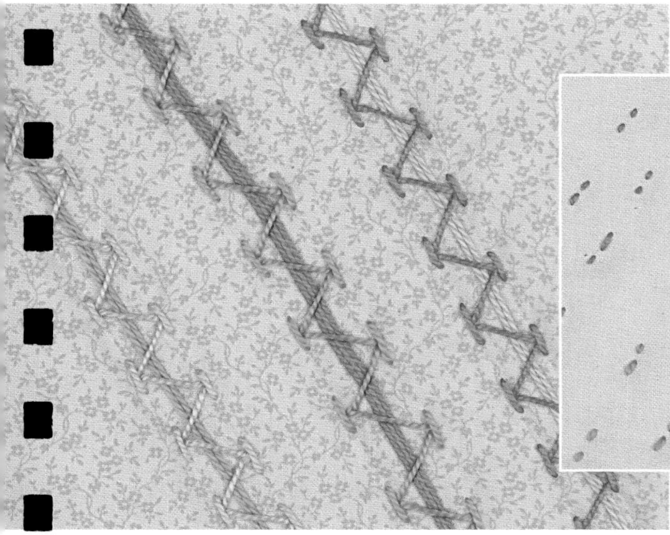

REVERSE OF WORK

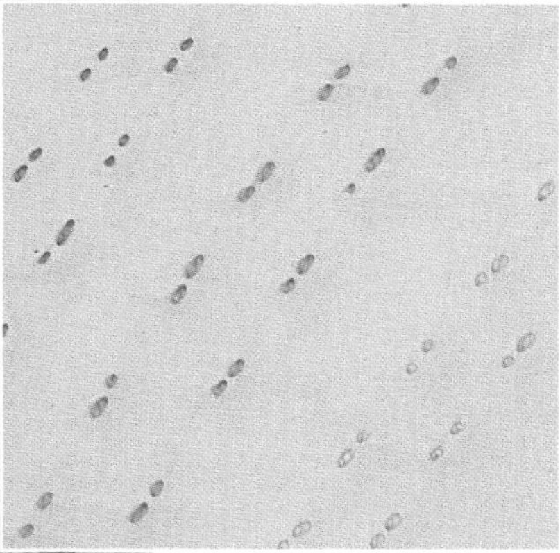

CHEVRON STITCH *Couching using basic chevron stitch (see page 132) over multiple threads.*

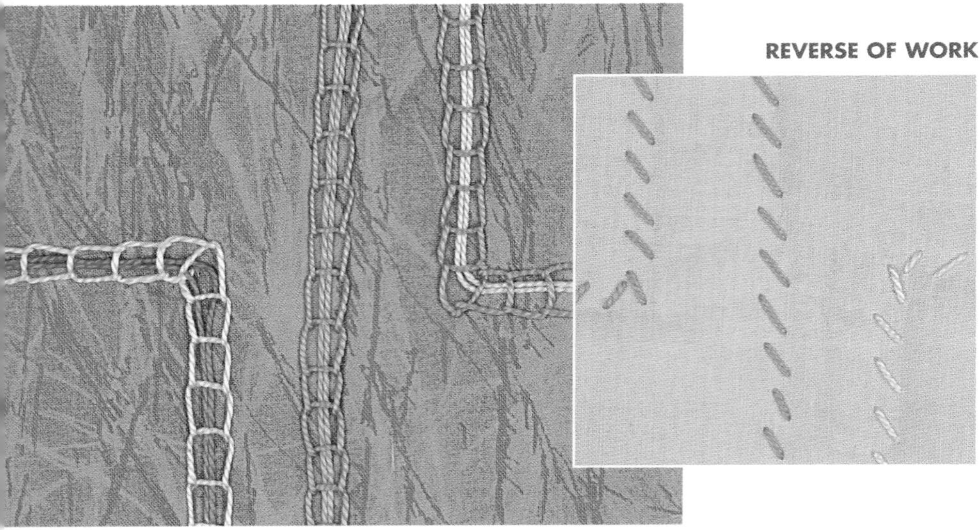

OPEN CHAIN *Couching with basic open chain stitch (see page 81) over multiple threads.*

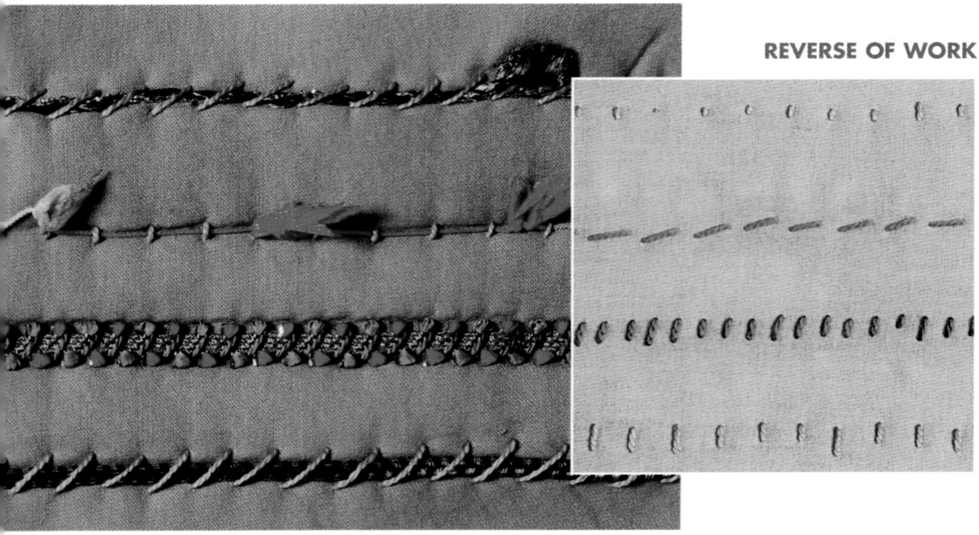

EMBELLISHMENT *Couching with single diagonal or straight stitches over fancy threads, yarns, metallics, wool and ribbons.*

Hand-sewn Insertion Stitches

Insertion stitches provide an interesting alternative method of joining multiple panels to form a quilt. Each individual panel needs a finished edge that is then joined to its neighboring finished panel with a decorative stitch. Insertion stitches can be worked tightly, so that the panels are next to each other, or worked in a looser fashion, providing a delicate trelliswork of stitching for more decorative projects.

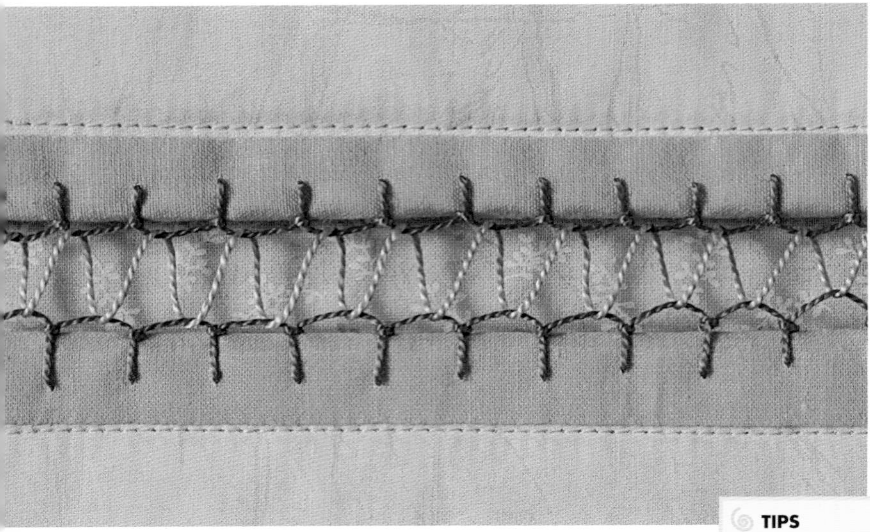

Laced insertion

This stitch is also known as laced faggot stitch. A looped and knotted stitch is worked along each of the quilt edges, and the lacing is then worked through the loops.

TIPS

- This stitch can be worked in one color of thread or multiple colors for added interest.
- Using a blunt needle for the lacing process is quicker.

STEP 1

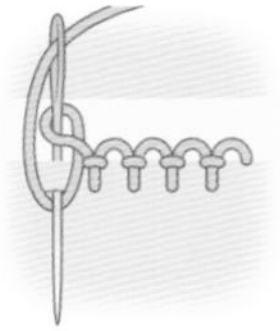

First, work a row of knotted and looped stitches along each of the quilt edges to be joined. Bring the thread to the surface of the fabric. Hold the thread forward and wrap the thread around the back of the needle from left to right. Hold this wrapped thread while inserting the needle into the fabric. Before pulling the needle and thread through, wrap the thread around the back of the needle a second time, from right to left. Pull the thread through and a knot will form. Continue along edge of the fabric. Work a matching set of edging stitches on the second quilt edge.

STEP 2

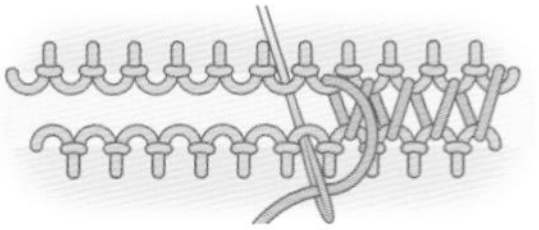

Take a second thread and lace this through the edging stitches, running the needle in and out of the stitches without catching up any fabric as you progress along the line. Secure the lacing thread at the end of the work.

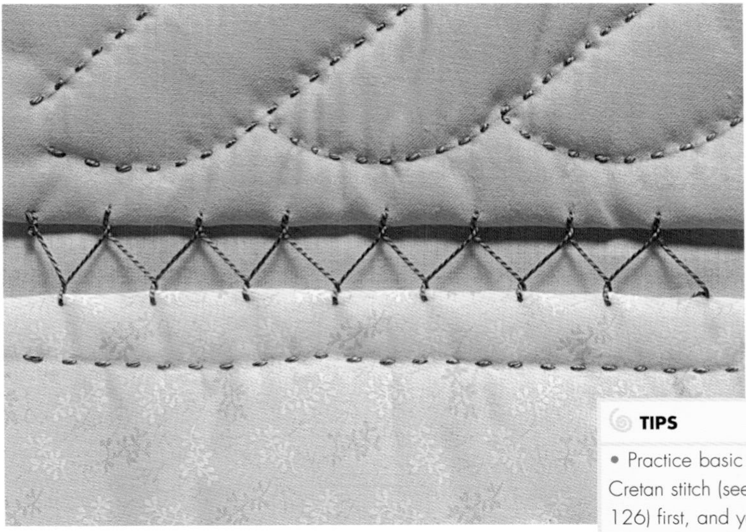

> **TIPS**
> - Practice basic open Cretan stitch (see page 126) first, and you will find it easy to use it for joining two edges of fabric.
> - The wrapping of the thread relies on the way the thread is held prior to passing the needle through the fabric.

Open Cretan stitch

Open Cretan stitch makes an easy-to-work and attractive insertion stitch. It is also known as faggoting and herringbone insertion stitch.

STEP 1

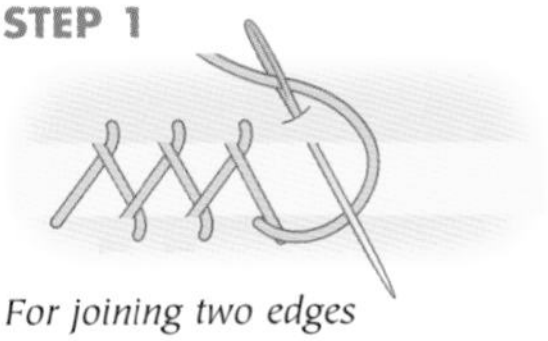

For joining two edges of fabric, bring the thread to the surface at the lower of the two edges. Hold the thread forward and upward along the line of work. Make a small, vertical stitch downward in the upper edge of fabric, bringing the needle into the waiting loop of thread.

STEP 2

Hold the thread forward and downward along the line of work. Make a small, vertical stitch upward in the lower edge of fabric, bringing the needle into the waiting loop of thread. Continue in this way along the line of work.

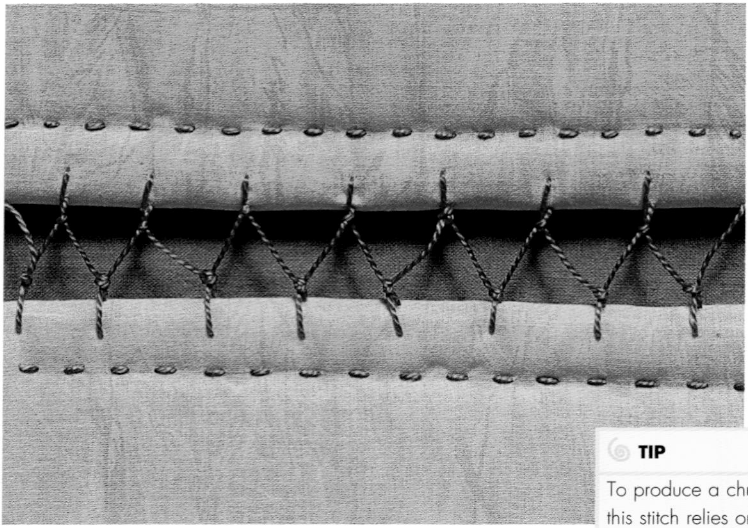

Knotted insertion

Knotted insertion stitch is also known as knotted faggot stitch. It produces an attractive joining stitch with a pretty knotted finish.

TIP

To produce a chunky knot, this stitch relies on the placement of the thread before and after each stitch is taken.

STEP 1

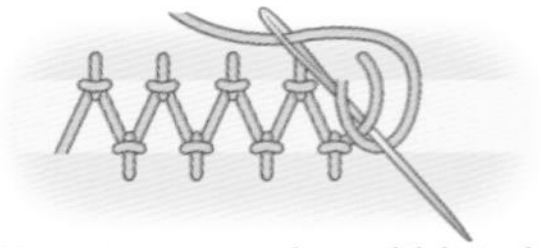

For joining two edges of fabric, bring the thread to the surface of the fabric at the lower of the two edges. Hold the thread forward and upward along the line of work. Make a vertical stitch downward in the upper edge of fabric and into the waiting loop of thread. Holding the thread forward once more, take the needle behind the threads of the stitch without catching up any fabric and bring it into the waiting loop of thread for a second time. This will form the knot.

STEP 2

Hold the thread forward and downward along the line of work. Make a vertical stitch upward in the lower edge of fabric and into the waiting loop of thread. Holding the thread forward and downward once more, take the needle behind the threads of the stitch without catching any fabric and bring it into the waiting loop of thread for a second time. Continue along the line of work.

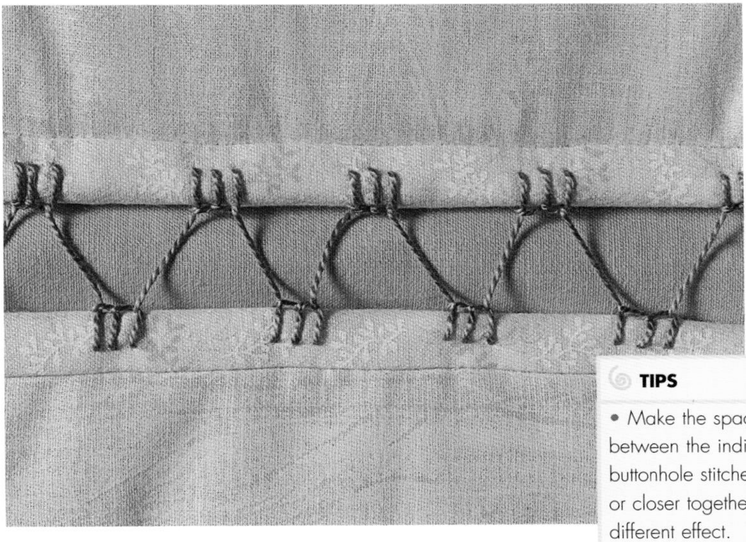

> **TIPS**
> - Make the spaces between the individual buttonhole stitches wider or closer together for a different effect.
> - You can vary the number of buttonhole stitches from two up to four or five.

Buttonhole insertion

Buttonhole insertion stitch makes an attractive and strong stitch for joining two quilt edges. Practice basic buttonhole stitch (worked in the same way as blanket stitch, see page 104) first.

STEP 1

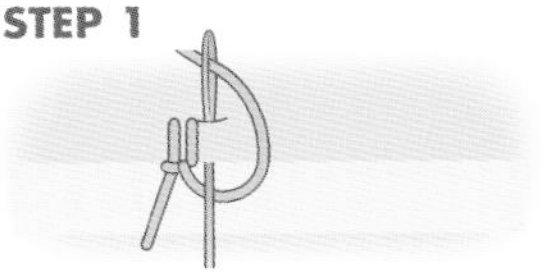

For joining two edges of fabric, bring the thread to the surface of the fabric at the lower of the two edges. Hold the thread forward and upward along the line of work. Make a vertical stitch downward in the upper edge of fabric, bringing the needle into the waiting loop of thread. Repeat this twice more.

STEP 2

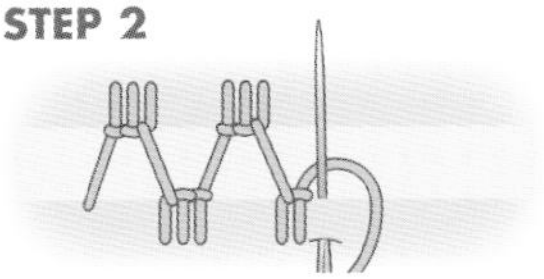

Hold the thread forward and downward along the line of work. Make a vertical stitch upward in the lower edge of fabric, bringing the needle into the waiting loop of thread. Repeat this twice more. Repeat steps 1 and 2 to continue along the line of work.

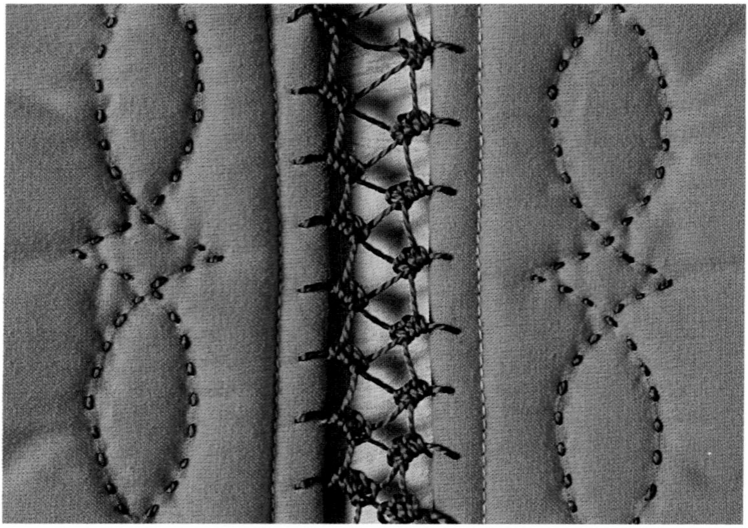

Italian insertion

Italian insertion stitch is also known as Italian buttonhole insertion stitch. When used to join two edges of quilt work together, it provides a decorative latticework of stitches.

STEP 1

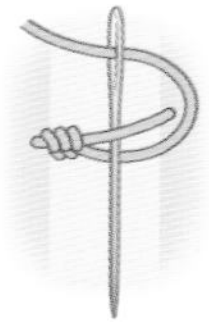

Working vertically and down toward you, bring the thread to the surface of the fabric on the right-hand quilt edge. Make a small stitch to the fabric on the left-hand quilt edge. Work four buttonhole stitches along the bar of thread between the two edges of fabric, working from left to right.

STEP 2

Hold the thread below the work, move further down the line and make a stitch from the right-hand quilt edge, bringing the needle into a loop of thread. Follow this with a stitch from the left-hand quilt edge, further down the work, bringing the needle into a loop of thread.

STEP 3

Work four buttonhole stitches over the two threads on the right-hand side of the insertion space, working from center to right. Make a stitch into a loop of thread on the right-hand quilt edge. Work four buttonhole stitches over the two threads on the left-hand side of the insertion space, working from center to left. Make a stitch into a loop of thread on the left-hand quilt edge and repeat steps 2 and 3 to continue along the line of work.

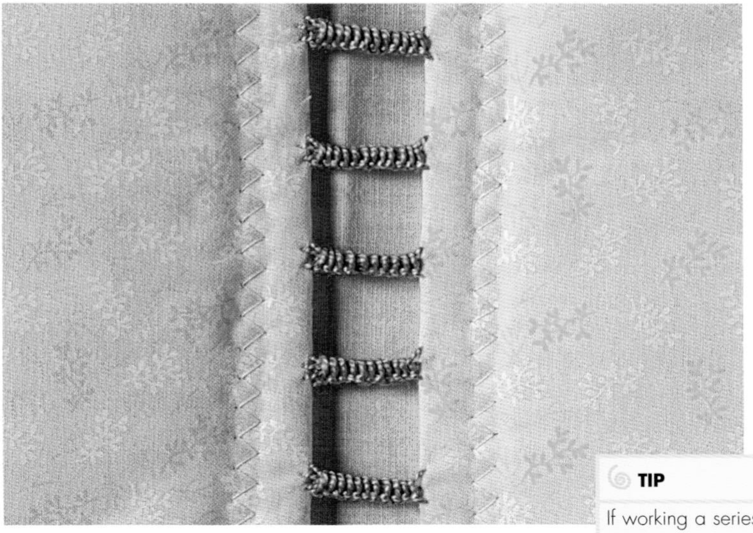

TIP

If working a series of buttonhole bar stitches, run the thread between the bars through the batting and/or fabrics of the two quilt edges for added strength.

Buttonhole bar

A strong, individual linking stitch suitable for joining two quilt edges. Each bar is constructed from two lengths of thread, covered with basic buttonhole stitch (worked in the same way as blanket stitch, see page 104).

STEP 1

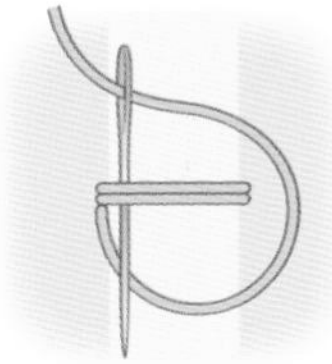

Bring the thread to the surface of the fabric on the left-hand quilt edge. Form a bar between the two edges. Make a small stitch from the right-hand quilt edge, followed by a second stitch from the left-hand quilt edge (make between two and five stitches, depending on how heavy you would like the bar to appear).

STEP 2

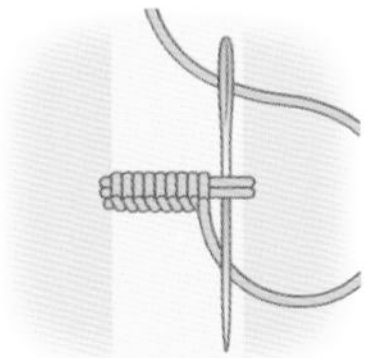

Cover each set of long base stitches with a row of tightly worked basic buttonhole stitch (sewn in the same way as blanket stitch, see page 104). If working several bars in a row, run the thread through the fabric and/or batting of the quilt edges in order to move to the next area to be worked.

Stitches for Machine Quilting

It is possible to machine quilt a project with a simple running stitch or zigzag stitch, however many modern sewing machines come with a selection of decorative stitches that can all be used for quilting.

It's important to check what is happening on the reverse of your quilt, whether you are quilting by hand or by machine. A row of machined stitches is heavier, stiffer and more densely worked than hand-sewn stitches.

USE THIS STITCH FOR

- straight lines
- curved lines
- geometric designs
- corners

Straight stitch

Straight stitch is the most versatile of all the stitches that a sewing machine will do. The stitch length can be elongated or reduced to suit the required end appearance. It is just as easy to sew a straight line as it is to sew a curved line or a corner.

STRAIGHT LINE

CURVED LINE

GEOMETRIC/CORNER

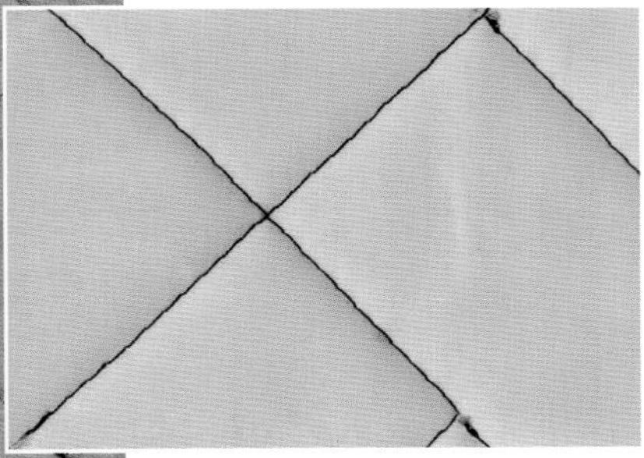

REVERSE OF WORK

Zigzag stitch

The width and length of zigzag stitch can be adjusted to vary its appearance. For a gently tapering result, reduce the width of the stitch as it is being sewn. Keep the needle in the fabric and pivot the work to turn corners.

USE THIS STITCH FOR

- straight lines
- curved lines
- geometric designs
- corners

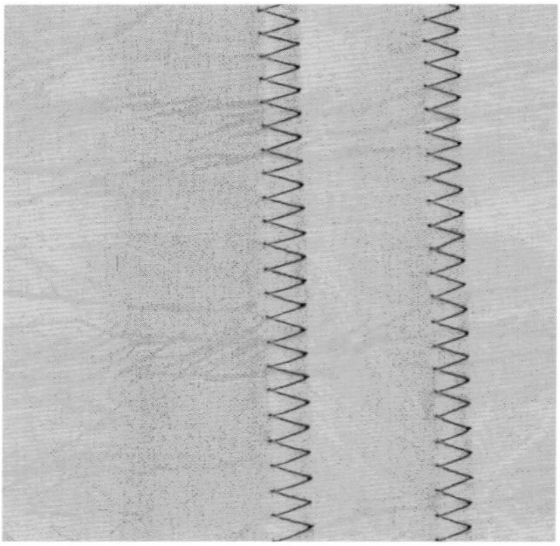

STRAIGHT LINE

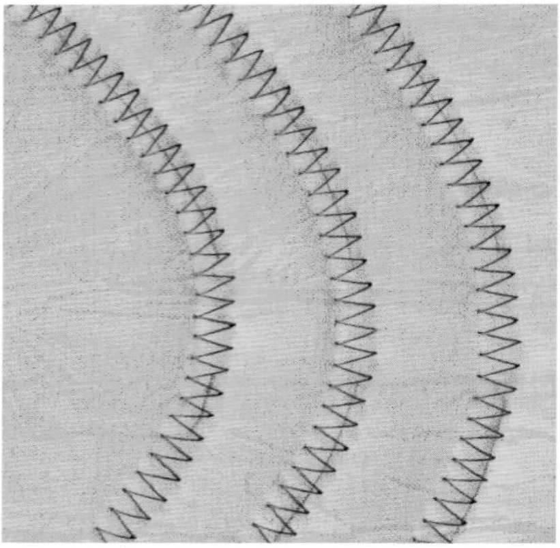

CURVED LINE

REVERSE OF WORK

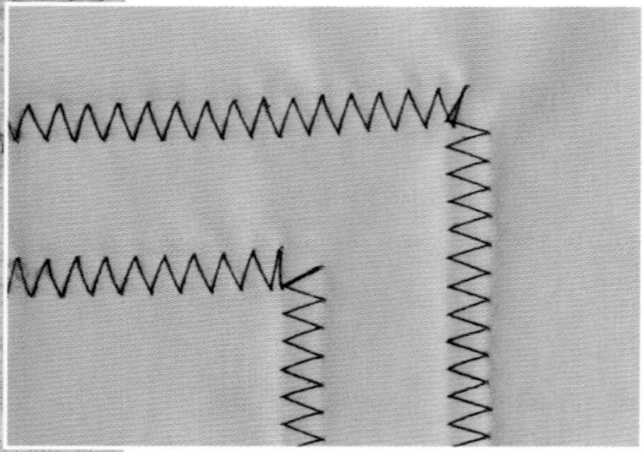

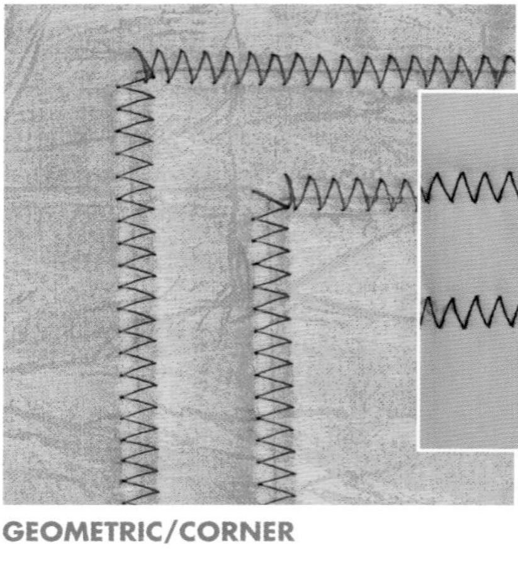

GEOMETRIC/CORNER

USE THIS STITCH FOR

- straight lines
- curved lines
- geometric designs
- corners
- decorative alternative to zigzag

Elastic blind hem

This stitch is generally provided for hemming stretchy fabrics, but it offers a decorative alternative to ordinary zigzag stitch when worked on woven fabrics and quilt projects. Reducing the length of the stitch will bring the peaks of the stitch closer together.

STRAIGHT LINE

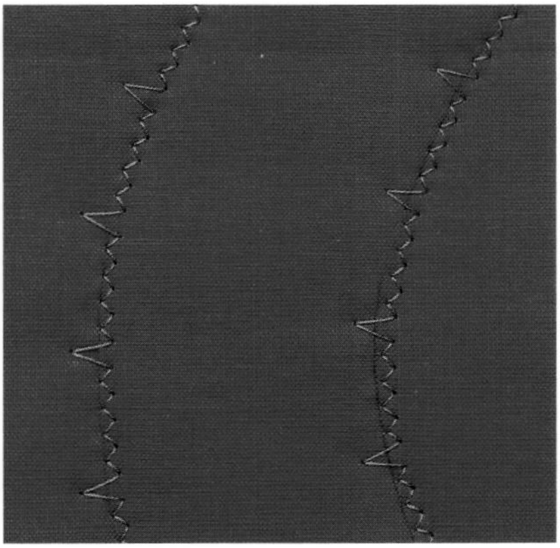

CURVED LINE

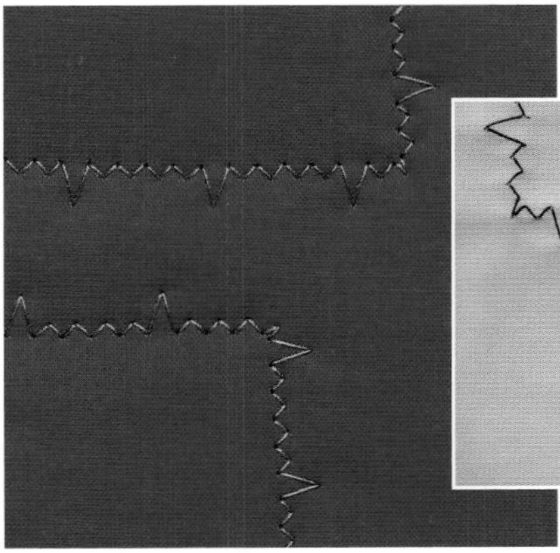

GEOMETRIC/CORNER

REVERSE OF WORK

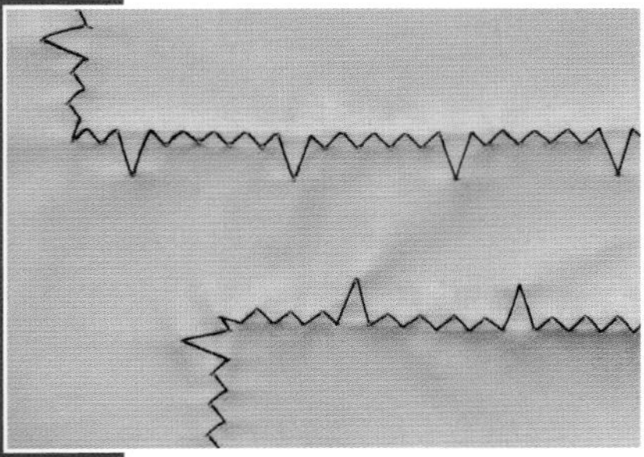

Elastic stitch

Elastic stitch is primarily provided for sewing elastic to garments—the stitch will stretch with the elastic when it is pulled. This stitch provides an alternative to ordinary zigzag stitch and can be used when a firmer zigzag stitch is required.

USE THIS STITCH FOR

- straight lines
- curved lines
- geometric designs
- corners
- a firmer alternative to zigzag stitch

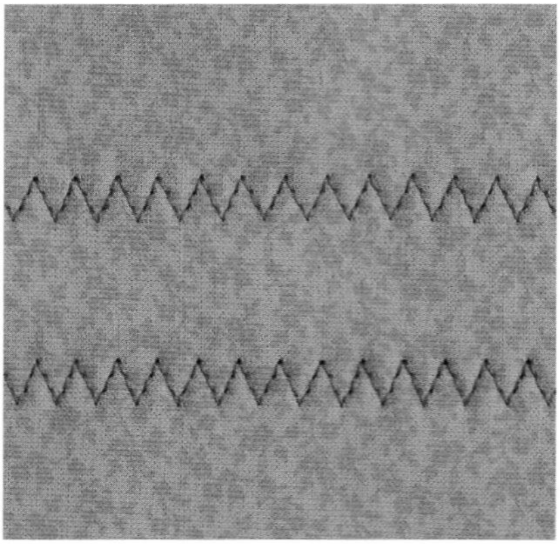

STRAIGHT LINE

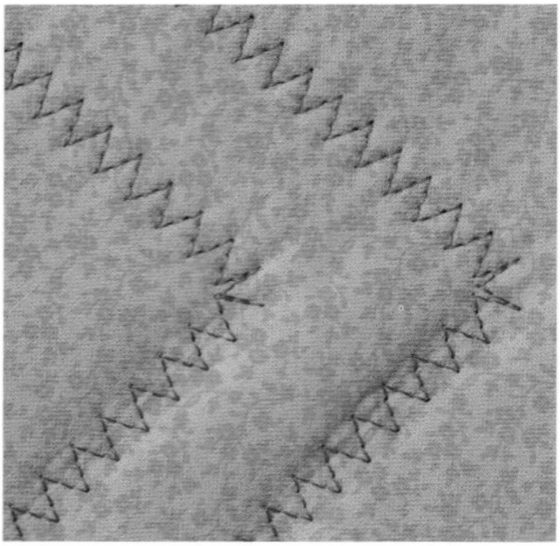

GEOMETRIC/CORNER

REVERSE OF WORK

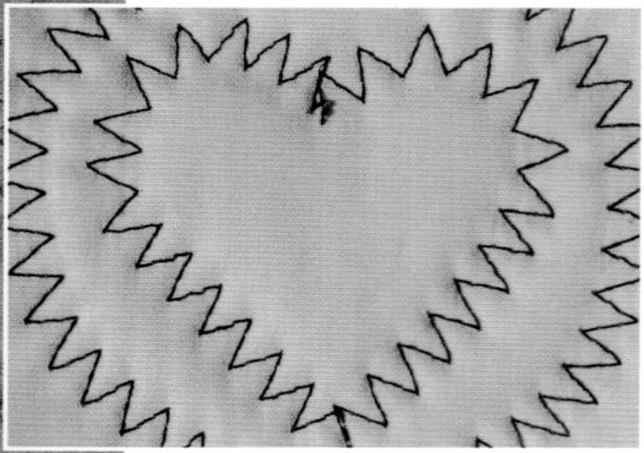

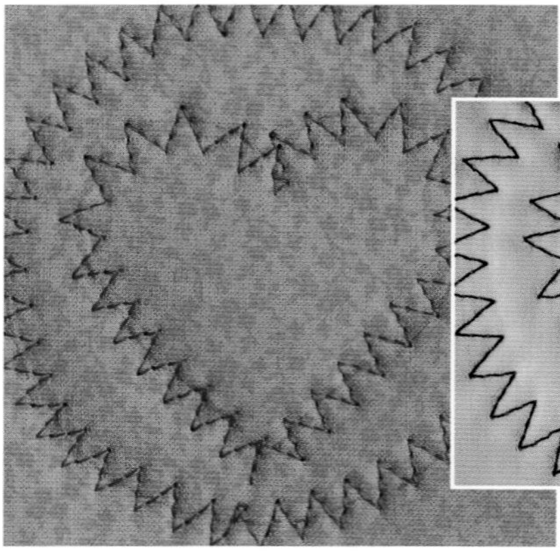

CURVED LINE

USE THIS STITCH FOR

- straight lines
- curved lines
- geometric designs
- corners
- bold quilting lines

Closed overlock stitch

Closed overlock stitch is another stitch that is primarily provided as a stretch stitch for elastic or jersey fabrics. It makes a useful quilting stitch and gives a dense and busy finish to the quilting line.

STRAIGHT LINE

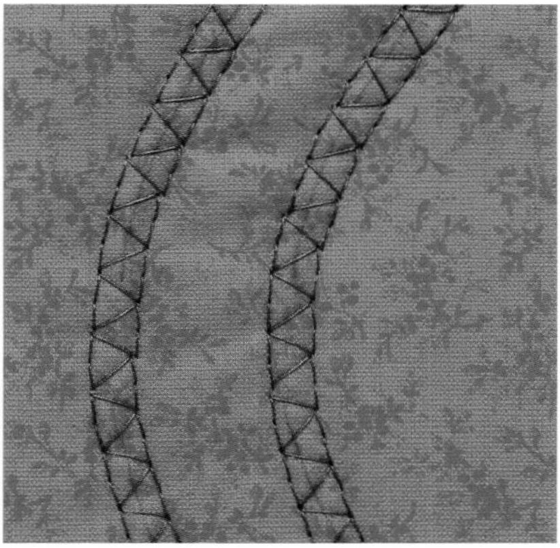
CURVED LINE

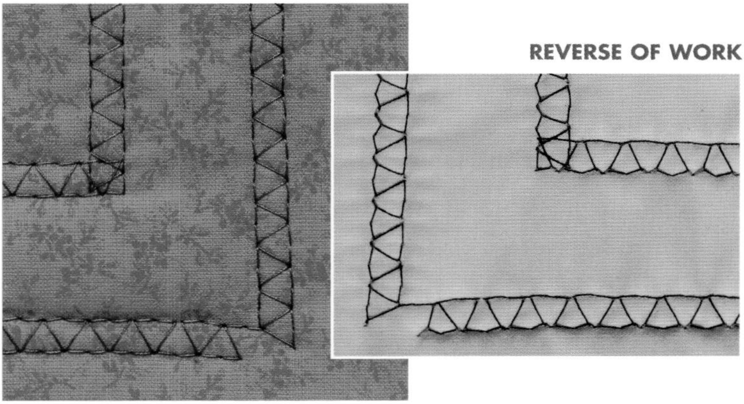
REVERSE OF WORK

GEOMETRIC/CORNER

Buttonhole stitch

Machine-sewn buttonhole stitch closely resembles hand-sewn blanket stitch (see page 104). It is as easy to sew this stitch on a curve or corner as it is to sew it on a straight line, although care must be taken when pivoting the work around the needle on a sharp corner.

USE THIS STITCH FOR

- straight lines
- curved lines
- geometric designs
- corners

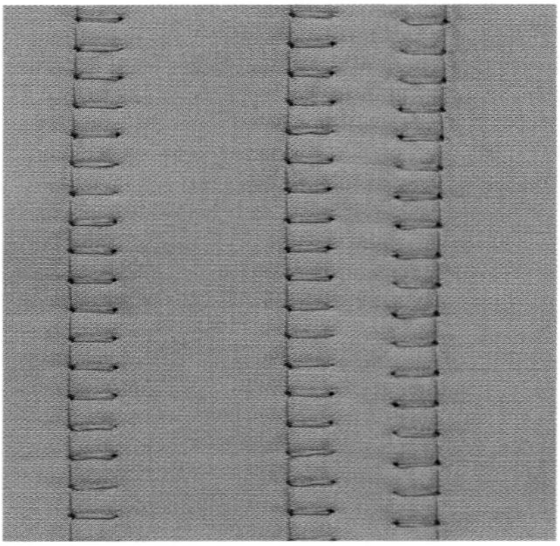

STRAIGHT LINE

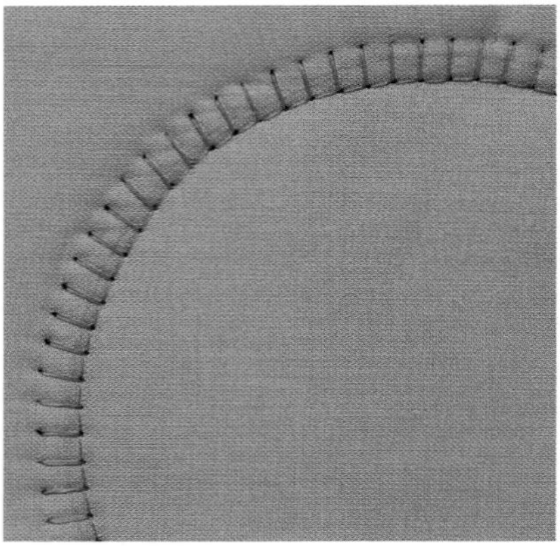

CURVED LINE

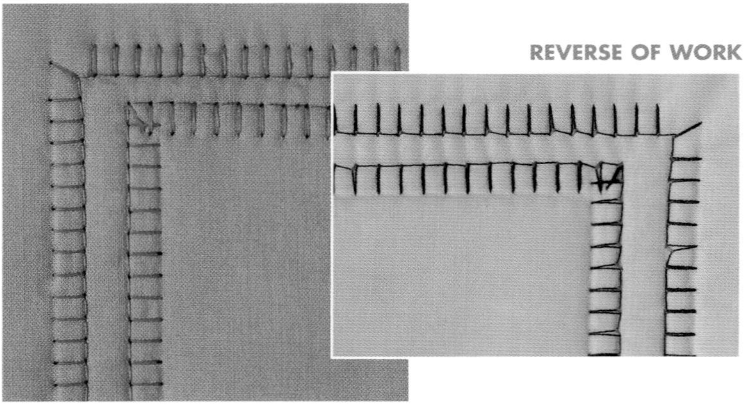

REVERSE OF WORK

GEOMETRIC/CORNER

USE THIS STITCH FOR

- straight lines
- curved lines
- geometric designs
- corners
- decorative feathered effect

Bridging stitch

Bridging stitch is primarily provided on a sewing machine for joining two pieces of fabric together with a decorative stitch rather than a seam. Used as a quilting stitch, it has a similar finished appearance to the hand-sewn single feather stitch (see page 95).

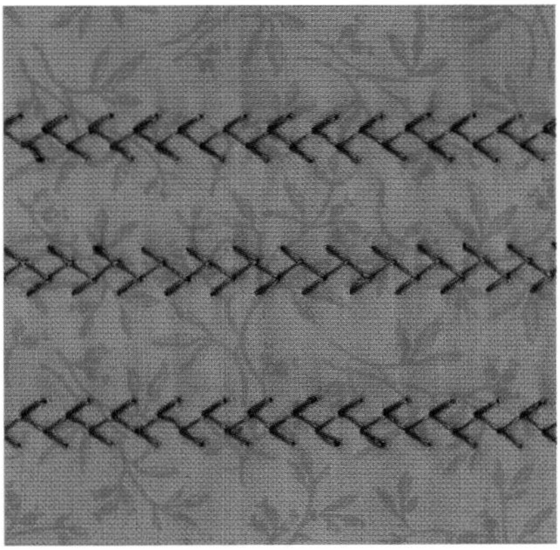

STRAIGHT LINE

GEOMETRIC/CORNER

REVERSE OF WORK

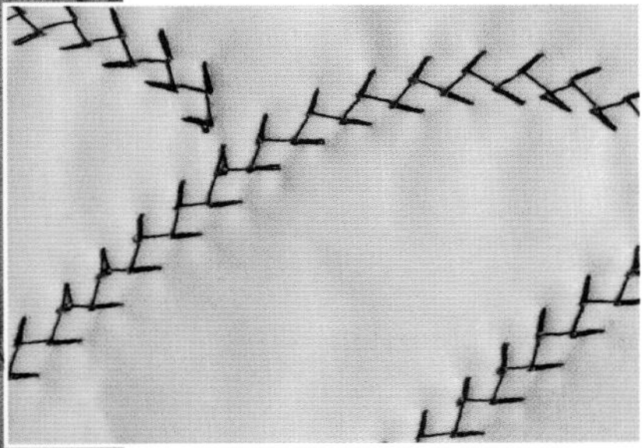

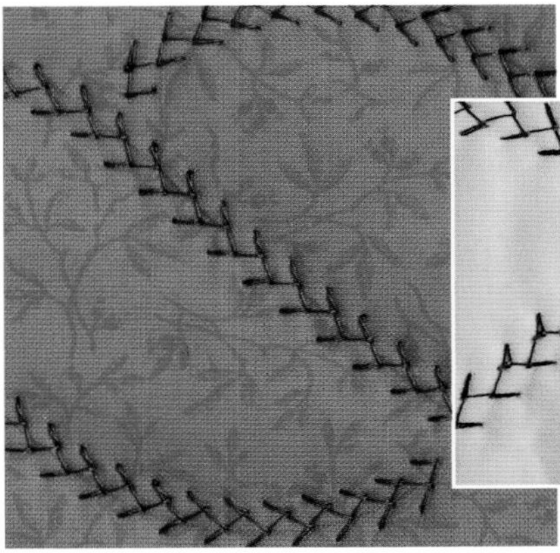

CURVED LINE

Pullover stitch

This standard utility stitch is offered for joining open-knit and heavy knit fabrics, but it also creates a very attractive quilting stitch. It is easy to sew on curves and corners, as well as on straight lines.

USE THIS STITCH FOR

- straight lines
- curved lines
- geometric designs
- corners

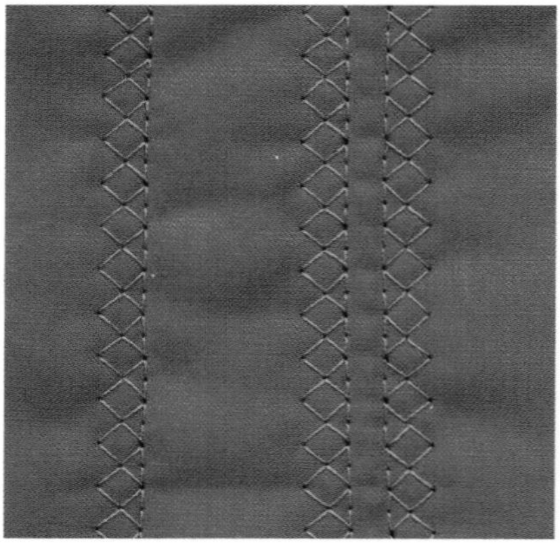

STRAIGHT LINE

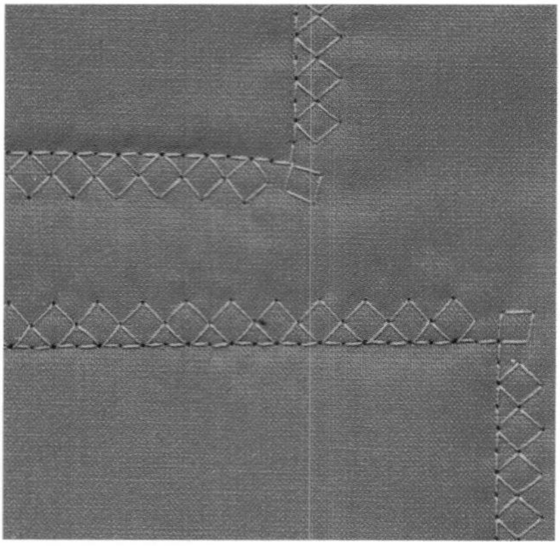

GEOMETRIC/CORNER

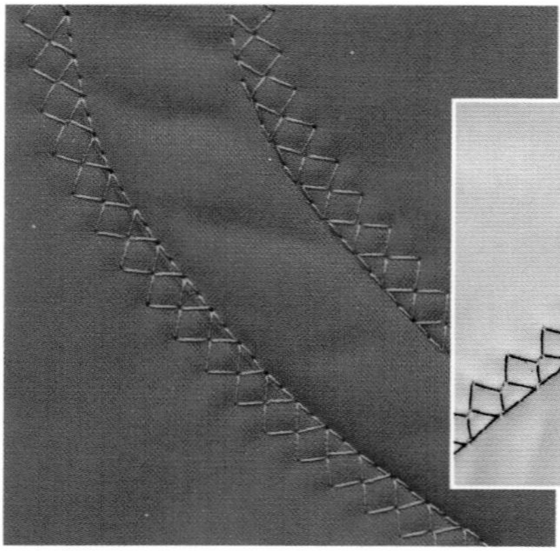

CURVED LINE

REVERSE OF WORK

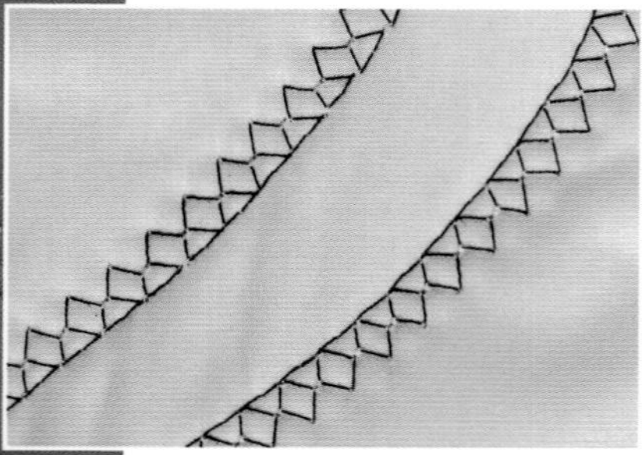

USE THIS STITCH FOR

- straight lines
- curved lines
- geometric designs
- corners
- adding movement to a design

Open overlock stitch

Another utility stitch, primarily offered for joining fabric edges or overlocking the edges of fabrics that do not fray excessively. For quilters, it provides a diagonal variation on buttonhole/blanket stitch which, in itself, adds movement to a quilting design.

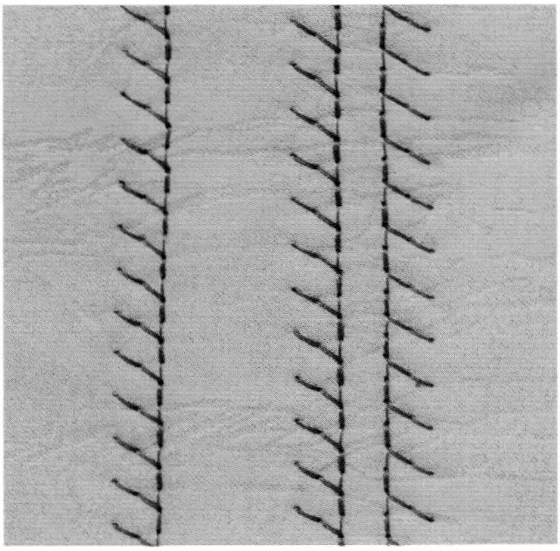

STRAIGHT LINE

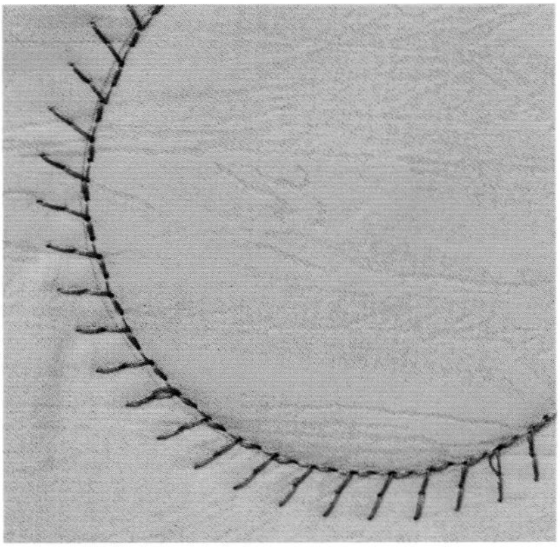

CURVED LINE

REVERSE OF WORK

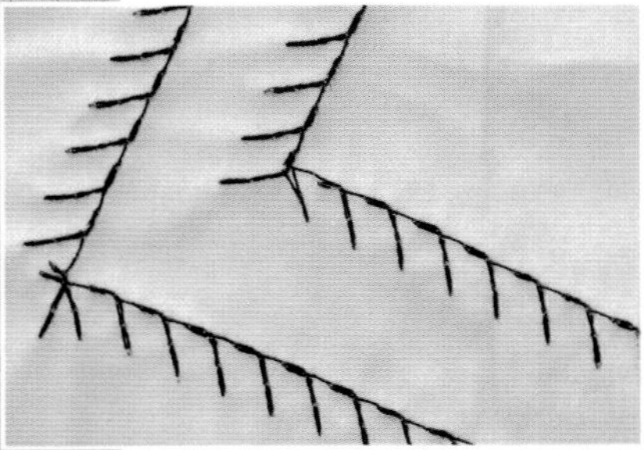

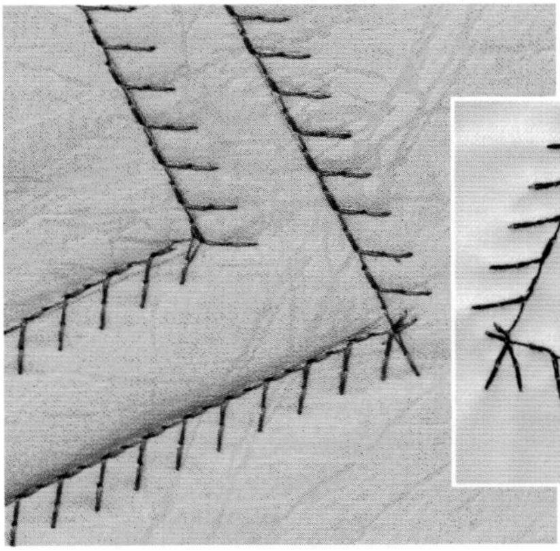

GEOMETRIC/CORNER

Waves stitch (preset)

Some of the more curvilinear stitches found in the preset selection on sewing machines can add a lot of extra movement to a quilting design, whether used on a straight line, curved line, or geometric line. This pattern of waves is fun to use for quilting.

USE THIS STITCH FOR

- straight lines
- curved lines
- geometric designs
- corners
- decorative effect

STRAIGHT LINE

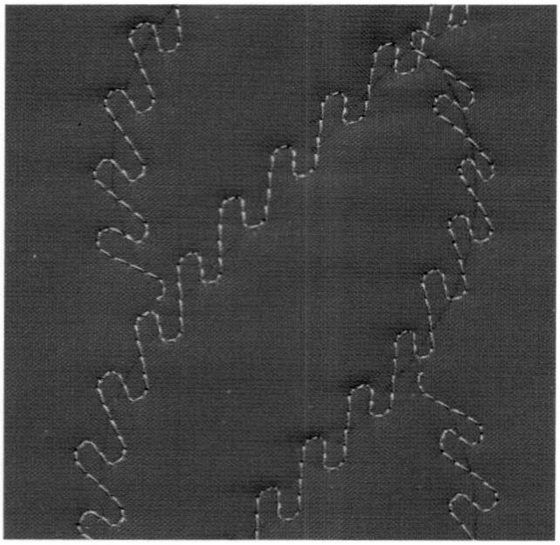

CURVED LINE

REVERSE OF WORK

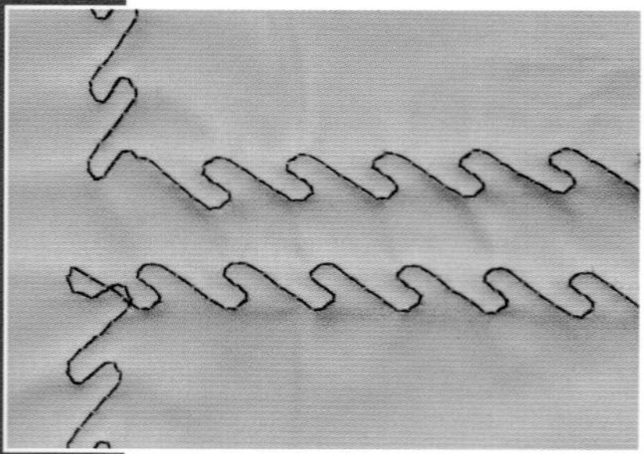

GEOMETRIC/CORNER

USE THIS STITCH FOR

- straight lines
- curved lines
- geometric designs
- corners
- textural interest
- eye-catching repeated motif

Stars stitch (preset)

Motif stitches such as these stars can be found among the preset stitch selection on a sewing machine. When used as a quilting stitch, they can add extra textural interest as well as visual appeal to your quilt work.

STRAIGHT LINE

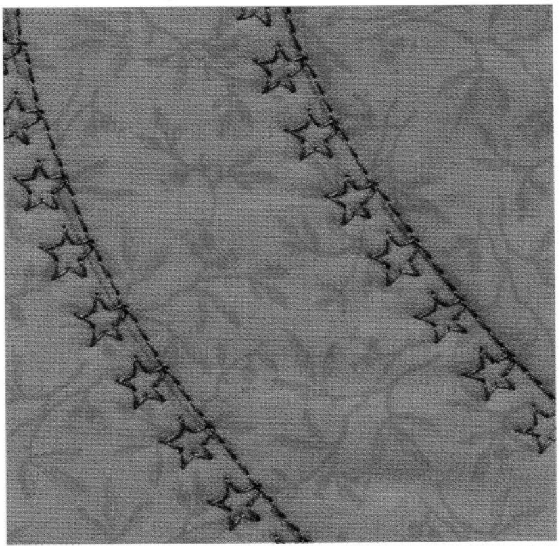

CURVED LINE

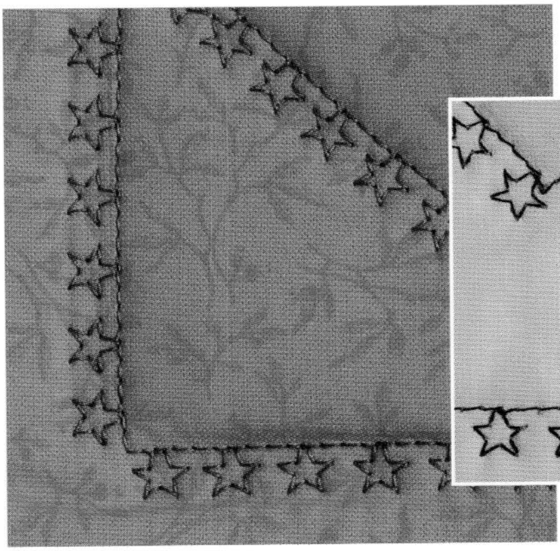

GEOMETRIC/CORNER

REVERSE OF WORK

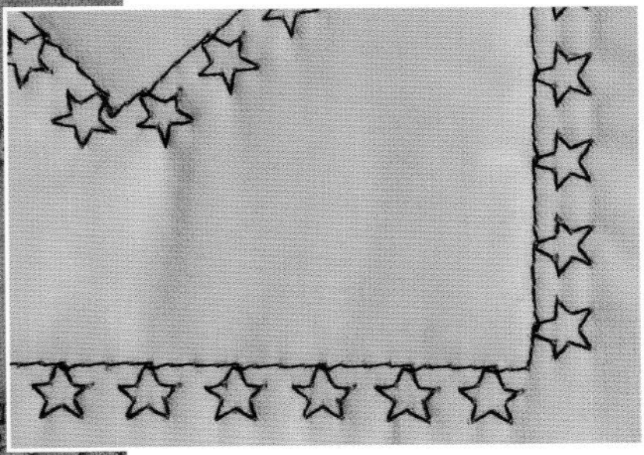

Hearts stitch (preset)

Some of the wider stitches in the preset selection of machine stitches, such as this heart, make decorative quilting stitches. If a stitch is "one-sided," as the heart motif is, you need to consider which side of the quilting line you would like the motif to sit on.

USE THIS STITCH FOR

- straight lines
- curved lines
- geometric designs
- corners
- family heritage designs

STRAIGHT LINE

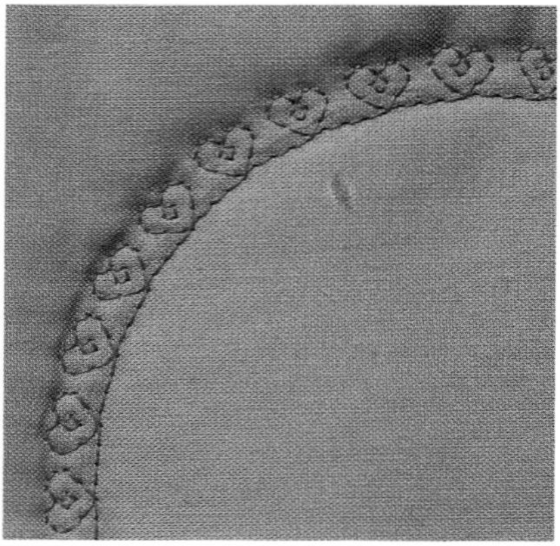

CURVED LINE

GEOMETRIC/CORNER

REVERSE OF WORK

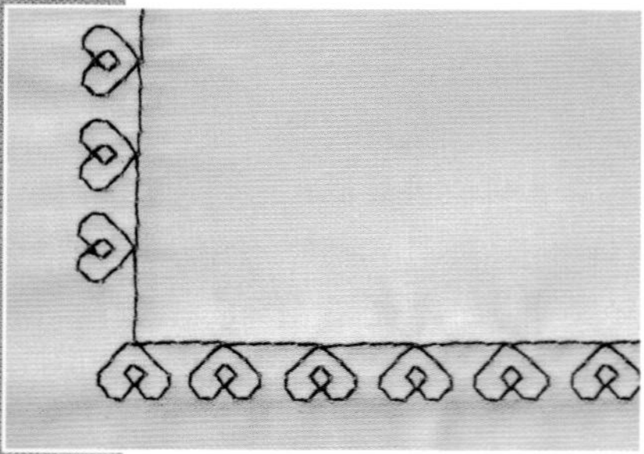

USE THIS STITCH FOR

- straight lines
- curved lines
- geometric designs
- corners
- simple quilting designs

Geometric stitch (preset)

Some preset stitches are wide and dense in appearance, as demonstrated by the geometric "Roman key" stitch shown here. These wide and heavier stitches are better used for more open and basic quilt designs, rather than smaller, intricate patterns.

STRAIGHT LINE

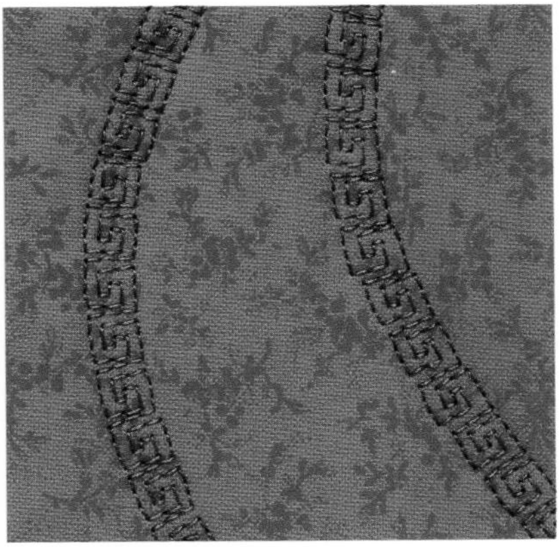

CURVED LINE

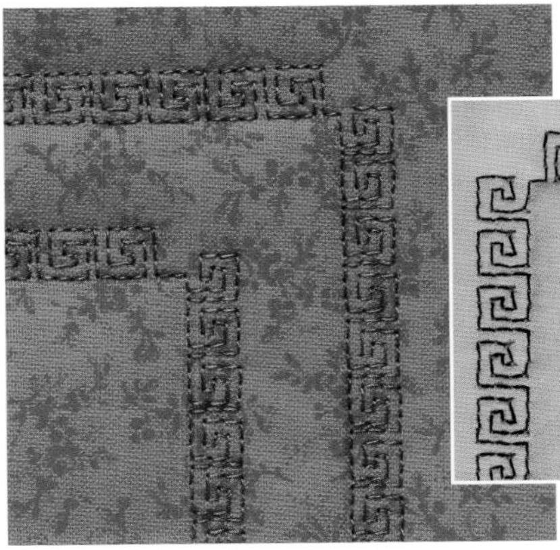

GEOMETRIC/CORNER

REVERSE OF WORK

Twin-needle zigzag

Using the twin-needle facility on your sewing machine can add fun and color to a quilting project. It adds extra definition to the chosen stitches. Use the same color thread in each needle, or two contrasting threads for greater effect.

USE THIS STITCH FOR

- straight lines
- curved lines
- geometric designs
- corners

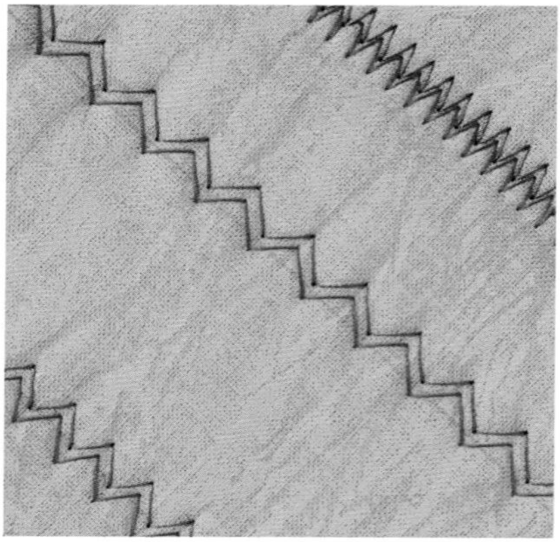

STRAIGHT LINE

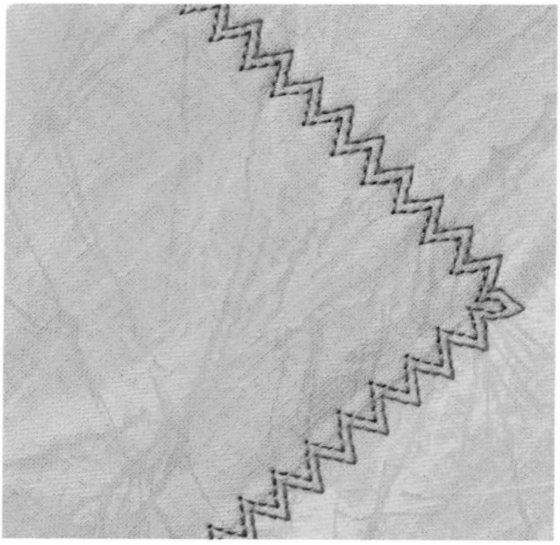

GEOMETRIC/CORNER

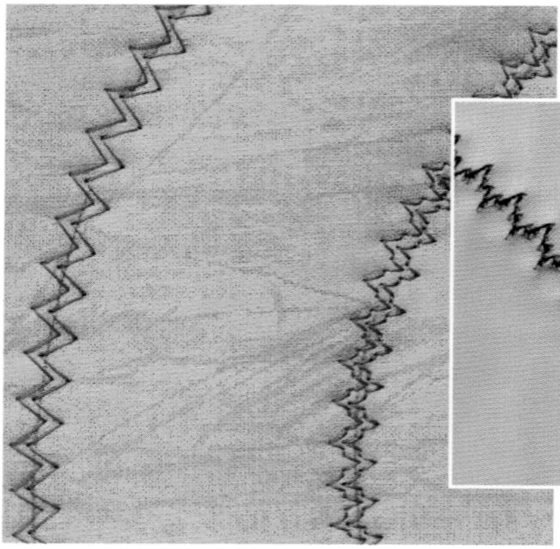

CURVED LINE

REVERSE OF WORK

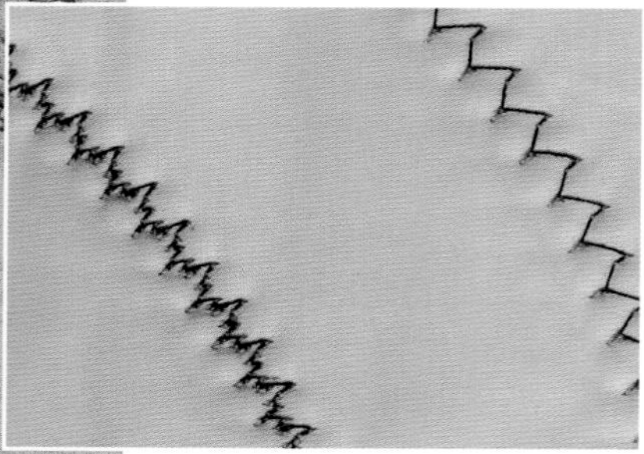

USE THIS STITCH FOR

- straight lines
- curved lines
- geometric designs
- corners

Twin-needle decorative stitches

The twin-needle facility on a sewing machine does not have to be used purely for simple stitches; it can also be used to great effect for a selection of preset stitches. Using two different colored threads will provide a "shadow" effect to the line of quilting.

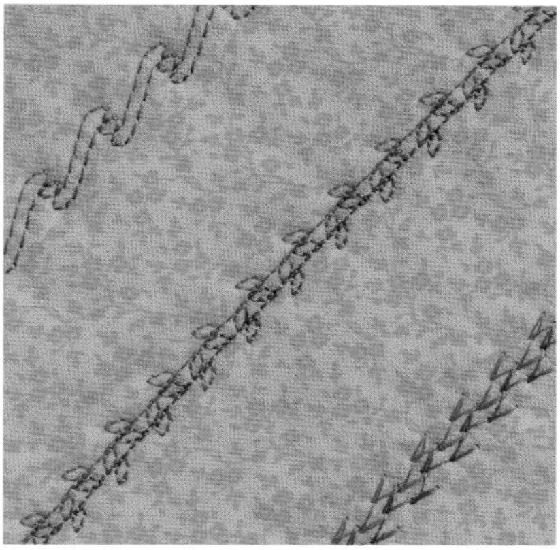

STRAIGHT LINE

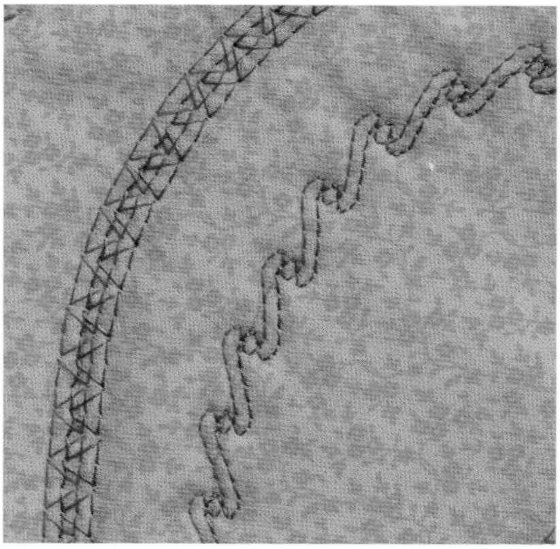

CURVED LINE

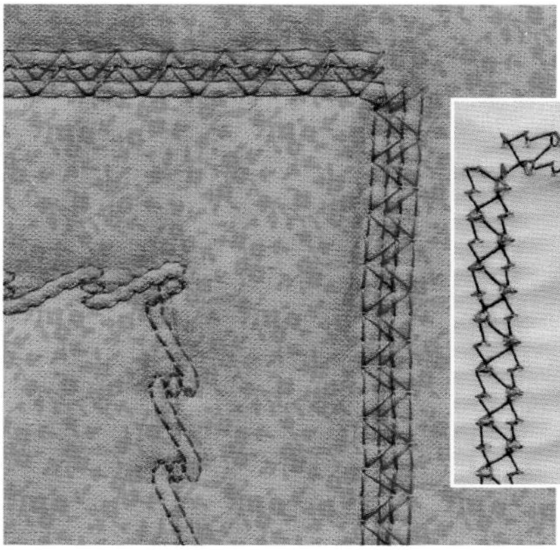

GEOMETRIC/CORNER

REVERSE OF WORK

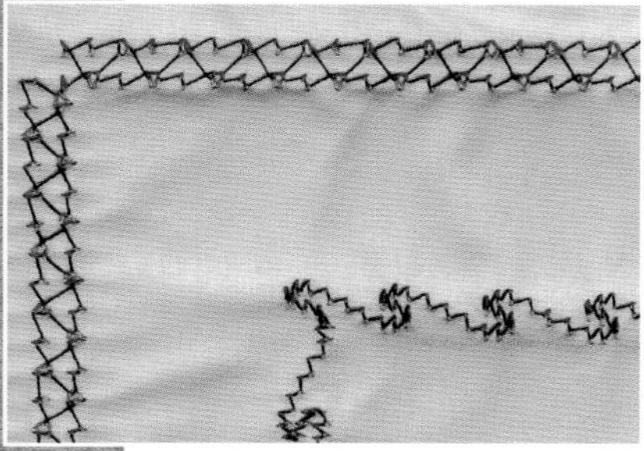

Machine-sewn Surface Embellishment

Embellishments can be added to your project at different stages during quilt construction. If the quilt top is a single layer, the added embellishment will appear only on the surface of the work. If the quilt layers have already been put together, the machined stitches will pass through all layers and also be seen on the back of the work—an important consideration in some projects.

If further embellishment is needed at the quilting stage of a project, decorative thread and fabric scraps can be anchored by machine quilting.

MATERIALS

- cord
- braid
- yarn
- metallic thread

Couching

Add extra textural interest to quilt work by "couching" a ribbon or thread—lay it on top of the quilt and couch it in place with a decorative stitch such as zigzag, elastic stitch, overlocking stitch, or any of the wider, preset decorative stitches.

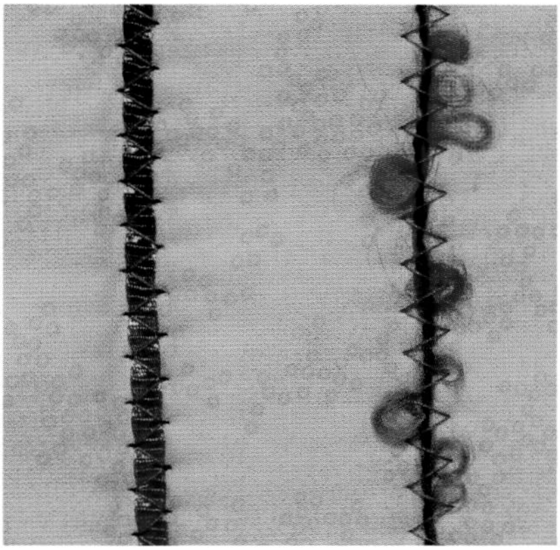

STRAIGHT LINE

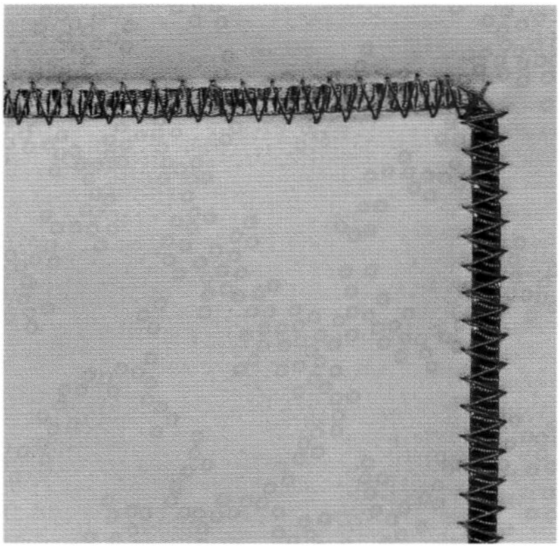

GEOMETRIC/CORNER

REVERSE OF WORK

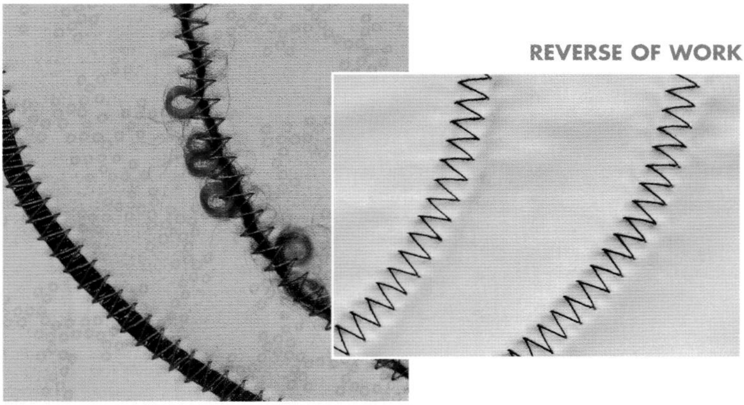

CURVED LINE

Fabric manipulation

Use fabric manipulation to add extra textural interest. Try slashing—layer different colored fabrics, sew together in channels, then cut the top fabrics between the channels to reveal the layered colors. The raw edges of fabric provide surface interest.

TIP

Small sharp scissors or a specialist slashing tool can be used for cutting through fabric layers. A soft brush or the use of a washing machine can also add extra texture to slashed areas.

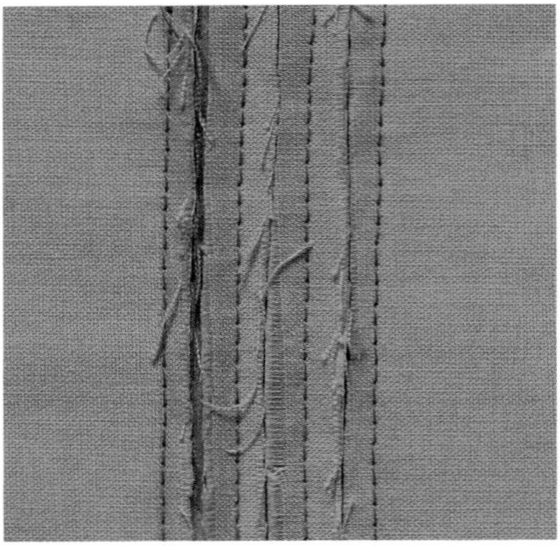

STRAIGHT LINE

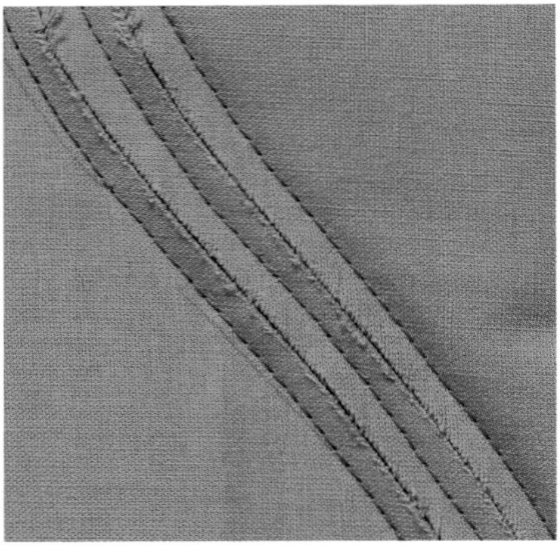

CURVED LINE

GEOMETRIC/CORNER AND STRAIGHT LINE WITH PRESET WAVE STITCH

REVERSE OF WORK

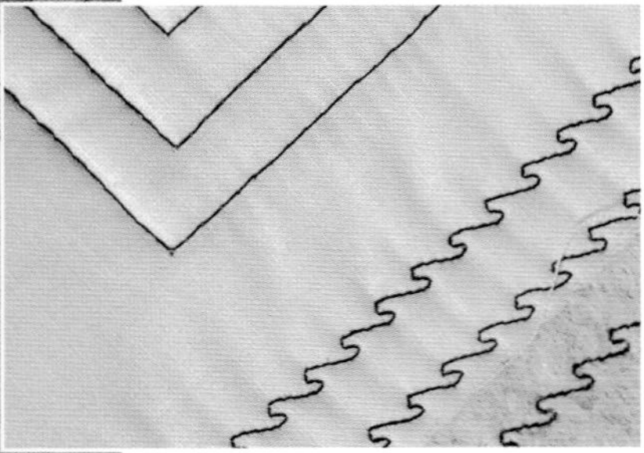

TIP

Turned-edge appliqué does not need additional stitching to reinforce the edges. Use reinforcing stitches for raw edge appliqué and/or fabric that has been bonded into place.

Machine-sewn appliqué

Motifs can be appliquéd to a quilt: Stitch them during construction, or at the quilting stage (when the stitches can be taken through all layers to do the job of quilting in addition to actually reinforcing the appliqué shapes). Use a straight stitch or a decorative stitch.

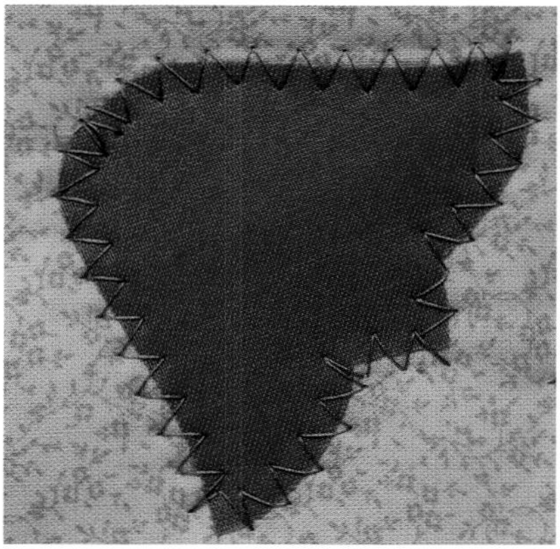

ZIGZAG STITCH

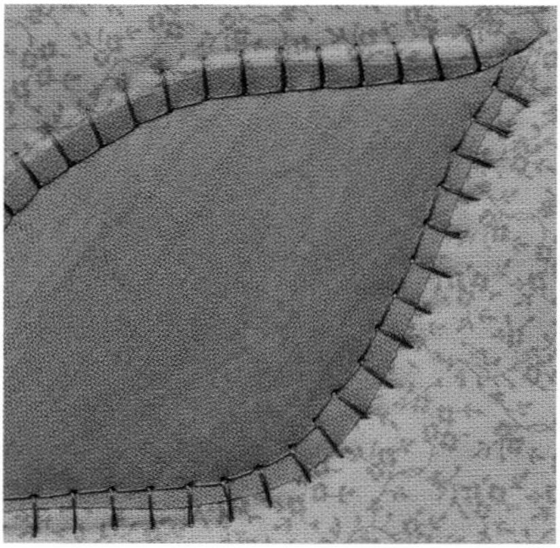

BLANKET STITCH

REVERSE OF WORK

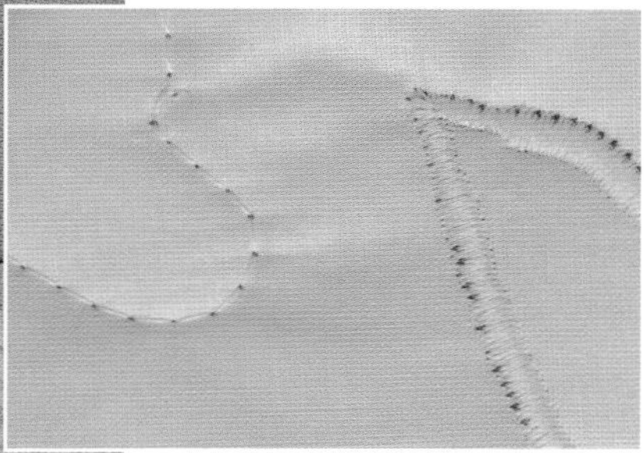

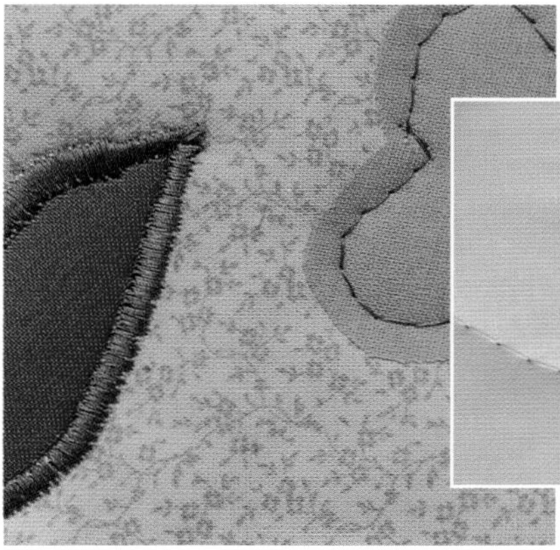

SATIN STITCH AND STRAIGHT STITCH

Machine-sewn Construction and Insertion Stitches

Any of the more decorative and wider stitches to be found on modern sewing machines can be used for joining together multiple panels to make a quilt. Each individual panel will need a finished edge before it can be joined to its neighboring panel. The panels need to be close together as sewing machine stitches are limited in how wide they can be worked—the maximum width is generally ⅜ in. (1 cm).

ENLARGED VIEW

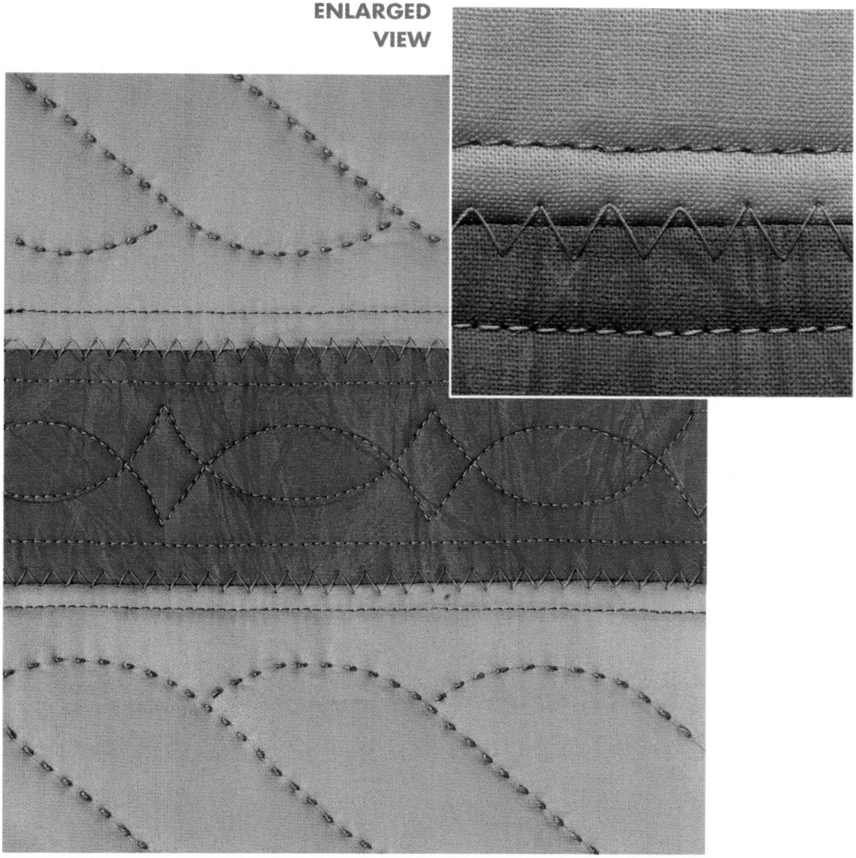

Zigzag stitch

Zigzag stitch and its variations can all be used to join blocks of patchwork that have a finished edge. Construction stitches need to be wide enough to secure the two edges firmly—you will probably need to set the stitch width to its widest setting. The two edges to be joined need to butt up close together without overlapping.

USE THIS STITCH FOR

Joining neatened edges of quilt blocks where no gap is required between edges.

ENLARGED VIEW

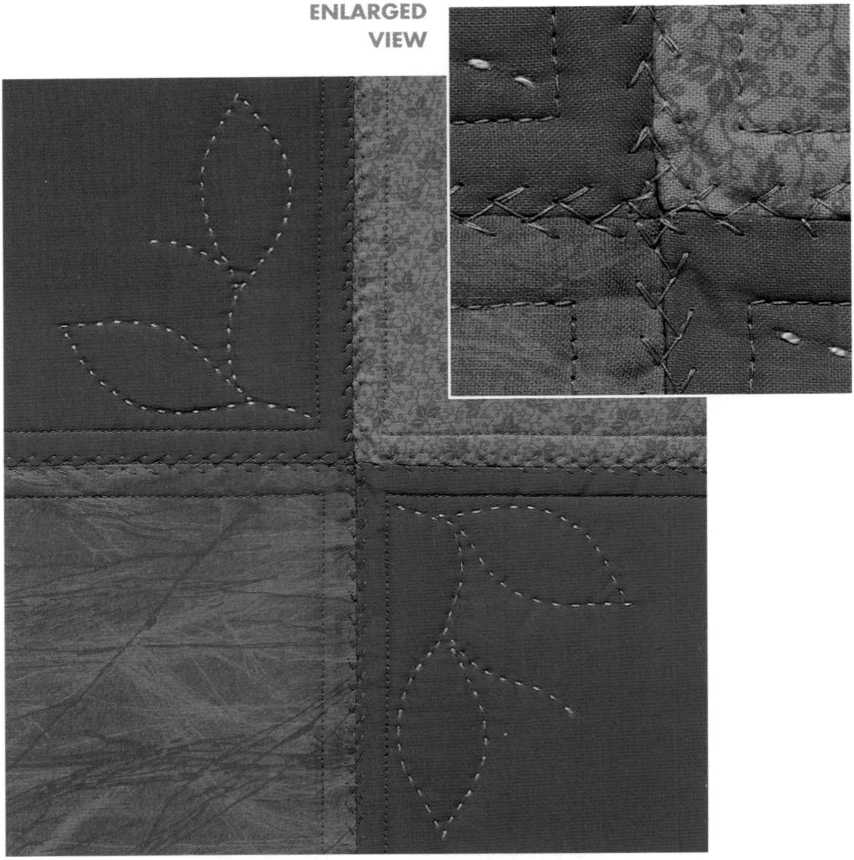

Bridging stitch

Many sewing machines come with a selection of stitches known as bridging stitches—these are specifically designed for joining two pieces of fabric together. Set the stitch width to its widest setting; the stitch length can be reduced or elongated for a different effect. The two finished edges of the quilt blocks need to butt up against each other.

USE THIS STITCH FOR

- Joining multiple quilt blocks with neatened edges.
- When a more decorative effect is required.
- Where a stronger stitch is required.

ENLARGED VIEW

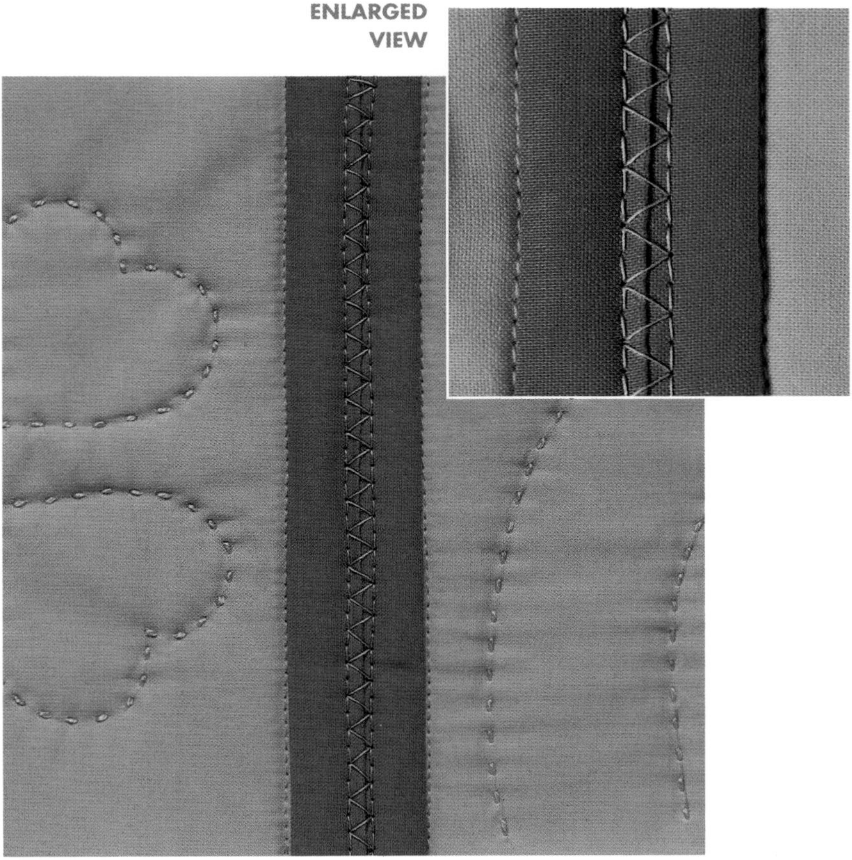

Closed overlock stitch

Most sewing machines offer some sort of overlocking stitch—these stitches are wide enough to be used for joining two finished quilt edges together. Set the stitch width to its widest setting; the stitch length can be altered to suit the required finished effect. The edges of the fabric must butt up against each other.

USE THIS STITCH FOR

- Joining quilt blocks with finished edges.
- When a stronger stitch is required.

Quilting Your Patchwork

Your chosen quilting design should enhance the patchwork in your quilt project, but not overwhelm it. Choose a quilting pattern that reflects the design of your entire quilt.

Interesting contrasts can be provided by working geometric patterns on curves and vice versa, adding movement and visual interest to what might be an otherwise unexciting quilt. Quilt "in the ditch" with a traditional quilting stitch if you don't want the quilting to detract from the design of the patchwork.

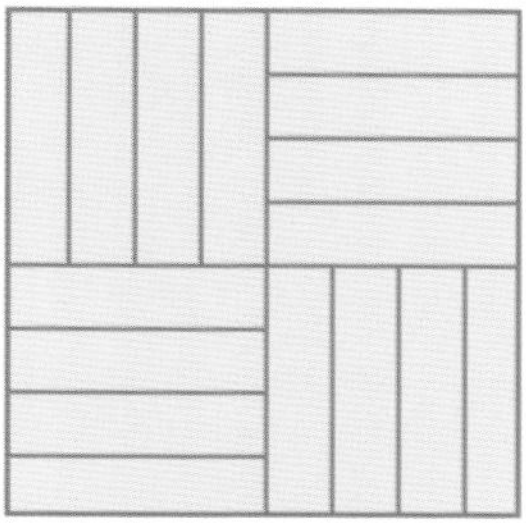

PATCHWORK BLOCK

Rail fence

Rail fence is based on strips of patchwork. Long strips of fabric are joined together; the resulting fabric "scarf" is then cut across to make units for piecing together to form various patterns. The simplicity of the patchwork pattern allows scope for a variety of quilting designs.

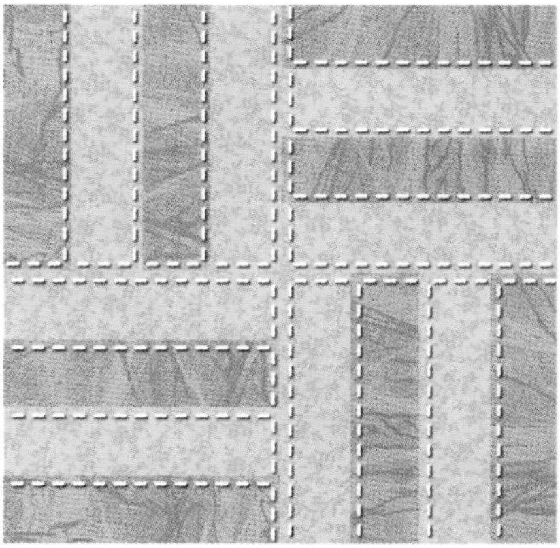

CONTOUR-QUILTING

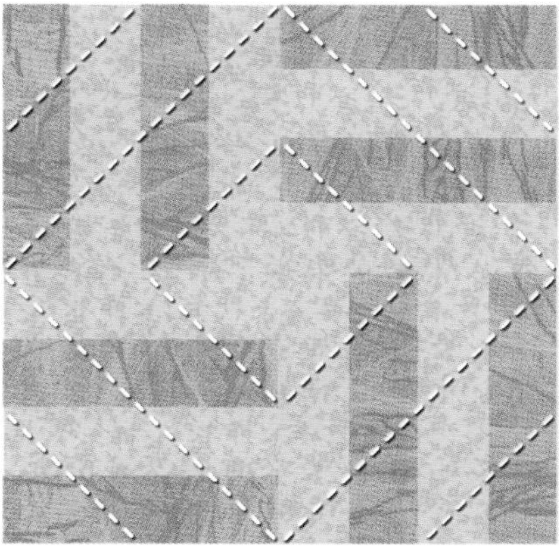

GEOMETRIC DESIGN

CURVILINEAR DESIGN: SPIRAL

TIP
A simple quilting design is all that is required to highlight the simplicity of this strip-patchwork technique.

Log cabin

Log cabin patchwork is one of the oldest patterns and has been used extensively, both historically and geographically. This block is constructed using strips of fabric and working in a circular direction emanating outward from the central square.

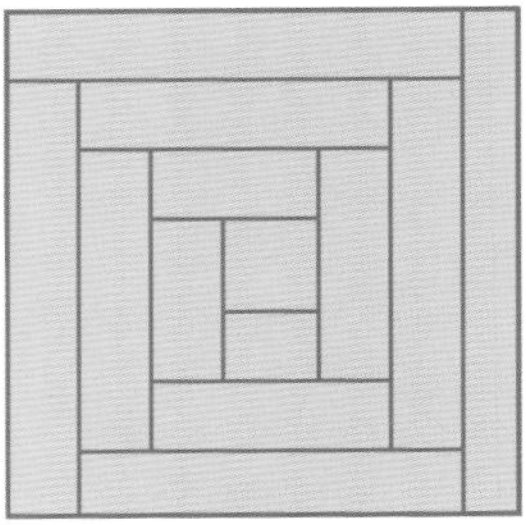

PATCHWORK BLOCK

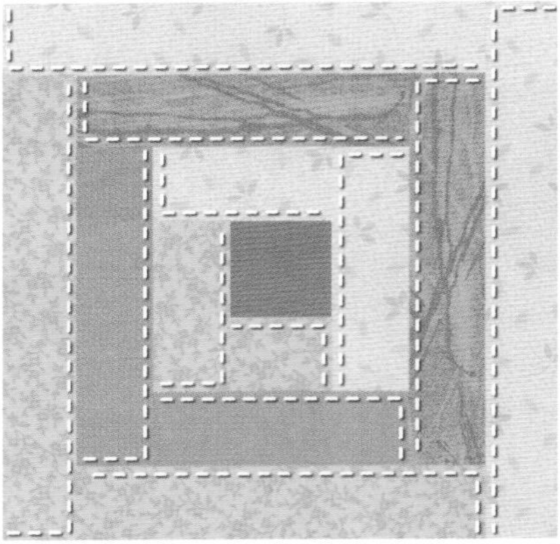

CONTOUR-QUILTING

GEOMETRIC DESIGN: STRAIGHT LINE SPIRAL

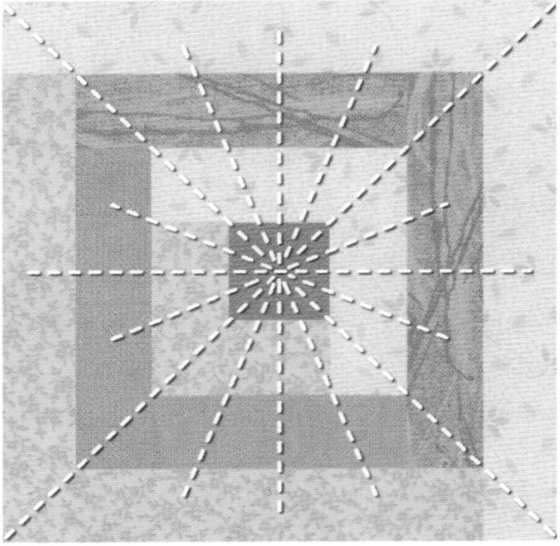

GEOMETRIC DESIGN: STARBURST

TIP

The quilting designs and stitches chosen will depend on the width of the "logs" sewn and the number of seams present to be quilted through.

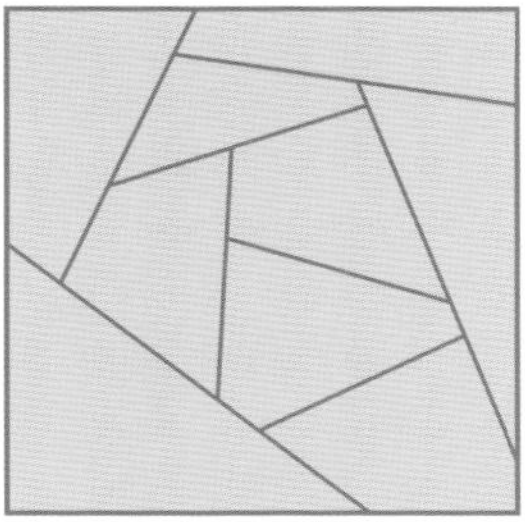

PATCHWORK BLOCK

Crazy patchwork

Crazy patchwork was a favorite of nineteenth-century quilters. Quilts using this design would often incorporate heavy, textured fabrics, such as velvets and brocades, and the use of surface embellishment. Crazy patchwork can be hand-sewn or machine-sewn.

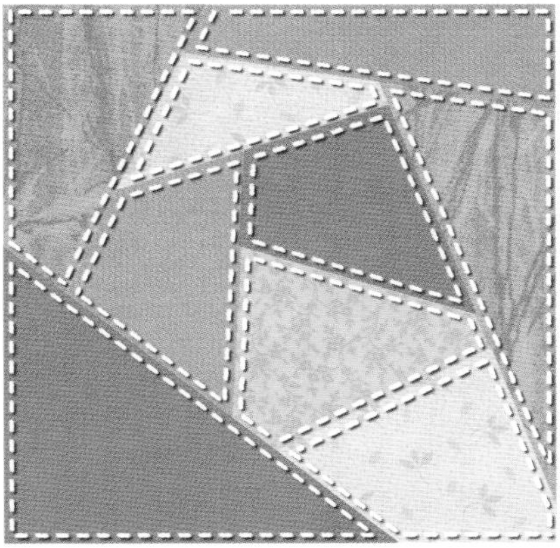

CONTOUR-QUILTING

TIP

Crazy patchwork involves a lot of seams and bulky areas—both factors that will determine the method of quilting, quilting design, and the stitches that you choose to use.

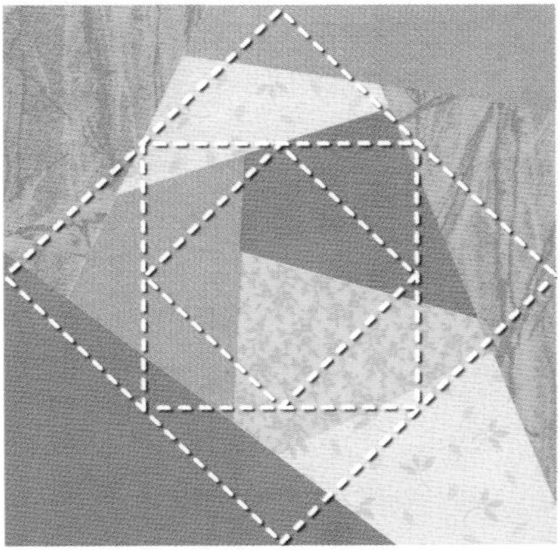

GEOMETRIC DESIGN: SQUARE WITHIN A SQUARE

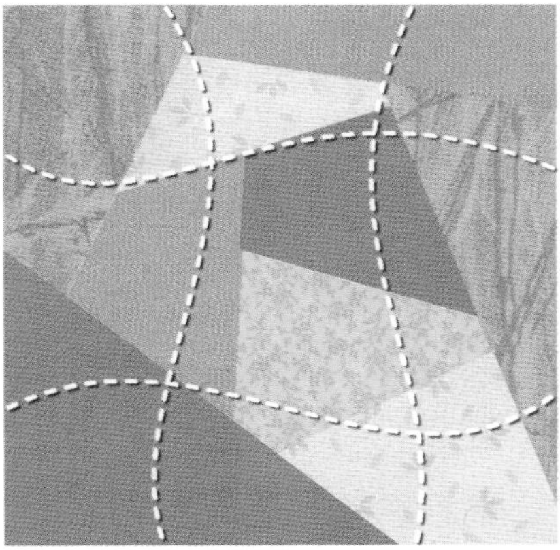

CURVILINEAR DESIGN: FREEHAND CURVES

Pinwheel (2 x 2 grid)

"Pinwheel" is a patchwork block designed on a 2 x 2 grid (four squares in total). With careful fabric placement, an optical illusion of movement can be achieved, making it look like a rotating windmill. Quilting designs can be simple, such as quilting in the ditch, or contour-quilting around the individual patches.

PATCHWORK BLOCK

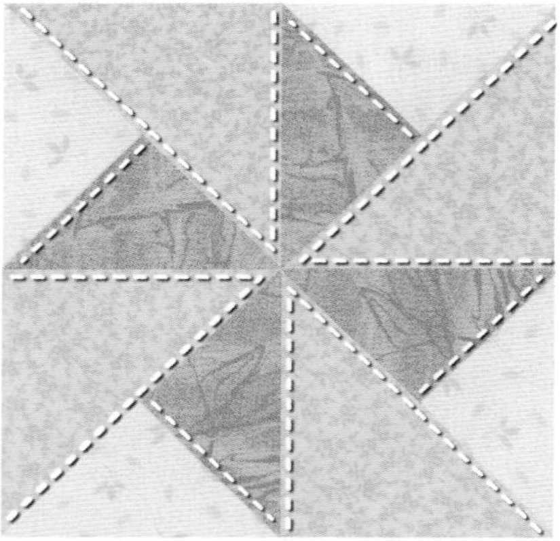

CONTOUR-QUILTING

TIP

The "movement" can be highlighted further by the use of circles or spirals. This simple patchwork block provides an ideal canvas for trying out different types of quilting and different stitches.

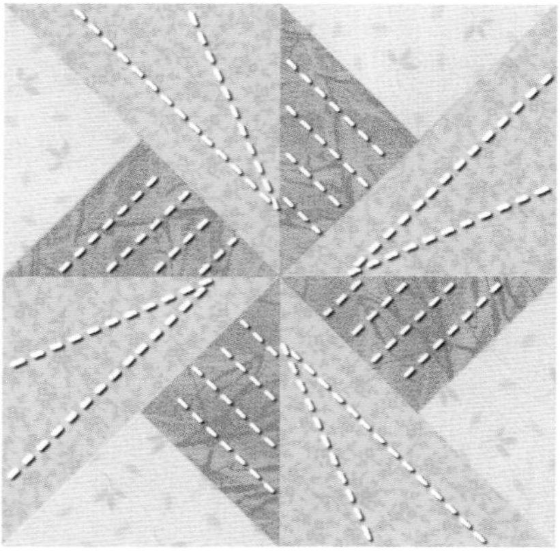

GEOMETRIC DESIGN: ECHOING MOVEMENT

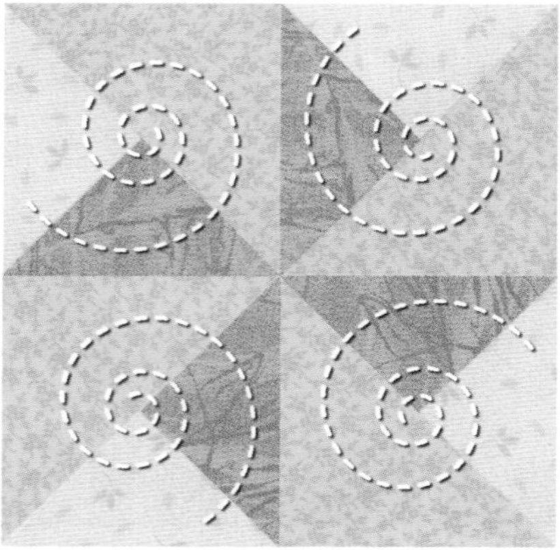

CURVILINEAR DESIGN: QUARTERED SPIRALS

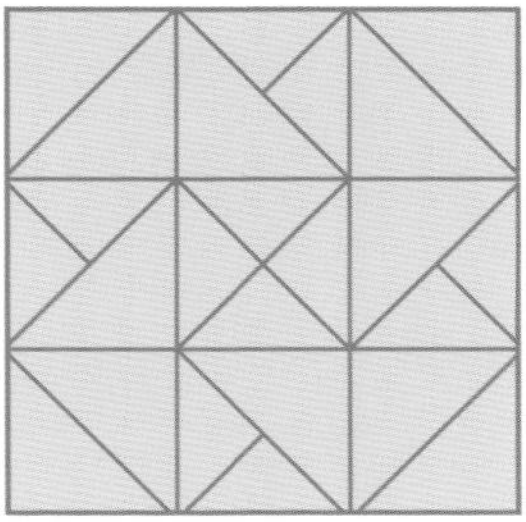

PATCHWORK BLOCK

Card trick (3 x 3 grid)

This ever-popular patchwork pattern uses an optical illusion to place four "playing cards" within a square. Careful fabric placement ensures that the cards seem to overlap one another.

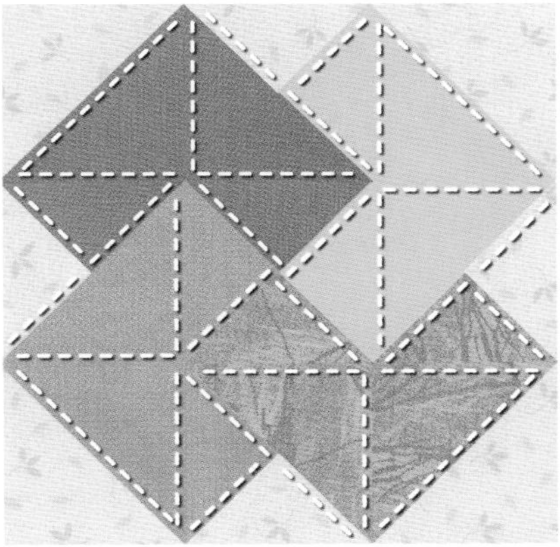

CONTOUR-QUILTING

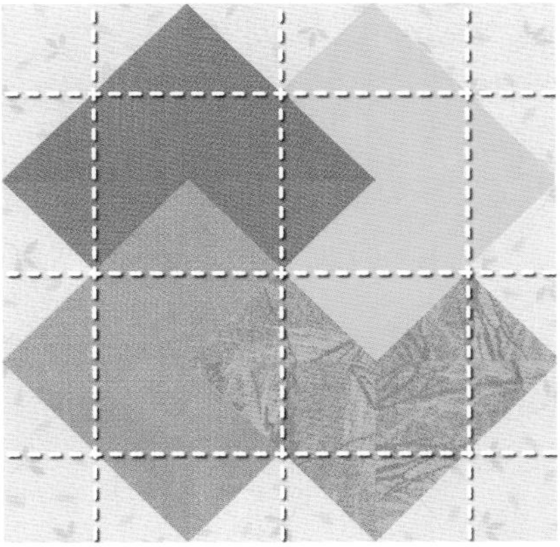

GEOMETRIC DESIGN: GRID

CURVILINEAR DESIGN: HEARTS STENCIL

TIP

There are a lot of seams used to construct this block, and this will determine which method of quilting and which stitches you choose.

Star (4 x 4 grid)

There are an endless variety of patchwork blocks offering "star" patterns. This interesting variation is based on a geometric 4 x 4 grid (sixteen squares in total). More emphasis can be placed on the star by quilting in the ditch or contour-quilting around the individual patches that represent the star itself.

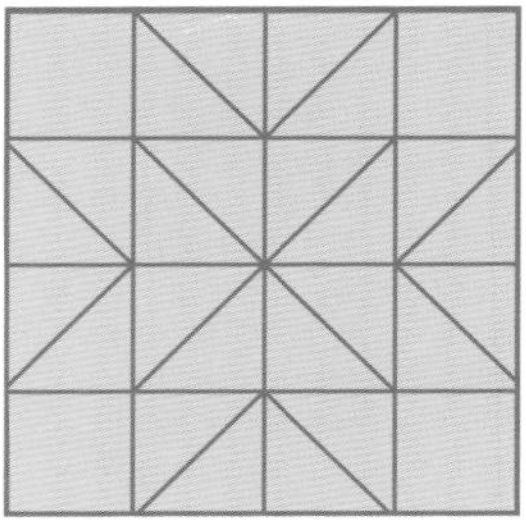

PATCHWORK BLOCK

CONTOUR-QUILTING

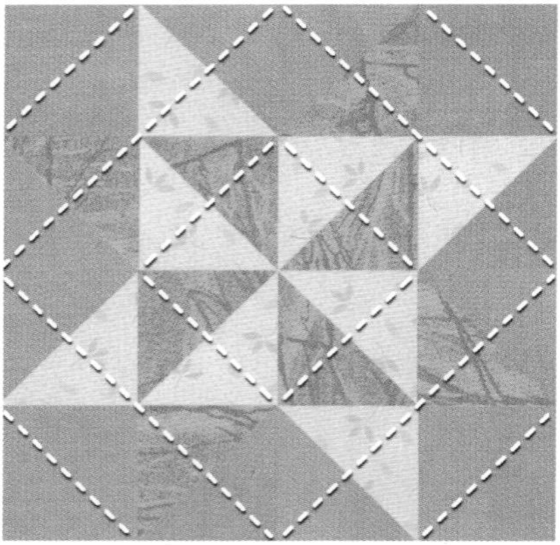

GEOMETRIC DESIGN

TIP

As an alternative, place a quilt stencil design over the entire block to add further visual interest.

CURVILINEAR DESIGN: FLEUR-DE-LYS STENCIL

Mariner's compass (no grid)

Many patchwork blocks, such as this one, are not designed on a formal grid. The "compass" can be kept fairly simple, or added to with extra "spikes" at additional "compass settings," along with intricate piecing of the central circle. A simple quilting design is all that is necessary for this patchwork block.

PATCHWORK BLOCK

TIP

Use busy quilting stitches in moderation so they do not detract from the pattern itself.

CONTOUR-QUILTING

GEOMETRIC DESIGN: STARBURST

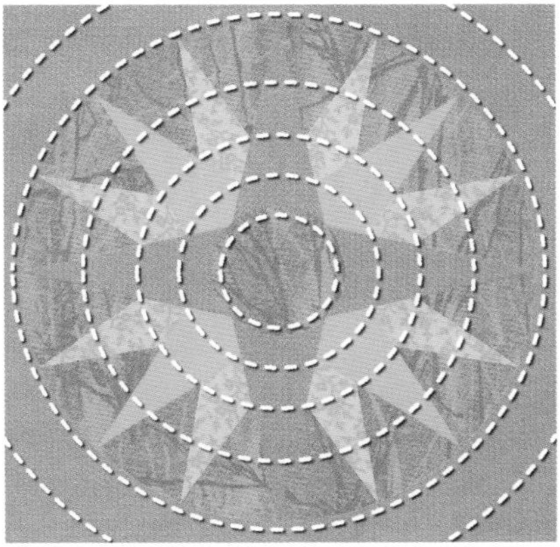

CURVILINEAR DESIGN: CIRCLES

Drunkard's path (curved-seam patchwork)

Sewing curved-seam patchwork is just as easy to do by hand as by machine. The seam allowance will naturally fall to one side of the curve and this may dictate how and where you quilt this block. A quilting design that uses curves will accentuate the visual "movement" provided by the curved-seam patchwork.

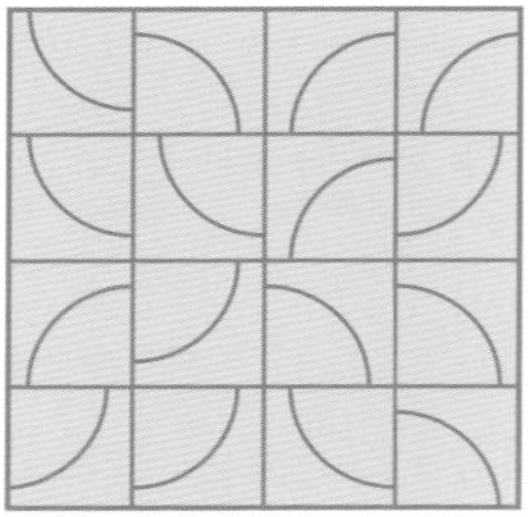

PATCHWORK BLOCK

TIP

There is plenty of scope for quilting with different stitches within this block, which will add further textural interest.

CONTOUR-QUILTING

GEOMETRIC DESIGN: DIRECTIONAL

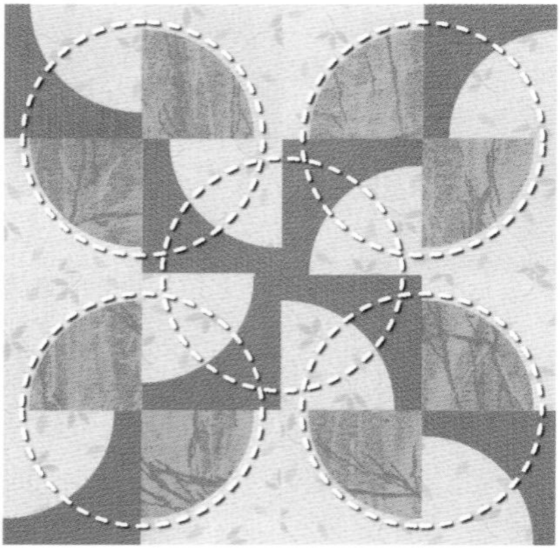

CURVILINEAR DESIGN: OVERLAPPING CIRCLES

Dutchman's puzzle (triangles)

Many patchwork patterns, such as this one, are constructed using triangles only. In this block, "geese" are clearly seen flying outward from the center of the block, in four different directions. The emphasis of the pattern can change according to fabric placement.

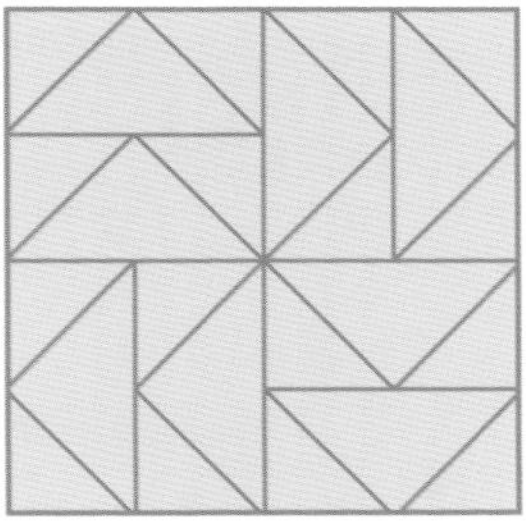

PATCHWORK BLOCK

TIP

Place a curved quilting design over the complete block to add an interesting contrast to the geometric patchwork piecing.

CONTOUR-QUILTING

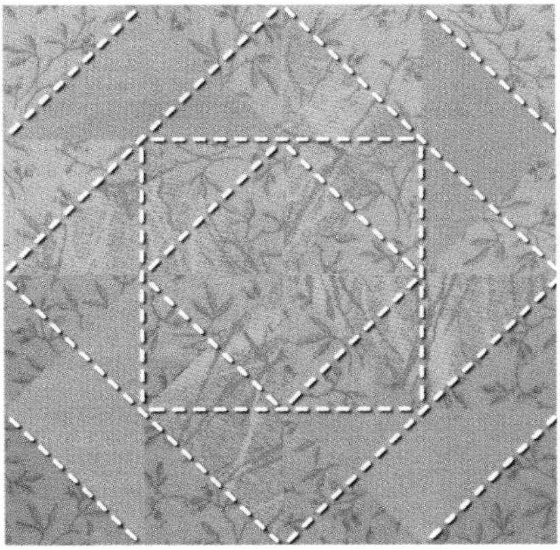

GEOMETRIC DESIGN: SQUARE WITHIN A SQUARE

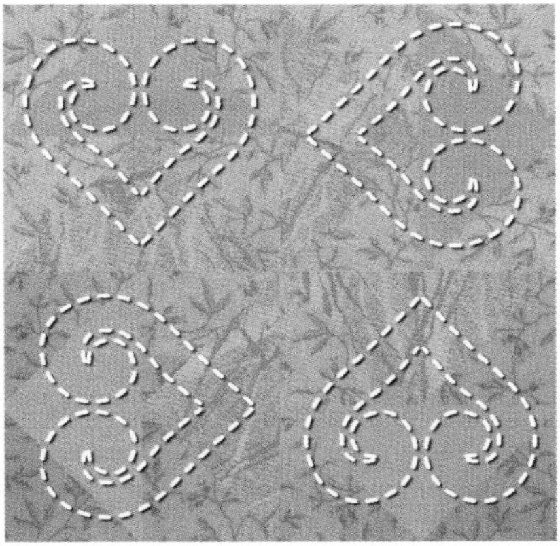

CURVILINEAR DESIGN: HEARTS STENCIL

Trip around the world (squares)

Many patchwork quilts are constructed entirely from squares of fabric. This idea can also be interpreted within one patchwork block, as shown here. The geometric pattern lends itself well to a variety of straight-line quilting designs.

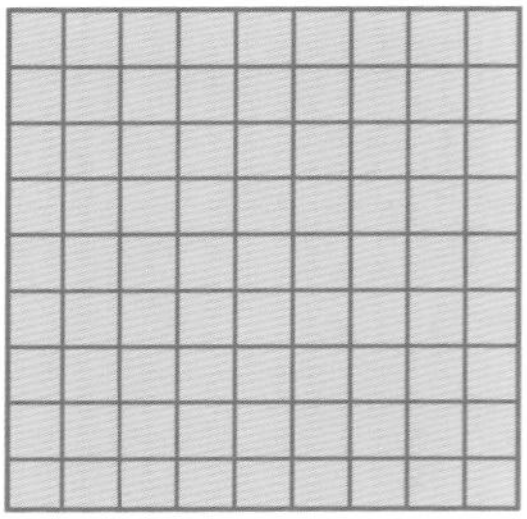

PATCHWORK BLOCK

TIP

The high number of closely spaced seam allowances and small squares of different fabrics will require the use of simple quilting stitches.

CONTOUR-QUILTING

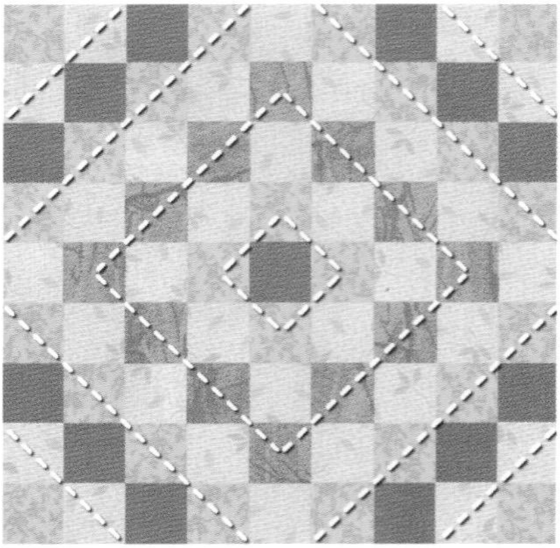

GEOMETRIC DESIGN: FOLLOWING COLORWAY

GEOMETRIC DESIGN: DIRECTIONAL

Tumbling blocks (hexagons and diamonds)

This is just one of numerous patchwork patterns that are constructed using either hexagons or diamonds, or a combination of both. The optical illusion of cubes placed on top of each other is achieved by careful fabric placement, making use of tonal values in the fabrics. Use a curved quilting design to add visual "movement."

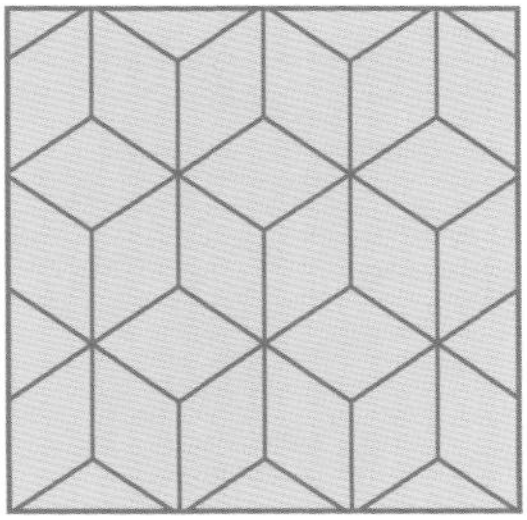

PATCHWORK BLOCK

TIP

This design is generally quilted in the ditch, or the individual patches are contour-quilted to emphasize the pattern.

CONTOUR-QUILTING

GEOMETRIC DESIGN: HIGHLIGHTING THE PATTERN

CURVILINEAR DESIGN: WAVES/CURVES

Flying geese (three-dimensional patchwork)

Three-dimensional patchwork is achieved by fabric manipulation. The "geese" triangles are raised and sit above the surrounding pieced fabrics. Care needs to be taken when quilting three-dimensional patchwork. The raised fabric is often on the bias and, therefore, easy to stretch out of shape.

PATCHWORK BLOCK

TIP

Ensure that any chosen quilting design will fit within the areas surrounding (or behind) the raised fabrics.

CONTOUR-QUILTING

GEOMETRIC DESIGN: DIRECTIONAL

CURVILINEAR DESIGN: STIPPLE (FREE-FORM)

Secret garden (folded patchwork)

Folded patchwork patterns rely on fabric manipulation. The raised areas of folded fabric add extra textural interest to the patchwork block and will determine how and where the block is quilted. Contour-quilt around the raised fabric areas to add emphasis to them.

PATCHWORK BLOCK

TIP

Quilting across the "background" fabric and over the areas where the squares are joined together will strengthen the seams.

CONTOUR-QUILTING

GEOMETRIC DESIGN: DIAGONAL LINES

CURVILINEAR DESIGN: STIPPLE (FREE-FORM)

Wholecloth border

A simple border of plain fabric can be added to any quilt, whether it has a busy, pieced patchwork center, or not. Further interest can be added to a plain fabric border by the use of a variety of quilting designs and stitches.

BORDER PATTERN

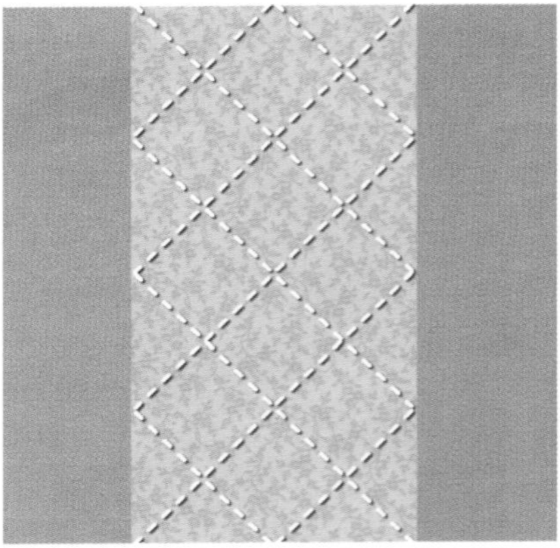

GEOMETRIC DESIGN: CROSSHATCHING

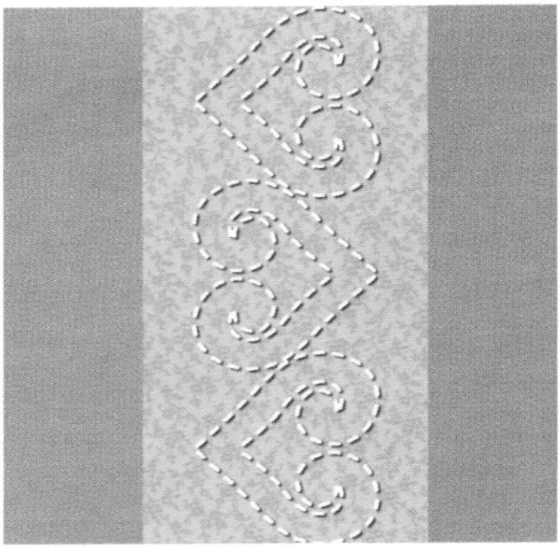

CURVILINEAR DESIGN: HEARTS STENCIL

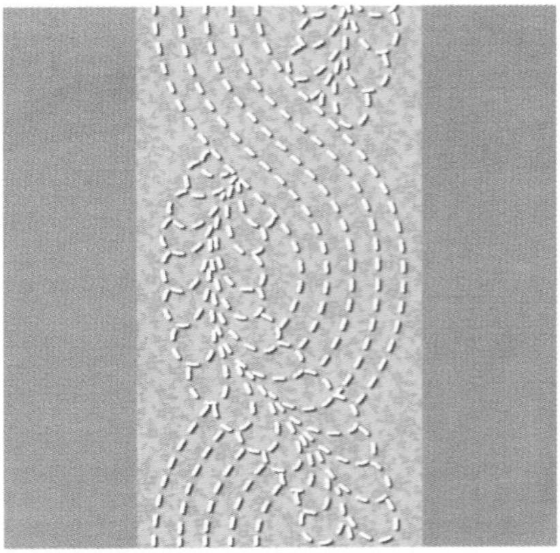

CURVILINEAR DESIGN: FEATHER AND CABLE STENCIL

TIP

The lack of patchwork seams within the plain fabric border provides a wonderful canvas for endless creativity and the use of experimental quilting.

Pieced checkerboard border

If further interest is required at the outer edge of a quilt, or the quilt needs to be made bigger, one or two (or more) patchwork-pieced borders can be added. These can be made from simple squares, or can be more complex. The design should highlight the pieced border pattern, thereby carrying the design of the quilt outward to its edges.

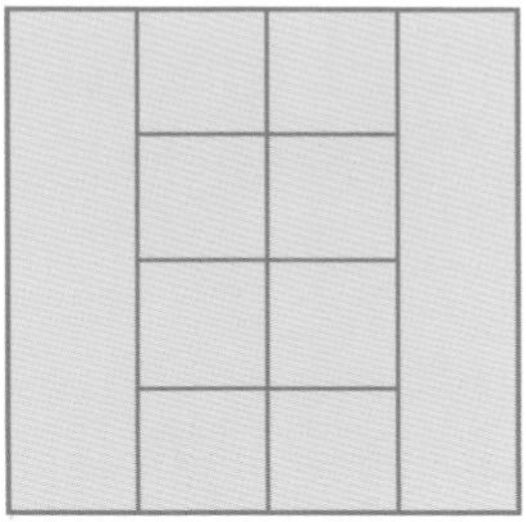

BORDER PATTERN

TIP

Choose a quilting design that accentuates the patchwork piecing.

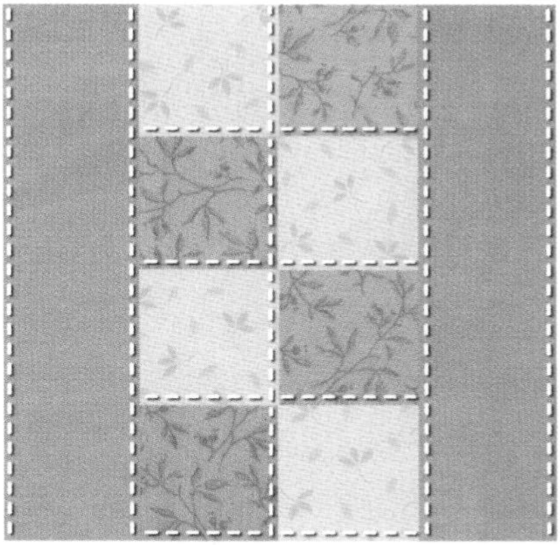

CONTOUR-QUILTING

GEOMETRIC DESIGN

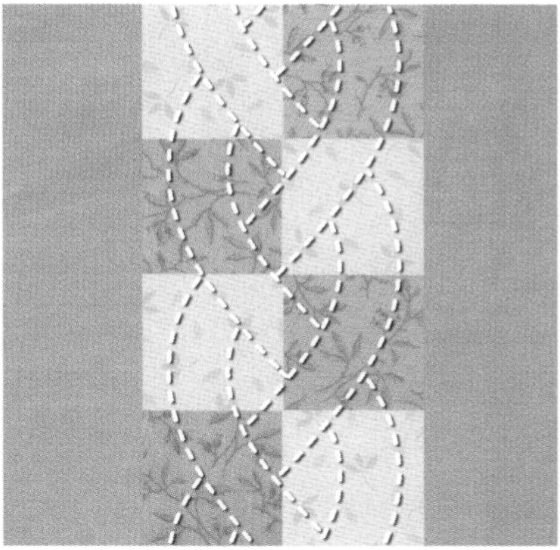

CURVILINEAR DESIGN: PLAITED DESIGN STENCIL

Quilting Your Appliqué

Appliquéd motifs can be further enhanced by quilting around the motif outline. This will add dimension to the quilt.

If the appliqué shapes are quite small, outline quilting will be sufficient. If the shapes are on the large side, they may require quilting inside the shapes themselves. The method of appliqué used and any resulting bulky areas of fabric will determine if you use hand or machine quilting.

APPLIQUÉ BLOCK

Dresden plate

The Dresden plate pattern is one of the most popular and recognizable appliqué patterns in quilt-making. The number of "petals" can range from as few as twelve up to as many as twenty. Contour-quilt each individual petal to emphasize the pattern.

CONTOUR-QUILTING

GEOMETRIC DESIGN: RADIATING LINES

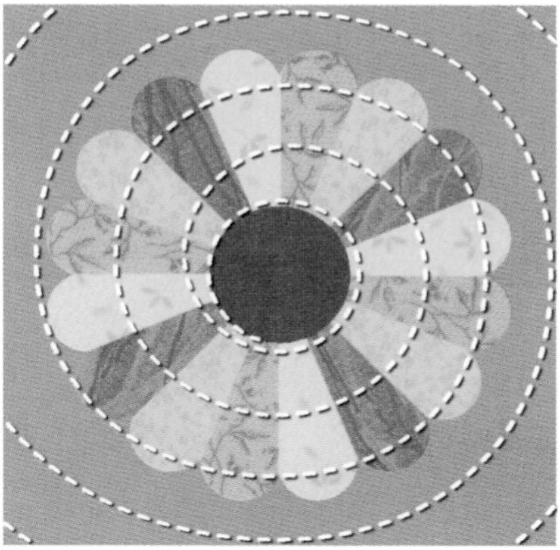

CURVILINEAR DESIGN: SPIRAL

TIP

A design that is taken outside the ring of "petals" can effectively quilt the background fabric at the same time.

Wreath

There are numerous "wreath" patterns to be found among appliqué designs. Variations can be made in the number and style of flowers and leaves, and whether or not a circular "vine" is included. The style of the wreath can be highlighted effectively by contour-quilting the flowers, leaves etc.

APPLIQUÉ BLOCK

CONTOUR-QUILTING

TIP

Use an infill pattern to quilt the background fabric and add emphasis to the appliqué.

GEOMETRIC DESIGN: DIAGONAL INFILL LINES

CURVILINEAR DESIGN: ECHO QUILTING

APPLIQUÉ BLOCK

Celtic knot (bias strip)

A Celtic knot design is based on overlapping curves and circles, and the appliquéd knot is formed by a series of "under and over" junctions using bias-cut fabric strips. Celtic knots can be simple or very elaborate. Choose a quilting design that accentuates the flowing lines of the pattern.

CONTOUR-QUILTING

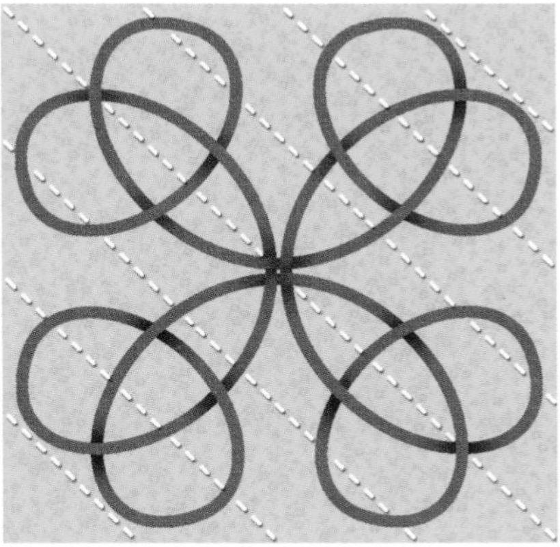

GEOMETRIC DESIGN: DIAGONAL INFILL LINES

CURVILINEAR DESIGN: STIPPLE (FREE-FORM)

TIP

Bias strip appliqué can be used for curved designs where a prominent line is needed. Use the areas of background fabric for interesting quilting designs and/or stitches.

Tulip (stained glass appliqué)

Highlight the use of bias-cut fabric strips by adding patches of extra "background" fabric within the spaces of the pattern, thereby giving the illusion of stained glass. This form of appliqué lends itself to contour-quilting and echo quilting, which emphasize the raised edges of the fabric strips and make the stained glass effect more realistic.

APPLIQUÉ BLOCK

TIP

Use interesting stitches to quilt the surrounding background fabric.

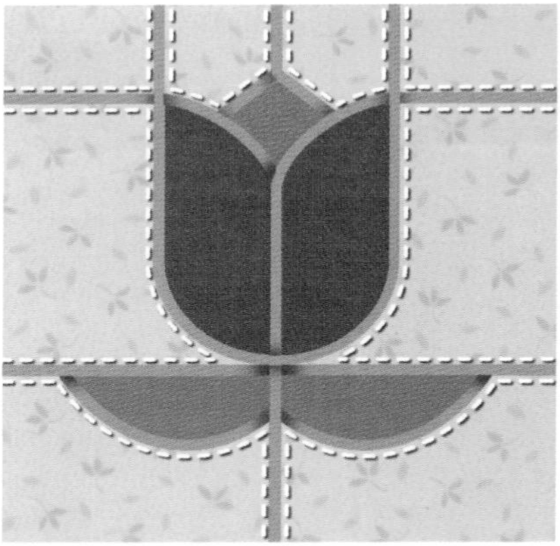

CONTOUR-QUILTING

GEOMETRIC DESIGN: CROSSHATCHED INFILL

CURVILINEAR DESIGN: ECHO QUILTING

APPLIQUÉ BLOCK

Hawaiian appliqué

Patterns for Hawaiian appliqué are numerous and individual to the maker. They are achieved by folding paper and cutting out designs (similar to the snowflake cutouts that children love to make in winter), which are then interpreted in fabric.

CONTOUR-QUILTING

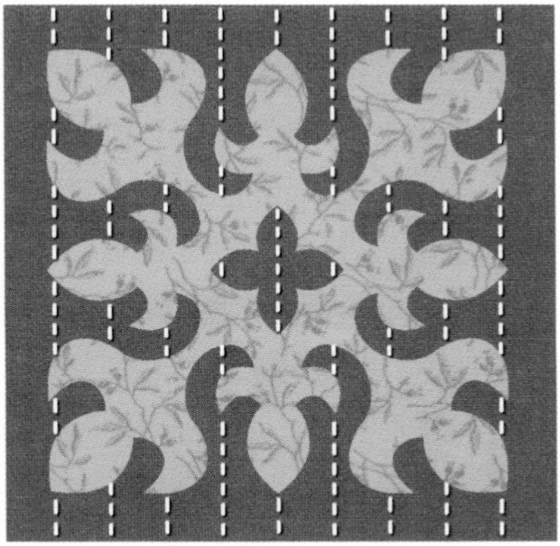

GEOMETRIC DESIGN: INFILL LINES

CURVILINEAR DESIGN: ECHO QUILTING

TIP

Intricate patterns require simple contour-quilting or echo quilting, which does not detract from the elaborate design of the appliqué.

Broderie Perse appliqué

Broderie Perse appliqué is achieved by cutting large motifs from printed fabric and placing them on a contrasting background fabric. It usually takes the form of a display of flowers within a basket or vase. The raw edges of the motifs are secured with a variety of decorative embroidery stitches.

APPLIQUÉ BLOCK

CONTOUR-QUILTING

TIP

Simple quilting designs will help to emphasize the appliqué. Knotting and tufting can add extra textural interest to the background areas.

GEOMETRIC DESIGN: INFILL LINES, CONTRASTING DIRECTIONS

CURVILINEAR DESIGN: ECHO QUILTING WITH KNOTTING AND TUFTING

APPLIQUÉ BLOCK

Appliqué on pieced patchwork block

Mixing appliquéd shapes with a pieced patchwork block can add dimension and interest to simple patchwork. Contour-quilting or echo quilting around the areas of additional appliqué will add definition.

CONTOUR-QUILTING

TIP

If an overall design is preferred, sew simple quilting designs over the seams of both the patchwork and the appliqué. Use simple quilting stitches that won't detract from the patchwork/appliqué pattern.

GEOMETRIC DESIGN: "TRIP AROUND THE WORLD" DESIGN

CURVILINEAR DESIGN: DAISY STENCIL

Quilt Edge Finishings

There are several ways to complete the final edge of your quilt and it's worth giving this some time and thought.

Adding the right binding fabric can soften the effect of an over vibrant quilt or, in turn, give the required visual lift to a mediocre or subdued quilt.

If a binding fabric is too intrusive for your quilt design, the quilt edges can be turned inward and the quilt finished with no additional binding.

Whichever way you choose to finish your quilt, try to ensure that the finishing edge is sympathetic to the overall design of the quilt.

Binding using backing fabric

The backing fabric on a quilt can be folded forward and used to provide an attractive binding that is already part of the quilt. Bear this in mind when selecting backing fabric.

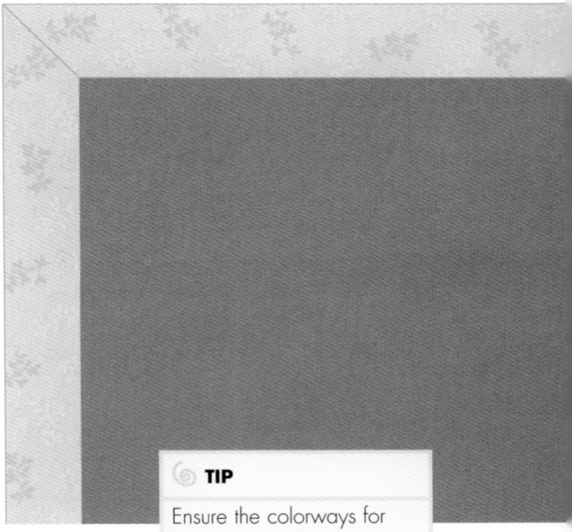

TIP

Ensure the colorways for the quilt front and back harmonize.

STEP 1

When the quilting is finished, trim the batting back to the same size as the quilt top. Leave the backing fabric at least 1 in. (2.5 cm) wider than the quilt top and batting on all edges of the quilt.

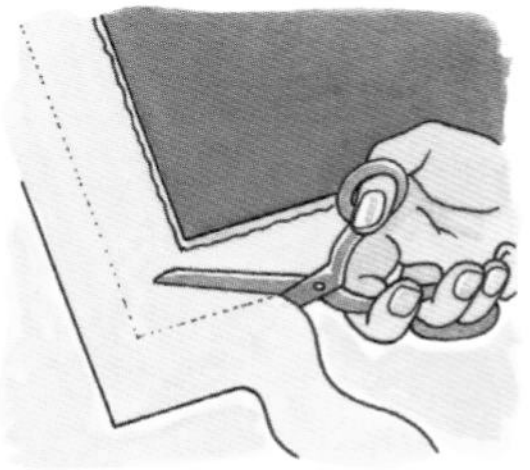

STEP 2

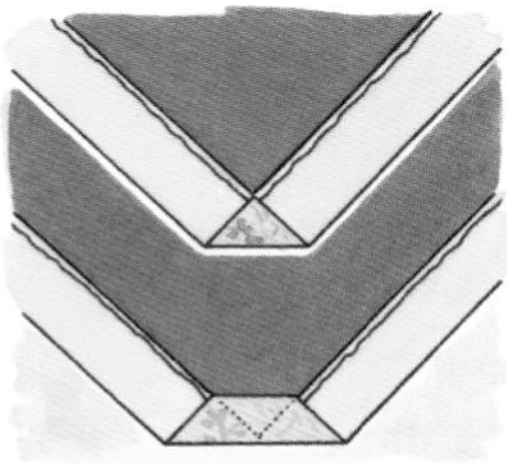

At each corner of the quilt, make one fold in the backing fabric so the point of the fold touches the corner of the quilt top. Make a second fold equal to the first.

STEP 3

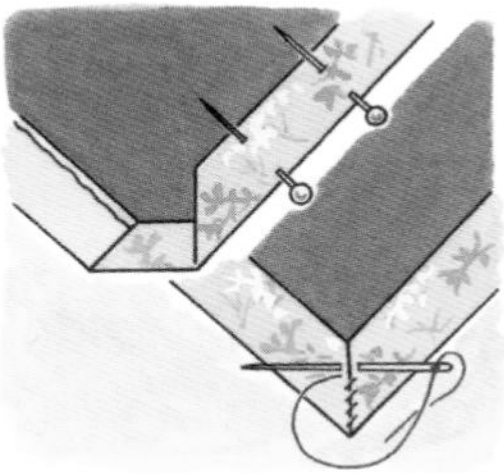

Fold in the raw edge of the binding on one edge of the quilt; fold in the binding toward the quilt top and pin in place. Repeat with the second side of the binding, so the two edges of binding meet diagonally at the corner of the quilt. Pin and stitch in place. Repeat on all corners of the quilt.

Folded-in edges

Achieve a neat, unobtrusive finish by folding the raw edges of the backing and quilt top fabrics inward. Secure the raw edges with a quilting stitch just inside the folded edge.

STEP 1

Trim the batting back to fit the quilt top. Leave the backing fabric and quilt top fabric approximately ½ in. (1 cm) larger than the actual quilt top on all sides of the quilt. Fold the backing fabric inward, and the quilt top fabrics inward, so they both sit behind the batting.

TIP

Use this method if your quilt design does not need the addition of a binding.

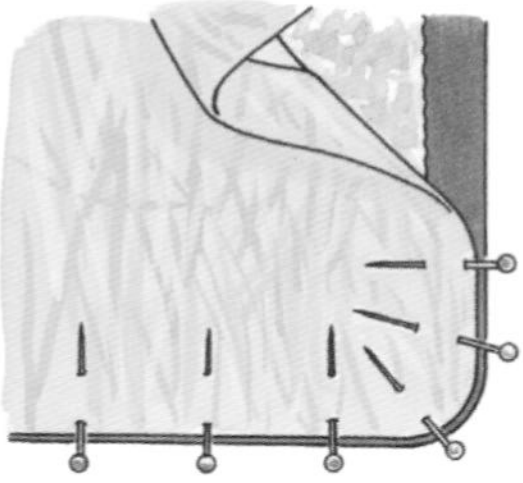

STEP 2

Gently curve the corners. Pin the fabrics in place as you go.

STEP 3

Make a quilting stitch just inside the folded edges of the quilt to secure the raw edges.

Separate fabric binding

Choose the binding fabric once all the quilt-making has been finished: it can make a calming or vibrant addition to a quilt at this stage, depending on what is needed.

STEP 1

Trim the quilt top fabric, backing fabric, and batting so all the quilt edges are even. Cut strips of binding fabric on the straight grain (if longer lengths are needed, join the strips on the diagonal).

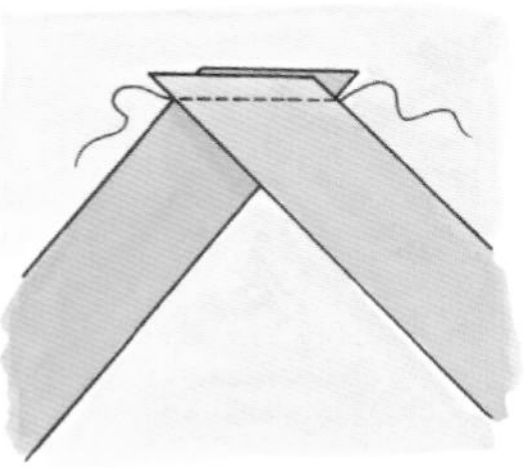

STEP 2

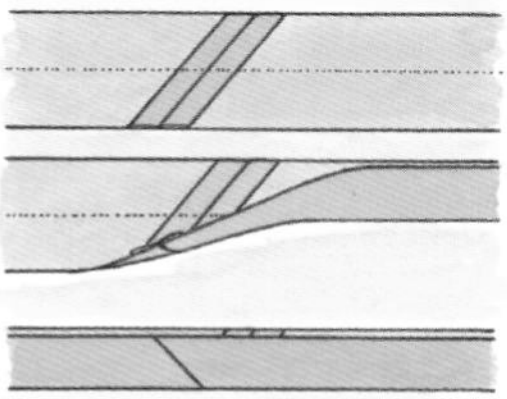

Press all binding strips in half lengthways.

STEP 3

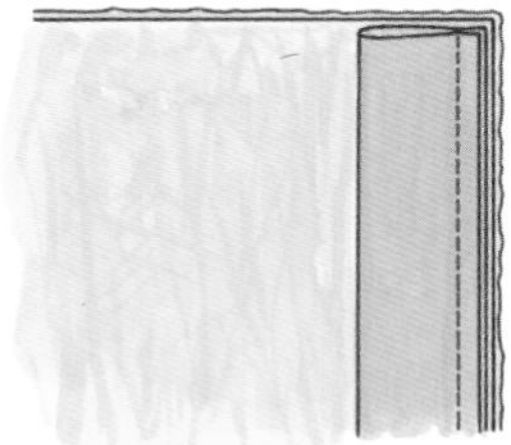

On the two side edges of the quilt, place binding strips on top of the quilt top, matching raw edges, and stitch in place.

STEP 4

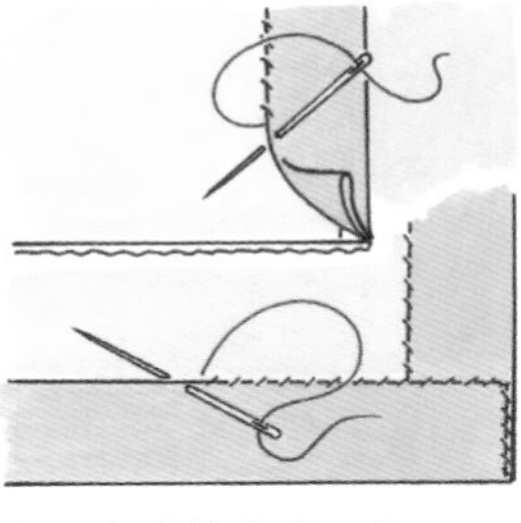

Turn the folded edge of binding to the back of the quilt and slipstitch in place. Repeat step 3 on the other edges, leaving excess binding at each end of the quilt edge. Turn in this excess fabric when folding the binding to the back of the quilt, then stitch in place.

Mitered corners

A squared quilt corner can be mitered if a fabric print needs to continue around the corner. It is better to use one continuous strip of binding fabric here.

STEP 1

Trim the batting, backing fabric and quilt top fabrics so all quilt edges are even. Begin in the center of one side of the quilt, placing the raw edge of one side of the binding (right side down) against the raw edges of the quilt and folding in a small excess of fabric before beginning to stitch the fabric layers together.

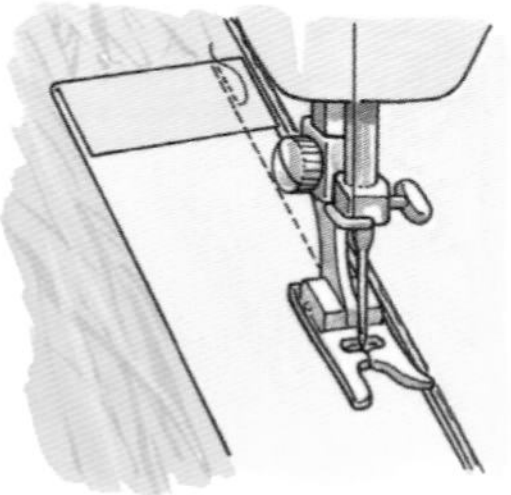

STEP 2

Continue stitching until you reach the corner of the quilt, then stop stitching with the needle in the "down" position, a seam's length from the edge of the quilt. Pivot the work around the needle and continue stitching along the next quilt edge.

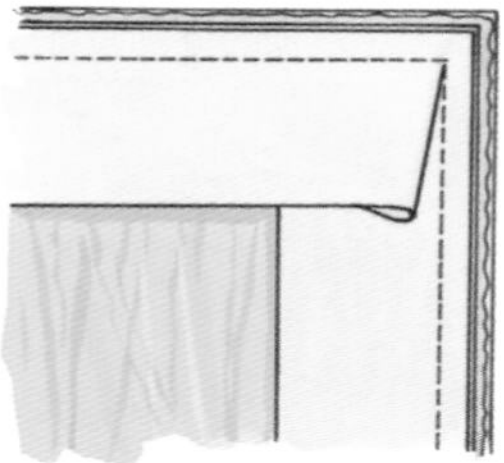

STEP 3

Continue stitching the binding until you reach the point where you began. Join the two ends neatly.

STEP 4

Turn the opposite raw edge of binding fabric under and fold all binding to the back of the quilt. Slipstitch in place. Fold the corner tucks diagonally and slipstitch to neaten.

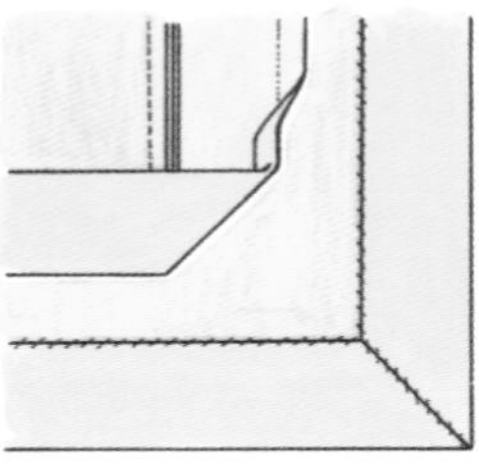

Binding a curved quilt corner

If a separate binding fabric is required to continue around a curved quilt corner, cut the binding fabric strips on the bias to give them stretch and prevent the fabric puckering.

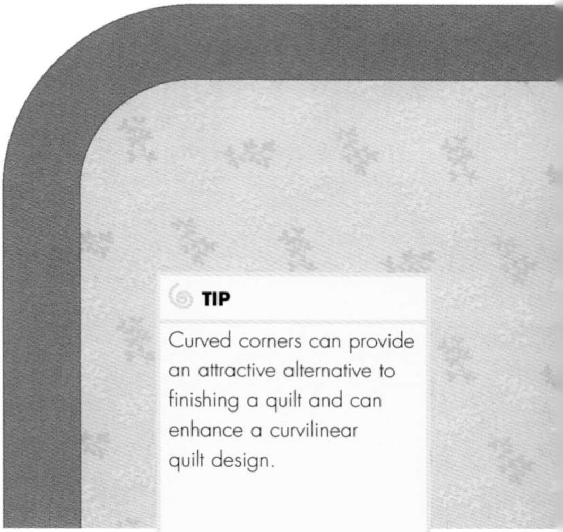

TIP

Curved corners can provide an attractive alternative to finishing a quilt and can enhance a curvilinear quilt design.

STEP 1

Trim the batting, backing fabric and quilt top fabric so that all the quilt edges are even. Use a dinner plate or something similar to draw a large curve at the corners of the quilt; trim the fabrics back to this curve.

STEP 2

Using one continuous strip of binding fabric and beginning halfway along one of the quilt edges, lay the binding right side down, raw edge to raw edge, on the quilt top and begin stitching in place, turning in a small amount of excess fabric to begin.

STEP 3

Gently ease the stretchy, bias-cut fabric around the curve when you reach it. Finish the binding where it meets the point you began. Slipstitch to neaten. Fold the raw edge of the binding inward and fold all the binding to the back of the quilt. Slipstitch in place.

Binding shaped quilt edges

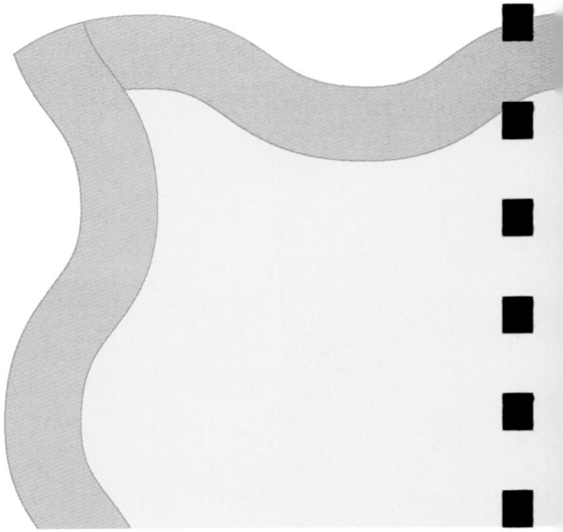

Quilt edges can be shaped to follow the quilt top design or be cut freehand. To achieve a squared-off corner, use four separate bias-cut binding strips, one for each quilt edge.

STEP 1

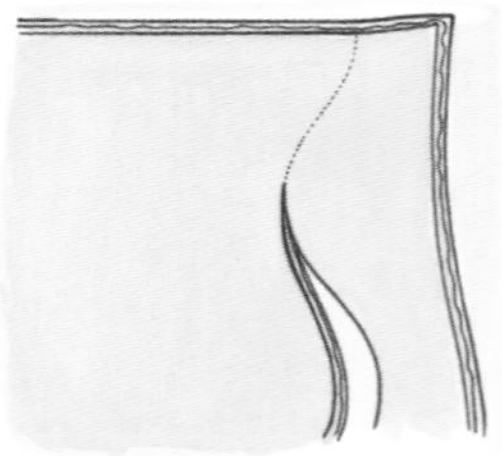

Trim the quilt edge, batting and backing fabric to neaten the quilt edges and follow the shape required.

TIP

Cut fabric strips on the bias so they stretch and curve easily.

STEP 2

Fold the binding strips in half down their length. Working on two side edges of the quilt first, place the binding on the quilt top, raw edge to raw edge and stitch in place, gently easing the binding fabric to follow the shape of the quilt edge. Turn the folded edges of the binding to the back of the quilt and slipstitch in place. Repeat with the top and bottom edges, leaving excess fabric at either end of the quilt edge—this is turned in before folding the binding to the back.

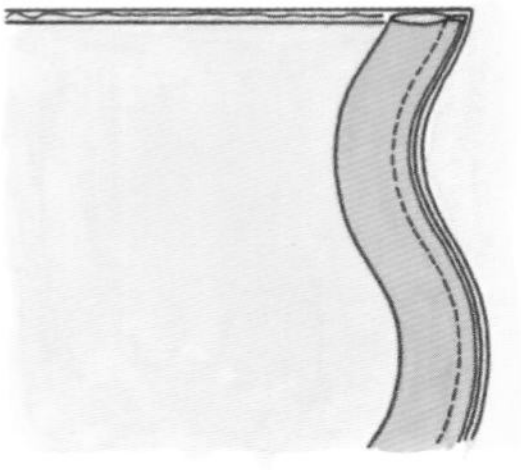

Binding a scalloped edge

A scalloped quilt edge requires a continuous length of binding fabric that has been cut on the bias to allow it to stretch around the curves.

STEP 1

Mark the scalloped edge on the quilt top or follow the pattern of the quilt itself. Leave the batting and backing fabric untrimmed until the binding has been sewn in place. Place the binding strip, right side down and raw edge to raw edge, on the quilt top. At each valley in the scalloped shape, make a small cut into the seam allowance of the binding fabric to help release any tension. Stitch the binding in place, keeping the needle in a "down" position when you pivot at each valley section. Continue until the binding meets the point where you started and fold in the two raw edges to neaten.

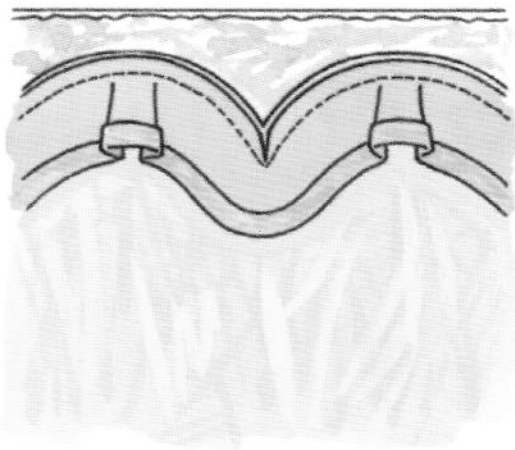

STEP 2

Trim the batting and backing fabric so they are even with the quilt top. Fold the complete binding strip to the back of the quilt, helping the fabric tuck into a fold at each valley. Slipstitch the binding in place.

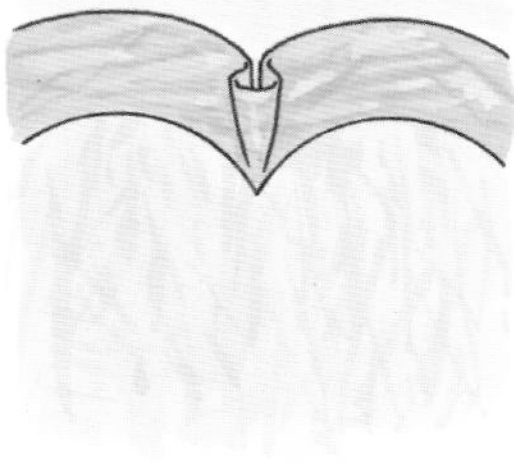

TIP

Use an object such as a dinner plate to mark an even scalloped edge.

STEP 3

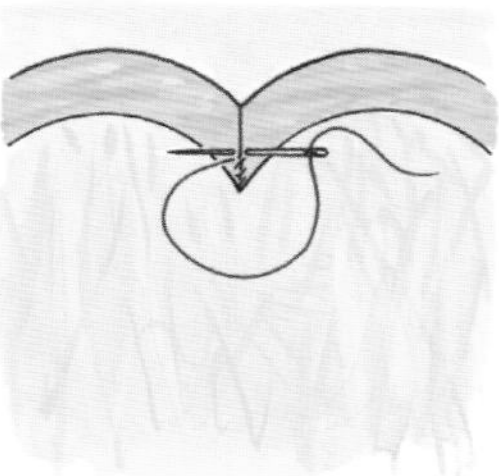

Neaten the fabric folds at each valley and carefully slipstitch the folds in place.

Folded-in handkerchief edge

A quilt with a pennant-shaped, handkerchief edge is difficult to add a binding to. The best way to finish it off is to fold in the two fabrics and not use a binding.

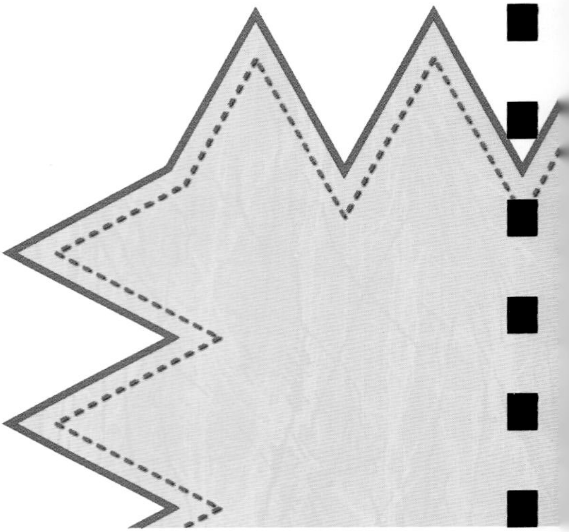

STEP 1

Trim the batting, backing fabric and quilt top fabrics to the shape required, then trim the batting to approximately ½ in. (1 cm) smaller than the two fabric edges.

STEP 2

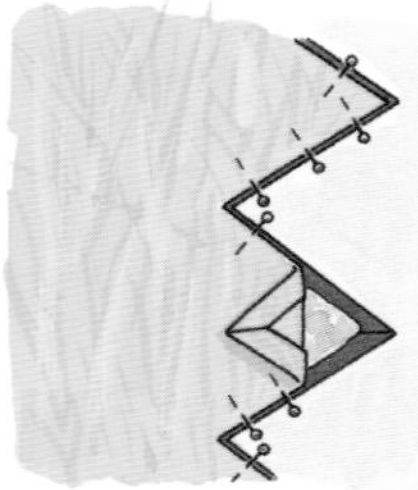

Fold the backing fabric and the quilt top fabrics inward evenly, pushing them behind the batting. Pin in place as you go.

TIP

Alter the width or length of the spikes to fit in with the quilt measurements.

STEP 3

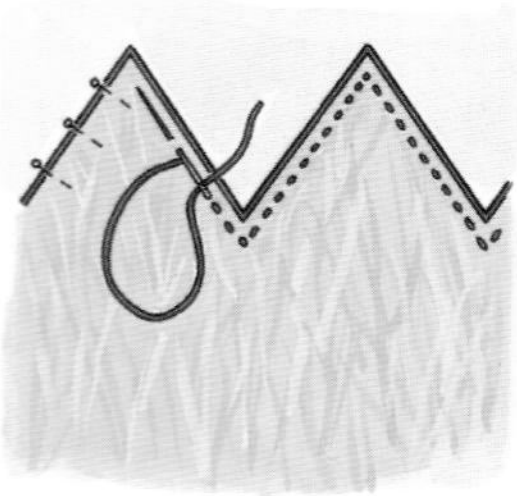

Stitch all the layers together with a quilting stitch made just inside the folded-in quilt edges.

Inset piping

Adding an inset fabric-covered piping can provide an attractive alternative to both binding and folding in a quilt edge.

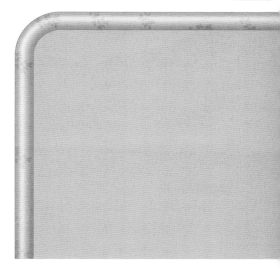

STEP 1

Trim the batting, backing fabric and quilt top fabric so each quilt edge is even. Cover the length of piping cord in bias-cut fabric and stitch the piping to the quilt backing fabric, neatening the point at which the two raw edges meet.

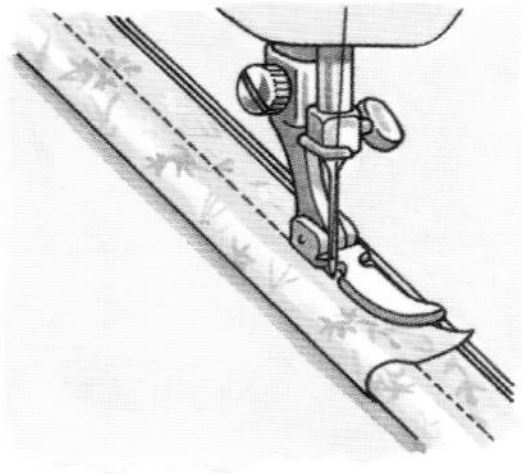

TIP

The piping fabric can be a subtle color that harmonizes with the quilt top, or a strongly contrasting color.

STEP 2

Fold in the raw edges of the quilt backing so the piping is on the outside of the quilt and the raw edges are inside the quilt. Fold the raw edge of the quilt top inward evenly. Pin as you go along. Slipstitch the quilt top in place so it meets the inside edge of the piping and covers the row of stitching.

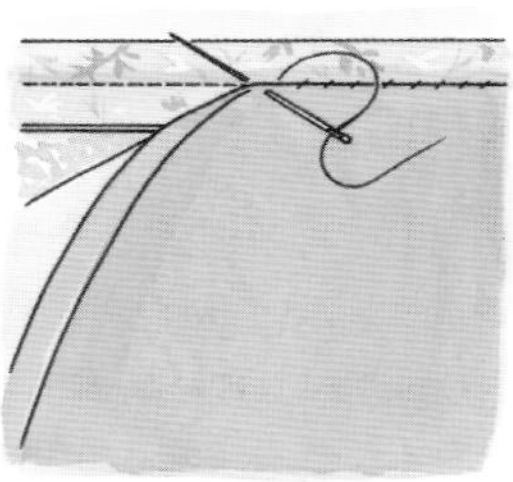

Inset sawtooth triangles

Adding sawtooth triangles to the folded-in edge of a quilt can give the illusion of a handkerchief edging without the need to shape the quilt itself.

STEP 1

Trim the batting, quilt top and backing fabric so all quilt edges are even. Trim the batting so it is approximately ½ in. (1 cm) shorter than the quilt fabrics.

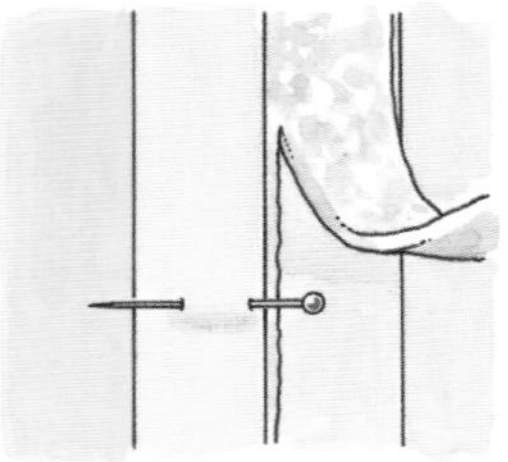

STEP 2

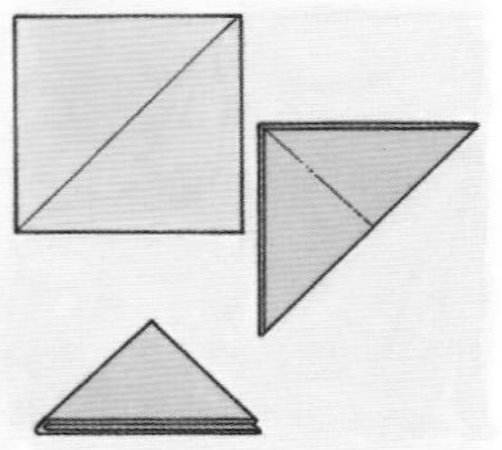

Cut and fold several sawtooth triangles of fabric.

STEP 3

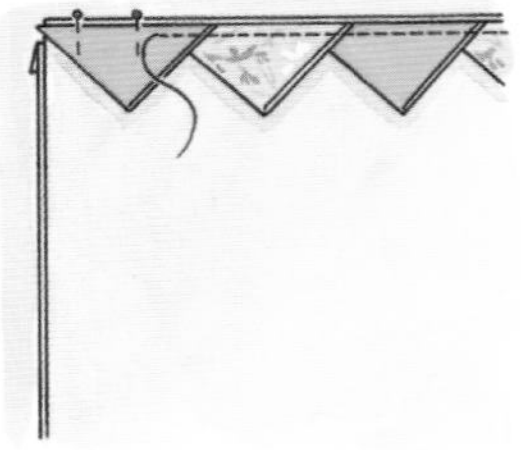

Position these along the edge of the quilt backing fabric, ensuring that each triangle sits inside the previous one. Space the triangles evenly along the quilt edge, pin and stitch in place. Repeat on all sides of the quilt.

STEP 4

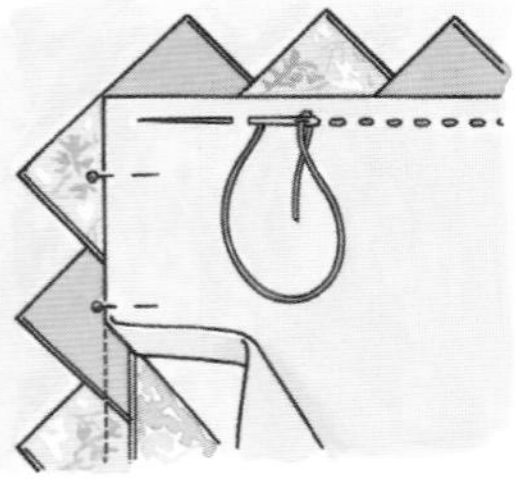

Fold the backing fabric inward, ensuring that the raw edges are inside the quilt and the triangles are sitting outside the quilt. Fold the quilt top fabrics inward neatly, pin in place and slipstitch or secure with quilting stitches to finish.

Inset prairie point triangles

Inset these triangles into a folded-in edge to add another dimension to a quilt. Try using a striped fabric, or scraps of different fabrics that have been used throughout the quilt.

STEP 1

Trim the batting, quilt top and backing fabric so all the quilt edges are even. Trim the batting so it is approximately ½ in. (1 cm) shorter than the quilt fabrics.

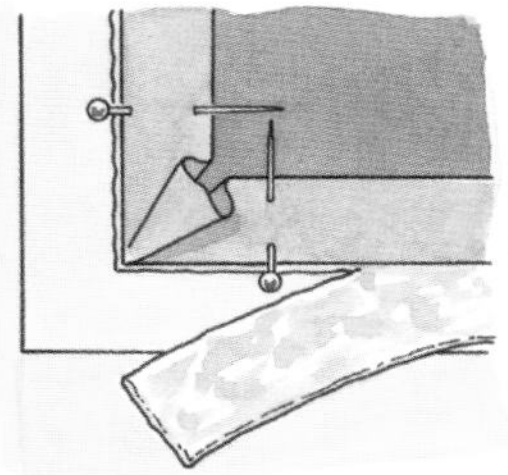

STEP 2

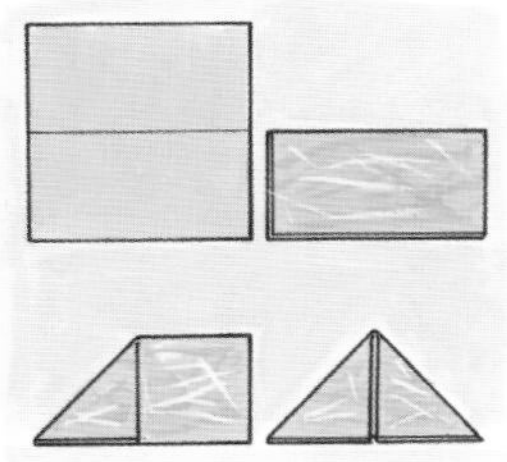

Cut and fold several prairie point triangles.

STEP 3

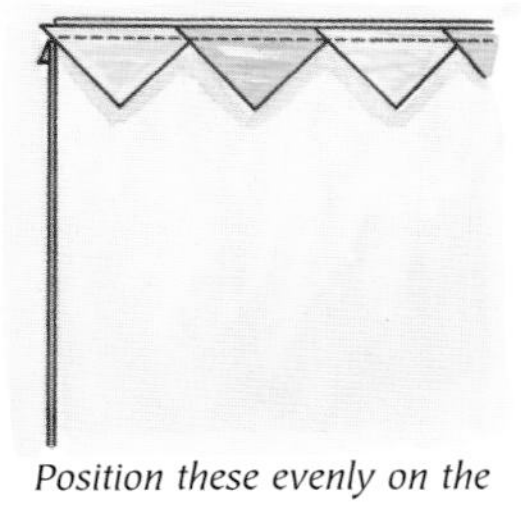

Position these evenly on the right side of the backing fabric, matching raw edges. Pin and stitch in place.

STEP 4

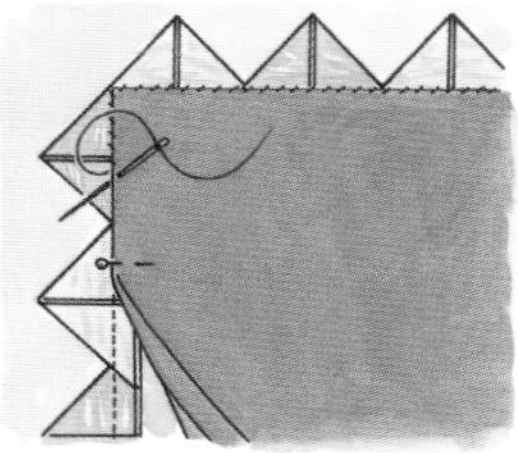

Fold backing fabric inward so that the triangles point outward. Fold quilt top fabrics inward. Pin and slipstitch to finish.

Cleaning, Storage and Display

The aftercare and presentation of your quilt is important if it is expected to last and, hopefully, be passed down through the generations to follow.

CLEANING

At some stage you'll have to think about cleaning your quilt. You need to consider the fabrics used in the quilt, including the batting. Don't resort to professional dry-cleaning unless you are sure of the fiber content of the quilt and can discuss this with the dry-cleaners beforehand.

Machine washing If the quilt is quite robust—made from new, prewashed 100 percent cotton fabrics, machine quilted, and it contains a batting such as polyester—you can launder it in a washing machine. Choose mild soapflakes rather than a detergent, and a cool wash setting. Tumble-dry the quilt afterward, or lay it flat on a sheet to dry. Do not hang it on a clothes line—the weight of damp fabric and batting could pull on the stitching.

Delicate quilts If a quilt is hand quilted, made from fragile or less robust fabrics (such as silks or pieces cut from old clothing), or if the content of fabrics and/or batting is unknown, it is probably better to treat the quilt gently. Antique quilts or quilts with mixed and fragile fibers can be cleaned by covering the quilt with a length of calico or net and vacuuming through it, with the vacuum cleaner set to the lowest strength and held above the fabric fibers so that they are not sucked upward.

DOWEL

There are several ways to display wall quilts: The most common method is to sew a tube of fabric to the top edge of the quilt, on the reverse side, where a length of dowel can be inserted. This is a requirement for exhibition quilts, but also means that the quilt can be displayed so that the dowel or hanging pole is not on show.

Washing by hand If the quilt really does need a good but gentle wash, fill a bathtub with warm water and dissolve some mild soapflakes in it. Immerse the quilt in the water, gently pushing it downward until the layers are soaked through. Knead very carefully to clean it. Leaving the quilt in the bath, let the soapy water drain away and refill the bath a couple of times with clean rinsing water. Once the water runs clear, empty the bath. Using a large sheet or towel, roll the wet quilt onto the sheet and lift it out of the bath. Lay the quilt out flat on top of the sheet, either on a suitable floor or outdoors on a warm day, to dry naturally.

STORAGE

Be careful about where and how your quilt is stored. Buy plenty of acid-free tissue paper; if the quilt has to be folded, pad the folds with the tissue paper to avoid permanent creasing. Add more sheets of tissue between the layers and around the outside. Wrap the complete quilt in a cotton sheet or, if smaller, put it inside a pillowcase and store it away from direct sunlight and damp conditions.

DISPLAY

If your quilt is to be displayed on a bed, make sure it is turned regularly. If direct sunlight shines in, turn the quilt face down so that it doesn't fade, or cover with an additional sheet to protect the fabrics.

Some quilts are intended to be displayed on a wall, either at home or in an exhibition. Again, try to avoid hanging the quilt in direct sunlight. Take it down at regular intervals and lay it flat for a few days to alleviate the stress on the fabrics and stitching.

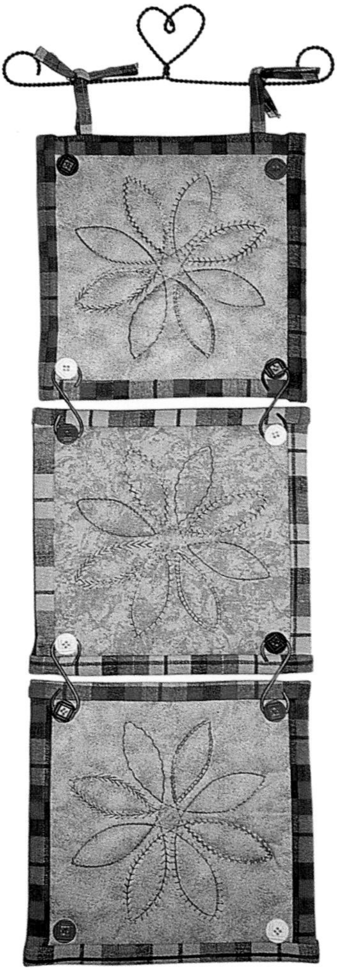

QUILT-HANGERS

You can buy decorative quilt-hangers made from wire or wood, or just use a brass pole and some fancy cord, to make a feature of your quilt-hanging system. These can be used either with the tubular hanging sleeve, or you might like to add some hanging loops at the top of your project specifically for this purpose.

Glossary

ACID-FREE TISSUE PAPER
Used for storing textiles and quilts.

APPLIQUÉ
Attaching shapes and motifs of fabric to another fabric for surface embellishment.

BACKING FABRIC
A material used on the reverse side of a quilt.

BASTING
A large, temporary stitch, used to hold layers of fabric together. In quilting, used to secure layers of fabric (or fabric and batting) together prior to quilting.

BATTING
A material used for padding or insulation. In quilt-making, it is used to fill the area between layers of fabric to provide surface relief.

BEARDING
The word used to describe the appearance of a fabric when a fluffy batting has worked its way through the fibers of the fabric or emerged through the seams of patchwork.

BETWEENS
Specialist needles for hand quilting.

BIAS-CUT FABRIC
Fabric that is cut at an angle of approximately 45° to the straight grain and is very stretchy.

BINDING
Fabric added to the edge of a quilt to neaten it and hide the raw edges of all the layers.

BODKIN
A sewing needle with a blunt point and a large eye, for use with thick thread. It is used for corded quilting.

BONDING WEB
A web of adhesive presented in sheet form, which is used to glue two pieces of fabric together.

CALICO OR CHEESECLOTH
A very open-weave, lightweight cloth used as an interlining when working stuffed or corded quilting.

COLORFAST FABRIC
Fabric where the dye does not run when it is immersed in water.

CORDED QUILTING
Also known as Italian quilting. A length of cord, yarn, or wool is passed between two layers of fabric to provide dimensional interest to a quilted surface.

COTTON
Natural fiber, even-weave fabric or natural fiber thread.

COUCHING
Stitching down a length of thread, yarn or cord on a fabric for surface embellishment.

ECHO QUILTING
Stitching around a quilting design at a regular interval from the edge of the design to echo the design further.

FRAME/HOOP
A wooden or plastic structure used to support work that is being quilted or embroidered.

HAND QUILTING
Stitches that hold the layers of a quilt together and are sewn by hand.

INSERTION STITCHES
Decorative stitches sewn as a means of joining two neatened edges of fabric together.

INTERFACING
A stabilizing fabric that is ironed or sewn to the reverse side of a material which requires support.

ITALIAN QUILTING
Also known as corded quilting. A length of cord, yarn or wool is passed between two layers of fabric to provide dimensional interest to a quilted surface.

KANTHA QUILTING
A style of quilting originating in Bangladesh, which consists of running stitches in colored threads.

LIGHTBOX
An illuminated box that allows designs to be traced onto fabric with ease.

MACHINE QUILTING
Stitching that holds the layers of a quilt together and is sewn on a sewing machine.

METALLICS
Fabrics or thread which contain a manmade fiber with a high-gloss sheen.

MITERED CORNERS
Corners that have been folded and sewn at an angle of 45°.

MUSLIN
An even-weave fabric with a homespun appearance. Cream or bleached white in color.

PATCHWORK
Patches of fabric that have been joined together to form a pattern.

PIECING
The sewing together of patchwork shapes.

POLYESTER
A manmade synthetic fiber used in fabric, threads and batting.

POUNCING
Transferring a design onto fabric through holes in paper using a cloth filled with powder or chalk.

QUILT
Two layers of fabric with padding in between, stitched together. Commonly used as a bed covering.

QUILTING
Utility and/or decorative stitching that holds the three layers of a quilt together.

ROTARY CUTTING EQUIPMENT
A safety mat, a safety ruler and a cutting wheel with a sharp blade.

SASHIKO
A style of quilting originating in Japan, which is usually stitched in designs based on a grid.

STABILIZING FABRIC
A fabric that is ironed on or sewn to the reverse side of a material which requires additional support. In quilt-making, usually a nonwoven interfacing.

STRAIGHT GRAIN
The fibers that run across the width, or down the length, of a piece of fabric.

TEMPLATE
A shape used for making patches to be used for patchwork or appliqué, or a motif for a quilting design.

TRAPUNTO
A form of quilting where areas of the design are padded with stuffing.

WALKING/EVEN-FEED FOOT
A sewing machine foot that is used to help ensure that the top and bottom fabrics in a quilt are fed through the machine at the same speed.

WATER-SOLUBLE PEN
A fabric-marking tool with ink that is removable in cold water.

WHOLECLOTH QUILT
A quilt where the top is made using a whole length of fabric, rather than being pieced together.

Further reading

EMBROIDERY

Barnden, B. *The Embroidery Stitch Bible* (KP books, 2003)

Eaton, J. *Mary Thomas's Dictionary of Embroidery Stitches* (Trafalgar Square Publishing, 1998)

Harlow, E. *The Anchor Book of Free-Style Embroidery Stitches* (David & Charles Publishers, 1997)

QUILTS AND QUILTING

Donaldson, J. *Add-A-Line: Continuous Quilting Patterns* (American Quilter's Society, 2002)

Eddy, C. *Quilting Basics* (Barron's Educational Series, 2003)

Finley, R. *Old Patchwork Quilts and the Women Who Made Them* (Charles T. Branford, 1971)

Gaudynski, D. *Guide to Machine Quilting* (American Quilter's Society, 2002)

Jenkins, S. and Seward, L. *The American Quilt Story* (Rodale, 1992)

Poe, A. *Quilting School* (Reader's Digest, 2003)

Sandbach, K. *Show Me How To Create Quilting Designs* (C & T Publishing, 2004)

Seward, L. *The Complete Book of Patchwork, Quilting and Appliqué* (Mitchell Beazley, 1997)

Tinkler, N. *The Essential Sampler Quilt* (Teamwork Craftbooks, 2005)

Tinkler, N. *Quilting With A Difference* (Traplet Publications, 2002)

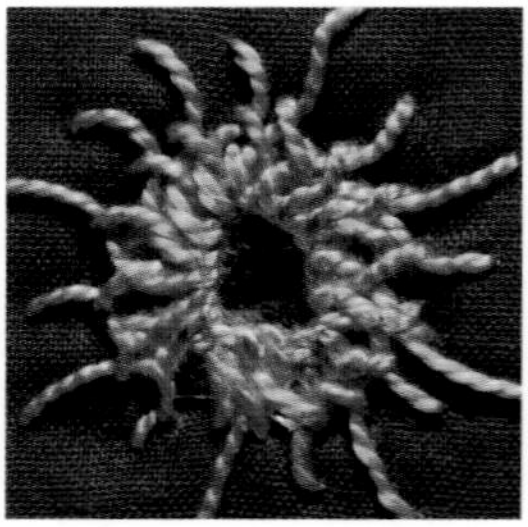

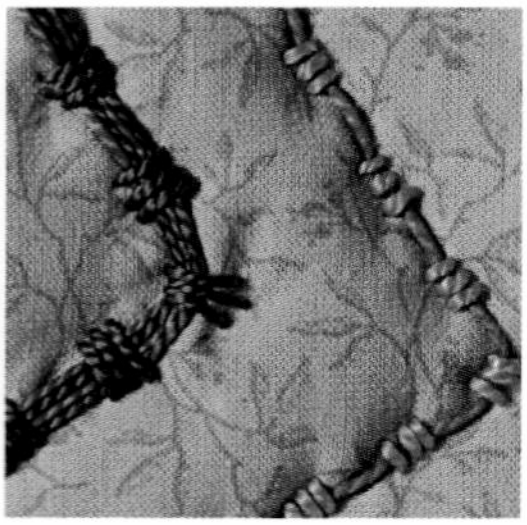

Suppliers

U.S SUPPLIERS

CLASSIC COTTONS
Customer Service Dept.
1384 Broadway
New York
NY 10018
Tel: 212 391-2300
Email: customerservice@classiccottons.com
Web site: www.classiccottons.com

FABRIC TRADITIONS
1350 Broadway
Suite 2106
New York
NY 10018
Tel: 212 279-5710
Web site: http://fabrictraditions.com

U.K SUPPLIERS

COATS CRAFTS
PO Box 22
Lingfield House
McMullen Road
Darlington, County Durham DL1 1YQ
Tel: 0044 (0)1325 394237
Email: consumer.ccuk@coats.com
Web site: www.coats.crafts.co.uk

CREATIVE GRIDS (UK) LTD.
Unit 4, Swannington Road
Broughton Astley
Leicester LE9 6TU
Tel: 0044 (0)845 450 7722/7733
Email: sales@creativegrids.com
Web site: www.creativegrids.com

THE COTTON PATCH
1285 Stratford Road
Hall Green, Birmingham B28 9AJ
Tel: 0044 (0)121 7022840
Email: mailorder@cottonpatch.net
Web site: www.cottonpatch.net

THE QUILT ROOM
20 West Street
Dorking, Surrey RH4 1BL
Shop: 0044 (0)1306 740739
Mail order: 0044 (0)1306 877307
Web site: www.quiltroom.co.uk

WHALEYS (BRADFORD) LTD
Harris Court
Great Horton, Bradford
West Yorkshire, BD7 4EQ
Tel: 0044 (0)1274 576718
Email: info@whaleys-bradford.ltd.uk
Web site: www.whaleys-bradford.ltd.uk

Index

Page numbers in *italics* refer to captions

D

E

F

G

H

I

K

L

M

N

O

P

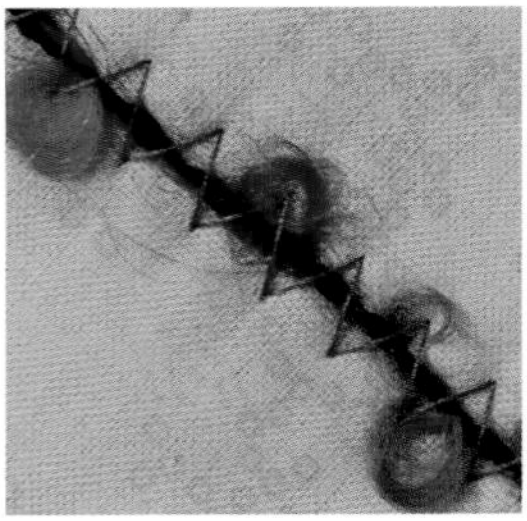

Q

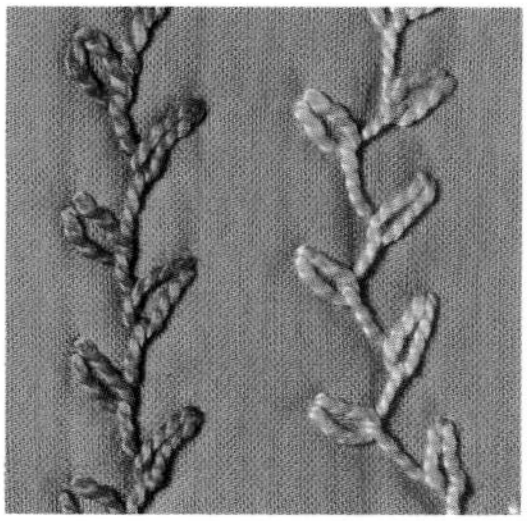

Picture Credits

Quarto would like to thank Nikki Tinkler for supplying the photographs that appear on page 6, 7 (top left), 9 and 247.

While every effort has been made to credit contributors, Quarto would like to apologize should there have been any omissions or errors—and would be pleased to make the appropriate correction for future editions of the book.

Author Acknowledgments

I would like to thank all my family for their support and encouragement, and also Liz Pasfield and Penny Cobb at Quarto for their input and advice. Thanks also to Classic Cottons, Coats Crafts UK, Whaley's of Bradford, The Quilt Room and The Cotton Patch for generously supplying many of the fabrics and threads used in the book.

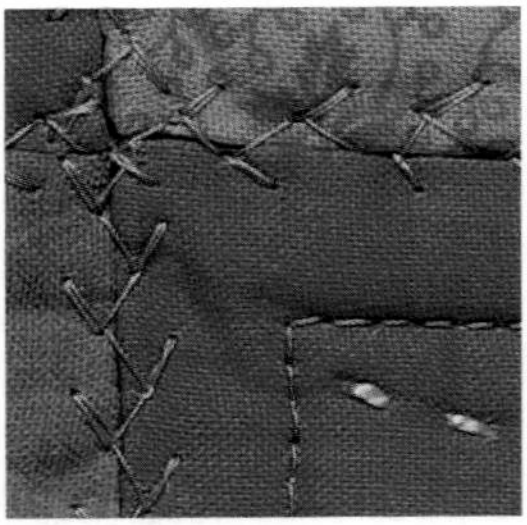

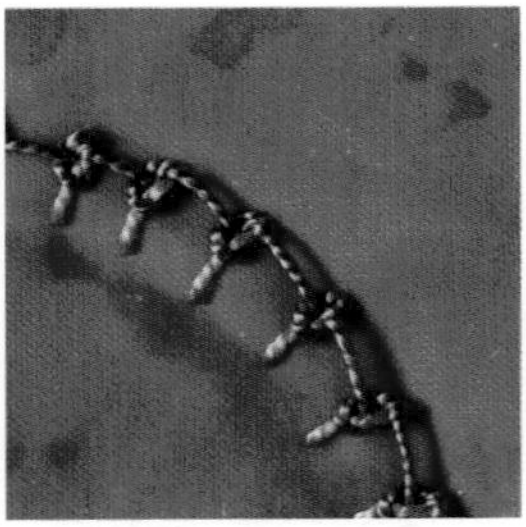

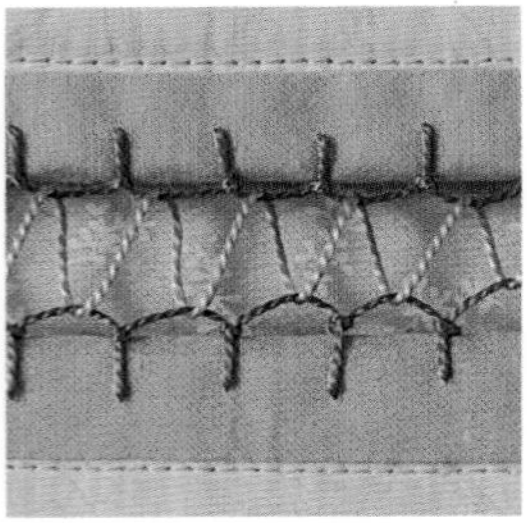

PHILIP'S

ROAD ATLAS

France

Belgium and The Netherlands

C000215833

www.philips-maps.co.uk

First published in 2009 by Philip's,
a division of Octopus Publishing Group Ltd
www.octopusbooks.co.uk
Endeavour House, 189 Shaftesbury Avenue
London WC2H 8JY
An Hachette UK Company
www.hachette.co.uk

Second edition 2013
Second impression 2014

ISBN 978-1-84907-291-5

Cartography by Philip's

Printed in China

Contents

Legend

Route planning map pages VI–VII

Symbol	Meaning
	Motorway with selected junctions
	tunnel, under construction
	Toll motorway
	Pre-pay motorway
	Main through route
	Other major road
	Other road
25	**European road number**
56	**Motorway number**
55	**National road number**
56	**Distances** – in kilometres
	International boundary
	National boundary
LE HAVRE	**Car ferry and destination**
	International airport
	Town – population
PARIS	5 million +
LYON	1–2 million
Toulouse	500000–1million
Dijon	200000-500000
Caen	100000–200000
Niort	50000–100000
Beune	20000–50000
Lunel	10000–20000
Tonnerre	5000–10000
Vienne	0–5000
	Town – Low Emission Zone
	5 million +
	1–2 million
	500000–1million
	200000–500000
	100000–200000
	50000–100000
	20000–50000
	10000–20000
	5000–10000
	0–5000

Scales

Pages VI–VII • 1:4 730 396, 1cm = 47.3km, 1 in = 74.65 miles

0 20 40 60 80 miles

0 40 80 120 km

Pages 2–38 • 1:1 066 044, 1cm = 10.66km, 1 inch = 16.8 miles

0 5 10 15 20 miles

0 10 20 30 km

Road maps pages 2–38

Symbol	Meaning
7 8	**Motorway with junctions** – full, restricted access
	services, rest or parking area
	tunnel
	under construction
	Toll motorway – with toll barrier
	Pre-pay motorway – 'Vignette' must be purchased before travel
	Principal trunk highway – single / dual carriageway
	Tunnel
	Under construction
	Other main highway – single / dual carriageway
	Other important road
	Other road
E25	**European road number**
A49	**Motorway number**
135	**National road number**
	Distances – in kilometres
143	major
28	minor
Col Bayard 1248	**Mountain pass**
	Scenic route, gradient – arrow points uphill
	Principal railway
	tunnel
Bastia 8:30	**Ferry route with journey time** – hours : minutes
	Short ferry route
	International boundary
	National boundary
	National park
	Natural park
ORLY	**Airport**
AQUEDUC ROMAINE	**Ancient monument**
	Beach
CHÂTEAU DU LUDE	**Castle or house**
GROTTE DU GRAND ROC	**Cave**
VULCANIA	**Other place of interest**
GIVERNY	**Park or garden**
ST CHRISTOL	**Religious building**
	Ski resort
DISNEYLAND PARIS	**Theme park**
VERSAILLES	**World Heritage site**
1754	**Spot height**
Bordeaux	**World Heritage town**
Toulouse	**Town of tourist interest**
	Town with Low Emission Zone

In France, some national routes have become departmental roads and have been assigned new road numbers. This means that road signs are subject to change. The new road numbers are shown in this atlas

Driving regulations

Belgium (B)

120*	120*	90	50**
If towing trailer			
90	90	60	50
Over 3.5 tonnes			
90	90	60	50

*Minimum speed of 70kph may be applied in certain conditions on motorways and some dual carriageways **Near schools, hospitals and churches the limit may be 30kph

- Compulsory
- All under 19s under 135 cm must wear an appropriate child restraint. Airbags must be deactivated if a rear-facing child seat is used in the front
- 0.05%
- Compulsory
- Compulsory
- Recommended Compulsory
- Compulsory for all riders 18
- Third party insurance
- Only allowed with a hands-free kit
- ★ Cruise control is not permitted on motorways
- ★ Dipped headlights compulsory for motorcycles during day and other vehicles during poor daytime visibility
- ★ On-the-spot fines imposed
- ★ Radar detectors prohibited
- ★ Sticker indicating maximum recommended speed for winter tyres must be displayed on dashboard if using them
- ★ Visibility vest compulsory

France (F)

130	110	90	50
On wet roads or if full driving licence held for less than 2 years			
110	100	80	50
If towing below 3.5 tonnes gross / above 3.5 tonnes gross			
110/90	100/90	90/80	50

50kph on all roads if fog reduces visibility to less than 50m • Licence will be lost and driver fined for exceeding speed limit by over 40kph

- Compulsory in front seats and, if fitted, rear
- Under 10 not allowed in front seats; in rear, if 4 or under, must have a child safety seat (rear facing if up to 9 months); if 5 to 10 must use an appropriate restraint system. Under 10 permitted in the front only if rear seats are fully occupied by other under 10s or there are no rear seat belts. In front if child is in rear-facing child seat, any airbags must be deactivated.
- 0.05%. If towing or with less than 2 years with full driving licence, 0.00% • All drivers/motorcyclists must carry 2 unused breathalysers to French certification standards, showing an NF number.
- Compulsory
- Recommended
- Recommended
- Compulsory for all riders
- 18 (16 for motorbikes under 80 cc)
- Use not permitted whilst driving
- ★ Dipped headlights compulsory in poor daytime visibility and at all times for motorcycles over 125cc
- ★ GPS must have fixed speed camera function deactivated; radar-detection equipment is prohibited
- ★ On-the-spot fines imposed
- ★ Tolls on motorways. Electronic tag needed if using automatic tolls.
- ★ Visibility vests must be worn at all times by motorcyclists and passengers; compulsory in other vehicles
- ★ Winter tyres - recommended. Carrying snow chains recommended in winter

Netherlands (NL)

120/100	80/100	80/100	50

- Compulsory in front seats and, if fitted, rear
- Under 135cm must use appropriate child restraint; if no seat belts, under 3s not permitted in vehicle; rear-facing child seat permitted in the front only if airbags deactivated
- 0.05%, 0.02% with less than 5 years experience or moped riders under 24
- Recommended Recommended
- Recommended Recommended
- Compulsory 18
- Third party insurance
- Only allowed with a hands-free kit
- LEZ About 20 cities operate or are planning LEZs. Permit system/number plate recognition.
- ★ Dipped headlights compulsory for motorcycles
- ★ Radar-detection equipment is prohibited

Tourist sights

Belgium Belgique

www.visitbelgium.com

Antwerp Antwerpen

City with many tall gabled Flemish houses on the river. Heart of the city is Great Market with 16–17c guildhouses and Town Hall. Charles Borromeus Church (Baroque). 14–16c Gothic cathedral has Rubens paintings. Rubens also at the Rubens House and his burial place in St Jacob's Church. Excellent museums: Mayer van den Bergh Museum (applied arts); Koninklijk Museum of Fine Arts (Flemish, Belgian); MAS (ethnography, folklore, shipping).
www.antwerpen.be **5 A4**

Bruges Brugge

Well-preserved medieval town with narrow streets and canals. Main squares: the Market with 13c Belfort and covered market; the Burg with Basilica of the Holy Blood and Town Hall. The collections of Groeninge Museum and Memling museum in St Jans Hospital include 15c Flemish masters. The Onze Lieve Vrouwekerk has a famous *Madonna and Child* by Michelangelo www.brugge.be **4 A3**

Brussels Bruxelles

Capital of Belgium. The Lower Town is centred on the enormous Grand Place with Hôtel de Ville and rebuilt guildhouses. Symbols of the city include the 'Manneken Pis' and Atomium (giant model of a molecule). The 13c Notre Dame de la Chapelle is the oldest church. The Upper Town contains: Gothic cathedral; Neoclassical Place Royale; 18c King's Palace; Royal Museums of Fine Arts (old and modern masters) Magritte Museum; MRAH (art and historical artefacts); BELvue museum (in the Bellevue Residence). Also: much Art Nouveau (Bozar, Hôtel Tassel, Hôtel Solvay); Place du Petit Sablon and Place du Grand Sablon; 19c Palais de Justice.
http://visitbrussels.be **5 B4**

Ghent Gent

Medieval town built on islands surrounded by canals and rivers. Views from Pont St-Michel. The Graslei and Koornlei quays have Flemish guild houses. The Gothic cathedral has famous Van Eyck altarpiece. Also: Belfort; Cloth Market; Gothic Town Hall; Gravensteen. Museums: STAM Museum in Bijloke Abbey (provincial and applied art); Museum of Fine Arts (old masters). www.visitgent.be **5 A3**

Namur

Reconstructed medieval citadel is the major sight of Namur, which also has a cathedral and provincial museums.
www.namurtourisme.be/index.php **5 B4**

Tournai

The Romanesque-Gothic cathedral is Belgium's finest (much excellent art). Fine Arts Museum has a good collection (15–20c).
www.tournai.be/en/officiel **4 B3**

France

http://us.franceguide.com

Albi

Old town with rosy brick architecture. The vast Cathédrale Ste-Cécile (begun 13c) holds some good art. The Berbie Palace houses the Toulouse-Lautrec museum.
www.albi-tourisme.fr **30 B1**

Alps

Grenoble, capital of the French Alps, has a good 20c collection in the Museum of Grenoble. The Vanoise Massif has the greatest number of resorts (Val d'Isère, Courchevel). Chamonix has spectacular views on Mont Blanc, France's and Europe's highest peak. www.thealps.com **26 B2**

Amiens

France's largest Gothic cathedral has beautiful decoration. The Museum of Picardy has unique 16c panel paintings. www.visit-amiens.com
www.amiens-tourisme.com **10 B2**

Arles
Ancient, picturesque town with Roman relics (1c amphitheatre), 11c cathedral, Archaeological Museum (Roman art); Van Gogh centre. www.arlestourisme.com 31 B3

Avignon
Medieval papal capital (1309–77) with 14c walls and many ecclesiastical buildings. Vast Palace of the Popes has stunning frescoes. The Little Palace has fine Italian Renaissance painting. The 12–13c Bridge of St Bénézet is famous. www.ot-avignon.fr 31 B3

Bourges
The Gothic Cathedral of St Etienne, one of the finest in France, has a superb sculptured choir. Also notable is the House of Jacques Coeur. www.bourgestourisme.com 17 B4

Burgundy Bourgogne
Rural wine region with a rich Romanesque, Gothic and Renaissance heritage. The 12c cathedral in Autun and 12c basilica in Vézelay have fine Romanesque sculpture. Monasteries include 11c L'Abbaye de Cluny (ruins) and L'Abbaye de Fontenay. Beaune has beautiful Gothic Hôtel-Dieu and 15c Nicolas Rolin hospices. www.burgundy-tourism.com 18 B3

Brittany Bretagne
Brittany is famous for cliffs, sandy beaches and wild landscape. It is also renowned for megalithic monuments (Carnac) and Celtic culture. Its capital, Rennes, has the Palais de Justice and good collections in the Museum of Brittany (history) and Museum of Fine Arts. Also: Nantes; St-Malo. www.bretagne.com

Caen
City with two beautiful Romanesque buildings: Abbaye aux Hommes; Abbaye aux Dames. The château has two museums (15–20c painting; history). The *Bayeux Tapestry* is displayed in nearby Bayeux. www.tourisme.caen.fr 9 A3

Carcassonne
Unusual double-walled fortified town of narrow streets with an inner fortress. The fine Romanesque Church of St Nazaire has superb stained glass. www.carcassonne.fr 30 B1

Chartres
The 12–13c cathedral is an exceptionally fine example of Gothic architecture (Royal Doorway, stained glass, choir screen). The Fine Arts Museum has a good collection. www.chartres.com 10 C1

Clermont-Ferrand
The old centre contains the cathedral built out of lava and Romanesque basilica. The Puy de Dôme and Puy de Sancy give spectacular views over some 60 extinct volcanic peaks (*puys*). www.clermont-ferrand.fr 24 B3

Colmar
Town characterised by Alsatian half-timbered houses. The Unterlinden Museum has excellent German religious art including the famous Isenheim altarpiece. The Dominican church also has a fine altarpiece. Espace André Malraux (contemporary arts). www.ot-colmar.fr 20 A2

Corsica Corse
Corsica has a beautiful rocky coast and mountainous interior. Napoleon's birthplace of Ajaccio has: Fesch Museum with Imperial Chapel and a large collection of Italian art; Maison Bonaparte; cathedral. Bonifacio, a medieval town, is spectacularly set on a rock over the sea. www.visit-corsica.com

Côte d'Azur
The French Riviera is best known for its coastline and glamorous resorts. There are many relics of artists who worked here: St-Tropez has Musée de l'Annonciade; Antibes has 12c Château Grimaldi with the Picasso Museum; Cagnes has the Renoir House and Mediterranean Museum of Modern Art; St-Paul-de-Vence has the excellent Maeght Foundation and Matisse's Chapelle du Rosaire. Cannes is famous for its film festival. Also: Marseille, Monaco, Nice. www.frenchriviera-tourism.com 33 B3

Dijon
Great 15c cultural centre. The Palais des Ducs et des Etats is the most notable monument and contains the Museum of Fine Arts. Also: the Charterhouse of Champmol. www.visitdijon.com 19 B4

Disneyland Paris
Europe's largest theme park follows in the footsteps of its famous predecessors in the United States. www.disneylandparis.com 10 C2

Le Puy-en-Velay
Medieval town bizarrely set on the peaks of dead volcanoes. It is dominated by the Romanesque cathedral (cloisters). The Romanesque chapel of St-Michel is dramatically situated on the highest rock. www.ot-lepuyenvelay.fr 25 B3

Loire Valley
The Loire Valley has many 15–16c châteaux built amid beautiful scenery by French monarchs and members of their courts. Among the most splendid are Azay-le-Rideau, Chenonceaux and Loches. Also: Abbaye de Fontévraud. www.lvo.com 16 B2

Lyon
France's third largest city has an old centre and many museums including the Museum of the History of Textiles and the Museum of Fine Arts (old masters). www.lyon-france.com 25 B4

Marseilles Marseille
Second lagest city in France. Spectacular views from the 19c Notre-Dame-de-la-Garde. The Old Port has 11-12c Basilique St Victor (crypt, catacombs). Cantini Museum has major collection of 20c French art. Château d'If was the setting of Dumas' *The Count of Monte Cristo*. www.marseille-tourisme.com 31 B4

Mont-St-Michel
Gothic pilgrim abbey (11–12c) set dramatically on a steep rock island rising from mud flats and connected to the land by a road covered by the tide. The abbey is made up of a complex of buildings. www.ot-montsaintmichel.com 15 A4

Nancy
A centre of Art Nouveau. The 18c Place Stanislas was constructed by dethroned Polish king Stanislas. Museums: School of Nancy Museum (Art Nouveau furniture); Fine Arts Museum. www.ot-nancy.fr 12 C2

Nantes
Former capital of Brittany, with the 15c Château des ducs de Bretagne. The cathedral has a striking interior. www.nantes-tourisme.com 15 B4

Nice
Capital of the Côte d'Azur, the old town is centred on the old castle on the hill. The seafront includes the famous 19c Promenade des Anglais. The aristocratic quarter of the Cimiez Hill has the Marc Chagall Museum and the Matisse Museum. Also: Museum of Modern and Contemporary Art (especially neo-Realism and Pop Art). www.nicetourism.com 33 B3

Paris
Capital of France, one of Europe's most interesting cities. The Île de la Cité area, an island in the River Seine has the 12–13c Gothic Notre Dame (wonderful stained glass) and La Sainte-Chapelle (1240–48), one of the jewels of Gothic art. The Left Bank area: Latin Quarter with the famous Sorbonne university; Museum of Cluny housing medieval art; the Panthéon; Luxembourg Palace and Gardens; Montparnasse, interwar artistic and literary centre; Eiffel Tower; Hôtel des Invalides with Napoleon's tomb. Right Bank: the great boulevards (Avenue des Champs-Élysées joining the Arc de Triomphe and Place de la Concorde); 19c Opéra Quarter; Marais, former aristocratic quarter of elegant mansions (Place des Vosges); Bois de Boulogne, the largest park in Paris; Montmartre, centre of 19c bohemianism, with the Basilique Sacré-Coeur. The Church of St Denis is the first gothic church and the mausoleum of the French monarchy. Paris has three of the world's greatest art collections: The Louvre (to 19c, *Mona Lisa*), Musée d'Orsay (19–20c) and National Modern Art Museum in the Pompidou Centre. Other major museums include: Orangery Museum; Paris Museum of Modern Art; Rodin Museum; Picasso Museum. Notable cemeteries with graves of the famous: Père-Lachaise, Montmartre, Montparnasse. Near Paris are the royal residences of Fontainebleau and Versailles. www.parisinfo.com 10 C2

Pyrenees
Beautiful unspoiled mountain range. Towns include: delightful sea resorts of St-Jean-de-Luz and Biarritz; Pau, with access to the Pyrenees National Park; pilgrimage centre Lourdes. www.pyrenees-online.fr

Reims
Together with nearby Epernay, the centre of champagne production. The 13c Gothic cathedral is one of the greatest architectural achievements in France (stained glass by Chagall). Other sights: Palais du Tau with cathedral sculpture, 11c Basilica of St Rémi; cellars on Place St-Niçaise and Place des Droits-des-Hommes. www.reims-tourisme.com 11 B4

Rouen
Old centre with many half-timbered houses and 12–13c Gothic cathedral and the Gothic Church of St Maclou with its fascinating remains of a dance macabre on the former cemetery of Aître St-Maclou. The Fine Arts Museum has a good collection. www.rouentourisme.com 9 A5

St-Malo
Fortified town (much rebuilt) in a fine coastal setting. There is a magnificent boat trip along the river Rance to Dinan, a splendid well-preserved medieval town. www.saint-malo-tourisme.com 15 A3

Strasbourg
Town whose historic centre includes a well-preserved quarter of medieval half-timbered Alsatian houses, many of them set on the canal. The cathedral is one of the best in France. The Palais Rohan contains several museums. www.otstrasbourg.fr 13 C3

Toulouse
Medieval university town characterised by flat pink brick (Hôtel Assézat). The Basilique St Sernin, the largest Romanesque church in France, has many art treasures. Marvellous Church of the Jacobins holds the body of St Thomas Aquinas. www.toulouse-tourisme.com 29 C4

Tours
Historic town centred on Place Plumereau. Good collections in the Guilds Museum and Fine Arts Museum. www.tours-tourisme.fr 16 B2

Versailles
Vast royal palace built for Louis XIV, primarily by Mansart, set in large formal gardens with magnificent fountains. The extensive and much-imitated state apartments include the famous Hall of Mirrors and the exceptional Baroque chapel. www.chateauversailles.fr **10 C2**

Vézère Valley Caves
A number of prehistoric sites, most notably the cave paintings of Lascaux (some 17,000 years old), now only seen in a duplicate cave, and the cave of Font de Gaume. The National Museum of Prehistory is in Les Eyzies. www.tourisme-vezere.com **29 B4**

Netherlands Nederland

http://holland.com

Amsterdam
Capital of the Netherlands. Old centre has picturesque canals lined with distinctive elegant 17–18c merchants' houses. Dam Square has 15c New Church and Royal Palace. Other churches include Westerkerk. The Museumplein has three world-famous museums: Rijksmuseum (several art collections including 15–17c painting); Van Gogh Museum; Municipal Museum (art from 1850 on). Other museums: Anne Frank House; Jewish Historical Museum; Rembrandt House; Hermitage Museum (exhibitions). http://holland.com **2 B1**

Delft
Well-preserved old Dutch town with gabled red-roofed houses along canals. Gothic churches: New Church; Old Church. Famous for Delftware (two museums). www.delft.nl **2 B1**

Haarlem
Many medieval gabled houses centred on the Great Market with 14c Town Hall and 15c Church of St Bavon. Museums: Frans Hals Museum; Teylers Museum. www.haarlemmarketing.nl/servicelinks/international_visitors/english **2 B1**

The Hague Den Haag
Seat of Government and of the royal house of the Netherlands. The 17c Mauritshuis houses the Royal Picture Gallery (excellent 15–18c Flemish and Dutch). Other good collections: Escher Museum; Hesdag Museum; Municipal Museum www.denhaag.nl **2 B1**

Het Loo
Former royal palace and gardens set in a vast landscape (commissioned by future the future King and Queen of England, William and Mary). www.paleishetloo.nl **2 B2**

Keukenhof
In spring, landscaped gardens, planted with bulbs of many varieties, are the largest flower gardens in the world. www.keukenhof.nl **2 B1**

Leiden
University town of beautiful gabled houses set along canals. The Rijksmuseum Van Oudheden is Holland's most important home to archaeological artefacts from the Antiquity. The 16c Hortus Botanicus is one of the oldest botanical gardens in Europe. The Cloth Hall with van Leyden's *Last Judgement*. http://leidenholland.com **2 B1**

Rotterdam
The largest port in the world. The Boymans-van Beuningen Museum has a huge and excellent decorative and fine art collection (old and modern). Nearby: 18c Kinderdijk with 19 windmills. www.rotterdam.info **5 A4**

Utrecht
Delightful old town centre along canals with the Netherlands' oldest university and Gothic cathedral. Good art collections: Central Museum; National Museum. www.utrecht.nl **2 B2**

Ski resorts

Alps

Alpe d'Huez 26 B3 1860m 85 lifts Dec–Apr •Grenoble (63km) ☎+33 4 76 11 44 44 🖳www.alpedhuez.com *Snow chains may be required on access road to resort.*

Avoriaz 26 A3 2277m 35 lifts Dec–May •Morzine (14km) ☎+33 4 50 74 02 11 🖳www.avoriaz.com *Chains may be required for access road from Morzine. Car-free resort, park on edge of village. Horse-drawn sleigh service available.*

Chamonix-Mont-Blanc 27 B3 1035m 49 lifts Dec–Apr •Martigny (38km) ☎+33 4 50 53 00 24 🖳www.chamonix.com

Chamrousse 26 B2 1700m 26 lifts Dec–Apr •Grenoble (30km) ☎+33 4 76 89 92 65 🖳www.chamrousse.com *Roads normally cleared, keep chains accessible because of altitude.*

Châtel 27 A3 2200m 41 lifts Dec–Apr •Thonon-Les-Bains (35km) ☎+33 4 50 73 22 44 🖳http://info.chatel.com/english-version.html

Courchevel 26 B3 1850m 67 lifts Dec–Apr •Moûtiers (23km) ☎+33 4 79 08 00 29 🖳www.courchevel.com *Roads normally cleared but keep chains accessible. Traffic 'discouraged' within the four resort bases.*

Flaine 26 A3 1800m 26 lifts Dec–Apr •Cluses (25km) ☎+33 4 50 90 80 🖳www.flaine.com *Keep chains accessible for D6 from Cluses to Flaine. Car access for depositing luggage and passengers only. 1500-space car park outside resort. Near Sixt-Fer-á-Cheval.*

La Clusaz 26 B3 1100m 55 lifts Dec–Apr •Annecy (32km) 🖳www.laclusaz.com *Roads normally clear but keep chains accessible for final road from Annecy.*

La Plagne 26 B3 2100m 109 lifts Dec–Apr Moûtiers (32km) ☎+33 4 79 09 79 79 🖳www.la-plagne.com *Ten different centres up to 2100m altitude. Road access via Bozel, Landry or Aime normally cleared. Linked to Les Arcs by cablecar*

Les Arcs 27 B3 2600m 77 lifts Dec–May •Bourg-St-Maurice (15km) ☎+33 4 79 07 12 57 🖳www.lesarcs.com *Three base areas up to 2000 metres; keep chains accessible. Pay parking at edge of each base resort. Linked to La Plagne by cablecar*

Les Carroz d'Araches 26 A3 1140m 80 lifts Dec–Apr •Cluses (13km) ☎+ 33 4 50 90 00 04 🖳www.lescarroz.com

Les Deux-Alpes 26 C3 1650m 55 lifts Dec–Apr •Grenoble (75km) ☎+33 4 76 79 22 00 🖳www.les2alpes.com *Roads normally cleared, however snow chains recommended for D213 up from valley road (D1091).*

Les Gets 26 A3 1172m 52 lifts Dec–Apr •Cluses (18km) ☎+33 4 50 75 80 80 🖳www.lesgets.com

Les Ménuires 26 B3 1815m 40 lifts Dec–Apr •Moûtiers (27km) ☎+33 4 79 00 73 00 🖳www.lesmenuires.com *Keep chains accessible for D117 from Moûtiers.*

Les Sept Laux Prapoutel 26 B3 1350m, 24 lifts Dec–Apr •Grenoble (38km) ☎+33 4 76 08 17 86 🖳www.les7laux.com *Roads normally cleared, however keep chains accessible for mountain road up from the A41 motorway. Near St Sorlin d'Arves.*

Megève 26 B3 2350m 79 lifts Dec–Apr •Sallanches (12km) ☎+ 33 4 50 21 28 🖳www.megeve.com *Horse-drawn sleigh rides available.*

Méribel 26 B3 1400m 61 lifts Dec–May •Moûtiers (18km) ☎+33 4 79 08 60 01 🖳www.meribel.net *Keep chains accessible for 18km to resort on D90 from Moûtiers.*

Morzine 26 A3 1000m 67 lifts, Dec–Apr •Thonon-Les-Bains (30km) ☎+33 4 50 74 72 72 🖳www.morzine-avoriaz.com

Pra Loup 32 A2 1600m 53 lifts Dec–Apr •Barcelonnette (10km) ☎+33 4 92 84 10 04 🖳www.praloup.com *Roads normally cleared but chains accessibility recommended.*

Risoul 26 C3 1850m 52 lifts Dec–Apr •Briançon (40km) 🖳www.risoul.com *Keep chains accessible. Near Guillestre. Linked with Vars Les Claux*

St-Gervais Mont-Blanc 26 B3 850m 27 lifts Dec–Apr •Sallanches (10km) ☎+33 4 50 47 76 08 🖳www.st-gervais.com

Serre Chevalier 26 C3 1350m 77 lifts Dec–Apr •Briançon (10km) ☎+ 33 4 92 24 98 98 🖳www.serre-chevalier.com *Made up of 13 small villages along the valley road, which is normally cleared.*

Tignes 27 B3 2100m 47 lifts Jan–Dec •Bourg St Maurice (26km) ☎+33 4 79 40 04 40 🖳www.tignes.net *Keep chains accessible because of altitude.*

Val d'Isère 27 B3 1850m 50 lifts Dec–Apr •Bourg-St-Maurice (30km) ☎+33 4 79 06 06 60 🖳www.valdisere.com *Roads normally cleared but keep chains accessible.*

Val Thorens 26 B3 2300m 29 lifts Dec–Apr •Moûtiers (37km) ☎+33 4 79 00 08 08 🖳www.valthorens.com *Chains essential – highest ski resort in Europe. Obligatory paid parking on edge of resort.*

Valloire 26 B3 1430m 34 lifts Dec–Apr •Modane (20km) ☎+33 4 79 59 03 96 🖳www.valloire.net *Road normally clear up to the Col du Galbier, to the south of the resort, which is closed from 1st November to 1st June. Linked to Valmeinier.*

Valmeinier 26 B3 2600m 34 lifts Dec–Apr •St Michel de Maurienne (47km) ☎+33 4 79 59 53 69 🖳www.valmeinier.com *Access from north on D1006 / D902. Col du Galbier, to the south of the resort closed from 1st November to 1st June. Linked to Valloire.*

Valmorel 26 B3 1400m 38 lifts Dec–Apr •Moûtiers (15km) ☎+33 4 79 09 85 55 🖳www.valmorel.com *Near St Jean-de-Belleville. Linked with ski areas of Doucy-Combelouvière and St François-Longchamp.*

Vars Les Claux 26 C3 1850m 52 lifts Dec–Apr •Briançon (40km) ☎+33 4 92 46 51 31 🖳www.vars-ski.com *Four base resorts up to 1850 metres. Keep chains accessible. Linked with Risoul.*

Villard de Lans 26 B2 1050m 28 lifts Dec–Apr •Grenoble (32km) ☎+33 4 76 95 10 38 🖳www.villarddelans.com

Pyrenees

Font-Romeu 36 B3 1800m 25 lifts Nov–Apr •Perpignan (87km) ☎+33 4 68 30 68 30 🖳www.font-romeu.fr *Roads normally cleared but keep chains accessible.*

Saint-Lary Soulan 35 B4 830m 31 lifts Dec–Mar •Tarbes (75km) ☎+33 5 62 39 50 81 🖳www.saintlary.com *Access roads constantly cleared of snow.*

Vosges

La Bresse-Hohneck 20 A1 900m 33 lifts Dec–Mar •Cornimont (6km) ☎+33 3 29 25 41 29 🖳www.labresse.net

English Channel
La Manche
Channel Is. (U.K.)
Guernsey
Jersey
Isle of Wight
Baie de la Seine
CÔTE DE NACRE
G. de St.-Malo
CÔTE D'EMERAUDE
CÔTE DE CORNOUAILLE
CÔTE D'AMOUR
CÔTE DE JADE
CÔTE DES LANDES
CÔTE D'ARGENT
CÔTE BASQUE
COSTA VASCA
COSTA MONTAÑESA
Bay of Biscay
Golfe de Gascogne
F R A N C E
S P A I N
ANDORRA
Corse
Corsica
Belle-Île
Î. d' Oléron
Plymouth
Southampton
Portsmouth
Brighton
Dover
Calais
Dunkerque
Lille
Amiens
Rouen
Le Havre
Caen
Cherbourg-Octeville
St.-Malo
Brest
Quimper
Lorient
Rennes
Laval
Le Mans
PARIS
Versailles
Orléans
Tours
Angers
Nantes
St.-Nazaire
Poitiers
La Rochelle
Limoges
Angoulême
Bordeaux
Bayonne
Pau
Toulouse
Donostia-San Sebastián
Bilbao
Santander
Vitoria-Gasteiz
Pamplona
Burgos
Logroño
Ajaccio
Bastia
0 20 40 60 80 100 miles
0 40 80 120 160 km

NETHERLANDS
BELGIUM
LUX.
FRANCE
SWITZERLAND
LIECHTENSTEIN
ITALY
MONACO
MARE LIGURE
LIGURIAN SEA
Golfe du Lion
Golfo di Génova
Corse
Corsica
AMSTERDAM
ROTTERDAM
BRUXELLES
BRUSSELS
LYON
MARSEILLE
MARSEILLES
TORINO
TURIN
MILANO
MILAN
Genève
Zürich
Bern
Strasbourg
Nice
Génova

Distances

How to use this table

Distances are shown in miles and, in light type, kilometres. For example, the distance between Antwerp and Dieppe is **232** miles or 374 kilometres.

	Amsterdam	Antwerp	Bordeaux	Boulogne	Brest	Brussels	Calais	Cherbourg-Octeville	Clermont-Ferrand	Dieppe	Eindhoven	Grenoble	La Rochelle	Le Havre	Le Mans	Liege	Lille	Limoges	Luxembourg	Lyon	Marseilles	Montpellier	Nancy	Nantes	Nice	Oostende	Paris	Reims	Rennes	Rotterdam	Strasbourg	Toulouse
Amsterdam																																
Antwerp	99 / 159																															
Bordeaux	662 / 1065	573 / 922																														
Boulogne	242 / 390	145 / 233	539 / 867																													
Brest	646 / 1040	547 / 881	398 / 641	421 / 678																												
Brussels	127 / 205	28 / 45	545 / 877	140 / 226	525 / 845																											
Calais	227 / 366	126 / 203	533 / 857	22 / 35	442 / 712	122 / 196																										
Cherbourg-Octeville	505 / 812	388 / 624	431 / 694	273 / 439	262 / 422	370 / 596	291 / 468																									
Clermont-Ferrand	574 / 924	474 / 763	230 / 370	422 / 679	513 / 825	447 / 720	442 / 711	446 / 717																								
Dieppe	334 / 538	232 / 374	439 / 706	85 / 137	339 / 545	180 / 290	109 / 176	184 / 296	344 / 554																							
Eindhoven	77 / 124	55 / 89	607 / 977	199 / 321	595 / 958	79 / 127	181 / 291	441 / 709	516 / 831	247 / 397																						
Grenoble	641 / 1032	495 / 797	419 / 674	513 / 826	678 / 1091	500 / 804	530 / 853	575 / 926	185 / 297	474 / 763	539 / 867																					
La Rochelle	604 / 972	511 / 823	113 / 182	413 / 665	273 / 439	478 / 769	431 / 694	293 / 472	295 / 475	337 / 543	560 / 902	462 / 743																				
Le Havre	375 / 604	275 / 442	418 / 673	151 / 243	288 / 463	250 / 402	172 / 277	135 / 217	366 / 589	68 / 110	328 / 528	478 / 770	314 / 506																			
Le Mans	438 / 705	341 / 548	269 / 433	244 / 392	243 / 391	314 / 505	267 / 430	176 / 283	270 / 435	169 / 272	395 / 636	446 / 717	178 / 286	153 / 246																		
Liege	152 / 244	77 / 124	566 / 911	194 / 313	559 / 899	60 / 96	185 / 297	402 / 647	478 / 770	239 / 385	67 / 108	489 / 787	519 / 835	288 / 464	350 / 564																	
Lille	176 / 283	78 / 125	488 / 786	71 / 115	460 / 741	68 / 109	69 / 111	305 / 491	398 / 640	115 / 185	130 / 210	493 / 793	425 / 684	132 / 213	263 / 423	126 / 202																
Limoges	542 / 872	463 / 745	137 / 221	401 / 646	373 / 600	434 / 699	421 / 678	371 / 597	113 / 182	341 / 549	508 / 817	330 / 531	137 / 220	334 / 537	184 / 296	469 / 755	375 / 604															
Luxembourg	233 / 375	159 / 256	544 / 875	252 / 405	612 / 985	132 / 212	249 / 401	426 / 686	367 / 590	264 / 425	166 / 267	371 / 597	485 / 781	321 / 516	88 / 142	87 / 140	174 / 280	473 / 762														
Lyon	575 / 925	473 / 761	347 / 558	442 / 712	629 / 1013	446 / 717	464 / 746	493 / 794	106 / 170	389 / 626	492 / 792	66 / 106	459 / 739	411 / 662	331 / 533	413 / 665	426 / 685	260 / 418	318 / 511													
Marseilles	768 / 1236	670 / 1079	393 / 632	640 / 1030	786 / 1265	643 / 1035	581 / 935	700 / 1127	255 / 410	600 / 966	699 / 1125	180 / 290	516 / 830	595 / 958	546 / 878	615 / 990	609 / 980	366 / 589	518 / 833	187 / 301												
Montpellier	760 / 1223	662 / 1066	303 / 488	626 / 1008	696 / 1120	641 / 1031	643 / 1034	643 / 1035	207 / 333	548 / 882	678 / 1091	183 / 295	413 / 665	564 / 908	470 / 756	609 / 980	606 / 975	270 / 434	506 / 814	188 / 302	103 / 165											
Nancy	327 / 527	228 / 367	547 / 880	324 / 521	598 / 962	203 / 326	321 / 517	460 / 740	342 / 550	321 / 517	249 / 401	318 / 512	491 / 790	357 / 574	362 / 582	175 / 282	260 / 418	409 / 659	72 / 116	254 / 409	445 / 716	439 / 707										
Nantes	548 / 882	449 / 723	219 / 352	353 / 568	185 / 297	428 / 688	373 / 601	211 / 339	333 / 536	278 / 448	505 / 813	506 / 815	87 / 140	239 / 385	115 / 185	465 / 749	374 / 602	217 / 350	465 / 748	451 / 725	613 / 987	511 / 823	469 / 755									
Nice	865 / 1392	767 / 1235	499 / 803	737 / 1186	894 / 1438	743 / 1195	761 / 1225	798 / 1284	393 / 633	698 / 1124	784 / 1261	204 / 328	608 / 979	699 / 1125	652 / 1050	713 / 1148	716 / 1153	527 / 848	611 / 984	293 / 471	127 / 204	202 / 325	542 / 872	710 / 1142								
Oostende	175 / 282	75 / 121	550 / 885	78 / 126	501 / 807	70 / 113	60 / 97	347 / 558	452 / 727	172 / 277	128 / 206	551 / 886	481 / 774	227 / 365	321 / 516	131 / 211	55 / 89	432 / 695	207 / 333	484 / 779	677 / 1090	670 / 1079	278 / 447	429 / 690	774 / 1245							
Paris	312 / 502	212 / 341	364 / 585	158 / 255	367 / 591	190 / 305	180 / 290	221 / 355	263 / 423	121 / 195	265 / 427	355 / 571	293 / 471	122 / 196	129 / 208	228 / 367	137 / 220	244 / 392	232 / 373	289 / 465	482 / 775	466 / 750	240 / 386	240 / 386	579 / 932	191 / 307						
Reims	296 / 477	199 / 321	447 / 720	171 / 275	451 / 726	167 / 269	166 / 267	313 / 503	331 / 532	176 / 284	241 / 388	373 / 600	377 / 606	217 / 349	213 / 342	164 / 264	126 / 202	327 / 526	145 / 233	303 / 488	496 / 799	489 / 787	129 / 208	323 / 520	593 / 955	180 / 289	89 / 143					
Rennes	532 / 856	432 / 695	289 / 465	309 / 498	150 / 241	409 / 659	329 / 530	145 / 234	368 / 592	230 / 370	485 / 781	546 / 878	158 / 255	174 / 280	96 / 155	449 / 722	356 / 573	287 / 462	444 / 715	478 / 770	652 / 1050	570 / 918	451 / 725	67 / 108	749 / 1206	387 / 622	219 / 352	302 / 486				
Rotterdam	46 / 74	62 / 99	635 / 1022	210 / 338	612 / 985	94 / 151	193 / 310	454 / 731	537 / 864	294 / 473	69 / 111	606 / 976	568 / 914	337 / 543	404 / 650	135 / 218	142 / 228	519 / 835	215 / 346	538 / 866	731 / 1177	724 / 1165	290 / 466	514 / 827	829 / 1334	139 / 223	279 / 449	261 / 420	496 / 799			
Strasbourg	378 / 608	293 / 472	593 / 954	387 / 623	666 / 1071	268 / 432	385 / 620	528 / 850	375 / 604	392 / 631	301 / 484	330 / 531	584 / 940	432 / 696	426 / 686	240 / 386	342 / 550	457 / 735	137 / 220	308 / 495	500 / 805	493 / 793	97 / 156	536 / 863	489 / 787	342 / 550	303 / 487	216 / 347	515 / 828	357 / 575		
Toulouse	732 / 1178	632 / 1017	152 / 244	579 / 932	548 / 882	609 / 980	601 / 967	578 / 930	232 / 374	534 / 860	685 / 1103	330 / 531	262 / 421	536 / 862	378 / 608	647 / 1042	556 / 895	179 / 288	654 / 1052	334 / 538	252 / 405	150 / 241	585 / 941	364 / 585	349 / 562	610 / 982	422 / 679	505 / 812	434 / 699	696 / 1120	639 / 1028	
Tours	459 / 738	359 / 577	216 / 347	305 / 491	308 / 496	336 / 541	325 / 523	237 / 382	211 / 339	230 / 370	413 / 664	384 / 618	146 / 235	211 / 340	63 / 102	375 / 603	283 / 456	140 / 225	378 / 609	328 / 528	496 / 799	413 / 664	346 / 557	134 / 215	593 / 955	337 / 543	149 / 239	232 / 374	157 / 253	423 / 681	430 / 692	318 / 511

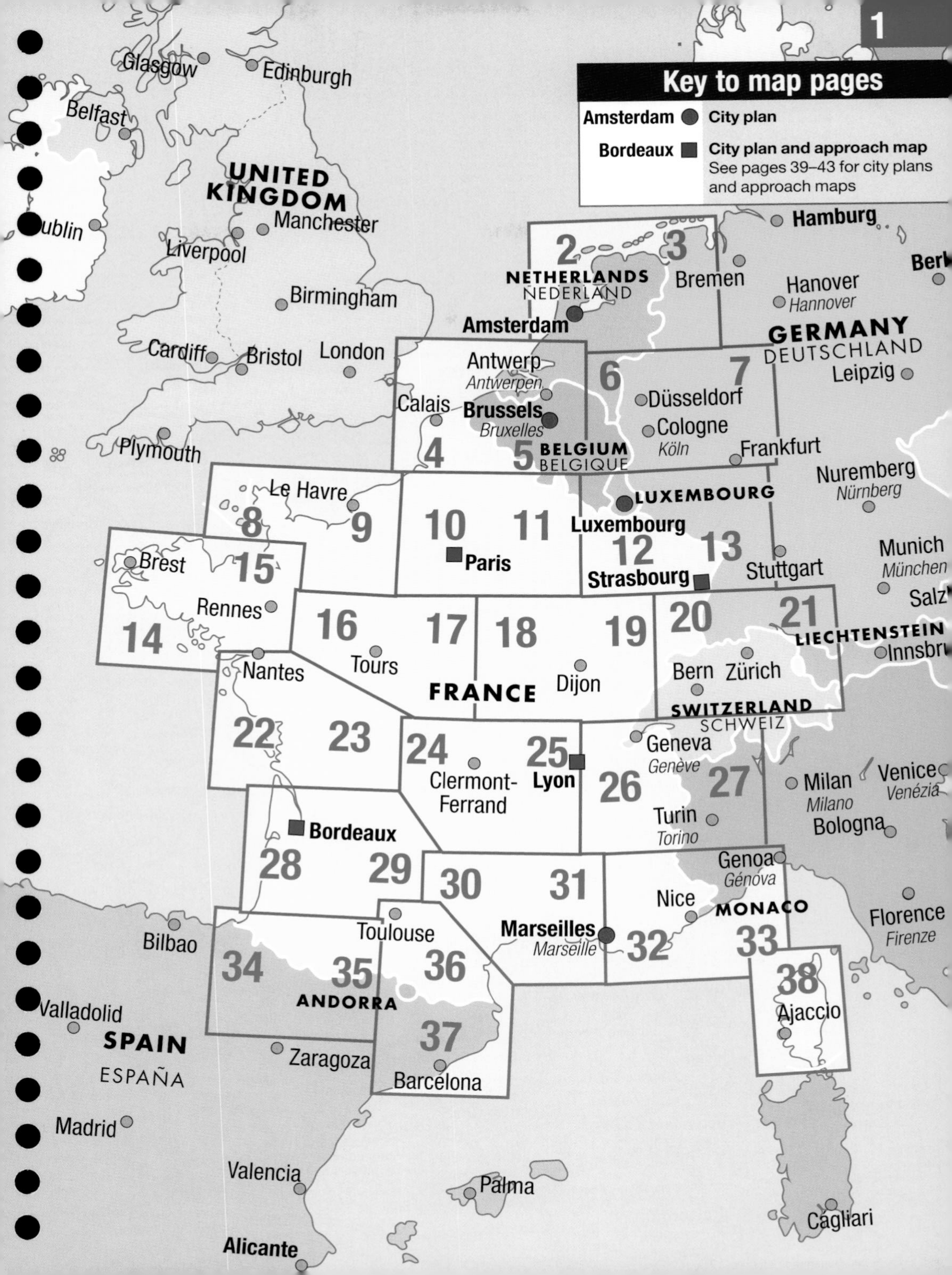
Key to map pages
Amsterdam City plan
Bordeaux City plan and approach map
See pages 39–43 for city plans and approach maps
Glasgow
Edinburgh
Belfast
UNITED KINGDOM
Dublin
Manchester
Liverpool
Birmingham
Cardiff
Bristol
London
Plymouth
Hamburg
Berl
Bremen
Hanover
Hannover
NETHERLANDS
NEDERLAND
Amsterdam
GERMANY
DEUTSCHLAND
Leipzig
Antwerp
Antwerpen
Calais
Brussels
Bruxelles
Düsseldorf
Cologne
Köln
Frankfurt
BELGIUM
BELGIQUE
Nuremberg
Nürnberg
LUXEMBOURG
Luxembourg
Le Havre
Paris
Brest
Rennes
Strasbourg
Stuttgart
Munich
München
Salz
LIECHTENSTEIN
Innsbr
Nantes
Tours
FRANCE
Dijon
Bern
Zürich
SWITZERLAND
SCHWEIZ
Geneva
Genève
Clermont-Ferrand
Lyon
Milan
Milano
Venice
Venézia
Turin
Torino
Bologna
Bordeaux
Genoa
Génova
Nice
MONACO
Florence
Firenze
Bilbao
Toulouse
Marseilles
Marseille
ANDORRA
Ajaccio
Valladolid
SPAIN
ESPAÑA
Zaragoza
Barcelona
Madrid
Valencia
Palma
Cagliari
Alicante
2 3 4 5 6 7 8 9 10 11 12 13 14 15 16 17 18 19 20 21 22 23 24 25 26 27 28 29 30 31 32 33 34 35 36 37 38

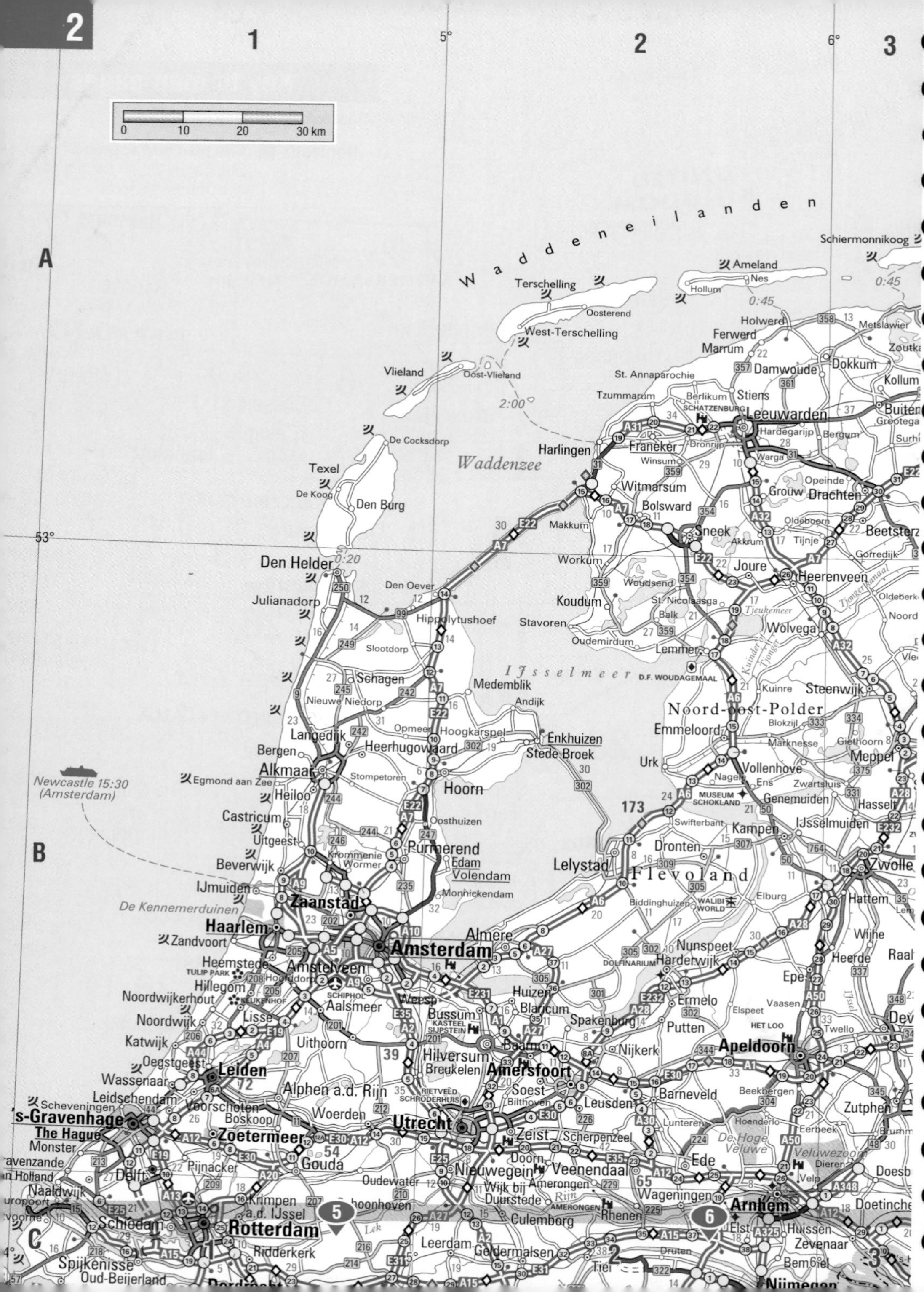

1
2
3
5°
6°
A
B
C
53°
0
10
20
30 km
Waddeneilanden
Schiermonnikoog
Ameland
Nes
Hollum
Terschelling
Oosterend
West-Terschelling
Vlieland
Oost-Vlieland
De Cocksdorp
Texel
De Koog
Den Burg
Waddenzee
Den Helder
Julianadorp
Den Oever
Hippolytushoef
Slootdorp
Schagen
Nieuwe Niedorp
Medemblik
Andijk
Enkhuizen
Stede Broek
Hoogkarspel
Opmeer
Langedijk
Heerhugowaard
Bergen
Alkmaar
Egmond aan Zee
Heiloo
Stompetoren
Hoorn
Castricum
Uitgeest
Beverwijk
Krommenie
Wormer
Purmerend
Oosthuizen
Edam
Volendam
Monnickendam
IJmuiden
Zaanstad
De Kennemerduinen
Newcastle 15:30
(Amsterdam)
Haarlem
Zandvoort
Amsterdam
Amstelveen
Heemstede
Hoofddorp
Schiphol
TULIP PARK
Hillegom
KEUKENHOF
Noordwijkerhout
Noordwijk
Lisse
Aalsmeer
Weesp
Bussum
KASTEEL SIJPSTEIN
Huizen
Blaricum
Katwijk
Oegstgeest
Uithoorn
Hilversum
Breukelen
Baarn
Amersfoort
Soest
Wassenaar
Leiden
Leidschendam
Scheveningen
Voorschoten
Alphen a.d. Rijn
RIETVELD SCHRÖDERHUIS
Bilthoven
Leusden
's-Gravenhage
The Hague
Boskoop
Woerden
Utrecht
Zeist
Scherpenzeel
Monster
Zoetermeer
Gouda
Delft
Pijnacker
Naaldwijk
Schiedam
Rotterdam
Krimpen a.d. IJssel
Schoonhoven
Oudewater
Nieuwegein
Veenendaal
Doorn
Wijk bij Duurstede
Amerongen
Rhenen
Culemborg
Leerdam
Geldermalsen
Ridderkerk
Spijkenisse
Oud-Beijerland
Dordrecht
Lek
Rijn
Harlingen
Franeker
Winsum
Witmarsum
Bolsward
Makkum
Workum
Koudum
Stavoren
Oudemirdum
Woudsend
St. Nicolaasga
Balk
Lemmer
IJsselmeer
D.F. WOUDAGEMAAL
Tzummarum
St. Annaparochie
Berlikum
SCHATZENBURG
Stiens
Leeuwarden
Dronrijp
Hardegarijp
Bergum
Warga
Holwerd
Ferwerd
Marrum
Damwoude
Dokkum
Kollum
Metslawier
Grouw
Opeinde
Drachten
Sneek
Akkrum
Oldeboorn
Tijnje
Beetsterz
Joure
Heerenveen
Gorredijk
Tjeukemeer
Oldeberkoop
Wolvega
Noord
Kuinre
Steenwijk
Noord-oost-Polder
Emmeloord
Blokzijl
Marknesse
Giethoorn
Meppel
Urk
Vollenhove
Nagele
Ens
Zwartsluis
MUSEUM SCHOKLAND
Genemuiden
Hasselt
Kampen
IJsselmuiden
Swifterbant
Dronten
Lelystad
Flevoland
Zwolle
Biddinghuizen
WALIBI WORLD
Elburg
Hattem
Almere
Nunspeet
Harderwijk
DOLFINARIUM
Heerde
Epe
Wijhe
Raalte
Ermelo
Spakenburg
Putten
Vaassen
HET LOO
Twello
Elspeet
Nijkerk
Apeldoorn
Deventer
Barneveld
Beekbergen
Zutphen
Lunteren
De Hoge Veluwe
Veluwezoom
Hoenderloo
Eerbeek
Ede
Wageningen
Dieren
Doesburg
Velp
Arnhem
Doetinchem
Elst
Huissen
Zevenaar
Druten
Bemmel
Nijmegen
0:45
2:00
0:20

Ostfriesische Inseln
Niedersächsisches Wattenmeer
3
4
5
7°
8°
Borkum
Juist
Norderney
Baltrum
Langeoog
Spiekeroog
Wangerooge
Mellum
Memmert
Rottumerplaat
Rottumeroog
0:55
1:00
Norddeich
Norden
Hage
Dornum
Esens
Nessmersiel
Neuharlingersiel
Carolinensiel
Minsen
Hohenkirchen
Hooksiel
Westerholt
Wittmund
Jever
Schortens
Wilhelmshaven
Sande
Jade-busen
Sengwarden
Langwarden
Burhave
Nordenham
Stollhamm
Abbehausen
Seefeld
Ostfriesland
Aurich
Moordorf
Sandhorst
Friedeburg
Horsten
Zetel
Varel
Wiesmoor
Pewsum
Emden
Landesmuseum & Rathaus
Eemshaven
Uithuizermeeden
Uithuizen
Usquert
Spijk
Menkemaborg
Delfzijl
Appingedam
Loppersum
Middelstum
Baflo
Winsum
Bedum
Ulrum
Leens
Groningen
Slochteren
Zuidhorn
Hoogkerk
Leek
Roden
Haren
Hoogezand-Sappemeer
Midlaaren
Zuidlaren
Borg Nienoord & National Rijtuigmuseum
Veendam
Scheemda
Winschoten
Midwolda
Finsterwolde
Nieuweschans
Bunde
Weener
Dollard
Jemgum
Leer
Neermoor
Hesel
Remels
Westerstede
Bad Zwischenahn
Wiefelstede
Rastede
Oldenburg
Edewecht
Augustfehn
Apen
Barssel
Collinghorst
Ostrhauderfehn
Papenburg
Aschendorf
Rhede
Friesoythe
Küstenkanal
Hatten
Ganderkesee
Wardenburg
Hude
Elsfleth
Brake
Ovelgönne
Schwanewede
Bockhorn
Neuenburg
Jade
Strackholt
Warsingsfehn
Oude-Pekela
Nieuwe-Pekela
Vlagtwedde
Stadskanaal
Assen
Gieten
Rolde
Norg
Eext
Tynaarlo
Annen
Borger
Drouwen
Musselkanaal
Ter Apel
Dörpen
Heede
Surwold
Esterwegen
Börger
Lorup
Hümmling
Werlte
Sögel
Jagdschloss Clemenswerth & Emslands Museum
Lathen
Molbergen
Cloppenburg
Lindern
Garrel
Grossenkneten
Ahlhorn
Wildeshauser Geest
Visbek
Emstek
Cappeln
Lastrup
Löningen
Essen
Quakenbrück
Vechta
Bakum
Lohne
Dinklage
Diepholz
Goldenstedt
Beilen
Westerbork
Emmen
Emmer-Compascuum
Klazienaveen
Hoogeveen
Coevorden
Zuidwolde
Schoonebeek
Nieuw-Amsterdam
Twist
Haren
Meppen
Haselünne
Herzlake
Menslage
Berge
Bersenbrück
Ankum
Fürstenau
Lingen
Dalum
Lengerich
Bawinkel
Emlichheim
Hardenberg
Dedemsvaart
Ommen
Staphorst
Den Ham
Vroomshoop
Uelsen
Neuenhaus
Wietmarschen
Nordhorn
Wilsum
Freren
Messingen
Merzen
Neuenkirchen
Vörden
Damme
Dümmer
Bramsche
Hopsten
Recke
Wiehengebirge
Wallenhorst
Ostercappeln
Bad Essen
Osnabrück
Mettingen
Westerkappeln
Ibbenbüren
Hörstel
Rheine
Emsbüren
Schüttorf
Bad Bentheim
Oldenzaal
Almelo
Wierden
Tubbergen
Denekamp
Ootmarsum
Nijverdal
Rijssen
Holten
Goor
Borne
Hengelo
Enschede
Losser
Gronau
Ochtrup
Neuenkirchen
Wettringen
Steinfurt
Emsdetten
Tecklenburg
Georgsmarienhütte
Lengerich
Teutoburger Wald
Ladbergen
Lienen
Greven
Saerbeck
Bad Iburg
Bissendorf
Melle
Dissen
Halle
Versmold
Glandorf
Bielefeld
Steinhagen
Münster
Münsterland
Telgte
Ostbevern
Warendorf
Sassenberg
Harsewinkel
Gütersloh
Herzebrock
Rheda-Wiedenbrück
Beelen
Everswinkel
Freckenhorst
Albersloh
Ennigerloh
Sendenhorst
Senden
Nottuln
Havixbeck
Billerbeck
Coesfeld
Altenberge
Nordwalde
Laer
Horstmar
Metelen
Heek
Ahaus
Vreden
Stadtlohn
Gescher
Velen
Borken
Bocholt
Winterswijk
Groenlo
Eibergen
Haaksbergen
Neede
Borculo
Lochem
Ruurlo
Lichtenvoorde
Aalten
Varsseveld
Terborg
Dinxperlo
Markelo
Deventer
Raalte
Havelte
Ruinen
Smilde
Oosterwolde
Diever
A
B
C
6
7
52°
53°

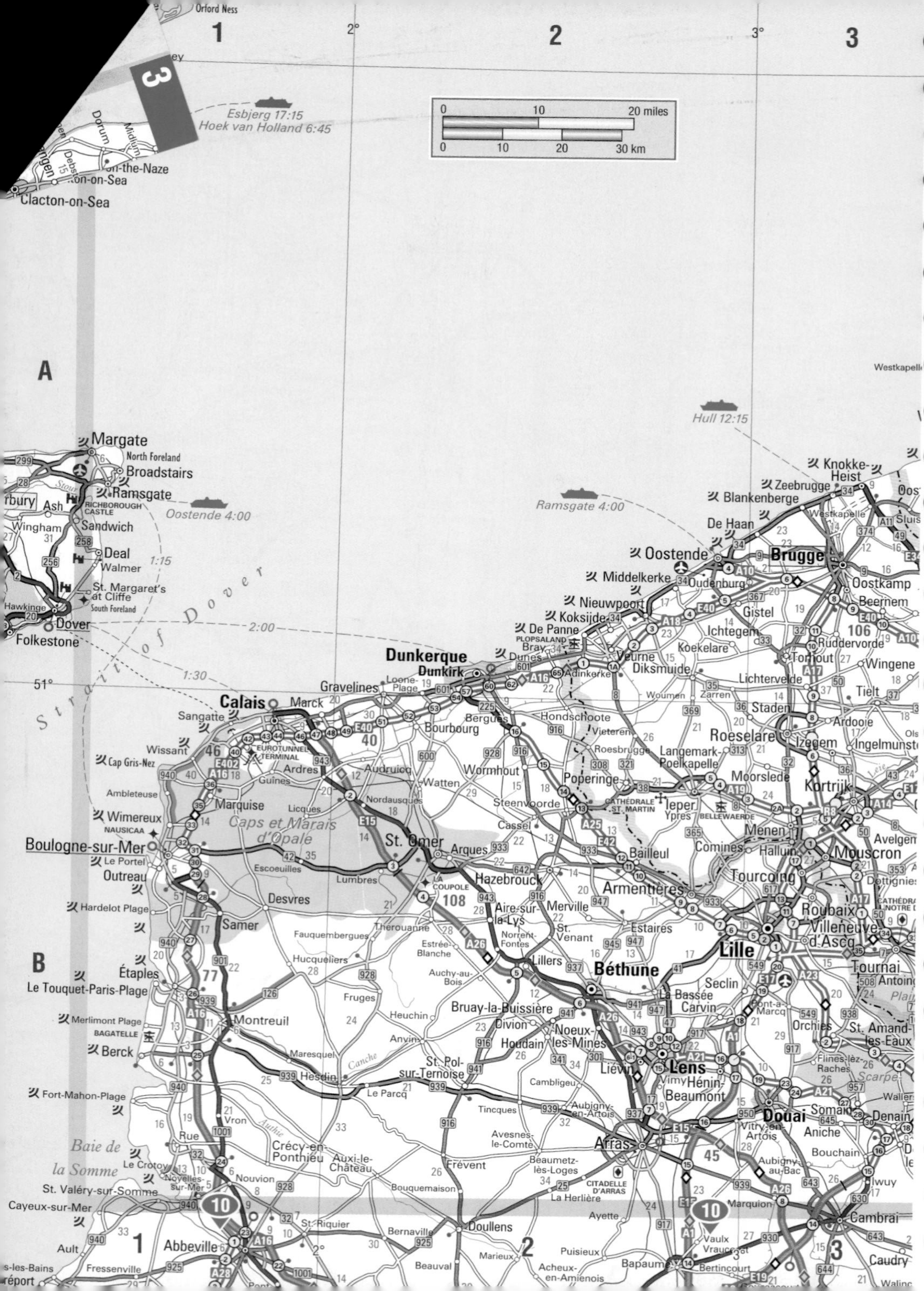
1
2
3
A
B
2°
3°
51°
0 10 20 miles
0 10 20 30 km
Orford Ness
Esbjerg 17:15
Hoek van Holland 6:45
Hull 12:15
Oostende 4:00
Ramsgate 4:00
Strait of Dover
1:15
2:00
1:30
Clacton-on-Sea
Margate
North Foreland
Broadstairs
Ramsgate
RICHBOROUGH CASTLE
Sandwich
Ash
Wingham
Deal
Walmer
St. Margaret's at Cliffe
South Foreland
Hawkinge
Dover
Folkestone
Knokke-Heist
Zeebrugge
Blankenberge
De Haan
Oostende
Brugge
Middelkerke
Oudenburg
Nieuwpoort
Koksijde
De Panne
PLOPSALAND
Bray-Dunes
Dunkerque
Dunkirk
Adinkerke
Veurne
Diksmuide
Gistel
Ichtegem
Koekelare
Torhout
Oostkamp
Beernem
Ruddervorde
Wingene
Lichtervelde
Tielt
Woumen
Zarren
Staden
Ardooie
Roeselare
Izegem
Ingelmunster
Langemark-Poelkapelle
Moorslede
Kortrijk
Westkapelle
Sluis
Gravelines
Loone-Plage
Calais
Marck
Sangatte
Wissant
Cap Gris-Nez
EUROTUNNEL TERMINAL
Ardres
Guînes
Bourbourg
Bergues
Hondschoote
Vleteren
Roesbrugge
Poperinge
Ieper
Ypres
BELLEWAERDE
CATHÉDRALE ST. MARTIN
Menen
Halluin
Mouscron
Avelgem
Dottignies
Tourcoing
Roubaix
Villeneuve-d'Ascq
Tournai
Antoing
Audruicq
Watten
Wormhout
Steenvoorde
Cassel
Bailleul
Comines
Armentières
Ambleteuse
Marquise
Licques
Nordausques
Caps et Marais d'Opale
Wimereux
NAUSICAA
Boulogne-sur-Mer
Le Portel
Outreau
Escoeuilles
Lumbres
St. Omer
Arques
Hazebrouck
LA COUPOLE
Desvres
Hardelot Plage
Samer
Aire-sur-la-Lys
Merville
St. Venant
Estaires
Lille
Thérouanne
Fauquembergues
Estrée-Blanche
Norrent-Fontes
Lillers
Béthune
Hucqueliers
Étaples
Le Touquet-Paris-Plage
Auchy-au-Bois
Fruges
Heuchin
Seclin
La Bassée
Carvin
Pont-à-Marcq
Orchies
St. Amand-les-Eaux
Bruay-la-Buissière
Divion
Houdain
Noeux-les-Mines
Liévin
Lens
Vimy
Hénin-Beaumont
Flines-lez-Raches
Scarpe
Merlimont Plage
BAGATELLE
Montreuil
Berck
Anvin
Maresquel
Hesdin
Canche
St. Pol-sur-Ternoise
Cambligeu
Douai
Somain
Denain
Wallers
Fort-Mahon-Plage
Le Parcq
Tincques
Aubigny-en-Artois
Vitry-en-Artois
Aniche
Bouchain
Vron
Authie
Rue
Baie de la Somme
Le Crotoy
Crécy-en-Ponthieu
Auxi-le-Château
Avesnes-le-Comte
Arras
Aubigny-au-Bac
Frévent
Beaumetz-lès-Loges
CITADELLE D'ARRAS
Iwuy
St. Valéry-sur-Somme
Noyelles-sur-Mer
Nouvion
Bouquemaison
La Herlière
Marquion
Cambrai
Cayeux-sur-Mer
St. Riquier
Doullens
Bernaville
Ayette
Vaulx Vraucourt
Caudry
Ault
Abbeville
Fressenville
Beauval
Marieux
Puisieux
Acheux-en-Amiénois
Bapaume
Bertincourt
Walincourt
Mers-les-Bains
Le Tréport
Doorum
Midlum
Debstedt
Langen
Walton-on-the-Naze
Frinton-on-Sea
E40
A16
A26
A25
A1
A21
E15
E17
E19
A10
A17
A18
A19
A14
A23
A28
E42
E402
10

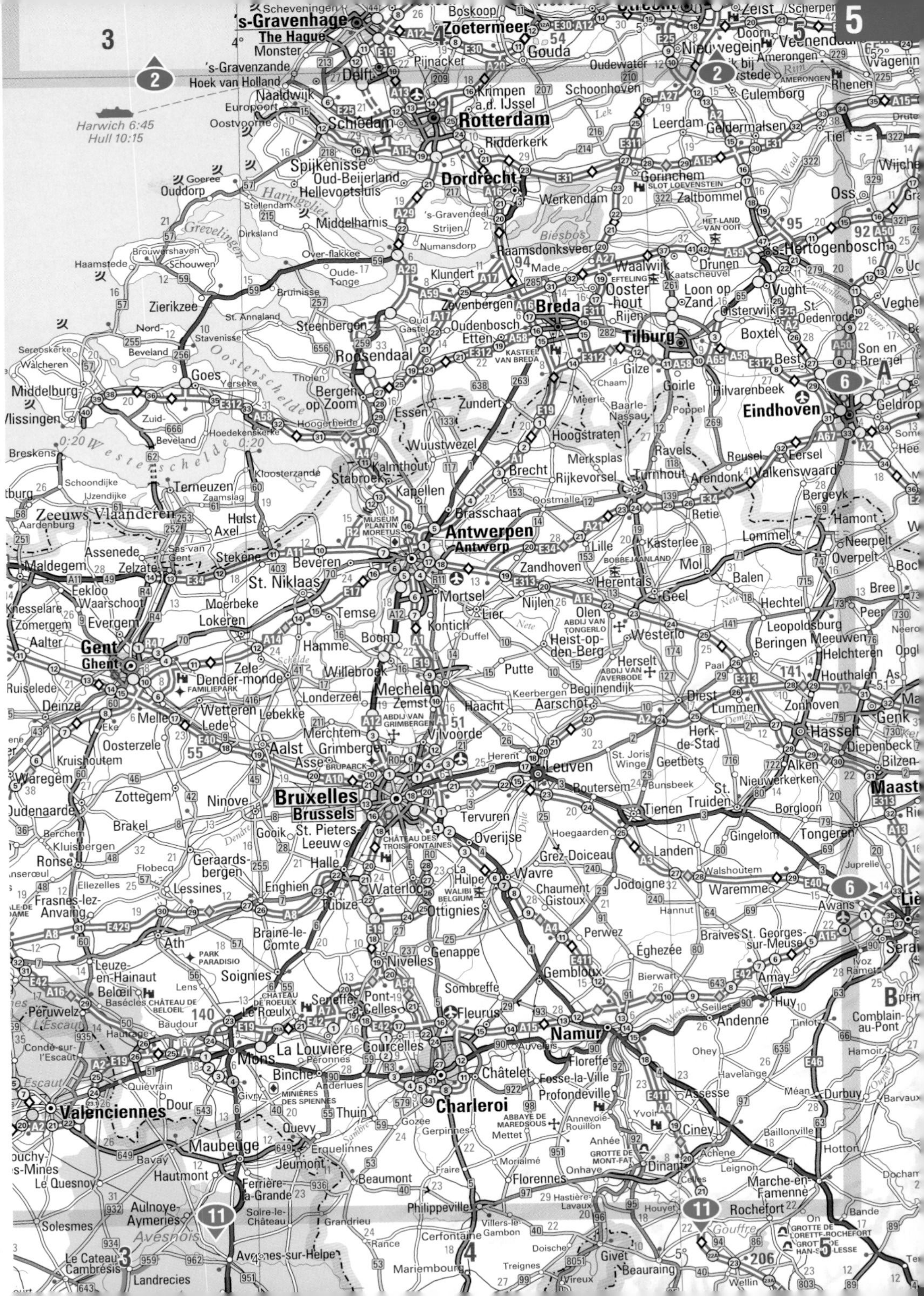
3
's-Gravenhage
The Hague
Scheveningen
Monster
's-Gravenzande
Hoek van Holland
Naaldwijk
Delft
Zoetermeer
Gouda
Pijnacker
Boskoop
Zeist
Nieuwegein
Veenendaal
Rhenen
Culemborg
Schoonhoven
Krimpen a.d. IJssel
Europoort
Oostvoorne
Schiedam
Rotterdam
Ridderkerk
Harwich 6:45
Hull 10:15
Spijkenisse
Oud-Beijerland
Hellevoetsluis
Dordrecht
Gorinchem
Leerdam
Geldermalsen
Tiel
Zaltbommel
Werkendam
Oss
Goeree
Ouddorp
Haringvliet
Middelharnis
'S-Gravendeel
Strijen
Numansdorp
Biesbos
Greveling
Dirksland
Brouwershaven
Schouwen
Haamstede
Zierikzee
Over-flakkee
Oude-Tonge
Bruinisse
Klundert
Raamsdonksveer
Made
Waalwijk
Drunen
's-Hertogenbosch
Vught
Oosterhout
Loon op Zand
Oisterwijk
Zevenbergen
Breda
Tilburg
Boxtel
St. Oedenrode
Steenbergen
Oudenbosch
Etten
Roosendaal
Gilze
Goirle
Best
Son en Breugel
Eindhoven
Geldrop
Hilvarenbeek
St. Annaland
Stavenisse
Noord-Beveland
Serooskerke
Walcheren
Middelburg
Vlissingen
Goes
Yerseke
Oosterschelde
Tholen
Bergen op Zoom
Zundert
Essen
Hoogerheide
Zuid-Beveland
Westerschelde
Breskens
Schoondijke
Terneuzen
Zeeuws Vlaanderen
Aardenburg
Hulst
Axel
Kalmthout
Wuustwezel
Hoogstraten
Baarle-Nassau
Merksplas
Ravels
Turnhout
Arendonk
Reusel
Eersel
Valkenswaard
Bergeyk
Brecht
Rijkevorsel
Stabroek
Kapellen
Brasschaat
Antwerpen
Antwerp
Retie
Lommel
Neerpelt
Overpelt
Hamont
Assenede
Maldegem
Zelzate
Eekloo
Waarschoot
Stekene
Beveren
St. Niklaas
Zandhoven
Lille
Kasterlee
Mol
Balen
Herentals
Geel
Mortsel
Nijlen
Lier
Olen
Hechtel
Bree
Peer
Knesselare
Zomergem
Evergem
Aalter
Moerbeke
Lokeren
Temse
Boom
Kontich
Duffel
Heist-op-den-Berg
Westerlo
Leopoldsburg
Beringen
Meeuwen
Helchteren
Gent
Ghent
Zele
Dendermonde
Hamme
Willebroek
Putte
Herselt
Houthalen
Ruiselede
Deinze
Mechelen
Keerbergen
Begijnendijk
Diest
Lummen
Zonhoven
Genk
Melle
Wetteren
Lede
Londerzeel
Zemst
Haacht
Aarschot
Hasselt
Merchtem
Vilvoorde
Herk-de-Stad
Diepenbeek
Alken
Oosterzele
Aalst
Grimbergen
Asse
Leuven
St. Joris Winge
Geetbets
Bilzen
Kruishoutem
Waregem
Zottegem
Ninove
Bruxelles
Brussels
Boutersem
Tienen
St. Truiden
Nieuwerkerken
Maastricht
Oudenaarde
Brakel
Gooik
St. Pieters-Leeuw
Tervuren
Overijse
Hoegaarden
Borgloon
Tongeren
Gingelom
Landen
Kluisbergen
Ronse
Geraardsbergen
Halle
La Hulpe
Wavre
Grez-Doiceau
Jodoigne
Flobecq
Ellezelles
Lessines
Enghien
Waterloo
Chaumont Gistoux
Waremme
Awans
Liège
Frasnes-lez-Anvaing
Tubize
Ottignies
Hannut
Perwez
Braives
St. Georges-sur-Meuse
Seraing
Ath
Braine-le-Comte
Genappe
Nivelles
Éghezée
Leuze-en-Hainaut
Soignies
Gembloux
Amay
Beloeil
Sombreffe
Huy
Péruwelz
Le Roeulx
Seneffe
Pont-à-Celles
Fleurus
Andenne
Comblain-au-Pont
Condé-sur-l'Escaut
Mons
La Louvière
Courcelles
Namur
Ohey
Hamoir
Valenciennes
Quiévrain
Dour
Binche
Anderlues
Charleroi
Châtelet
Fosse-la-Ville
Profondeville
Assesse
Durbuy
Thuin
Gerpinnes
Mettet
Yvoir
Ciney
Maubeuge
Quevy
Erquelinnes
Jeumont
Anhée
Dinant
Achêne
Hotton
Bavay
Hautmont
Beaumont
Florennes
Onhaye
Marche-en-Famenne
Le Quesnoy
Ferrière-la-Grande
Philippeville
Rochefort
Aulnoye-Aymeries
Solre-le-Château
Solesmes
Avesnois
Le Cateau Cambrésis
Landrecies
Avesnes-sur-Helpe
Cerfontaine
Mariembourg
Givet
Beauraing
Wellin
Treignes

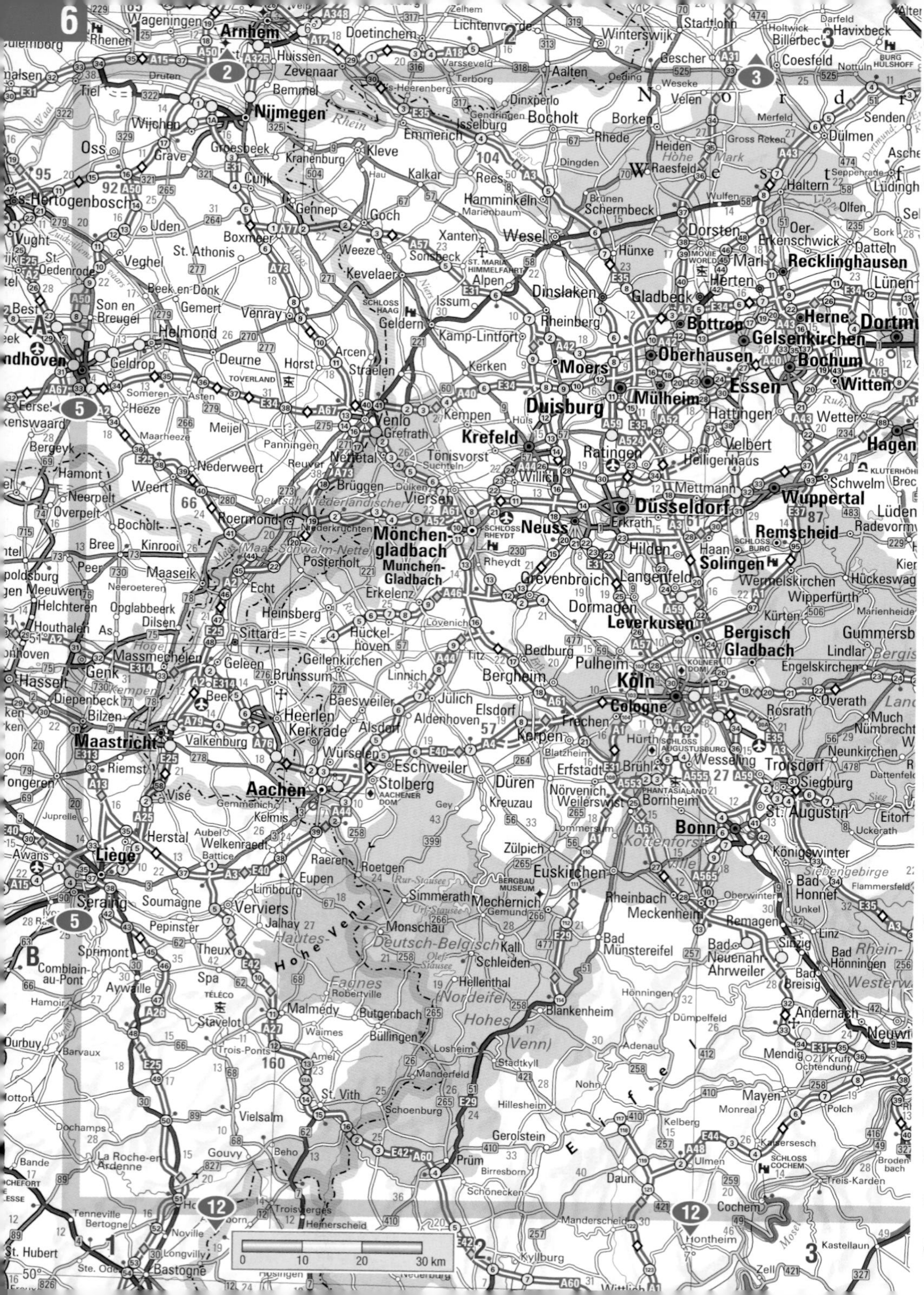

Wageningen
Arnhem
Rhenen
Doetinchem
Lichtenvoorde
Winterswijk
Stadtlohn
Darfeld
Havixbeck
Billerbeck
Coesfeld
Huissen
Zevenaar
Varsseveld
Terborg
Aalten
Gescher
Oeding
Weseke
Nottuln
Tiel
Druten
Bemmel
's-Heerenberg
Dinxperlo
Bocholt
Borken
Velen
Merfeld
Senden
Nijmegen
Wijchen
Emmerich
Isselburg
Rhede
Heiden
Gross Reken
Dülmen
Oss
Grave
Groesbeek
Kranenburg
Kleve
Hohe Mark
Raesfeld
Haltern
Lüdinghausen
's-Hertogenbosch
Cuijk
Kalkar
Rees
Dingden
Hamminkeln
Schermbeck
Wulfen
Olfen
Uden
Gennep
Goch
Xanten
Wesel
Dorsten
Oer-Erkenschwick
Datteln
Vught
Boxmeer
St. Athonis
Weeze
Sonsbeck
Hünxe
Marl
Recklinghausen
St. Oedenrode
Veghel
Kevelaer
Alpen
Herten
Beek en Donk
Gemert
Issum
Dinslaken
Gladbeck
Lünen
Best
Son en Breugel
Venray
Geldern
Kamp-Lintfort
Rheinberg
Bottrop
Herne
Dortmund
Helmond
Deurne
Horst
Arcen
Straelen
Kerken
Oberhausen
Gelsenkirchen
Bochum
Eindhoven
Geldrop
Moers
Essen
Witten
Someren
Asten
Duisburg
Mülheim
Hattingen
Wetter
Eersel
Heeze
Venlo
Kempen
Krefeld
Ratingen
Velbert
Hagen
Meijel
Panningen
Grefrath
Tönisvorst
Heiligenhaus
Bergeyk
Nederweert
Nettetal
Brüggen
Willich
Mettmann
Schwelm
Wuppertal
Hamont
Weert
Neerpelt
Viersen
Düsseldorf
Erkrath
Lüdenscheid
Overpelt
Roermond
Mönchengladbach
Neuss
Remscheid
Bocholt
Bree
Kinrooi
Niederkrüchten
Hilden
Haan
Solingen
Radevormwald
Peer
Maaseik
Posterholt
Rheydt
Grevenbroich
Langenfeld
Wermelskirchen
Hückeswagen
Echt
Erkelenz
Dormagen
Wipperfürth
Helchteren
Opglabbeek
Heinsberg
Leverkusen
Kürten
Houthalen
Dilsen
Sittard
Hückelhoven
Bedburg
Pulheim
Bergisch Gladbach
Gummersbach
Lindlar
Genk
Massmechelen
Geleen
Geilenkirchen
Linnich
Titz
Bergheim
Köln
Cologne
Engelskirchen
Hasselt
Diepenbeek
Brunssum
Beek
Heerlen
Baesweiler
Jülich
Elsdorf
Overath
Bilzen
Maastricht
Valkenburg
Kerkrade
Alsdorf
Aldenhoven
Kerpen
Frechen
Hürth
Rösrath
Much
Nümbrecht
Würselen
Eschweiler
Brühl
Wesseling
Troisdorf
Riemst
Tongeren
Visé
Aachen
Stolberg
Düren
Erftstadt
Siegburg
Kreuzau
Nörvenich
Weilerswist
Bornheim
St. Augustin
Eitorf
Herstal
Aubel
Welkenraedt
Kelmis
Zülpich
Euskirchen
Bonn
Königswinter
Liège
Awans
Raeren
Roetgen
Eupen
Rheinbach
Meckenheim
Bad Honnef
Seraing
Soumagne
Limbourg
Verviers
Simmerath
Mechernich
Remagen
Pepinster
Jalhay
Monschau
Sinzig
Linz
Sprimont
Theux
Schleiden
Bad Münstereifel
Bad Neuenahr Ahrweiler
Bad Breisig
Bad Hönningen
Comblain-au-Pont
Spa
Aywaille
Hellenthal
Hohe Venn
Hamoir
Malmedy
Stavelot
Bütgenbach
Blankenheim
Andernach
Neuwied
Durbuy
Trois-Ponts
Büllingen
Losheim
Adenau
Mendig
Stadtkyll
Amel
Manderfeld
Nohn
Mayen
St. Vith
Vielsalm
Schoenburg
Hillesheim
Polch
Gerolstein
Kelberg
Kaisersesch
Gouvy
Beho
Prüm
Ulmen
Daun
La Roche-en-Ardenne
Birresborn
Treis-Karden
Cochem
Schönecken
Troisvierges
Tenneville
Bertogne
Noville
Manderscheid
Hontheim
St. Hubert
Longvilly
Bastogne
Kyllburg
Kastellaun
Zell
Eifel
Nord
Westfalen
0
10
20
30 km

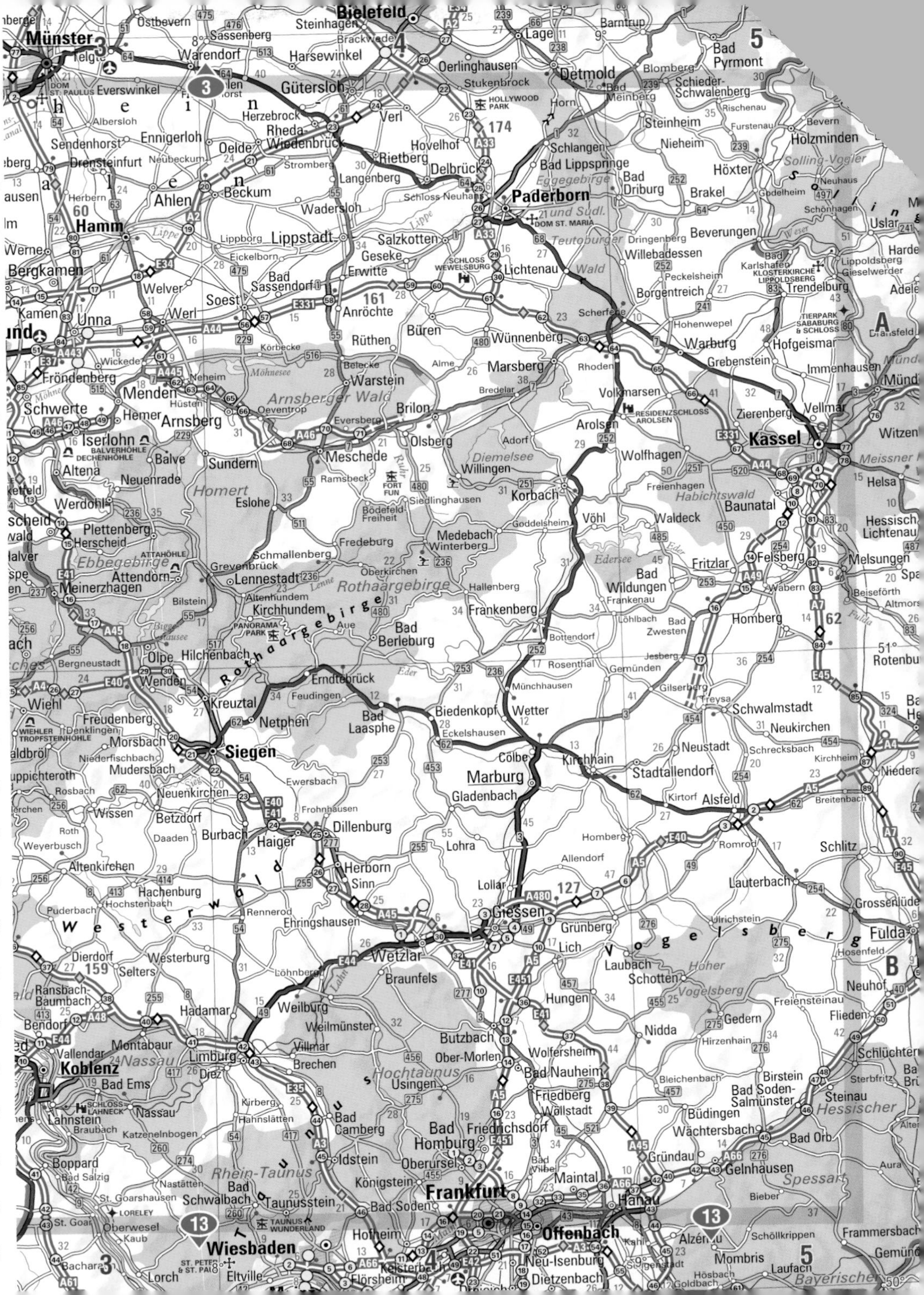

Bielefeld
Münster
Telgte
Ostbevern
Sassenberg
Warendorf
Steinhagen
Brackwede
Harsewinkel
Gütersloh
Oerlinghausen
Lage
Barntrup
Bad Pyrmont
Detmold
Blomberg
Schieder-Schwalenberg
Stukenbrock
Hollywood Park
Everswinkel
Herzebrock
Rheda-Wiedenbrück
Verl
Hovelhof
Horn
Steinheim
Nieheim
Holzminden
Sendenhorst
Ennigerloh
Oelde
Rietberg
Delbrück
Schlangen
Bad Lippspringe
Eggegebirge
Bad Driburg
Höxter
Solling-Vogler
Drensteinfurt
Stromberg
Langenberg
Beckum
Ahlen
Hamm
Wadersloh
Schloss Neuhaus
Paderborn
Brakel
Dom St. Maria
Lippborg
Lippstadt
Salzkotten
Geseke
Teutoburger Wald
Dringenberg
Beverungen
Uslar
Werne
Bergkamen
Eickelborn
Bad Sassendorf
Erwitte
Schloss Wewelsburg
Lichtenau
Willebadessen
Borgentreich
Bad Karlshafen
Trendelburg
Welver
Soest
Anröchte
Kamen
Unna
Werl
Büren
Rüthen
Wünnenberg
Scherfede
Warburg
Hofgeismar
Tierpark Sababurg
Fröndenberg
Wickede
Neheim
Möhnesee
Belecke
Warstein
Alme
Marsberg
Rhoden
Grebenstein
Immenhausen
Schwerte
Menden
Hüsten
Arnsberger Wald
Brilon
Volkmarsen
Zierenberg
Vellmar
Hemer
Arnsberg
Oeventrop
Eversberg
Arolsen
Residenzschloss Arolsen
Kassel
Iserlohn
Balve
Sundern
Meschede
Olsberg
Adorf
Diemelsee
Wolfhagen
Altena
Neuenrade
Homert
Ramsbeck
Fort Fun
Willingen
Habichtswald
Baunatal
Helsa
Werdohl
Eslohe
Siedlinghausen
Korbach
Freienhagen
Plettenberg
Herscheid
Bödefeld-Freiheit
Goddelsheim
Vöhl
Waldeck
Hessisch Lichtenau
Attahöhle
Schmallenberg
Fredeburg
Medebach
Winterberg
Edersee
Felsberg
Melsungen
Ebbegebirge
Attendorn
Grevenbrück
Lennestadt
Oberkirchen
Rothaargebirge
Hallenberg
Bad Wildungen
Fritzlar
Wabern
Meinerzhagen
Bilstein
Altenhundem
Kirchhundem
Panorama Park
Aue
Frankenberg
Frankenau
Löhlbach
Bad Zwesten
Homberg
Bad Berleburg
Bottendorf
Jesberg
Rotenburg
Bergneustadt
Olpe
Hilchenbach
Rosenthal
Gemünden
Wenden
Erndtebrück
Münchhausen
Gilserberg
Wiehl
Kreuztal
Feudingen
Treysa
Schwalmstadt
Freudenberg
Bad Laasphe
Biedenkopf
Wetter
Neukirchen
Wiehler Tropfsteinhöhle
Denklingen
Morsbach
Netphen
Eckelshausen
Neustadt
Schrecksbach
Kirchheim
Siegen
Niederfischbach
Mudersbach
Cölbe
Kirchhain
Stadtallendorf
Marburg
Eversbach
Neuenkirchen
Gladenbach
Kirtorf
Alsfeld
Breitenbach
Rosbach
Wissen
Betzdorf
Frohnhausen
Dillenburg
Daaden
Burbach
Haiger
Lohra
Homberg
Romrod
Schlitz
Altenkirchen
Herborn
Sinn
Allendorf
Hachenburg
Hochstenbach
Lollar
Lauterbach
Puderbach
Rennerod
Ehringshausen
Giessen
Grünberg
Ulrichstein
Grossenlüder
Fulda
Westerwald
Wetzlar
Lich
Vogelsberg
Laubach
Dierdorf
Westerburg
Selters
Löhnberg
Braunfels
Hungen
Schotten
Hoher Vogelsberg
Hosenfeld
Neuhof
Ransbach-Baumbach
Hadamar
Weilburg
Weilmünster
Freiensteinau
Flieden
Bendorf
Montabaur
Villmar
Butzbach
Nidda
Gedern
Hirzenhain
Vallendar
Nassau
Limburg
Diez
Brechen
Ober-Morlen
Wolfersheim
Schlüchtern
Koblenz
Bad Ems
Hochtaunus
Bad Nauheim
Bleichenbach
Birstein
Steinau
Usingen
Friedberg
Bad Soden-Salmünster
Lahnstein
Schloss Lahneck
Kirberg
Wöllstadt
Büdingen
Hessischer
Braubach
Hahnstätten
Bad Camberg
Bad Homburg
Friedrichsdorf
Wächtersbach
Bad Orb
Katzenelnbogen
Boppard
Bad Salzig
Idstein
Oberursel
Bad Vilbel
Gründau
Gelnhausen
Rhein-Taunus
Nastätten
Königstein
Maintal
Spessart
St. Goarshausen
Loreley
Schwalbach
Bad Schwalbach
Taunusstein
Frankfurt
Bad Soden
Hanau
Bieber
St. Goar
Oberwesel
Kaub
Taunus Wunderland
Hofheim
Offenbach
Alzenau
Schöllkrippen
Frammersbach
Wiesbaden
Kelsterbach
Neu-Isenburg
Mombris
Bacharach
Lorch
Eltville
Flörsheim
Dietzenbach
Laufach
Gemünden
Bayerischer

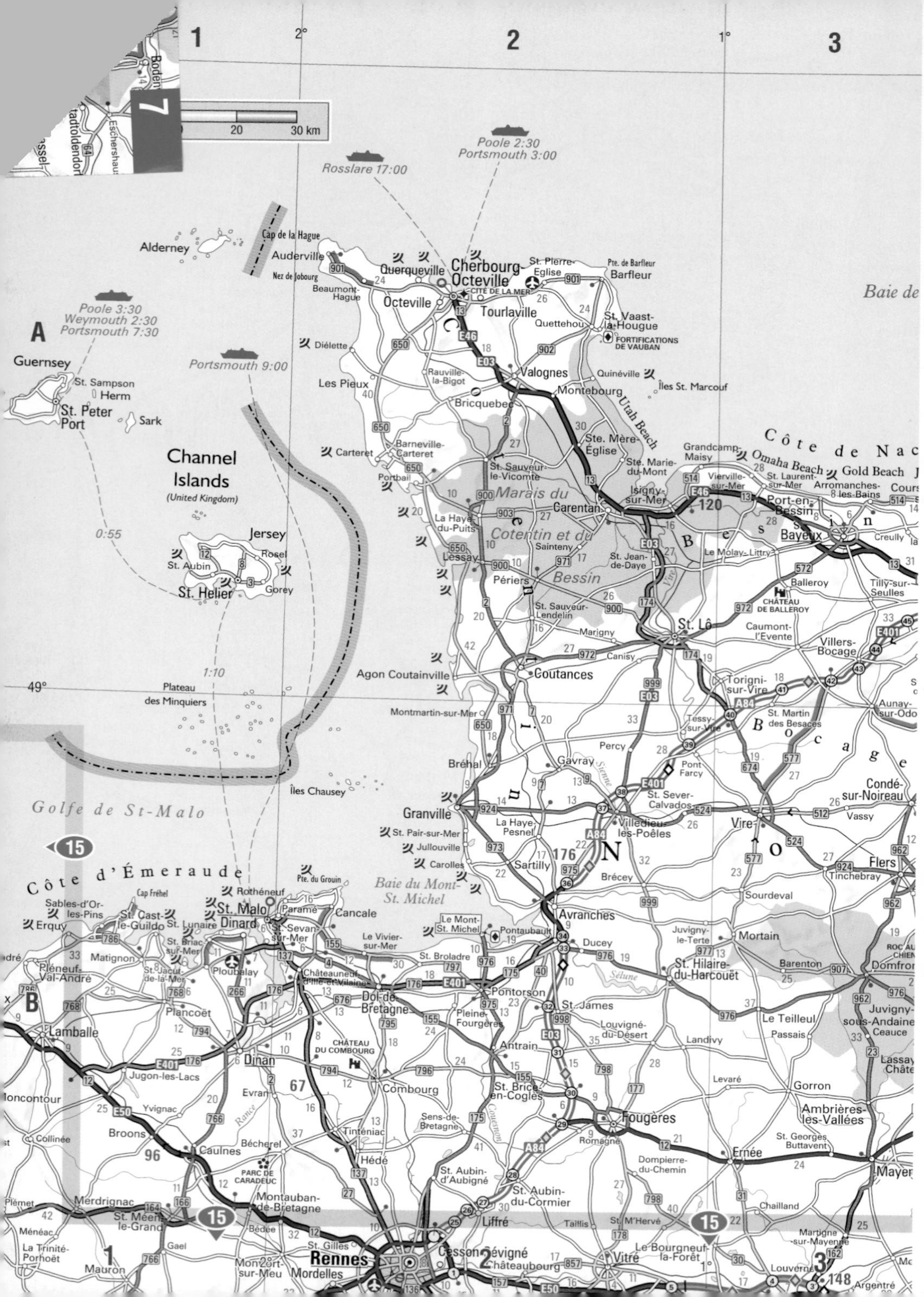

1
2
3
7
20
30 km
Poole 2:30
Portsmouth 3:00
Rosslare 17:00
Poole 3:30
Weymouth 2:30
Portsmouth 7:30
Portsmouth 9:00
A
B
Alderney
Cap de la Hague
Auderville
Nez de Jobourg
Beaumont-Hague
Querqueville
Cherbourg-Octeville
Octeville
Tourlaville
St. Pierre-Eglise
Pte. de Barfleur
Barfleur
Cité de la Mer
St. Vaast-la-Hougue
Quettehou
Fortifications de Vauban
Diélette
Les Pieux
Rauville-la-Bigot
Valognes
Bricquebec
Montebourg
Quinéville
Îles St. Marcouf
Utah Beach
Guernsey
St. Sampson
Herm
St. Peter Port
Sark
Channel Islands
(United Kingdom)
Jersey
Rosel
St. Aubin
St. Helier
Gorey
0:55
1:10
Carteret
Barneville-Carteret
Portbail
Ste. Mère-Église
St. Sauveur-le-Vicomte
Marais du Cotentin et du Bessin
Ste. Marie-du-Mont
Grandcamp-Maisy
Omaha Beach
Vierville-sur-Mer
St. Laurent-sur-Mer
Gold Beach
Arromanches-les-Bains
Port-en-Bessin
Bayeux
Creully
Côte de Nac
Baie de
Isigny-sur-Mer
Carentan
La Haye-du-Puits
Lessay
Sainteny
St. Jean-de-Daye
Le Molay-Littry
Balleroy
Château de Balleroy
Tilly-sur-Seulles
Périers
St. Sauveur-Lendelin
Marigny
St. Lô
Caumont-l'Evente
Villers-Bocage
Canisy
Coutances
Agon Coutainville
49°
Plateau des Minquiers
Torigni-sur-Vire
Aunay-sur-Odon
Montmartin-sur-Mer
Tessy-sur-Vire
St. Martin des Besaces
Percy
Gavray
Bréhal
Pont Farcy
Bocage
Condé-sur-Noireau
Îles Chausey
Golfe de St-Malo
Granville
St. Sever-Calvados
Villedieu-les-Poêles
Vire
Vassy
La Haye-Pesnel
St. Pair-sur-Mer
Jullouville
Carolles
Sartilly
Flers
Tinchebray
Brécey
Côte d'Émeraude
Pte. du Grouin
Baie du Mont-St. Michel
Sourdeval
Cap Fréhel
Rothéneuf
Sables-d'Or-les-Pins
St. Cast-le-Guildo
St. Malo
Paramé
Cancale
Erquy
St. Lunaire
Dinard
St. Servan-sur-Mer
Le Vivier-sur-Mer
Le Mont-St. Michel
Pontaubault
Avranches
Mortain
Juvigny-le-Tertre
Ducey
St. Briac-sur-Mer
Matignon
Pléneuf-Val-André
St. Jacut-de-la-Mer
Ploubalay
St. Broladre
Châteauneuf-d'Ille-et-Vilaine
St. Hilaire-du-Harcouët
Barenton
Domfront
Pontorson
Dol-de-Bretagne
Plancoët
Pleine-Fougères
St. James
Juvigny-sous-Andaine
Ceauce
Le Teilleul
Passais
Lamballe
Louvigné-du-Désert
Landivy
Antrain
Dinan
Château du Combourg
Jugon-les-Lacs
Lassay
Levaré
Gorron
Moncontour
Evran
Combourg
St. Brice-en-Coglès
Yvignac
Ambrières-les-Vallées
Broons
Tinténiac
Sens-de-Bretagne
Fougères
Collinée
Bécherel
Romagné
St. Georges-Buttavent
Caulnes
Ernée
Hédé
Parc de Caradeuc
St. Aubin-d'Aubigné
Dompierre-du-Chemin
Mayenne
Montauban-de-Bretagne
St. Aubin-du-Cormier
Plémet
Merdrignac
St. Méen-le-Grand
Chailland
Ménéac
Bédée
Liffré
Taillis
St. M'Hervé
Martigné-sur-Mayenne
La Trinité-Porhoët
Gael
St. Gilles
Le Bourgneuf-la-Forêt
Mauron
Montfort-sur-Meu
Rennes
Cesson-Sévigné
Châteaubourg
Vitré
Louverné
Mordelles
Argentré
Sélune
Couesnon
Rance
Vire
Sienne
E401
E50
E46
E03
A84
15

3
4
5
0°
1°
50°
Newhaven 4:00
Portsmouth 3:15
Portsmouth 5:30
la Seine
Mers-les-Bains
Le Tréport
Eu
Criel-sur-Mer
Biville-sur-Mer
Gamaches
Bouttencourt
Blangy-sur-Bresle
Dieppe
Varengeville-sur-Mer
Quiberville
CHÂTEAU DE DIEPPE
Envermeu
Arques-la-Bataille
Fresnoy-Folny
St. Valery-en-Caux
Veulettes-sur-Mer
Veules-les-Roses
Offranville
Bacqueville-en-Caux
Londinières
Les Grandes-Ventes
St. Pierre-en-Port
Fontaine-le-Dun
Torcy-le-Petit
Béthune
Fécamp
Yport
Cany-Barville
Valmont
ST. JOSEPH
PALAIS BÉNÉDICTINE
St. Laurent-en-Caux
Neufchâtel-en-Bray
Étretat
Cap d'Antifer
Héricourt-en-Caux
Doudeville
Yerville
Tôtes
St. Saëns
Gaillefontaine
Fauville-en-Caux
St. Martin-Osmonville
Pays de Caux
Criquetot-l'Esneval
Goderville
Yvetot
Limésy
Pavilly
Clères
Buchy
Forges-les-Eaux
Heuqueville
Alvimare
Quincampoix
Malaunay
Argueil
Montivilliers
Bolbec
Caudebec-en-Caux
Barentin
ABBAYE ST. WANDRILLE
Ste. Adresse
Harfleur
St. Romain-de-Colbosc
Tancarville
Lillebonne
Duclair
La Feuillie
Le Havre
Boucles de Seine Normande
La Mailleraye-sur-Seine
Maromme
Mont-St. Aignan
ST. JOSEPH
CHÂTEAU DE TANCARVILLE
Quillebeuf
ABBAYE DE JUMIÈGES
Jumièges
Rouen
Lyons-la-Forêt
Honfleur
Berville-sur-Mer
Seine
Le Grand-Quevilly
Boos
Côte Fleurie
Villerville
Bourneville
Fleury-sur-Andelle
Trouville-sur-Mer
Deauville
St. Maclou
Grand Couronne
St. Étienne-du-Rouvray
Juno Beach
Sword Beach
Blonville-sur-Mer
Beuzeville
Pont-Audemer
Bourg-Achard
Ecouis
St. Aubin-sur-Mer
Houlgate
Villers-sur-Mer
Bourgtheroulde
Pont-de-l'Arche
CHÂTEAU GAILLARD
Luc-sur-Mer
Lion-sur-Mer
Cabourg
Douvres-la-Délivrande
Dives-sur-Mer
Pont-l'Évêque
Montfort-sur-Risle
Elbeuf
Les Andelys
Ouistreham
Cormeilles
Lieurey
ABBAYE DE NOTRE DAME DU BEC
Louviers
Gaillon
Dozulé
Le Breuil-en-Auge
Brionne
Caen
Troarn
Lisieux
Le Neubourg
Acquigny
La Boissière
Thiberville
La Rivière-Thibouville
Autheuil-Authouillet
Vernon
GIVERNY
Fleury-sur-Orne
Moult
Bernay
Beaumont-le-Roger
Bonnières-sur-Seine
Evrecy
Orne
Mézidon-Canon
Touques
CHÂTEAU ST. GERMAIN-DE-LIVET
Évreux
Pacy-sur-Eure
St. Laurent-de-Condel
Bretteville-sur-Laize
St. Pierre-sur-Dives
Orbec
CHÂTEAU BEAUMESNIL
Beaumesnil
Livarot
Broglie
Thury-Harcourt
Potigny
La Barre-en-Ouche
Conches-en-Ouche
Iton
Vimoutiers
Normandie
Eure
ST. MARTIN
Falaise
Trun
La Neuve-Lyre
St. André-de-l'Eure
Ivry-la-Bataille
Pont d'Ouilly
Nècy
Damville
CHÂTEAU D'ANET
Anet
Rugles
Risle
La Ferté-Frênel
Breteuil
Chambois
Gacé
Exmes
L'Aigle
Verneuil-sur-Avre
Nonancourt
Putanges-Pont-Ecrepin
Argentan
Ste. Gauburge-Ste. Colombe
Dreux
Messei
Écouché
Nonant-le-Pin
Le Merlerault
Avre
Brezolles
Laons
Le Boullay-Mivoye
Briouze
Rânes
Moulins-la-Marche
Tremblay-le-Vicomte
Mortrée
Courtomer
Perche
Tourouvre
Ste. Anne
La Ferté-Vidame
Châteauneuf-en-Thymerais
Maintenon
La Ferté-Macé
Carrouges
Sées
Senonches
Bagnoles-de-l'Orne
STATION THERMALE
CHÂTEAU DE CARROUGES
Essay
Bazoches-sur-Hoëne
Mortagne-au-Perche
Longny-au-Perche
Digny
Dangers
CATHÉDRALE DE CHARTRES
Normandie Maine
Couterne
Mayenne
Le Mêle-sur-Sarthe
La Loupe
Mainvilliers
Couptrain
Pré-en-Pail
Rémalard
Courville
Alençon
Champrond-en-Gâtine
Lucé
Thivars
Javron
Sarthe
St. Rémy-du-Val
Bellême
Villaines-la-Juhel
Mamers
Thiron-Gardais
Illiers-Combray
Nogent-le-Rotrou
Huisne
Montainville
La Hutte
St. Cosme-en-Vairais
Fresnay-sur-Sarthe
Dangeul
Le Theil
Bais
Marolles-les-Braults
Brou
Bonneval
Beaumont-sur-Sarthe
La Ferté-Bernard
Authon-du-Perche
Bonnétable
Évron
Sillé-le-Guillaume
Ballon
Chapelle Royale
La Bazoche-Gouet
Tuffé
Ste. Suzanne
Conlie
Domfront-en-Champagne
Parennes
Montmirail
Arrou
CHÂTEAU DE CHÂTEAUDUN
Châteaudun
Cormainville
A
B
10
16
E46
E44
E05
E402
E50
A28
A29
A13
A131
A151
A150
A84
A88
A11
A154
167
107
130
200
204
69
55
36

Abbeville
Le Tréport
Mers-les-Bains
Criel-sur-Mer
Eu
Doullens
Amiens
Albert
Bapaume
Cambrai
Péronne
Corbie
Plaine de Picardie
Airaines
Flixecourt
Picquigny
Poix-de-Picardie
Aumale
Blangy-sur-Bresle
Neufchâtel-en-Bray
Pays de Bray
Moreuil
Montdidier
Roye
Ham
Nesle
Tergnier
Chauny
Noyon
Breteuil
Grandvilliers
Crèvecœur-le-Grand
Songeons
Gournay-en-Bray
Beauvais
St. Just-en-Chaussée
Clermont
Compiègne
Soissons
Creil
Senlis
Chantilly
Pont Ste. Maxence
Crépy-en-Valois
Villers-Cotterêts
Les Andelys
Gisors
Vernon
Mantes-la-Jolie
Vexin Français
Pontoise
Cergy
L'Isle-Adam
Méru
Chaumont-en-Vexin
Magny-en-Vexin
Sarcelles
Montmorency
Argenteuil
St. Denis
Nanterre
PARIS
Bobigny
Montreuil
Chelles
Meaux
Versailles
St. Germain-en-Laye
Poissy
Rambouillet
Dreux
Chartres
Étampes
Dourdan
Évry
Corbeil-Essonnes
Melun
Fontainebleau
Forêt de Fontainebleau
Nemours
Montereau-Fault-Yonne
Provins
Coulommiers
Château-Thierry
Malesherbes
Pithiviers
Vitry-sur-Seine
Créteil
Orly
Massy
Palaiseau
Orsay
Trappes
Élancourt
Montlhéry
Brétigny-sur-Orge
La Haute Vallée de Chevreuse
Gâtinais Français
Disneyland Paris & Walt Disney Studios
Parc Astérix
Charles de Gaulle
Château de Compiègne
Cathédrale de Amiens
Cathédrale de Chartres
Cathédrale St. Étienne
Château de Breteuil
Château d'Anet
Château Gaillard
Château de Courances
Giverny
Houdan
Maintenon
Auneau
Voves
Angerville
Milly-la-Forêt
Nangis
Lagny-sur-Marne
La Ferté-sous-Jouarre
0 10 20 30 km

Solesmes
Aymeries
Avesnois
Le Cateau-Cambrésis
Landrecies
Avesnes-sur-Helpe
Grandrieu
Rance
Cerfontaine
Villers-le-Gambon
Doische
Mariembourg
Treignes
Givet
Beauraing
Rochefort
Gouffre
Wellin
Caudry
Walincourt
Catillon
Le Nouvion-en-Thiérache
Etroeungt
Trélon
Fourmies
Chimay
Couvin
Baileux
Macon
Vireux
Hargnies
Haut-Fays
EUROSPACE CENTER
Libin
St. Hubert
Freux
Prémont
Bohain-en-Vermandois
La Capelle
Hirson
St. Michel
Signy-le-Petit
Rocroi
Revin
Fumay
Rienne
Gedinne
Bièvre
Paliseul
Recogne
Libramont
Guise
Etréaupont
Oise
Landouzy-la-Ville
Aubenton
Les Mazures
Maubert-Fontaine
Ardennes
Monthermé
Rimogne
Nouzonville
Gespunsart
Sugny
Corbion
Bouillon
Bertrix
Neufchâteau
Herbeumont
St. Quentin
Thiérache
Origny-Ste Benoite
Vervins
Rumigny
Rouvroy-sur-Audry
Charleville-Mézières
Vrigne-aux-Bois
St. Menges
Sedan
Semois
Ribemont
Sains Richaumont
Liart
Brunehamel
Rozoy-sur-Serre
Marle
Signy-l'Abbaye
Rossignol
Jamoigne
Florenville
Vendeuil
Crécy-sur-Serre
l'Espérance
Montcornet
Chaumont-Porcien
Flize
Douzy
Carignan
Pierrepont
Launois-sur-Vence
Poix-Terron
Mouzon
Meix-devant-Virton
La Fère
Crépy
Bucy-lès-Pierrepont
Dizy-le-Gros
Seraincourt
Novion-Porcien
Chemery-sur-Bar
Raucourt-et-Flaba
Chiers
Margut
NOTRE-DAME AVIOTH
Virton
Avioth
St. Gobain
Laon
Athies-sous-Laon
Sévigny
Saulces Monclin
Montmédy
Sissonne
Château-Porcien
Novy-Chevrières
Tourteron
Beaumont-en-Argonne
Anizy-le-Château
CATHÉDRALE NOTRE-DAME DE LAON
Festieux
Lor
Rethel
Le Chesne
Tannay
Stenay
Coucy-Château-Auffrique
Chavignon
Corbeny
Asfeld
Attigny
Quatre-Champs
Lanneuville-sur-Meuse
Marville
Tagnon
Neuflize
Craonne
Neufchâtel-sur-Aisne
Juniville
Vouziers
Buzancy
Dun-sur-Meuse
Damvillers
Vailly-sur-Aisne
Bourg-et-Comin
Braine
Machault
Semide
Grandpré
Bantheville
Aisne
Bourgogne
Hermonville
Vesle
Witry-lès-Reims
Béthenville
Monthois
Consenvoye
Samogneux
Fismes
Jonchery-sur-Vesle
Pontfaverger-Moronvillers
Séchault
Montfaucon-d'Argonne
Aire
Meuse
Hartennes
Courville
Reims
Beine-Nauroy
Sommepy-Tahure
Varennes-en-Argonne
Fère-en-Tardenois
Souain
Argonne
Oulchy-le-Château
Mourmelon-le-Grand
Ville-sur-Tourbe
Verdun
Haudainville
Pourcy
Montagne de Reims
Verzy
Suippes
Clermont-en-Argonne
Livry-Louvercy
Louvois
Ste. Ménéhould
Dugny-sur-Meuse
Verneuil
Châtillon-sur-Marne
Somme-Tourbe
Trélou-sur-Marne
Ay
Condé-sur-Marne
La Cheppe
Souilly
Port-à-Binson
Dormans
Marne
Épernay
Châlons-en-Champagne
Tilloy Bellay
Dommartin
Isssoncourt
Triaucourt-en-Argonne
Condé-en-Brie
Igny-Comblizy
St. Martin-d'Ablois
Chouilly
Jâlons
Fagnières
Givry-en-Argonne
Rembercourt-aux-Pots
Chaumont-sur-Aire
Orbais
Mareuil-en-Brie
Avize
Le Mesnil-sur-Oger
CATHÉDRALE ST. ETIENNE
Marson
Sommeilles
Montmort-Lucy
Vertus
Thibie
Coupéville
Possesse
Laheycourt
Pierrefitte-sur-Aire
Vauchamps
Etoges
Vanault-les-Dames
Nettancourt
Montmirail
Champaubert
Bergères-lès-Vertus
Villeseneux
Soudron
Pogny
La Chaussée-sur-Marne
Revigny-sur-Ornain
Rumont
Le Gault-Soigny
Bannes
Vatry
Fontaine
Fains-Véel
Bar-le-Duc
Fère-Champenoise
Pargny-sur-Saulx
Sermaize-les-Bains
St. Aubin-sur-Aire
Sézanne
Connantre
Sommesous
Coole
Blacy
Vitry-le-François
Thiéblemont-Farémont
Brillon-en-Barrois
Ligny-en-Barrois
Esternay
Gourgançon
Sompuis
Stainville
Barbonne-Fayel
Pleurs
Mailly-le-Camp
Ancerville
Villiers-St. Georges
St. Dizier
St. Remy-en-Bouzemont
Villenauxe-la-Grande
Anglure
Plancy-l'Abbaye
Herbisse
Eclaron
Morley
Houdelaincourt
Lhuître
Lac du Der Chantecoq
Marcilly-sur-Seine
Aube
Margerie-Hancourt
Giffaumont-Champaubert
Romilly-sur-Seine
Arcis-sur-Aube
Vinets
Rachecourt-sur-Marne
Chevillon
Ramerupt
Wassy
Méry-sur-Seine
Chaudrey
Chavanges
Thonnance-les-Joinville
Pancey
Châtres
Montier-en-Der
Joinville
St. Martin-de-Bossenay
Voué
Lesmont
Poissons
Trainel
Savières
Brienne-le-Château
Doulevant-le-Château
Dommartin-le-Franc
Marigny-le-Châtel
Feuges
Lac du Temple
Piney
Soulaines-Dhuys
Doulaincourt-Saucourt
Marcilly-le-Hayer
Forêt d'Orient
Bercenay-le-Hayer
La Chapelle-St. Luc
Creney
Géraudot
Lac d'Orient
Vignory
St. Blin
Thorigny-sur-Oreuse
Ste. Savine
NIGLOLAND
Dolancourt
Estissac
Troyes
Lusigny-sur-Barse
Bar-sur-Aube
Andelot Blanchville
Villemaur-sur-Vanne
Bréviandes
Bucheres
Vendeuvre-sur-Barse
Colombey-les-deux-Églises
Briaucourt
Soucy
Villeneuve-l'Archevêque
Aix-en-Othe
Vauchassis
Bayel
Juzennecourt
Bologne
Burdons-sur-Rognon

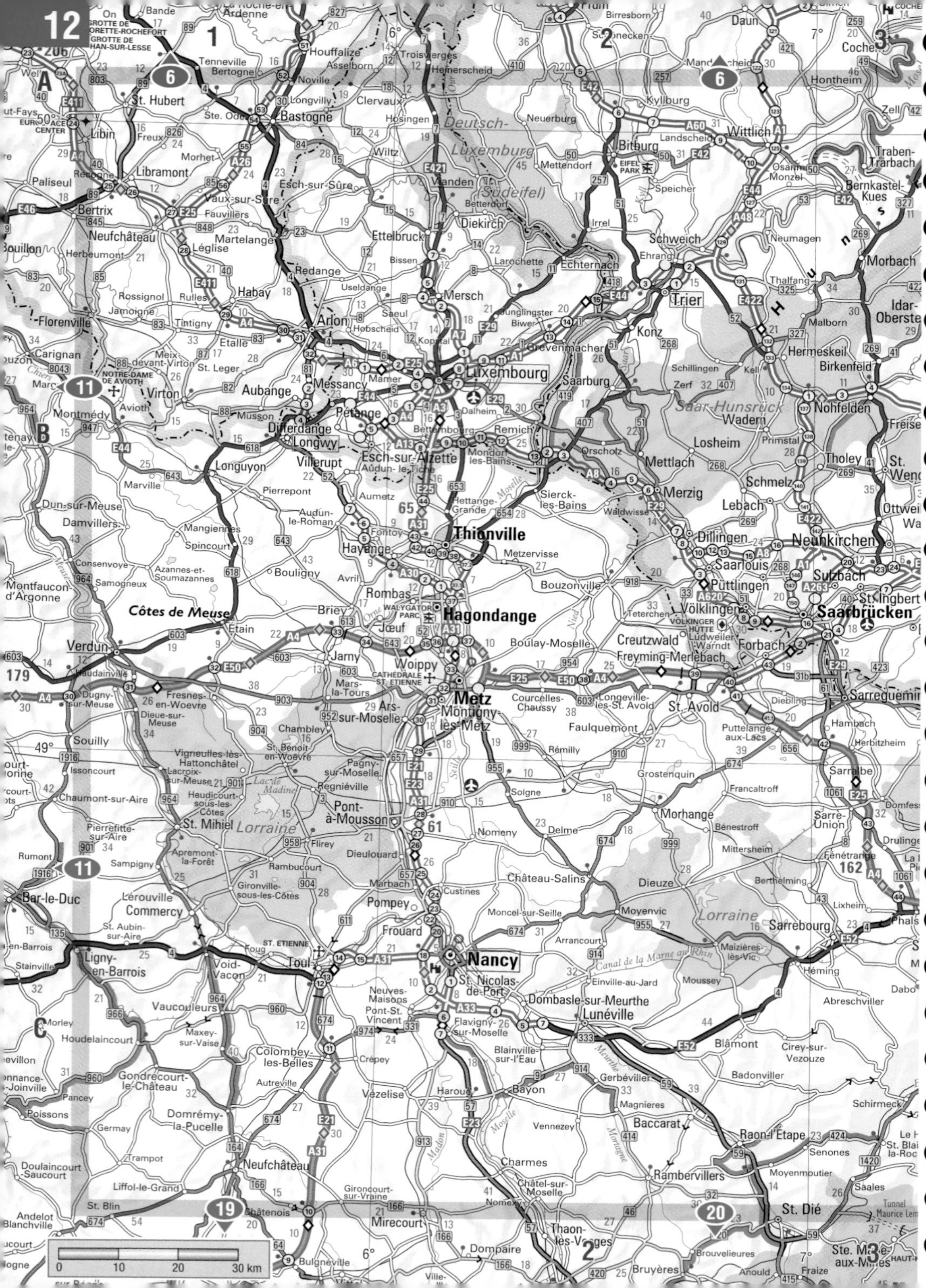
Houffalize
Bastogne
St. Hubert
Libin
Libramont
Paliseul
Bertrix
Neufchâteau
Bouillon
Herbeumont
Léglise
Martelange
Habay
Rossignol
Florenville
Carignan
Arlon
Tintigny
Etalle
Virton
Aubange
Messancy
Montmédy
Avioth
Longwy
Differdange
Pétange
Esch-sur-Alzette
Villerupt
Longuyon
Marville
Dun-sur-Meuse
Damvillers
Wiltz
Clervaux
Troisvierges
Vianden
Diekirch
Ettelbruck
Mersch
Redange
Luxembourg
Bettembourg
Mondorf-les-Bains
Remich
Grevenmacher
Echternach
Deutsch-Luxemburg
(Südeifel)
Bitburg
Daun
Wittlich
Kyllburg
Speicher
Schweich
Trier
Konz
Saarburg
Bernkastel-Kues
Traben-Trarbach
Morbach
Hermeskeil
Birkenfeld
Idar-Oberstein
Nohfelden
Saar-Hunsrück
Wadern
Losheim
Mettlach
Merzig
Lebach
Schmelz
Tholey
Dillingen
Saarlouis
Püttlingen
Völklingen
Neunkirchen
Sulzbach
Saarbrücken
St. Ingbert
Forbach
Creutzwald
Freyming-Merlebach
St. Avold
Sarreguemines
Puttelange-aux-Lacs
Sarralbe
Thionville
Hayange
Sierck-les-Bains
Bouzonville
Hagondange
Rombas
Briey
Jarny
Woippy
Metz
Montigny-lès-Metz
Boulay-Moselle
Faulquemont
Courcelles-Chaussy
Rémilly
Grostenquin
Morhange
Delme
Nomeny
Pont-à-Mousson
Château-Salins
Dieuze
Sarre-Union
Fénétrange
Sarrebourg
Lorraine
Étain
Côtes de Meuse
Verdun
Fresnes-en-Woëvre
Souilly
St. Mihiel
Lac de Madine
Commercy
Bar-le-Duc
Ligny-en-Barrois
Void-Vacon
Toul
Vaucouleurs
Pompey
Frouard
Nancy
St. Nicolas-de-Port
Dombasle-sur-Meurthe
Lunéville
Blâmont
Baccarat
Raon-l'Étape
Schirmeck
Senones
Moyenmoutier
St. Dié
Rambervillers
Charmes
Bayon
Vézelise
Colombey-les-Belles
Gondrecourt-le-Château
Domrémy-la-Pucelle
Neufchâteau
Mirecourt
Châtenois
Bulgnéville
Dompaire
Thaon-les-Vosges
Bruyères
Ste. Marie-aux-Mines
Fraize
0 10 20 30 km

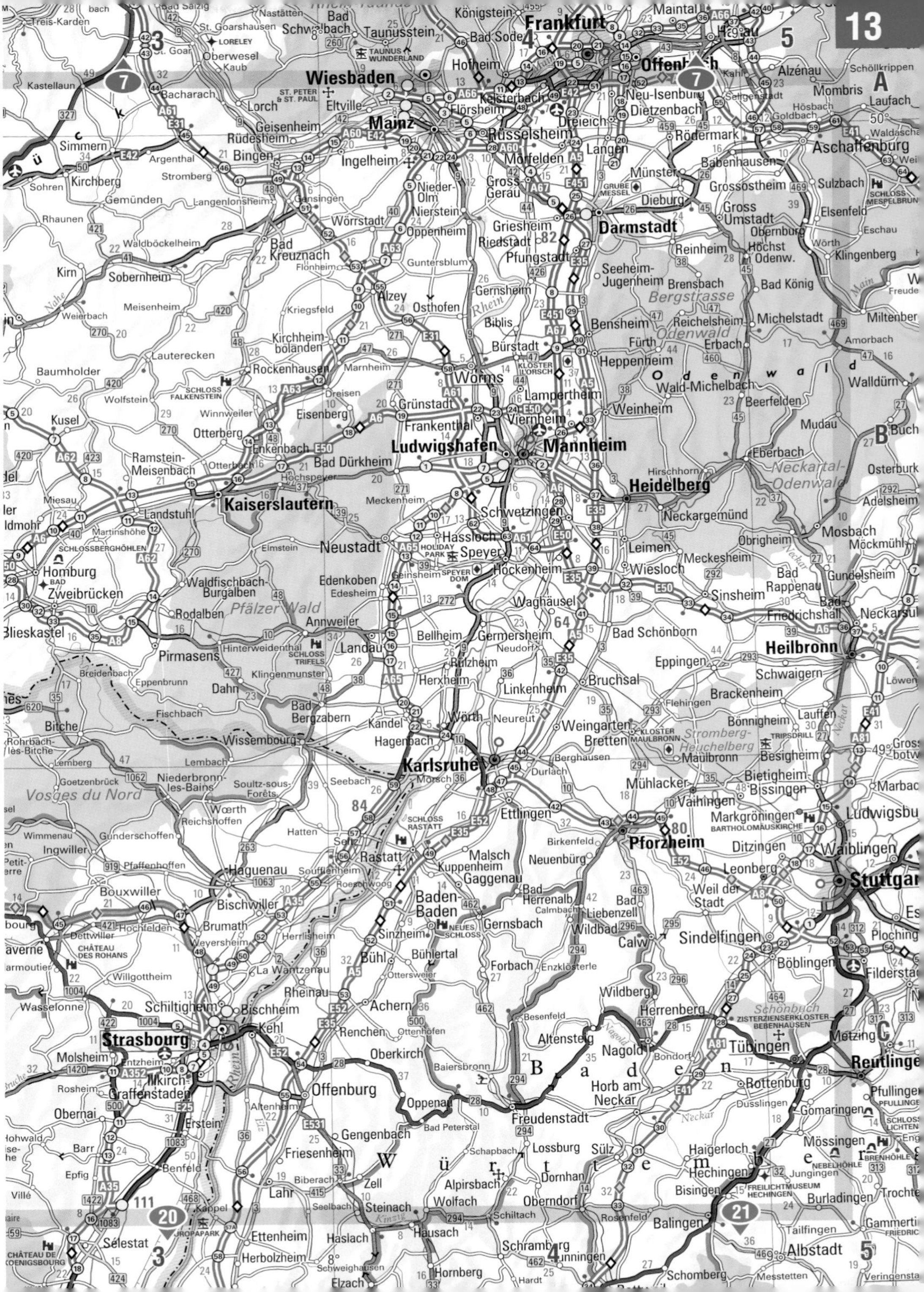
Treis-Karden
Bad Salzig
Nastätten
Bad Schwalbach
Taunusstein
Königstein
Frankfurt
Maintal
Hanau
St. Goarshausen
St. Goar
LORELEY
Oberwesel
Kaub
TAUNUS WUNDERLAND
Bad Soden
Offenbach
Kahl
Alzenau
Schöllkrippen
Kastellaun
Wiesbaden
Hofheim
ST. PETER & ST. PAUL
Bacharach
Lorch
Eltville
Kelsterbach
Flörsheim
Neu-Isenburg
Seligenstadt
Mombris
Laufach
Hösbach
Goldbach
Simmern
Geisenheim
Rüdesheim
Bingen
Mainz
Rüsselsheim
Dreieich
Dietzenbach
Rödermark
Langen
Aschaffenburg
Argenthal
Stromberg
Ingelheim
Mörfelden
Babenhausen
Kirchberg
Sohren
Gemünden
Langenlonsheim
Gensingen
Nieder-Olm
Nierstein
Gross Gerau
Münster
GRUBE MESSEL
Dieburg
Grossostheim
Sulzbach
SCHLOSS MESPELBRUNN
Elsenfeld
Eschau
Rhaunen
Wörrstadt
Oppenheim
Griesheim
Riedstadt
Darmstadt
Gross Umstadt
Obernburg
Höchst Odenw.
Wörth
Klingenberg
Waldböckelheim
Bad Kreuznach
Guntersblum
Pfungstadt
Reinheim
Kirn
Sobernheim
Flonheim
Seeheim-Jugenheim
Brensbach
Bad König
Alzey
Osthofen
Gernsheim
Bergstrasse
Nahe
Meisenheim
Kriegsfeld
Weierbach
Biblis
Bensheim
Reichelsheim
Michelstadt
Miltenberg
Kirchheimbolanden
Bürstadt
Fürth
Odenwald
Erbach
Amorbach
Lauterecken
Baumholder
Rockenhausen
Marnheim
Worms
KLOSTER LORSCH
Heppenheim
Odenwald
Walldürn
SCHLOSS FALKENSTEIN
Dreisen
Lampertheim
Wald-Michelbach
Beerfelden
Wolfstein
Grünstadt
Eisenberg
Kusel
Winnweiler
Frankenthal
Viernheim
Weinheim
Mudau
Otterberg
Enkenbach
Ludwigshafen
Mannheim
Ramstein-Meisenbach
Otterbach
Bad Dürkheim
Eberbach
Neckartal-Odenwald
Osterburken
Hochspeyer
Hirschhorn
Heidelberg
Miesau
Kaiserslautern
Meckenheim
Adelsheim
Landstuhl
Schwetzingen
Neckargemünd
Martinshöhe
Mosbach
SCHLOSSBERGHÖHLEN
Elmstein
Neustadt
Hassloch
HOLIDAY PARK
Speyer
Obrigheim
Leimen
Möckmühl
Homburg
SPEYER DOM
Hockenheim
Wiesloch
Meckesheim
Bad Rappenau
Gundelsheim
Waldfischbach-Burgalben
Edenkoben
Edesheim
Geinsheim
Bad Zweibrücken
Waghäusel
Sinsheim
Bad Friedrichshall
Neckarsulm
Pfälzer Wald
Rodalben
Annweiler
Blieskastel
Bellheim
Germersheim
Neudorf
Bad Schönborn
Heilbronn
Hinterweidenthal
SCHLOSS TRIFELS
Landau
Pirmasens
Rülzheim
Eppingen
Schwaigern
Breidenbach
Eppenbrunn
Dahn
Klingenmünster
Herxheim
Linkenheim
Bruchsal
Brackenheim
Bad Bergzabern
Fischbach
Flehingen
Bitche
Kandel
Wörth
Neureut
Weingarten
Bretten
KLOSTER MAULBRONN
Stromberg-Heuchelberg
Bönnigheim
Lauffen
TRIPSDRILL
Rohrbach-lès-Bitche
Wissembourg
Hagenbach
Lemberg
Lembach
Karlsruhe
Berghausen
Maulbronn
Besigheim
Goetzenbrück
Niederbronn-les-Bains
Soultz-sous-Forêts
Seebach
Mörsch
Durlach
Mühlacker
Bietigheim-Bissingen
Vosges du Nord
Wœrth
Reichshoffen
SCHLOSS RASTATT
Ettlingen
Vaihingen
Markgröningen
BARTHOLOMÄUSKIRCHE
Ludwigsburg
Wimmenau
Ingwiller
Gunderschoffen
Hatten
Selz
Birkenfeld
Pforzheim
Ditzingen
Waiblingen
Pfaffenhoffen
Haguenau
Soufflenheim
Rastatt
Malsch
Kuppenheim
Neuenbürg
Leonberg
Roeschwoog
Gaggenau
Stuttgart
Bouxwiller
Bischwiller
Baden-Baden
Bad Herrenalb
Calmbach
Bad Liebenzell
Weil der Stadt
Dettwiller
Hochfelden
Brumath
Herrlisheim
NEUES SCHLOSS
Gernsbach
Wildbad
Calw
Sindelfingen
Plochingen
CHÂTEAU DES ROHANS
Weyersheim
Sinzheim
Bühlertal
Böblingen
Filderstadt
Saverne
Marmoutier
Willgottheim
La Wantzenau
Bühl
Ottersweier
Forbach
Enzklösterle
Wildberg
Rheinau
Achern
Wasselonne
Schiltigheim
Bischheim
Kehl
Herrenberg
Schönbuch
ZISTERZIENSERKLOSTER BEBENHAUSEN
Strasbourg
Renchen
Ottenhofen
Besenfeld
Altensteig
Nagold
Tübingen
Metzingen
Molsheim
Entzheim
Illkirch-Graffenstaden
Oberkirch
Baiersbronn
Baden
Bondorf
Rottenburg
Reutlingen
Rosheim
Offenburg
Horb am Neckar
Pfullingen
PFULLINGEN
Obernai
Erstein
Altenheim
Oppenau
Bad Peterstal
Freudenstadt
Dusslingen
Gomaringen
SCHLOSS LICHTENSTEIN
Hohwald
Barr
Gengenbach
Friesenheim
Schapbach
Lossburg
Sülz
Haigerloch
Mössingen
BRENHÖHLE
NEBELHÖHLE
Württemberg
Epfig
Benfeld
Biberach
Zell
Alpirsbach
Dornhan
Hechingen
Jungingen
Villé
Lahr
Seelbach
Steinach
Wolfach
Oberndorf
Bisingen
FREILICHTMUSEUM HECHINGEN
Burladingen
Trochtelfingen
Kappel
EUROPAPARK
Kinzig
Schiltach
Rosenfeld
Balingen
Gammertingen
Sélestat
Ettenheim
Haslach
Hausach
Tailfingen
CHÂTEAU DE KOENIGSBOURG
Herbolzheim
Schramberg
Dunningen
Albstadt
Schweighausen
Hornberg
Schömberg
Messtetten
Elzach
Hardt
Veringenstadt

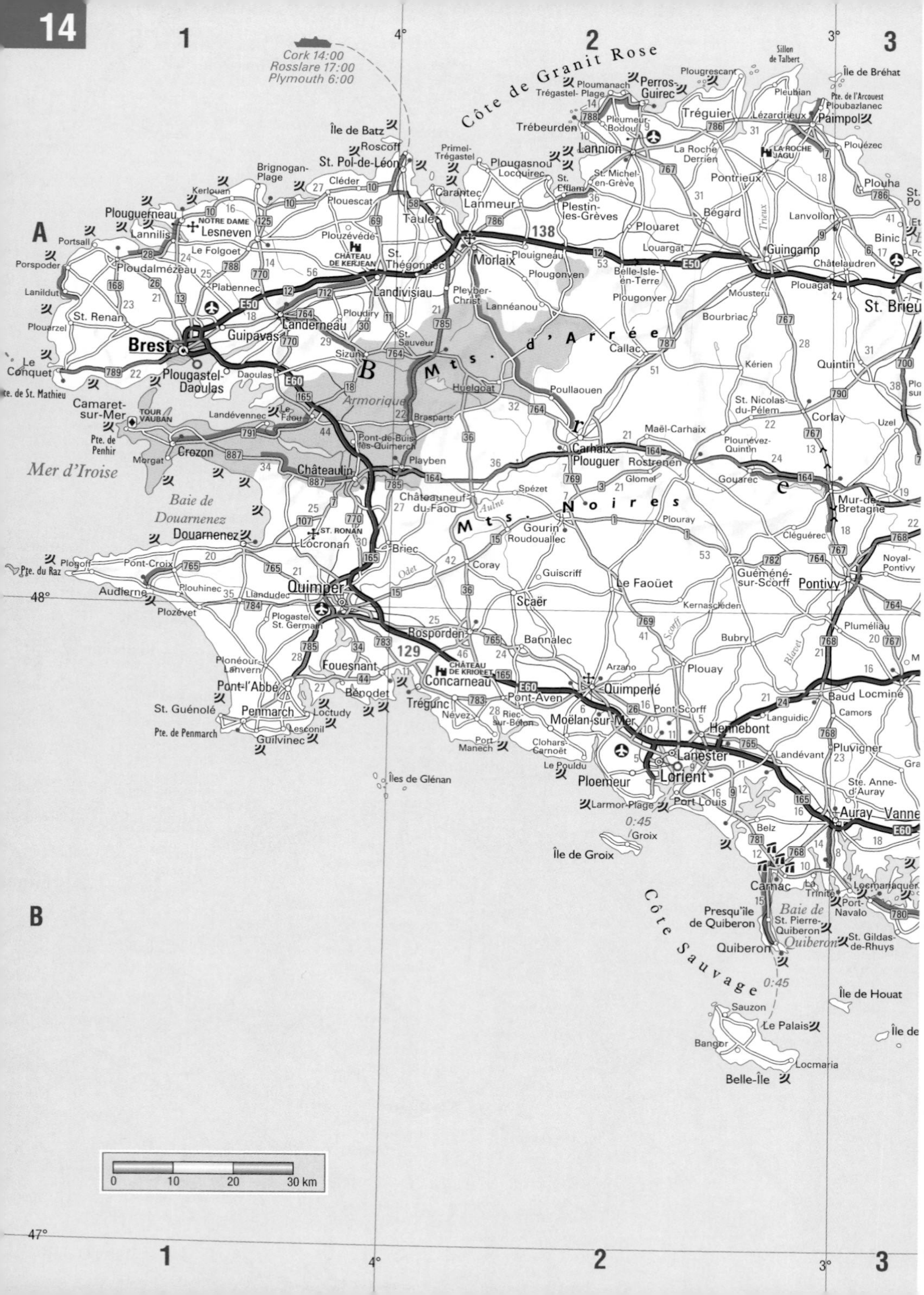

1
2
3
A
B
4°
3°
48°
47°
Cork 14:00
Rosslare 17:00
Plymouth 6:00
Côte de Granit Rose
Sillon de Talbert
Île de Bréhat
Pte. de l'Arcouest
Ploubazlanec
Paimpol
Plougrescant
Pleubian
Lézardrieux
Tréguier
Perros-Guirec
Ploumanach
Trégastel-Plage
Trébeurden
Pleumeur-Bodou
Lannion
La Roche Derrien
LA ROCHE JAGU
Plouézec
Plouha
Île de Batz
Roscoff
St. Pol-de-Léon
Primel-Trégastel
Plougasnou
Locquirec
St. Efflam
St. Michel-en-Grève
Pontrieux
Brignogan-Plage
Kerlouan
Cléder
Plouescat
Carantec
Lanmeur
Plestin-les-Grèves
Plouaret
Bégard
Lanvollon
Plouguerneau
NOTRE DAME
Lesneven
Lannilis
Portsall
Porspoder
Le Folgoet
Plouzévédé
CHÂTEAU DE KERJEAN
Taulé
Morlaix
Plouigneau
Louargat
Guingamp
Binic
Châtelaudren
Plouagat
St. Brieuc
Ploudalmézeau
Plabennec
St. Thégonnec
Landivisiau
Pleyber-Christ
Lannéanou
Plougonven
Belle-Isle-en-Terre
Plougonver
Mousteru
Bourbriac
Lanildut
St. Renan
Plouarzel
Brest
Guipavas
Landerneau
Ploudiry
St. Sauveur
Sizun
Mts. d'Arrée
Callac
Kérien
Quintin
Le Conquet
Pte. de St. Mathieu
Plougastel-Daoulas
Daoulas
Huelgoat
Poullaouen
Armorique
Camaret-sur-Mer
TOUR VAUBAN
Pte. de Penhir
Landévennec
Le Faou
Brasparts
Pont-de-Buis-lès-Quimerch
Carhaix-Plouguer
Maël-Carhaix
St. Nicolas-du-Pélem
Corlay
Uzel
Plounévez-Quintin
Rostrenen
Glomel
Gouarec
Mur-de-Bretagne
Crozon
Morgat
Mer d'Iroise
Châteaulin
Playben
Spézet
Châteauneuf-du-Faou
Aulne
Mts. Noires
Plouray
Cléguérec
Noyal-Pontivy
Baie de Douarnenez
Douarnenez
ST. RONAN
Locronan
Briec
Gourin
Roudouallec
Plogoff
Pte. du Raz
Pont-Croix
Audierne
Plouhinec
Coray
Guiscriff
Le Faoüet
Guémené-sur-Scorff
Pontivy
Odet
Quimper
Plozévet
Llandudec
Plogastel-St. Germain
Scaër
Kernascléden
Rosporden
Bannalec
Bubry
Pluméliau
Plonéour-Lanvern
Fouesnant
CHÂTEAU DE KRIOLET
Concarneau
Arzano
Quimperlé
Plouay
Scorff
Blavet
Pont-l'Abbé
Bénodet
Trégunc
Pont-Aven
Baud
Locminé
Camors
St. Guénolé
Penmarch
Loctudy
Pte. de Penmarch
Lesconil
Guilvinec
Névez
Riec-sur-Belon
Moëlan-sur-Mer
Pont Scorff
Languidic
Hennebont
Port Manech
Clohars-Carnoët
Lanester
Landévant
Pluvigner
Le Pouldu
Îles de Glénan
Ploemeur
Lorient
Port Louis
Larmor-Plage
Ste. Anne-d'Auray
Auray
Vannes
0:45
Groix
Île de Groix
Belz
Carnac
La Trinité
Locmariaquer
Côte Sauvage
Presqu'île de Quiberon
St. Pierre-Quiberon
Baie de Quiberon
Port-Navalo
St. Gildas-de-Rhuys
Quiberon
Île de Houat
Sauzon
Le Palais
Bangor
Locmaria
Belle-Île
Île de
E50
E60
138
129
0
10
20
30 km

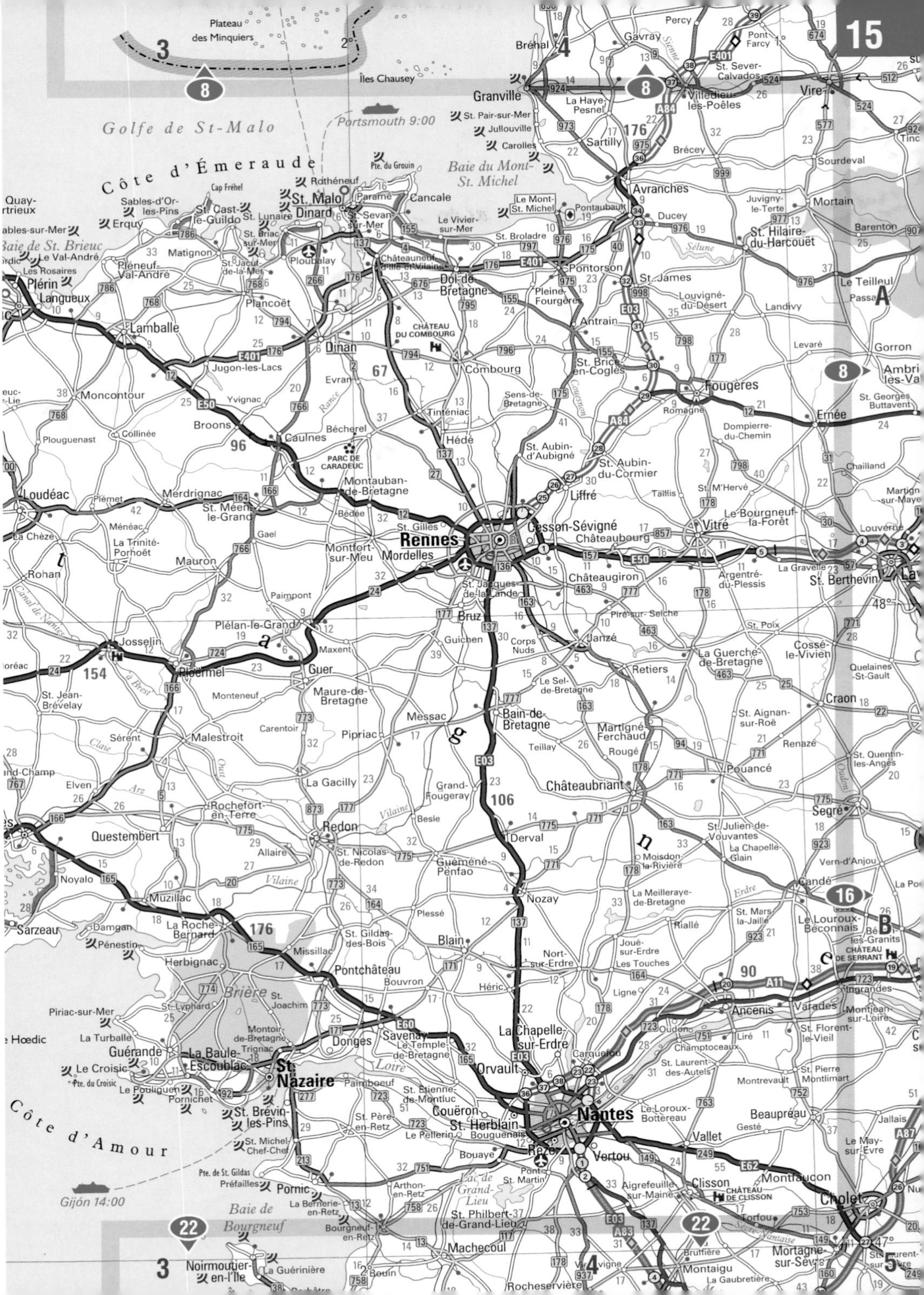

Plateau des Minquiers
Îles Chausey
Golfe de St-Malo
Portsmouth 9:00
Côte d'Émeraude
Baie du Mont-St. Michel
Granville
St. Pair-sur-Mer
Jullouville
Carolles
Bréhal
Gavray
Percy
Pont Farcy
St. Sever-Calvados
Villedieu-les-Poêles
La Haye-Pesnel
Sartilly
Brécey
Vire
Sourdeval
Mortain
Juvigny-le-Tertre
Avranches
Ducey
Le Mont-St. Michel
Pontaubault
St. Hilaire-du-Harcouët
Barenton
Le Teilleul
Passa
Pontorson
St. James
Louvigné-du-Désert
Landivy
Antrain
St. Brice-en-Coglès
Fougères
Romagné
Levaré
Gorron
Ambri les-Va
St. Georges Buttavent
Ernée
Pte. du Grouin
Rothéneuf
Cancale
St. Malo
Paramé
Dinard
St. Lunaire
St. Servan-sur-Mer
Le Vivier-sur-Mer
St. Broladre
Cap Fréhel
Sables-d'Or-les-Pins
St. Cast-le-Guildo
Erquy
Baie de St. Brieuc
Le Val-André
Les Rosaires
Pléneuf-Val-André
Matignon
St. Jacut-de-la-Mer
St. Briac-sur-Mer
Ploubalay
Châteauneuf-d'Ille-et-Vilaine
Dol-de-Bretagne
Pleine-Fougères
Plérin
Langueux
Plancoët
Lamballe
Dinan
Château du Combourg
Combourg
Jugon-les-Lacs
Evran
Moncontour
Yvignac
Broons
Tinténiac
Sens-de-Bretagne
Hédé
Bécherel
Parc de Caradeuc
Caulnes
Plouguenast
Collinée
St. Aubin-d'Aubigné
St. Aubin-du-Cormier
Dompierre-du-Chemin
Chailland
Loudéac
Merdrignac
St. Méen-le-Grand
Montauban-de-Bretagne
Liffré
St. M'Hervé
Martign-sur-Maye
Plémet
Ménéac
La Trinité-Porhoët
La Chèze
Bédée
St. Gilles
Rennes
Cesson-Sévigné
Châteaubourg
Vitré
Le Bourgneuf-la-Forêt
Louverné
Gael
Montfort-sur-Meu
Mordelles
Mauron
Rohan
Châteaugiron
Argentré-du-Plessis
La Gravelle
St. Berthevin
Paimpont
St. Jacques-de-la-Lande
Bruz
Piré-sur-Seiche
Janzé
Plélan-le-Grand
Josselin
Ploërmel
Guer
Maxent
Guichen
Corps-Nuds
La Guerche-de-Bretagne
Cossé-le-Vivien
St. Poix
Retiers
Quelaines-St-Gault
St. Jean-Brévelay
Monteneuf
Maure-de-Bretagne
Le Sel-de-Bretagne
Craon
Messac
Bain-de-Bretagne
Martigné-Ferchaud
St. Aignan-sur-Roë
Sérent
Malestroit
Carentoir
Pipriac
Teillay
Rougé
Renazé
St. Quentin-les-Anges
Elven
La Gacilly
Grand-Fougeray
Châteaubriant
Pouancé
Rochefort-en-Terre
Questembert
Redon
Besle
Derval
Segré
St. Nicolas-de-Redon
Allaire
Guémené-Penfao
St. Julien-de-Vouvantes
La Chapelle-Glain
Moisdon-la-Rivière
Vern-d'Anjou
Noyalo
Muzillac
Nozay
La Meilleraye-de-Bretagne
Candé
Sarzeau
Damgan
Pénestin
La Roche-Bernard
Plessé
St. Gildas-des-Bois
Blain
Riaillé
St. Mars-la-Jaillé
Le Louroux-Béconnais
Château de Serrant
Herbignac
Missillac
Pontchâteau
Bouvron
Nort-sur-Erdre
Joué-sur-Erdre
Les Touches
Héric
Ligné
Ancenis
Varades
Ingrandes
Brière
St. Lyphard
St. Joachim
Piriac-sur-Mer
La Turballe
Montoir-de-Bretagne
Trignac
Donges
Savenay
Le Temple-de-Bretagne
La Chapelle-sur-Erdre
Oudon
Liré
Montjean-sur-Loire
St. Florent-le-Vieil
Hoedic
Guérande
La Baule-Escoublac
Le Croisic
Pte. du Croisic
Le Pouliguen
Pornichet
St. Nazaire
Paimboeuf
St. Etienne-de-Montluc
Orvault
Carquefou
Champtoceaux
St. Laurent-des-Autels
Montrevault
St. Pierre Montlimart
Côte d'Amour
St. Brévin-les-Pins
St. Père-en-Retz
Couëron
St. Herblain
Nantes
Le Loroux-Bottereau
Beaupréau
Gesté
Jallais
St. Michel-Chef-Chef
Le Pellerin
Bouguenais
Rezé
Vertou
Vallet
Le May-sur-Evre
Bouaye
Pont-St. Martin
Aigrefeuille-sur-Maine
Clisson
Château de Clisson
Montfaucon
Cholet
Pte. de St. Gildas
Préfailles
Pornic
Arthon-en-Retz
Lac de Grand-Lieu
Gijón 14:00
Baie de Bourgneuf
La Bernerie-en-Retz
Bourgneuf-en-Retz
St. Philbert-de-Grand-Lieu
Machecoul
Torfou
Mortagne-sur-Sèvre
Noirmoutier-en-l'Île
La Guérinière
Bouin
Rocheservière
Montaigu
La Gaubretière
Vieillevigne
Canal de Nantes à Brest
Vilaine
Loire
Erdre
Oust
Rance
Sélune
Couesnon
Oudon
Sèvre Nantaise

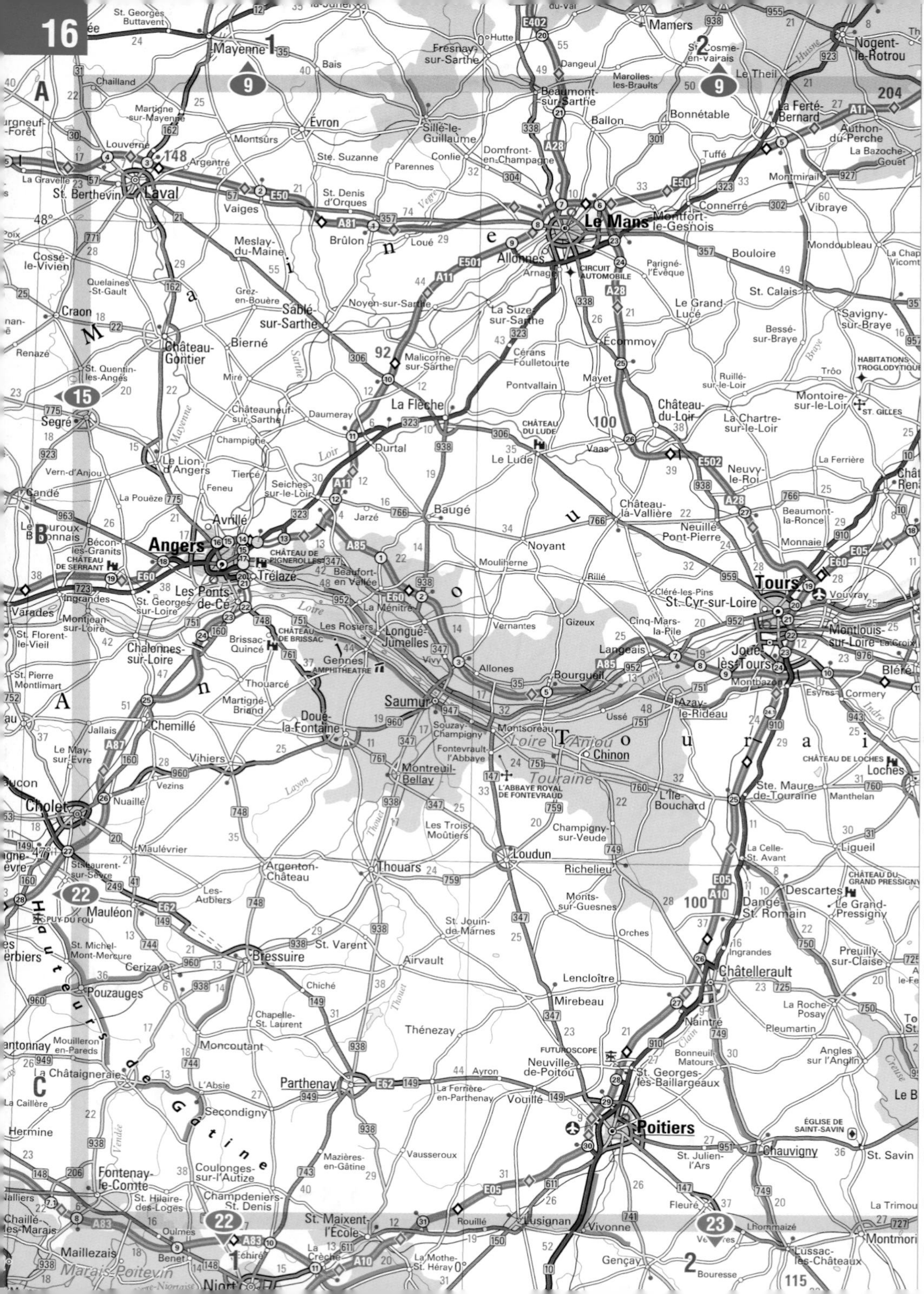
St. Georges Buttavent
Mayenne
Hutte
Fresnay-sur-Sarthe
Mamers
St. Cosme-en-vairais
Nogent-le-Rotrou
Bais
Chailland
Dangeul
Marolles-les-Braults
Le Theil
Beaumont-sur-Sarthe
Martigné-sur-Mayenne
Évron
Sillé-le-Guillaume
Ballon
Bonnétable
La Ferté-Bernard
Authon-du-Perche
Montsûrs
Louverné
Ste. Suzanne
Conlie
Domfront-en-Champagne
Tuffé
La Bazoche-Gouet
Argentré
Parennes
Montmirail
La Gravelle
St. Berthevin
Laval
Vaiges
St. Denis d'Orques
Connerré
Vibraye
Le Mans
Montfort-le-Gesnois
Brûlon
Loué
Meslay-du-Maine
Cossé-le-Vivien
Allonnes
Arnage
CIRCUIT AUTOMOBILE
Parigné-l'Évêque
Bouloire
Mondoubleau
Quelaines-St-Gault
Grez-en-Bouère
St. Calais
Craon
Sablé-sur-Sarthe
Noyen-sur-Sarthe
La Suze-sur-Sarthe
Le Grand-Lucé
Savigny-sur-Braye
Bessé-sur-Braye
Château-Gontier
Bierné
Écommoy
Renazé
Malicorne-sur-Sarthe
Cérans Foulletourte
St. Quentin-les-Anges
Miré
HABITATIONS TROGLODYTIQUES
Trôo
Ruillé-sur-le-Loir
Pontvallain
Mayet
Montoire-sur-le-Loir
ST. GILLES
Segré
Châteauneuf-sur-Sarthe
Daumeray
La Flèche
CHÂTEAU DU LUDE
Château-du-Loir
La Chartre-sur-le-Loir
Champigné
Durtal
Le Lude
Vaas
Le Lion-d'Angers
Vern-d'Anjou
Tiercé
La Ferrière
Neuvy-le-Roi
Seiches-sur-le-Loir
Feneu
Candé
La Pouëze
Baugé
Jarzé
Château-la-Vallière
Beaumont-la-Ronce
Avrillé
Neuillé-Pont-Pierre
Noyant
Monnaie
Angers
Bécon-les-Granits
CHÂTEAU DE SERRANT
CHÂTEAU DE PIGNEROLLES
Beaufort-en Vallée
Mouliherne
Rillé
Trélazé
Tours
Vouvray
Les Ponts-de-Cé
Ingrandes
St. Georges-sur-Loire
Cléré-les-Pins
St.-Cyr-sur-Loire
Varades
La Ménitré
Montjean-sur-Loire
Les Rosiers
Vernantes
Gizeux
Cinq-Mars-la-Pile
Montlouis-sur-Loire
St. Florent-le-Vieil
CHÂTEAU DE BRISSAC
Brissac-Quincé
Longué-Jumelles
Langeais
Joué-lès-Tours
Chalonnes-sur-Loire
Gennes
AMPHITHÉÂTRE
Vivy
Allonnes
Bourgueil
Bléré
St. Pierre Montlimart
Thouarcé
Montbazon
Esvres
Cormery
Martigné-Briand
Saumur
Azay-le-Rideau
Doué-la-Fontaine
Souzay-Champigny
Ussé
Chemillé
Jallais
Montsoreau
Loire
Anjou
Chinon
Le May-sur-Èvre
Vihiers
Fontevrault-l'Abbaye
CHÂTEAU DE LOCHES
Loches
Montreuil-Bellay
Touraine
Cholet
Vezins
Nuaillé
L'ABBAYE ROYAL DE FONTEVRAUD
L'Ile-Bouchard
Ste. Maure-de-Touraine
Manthelan
Les Trois-Moûtiers
Champigny-sur-Veude
Maulévrier
Loudun
Ligueil
La Celle-St. Avant
St. Laurent-sur-Sèvre
Argenton-Château
Thouars
Richelieu
CHÂTEAU DU GRAND PRESSIGNY
Les Aubiers
Monts-sur-Guesnes
Descartes
Mauléon
PUY DU FOU
Dangé-St. Romain
Le Grand-Pressigny
St. Jouin-de-Marnes
St. Michel-Mont-Mercure
St. Varent
Orches
Ingrandes
Preuilly-sur-Claise
Cerizay
Bressuire
Airvault
Châtellerault
Pouzauges
Chiché
Lencloître
La Roche-Posay
Mirebeau
Chapelle-St. Laurent
Thénezay
Naintré
Pleumartin
Moncoutant
Mouilleron en-Pareds
FUTUROSCOPE
Bonneuil-Matours
Angles sur l'Anglin
La Châtaigneraie
Ayron
Neuville-de-Poitou
St. Georges-lès-Baillargeaux
L'Absie
Parthenay
La Ferrière-en-Parthenay
Vouillé
La Caillère
Secondigny
Poitiers
Le B
Hermine
ÉGLISE DE SAINT-SAVIN
Chauvigny
St. Savin
St. Julien-l'Ars
Vasseroux
Mazières-en-Gâtine
Coulonges-sur-l'Autize
Fontenay-le-Comte
St. Hilaire-des-Loges
Champdeniers-St. Denis
Fleuré
La Trimouille
Chaillé-les-Marais
Oulmes
St. Maixent-l'École
Rouillé
Lusignan
Vivonne
Lhommaizé
Montmori
Maillezais
Benet
Échiré
La Crèche
La Mothe-St. Héray
Gençay
Lussac-les-Châteaux
Bouresse
Marais Poitevin
Niort
Hauteurs de Gâtine
Maine
Anjou
Touraine

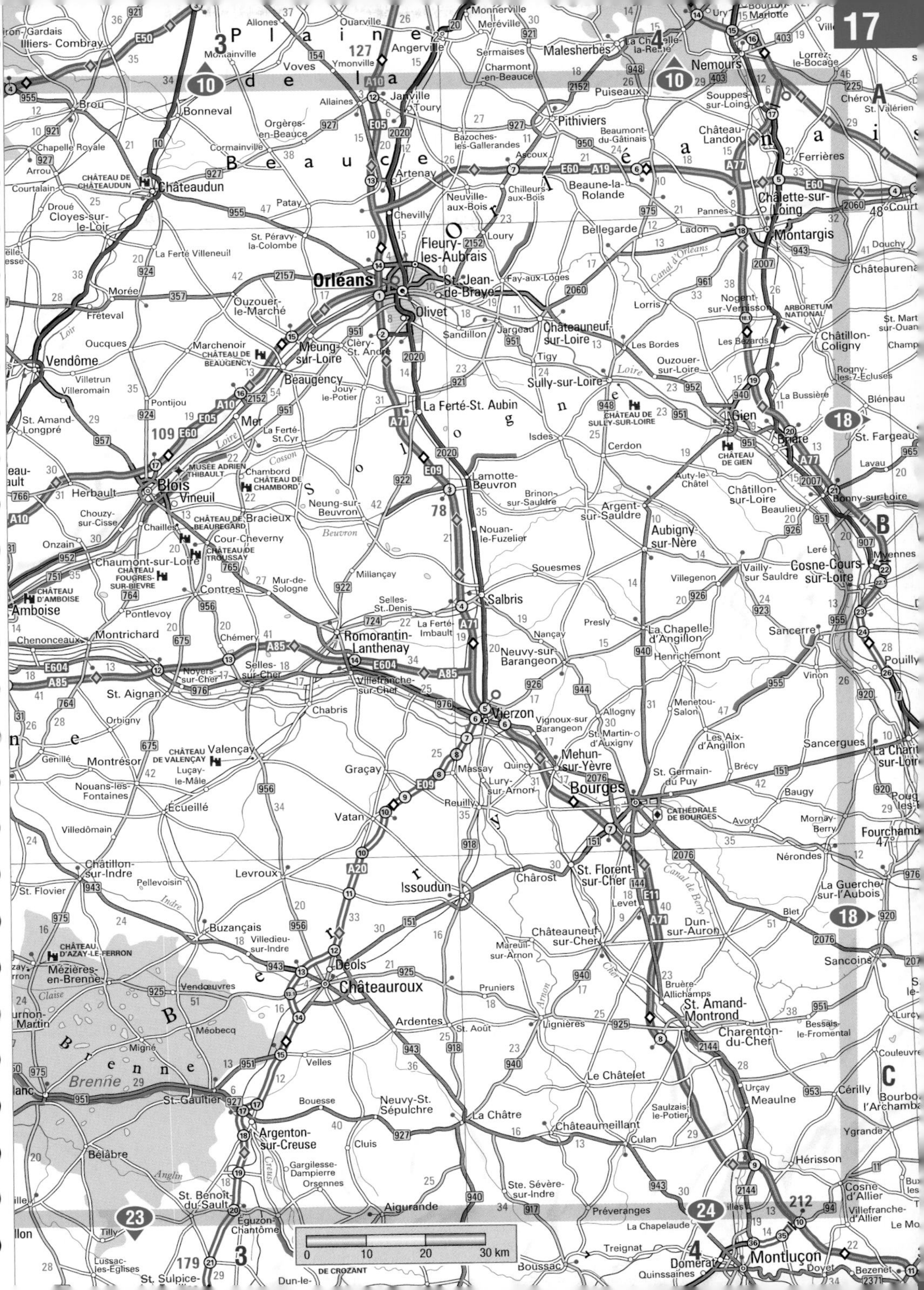
Plaine de la Beauce
Beauce
Orléans
Fleury-les-Aubrais
St. Jean-de-Braye
Olivet
Sologne
Berry
Brenne
Gâtinais
Châteaudun
CHÂTEAU DE CHÂTEAUDUN
Illiers-Combray
Bonneval
Brou
Cloyes-sur-le-Loir
Vendôme
Montargis
Châlette-sur-Loing
Pithiviers
Malesherbes
Nemours
Puiseaux
Beaune-la-Rolande
Bellegarde
Lorris
Châteauneuf-sur-Loire
Meung-sur-Loire
Beaugency
CHÂTEAU DE BEAUGENCY
Sully-sur-Loire
CHÂTEAU DE SULLY-SUR-LOIRE
Gien
CHÂTEAU DE GIEN
Briare
Blois
MUSÉE ADRIEN THIBAULT
CHÂTEAU DE CHAMBORD
CHÂTEAU DE BEAUREGARD
CHÂTEAU DE TROUSSAY
CHÂTEAU FOUGRES-SUR-BIEVRE
CHÂTEAU D'AMBOISE
Amboise
Chaumont-sur-Loire
Cour-Cheverny
Contres
Montrichard
Chenonceaux
La Ferté-St. Aubin
Lamotte-Beuvron
Nouan-le-Fuzelier
Salbris
Romorantin-Lanthenay
Selles-sur-Cher
St. Aignan
Vierzon
Mehun-sur-Yèvre
Bourges
CATHÉDRALE DE BOURGES
Aubigny-sur-Nère
Argent-sur-Sauldre
Cosne-Cours-sur-Loire
Sancerre
La Charité-sur-Loire
CHÂTEAU DE VALENÇAY
Valençay
Vatan
Issoudun
Levroux
Buzançais
CHÂTEAU D'AZAY-LE-FERRON
Mézières-en-Brenne
Châteauroux
Déols
Argenton-sur-Creuse
La Châtre
St. Amand-Montrond
Dun-sur-Auron
Sancoins
Châteaumeillant
Montluçon
Cosne-d'Allier
Aigurande
St. Benoît-du-Sault
ARBORETUM NATIONAL
Canal d'Orléans
Canal de Berry
Loire
Cher
Indre
Creuse
Beuvron
Cosson
A10
A71
A19
A20
A77
A85
E09
E11
E05
E60
E604
E50
0 10 20 30 km

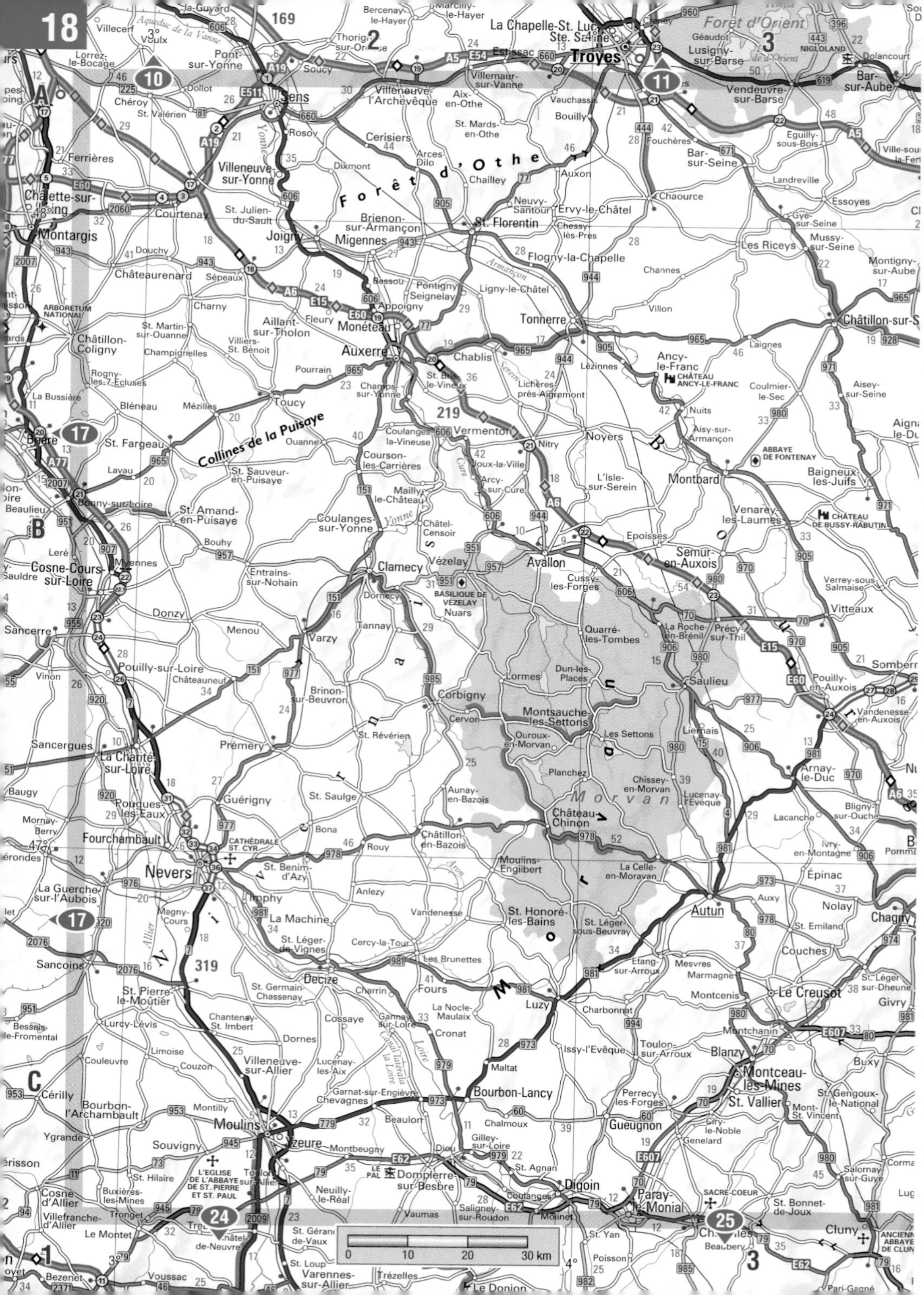
Troyes
La Chapelle-St. Luc
Ste. Savine
Forêt d'Orient
Géaudot
Lusigny-sur-Barse
Nigloland
Dolancourt
Bar-sur-Aube
Vendeuvre-sur-Barse
Estissac
Villemaur-sur-Vanne
Bercenay-le-Hayer
Marcilly-le-Hayer
Thorigny-sur-Oreuse
Soucy
Sens
Villeneuve-l'Archevêque
Aix-en-Othe
Vauchassis
Bouilly
St. Mards-en-Othe
Cerisiers
Arces-Dilo
Dixmont
Rosoy
Forêt d'Othe
Chailley
Auxon
Fouchères
Bar-sur-Seine
Eguilly-sous-Bois
Ville-sous-la-Ferté
Landreville
Chaource
Essoyes
Gyé-sur-Seine
Mussy-sur-Seine
Les Riceys
Montigny-sur-Aube
Villecerf
Voulx
Lorrez-le-Bocage
Pont-sur-Yonne
Dollot
Chéroy
St. Valérien
Ferrières
Villeneuve-sur-Yonne
Châlette-sur-Loing
Montargis
Courtenay
St. Julien-du-Sault
Joigny
Brienon-sur-Armançon
Migennes
St. Florentin
Neuvy-Santour
Ervy-le-Châtel
Chessy-lès-Pres
Flogny-la-Chapelle
Channes
Douchy
Châteaurenard
Sépeaux
Charny
Bassou
Pontigny
Seignelay
Appoigny
Ligny-le-Châtel
Tonnerre
Villon
Châtillon-sur-Seine
Laignes
Arboretum National
Châtillon-Coligny
St. Martin-sur-Ouanne
Aillant-sur-Tholon
Fleury
Monéteau
Villiers-St. Benoit
Champignelles
Auxerre
Chablis
St. Bris-le-Vineux
Lichères-près-Aigremont
Lézinnes
Ancy-le-Franc
Château Ancy-le-Franc
Coulmier-le-Sec
Aisey-sur-Seine
Rogny-les-7-Écluses
Pourrain
Champs-sur-Yonne
La Bussière
Bléneau
Mézilles
Toucy
Nuits
Aisy-sur-Armançon
Briare
St. Fargeau
Collines de la Puisaye
Ouanne
Coulanges-la-Vineuse
Vermenton
Nitry
Noyers
Abbaye de Fontenay
Aignay-le-Duc
Lavau
St. Sauveur-en-Puisaye
Courson-les-Carrières
Joux-la-Ville
Arcy-sur-Cure
L'Isle-sur-Serein
Montbard
Baigneux-les-Juifs
Bonny-sur-Loire
St. Amand-en-Puisaye
Mailly-le-Château
Châtel-Censoir
Venarey-les-Laumes
Château de Bussy-Rabutin
Coulanges-sur-Yonne
Epoisses
Semur-en-Auxois
Verrey-sous-Salmaise
Leré
Myennes
Cosne-Cours-sur-Loire
Bouhy
Entrains-sur-Nohain
Clamecy
Vézelay
Avallon
Cussy-les-Forges
Basilique de Vézelay
Dornecy
Nuars
Vitteaux
Sancerre
Donzy
Menou
Tannay
Varzy
Quarré-les-Tombes
La Roche-en-Brénil
Précy-sous-Thil
Pouilly-sur-Loire
Vinon
Châteauneuf
Brinon-sur-Beuvron
Corbigny
Lormes
Dun-les-Places
Saulieu
Sombernon
Pouilly-en-Auxois
Vandenesse-en-Auxois
Cervon
Montsauche-les-Settons
Les Settons
Ouroux-en-Morvan
Liernais
Sancergues
La Charité-sur-Loire
Prémery
St. Révérien
Planchez
Arnay-le-Duc
Baugy
Pougues-les-Eaux
Guérigny
St. Saulge
Aunay-en-Bazois
Chissey-en-Morvan
Lucenay-l'Evêque
Morvan
Château-Chinon
Lacanche
Bligny-sur-Ouche
Mornay-Berry
Fourchambault
Cathédrale St. Cyr
Bona
Rouy
Châtillon-en-Bazois
Ivry-en-Montagne
Nevers
St. Benim-d'Azy
Moulins-Engilbert
La Celle-en-Moravan
Épinac
La Guerche-sur-l'Aubois
Imphy
Anlezy
Autun
Auxy
Nolay
Chagny
Magny-Cours
La Machine
Vandenesse
St. Honoré-les-Bains
St. Léger-sous-Beuvray
St. Emiland
St. Léger-de-Vignes
Cercy-la-Tour
Couches
Sancoins
Les Brunettes
Etang-sur-Arroux
Mesvres
Marmagne
St. Pierre-le-Moûtier
Decize
St. Germain-Chassenay
Charrin
Fours
Luzy
Montcenis
Le Creusot
St. Léger-sur-Dheune
Givry
Bessais-le-Fromental
Lurcy-Lévis
Chantenay-St. Imbert
Cossaye
Gannay-sur-Loire
La Nocle-Maulaix
Cronat
Charbonnat
Montchanin
Dornes
Issy-l'Evêque
Toulon-sur-Arroux
Blanzy
Couleuvre
Limoise
Couzon
Villeneuve-sur-Allier
Lucenay-les-Aix
Maltat
Montceau-les-Mines
Buxy
Cérilly
Bourbon-l'Archambault
Montilly
Garnat-sur-Engièvre
Chevagnes
Bourbon-Lancy
Perrecy-les-Forges
St. Vallier
Mont-St. Vincent
St. Gengoux-le-National
Moulins
Yzeure
Beaulon
Chalmoux
Gueugnon
Genelard
Ygrande
Souvigny
Montbeugny
Gilley-sur-Loire
Diou
St. Agnan
Cirey-le-Noble
St. Hilaire
L'Eglise de l'Abbaye de St. Pierre et St. Paul
Toulon-sur-Allier
Le Pal
Dompierre-sur-Besbre
Digoin
Paray-le-Monial
Salornay-sur-Guye
Cosne-d'Allier
Buxières-les-Mines
Neuilly-le-Réal
Coulanges
Sacre-Coeur
St. Bonnet-de-Joux
Villefranche-d'Allier
Tronget
Vaumas
Saligny-sur-Roudon
Molinet
Charolles
Le Montet
St. Gérand-de-Vaux
St. Yan
Beaubery
Cluny
Ancienne Abbaye de Cluny
Châtel-de-Neuvre
St. Loup
Poisson
Bezenet
Voussac
Varennes-sur-Allier
Trézelles
Le Donjon
Paris-Gagné
0
10
20
30 km

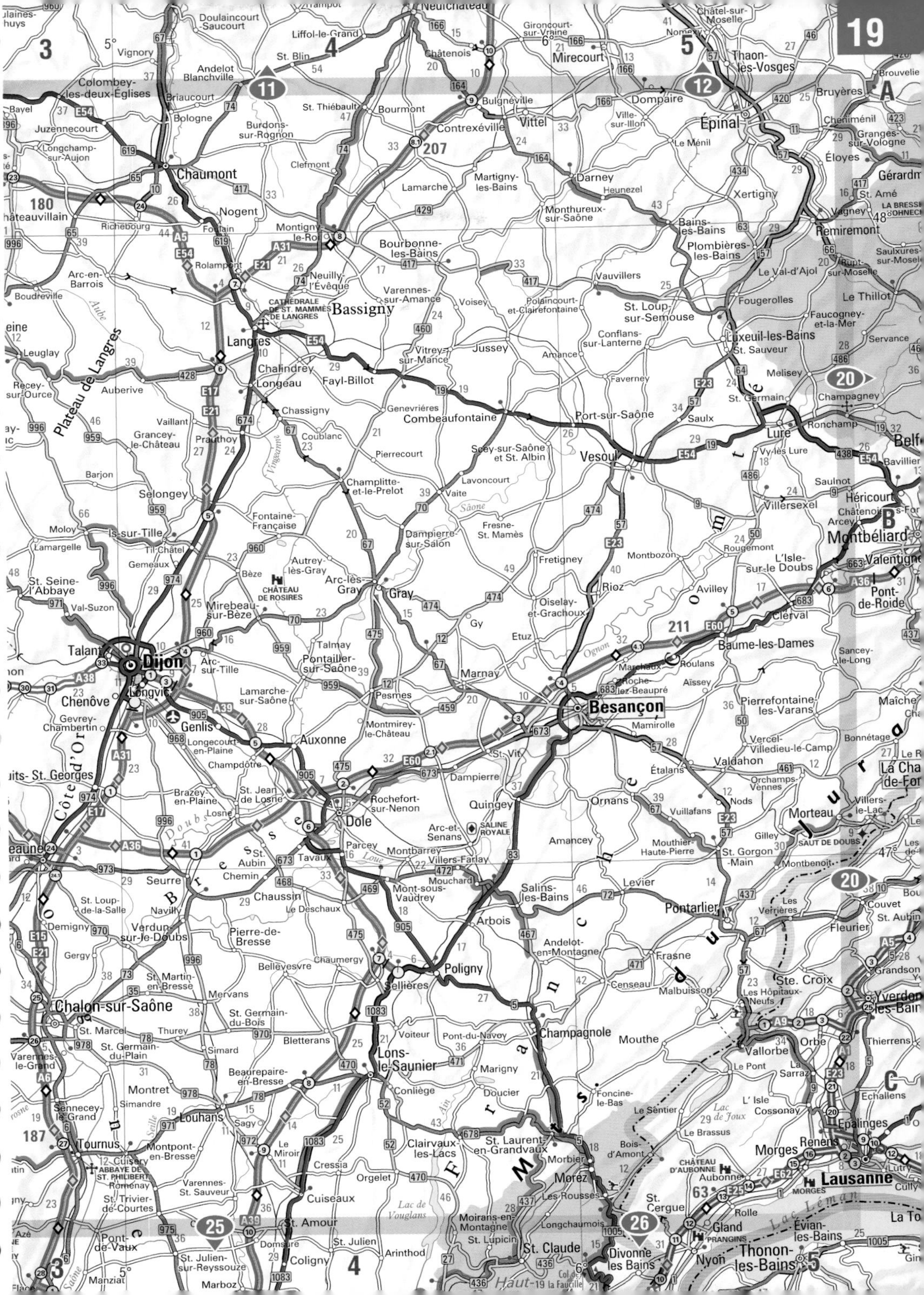
Neufchâteau
Doulaincourt-Saucourt
Liffol-le-Grand
Châtenois
Gironcourt-sur-Vraine
Mirecourt
Châtel-sur-Moselle
Nomexy
Thaon-les-Vosges
Vignory
Andelot Blanchville
St. Blin
Colombey-les-deux-Églises
Briaucourt
Bologne
St. Thiébault
Bourmont
Bulgnéville
Vittel
Contrexéville
Dompaire
Épinal
Bruyères
Brouvelie
Bayel
Juzennecourt
Burdons-sur-Rognon
Ville-sur-Illon
Le Ménil
Chenimenil
Granges-sur-Vologne
Longchamp-sur-Aujon
Chaumont
Clefmont
Martigny-les-Bains
Darney
Heunezel
Éloyes
Gérardmer
St. Amé
Lamarche
Xertigny
Vagney
Remiremont
Châteauvillain
Richebourg
Nogent
Montigny-le-Roi
Monthureux-sur-Saône
Bains-les-Bains
Plombières-les-Bains
Foulain
Rolampont
Bourbonne-les-Bains
Saulxures-sur-Moselle
Arc-en-Barrois
Neuilly-l'Évêque
Varennes-sur-Amance
Vauvillers
Le Val-d'Ajol
Rupt-sur-Moselle
Boudreville
CATHÉDRALE DE ST. MAMMÈS DE LANGRES
Bassigny
Voisey
Polaincourt-et-Clairefontaine
St. Loup-sur-Semouse
Fougerolles
Le Thillot
Faucogney-et-la-Mer
Langres
Conflans-sur-Lanterne
Luxeuil-les-Bains
Servance
Leuglay
Vitrey-sur-Mance
Jussey
Amance
St. Sauveur
Plateau de Langres
Chalindrey
Longeau
Fayl-Billot
Faverney
Melisey
Recey-sur-Ource
Auberive
Chassigny
Genevrières
Combeaufontaine
Port-sur-Saône
Saulx
St. Germain
Champagney
Ronchamp
Lure
Vaillant
Grancey-le-Château
Prauthoy
Coublanc
Pierrecourt
Scey-sur-Saône et St. Albin
Vesoul
Vy-lès-Lure
Belfort
Bavilliers
Barjon
Selongey
Champlitte-et-le-Prelot
Lavoncourt
Vaite
Saulnot
Villersexel
Héricourt
Châtenois
Arcey
Montbéliard
Moloy
Is-sur-Tille
Til-Châtel
Lamargelle
Gemeaux
Fontaine-Française
Dampierre-sur-Salon
Fresne-St. Mamès
Fretigney
Montbozon
Rougemont
L'Isle-sur-le-Doubs
Valentigney
St. Seine-l'Abbaye
Bèze
Autrey-lès-Gray
Arc-lès-Gray
CHÂTEAU DE ROSIRES
Gray
Rioz
Avilley
Pont-de-Roide
Val-Suzon
Mirebeau-sur-Bèze
Oiselay-et-Grachaux
Clerval
Gy
Talant
Dijon
Arc-sur-Tille
Talmay
Pontailler-sur-Saône
Etuz
Baume-les-Dames
Sancey-le-Long
Marnay
Marchaux
Roulans
Chenôve
Longvic
Lamarche-sur-Saône
Pesmes
Roche-lez-Beaupré
Aïssey
Gevrey-Chambertin
Genlis
Montmirey-le-Château
Besançon
Pierrefontaine-les-Varans
Maîche
Mamirolle
Longecourt-en-Plaine
Auxonne
Vercel-Villedieu-le-Camp
Bonnétage
Champdôtre
St. Vit
Étalans
Valdahon
Nuits-St. Georges
Côte d'Or
Dampierre
Orchamps-Vennes
La Chaux-de-Fonds
Brazey-en-Plaine
St. Jean de Losne
Rochefort-sur-Nenon
Quingey
Ornans
Nods
Villers-le-Lac
Losne
Dole
Arc-et-Senans
SALINE ROYALE
Vuillafans
Morteau
Beaune
Bresse
Parcey
Montbarrey
Amancey
Mouthier-Haute-Pierre
Gilley
SAUT DE DOUBS
St. Aubin
Tavaux
Villers-Farlay
St. Gorgon-Main
Montbenoît
Seurre
Chemin
Mouchard
Levier
Mont-sous-Vaudrey
Salins-les-Bains
Pontarlier
Les Verrières
Couvet
St. Loup-de-la-Salle
Navilly
Chaussin
Le Deschaux
Fleurier
Demigny
Verdun-sur-le-Doubs
Pierre-de-Bresse
Arbois
Andelot-en-Montagne
Frasne
Gergy
Bellevesvre
Chaumergy
Poligny
Ste. Croix
St. Martin-en-Bresse
Sellières
Censeau
Malbuisson
Grandson
Yverdon-les-Bains
Mervans
Les Hôpitaux-Neufs
Chalon-sur-Saône
St. Germain-du-Bois
St. Marcel
Thurey
St. Germain-du-Plain
Bletterans
Voiteur
Pont-du-Navoy
Champagnole
Mouthe
Vallorbe
Orbe
Thierrens
Varennes-le-Grand
Simard
Lons-le-Saunier
Marigny
Le Pont
La Sarraz
Montret
Beaurepaire-en-Bresse
Conliège
Doucier
Foncine-le-Bas
Echallens
Sennecey-le-Grand
Simandre
Louhans
Sagy
L'Isle
Cossonay
Le Sentier
Lac de Joux
Epalinges
Tournus
Montpont-en-Bresse
Le Miroir
Clairvaux-les-Lacs
St. Laurent-en-Grandvaux
Le Brassus
Morbier
Bois-d'Amont
Morges
Renens
Cuiseaux
ABBAYE DE ST. PHILIBERT
Romenay
Cressia
Orgelet
CHÂTEAU D'AUBONNE
Aubonne
Lausanne
Lutry
Cully
St. Trivier-de-Courtes
Varennes-St. Sauveur
Morez
Les Rousses
MORGES
Lac de Vouglans
St. Cergue
Lac Léman
Rolle
St. Amour
Moirans-en-Montagne
Longchaumois
Gland
La Tour
Pont-de-Vaux
Domsure
St. Julien
Arinthod
St. Lupicin
PRANGINS
Évian-les-Bains
St. Julien-sur-Reyssouze
Coligny
St. Claude
Divonne-les-Bains
Nyon
Thonon-les-Bains
Manziat
Marboz
Haut-Jura
Col de la Faucille
Monts Jura
Franche-Comté
Plateau de Langres
Saône
Doubs
Ognon
Aube
Vingeanne
Loue
Ain
Seille

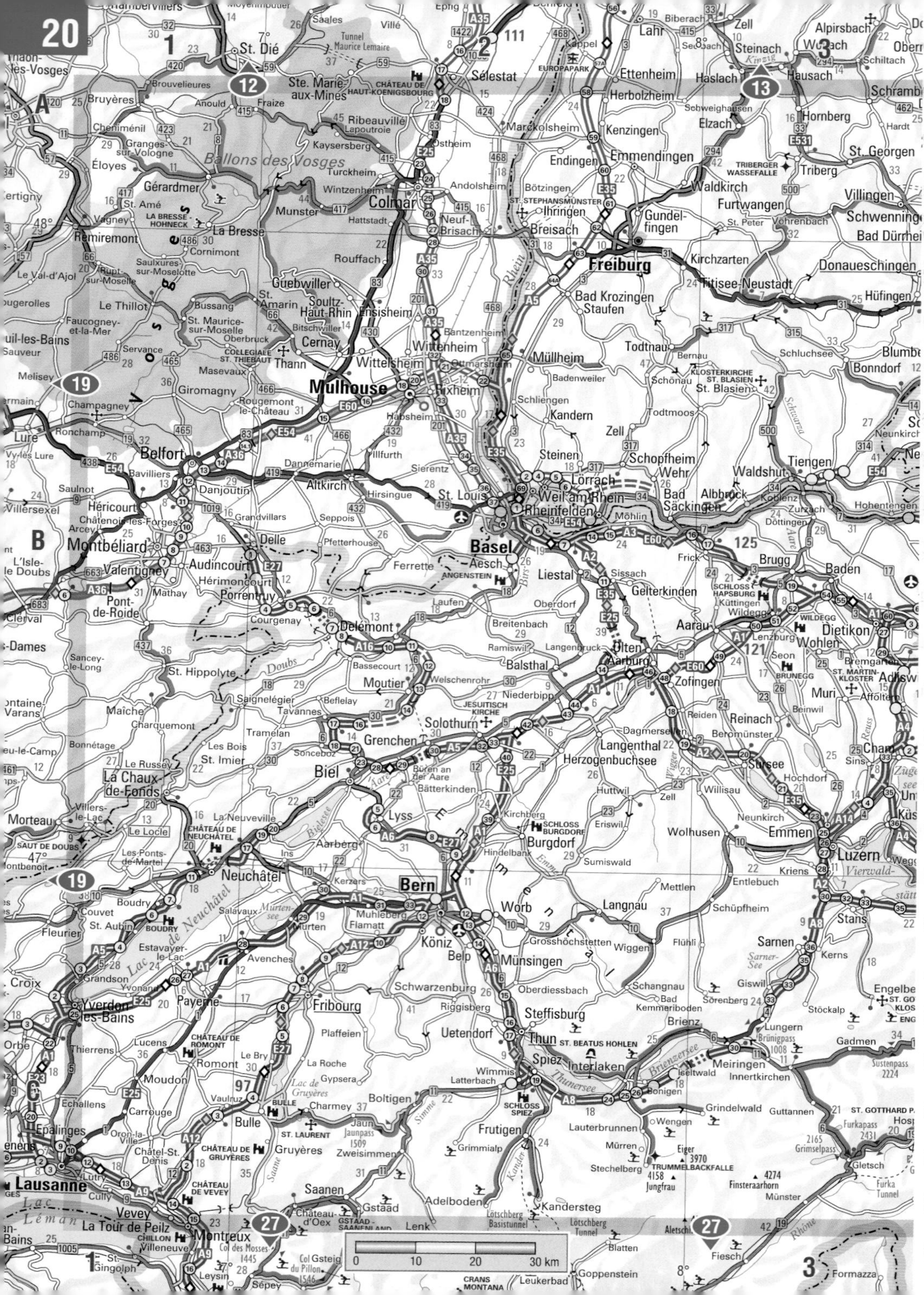
St. Dié
Sélestat
Lahr
Steinach
Hausach
Ste. Marie-aux-Mines
Ribeauvillé
Gérardmer
Colmar
Ballons des Vosges
Remiremont
La Bresse
Guebwiller
Freiburg
Breisach
Emmendingen
Waldkirch
Triberg
Villingen
Schwenningen
Donaueschingen
Titisee-Neustadt
Bad Krozingen
Staufen
Müllheim
Todtnau
St. Blasien
Mulhouse
Cernay
Thann
Belfort
Lure
Montbéliard
Héricourt
Lörrach
Weil am Rhein
Rheinfelden
Basel
Bad Säckingen
Waldshut
Tiengen
Liestal
Delle
Porrentruy
Delémont
Laufen
Olten
Aarau
Brugg
Baden
Dietikon
Zofingen
Solothurn
Grenchen
Biel
Moutier
St. Imier
La Chaux-de-Fonds
Le Locle
Neuchâtel
Langenthal
Burgdorf
Lyss
Aarberg
Bern
Köniz
Worb
Münsingen
Langnau
Emmen
Luzern
Sursee
Stans
Sarnen
Fribourg
Murten
Payerne
Yverdon-les-Bains
Avenches
Estavayer-le-Lac
Romont
Bulle
Gruyères
Thun
Spiez
Interlaken
Brienz
Meiringen
Grindelwald
Lauterbrunnen
Frutigen
Kandersteg
Adelboden
Saanen
Gstaad
Lausanne
Vevey
Montreux
Villeneuve
Lac Léman
0 10 20 30 km

Hechingen
Jungingen
Balingen
Bisingen
Burladingen
Trochtelfingen
Gammertingen
Erbach
Senden
Weissenhorn
Ehingen
Vöhringen
Laupheim
Dietenheim
Illertissen
Krumbach
Albstadt
Tailfingen
Zwiefalten
Munderkingen
Rottweil
Schomberg
Messtetten
Veringenstadt
Riedlingen
Uttenweiler
Babenhausen
Sigmaringen
Biberach
Ochsenhausen
Trossingen
Spaichingen
Donau
Mengen
Saulgau
Bad Buchau
Mindelheim
Memmingen
Tuttlingen
Messkirch
Ostrach
Aulendorf
Bad Schussenried
Ottobeuren
Pfullendorf
Bad Waldsee
Bad Wurzach
Geisingen
Stockach
Engen
Salem
Leutkirch
Obergünzburg
Weingarten
Ravensburg
Kisslegg
Radolfzell
Singen
Überlingen
Kempten
Schaffhausen
Meersburg
Wangen im Allgäu
Konstanz
Friedrichshafen
Tettnang
Allgäu
Immenstadt
Frauenfeld
Weinfelden
Kreuzlingen
Bodensee
Romanshorn
Lindau
Sonthofen
Bregenz
Winterthur
Bülach
Kloten
Wil
St. Gallen
Rorschach
Lustenau
Dornbirn
Oberstdorf
Zürich
Dübendorf
Uster
Herisau
Altstätten
Hohenems
Appenzell
Mittelberg
Allgäuer Alpen
Thalwil
Meilen
Wattwil
Rankweil
Horgen
Feldkirch
Wädenswil
Rapperswil
Zürichsee
Bludenz
St. Anton am Arlberg
Zug
Vaduz
Walensee
Walenstadt
Einsiedeln
Rätikon
Schruns
Glarus
Sargans
Schwyz
Bad Ragaz
Maienfeld
Ischgl
Landquart
Klosters
Altdorf
Chur
Davos
Flims
Ilanz
Arosa
Scuol
Thusis
Tiefencastel
Zernez
Andermatt
St. Gotthard Tunnel
Splügen
Airolo
Samedan
Pontresina
St. Moritz
Livigno
Bórmio
Biasca
Mesocco
Rhätische Alpen
Piz Bernina
4049
3
4
5
A
B
C

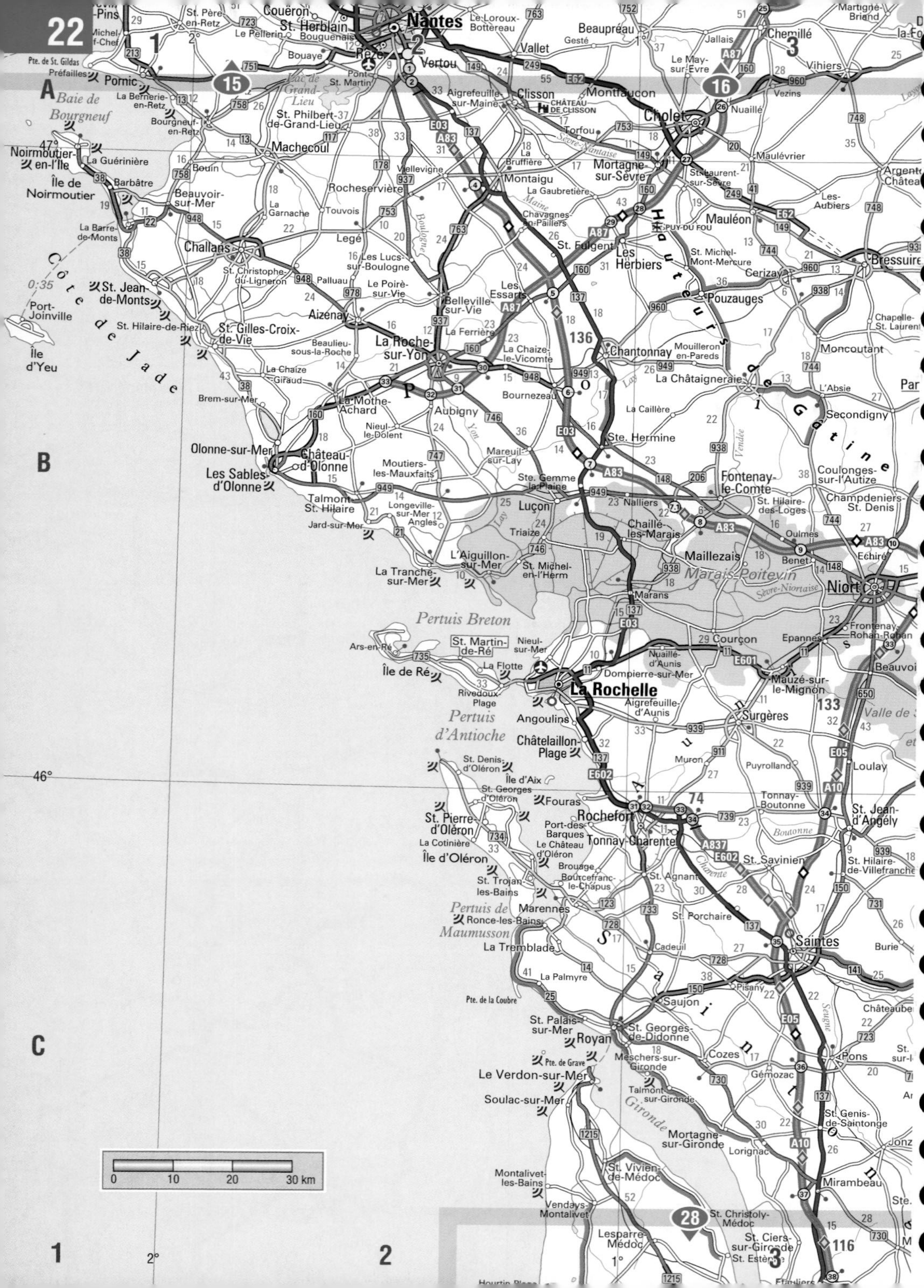
Nantes
St. Herblain
Couëron
Rezé
Vertou
Bouguenais
Le Pellerin
Bouaye
Pornic
Préfailles
Pte. de St. Gildas
Baie de Bourgneuf
La Bernerie-en-Retz
Bourgneuf-en-Retz
St. Philbert-de-Grand-Lieu
Lac de Grand-Lieu
Machecoul
Noirmoutier-en-l'Île
La Guérinière
Île de Noirmoutier
Barbâtre
Beauvoir-sur-Mer
Bouin
La Garnache
Challans
Rocheservière
Touvois
Legé
Vieillevigne
Montaigu
Clisson
Aigrefeuille-sur-Maine
Vallet
Beaupréau
Montfaucon
Cholet
Chemillé
Vihiers
Torfou
Mortagne-sur-Sèvre
Maulévrier
St. Laurent-sur-Sèvre
Les Aubiers
Mauléon
Bressuire
Cerizay
Pouzauges
St. Michel-Mont-Mercure
Les Herbiers
St. Fulgent
Chavagnes-en-Paillers
La Gaubretière
Les Essarts
Chantonnay
Mouilleron-en-Pareds
La Châtaigneraie
Moncoutant
L'Absie
Secondigny
Coulonges-sur-l'Autize
Champdeniers-St. Denis
Fontenay-le-Comte
St. Hilaire-des-Loges
Côte de Jade
St. Jean-de-Monts
Port-Joinville
Île d'Yeu
St. Hilaire-de-Riez
St. Gilles-Croix-de-Vie
Aizenay
Palluau
Le Poiré-sur-Vie
Belleville-sur-Vie
Les Lucs-sur-Boulogne
La Roche-sur-Yon
Beaulieu-sous-la-Roche
La Ferrière
La Chaize-le-Vicomte
La Chaize-Giraud
Brem-sur-Mer
La Mothe-Achard
Aubigny
Nieul-le-Dolent
Bournezeau
Ste. Hermine
Olonne-sur-Mer
Château-d'Olonne
Les Sables-d'Olonne
Talmont-St. Hilaire
Moutiers-les-Mauxfaits
Mareuil-sur-Lay
Ste. Gemme-la-Plaine
Luçon
Longeville-sur-Mer
Angles
Jard-sur-Mer
La Tranche-sur-Mer
L'Aiguillon-sur-Mer
St. Michel-en-l'Herm
Triaize
Nalliers
Chaillé-les-Marais
Maillezais
Marais Poitevin
Benet
Oulmes
Echiré
Niort
Marans
Pertuis Breton
St. Martin-de-Ré
Ars-en-Ré
Île de Ré
La Flotte
Rivedoux-Plage
Nieul-sur-Mer
La Rochelle
Dompierre-sur-Mer
Nuaillé-d'Aunis
Courçon
Epannes
Frontenay-Rohan-Rohan
Mauzé-sur-le-Mignon
Aigrefeuille-d'Aunis
Surgères
Angoulins
Pertuis d'Antioche
Châtelaillon-Plage
St. Denis-d'Oléron
Île d'Aix
St. Georges-d'Oléron
Fouras
St. Pierre-d'Oléron
La Cotinière
Île d'Oléron
St. Trojan-les-Bains
Rochefort
Port-des-Barques
Tonnay-Charente
Le Château-d'Oléron
Brouage
Bourcefranc-le-Chapus
Marennes
Pertuis de Maumusson
Ronce-les-Bains
La Tremblade
La Palmyre
Pte. de la Coubre
Muron
Puyrolland
Loulay
Tonnay-Boutonne
St. Jean-d'Angély
St. Savinien
St. Hilaire-de-Villefranche
St. Agnant
St. Porchaire
Saintes
Burie
Cadeuil
Pisany
Saujon
St. Palais-sur-Mer
Royan
St. Georges-de-Didonne
Meschers-sur-Gironde
Cozes
Gémozac
Pons
Pte. de Grave
Le Verdon-sur-Mer
Soulac-sur-Mer
Talmont-sur-Gironde
Gironde
Mortagne-sur-Gironde
Lorignac
St. Genis-de-Saintonge
Mirambeau
St. Vivien-de-Médoc
Montalivet-les-Bains
Vendays-Montalivet
St. Christoly-Médoc
Lesparre-Médoc
St. Ciers-sur-Gironde
St. Estèphe
Hauteurs de la Gâtine
Aunis
Saintonge
0
10
20
30 km
47°
46°
2°
1°
A
B
C
1
2
3
15
16
28
E03
A83
A87
E62
E601
E602
E05
A10
A837

Chinon
Loches
Loudun
Thouars
Richelieu
Châtellerault
Poitiers
Chauvigny
Le Blanc
Brenne
Montmorillon
Lussac-les-Châteaux
Bellac
Limoges
Confolens
Ruffec
Civray
Angoulême
Cognac
Angoumois
St. Junien
Rochechouart
Aixe-sur-Vienne
Périgord-Limousin
Nontron
Brantôme
Montmoreau-St. Cybard
Barbezieux-St. Hilaire
St. Maixent-l'École
Melle
Parthenay
Argenton-sur-Creuse
La Souterraine
St. Yrieix-la-Perche
Excideuil
Ribérac
Chalus

Aigurande
Ste. Sévère-sur-Indre
Préveranges
La Chapelaude
Estivareilles
Cosne-d'Allier
Villefranche-d'Allier
Buxières-les-Mines
St. Hilaire
L'EGLISE DE L'ABBAYE DE ST. PIERRE ET ST. PAUL
Tronget
Treban
Le Montet
Châtel-de-Neuvre
Eguzon-Chantôme
CHÂTEAU DE CROZANT
Dun-le-Palestel
Bonnat
Boussac
Treignat
Domérat
Montluçon
Quinssaines
Doyet
Bezenet
Voussac
St. Pourçain-sur-Sioule
Sulpice-Feuilles
Châtelus-Malvaleix
Néris-les Bains
Commentry
Montmarault
Chantelle
La Souterraine
St. Vaury
Ajain
Gouzon
Chambon-sur-Voueize
Lapeyrouse
Bellenaves
St. Etienne-de-Fursac
Guéret
Evaux-les-Bains
Marcillat-en-Combraille
Fontanières
Montaigut
St. Eloy-les-Mines
Lalizolle
Broût-Vernet
Bénévent-l'Abbaye
Le-Grand-Bourg
Laurière
Chénerailles
Pionsat
Menat
Ebreuil
Gannat
St. Sulpice-Laurière
Ahun
Auzances
St. Gervais-d'Auvergne
Effiat
St. Dizier-Leyrenne
Aigueperse
La Jonchère-St. Maurice
Pontarion
Combronde
Thuret
Ambazac
Bourganeuf
Aubusson
Bellegarde-en-Marche
Montel-de-Gelat
St. Georges-de Mons
Manzat
Maringues
Ennezat
Sauviat-sur-Vige
Felletin
Châtelguyon
Riom
St. Léonard-de-Noblat
Royère-de-Vassivière
Crocq
St. Avit
Les Ancizes-Comps
Pontaumur
Volvic
Joze
Peyrat-le-Château
L. de Vassivière
Gentioux
Giat
Bromont-Lamothe
Pontgibaud
Clermont-Ferrand
Gerzat
Pont-du-Château
St Bonnet Briance
Eymoutiers
Millevaches
Sauvagnat
VULCANIA
Royat
Herment
1464 Puy-de-Dôme
Rochefort-Montagne
Ceyrat
Cournon-d'Auvergne
Châteauneuf-la-Forêt
La Courtine
TEMPLE DE MERCURE
ST. JEAN
Plateau de Millevaches
Sornac
Eygurande
Bourg-Lastic
Veyre-Monton
St. Amant-Tallende
Vic-le-Comte
Mt. Gargan 731
Limousin
Millevaches
La Bourboule
Magnac-Bourg
St. Germain-les-Belles
Bugeat
Tauves
Le Mont-Dore
Chambon-sur-Lac
Murol
St. Nectaire
Champeix
Meuzac
Chamberet
Masseret
Treignac
Meymac
Ussel
L'EGLISE HAUTE
Issoire
1885 Puy de Sancy
Besse-en-Chandesse
Peyrissac
St. Angel
Mts. Dore
St. Germain-Lembron
Limousin
Uzerche
Arnac-Pompadour
Chamboulive
Egletons
Champs-sur-Tarentaine
Egliseneuve-d'Entraigues
Ardes
Vigeois
Seilhac
Corrèze
Neuvic
Bort-les-Orgues
Lempdes
Ydes
Condat
Monts du Cantal
Saignes
Anzat-le-Luguet
Blesle
Brioude
Allassac
Tulle
Marcillac-la-Croisille
Marcenat
Riom-ès-Montagnes
Donzenac
Laguenne
Trizac
Volcans d'Auvergne
Massiac
Molompize
La Roche-Canillac
Mauriac
Allanche
Malemort
St. Martin-la-Méanne
Ségur-les-Villas
Neussargues-Moissac
La Chapelle-Laurent
Brive-la-Gaillarde
Beynat
St. Chamant
Pléaux
Salers
Larche
Argentat
St. Privat
St. Martin-Valmeroux
Talizat
Vieillespesse
Meyssac
Murat
Ussel
1855 Plomb du Cantal
Roffiac
Cressensac
St. Cernin
Thiezac
St. Flour
Les Ternes
Vayrac
Beaulieu-sur-Dordogne
Laroquebrou
Jussac
Vic-sur-Cère
Ruynes-en-Margeride
Martel
Souillac
Bretenoux
Aurillac
Polminhac
Pierrefort
CHÂTEAU DE CASTELNAU-BRETENOUX
Sousceyrac
Arpajon-sur-Cère
Raulhac
GROTTE DE LANCAVE
St. Céré
CHÂTEAU DE MONTAL
Le Rouget
St. Mamet-la-Salvetat
Alvignac
Mur-de-Barrez
Chaudes-Aigues
Termes
Payrac
Rocamadour
Gramat
Fournels
Latronquière
Lacroix-Barrez
St. Chély-d'Apcher
Calvinet
Mts. d'Aubrac
Causses de Quercy
Le Bourg
Lacapelle-Marival
Maurs
Cassuéjouls
Montsalvy
St. Hippolyte
Laguiole
Nasbinals
Labastide-Murat
Livernon
Figeac
Entraygues-sur-Truyère
Conques
Aubrac
Lamothe-Cassel
Grèzec
Lauzès
Capdenac-Gare
Decazeville
Firmi
Le Cayrol
St. Chély-d'Aubrac
Aubin
Espalion
St. Come-d'Olt
Montbazens
Chirac
Massif Central
Marche
Combrailles
Bourbonnais
Monts d'Auvergne
Limousin
0 10 20 30 km

Neuilly-le-Réal
Dompierre-sur-Besbre
Digoin
Paray-le-Monial
SACRE-COEUR
St. Bonnet-de-Joux
Cluny
ANCIENNE ABBAYE DE CLUNY
Lugny
St. Trivier-de-Courtes
Jaligny-sur-Besbre
Saligney-sur-Roudon
Coulanges
Molinet
St. Gérand-de-Vaux
St. Yan
Charolles
Beaubery
Azé
Pont-de-Vaux
St. Julien-sur-Reyssouze
Poisson
Manziat
Marboz
St. Loup
Varennes-sur-Allier
Trézelles
Le Donjon
Pari-Gagné
Mâcon
Montrevel-en-Bresse
CHÂTEAU DE LAPALISSE
Montaiguët-en-Forez
Matour
La Clayette
Marcigny
Chambilly
St. Christophe-en-Brionnais
Crèches-sur-Saône
Pont-de-Veyle
St. Cyr-sur-Menthon
Bourg-en-Bresse
St. Gérand-le-Puy
Lapalisse
St. Germain-des-Fossés
St. Martin-d'Estreaux
Châteauneuf
Iguerande
Chauffailles
Romanèche-Thorins
Mézériat
La Pacaudière
Le Breuil
Arfeuilles
Pouilly-sous-Charlieu
Belmont-de-la-Loire
Beaujeu
St. Didier
Châtillon-sur-Chalaronne
Neuville-les-Dames
Vichy
Cusset
Changy
Châtel-Montagne
Charlieu
Cuinzier
St. Germain-Lespinasse
ST. PHILIBERT
Mably
Cours-la-Ville
Belleville
St. Paul-de-Varax
Abrest
Le Mayet-de-Montagne
STE. MADELEINE
Roanne
Bourg-de-Thizy
Lamure-sur-Azergues
St. Georges-de-Reneins
St. Trivier-sur-Moignans
Marlieux
St. Yorre
Ferrières-sur-Sichon
Renaison
Ambérieux-en-Dombes
Villars-les-Dombes
Chalamont
Randan
Thizy
Arnas
Regny
Villemontais
Villefranche-sur-Saône
Trévoux
Limons
Puy-Guillaume
Amplepuis
Valsonne
St. Just-en-Chevalet
Cremeaux
St. Polgues
St. Symphorien-de-Lay
Tarare
Anse
St. André-de-Corcy
Meximieux
Lagnieu
Chabreloche
Neulise
Pontcharra-sur-Turdine
Montluel
Thiers
La Monnerie-le-Montel
Champoly
Violay
L'Arbresle
Neuville-sur-Saône
Miribel
Pont de Dore
Noirétable
St. Germain-Laval
Néronde
Balbigny
Caluire-et-Cuire
Villeurbanne
Lezoux
Vollore-Montagne
St. Julien-la-Vêtre
Panissières
Pont-de-Chéruy
Courpière
Boën
Feurs
St. Laurent-de-Chamousset
Craponne
AQUEDUC ROMAIN
Lyon
Meyzieu
St. Priest
Crémieu
Billom
CHÂTEAU DE LA BASTIE D'URFÉ
Ste. Foy-l'Argentière
Oullins
Olliergues
Chalmazel
St. Georges-en-Couzan
Vénissieux
Montrond-les-Bains
St. Symphorien-sur-Coise
Thurins
St. Dier-d'Auvergne
St. Martin-en-Haut
St. Symphorien-d'Ozon
Villefontaine
Comte
Champdieu
Chazelles-sur-Lyon
Mornant
Cunlhat
St. Amant-Roche-Savine
Montbrison
St. Galmier
Givors
Bourgoin-Jallieu
Diémoz
Sugères
Andrézieux-Bouthéon
Vienne
St. Jean-de-Bournay
AUSTREMOINE
Sauxillanges
Livradois-Forez
Ambert
Sury-le-Comtal
Fournols
Rive-de-Gier
St. Anthème
St. Chamond
Sarpoil
Marsac-en-Livradois
St. Marcellin-sur-Loire
Condrieu
La Grande-Croix
St. Just-St. Rambert
Les Roches
Cour-et-Buis
Jumeaux
St. Germain-l'Herm
St. Étienne
La Côte-St. André
Brassac-les-Mines
Arlanc
Viverols
Pilat
Pelussin
Champagnac-le-Vieux
St. Bonnet-le-Château
Le Chambon-Feugerolles
Roussillon
Auzon
Usson-en-Forez
Le Péage-de-Roussillon
Beaurepaire
Marcilloles
Firminy
Le Bessat
Craponne-sur-Arzon
St. Genest-Malifaux
Serrières
Monistrol-sur-Loire
St. Didier-en-Velay
St. Rambert-d'Albon
Lens Lestang
La Chaise-Dieu
L'EGLISE DE L'ABBAYE DE ST. ROBERT
St. Sauveur-en-Rue
Bourg-Argental
Roybon
Vieille-Brioude
Andance
Hauterives
Collat
Ste. Sigolène
Villevocance
Paulhaguet
Allègre
Bellevue-la-Montagne
Riotord
Annonay
Sarras
Montmiral
Vorey
Retournac
Montfaucon-en-Velay
St. Vallier
St. Marcellin
St. Georges-d'Aurac
Margès
Langeac
St. Paulien
Yssingeaux
Satillieu
St. Hilaire-Rosier
Saugues-St. Romain
CHÂTEAU DE LAVOTE-POLIGNAC
St. Bonnet-le-Froid
Tain-l'Hermitage
Peyrins
Romans-sur-Isère
Le Pertuis
Tence
Le Chambon-sur-Lignon
St. Félicien
CHÂTEAU CHAZOTTE
Chanteuges
Pinols
CHAPELLE ST. MICHEL D'AIGUILHE
Le Puy-en-Velay
St. Julien-Chapteuil
Arlebosc
Tournon-sur-Rhône
Bourg-de-Péage
St. Nazaire-en-Royans
St. Agrève
Alixan
Bains
Laussonne
Lamastre
St. Péray
Monistrol-d'Allier
Le Monastier-sur-Gazeille
St. Martin-de-Valamas
Montelier
Saugues
Cayres
Mt. Mézenc 1754
Valence
Léoncel
Costaros
Les Estables
Le Cheylard
Vernoux-en-Vivarais
Chabeuil
Portes-lès-Valence
Le Malzieu-Ville
Chanaleilles
Landos
Le Béage
Charmes-sur-Rhône
Montmeyran
St. Pierreville
St. Sauveur-de-Montagut
La Voulte-sur-Rhône
Plan-de-Baix
Grandrieu
Mézilhac
St. Alban-sur-Limagnole
Pradelles
Coucouron
Livron-sur-Drôme
Auroux
Monts
Privas
Crest
Langogne
Montpezat-sous-Bauzon
Loriol-sur-Drôme
Serverette
Lanarce
Chomérac
Saillans
St. Amans
Thueyts
Pont-de-Labeaume
Châteauneuf-de-Randon
Cruas
Mayres
Vals-les-Bains
Luc
La Bastide-Puylaurent
D'Ardèche
Aubenas
Meysse
Cléon-d'Andran
Pradelle
Bourdeaux
Rochemaure
Sauzet
Laubert
Lavilledieu
Le Teil
Montélimar
Valgorge
Villeneuve-de-Berg
La Bégude-de-Mazenc
Marvejols
Belvezet
Largentière
Vogüé
CHÂTEAU DE VOGUÉ
Espeluche
Dieulefit
Mende
Prevenchères
Aleyrac
Bouvières
ERMITAGE DE ST. PRIVAT
Le Bleymard
Joyeuse
BAPTISTRE DE MÉLAS
Viviers
Beaujolais
Monts du Forez
Mts du Velay
Monts de la Margeride
Lyonnais
Dombes
Loire
Rhône
Isère
Drôme
Ardèche
Ain

Lausanne
Genève
Geneva
Thonon-les-Bains
Évian-les-Bains
Nyon
Lac Léman
Annemasse
Bonneville
Cluses
Sallanches
Annecy
Lac d'Annecy
Thônes
Megève
Ugine
Faverges
Albertville
Massif des Bauges
Aix-les-Bains
L. du Bourget
Chambéry
Montmélian
Moûtiers
Bourg-St. Maurice
Aime
Maurienne
St. Jean-de-Maurienne
St. Michel-de-Maurienne
Modane
Val Thorens
Méribel
Courchevel
Grenoble
St. Martin-d'Hères
Échirolles
Meylan
Voiron
Vizille
Chartreuse
Belledonne
Vercors
Villard-de-Lans
Valence
Romans-sur-Isère
Die
Crest
Écrins
Massif du Pelvoux
Briançon
La Grave
Les Deux-Alpes
L'Alpe-d'Huez
Gap
Embrun
Veynes
Lyon
Villeurbanne
Vénissieux
Vienne
Bourgoin-Jallieu
La Tour-du-Pin
Bourg-en-Bresse
Ambérieu-en-Bugey
Oyonnax
Nantua
Bellegarde-sur-Valserine
St. Claude
Haut-Jura
Gex
Ferney-Voltaire
Rumilly
Belley
Dombes
Chablais
Montélimar
Lac de Vouglans
Mt. Thabor 3181
Tunnel du Fréjus
Col du Galibier 2646
Col du Lautaret 2058
Col Bayard 1248
Col de Vars 2109
Col de Rousset 1254
Col de la Croix Haute 1179
0 10 20 30 km

Vevey
Montreux
Villeneuve
Château-d'Œx
Saanen
Gstaad
Adelboden
Lenk
Kandersteg
Jungfrau
Finsteraarhorn
Aletschhorn
Münster
Furka Tunnel
Bedretto
Col des Mosses
Col du Pillon
Gsteig
Leysin
Aigle
Sépey
Les Diablerets
VILLARS
Lötschberg Basistunnel
Lötschberg Tunnel
Blatten
Goppenstein
Leukerbad
CRANS MONTANA
Montana-Vermala
Leuk
Fiesch
Naters
Brig
Visp
STOCKALPER
Sierre
Turtmann
Sion
Conthey
Vétroz
Monthey
Châtel
Vouvry
Bex
St. Maurice
L'EGLISE DE L'ABBAYE DE ST. MAURICE
Champéry
Vex
NENDAZ
Riddes
Fully
Vernayaz
Martigny
Verbier
Evolène
Les Haudères
Ferpècle
Arolla
Ayer
Zinal
Stalden
St. Niklaus
Täsch
Zermatt
Saas-Fee
Simplon P. 2005
Simplon Tunnel
Simplon
Iselle
Varzo
Gondo
Crévola d'Ossola
Crodo
Prémia
Góglio
Formazza
San Carlo
Bignasco
Cévio
Cimalmotto
Vergeletto
Intragna
Ascona
Brissago
Masera
Santa Maria Maggiore
Bognanco Fonti
Domodóssola
Villadóssola
Antronapiana
Piedimulera
Vogogna
Val Grande
Cannóbio
Cánnero Riviera
Verbánia
Pallanza
Gravellona Toce
Forno
Macugnaga
Dufourspitze 4634
Monte Rosa
Matterhorn 4482
Breuil-Cervínia
Valtournenche
Champoluc
Gressoney-la-Trinité
Alagna Valsésia
Balmuccia
MADONNA DI LORETO
Varallo
Omegna
Stresa
Armeno
L. d'Orta
Laveno
L. Maggiore
Meina
Arona
Angera
Vergiate
Sesto Calende
Somma Lombardo
Orsières
Sixt-Fer-à-Cheval
Chamonix-Mont Blanc
St. Gervais-les-Bains
Tunnel du Mt. Blanc
Mont Blanc 4807
COURMAYEUR
Courmayeur
Ferret
Tunnel du Grd. St. Bernard
Étroubles
Bionaz
Valpelline
Aosta
Nus
Châtillon
Brusson
St. Vincent
Gressoney-St.-Jean
Scopello
Morgex
La Thuile
Sarre
Col du Petit Saint Bernard 2188
Mte. Emilius 3559
CHÂTEAU DE CHÂTILLON
CHÂTEAU DE VERRÈS
Verrès
Issogne
Gaby
Piedicavallo
Trivero
Borgosésia
Borgomanero
Serravalle
SANTUARIO DI MARIA SANTISSIMA
Oropa
Valle Mosso
Gattinara
Romagnano Sésia
Oléggio
Cogne
Champorcher
Pont-St. Martin
Settimo Vittone
ABBAZIA DI SETTIMO VITTONE
Biella
Cossato
Carpignano Sésia
Fara Novarese
Momo
Valgrisenche
Les Arcs
Peisey-Nancroix
Valsavarenche
Rhêmes-Notre-Dame
Gran Paradiso
Gran Paradiso 4061
Pont
Ronco Canavese
Borgofranco d'Ivrea
Arbório
Ivrea
Salussola
Buronzo
Biandrate
Novara
Tignes
Val-d'Isère
Col de l'Iseran 2764
Vanoise
Grande Casse 3852
Bonneval-sur-Arc
Ceresole-Reale
Locana
Pont Canavese
Cavaglia
Formigliana
Santhià
San Germano Vercellese
Borgo Vercelli
Vespolate
Forno Alpi-Gráie
Chialamberto
Cuorgnè
Castellamonte
Borgomasino
Caluso
Lanslebourg-Mont-Cenis
Ala di Stura
Ceres
Busano
Rivarolo Canavese
Tronzano Vercellese
Livorno Ferraris
Vercelli
Róbbio
Balme
Cório
Col du Mt. Cenis 2084
Lanzo Torinese
Front
Ciriè
Cigliano
Desana
Stroppiana
Usséglio
Viù
Fiano
Crescentino
Trino
Margone
Caselle Torinese
Chivasso
Molaretto
Venaría
Brusasco
SAN GENUARIO
Casale Monferrato
Cándia Lomellina
Bussoleno
Susa
Condove
Almese
Alpignano
Séttimo Torinese
Casalborgone
ABBAZIA DI VEZZOLANO
Sartirana Lomellina
Salbertrand
Chiomonte
Avigliana
Rívoli
Torino
Turin
Castelnuovo Don Bosco
Montiglio
Moncalvo
Ozzano Monferrato
Occimiano
Oulx
Fenestrelle
Forno
Giaveno
Trana
Orbassano
Chieri
Montechiaro d'Asti
Calliano
Vignale
Pragelato
Villaretto
Moncalieri
Cumiana
Montafia
SAN PIETRO
Montemagno
Quargnento
Alessandria
Sestriere
Perosa Argentina
Villar Perosa
None
Poirino
Villanova d'Asti
Felizzano
Perrero
Carignano
Villastellone
DUOMO DI SANTA MARIA ASSUNTA
Asti
Ghigo
Pinerolo
Carmagnola
San Damiano d'Asti
Isola d'Asti
Oviglio
Bosco
Col d'Izoard 2360
Bóbbio Pellice
Torre Péllice
Vigone
Pancalieri
Canale
Nizza Monferrato
Abriès
Cavour
Aiguilles
Arvieux
Moretta
Racconigi
Sommariva del Bosco
Costigliole d'Asti
Cassine
Barge
ABBAZIA DI SANTA MARIA DI STAFFARDA
Cavallermaggiore
Bra
Canelli
Acqui Terme
DUOMO
Crissolo
Néive
Alba
Bubbio
Bistango
Visone
Ovada
St. Véran
Mte. Viso 3841
Paesana
Revello
Chianale
Saluzzo
Savigliano
Cherasco
Diano d'Alba
Vésime
Molare
CASTELLO DI MOLARE
Casteldelfino
Verzuolo
Genola
Narzole
Monforte d'Alba
Cortemilia
Sampéyre
Costigliole Saluzzo
Fossano
Bene Vagienna
Dogliani
Bossolasco
Spigno Monferrato
Venasca
Busca
Alpes Pennine
Alpi Pennine
Alpi Graie
Berner Alpen
Piemonte
Queyras
Rhône
Dora Báltea
Dora Ripária
Orco
Po
Sesia
Tánaro
Chisone
Pellice
Máira
Varáita
Bormida
Orba
Toce
Cervo
Elvo
Stura di Lanzo
Belbo
A
B
C
3
4
5
20
33
7°
8°
46°
45°

0 10 20 30 km
22
23
34
35
Bordeaux
Mérignac
Pessac
St. Médard-en-Jalles
Blanquefort
Villenave-d'Ornon
Cestas
La Brède
CHATEAU DE LA BRÈDE
CATHÉDRAL ST-ANDRÉ
Libourne
St. Émilion
St. André-de-Cubzac
Bourg
Blaye
Pauillac
St. Estèphe
St. Ciers-sur-Gironde
Lesparre-Médoc
St. Christoly-Médoc
Vendays-Montalivet
Hourtin-Plage
Hourtin
Étang d'Hourtin-Carcans
Carcans-Plage
Carcans
Lacanau-Océan
Lacanau
Étang de Lacanau
Le Porge-Océan
Le Porge
Saumos
Castelnau-de-Médoc
Listrac-Médoc
St. Laurent-Médoc
Beychevelle
FORT MÉDOC
Lamarque
Margaux
Macau
Arsac
Ste. Hélène
Cissac-Médoc
Mirambeau
Baignes-Ste. Radegonde
Montendre
Chevanceaux
Brossac
Montmoreau-St. Cybard
Aubeterre-sur-Dronne
Chalais
Montlieu-la-Garde
Montguyon
St. Aulaye
La Roche-Chalais
St. Savin
Cavignac
Guîtres
Coutras
St. Médard-de-Guizières
Montpon-Ménesterol
Galgon
Lussac
Villefranche-de-Lonchat
Fronsac
Arveyres
Castillon-la-Bataille
Lamothe-Montravel
Branne
Pujols
Créon
Rauzan
Targon
Pellegrue
Sauveterre-de-Guyenne
Portets
Podensac
Cadillac
Cérons
Saucats
Cabanac-et-Villagrains
Villagrains
Illats
Monségur
La Réole
St. Macaire
Langon
Marmande
Auros
Mitton
Bazas
Grignols
Casteljaloux
Damazan
Captieux
Lège-Cap-Ferret
Arès
Andernos-les-Bains
Lanton
Ile aux Oiseaux
Bassin d'Arcachon
Audenge
Biganos
Marcheprime
Arcachon
Cap Ferret
Pyla-sur-Mer
La Teste
Gujan-Mestras
Mios
Le Barp
Salles
Cazaux
Étang de Cazaux et de Sanguinet
Sanguinet
Biscarrosse-Plage
Biscarrosse
Parentis-en-Born
Étang de Biscarrosse et de Parentis
Gastes
Belin-Béliet
Hostens
Guillos
Balizac
Villandraut
St. Symphorien
Préchac
Le Muret
Belhade
Moustey
Landes de Gascogne
Liposthey
Pissos
Sore
Luxey
Pontenx-les-Forges
Mimizan-Plage
Mimizan
Labouheyre
Commensacq
Trensacq
Escource
Bias
Cap-de-Pin
Sabres
Labrit
Contis-Plage
Onesse-et-Laharie
Laharie
St. Julien-en-Born
Mézos
Lit-et-Mixe
Uza
Morcenx
Arengosse
Garein
Brocas
Roquefort
Ygos-St. Saturnin
Le Souquet
Rion-des-Landes
St. Girons-Plage
St. Girons
Castets
Léon
Le Caloy
Mont-de-Marsan
Villeneuve-de-Marsan
St. Justin
Gabarret
Barbotan-les-Thermes
Cazaubon
Estang
Eauze
Laluque
Tartas
Meilhan
Pontonx-sur-l'Adour
Vieux-Boucau-les-Bains
Azur
Magescq
Soustons
St. Paul-lès-Dax
Dax
Souprosse
St. Sever
Grenade-sur-l'Adour
Le Houga
Nogaro
Manciet
Vic-Fézensac
Mugron
Aire-sur-l'Adour
Hossegor
Tosse
Capbreton
St. Geours-de-Maremne
St. Vincent-de-Tyrosse
Labenne
Montfort-en-Chalosse
Hagetmau
Samadet
Geaune
Riscle
Aignan
Plaisance
Bassoues
Marciac
St. Lon-les-Mines
Pomarez
Puillon
Amou
Tarnos
Boucau
Anglet
Biarritz
Bayonne
Port-de-Lanne
Peyrehorade
Habas
Tilh
Puyôo
Sault-de-Navailles
Salies-de-Béarn
Orthez
Bidache
Briscous
Hasparren
Ustaritz
Sauveterre-de-Béarn
Masiacq
Arthez-de-Béarn
Arzacq-Arraziguet
Garlin
Sarron
Thèze
Lembeye
Maubourguet
Vic-en-Bigorre
Uzein
Côte des Landes
Côte d'Argent
Aquitaine
Gascogne
Médoc
Landes
45°
44°
A
B
C
1
2
3

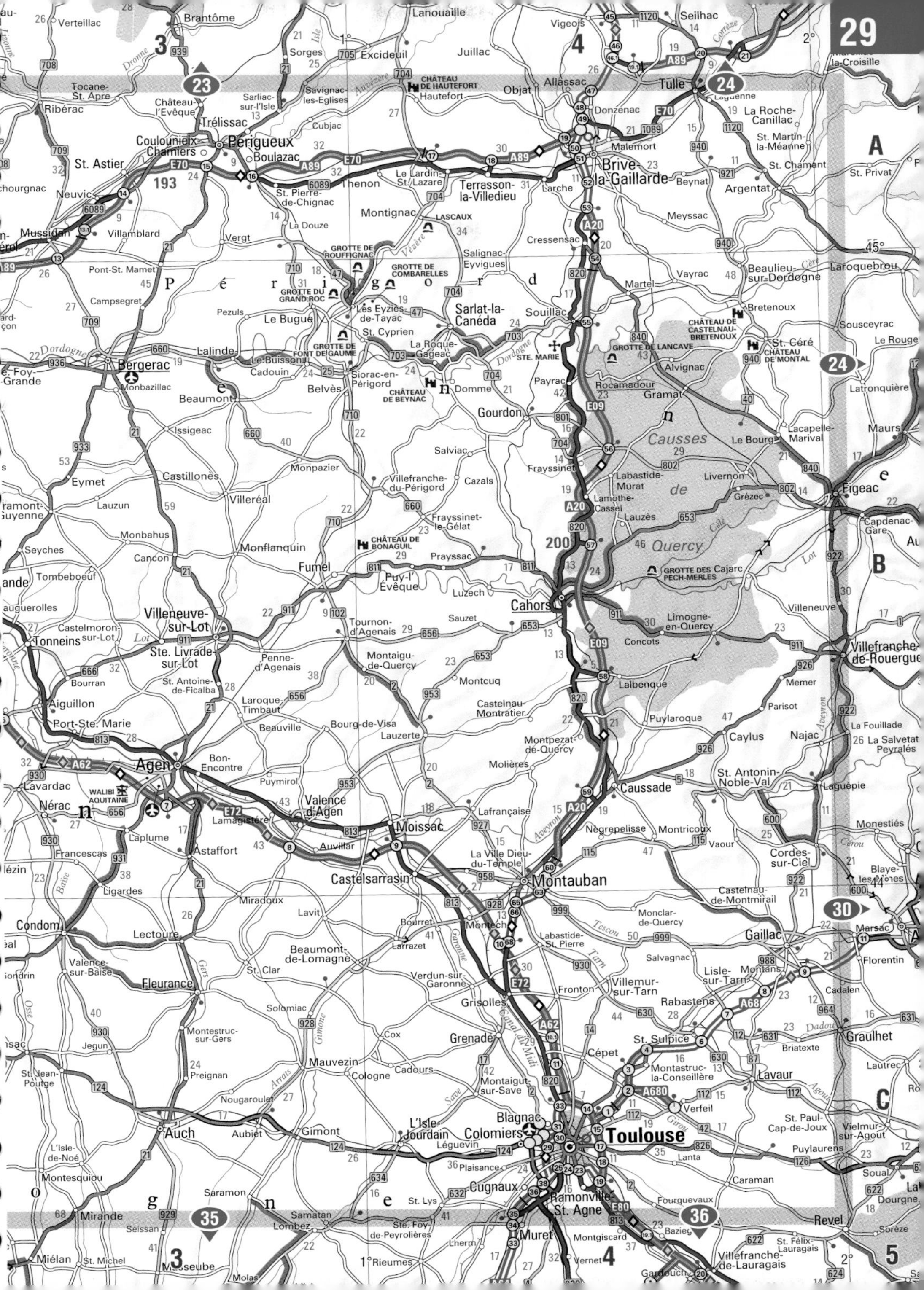
Verteillac
Brantôme
Lanouaille
Vigeois
Seilhac
Sorges
Excideuil
Juillac
Tocane-St. Apre
Ribérac
Château-l'Evêque
Sarliac-sur-l'Isle
Savignac-les-Eglises
CHÂTEAU DE HAUTEFORT
Hautefort
Objat
Allassac
Tulle
La Croisille
Trélissac
Cubjac
Donzenac
La Roche-Canillac
Coulounieix-Chamiers
Périgueux
Boulazac
Malemort
St. Martin-la-Méanne
St. Astier
Brive-la-Gaillarde
St. Chamant
St. Privat
Neuvic
St. Pierre-de-Chignac
Thenon
Le Lardin-St. Lazare
Terrasson-la-Villedieu
Larche
Beynat
Argentat
Mussidan
Villamblard
La Douze
Montignac
LASCAUX
Meyssac
Vergt
GROTTE DE ROUFFIGNAC
GROTTE DE COMBARELLES
Cressensac
Salignac-Eyvigues
Pont-St. Mamet
Vayrac
Beaulieu-sur-Dordogne
Laroquebrou
Martel
GROTTE DU GRAND ROC
Périgord
Campsegret
Pezuls
Le Bugue
Les Eyzies-de-Tayac
Sarlat-la-Canéda
Souillac
Bretenoux
Sousceyrac
St. Cyprien
CHÂTEAU DE CASTELNAU-BRETENOUX
GROTTE DE FONT DE GAUME
La Roque-Gageac
GROTTE DE LANCAVE
St. Céré
CHÂTEAU DE MONTAL
Le Rouget
Dordogne
Bergerac
Lalinde
Le Buisson
Cadouin
STE. MARIE
Ste. Foy-la-Grande
Monbazillac
Belvès
Siorac-en-Périgord
Domme
Payrac
Alvignac
Rocamadour
Gramat
CHÂTEAU DE BEYNAC
Beaumont
Gourdon
Latronquière
Issigeac
Causses de Quercy
Lacapelle-Marival
Maurs
Le Bourg
Salviac
Frayssinet
Labastide-Murat
Livernon
Eymet
Monpazier
Castillonès
Villefranche-du-Périgord
Cazals
Figeac
Lauzun
Villeréal
Lamothe-Cassel
Grèzec
Capdenac-Gare
Lauzès
Frayssinet-le-Gélat
Monbahus
Seyches
Monflanquin
CHÂTEAU DE BONAGUIL
Cancon
Prayssac
GROTTE DES PECH-MERLES
Cajarc
Tombeboeuf
Fumel
Puy-l'Evêque
Luzech
Cahors
Villeneuve
Villeneuve-sur-Lot
Sauzet
Limogne-en-Quercy
Castelmoron-sur-Lot
Tonneins
Tournon-d'Agenais
Concots
Villefranche-de-Rouergue
Ste. Livrade-sur-Lot
Penne-d'Agenais
Montaigu-de-Quercy
Bourran
St. Antoine-de-Ficalba
Montcuq
Lalbenque
Memer
Aiguillon
Laroque-Timbaut
Castelnau-Montratier
Parisot
Port-Ste. Marie
Beauville
Bourg-de-Visa
Lauzerte
Puylaroque
Caylus
Najac
La Fouillade
La Salvetat Peyralès
Montpezat-de-Quercy
Agen
Bon-Encontre
Puymirol
Molières
Caussade
St. Antonin-Noble-Val
Laguépie
Lavardac
WALIBI AQUITAINE
Nérac
Valence-d'Agen
Lafrançaise
Lamagistère
Moissac
Nègrepelisse
Montricoux
Monestiés
Laplume
Francescas
Astaffort
Auvillar
La Ville Dieu-du-Temple
Vaour
Cordes-sur-Ciel
Blaye-les-Mines
Castelsarrasin
Montauban
Ligardes
Castelnau-de-Montmirail
Miradoux
Lavit
Monclar-de-Quercy
Condom
Lectoure
Bourret
Montech
Labastide-St. Pierre
Gaillac
Marsac
Larrazet
Beaumont-de-Lomagne
Salvagnac
Florentin
Valence-sur-Baïse
St. Clar
Verdun-sur-Garonne
Villemur-sur-Tarn
Lisle-sur-Tarn
Montans
Fleurance
Fronton
Cadalen
Rabastens
Solomiac
Grisolles
Montestruc-sur-Gers
Jegun
Cox
Grenade
St. Sulpice
Graulhet
Briatexte
Mauvezin
Cadours
Cépet
Montastruc-la-Conseillère
Lavaur
St. Jean-Poutge
Cologne
Preignan
Montaigut-sur-Save
Lautrec
Nougaroulet
Verfeil
Blagnac
Auch
Aubiet
Gimont
L'Isle-Jourdain
Colomiers
Toulouse
St. Paul-Cap-de-Joux
Vielmur-sur-Agout
L'Isle-de-Noé
Léguevin
Lanta
Puylaurens
Montesquiou
Plaisance
Soual
Saramon
Cugnaux
Caraman
Dourgne
St. Lys
Ramonville-St. Agne
Fourquevaux
Mirande
Samatan
Lombez
Ste. Foy-de-Peyrolières
Muret
Revel
Seissan
Montgiscard
Baziège
Sorèze
St. Félix-Lauragais
L'herm
Miélan
St. Michel
Masseube
Rieumes
Vernet
Villefranche-de-Lauragais
Gardouch
Canal du Midi
Garonne
Tarn
Aveyron
Lot
Gers
Baïse
Save
Gimone
Arrats
Tescou
Agout
Dadou
Cère
Célé
Vézère
Isle
Dronne
Auvézère
Corrèze
A20
A62
A68
A680
A89
E09
E70
E72
E80
23
24
30
35
36

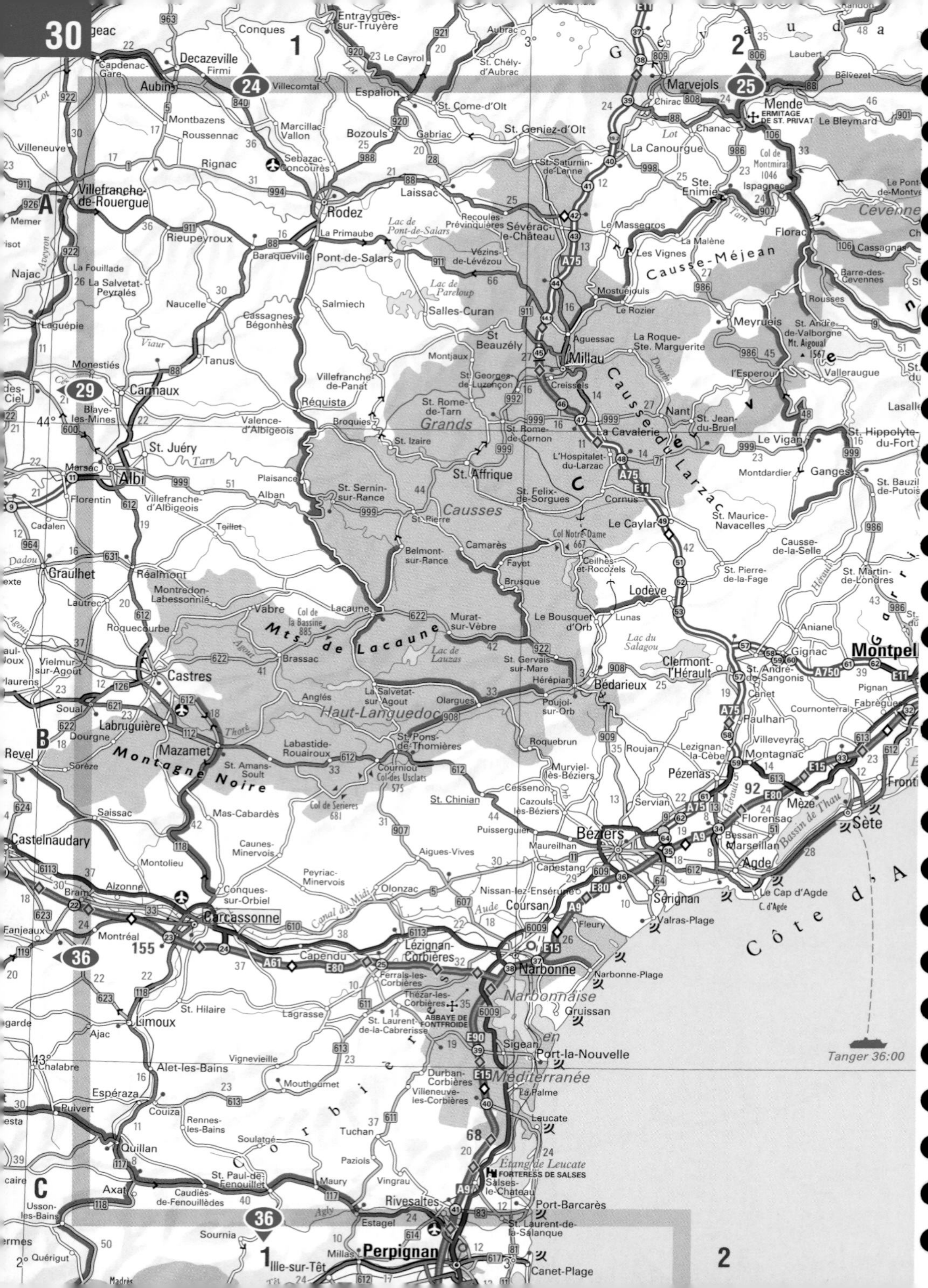

Conques
Entraygues-sur-Truyère
Decazeville
Capdenac-Gare
Aubin
Firmi
24
Villecomtal
Espalion
Aubrac
St. Chély-d'Aubrac
Le Cayrol
Marvejols
25
Mende
Chirac
ERMITAGE DE ST. PRIVAT
Le Bleymard
Laubert
Bleymard
St. Come-d'Olt
Montbazens
Roussennac
Marcillac-Vallon
Bozouls
Gabriac
St. Geniez-d'Olt
Chanac
La Canourgue
Col de Montmirat 1046
Villeneuve
Rignac
Sebazac-Concourès
St. Saturnin-de-Lenne
Ste. Enimie
Ispagnac
Villefranche-de-Rouergue
Rodez
Laissac
Recoules-Prévinquières
Sévérac-le-Château
Le Massegros
Le Pont-de-Montvert
Cévennes
Memer
Rieupeyroux
Baraqueville
La Primaube
Lac de Pont-de-Salars
Pont-de-Salars
Vézins-de-Lévézou
Les Vignes
La Malène
Causse-Méjean
Florac
Cassagnas
Najac
La Fouillade
La Salvetat-Peyralès
Naucelle
Salmiech
Lac de Pareloup
Salles-Curan
Mostuéjouls
Le Rozier
Barre-des-Cevennes
Rousses
Laguépie
Cassagnes-Bégonhès
St Beauzély
Aguessac
La Roque-Ste. Marguerite
Meyrueis
St. Andre-de-Valborgne
Mt. Aigoual 1567
Tanus
Monestiés
Montjaux
Millau
l'Esperou
Valleraugue
29
Carmaux
Villefranche-de-Panat
St. Georges-de-Luzençon
Creissels
Causse du Larzac
Blaye-les-Mines
Réquista
St. Rome-de-Tarn
Grands
Nant
St. Jean-du-Bruel
Lasalle
Valence-d'Albigeois
Broquies
St. Rome-de-Cernon
La Cavalerie
St. Izaire
L'Hospitalet-du-Larzac
Le Vigan
St. Hippolyte-du-Fort
St. Juéry
Marsac
Albi
Plaisance
Alban
St. Sernin-sur-Rance
St. Affrique
St. Felix-de-Sorgues
Cornus
Montdardier
Ganges
St. Bauzil-de-Putois
Florentin
Villefranche-d'Albigeois
St. Pierre
Causses
Le Caylar
St. Maurice-Navacelles
Cadalen
Teillet
Col Notre-Dame 667
Camarès
Belmont-sur-Rance
Fayet
Ceilhes-et-Rocozels
Causse-de-la-Selle
St. Martin-de-Londres
Graulhet
Réalmont
Brusque
St. Pierre-de-la-Fage
Lodève
Montredon-Labessonnié
Lautrec
Vabre
Col de la Bassine 885
Lacaune
Murat-sur-Vèbre
Le Bousquet-d'Orb
Lunas
Roquecourbe
Mts. de Lacaune
Lac de Lauzas
Lac du Salagou
Aniane
Gignac
Montpel
Vielmur-sur-Agout
Brassac
St. Gervais-sur-Mare
Hérépian
Clermont-l'Hérault
St. André-de-Sangonis
Castres
Anglès
La Salvetat-sur-Agout
Olargues
Bédarieux
Pignan
Soual
Labruguière
Haut-Languedoc
Poujol-sur-Orb
Canet
Cournonterral
Fabrègues
Dourgne
Mazamet
St. Pons-de-Thomières
Paulhan
Revel
Sorèze
Montagne Noire
Labastide-Rouairoux
Roquebrun
Roujan
Lezignan-la-Cèbe
Villeveyrac
St. Amans-Soult
Courniou
Col des Usclats 575
Murviel-lès-Béziers
Montagnac
Pézenas
Frontignan
Saissac
Col de Serieres 681
Cessenon
St. Chinian
Cazouls-les-Béziers
Servian
Florensac
Mèze
Sète
Bassin de Thau
Mas-Cabardès
Puisserguier
Béziers
Bessan
Marseillan
Castelnaudary
Caunes-Minervois
Aigues-Vives
Maureilhan
Montolieu
Capestang
Agde
Alzonne
Peyriac-Minervois
Bram
Conques-sur-Orbiel
Olonzac
Nissan-lez-Ensérune
Sérignan
Le Cap d'Agde
C. d'Agde
Canal du Midi
Coursan
Fanjeaux
Carcassonne
Valras-Plage
Côte d'A
Montréal
Lézignan-Corbières
Fleury
36
Capendu
Narbonne
Narbonne-Plage
Ferrals-les-Corbières
Narbonnaise
Thézar-les-Corbières
Gruissan
St. Hilaire
Lagrasse
ABBAYE DE FONTFROIDE
Limoux
St. Laurent-de-la-Cabrerisse
Ajac
Sigean
en
Port-la-Nouvelle
Vignevieille
Tanger 36:00
Chalabre
Alet-les-Bains
Méditerranée
Mouthoumet
Durban-Corbières
Espéraza
Villeneuve-les-Corbières
La Palme
Puivert
Couiza
Rennes-les-Bains
Leucate
Corbières
Tuchan
Soulatgé
Quillan
Paziols
Étang de Leucate
FORTERESSE DE SALSES
St. Paul-de-Fenouillet
Vingrau
Maury
Salses-le-Château
Axat
Caudiès-de-Fenouillèdes
Rivesaltes
Port-Barcarès
Usson-les-Bains
Agly
Estagel
St. Laurent-de-la-Salanque
Sournia
Millas
Perpignan
Quérigut
Ille-sur-Têt
Canet-Plage
Madrès
A75
A9
A61
A750
E11
E15
E80
E90

Aubenas
Vals-les-Bains
D'Ardêche
La Bastide-Puylaurent
Largentière
Joyeuse
Lablachère
Villefort
Les Vans
Valgorge
Prevenchères
Ruoms
Villeneuve-de-Berg
Vogué
CHÂTEAU DE VOGUÉ
BAPTISTRE DE MÉLAS
Viviers
Le Teil
Rochemaure
Meysse
Lavilledieu
Montélimar
Sauzet
La Bégude-de-Mazenc
Espeluche
Cléon-d'Andran
Pradelle
Bourdeaux
Dieulefit
Bouvières
Aleyrac
Taulignan
CHÂTEAU DE GRIGNAN
Grignan
Donzère
St. Montant
Pierrelatte
Vallon-Pont-d'Arc
Bourg-St. Andéol
St. Paul-Trois-Châteaux
Valréas
Nyons
Luc-en-Diois
St. Nazaire-le-Désert
Bellegarde-en-Diois
La Motte-Chalançon
La Charce
Aspres-sur-Buëch
Serres
Rosans
Rémuzat
Verclause
L'Epine
Ste. Jalle
Laragne-Montéglin
Barret-le-Bas
La Rochette
Buis-les-Baronnies
Mirabel-aux-Baronnies
Vaison-la-Romaine
VILLE ROMAINE RUIN
Séderon
Montbrun-les-Bains
Les Omergues
Malaucène
1909 Mt. Ventoux
Bédoin
Sault
Revest-du-Bion
Banon
ST. CHRISTOL
St. Christol
St. Etienne-les-Orgues
St. Saturnin-lès-Apt
Rustrel
Reillanne
Manosque
Apt
Céreste
Luberon
Bonnieux
La Bastide-des-Jourdans
Cucuron
Lourmarin
Cadenet
La Tour d'Aigues
Pertuis
Durance
Mallemort
Lambesc
Rognes
Le Puy-Ste. Réparade
Meyrargues
Peyrolles-en-Provence
Venelles
Vauvenargues
Aix-en-Provence
Eguilles
St. Cannat
Pélissanne
Salon-de-Provence
Lançon-Provence
Gardanne
Trets
St. Savournin
Roquevaire
Auriol
Allauch
Aubagne
Gémenos
Marseille
Marseilles
CHÂTEAU D'IF
Cap Croisette
Cassis
Calanques
La Ciotat
St. Cyr-sur-Mer
Bandol
Carry-le-Rouet
Sausset-les-Pins
Carro
C. Couronne
Martigues
Marignane
Berre-l'Etang
Etang de Berre
Istres
St. Chamas
Miramas
Port-de-Bouc
Fos-sur-Mer
La Crau
Port-St.-Louis-du-Rhône
Camargue
Etang de Vaccarès
Stes. Maries-de-la-Mer
STES. MARIES DE LA MER
Arles
St. Martin-de-Crau
Mouriès
Maussane-les-Alpilles
Eyguières
Alpilles
Les Baux-de-Provence
RUINES ROMAINES DE GLANUM
St. Rémy-de-Provence
Orgon
Sénas
Plan-d'Orgon
Cavaillon
Noves
Graveson
Tarascon
CHÂTEAU DE TARASCON
Barbentane
Châteaurenard
Avignon
Villeneuve-lès-Avignon
Aramon
Sorgues
Bédarrides
Châteauneuf-du-Pape
Carpentras
Mazan
Pernes-les-Fontaines
L'Isle-sur-la-Sorgue
Fontaine de Vaucluse
Orange
Camaret-sur-Aigues
Vacqueyras
Mondragon
Bollène
Suze-la-Rousse
Tulette
Roquemaure
Bagnols-sur-Cèze
Pont-St. Esprit
St. Just
AVEN MARZAL-GROTTE MUSÉE ET ZOO PREHISTORIQUE
Orgnac-l'Aven
Barjac
St. Paul-le-Jeune
Bessèges
Le Collet-de-Deze
St. Ambroix
St. André-de-Roquepertuis
Les Mages
St. Germain-de-Calberte
La Grand-Combe
Salindres
Lussan
Seynes
Connaux
Alès
St. Christol-lès-Alès
Vézenobres
St. Quentin-la-Poterie
Serviers
Uzès
Anduze
Lédignan
Moussac
PONT DU GARD
Remoulins
La Calmette
Quissac
Sauve
Montmirat
Sauteyrargues
Marguerittes
Nîmes
Beaucaire
Bouillargues
Bellegarde
Calvisson
Sommières
Vaflaunes
St. Mathieu-de-Tréviers
Boisseron
Uchaud
Vauvert
St. Gilles
L'EGLISE DE L'ABBAYE DE ST. GILLES
Aimargues
Lunel
Castries
MURS DU MOYEN-AGE
Mauguio
St. Laurent-d'Aigouze
Aigues-Mortes
Pérols
Carnon-Plage
Palavas-les-Flots
La Grande-Motte
Le Grau-du-Roi
Port-Camargue
Golfe d'Aigues-Mortes
Etang de Vic
Golfe du Lion
Alicante
Oran 23:00
Alger 18:00
Annaba 23:00
Bejaia 21:00
Skikda 23:00
Tunis 20:00
Porto Tórres 14:15
Ajaccio 8:30
Bastia 10:00
Calvi 12:00
l'Ile Rousse 11:30
Porto-Vecchio 13:30
Propriano 8:30
0 10 20 30 km
4°
5°
44°
43°
2
3
4
A
B
C

Luc-en-Diois
St. Nazaire-le-Désert
Bellegarde-en-Diois
La Motte-Chalançon
La Charce
Aspres-sur-Buëch
Veynes
Gap
La Roche-des-Arnauds
Col Bayard 1248
St. Bonnet
Orcières
Mont Dauphin
Guillestre
St. Véran
Mte. Viso 3841
Châteauroux-les-Alpes
Risoul
Embrun
Vars
Vars les Claux
Col de Vars 2109
Chorges
Les Orres
Savines-le-lac
Lac de Serre-Ponçon
Espinasses
Tallard
St. Paul
Acceglio
Prazzo
La Condamine-Châtelard
Larche
Col de Larche 1948
Argentera
Campo
Serres
Rosans
L'Epine
Rémuzat
Savournon
Verclause
Jalle
Eyguians
Ventavon
Durance
La Motte-du-Caire
Bréziers
Turriers
Selonnet
Le Lauzet-Ubaye
Seyne
Jausiers
Barcelonnette
Pra Loup
Col de la Bonette 2802
Col de Maure 1347
Col d'Allos 2247
Super Sauze
Bayons
Laragne-Montéglin
Le Poët
Buis-les-Baronnies
La Rochette
Barret-le-Bas
Le Vernet
Mt. Pelat 3052
Col de la Cayolle 2326
St. Étienne-de-Tinée
Allos
Barles
St. Geniez
Authon
Ribiers
Séderon
Les Omergues
Sisteron
Beaujeu
La Javie
Colmars
Mercantour
Isola
St. Martin-d'Entraunes
Montbrun-les-Bains
Noyers-sur-Jabron
Le Brusquet
Thorame-Haute
Château-Arnoux
Sault
Revest-du-Bion
St. Etienne-les-Orgues
Cruis
Digne-les-Bains
Thorame-Basse
Guillaumes
Valberg
Beuil
Malijai
Peyruis
Banon
St. Christol
Les Mées
Châteauredon
Daluis
St. Saturnin-lès-Apt
Forcalquier
Puimichel
St. André-les-Alpes
Le Fugeret
Annot
Puget-Théniers
Entrevaux
Mane
La Brillanne
Bras d'Asse
Estoublon
Barrême
Rustrel
Reillanne
Oraison
Senez
St. Julien-du-Verdon
Apt
Céreste
Volx
Puimoisson
Castellane
Roquesteron
Brianconnet
Luberon
Manosque
Valensole
Moustiers-Ste. Marie
St. Auban
Mt. Cheiron 1776
Var
La Bastide-des-Jourdans
Ste. Tulle
Riez
Soleils
Cucuron
Lourmarin
Gréoux-les-Bains
Verdon
Cadenet
La Tour d'Aigues
Lac de Ste. Croix
Bramafan
Vence
Le Bar-sur-Loup
Escragnolles
Pertuis
Vinon-sur-Verdon
Quinson
Comps-sur-Artuby
St. Vallier-de-Thiey
Grasse
Cagnes-sur-Mer
Rognes
Le Puy-Ste. Réparade
Peyrolles-en-Provence
Ginasservis
Montmeyan
Aups
Fayence
Meyrargues
Venelles
Montferrat
Bargemon
Callas
Mougins
Eguilles
Vauvenargues
Rians
Esparron
Varages
Salernes
Aix-en-Provence
Brue-Auriac
Barjols
Draguignan
Bagnols-en-Forêt
Cannes
Châteauneuf-le-Rouge
Flayosc
Trans-en-Provence
Gardanne
Lorgues
Le Muy
Mandelieu-la-Napoule
Trets
St. Maximin-la-Ste. Baume
Carcès
Le Val
Les Arcs
Puget-sur-Argens
Cabasse
Abbaye du Thoronet
Vidauban
Fréjus
St. Raphaël
Savournin
Tourves
Brignoles
Le Luc
Agay
Auriol
Roquevaire
Flassans-sur-Issole
St. Aygulf
Côte de l'Esterel
Allauch
La Roquebrussanne
Gonfaron
La Garde-Freinet
Val d'Esquières
Aubagne
Gémenos
Garéoult
Ste. Maxime
Marseille
Marseilles
Cuges-les-Pins
Signes
Puget-ville
Grimaud
OK Corral
Méounes-les-Montrieux
Belgentier
Cuers
Collobrières
Cogolin
St. Tropez
Cap Croisette
Cassis
Le Beausset
Pierrefeu-du-Var
La Mole
Solliès-Pont
La Croix-Valmer
Cap Camarat
La Ciotat
St. Cyr-sur-Mer
Bandol
Toulon
La Crau
Maures
Bormes-les-Mimosas
Cavalaire-sur-Mer
Le Rayol
Sanary-sur-Mer
La Seyne-sur-Mer
Carqueiranne
Hyères
La Londe-les-Maures
Le Lavandou
Hyères Plage
C. Bénat
St. Mandrier-sur-Mer
Giens
Î. du Levant
Îs. d'Hyères
Porquerolles
Î. de Porquerolles
Parc National de Port-Cros
Î. de Port-Cros
Ajaccio 8:30
Bastia 10:00
Calvi 12:00
l'Ile Rousse 11:30
Porto-Vecchio 13:30
Propriano 8:30
Ajaccio 8:00
Bastia 8:30
Civitavecchia 14:00
Porto Tórres 9:30
44°
43°
6°
7°
A
B
C
1
2
3

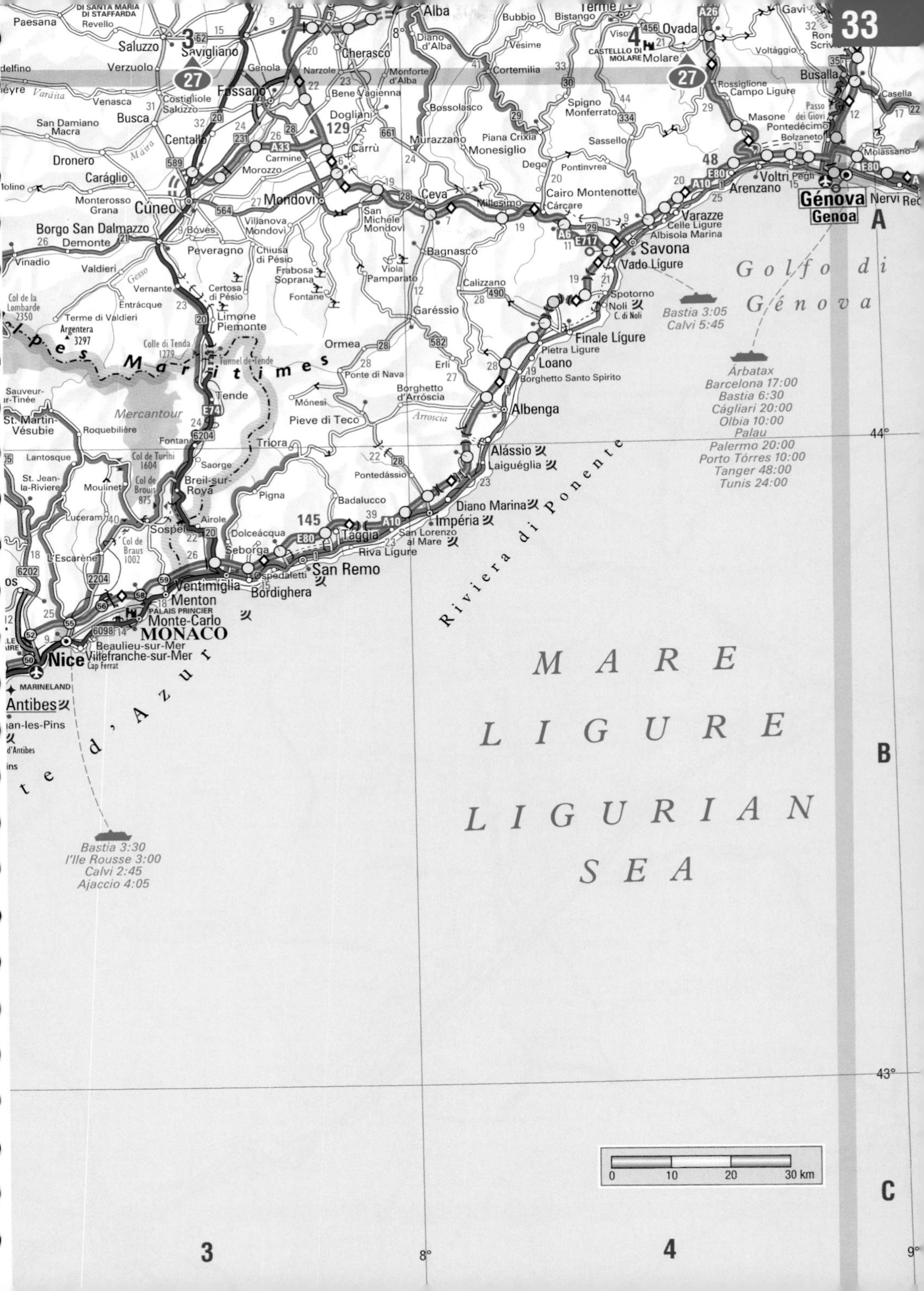
Paesana
Revello
Saluzzo
Savigliano
Verzuolo
Costigliole Saluzzo
Venasca
Busca
San Damiano Macra
Centallo
Dronero
Caráglio
Monterosso Grana
Cúneo
Borgo San Dalmazzo
Demonte
Vinadio
Valdieri
Vernante
Entrácque
Terme di Valdieri
Argentera 3297
Col de la Lombarde 2350
Peveragno
Bóves
Chiusa di Pésio
Certosa di Pésio
Limone Piemonte
Colle di Tenda 1279
Tunnel de Tende
Alpes Maritimes
Tende
Mercantour
St. Martin-Vésubie
Roquebilière
Fontan
Lantosque
Col de Turini 1604
Saorge
Breil-sur-Roya
Col de Brouis 875
St. Jean-la-Riviere
Moulinet
Luceram
Sospel
Airole
Col de Braus 1002
L'Escarène
Ventimiglia
Menton
Monte-Carlo
MONACO
Beaulieu-sur-Mer
Villefranche-sur-Mer
Cap Ferrat
Nice
MARINELAND
Antibes
Fossano
Genola
Cherasco
Narzole
Bene Vagienna
Monforte d'Alba
Dogliani
Carrù
Carmine
Morozzo
Mondovì
Villanova Mondovì
Frabosa Soprana
Fontane
San Michele Mondovì
Viola
Pamparato
Ceva
Bagnasco
Garéssio
Ormea
Ponte di Nava
Mónesi
Pieve di Teco
Triora
Pigna
Badalucco
Dolceácqua
Seborga
Ospedaletti
Bordighera
San Remo
Tággia
Riva Ligure
San Lorenzo al Mare
Impéria
Diano Marina
Pontedássio
Alássio
Laiguéglia
Albenga
Borghetto d'Arróscia
Arroscia
Erli
Calizzano
Loano
Borghetto Santo Spirito
Pietra Ligure
Finale Lígure
Noli
C. di Noli
Spotorno
Vado Lígure
Savona
Albisola Marina
Celle Ligure
Varazze
Cárcare
Cairo Montenotte
Millesimo
Dego
Pontinvrea
Sassello
Piana Crixia
Monesiglio
Murazzano
Bossolasco
Cortemilia
Vésime
Bubbio
Bistango
Spigno Monferrato
Alba
Diano d'Alba
Ovada
Molare
CASTELLO DI MOLARE
Rossiglione
Campo Ligure
Masone
Passo dei Giovi
Pontedécimo
Bolzaneto
Busalla
Voltággio
Gavi
Casella
Arenzano
Voltri
Pegli
Génova
Genoa
Nervi
Molassano
Golfo di Génova
Riviera di Ponente
Côte d'Azur
Bastia 3:05
Calvi 5:45
Árbatax
Barcelona 17:00
Bastia 6:30
Cágliari 20:00
Olbia 10:00
Palau
Palermo 20:00
Porto Tórres 10:00
Tanger 48:00
Tunis 24:00
Bastia 3:30
l'Ile Rousse 3:00
Calvi 2:45
Ajaccio 4:05
MARE LIGURE
LIGURIAN SEA
0 10 20 30 km
A
B
C
3
4
8°
9°
44°
43°

0 10 20 30 km
2°
43°
42°
Bayonne
Biarritz
Anglet
Tarnos
Boucau
Peyrehorade
Salies-de-Béarn
Orthez
Bidache
Sauveterre-de-Béarn
Hasparren
St. Jean-de-Luz
Hendaye
Hondarribia
Irun
Donostia-San Sebastián
Renteria
Oiartzun
Hernani
Lasarte
Andoain
Zarautz
Zumaia
Mutriku
Deba
Ondarroa
Lekeitio
Eibar
Elgoibar
Zestoa
Azpeitia
Azcoitia
Placencia
Elorrio
Bergara
Zumárraga
Oñati
Tolosa
Villabona
Ordizia
Beasain
Lazkao
Idiazábal
Segura
Alsasua
Etxarri-Aranatz
Olazagutia
Salvatierra
Sierra de Urbasa
Sierra de Andía
Irurzun
Lekunberri
Leitza
Goizueta
Zubieta
Donestebe-Santesteban
Sunbilla
Elizondo
Lesaka
Cambo-les-Bains
Ainhoa
Sare
St. Etienne-de-Baigorry
St. Jean-Pied-de-Port
St. Palais
Mauléon-Licharre
Tardets-Sorholus
Larrau
Ste. Engrâce
Orreaga-Roncesvalles
Auritz-Burguette
Pyrénées Occidentales
Pays Basque
Ochagavía
Ezcároz
Isaba
Roncal
Ansó
Hecho
Burgui
Navascués
Lumbier
Monasterio de Leyre
Sangüesa
Javier
Embalse de Yesa
Tiermas
Sigües
Berdún
Embún
Puente la Reina de Jaca
Sierra de
Aoiz
Zubiri
Ansoain
Burlada
Barañain
Pamplona
Noain
Cizur Mayor
Echauri
Puente la Reina
Estella
Monreal
Tafalla
Olite
Eslava
Sos del Rey Católico
Uncastillo
Sádaba
Ejea de los Caballeros
Luna
Erla
Los Arcos
Viana
Logroño
Lodosa
Mendavia
Sesma
Lerin
Andosilla
San Adrián
Peralta
Marcilla
Falces
Caparroso
Carcastillo
Murillo el Fruto
Calahorra
Villafranca
Milagro
Rincón de Soto
Alfaro
Arnedo
Quel
Autol
Adeanueva de Ebro
Corella
Cintruénigo
Fitero
Castejón
Valtierra
Arguedas
Doña Blanca de Navarra
Tudela
Cabanillas
Fustiñana
Ribaforada
Buñuel
Cortes
Mallén
Tauste
Gallur
Cascante
Murchante
Tarazona
Borja
Magallon
Agreda
Sierra del Madero
Sierra del Moncayo
Olvega
Soria
Numancia Antiquisima
Almajano
Pedrola
Alagón
Utebo
Zaragoza
Zuera
Villanueva de Gállego
Epila
La Muela
Rueda de Jalón
Lumpiaque
Tabuenca
Calcena
Borobia
Ciria
Aranda de Moncayo
Tierga
Tejado
Almazul
Torrelapaja
Gómara
Cubo de la Solana
Los Rábanos
Almenar de Soria
Aldeapozo
Matalebreras
Enciso
Arnedillo
Cervera del Río Alhama
San Pedro Manrique
Ventosa de la Sierra
Castilfrio de la Sierra
La Rubia
Alcalá de Gurrea
Gurrea de Gállego
El Temple
Castejón de Valdejasa
Remolinos
Sierra de Luna
Biel
Santa María
Luesia

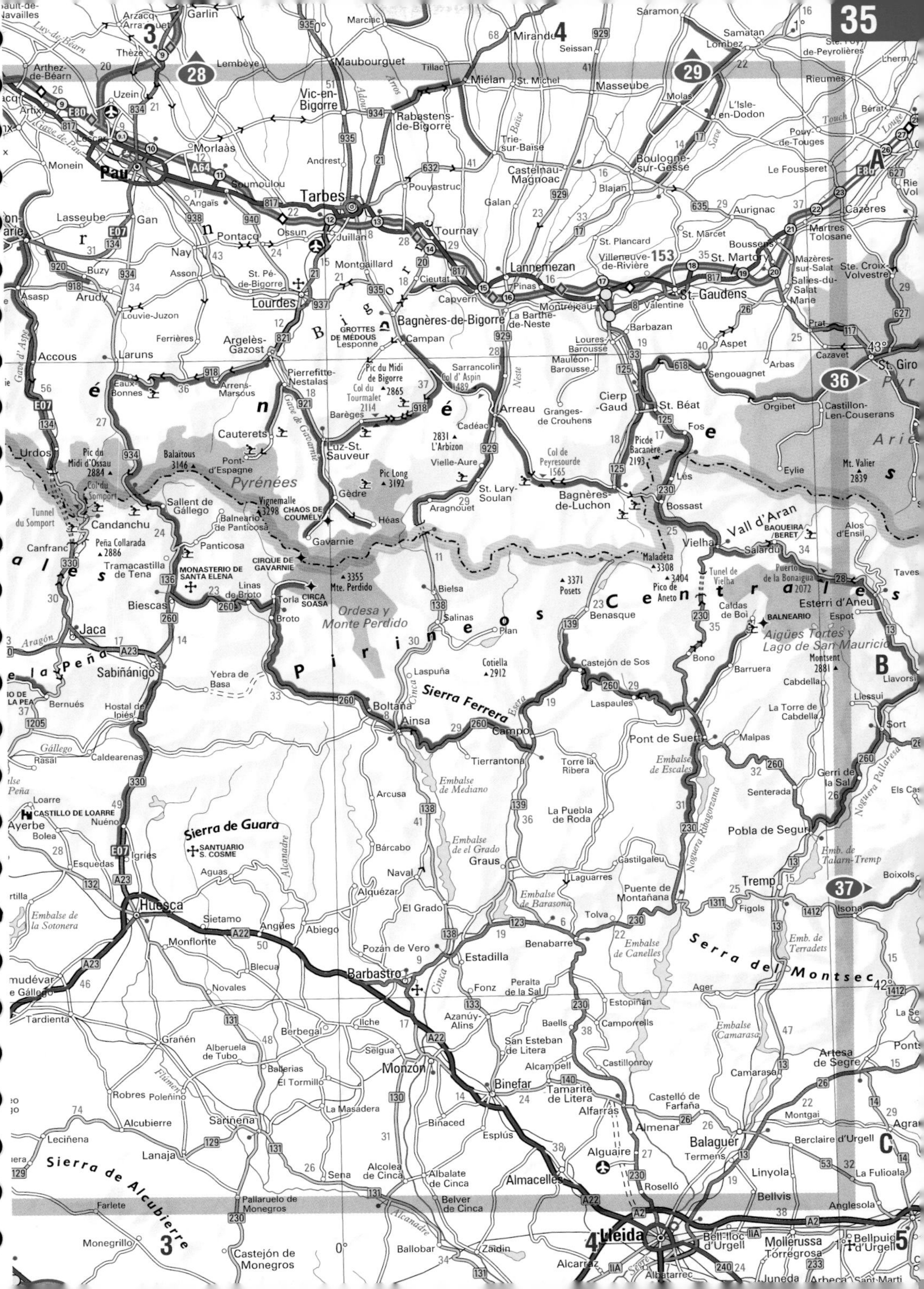

Pau
Tarbes
Lourdes
Bagnères-de-Bigorre
Lannemezan
St. Gaudens
Montréjeau
Vic-en-Bigorre
Maubourguet
Rabastens-de-Bigorre
Mielan
Mirande
Masseube
Boulogne-sur-Gesse
Castelnau-Magnoac
Trie-sur-Baïse
Morlaàs
Soumoulou
Nay
Arudy
Oloron
Argelès-Gazost
Pierrefitte-Nestalas
Cauterets
Luz-St. Sauveur
Barèges
Gavarnie
Arreau
St. Lary-Soulan
Bagnères-de-Luchon
Cierp-Gaud
St. Béat
Aspet
Cazères
Martres Tolosane
St. Martory
Salies-du-Salat
St. Girons
Castillon-Len-Couserans
Pyrénées
Pic du Midi de Bigorre 2865
Col du Tourmalet 2114
Col d' Aspin 1489
Col de Peyresourde 1565
Pic du Midi d'Ossau 2884
Balaïtous 3146
Vignemalle 3298
Pic Long 3192
L'Arbizon 2831
Mt. Valier 2839
Pic de Bacanère 2193
Tunnel du Somport
Col du Somport
Canfranc
Candanchu
Jaca
Sabiñánigo
Biescas
Sallent de Gállego
Panticosa
Torla
Broto
Bielsa
Benasque
Vielha
Vall d'Aran
Tunel de Vielha
Salardú
Baqueira / Beret
Maladeta 3308
Pico de Aneto 3404
Posets 3371
Mte. Perdido 3355
Ordesa y Monte Perdido
Cotiella 2912
Aigües Tortes y Lago de San Mauricio
Esterri d'Aneu
Sierra Ferrera
Boltaña
Ainsa
Campo
Castejón de Sos
Pont de Suert
Pobla de Segur
Sort
Tremp
Serra del Montsec
Graus
Barbastro
Monzón
Binefar
Huesca
Sierra de Guara
Balaguer
Lleida
Almacelles
Tamarite de Litera
Sariñena
Sierra de Alcubierre
Alcubierre
Lanaja
Grañén
Tardienta
Ayerbe
Castillo de Loarre
Mollerussa
Bellpuig d'Urgell
Artesa de Segre
Alcarràs
Fraga
Pirineos Centrales
Pyrénées
28
29
36
37
3
4
5
A
B
C

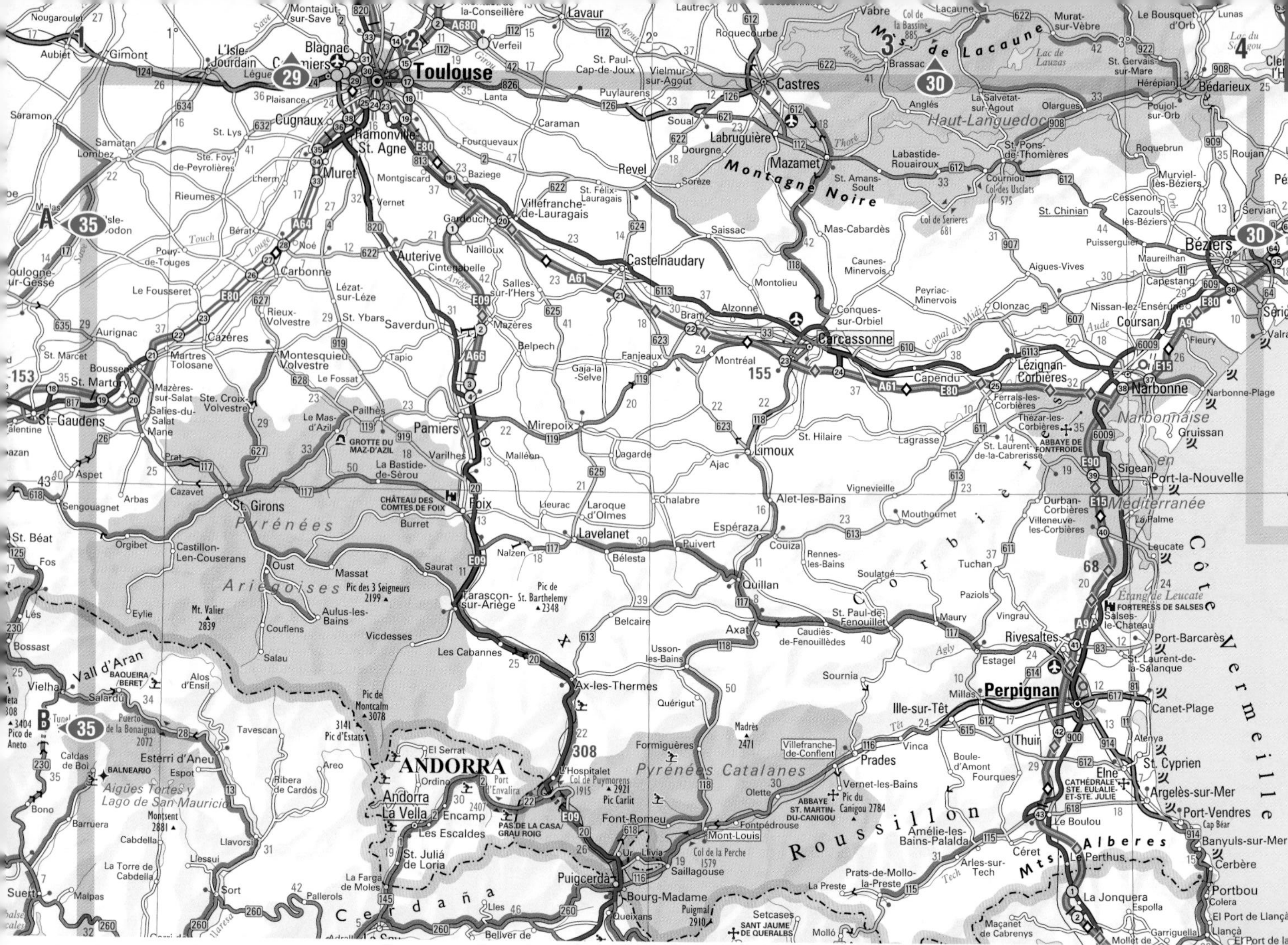

Toulouse
Blagnac
Colomiers
L'Isle-Jourdain
Cugnaux
Ramonville-St. Agne
Muret
Lavaur
Castres
Mazamet
Labruguière
Revel
Castelnaudary
Villefranche-de-Lauragais
Carcassonne
Limoux
Lézignan-Corbières
Narbonne
Béziers
Bédarieux
St. Pons-de-Thomières
Pamiers
Foix
Mirepoix
Lavelanet
Quillan
St. Girons
St. Gaudens
Tarascon-sur-Ariège
Ax-les-Thermes
Perpignan
Rivesaltes
Ille-sur-Têt
Prades
Thuir
Elne
Céret
Le Boulou
Le Perthus
Argelès-sur-Mer
Port-Vendres
Banyuls-sur-Mer
Cerbère
Portbou
La Jonquera
Puigcerdà
Bourg-Madame
Font-Romeu
Mont-Louis
ANDORRA
Andorra La Vella
Vall d'Aran
Vielha
Montagne Noire
Mts. de Lacaune
Haut-Languedoc
Corbières
Pyrénées
Ariégoises
Pyrénées Catalanes
Roussillon
Mts. Albères
Cerdaña
Côte Vermeille
Méditerranée
Narbonnaise en Méditerranée
Étang de Leucate
FORTERESS DE SALSES
ABBAYE DE FONTFROIDE
CHÂTEAU DES COMTES DE FOIX
GROTTE DU MAZ-D'AZIL
ABBAYE ST. MARTIN-DU-CANIGOU
CATHÉDRALE STE. EULALIE-ET-STE. JULIE
Pic du Canigou 2784
Pic Carlit
Pic d'Estats 3141
Pic de Montcalm 3078
Pic de Aneto 3404
Mt. Valier 2839
Puigmal 2910
Canal du Midi
43°
A
B
1
2
3
4
29
30
35
153
155
308

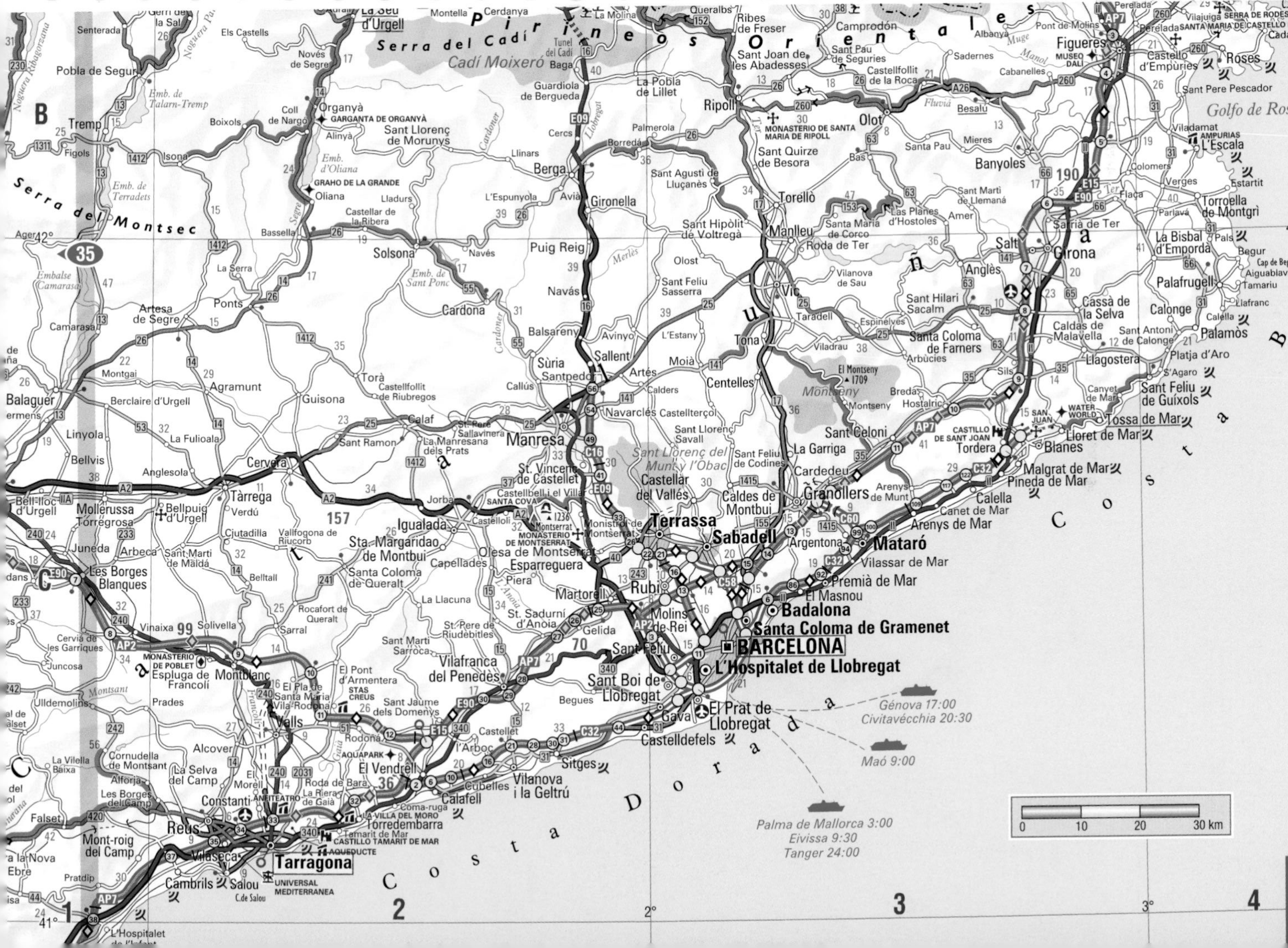
Pirineos Orientales
Serra del Cadí
Cadí Moixeró
Serra del Montsec
Golfo de Roses
Costa Brava
Costa Dorada
BARCELONA
L'Hospitalet de Llobregat
Santa Coloma de Gramenet
Badalona
Mataró
Sabadell
Terrassa
Granollers
Manresa
Vic
Girona
Figueres
Tarragona
Reus
Lleida
Igualada
Vilafranca del Penedès
Vilanova i la Geltrú
Sitges
Castelldefels
El Prat de Llobregat
Blanes
Lloret de Mar
Tossa de Mar
Sant Feliu de Guíxols
Palamós
Palafrugell
Roses
L'Escala
Olot
Ripoll
Berga
Solsona
Cervera
Tàrrega
Valls
El Vendrell
Salou
Cambrils
Tremp
Balaguer
Génova 17:00
Civitavécchia 20:30
Maó 9:00
Palma de Mallorca 3:00
Eivissa 9:30
Tanger 24:00
0 10 20 30 km
B
C
1
2
3
4
42°
41°
2°
3°

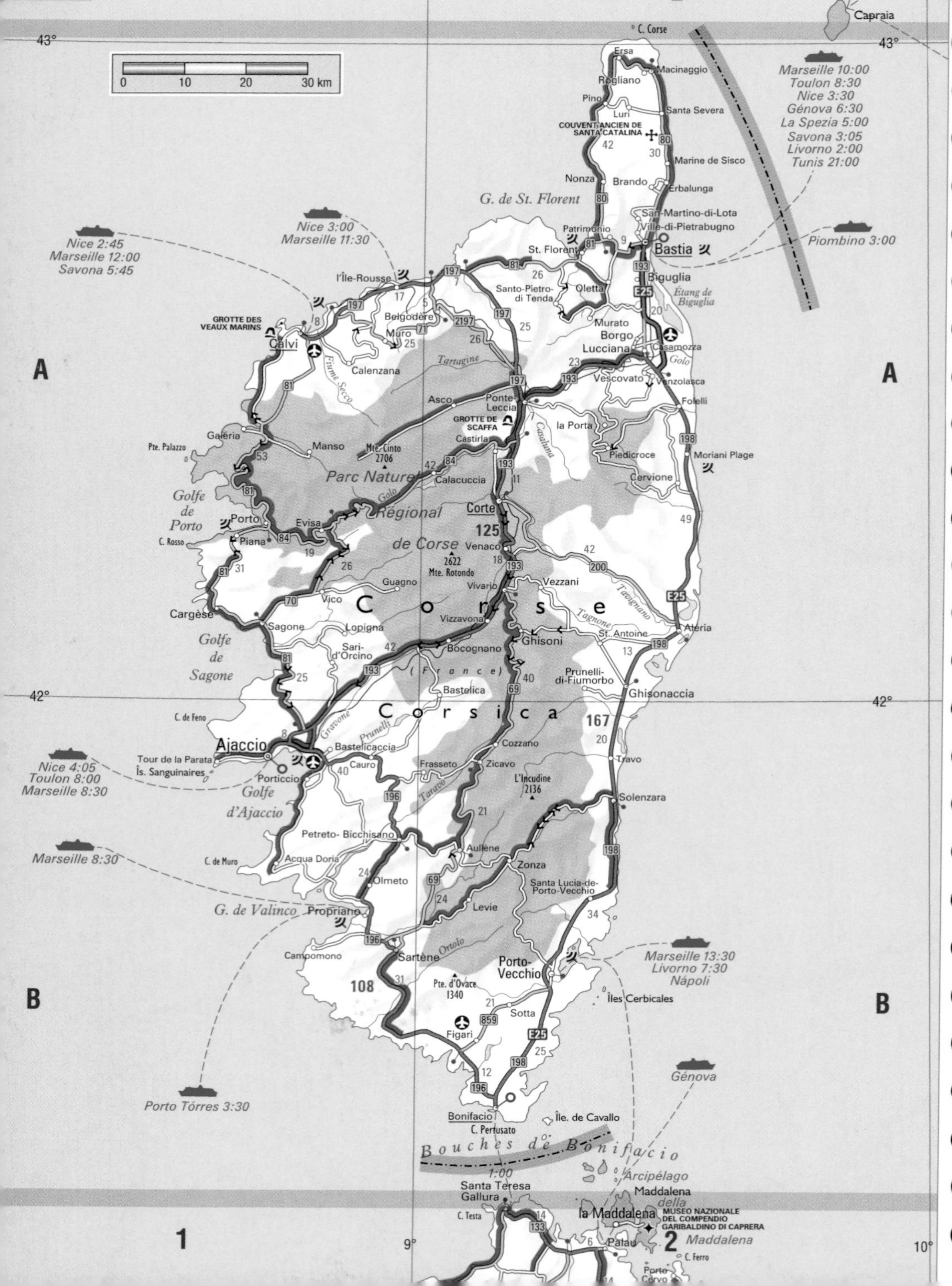

1
2
A
B
9°
10°
43°
42°
0 10 20 30 km
C. Corse
Capraia
Marseille 10:00
Toulon 8:30
Nice 3:30
Génova 6:30
La Spezia 5:00
Savona 3:05
Livorno 2:00
Tunis 21:00
Ersa
Macinaggio
Rogliano
Pino
Luri
Santa Severa
COUVENT ANCIEN DE SANTA CATALINA
Marine de Sisco
Nonza
Brando
Erbalunga
G. de St. Florent
San-Martino-di-Lota
Ville-di-Pietrabugno
Patrimonio
Bastia
Piombino 3:00
St. Florent
Biguglia
Étang de Biguglia
Nice 3:00
Marseille 11:30
Nice 2:45
Marseille 12:00
Savona 5:45
l'Île-Rousse
Santo-Pietro-di Tenda
Oletta
Belgodère
Muro
GROTTE DES VEAUX MARINS
Calvi
Murato
Borgo
Lucciana
Casamozza
Golo
Calenzana
Tartagine
Fiume Secco
Vescovato
Venzolasca
Asco
Ponte-Leccia
Folelli
GROTTE DE SCAFFA
la Porta
Castirla
Galéria
Pte. Palazzo
Manso
Mte. Cinto 2706
Piedicroce
Moriani Plage
Calacuccia
Cervione
Parc Naturel Régional de Corse
Golfe de Porto
Porto
Evisa
Corte
C. Rosso
Piana
Venaco
Mte. Rotondo 2622
Vezzani
Guagno
Vivario
Tavignano
Cargèse
Vico
Corse
Vizzavona
Tagnone
Sagone
Lopigna
Aléria
Ghisoni
St. Antoine
Golfe de Sagone
Sari-d'Orcino
Bocognano
(France)
Prunelli-di-Fiumorbo
Bastelica
Ghisonaccia
C. de Feno
Corsica
Gravone
Prunelli
Ajaccio
Bastelicaccia
Cozzano
Tour de la Parata
Îs. Sanguinaires
Nice 4:05
Toulon 8:00
Marseille 8:30
Porticcio
Cauro
Frasseto
Zicavo
Travo
Golfe d'Ajaccio
Taravo
L'Incudine 2136
Solenzara
Petreto-Bicchisano
Marseille 8:30
C. de Muro
Acqua Doria
Aullène
Zonza
Olmeto
Santa Lucia-de-Porto-Vecchio
G. de Valinco
Propriano
Levie
Campomono
Sartène
Ortolo
Porto-Vecchio
Marseille 13:30
Livorno 7:30
Nápoli
Pte. d'Ovace 1340
Îles Cerbicales
Sotta
Figari
Porto Tórres 3:30
Génova
Bonifacio
C. Pertusato
Île. de Cavallo
Bouches de Bonifacio
1:00
Arcipélago della Maddalena
Santa Teresa Gallura
C. Testa
la Maddalena
MUSEO NAZIONALE DEL COMPENDIO GARIBALDINO DI CAPRERA
Palau
Maddalena
C. Ferro
Porto Cervo
125
167
108
E25

City plans

Motorway	Destination (GENT)
Major through route	Railway
Through route	Rail / bus station
Secondary road	Underground, metro station
Dual carriageway	Cable car
Other road	Abbey, cathedral
Tunnel	Church of interest
Limited access / pedestrian road	Synagogue
One-way street	Hospital
Parking	Police station (POL)
Motorway number (A7)	Post office
National road number (447)	Tourist information
European road number (E45)	Place of interest (Theatre)
Car ferry	Public Building (Sorbonne)

Approach maps

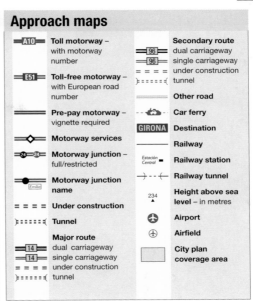

Toll motorway – with motorway number (A10)	Secondary route: dual carriageway (96), single carriageway (96), under construction, tunnel
Toll-free motorway – with European road number (E51)	Other road
Pre-pay motorway – vignette required	Car ferry
Motorway services	Destination (GIRONA)
Motorway junction – full/restricted (24)	Railway
Motorway junction name (Emilia)	Railway station (Estación Central)
Under construction	Railway tunnel
Tunnel	Height above sea level – in metres (234)
Major route: dual carriageway (14), single carriageway (14), under construction, tunnel	Airport
	Airfield
	City plan coverage area

Amsterdam

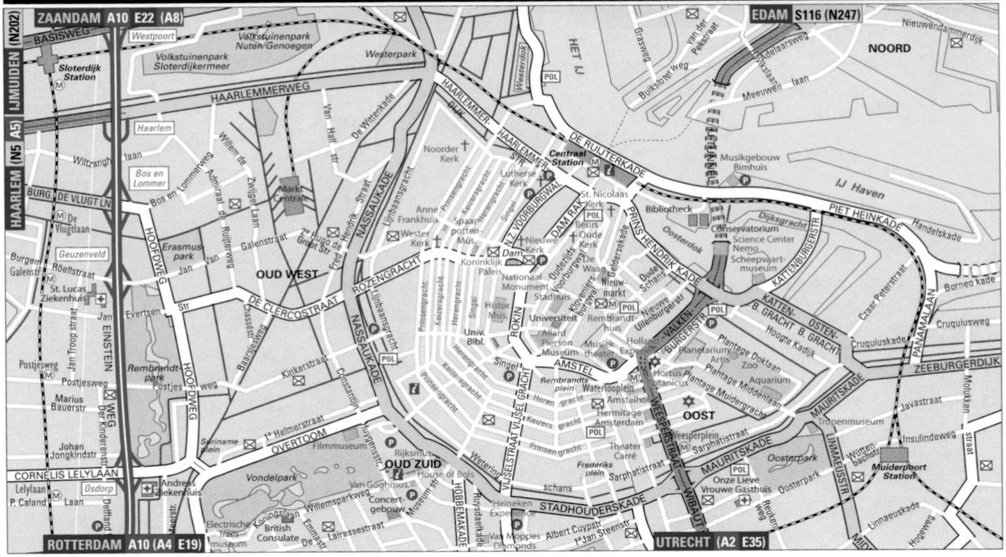

Bruxelles Brussels

0 km 1

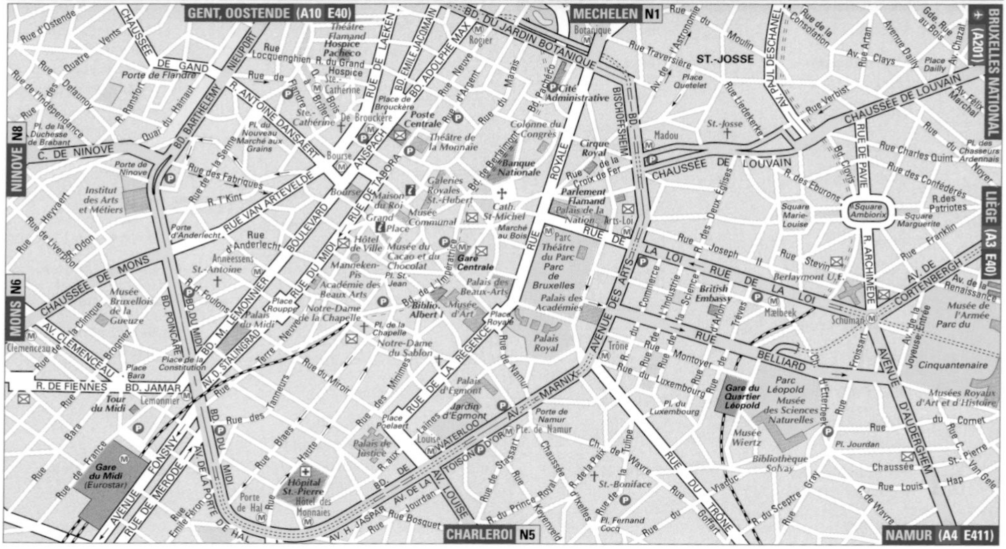

Bordeaux

0 km 1

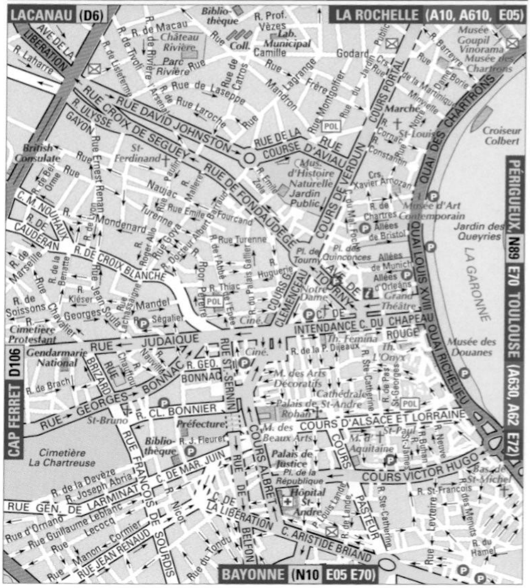

Bordeaux

0 km 5

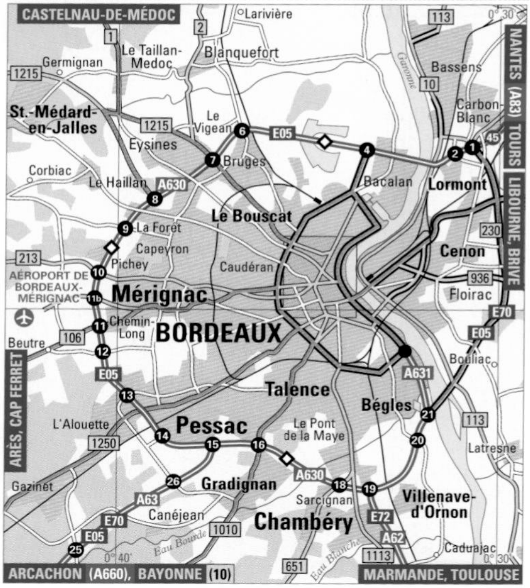

Lyon

0 km 5

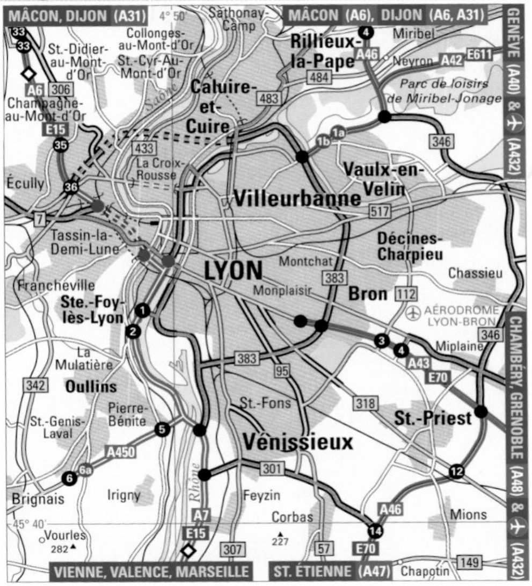

Lyon

0 km 1

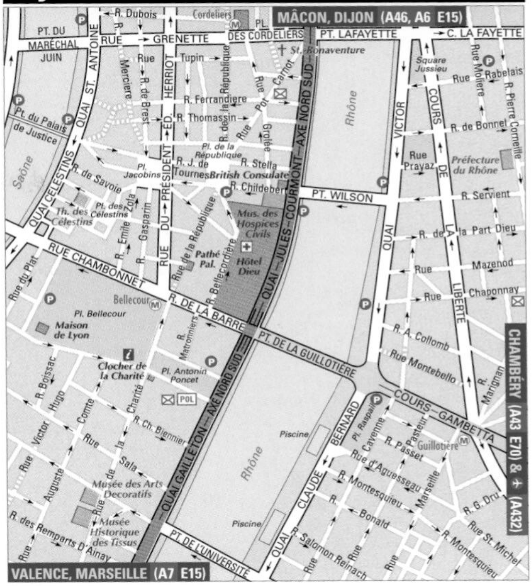

Luxembourg

0 km 0.5

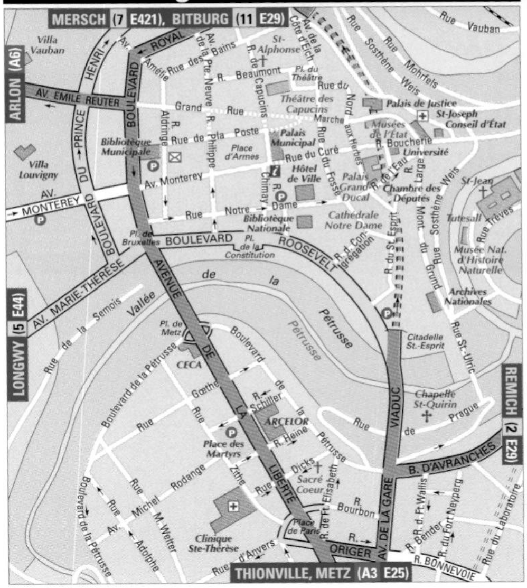

Marseille Marseilles

0 km 0.5

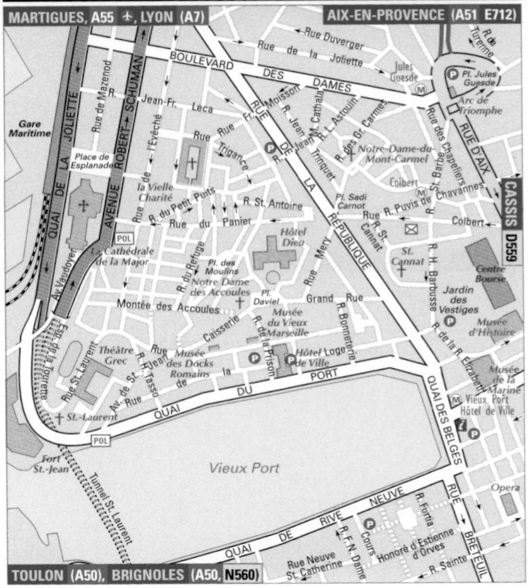

Paris

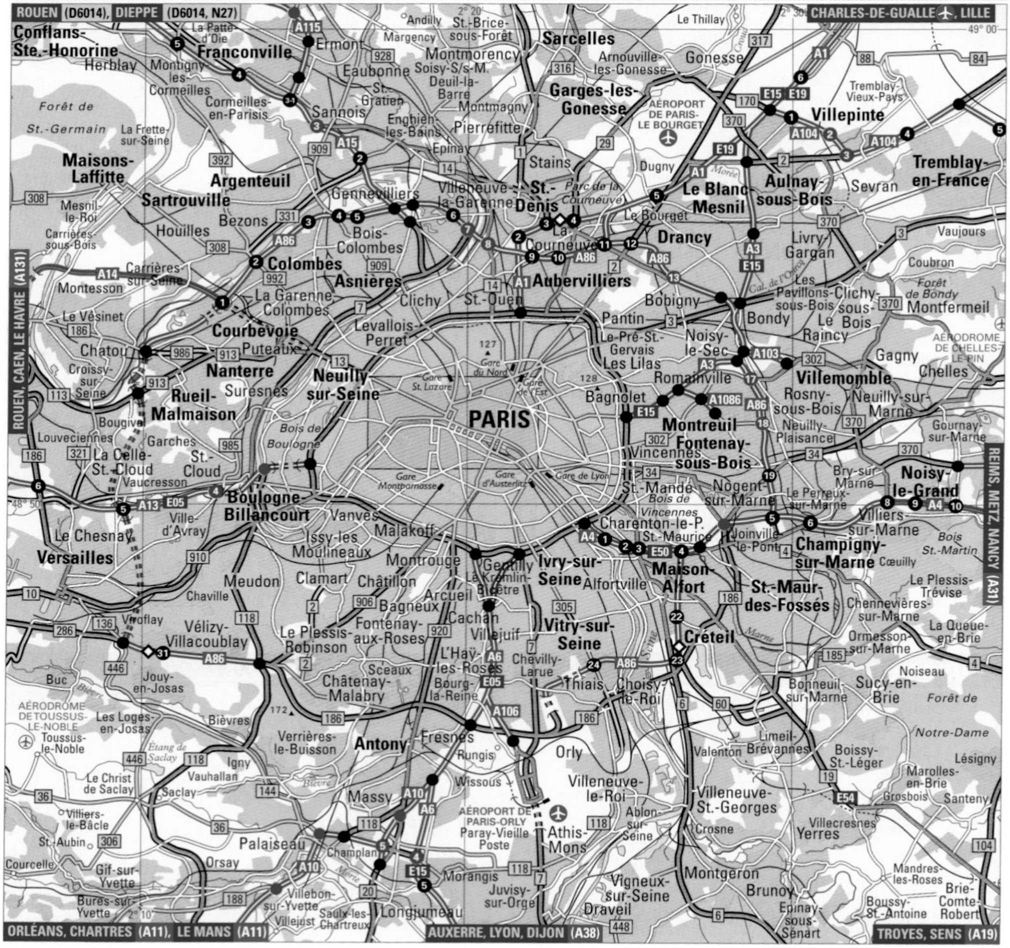
0 km 5
ROUEN (D6014), DIEPPE (D6014, N27)
CHARLES-DE-GUALLE, LILLE
ROUEN, CAEN, LE HAVRE (A131)
REIMS, METZ, NANCY (A31)
ORLÉANS, CHARTRES (A11), LE MANS (A11)
AUXERRE, LYON, DIJON (A38)
TROYES, SENS (A19)
PARIS
Conflans-Ste.-Honorine
Franconville
Herblay
Montigny-les-Cormeilles
Ermont
Andilly
Margency
St.-Brice-sous-Forêt
Sarcelles
Le Thillay
Gonesse
Arnouville-les-Gonesse
Eaubonne
Montmorency
Soisy-S/s-M.
Deuil-la-Barre
Montmagny
St.-Gratien
Sannois
Cormeilles-en-Parisis
Forêt de St.-Germain
La Frette-sur-Seine
Enghien-les-Bains
Pierrefitte
Epinay
Garges-les-Gonesse
AÉROPORT DE PARIS-LE BOURGET
Villepinte
Tremblay-Vieux-Pays
Tremblay-en-France
Sevran
Aulnay-sous-Bois
Le Blanc-Mesnil
Dugny
Stains
Maisons-Laffitte
Argenteuil
Sartrouville
Mesnil-le-Roi
Carrières-sous-Bois
Houilles
Bezons
Gennevilliers
Villeneuve-la-Garenne
St.-Denis
Parc de la Courneuve
La Courneuve
Le Bourget
Drancy
Livry-Gargan
Vaujours
Coubron
Forêt de Bondy
Montfermeil
Colombes
Bois-Colombes
Asnières
Aubervilliers
Bobigny
Les Pavillons-sous-Bois
Clichy-sous-Bois
Le Raincy
Bondy
Montesson
Carrières-sur-Seine
La Garenne-Colombes
Clichy
St.-Ouen
Pantin
Le Vésinet
Courbevoie
Levallois-Perret
Le-Pré-St.-Gervais
Les Lilas
Noisy-le-Sec
AÉRODROME DE CHELLES-LE PIN
Gagny
Chelles
Chatou
Puteaux
Nanterre
Croissy-sur-Seine
Rueil-Malmaison
Suresnes
Neuilly-sur-Seine
Gare du Nord
Gare de l'Est
Gare St. Lazare
Bagnolet
Romainville
Villemomble
Rosny-sous-Bois
Neuilly-sur-Marne
Montreuil
Neuilly-Plaisance
Gournay-sur-Marne
Bougival
Louveciennes
Garches
Bois de Boulogne
La Celle-St.-Cloud
St.-Cloud
Vaucresson
Fontenay-sous-Bois
Vincennes
St.-Mandé
Bois de Vincennes
Nogent-sur-Marne
Bry-sur-Marne
Le Perreux-sur-Marne
Noisy-le-Grand
Gare Montparnasse
Gare d'Austerlitz
Gare de Lyon
Boulogne-Billancourt
Ville-d'Avray
Le Chesnay
Versailles
Vanves
Malakoff
Issy-les-Moulineaux
Charenton-le-P.
St.-Maurice
Joinville-le-Pont
Villiers-sur-Marne
Bois St.-Martin
Champigny-sur-Marne
Cœuilly
Montrouge
Gentilly
Le Kremlin-Bicêtre
Ivry-sur-Seine
Alfortville
Maison-Alfort
St.-Maur-des-Fossés
Meudon
Clamart
Châtillon
Chaville
Bagneux
Arcueil
Cachan
Le Plessis-Trévise
Chennevières-sur-Marne
La Queue-en-Brie
Viroflay
Vélizy-Villacoublay
Fontenay-aux-Roses
Villejuif
Vitry-sur-Seine
Créteil
Ormesson-sur-Marne
Le Plessis-Robinson
L'Haÿ-les-Roses
Chevilly-Larue
Noiseau
Buc
Jouy-en-Josas
Sceaux
Châtenay-Malabry
Bourg-la-Reine
Thiais
Choisy-le-Roi
Bonneuil-sur-Marne
Sucy-en-Brie
Forêt de Notre-Dame
AÉRODROME DE TOUSSUS-LE-NOBLE
Toussus-le-Noble
Les Loges-en-Josas
Bièvres
Verrières-le-Buisson
Antony
Fresnes
Rungis
Orly
Limeil-Brévannes
Valenton
Boissy-St.-Léger
Lésigny
Marolles-en-Brie
Santeny
Grosbois
Étang de Saclay
Igny
Vauhallan
Le Christ de Saclay
Saclay
Massy
Wissous
Villeneuve-le-Roi
Villeneuve-St.-Georges
Villecresnes
Yerres
Villiers-le-Bâcle
St.-Aubin
AÉROPORT DE PARIS-ORLY
Paray-Vieille Poste
Athis-Mons
Ablon-sur-Seine
Crosne
Palaiseau
Champlan
Orsay
Courcelle
Gif-sur-Yvette
Bures-sur-Yvette
Villebon-sur-Yvette
Villejust
Saulx-les-Chartreux
Longjumeau
Morangis
Juvisy-sur-Orge
Vigneux-sur-Seine
Draveil
Montgeron
Brunoy
Epinay-sous-Sénart
Mandres-les-Roses
Boussy-St.-Antoine
Brie-Comte-Robert

Paris

0 km 1

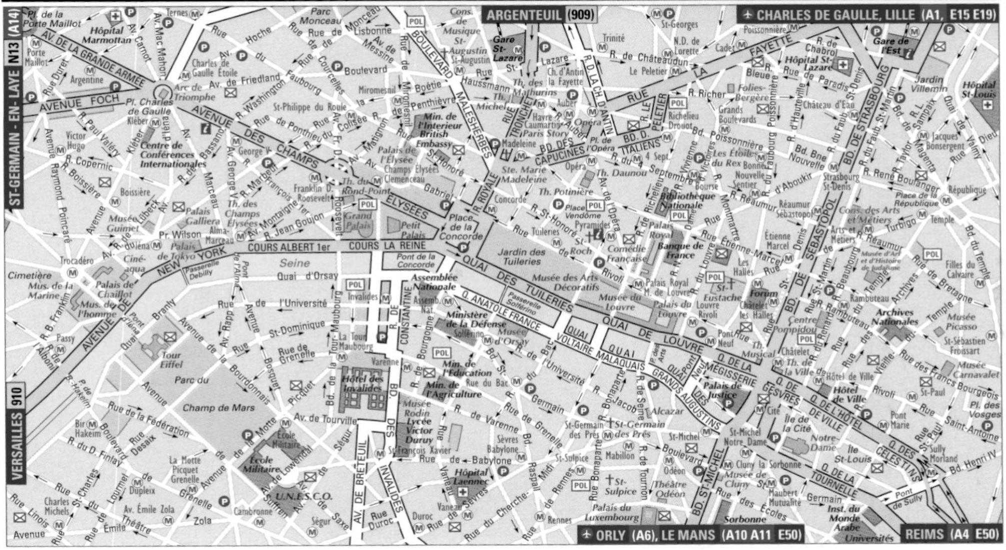
ARGENTEUIL (909)
CHARLES DE GAULLE, LILLE (A1, E15 E19)
ST-GERMAIN - EN - LAYE N13 (A14)
VERSAILLES 910
ORLY (A6), LE MANS (A10 A11 E50)
REIMS (A4 E50)
AVENUE FOCH
AV. DE LA GRANDE ARMEE
AVENUE DES CHAMPS ELYSÉES
COURS ALBERT 1er
COURS LA REINE
QUAI DES TUILERIES
QUAI DE LOUVRE
QUAI VOLTAIRE
Q. ANATOLE FRANCE
Seine
Quai d'Orsay
Arc de Triomphe
Jardin des Tuileries
Champ de Mars
Parc du
Tour Eiffel
Palais de Chaillot
Trocadéro
Place de la Concorde
Gare St-Lazare
Gare de l'Est
Hôtel des Invalides
École Militaire
U.N.E.S.C.O.
Palais de Justice
Bibliothèque Nationale
Forum
Notre Dame
Sorbonne
Palais du Luxembourg
BD. DE SEBASTOPOL
BD. ST-MICHEL
BD. DE STRASBOURG
BD. HAUSSMANN
BOULEVARD MALESHERBES
RUE LA FAYETTE
Archives Nationales
Assemblée Nationale
Musée des Arts Décoratifs
Grand Palais
Petit Palais

Strasbourg

0 km 5

METZ
OFFENBURG
OFFENBURG (33), A5
OFFENBURG (33a), A5
NANCY (A33)
MOLSHEIM, ST. DIÉ (D1420 A352)
SÉLESTAT
BASEL (A5)
STRASBOURG
Schiltigheim
Bischheim
Hoenheim
Souffelweyersheim
Mundolsheim
Griesheim-sur-Souffel
Dingsheim
Stutzheim-Offenheim
Niederhausbergen
Mittelhausbergen
Oberhausbergen
Oberschaeffolsheim
Achenheim
Wolfisheim
Eckbolsheim
Holtzheim
Hangenbieten
Lingolsheim
Ostwald
Illkirch-Graffenstaden
Entzheim
Kratz
Geispolsheim
Lipsheim
Eschau
Fegersheim
Ichtratzheim
Hindisheim
Plobsheim
Müllen
Goldscheuer
Marlen
Eckartsweier
Stockfeld
Neuhof
La Meinau
Neudorf
Kehl
Auenheim
La Robertsau
Elsau
AÉRODROME DE POLYGONE
AÉROPORT DE STRASBOURG-INTERNATIONAL
FRANCE
DEUTSCHLAND
Rhin
Rhine
Bruche
Souffel
Andlau
Canal du Rhône au Rhin
Mühlbach
A4
E25
A35
A351
A354
E25
1004
468
41
222
221
392
400
28
36
353
1083
7° 40
7° 50
48° 30

Strasbourg

0 km 0.5

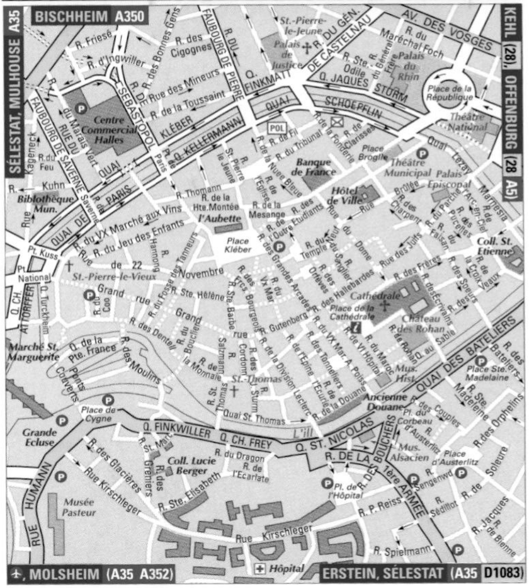
BISCHHEIM A350
SÉLESTAT, MULHOUSE A35
KEHL (28), OFFENBURG (28 A5)
MOLSHEIM (A35 A352)
ERSTEIN, SÉLESTAT (A35 D1083)
AV. DES VOSGES
Place de la République
Centre Commercial Halles
QUAI KLÉBER
Q. KELLERMANN
QUAI DE PARIS
QUAI SCHOEPFLIN
Banque de France
Théâtre Municipal
Hôtel de Ville
Place Kléber
l'Aubette
Cathédrale
Château des Rohan
Place Broglie
Ancienne Douane
Q. FINKWILLER
Q. CH. FREY
Q. ST. NICOLAS
QUAI DES BATELIERS
Grande Ecluse
Musée Pasteur
Coll. Lucie Berger
Bibliothèque Mun.
Marché St. Marguerite
L'Ill
Hôpital
Place d'Austerlitz
RUE HUMANN
FAUBOURG DE SAVERNE
FAUBOURG DE PIERRE
BD. DU PRÉSIDENT WILSON

A

Aach D 21 B4
Aachen D 6 B2
Aalsmeer NL 2 B1
Aalst B 5 B4
Aalten NL 3 C3
Aalter B 5 A3
Aarau CH 20 B3
Aarberg CH 20 B2
Aarburg CH 20 B2
Aardenburg NL 5 A3
Aarschot B 5 B4
Abbeville F 10 A1
Abiego E 35 B3
Ablis F 10 C1
Abondance F 26 A3
Abreschviller F 12 C3
Abrest F 25 A3
Abriès F 27 C3
Accéglio I 32 A2
Accous F 35 A3
Achene B 5 B5
Achern D 13 C4
Acheux-en-Amienois F 10 A2
Acqua Doria F 38 B1
Acqui Terme I 27 C5
Acquigny F 9 A5
Acy-en-Multien F 10 B2
Adeanueva de Ebro E 34 B2
Adelboden CH 20 C2
Adenau D 6 B2
Adinkerke B 4 A2
Adliswil CH 21 B3
Adorf, *Hessen* D 7 A4
Adrall E 37 B2
Aesch CH 20 B2
Affoltern CH 20 B3
Agay F 32 B2
Agde F 30 B2
Agen F 29 B3
Ager E 35 C4
Agnières F 26 C2
Agon Coutainville F 8 A2
Agramunt E 37 C2
Agreda E 34 C2
Aguas E 35 B3
Aguessac F 30 A2
Ahaus D 3 B3
Ahlen D 7 A3
Ahlhorn D 3 B5
Ahun F 24 A2
Aibar E 34 B2
Aigle CH 27 A3
Aignan F 28 C3
Aignay-le-Duc F 18 B3
Aigre F 23 C4
Aigrefeuille-d'Aunis F 22 B3
Aigrefeuille-sur-Maine F 15 B4
Aiguablava E 37 C4
Aiguebelle F 26 B3
Aigueperse F 24 A3
Aigues-Mortes F 31 B3
Aigues-Vives F 30 B1
Aiguilles F 27 C3
Aiguillon F 29 B3
Aigurande F 17 C3
Ailefroide F 26 C3
Aillant-sur-Tholon F 18 B2
Ailly-sur-Noye F 10 B2
Ailly-sur-Somme F 10 B2
Aimargues F 31 B3
Aime F 26 B3
Ainhoa F 34 A2
Ainsa E 35 B4
Airaines F 10 B1
Aire-sur-la-Lys F 4 B2
Aire-sur-l'Adour F 28 C2
Airole I 33 B3
Airolo CH 21 C3
Airvault F 16 C1
Aisey-sur-Seine F 18 B3
Aissey F 19 B5
Aisy-sur-Armançon F 18 B3
Aitrach D 21 B5
Aix-en-Othe F 18 A2
Aix-en-Provence F 31 B4
Aix-les-Bains F 26 B2
Aixe-sur-Vienne F 23 C5
Aizenay F 22 B2
Ajac F 36 A3
Ajaccio F 38 B1
Ajain F 24 A1
Akkrum NL 2 A2
Ala di Stura I 27 B4
Alagna Valsésia I 27 B4
Alagón E 34 C2
Alássio I 33 A4
Alba I 27 C5
Albalate de Cinca E 35 C4
Alban F 30 B1
Albanyà E 37 B3
Albbruck D 20 B3
Albenga I 33 A4
Albens F 26 B2
Albersloh D 7 A3
Albert F 10 A2
Albertville F 26 B3
Alberuela de Tubo E 35 C3
Albi F 30 B1
Albisola Marina I 33 A4
Albstadt D 21 A4
Alcalá de Gurrea E 34 B3
Alcampell E 35 C4
Alcanadre E 34 B1
Alcolea de Cinca E 35 C4
Alcover E 37 C2
Alcubierre E 35 C3
Aldeapozo E 34 C1
Aldenhoven D 6 B2
Aldudes F 34 A2
Alençon F 9 B4
Alenya F 36 B3
Aléria F 38 A2
Alès F 31 A3
Alet-les-Bains F 36 B3
Aleyrac F 31 A3
Alfaro E 34 B2
Alfarrás E 35 C4
Alfhausen D 3 B4
Alforja E 37 C1
Alguaire E 35 C4
Alinyà E 37 B2
Alixan F 25 C5
Alken B 5 B5
Alkmaar NL 2 B1
Allaines F 17 A3
Allaire F 15 B3
Allanche F 24 B2
Allassac F 29 A4
Allauch F 31 B4
Allègre F 25 B3
Allemont F 26 B3
Allendorf D 7 B4
Allevard F 26 B3
Allmannsdorf D 21 B4
Allo E 34 B1
Allogny F 17 B4
Allones, *Eure et Loire* F 10 C1
Allones, *Maine-et-Loire* F 16 B2
Allonnes F 16 B2
Allons F 28 B2
Allos F 32 A2
Almacelles E 35 C4
Almajano E 34 C1
Alme D 7 A4
Almelo NL 3 B3
Almenar E 35 C4
Almere NL 2 B2
Almese I 27 B4
Almudévar E 35 B3
Alos d'Ensil E 36 B2
Alpen D 6 A2
Alphen aan de Rijn NL 2 B1
Alpignano I 27 B4
Alpirsbach D 13 C4
Alquézar E 35 B4
Alsasua E 34 B1
Alsdorf D 6 B2
Alsfeld D 7 B5
Alstätte D 3 B3
Altdorf CH 21 C3
Altena D 7 A3
Altenberge D 3 B4
Altenheim D 13 C3
Altenhundem D 7 A4
Altenkirchen, *Radom* D 7 B3
Altensteig D 13 C4
Altkirch F 20 B2
Altshausen D 21 B4
Altstätten CH 21 B4
Altusried D 21 B5
Alvignac F 29 B4
Alvimare F 9 A4
Alzénau D 13 A5
Alzey D 13 B4
Alzonne F 36 A3
Amance F 19 B5
Amancey F 19 B5
Amay B 5 B5
Ambazac F 23 C5
Ambérieu-en-Bugey F 26 B2
Ambérieux-en-Dombes F 25 A4
Ambert F 25 B3
Ambès F 28 A2
Ambleteuse F 4 B1
Amboise F 16 B2
Ambrières-les-Vallées F 8 B3
Amden CH 21 B4
Amel B 6 B2
Amélie-les-Bains-Palalda F 36 B3
Amer E 37 B3
Amerongen NL 2 B2
Amersfoort NL 2 B2
Amiens F 10 B2
Amou F 28 C2
Amplepuis F 25 B4
Amriswil CH 21 B4
Amstelveen NL 2 B1
Amsterdam NL 2 B1
Amtzell D 21 B4
Ancenis F 15 B4
Ancerville F 11 C5
Ancy-le-Franc F 18 B3
Andance F 25 B4
Andeer CH 21 C4
Andelfingen CH 21 B3
Andelot F 19 A4
Andelot-en-Montagne F 19 C4
Andenne B 5 B5
Anderlues B 5 B4
Andermatt CH 21 C3
Andernach D 6 B3
Andernos-les-Bains F 28 B1
Andijk NL 2 B2
Andoain E 34 A1
Andolsheim F 20 A2
Andorra La Vella AND 36 B2
Andosilla E 34 B2
Andrest F 35 A4
Andrezieux-Bouthéon F 25 B4
Anduze F 31 A2
Anet F 10 C1
Angaïs F 35 A3
Angers F 16 B1
Angerville F 10 C2
Anglès E 37 C3
Anglés, *Tarn* F 30 B1
Angles, *Vendée* F 22 B2
Angles sur l'Anglin F 23 B4
Anglesola E 37 C2
Anglet F 28 C1
Anglure F 11 C3
Angoulême F 23 C4
Angoulins F 22 B2
Angües E 35 B3
Anhée B 5 B4
Aniane F 30 B2
Aniche F 4 B3
Anizy-le-Château F 11 B3
Ankum D 3 B4
Anlezy F 18 C2
Annecy F 26 B3
Annemasse F 26 A3
Annevoie-Rouillon B 5 B4
Annonay F 25 B4
Annot F 32 B2
Annweiler D 13 B3
Anould F 20 A1
Anröchte D 7 A4
Anse F 25 B4
Anserœul B 5 B3
Ansó E 34 B3
Ansoain E 34 B2
Antibes F 32 B3
Antoing B 5 B3
Antrain F 8 B2
Antronapiana I 27 A5
Antwerp = Antwerpen B 5 A4
Antwerpen = Antwerp B 5 A4
Anvin F 4 B2
Anzat-le-Luguet F 24 B3
Anzón E 34 C2
Aoiz E 34 B2
Aosta I 27 B4
Apeldoorn NL 2 B2
Apen D 3 A4
Appenzell CH 21 B4
Appingedam NL 3 A3
Appoigny F 18 B2
Apremont-la-Forêt F 12 C1
Apt F 31 B4
Aragnouet F 35 B4
Aramits F 34 A3
Aramon F 31 B3
Arbas F 35 B4
Arbeca E 37 C1
Arbois F 19 C4
Arbon CH 21 B4
Arbório I 27 B5
Arbúcies E 37 C3
Arc-en-Barrois F 19 B3
Arc-et-Senans F 19 B4
Arc-lès-Gray F 19 B4
Arc-sur-Tille F 19 B4
Arcachon F 28 B1
Arcen NL 6 A2
Arces-Dilo F 18 A2
Arcey F 20 B1
Archiac F 23 C3
Arcis-sur-Aube F 11 C4
Arcusa E 35 B4
Arcy-sur-Cure F 18 B2
Ardentes F 17 C3
Ardes F 24 B3
Ardez CH 21 C5
Ardisa E 34 B3
Ardooie B 4 B3
Ardres F 4 B1
Arendonk B 5 A5
Arengosse F 28 B2
Arenys de Mar E 37 C3
Arenys de Munt E 37 C3
Arenzano I 33 A4
Areo E 36 B2
Arès F 28 B1
Arette F 34 A3
Arfeuilles F 25 A3
Argelès-Gazost F 35 A3
Argelès-sur-Mer F 36 B4
Argent-sur-Sauldre F 17 B4
Argentan F 9 B3
Argentat F 24 B1
Argentera I 32 A2
Argenteuil F 10 C2
Argenthal D 13 B3
Argenton-Château F 16 C1
Argenton-sur-Creuse F 17 C3
Argentona E 37 C3
Argentré F 16 A1
Argentré-du-Plessis F 15 A4
Arguedas E 34 B2
Argueil F 10 B1
Aribe E 34 B2
Arinthod F 26 A2
Arlanc F 25 B3
Arlebosc F 25 B4
Arles F 31 B3
Arles-sur-Tech F 36 B3
Arlon B 12 B1
Armeno I 27 B5
Armentières F 4 B2
Arnac-Pompadour F 23 C5
Arnage F 16 B2
Arnas F 25 A4
Arnay-le-Duc F 18 B3
Arnedillo E 34 B1
Arnedo E 34 B1
Arneguy F 34 A2
Arnhem NL 2 C2
Arnsberg D 7 A4
Arolla CH 27 A4
Arolsen D 7 A5
Arona I 27 B5
Arosa CH 21 C4
Arpajon F 10 C2
Arpajon-sur-Cère F 24 C2
Arques F 4 B2
Arques-la-Bataille F 9 A5
Arracourt F 12 C2
Arras F 4 B2
Arreau F 35 B4
Arrens-Marsous F 35 B3
Arromanches-les-Bains F 8 A3
Arroniz E 34 B1
Arrou F 17 A3
Ars-en-Ré F 22 B2
Ars-sur-Moselle F 12 B2
Arsac F 28 B2
Artajona E 34 B2
Artemare F 26 B2
Artenay F 17 A3
Artés E 37 C2
Artesa de Segre E 37 C2
Arth CH 21 B3
Arthez-de-Béarn F 35 A3
Arthon-en-Retz F 15 B4
Artieda E 34 B3
Artix F 35 A3
Arudy F 35 A3
Arveyres F 28 B2
Arvieux F 26 C3
Arzacq-Arraziguet F 28 C2
Arzano F 14 B2
As B 6 A1
Asasp F 35 A3
Ascain F 34 A2
Aschaffenburg D 13 B5
Ascheberg, *Nordrhein-Westfalen* D 7 A3
Aschendorf D 3 A4
Asco F 38 A2
Ascoux F 17 A4
Asfeld F 11 B4
Aspet F 35 A4
Aspres-sur-Buëch F 32 A1
Asse B 5 B4
Asselborn L 12 A1
Assen NL 3 B3
Assenede B 5 A3
Assesse B 5 B5
Asson F 35 A3
Astaffort F 29 B3
Asten NL 6 A1
Asti I 27 C5
Ath B 5 B3
Athies F 10 B2
Athies-sous-Laon F 11 B3
Attendorn D 7 A3
Attichy F 10 B3
Attigny F 11 B4
Au, *Vorarlberg* A 21 B4
Aubagne F 32 B1
Aubange B 12 B1
Aubel B 6 B1
Aubenas F 25 C4
Aubenton F 11 B4
Auberive F 19 B4
Aubeterre-sur-Dronne F 28 A3
Aubiet F 29 C3
Aubigné F 23 B3
Aubigny F 22 B2
Aubigny-au-Bac F 4 B3
Aubigny-en-Artois F 4 B2
Aubigny-sur-Nère F 17 B4
Aubin F 30 A1
Aubonne CH 19 C5
Aubrac F 24 C2
Aubusson F 24 B2
Auch F 29 C3
Auchy-au-Bois F 4 B2
Audenge F 28 B1
Auderville F 8 A2
Audierne F 14 A1
Audincourt F 20 B1
Audruicq F 4 B2
Audun-le-Roman F 12 B1
Audun-le-Tiche F 12 B1
Aue, *Nordrhein-Westfalen* D 7 A4
Augignac F 23 C4
Augustfehn D 3 A4
Aulendorf D 21 B4
Aullène F 38 B2
Aulnay F 23 B3
Aulnoye-Aymeries F 5 B3
Ault F 10 A1
Aulus-les-Bains F 36 B2
Aumale F 10 B1
Aumetz F 12 B1
Aumont-Aubrac F 24 C3
Aunay-en-Bazois F 18 B2
Aunay-sur-Odon F 8 A3
Auneau F 10 C1
Auneuil F 10 B1
Aups F 32 B2
Auray F 14 B3
Aurich D 3 A4
Aurignac F 35 A4
Aurillac F 24 C2
Auriol F 32 B1
Auritz-Burguette E 34 B2
Auros F 28 B2
Auroux F 25 C3
Auterive F 36 A2
Autheuil-Authouillet F 9 A5
Authon F 32 A2
Authon-du-Perche F 16 A2
Autol E 34 B2
Autreville F 12 C1
Autrey-lès-Gray F 19 B4
Autun F 18 C3
Auty-le-Châtel F 17 B4
Auvelais B 5 B4
Auvillar F 29 B3
Auxerre F 18 B2
Auxi-le-Château F 4 B2
Auxon F 18 A2
Auxonne F 19 B4
Auxy F 18 C3
Auzances F 24 A2
Auzon F 25 B3
Availles-Limouzine F 23 B4
Avallon F 18 B2
Avelgem B 5 B3
Avenches CH 20 C2
Avesnes-le-Comte F 4 B2
Avesnes-sur-Helpe F 11 A3
Avià E 37 B2
Avigliana I 27 B4
Avignon F 31 B3
Avilley F 19 B5
Avinyo E 37 C2
Avioth F 12 B1
Avize F 11 C4
Avon F 10 C2
Avord F 17 B4
Avranches F 8 B2
Avril F 12 B1
Avrillé F 16 B1
Awans B 5 B5
Ax-les-Thermes F 36 B2
Axat F 36 B3
Axel NL 5 A3
Ay F 11 B4
Aya E 34 A1
Ayer CH 27 A4
Ayerbe E 34 B3
Ayette F 4 B2
Ayron F 23 B4
Aywaille B 6 B1
Azannes-et-Soumazannes F 12 B1
Azanúy-Alins E 35 C4
Azay-le-Ferron F 23 B5
Azay-le-Rideau F 16 B2
Azé F 25 A4
Azpeitia E 34 A1
Azur F 28 C1

B

Baad A 21 B5
Baar CH 21 B3
Baarle-Nassau B 5 A4
Baarn NL 2 B2
Babenhausen, *Bayern* D 21 A5
Babenhausen, *Hessen* D 13 B4
Baccarat F 12 C2
Bacharach D 13 A3
Bacqueville-en-Caux F 9 A5
Bad Bentheim D 3 B4
Bad Bergzabern D 13 B3
Bad Berleburg D 7 A4
Bad Breisig D 6 B3
Bad Buchau D 21 A4
Bad Camberg D 7 B4
Bad Driburg D 7 A5
Bad Dürkheim D 13 B4
Bad Dürrheim D 21 A3
Bad Ems D 7 B3
Bad Essen D 3 B5
Bad Friedrichshall D 13 B5
Bad Herrenalb D 13 C4
Bad Homburg D 7 B4
Bad Honnef D 6 B3
Bad Hönningen D 6 B3
Bad Iburg D 3 B5
Bad Inner-laterns A 21 B4
Bad Karlshafen D 7 A5
Bad Kemmeriboden CH 20 C2
Bad König D 13 B5
Bad Kreuznach D 13 B3
Bad Krozingen D 20 B2
Bad Laasphe D 7 B4
Bad Liebenzell D 13 C4
Bad Lippspringe D 7 A4
Bad Meinberg D 7 A4
Bad Münstereifel D 6 B2
Bad Nauheim D 7 B4
Bad Neuenahr-Ahrweiler D 6 B3
Bad Orb D 7 B5
Bad Peterstal D 13 C4
Bad Ragaz CH 21 C4
Bad Rappenau D 13 B5
Bad Säckingen D 20 B2
Bad Salzig D 7 B3
Bad Sassendorf D 7 A4
Bad Schönborn D 13 B4
Bad Schussenried D 21 A4
Bad Schwalbach D 7 B4
Bad Soden D 7 B4
Bad Soden-Salmünster D 7 B5
Bad Vilbel D 7 B4
Bad Waldsee D 21 B4
Bad Wildungen D 7 A5
Bad Wurzach D 21 B4
Bad Zwesten D 7 A5
Bad Zwischenahn D 3 A5
Badalona E 37 C3
Badalucco I 33 B3
Baden CH 20 B3
Baden-Baden D 13 C4
Badenweiler D 20 B2
Badonviller F 12 C2
Baells E 35 C4
Baesweiler D 6 B2
Baflo NL 3 A3
Baga E 37 B2
Bagnasco I 33 A4
Bagnères-de-Bigorre F 35 A4
Bagnères-de-Luchon F 35 B4
Bagnoles-de-l'Orne F 9 B3
Bagnols-en-Forêt F 32 B2
Bagnols-sur-Cèze F 31 A3
Baiersbronn D 13 C4
Baignes-Ste. Radegonde F 23 C3
Baigneux-les-Juifs F 18 B3
Baileux B 11 A4
Bailleul F 4 B2
Baillonville B 5 B5
Bailó E 34 B3
Bain-de-Bretagne F 15 B4
Bains F 25 B3
Bains-les-Bains F 19 A5
Bais F 9 B3
Bakum D 3 B5
Balaguer E 35 C4
Balbigny F 25 B4
Balen B 5 A5
Balingen D 21 A3
Balizac F 28 B2
Balk NL 2 B2
Balkbrug NL 3 B3
Ballancourt-sur-Essonne F 10 C2
Ballerias E 35 C3
Balleroy F 8 A3
Ballon F 16 A2
Balme I 27 B4
Balmuccia I 27 B5
Balneario de Panticosa E 35 B3
Balsareny E 37 C2
Balsthal CH 20 B2
Balve D 7 A3
Bande B 5 B5
Bandol F 32 B1
Bangor F 14 B2
Bannalec F 14 B2
Bannes F 11 C3
Banon F 32 A1
Bantheville F 11 B5
Bantzenheim F 20 B2
Banyoles E 37 B3
Banyuls-sur-Mer F 36 B4
Bapaume F 10 A2
Bar-le-Duc F 11 C5
Bar-sur-Aube F 18 A3
Bar-sur-Seine F 18 A3
Barañain E 34 B2
Baraqueville F 30 A1
Barasoain E 34 B2
Barastro E 35 B4
Barbâtre F 22 B1
Barbazan F 35 A4
Barbentane F 31 B3
Barbezieux-St. Hilaire F 23 C3
Barbonne-Fayel F 11 C3
Barbotan-les-Thermes F 28 C2
Bárcabo E 35 B4
Barcelona E 37 C3
Barcelonette F 32 A2
Barcus F 34 A3
Bardonécchia I 26 B3
Barèges F 35 B4
Barentin F 9 A4
Barenton F 8 B3
Barfleur F 8 A2
Barge I 27 C4
Bargemon F 32 B2
Barjac F 31 A3
Barjols F 32 B1
Barjon F 19 B3
Barles F 32 A2
Barneveld NL 2 B2
Barneville-Carteret F 8 A2
Baron F 10 B2
Barr F 13 C3
Barre-des-Cevennes F 30 A2
Barrême F 32 B2
Barret-le-Bas F 32 A1
Barruera E 35 B4
Barssel D 3 A4
Barvaux B 6 B1
Bas E 37 B3
Basécles B 5 B3
Basel CH 20 B2
Bassecourt CH 20 B2
Bassella E 37 B2
Bassou F 18 B2
Bassoues F 28 C3
Bastelica F 38 A2
Bastelicaccia F 38 B1
Bastia F 38 A2
Bastogne B 12 A1

Bätterkinden	CH	20	B2
Battice	B	6	B1
Baud	F	14	B2
Baudour	B	5	B3
Baugé	F	16	B1
Baugy	F	17	B4
Bauma	CH	21	B3
Baume-les-Dames	F	19	B5
Baumholder	D	13	B3
Baunatal	D	7	A5
Bavay	F	5	B3
Bavilliers	F	20	B1
Bawinkel	D	3	B4
Bayel	F	19	A3
Bayeux	F	8	A3
Bayon	F	12	C2
Bayonne	F	28	C1
Bayons	F	32	A2
Bazas	F	28	B2
Baziege	F	36	A2
Bazoches-les-Gallerandes	F	17	A4
Bazoches-sur-Hoëne	F	9	B4
Beasain	E	34	A1
Beaubery	F	25	A4
Beaucaire	F	31	B3
Beaufort	F	26	B3
Beaufort-en Vallée	F	16	B1
Beaugency	F	17	B3
Beaujeu, *Alpes-de-Haute-Provence*	F	32	A2
Beaujeu, *Rhône*	F	25	A4
Beaulac	F	28	B2
Beaulieu	F	17	B4
Beaulieu-sous-la-Roche	F	22	B2
Beaulieu-sur-Dordogne	F	29	B4
Beaulieu-sur-Mer	F	33	B3
Beaulon	F	18	C2
Beaumesnil	F	9	A4
Beaumetz-lès-Loges	F	4	B2
Beaumont	B	5	B4
Beaumont	F	29	B3
Beaumont-de-Lomagne	F	29	C3
Beaumont-du-Gâtinais	F	17	A4
Beaumont-en-Argonne	F	11	B5
Beaumont-Hague	F	8	A2
Beaumont-la-Ronce	F	16	B2
Beaumont-le-Roger	F	9	A4
Beaumont-sur-Oise	F	10	B2
Beaumont-sur-Sarthe	F	16	A2
Beaune	F	19	B3
Beaune-la-Rolande	F	17	A4
Beaupréau	F	15	B5
Beauraing	B	11	A4
Beaurepaire	F	25	B5
Beaurepaire-en-Bresse	F	19	C4
Beaurières	F	32	A1
Beauvais	F	10	B2
Beauval	F	10	A2
Beauville	F	29	B3
Beauvoir-sur-Mer	F	22	B1
Beauvoir-sur-Niort	F	22	B3
Bécherel	F	15	A4
Beckum	D	7	A4
Bécon-les-Granits	F	16	B1
Bédarieux	F	30	B2
Bédarrides	F	31	A3
Bedburg	D	6	B2
Bédée	F	15	A4
Bédoin	F	31	A4
Bedretto	CH	21	C3
Bedum	NL	3	A3
Beek en Donk	NL	6	A1
Beekbergen	NL	2	B2
Beelen	D	3	C5
Beerfelden	D	13	B4
Beernem	B	4	A3
Beetsterzwaag	NL	2	A3
Beflelay	CH	20	B2
Bégard	F	14	A2
Begijnendijk	B	5	A4
Begues	E	37	C2
Begur	E	37	C4
Beho	B	6	B1
Beilen	NL	3	B3
Beine-Nauroy	F	11	B4
Beinwil	CH	20	B3
Bélâbre	F	23	B5
Belcaire	F	36	B2
Belecke	D	7	A4
Bélesta	F	36	B2
Belfort	F	20	B1
Belgentier	F	32	B1
Belgodère	F	38	A2
Belhade	F	28	B2
Belin-Bèliet	F	28	B2
Bellac	F	23	B5
Belle-Isle-en-Terre	F	14	A2
Belleau	F	10	B3
Bellegarde, *Gard*	F	31	B3
Bellegarde, *Loiret*	F	17	B4
Bellegarde-en-Diois	F	32	A1
Bellegarde-en-Marche	F	24	B2
Bellegarde-sur-Valserine	F	26	A2
Bellême	F	9	B4
Bellenaves	F	24	A3
Bellentre	F	26	B3
Bellevaux	F	26	A3
Bellevesvre	F	19	C4
Belleville	F	25	A4
Belleville-sur-Vie	F	22	B2
Bellevue-la-Montagne	F	25	B3
Belley	F	26	B2
Bellheim	D	13	B4
Bellpuig d'Urgell	E	37	C2
Belltall	E	37	C2
Bellver de Cerdanya	E	36	B2
Bellvis	E	37	C1
Belmont-de-la-Loire	F	25	A4
Belmont-sur-Rance	F	30	B1
Belœil	B	5	B3
Belp	CH	20	C2
Belpech	F	36	A2
Belvès	F	29	B3
Belvezet	F	30	A2
Belz	F	14	B2
Bemmel	NL	6	A1
Benabarre	E	35	B4
Benasque	E	35	B4
Bendorf	D	7	B3
Bene Vagienna	I	33	A3
Bénestroff	F	12	C2
Benet	F	22	B3
Bénévent-l'Abbaye	F	24	A1
Benfeld	F	13	C3
Bénodet	F	14	B1
Bensheim	D	13	B4
Bérat	F	36	A2
Berbegal	E	35	C3
Bercenay-le-Hayer	F	11	C3
Berchem	B	5	B3
Berck	F	4	B1
Berclaire d'Urgell	E	37	C1
Berdún	E	34	B3
Berga	E	37	B2
Berge, *Niedersachsen*	D	3	B4
Bergen	NL	2	B1
Bergen op Zoom	NL	5	A4
Bergerac	F	29	B3
Bergères-lés-Vertus	F	11	C4
Bergeyk	NL	5	A5
Berghausen	D	13	C4
Bergheim	D	6	B2
Bergisch Gladbach	D	6	B3
Bergkamen	D	7	A3
Bergneustadt	D	7	A3
Bergues	F	4	B2
Bergum	NL	2	A2
Bergün Bravuogn	CH	21	C4
Beringen	B	5	A5
Berkheim	D	21	A5
Berlikum	NL	2	A2
Bern	CH	20	C2
Bernau, *Baden-Württemberg*	D	20	B3
Bernaville	F	10	A2
Bernay	F	9	A4
Bernkastel-Kues	D	12	B3
Bernués	E	35	B3
Beromünster	CH	20	B3
Berre-l'Etang	F	31	B4
Bersenbrück	D	3	B4
Berthelming	F	12	C2
Bertincourt	F	10	A2
Bertogne	B	12	A1
Bertrix	B	11	B5
Berville-sur-Mer	F	9	A4
Besalú	E	37	B3
Besançon	F	19	B5
Besenfeld	D	13	C4
Besigheim	D	13	C5
Besle	F	15	B4
Bessais-le-Fromental	F	17	C4
Bessan	F	30	B2
Besse-en-Chandesse	F	24	B2
Bessé-sur-Braye	F	16	B2
Bességes	F	31	A3
Bessines-sur-Gartempe	F	23	B5
Best	NL	5	A5
Betelu	E	34	A2
Béthenville	F	11	B4
Béthune	F	4	B2
Beton-Bazoches	F	10	C3
Bettembourg	L	12	B2
Betterdorf	L	12	B2
Betz	F	10	B2
Betzdorf	D	7	B3
Beuil	F	32	A2
Beuzeville	F	9	A4
Beveren	B	5	A4
Bevern	D	7	A5
Beverungen	D	7	A5
Beverwijk	NL	2	B1
Bex	CH	27	A4
Beychevelle	F	28	A2
Beynat	F	29	A4
Bezau	A	21	B4
Bèze	F	19	B4
Bezenet	F	24	A2
Béziers	F	30	B2
Biandrate	I	27	B5
Biarritz	F	34	A2
Bias	F	28	B1
Biberach, *Baden-Württemberg*	D	21	A4
Biberach, *Baden-Württemberg*	D	13	C4
Biblis	D	13	B4
Bidache	F	28	C1
Bidart	F	34	A2
Biddinghuizen	NL	2	B2
Bieber	D	7	B5
Biedenkopf	D	7	B4
Biel	CH	20	B2
Biel	E	34	B3
Biella	I	27	B5
Bielsa	E	35	B4
Bierné	F	16	B1
Bierwart	B	5	B5
Biescas	E	35	B3
Bietigheim-Bissingen	D	13	C5
Bièvre	B	11	B5
Biganos	F	28	B2
Bignasco	CH	27	A5
Biguglia	F	38	A2
Billerbeck	D	3	C4
Billom	F	24	B3
Bilstein	D	7	A4
Bilthoven	NL	2	B2
Bilzen	B	6	B1
Binaced	E	35	C4
Binche	B	5	B4
Binefar	E	35	C4
Bingen	D	13	B3
Binic	F	14	A3
Bionaz	I	27	B4
Birkenfeld, *Baden-Württemberg*	D	13	C4
Birkenfeld, *Rheinland-Pfalz*	D	12	B3
Birresborn	D	6	B2
Birstein	D	7	B5
Biscarosse	F	28	B1
Biscarosse Plage	F	28	B1
Biscarrués	E	34	B3
Bischheim	F	13	C3
Bischofszell	CH	21	B4
Bischwiller	F	13	C3
Bisingen	D	13	C4
Bissen	L	12	B2
Bissendorf	D	3	B5
Bistango	I	27	C5
Bitburg	D	12	B2
Bitche	F	13	B3
Bitschwiller	F	20	B2
Biville-sur-Mer	F	9	A5
Biwer	L	12	B2
Blacy	F	11	C4
Blagnac	F	29	C4
Blaichach	D	21	B5
Blain	F	15	B4
Blainville-sur-l'Eau	F	12	C2
Blajan	F	35	A4
Blâmont	F	12	C2
Blanes	E	37	C3
Blangy-sur-Bresle	F	10	B1
Blankenberge	B	4	A3
Blankenheim	D	6	B2
Blanquefort	F	28	B2
Blanzac	F	23	C4
Blanzy	F	18	C3
Blaricum	NL	2	B2
Blatten	CH	27	A4
Blatzheim	D	6	B2
Blaye	F	28	A2
Blaye-les-Mines	F	30	A1
Blecua	E	35	B3
Bleichenbach	D	7	B5
Bléneau	F	18	B1
Blérancourt	F	10	B3
Bléré	F	16	B2
Blesle	F	24	B3
Blet	F	17	C4
Bletterans	F	19	C4
Blieskastel	D	12	B3
Bligny-sur-Ouche	F	18	B3
Blois	F	17	B3
Blokzijl	NL	2	B2
Blonville-sur-Mer	F	9	A4
Bludenz	A	21	B4
Blumberg	D	21	B3
Bòbbio Pellice	I	27	C4
Bobigny	F	10	C2
Böblingen	D	13	C5
Bocholt	B	6	A1
Bocholt	D	6	A2
Bochum	D	6	A3
Bockhorn	D	3	A5
Bocognano	F	38	A2
Bödefeld-Freiheit	D	7	A4
Boëge	F	26	A3
Boën	F	25	B3
Bognanco Fonti	I	27	A5
Bohain-en-Vermandois	F	11	B3
Bohmte	D	3	B5
Bois-d'Amont	F	19	C5
Boisseron	F	31	B3
Boixols	E	37	B2
Bolbec	F	9	A4
Bolea	E	35	B3
Bollène	F	31	A3
Bologne	F	19	A4
Bolsward	NL	2	A2
Boltaña	E	35	B4
Boltigen	CH	20	C2
Bolzaneto	I	33	A4
Bon-Encontre	F	29	B3
Bona	F	18	B2
Bonaduz	CH	21	C4
Bondorf	D	13	C4
Bonifacio	F	38	B2
Bonigen	CH	20	C2
Bonn	D	6	B3
Bonnat	F	24	A1
Bonndorf	D	20	B3
Bonnétable	F	16	A2
Bonnétage	F	20	B1
Bonneuil-les-Eaux	F	10	B2
Bonneuil-Matours	F	23	B4
Bonneval	F	17	A3
Bonneval-sur-Arc	F	27	B4
Bonneville	F	26	A3
Bonnières-sur-Seine	F	10	B1
Bonnieux	F	31	B4
Bönnigheim	D	13	B5
Bonny-sur-Loire	F	17	B4
Bono	E	35	B4
Boom	B	5	A4
Boos	F	9	A5
Boppard	D	7	B3
Boran-sur-Oise	F	10	B2
Borculo	NL	3	B3
Bordeaux	F	28	B2
Bordighera	I	33	B3
Borgentreich	D	7	A5
Börger	D	3	B4
Borger	NL	3	B3
Borghetto d'Arróscia	I	33	A3
Borghetto Santo Spirito	I	33	A4
Borghorst	D	3	B4
Borgloon	B	5	B5
Borgo	F	38	A2
Borgo San Dalmazzo	I	33	A3
Borgo Vercelli	I	27	B5
Borgofranco d'Ivrea	I	27	B4
Borgomanero	I	27	B5
Borgomasino	I	27	B4
Borgosésia	I	27	B5
Borja	E	34	C2
Bork	D	6	A3
Borken	D	6	A2
Borkum	D	3	A3
Bormes-les-Mimosas	F	32	B2
Bórmio	I	21	C5
Borne	NL	3	B3
Bornheim	D	6	B2
Borredá	E	37	B2
Bort-les-Orgues	F	24	B2
Bösel	D	3	A4
Boskoop	NL	2	B1
Bossast	E	35	B4
Bossolasco	I	33	A4
Bottendorf	D	7	A4
Bottrop	D	6	A2
Bötzingen	D	20	A2
Bouaye	F	15	B4
Boucau	F	28	C1
Bouchain	F	4	B3
Bouchoir	F	10	B2
Boudreville	F	19	B3
Boudry	CH	20	C1
Bouesse	F	17	C3
Bouguenais	F	15	B4
Bouhy	F	18	B2
Bouillargues	F	31	B3
Bouillon	B	11	B5
Bouilly	F	18	A2
Bouin	F	22	B2
Boulay-Moselle	F	12	B2
Boulazac	F	29	A3
Boule-d'Amont	F	36	B3
Bouligny	F	12	B1
Boulogne-sur-Gesse	F	35	A4
Boulogne-sur-Mer	F	4	B1
Bouloire	F	16	B2
Bouquemaison	F	4	B2
Bourbon-Lancy	F	18	C2
Bourbon-l'Archambault	F	18	C2
Bourbonne-les-Bains	F	19	B4
Bourbourg	F	4	B2
Bourbriac	F	14	A2
Bourcefranc-le-Chapus	F	22	C2
Bourdeaux	F	31	A4
Bouressé	F	23	B4
Bourg	F	28	A2
Bourg-Achard	F	9	A4
Bourg-Argental	F	25	B4
Bourg-de-Péage	F	25	B5
Bourg-de-Thizy	F	25	A4
Bourg-de-Visa	F	29	B3
Bourg-en-Bresse	F	26	A2
Bourg-et-Comin	F	11	B3
Bourg-Lastic	F	24	B2
Bourg-Madame	F	36	B2
Bourg-St. Andéol	F	31	A3
Bourg-St. Maurice	F	27	B3
Bourganeuf	F	24	B1
Bourges	F	17	B4
Bourgneuf-en-Retz	F	22	A2
Bourgogne	F	11	B4
Bourgoin-Jallieu	F	26	B2
Bourgtheroulde	F	9	A4
Bourgueil	F	16	B2
Bourmont	F	19	A4
Bourneville	F	9	A4
Bournezeau	F	22	B2
Bourran	F	29	B3
Bourret	F	29	C4
Bourron-Marlotte	F	10	C2
Boussac	F	24	A2
Boussens	F	35	A4
Boutersem	B	5	B4
Bouttencourt	F	10	B1
Bouvières	F	31	A4
Bouvron	F	15	B4
Bouxwiller	F	13	C3
Bouzonville	F	12	B2
Bóves	I	33	A3
Boxmeer	NL	6	A1
Boxtel	NL	5	A5
Bozouls	F	30	A1
Bra	I	27	C4
Bracieux	F	17	B3
Brackenheim	D	13	B5
Braine	F	11	B3
Braine-le-Comte	B	5	B4
Braives	B	5	B5
Brakel	B	5	B3
Brakel	D	7	A5
Bram	F	36	A3
Bramafan	F	32	B2
Bramsche	D	3	B4
Brand, *Vorarlberg*	A	21	B4
Brando	F	38	A2
Branne	F	28	B2
Brantôme	F	23	C4
Bras d'Asse	F	32	B2
Brasparts	F	14	A2
Brassac, *Charente*	F	23	C3
Brassac, *Tarn*	F	30	B1
Brassac-les-Mines	F	24	B3
Brasschaat	B	5	A4
Braubach	D	7	B3
Braunfels	D	7	B4
Bray Dunes	F	4	A2
Bray-sur-Seine	F	10	C3
Bray-sur-Somme	F	10	B2
Brazey-en-Plaine	F	19	B4
Brécey	F	8	B2
Brechen	D	7	B4
Brecht	B	5	A4
Brecketfeld	D	6	A3
Brécy	F	17	B4
Breda	E	37	C3
Breda	NL	5	A4
Bredelar	D	7	A4
Bree	B	6	A1
Bregenz	A	21	B4
Bréhal	F	8	B2
Breidenbach	F	13	B3
Breil-sur-Roya	F	33	B3
Breisach	D	20	A2
Breitenbach	CH	20	B2
Breitenbach	D	7	B5
Brem-sur-Mer	F	22	B2
Bremgarten	CH	20	B3
Brénod	F	26	A2
Brensbach	D	13	B4
Breskens	NL	5	A3
Bresles	F	10	B2
Bressuire	F	16	C1
Brest	F	14	A1
Bretenoux	F	29	B4
Breteuil, *Eure*	F	9	B4
Breteuil, *Oise*	F	10	B2
Brétigny-sur-Orge	F	10	C2
Bretten	D	13	B4
Bretteville-sur-Laize	F	9	A3
Breuil-Cervínia	I	27	B4
Breukelen	NL	2	B2
Bréziers	F	32	A2
Brezolles	F	9	B5
Briançon	F	26	C3
Brianconnet	F	32	B2
Briare	F	17	B4
Briatexte	F	29	C4
Briaucourt	F	19	A4
Bricquebec	F	8	A2
Brie-Comte-Robert	F	10	C2
Briec	F	14	A1
Brienne-le-Château	F	11	C4
Brienon-sur-Armançon	F	18	B2
Brienz	CH	20	C3
Briey	F	12	B1
Brig	CH	27	A5
Brignogan-Plage	F	14	A1
Brignoles	F	32	B2
Brillon-en-Barrois	F	11	C5
Brilon	D	7	A4
Brinon-sur-Beuvron	F	18	B2
Brinon-sur-Sauldre	F	17	B4
Brionne	F	9	A4
Brioude	F	25	B3
Brioux-sur-Boutonne	F	23	B3
Briouze	F	9	B3
Briscous	F	34	A2
Brissac-Quincé	F	16	B1
Brive-la-Gaillarde	F	29	A4
Brocas	F	28	B2
Brock	D	3	B4
Broden-bach	D	6	B3
Broglie	F	9	B4
Bromont-Lamothe	F	24	B2
Broons	F	15	A3
Broquies	F	30	A1
Broto	E	35	B3
Brou	F	17	A3
Brouage	F	22	C2
Broût-Vernet	F	24	A3
Brouvelieures	F	20	A1
Brouwershaven	NL	5	A3
Bruay-la-Buissière	F	4	B2
Bruchsal	D	13	B4
Brue-Auriac	F	32	B1
Bruen	CH	21	C3
Bruère-Allichamps	F	17	C4
Brugg	CH	20	B3
Brugge	B	4	A3
Brüggen	D	6	A2
Brühl	D	6	B2
Bruinisse	NL	5	A4
Brûlon	F	16	B1
Brumath	F	13	C3
Brummen	NL	2	B3
Brunehamel	F	11	B4
Brünen	D	6	A2
Brunnen	CH	21	C3
Brunssum	NL	6	B1
Brusasco	I	27	B5
Brusque	F	30	B1
Brussels = Bruxelles	B	5	B4
Brusson	I	27	B4
Bruxelles = Brussels	B	5	B4
Bruyères	F	20	A1
Bruz	F	15	A4
Bubbio	I	27	C5
Bubry	F	14	B2
Buchboden	A	21	B4
Buchenberg	D	21	B5
Buchères	F	18	A3
Buchs	CH	21	B4
Buchy	F	9	A5
Bucy-lés-Pierreport	F	11	B3
Büdingen	D	7	B5
Bugeat	F	24	B1
Bühl, *Baden-Württemberg*	D	13	C4
Bühl, *Bayern*	D	21	B5
Bühlertal	D	13	C4
Buis-les-Baronnies	F	31	A4
Buitenpost	NL	2	A3
Bülach	CH	21	B3
Bulgnéville	F	19	A4
Bulle	CH	20	C2
Büllingen	B	6	B2
Bunde, *Niedersachsen*	D	3	A4
Bunsbeek	B	5	B4
Buñuel	E	34	C2
Burbach	D	7	B4
Burdons-sur-Rognon	F	19	A4
Büren	D	7	A4
Büren an der Aare	CH	20	B2
Burgdorf	CH	20	B2
Burgui	E	34	B3
Burhave	D	3	A5
Burie	F	22	C3
Burlada	E	34	B2
Burladingen	D	21	A4
Burlage	D	3	A4
Buronzo	I	27	B5
Burret	F	36	B2
Bürs	A	21	B4
Bürstadt	D	13	B4
Busano	I	27	B4
Busca	I	33	A3
Bussang	F	20	B1
Bussière-Badil	F	23	C4
Bussière-Poitevine	F	23	B4
Bussoleno	I	27	B4
Bussum	NL	2	B2
Butgenbach	B	6	B2
Bütschwil	CH	21	B4
Butzbach	D	7	B4
Buxières-les-Mines	F	18	C1
Buxy	F	18	C3
Buzançais	F	17	C3
Buzancy	F	11	B4
Buzy	F	35	A3

C

Cabanac-et-Villagrains	F	28	B2
Cabanelles	E	37	B3
Cabanillas	E	34	B2
Cabasse	F	32	B2
Cabdella	E	36	B2
Cabourg	F	9	A3
Cadalen	F	29	C5
Cadaqués	E	37	B4
Cadéac	F	35	B4
Cadenet	F	31	B4
Cadeuil	F	22	C3
Cadillac	F	28	B2
Cadouin	F	29	B3
Cadours	F	29	C4
Caen	F	9	A3
Cagnes-sur-Mer	F	32	B3
Cahors	F	29	B4
Cairo Montenotte	I	33	A4
Cajarc	F	29	B4
Calacuccia	F	38	A2
Calaf	E	37	C2
Calafell	E	37	C2
Calahorra	E	34	B2
Calais	F	4	B1
Caldas de Boì	E	35	B4
Caldas de Malavella	E	37	C3
Caldearenas	E	35	B3
Calders	E	37	C2
Caldes de Montbui	E	37	C3
Calella, *Barcelona*	E	37	C3
Calella, *Girona*	E	37	C4
Calenzana	F	38	A1
Calizzano	I	33	A4
Callac	F	14	A2
Callas	F	32	B2

Calliano, *Piemonte* I 27 B5
Callús E 37 C2
Calmbach D 13 C4
Calonge E 37 C4
Caluire-et-Cuire F 25 B4
Caluso I 27 B4
Calvi F 38 A1
Calvinet F 24 C2
Calvisson F 31 B3
Calw D 13 C4
Camarasa E 35 C4
Camarès F 30 B1
Camaret-sur-Aigues F 31 A3
Camaret-sur-Mer F 14 A1
Cambligeu F 4 B2
Cambo-les-Bains F 34 A2
Cambrai F 4 B3
Cambrils E 37 C2
Camors F 14 B3
Campan F 35 A4
Campo E 35 B4
Campo Ligure I 33 A4
Campo Molino I 33 A3
Campomono F 38 B1
Camporrells E 35 C4
Camprodón E 37 B3
Campsegret F 29 B3
Canale I 27 C4
Cancale F 8 B2
Cancon F 29 B3
Candanchu E 35 B3
Candé F 15 B4
Canelli I 27 C5
Canet F 30 B2
Canet de Mar E 37 C3
Canet-Plage F 36 B4
Canfranc E 35 B3
Canisy F 8 A2
Cannes F 32 B3
Cany-Barville F 9 A4
Canyet de Mar E 37 C3
Cap-de-Pin F 28 B2
Cap Ferret F 28 B1
Caparroso E 34 B2
Capbreton F 28 C1
Capdenac-Gare F 24 C2
Capellades E 37 C2
Capendu F 36 A3
Capestang F 30 B2
Cappeln D 3 B5
Captieux F 28 B2
Capvern F 35 A4
Caráglio I 33 A3
Caraman F 36 A2
Carantec F 14 A2
Carbon-Blanc F 28 B2
Carbonne F 36 A2
Carcans F 28 A1
Carcans-Plage F 28 A1
Carcar E 34 B2
Cárcare I 33 A4
Carcassonne F 36 A3
Carcastillo E 34 B2
Carcès F 32 B2
Cardedeu E 37 C3
Cardona E 37 C2
Carentan F 8 A2
Carentoir F 15 B3
Cargèse F 38 A1
Carhaix-Plouguer F 14 A2
Carignan F 11 B5
Carignano I 27 C4
Carlepont F 10 B3
Carmagnola I 27 C4
Carmaux F 30 A1
Carmine I 33 A3
Carnac F 14 B2
Carnon Plage F 31 B2
Carolinensiel D 3 A4
Carolles F 8 B2
Carpentras F 31 A4
Carpignano Sésia I 27 B5
Carquefou F 15 B4
Carqueiranne F 32 B2
Carro F 31 B4
Carros F 33 B3
Carrouge CH 20 C1
Carrouges F 9 B3
Carrù I 33 A3
Carry-le-Rouet F 31 B4
Carteret F 8 A2
Carvin F 4 B2
Casalborgone I 27 B4
Casale Monferrato I 27 B5
Casamozza F 38 A2
Cascante E 34 C2
Cáseda E 34 B2
Caselle Torinese I 27 B4
Cassà de la Selva E 37 C3
Cassagnas F 30 A2
Cassagnes-Bégonhès F 30 A1
Cassel F 4 B2
Cassine I 27 C5
Cassis F 32 B1
Cassuéjouls F 24 C2
Castejón E 34 B2
Castejón de Sos E 35 B4
Castejón de Valdejasa E 34 C3
Casteldelfino I 32 A3
Casteljaloux F 28 B3
Castellamonte I 27 B4
Castellane F 32 B2
Castellar de la Ribera E 37 B2
Castellar del Vallés E 37 C3
Castellbell i Vilar E 37 C2
Castelldefels E 37 C2
Castellet E 37 C2
Castellfollit de la Roca E 37 B3
Castellfollit de Riubregos E 37 C2
Castelló de Farfaña E 35 C4
Castello d'Empùries E 37 B4
Castelloli E 37 C2
Castellterçol E 37 C3
Castelmoron-sur-Lot F 29 B3
Castelnau-de-Médoc F 28 A2
Castelnau-de-Montmirail F 29 C4
Castelnau-Magnoac F 35 A4
Castelnau-Montratier F 29 B4
Castelnaudary F 36 A2
Castelnuovo Don Bosco I 27 B4
Castelsarrasin F 29 B4
Castets F 28 C1
Castilfrio de la Sierra E 34 C1
Castilgaleu E 35 B4
Castilisar E 34 B2
Castillon-la-Bataille F 28 B2
Castillon-Len-Couserans F 36 B2
Castillonès F 29 B3
Castillonroy E 35 C4
Castilruiz E 34 C1
Castirla F 38 A2
Castres F 30 B1
Castricum NL 2 B1
Castries F 31 B2
Catillon F 11 A3
Caudebec-en-Caux F 9 A4
Caudiès-de-Fenouillèdes F 36 B3
Caudry F 11 A3
Caulnes F 15 A3
Caumont-l'Evente F 8 A3
Caunes-Minervois F 36 A3
Cauro F 38 B1
Caussade F 29 B4
Causse-de-la-Selle F 30 B2
Cauterets F 35 B3
Cavaglia I 27 B5
Cavaillon F 31 B4
Cavalaire-sur-Mer F 32 B2
Cavallermaggiore I 27 C4
Cavignac F 28 A2
Cavour I 27 C4
Cayeux-sur-Mer F 4 B1
Caylus F 29 B4
Cayres F 25 C3
Cazals F 29 B4
Cazaubon F 28 C2
Cazaux F 28 B1
Cazavet F 36 A2
Cazères F 36 A2
Cazis CH 21 C4
Cazouls-lès-Béziers F 30 B2
Ceauce F 8 B3
Ceilhes-et-Rocozels F 30 B2
Celle Ligure I 33 A4
Celles B 5 B4
Celles-sur-Belle F 23 B3
Censeau F 19 C5
Centallo I 33 A3
Centelles E 37 C3
Cépet F 29 C4
Cérans Foulletourte F 16 B2
Cerbère F 36 B4
Cercs E 37 B2
Cercy-la-Tour F 18 C2
Cerdon F 17 B4
Ceres I 27 B4
Ceresole-Reale I 27 B4
Cereste F 32 B1
Céret F 36 B3
Cerfontaine B 5 B4
Cergy F 10 B2
Cérilly F 17 C4
Cerisiers F 18 A2
Cerizay F 22 B3
Cernay F 20 B2
Cérons F 28 B2
Certosa di Pésio I 33 A3
Cervera E 37 C2
Cervera del Río Alhama E 34 B2
Cerviá de les Garriques E 37 C1
Cervione F 38 A2
Cervon F 18 B2
Cesana Torinese I 27 C3
Cessenon F 30 B2
Cesson-Sévigné F 15 A4
Cestas F 28 B2
Ceva I 33 A4
Cevins F 26 B3
Cévio CH 27 A5
Ceyrat F 24 B3
Ceyzériat F 26 A2
Chaam NL 5 A4
Chabanais F 23 C4
Chabeuil F 25 C5
Chablis F 18 B2
Châbons F 26 B2
Chabreloche F 25 B3
Chabris F 17 B3
Chagny F 19 C3
Chailland F 8 B3
Chaillé-les-Marais F 22 B2
Chailles F 17 B3
Chailley F 18 A2
Chalabre F 36 B3
Chalais F 28 A3
Chalamont F 26 B2
Châlette-sur-Loing F 17 A4
Chalindrey F 19 B4
Challans F 22 B2
Challes-les-Eaux F 26 B2
Chalmazel F 25 B3
Chalmoux F 18 C2
Chalon-sur-Saône F 19 C3
Chalonnes-sur-Loire F 16 B1
Châlons-en-Champagne F 11 C4
Châlus F 23 C4
Cham CH 20 B3
Chamberet F 24 B1
Chambéry F 26 B2
Chambilly F 25 A4
Chambley F 12 B1
Chambly F 10 B2
Chambois F 9 B4
Chambon-sur-Lac F 24 B2
Chambon-sur-Voueize F 24 A2
Chambord F 17 B3
Chamborigaud F 31 A2
Chamboulive F 24 B1
Chamonix-Mont Blanc F 27 B3
Chamoux-sur-Gelon F 26 B3
Champagnac-le-Vieux F 25 B3
Champagney F 20 B1
Champagnole F 19 C4
Champagny-Mouton F 23 B4
Champaubert F 11 C3
Champdeniers-St. Denis F 22 B3
Champdieu F 25 B4
Champdôtre F 19 B4
Champeix F 24 B3
Champéry CH 27 A3
Champigne F 16 B1
Champignelles F 18 B2
Champigny-sur-Veude F 16 B2
Champlitte-et-le-Prelot F 19 B4
Champoluc I 27 B4
Champoly F 25 B3
Champorcher I 27 B4
Champrond-en-Gâtine F 9 B5
Champs-sur-Tarentaine F 24 B2
Champs-sur-Yonne F 18 B2
Champtoceaux F 15 B4
Chamrousse F 26 B2
Chanac F 30 A2
Chanaleilles F 25 C3
Changy F 25 A3
Channes F 18 B3
Chantelle F 24 A3
Chantenay-St. Imbert F 18 C2
Chanteuges F 25 B3
Chantilly F 10 B2
Chantonnay F 22 B2
Chaource F 18 A3
Chapareillan F 26 B2
Chapelle Royale F 17 A3
Chapelle-St. Laurent F 16 C1
Charbonnat F 18 C3
Charenton-du-Cher F 17 C4
Charleroi B 5 B4
Charleville-Mézières F 11 B4
Charlieu F 25 A4
Charly F 10 C3
Charmes F 12 C2
Charmes-sur-Rhône F 25 C4
Charmey CH 20 C2
Charmont-en-Beauce F 17 A4
Charny F 18 B2
Charolles F 25 A4
Chârost F 17 C4
Charquemont F 20 B1
Charrin F 18 C2
Charroux F 23 B4
Chartres F 10 C1
Chasseneuil-sur-Bonnieure F 23 C4
Chassigny F 19 B4
Château-Arnoux F 32 A2
Château-Chinon F 18 B2
Château-d'Oex CH 20 C2
Château-d'Olonne F 22 B2
Château-du-Loir F 16 B2
Château-Gontier F 16 B1
Château-la-Vallière F 16 B2
Château-Landon F 17 A4
Château-l'Evêque F 29 A3
Château-Porcien F 11 B4
Château-Renault F 16 B2
Château-Salins F 12 C2
Château-Thierry F 11 B3
Châteaubernard F 23 C3
Châteaubourg F 15 A4
Châteaubriant F 15 B4
Châteaudun F 17 A3
Châteaugiron F 15 A4
Châteaulin F 14 A1
Châteaumeillant F 17 C4
Châteauneuf, *Nièvre* F 18 B2
Châteauneuf, *Saône-et-Loire* F 25 A4
Châteauneuf-de-Randon F 25 C3
Châteauneuf-d'Ille-et-Vilaine F 8 B2
Châteauneuf-du-Faou F 14 A2
Châteauneuf-du-Pape F 31 A3
Châteauneuf-en-Thymerais F 9 B5
Châteauneuf la-Forêt F 24 B1
Châteauneuf-le-Rouge F 32 B1
Châteauneuf-sur-Charente F 23 C3
Châteauneuf-sur-Cher F 17 C4
Châteauneuf-sur-Loire F 17 B4
Châteauneuf-sur-Sarthe F 16 B1
Châteauponsac F 23 B5
Châteauredon F 32 A2
Châteaurenard, *Bouches du Rhône* F 31 B3
Châteaurenard, *Loiret* F 18 B1
Châteauroux F 17 C3
Châteauroux-les-Alpes F 26 C3
Châteauvillain F 19 A3
Châtel F 27 A3
Châtel-Censoir F 18 B2
Châtel-de-Neuvre F 24 A3
Châtel-Montagne F 25 A3
Châtel-St. Denis CH 20 C1
Châtel-sur-Moselle F 12 C2
Châtelaillon-Plage F 22 B2
Châtelaudren F 14 A3
Châtelet B 5 B4
Châtelguyon F 24 B3
Châtellerault F 23 B4
Châtelus-Malvaleix F 24 A2
Châtenois F 19 A4
Châtenois-les-Forges F 20 B1
Châtillon I 27 B4
Châtillon-Coligny F 17 B4
Châtillon-en-Bazois F 18 B2
Châtillon-en-Diois F 26 C2
Châtillon-sur-Chalaronne F 25 A4
Châtillon-sur-Indre F 17 C3
Châtillon-sur-Loire F 17 B4
Châtillon-sur-Marne F 11 B3
Châtillon-sur-Seine F 18 B3
Châtres F 11 C3
Chaudes-Aigues F 24 C3
Chaudrey F 11 C4
Chauffailles F 25 A4
Chaulnes F 10 B2
Chaument Gistoux B 5 B4
Chaumergy F 19 C4
Chaumont F 19 A4
Chaumont-en-Vexin F 10 B1
Chaumont-Porcien F 11 B4
Chaumont-sur-Aire F 11 C5
Chaumont-sur-Loire F 17 B3
Chaunay F 23 B4
Chauny F 10 B3
Chaussin F 19 C4
Chauvigny F 23 B4
Chavagnes-en-Paillers F 22 B2
Chavanges F 11 C4
Chavignon F 11 B3
Chazelles-sur-Lyon F 25 B4
Chazey-Bons F 26 B2
Chef-Boutonne F 23 B3
Chelles F 10 C2
Chémery F 17 B3
Chemery-sur-Bar F 11 B4
Chemillé F 16 B1
Chemin F 19 C4
Chénerailles F 24 A2
Cheniménil F 19 A5
Chenonceaux F 17 B3
Chenôve F 19 B3
Cherasco I 27 C4
Cherbonnières F 23 C3
Cherbourg-Octeville F 8 A2
Chéroy F 18 A1
Chessy-lès-Pres F 18 A2
Chevagnes F 18 C2
Chevanceaux F 23 C3
Chevillon F 11 C5
Chevilly F 17 A3
Chézery-Forens F 26 A2
Chialamberto I 27 B4
Chianale I 27 C4
Chiché F 16 C1
Chieri I 27 B4
Chilleurs-aux-Bois F 17 A4
Chimay B 11 A4
Chinon F 16 B2
Chiomonte I 27 B3
Chirac F 30 A2
Chirens F 26 B2
Chissey-en-Morvan F 18 B3
Chiusa di Pésio I 33 A3
Chivasso I 27 B4
Cholet F 22 A3
Chomérac F 25 C4
Chorges F 32 A2
Chouilly F 11 B4
Chouzy-sur-Cisse F 17 B3
Chur CH 21 C4
Churwalden CH 21 C4
Cierp F 35 B4
Cieutat F 35 A4
Cigliano I 27 B5
Cimalmotto CH 27 A5
Ciney B 5 B5
Cinq-Mars-la-Pile F 16 B2
Cintegabelle F 36 A2
Cintruénigo E 34 B2
Cirey-sur-Vezouze F 12 C2
Ciriè I 27 B4
Ciry-le-Noble F 18 C3
Cissac-Médoc F 28 A2
Civray F 23 B4
Cizur Mayor E 34 B2
Cjutadilla E 37 C2
Clairvaux-les-Lacs F 19 C4
Clamecy F 18 B2
Claye-Souilly F 10 C2
Cléder F 14 A1
Clefmont F 19 A4
Cléguérec F 14 A2
Clelles F 26 C2
Cléon-d'Andran F 25 C4
Cléré-les-Pins F 16 B2
Clères F 9 A5
Clermont F 10 B2
Clermont-en-Argonne F 11 B5
Clermont-Ferrand F 24 B3
Clermont-l'Hérault F 30 B2
Clerval F 19 B5
Clervaux L 12 A2
Cléry-St. André F 17 B3
Clisson F 15 B4
Clohars-Carnoët F 14 B2
Cloppenburg D 3 B5
Cloyes-sur-le-Loir F 17 B3
Cluis F 17 C3
Cluny F 25 A4
Cluses F 26 A3
Cochem D 6 B3
Coesfeld D 3 C4
Coevorden NL 3 B3
Cognac F 23 C3
Cogne I 27 B4
Cognin F 26 B2
Cogolin F 32 B2
Cölbe D 7 B4
Colera E 36 B4
Coligny F 26 A2
Coll de Nargó E 37 B2
Collat F 25 B3
Collinée F 15 A3
Collinghorst D 3 A4
Collobrières F 32 B2
Colmar F 20 A2
Colmars F 32 A2
Cologne = Köln D 6 B2
Cologne F 29 C3
Colombey-les-Belles F 12 C1
Colombey-les-deux-Églises F 19 A3
Colomers E 37 B3
Colomiers F 29 C4
Coma-ruga E 37 C2
Combeaufontaine F 19 B4
Comblain-au-Pont B 6 B1
Combloux F 26 B3
Combourg F 8 B2
Combronde F 24 B3
Comines F 4 B3
Commensacq F 28 B2
Commentry F 24 A2
Commercy F 12 C1
Compiègne F 10 B2
Comps-sur-Artuby F 32 B2
Concarneau F 14 B2
Conches-en-Ouche F 9 B4
Concots F 29 B4
Condat F 24 B2
Condé-en-Brie F 11 C3
Condé-sur-l'Escaut F 5 B3
Conde-sur-Marne F 11 B4
Condé-sur-Noireau F 8 B3
Condom F 29 C3
Condove I 27 B4
Condrieu F 25 B4
Conflans-sur-Lanterne F 19 B5
Confolens F 23 B4
Conlie F 16 A1
Conliège F 19 C4
Connantre F 11 C3
Connaux F 31 A3
Connerré F 16 A2
Conques F 24 C2
Conques-sur-Orbiel F 36 A3
Consenvoye F 11 B5
Constanti E 37 C2
Contay F 10 B2
Conthey CH 27 A4
Contis-Plage F 28 B1
Contres F 17 B3
Contrexéville F 19 A4
Conty F 10 B2
Coole F 11 C4
Coray F 14 A2
Corbeil-Essonnes F 10 C2
Corbeny F 11 B3
Corbie F 10 B2
Corbigny F 18 B2
Corbion B 11 B4
Cordes-sur-Ciel F 29 B4
Corella E 34 B2
Cório I 27 B4
Corlay F 14 A2
Cormainville F 17 A3
Cormatin F 18 C3
Cormeilles F 9 A4
Cormery F 16 B2
Cormoz F 26 A2
Cornago E 34 B1
Cornimont F 20 B1
Cornudella de Montsant E 37 C1
Cornus F 30 B2
Corps F 26 C2
Corps Nuds F 15 B4
Corrèze F 24 B1
Corte F 38 A2
Cortemilia I 33 A4
Cortes E 34 C2
Cosne-Cours-sur-Loire F 18 B1
Cosne d'Allier F 17 C4
Cossato I 27 B5
Cossaye F 18 C2
Cossé-le-Vivien F 15 B5
Cossonay CH 19 C5
Costaros F 25 C3
Costigliole d'Asti I 27 C5
Costigliole Saluzzo I 33 A3
Coublanc F 19 B4
Couches F 18 C3
Coucouron F 25 C3
Coucy-le-Château-Auffrique F 10 B3
Couëron F 15 B4
Couflens F 36 B2
Couhé F 23 B4
Couiza F 36 B3
Coulanges F 18 C2
Coulanges-la-Vineuse F 18 B2
Coulanges-sur-Yonne F 18 B2
Couleuvre F 18 C1
Coulmier-le-Sec F 18 B3
Coulommiers F 10 C3
Coulonges-sur-l'Autize F 22 B3
Coulounieix-Chamiers F 29 A3
Coupéville F 11 C4
Couptrain F 9 B3
Cour-Cheverny F 17 B3
Cour-et-Buis F 25 B4
Courcelles B 5 B4
Courcelles-Chaussy F 12 B2
Courchevel F 26 B3
Courcôme F 23 C4
Courçon F 22 B3
Courgenay CH 20 B2
Courmayeur I 27 B3
Courniou F 30 B1
Cournon-d'Auvergne F 24 B3
Cournonterral F 30 B2
Courpière F 25 B3
Cours-la-Ville F 25 A4
Coursan F 30 B2
Courseulles-sur-Mer F 9 A3
Courson-les-Carrières F 18 B2
Courtalain F 17 A3
Courtenay F 18 A2
Courtomer F 9 B4
Courville, *Eure-et-Loire* F 9 B5
Courville, *Marne* F 11 B3
Coussac-Bonneval F 23 C5
Coutances F 8 A2
Couterne F 9 B3
Coutras F 28 A2
Couvet CH 20 C1
Couvin B 11 A4
Couzon F 18 C2
Cox F 29 C4
Cozes F 22 C3
Cozzano F 38 B2
Craon F 15 B5
Craonne F 11 B3
Craponne F 25 B4
Craponne-sur-Arzon F 25 B3
Crèches-sur-Saône F 25 A4
Crécy-en-Ponthieu F 4 B1

Crécy-la-Chapelle F 10 C2
Crécy-sur-Serre F 11 B3
Creil F 10 B2
Creissels F 30 A2
Cremeaux F 25 B3
Crémieu F 26 B2
Creney F 11 C4
Créon F 28 B2
Crépey F 12 C1
Crépy F 11 B3
Crépy-en-Valois F 10 B2
Crescentino I 27 B5
Cressensac F 29 A4
Cressia F 19 C4
Crest F 25 C5
Cresta CH 21 C4
Créteil F 10 C2
Creully F 8 A3
Creutzwald F 12 B2
Crèvecœur-le-Grand F 10 B2
Crévola d'Ossola I 27 A5
Criel-sur-Mer F 10 A1
Crillon F 10 B1
Criquetot-l'Esneval F 9 A4
Crissolo I 27 C4
Crocq F 24 B2
Crodo I 27 A5
Cronat F 18 C2
Crouy F 10 B3
Crozon F 14 A1
Cruas F 25 C4
Cruis F 32 A1
Cruseilles F 26 A3
Cubelles E 37 C2
Cubjac F 29 A3
Cucuron F 31 B4
Cuers F 32 B2
Cueva de Agreda E 34 C2
Cuges-les-Pins F 32 B1
Cugnaux F 29 C4
Cuijk NL 6 A1
Cuinzier F 25 A4
Cuiseaux F 19 C4
Cuisery F 19 C4
Culan F 17 C4
Culemborg NL 5 A5
Cully CH 20 C1
Culoz F 26 B2
Cumiana I 27 C4
Cúneo I 33 A3
Cunlhat F 25 B3
Cuorgnè I 27 B4
Cusset F 25 A3
Cussy-les-Forges F 18 B3
Custines F 12 C2
Cuts F 10 B3
Cuvilly F 10 B2

D

Daaden D 7 B3
Dabo F 12 C3
Dagmersellen CH 20 B2
Dahn D 13 B3
Dalaas A 21 B5
Dalheim L 12 B2
Daluis F 32 A2
Dalum D 3 B4
Damazan F 29 B3
Dammarie-les-Lys F 10 C2
Dammartin-en-Goële F 10 B2
Damme D 3 B5
Dampierre F 19 B4
Dampierre-sur-Salon F 19 B4
Damüls A 21 B4
Damville F 9 B5
Damvillers F 12 B1
Damwoude NL 2 A2
Dangé-St. Romain F 16 C2
Dangers F 9 B5
Dangeul F 9 B4
Danjoutin F 20 B1
Dannemarie F 20 B2
Daoulas F 14 A1
Darfeld D 3 B4
Darmstadt D 13 B4
Darney F 19 A5
Datteln D 6 A3
Dattenfeld D 7 B3
Daumeray F 16 B1
Daun D 6 B2
Davos CH 21 C4
Dax F 28 C1
De Cocksdorp NL 2 A1
De Haan B 4 A3
De Koog NL 2 A1
De Panne B 4 A2
De Wijk NL 3 B3
Deauville F 9 A4
Decazeville F 30 A1
Decize F 18 C2
Dedemsvaart NL 3 B3
Dego I 33 A4
Deinze B 5 B3
Delbrück D 7 A4
Delden NL 3 B3
Delémont CH 20 B2
Delft NL 2 B1
Delfzijl NL 3 A3
Delle F 20 B2
Delme F 12 C2
Demigny F 19 C3
Demonte I 33 A3
Den Burg NL 2 A1
Den Ham NL 3 B3
Den Helder NL 2 B1
Den Oever NL 2 B2
Denain F 4 B3
Dender-monde B 5 A4
Denekamp NL 3 B4
Denklingen D 7 B3
Déols F 17 C3
Derval F 15 B4
Desana I 27 B5
Descartes F 16 C2
Desvres F 4 B1
Dettingen, *Baden-Württemberg* D 21 B4
Dettwiller F 13 C3
Deurne NL 6 A1
Deventer NL 2 B3
Diano d'Alba I 27 C5
Diano Marina I 33 B4
Die F 26 C2
Diebling F 12 B2
Dieburg D 13 B4
Diekirch L 12 B2
Diélette F 8 A2
Diémoz F 26 B2
Diepenbeck B 5 B5
Diepholz D 3 B5
Dieppe F 9 A5
Dierdorf D 7 B3
Dieren NL 2 B3
Diest B 5 B5
Dietikon CH 20 B3
Dietzenbach D 13 A4
Dieue-sur-Meuse F 12 B1
Dieulefit F 31 A4
Dieulouard F 12 C2
Dieuze F 12 C2
Diever NL 3 B3
Diez D 7 B4
Differdange L 12 B1
Dignac F 23 C4
Digne-les-Bains F 32 A2
Digny F 9 B5
Digoin F 18 C2
Dijon F 19 B4
Diksmuide B 4 A2
Dillenburg D 7 B4
Dillingen, *Saarland* D 12 B2
Dilsen B 6 A1
Dinan F 15 A3
Dinant B 5 B4
Dinard F 15 A3
Dingden D 6 A2
Dinklage D 3 B5
Dinslaken D 6 A2
Dinxperlo NL 6 A2
Diou F 18 C2
Dirksland NL 5 A4
Disentis CH 21 C3
Dissen D 3 B5
Ditzingen D 13 C5
Ditzum D 3 A4
Dives-sur-Mer F 9 A3
Divion F 4 B2
Divonne les Bains F 26 A3
Dixmont F 18 A2
Dizy-le-Gros F 11 B4
Dochamps B 6 B1
Doesburg NL 2 B3
Doetinchem NL 3 C3
Dogliani I 33 A3
Doische B 11 A4
Dokkum NL 2 A2
Dol-de-Bretagne F 8 B2
Dolancourt F 18 A3
Dolceácqua I 33 B3
Dole F 19 B4
Dollot F 18 A2
Domat-Ems CH 21 C4
Dombasle-sur-Meurthe F 12 C2
Domène F 26 B2
Domérat F 24 A2
Domfessel F 12 C3
Domfront F 8 B3
Domfront-en-Champagne F 16 A2
Dommartin F 11 C4
Dommartin-le-Franc F 11 C4
Domme F 29 B4
Domodóssola I 27 A5
Dompaire F 19 A5
Dompierre-du-Chemin F 8 B2
Dompierre-sur-Besbre F 18 C2
Dompierre-sur-Mer F 22 B2
Domrémy-la-Pucelle F 12 C1
Domsure F 26 A2
Donaueschingen D 20 B3
Donestebe-Santesteban E 34 A2
Donges F 15 B3
Donnemarie-Dontilly F 10 C3
Donostia-San Sebastián E 34 A2
Donzenac F 29 A4
Donzère F 31 A3
Donzy F 18 B2
Doorn NL 2 B2
Dordrecht NL 5 A4
Dörenthe D 3 B4
Dormagen D 6 A2
Dormans F 11 B3
Dornbirn A 21 B4
Dornecy F 18 B2
Dornes F 18 C2
Dornhan D 13 C4
Dornum D 3 A4
Dörpen D 3 B4
Dorsten D 6 A2
Dortan F 26 A2
Dortmund D 6 A3
Dottignies B 4 B3
Döttingen CH 20 B3
Douai F 4 B3
Douarnenez F 14 A1
Douchy F 18 B2
Douchy-les-Mines F 4 B3
Doucier F 19 C4
Doudeville F 9 A4
Doué-la-Fontaine F 16 B1
Doulaincourt F 11 C5
Doulevant-le-Château F 11 C4
Doullens F 10 A2
Dour B 5 B3
Dourdan F 10 C2
Dourgne F 36 A3
Dournazac F 23 C4
Douvaine F 26 A3
Douvres-la-Délivrande F 9 A3
Douzy F 11 B5
Doyet F 24 A2
Dozule F 9 A3
Drachten NL 2 A3
Draguignan F 32 B2
Dreieich D 13 A4
Dreisen D 13 B4
Drensteinfurt D 7 A3
Dreux F 9 B5
Dringenberg D 7 A5
Dronero I 33 A3
Dronrijp NL 2 A2
Dronten NL 2 B2
Droué F 17 A3
Drulingen F 12 C3
Drunen NL 5 A5
Druten NL 6 A1
Dübendorf CH 21 B3
Ducey F 8 B2
Duclair F 9 A4
Duffel B 5 A4
Dugny-sur-Meuse F 12 B1
Duisburg D 6 A2
Dülken D 6 A2
Dülmen D 6 A3
Dümpelfeld D 6 B2
Dun-le-Palestel F 24 A1
Dun-les-Places F 18 B3
Dun-sur-Auron F 17 C4
Dun-sur-Meuse F 11 B5
Dunkerque = Dunkirk F 4 A2
Dunkirk = Dunkerque F 4 A2
Dunningen D 21 A3
Durach D 21 B5
Durance F 28 B3
Duras F 28 B3
Durban-Corbières F 36 B3
Dürbheim D 21 A3
Durbuy B 5 B5
Düren D 6 B2
Durlach D 13 C4
Dürrboden CH 21 C4
Dürrenboden CH 21 C3
Durtal F 16 B1
Düsseldorf D 6 A2
Dusslingen D 13 C5

E

Eaux-Bonnes F 35 B3
Eauze F 28 C3
Eberbach D 13 B4
Ebnat-Kappel CH 21 B4
Ebreuil F 24 A3
Echallens CH 20 C1
Echauri E 34 B2
Echiré F 22 B3
Échirolles F 26 B2
Echourgnac F 28 A3
Echt NL 6 A1
Echternach L 12 B2
Eckelshausen D 7 B4
Éclaron F 11 C4
Écommoy F 16 B2
Écouché F 9 B3
Ecouis F 10 B1
Écueillé F 17 B3
Edam NL 2 B2
Ede NL 2 B2
Edenkoben D 13 B4
Edesheim D 13 B4
Edewecht D 3 A4
Eekloo B 5 A3
Eemshaven NL 3 A3
Eerbeek NL 2 B3
Eersel NL 5 A5
Effiat F 24 A3
Egg A 21 B4
Egg D 21 A5
Éghezée B 5 B4
Égletons F 24 B2
Eglisau CH 21 B3
Égliseneuve-d'Entraigues F 24 B2
Eglofs D 21 B4
Egmond aan Zee NL 2 B1
Eguilles F 31 B4
Eguilly-sous-Bois F 18 A3
Éguzon-Chantôme F 17 C3
Ehrang D 12 B2
Ehringshausen D 7 B4
Eibergen NL 3 B3
Eickelborn D 7 A4
Eindhoven NL 5 A5
Einsiedeln CH 21 B3
Einville-au-Jard F 12 C2
Eisenberg, *Rheinland-Pfalz* D 13 B4
Eitorf D 6 B3
Ejea de los Caballeros E 34 B2
Eke B 5 B3
El Buste E 34 C2
El Frago E 34 B3
El Grado E 35 B4
El Masnou E 37 C3
El Morell E 37 C2
El Pla de Santa Maria E 37 C2
El Pont d'Armentera E 37 C2
El Port de la Selva E 37 B4
El Port de Llançà E 36 B4
El Prat de Llobregat E 37 C3
El Serrat AND 36 B2
El Temple E 34 C3
El Tormillo E 35 C3
El Vendrell E 37 C2
El Villar de Arnedo E 34 B1
Élancourt F 10 C1
Elbeuf F 9 A4
Elburg NL 2 B2
Elizondo E 34 A2
Ellezelles B 5 B3
Elm CH 21 C4
Elmstein D 13 B3
Elne F 36 B3
Éloyes F 19 A5
Els Castells E 37 B2
Elsdorf D 6 B2
Elsenfeld D 13 B5
Elspeet NL 2 B2
Elst NL 2 C2
Eltville D 13 A4
Elven F 15 B3
Elzach D 20 A3
Embrun F 32 A2
Embún E 34 B3
Emden D 3 A4
Emlichheim D 3 B3
Emmeloord NL 2 B2
Emmen CH 20 B3
Emmen NL 3 B3
Emmendingen D 20 A2
Emmer-Compascuum NL 3 B4
Emmerich D 6 A2
Emsbüren D 3 B4
Emsdetten D 3 B4
Emstek D 3 B5
Encamp AND 36 B2
Enciso E 34 B1
Endingen D 20 A2
Engelberg CH 20 C3
Engelskirchen D 6 B3
Engen D 21 B3
Enghien B 5 B4
Engter D 3 B5
Enkenbach D 13 B3
Enkhuizen NL 2 B2
Ennezat F 24 B3
Ennigerloh D 7 A4
Ens NL 2 B2
Enschede NL 3 B3
Ensisheim F 20 B2
Entlebuch CH 20 B3
Entrácque I 33 A3
Entrains-sur-Nohain F 18 B2
Entraygues-sur-Truyère F 24 C2
Entrevaux F 32 B2
Entzheim F 13 C3
Envermeu F 9 A5
Enzklösterle D 13 C4
Épagny F 10 B3
Epalinges CH 20 C1
Epannes F 22 B3
Epe D 3 B4
Epe NL 2 B2
Épernay F 11 B3
Épernon F 10 C1
Epfig F 13 C3
Epierre F 26 B3
Épinac F 18 C3
Épinal F 19 A5
Epoisses F 18 B3
Eppenbrunn D 13 B3
Eppingen D 13 B4
Erbach, *Hessen* D 13 B4
Erbalunga F 38 A2
Erfstadt D 6 B2
Eriswil CH 20 B2
Erkelenz D 6 A2
Erkrath D 6 A2
Erla E 34 B3
Erli I 33 A4
Ermelo NL 2 B2
Ermenonville F 10 B2
Erndtebrück D 7 B4
Ernée F 8 B3
Erolzheim D 21 A5
Erquelinnes B 5 B4
Erquy F 15 A3
Erratzu E 34 A2
Erro E 34 B2
Ersa F 38 A2
Erstein F 13 C3
Erstfeld CH 21 C3
Ertingen D 21 A4
Ervy-le-Châtel F 18 A2
Erwitte D 7 A4
Esbly F 10 C2
Esch-sur-Alzette L 12 B1
Esch-sur-Sûre L 12 B1
Eschach D 21 B4
Eschenz CH 21 B3
Eschweiler D 6 B2
Escoeuilles F 4 B1
Escos F 34 A2
Escource F 28 B1
Escragnolles F 32 B2
Esens D 3 A4
Eslava E 34 B2
Eslohe D 7 A4
Espalion F 30 A1
Esparreguera E 37 C2
Esparron F 32 B1
Espeluche F 31 A3
Espéraza F 36 B3
Espinasses F 32 A2
Espinelves E 37 C3
Espluga de Francolí E 37 C2
Esplús E 35 C4
Espolla E 36 B3
Espot E 36 B2
Esquedas E 35 B3
Essay F 9 B4
Essen B 5 A4
Essen, *Niedersachsen* D 3 B4
Essen, *Nordrhein-Westfalen* D 6 A3
Essertaux F 10 B2
Essoyes F 18 A3
Estadilla E 35 B4
Estagel F 36 B3
Estaires F 4 B2
Estang F 28 C2
Estartit E 37 B4
Estavayer-le-Lac CH 20 C1
Estella E 34 B1
Esternay F 11 C3
Esterri d'Aneu E 36 B2
Esterwegen D 3 B4
Estissac F 18 A2
Estivareilles F 24 A2
Estopiñán E 35 C4
Estoublon F 32 B2
Estrée-Blanche F 4 B2
Estrées-St. Denis F 10 B2
Esyres F 16 B2
Etables-sur-Mer F 14 A3
Étain F 12 B1
Étalans F 19 B5
Etalle B 12 B1
Étampes F 10 C2
Etang-sur-Arroux F 18 C3
Étaples F 4 B1
Etauliers F 28 A2
Etoges F 11 C3
Etréaupont F 11 B3
Étréchy F 10 C2
Étrépagny F 10 B1
Étretat F 9 A4
Étrœungt F 11 A3
Étroubles I 27 B4
Ettelbruck L 12 B2
Etten NL 5 A4
Ettenheim D 20 A2
Ettlingen D 13 C4
Etuz F 19 B4
Etxarri-Aranatz E 34 B1
Eu F 10 A1
Eulate E 34 B1
Eupen B 6 B2
Europoort NL 5 A4
Euskirchen D 6 B2
Évaux-les-Bains F 24 A2
Evergem B 5 A3
Eversberg D 7 A4
Everswinkel D 3 C4
Évian-les-Bains F 26 A3
Evisa F 38 A1
Evolène CH 27 A4
Evran F 15 A4
Evrecy F 9 A3
Évreux F 9 A5
Évron F 16 A1
Évry F 10 C2
Ewersbach D 7 B4
Excideuil F 23 C5
Exmes F 9 B4
Eyguians F 32 A1
Eyguières F 31 B4
Eygurande F 24 B2
Eylie F 35 B4
Eymet F 29 B3
Eymoutiers F 24 B1
Ezcároz E 34 B2

F

Fabrègues F 30 B2
Fagnières F 11 C4
Faido CH 21 C3
Fains F 11 C5
Falaise F 9 B3
Falces E 34 B2
Falset E 37 C1
Fanjeaux F 36 A3
Fara Novarese I 27 B5
Farasdues E 34 B2
Faucogney-et-la-Mer F 19 B5
Fauguerolles F 28 B3
Faulquemont F 12 B2
Fauquembergues F 4 B2
Fauville-en-Caux F 9 A4
Fauvillers B 12 B1
Faverges F 26 B3
Faverney F 19 B5
Fay-aux-Loges F 17 B4
Fayence F 32 B2
Fayet F 30 B1
Fayl-Billot F 19 B4
Fécamp F 9 A4
Feldkirch A 21 B4
Felizzano I 27 C5
Felletin F 24 B2
Felsberg D 7 A5
Fenestrelle I 27 B4
Fénétrange F 12 C3
Feneu F 16 B1
Fère-Champenoise F 11 C3
Fère-en-Tardenois F 11 B3
Fernay-Voltaire F 26 A3
Ferpècle CH 27 A4
Ferrals-les-Corbières F 36 A3
Ferret CH 27 B4
Ferrette F 20 B2
Ferrière-la-Grande F 5 B3
Ferrières, *Hautes-Pyrénées* F 35 A3
Ferrières, *Loiret* F 17 A4
Ferrières, *Oise* F 10 B2
Ferrières-sur-Sichon F 25 A3
Ferwerd NL 2 A2
Festieux F 11 B3
Feudingen D 7 B4
Feuges F 11 C4
Feuquières F 10 B1
Feurs F 25 B4
Fiano I 27 B4
Fiesch CH 27 A5
Figari F 38 B2
Figeac F 24 C2
Figols E 35 B4
Figueres E 37 B3
Filisur CH 21 C4
Finale Ligure I 33 A4
Finsterwolde NL 3 A4
Firmi F 30 A1
Firminy F 25 B4
Fischbach D 13 B3
Fischen D 21 B5
Fismes F 11 B3
Fitero E 34 B2
Flaça E 37 B3
Flace F 25 A4
Flaine F 26 A3
Flamatt CH 20 C2
Flammersfeld D 7 B3
Flassans-sur-Issole F 32 B2
Flavigny-sur-Moselle F 12 C2
Flavy-le-Martel F 10 B3
Flawil CH 21 B4
Flayosc F 32 B2
Flehingen D 13 B4
Flers F 8 B3
Fleurance F 29 C3
Fleuré F 23 B4
Fleurier CH 19 C5
Fleurus B 5 B4
Fleury, *Hérault* F 30 B2
Fleury, *Yonne* F 18 B2
Fleury-les-Aubrais F 17 B3
Fleury-sur-Andelle F 9 A5
Fleury-sur-Orne F 9 A3
Flieden D 7 B5
Flims CH 21 C4
Flines-lèz-Raches F 4 B3
Flirey F 12 C1
Flixecourt F 10 A2
Flize F 11 B4
Flobecq B 5 B3
Flogny-la-Chapelle F 18 B2
Flonheim D 13 B4
Florac F 30 A2
Floreffe B 5 B4
Florennes B 5 B4
Florensac F 30 B2
Florentin F 29 C5
Florenville B 11 B5
Flörsheim D 13 A4
Flühli CH 20 C3
Flumet F 26 B3
Flums CH 21 B4
Foix F 36 B2
Folelli F 38 A2
Foncine-le-Bas F 19 C5
Font-Romeu F 36 B3
Fontaine F 11 C4
Fontaine de Vaucluse F 31 B4
Fontaine-Française F 19 B4
Fontaine-le-Dun F 9 A4
Fontainebleau F 10 C2
Fontan F 33 A3
Fontane I 33 A3
Fontanières F 24 A2
Fontenay-le-Comte F 22 B3
Fontenay-Trésigny F 10 C2
Fontevrault-l'Abbaye F 16 B2
Fontoy F 12 B1
Fontpédrouse F 36 B3
Fonz E 35 B4
Forbach D 13 C4
Forbach F 12 B2
Forcalquier F 32 B1
Forges-les-Eaux F 10 B1
Formazza I 27 A5
Formerie F 10 B1
Formigliana I 27 B5
Formiguères F 36 B3

Forno, *Piemonte* I 27 B5
Forno, *Piemonte* I 27 B4
Forno Alpi-Gráie I 27 B4
Fort-Mahon-Plage F 4 B1
Fos F 35 B4
Fos-sur-Mer F 31 B3
Fossano I 33 A3
Fosse-la-Ville B 5 B4
Fouchères F 18 A3
Fouesnant F 14 B1
Foug F 12 C1
Fougères F 8 B2
Fougerolles F 19 B5
Foulain F 19 A4
Fouras F 22 C2
Fourchambault F 18 B2
Fourmies F 11 A4
Fournels F 24 C3
Fournols F 25 B3
Fourques F 36 B3
Fourquevaux F 36 A2
Fours F 18 C2
Frabosa Soprana I 33 A3
Fraire B 5 B4
Fraize F 20 A1
Francaltroff F 12 C2
Francescas F 29 B3
Franeker NL 2 A2
Frangy F 26 A2
Frankenau D 7 A4
Frankenberg, *Hessen* D 7 A4
Frankenthal D 13 B4
Frankfurt, *Hessen* D 7 B4
Frasne F 19 C5
Frasnes-lez-Anvaing B 5 B3
Frasseto F 38 B2
Frastanz A 21 B4
Frauenfeld CH 21 B3
Frayssinet F 29 B4
Frayssinet-le-Gélat F 29 B4
Frechen D 6 B2
Freckenhorst D 3 C4
Fredeburg D 7 A4
Freiburg, *Baden-Württemberg* D 20 B2
Freienhagen D 7 A5
Freiensteinau D 7 B5
Freisen D 12 B3
Fréjus F 32 B2
Freren D 3 B4
Fresnay-sur-Sarthe F 9 B4
Fresne-St. Mamès F 19 B4
Fresnes-en-Woevre F 12 B1
Fresnoy-Folny F 10 B1
Fresnoy-le-Grand F 11 B3
Fressenville F 10 A1
Fréteval F 17 B3
Fretigney F 19 B4
Freudenberg, *Nordrhein-Westfalen* D 7 B3
Freudenstadt D 13 C4
Freux B 12 B1
Frévent F 4 B2
Freyming-Merlebach F 12 B2
Fribourg CH 20 C2
Frick CH 20 B3
Friedberg, *Hessen* D 7 B4
Friedeburg D 3 A4
Friedrichsdorf D 7 B4
Friedrichshafen D 21 B4
Friesenheim D 13 C3
Friesoythe D 3 A4
Fritzlar D 7 A5
Froges F 26 B2
Frohnhausen D 7 B4
Froissy F 10 B2
Fröndenberg D 7 A3
Fronsac F 28 B2
Front I 27 B4
Frontenay-Rohan-Rohan F 22 B3
Frontignan F 30 B2
Fronton F 29 C4
Frouard F 12 C2
Fruges F 4 B2
Frutigen CH 20 C2
Fuendejalón E 34 C2
Fully CH 27 A4
Fumay F 11 B4
Fumel F 29 B3
Fürstenau, *Niedersachsen* D 3 B4
Furstenau, *Nordrhein-Westfalen* D 7 A5
Fürth, *Hessen* D 13 B4
Furtwangen D 20 A3
Fusio CH 21 C3
Fustiñana E 34 B2

G

Gabarret F 28 C2
Gabriac F 30 A1
Gaby I 27 B4
Gacé F 9 B4
Gadmen CH 20 C3
Gael F 15 A3
Gaggenau D 13 C4
Gaillac F 29 C4
Gaillefontaine F 10 B1
Gaillon F 9 A5
Gaja-la-Selve F 36 A2
Galan F 35 A4
Galéria F 38 A1
Galgon F 28 B2
Gallardon F 10 C1
Gallur E 34 C2
Galtür A 21 C5
Gamaches F 10 B1
Gammertingen D 21 A4
Gams CH 21 B4
Gan F 35 A3
Ganges F 30 B2
Gannat F 24 A3
Gannay-sur-Loire F 18 C2
Gap F 32 A2
Gardanne F 31 B4
Gardouch F 36 A2
Garein F 28 B2
Garéoult F 32 B2
Garéssio I 33 A4
Gargellen A 21 C4
Gargilesse-Dampierre F 17 C3
Garlin F 28 C2
Garnat-sur-Engièvre F 18 C2
Garrel D 3 B5
Garriguella E 36 B4
Gaschurn A 21 C5
Gasny F 10 B1
Gastes F 28 B1
Gattinara I 27 B5
Gava E 37 C3
Gavarnie F 35 B3
Gavray F 8 B2
Géaudot F 11 C4
Geaune F 28 C2
Gedern D 7 B5
Gedinne B 11 B4
Gèdre F 35 B4
Geel B 5 A4
Geetbets B 5 B5
Geilenkirchen D 6 B2
Geinsheim D 13 B4
Geisenheim D 13 B4
Geisingen D 21 B3
Geldermalsen NL 5 A5
Geldern D 6 A2
Geldrop NL 6 A1
Geleen NL 6 B1
Gelida E 37 C2
Gelnhausen D 7 B5
Gelsenkirchen D 6 A3
Gelterkinden CH 20 B2
Gembloux B 5 B4
Gemeaux F 19 B4
Gémenos F 32 B1
Gemert NL 6 A1
Gemmenich B 6 B1
Gémozac F 22 C3
Gemund D 6 B2
Gemünden, *Hessen* D 7 B4
Gemünden, *Rheinland-Pfalz* D 13 B3
Genappe B 5 B4
Gençay F 23 B4
Gendringen NL 6 A2
Genelard F 18 C3
Genemuiden NL 2 B3
Geneva = Genève CH 26 A3
Genève = Geneva CH 26 A3
Genevriéres F 19 B4
Gengenbach D 13 C4
Genillé F 17 B3
Genk B 6 B1
Genlis F 19 B4
Gennep NL 6 A1
Gennes F 16 B1
Genola I 33 A3
Gensingen D 13 B3
Gent = Ghent B 5 A3
Gentioux F 24 B1
Georgsmarienhütte D 3 B5
Geraards-bergen B 5 B3
Gérardmer F 20 A1
Gerbéviller F 12 C2
Gergy F 19 C3
Germay F 12 C1
Germersheim D 13 B4
Gernsbach D 13 C4
Gernsheim D 13 B4
Gerolstein D 6 B2
Gerpinnes B 5 B4
Gerri de la Sal E 37 B2
Gerzat F 24 B3
Gescher D 3 C4
Geseke D 7 A4
Gespunsart F 11 B4
Gesté F 15 B4
Gevrey-Chambertin F 19 B3
Gex F 26 A3
Gey D 6 B2
Ghent = Gent B 5 A3
Ghigo I 27 C4
Ghisonaccia F 38 A2
Ghisoni F 38 A2
Giat F 24 B2
Giaveno I 27 B4
Gien F 17 B4
Giens F 32 B2
Giesselwerder D 7 A5
Giessen D 7 B4
Gieten NL 3 A3
Giethoorn NL 2 B3
Giffaumont-Champaubert F 11 C4
Gignac F 30 B2
Gilley F 19 B5
Gilley-sur-Loire F 18 C2
Gilocourt F 10 B2
Gilserberg D 7 B5
Gilze NL 5 A4
Gimont F 29 C3
Ginasservis F 32 B1
Gingelom B 5 B5
Giromagny F 20 B1
Girona E 37 C3
Gironcourt-sur-Vraine F 12 C1
Gironella E 37 B2
Gironville-sous-les-Côtes F 12 C1
Gisors F 10 B1
Gistel B 4 A2
Giswil CH 20 C3
Givet F 11 A4
Givors F 25 B4
Givry B 5 B4
Givry F 18 C3
Givry-en-Argonne F 11 C4
Gizeux F 16 B2
Gladbeck D 6 A2
Gladenbach D 7 B4
Gland CH 19 C5
Glandorf D 3 B4
Glarus CH 21 B4
Gletsch CH 20 C3
Glomel F 14 A2
Goch D 6 A2
Goddelsheim D 7 A4
Godelheim D 7 A5
Goderville F 9 A4
Goes NL 5 A3
Goetzenbrück F 13 C3
Góglio I 27 A5
Goirle NL 5 A5
Goizueta E 34 A2
Goldach CH 21 B4
Goldbach D 13 A5
Gomaringen D 13 C5
Goncelin F 26 B2
Gondrecourt-le-Château F 12 C1
Gondrin F 28 C3
Gonfaron F 32 B2
Goñi E 34 B2
Gooik B 5 B4
Goor NL 3 B3
Goppenstein CH 27 A4
Gorey GB 8 A1
Gorinchem NL 5 A4
Gorredijk NL 2 A3
Gorron F 8 B3
Gossau CH 21 B4
Götzis A 21 B4
Gouarec F 14 A2
Gouda NL 2 B1
Gourdon F 29 B4
Gourgançon F 11 C4
Gourin F 14 A2
Gournay-en-Bray F 10 B1
Gouvy B 6 B1
Gouzeaucourt F 10 A3
Gouzon F 24 A2
Gozee B 5 B4
Grabs CH 21 B4
Graçay F 17 B3
Gramat F 29 B4
Grancey-le-Château F 19 B4
Grand-Champ F 14 B3
Grand Couronne F 9 A5
Grand-Fougeray F 15 B4
Grandcamp-Maisy F 8 A2
Grandpré F 11 B4
Grandrieu B 5 B4
Grandrieu F 25 C3
Grandson CH 20 C1
Grandvillars F 20 B1
Grandvilliers F 10 B1
Grañén E 35 C3
Granges-de-Crouhens F 35 B4
Granges-sur-Vologne F 20 A1
Granollers E 37 C3
Granville F 8 B2
Grasse F 32 B2
Graulhet F 29 C4
Graus E 35 B4
Grávalos E 34 B2
Grave NL 6 A1
Gravelines F 4 A2
Gravellona Toce I 27 B5
's-Gravendeel NL 5 A4
's-Gravenhage = The Hague NL 2 B1
's-Gravenzande NL 5 A4
Graveson F 31 B3
Gray F 19 B4
Grebenstein D 7 A5
Grefrath D 6 A2
Grenade F 29 C4
Grenade-sur-l'Adour F 28 C2
Grenchen CH 20 B2
Grenoble F 26 B2
Gréoux-les-Bains F 32 B1
Gressoney-la-Trinité I 27 B4
Gressoney-St.-Jean I 27 B4
Greven, *Nordrhein-Westfalen* D 3 B4
Grevenbroich D 6 A2
Grevenbrück D 7 A4
Grevenmacher L 12 B2
Grez-Doiceau B 5 B4
Grez-en-Bouère F 16 B1
Grèzec F 29 B4
Griesheim D 13 B4
Grignan F 31 A3
Grignols F 28 B2
Grignon F 26 B3
Grijpskerk NL 3 A3
Grimaud F 32 B2
Grimbergen B 5 B4
Grimmialp CH 20 C2
Grindelwald CH 20 C3
Grisolles F 29 C4
Groenlo NL 3 B3
Groesbeek NL 6 A1
Groix F 14 B2
Gronau, *Nordrhein-Westfalen* D 3 B4
Grönenbach D 21 B5
Groningen NL 3 A3
Grootegast NL 3 A3
Gross-Gerau D 13 B4
Gross Reken D 6 A3
Gross Umstadt D 13 B4
Grossenkneten D 3 B5
Grossenlüder D 7 B5
Grosshöchstetten CH 20 C2
Grossostheim D 13 B5
Grostenquin F 12 C2
Grouw NL 2 A2
Gruissan F 30 B2
Grünberg D 7 B4
Gründau D 7 B5
Grünstadt D 13 B4
Gruyères CH 20 C2
Gstaad CH 20 C2
Gsteig CH 27 A4
Guagno F 38 A1
Guardiola de Bergueda E 37 B2
Guebwiller F 20 B2
Guéméné-Penfao F 15 B4
Guéméné-sur-Scorff F 14 A2
Guer F 15 B3
Guérande F 15 B3
Guéret F 24 A1
Guérigny F 18 B2
Guesa E 34 B2
Gueugnon F 18 C3
Guichen F 15 B4
Guignes F 10 C2
Guillaumes F 32 A2
Guillestre F 26 C3
Guillos F 28 B2
Guilvinec F 14 B1
Guînes F 4 B1
Guingamp F 14 A2
Guipavas F 14 A1
Guiscard F 10 B3
Guiscriff F 14 A2
Guise F 11 B3
Guisona E 37 C2
Guîtres F 28 A2
Gujan-Mestras F 28 B1
Gummersbach D 7 A3
Gundel-fingen D 20 A2
Gundelsheim D 13 B5
Gunderschoffen F 13 C3
Guntersblum D 13 B4
Gurrea de Gállego E 34 B3
Gütersloh D 7 A4
Guttannen CH 20 C3
Güttingen CH 21 B4
Gy F 19 B4
Gyé-sur-Seine F 18 A3
Gypsera CH 20 C2

H

Haacht B 5 B4
Haaksbergen NL 3 B3
Haamstede NL 5 A3
Haan D 6 A3
Haarlem NL 2 B1
Habas F 28 C2
Habay B 12 B1
Habsheim F 20 B2
Hachenburg D 7 B3
Hadamar D 7 B4
Hage D 3 A4
Hagen, *Nordrhein-Westfalen* D 6 A3
Hagenbach D 13 B4
Hagetmau F 28 C2
Hagondange F 12 B2
Haguenau F 13 C3
Hahnslätten D 7 B4
Haiger D 7 B4
Haigerloch D 13 C4
Haldem D 3 B5
Halle B 5 B4
Hallenberg D 7 A4
Halluin F 4 B3
Haltern D 6 A3
Halver D 6 A3
Ham F 10 B3
Hambach F 12 B3
Hamm D 7 A3
Hamme B 5 A4
Hamminkeln D 6 A2
Hamoir B 6 B1
Hamont B 6 A1
Hanau D 7 B4
Hannut B 5 B5
Hardegarijp NL 2 A2
Hardelot Plage F 4 B1
Hardenberg NL 3 B3
Harderwijk NL 2 B2
Hardt D 20 A3
Haren D 3 B4
Haren NL 3 A3
Harfleur F 9 A4
Hargicourt F 10 B3
Hargnies F 11 A4
Harkebrügge D 3 A4
Harlingen NL 2 A2
Haroué F 12 C2
Harsewinkel D 3 C5
Hartennes F 10 B3
Haselünne D 3 B4
Haslach D 20 A3
Hasparren F 34 A2
Hasselt B 5 B5
Hasselt NL 2 B3
Hassloch D 13 B4
Hastière-Lavaux B 5 B4
Hattem NL 2 B3
Hatten D 3 A5
Hatten F 13 C3
Hattingen D 6 A3
Hattstadt F 20 A2
Hau D 6 A2
Haudainville F 12 B1
Haulerwijk NL 3 A3
Hausach D 20 A3
Haut-Fays B 11 A5
Hautefort F 29 A4
Hauterives F 25 B5
Hauteville-Lompnès F 26 B2
Hautmont F 5 B3
Hautrage B 5 B3
Havelange B 5 B5
Havelte NL 2 B3
Havixbeck D 3 C4
Hayange F 12 B2
Hazebrouck F 4 B2
Héas F 35 B4
Hechingen D 13 C4
Hecho E 34 B3
Hechtel B 5 A5
Hédé F 15 A4
Heede D 3 B4
Heek D 3 B4
Heemstede NL 2 B1
Heerde NL 2 B3
Heerenveen NL 2 B2
Heerhugowaard NL 2 B1
Heerlen NL 6 B1
Heeze NL 6 A1
Heidelberg D 13 B4
Heiden D 6 A2
Heilbronn D 13 B5
Heiligenhaus D 6 A2
Heiloo NL 2 B1
Heinerscheid L 12 A2
Heinsberg D 6 A2
Heist-op-den-Berg B 5 A4
Helchteren B 5 A5
Hellendoorn NL 3 B3
Hellenthal D 6 B2
Hellevoetsluis NL 5 A4
Helmond NL 6 A1
Hemer D 7 A3
Héming F 12 C2
Hendaye F 34 A2
Hengelo, *Gelderland* NL 3 B3
Hengelo, *Overijssel* NL 3 B3
Hénin-Beaumont F 4 B2
Hennebont F 14 B2
Henrichemont F 17 B4
Heppenheim D 13 B4
Herbault F 17 B3
Herbern D 7 A3
Herbeumont B 11 B5
Herbignac F 15 B3
Herbisse F 11 C4
Herbitzheim F 12 B3
Herbolzheim D 20 A2
Herborn D 7 B4
Herchen D 6 B3
Herent B 5 B4
Herentals B 5 A4
Hérépian F 30 B2
Héric F 15 B4
Héricourt F 20 B1
Héricourt-en-Caux F 9 A4
Hérimoncourt F 20 B1
Herisau CH 21 B4
Hérisson F 17 C4
Herk-de-Stad B 5 B5
Herment F 24 B2
Hermeskeil D 12 B2
Hermonville F 11 B3
Hernani E 34 A2
Herne D 6 A3
Herrenberg D 13 C4
Herrlisheim F 13 C3
Herscheid D 7 A3
Herselt B 5 A4
Herstal B 6 B1
Herten D 6 A3
's-Hertogenbosch NL 5 A5
Herxheim D 13 B4
Herzebrock D 7 A4
Herzlake D 3 B4
Herzogenbuchsee CH 20 B2
Hesdin F 4 B2
Hesel D 3 A4
Hettange-Grande F 12 B2
Heuchin F 4 B2
Heudicourt-sous-les-Côtes F 12 C1
Heunezel F 19 A5
Heuqueville F 9 A4
Hiersac F 23 C4
Hilchenbach D 7 A3
Hilden D 6 A2
Hillegom NL 2 B1
Hillesheim D 6 B2
Hilvarenbeek NL 5 A5
Hilversum NL 2 B2
Hindelbank CH 20 B2
Hinterweidenthal D 13 B3
Hinwil CH 21 B3
Hippolytushoef NL 2 B1
Hirschhorn D 13 B4
Hirsingue F 20 B2
Hirson F 11 B4
Hirzenhain D 7 B5
Hittisau A 21 B4
Hobscheid L 12 B1
Hochdorf CH 20 B3
Hochfelden F 13 C3
Hochspeyer D 13 B3
Höchst im Odenwald D 13 B5
Hochstenbach D 7 B3
Hockenheim D 13 B4
Hoedekenskerke NL 5 A3
Hoegaarden B 5 B4
Hoek van Holland NL 5 A4
Hoenderlo NL 2 B2
Hofgeismar D 7 A5
Hofheim, *Hessen* D 13 A4
Hohenems A 21 B4
Hohenkirchen D 3 A4
Hohentengen D 20 B3
Hohenwepel D 7 A5
Holdorf D 3 B5
Hollum NL 2 A2
Holten NL 3 B3
Holtwick D 3 B4
Holwerd NL 2 A2
Holzminden D 7 A5
Homberg, *Hessen* D 7 A5
Homberg, *Hessen* D 7 B5
Homburg D 13 B3
Hondarribia E 34 A2
Hondschoote F 4 B2
Honfleur F 9 A4
Hönningen D 6 B2
Hontheim D 12 A2
Hoofddorp NL 2 B1
Hoogerheide NL 5 A4
Hoogeveen NL 3 B3
Hoogezand-Sappemeer NL 3 A3
Hoogkarspel NL 2 B2
Hoogkerk NL 3 A3
Hoogstede D 3 B3
Hoogstraten B 5 A4
Hooksiel D 3 A5
Hoorn NL 2 B2
Hopsten D 3 B4
Horb am Neckar D 13 C4
Horgen CH 21 B3
Horn D 7 A4
Hornberg D 20 A3
Hornoy-le-Bourg F 10 B1
Horst NL 6 A2
Horstel D 3 B4
Horsten D 3 A4
Horstmar D 3 B4
Hösbach D 13 A5
Hosenfeld D 7 B5
Hosingen L 12 A2
Hospental CH 21 C3
Hossegor F 28 C1
Hostal de Ipiés E 35 B3
Hostalric E 37 C3
Hostens F 28 B2
Hotton B 5 B5
Houdain F 4 B2
Houdan F 10 C1
Houdelaincourt F 12 C1
Houeillès F 28 B3
Houffalize B 12 A1
Houlgate F 9 A3
Hourtin F 28 A1
Hourtin-Plage F 28 A1
Houthalen B 5 A5
Houyet B 5 B4
Hovelhof D 7 A4
Höxter D 7 A5
Hückel-hoven D 6 A2
Hückeswagen D 6 A3
Hucqueliers F 4 B1
Huelgoat F 14 A2
Huesca E 35 B3
Hüfingen D 20 B3
Huissen NL 2 C2
Huizen NL 2 B2
Hüls D 6 A2
Hulst NL 5 A4
Hungen D 7 B4
Hünxe D 6 A2
Hürbel D 21 A4
Hürth D 6 B2
Hüsten D 7 A3
Huttwil CH 20 B2
Huy B 5 B5
Hyères F 32 B2
Hyéres Plage F 32 B2

I

Ibbenbüren D 3 B4
Ichtegem B 4 A3
Idar-Oberstein D 13 B3
Idiazábal E 34 B1
Idstein D 7 B4
Ieper = Ypres B 4 B2
Igea E 34 B1
Igny-Comblizy F 11 B3
Igries E 35 B3
Igualada E 37 C2
Iguerande F 25 A4
Ihringen D 20 A2

Le Cayrol F 24 C2
Le Chambon-Feugerolles F 25 B4
Le Chambon-sur-Lignon F 25 B4
Le Château d'Oléron F 22 C2
Le Châtelard F 26 B3
Le Châtelet F 17 C4
Le Chatelet-en-Brie F 10 C2
Le Chesne F 11 B4
Le Cheylard F 25 C4
Le Collet-de-Deze F 31 A2
Le Conquet F 14 A1
Le Creusot F 18 C3
Le Croisic F 15 B3
Le Crotoy F 4 B1
Le Deschaux F 19 C4
Le Donjon F 25 A3
Le Dorat F 23 B5
Le Faou F 14 A1
Le Faoüet F 14 A2
Le Folgoet F 14 A1
Le Fossat F 36 A2
Le Fousseret F 36 A2
Le Fugeret F 32 A2
Le Gault-Soigny F 11 C3
Le Grand-Bornand F 26 B3
Le-Grand-Bourg F 24 A1
Le Grand-Lucé F 16 B2
Le Grand-Pressigny F 16 C2
Le Grand-Quevilly F 9 A5
Le Grau-du-Roi F 31 B3
Le Havre F 9 A4
Le Hohwald F 13 C3
Le Houga F 28 C2
Le Lardin-St. Lazare F 29 A4
Le Lauzet-Ubaye F 32 A2
Le Lavandou F 32 B2
Le Lion-d'Angers F 16 B1
Le Locle CH 20 B1
Le Loroux-Bottereau F 15 B4
Le Louroux-Béconnais F 15 B5
Le Luc F 32 B2
Le Lude F 16 B2
Le Malzieu-Ville F 24 C3
Le Mans F 16 A2
Le Mas-d'Azil F 36 A2
Le Massegros F 30 A2
Le May-sur-Evre F 15 B5
Le Mayet-de-Montagne F 25 A3
Le Mêle-sur-Sarthe F 9 B4
Le Ménil F 19 A5
Le Merlerault F 9 B4
Le Mesnil-sur-Oger F 11 C4
Le Miroir F 19 C4
Le Molay-Littry F 8 A3
Le Monastier-sur-Gazeille F 25 C3
Le Monêtier-les-Bains F 26 C3
Le Mont-Dore F 24 B2
Le Mont-St. Michel F 8 B2
Le Montet F 24 A3
Le Muret F 28 B2
Le Muy F 32 B2
Le Neubourg F 9 A4
Le Nouvion-en-Thiérache F 11 A3
Le Palais F 14 B2
Le Parcq F 4 B2
Le Péage-de-Roussillon F 25 B4
Le Pellerin F 15 B4
Le Perthus F 36 B3
Le Pertuis F 25 B4
Le Petit-Bornand F 26 B3
Le Poët F 32 A1
Le Poirè-sur-Vie F 22 B2
Le Pont CH 19 C5
Le Pont-de-Montvert F 30 A2
Le Porge F 28 B1
Le Porge-Océan F 28 B1
Le Portel F 4 B1
Le Pouldu F 14 B2
Le Pouliguen F 15 B3
Le Puy-en-Velay F 25 B3
Le Puy-Ste. Réparade F 31 B4
Le Quesnoy F 5 B3
Le Rayol F 32 B2
Le Rœulx B 5 B4
Le Rouget F 24 C2
Le Rozier F 30 A2
Le Russey F 20 B1
Le Sel-de-Bretagne F 15 B4
Le Sentier CH 19 C5
Le Souquet F 28 C1
Le Teil F 31 A3
Le Teilleul F 8 B3
Le Temple-de-Bretagne F 15 B4
Le Theil F 9 B4
Le Thillot F 20 B1
Le Touquet-Paris-Plage F 4 B1
Le Touvet F 26 B2
Le Translay F 10 B1
Le Tréport F 10 A1
Le Val F 32 B2
Le Val-André F 15 A3
Le Val-d'Ajol F 19 B5
Le Verdon-sur-Mer F 22 C2
Le Vernet F 32 A2
Le Vigan F 30 B2
Le Vivier-sur-Mer F 8 B2
Lebach D 12 B2
Lebekke B 5 A4
Lech A 21 B5
Leciñena E 35 C3
Lectoure F 29 C3
Lede B 5 B3
Lédignan F 31 B3
Leek NL 3 A3
Leens NL 3 A3
Leer D 3 A4
Leerdam NL 5 A5
Leerhafe D 3 A4
Leeuwarden NL 2 A2
Legau D 21 B5
Legé F 22 B2
Lège-Cap-Ferret F 28 B1
Léglise B 12 B1
Léguevin F 29 C4
Leiden NL 2 B1
Leidschendam NL 2 B1
Leignon B 5 B5
Leimen D 13 B4
Leitza E 34 A2
Lekunberri E 34 A2
Lelystad NL 2 B2
Lembach F 13 B3
Lemberg F 13 B3
Lembèye F 35 A3
Lemelerveld NL 3 B3
Lemförde D 3 B5
Lemmer NL 2 B2
Lempdes F 24 B3
Lencloître F 16 C2
Lengerich, *Niedersachsen* D 3 B4
Lengerich, *Nordrhein-Westfalen* D 3 B4
Lenk CH 20 C2
Lennestadt D 7 A4
Lens B 5 B3
Lens F 4 B2
Lens Lestang F 25 B5
Lenzburg CH 20 B3
Lenzerheide CH 21 C4
Léon F 28 C1
Leonberg D 13 C5
Léoncel F 26 C2
Leopoldsburg B 5 A5
L'Epine F 32 A1
Leré F 17 B4
Lerin E 34 B2
Lerm-et-Musset F 28 B2
Lérouville F 12 C1
Lés E 35 B4
Les Abrets F 26 B2
Les Aix-d'Angillon F 17 B4
Les Ancizes-Comps F 24 B2
Les Andelys F 10 B1
Les Arcs, *Savoie* F 27 B3
Les Arcs, *Var* F 32 B2
Les-Aubiers F 16 C1
Les Baux-de-Provence F 31 B3
Les Bézards F 17 B4
Les Bois CH 20 B1
Les Bordes F 17 B4
Les Borges Blanques E 37 C1
Les Borges del Camp E 37 C2
Les Brunettes F 18 C2
Les Cabannes F 36 B2
Les Contamines-Montjoie F 26 B3
Les Déserts F 26 B2
Les Deux-Alpes F 26 C3
Les Diablerets CH 27 A4
Les Echelles F 26 B2
Les Escaldes AND 36 B2
Les Essarts F 22 B2
Les Estables F 25 C4
Les Eyzies-de-Tayac F 29 B4
Les Gets F 26 A3
Les Grandes-Ventes F 9 A5
Les Haudères CH 27 A4
Les Herbiers F 22 B2
Les Hôpitaux-Neufs F 19 C5
Les Lucs-sur-Boulogne F 22 B2
Les Mages F 31 A3
Les Mazures F 11 B4
Les Mées F 32 A1
Les Mureaux F 10 C1
Les Omergues F 32 A1
Les Ormes-sur-Voulzie F 10 C3
Les Orres F 32 A2
Les Pieux F 8 A2
Les Ponts-de-Cé F 16 B1
Les Ponts-de-Martel CH 20 C1
Les Praz F 27 B3
Les Riceys F 18 B3
Les Roches F 25 B4
Les Rosaires F 15 A3
Les Rosiers F 16 B1
Les Rousses F 19 C5
Les Sables-d'Olonne F 22 B2
Les Settons F 18 B3
Les Ternes F 24 B2
Les Thilliers en-Vexin F 10 B1
Les Touches F 15 B4
Les Trois Moûtiers F 16 B2
Les Vans F 31 A3
Les Verrières CH 19 C5
Les Vignes F 30 A2
Lesaka E 34 A2
L'Escala E 37 B4
Lescar F 35 A3
L'Escarène F 33 B3
Lescheraines F 26 B3
Lesconil F 14 B1
Lesdins F 10 B3
Lesmont F 11 C4
Lesneven F 14 A1
Lesparre-Médoc F 28 A2
l'Espérance F 11 B3
l'Esperou F 30 A2
Lesponne F 35 A4
L'Espunyola E 37 B2
Lessay F 8 A2
Lessines B 5 B3
L'Estany E 37 C3
Lesterps F 23 B4
Leucate F 36 B4
Leuglay F 19 B3
Leuk CH 27 A4
Leukerbad CH 27 A4
Leusden NL 2 B2
Leutkirch D 21 B5
Leuven B 5 B4
Leuze-en-Hainaut B 5 B3
Levaré F 8 B3
Leverkusen D 6 A2
Levet F 17 C4
Levie F 38 B2
Levier F 19 C5
Lévignen F 10 B2
Levroux F 17 C3
Leysin CH 27 A4
Lézardrieux F 14 A2
Lézat-sur-Léze F 36 A2
Lezay F 23 B3
Lézignan-Corbières F 30 B1
Lezignan-la-Cèbe F 30 B2
Lézinnes F 18 B3
Lezoux F 25 B3
Lherm F 36 A2
Lhommaizé F 23 B4
L'Hospitalet F 36 B2
L'Hospitalet de l'Infant E 37 D1
L'Hospitalet de Llobregat E 37 C3
L'Hospitalet-du-Larzac F 30 B2
Lhuître F 11 C4
Liancourt F 10 B2
Liart F 11 B4
Libourne F 28 B2
Libramont B 12 B1
Lich D 7 B4
Lichères-près-Aigremont F 18 B2
Lichtenau D 7 A4
Lichtensteig CH 21 B4
Lichtenvoorde NL 3 C3
Lichtervelde B 4 A3
Licques F 4 B1
Liège B 6 B1
Lienen D 3 B4
Lier B 5 A4
Liernais F 18 B3
Liestal CH 20 B2
Lieurac F 36 B2
Lieurey F 9 A4
Liévin F 4 B2
Liffol-le-Grand F 12 C1
Liffré F 15 A4
Ligardes F 29 B3
Ligne F 15 B4
Lignières F 17 C4
Ligny-en-Barrois F 12 C1
Ligny-le-Châtel F 18 B2
Ligueil F 16 B2
L'Île-Bouchard F 16 B2
l'Île-Rousse F 38 A1
Lille B 5 A4
Lille F 4 B3
Lillebonne F 9 A4
Lillers F 4 B2
Limbourg B 6 B1
Limburg D 7 B4
Limésy F 9 A4
Limoges F 23 C5
Limogne-en-Quercy F 29 B4
Limoise F 18 C2
Limone Piemonte I 33 A3
Limons F 25 B3
Limours F 10 C2
Limoux F 36 A3
Linas de Broto E 35 B3
Lindau D 21 B4
Lindenberg im Allgäu D 21 B4
Lindern D 3 B4
Lindlar D 6 A3
Lingen D 3 B4
Linkenheim D 13 B4
Linnich D 6 B2
Linthal CH 21 C4
Linyola E 37 C1
Linz D 6 B3
Lion-sur-Mer F 9 A3
Liposthey F 28 B2
Lippborg D 7 A4
Lippoldsberg D 7 A5
Lippstadt D 7 A4
Liré F 15 B4
Lisieux F 9 A4
L'Isle CH 19 C5
L'Isle-Adam F 10 B2
L'Isle-de-Noé F 29 C3
L'Isle-en-Dodon F 35 A4
L'Isle-Jourdain, *Gers* F 29 C4
L'Isle-Jourdain, *Vienne* F 23 B4
L'Isle-sur-la-Sorgue F 31 B4
L'Isle-sur-le Doubs F 19 B5
L'Isle-sur-Serein F 18 B3
Lisle-sur-Tarn F 29 C4
Lisse NL 2 B1
Listrac-Médoc F 28 A2
Lit-et-Mixe F 28 B1
Livarot F 9 B4
Livernon F 29 B4
Livigno I 21 C5
Livorno Ferraris I 27 B5
Livron-sur-Drôme F 25 C4
Livry-Louvercy F 11 B4
Lixheim F 12 C3
Lizy-sur-Ourcq F 10 B3
Lladurs E 37 B2
Llafranc E 37 C4
Llagostera E 37 C3
Llançà E 36 B4
Llandudec F 14 A1
Llavorsi E 36 B2
Lles E 36 B2
Llessui E 36 B2
Llinars E 37 B2
Llivia E 36 B2
Lloret de Mar E 37 C3
Loano I 33 A4
Loarre E 35 B3
Locana I 27 B4
Lochau A 21 B4
Lochem NL 3 B3
Loches F 16 B2
Locmaria F 14 B2
Locmariaquer F 14 B3
Locminé F 14 B3
Locquirec F 14 A2
Locronan F 14 A1
Loctudy F 14 B1
Lodève F 30 B2
Lodosa E 34 B1
Löhlbach D 7 A4
Löhnberg D 7 B4
Lohne, *Niedersachsen* D 3 B5
Lohra D 7 B4
Lokeren B 5 A3
Lollar D 7 B4
Lombez F 36 A1
Lommel B 5 A5
Lommersum D 6 B2
Londerzeel B 5 A4
Londinières F 9 A5
Longchamp-sur-Aujon F 19 A3
Longchaumois F 26 A2
Longeau F 19 B4
Longecourt-en-Plaine F 19 B4
Longeville-les-St. Avold F 12 B2
Longeville-sur-Mer F 22 B2
Longny-au-Perche F 9 B4
Longré F 23 B3
Longué-Jumelles F 16 B1
Longueau F 10 B2
Longuyon F 12 B1
Longvic F 19 B4
Longvilly B 12 A1
Longwy F 12 B1
Löningen D 3 B4
Lons-le-Saunier F 19 C4
Loon op Zand NL 5 A5
Loone-Plage F 4 A2
Lopigna F 38 A1
Loppersum NL 3 A3
Lor F 11 B4
Lorch D 13 A3
Lorgues F 32 B2
Lorient F 14 B2
Lorignac F 22 C3
Loriol-sur-Drôme F 25 C4
Lormes F 18 B2
Lörrach D 20 B2
Lorrez-le-Bocage F 17 A4
Lorris F 17 B4
Lorup D 3 B4
Los Arcos E 34 B1
Losheim, *Nordrhein-Westfalen* D 6 B2
Losheim, *Saarland* D 12 B2
Losne F 19 B4
Lossburg D 13 C4
Losse F 28 B2
Losser NL 3 B4
Louargat F 14 A2
Loudéac F 15 A3
Loudun F 16 B2
Loué F 16 B1
Louhans F 19 C4
Loulay F 22 B3
Lourdes F 35 A3
Loures-Barousse F 35 A4
Lourmarin F 31 B4
Loury F 17 B4
Louverné F 16 A1
Louvie-Juzon F 35 A3
Louviers F 9 A5
Louvigné-du-Désert F 8 B2
Louvois F 11 B4
Lövenich D 6 A2
Lubersac F 23 C5
Luc F 25 C3
Luc-en-Diois F 26 C2
Luc-sur-Mer F 9 A3
Luçay-le-Mâle F 17 B3
Lucciana F 38 A2
Lucé F 10 C1
Lucenay-les-Aix F 18 C2
Lucenay-l'Evéque F 18 B3
Luceni E 34 C2
Lucens CH 20 C1
Luceram F 33 B3
Luçon F 22 B2
Lüdenscheid D 7 A3
Lüdinghausen D 6 A3
Ludweiler Warndt D 12 B2
Ludwigshafen D 13 B4
Luesia E 34 B2
Lugny F 19 C3
Lumbier E 34 B2
Lumbres F 4 B2
Lummen B 5 B5
Luna E 34 B3
Lunas F 30 B2
Lunel F 31 B3
Lünen D 7 A3
Lunéville F 12 C2
Lungern CH 20 C3
Lünne D 3 B4
Lunteren NL 2 B2
Lurcy-Lévis F 18 C1
Lure F 19 B5
Luri F 38 A2
Lury-sur-Arnon F 17 B4
Lusignan F 23 B4
Lusigny-sur-Barse F 18 A3
Lussac F 28 B2
Lussac-les-Châteaux F 23 B4
Lussac-les-Eglises F 23 B5
Lussan F 31 A3
Lustenau A 21 B4
Lutry CH 20 C1
Luxembourg L 12 B2
Luxeuil-les-Bains F 19 B5
Luxey F 28 B2
Luz-St. Sauveur F 35 B3
Luzarches F 10 B2
Luzech F 29 B4
Luzern CH 20 B3
Luzy F 18 C2
Lyon F 25 B4
Lyons-la-Forêt F 10 B1
Lyss CH 20 B2

M

Maarheeze NL 6 A1
Maaseik B 6 A1
Maastricht NL 6 B1
Mably F 25 A4
Maçanet de Cabrenys E 36 B3
Macau F 28 A2
Machault F 11 B4
Machecoul F 22 B2
Macinaggio F 38 A2
Macon B 11 A4
Mâcon F 25 A4
Macugnaga I 27 B4
Made NL 5 A4
Maël-Carhaix F 14 A2
Magallon E 34 C2
Magaña E 34 C1
Magescq F 28 C1
Magnac-Bourg F 23 C5
Magnac-Laval F 23 B5
Magnieres F 12 C2
Magny-Cours F 18 C2
Magny-en-Vexin F 10 B1
Maia E 34 A2
Maîche F 20 B1
Maienfeld CH 21 B4
Maignelay Montigny F 10 B2
Maillezais F 22 B3
Mailly-le-Camp F 11 C4
Mailly-le-Château F 18 B2
Maintal D 7 B4
Maintenon F 10 C1
Mainvilliers F 10 C1
Mainz D 13 A4
Maison-Rouge F 10 C3
Maisse F 10 C2
Maizières-lès-Vic F 12 C2
Makkum NL 2 A2
Malaucène F 31 A4
Malaunay F 9 A5
Malborn D 12 B2
Malbuisson F 19 C5
Maldegem B 5 A3
Malemort F 29 A4
Malesherbes F 10 C2
Malestroit F 15 B3
Malgrat de Mar E 37 C3
Malicorne-sur-Sarthe F 16 B1
Malijai F 32 A2
Mallemort F 31 B4
Mallén E 34 C2
Malléon F 36 A2
Malmédy B 6 B2
Malpas E 35 B4
Malsch D 13 C4
Maltat F 18 C2
Mamer L 12 B2
Mamers F 9 B4
Mamirolle F 19 B5
Manciet F 28 C3
Mandelieu-la-Napoule F 32 B2
Manderfeld B 6 B2
Manderscheid D 6 B2
Mane, *Alpes-de-Haute-Provence* F 32 B1
Mane, *Haute-Garonne* F 35 A4
Mañeru E 34 B2
Mangiennes F 12 B1
Manlleu E 37 C3
Männedorf CH 21 B3
Mannheim D 13 B4
Manosque F 32 B1
Manresa E 37 C2
Mansle F 23 C4
Manso F 38 A1
Mantes-la-Jolie F 10 C1
Mantes-la-Ville F 10 C1
Manthelan F 16 B2
Manzat F 24 B2
Manziat F 25 A4
Marans F 22 B2
Marbach F 12 C2
Marboz F 26 A2
Marburg D 7 B4
Marcenat F 24 B2
Marchaux F 19 B5
Marche-en-Famenne B 5 B5
Marchenoir F 17 B3
Marcheprime F 28 B2
Marciac F 28 C3
Marcigny F 25 A4
Marcilla E 34 B2
Marcillac-la-Croisille F 24 B2
Marcillac-Vallon F 30 A1
Marcillat-en-Combraille F 24 A2
Marcille-sur-Seine F 11 C3
Marcilloles F 26 B2
Marcilly-le-Hayer F 11 C3
Marck F 4 B1
Marckolsheim F 20 A2
Marennes F 22 C2
Maresquel F 4 B1
Mareuil F 23 C4
Mareuil-en-Brie F 11 C3
Mareuil-sur-Arnon F 17 C4
Mareuil-sur-Lay F 22 B2
Mareuil-sur-Ourcq F 10 B3
Margaux F 28 A2
Margerie-Hancourt F 11 C4
Margès F 25 B5
Margone I 27 B4
Marguerittes F 31 B3
Margut F 11 B5
Mariembourg B 11 A4
Marienbaum D 6 A2
Marienheide D 7 A3
Marieux F 10 A2
Marignane F 31 B4
Marigny, *Jura* F 19 C4
Marigny, *Manche* F 8 A2
Marigny-le-Châtel F 11 C3
Marine de Sisco F 38 A2
Marines F 10 B1
Maringues F 24 B3
Markdorf D 21 B4
Markelo NL 3 B3
Markgröningen D 13 C5
Markhausen D 3 B4
Marknesse NL 2 B2
Marl D 6 A3
Marle F 11 B3
Marlieux F 25 A5
Marmagne F 18 C3
Marmande F 28 B3
Marmoutier F 13 C3
Marnay F 19 B4
Marnheim D 13 B4
Marolles-les-Braults F 9 B4
Maromme F 9 A5
Marquion F 4 B3
Marquise F 4 B1
Marrum NL 2 A2
Mars-la-Tours F 12 B1
Marsac F 29 C5
Marsac-en-Livradois F 25 B3
Marsberg D 7 A4
Marseillan F 30 B2
Marseille = Marseilles F 31 B4
Marseille en Beauvaisis F 10 B1
Marseilles = Marseille F 31 B4
Marson F 11 C4
Martel F 29 B4
Martelange B 12 B1
Marthon F 23 C4
Martigné-Briand F 16 B1
Martigné-Ferchaud F 15 B4
Martigne-sur-Mayenne F 16 A1
Martigny CH 27 A4
Martigny-les-Bains F 19 A4
Martigues F 31 B4
Martinshöhe D 13 B3
Martinszell D 21 B5
Martorell E 37 C2
Martres Tolosane F 36 A1

Marvejols F 30 A2
Marville F 12 B1
Mas-Cabardès F 36 A3
Masera I 27 A5
Masevaux F 20 B1
Maslacq F 34 A3
Masone I 33 A4
Massat F 36 B2
Massay F 17 B3
Masseret F 24 B1
Masseube F 35 A4
Massiac F 24 B3
Massignac F 23 C4
Massmechelen B 6 B1
Matalebreras E 34 C1
Mataró E 37 C3
Matha F 23 C3
Mathay F 20 B1
Matignon F 15 A3
Matour F 25 A4
Maubert-Fontaine F 11 B4
Maubeuge F 5 B3
Maubourguet F 35 A4
Mauguio F 31 B3
Maulbronn D 13 C4
Maule F 10 C1
Mauléon F 22 B3
Mauléon-Barousse F 35 B4
Mauléon-Licharre F 34 A3
Maulévrier F 22 A3
Maure-de-Bretagne F 15 B4
Maureilhan F 30 B2
Mauriac F 24 B2
Mauron F 15 A3
Maurs F 24 C2
Maury F 36 B3
Maussane-les-Alpilles F 31 B3
Mauvezin F 29 C3
Mauzé-sur-le-Mignon F 22 B3
Maxent F 15 B3
Maxey-sur-Vaise F 12 C1
Mayen D 6 B3
Mayenne F 8 B3
Mayet F 16 B2
Mayres F 25 C4
Mazamet F 30 B1
Mazan F 31 A4
Mazères F 36 A2
Mazères-sur-Salat F 35 A4
Mazières-en-Gâtine F 23 B3
Méan B 5 B5
Meaulne F 17 C4
Meaux F 10 C2
Mechelen B 5 A4
Mechernich D 6 B2
Meckenbeuren D 21 B4
Meckenheim, *Rheinland-Pfalz* D 6 B3
Meckenheim, *Rheinland-Pfalz* D 13 B4
Meckesheim D 13 B4
Medebach D 7 A4
Medemblik NL 2 B2
Meerle B 5 A4
Meersburg D 21 B4
Meeuwen B 5 A5
Megève F 26 B3
Mehun-sur-Yèvre F 17 B4
Meijel NL 6 A1
Meilen CH 21 B3
Meilhan F 28 C2
Meina I 27 B5
Meinerzhagen D 7 A3
Meiringen CH 20 C3
Meisenheim D 13 B3
Meix-devant-Virton B 12 B1
Melisey F 19 B5
Melle B 5 A3
Melle D 3 B5
Melle F 23 B3
Mels CH 21 B4
Melun F 10 C2
Memer F 29 B4
Memmingen D 21 B5
Menat F 24 A2
Mendavia E 34 B1
Mendaza E 34 B1
Mende F 30 A2
Menden D 7 A3
Mendig D 6 B3
Ménéac F 15 A3
Menen B 4 B3
Menetou-Salon F 17 B4
Mengen D 21 A4
Menou F 18 B2
Mens F 26 C2
Menslage D 3 B4
Menton F 33 B3
Méobecq F 23 B5
Méounes-les-Montrieux F 32 B1
Meppel NL 2 B3
Meppen D 3 B4
Mer F 17 B3
Merchtem B 5 B4
Merdrignac F 15 A3
Meréville F 10 C2
Merfeld D 6 A3
Méribel F 26 B3
Méribel Motraret F 26 B3
Mérignac F 28 B2
Merksplas B 5 A4
Merlimont Plage F 4 B1
Mers-les-Bains F 10 A1
Mersch L 12 B2
Méru F 10 B2
Mervans F 19 C4
Merville F 4 B2
Méry-sur-Seine F 11 C3
Merzen D 3 B4
Merzig D 12 B2
Meschede D 7 A4
Meschers-sur-Gironde F 22 C3
Meslay-du-Maine F 16 B1
Messac F 15 B4
Messancy B 12 B1
Messei F 8 B3
Messingen D 3 B4
Messkirch D 21 B4
Messtetten D 21 A3
Mesvres F 18 C3
Metelen D 3 B4
Metslawier NL 2 A3
Mettendorf D 12 B2
Mettet B 5 B4
Mettingen D 3 B4
Mettlach D 12 B2
Mettlen CH 20 C2
Mettmann D 6 A2
Metz F 12 B2
Metzervisse F 12 B2
Meulan F 10 B1
Meung-sur-Loire F 17 B3
Meuzac F 23 C5
Meximieux F 26 B2
Meyerhöfen D 3 B5
Meylan F 26 B2
Meymac F 24 B2
Meyrargues F 32 B1
Meyrueis F 30 A2
Meyssac F 29 A4
Meysse F 25 C4
Meyzieu F 25 B4
Mèze F 30 B2
Mézériat F 25 A5
Mézidon-Canon F 9 A3
Mézières-en-Brenne F 23 B5
Mézières-sur-Issoire F 23 B4
Mézilhac F 25 C4
Mézilles F 18 B2
Mézin F 28 B3
Mézos F 28 B1
Michelstadt D 13 B5
Middelburg NL 5 A3
Middelharnis NL 5 A4
Middelkerke B 4 A2
Middelstum NL 3 A3
Midwolda NL 3 A4
Miélan F 35 A4
Mieres, *Girona* E 37 B3
Miesau D 13 B3
Migennes F 18 B2
Migné F 23 B5
Milagro E 34 B2
Millançay F 17 B3
Millas F 36 B3
Millau F 30 A2
Millesimo I 33 A4
Millevaches F 24 B2
Milly-la-Forêt F 10 C2
Mimizan F 28 B1
Mimizan-Plage F 28 B1
Minsen D 3 A4
Mios F 28 B2
Mirabel-aux-Baronnies F 31 A4
Miradoux F 29 B3
Miramas F 31 B3
Mirambeau F 22 C3
Miramont-de-Guyenne F 29 B3
Miranda de Arga E 34 B2
Mirande F 29 C3
Miré F 16 B1
Mirebeau F 16 C2
Mirebeau-sur-Bèze F 19 B4
Mirecourt F 19 A5
Mirepoix F 36 A2
Miribel F 25 B4
Missillac F 15 B3
Mittelberg, *Vorarlberg* A 21 B5
Mittersheim F 12 C2
Mitton F 28 B2
Modane F 26 B3
Moëlan-sur-Mer F 14 B2
Moerbeke B 5 A3
Moers D 6 A2
Möhlin CH 20 B2
Moià E 37 C3
Moirans F 26 B2
Moirans-en-Montagne F 26 A2
Moisdon-la-Rivière F 15 B4
Moissac F 29 B4
Mol B 5 A5
Molare I 33 A4
Molaretto I 27 B4
Molas F 35 A4
Molbergen D 3 B4
Molières F 29 B4
Molinet F 18 C2
Molins de Rei E 37 C3
Mollerussa E 37 C1
Mollet de Perelada E 36 B3
Molló E 36 B3
Molompize F 24 B3
Moloy F 19 B3
Molsheim F 13 C3
Mombris D 13 A5
Momo I 27 B5
Monbahus F 29 B3
Monbazillac F 29 B3
Moncalieri I 27 B4
Moncalvo I 27 B5
Moncel-sur-Seille F 12 C2
Mönchen-gladbach = Munchen-Gladbach D 6 A2
Monclar-de-Quercy F 29 C4
Moncontour F 15 A3
Moncoutant F 22 B3
Mondorf-les-Bains L 12 B2
Mondoubleau F 16 B2
Mondovi I 33 A3
Mondragon F 31 A3
Monein F 35 A3
Mónesi I 33 A3
Monesiglio I 33 A4
Monestier-de-Clermont F 26 C2
Monestiés F 30 A1
Monéteau F 18 B2
Monflanquin F 29 B3
Monflorite E 35 B3
Monforte d'Alba I 33 A3
Monistrol-d'Allier F 25 C3
Monistrol de Montserrat E 37 C2
Monistrol-sur-Loire F 25 B4
Monnaie F 16 B2
Monnerville F 10 C2
Monnickendam NL 2 B2
Monpazier F 29 B3
Monreal D 6 B3
Monreal E 34 B2
Mons B 5 B3
Monschau D 6 B2
Monségur F 28 B3
Monster NL 2 B1
Mont-de-Marsan F 28 C2
Mont-Louis F 36 B3
Mont-roig del Camp E 37 C1
Mont-St. Aignan F 9 A5
Mont-St. Vincent F 18 C3
Mont-sous-Vaudrey F 19 C4
Montabaur D 7 B3
Montafia I 27 C5
Montagnac F 30 B2
Montaigu F 22 B2
Montaigu-de-Quercy F 29 B4
Montaiguët-en-Forez F 25 A3
Montaigut F 24 A2
Montaigut-sur-Save F 29 C4
Montainville F 10 C1
Montalieu-Vercieu F 26 B2
Montalivet-les-Bains F 22 C2
Montana-Vermala CH 27 A4
Montans F 29 C4
Montargis F 17 B4
Montastruc-la-Conseillère F 29 C4
Montauban F 29 B4
Montauban-de-Bretagne F 15 A3
Montbard F 18 B3
Montbarrey F 19 B4
Montbazens F 30 A1
Montbazon F 16 B2
Montbéliard F 20 B1
Montbenoit F 19 C5
Montbeugny F 18 C2
Montblanc E 37 C2
Montbozon F 19 B5
Montbrison F 25 B4
Montbron F 23 C4
Montbrun-les-Bains F 31 A4
Montceau-les-Mines F 18 C3
Montcenis F 18 C3
Montchanin F 18 C3
Montcornet F 11 B4
Montcuq F 29 B4
Montdardier F 30 B2
Montdidier F 10 B2
Monte-Carlo MC 33 B3
Montebourg F 8 A2
Montech F 29 C4
Montechiaro d'Asti I 27 B5
Montel-de-Gelat F 24 B2
Montelier F 25 C5
Montélimar F 31 A3
Montella E 36 B2
Montemagno I 27 C5
Montendre F 28 A2
Monteneuf F 15 B3
Montereau-Faut-Yonne F 10 C2
Monterosso Grana I 33 A3
Montesquieu-Volvestre F 36 A2
Montesquiou F 29 C3
Montestruc-sur-Gers F 29 C3
Montfaucon F 15 B4
Montfaucon-d'Argonne F 11 B5
Montfaucon-en-Velay F 25 B4
Montferrat, *Isère* F 26 B2
Montferrat, *Var* F 32 B2
Montfort-en-Chalosse F 28 C2
Montfort-l'Amaury F 10 C1
Montfort-le-Gesnois F 16 A2
Montfort-sur-Meu F 15 A4
Montfort-sur-Risle F 9 A4
Montgai E 37 C1
Montgaillard F 35 A4
Montgenèvre F 26 C3
Montgiscard F 36 A2
Montguyon F 28 A2
Monthermé F 11 B4
Monthey CH 27 A3
Monthois F 11 B4
Monthureux-sur-Saône F 19 A4
Montier-en-Der F 11 C4
Montiglio I 27 B5
Montignac F 29 A4
Montigny-le-Roi F 19 B4
Montigny-lès-Metz F 12 B2
Montigny-sur-Aube F 19 B3
Montilly F 18 C2
Montivilliers F 9 A4
Montjaux F 30 A1
Montjean-sur-Loire F 16 B1
Montlhéry F 10 C2
Montlieu-la-Gard F 28 A2
Montlouis-sur-Loire F 16 B2
Montluçon F 24 A2
Montluel F 25 B5
Montmarault F 24 A2
Montmartin-sur-Mer F 8 B2
Montmédy F 12 B1
Montmélian F 26 B3
Montmeyan F 32 B2
Montmeyran F 25 C4
Montmirail, *Marne* F 11 C3
Montmirail, *Sarthe* F 16 A2
Montmiral F 26 B2
Montmirat F 31 B3
Montmirey-le-Château F 19 B4
Montmoreau-St. Cybard F 23 C4
Montmorency F 10 C2
Montmorillon F 23 B4
Montmort-Lucy F 11 C3
Montoir-de-Bretagne F 15 B3
Montoire-sur-le-Loir F 16 B2
Montolieu F 36 A3
Montpellier F 31 B2
Montpezat-de-Quercy F 29 B4
Montpezat-sous-Bouzon F 25 C4
Montpon-Ménestérol F 28 A3
Montpont-en-Bresse F 19 C4
Montréal, *Aude* F 36 A3
Montréal, *Gers* F 28 C3
Montredon-Labessonnié F 30 B1
Montréjeau F 35 A4
Montrésor F 17 B3
Montret F 19 C4
Montreuil, *Pas de Calais* F 4 B1
Montreuil, *Seine St. Denis* F 10 C2
Montreuil-aux-Lions F 10 B3
Montreuil-Bellay F 16 B1
Montreux CH 20 C1
Montrevault F 15 B4
Montrevel-en-Bresse F 26 A2
Montrichard F 17 B3
Montricoux F 29 B4
Montrond-les-Bains F 25 B4
Monts-sur-Guesnes F 16 C2
Montsalvy F 24 C2
Montsauche-les-Settons F 18 B3
Montseny E 37 C3
Montsoreau F 16 B2
Montsûrs F 16 A1
Monzón E 35 C4
Moordorf D 3 A4
Moorslede B 4 B3
Moos D 21 B3
Morbach D 12 B3
Morbier F 19 C5
Morcenx F 28 B2
Mordelles F 15 A4
Moréac F 14 B3
Morée F 17 B3
Morestel F 26 B2
Moret-sur-Loing F 10 C2
Moretta I 27 C4
Moreuil F 10 B2
Morez F 19 C5
Mörfelden D 13 B4
Morgat F 14 A1
Morges CH 19 C5
Morgex I 27 B4
Morhange F 12 C2
Morhet B 12 B1
Morialmé B 5 B4
Moriani Plage F 38 A2
Morlaàs F 35 A3
Morlaix F 14 A2
Morley F 11 C5
Mormant F 10 C2
Mornant F 25 B4
Mornay-Berry F 17 B4
Morozzo I 33 A3
Morsbach D 7 B3
Mörsch D 13 C4
Mortagne-au-Perche F 9 B4
Mortagne-sur-Gironde F 22 C3
Mortagne-sur-Sèvre F 22 B3
Mortain F 8 B3
Morteau F 19 B5
Mortemart F 23 B4
Mortrée F 9 B4
Mortsel B 5 A4
Morzine F 26 A3
Mosbach D 13 B5
Mössingen D 13 C5
Mostuéjouls F 30 A2
Mouchard F 19 C4
Moudon CH 20 C1
Mougins F 32 B2
Mouilleron en-Pareds F 22 B3
Mouliherne F 16 B2
Moulinet F 33 B3
Moulins F 18 C2
Moulins-Engilbert F 18 C2
Moulins-la-Marche F 9 B4
Moulismes F 23 B4
Moult F 9 A3
Mourenx F 35 A3
Mouriés F 31 B3
Mourmelon-le-Grand F 11 B4
Mouscron B 4 B3
Moussac F 31 B3
Moussey F 12 C2
Mousteru F 14 A2
Moustey F 28 B2
Moustiers-Ste. Marie F 32 B2
Mouthe F 19 C5
Mouthier-Haute-Pierre F 19 B5
Mouthoumet F 36 B3
Moutier CH 20 B2
Moûtiers F 26 B3
Moutiers-les-Mauxfaits F 22 B2
Mouy F 10 B2
Mouzon F 11 B5
Moyenmoutier F 12 C2
Moyenvic F 12 C2
Much D 6 B3
Mudau D 13 B5
Mudersbach D 7 B3
Mugron F 28 C2
Mühlacker D 13 C4
Muhleberg CH 20 C2
Mühleim D 21 A3
Mulegns CH 21 C4
Mülheim D 6 A2
Mulhouse F 20 B2
Müllheim D 20 B2
Munchen-Gladbach = Mönchen-gladbach D 6 A2
Münchhausen D 7 B4
Munderkingen D 21 A4
Münsingen CH 20 C2
Münster CH 20 C3
Münster, *Hessen* D 13 B4
Münster, *Nordrhein-Westfalen* D 3 C4
Munster F 20 A2
Muotathal CH 21 C3
Mur-de-Barrez F 24 C2
Mur-de-Bretagne F 14 A2
Mur-de-Sologne F 17 B3
Murat F 24 B2
Murat-sur-Vèbre F 30 B1
Murato F 38 A2
Murazzano I 33 A4
Murchante E 34 B2
Muret F 36 A2
Murg CH 21 B4
Muri CH 20 B3
Murillo el Fruto E 34 B2
Muro F 38 A1
Murol F 24 B2
Muron F 22 B3
Mürren CH 20 C2
Murten CH 20 C2
Murviel-lès-Béziers F 30 B2
Musculdy F 34 A3
Musselkanaal NL 3 B4
Mussidan F 29 A3
Musson B 12 B1
Mussy-sur-Seine F 18 B3
Muzillac F 15 B3
Myennes F 18 B1

N

Naaldwijk NL 5 A4
Näfels CH 21 B4
Nagele NL 2 B2
Nagold D 13 C4
Nagore E 34 B2
Nailloux F 36 A2
Naintré F 23 B4
Najac F 29 B4
Nalliers F 22 B2
Nalzen F 36 B2
Namur B 5 B4
Nançay F 17 B4
Nancy F 12 C2
Nangis F 10 C3
Nant F 30 A2
Nanterre F 10 C2
Nantes F 15 B4
Nanteuil-le-Haudouin F 10 B2
Nantiat F 23 B5
Nantua F 26 A2
Narbonne F 30 B1
Narbonne-Plage F 30 B2
Narzole I 33 A3
Nasbinals F 24 C3
Nassau D 7 B3
Nastätten D 7 B3
Naters CH 27 A5
Naucelle F 30 A1
Naval E 35 B4
Navarclés E 37 C2
Navarrenx F 34 A3
Navás E 37 C2
Navascués E 34 B2
Navés E 37 C2
Navilly F 19 C4
Nay F 35 A3
Neckargemünd D 13 B4
Nederweert NL 6 A1
Neede NL 3 B3
Neermoor D 3 A4
Neeroeteren B 6 A1
Neerpelt B 5 A5
Nègrepelisse F 29 B4
Neheim D 7 A3
Néive I 27 C5
Nemours F 17 A4
Nenzing A 21 B4
Nérac F 29 B3
Néré F 23 C3
Néris-les Bains F 24 A2
Néronde F 25 B4
Nérondes F 17 C4
Nes NL 2 A2
Nesle F 10 B2
Nesslau CH 21 B4
Nessmersiel D 3 A4
Netphen D 7 B4
Netstal CH 21 B4
Nettancourt F 11 C4
Nettetal D 6 A2
Neu-Isenburg D 13 A4
Neubeckum D 7 A4
Neuchâtel CH 20 C1
Neudorf D 13 B4
Neuenbürg, *Baden-Württemberg* D 13 C4
Neuenburg, *Niedersachsen* D 3 A4
Neuenhaus D 3 B3
Neuenkirchen, *Niedersachsen* D 3 B5
Neuenkirchen, *Nordrhein-Westfalen* D 3 B4
Neuenkirchen, *Nordrhein-Westfalen* D 7 B3
Neuenrade D 7 A3
Neuerburg D 12 A2
Neuf-Brisach F 20 A2
Neufchâteau B 12 B1
Neufchâteau F 12 C1
Neufchâtel-en-Bray F 10 B1
Neufchâtel-sur-Aisne F 11 B4
Neuflize F 11 B4
Neuharlingersiel D 3 A4
Neuhaus, *Niedersachsen* D 7 A5
Neuhausen CH 21 B3
Neuhausen ob Eck D 21 B3
Neuillé-Pont-Pierre F 16 B2
Neuilly-en-Thelle F 10 B2
Neuilly-le-Réal F 18 C2
Neuilly-l'Évêque F 19 B4
Neuilly-St. Front F 10 B3
Neukirchen, *Hessen* D 7 B5
Neulise F 25 B4
Neumagen D 12 B2
Neung-sur-Beuvron F 17 B3
Neunkirch, *Luzern* CH 20 B3
Neunkirch, *Schaffhausen* CH 21 B3
Neunkirchen, *Nordrhein-Westfalen* D 6 B3
Neunkirchen, *Saarland* D 12 B3
Neuravensburg D 21 B4
Neureut D 13 B4
Neuss D 6 A2
Neussargues-Moissac F 24 B2
Neustadt, *Hessen* D 7 B5
Neustadt, *Rheinland-Pfalz* D 13 B4
Neuves-Maisons F 12 C2
Neuvic, *Corrèze* F 24 B2
Neuvic, *Dordogne* F 29 A3
Neuville-aux-Bois F 17 A4
Neuville-de-Poitou F 23 B4

O

P

Pressac F 23 B4
Preuilly-sur-Claise F 23 B4
Prevenchères F 31 A2
Préveranges F 24 A2
Priay F 26 A2
Primel-Trégastel F 14 A2
Primstal D 12 B2
Privas F 25 C4
Profondeville B 5 B4
Propriano F 38 B1
Provins F 10 C3
Prüm D 6 B2
Prunelli-di-Fiumorbo F 38 A2
Pruniers F 17 C4
Puchevillers F 10 A2
Puderbach D 7 B3
Puente de Montañana E 35 B4
Puente la Reina E 34 B2
Puente la Reina de Jaca E 34 B3
Puget-Sur-Argens F 32 B2
Puget-Théniers F 32 B2
Puget-ville F 32 B2
Puig Reig E 37 C2
Puigcerdà E 36 B2
Puillon F 28 C2
Puimichel F 32 B2
Puimoisson F 32 B2
Puiseaux F 17 A4
Puisieux F 10 A2
Puisserguier F 30 B2
Puivert F 36 B3
Pujols F 28 B2
Pulheim D 6 A2
Purmerend NL 2 B1
Putanges-Pont-Ecrepin F 9 B3
Putte B 5 A4
Puttelange-aux-Lacs F 12 B2
Putten NL 2 B2
Püttlingen D 12 B2
Puy-Guillaume F 25 B3
Puy-l'Évêque F 29 B4
Puylaroque F 29 B4
Puylaurens F 36 A3
Puymirol F 29 B3
Puyôo F 28 C2
Puyrolland F 22 B3
Pyla-sur-Mer F 28 B1

Q

Quakenbrück D 3 B4
Quargnento I 27 C5
Quarré-les-Tombes F 18 B2
Quatre-Champs F 11 B4
Queige F 26 B3
Queixans E 36 B2
Quel E 34 B1
Quelaines-St-Gault F 16 B1
Queralbs E 37 B3
Quérigut F 36 B3
Querqueville F 8 A2
Questembert F 15 B3
Quettehou F 8 A2
Quevauvillers F 10 B2
Quevy B 5 B4
Quiberon F 14 B2
Quiberville F 9 A4
Quiévrain B 5 B3
Quillan F 36 B3
Quillebeuf F 9 A4
Quimper F 14 A1
Quimperlé F 14 B2
Quincampoix F 9 A5
Quincy F 17 B4
Quinéville F 8 A2
Quingey F 19 B4
Quinson F 32 B2
Quinssaines F 24 A2
Quintin F 14 A3
Quissac F 31 B2

R

Raalte NL 3 B3
Raamsdonksveer NL 5 A4
Rabastens F 29 C4
Rabastens-de-Bigorre F 35 A4
Racconigi I 27 C4
Rachecourt-sur-Marne F 11 C5
Radevormwald D 6 A3
Radolfzell D 21 B3
Raeren B 6 B2
Raesfeld D 6 A2
Rambervillers F 12 C2
Rambouillet F 10 C1
Rambucourt F 12 C1
Ramerupt F 11 C4
Ramiswil CH 20 B2
Ramonville-St. Agne F 29 C4
Ramsbeck D 7 A4
Ramstein-Meisenbach D 13 B3
Rance B 11 A4
Randan F 25 A3
Rânes F 9 B3
Rankweil A 21 B4
Ransbach-Baumbach D 7 B3
Raon-l'Étape F 12 C2
Rapperswil CH 21 B3
Rasal E 35 B3
Rastatt D 13 C4
Rastede D 3 A5
Ratingen D 6 A2
Raucourt-et-Flaba F 11 B4
Raulhac F 24 C2
Rauville-la-Bigot F 8 A2
Rauzan F 28 B2
Ravels B 5 A4
Ravensburg D 21 B4
Razes F 23 B5
Réalmont F 30 B1
Rebais F 10 C3
Recey-sur-Ource F 19 B3
Recke D 3 B4
Recklinghausen D 6 A3
Recogne B 12 B1
Recoules-Prévinquières F 30 A1
Redange L 12 B1
Redon F 15 B3
Rees D 6 A2
Régil E 34 A1
Regniéville F 12 C1
Regny F 25 B4
Reichelsheim D 13 B4
Reichshoffen F 13 C3
Reiden CH 20 B2
Reillanne F 32 B1
Reims F 11 B4
Reinach CH 20 B3
Reinheim D 13 B4
Remagen D 6 B3
Rémalard F 9 B4
Rembercourt-aux-Pots F 11 C5
Remels D 3 A4
Remich L 12 B2
Rémilly F 12 B2
Remiremont F 19 A5
Remolinos E 34 C2
Remoulins F 31 B3
Remscheid D 6 A3
Rémuzat F 31 A4
Renaison F 25 A3
Renazé F 15 B4
Renchen D 13 C4
Rencurel F 26 B2
Renens CH 19 C5
Rennerod D 7 B4
Rennes F 15 A4
Rennes-les-Bains F 36 B3
Rentería E 34 A2
Réquista F 30 A1
Ressons-sur-Matz F 10 B2
Rethel F 11 B4
Retie B 5 A5
Retiers F 15 B4
Retournac F 25 B4
Reuilly F 17 B4
Reus E 37 C2
Reusel NL 5 A5
Reuver NL 6 A2
Revel F 36 A2
Revello I 27 C4
Revest-du-Bion F 32 A1
Revigny-sur-Ornain F 11 C4
Revin F 11 B4
Rezé F 15 B4
Rhaunen D 13 B3
Rheda-Wiedenbrück D 7 A4
Rhede, *Niedersachsen* D 3 A4
Rhede, *Nordrhein-Westfalen* D 6 A2
Rheinau D 13 C3
Rheinbach D 6 B2
Rheinberg D 6 A2
Rheine D 3 B4
Rheinfelden D 20 B2
Rhêmes-Notre-Dame I 27 B4
Rhenen NL 2 C2
Rhens D 7 B3
Rheydt D 6 A2
Rhoden D 7 A5
Riallé F 15 B4
Rians F 32 B1
Ribaforada E 34 C2
Ribeauvillé F 20 A2
Ribécourt-Dreslincourt F 10 B2
Ribemont F 11 B3
Ribera de Cardós E 36 B2
Ribérac F 29 A3
Ribes de Freser E 37 B3
Ribiers F 32 A1
Richebourg F 19 A4
Richelieu F 16 B2
Richisau CH 21 B3
Richterswil CH 21 B3
Ridderkerk NL 5 A4
Riddes CH 27 A4
Riec-sur-Bélon F 14 B2
Riedlingen D 21 A4
Riedstadt D 13 B4
Riemst B 6 B1
Rienne B 11 B4
Rietberg D 7 A4
Rieumes F 36 A2
Rieupeyroux F 30 A1
Rieux F 36 A2
Riez F 32 B2
Riggisberg CH 20 C2
Rignac F 30 A1
Rijen NL 5 A4
Rijkevorsel B 5 A4
Rijssen NL 3 B3
Rillé F 16 B2
Rimogne F 11 B4
Rincón de Soto E 34 B2
Riom F 24 B3
Riom-ès-Montagnes F 24 B2
Rion-des-Landes F 28 C2
Riotord F 25 B4
Rioz F 19 B5
Ripoll E 37 B3
Rischenau D 7 A5
Riscle F 28 C2
Riva Lígure I 33 B3
Rivarolo Canavese I 27 B4
Rive-de-Gier F 25 B4
Rivedoux-Plage F 22 B2
Rives F 26 B2
Rivesaltes F 36 B3
Rívoli I 27 B4
Rixheim F 20 B2
Roanne F 25 A4
Robertville B 6 B2
Robres E 35 C3
Robres del Castillo E 34 B1
Rocafort de Queralt E 37 C2
Rocamadour F 29 B4
Roche-lez-Beaupré F 19 B5
Rochechouart F 23 C4
Rochefort B 5 B5
Rochefort F 22 C3
Rochefort-en-Terre F 15 B3
Rochefort-Montagne F 24 B2
Rochefort-sur-Nenon F 19 B4
Rochemaure F 31 A3
Rocheservière F 22 B2
Rockenhausen D 13 B3
Rocroi F 11 B4
Roda de Bara E 37 C2
Roda de Ter E 37 C3
Rodalben D 13 B3
Roden NL 3 A3
Rödermark D 13 B4
Rodez F 30 A1
Rodoñá E 37 C2
Roermond NL 6 A1
Roesbrugge B 4 B2
Roeschwoog F 13 C4
Roeselare B 4 B3
Roetgen D 6 B2
Roffiac F 24 B3
Rogliano F 38 A2
Rognes F 31 B4
Rogny-les-7-Ecluses F 17 B4
Rohan F 15 A3
Rohrbach-lès-Bitche F 12 B3
Roisel F 10 B3
Rolampont F 19 B4
Rolde NL 3 B3
Rolle CH 19 C5
Romagnano Sésia I 27 B5
Romagné F 8 B2
Romanèche-Thorins F 25 A4
Romans-sur-Isère F 26 B2
Romanshorn CH 21 B4
Rombas F 12 B2
Romenay F 19 C4
Romilly-sur-Seine F 11 C3
Romont CH 20 C1
Romorantin-Lanthenay F 17 B3
Romrod D 7 B5
Roncal E 34 B3
Ronce-les-Bains F 22 C2
Ronchamp F 20 B1
Ronco Canavese I 27 B4
Ronse B 5 B3
Roosendaal NL 5 A4
Roquebillière F 33 A3
Roquebrun F 30 B2
Roquecourbe F 30 B1
Roquefort F 28 B2
Roquemaure F 31 A3
Roquesteron F 32 B3
Roquevaire F 32 B1
Rorschach CH 21 B4
Rosans F 32 A1
Rosbach D 7 B3
Roscoff F 14 A2
Rosel GB 8 A1
Rosenfeld D 13 C4
Rosenthal D 7 A4
Roses E 37 B4
Rosheim F 13 C3
Rosières-en-Santerre F 10 B2
Rosoy F 18 A2
Rosporden F 14 B2
Rosrath D 6 B3
Rossiglione I 33 A4
Rossignol B 12 B1
Rostrenen F 14 A2
Roth, *Rheinland-Pfalz* D 7 B3
Rothéneuf F 8 B2
Rottenburg, *Baden-Württemberg* D 13 C4
Rotterdam NL 5 A4
Rottweil D 21 A3
Roubaix F 4 B3
Roudouallec F 14 A2
Rouen F 9 A5
Rouffach F 20 B2
Rougé F 15 B4
Rougemont F 19 B5
Rougemont le-Château F 20 B1
Rouillac F 23 C3
Rouillé F 23 B4
Roujan F 30 B2
Roulans F 19 B5
Roussac F 23 B5
Roussennac F 30 A1
Rousses F 30 A2
Roussillon F 25 B4
Rouvroy-sur-Audry F 11 B4
Rouy F 18 B2
Royan F 22 C2
Royat F 24 B3
Roybon F 26 B2
Roye F 10 B2
Royère-de-Vassivière F 24 B1
Rozay-en-Brie F 10 C2
Rozoy-sur-Serre F 11 B4
Rubí E 37 C3
Ruddervorde B 4 A3
Rüdesheim D 13 B3
Rue F 4 B1
Ruelle-sur-Touvre F 23 C4
Ruffec F 23 B4
Rugles F 9 B4
Ruhle D 3 B4
Ruillé-sur-le-Loir F 16 B2
Ruinen NL 3 B3
Ruiselede B 4 A3
Rulles B 12 B1
Rülzheim D 13 B4
Rumigny F 11 B4
Rumilly F 26 B2
Rumont F 11 C5
Ruoms F 31 A3
Ruppichteroth D 6 B3
Rupt-sur-Moselle F 20 B1
Rüsselsheim D 13 B4
Rustrel F 31 B4
Rüthen D 7 A4
Rüti CH 21 B3
Ruurlo NL 3 B3
Ruynes-en-Margeride F 24 C3

S

Saales F 12 C3
Saanen CH 20 C2
Saarbrücken D 12 B2
Saarburg D 12 B2
Saarlouis D 12 B2
Saas-Fee CH 27 A4
Sabadell E 37 C3
Sabiñánigo E 35 B3
Sablé-sur-Sarthe F 16 B1
Sables-d'Or-les-Pins F 15 A3
Sabres F 28 B2
Sádaba E 34 B2
Sadernes E 37 B3
Saerbeck D 3 B4
Saeul L 12 B1
S'Agaro E 37 C4
Sagone F 38 A1
Sagy F 19 C4
Saignelégier CH 20 B1
Saignes F 24 B2
Saillagouse F 36 B3
Saillans F 26 C2
Sains F 11 B3
St. Affrique F 30 B1
St. Agnan F 18 C2
St. Agnant F 22 C3
St. Agrève F 25 B4
St. Aignan F 17 B3
St. Aignan-sur-Roë F 15 B4
St. Alban-sur-Limagnole F 25 C3
St. Amand-en-Puisaye F 18 B2
St. Amand-les-Eaux F 5 B3
St. Amand-Longpré F 17 B3
St. Amand-Montrond F 17 C4
St. Amans F 25 C3
St. Amans-Soult F 30 B1
St. Amant-Roche-Savine F 25 B3
St. Amarin F 20 B1
St. Ambroix F 31 A3
St. Amé F 20 A1
St. Amour F 26 A2
St. André-de-Corcy F 25 B4
St. André-de-Cubzac F 28 B2
St. André-de-l'Eure F 9 B5
St. André-de-Roquepertuis F 31 A3
St. André-de-Sangonis F 30 B2
St. André-de-Valborgne F 30 A2
St. André-les-Alpes F 32 B2
St. Angel F 24 B2
St. Anthème F 25 B3
St. Antoine F 38 A2
St. Antoine-de-Ficalba F 29 B3
St. Antönien CH 21 C4
St. Antonin-Noble-Val F 29 B4
St. Août F 17 C3
St. Armant-Tallende F 24 B3
St. Arnoult F 10 C1
St. Astier F 29 A3
St. Auban F 32 B2
St. Aubin CH 20 C1
St. Aubin F 19 B4
St. Aubin GB 8 A1
St. Aubin-d'Aubigné F 15 A4
St. Aubin-du-Cormier F 15 A4
St. Aubin-sur-Aire F 12 C1
St. Aubin-sur-Mer F 9 A3
St. Aulaye F 28 A3
St. Avit F 24 B2
St. Avold F 12 B2
St. Aygulf F 32 B2
St. Bauzille-de-Putois F 30 B2
St. Béat F 35 B4
St. Beauzély F 30 A1
St. Benim-d'Azy F 18 C2
St. Benoît-du-Sault F 23 B5
St. Benoit-en-Woëvre F 12 C1
St. Berthevin F 16 A1
St. Blaise-la-Roche F 12 C3
St. Blin F 19 A4
St. Bonnet F 26 C3
St. Bonnet Briance F 23 C5
St. Bonnet-de-Joux F 18 C3
St. Bonnet-le-Château F 25 B4
St. Bonnet-le-Froid F 25 B4
St. Brévin-les-Pins F 15 B3
St. Briac-sur-Mer F 15 A3
St. Brice-en-Coglès F 8 B2
St. Brieuc F 15 A3
St. Bris-le-Vineux F 18 B2
St. Broladre F 8 B2
St. Calais F 16 B2
St. Cannat F 31 B4
St. Cast-le-Guildo F 15 A3
St. Céré F 29 B4
St. Cergue CH 26 A3
St. Cergues F 26 A3
St. Cernin F 24 B2
St. Chamant F 24 B1
St. Chamas F 31 B4
St. Chamond F 25 B4
St. Chély-d'Apcher F 24 C3
St. Chély-d'Aubrac F 24 C2
St. Chinian F 30 B1
St. Christol F 31 A4
St. Christol-lès-Alès F 31 A3
St. Christoly-Médoc F 22 C3
St. Christophe-du-Ligneron F 22 B2
St. Christophe-en-Brionnais F 25 A4
St. Ciers-sur-Gironde F 28 A2
St. Clair-sur-Epte F 10 B1
St. Clar F 29 C3
St. Claud F 23 C4
St. Claude F 26 A2
St. Come-d'Olt F 30 A1
St. Cosme-en-Vairais F 9 B4
St. Cyprien, *Dordogne* F 29 B4
St. Cyprien, *Pyrenées-Orientales* F 36 B4
St. Cyr-sur-Loire F 16 B2
St. Cyr-sur-Mer F 32 B1
St. Cyr-sur-Methon F 25 A4
St. Denis F 10 C2
St. Denis-d'Oléron F 22 B2
St. Denis d'Orques F 16 A1
St. Didier F 25 A4
St. Didier-en-Velay F 25 B4
St. Dié F 12 C2
St. Dier-d'Auvergne F 25 B3
St. Dizier F 11 C4
St. Dizier-Leyrenne F 24 A1
St. Efflam F 14 A2
St. Égrève F 26 B2
St. Eloy-les-Mines F 24 A2
St. Emiland F 18 C3
St. Émilion F 28 B2
St. Esteben F 34 A2
St. Estèphe F 28 A2
St. Étienne F 25 B4
St. Etienne-de-Baigorry F 34 A2
St. Étienne-de-Cuines F 26 B3
St. Etienne-de-Fursac F 24 A1
St. Etienne-de-Montluc F 15 B4
St. Etienne-de-St. Geoirs F 26 B2
St. Étienne-de-Tinée F 32 A2
St. Étienne-du-Bois F 26 A2
St. Étienne-du-Rouvray F 9 A5
St. Etienne-les-Orgues F 32 A1
St. Fargeau F 18 B2
St. Félicien F 25 B4
St. Felix-de-Sorgues F 30 B1
St. Félix-Lauragais F 36 A2
St. Firmin F 26 C3
St. Florent F 38 A2
St. Florent-le-Vieil F 15 B4
St. Florent-sur-Cher F 17 C4
St. Florentin F 18 B2
St. Flour F 24 B3
St. Flovier F 17 C3
St. Fort-sur-le-Né F 23 C3
St. Fulgent F 22 B2
St. Galmier F 25 B4
St. Gaudens F 35 A4
St. Gaultier F 23 B5
St. Gély-du-Fesc F 30 B2
St. Genest-Malifaux F 25 B4
St. Gengoux-le-National F 18 C3
St. Geniez F 32 A2
St. Geniez-d'Olt F 30 A1
St. Genis-de-Saintonge F 22 C3
St. Genis-Pouilly F 26 A3
St. Genix-sur-Guiers F 26 B2
St. Georges Buttavent F 8 B3
St. Georges-d'Aurac F 25 B3
St. Georges-de-Commiers F 26 B2
St. Georges-de-Didonne F 22 C3
St. Georges-de-Luzençon F 30 A1
St. Georges-de Mons F 24 B2
St. Georges-de-Reneins F 25 A4
St. Georges d'Oléron F 22 C2
St. Georges-en-Couzan F 25 B3
St. Georges-lès-Baillargeaux F 23 B4
St. Georges-sur-Loire F 16 B1
St. Georges-sur-Meuse B 5 B5
St. Geours-de-Maremne F 28 C1
St. Gérand-de-Vaux F 25 A3
St. Gérand-le-Puy F 25 A3
St. Germain F 19 B5
St. Germain-Chassenay F 18 C2
St. Germain-de-Calberte F 30 A2
St. Germain-de-Confolens F 23 B4
St. Germain-de-Joux F 26 A2
St. Germain-des-Fossés F 25 A3
St. Germain-du-Bois F 19 C4
St. Germain-du-Plain F 19 C3
St. Germain-du Puy F 17 B4
St. Germain-en-Laye F 10 C2
St. Germain-Laval F 25 B4
St. Germain-Lembron F 24 B3
St. Germain-les-Belles F 24 B1
St. Germain-Lespinasse F 25 A3
St. Germain-l'Herm F 25 B3
St. Gervais-d'Auvergne F 24 A2
St. Gervais-les-Bains F 26 B3
St. Gervais-sur-Mare F 30 B2
St. Gildas-de-Rhuys F 14 B3
St. Gildas-des-Bois F 15 B3
St. Gilles, *Gard* F 31 B3
St. Gilles, *Ille-et-Vilaine* F 15 A4
St. Gilles-Croix-de-Vie F 22 B2
St. Gingolph F 27 A3
St. Girons, *Ariège* F 36 B2
St. Girons, *Landes* F 28 C1
St. Girons-Plage F 28 C1
St. Gobain F 11 B3
St. Gorgon-Main F 19 B5
St. Guénolé F 14 B1

St. Helier GB 8 A1
St. Herblain F 15 B4
St. Hilaire, *Allier* F 18 C2
St. Hilaire, *Aude* F 36 A3
St. Hilaire-de-Riez F 22 B2
St. Hilaire-de-Villefranche F 22 C3
St. Hilaire-des-Loges F 22 B3
St. Hilaire-du-Harcouët F 8 B2
St. Hilaire-du-Rosier F 26 B2
St. Hippolyte, *Aveyron* F 24 C2
St. Hippolyte, *Doubs* F 20 B1
St. Hippolyte-du-Fort F 30 B2
St. Honoré-les-Bains F 18 C2
St. Hubert B 12 A1
St. Imier CH 20 B2
St. Izaire F 30 B1
St. Jacques-de-la-Lande F 15 A4
St. Jacut-de-la-Mer F 15 A3
St. James F 8 B2
St. Jean-Brévelay F 15 B3
St. Jean-d'Angély F 22 C3
St. Jean-de-Belleville F 26 B3
St. Jean-de-Bournay F 26 B2
St. Jean-de-Braye F 17 B3
St. Jean-de-Côle F 23 C4
St. Jean-de-Daye F 8 A2
St. Jean de Losne F 19 B4
St. Jean-de-Luz F 34 A2
St. Jean-de-Maurienne F 26 B3
St. Jean-de-Monts F 22 B1
St. Jean-d'Illac F 28 B2
St. Jean-du-Bruel F 30 A2
St. Jean-du-Gard F 31 A2
St. Jean-en-Royans F 26 B2
St. Jean-la-Riviere F 33 B3
St. Jean-Pied-de-Port F 34 A2
St. Jean-Poutge F 29 C3
St. Jeoire F 26 A3
St. Joachim F 15 B3
St. Jorioz F 26 B3
St. Joris Winge B 5 B4
St. Jouin-de-Marnes F 16 C1
St. Juéry F 30 B1
St. Julien F 26 A2
St. Julien-Chapteuil F 25 B4
St. Julien-de-Vouvantes F 15 B4
St. Julien-du-Sault F 18 A2
St. Julien-du-Verdon F 32 B2
St. Julien-en-Born F 28 B1
St. Julien-en-Genevois F 26 A3
St. Julien la-Vêtre F 25 B3
St. Julien-l'Ars F 23 B4
St. Julien-Mont-Denis F 26 B3
St. Julien-sur-Reyssouze F 26 A2
St. Junien F 23 C4
St. Just F 31 A3
St. Just-en-Chaussée F 10 B2
St. Just-en-Chevalet F 25 B3
St. Just-St. Rambert F 25 B4
St. Justin F 28 C2
St. Lary-Soulan F 35 B4
St. Laurent-d'Aigouze F 31 B3
St. Laurent-de-Chamousset F 25 B4
St. Laurent-de-Condel F 9 A3
St. Laurent-de-la-Cabrerisse F 36 A3
St. Laurent-de-la-Salanque F 36 B3
St. Laurent-des-Autels F 15 B4
St. Laurent-du-Pont F 26 B2
St. Laurent-en-Caux F 9 A4
St. Laurent-en-Grandvaux F 19 C4
St. Laurent-Médoc F 28 A2
St. Laurent-sur-Gorre F 23 C4
St. Laurent-sur-Mer F 8 A3
St. Laurent-sur-Sèvre F 22 B3
St. Leger B 12 B1
St. Léger-de-Vignes F 18 C2
St. Léger-sous-Beuvray F 18 C3
St. Léger-sur-Dheune F 18 C3
St. Léonard-de-Noblat F 24 B1
St. Lô F 8 A2
St. Lon-les-Mines F 28 C1
St. Louis F 20 B2
St. Loup F 25 A3
St. Loup-de-la-Salle F 19 C3
St. Loup-sur-Semouse F 19 B5
St. Lunaire F 15 A3
St. Lupicin F 26 A2
St. Lyphard F 15 B3
St. Lys F 36 A2
St. Macaire F 28 B2
St. Maclou F 9 A4
St. Maixent-l'École F 23 B3
St. Malo F 8 B1
St. Mamet-la-Salvetat F 24 C2
St. Mandrier-sur-Mer F 32 B1
St. Marcel, *Drôme* F 25 C4
St. Marcel, *Saône-et-Loire* F 19 C3
St. Marcellin F 26 B2
St. Marcellin sur Loire F 25 B4
St. Marcet F 35 A4
St. Mards-en-Othe F 18 A2
St. Mars-la-Jaille F 15 B4
St. Martin-d'Ablois F 11 C3
St. Martin-d'Auxigny F 17 B4
St. Martin-de-Belleville F 26 B3
St. Martin-de-Bossenay F 11 C3
St. Martin-de-Crau F 31 B3
St. Martin-de-Londres F 30 B2
St. Martin-de-Queyrières F 26 C3
St. Martin-de-Ré F 22 B2
St. Martin-de-Valamas F 25 C4
St. Martin-d'Entraunes F 32 A2
St. Martin des Besaces F 8 A3
St. Martin-d'Estreaux F 25 A3
St. Martin-d'Hères F 26 B2
St. Martin-du-Frêne F 26 A2
St. Martin-en-Bresse F 19 C4
St. Martin-en-Haut F 25 B4
St. Martin-la-Méanne F 24 B1
St. Martin-sur-Ouanne F 18 B2
St. Martin-Valmeroux F 24 B2
St. Martin-Vésubie F 33 A3
St. Martory F 35 A4
St. Mathieu F 23 C4
St. Mathieu-de-Tréviers F 31 B2
St. Maurice CH 27 A3
St. Maurice-Navacelles F 30 B2
St. Maurice-sur-Moselle F 20 B1
St. Maximin-la-Ste. Baume F 32 B1
St. Méard-de-Gurçon F 28 B3
St. Médard-de-Guizières F 28 A2
St. Médard-en-Jalles F 28 B2
St. Méen-le-Grand F 15 A3
St. Menges F 11 B4
St. M'Hervé F 15 A4
St. Michel, *Aisne* F 11 B4
St. Michel, *Gers* F 35 A4
St. Michel-Chef-Chef F 15 B3
St. Michel-de-Castelnau F 28 B2
St. Michel-de-Maurienne F 26 B3
St. Michel-en-Grève F 14 A2
St. Michel-en-l'Herm F 22 B2
St. Michel-Mont-Mercure F 22 B3
St. Mihiel F 12 C1
St. Montant F 31 A3
St. Moritz CH 21 C4
St. Nazaire F 15 B3
St. Nazaire-en-Royans F 26 B2
St. Nazaire-le-Désert F 31 A4
St. Nectaire F 24 B2
St. Nicolas-de-Port F 12 C2
St. Nicolas-de-Redon F 15 B3
St. Nicolas-du-Pélem F 14 A2
St. Niklaas B 5 A4
St. Omer F 4 B2
St. Pair-sur-Mer F 8 B2
St. Palais F 34 A2
St. Palais-sur-Mer F 22 C2
St. Pardoux-la-Rivière F 23 C4
St. Paul-Cap-de-Joux F 29 C4
St. Paul-de-Fenouillet F 36 B3
St. Paul-de-Varax F 26 A2
St. Paul-le-Jeune F 31 A3
St. Paul-lès-Dax F 28 C1
St. Paul-Trois-Châteaux F 31 A3
St. Paulien F 25 B3
St. Pé-de-Bigorre F 35 A3
St. Pée-sur-Nivelle F 34 A2
St. Péravy-la-Colombe F 17 B3
St. Péray F 25 C4
St. Père-en-Retz F 15 B3
St. Peter Port GB 8 A1
St. Philbert-de-Grand-Lieu F 22 A2
St. Pierre F 30 B1
St. Pierre-d'Albigny F 26 B3
St. Pierre-d'Allevard F 26 B3
St. Pierre-de-Chartreuse F 26 B2
St. Pierre-de-Chignac F 29 A3
St. Pierre-de-la-Fage F 30 B2
St. Pierre-d'Entremont F 26 B2
St. Pierre-d'Oléron F 22 C2
St. Pierre-Eglise F 8 A2
St. Pierre-en-Port F 9 A4
St. Pierre-le-Moûtier F 18 C2
St. Pierre Montlimart F 15 B4
St. Pierre-Quiberon F 14 B2
St. Pierre-sur-Dives F 9 A3
St. Pierreville F 25 C4
St. Pieters-Leeuw B 5 B4
St. Plancard F 35 A4
St. Poix F 15 B4
St. Pol-de-Léon F 14 A2
St. Pol-sur-Ternoise F 4 B2
St. Polgues F 25 B3
St. Pons-de-Thomières F 30 B1
St. Porchaire F 22 C3
St. Pourçain-sur-Sioule F 24 A3
St. Priest F 25 B4
St. Privat F 24 B2
St. Quay-Portrieux F 14 A3
St. Quentin F 10 B3
St. Quentin-la-Poterie F 31 A3
St. Quentin-les-Anges F 16 B1
St. Rambert-d'Albon F 25 B4
St. Rambert-en-Bugey F 26 B2
St. Raphaël F 32 B2
St. Rémy-de-Provence F 31 B3
St. Rémy-du-Val F 9 B4
St. Remy-en-Bouzemont F 11 C4
St. Renan F 14 A1
St. Révérien F 18 B2
St. Riquier F 10 A1
St. Romain-de-Colbosc F 9 A4
St. Rome-de-Cernon F 30 A1
St. Rome-de-Tarn F 30 A1
St. Sadurní d'Anoia E 37 C2
St. Saëns F 9 A5
St. Sampson GB 8 A1
St. Samson-la-Poterie F 10 B1
St. Saturnin-de-Lenne F 30 A2
St. Saturnin-lès-Apt F 31 B4
St. Sauflieu F 10 B2
St. Saulge F 18 B2
St. Sauveur, *Finistère* F 14 A2
St. Sauveur, *Haute-Saône* F 19 B5
St. Sauveur-de-Montagut F 25 C4
St. Sauveur-en-Puisaye F 18 B2
St. Sauveur-en-Rue F 25 B4
St. Sauveur-le-Vicomte F 8 A2
St. Sauveur-Lendelin F 8 A2
St. Sauveur-sur-Tinée F 32 A3
St. Savin, *Gironde* F 28 A2
St. Savin, *Vienne* F 23 B4
St. Savinien F 22 C3
St. Savournin F 31 B4
St. Seine-l'Abbaye F 19 B3
St. Sernin-sur-Rance F 30 B1
St. Sevan-sur-Mer F 8 B1
St. Sever F 28 C2
St. Sever-Calvados F 8 B2
St. Sorlin-d'Arves F 26 B3
St. Soupplets F 10 B2
St. Sulpice F 29 C4
St. Sulpice-Laurière F 24 A1
St. Sulpice-les-Feuilles F 23 B5
St. Symphorien F 28 B2
St. Symphorien-de-Lay F 25 B4
St. Symphorien d'Ozon F 25 B4
St. Symphorien-sur-Coise F 25 B4
St. Thégonnec F 14 A2
St. Thiébault F 19 A4
St. Trivier-de-Courtes F 26 A2
St. Trivier sur-Moignans F 25 A4
St. Trojan-les-Bains F 22 C2
St. Tropez F 32 B2
St. Truiden B 5 B5
St. Vaast-la-Hougue F 8 A2
St. Valérien F 18 A2
St. Valery-en-Caux F 9 A4
St. Valéry-sur-Somme F 4 B1
St. Vallier, *Drôme* F 25 B4
St. Vallier, *Saône-et-Loire* F 18 C3
St. Vallier-de-Thiey F 32 B2
St. Varent F 16 C1
St. Vaury F 24 A1
St. Venant F 4 B2
St. Véran F 27 C3
St. Vincent I 27 B4
St. Vincent-de-Tyrosse F 28 C1
St. Vit F 19 B4
St. Vith B 6 B2
St. Vivien-de-Médoc F 22 C2
St. Yan F 25 A4
St. Ybars F 36 A2
St. Yorre F 25 A3
St. Yrieix-la-Perche F 23 C5
Ste. Adresse F 9 A4
Ste. Anne F 9 B4
Ste. Anne-d'Auray F 14 B3
Ste. Croix CH 19 C5
Ste. Croix-Volvestre F 36 A2
Ste. Engrâce F 34 A3
Ste. Enimie F 30 A2
Ste. Foy-de-Peyrolières F 36 A2
Ste. Foy-la-Grande F 28 B3
Ste. Foy l'Argentiere F 25 B4
Ste. Gauburge-Ste. Colombe F 9 B4
Ste. Gemme la Plaine F 22 B2
Ste. Geneviève F 10 B2
Ste. Hélène F 28 B2
Ste. Hélène-sur-Isère F 26 B3
Ste. Hermine F 22 B2
Ste. Jalle F 31 A4
Ste. Livrade-sur-Lot F 29 B3
Ste. Marie-aux-Mines F 20 A2
Ste. Marie-du-Mont F 8 A2
Ste. Maure-de-Touraine F 16 B2
Ste. Maxime F 32 B2
Ste. Ménéhould F 11 B4
Ste. Mère-Église F 8 A2
Ste. Ode B 12 A1
Ste. Savine F 11 C4
Ste. Sévère-sur-Indre F 17 C4
Ste. Sigolène F 25 B4
Ste. Suzanne F 16 A1
Ste. Tulle F 32 B1
Sainteny F 8 A2
Saintes F 22 C3
Stes. Maries-de-la-Mer F 31 B3
Saissac F 36 A3
Salardú E 35 B4
Salau F 36 B2
Salavaux CH 20 C2
Salbertrand I 27 B3
Salbris F 17 B4
Salem D 21 B4
Salernes F 32 B2
Salers F 24 B2
Salies-de-Béarn F 34 A3
Salies-du-Salat F 35 A4
Salignac-Eyvigues F 29 B4
Saligney-sur-Roudon F 18 C2
Salinas, *Huesca* E 35 B4
Salindres F 31 A3
Salins-les-Bains F 19 C4
Sallanches F 26 B3
Sallent E 37 C2
Sallent de Gállego E 35 B3
Salles F 28 B2
Salles-Curan F 30 A1
Salles-sur-l'Hers F 36 A2
Salmiech F 30 A1
Salon-de-Provence F 31 B4
Salornay-sur-Guye F 18 C3
Salou E 37 C2
Salses-le-Chateau F 36 B3
Salt E 37 C3
Salussola I 27 B5
Saluzzo I 27 C4
Salvagnac F 29 C4
Salviac F 29 B4
Salzkotten D 7 A4
Samadet F 28 C2
Samatan F 36 A1
Samedan CH 21 C4
Samer F 4 B1
Samnaun CH 21 C5
Samoëns F 26 A3
Samogneux F 12 B1
Sampéyre I 33 A3
Sampigny F 12 C1
San Adrián E 34 B2
San Carlo CH 27 A5
San Damiano d'Asti I 27 C5
San Damiano Macra I 33 A3
San Esteban de Litera E 35 C4
San Germano Vercellese I 27 B5
San Lorenzo al Mare I 33 B3
San Martin de Unx E 34 B2
San-Martino-di-Lota F 38 A2
San Mateo de Gallego E 34 C3
San Michele Mondovì I 33 A3
San Pedro Manrique E 34 B1
San Remo I 33 B3
San Vicente de Arana E 34 B1
Sanary-sur-Mer F 32 B1
Sancergues F 18 B1
Sancerre F 17 B4
Sancey-le-Long F 19 B5
Sancoins F 18 C1
Sande D 3 A5
Sandhorst D 3 A4
Sandillon F 17 B4
Sangatte F 4 B1
Sangüesa E 34 B2
Sanguinet F 28 B1
Sankt Anton am Arlberg A 21 B5
Sankt Augustin D 6 B3
Sankt Blasien D 20 B3
Sankt Gallen CH 21 B4
Sankt Gallenkirch A 21 B4
Sankt Georgen D 20 A3
Sankt Goar D 7 B3
Sankt Goarshausen D 7 B3
Sankt Ingbert D 12 B3
Sankt Margrethen CH 21 B4
Sankt Niklaus CH 27 A4
Sankt Paul F 32 A2
Sankt Peter D 20 A3
Sankt Wendel D 12 B3
Sant Agustí de Lluçanès E 37 B3
Sant Antoni de Calonge E 37 C4
Sant Boi de Llobregat E 37 C3
Sant Celoni E 37 C3
Sant Feliu E 37 C3
Sant Feliu de Codines E 37 C3
Sant Feliu de Guíxols E 37 C4
Sant Feliu Sasserra E 37 C3
Sant Hilari Sacalm E 37 C3
Sant Hipòlit de Voltregà E 37 B3
Sant Jaume dels Domenys E 37 C2
Sant Joan de les Abadesses E 37 B3
Sant Julià de Loria AND 36 B2
Sant Llorenç de Morunys E 37 B2
Sant Llorenç Savall E 37 C3
Sant Martí de Llemaná E 37 B3
Sant Marti de Maldá E 37 C2
Sant Marti Sarroca E 37 C2
Sant Pau de Seguries E 37 B3
Sant Pere de Riudebitles E 37 C2
Sant Pere Pescador E 37 B4
Sant Pere Sallavinera E 37 C2
Sant Quirze de Besora E 37 B3
Sant Ramon E 37 C2
Sant Vincenç de Castellet E 37 C2
Santa Coloma de Farners E 37 C3
Santa Coloma de Gramenet E 37 C3
Santa Coloma de Queralt E 37 C2
Santa Lucia-de-Porto-Vecchio F 38 B2
Santa Margaridao de Montbui E 37 C2
Santa Maria E 34 B3
Santa Maria de Corco E 37 B3
Santa Maria Maggiore I 27 A5
Santa Pau E 37 B3
Santa Severa F 38 A2
Santacara E 34 B2
Santhià I 27 B5
Santo-Pietro-di Tenda F 38 A2
Santpedor E 37 C2
Saorge F 33 B3
Saramon F 29 C3
Sarcelles F 10 B2
Sare F 34 A2
Sargans CH 21 B4
Sari-d'Orcino F 38 A1
Sariñena E 35 C3
Sarlat-la-Canéda F 29 B4
Sarliac-sur-l'Isle F 29 A3
Sarnen CH 20 C3
Sarpoil F 25 B3
Sarral E 37 C2
Sarralbe F 12 B3
Sarrancolin F 35 B4
Sarras F 25 B4
Sarre I 27 B4
Sarre-Union F 12 C3
Sarrebourg F 12 C3
Sarreguemines F 12 B3
Sarrià de Ter E 37 B3
Sarron F 28 C2
Sartène F 38 B1
Sartilly F 8 B2
Sarzeau F 15 B3
Sas van Gent NL 5 A3
Sassello I 33 A4
Sassenberg D 3 C5
Satillieu F 25 B4
Satteins A 21 B4
Saucats F 28 B2
Saugues F 25 C3
Saujon F 22 C3
Saulces Monclin F 11 B4
Saulgau D 21 A4
Saulieu F 18 B3
Saulnot F 20 B1
Sault F 31 A4
Sault-Brénaz F 26 B2
Sault-de-Navailles F 28 C2
Saulx F 19 B5
Saulxures-sur-Moselotte F 20 B1
Saulzais-le-Potier F 17 C4
Saumos F 28 B1
Saumur F 16 B1
Saurat F 36 B2
Sausset-les-Pins F 31 B4
Sauteyrargues F 31 B2
Sauvagnat F 24 B2
Sauve F 31 B2
Sauveterre-de-Béarn F 34 A3
Sauveterre-de-Guyenne F 28 B2
Sauviat-sur-Vige F 24 B1
Sauxillanges F 25 B3
Sauzé-Vaussais F 23 B4
Sauzet, *Drôme* F 25 C4
Sauzet, *Lot* F 29 B4
Sauzon F 14 B2
Savenay F 15 B4
Saverdun F 36 A2
Saverne F 13 C3
Savières F 11 C3
Savigliano I 27 C4
Savignac-les-Eglises F 29 A3
Savigny-sur-Braye F 16 B2
Savines-le-lac F 32 A2
Savognin CH 21 C4
Savona I 33 A4
Savournon F 32 A1
Scaër F 14 A2
Scey-sur-Saône et St. Albin F 19 B4
Schaffhausen CH 21 B3
Schagen NL 2 B1
Schangnau CH 20 C2
Schapbach D 13 C4
Scharrel D 3 A4
Scheemda NL 3 A3
Scheidegg D 21 B4
Scherfede D 7 A5
Schermbeck D 6 A2
Scherpenzeel NL 2 B2
Scheveningen NL 2 B1
Schiedam NL 5 A4
Schiers CH 21 C4
Schillingen D 12 B2
Schiltach D 13 C4
Schiltigheim F 13 C3
Schirmeck F 12 C3
Schlangen D 7 A4
Schleiden D 6 B2
Schliengen D 20 B2

Schlitz D 7 B5
Schloss Neuhans D 7 A4
Schluchsee D 20 B3
Schlüchtern D 7 B5
Schmallenberg D 7 A4
Schmelz D 12 B2
Schoenburg B 6 B2
Schöllkrippen D 7 B5
Schomberg D 21 A3
Schönau, *Baden-Württemberg* D 20 B2
Schönecken- D 6 B2
Schönhagen D 7 A5
Schoondijke NL 5 A3
Schoonebeek NL 3 B3
Schoonhoven NL 5 A4
Schopfheim D 20 B2
Schortens D 3 A4
Schotten D 7 B5
Schramberg D 20 A3
Schrecksbach D 7 B5
Schröcken A 21 B5
Schruns A 21 B4
Schüpfheim CH 20 C3
Schüttorf D 3 B4
Schwagstorf D 3 B4
Schwaigern D 13 B5
Schwalmstadt D 7 B5
Schwanden CH 21 C4
Schwarzenburg CH 20 C2
Schwei D 3 A5
Schweich D 12 B2
Schweighausen D 20 A2
Schwelm D 6 A3
Schwenningen D 21 A3
Schwerte D 7 A3
Schwetzingen D 13 B4
Schwyz CH 21 B3
Scionzier F 26 A3
Scopello, *Piemonte* I 27 B5
Scuol CH 21 C5
Sebazac-Concourès F 30 A1
Seborga I 33 B3
Séchault F 11 B4
Seclin F 4 B3
Secondigny F 22 B3
Sedan F 11 B4
Séderon F 31 A4
Seebach F 13 C3
Seefeld, *Niedersachsen* D 3 A5
Seeheim-Jugenheim D 13 B4
Seelbach D 13 C3
Sées F 9 B4
Segonzac F 23 C3
Segré F 15 B5
Ségur-les-Villas F 24 B2
Segura E 34 B1
Seiches-sur-le-Loir F 16 B1
Seignelay F 18 B2
Seilhac F 24 B1
Seilles B 5 B5
Seissan F 35 A4
Sélestat F 20 A2
Selgua E 35 C4
Seligenstadt D 13 A4
Selles-St. Denis F 17 B3
Selles-sur-Cher F 17 B3
Sellières F 19 C4
Selm D 6 A3
Selongey F 19 B4
Selonnet F 32 A2
Selters D 7 B3
Seltz F 13 C4
Semide F 11 B4
Semur-en-Auxois F 18 B3
Sena E 35 C3
Senarpont F 10 B1
Sénas F 31 B4
Senden, *Nordrhein-Westfalen* D 6 A3
Sendenhorst D 7 A3
Seneffe B 5 B4
Senez F 32 B2
Sengouagnet F 35 B4
Sengwarden D 3 A5
Senlis F 10 B2
Sennecey-le-Grand F 19 C3
Sennwald CH 21 B4
Senonches F 9 B5
Senones F 12 C2
Sens F 18 A2
Sens-de-Bretagne F 15 A4
Senterada E 35 B4
Seon CH 20 B3
Sépeaux F 18 B2
Sépey CH 27 A4
Seppenrade D 6 A3
Seppois F 20 B2
Septeuil F 10 C1
Seraincourt F 11 B4
Seraing B 6 B1
Sérent F 15 B3
Sérifontaine F 10 B1
Sérignan F 30 B2
Sermaises F 10 C2
Sermaize-les-Bains F 11 C4
Serooskerke NL 5 A3
Serravalle, *Piemonte* I 27 B5
Serres F 32 A1
Serrières F 25 B4
Serrières-de-Briord F 26 B2
Sertig Dörfli CH 21 C4
Servance F 20 B1
Serverette F 25 C3
Servian F 30 B2
Serviers F 31 A3
Sesma E 34 B1
Sestriere I 27 C3
Setcases E 36 B3
Sète F 30 B2
Séttimo Torinese I 27 B4
Settimo Vittone I 27 B4
Seurre F 19 C4
Sévérac-le-Château F 30 A2
Sévigny F 11 B4
Sevrier F 26 B3
Seyches F 29 B3
Seyne F 32 A2
Seynes F 31 A3
Seyssel F 26 B2
Sézanne F 11 C3
'sHeerenberg NL 6 A2
Siauges-St. Romain F 25 B3
Siddeburen NL 3 A3
Siedlinghausen D 7 A4
Siegburg D 6 B3
Siegen D 7 B4
Sierck-les-Bains F 12 B2
Sierentz F 20 B2
Sierra de Luna E 34 B3
Sierre CH 27 A4
Sietamo E 35 B3
Sigean F 30 B1
Sigmaringen D 21 A4
Signes F 32 B1
Signy-l'Abbaye F 11 B4
Signy-le-Petit F 11 B4
Sigogne F 23 C3
Sigües E 34 B2
Sillé-le-Guillaume F 16 A1
Sillenstede D 3 A4
Sils E 37 C3
Silvaplana CH 21 C4
Simandre F 19 C3
Simard F 19 C4
Simmerath D 6 B2
Simmerberg D 21 B4
Simmern D 13 B3
Simplon CH 27 A5
Sindelfingen D 13 C5
Singen D 21 B3
Sinn D 7 B4
Sins CH 20 B3
Sinsheim D 13 B4
Sint Annaland NL 5 A4
Sint Annaparochie NL 2 A2
Sint Athonis NL 6 A1
Sint Nicolaasga NL 2 B2
Sint Oedenrode NL 5 A5
Sinzheim D 13 C4
Sinzig D 6 B3
Sion CH 27 A4
Siorac-en-Périgord F 29 B3
Sissach CH 20 B2
Sissonne F 11 B3
Sisteron F 32 A1
Sitges E 37 C2
Sittard NL 6 A1
Sixt-Fer-á-Cheval F 27 A3
Sizun F 14 A1
Slagharen NL 3 B3
Slochteren NL 3 A3
Slootdorp NL 2 B1
Sluis NL 4 A3
Smilde NL 3 B3
Sneek NL 2 A2
Sobernheim D 13 B3
Soest D 7 A4
Soest NL 2 B2
Sögel D 3 B4
Sohren D 13 B3
Soignies B 5 B4
Soissons F 10 B3
Soleils F 32 B2
Solenzara F 38 B2
Solesmes F 5 B3
Solgne F 12 C2
Solignac F 23 C5
Solingen D 6 A3
Solivella E 37 C2
Solliès-Pont F 32 B2
Solomiac F 29 C3
Solothurn CH 20 B2
Solre-le-Château F 5 B4
Solsona E 37 C2
Somain F 4 B3
Sombernon F 18 B3
Sombreffe B 5 B4
Someren NL 6 A1
Sommariva del Bosco I 27 C4
Somme-Tourbe F 11 B4
Sommeilles F 11 C4
Sommepy-Tahure F 11 B4
Sommesous F 11 C4
Sommières F 31 B3
Sommières-du-Clain F 23 B4
Sompuis F 11 C4
Son en Breugel NL 6 A1
Sonceboz CH 20 B2
Songeons F 10 B1
Sonsbeck D 6 A2
Sonthofen D 21 B5
Sore F 28 B2
Sörenberg CH 20 C3
Sorèze F 36 A3
Sorges F 23 C4
Sorgues F 31 A3
Sornac F 24 B2
Sort E 36 B2
Sos F 28 B3
Sos del Rey Católico E 34 B2
Sospel F 33 B3
Sotta F 38 B2
Souain F 11 B4
Soual F 36 A3
Soucy F 18 A2
Soudron F 11 C4
Souesmes F 17 B4
Soufflenheim F 13 C3
Souillac F 29 B4
Souilly F 11 B5
Soulac-sur-Mer F 22 C2
Soulaines-Dhuys F 11 C4
Soulatgé F 36 B3
Soultz-Haut-Rhin F 20 B2
Soultz-sous-Forêts F 13 C3
Soumagne B 6 B1
Soumoulou F 35 A3
Souppes-sur-Loing F 17 A4
Souprosse F 28 C2
Sourdeval F 8 B3
Sournia F 36 B3
Sours F 10 C1
Sousceyrac F 24 C2
Soustons F 28 C1
Souvigny F 18 C2
Souzay-Champigny F 16 B1
Soyaux F 23 C4
Spa B 6 B1
Spaichingen D 21 A3
Spakenburg NL 2 B2
Speicher D 12 B2
Speyer D 13 B4
Spézet F 14 A2
Spiekeroog D 3 A4
Spiez CH 20 C2
Spigno Monferrato I 33 A4
Spijk NL 3 A3
Spijkenisse NL 5 A4
Spincourt F 12 B1
Splügen CH 21 C4
Spohle D 3 A5
Spotorno I 33 A4
Sprimont B 6 B1
Stabroek B 5 A4
Staden B 4 B3
Stadskanaal NL 3 B3
Stadtallendorf D 7 B5
Stadtkyll D 6 B2
Stadtlohn D 3 C3
Stäfa CH 21 B3
Stainville F 11 C5
Stalden CH 27 A4
Stans CH 20 C3
Staphorst NL 2 B3
Staufen D 20 B2
Stavelot B 6 B1
Stavenisse NL 5 A4
Stavoren NL 2 B2
Stechelberg CH 20 C2
Steckborn CH 21 B3
Stede Broek NL 2 B2
Steeg A 21 B5
Steenbergen NL 5 A4
Steenvoorde F 4 B2
Steenwijk NL 2 B3
Steffisburg CH 20 C2
Stein an Rhein CH 21 B3
Steinach, *Baden-Württemberg* D 20 A3
Steinau, *Bayern* D 7 B5
Steinen D 20 B2
Steinfeld D 3 B5
Steinfurt D 3 B4
Steinheim, *Bayern* D 21 A5
Steinheim, *Nordrhein-Westfalen* D 7 A5
Stekene B 5 A4
Stellendam NL 5 A4
Stenay F 11 B5
Stiens NL 2 A2
Stockach D 21 B4
Stöckalp CH 20 C3
Stolberg D 6 B2
Stollhamm D 3 A5
Stompetoren NL 2 B1
Strackholt D 3 A4
Straelen D 6 A2
Strasbourg F 13 C3
Stresa I 27 B5
Strijen NL 5 A4
Stromberg, *Nordrhein-Westfalen* D 7 A4
Stromberg, *Rheinland-Pfalz* D 13 B3
Stroppiana I 27 B5
Strücklingen D 3 A4
Stuben A 21 B5
Stukenbrock D 7 A4
Suchteln D 6 A2
Sugères F 25 B3
Sugny B 11 B4
Suippes F 11 B4
Sulgen CH 21 B4
Sully-sur-Loire F 17 B4
Sülz D 13 C4
Sulzbach, *Bayern* D 13 B5
Sulzbach, *Saarland* D 12 B3
Sumiswald CH 20 B2
Sunbilla E 34 A2
Sundern D 7 A4
Super Sauze F 32 A2
Surgères F 22 B3
Surhuisterveen NL 2 A3
Sùria E 37 C2
Surin F 23 B4
Sursee CH 20 B3
Surwold D 3 B4
Sury-le-Comtal F 25 B4
Susa I 27 B4
Susch CH 21 C5
Suze-la-Rousse F 31 A3
Swifterbant NL 2 B2

T

Tafalla E 34 B2
Tàggia I 33 B3
Tagnon F 11 B4
Tailfingen D 21 A4
Taillis F 15 A4
Tain-l'Hermitage F 25 B4
Talant F 19 B3
Talizat F 24 B3
Tallard F 32 A2
Talloires F 26 B3
Talmay F 19 B4
Talmont-St. Hilaire F 22 B2
Talmont-sur-Gironde F 22 C3
Tamarit de Mar E 37 C2
Tamarite de Litera E 35 C4
Tamariu E 37 C4
Tancarville F 9 A4
Taninges F 26 A3
Tannay, *Ardennes* F 11 B4
Tannay, *Nièvre* F 18 B2
Tanus F 30 A1
Tapio E 36 A2
Taradell E 37 C3
Tarare F 25 B4
Tarascon F 31 B3
Tarascon-sur-Ariège F 36 B2
Tarazona E 34 C2
Tarbes F 35 A4
Tardets-Sorholus F 34 A3
Tardienta E 35 C3
Targon F 28 B2
Tarnos F 28 C1
Tarragona E 37 C2
Tàrrega E 37 C2
Tartas F 28 C2
Täsch CH 27 A4
Taulé F 14 A2
Taulignan F 31 A3
Taunusstein D 7 B4
Tauste E 34 C2
Tauves F 24 B2
Tavannes CH 20 B2
Tavaux F 19 B4
Taverny F 10 B2
Tavescan E 36 B2
Tecklenburg D 3 B4
Teillay F 15 B4
Teillet F 30 B1
Telgte D 3 C4
Temse B 5 A4
Ten Boer NL 3 A3
Tenay F 26 B2
Tence F 25 B4
Tende F 33 A3
Tenneville B 12 A1
Ter Apel NL 3 B4
Terborg NL 3 C3
Tergnier F 10 B3
Terme di Valdieri I 33 A3
Termens E 35 C4
Termes F 24 C3
Terneuzen NL 5 A3
Terrassa E 37 C3
Terrasson-la-Villedieu F 29 A4
Tervuren B 5 B4
Tessy-sur-Vire F 8 B2
Teterchen F 12 B2
Tettnang D 21 B4
Thalfang D 12 B2
Thalkirch CH 21 C4
Thalwil CH 21 B3
Thann F 20 B2
Thaon-les-Vosges F 19 A5
Thayngen CH 21 B3
The Hague = 's-Gravenhage NL 2 B1
Thénezay F 16 C1
Thenon F 29 A4
Therouanne F 4 B2
Theux B 6 B1
Thézar-les-Corbières F 36 A3
Thèze F 35 A3
Thiberville F 9 A4
Thibie F 11 C4
Thiéblemont-Farémont F 11 C4
Thierrens CH 20 C1
Thiers F 25 B3
Thiezac F 24 B2
Thionville F 12 B2
Thiron-Gardais F 9 B4
Thivars F 10 C1
Thiviers F 23 C4
Thizy F 25 A4
Tholen NL 5 A4
Tholey D 12 B3
Thônes F 26 B3
Thonnance-les-Joinville F 11 C5
Thonon-les-Bains F 26 A3
Thorame-Basse F 32 A2
Thorame-Haute F 32 A2
Thorens-Glières F 26 A3
Thorigny-sur-Oreuse F 11 C3
Thouarcé F 16 B1
Thouars F 16 C1
Thueyts F 25 C4
Thuin B 5 B4
Thuir F 36 B3
Thun CH 20 C2
Thuret F 24 B3
Thurey F 19 C4
Thüringen A 21 B4
Thurins F 25 B4
Thury-Harcourt F 9 B3
Thusis CH 21 C4
Tiefencastel CH 21 C4
Tiel NL 5 A5
Tielt B 4 A3
Tienen B 5 B4
Tiengen D 20 B3
Tiercé F 16 B1
Tiermas E 34 B2
Tierrantona E 35 B4
Tignes F 27 B3
Tigy F 17 B4
Tijnje NL 2 A2
Til Châtel F 19 B4
Tilburg NL 5 A5
Tilh F 28 C2
Tillac F 35 A4
Tille F 10 B2
Tilloy Bellay F 11 B4
Tilly F 23 B5
Tilly-sur-Seulles F 8 A3
Tinchebray F 8 B3
Tincques F 4 B2
Tinlot B 5 B5
Tinténiac F 15 A4
Tintigny B 12 B1
Titisee-Neustadt D 20 B3
Titz D 6 A2
Tocane-St. Apre F 29 A3
Todtmoos D 20 B3
Todtnau D 20 B2
Tolosa E 34 A1
Tolva E 35 B4
Tombeboeuf F 29 B3
Tona E 37 C3
Tongeren B 5 B5
Tönisvorst D 6 A2
Tonnay-Boutonne F 22 C3
Tonnay-Charente F 22 C3
Tonneins F 29 B3
Tonnerre F 18 B2
Torà E 37 C2
Torcy-le-Petit F 9 A5
Tordera E 37 C3
Torellò E 37 B3
Torfou F 22 A2
Torhout B 4 A3
Torigni-sur-Vire F 8 A3
Torino = Turin I 27 B4
Torla E 35 B3
Torre la Ribera E 35 B4
Torre Pèllice I 27 C4
Torredembarra E 37 C2
Torregrosa E 37 C1
Torroella de Montgrì E 37 B4
Tossa de Mar E 37 C3
Tosse F 28 C1
Tôtes F 9 A5
Toucy F 18 B2
Toul F 12 C1
Toulon F 32 B1
Toulon-sur-Allier F 18 C2
Toulon-sur-Arroux F 18 C3
Toulouse F 29 C4
Tour de la Parata F 38 B1
Tourcoing F 4 B3
Tourlaville F 8 A2
Tournai B 4 B3
Tournan-en-Brie F 10 C2
Tournay F 35 A4
Tournon-d'Agenais F 29 B3
Tournon-St. Martin F 23 B4
Tournon-sur-Rhône F 25 B4
Tournus F 19 C3
Tourouvre F 9 B4
Tourriers F 23 C4
Tours F 16 B2
Tourteron F 11 B4
Tourves F 32 B1
Toury F 17 A3
Touvois F 22 B2
Traben-Trarbach D 12 B3
Trainel F 11 C3
Tramacastilla de Tena E 35 B3
Tramelan CH 20 B2
Trampot F 12 C1
Trana I 27 B4
Trans-en-Provence F 32 B2
Trappes F 10 C2
Travo F 38 B2
Treban F 24 A3
Trébeurden F 14 A2
Treffort F 26 A2
Trégastel-Plage F 14 A2
Tréguier F 14 A2
Trégunc F 14 B2
Treignac F 24 B1
Treignat F 24 A2
Treignes B 11 A4
Treis-Karden D 6 B3
Trélazé F 16 B1
Trélissac F 29 A3
Trélon F 11 A4
Trélou-sur-Marne F 11 B3
Tremblay-le-Vicomte F 9 B5
Tremp E 35 B4
Trendelburg D 7 A5
Trensacq F 28 B2
Trept F 26 B2
Trets F 32 B1
Trévoux F 25 B4
Treysa D 7 B5
Trézelles F 25 A3
Triaize F 22 B2
Triaucourt-en-Argonne F 11 C5
Triberg D 20 A3
Trie-sur-Baïse F 35 A4
Trier D 12 B2
Trignac F 15 B3
Trilport F 10 C2
Trino I 27 B5
Triora I 33 B3
Triste E 34 B3
Trivero I 27 B5
Troarn F 9 A3
Trois-Ponts B 6 B1
Troisdorf D 6 B3
Troisvierges L 12 A2
Tronget F 24 A3
Tronzano-Vercellese I 27 B5
Trôo F 16 B2
Trosly-Breuil F 10 B3
Trossingen D 21 A3
Trouville-sur-Mer F 9 A4
Troyes F 18 A3
Trun CH 21 C3
Trun F 9 B4
Tschagguns A 21 B4
Tubbergen NL 3 B3
Tübingen D 13 C5
Tubize B 5 B4
Tuchan F 36 B3
Tudela E 34 B2
Tuffé F 16 A2
Tulette F 31 A3
Tulle F 24 B1
Tullins F 26 B2
Turbenthal CH 21 B3
Turckheim F 20 A2
Turin = Torino I 27 B4
Turnhout B 5 A4
Turries F 32 A2
Turtmann CH 27 A4
Tuttlingen D 21 B3
Twello NL 2 B3
Twist D 3 B4
Tzummarum NL 2 A2

U

Überlingen D 21 B4
Uchaud F 31 B3
Uckerath D 6 B3
Uden NL 6 A1
Uelsen D 3 B3
Uetendorf CH 20 C2
Ugine F 26 B3
Uitgeest NL 2 B1
Uithoorn NL 2 B1
Uithuizen NL 3 A3
Uithuizermeeden NL 3 A3
Ujué E 34 B2
Ulldemolins E 37 C1
Ulmen D 6 B2
Ulrichstein D 7 B5
Ulrum NL 3 A3
Uncastillo E 34 B2
Unkel D 6 B3
Unna D 7 A3
Unterägeri CH 21 B3
Unteriberg CH 21 B3
Unterschächen CH 21 C3
Ur F 36 B2
Urçay F 17 C4
Urdax E 34 A2
Urdos F 35 B3
Urk NL 2 B2
Urnäsch CH 21 B4
Urries E 34 B2
Urroz E 34 B2
Ury F 10 C2
Useldange L 12 B1
Usingen D 7 B4
Usquert NL 3 A3
Ussé F 16 B2
Usséglio I 27 B4
Ussel, *Cantal* F 24 B2
Ussel, *Corrèze* F 24 B2
Usson-du-Poitou F 23 B4
Usson-en-Forez F 25 B3
Usson-les-Bains F 36 B3
Ustaritz F 34 A2
Uster CH 21 B3
Utrecht NL 2 B2
Uttenweiler D 21 A4
Uza F 28 B1
Uzein F 35 A3
Uzel F 14 A3
Uzerche F 24 B1
Uzès F 31 A3
Uznach CH 21 B3

V

Vaas F 16 B2
Vaasen NL 2 B2
Vabre F 30 B1
Vacqueyras F 31 A3
Vado Ligure I 33 A4
Vaduz FL 21 B4

Vagney F 20 A1
Vaiges F 16 A1
Vaihingen D 13 C4
Vaillant F 19 B4
Vailly-sur-Aisne F 11 B3
Vailly-sur Sauldre F 17 B4
Vaison-la-Romaine F 31 A4
Vaite F 19 B4
Val d'Esquières F 32 B2
Val-d'Isère F 27 B3
Val-Suzon F 19 B3
Val Thorens F 26 B3
Valberg F 32 A2
Valbonnais F 26 C2
Valdahon F 19 B5
Valdieri I 33 A3
Valençay F 17 B3
Valence, *Charente* F 23 C4
Valence, *Drôme* F 25 C4
Valence d'Agen F 29 B3
Valence-d'Albigeois F 30 A1
Valence-sur-Baise F 29 C3
Valenciennes F 5 B3
Valensole F 32 B1
Valentigney F 20 B1
Valentine F 35 A4
Valflaunes F 31 B2
Valgorge F 31 A3
Valgrisenche I 27 B4
Valkenburg NL 6 B1
Valkenswaard NL 5 A5
Valle Mosso I 27 B5
Vallendar D 7 B3
Valleraugue F 30 A2
Vallet F 15 B4
Vallfogona de Riucorb E 37 C2
Valloire F 26 B3
Vallon-Pont-d'Arc F 31 A3
Vallorbe CH 19 C5
Vallouise F 26 C3
Valls E 37 C2
Valmont F 9 A4
Valognes F 8 A2
Valpelline I 27 B4
Valras-Plage F 30 B2
Valréas F 31 A3
Vals CH 21 C4
Vals-les-Bains F 25 C4
Valsavarenche I 27 B4
Valsonne F 25 B4
Valtierra E 34 B2
Valtournenche I 27 B4
Valverde E 34 C2
Vanault-les-Dames F 11 C4
Vandenesse F 18 C2
Vandenesse-en-Auxois F 18 B3
Vannes F 15 B3
Vaour F 29 B4
Varacieux F 26 B2
Varades F 15 B4
Varages F 32 B1
Varallo I 27 B5
Varazze I 33 A4
Varel D 3 A5
Varengeville-sur-Mer F 9 A4
Varennes-en-Argonne F 11 B5
Varennes-le-Grand F 19 C3
Varennes-St. Sauveur F 19 C4
Varennes-sur-Allier F 25 A3
Varennes-sur-Amance F 19 B4
Varilhes F 36 A2
Varreddes F 10 C2
Vars F 26 C3
Varsseveld NL 3 C3
Varzo I 27 A5
Varzy F 18 B2
Vassieux-en-Vercors F 26 C2
Vassy F 8 B3
Vatan F 17 B3
Vatry F 11 C4
Vättis CH 21 C4
Vauchamps F 11 C3
Vauchassis F 18 A2
Vaucouleurs F 12 C1
Vaudoy-en-Brie F 10 C3
Vaulruz CH 20 C1
Vaulx Vraucourt F 10 A2
Vaumas F 18 C2
Vausseroux F 23 B3
Vauvenargues F 32 B1
Vauvert F 31 B3
Vauvillers F 19 B5
Vaux-sur-Sure B 12 B1
Vayrac F 29 B4
Vechta D 3 B5
Veendam NL 3 A3
Veenendaal NL 2 B2
Veghel NL 6 A1
Velbert D 6 A3
Velen D 6 A2
Velles F 17 C3
Vellmar D 7 A5
Velp NL 2 B2
Venaco F 38 A2
Venarey-les-Laumes F 18 B3
Venaria I 27 B4
Venasca I 33 A3
Vence F 32 B3
Vendays-Montalivet F 22 C2
Vendeuil F 11 B3
Vendeuvre-sur-Barse F 18 A3
Vendœuvres F 23 B5
Vendôme F 17 B3
Venelles F 31 B4
Vénissieux F 25 B4
Venlo NL 6 A2
Vennezey F 12 C2
Venray NL 6 A1
Ventavon F 32 A1
Ventimíglia I 33 B3
Venzolasca F 38 A2
Vera de Bidasoa E 34 A2
Vera de Moncayo E 34 C2
Verbánia I 27 B5
Verberie F 10 B2
Verbier CH 27 A4
Vercel-Villedieu-le-Camp F 19 B5
Vercelli I 27 B5
Vercheny F 26 C2
Verclause F 31 A4
Verdille F 23 C3
Verdú E 37 C2
Verdun F 12 B1
Verdun-sur-Garonne F 29 C4
Verdun-sur-le-Doubs F 19 C4
Verfeil F 29 C4
Verges E 37 B4
Vergt F 29 A3
Veringenstadt D 21 A4
Verl D 7 A4
Vermand F 10 B3
Vermenton F 18 B2
Vern-d'Anjou F 16 B1
Vernante I 33 A3
Vernantes F 16 B2
Vernayaz CH 27 A4
Vernet F 36 A2
Vernet-les-Bains F 36 B3
Verneuil F 11 B3
Verneuil-sur-Avre F 9 B4
Vernier CH 26 A3
Vernon F 10 B1
Vernoux-en-Vivarais F 25 C4
Verrès I 27 B4
Verrey-sous-Salmaise F 18 B3
Verrières F 23 B4
Versailles F 10 C2
Versam CH 21 C4
Versmold D 3 B5
Versoix CH 26 A3
Verteillac F 23 C4
Vertou F 15 B4
Vertus F 11 C3
Verviers B 6 B1
Vervins F 11 B3
Verzuolo I 33 A3
Verzy F 11 B4
Vescovato F 38 A2
Vésime I 27 C5
Vesoul F 19 B5
Vétroz CH 27 A4
Veules-les-Roses F 9 A4
Veulettes-sur-Mer F 9 A4
Veurne B 4 A2
Vevey CH 20 C1
Vex CH 27 A4
Veynes F 32 A1
Veyre-Monton F 24 B3
Veyrier F 26 B3
Vézelay F 18 B2
Vézelise F 12 C2
Vézenobres F 31 A3
Vezins F 16 B1
Vézins-de-Lévézou F 30 A1
Vezzani F 38 A2
Vianden L 12 B2
Vibraye F 16 A2
Vic E 37 C3
Vic-en-Bigorre F 35 A4
Vic-Fézensac F 29 C3
Vic-le-Comte F 24 B3
Vic-sur-Aisne F 10 B3
Vic-sur-Cère F 24 C2
Vicdesses F 36 B2
Vichy F 25 A3
Vico F 38 A1
Vidauban F 32 B2
Vieille-Brioude F 25 B3
Vielha E 35 B4
Vielle-Aure F 35 B4
Viellespesse F 24 B3
Viellevigne F 22 B2
Vielmur-sur-Agout F 30 B1
Viels Maison F 11 C3
Vielsalm B 6 B1
Vienne F 25 B4
Viernheim D 13 B4
Viersen D 6 A2
Vierville-sur-Mer F 8 A3
Vierzon F 17 B4
Vieteren B 4 B2
Vieux-Boucau-les-Bains F 28 C1
Vif F 26 B2
Vigeois F 24 B1
Vignale I 27 B5
Vigneulles-lès-Hattonchâtel F 12 C1
Vignevieille F 36 B3
Vignory F 19 A4
Vignoux-sur Barangeon F 17 B4
Vigone I 27 C4
Vihiers F 16 B1
Vila-Rodona E 37 C2
Viladamat E 37 B4
Viladrau E 37 C3
Vilafranca del Penedès E 37 C2
Vilajuiga E 37 B4
Vilanova de Sau E 37 C3
Vilanova i la Geltrú E 37 C2
Vilaseca E 37 C2
Vilassar de Mar E 37 C3
Villabona E 34 A1
Villadóssola I 27 A5
Villafranca, *Navarra* E 34 B2
Villagrains F 28 B2
Villaines-la-Juhel F 9 B3
Villamblard F 29 A3
Villandraut F 28 B2
Villanova d'Asti I 27 C4
Villanova Mondovì I 33 A3
Villanueva de Gállego E 34 C3
Villar Perosa I 27 C4
Villard-de-Lans F 26 B2
Villaretto I 27 B4
Villars-les-Dombes F 25 A5
Villastellone I 27 C4
Villé F 13 C3
Ville-di-Pietrabugno F 38 A2
Ville-sous-la-Ferté F 19 A3
Ville-sur-Illon F 19 A5
Ville-sur-Tourbe F 11 B4
Villebois-Lavalette F 23 C4
Villecerf F 10 C2
Villecomtal F 30 A1
Villedieu-les-Poêles F 8 B2
Villedieu-sur-Indre F 17 C3
Villedômain F 17 B3
Villefagnan F 23 B4
Villefontaine F 26 B2
Villefort F 31 A2
Villefranche-d'Albigeois F 30 B1
Villefranche-d'Allier F 24 A2
Villefranche-de-Lauragais F 36 A2
Villefranche-de-Lonchat F 28 B3
Villefranche-de-Panat F 30 A1
Villefranche-de-Rouergue F 30 A1
Villefranche-du-Périgord F 29 B4
Villefranche-sur-Cher F 17 B3
Villefranche-sur-Mer F 33 B3
Villefranche-sur-Saône F 25 A4
Villegenon F 17 B4
Villemaur-sur-Vanne F 18 A2
Villemur-sur-Tarn F 29 C4
Villenauxe-la-Grande F 11 C3
Villenave-d'Ornon F 28 B2
Villeneuve CH 27 A3
Villeneuve F 29 B5
Villeneuve-d'Ascq F 4 B3
Villeneuve-de-Berg F 31 A3
Villeneuve-de-Marsan F 28 C2
Villeneuve-de-Rivière F 35 A4
Villeneuve-la-Guyard F 10 C3
Villeneuve-l'Archevêque F 18 A2
Villeneuve-le-Comte F 10 C2
Villeneuve-lès-Avignon F 31 B3
Villeneuve-les-Corbières F 36 B3
Villeneuve-St. Georges F 10 C2
Villeneuve-sur-Allier F 18 C2
Villeneuve-sur-Lot F 29 B3
Villeneuve-sur-Yonne F 18 A2
Villeréal F 29 B3
Villeromain F 17 B3
Villers-Bocage, *Calvados* F 8 A3
Villers-Bocage, *Somme* F 10 B2
Villers-Bretonneux F 10 B2
Villers-Carbonnel F 10 B2
Villers-Cotterêts F 10 B3
Villers-Farlay F 19 C4
Villers-le-Gambon B 5 B4
Villers-le-Lac F 20 B1
Villers-sur-Mer F 9 A3
Villersexel F 19 B5
Villerupt F 12 B1
Villerville F 9 A4
Villeseneux F 11 C4
Villetrun F 17 B3
Villeurbanne F 25 B4
Villeveyrac F 30 B2
Villevocance F 25 B4
Villiers-St. Benoit F 18 B2
Villiers-St. Georges F 11 C3
Villingen D 20 A3
Villmar D 7 B4
Villon F 18 B3
Vilvoorde B 5 B4
Vimoutiers F 9 B4
Vimy F 4 B2
Vinadio I 33 A3
Vinaixa E 37 C1
Vinay F 26 B2
Vinca F 36 B3
Vinets F 11 C4
Vineuil F 17 B3
Vingrau F 36 B3
Vinon F 17 B4
Vinon-sur-Verdon F 32 B1
Viola I 33 A3
Violay F 25 B4
Vire F 8 B3
Vireux F 11 A4
Virieu F 26 B2
Virieu-le-Grand F 26 B2
Virton B 12 B1
Viry F 26 A3
Visbek D 3 B5
Visé B 6 B1
Visone I 27 C5
Visp CH 27 A4
Vitré F 15 A4
Vitrey-sur-Mance F 19 B4
Vitry-en-Artois F 4 B2
Vitry-le-François F 11 C4
Vitry-sur-Seine F 10 C2
Vitteaux F 18 B3
Vittel F 19 A4
Viù I 27 B4
Vivario F 38 A2
Viverols F 25 B3
Viviers F 31 A3
Vivonne F 23 B4
Vivy F 16 B1
Vizille F 26 B2
Vizzavona F 38 A2
Vlagtwedde NL 3 A4
Vledder NL 2 B3
Vlissingen NL 5 A3
Vogogna I 27 A5
Vogué F 31 A3
Vöhl D 7 A4
Vöhrenbach D 20 A3
Void-Vacon F 12 C1
Voiron F 26 B2
Voise F 10 C1
Voisey F 19 B4
Voiteur F 19 C4
Volendam NL 2 B2
Völklingen D 12 B2
Volkmarsen D 7 A5
Vollenhove NL 2 B2
Vollore-Montagne F 25 B3
Voltri I 33 A4
Volvic F 24 B3
Volx F 32 B1
Voorschoten NL 2 B1
Vorden D 3 B5
Vorden NL 3 B3
Voreppe F 26 B2
Vorey F 25 B3
Voué F 11 C4
Vouillé F 23 B4
Voulx F 10 C2
Voussac F 24 A3
Vouvray F 16 B2
Vouvry CH 27 A3
Vouziers F 11 B4
Voves F 17 A3
Vreden D 3 B3
Vriezenveen NL 3 B3
Vrigne-aux-Bois F 11 B4
Vron F 4 B1
Vroomshoop NL 3 B3
Vught NL 5 A5
Vuillafans F 19 B5
Vy-lès Lure F 19 B5

W

Waalwijk NL 5 A5
Waarschoot B 5 A3
Wabern D 7 A5
Wächtersbach D 7 B5
Wädenswil CH 21 B3
Wadern D 12 B2
Wadersloh D 7 A4
Wageningen NL 2 C2
Waghäusel D 13 B4
Waimes B 6 B2
Wald CH 21 B3
Wald-Michelbach D 13 B4
Waldböckelheim D 13 B3
Waldbröl D 7 B3
Waldeck D 7 A5
Waldfischbach-Burgalben D 13 B3
Waldkirch D 20 A2
Waldmohr D 13 B3
Waldshut D 20 B3
Waldstatt CH 21 B4
Waldwisse F 12 B2
Walenstadt CH 21 B4
Walincourt F 10 A3
Wallenhorst D 3 B5
Wallers F 4 B3
Walshoutem B 5 B5
Waltenhofen D 21 B5
Wangen im Allgäu D 21 B4
Wangerooge D 3 A4
Wängi CH 21 B3
Warburg D 7 A5
Wardenburg D 3 A5
Waregem B 5 B3
Waremme B 5 B5
Warendorf D 3 C4
Warga NL 2 A2
Warnsveld NL 2 B3
Warsingsfehn D 3 A4
Warstein D 7 A4
Warth A 21 B5
Wasselonne F 13 C3
Wassen CH 21 C3
Wassenaar NL 2 B1
Wasserauen CH 21 B4
Wassy F 11 C4
Waterloo B 5 B4
Watten F 4 B2
Wattwil CH 21 B4
Wavignies F 10 B2
Wavre B 5 B4
Weener D 3 A4
Weert NL 6 A1
Weesp NL 2 B2
Weeze D 6 A2
Weggis CH 20 B3
Wehr D 20 B2
Weierbach D 13 B3
Weil am Rhein D 20 B2
Weil der Stadt D 13 C4
Weilburg D 7 B4
Weilerswist D 6 B2
Weilmünster D 7 B4
Weinfelden CH 21 B4
Weingarten, *Baden-Württemberg* D 13 B4
Weingarten, *Baden-Württemberg* D 21 B4
Weinheim D 13 B4
Weisstannen CH 21 C4
Weitnau D 21 B5
Welkenraedt B 6 B1
Wellin B 11 A5
Welschenrohr CH 20 B2
Welver D 7 A3
Wenden D 7 B3
Wengen CH 20 C2
Werdohl D 7 A3
Werkendam NL 5 A4
Werl D 7 A3
Werlte D 3 B4
Wermelskirchen D 6 A3
Werne D 7 A3
Weseke D 6 A2
Wesel D 6 A2
Wesseling D 6 B2
West-Terschelling NL 2 A2
Westerbork NL 3 B3
Westerburg D 7 B3
Westerhaar NL 3 B3
Westerholt D 3 A4
Westerkappeln D 3 B4
Westerlo B 5 A4
Westerstede D 3 A4
Westkapelle B 4 A3
Westkapelle NL 5 A3
Wetter, *Hessen* D 7 B4
Wetter, *Nordrhein-Westfalen* D 6 A3
Wetteren B 5 A3
Wettringen D 3 B4
Wetzikon CH 21 B3
Wetzlar D 7 B4
Weyerbusch D 7 B3
Weyersheim F 13 C3
Wickede D 7 A3
Wiefelstede D 3 A5
Wiehl D 7 B3
Wierden NL 3 B3
Wiesbaden D 13 A4
Wiesen CH 21 C4
Wiesloch D 13 B4
Wiesmoor D 3 A4
Wietmarschen D 3 B4
Wiggen CH 20 C2
Wijchen NL 6 A1
Wijhe NL 2 B3
Wijk bij Duurstede NL 2 C2
Wil CH 21 B4
Wildbad D 13 C4
Wildberg, *Baden-Württemberg* D 13 C4
Wildegg CH 20 B3
Wilhelmsdorf D 21 B4
Wilhelmshaven D 3 A5
Willebadessen D 7 A5
Willebroek B 5 A4
Willgottheim F 13 C3
Willich D 6 A2
Willingen D 7 A4
Willisau CH 20 B3
Wilsum D 3 B3
Wiltz L 12 B1
Wimereux F 4 B1
Wimmenau F 13 C3
Wimmis CH 20 C2
Wingene B 4 A3
Winnweiler D 13 B3
Winschoten NL 3 A4
Winsum, *Friesland* NL 2 A2
Winsum, *Groningen* NL 3 A3
Winterberg D 7 A4
Winterswijk NL 3 C3
Winterthur CH 21 B3
Wintzenheim F 20 A2
Wipperfürth D 6 A3
Wissant F 4 B1
Wissembourg F 13 B3
Wissen D 7 B3
Witmarsum NL 2 A2
Witry-les-Reims F 11 B4
Wittelsheim F 20 B2
Witten D 6 A3
Wittenheim F 20 B2
Wittlich D 12 B2
Wittmund D 3 A4
Woerden NL 2 B1
Wœrth F 13 C3
Wohlen CH 20 B3
Woippy F 12 B2
Wolfach D 13 C4
Wolfegg D 21 B4
Wolfersheim D 7 B4
Wolfhagen D 7 A5
Wolfstein D 13 B3
Wolfurt A 21 B4
Wolhusen CH 20 B3
Wöllstadt D 7 B4
Wolvega NL 2 B2
Worb CH 20 C2
Workum NL 2 B2
Wormer NL 2 B1
Wormhout F 4 B2
Worms D 13 B4
Wörrstadt D 13 B4
Wörth, *Bayern* D 13 B5
Wörth, *Rheinland-Pfalz* D 13 B4
Woudsend NL 2 B2
Woumen B 4 A2
Wulfen, *Nordrhein-Westfalen* D 6 A3
Wünnenberg D 7 A4
Wuppertal D 6 A3
Würselen D 6 B2
Wuustwezel B 5 A4

X

Xanten D 6 A2
Xertigny F 19 A5

Y

Yebra de Basa E 35 B3
Yenne F 26 B2
Yerseke NL 5 A4
Yerville F 9 A4
Ygos-St. Saturnin F 28 C2
Ygrande F 18 C1
Ymonville F 17 A3
Yport F 9 A4
Ypres = Ieper B 4 B2
Yssingeaux F 25 B4
Yverdon-les-Bains CH 20 C1
Yvetot F 9 A4
Yvignac F 15 A3
Yvoir B 5 B4
Yvonand CH 20 C1
Yzeure F 18 C2

Z

Zaamslag NL 5 A3
Zaanstad NL 2 B1
Zaltbommel NL 5 A5
Zandhoven B 5 A4
Zandvoort NL 2 B1
Zarautz E 34 A1
Zarren B 4 A2
Zeebrugge B 4 A3
Zeist NL 2 B2
Zele B 5 A4
Zelhem NL 3 B3
Zell CH 20 B2
Zell, *Baden-Württemberg* D 20 B2
Zell, *Baden-Württemberg* D 13 C4
Zell, *Rheinland-Pfalz* D 12 A3
Zelzate B 5 A3
Zemst B 5 B4
Zerf D 12 B2
Zermatt CH 27 A4
Zernez CH 21 C5
Zestoa E 34 A1
Zetel D 3 A4
Zevenaar NL 2 C3
Zevenbergen NL 5 A4
Zicavo F 38 B2
Zierenberg D 7 A5
Zierikzee NL 5 A3
Zinal CH 27 A4
Zoetermeer NL 2 B1
Zofingen CH 20 B2
Zomergem B 5 A3
Zonhoven B 5 B5
Zonza F 38 B2
Zottegem B 5 B3
Zoutkamp NL 3 A3
Zubieta E 34 A2
Zubiri E 34 B2
Zuera E 34 C3
Zug CH 21 B3
Zuidhorn NL 3 A3
Zuidlaren NL 3 A3
Zuidwolde NL 3 B3
Zülpich D 6 B2
Zumaia E 34 A1
Zundert NL 5 A4
Zürich CH 21 B3
Zurzach CH 20 B3
Zutphen NL 2 B3
Zwartsluis NL 2 B3
Zweibrücken D 13 B3
Zweisimmen CH 20 C2
Zwiefalten D 21 A4
Zwolle NL 2 B3

A-Z NOTTINGHAMSHIRE

CONTENTS

C008215377

REFERENCE

Motorway	M1
Primary Route	A52
A Road	A612
Under Construction	
Proposed	
B Road	B6004
Dual Carriageway	
One-way Street	→
Traffic flow on A Roads is also indicated by a heavy line on the driver's left.	⇨
Restricted Access	
Pedestrianized Road	
Track / Footpath	
Residential Walkway	
Railway	Station / Level Crossing / Heritage Station / Tunnel
Nottingham Express Transit (NET)	Stop
Local Authority Boundary	
Posttown Boundary	
Postcode Boundary (within Posttown)	
Forest Park Boundary	
Built-up Area	LION CLOSE
Map Continuation 58	Large Scale City Centre 6 Road Map Pages 148

Car Park (Selected)	P
Church or Chapel	†
Cycleway (Selected)	
Fire Station	■
Hospital	H
House Numbers (A & B Roads only)	13 8
Information Centre	i
National Grid Reference	450
Park & Ride (Bus)	Queen's Drive P+
Park & Ride (NET)	P+
Police Station	▲
Post Office	★
Toilet:	
without facilities for the Disabled	▽
with facilities for the Disabled	▽
Disabled facilities only	▽
Educational Establishment	
Hospital or Hospice	
Industrial Building	
Leisure or Recreational Facility	
Place of Interest	
Public Building	
Shopping Centre or Market	
Other Selected Buildings	

SCALE

Map Pages 8-143	Large Scale City Centre Pages 6-7
1:16,896 3¾ inches (9.53 cm) to 1 mile 5.9cm to 1km	1:8,448 7½ inches (19.05 cm) to 1 mile 11.8cm to 1km
0 ¼ ½ Mile	0 ⅛ ¼ Mile
0 250 500 750 1 km	0 125 250 375 500m

Copyright of Geographers' A-Z Map Company Ltd.

Fairfield Road, Borough Green, Sevenoaks, Kent TN15 8PP
Telephone: 01732 781000 (Enquiries & Trade Sales)
01732 783422 (Retail Sales)
www.a-zmaps.co.uk
Copyright © Geographers' A-Z Map Co. Ltd.

Ordnance Survey®   This product includes mapping data licensed from Ordnance Survey® with the permission of the Controller of Her Majesty's Stationery Office.

© Crown Copyright 2005. All rights reserved. Licence number 100017302
EDITION 1   2006

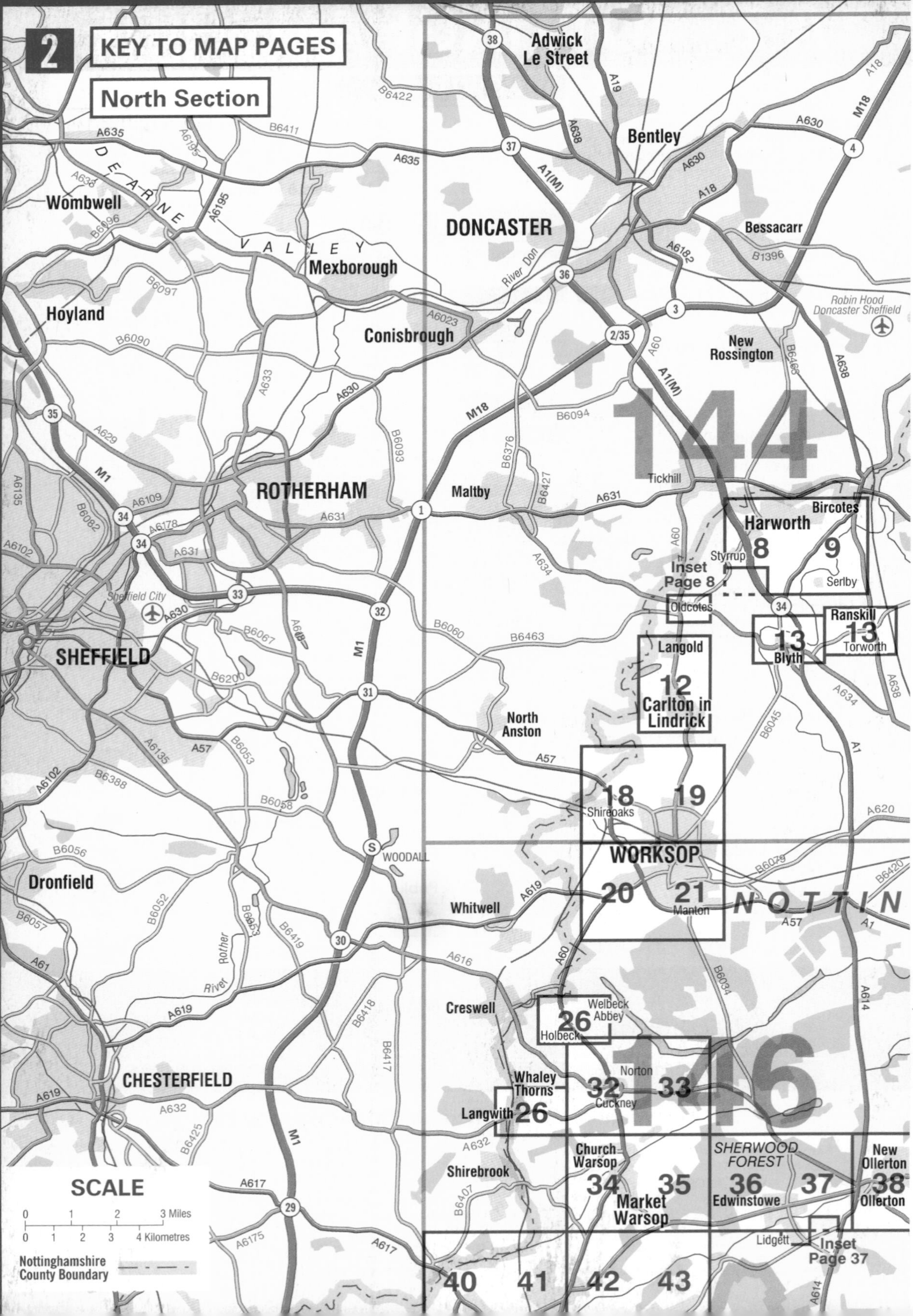
2
KEY TO MAP PAGES
North Section
Adwick Le Street
Bentley
Wombwell
DEARNE VALLEY
DONCASTER
Bessacarr
Mexborough
River Don
Hoyland
Conisbrough
Robin Hood Doncaster Sheffield
New Rossington
144
ROTHERHAM
Maltby
Tickhill
Harworth
Bircotes
8
9
Styrrup
Inset Page 8
Serlby
Oldcotes
Ranskill
13
Blyth
Torworth
Sheffield City
SHEFFIELD
Langold
12
Carlton in Lindrick
North Anston
18
19
Shireoaks
WOODALL
WORKSOP
20
21
Manton
Dronfield
Whitwell
NOTTIN
River Rother
Creswell
Welbeck Abbey
26
Holbeck
146
Whaley Thorns
Norton
32
33
Cuckney
CHESTERFIELD
Langwith
26
Church Warsop
Shirebrook
SHERWOOD FOREST
New Ollerton
34
35
36
37
38
Market Warsop
Edwinstowe
Ollerton
Lidgett
Inset Page 37
40
41
42
43
SCALE
0 1 2 3 Miles
0 1 2 3 4 Kilometres
Nottinghamshire County Boundary
M1
M18
A1(M)
A1
A57
A60
A614
A616
A619
A630
A631
A634
A635
A638

SCUNTHORPE
M180
2
Burringham
M181
B1450
3
Bottesford
A159
A18
B1207
M180
4
A614
ISLE OF AXHOLME
Epworth
B1398
Messingham
B1400
A161
River Trent
A15
B1206
B1396
Finningley
Haxey
Kirton in Lindsey
B1205
B1205
145
Blyton
10 Misson
Misterton
11
Walkeringham
A159
B1398
Everton
10
Gringley on the Hill 16
Beckingham
16
Gainsborough
A631
A631
A631
Mattersey Thorpe
15
Mattersey
Clayworth
15
A620
Lound
14
Sutton cum Lound
B1403
North Wheatley
17
South Wheatley
Hayton
17
Clarborough
Sturton le Steeple
24
Habblesthorpe
North Leverton
A156
Ingham
Marton
B1241
Sturton by Stow
Babworth
RETFORD
22
23
Ordsall
South Leverton
25
Treswell
A1500
Rampton
GHAMSHIRE
Woodbeck
Inset Page 25
Church Laneham
Laneham
29
Dunham on Trent
B1398
A15
27
Elkesley
A638
Saxilby
A57
A1
A57
East Markham
28
Tuxford
Thorney
31
North Clifton
30
High Marnham
South Clifton
147
LINCOLN
Harby
31
Wigsley
Walesby
27
A6075
A46
B1378
B1190
A15
B1003
Kirton
Boughton
39
Egmanton
124
Laxton
B1164
A1
Normanton on Trent
125
Weston
River Trent
A1133
A1434
A607
Wellow
Sutton on Trent
128
Girton
125
Besthorpe
Waddington

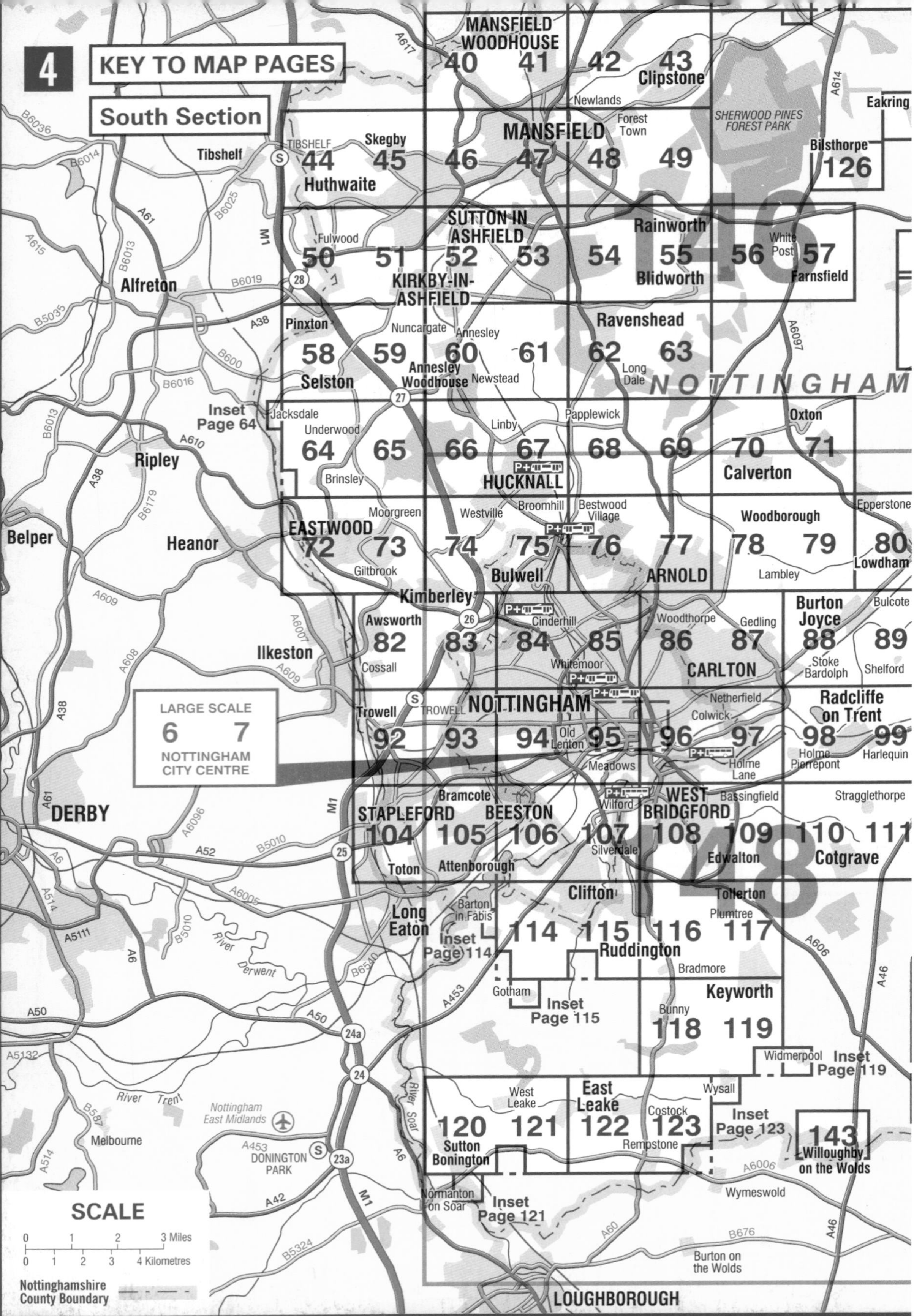

4
KEY TO MAP PAGES
South Section
MANSFIELD WOODHOUSE
40 41 42 43
Clipstone
Newlands
Forest Town
MANSFIELD
SHERWOOD PINES FOREST PARK
Eakring
Bilsthorpe
126
Tibshelf
TIBSHELF
Skegby
44 45 46 47 48 49
Huthwaite
SUTTON IN ASHFIELD
Rainworth
Fulwood
50 51 52 53 54 55 56 57
White Post
Blidworth
Farnsfield
KIRKBY-IN-ASHFIELD
Alfreton
Pinxton
Nuncargate
Annesley
Ravenshead
58 59 60 61 62 63
Selston
Annesley Woodhouse
Newstead
Long Dale
NOTTINGHAM
Inset Page 64
Jacksdale
Underwood
Linby
Papplewick
Oxton
64 65 66 67 68 69 70 71
Ripley
Brinsley
HUCKNALL
Calverton
Moorgreen
Westville
Broomhill
Bestwood Village
Woodborough
Epperstone
Belper
Heanor
EASTWOOD
72 73 74 75 76 77 78 79 80
Giltbrook
Bulwell
ARNOLD
Lambley
Lowdham
Kimberley
Awsworth
Cinderhill
Woodthorpe
Gedling
Burton Joyce
Bulcote
82 83 84 85 86 87 88 89
Ilkeston
Cossall
Whitemoor
CARLTON
Stoke Bardolph
Shelford
LARGE SCALE
6 7
NOTTINGHAM CITY CENTRE
Trowell
TROWELL
NOTTINGHAM
Netherfield
Colwick
Radcliffe on Trent
92 93 94 95 96 97 98 99
Old Lenton
Meadows
Holme Lane
Holme Pierrepont
Harlequin
Bramcote
Wilford
WEST BRIDGFORD
Bassingfield
Stragglethorpe
DERBY
STAPLEFORD
BEESTON
104 105 106 107 108 109 110 111
Silverdale
Edwalton
Cotgrave
Toton
Attenborough
Clifton
Tollerton
Long Eaton
Barton in Fabis
Plumtree
114 115 116 117
Inset Page 114
Ruddington
Bradmore
Gotham
Inset Page 115
Keyworth
Bunny
118 119
Widmerpool
Inset Page 119
River Trent
River Derwent
River Soar
Nottingham East Midlands
Melbourne
DONINGTON PARK
West Leake
East Leake
Costock
Wysall
Inset Page 123
120 121 122 123
143
Sutton Bonington
Rempstone
Willoughby on the Wolds
Wymeswold
Normanton on Soar
Inset Page 121
Burton on the Wolds
LOUGHBOROUGH
SCALE
0 1 2 3 Miles
0 1 2 3 4 Kilometres
Nottinghamshire County Boundary

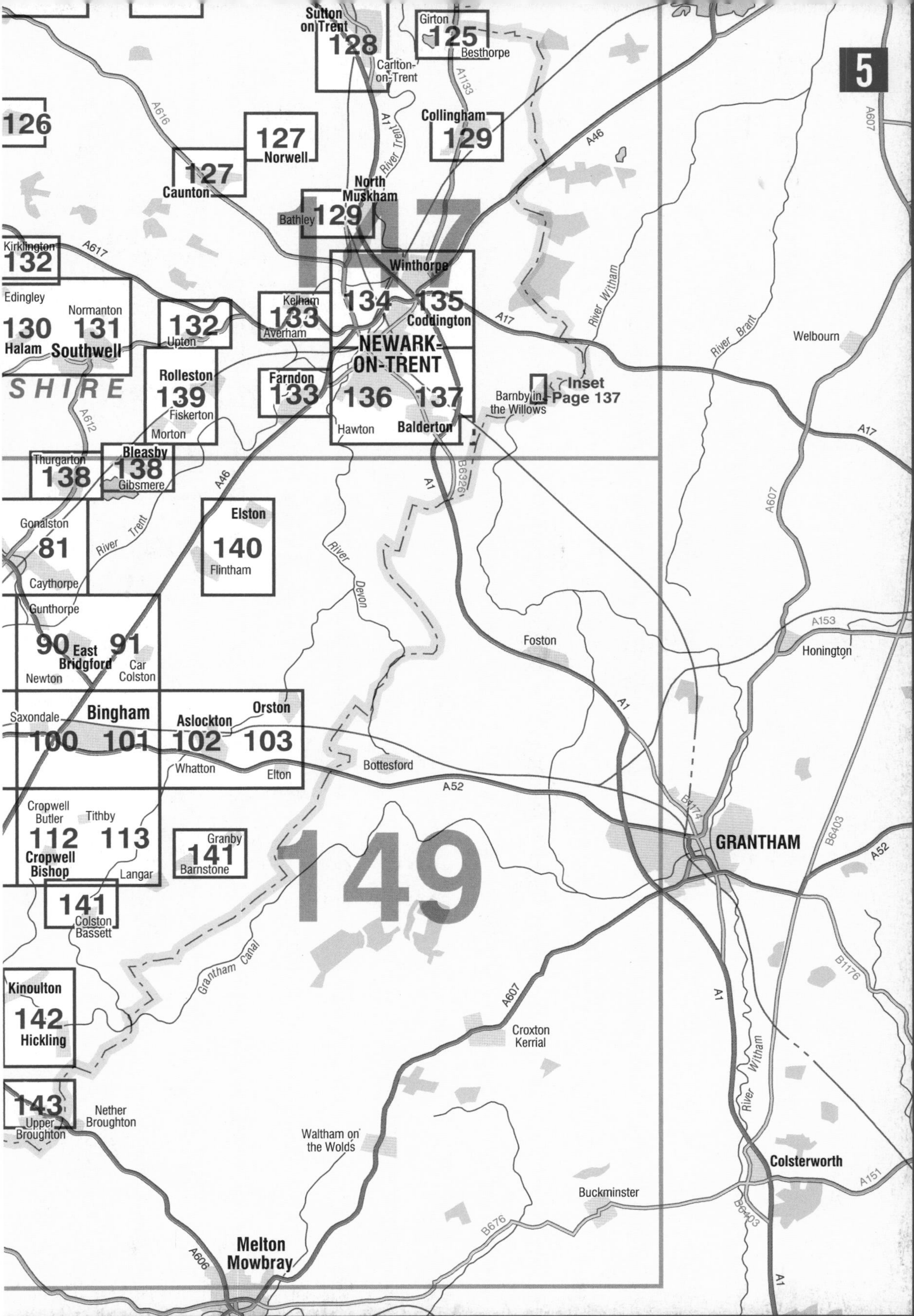
Sutton on Trent
128
Girton
125
Besthorpe
Carlton-on-Trent
A1133
A616
A1
River Trent
126
127
Norwell
127
Caunton
Collingham
129
A46
North Muskham
Bathley
129
147
Kirklington
132
A617
Winthorpe
Edingley
Normanton
130
131
Halam
Southwell
132
Upton
Kelham
133
Averham
134
135
Coddington
NEWARK-ON-TRENT
A17
River Witham
River Brant
Welbourn
A607
SHIRE
Rolleston
139
Fiskerton
Morton
A612
Farndon
133
136
137
Hawton
Balderton
Barnby in the Willows
Inset Page 137
A17
Thurgarton
138
Bleasby
138
Gibsmere
A46
B6326
A1
Gonalston
81
Caythorpe
River Trent
Elston
140
Flintham
River Devon
A607
Gunthorpe
90
East Bridgford
91
Car Colston
Newton
Foston
A153
Honington
Saxondale
Bingham
100
101
Aslockton
102
Orston
103
Whatton
Elton
Bottesford
A1
A52
B1174
Cropwell Butler
Tithby
112
113
Cropwell Bishop
Langar
Granby
141
Barnstone
149
GRANTHAM
B6403
A52
141
Colston Bassett
Grantham Canal
B1176
Kinoulton
142
Hickling
A607
Croxton Kerrial
A1
River Witham
143
Upper Broughton
Nether Broughton
Waltham on the Wolds
Colsterworth
A151
Buckminster
B6403
B676
A606
Melton Mowbray
A1

6
56
41
340
56
457
457
A
B
C
D
E
A
B
C
D
E
1
2
3
4
5
6
7
1
2
3
4
5
6
7
95
95
95
FOREST RECREATION GROUND
Site of Goose Fair
Church Cemetery
Nottingham High School
Nottingham High School for Girls
High School
Mount Hooton
Arboretum
Arboretum Nursery School
Bowling Green
Waverley House PNEU Sch.
Hollygrit School
Unity Primary Sch.
Comm. Cen.
Royal Victoria Ct.
General Cemetery
Nottingham Trent University
Halls of Residence
Nottingham
The Bonington Gall.
Library
Trent Uni.
Clarendon Chambers
College
Guildhall
Royal Cen.
Royal Concert Hall
Theatre Royal
Lawrence Ho. Council Offs.
RC Cathedral
Albert Hall
Playhouse
NG7
The Park
Tennis Cts.
Bowling Green
Odeon Cinema
Gall.
Old Market Square
Old Mkt. Sq.
NOTTINGHAM
Tales of Robin Hood
The Arena
City Point
Standard Hill
Castle Museum & Art Gallery
Nottingham Castle
Mortimer's Hole Cave
Robin Hood Statue
Bandstand Yard
Brewhouse Mus.
Lace Cen. & Costume Mus.
The People's College
Radio Trent
Fitness First
County Archives
Government Offices
New Lenton
Pelham Cottages
CASTLE MEADOW RETAIL PARK
Superstore
ALFRETON ROAD
ILKESTON ROAD
DERBY ROAD
DERBY (BRIAN CLOUGH WAY)
CANNING CIRCUS
WOLLATON ST.
UP. PARLIAMENT ST.
MAID MARIAN WAY
MANSFIELD RD.
HUNTINGDON ST.
BOULEVARD
CASTLE BOULEVARD
WILFORD RD.
WILFORD ST.
CANAL
A610
A609
A6200
A6008
A6005
A60
A453

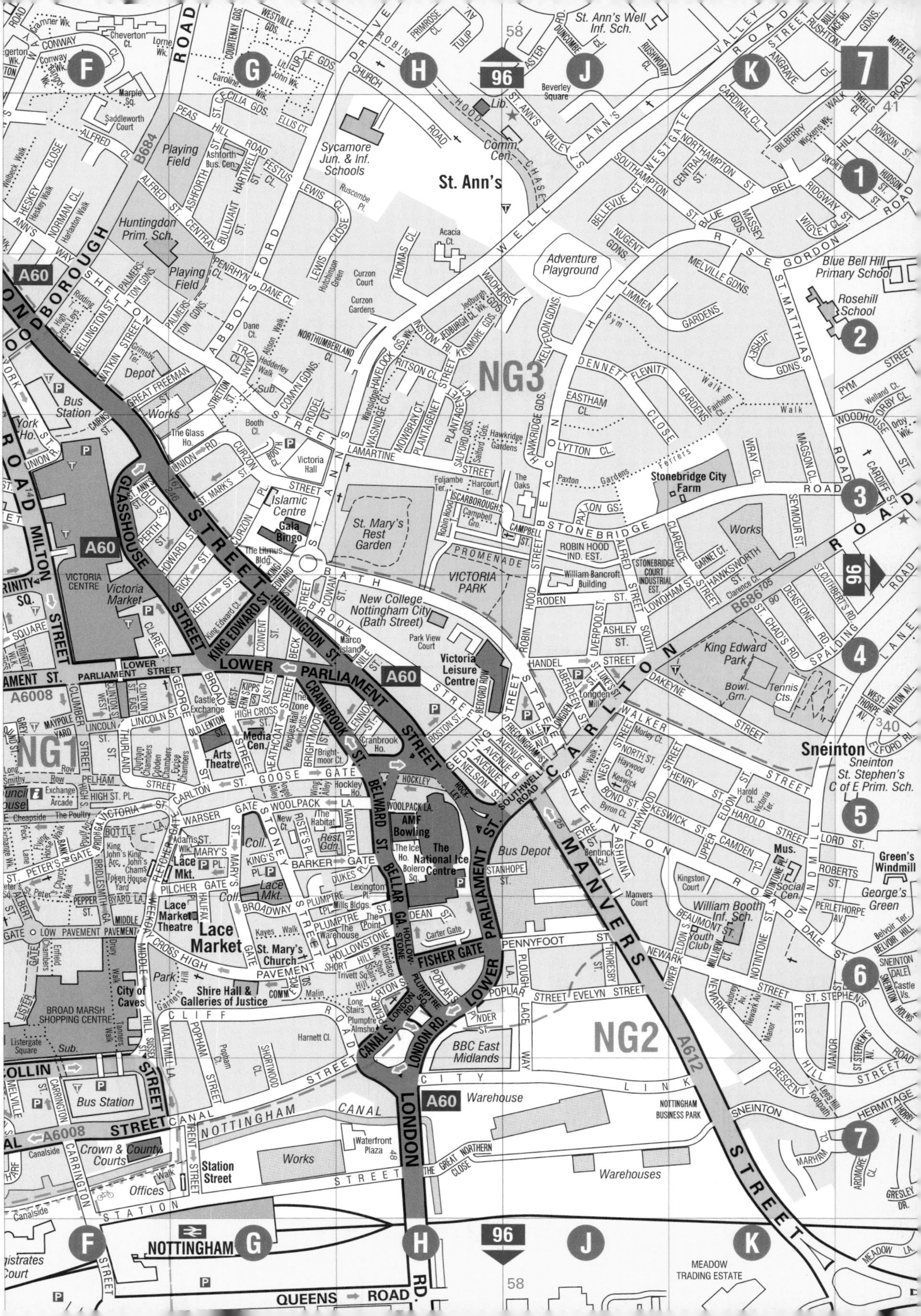
7
96
58
41
F
G
H
J
K
1
2
3
4
5
6
7
St. Ann's
NG3
NG1
NG2
A60
A6008
A612
B684
B686
St. Ann's Well Inf. Sch.
Sycamore Jun. & Inf. Schools
Huntingdon Prim. Sch.
Playing Field
Adventure Playground
Blue Bell Hill Primary School
Rosehill School
Stonebridge City Farm
St. Mary's Rest Garden
Victoria Park
Victoria Centre
Victoria Market
Bus Station
Islamic Centre
Gala Bingo
New College Nottingham City (Bath Street)
Victoria Leisure Centre
King Edward Park
Sneinton
Sneinton St. Stephen's C of E Prim. Sch.
Green's Windmill
George's Green
William Booth Inf. Sch.
Lace Market
Lace Market Theatre
St. Mary's Church
Shire Hall & Galleries of Justice
City of Caves
Broad Marsh Shopping Centre
AMF Bowling
The National Ice Centre
Bus Depot
BBC East Midlands
Arts Theatre
Media Cen.
Crown & County Courts
Station Street
Nottingham
Meadow Trading Estate
Nottingham Business Park
Warehouses
Works
Offices
Waterfront Plaza
Glasshouse Street
Huntingdon St.
Lower Parliament Street
Mansfield Road
Woodborough Road
Milton Street
Carlton Road
Manvers Street
London Road
Queens Road
Canal Street
Collin Street
Fisher Gate
Goose Gate
Hockley
Stoney Street
Bath Street
Stonebridge Road
Southwell Road
Sneinton Hill
City Link
Cliff Road
Hermitage
Meadow La.

HARWORTH
DN11
Doncaster
BAWTRY
A631
TICKHILL
BLYTH RD.
B6463
ROAD
MAIN ST.
A1(M) MOTORWAY
A1(M)
STYRRUP HALL
GOLF COURSE
Crow Wood
Club Ho.
Driving Range
STYRRUP CARR
Styrrup
STYRRUP
STREET
MAIN
SERLBY RD.
Sewage Works
Harworth Sewage Dike
Goole Dike or River Torne
DONCASTER
BASSETLAW
Doreen Villa
Rose Cottage
Grey Gables
Fernlea
Cemetery
Rec. Grd.
Play. Fld.
Well Hill Plantation
SCROOBY RD.
SCROOBY
Colliery
Cricket Grd.
Playing Field
Bircotes Leisure Centre
St. Patrick's Catholic Prim. Sch.
Snipe Park Wood
BRITISH COAL ENTERPRISE PARK
BRUNEL CLOSE
SNAPE LANE
BLYTH ROAD
Works
Lords Wood
Playing Fields
Triangle
HARWORTH PARK INDUSTRIAL ESTATE
Steer Bank Farm
Nook Flatt Wood
Sunny Nook
Elm Cottage
Kirk View
HARWORTH ROAD
A614
Worksop
S81
Deep Well Cottage
THE WOODLANDS
INSET
Oldcotes
A634
MALTBY RD.
BLYTH ROAD
DONCASTER
A60
LAMB B6463 LANE
Manor Farm
East Lodge
Nursery House Farm
Olde Mill
West Lodge
Weir
Oldcotes Dyke
Fishpond Plantation
Meadow Plantation
Hermeston Hall
Goldthorpe Farm
Goldthorpe Farm Cottage
144
A B C D E
1 2 3 4 5 6 7
61 62 91 92 88 59 460

9
144
91
92
90
89
63
64
465
F
G
H
J
K
1
2
3
4
5
6
7
ROAD
GAINSBOROUGH RD.
A631
A614
A638
GREAT NORTH RD.
BLYTH ROAD
GREAT NORTH ROAD
WEST WOOD ESTATE
BINBROOK CT.
LEEMING CT.
WESTWOOD RD.
Sports Field
Fish Pond
Fish Pond Wood
COCK HILL LA.
CHURCH CL.
ST.
COCK HILL CL.
PASTURES
Sports Grd.
Reservoir
PLUMTREE FARM INDUSTRIAL ESTATE
PLUMTREE RD.
PLUMTREE
Plumtree Farm
BIRCOTES
Serlby Park Senior Sch.
The Old Vicarage
Hall
WHITE HOUSE RD.
WHITE HOUSE CT.
WINCHESTER M.
WHITEHOUSE DR.
GALWAY AV.
GALWAY DR.
GALWAY RD.
ESSEX RD.
ESSEX DR.
SUFFOLK RD.
SUFFOLK GRO.
SUFFOLK AV.
NORFOLK DR.
NORFOLK ROAD
NORFOLK GRO.
NORFOLK AV.
CUMBERLAND CL.
CUMBERLAND HO.
WESTMORLAND HO.
MILNE DR.
MILNE AV.
MILNE GRO.
MILNE ROAD
HOWARD RD.
THE CRESCENT
CHURCH
MONCKTON RD.
DROVERSDALE ROAD
White House Plantation
Hawk's Nest Owl Sanctuary
LADY'S HOLT LANE
Nursery
GIBBET HILL LA.
LAKELAND CARAVAN SITE
Gibbet Hill
MILL LANE
ROAD
South Carr
Sowcarr
South Carr Farm
Sports Grd.
Football Grd.
Droversdale Wood
River Ryton
Ruins Plantation
Penny Acre
LOW
CHAPEL LA.
DOG LA.
HOLMFIELD CFT.
MANOR RD.
Manor House Farm
Ings Bank
Scrooby
CH. LA.
STATION RD.
CH. VW.
MAYFLOWER AV.
SARACENS LANE
Bawtry Lodge
Broom Hill
Coronation Clump
DN10
The Holt
Neale's Covert
Harworth Lodge
Round Holt
Kennel Cottage
River Ryton
Lodges
Meadowside Cottages
The Woodlands
Serlby
Serlby Hall
East Garden
Home Farm
The Laurels
SERLBY PARK
Golf Cottage
Club House
GREEN LANE
ROMAN BANK LANE
Black Cat Plantation
SERLBY PARK GOLF COURSE
LANE
Hollins Holt
Lodge Farm
Scrooby Top Ho.

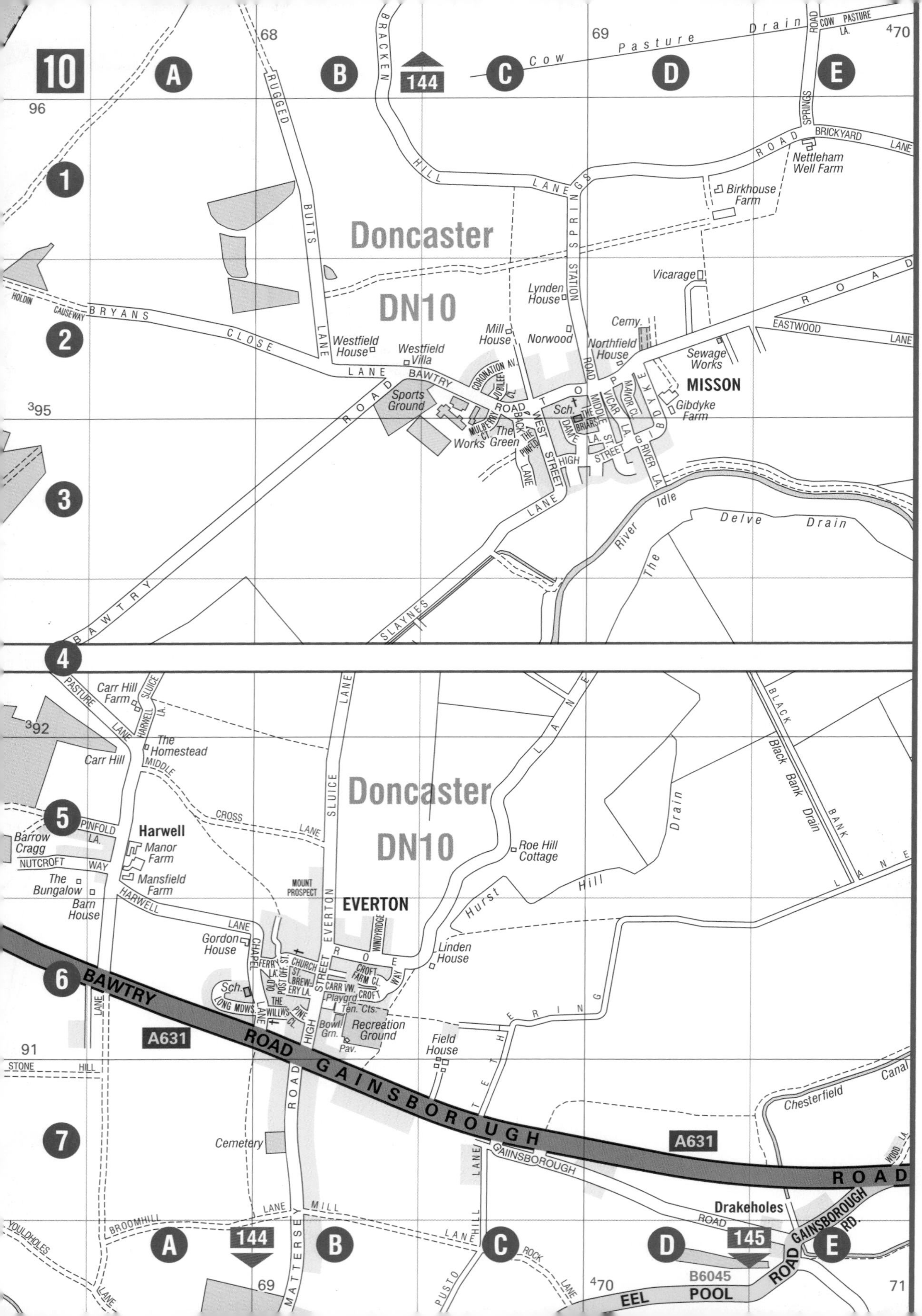
144
145
Doncaster
DN10
Doncaster
DN10
MISSON
EVERTON
Harwell
Drakeholes
Cow Pasture Drain
COW PASTURE LA.
BRACKEN HILL LANE
RUGGED BUTTS LANE
SPRINGS ROAD
BRICKYARD LANE
Nettleham Well Farm
Birkhouse Farm
Vicarage
Lynden House
STATION ROAD
HOLDIN CAUSEWAY
BRYANS CLOSE LANE
Westfield House
Westfield Villa
Mill House
Norwood
Northfield House
Cemy.
EASTWOOD LANE
Sewage Works
BAWTRY ROAD
Sports Ground
CORONATION AV.
JUBILEE CL.
MULBERRY CT.
The Works
The Green
BACK LANE
THE PINFOLD
WEST STREET
Sch.
DANE ST.
THE BRIARS
MIDDLE LA.
VICAR LA.
MANOR CL.
GIBDYKE
Gibdyke Farm
HIGH STREET
RIVER LA.
River Idle
Delve Drain
The
LANE
SLAYNES LANE
BAWTRY ROAD
PASTURE LANE
Carr Hill Farm
SLUICE LA.
HARWELL LA.
Carr Hill
The Homestead
MIDDLE CROSS LANE
PINFOLD LA.
Barrow Cragg
NUTCROFT WAY
Manor Farm
Mansfield Farm
The Bungalow
Barn House
HARWELL LANE
SLUICE LANE
BLACK BANK LANE
Black Bank Drain
Drain
Roe Hill Cottage
Hurst Hill
MOUNT PROSPECT
EVERTON
WINDYRIDGE
Gordon House
CHAPEL LANE
FERRY LA.
OLD POST OFF. ST.
CHURCH ST.
BREWERY LA.
CROFT FARM CL.
CARR VW.
CROFT
ROE WAY
Linden House
Sch.
LONG MDWS.
THE WILLWS.
PINE CL.
Playgrd.
Ten. Cts.
Bowl Grn.
Recreation Ground
Pav.
BAWTRY ROAD
GAINSBOROUGH ROAD
A631
Field House
TETHERING LANE
STONE HILL
HIGH ROAD
Cemetery
GAINSBOROUGH
HILL LANE
Chesterfield Canal
WOOD LA.
BROOMHILL LANE
MILL LANE
MATTERSEY ROAD
YOULDHOLES LANE
PUSTO ROCK LANE
GAINSBOROUGH RD.
ROAD
B6045
EEL POOL ROAD
A
B
C
D
E
1
2
3
4
5
6
7
68
69
470
96
395
392
91
71

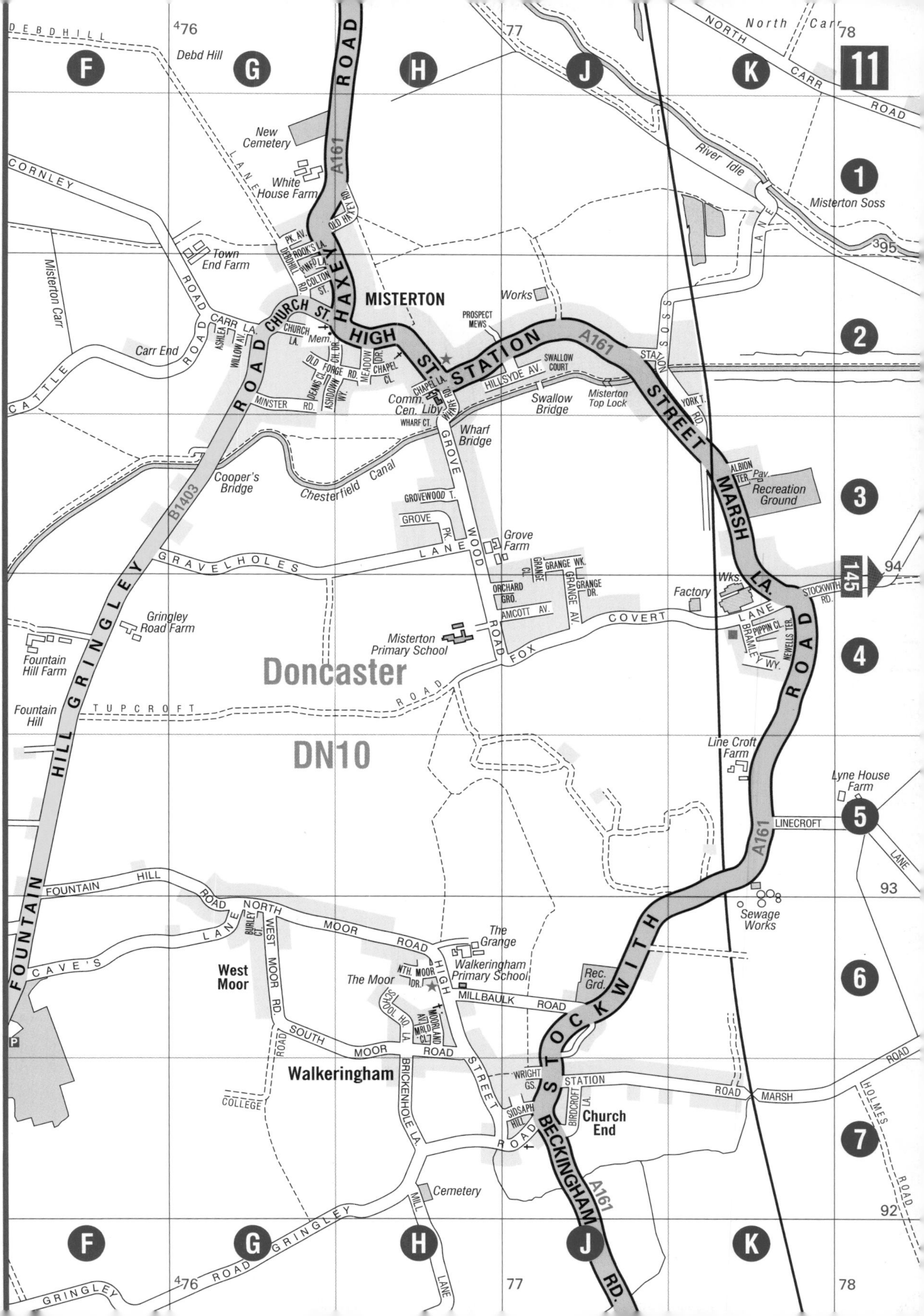

476
77
78
F
G
H
J
K
1
2
3
4
5
6
7
DEBDHILL
Debd Hill
NORTH CARR ROAD
North Carr
New Cemetery
A161
HAXEY ROAD
CORNLEY
White House Farm
OLD HAXEY RD.
River Idle
Misterton Soss
395
LANE
PK. AV.
ROOK'S LA.
DEBDHILL RD.
PINFOLD LA.
COLTON ST.
Town End Farm
Misterton Carr
CHURCH ST.
HIGH ST.
MISTERTON
Works
PROSPECT MEWS
STATION STREET
SOSS
STATION RD.
CARR LA.
ASHLEA
WILLOW AV.
CHURCH LA.
Mem.
OLD FORGE RD.
CH. DR.
MEADOW DR.
CHAPEL CL.
Carr End
CATTLE
ROAD
DEANS CL.
ASHDOWN WY.
CHAPEL LA.
WHARF RD.
HILLSYDE AV.
SWALLOW COURT
Comm. Cen.
Liby
Swallow Bridge
Misterton Top Lock
YORK T.
MINSTER RD.
WHARF CT.
Wharf Bridge
GROVE
Cooper's Bridge
Chesterfield Canal
B1403
GROVEWOOD T.
ALBION TER.
Pav.
Recreation Ground
MARSH LA.
GROVE PK.
Grove Farm
WOOD
GRAVELHOLES LANE
GRANGE CL.
GRANGE WK.
GRANGE DR.
GRANGE AV.
ORCHARD GRO.
AMCOTT AV.
Wks.
Factory
STOCKWITH RD.
145
94
COVERT LANE
BRAMLEY WY.
PIPPIN CL.
NEWELLS TER.
Gringley Road Farm
Misterton Primary School
FOX
ROAD
Fountain Hill Farm
Doncaster
TUPCROFT ROAD
Fountain Hill
GRINGLEY
HILL
DN10
Line Croft Farm
Lyne House Farm
LINECROFT
LANE
FOUNTAIN HILL ROAD
93
Sewage Works
NORTH MOOR ROAD
BURLEY CT.
WEST MOOR RD.
CAVE'S LANE
FOUNTAIN
The Grange
Walkeringham Primary School
West Moor
NTH. MOOR DR.
The Moor
HIGH STREET
Rec. Grd.
STOCKWITH
MILLBAULK ROAD
SCHOOL HO. LA.
MRLD CL.
MOORLAND AV.
SOUTH MOOR ROAD
ROAD
P
Walkeringham
BRICKENHOLE LA.
WRIGHT GS.
STATION ROAD
MARSH ROAD
HOLMES ROAD
COLLEGE
BIRDCROFT LA.
SIDSAPH HILL
Church End
BECKINGHAM RD.
Cemetery
MILL LANE
92
GRINGLEY ROAD

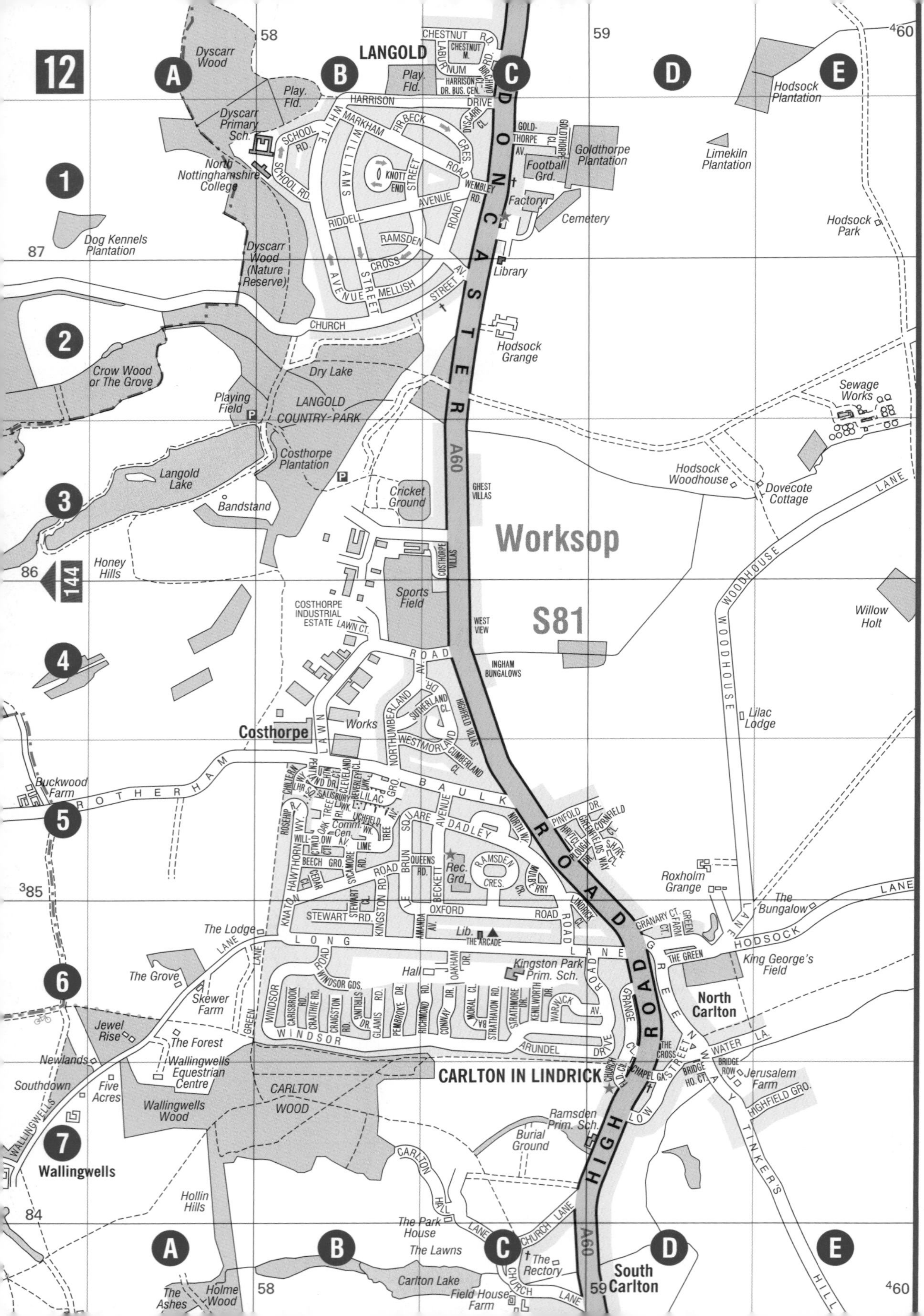
LANGOLD
Dyscarr Wood
Play. Fld.
Dyscarr Primary Sch.
North Nottinghamshire College
Dog Kennels Plantation
Dyscarr Wood (Nature Reserve)
CHESTNUT RD.
CHESTNUT M.
LABURNUM
HARRISON CL.
DR. BUS. CEN.
HARRISON DRIVE
SCHOOL RD.
WHITE
MARKHAM
FIR BECK
DYSCARR CL.
WILLIAMS
KNOTT END
STREET
CRES.
ROAD
WEMBLEY RD.
AVENUE
RIDDELL
RAMSDEN
CROSS
AVENUE
STREET
MELLISH
AV.
CHURCH
DONCASTER
GOLDTHORPE AV.
GOLDTHORPE CL.
Goldthorpe Plantation
Football Grd.
Factory
Cemetery
Library
Hodsock Grange
Hodsock Plantation
Limekiln Plantation
Hodsock Park
Crow Wood or The Grove
Dry Lake
Playing Field
LANGOLD COUNTRY PARK
Costhorpe Plantation
Langold Lake
Bandstand
Cricket Ground
Sewage Works
Hodsock Woodhouse
Dovecote Cottage
LANE
A60
GHEST VILLAS
Worksop
Honey Hills
144
COSTHORPE VILLAS
Sports Field
COSTHORPE INDUSTRIAL ESTATE
LAWN CT.
WEST VIEW
S81
INGHAM BUNGALOWS
Willow Holt
WOODHOUSE
ROAD
NORTHUMBERLAND AV.
SUTHERLAND DR.
SUTHERLAND CL.
HIGHFIELD VILLAS
Works
Costhorpe
LAWN
WESTMORLAND
CUMBERLAND CL.
Lilac Lodge
Buckwood Farm
ROTHERHAM
BAULK
CHILTERN
PENTLAND
CLEVELAND
BEVERLEY
SALISBURY
LILAC
GRO.
TREE
WILLOW AV.
LICHFIELD
Comm. Cen.
LIME
SQUARE
AVENUE
DADLEY
NORTH WY.
PINFOLD DR.
CORNFIELD
GREENFIELDS
PLOUGH DR.
SHIRE CL.
ROSEHIP
HAWTHORN
BEECH GRO.
CEDAR CL.
SYCAMORE RD.
BRUN
QUEENS RD.
BECKETT
Rec. Grd.
RAMSDEN CRES.
MULBERRY
Roxholm Grange
The Bungalow
KNATON
STEWART
STEWART RD.
KINGSTON RD.
AMANDA AV.
OXFORD
ROAD
LINDRICK CL.
GRANARY CT.
GREEN FARM CT.
The Lodge
LONG
Lib.
THE ARCADE
LANE
HODSOCK
THE GREEN
King George's Field
The Grove
Skewer Farm
WINDSOR GDS.
Hall
OAKHAM DR.
Kingston Park Prim. Sch.
North Carlton
WINDSOR
CARISBROOK RD.
CRAITHIE RD.
CRAGSTON RD.
STIRLING DR.
GLAMIS RD.
PEMBROKE DR.
RICHMOND RD.
CONWAY DR.
MORAL CL.
STRATHAVON RD.
STRATHMORE DR.
KENILWORTH DR.
WARWICK AV.
GRANGE CL.
Jewel Rise
The Forest
GREEN
Newlands
Wallingwells Equestrian Centre
ARUNDEL
DRIVE
THE CROSS
WATER LA.
BRIDGE ROW
BRIDGE HO. CT.
Jerusalem Farm
HIGHFIELD GRO.
Southdown
Five Acres
CARLTON WOOD
CARLTON IN LINDRICK
CHURCH
CHAPEL GA.
STREET
Wallingwells Wood
WALLINGWELLS
Wallingwells
Ramsden Prim. Sch.
Burial Ground
HIGH ROAD
LOW
TINKER'S HILL
CARLTON HALL LANE
Hollin Hills
The Park House
CHURCH LANE
The Lawns
The Rectory
South Carlton
Carlton Lake
Field House Farm
The Ashes
Holme Wood
58
59
460
87
86
385
84
A
B
C
D
E
1
2
3
4
5
6
7

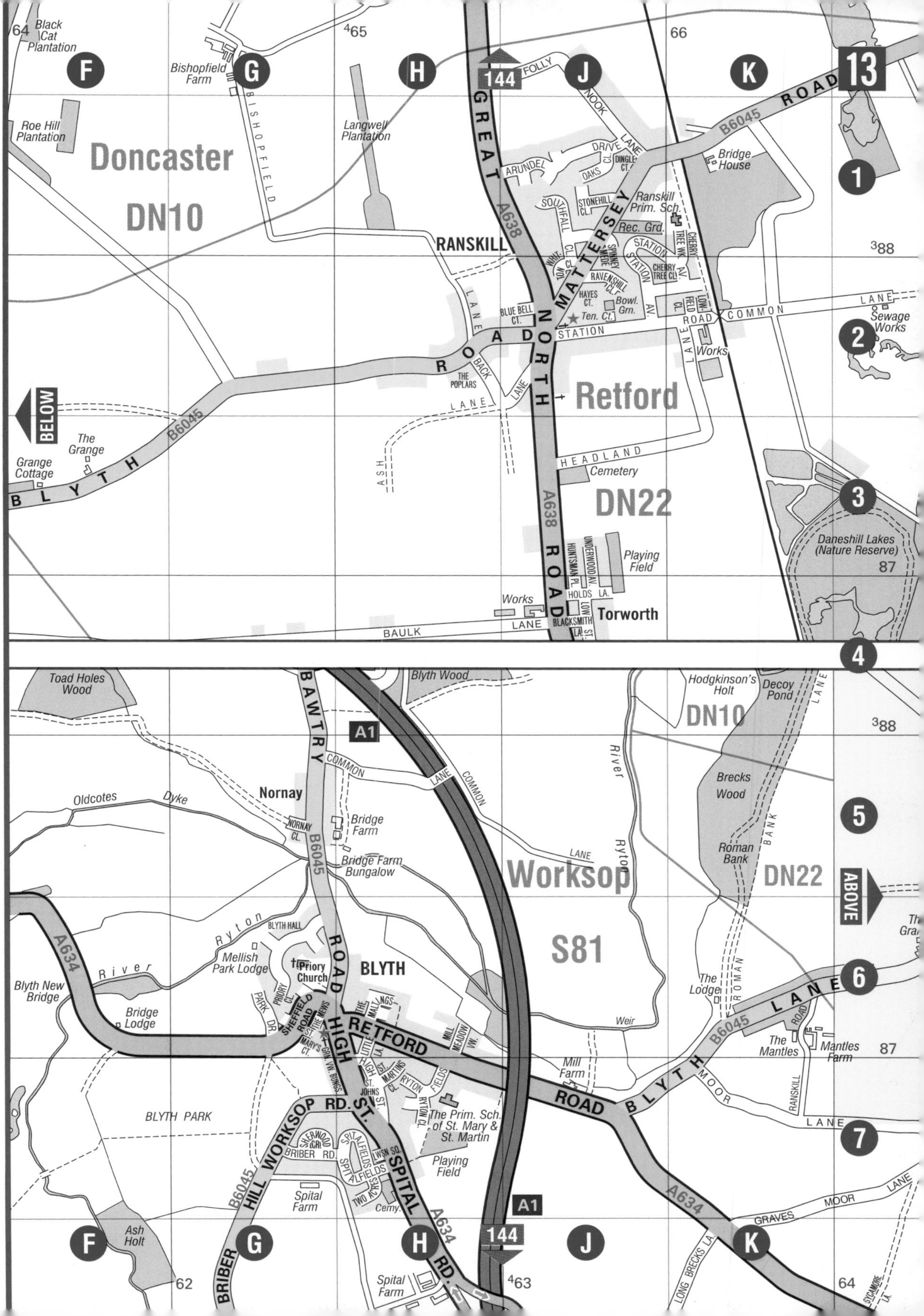

13
Doncaster
DN10
RANSKILL
Retford
DN22
Torworth
Black Cat Plantation
Bishopfield Farm
Roe Hill Plantation
Langwell Plantation
BISHOPFIELD
GREAT NORTH ROAD
A638
144
FOLLY NOOK LANE
B6045 ROAD
Bridge House
ARUNDEL DRIVE
OAKS CL.
DINGLE CT.
SOUTHFALL CL.
STONEHILL CL.
MATTERSEY
Ranskill Prim. Sch.
Rec. Grd.
WHITTON CL.
SPINNEY MEDE
STATION AV.
TREE WK.
CHERRY TREE CL.
RAVENSHILL CL.
HAYES CT.
Bowl. Grn.
Ten. Ct.
BLUE BELL CT.
LOW. FIELD CL.
COMMON LANE
Sewage Works
STATION ROAD
Works
BACK LANE
THE POPLARS
LANE
ASH
HEADLAND
Cemetery
BLYTH B6045 ROAD
The Grange
Grange Cottage
BELOW
Daneshill Lakes (Nature Reserve)
HUNTSMAN PL.
UNDERWOOD AV.
Playing Field
HOLDS LA.
BLACKSMITH LA.
LOW ST.
BAULK LANE
88
87
64
65
66
Toad Holes Wood
Blyth Wood
BAWTRY ROAD
A1
COMMON LANE
Hodgkinson's Holt
Decoy Pond
DN10
Brecks Wood
Roman Bank
DN22
ABOVE
Oldcotes Dyke
Nornay
NORNAY CL.
B6045
Bridge Farm
Bridge Farm Bungalow
River Ryton
Worksop
S81
A634
BLYTH HALL
Mellish Park Lodge
Priory Church
BLYTH
Blyth New Bridge
Bridge Lodge
PRIORY CL.
PARK DR.
SHEFFIELD ROAD
THE MEWS
ST. MARY'S CT.
HIGH ST.
THE MALTINGS
RETFORD ROAD
MILL MEADOW VW.
LITTLE LA.
HIGH ST. MEWS
ST. MARTINS CL.
RYTON FIELDS
ST. JOHNS ST.
RYTON CL.
Weir
Mill Farm
BLYTH ROAD
The Lodge
B6045 LANE
The Mantles
Mantles Farm
MOOR LANE
RANSKILL ROAD
BLYTH PARK
WORKSOP RD.
HILL
SHERWOOD CR.
BRIBER RD.
SPITALFIELDS
TWO ACRES
LWSN SQ.
SPITAL ROAD
The Prim. Sch. of St. Mary & St. Martin
Playing Field
Spital Farm
Cemy.
Ash Holt
BRIBER
GRAVES MOOR LANE
LONG BRECKS LA.
SYCAMORE LA.
62
63
64
F G H J K
1 2 3 4 5 6 7

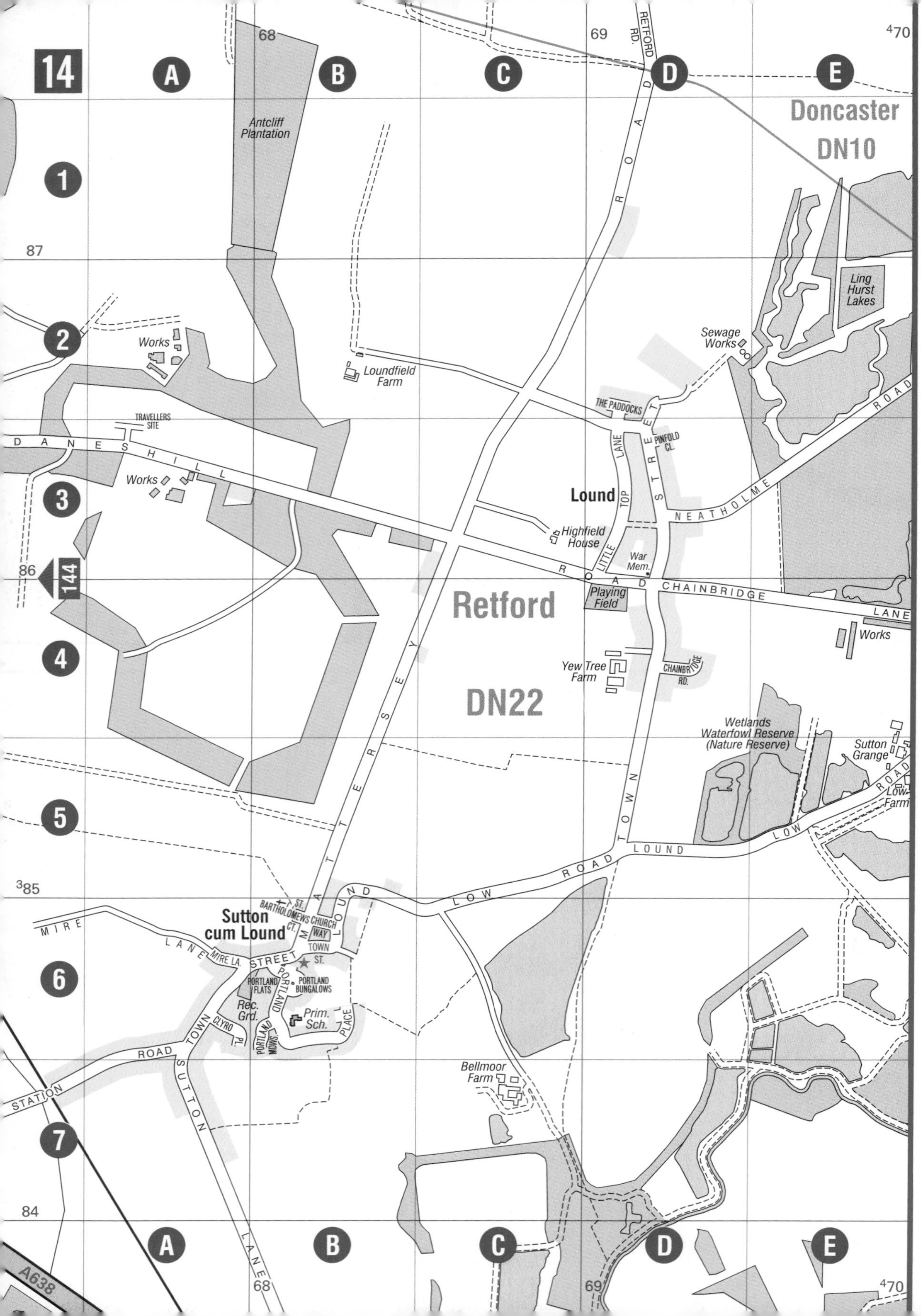
A
B
C
D
E
68
69
470
1
2
3
4
5
6
7
87
86
385
84
144
Doncaster
DN10
Antcliff Plantation
RETFORD RD.
ROAD
Ling Hurst Lakes
Sewage Works
Loundfield Farm
THE PADDOCKS
STREET
PINFOLD CL.
TRAVELLERS SITE
DANESHILL
ROAD
Works
Works
Lound
TOP LANE
NEATHOLME
ROAD
LITTLE
Highfield House
War Mem.
CHAINBRIDGE
LANE
Playing Field
Retford
Works
Yew Tree Farm
CHAINBRIDGE RD.
DN22
MATTERSEY
TOWN
Wetlands Waterfowl Reserve (Nature Reserve)
Sutton Grange
Low Farm
ROAD
LOW
LOUND
ROAD
LOW
LOUND
ST. BARTHOLOMEWS CT.
CHURCH
WAY
Sutton cum Lound
MIRE LANE
MIRE LA.
STREET
TOWN ST.
PORTLAND FLATS
PORTLAND
PORTLAND BUNGALOWS
Rec. Grd.
Prim. Sch.
PLACE
CLYRO PL.
PORTLAND MEWS
ROAD
TOWN
STATION
Bellmoor Farm
SUTTON LANE
A638

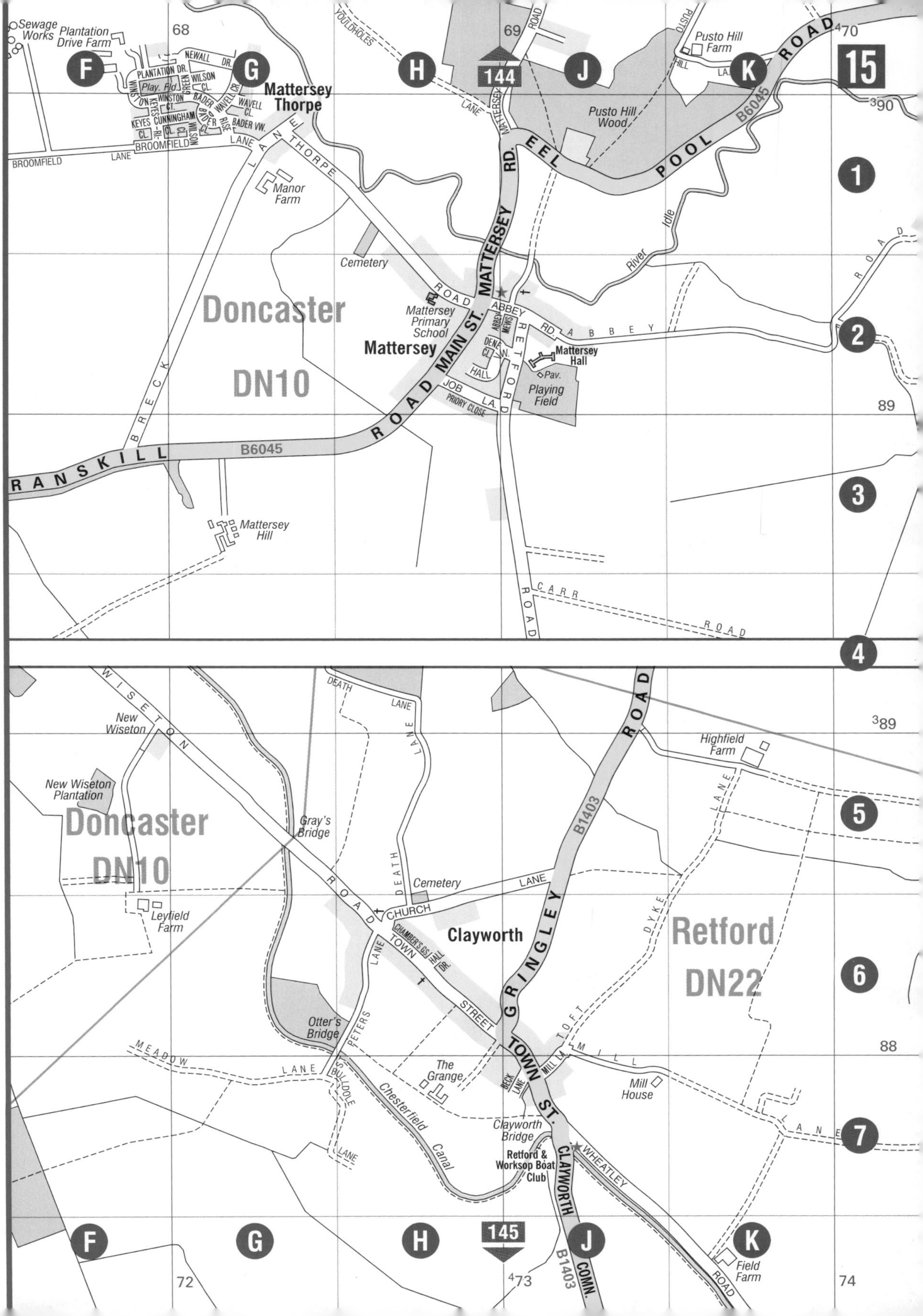
Sewage Works
Plantation Drive Farm
68
69
470
390
NEWALL DR.
PLANTATION DR.
Play. Fld.
GREEN WILSON CL.
WINSTON CT.
WINSTON
KEYES
CUNNINGHAM CL.
KEYES CL.
RI.
BADER RISE
BADER VW.
WAVELL CL.
WAVELL CR.
WILSON
BROOMFIELD
BROOMFIELD LANE
Mattersey Thorpe
THORPE LANE
YOULDHOLES LANE
MATTERSEY
144
Pusto Hill Wood
Pusto Hill Farm
PUSTO HILL LA.
EEL POOL ROAD
B6045
River Idle
Manor Farm
Cemetery
Doncaster
DN10
Mattersey Primary School
Mattersey
ROAD
MATTERSEY RD.
MAIN ST.
ABBEY RD.
ABBEY MEWS
ABBEY
DENE CL.
W.
HALL
RETFORD ROAD
Mattersey Hall
Pav.
Playing Field
JOB LA.
PRIORY CLOSE
89
RANSKILL ROAD
BECK LANE
Mattersey Hill
CARR ROAD
ROAD
F
G
H
J
K
1
2
3
4
5
6
7
WISETON ROAD
New Wiseton
New Wiseton Plantation
Doncaster
DN10
Gray's Bridge
DEATH LANE
LANE
Cemetery
CHURCH LANE
Leyfield Farm
CHAMBER'S GS
HALL DR.
TOWN STREET
Clayworth
GRINGLEY ROAD
B1403
Highfield Farm
389
DYKE
LANE
Retford
DN22
Otter's Bridge
PETERS LANE
MEADOW LANE
BULLDOLE LANE
TOFT
MILL LA.
MILL LANE
88
The Grange
BECK LANE
TOWN ST.
Mill House
Chesterfield Canal
Clayworth Bridge
Retford & Worksop Boat Club
CLAYWORTH COMN.
WHEATLEY ROAD
145
72
473
74
Field Farm

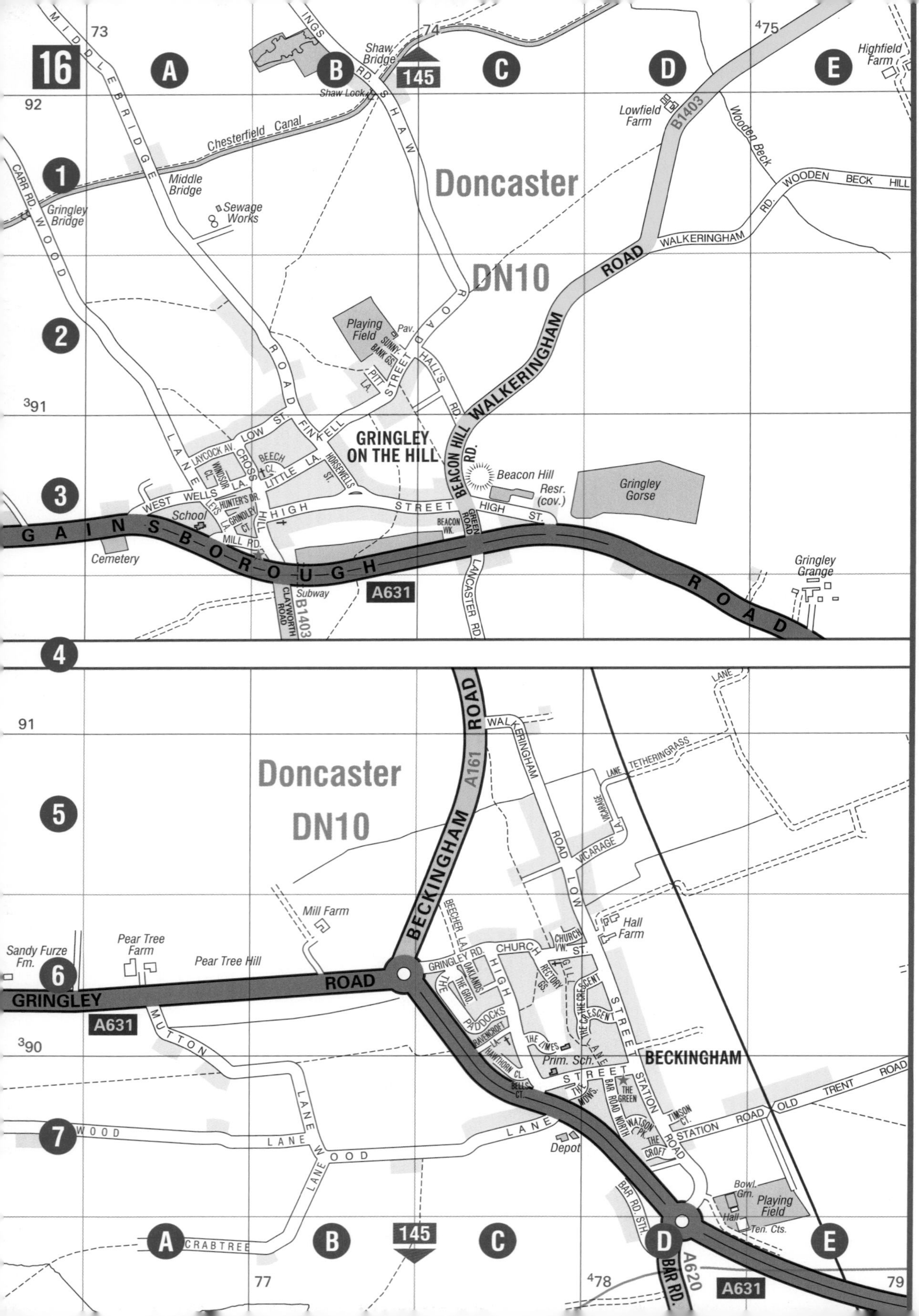
A
B
C
D
E
1
2
3
4
5
6
7
73
74
475
92
391
91
390
77
478
79
145
Shaw Bridge
Shaw Lock
INGS RD.
SHAW ROAD
MIDDLE BRIDGE ROAD
Chesterfield Canal
Middle Bridge
Gringley Bridge
CARR RD.
WOOD LANE
Sewage Works
Highfield Farm
Lowfield Farm
B1403
Wooden Beck
WOODEN BECK HILL
RD.
WALKERINGHAM ROAD
Doncaster
DN10
Playing Field
Pav.
SUNNY BANK GS.
PITT LA.
STREET
HALL'S RD.
BEACON HILL RD.
FINKELL
LOW ST.
LAYCOCK AV.
WINDSOR CL.
CROSS LA.
BEECH CL.
LITTLE LA.
HORSEWELLS ST.
GRINGLEY ON THE HILL
Beacon Hill
Resr. (cov.)
Gringley Gorse
WEST WELLS LA.
HUNTER'S DR.
GRINDLEY CT.
HIGH STREET
HIGH ST.
BEACON WK.
GREEN ROAD
School
MILL RD.
HILL
Cemetery
GAINSBOROUGH ROAD
A631
Subway
CLAYWORTH ROAD
B1403
LANCASTER RD.
Gringley Grange
Doncaster
DN10
BECKINGHAM ROAD
A161
WALKERINGHAM ROAD
LANE
TETHERINGRASS LANE
VICARAGE LA.
LOW
Mill Farm
Hall Farm
BECHER LA.
CHURCH ST.
CHURCH VW.
GILL ST.
Sandy Furze Fm.
Pear Tree Farm
Pear Tree Hill
GRINGLEY ROAD
A631
GRINGLEY RD.
OAKLANDS
THE GRO.
THE PADDOCKS
HIGH
RECTORY GS.
THE CRESCENT
STREET
RAVENSCROFT LA.
THE LIMES
Prim. Sch.
MUTTON LANE
HAWTHORN CL.
BELLS CT.
STREET
THE MDWS.
BAR ROAD NORTH
THE GREEN
BECKINGHAM
STATION ROAD
TIMSON CT.
STATION ROAD
OLD TRENT ROAD
WATSON PK.
THE CROFT
WOOD LANE
Depot
WOOD LANE
CRABTREE
BAR RD. STH.
Bowl. Grn.
Playing Field
Hall
Ten. Cts.
A620
BAR RD.
A631

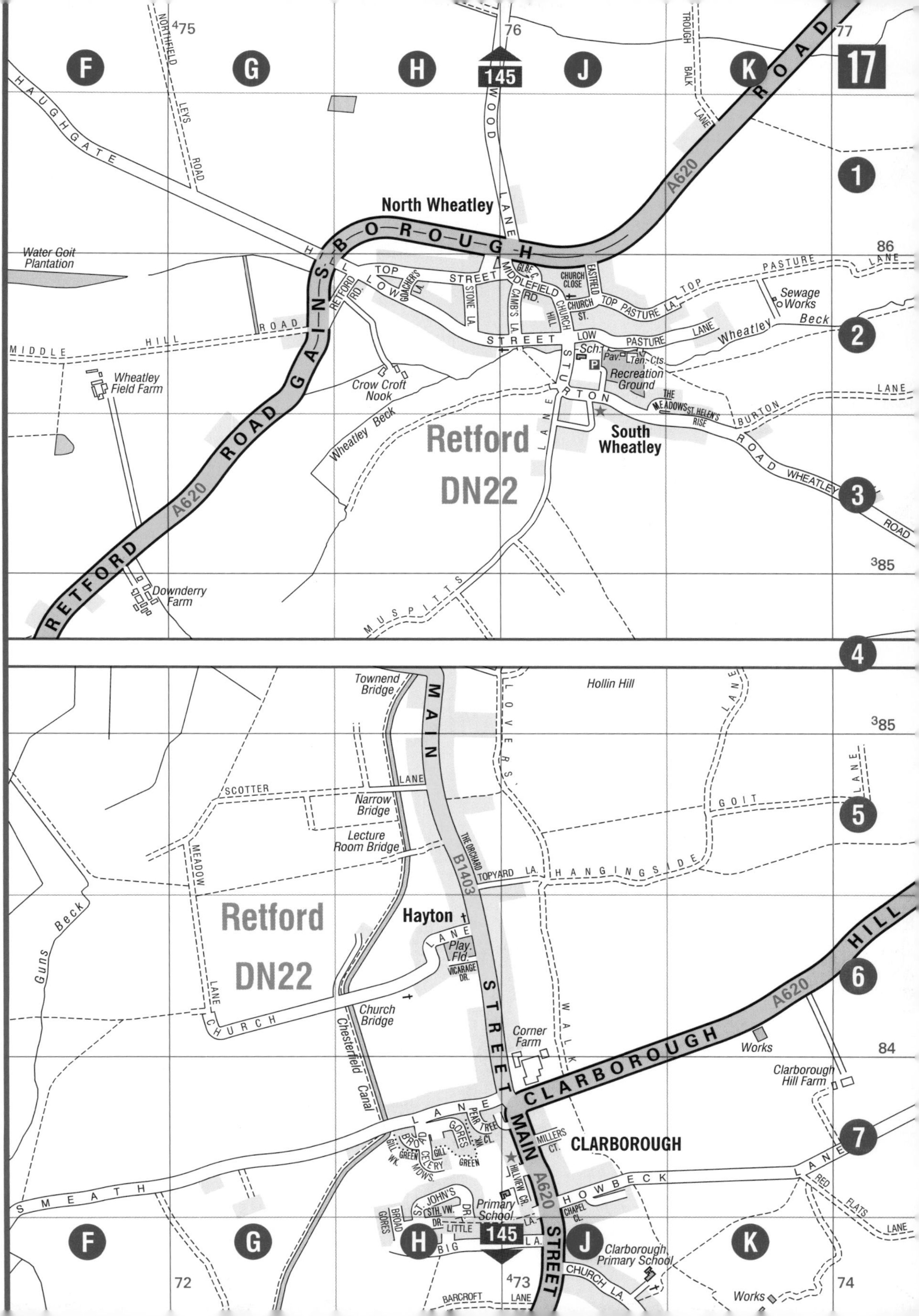

17
145
F
G
H
J
K
1
2
3
4
5
6
7
475
76
77
86
385
84
72
473
74
North Wheatley
South Wheatley
Retford
DN22
Hayton
CLARBOROUGH
HAUGHGATE
NORTHFIELD
LEYS ROAD
WOOD LANE
TROUGH BALK LANE
A620
RETFORD ROAD
GAINSBOROUGH ROAD
Water Goit Plantation
MIDDLE HILL ROAD
TOP STREET
LOW STREET
RETFORD RD.
GOACHER'S LA.
STONE LA.
CAMB'S LA.
MIDDLEFIELD RD.
GLEBE C.
HILL
CHURCH CLOSE
CHURCH HILL
CHURCH ST.
EASTFIELD
TOP PASTURE LA.
TOP PASTURE LANE
LOW PASTURE LANE
Sewage Works
Wheatley Beck
Sch.
Pav.
Ten. Cts.
Recreation Ground
STURTON LANE
BURTON LANE
THE MEADOWS
ST. HELEN'S RISE
BURTON ROAD
WHEATLEY ROAD
Wheatley Field Farm
Crow Croft Nook
Downderry Farm
MUSPITTS
Townend Bridge
Hollin Hill
MAIN STREET
LOVERS WALK
LANE
SCOTTER LANE
Narrow Bridge
Lecture Room Bridge
GOIT LANE
MEADOW LANE
THE ORCHARD
B1403
TOPYARD LA.
HANGINGSIDE
Guns Beck
Play. Fld.
VICARAGE DR.
CHURCH LANE
Church Bridge
Chesterfield Canal
Corner Farm
Works
CLARBOROUGH HILL
Clarborough Hill Farm
PEAR TREE CL.
GORES
MILLERS CT.
BROAD GORES
GILL WK.
GREEN
CELERY MDWS.
GILL GREEN
HILLVIEW CR.
HOWBECK LANE
RED FLATS LANE
SMEATH
ST. JOHN'S DR.
STH. VW. DR.
Primary School
LITTLE LA.
BIG LA.
CHAPEL CL.
Clarborough Primary School
CHURCH LA.
BARCROFT LANE

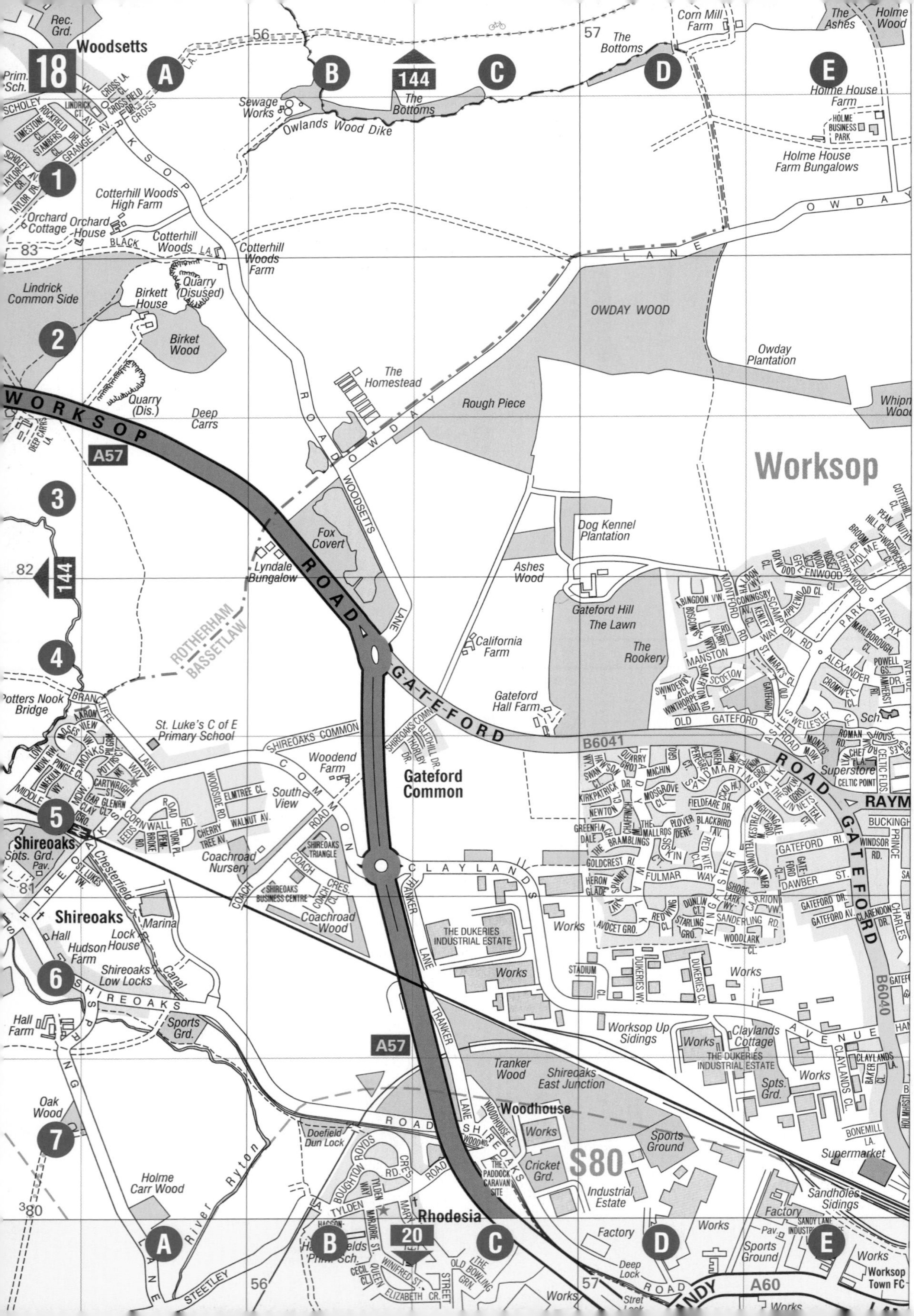

18
Woodsetts
A
B
C
D
E
144
1
2
3
4
5
6
7
56
57
83
82
81
80
Rec. Grd.
Prim. Sch.
Sewage Works
The Bottoms
Owlands Wood Dike
Corn Mill Farm
The Ashes
Holme Wood
Holme House Farm
HOLME BUSINESS PARK
Holme House Farm Bungalows
OWDAY LANE
Cotterhill Woods High Farm
Orchard Cottage
Orchard House
BLACK LA.
Cotterhill Woods
Cotterhill Woods Farm
Quarry (Disused)
Lindrick Common Side
Birkett House
Birket Wood
OWDAY WOOD
Owday Plantation
The Homestead
Rough Piece
Quarry (Dis.)
Deep Carrs
WORKSOP ROAD
A57
WOODSETTS LANE
Fox Covert
Lyndale Bungalow
ROTHERHAM
BASSETLAW
Worksop
Dog Kennel Plantation
Ashes Wood
Gateford Hill
The Lawn
The Rookery
California Farm
Gateford Hall Farm
GATEFORD ROAD
B6041
Potters Nook Bridge
St. Luke's C of E Primary School
SHIREOAKS COMMON
Woodend Farm
Gateford Common
South View
Coachroad Nursery
SHIREOAKS TRIANGLE
SHIREOAKS BUSINESS CENTRE
Coachroad Wood
CLAYLANDS
TRANKER LANE
THE DUKERIES INDUSTRIAL ESTATE
Works
STADIUM
Shireoaks
Spts. Grd.
Pav.
Chesterfield
Marina
Hall
Hudson Farm
Lock House
Shireoaks Low Locks
Canal
SHIREOAKS
Sports Grd.
Hall Farm
Worksop Up Sidings
Claylands Cottage
AVENUE
Tranker Wood
Shireoaks East Junction
Woodhouse
Sports Ground
Cricket Grd.
S80
Industrial Estate
Oak Wood
Doefield Dun Lock
Holme Carr Wood
River Ryton
Rhodesia
20
Factory
Deep Lock
Sports Ground
Supermarket
Sandholes Sidings
Worksop Town FC
A60
STEETLEY LANE
Superstore
RAYM
B6040
GATEFORD

58
59
460
South Carlton
Field House Farm
CHURCH LA.
F
G
H
J
K
19
144
21
WIGTHORPE LA.
LIQUORICE
Wigthorpe Hill
TINKER'S HILL LANE
CROSSLEY HILL
LANE
Kegham End Plantation
Owday Lodge
LANE
Wigthorpe
Wigthorpe Farm
Wigthorpe Cottage
Wigthorpe House
HUNDRED ACRE LANE
Forest Bungalow
1
Broom Covert
Hardwick Ashes
Toll Bar Cottage
Council Depot
83
Keepers Ashes
BRECK LANE
Roundwood House
Broom Farm
Broom Cottage
Round Wood
Little Broom Wood
Nab's Ashes Wood
2
Breck House
Black Wood
Equestrian Centre
Silverdale
Glebe House
LANE
Sand Hill Plantation
Peaks Hill
Kenwood
Lyn Dor
3
Carlton Forest Fm. Cotts.
Freshfields
Black Screed
Peaks Hill Farm
Eddison Plantation
Woodland Grove Farm
82
Carlton Forest Farm
Long Plantation
Gateford Hill
CARLTON ROAD
A60
B6045
4
S81
Thievesdale House
EDDISON PARK AVENUE
THIEVESDALE LANE
Playing Field
Gateford
St. John's C of E Prim. Sch.
B6041
THIEVESDALE LA.
FARMERS BRANCH
5
Recreation Ground
Lib.
81
Jun. & Inf. Schs.
Play. Fld.
Champion's Plantation
Club House
6
KILTON HILL
KILTON FOREST GOLF COURSE
Spts. Grd.
Worksop Leisure Cen.
Playing Field
Pav.
Resrs. (covered)
Greenacre Cen.
Sunnyside
BASSETLAW HOSPITAL
7
Valley Comp. Sch.
Playing Field
Wks.
Coll.
Play. Fld.
Prim. Sch.
BLYTH ROAD
380
TURNER RD.
SANDY LA. RETAIL PARK
TURNER RD. IND. EST.
Worksop
St. Augustine's

18
146
146
A
B
C
D
E
1
2
3
4
5
6
7
Rhodesia
WORKSOP
Worksop
S80
A57
A60
A619
MANSFIELD ROAD
SANDY LANE
NEWCASTLE
STEETLEY LANE
SPRING LANE
BROAD LANE
CASTLE FARM
Chesterfield
Doefield Dun Lock
Holme Carr
River Ryton
Haggonfields Prim. Sch.
TYLDEN WAY
MARJORIE ST.
MABLE ST.
WINIFRED ST.
QUEEN ELIZABETH CR.
CECIL CL.
MARY STREET
THE OLD BOWLING GRN.
SHIREOAKS
THE PADDOCK
Cricket Grd.
Industrial Estate
Sports Ground
Works
Factory
Supermarket
SANDY LANE INDUSTRIAL ESTATE
Pav.
Worksop Town FC
Deep Lock
Stret Lock
HIGH GROUNDS WAY
HIGH GROUNDS ROAD
STUBBING LANE
Depot
Sch.
Lady Lea
Lady Lee Quarry Nature Reserve
Lady Lea Farm
Darfoulds Dike
Morse Lock
Weir
Rugby Grd.
Sports Grd.
Meadowholme Farm
River Ryton
BEAUMONT RI.
BEAUMONT RISE
HESLOP CT.
ACKFORD DR.
CUSWORTH WY.
TEAGUE PL.
UNDERWOOD GDS.
Manor Lodge
Lodge Farm
ST. ANNES DRIVE
ST. ANNES WAY
ST. ANNES CL.
GLEBE CL.
OAKWOOD M.
WESTWOOD DR.
HAWTHORN CL.
ASHWOOD RD.
LINDBERGH CL.
MALLORY DR.
ACACIA CL.
BRIAR CL.
PASTURE CL.
MILL FIELD VW.
MILL GDS.
MEADOW DRIVE
LEA CT.
HAZELWOOD
BIRCHFIELD DR.
SPRUCE CT.
ALPINE CT.
NURSERY GDS.
MEADOW DR.
THE DENE
HALLIDAY CL.
CARLING
MILL HOUSE PARK
Park Cott.
The Old Vicarage
HALL DR.
WATER MEADOWS
SAXTON CL.
DEVONSHIRE
FEATHERBED LANE
Hill Top Cottage
Darfoulds
Darfoulds Farm
HIGH PK.
Nursery
The Croft
Harness Grove
Menagerie Cottage
Menagerie Wood
Manor Park House
WEST WOOD
WORKSOP MANOR
Lodge
Steetley Corner
MANOR PARK
Ratcliffe Grange Farm
Hawk's Nest
Hawk's Nest Screed
Pudding Hill Wood
Castle Farm
Oak Wood
Round Spinney
New Farm
Wallingbrook Wood
Ox Pastures Farm
Works
380
79
78
77
56
57

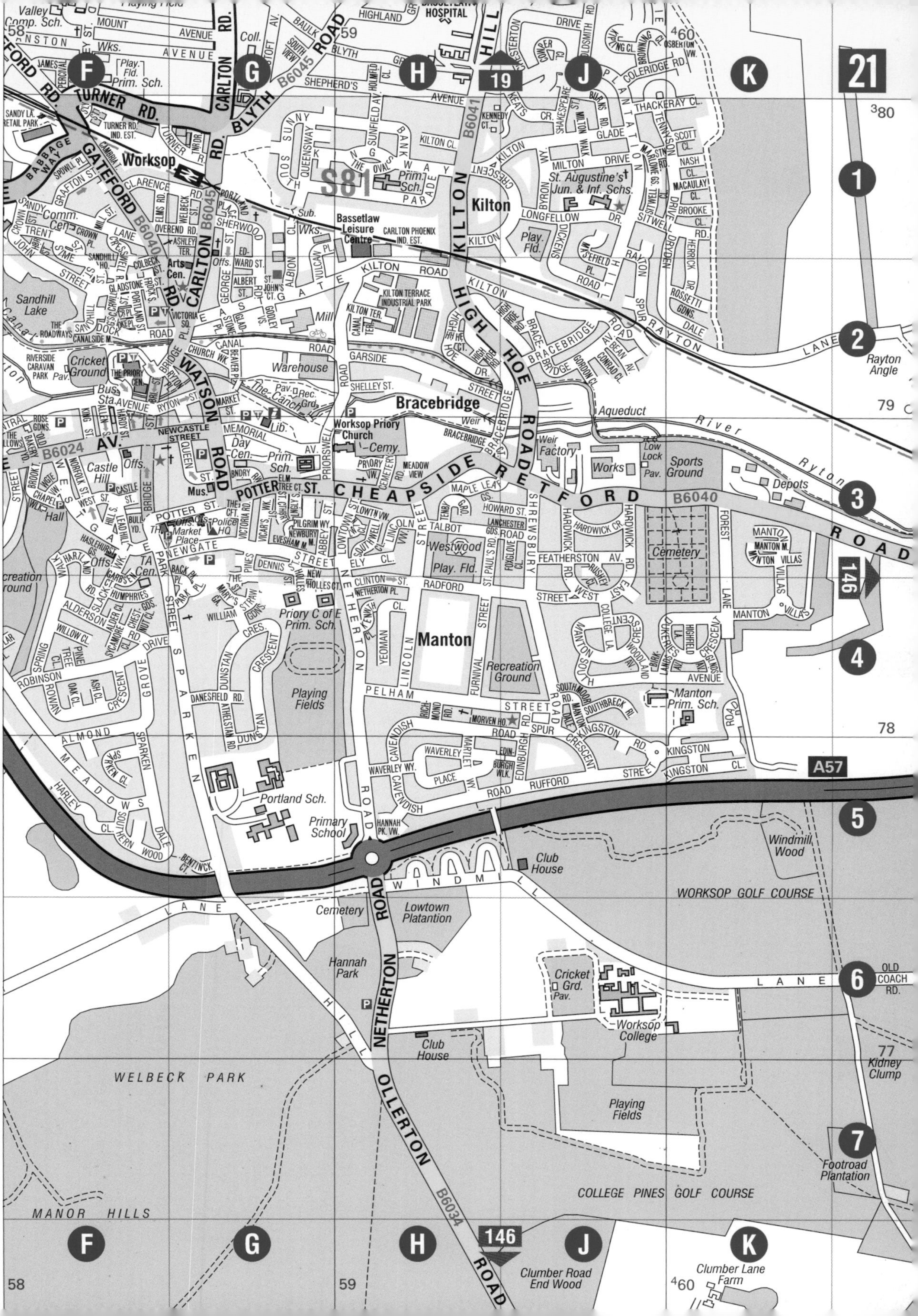
Worksop
S81
Kilton
Bracebridge
Manton
Bassetlaw Leisure Centre
Bassetlaw Hospital
Carlton Phoenix Ind. Est.
Kilton Terrace Industrial Park
Worksop Priory Church
Cemy.
Lib.
Mus.
Police HQ
Offs.
Market Place
Bus Sta.
The Priory Cen.
Arts Cen.
Cricket Ground
Riverside Caravan Park
Sandhill Lake
Canal
The Canch
Warehouse
Mill
Wks.
Sub.
Aqueduct
River Ryton
Weir
Factory
Works
Low Lock
Sports Ground
Depots
Cemetery
St. Augustine's Jun. & Inf. Schs.
Prim. Sch.
Play. Fld.
Priory C of E Prim. Sch.
Recreation Ground
Playing Fields
Portland Sch.
Primary School
Manton Prim. Sch.
Castle Hill
Westwood Play. Fld.
Day Cen.
Comm. Cen.
TA Cen.
Club House
Windmill Wood
WORKSOP GOLF COURSE
Lowtown Platantion
Hannah Park
Cricket Grd.
Pav.
Worksop College
WELBECK PARK
MANOR HILLS
Playing Fields
Footroad Plantation
Kidney Clump
COLLEGE PINES GOLF COURSE
Clumber Road End Wood
Clumber Lane Farm
Rayton Angle
CARLTON RD.
BLYTH RD.
GATEFORD RD.
TURNER RD.
WATSON RD.
KILTON HILL
HIGH HOE ROAD
KILTON ROAD
CHEAPSIDE
RETFORD ROAD
POTTER ST.
NEWCASTLE AV.
PARK STREET
SPARKEN
NETHERTON ROAD
OLLERTON ROAD
WINDMILL LANE
OLD COACH RD.
RAYTON LANE
RAYTON SPUR
SHREWSBURY ROAD
RADFORD STREET
PELHAM STREET
RUFFORD ROAD
KINGSTON RD.
MANTON VILLAS
ELY CL.
LINCOLN STREET
FURNIVAL STREET
ST. PAUL'S RD.
FEATHERSTON AV.
HARDWICK RD.
FOREST LANE
DUNSTAN CRESCENT
GROVE CRESCENT
MEADOWS
ALMOND
ROBINSON
SPRING
A57
B6040
B6041
B6045
B6024
B6034
19
146
F G H J K
1 2 3 4 5 6 7
58 59 460
380 79 78 77

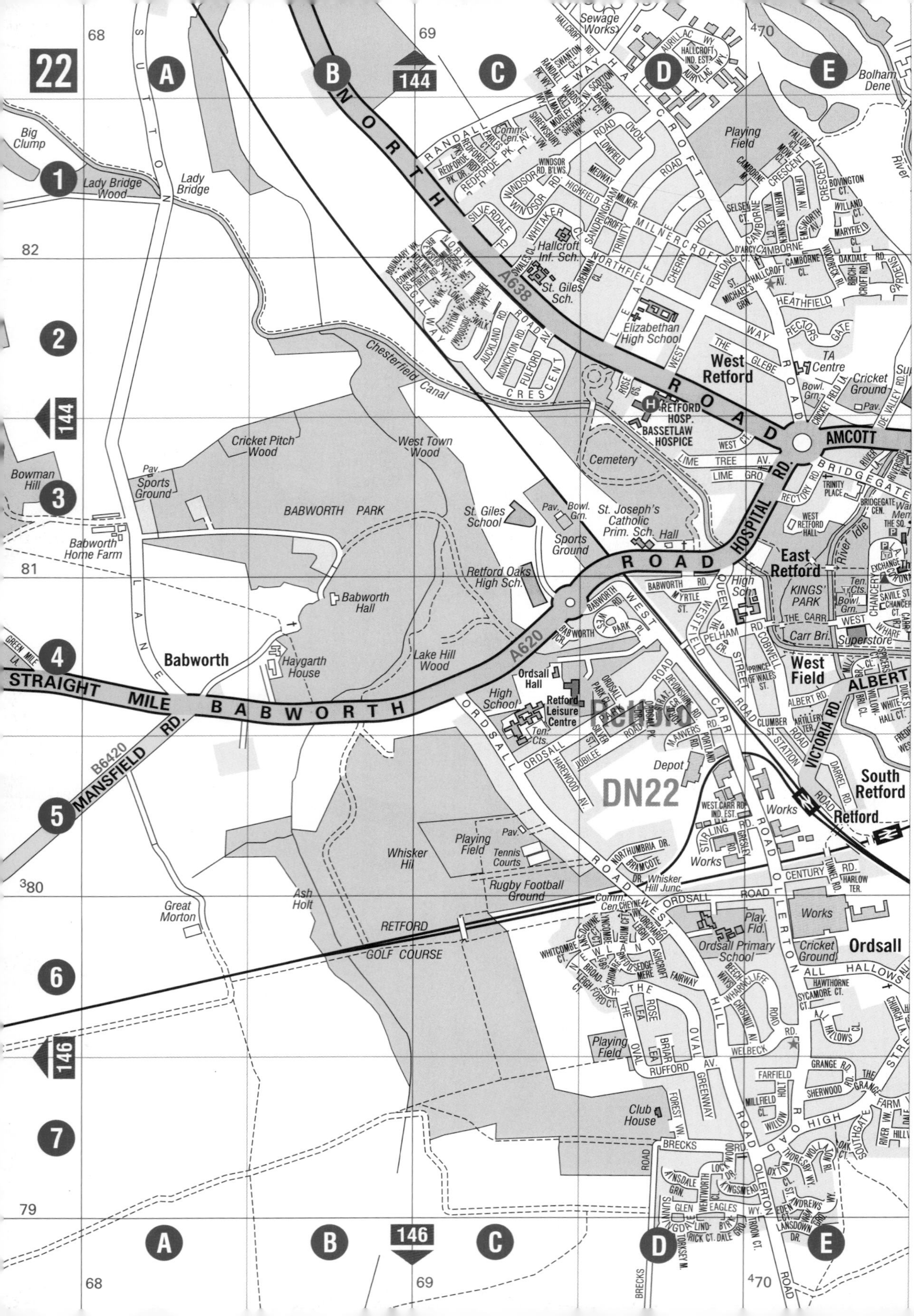

68
69
470
144
146
A
B
C
D
E
1
2
3
4
5
6
7
82
81
380
79
Big Clump
Lady Bridge Wood
Lady Bridge
SUTTON LANE
NORTH ROAD
A638
Sewage Works
Bolham Dene
River
Playing Field
Hallcroft Inf. Sch.
St. Giles Sch.
Elizabethan High School
West Retford
TA Centre
Cricket Ground
Chesterfield Canal
Cricket Pitch Wood
West Town Wood
RETFORD HOSP.
BASSETLAW HOSPICE
Cemetery
AMCOTT
BRIDGEGATE
HOSPITAL RD.
Bowman Hill
Sports Ground
BABWORTH PARK
St. Giles School
St. Joseph's Catholic Prim. Sch.
Hall
Babworth Home Farm
Retford Oaks High Sch.
Babworth Hall
ROAD
East Retford
KINGS' PARK
Carr Bri.
Superstore
Babworth
Haygarth House
Lake Hill Wood
A620
Ordsall Hall
Retford Leisure Centre
High School
West Field
ALBERT
STRAIGHT MILE
BABWORTH
MANSFIELD RD.
B6420
Retford
DN22
Depot
Works
South Retford
Retford
VICTORIA RD.
Playing Field
Whisker Hill
Tennis Courts
Ash Holt
Rugby Football Ground
Whisker Hill Junc.
Great Morton
RETFORD GOLF COURSE
Ordsall Primary School
Cricket Ground
Ordsall
ALL HALLOWS
Playing Field
Club House
OLLERTON ROAD
HIGH
BRECKS

23
RETFORD
Bolham
Bolham Manor
Moorgate Farm
Longholme Farm
Clarborough Hall
Welham
Welham Hall
THE GARDEN (CARAVAN PARK)
Little Gringley
Whitsunday Pie Lock
Carr Hill Prim. Sch.
Chesterfield Canal
Recreation Ground
Balk Field
Works
The Meadows
Playing Field
High Sch.
Bracken Lodge Farm
Newton Farm
Newtown
Thrumpton
Running Track
Sports Ground
Tennis Ct.
Bracken Lane Prim. Sch.
Bracken Lane Farm
Walmoor
Fairfield
Swindell Spring Wood
Morgan's Plantation
Top Lodge Plantation
GROVE PARK
The Rookery
Kennels Plantation
White Houses
Play. Fld.
Bowling Grn.
Play. Field
River Idle
MOORGATE
WELHAM ROAD
A620
LONDON ROAD
A638
ARLINGTON WAY
LEVERTON ROAD
GROVE LANE
BRACKEN LANE
GROVE COACH ROAD
SHADY LANE
PINFOLD LANE
LITTLE GRINGLEY LANE
BONE MILL LA.
BLACKSTOPE LANE
GOOSEMOOR LA.
WHITEHOUSES RD.
WHINNEY MOOR LA.
GROVE
145
147
F
G
H
J
K
1
2
3
4
5
6
7
71
72
73
79
80
81
82

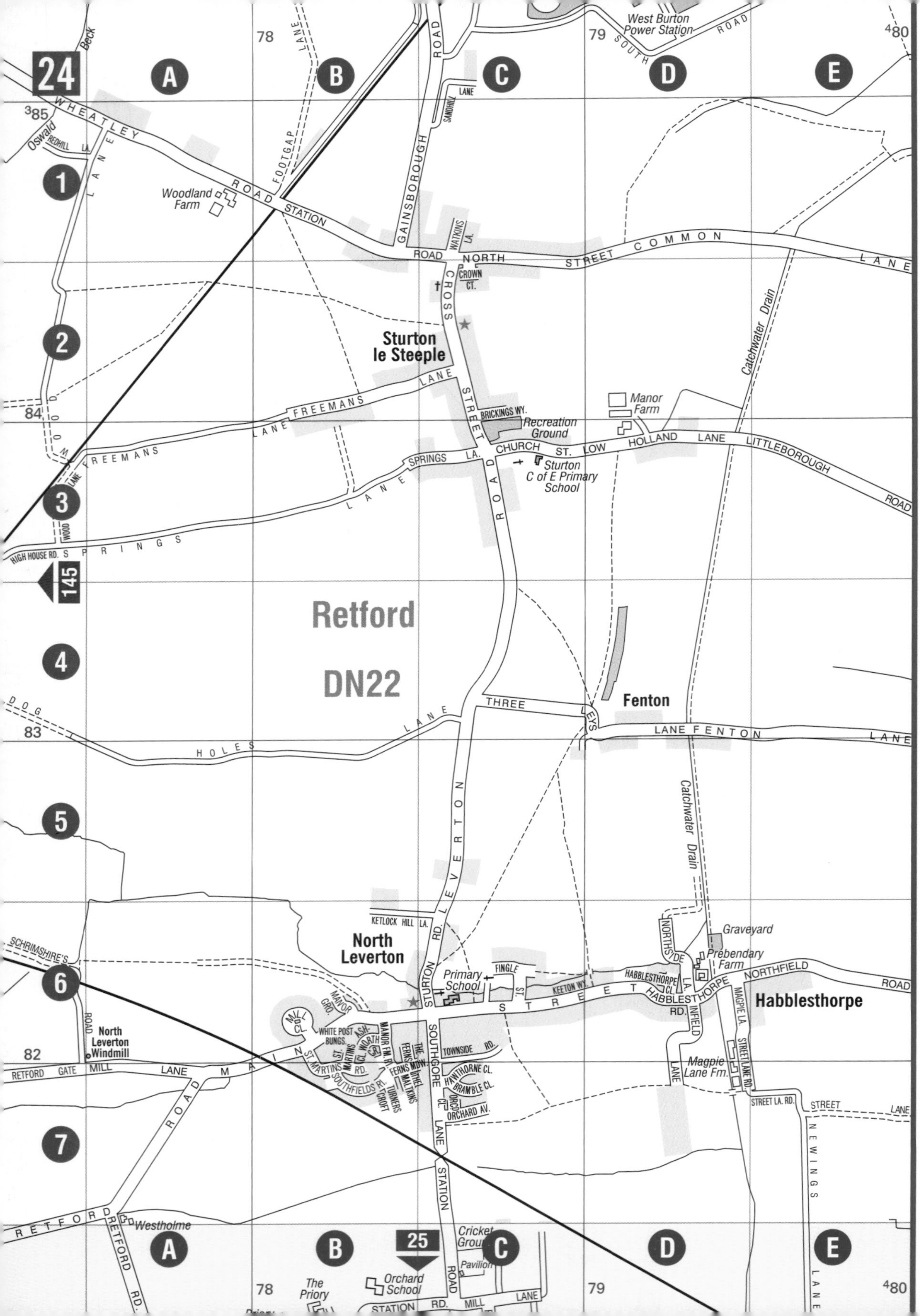

24
West Burton Power Station
Sturton le Steeple
Retford
DN22
Fenton
North Leverton
Habblesthorpe
North Leverton Windmill
Woodland Farm
Manor Farm
Recreation Ground
Sturton C of E Primary School
Primary School
Graveyard
Prebendary Farm
Magpie Lane Fm.
Westholme
Cricket Ground
Pavilion
The Priory
Orchard School
Catchwater Drain
WHEATLEY ROAD
STATION ROAD
GAINSBOROUGH ROAD
NORTH STREET
COMMON LANE
CROSS STREET
CHURCH ST.
LOW HOLLAND LANE
LITTLEBOROUGH ROAD
FREEMANS LANE
SPRINGS LANE
HIGH HOUSE RD.
WOOD LANE
THREE LEYS LANE
FENTON LANE
DOG HOLES LANE
LEVERTON ROAD
STURTON RD.
KETLOCK HILL LA.
MAIN STREET
NORTHFIELD ROAD
RETFORD GATE
MILL LANE
RETFORD ROAD
STATION LANE
SOUTHGORE LANE
NEWINGS LANE
FOOTGAP LANE
SANDHILL LANE
WATKINS LA.
CROWN CT.
BRICKINGS WY.
REDHILL LA.
Oswald
Beck
SCHRIMSHIRE'S
MANOR GRO.
MILL CL.
WHITE POST BUNGS.
TOWNSIDE RD.
HAWTHORNE CL.
BRAMBLE CL.
ORCHARD AV.
KEETON WY.
FINGLE ST.
HABBLESTHORPE CL.
HABBLESTHORPE RD.
NORTHSIDE LA.
INFIELD LANE
MAGPIE LA.
STREET LANE RD.
STREET LA. RD.
ST. MARTINS RD.
SOUTHFIELDS RI.
TURNERS CROFT
THE FERNS
MALTKINS
145
25
78
79
480
385
84
83
82

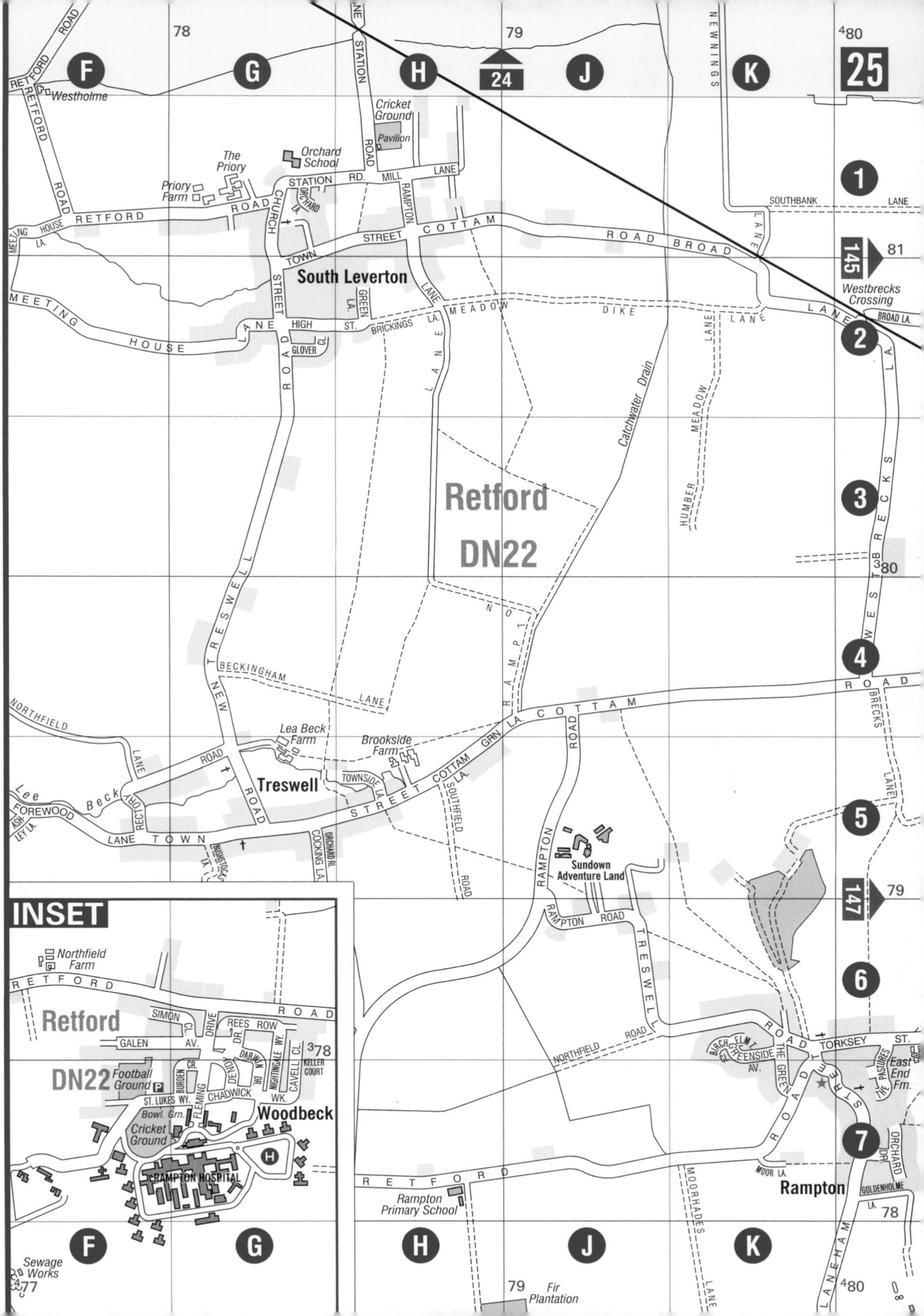
78
79
480
F
G
H
J
K
24
145
81
147
79
1
2
3
4
5
6
7
South Leverton
Treswell
Retford
DN22
Westholme
Cricket Ground
Pavilion
Orchard School
The Priory
Priory Farm
Westbrecks Crossing
Catchwater Drain
Lea Beck Farm
Brookside Farm
Lee Beck
Sundown Adventure Land
Rampton Primary School
Rampton
East End Fm.
Fir Plantation
380
RETFORD ROAD
STATION ROAD
STATION RD.
MILL LANE
RAMPTON LANE
CHURCH LA.
ORCHARD LA.
COTTAM ROAD
BROAD LANE
BROAD LA.
SOUTHBANK LANE
NEWNINGS LANE
TOWN STREET
MEETING HOUSE LA.
MEETING HOUSE LANE
HIGH ST.
GREEN LA.
GLOVER CL.
BRICKINGS LA.
MEADOW DIKE LANE
MEADOW LANE
HUMBER LANE
WESTBRECKS LA.
BRECKS LANE
TRESWELL ROAD
NEW LANE
BECKINGHAM LANE
NORTHFIELD LANE
RECTORY ROAD
FOREWOOD LANE
ASHLEY LA.
TOWN STREET
TOWNSIDE LA.
COTTAM GRN LA.
SOUTHFIELD LA.
SOUTHFIELD ROAD
COCKING LA.
ORCHARD RI.
BUSHSTOCKS
RAMPTON ROAD
TRESWELL ROAD
NORTHFIELD ROAD
TORKSEY ST.
BIRCH CL.
ELM T.
GREENSIDE AV.
THE GREEN
TORKSEY STREET
THE PASTURES
ORCHARD DR.
GOLDENHOLME LA.
MOOR LA.
MOORHADES LANE
LANEHAM ROAD
RETFORD ROAD
78
480
INSET
Northfield Farm
RETFORD ROAD
Retford
DN22
SIMON CL.
GALEN AV.
DRIVE
REES ROW
DENBY DR.
DARWIN DR.
NIGHTINGALE WY.
CAVELL CL.
KELLER COURT
378
Football Ground
BURDEN CR.
FLEMING
CHADWICK WK.
ST. LUKES WY.
Woodbeck
Bowl. Grn.
Cricket Ground
RAMPTON HOSPITAL
Sewage Works
477
F
G

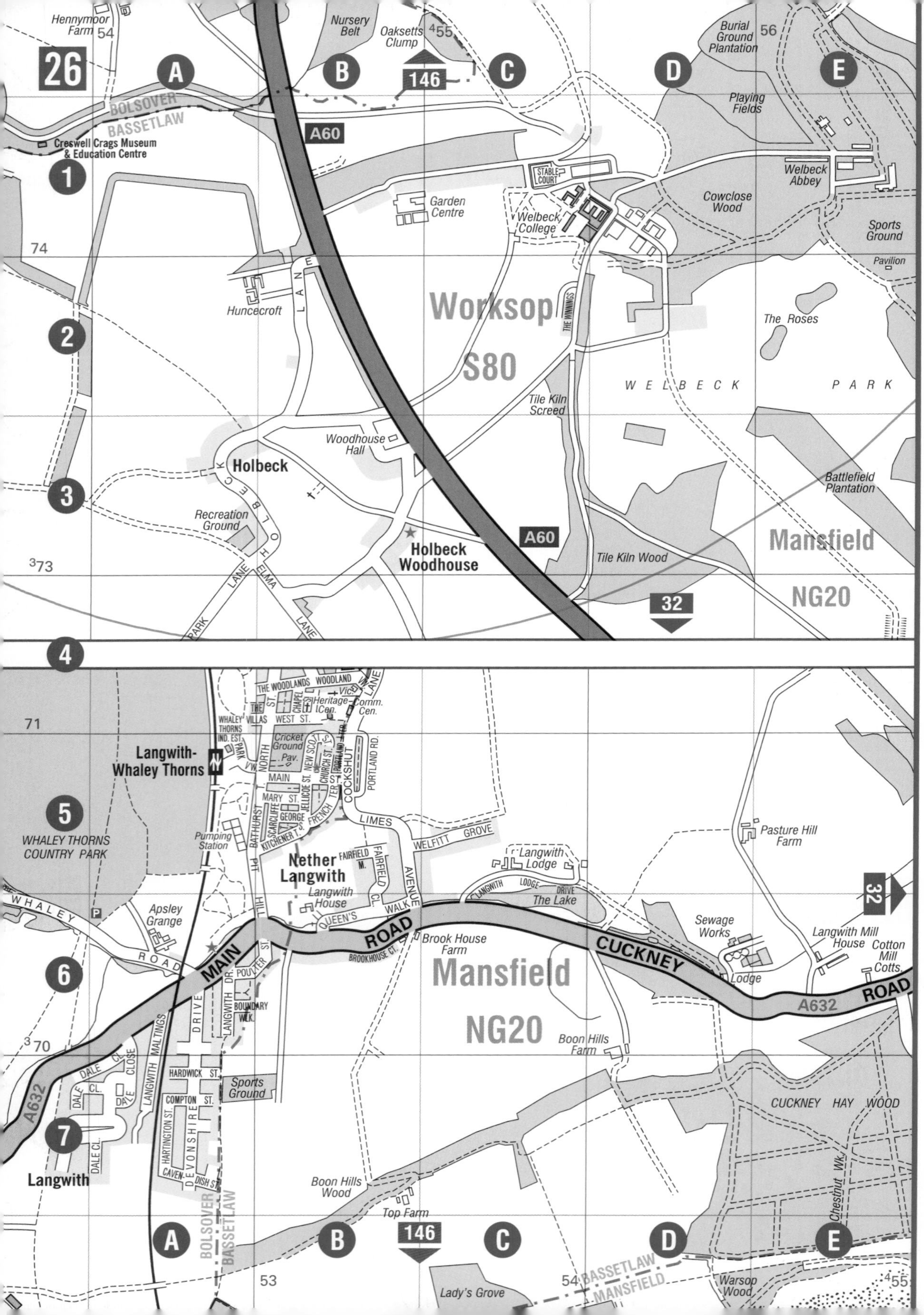
26
Hennymoor Farm
Nursery Belt
Oakstts Clump
Burial Ground Plantation
146
A60
BOLSOVER
BASSETLAW
Creswell Crags Museum & Education Centre
Playing Fields
STABLE COURT
Garden Centre
Welbeck College
Welbeck Abbey
Cowclose Wood
Sports Ground
Pavilion
Huncecroft
LANE
Worksop
S80
THE WINNINGS
The Roses
WELBECK PARK
Tile Kiln Screed
Woodhouse Hall
Holbeck
HOLBECK
Battlefield Plantation
Recreation Ground
Holbeck Woodhouse
Tile Kiln Wood
Mansfield
NG20
PARK LANE
ELMA LANE
32
THE WOODLANDS
WOODLAND
CHAPEL ST.
Vic.
Heritage Cen.
Comm. Cen.
WHALEY THORNS IND. EST.
THE VILLAS
WEST ST.
Cricket Ground
Pav.
NORTH ST.
MAIN ST.
NEW SCOT ST.
CHURCH ST.
PORTLAND TER.
COCKSHUT LANE
PORTLAND RD.
Langwith-Whaley Thorns
PARK VW.
MARY ST.
JELLICOE ST.
SCARCLIFFE
GEORGE ST.
FRENCH TER.
KITCHENER T.
BATHURST T.
LIMES AVENUE
WELFITT GROVE
Pumping Station
WHALEY THORNS COUNTRY PARK
Pasture Hill Farm
Langwith Lodge
Nether Langwith
FAIRFIELD
FAIRFIELD CL.
Langwith House
LANGWITH LODGE DRIVE
The Lake
QUEEN'S WALK
PIT HILL
WHALEY ROAD
Apsley Grange
Sewage Works
Langwith Mill House
Cotton Mill Cotts.
MAIN ROAD
Brook House Farm
BROOKHOUSE CT.
CUCKNEY ROAD
Lodge
A632
POUTER ST.
LANGWITH DR.
BOUNDARY WLK.
DRIVE
LANGWITH MALTINGS
Boon Hills Farm
DALE CL.
DALE CLOSE
HARDWICK ST.
Sports Ground
COMPTON ST.
CUCKNEY HAY WOOD
DEVONSHIRE
HARTINGTON ST.
CAVEN
DISH ST.
Langwith
Boon Hills Wood
Top Farm
Chestnut Wk.
BOLSOVER
BASSETLAW
MANSFIELD
Lady's Grove
Warsop Wood

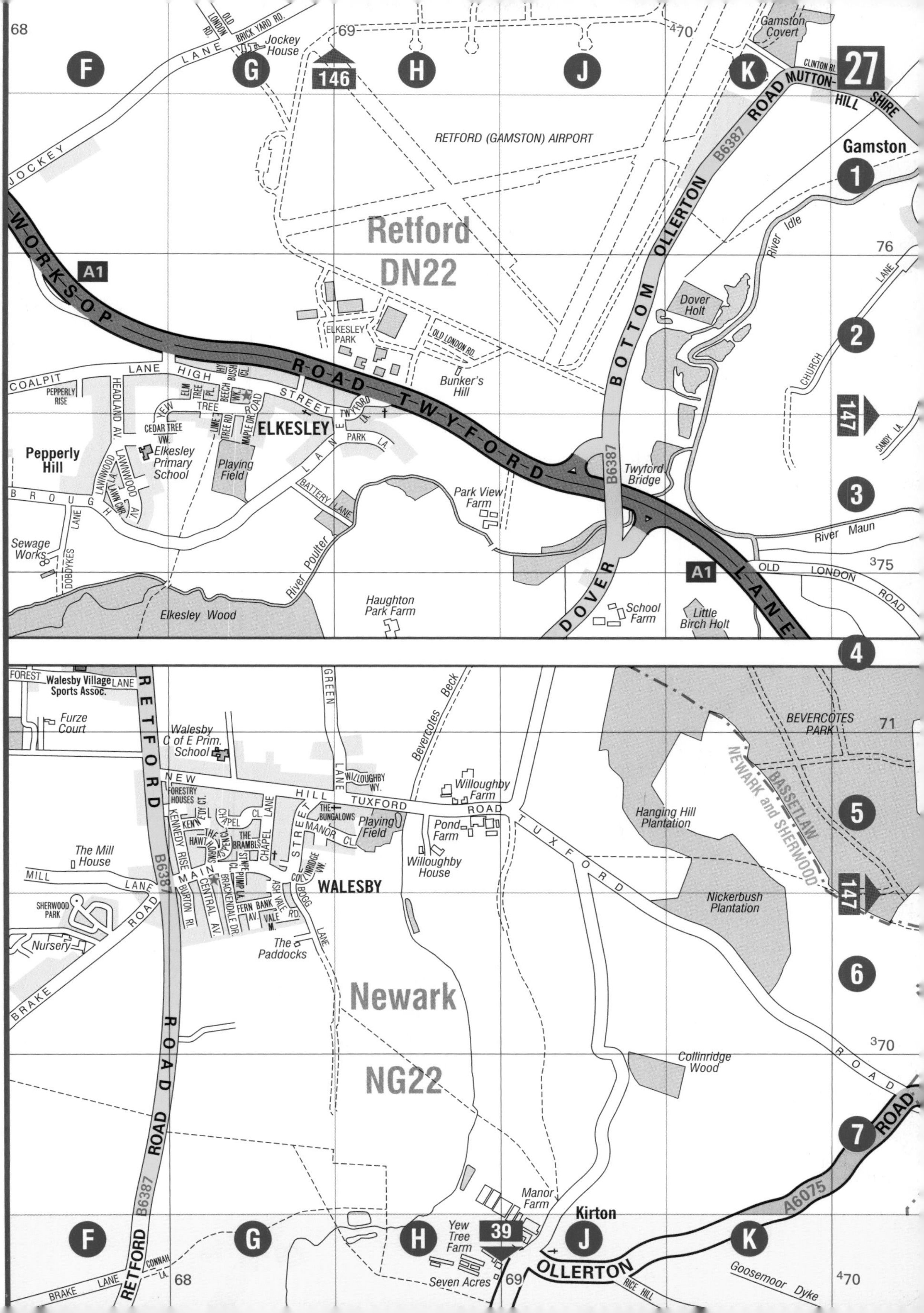

68
69
470
F
G
H
J
K
27
146
147
39
1
2
3
4
5
6
7
76
375
71
370
Jockey House
JOCKEY LANE
BRICK YARD RD.
OLD LONDON RD.
Gamston Covert
CLINTON RI.
MUTTON-HILL
SHIRE
ROAD
RETFORD (GAMSTON) AIRPORT
Gamston
B6387
BOTTOM OLLERTON
River Idle
Retford
DN22
A1
WORKSOP ROAD
TWYFORD
LANE
Dover Holt
CHURCH
ELKESLEY PARK
OLD LONDON RD.
Bunker's Hill
COALPIT LANE
HIGH STREET
PEPPERLY RISE
HEADLAND AV.
YEW TREE
ELM TREE PL.
BEECH WK.
BUSH CL.
CEDAR TREE VW.
LIME TREE RD.
MAPLE DR.
ELKESLEY
TWYFORD LA.
PARK LA.
SANDY LA.
Pepperly Hill
Elkesley Primary School
Playing Field
LAWNWOOD LA.
LAWNWOOD AV.
LAWN CHR.
BROUGH LANE
BATTERY LANE
Park View Farm
Twyford Bridge
River Maun
Sewage Works
DOBDYKES LANE
River Poulter
OLD LONDON ROAD
Haughton Park Farm
School Farm
Little Birch Holt
DOVER
Elkesley Wood
FOREST LANE
Walesby Village Sports Assoc.
Furze Court
RETFORD ROAD
GREEN LANE
Bevercotes Beck
BEVERCOTES PARK
Walesby C of E Prim. School
NEW HILL
WILLOUGHBY WY.
Willoughby Farm
FORESTRY HOUSES
TUXFORD ROAD
KENNEDY RISE
KEN'N EDY CT.
CHAPEL CL.
CHAPEL LANE
THE BUNGALOWS
Playing Field
Pond Farm
Hanging Hill Plantation
NEWARK and SHERWOOD
BASSETLAW
HAWTHORNS
THE BRAMBLS
STREET
MANOR CL.
The Mill House
MILL LANE
MAIN
BURTON RI.
CENTRAL AV.
PUMP LA.
BRACKENDALE DR.
FERN BANK AV.
ASH VALE
VALE M.
COLLINRIDGE VW.
BOGG LANE
RD.
Willoughby House
WALESBY
Nickerbush Plantation
SHERWOOD PARK
Nursery
The Paddocks
BRAKE ROAD
Newark
NG22
Collinridge Wood
Manor Farm
Kirton
Yew Tree Farm
OLLERTON
A6075
RICE HILL
Goosemoor Dyke
BRAKE LANE
CONNAH LA.
Seven Acres

28
Retford
DN22
CLIFF GATE
A57
A1
Beacon Hill
Sibthorpe
Cleveland Hill Farm
Sibthorpe Kennels
CLEVELAND HILL
PARSON LA.
West Markham
147
MAIN ST.
GT. NORTH ROAD
RETFORD ROAD
B1164
PRIESTGATE
HAROLD
HIGH
FINNEY LANE
ASKHAM ROAD
East Markham Primary School
Play. Fld.
GREAT LANE
YORK STREET
YORK PADOCK
FARM LA.
OLD HALL LA.
STOCKS FOLD
COLLEGE CT.
QUEENS CL.
THE HALL CL.
LOW STREET
HALL LA.
BECKLAND HILL
EAST MARKHAM
Markham Hall
CHURCH LANE
MARK LANE
EAST VIEW
TUXFORD ROAD
TOP CART GAPS
LINCOLN
PLANTATION ROAD
PLANTATION AV.
CROSSWAYS
BACK LA.
TRINITY CRES.
TRINITY CR.
KIRKE CL.
BACK LANE
BROAD GATE
Broad Gate Farm
OLD
MOORGATE
STREET
NOOKIN
QUAKEFIELD
Manor Farm
ROAD
Newark
NG22
Tuxford Windmill
MARKHAM ROAD
AMERICA GS.
BURLEIGH CT.
ELDON ST.
ELDON GRN.
Wks.
Hall
TUXFORD
MKT. PL.
BLUE BELL YD.
LINCOLN ROAD
Lib.
Comm. Cen.
NEWARK RD.
THE PASTURES
THE BEECH
BIRCH CT.
Prim. Sch.
PEEL AV.
ORCHARD CR.
CLARK LA.
NEWCASTLE ST.
LEXINGTON GS.
LEXINGTON CT.
Play. Fld.
Cemetery
EGMANTON RD.
LONG LANE
South Hills Farm
BEVERCOTES LANE
Depot
Works
BRITISH FIELDS
OLLERTON ROAD
A6075
Walks of Life Heritage Centre
LINCOLN ROAD
ASHVALE
FARADAY AV.
GILBERT
WELBECK PL.
LANDA GRO.
MACHIN CL.
FLEMING AV.
NICHOLAS PL.
HAYNES CL.
CHARTER PL.
WOODHOUSE PL.
AVENUE
CAPPS PL.
MAYFAIR PL.
LINDEN AV.
MAPLE CL.
ASPEN CL.
ASPEN CT.
CHESTNUT WY.
Tuxford School
MARNHAM ROAD
HILLSIDE CL.
DARLTON RD.
GREENACRES CARAVAN PARK
EASTFIELD PARK
LODGE LANE
LODGE LANE INDUSTRIAL EST.
GREAT NORTH RD.
ASHVALE
A B C D E
1 2 3 4 5 6 7
73
74
³74
⁴75
72
71

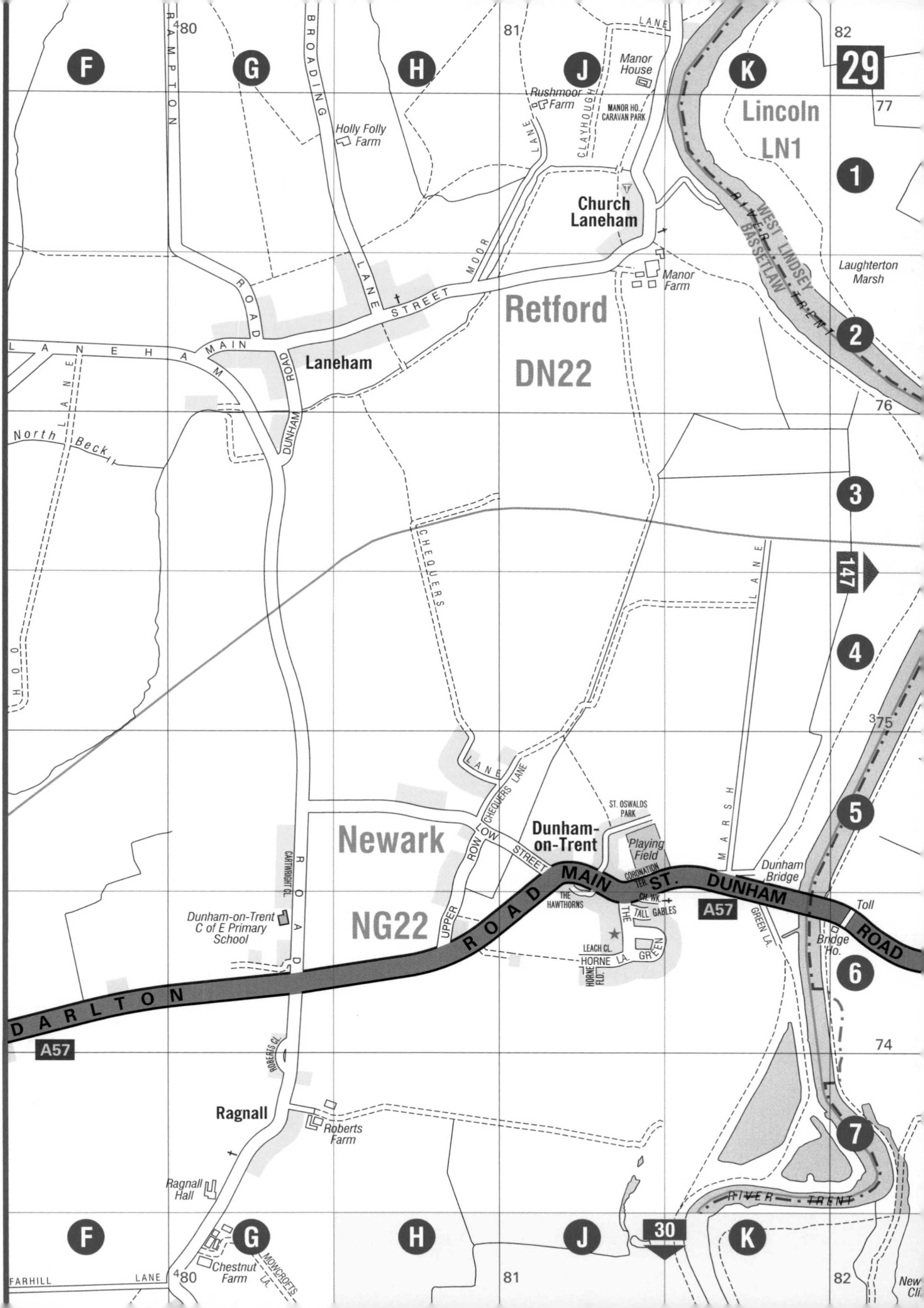

F
G
H
J
K
480
81
82
29
77
76
375
74
1
2
3
4
5
6
7
147
30
RAMPTON
BROADING LANE
LANE
Manor House
Rushmoor Farm
MANOR HO. CARAVAN PARK
CLAYHOUGH
Holly Folly Farm
Lincoln
LN1
Church Laneham
MOOR
STREET
Manor Farm
Laughterton Marsh
WEST LINDSEY
BASSETLAW
RIVER TRENT
Retford
DN22
ROAD
LANEHAM
MAIN
Laneham
North Beck
DUNHAM
CHEQUERS
HOO
MARSH LANE
LANE
CHEQUERS LANE
ST. OSWALDS PARK
Dunham-on-Trent
Playing Field
LOW STREET
ROW
Newark
NG22
UPPER
CORONATION TER.
CH. WK.
THE HAWTHORNS
THE TALL GABLES
MAIN ST. DUNHAM ROAD
Dunham Bridge
Toll
Bridge Ho.
A57
GREEN LA.
LEACH CL.
HORNE LA.
HORNE FLD.
THE GREEN
CARTWRIGHT CL.
Dunham-on-Trent C of E Primary School
DARLTON ROAD
ROBERTS CL.
Ragnall
Roberts Farm
Ragnall Hall
Chestnut Farm
MOWCROFTS LA.
FARHILL LANE
New Cli

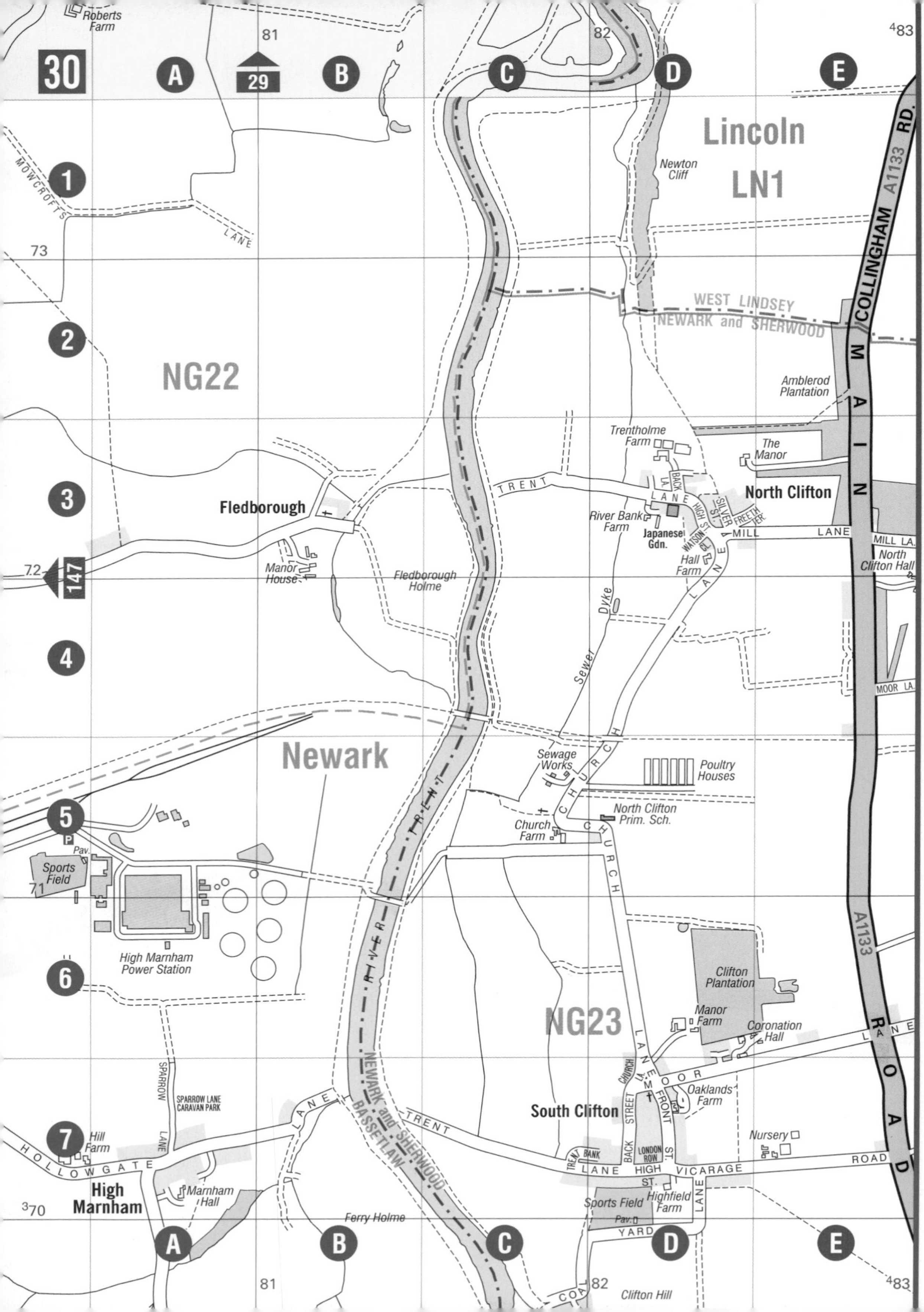
Roberts Farm
Lincoln
LN1
Newton Cliff
MOWCROFTS LANE
WEST LINDSEY
NEWARK and SHERWOOD
COLLINGHAM RD.
A1133
MAIN ROAD
NG22
Amblerod Plantation
Trentholme Farm
The Manor
TRENT LANE
BACK LA.
North Clifton
Fledborough
River Bank Farm
Japanese Gdn.
HIGH ST.
SILVER ST.
FREETH TER.
WATSON CL.
Hall Farm
MILL LANE
MILL LA.
North Clifton Hall
Manor House
Fledborough Holme
Sewer Dyke
MOOR LA.
Newark
Sewage Works
Poultry Houses
CHURCH LANE
North Clifton Prim. Sch.
Church Farm
Sports Field
Pav.
High Marnham Power Station
RIVER TRENT
Clifton Plantation
NG23
Manor Farm
Coronation Hall
MOOR LANE
Oaklands Farm
SPARROW LANE
SPARROW LANE CARAVAN PARK
South Clifton
CHURCH LA.
BACK STREET
FRONT ST.
LONDON ROW
Nursery
Hill Farm
HOLLOWGATE LANE
TRENT LANE
NEWARK and SHERWOOD
BASSETLAW
TRENT BANK
HIGH ST.
VICARAGE ROAD
High Marnham
Marnham Hall
Sports Field
Highfield Farm
Pav.
YARD
Ferry Holme
COAL
Clifton Hill
29
147
81
82
483
73
72
71
370

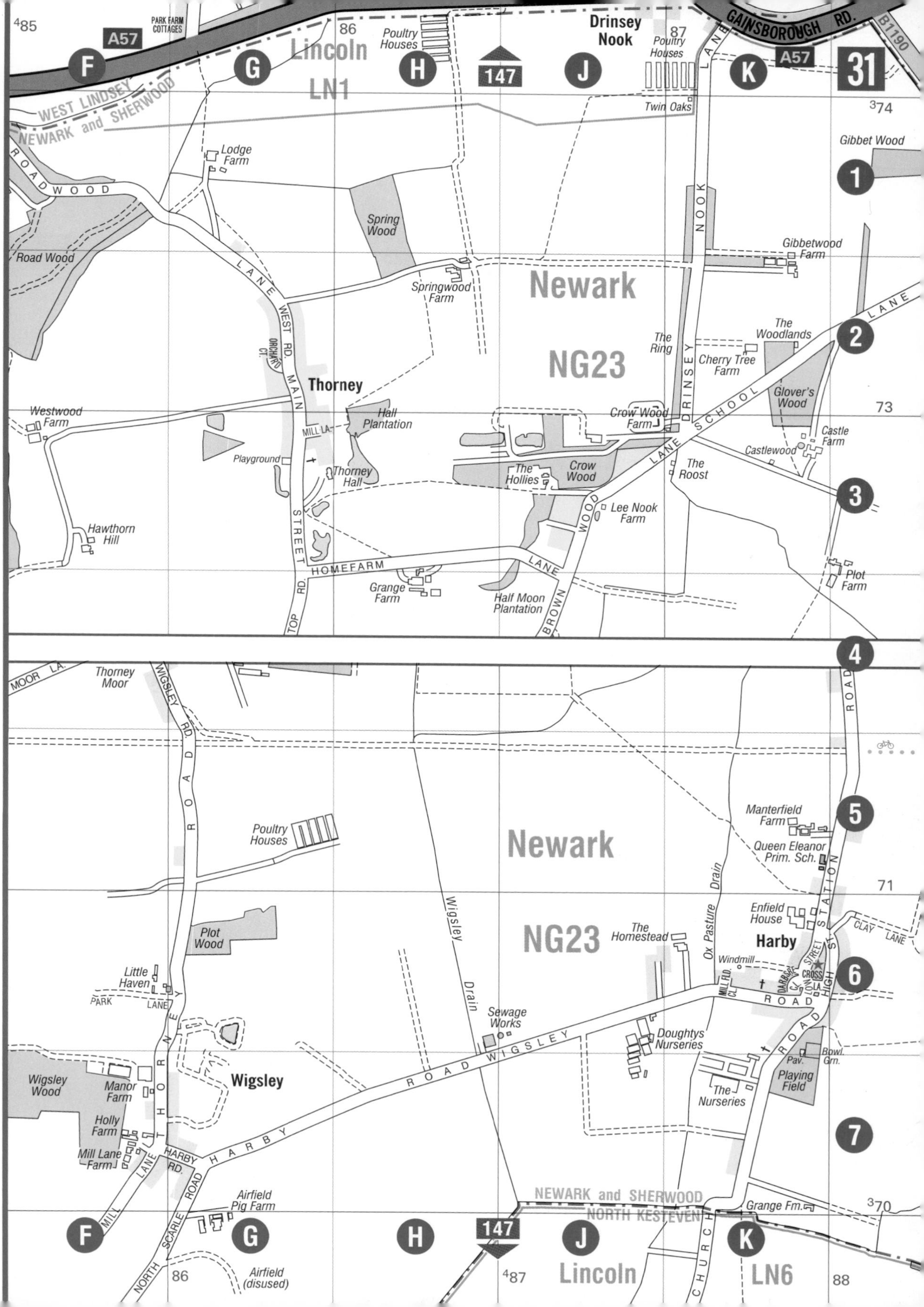

485
86
87
PARK FARM COTTAGES
A57
Lincoln
LN1
Poultry Houses
Drinsey Nook
147
GAINSBOROUGH RD.
B1190
F
G
H
J
K
WEST LINDSEY
NEWARK and SHERWOOD
Twin Oaks
374
Gibbet Wood
1
Lodge Farm
ROAD WOOD
Spring Wood
Road Wood
DRINSEY NOOK LANE
Gibbetwood Farm
LANE
Springwood Farm
Newark
WEST RD.
ORCHARD CT.
MAIN STREET
The Ring
The Woodlands
2
Cherry Tree Farm
NG23
Thorney
Glover's Wood
Westwood Farm
Hall Plantation
MILL LA.
Crow Wood Farm
73
SCHOOL LANE
Castle Farm
Castlewood
Playground
Thorney Hall
The Hollies
Crow Wood
The Roost
3
Lee Nook Farm
Hawthorn Hill
WOOD LANE
HOMEFARM LANE
Plot Farm
TOP RD.
Grange Farm
Half Moon Plantation
BROWN
4
MOOR LA.
Thorney Moor
WIGSLEY RD.
ROAD
Poultry Houses
Manterfield Farm
5
Queen Eleanor Prim. Sch.
STATION
71
Wigsley Drain
Ox Pasture Drain
Enfield House
CLAY LANE
Plot Wood
The Homestead
Harby
Little Haven
Windmill
STREET
PARK LANE
MILL FLD. CL.
DARBY CL.
LOW LA.
CROSS
HIGH ST.
6
Sewage Works
WIGSLEY ROAD
Doughtys Nurseries
Bowl. Grn.
Pav.
Playing Field
Wigsley Wood
Manor Farm
THORNEY
Wigsley
The Nurseries
Holly Farm
HARBY ROAD
7
Mill Lane Farm
HARBY RD.
MILL LANE
NORTH SCARLE ROAD
Airfield Pig Farm
NEWARK and SHERWOOD
NORTH KESTEVEN
Grange Fm.
370
CHURCH
Airfield (disused)
487
Lincoln
LN6
88

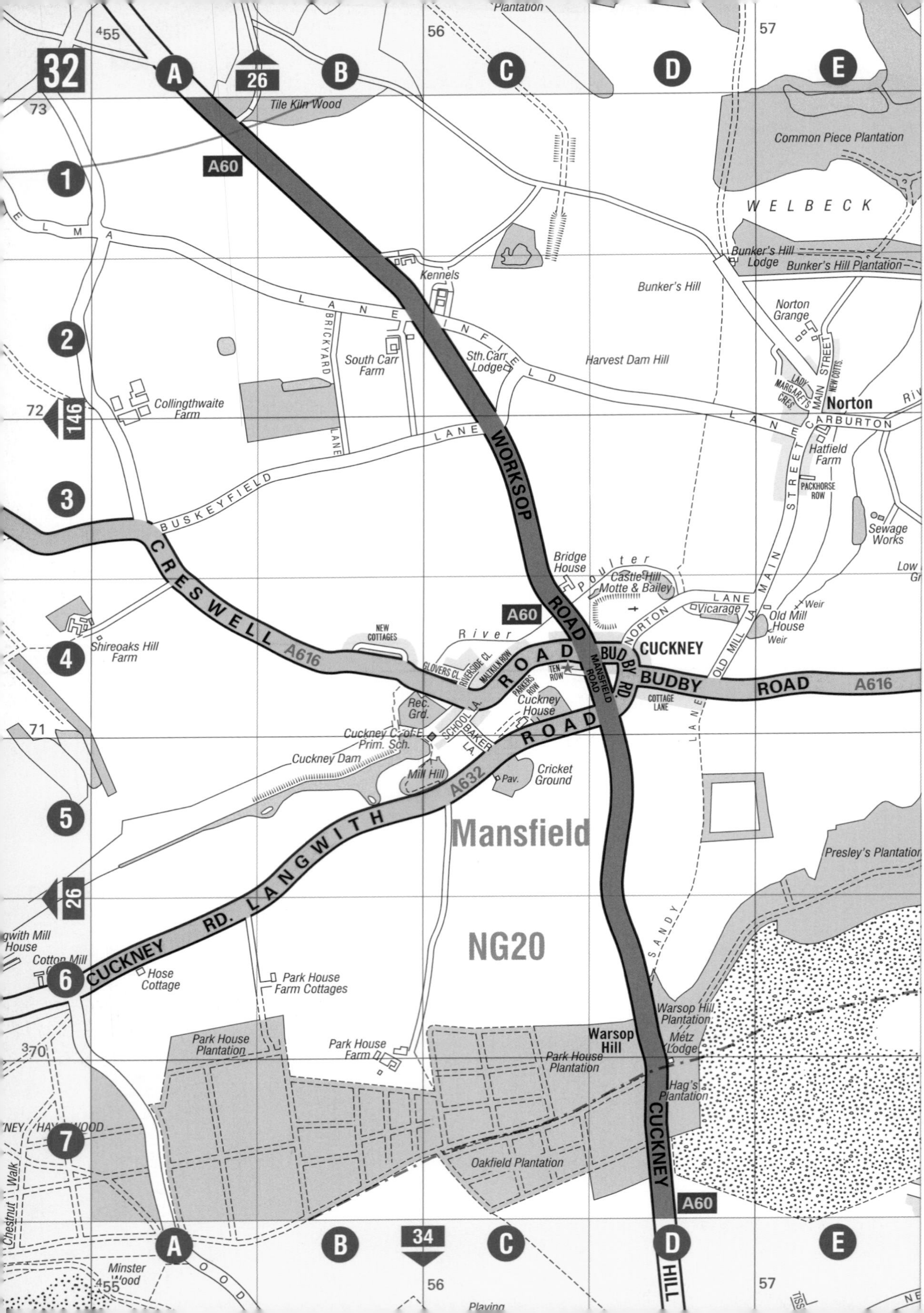

455
56
57
A
B
C
D
E
26
Plantation
73
Tile Kiln Wood
A60
Common Piece Plantation
1
ELMA
WELBECK
Bunker's Hill Lodge
Bunker's Hill Plantation
Kennels
Bunker's Hill
LANE
INFIELD
BRICKYARD LANE
Norton Grange
2
South Carr Farm
Sth.Carr Lodge
Harvest Dam Hill
LADY MARGARETS CRES.
MAIN STREET
NEW COTTS.
72
146
Collingthwaite Farm
Norton
CARBURTON LANE
Hatfield Farm
PACKHORSE ROW
3
BUSKEYFIELD LANE
WORKSOP ROAD
STREET
Sewage Works
Bridge House
Poulter
Castle Hill Motte & Bailey
Low
CRESWELL
LANE
Vicarage
NORTON
MAIN
Weir
Old Mill House
A60
NEW COTTAGES
River
CUCKNEY
OLD MILL LA.
4
Shireoaks Hill Farm
A616
GLOVERS CL.
RIVERSIDE CL.
MALTKILN ROW
ROAD
TEN ROW
BUDBY RD.
MANSFIELD ROAD
BUDBY ROAD
A616
PARKERS ROW
Rec. Grd.
Cuckney House
COTTAGE LANE
SCHOOL LA.
BAKER LA.
ROAD
71
Cuckney C. of E. Prim. Sch.
Cuckney Dam
Mill Hill
A632
Pav.
Cricket Ground
5
Mansfield
Presley's Plantation
26
LANGWITH
RD.
CUCKNEY
SANDY
NG20
Langwith Mill House
Cotton Mill
6
Hose Cottage
Park House Farm Cottages
Warsop Hill Plantation
Park House Plantation
Park House Farm
Warsop Hill
Park House Plantation
Metz Lodge
370
Hag's Plantation
HAYWOOD
7
Oakfield Plantation
CUCKNEY HILL
A60
Chestnut Walk
A
B
34
C
D
E
Minster Wood
455
56
57
Playing

Worksop
S80
A616
Moss Hall Plantation
Tichfield Hill
Pitiful Clump
Fox Hill Plantation
Youngrough Breck
Pitiful Hill Plantation
Mellish's Plantation
Kennel Plantation
Fox Covert Plantation
GREAT LAKE
PARK
Cat Hills Plantation
Fasque Plantation
Fasque Screed
Nightingale Plantation
Meadow Lodge
River Poulter
AVENUE
Weir
Milnthorpe Lodge
Carburton Forge Dam
Carburton Dam
LIMETREE
Poulter LANE
Forge Lodge
Works
Gibraltar Lodge
Bentinck Lodge
Corunna Lodge
Corunna Hill Plantation
Gibraltar Plantation
Battarain Plantation
Hazel Gap Wood
Burn's Breck
Lord Woodstock's Plantation
Hatfield Grange
Hazel Gap
Kingstand Lodge
Hazel Gap Farm
BUDBY DR.
High Hatfield
Sedan Lodge
Gleadthorpe Breck Plantation
BASSETLAW
MANSFIELD
Hatfield Plantation
Gleadthorpe Screed
Gleadthorpe Plantation
LANE
Welbeck Colliery
Gleadthorpe Lodge
Gleadthorpe Experimental Husbandry Farm
Elkesley Hill
Football Ground
BUDBY
HANGER HILL DRIVE
Cricket Ground
ELKESLEY PL.
CRESCENT
PORTLAND CR.
Gleadthorpe Grange
River Meden
KIRTON CL.
RUFFORD AV.
HATFIELD AV.
Sports Ground
BUDBY CRES.
PREST AV.
Gleadthorpe Cottage
JACKSON TER.
NETHERFIELD ROAD
EASTLAND TER.
CARBURTON AV.
BURTON AV.
TUXFORD AV.
LAXTON DR.
Eastlands Jun. Sch.
EGMANTON ROAD
MANBY
MARSTON AV.
OSSINGTON CL.
Netherfield Inf. Sch.
LANE
Assarts Farm
Holborn Hill Plantation
MELVILLE CT.
PERLETHORPE CL.
THORESBY ROAD
Meden Vale
Play. Fld.
KNEESALL CL.
NETHERFIELD CL.
MEDEN SIDE
Boundary Plantation
The Bottoms
F G H J K
1 2 3 4 5 6 7
58 59 460
73 72 71 370
146
35

Oakfield Plantation
32
A60
CUCKNEY
HILL
CHURCH
ROAD
Minster Wood
Collier Spring
Warsop Wood
WOOD
Playing Field
Church Vale Primary School
Church Warsop
Cemetery
Moorfield Farm
CRESCENT
STREET
LAUREL
LILAC GRO.
LIME
POPLAR GRO.
ELM GRO.
SYCAMORE
BIRCH
GROVE RD.
AVENUE
STREET
BISHOP'S
WALK
LANE
GIPSY
Bowl. Grn.
Hall
Football Ground
Springfields
War Memorial
ST. PETERS
HALIFAX AV.
WEETMAN AV.
CHURCH CL.
RECTORY RD.
GIGGS LA.
MANOR CT.
MANOR
ROAD
Manor Fm.
EASTLANDS LA.
BLANKLEYS YARD
BARN OWL CL.
TISSINGTON AV.
NETHERFIELD
MEDEN GLEN
DRONLEY DR.
GLAMIS
River Meden
Mill Pond
The Carrs
Recreation Ground
Playground
MARKET WARSOP
Play. Fld.
Meden Spts. Cen.
Meden Sch. & Technology College
Inf. Sch.
Playing Field
GEORGE SHOOTER CT.
NETHERCROSS
DERWENT CL.
DALE RD.
DRIVE
ROAD
SOUTHGATE
AVENUE
BURNS
B6031
LANE
CARTER
Rhein o' Thorns
Rock House
Hills and Holes
Hills & Holes
Warsop Vale
HEWETT ST.
KING ST.
WEST ST.
146
Askew Spa
Quarry (disused)
Stone Bridge
Sookholme Moor
Welfare Cen.
Sports Grd.
Bowl. Grn.
Pav.
Weir
Hills and Holes
Quarry (disused)
Hammerwater Bridge
THE WILLOWS
RIVER VIEW
EDWARD ST.
QUEEN ST.
WOOD ST.
ALEXANDRA ST.
VICTORIA ST.
ALBERT ST.
Town Hall
Recreation Ground
Pav.
CUMBERLAND AV.
ARGYLE CL.
HAMILTON
NORFOLK
SAVILE CL.
WAY
RUTLAND
DRIVE
CARR
KING RD.
YORK TER.
Bowl. Grn.
STONEBRIDGE
LANE
WINDSOR DR.
STONEBRIDGE RD.
THE HAWTHORNS
VALE
MEADOW
SOOKHOLME LA.
AVENUE
DR.
CHURCH ST.
HIGH ST.
Lib.
SHERWOOD
STREET
BIRKLAND
SANDY
LANE
EASTWOOD AV.
ENTERPRISE CEN.
Sch.
WOODLAND GRO.
APPLETON
MEDEN
FELL
WILSON GRO.
WILSON ST.
WILSON CT.
FITZHERBERT ST.
PRINCESS AV.
GEORGE ST.
SHORT ST.
CHERRY GROVE
UPPER
GLEBE
SANDY LA.
CROSS
CLUMBER
BAINBRIDGE
WATSON ST.
WELBECK ST.
PORTLAND ST.
THE HOMESTEADS
LONGDEN ST.
PAVILION CL.
OSBORNE
RIDGEWAY
FENWICK
VICKERS ST.
MUSCHAMP
MANVERS ST.
ROAD
TITCHFIELD
BENTINCK TER.
MORVEN TER.
MAYFIELD TER.
Sports Grd.
Pav.
Sch.
B6035
Mount Pleasant
LEA RD.
BRACKEN CL.
SANDY LANE
LINGS VIEW
WINDY RIDGE
TOP
MOUNT
CRES.
SOOKHOLME DR.
BLACKBERRY WY.
HAMMERWATER
ROAD
ASKEW
LANE
Depot
ELMFIELD
BULLY
SPRING
LANE
SOOKHOLME
LANE
NG19
SOOKHOLME
River Meden
Drain
Cleveland Villa
MOSSCAR
LANE
Play. Fld.
Works
Spion Kop
MOSSCAR CL.
Spion Kop
Rough Wood
Quarry (disused)
OAKFIELD AV.
ROBIN
HOOD
LITTLE JOHN AV.
COTTAGE LA.
FRIAR
LANE
AVENUE
FOREST RISE
STREET
Depot
Mineral Railway
COTTAGE
LANE
OAKFIELD
COACH
Poultry Houses
ROAD
B6407
Nettleworth Farm
ROAD
MANSFIELD
A60
42
Croft Plantation
OAKFIELD LANE
Nettleworth Manor
PEAF
A B C D E
1 2 3 4 5 6 7
455 56 57
369 68 67 66

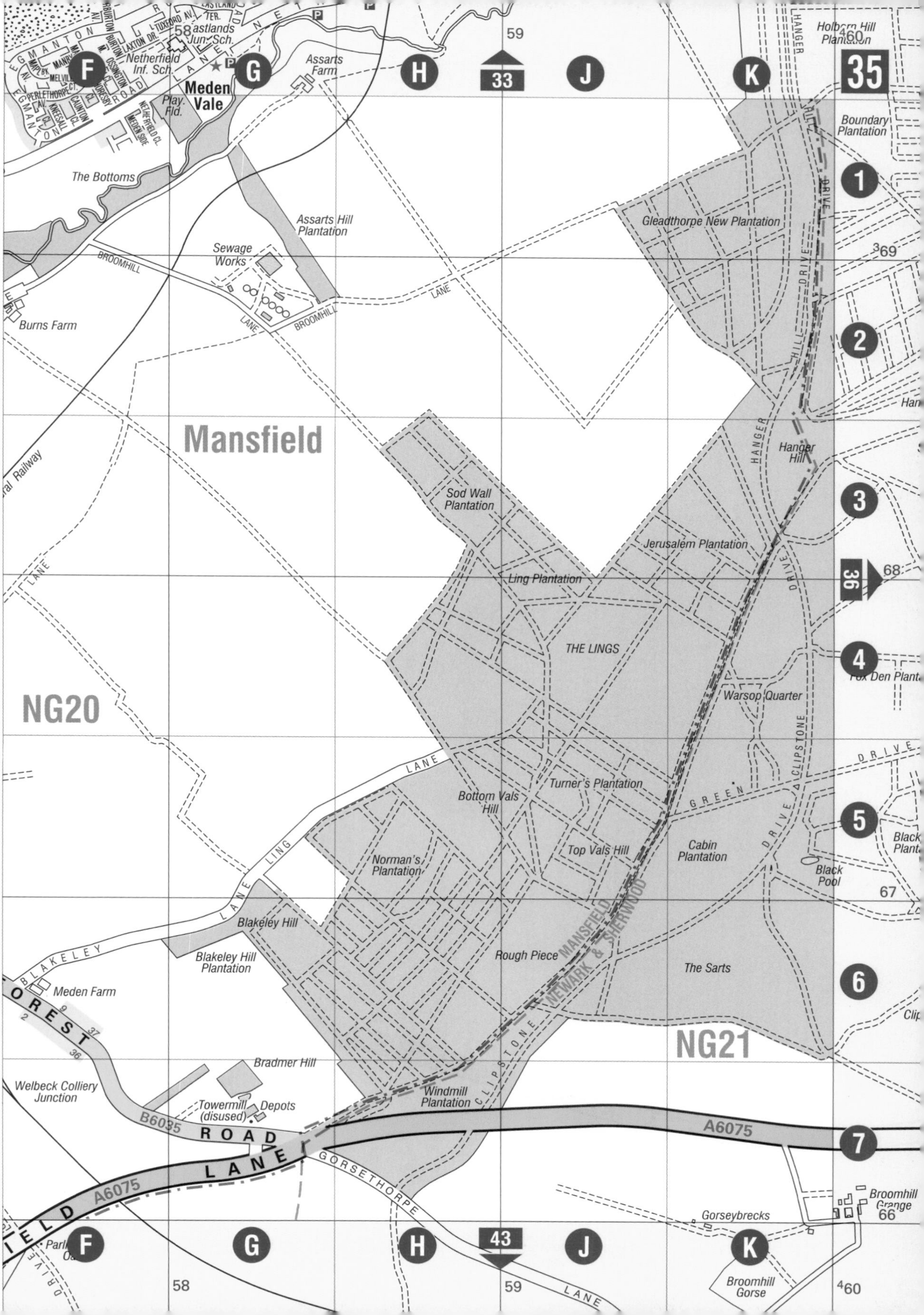

35
33
43
36
F
G
H
J
K
1
2
3
4
5
6
7
58
59
460
369
68
67
66
Meden Vale
Netherfield Inf. Sch.
Eastlands Jun. Sch.
Assarts Farm
Play. Fld.
Holborn Hill Plantation
Boundary Plantation
The Bottoms
Assarts Hill Plantation
Sewage Works
BROOMHILL LANE
Burns Farm
Gleadthorpe New Plantation
Mansfield
Hanger Hill
HANGER HILL DRIVE
Sod Wall Plantation
Jerusalem Plantation
Ling Plantation
THE LINGS
NG20
Warsop Quarter
Fox Den Plantation
CLIPSTONE DRIVE
GREEN DRIVE
Turner's Plantation
Bottom Vals Hill
LING LANE
Top Vals Hill
Cabin Plantation
Norman's Plantation
Black Pool
Blakeley Hill
BLAKELEY LANE
Blakeley Hill Plantation
Rough Piece
MANSFIELD NEWARK & SHERWOOD
The Sarts
Meden Farm
FOREST ROAD
NG21
Bradmer Hill
Welbeck Colliery Junction
Windmill Plantation
Towermill (disused)
Depots
B6035 ROAD
A6075
LANE
GORSETHORPE LANE
Broomhill Grange
Gorseybrecks
Broomhill Gorse

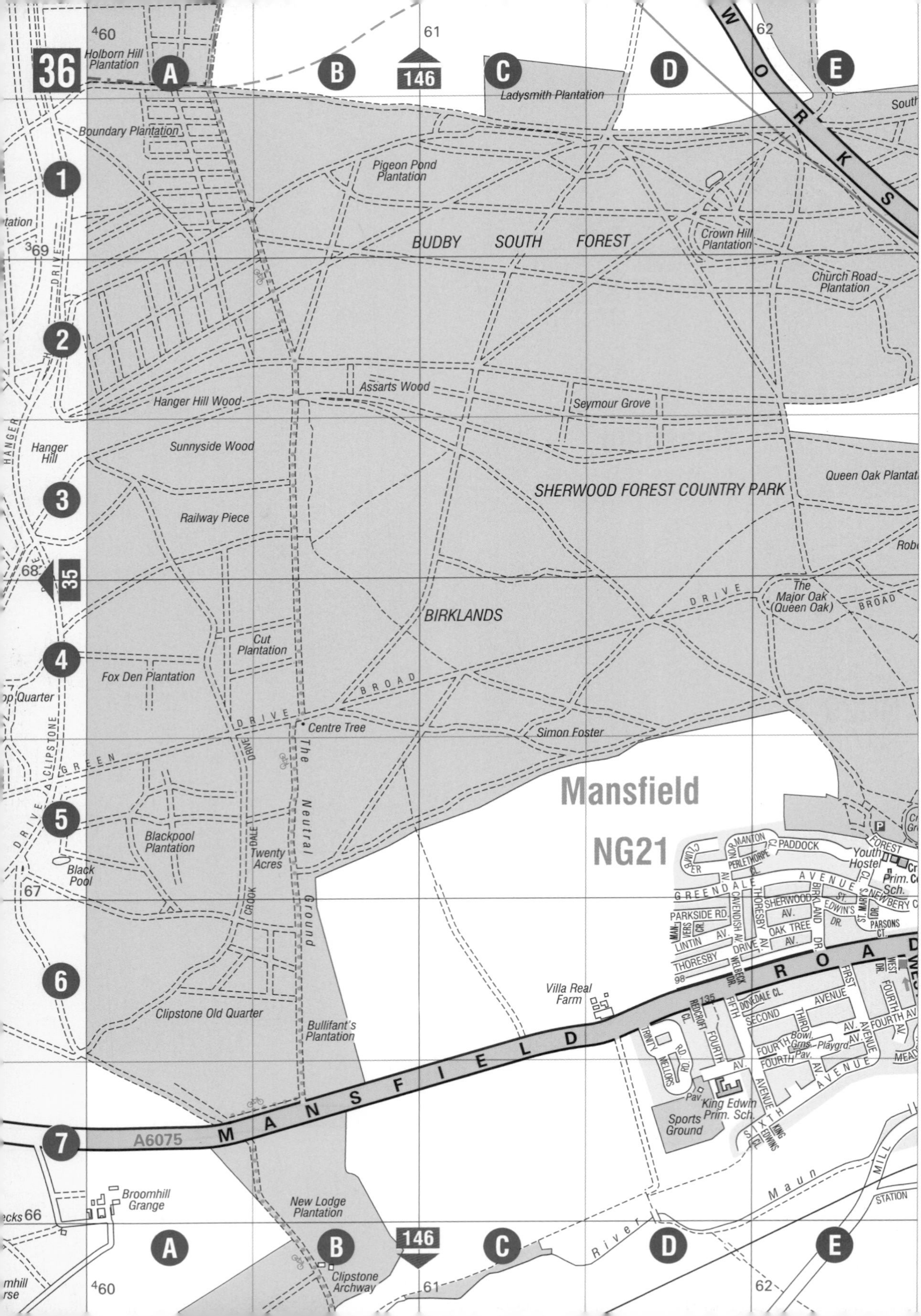
460
61
62
146
A
B
C
D
E
1
2
3
4
5
6
7
35
369
368
367
366
Holborn Hill Plantation
Ladysmith Plantation
WORKS
South
Boundary Plantation
Pigeon Pond Plantation
BUDBY SOUTH FOREST
Crown Hill Plantation
Church Road Plantation
Assarts Wood
Seymour Grove
Hanger Hill Wood
Hanger Hill
HANGER
DRIVE
Sunnyside Wood
SHERWOOD FOREST COUNTRY PARK
Queen Oak Plantat
Railway Piece
Rob
The Major Oak (Queen Oak)
BROAD DRIVE
BIRKLANDS
Cut Plantation
Fox Den Plantation
Quarter
BROAD DRIVE
Centre Tree
Simon Foster
CLIPSTONE DRIVE
GREEN
The Neutral Ground
CROOK DALE DRIVE
Mansfield
NG21
Blackpool Plantation
Twenty Acres
Black Pool
MANTON CRES.
PADDOCK
CLUMBER AV.
PERLETHORPE CL.
FOREST
Youth Hostel
Prim. Sch.
AVENUE
GREENDALE
SHERWOOD AV.
BIRKLAND DR.
ST. EDWIN'S DR.
NEWBERY CL.
PARKSIDE RD.
CAVENDISH AV.
THORESBY AV.
ST. MARY'S DR.
PARSONS CT.
MANVERS CR.
OAK TREE AV.
LINTIN AV.
DRIVE
THORESBY
WELBECK DR.
ROAD
WEST DR.
FOURTH AV.
Villa Real Farm
98
135
REDCROFT CL.
FIFTH
DOVEDALE CL.
AVENUE
FIRST
SECOND
THIRD AV.
AVENUE
FOURTH AV.
TRINITY
MELLORS RD.
FOURTH AV.
Bowl. Grns. Pav.
Playgrd.
FOURTH
AVENUE
MEAD
Clipstone Old Quarter
Bullifant's Plantation
MANSFIELD ROAD
A6075
Pav.
King Edwin Prim. Sch.
Sports Ground
SIXTH AVENUE
KING EDWINS CL.
MILL
STATION
River Maun
Broomhill Grange
New Lodge Plantation
Clipstone Archway

63
64
465
146
F
G
H
J
K
Ceres Lodge
Charles Wood
Grove
Works
Smiths Hill
Vincent Grove
CHESTNUT AVENUE
Old Oaks
Old Buck Gates
Proteus Camp
369
Clay Pits
THORESBY PARK
Postmans Wicket
Ollerton Assarts Plantation
Ollerton Corner
Stilehollow Plantation
Hawk Clump
A616
BILHAUGH
Shooting Range
B6034
ROAD
Sherwood Forest Visitors Centre
DRIVE
BEECH AVENUE
38
68
Burstheart Hill
Sherwood Heath Nature Reserve
Thoresby Colliery
OLLERTON ROAD
MANSFIELD RD.
NEWARK
Cockglode Cottages
A6075
SWINECOTE ROAD
ROAD
Weirs
Hamlyn Lodge
STATION
Maun
Carr Brecks Farm
CHURCH ST.
MAYTHORN GRO.
EDWINSTOWE
THE WHEELWRIGHTS
Black Hills Farm
Newark
COLLIERY VILLAS
Black Hills Plantation
Sewage Works
NG22
GREENWOOD AV.
LINDEN CT.
MAID MARION DR.
LYNDS CL.
Rainworth Water
RUFFORD
River
LANSBURY
Ollerton Station Farm
SAVILE ROW
Edwinstowe House
HIGH STREET
OLD RUFFORD
A614
Weir
LANE
CHAPEL CT.
FRIEND LA.
BOY
WOODHEAD CL.
HAZEL GROVE
DUKERIES CRES.
OCCUPATION LA.
RUFFORD ROAD
ABBEY RD.
BEARDSLEY ROAD
GAITSKILL CR.
HENTON RD.
Lidgett
Mansfield
MERRYWEATHER CL.
ROBIN HOOD AV.
SANDY LA.
NG21
GREENFIELD CL.
THORNE
BROCKLEHURST DR.
PINEWOOD AV.
Sth. Forest Leisure Cen.
OAKWOOD GRO.
PORTLAND ROW
Ollerton Hills
66
HENTON
ABBEY
CARVER CL.
BEARDSLEY
GAITSKILL CRES.
CLIPSTONE RD.
B6030
INSET
Holly Farm
SHERWOOD CASTLE HOLIDAY FOREST
465
ROBIN HOOD AV.
SANDY LA.
63
1
2
3
4
5
6
7

A
B
C
D
E
1
2
3
4
5
6
7
65
66
67
68
69
146
37
A614
A616
A6075
B6461
B6387
BLYTH ROAD
Boughton Brake
BRAKE
Boughton Pumping Sta.
New Zealand Cottage
WHINNEY LA.
BLACKBURN VW.
GOLDERE CL.
LITTLE JOHN CL.
KINGSWAY AV.
BIRKDALE AV.
BRAKE VW.
HALLAM ROAD
BRAMBLE CL.
STUART AV.
MAID MARION WAY
BRACKEN AV.
FERNDALE CL.
Playing Field
Comm. Cen.
STEPNALL HEIGHTS
TURNER LA.
BENTINCK CL.
KIRK DRIVE
SWINTON COPSE
MANVERS VW.
LINTON
THORNHILL
Games Cts.
The Dukeries College
Lib.
Dukeries Leisure Cen.
Playing Fields
Running Track
Ollerton Prim. Sch.
HOLLES CL.
EYELANDS
St. Josephs Catholic Prim. School
HEATHERS
GREENWOOD CRES.
GIBSON CT.
HAZEL ROAD
HAWTHORN DR.
HAWTHORN CL.
CLARK WOODS CL.
TUXFORD ROAD
MAIN ROAD
PETERSMITHS CL.
PETERSMITH CRES.
CEDAR LANE
CHESTNUT DRIVE
CHEST-NUT CL.
DRIVE
BIRKLANDS AV.
WATER
LANSBURY AV.
WHITE-WATER CL.
PETERSMITH DRIVE
MAUN CRES.
Works
BREK BANK
BREK BANK CRES.
JAMES
WHITEWATER RD.
WALKER CL.
PETERSMITH CL.
FIR VW.
HOLLY
LANE
ALDER GROVE
LIME TREE RD.
LIME TREE CL.
CHURCH CIRCLE
BRIAR RD.
Bowling Greens
LARCH
ROAD
AMBLESIDE
YEW TREE
YEW TREE RD.
ROAD
MIDDLETON CT.
BRIAR CT.
GREENFIELDS CRES.
River Maun
Sports Ground
Pav.
Maun Inf. Sch.
Forest View Sch.
GATTLYS LA.
DOVE LANE
DOVE CL.
BEECH AV.
YEW
FOREST VW.
WALESBY LA. COTTS.
WALESBY LANE
CROFT
DE LACY CT.
MAIDA
GLASBY CL.
Weir
Weirs
A6075 ROAD
Liby.
SHERWOOD DR.
SYCAMORE RD.
OAK AV.
PINE AV.
BIRCH
POPLAR STREET
RUFFORD AV.
SAVILE RW.
EDISON RI.
EDISON
Superstore
NEW OLLERTON
Newark
NG22
ST. PETERS CL.
THE MARKHAMS
MARKHAM CL.
Cemy.
LATIMER WY.
Offices
FOREST ROAD
OLLERTON ROAD
BACK LA.
HEREFORD
GRANGE AV.
Ollerton Hall
War Mem.
MAIN ST.
NEWARK RD.
FOREST HO. PARK HOMES
CHURCH VW.
CHURCH ST.
MKT. PL.
Ollerton Watermill
Hamlyn Lodge Cott. Industry
Ollerton
MANSFIELD RD.
Heath Reserve
Ollerton Corner
Clump
BEECH AVENUE
STATION ROAD
LANE
KINGSTON DR.
DEVONSHIRE DR.
CORNWALL DR.
HARDWICK DRIVE
TOR LANE
HAWKHILL CL.
BESCAR LANE
GRICESON CLOSE
MIDDLEFIELD LANE
FAIRHOLME PARK HOMES
SCHOOL LA.
CINDER LA.
MALT KILN CL.
WELLOW ROAD
A616
TOP ROW
RUFFORD ROAD
Ollerton Station Farm
Poultry Houses
Red House
BEACON CT.
Depot
Factory
NEWARK ROAD
WELLOW GRN.
Playing Field
PARK LANE
Wellow Dam
Crkt. Grd.
Pav.
Park Farm
Wellow
NEWARK ROAD
Wellow House School
Scotts Farm
GRN.
MAYPOLE RD.
CHURCH FARM GDNS.
LANE
Pinfold
Gorge Dyke
BOWMAN PL.
EAKRING
POTTER
MAYPOLE RD.
Ollerton Hills
SHERWOOD CASTLE HOLIDAY FOREST
RUFFORD LANE
Wellow Lodge
Brick Yard Farm
Brickyard Cottages
Caravan Site
LANE
110
15
62

39
27
146
147
F
G
H
J
K
1
2
3
4
5
6
7
68
69
470
369
68
67
66
Kirton
Boughton
RETFORD ROAD
B6387
LANE
CONNAH LA.
Manor Farm
Yew Tree Farm
THE HAVEN
Seven Acres
OLLERTON ROAD
A6075
RICE
Goosemoor Dyke
HILL LA.
Glebe Farm
Hall Farm
MAIN STREET
RECTORY GDS.
SANDFIELD LA.
WINDMILL CL.
CHARLOTTE CL.
KIRTON CT.
KIRTON PK.
THE FURZE
GOLDEN HILL LA.
Gate House Farm
BARONS DR.
Doncaster Farm
Playing Field
Doncaster Farm Cottages
CHURCH ROAD
MANOR CL.
PICKINS RW.
FAIRWEATHER CL.
CHURCH RD.
Manor Farm
Playing Field
PRIMROSE LA.
PRIMROSE LANE
The Willows
Pump House
Boughton Dyke
BOUGHTON INDUSTRIAL ESTATE (NORTH)
STATION RD.
A6075
ROAD
HARROW LA.
West View Farm
HARROW LANE CARAVAN SITE
VICTORIA
Cocking Hill Farm
WAY
MEDEN RD.
TRENT ROAD
BOUGHTON WY.
LEEN CT.
MAUN WAY
BOUGHTON INDUSTRIAL ESTATE (SOUTH)
Sewage Works
Works
Sports Ground
COCKING HILL ACRE EDGE ROAD
Norton Wood
Golden Hill
Reservoirs (covered)
WELLOW PARK
Laxton Common
The Holocaust Centre
Westwood Farm
Cocking Moor
Kennels Farm
Jordan Castle Lodge Farm
Jordan Castle
Jordan Castle Farm
COCKING MOOR LANE
Gallow Hole Dyke
LANE
SHORTWOOD
A616
Endeavour
Wood Close Farm

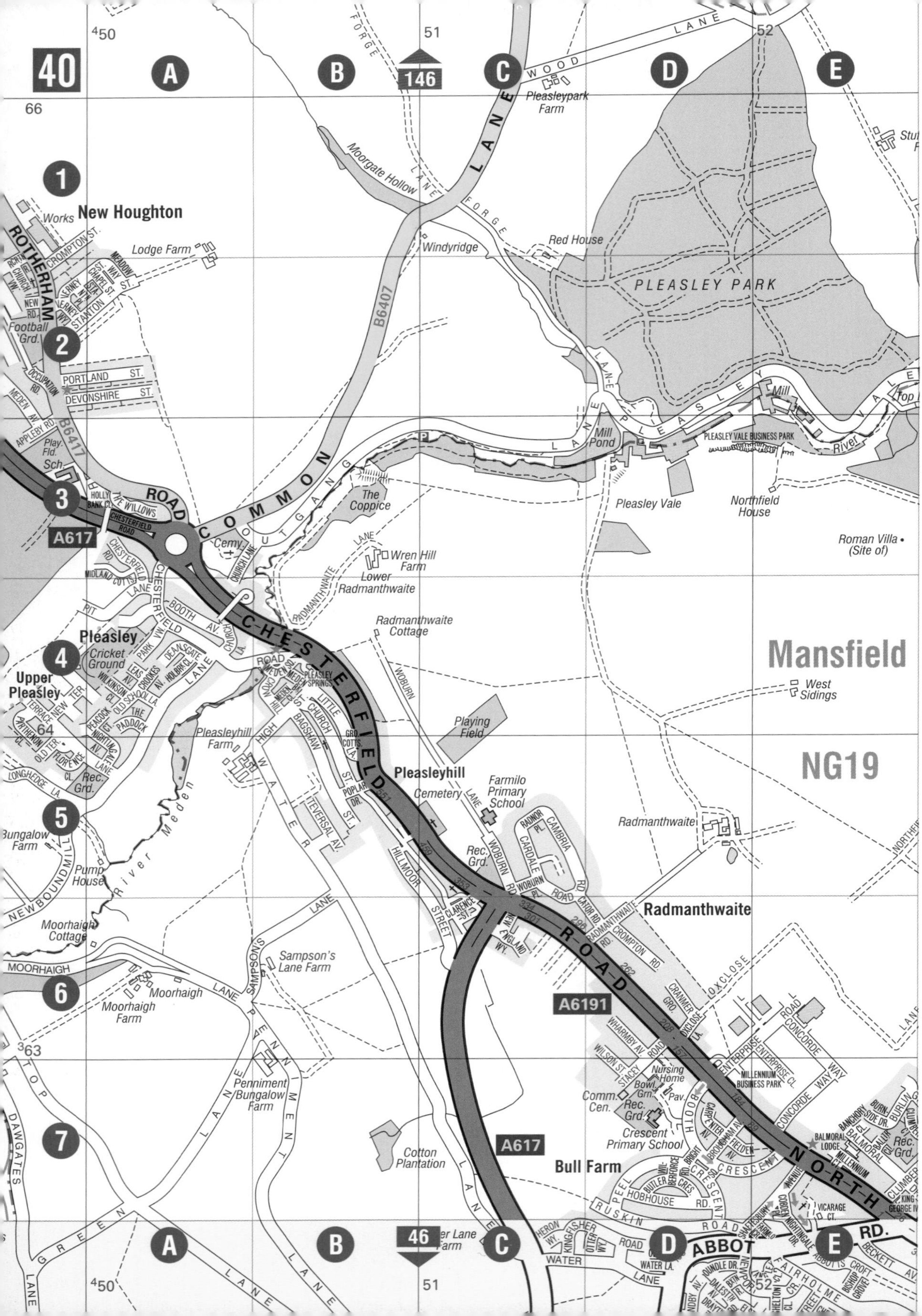

A
B
C
D
E
1
2
3
4
5
6
7
450
51
52
146
46
66
64
363
New Houghton
Works
ROTHERHAM
CROMPTON ST.
Lodge Farm
MEADOW WAY
CHAPEL ST.
STANTON ST.
VERNEY ST.
VERNEY WY.
CHURCH VW.
NEW RD.
Football Grd.
PORTLAND ST.
DEVONSHIRE ST.
OCCUPATION RD.
MEDEN W.
APPLEBY RD.
B6417
Play. Fld.
Sch.
HOLLY BANK CL.
THE WILLOWS
ROAD
CHESTERFIELD ROAD
A617
CHESTERFIELD RD.
MIDLAND COTTS.
LANE
RIT
BOOTH AV.
CHESTERFIELD
CHURCH LA.
CHURCH LANE
Cemy.
COMMON
OUTGANG
LANE
Pleasley
Cricket Ground
Upper Pleasley
WILKINSON CL.
PARK VW.
DEAN CL.
SGATE
LEAS AV.
CROOKES AV.
HOLBRK CL.
OLD SCHOOL LA.
THE PADDOCK
PEACOCK CT.
NEW TER.
TERRACE
PARTHENON CL.
OLD TER.
FLORENCE CL.
NIGHTINGALE AV.
Rec. Grd.
LONGHEDGE LA.
Bungalow Farm
Pump House
NEWBOUNDMILL
River Meden
Moorhaigh Cottage
MOORHAIGH
Moorhaigh
Moorhaigh Farm
LANE
TOP
DAWGATES
LANE
GREEN
LANE
FORGE
Moorgate Hollow
LANE
FORGE
B6407
Windyridge
WOOD LANE
Pleasleypark Farm
Red House
PLEASLEY PARK
LANE
PLEASLEY
VALE
Mill
Mill Pond
PLEASLEY VALE BUSINESS PARK
River
Top
The Coppice
Pleasley Vale
Northfield House
Roman Villa • (Site of)
Wren Hill Farm
Lower Radmanthwaite
RADMANTHWAITE LANE
Radmanthwaite Cottage
WOBURN
Mansfield
West Sidings
NG19
CHESTERFIELD
PLEASLEY SPRINGS
MEDEN ST.
HIGH
LITTLE
CHURCH
BAGSHAW
GRO. COTTS.
ST.
Pleasleyhill Farm
WATER
Playing Field
Pleasleyhill
Cemetery
LANE
Farmilo Primary School
POPLAR DR.
TEVERSAL AV.
HILLMOOR
STREET
CLARENCE ST.
Rec. Grd.
WOBURN RD.
RADNOR PL.
CAMBRIA RD.
CARDALE
WOBURN PL.
ROAD
CAYTOR RD.
Radmanthwaite
Radmanthwaite
RADMANTHWAITE RD.
CROMPTON RD.
NEW ENGLAND WY.
ROAD
A6191
CRANMER GRO.
OXCLOSE LA.
OXCLOSE
ROAD
CONCORDE
WAY
ENTERPRISE
ENTERPRISE CL.
MILLENNIUM BUSINESS PARK
WHARMBY AV.
WILSON ST.
STACEY
ROAD
Nursing Home
Bowl. Grn.
Pav.
Comm. Cen.
Rec. Grd.
Crescent Primary School
BOOTH
CARPENTER AV.
BROUGHAM AV.
FIELDEN AV.
CRESCENT
NORTH
Bull Farm
BALMORAL LODGE
BALMORAL
BANCHORY CL.
BURNSIDE DR.
BALLIR CL.
BURLIN
MILLENNIUM CT.
Rec. Grd.
CLUMBER
KING GEORGE IV
LANE
Sampson's Lane Farm
SAMPSON'S LANE
PENNIMENT
Penniment Bungalow Farm
LANE
LANE
Cotton Plantation
A617
er Lane Farm
LANE
PEEL
WILBERFORCE RD.
BUTLER CRES.
BRIGHT RD.
HOBHOUSE RD.
RUSKIN ROAD
HERON WY.
KINGFISHER WY.
OTTER WY.
ROAD
WATER
WATER LA.
LANE
ABBOT
ROAD
SHAFTESBURY AV.
CORDEN
NIGHTINGALE DR.
VICARAGE CT.
RD.
BECKETT AV.
ABBOTT'S CROFT
BISHOP GROVE
FAIRHOLME
OUNDLE DR.
DALESTH
NEWPORT
SHELTON CL.

41
146
47
42
F
G
H
J
K
1
2
3
4
5
6
7
53
54
55
66
65
64
63
Warsop Park Farm
Ox Pasture Wood
Spring Wood
Hop Yard
Nettleworth Manor
River Meden
Hind Car Wood
The Shrubbery
Littlewood
BOLSOVER
MANSFIELD
Hind Car
Home Farm
Park Hall
Fish Pond
Little Matlock
Meden
Works
Northfield Plantation
Meden Bank
Garden Plantation
Quarry (Disused)
Quarry Plantation
MANSFIELD WOODHOUSE GOLF COURSE
Club House
Cricket Grd.
Stone Quarry
Park Hall Farm
The Birches
Warehouse
The Bungalow
Stone Quarry
COMMON
MEDEN LANE
LITTLEWOOD LANE
The Bungalow
Sunnydale
North Lodge
North Lodge Cottage
Sunnydale Farm
Northfield Prim. Sch.
Fernlea
NORTHFIELD LANE
NORTHFIELD AVENUE
FELTON AVENUE
GUILDFORD AV.
FARM CROFT RD.
BERESFORD RD.
WORCESTER AVENUE
PARK HALL ROAD
MELBOURNE
CHESTNUT GROVE
BEECH TREE AV.
Bath House Farm
Manor Park Sports Complex
Playing Field
Games Ct.
Tennis Ct.
Bowl. Grns.
Works
Manor School
Playing Field
Tennis Courts
KINGSLEY AV.
LEAS ROAD
THE FAIRWAYS
LINDRICK CL.
NORTH
MARPLES
HAWTHORN AV.
PEAFIELD LA.
SHAKESPEARE AVENUE
VALE AVENUE
Playgrd.
Comm. Cen.
Rec. Grd.
Schools
Playing Field
OUTGANG LANE
RUSHPOOL
Works
OXCLOSE LANE
HIGH STREET
WARSOP RD.
WELBECK RD.
LEEMING LANE SOUTH
Mansfield Woodhouse
PRIORY RD.
PRIORY LANE
Burial Grd.
A60
Cemetery
MILL LANE
LOW
Sports Ground
Debdale Hall
Debdale Hall Farm
Debdale Hall Cottage
A6075
Yeoman Hill Park
MANSFIELD RD.
B6032
MANSFIELD WOODHOUSE
Maun Valley Park
FOREST PARK MOBILE HOMES
TALL TREE PARK HOMES
Hillcrest
OLD MILL LANE
A6117
DEBDALE
CHESTERFIELD
SHERWOOD RISE
Queen Elizabeth Endowed School
Oakdale Support Centre
Tennis Courts
Playing Fields
Sherwood Swim. Baths
OLD MILL LANE INDUSTRIAL ESTATE
Hallam's Grave
Sewage Treatment Works
Works
Maun View

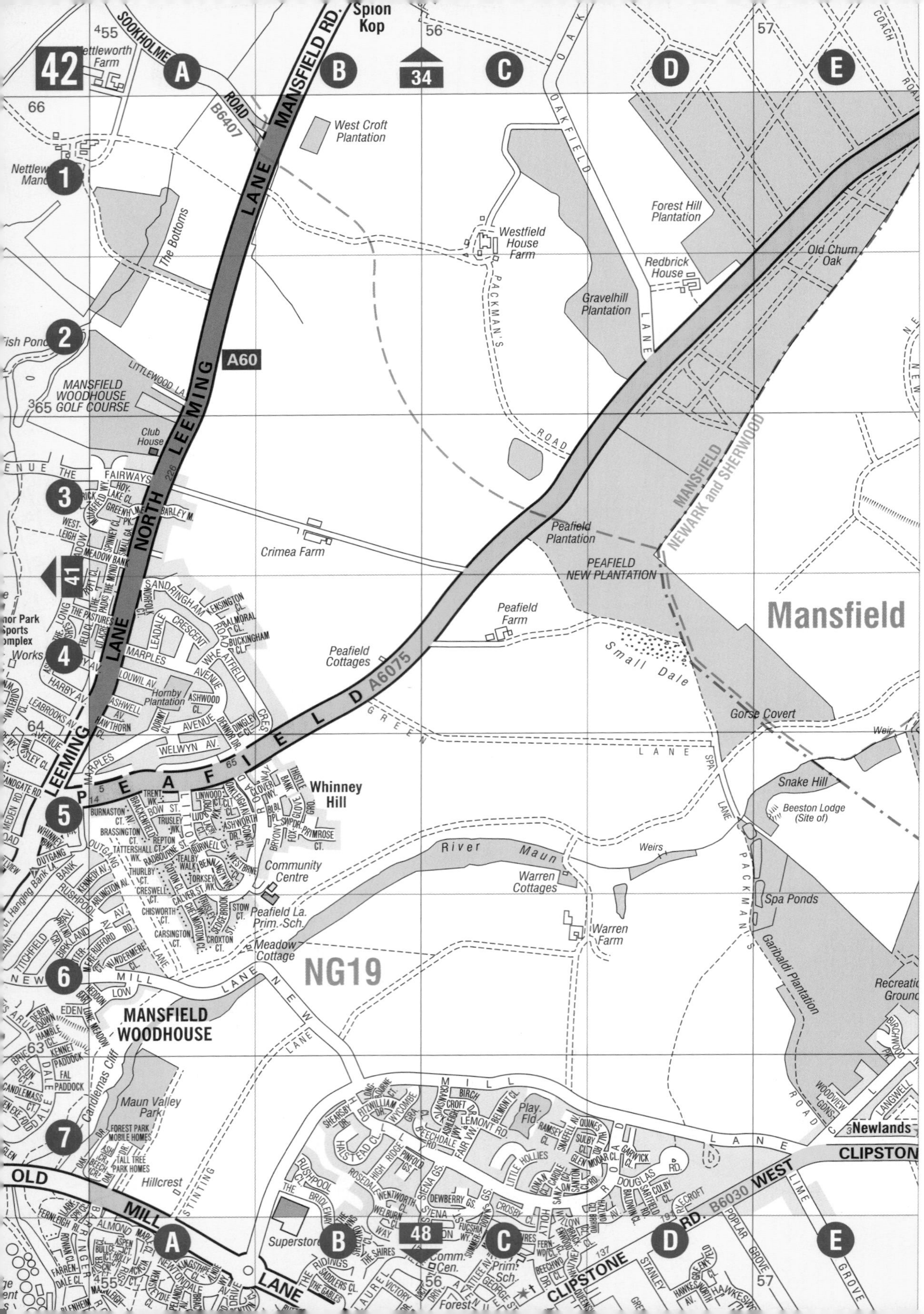
42
34
41
48
A
B
C
D
E
1
2
3
4
5
6
7
55
56
57
66
65
64
63
Spion Kop
Nettleworth Farm
SOOKHOLME ROAD
B6407
MANSFIELD RD.
West Croft Plantation
OAKFIELD LANE
LEEMING LANE NORTH
A60
The Bottoms
Fish Pond
MANSFIELD WOODHOUSE GOLF COURSE
LITTLEWOOD LA.
Club House
THE FAIRWAYS
Westfield House Farm
PACKMAN'S ROAD
Forest Hill Plantation
Redbrick House
Gravelhill Plantation
Old Churn Oak
COACH ROAD
Crimea Farm
Peafield Plantation
PEAFIELD NEW PLANTATION
MANSFIELD
NEWARK and SHERWOOD
Mansfield
Peafield Farm
Peafield Cottages
Small Dale
A6075
PEAFIELD LANE
GREEN LANE
SPA LANE
Gorse Covert
Weir
Snake Hill
Beeston Lodge (Site of)
Whinney Hill
River Maun
Weirs
Warren Cottages
Warren Farm
Community Centre
Peafield La. Prim. Sch.
Meadow Cottage
NG19
Spa Ponds
Garibaldi Plantation
Recreation Ground
MANSFIELD WOODHOUSE
NEW MILL LANE
LOW MILL LANE
Maun Valley Park
FOREST PARK MOBILE HOMES
TALL TREE PARK HOMES
Hillcrest
Candlemas Cliff
OLD MILL LANE
STINTING LANE
Superstore
Play. Fld.
Newlands
CLIPSTONE RD. WEST
B6030
LIME GROVE
POPLAR GROVE
Comm. Cen.
Prim. Sch.
Forest
WOODVIEW GDNS.
BIRCHWOOD PK.
LANGWELL

ROAD
LANE
A6075
F
G
H
J
K
58
59
460
35
43
Broomhill Grange
Gorseybrecks
66
Parliament Oak
DRIVE
Broomhill Gorse
1
GORSETHORPE LANE
GORSETHORPE COTTAGES
BUILDINGS
Sherwood Forest Farm Park
Lamb Pens Farm
NG20
2
Lawn Hills
SHERWOOD FOREST CARAVAN PARK
365
Cavendish Lodge
SQUIRES
HOLBROOK CR.
OLD BARN CT.
LANE
HILL TOP COTTS.
SQUIRES CFT.
3
Old Clipstone
River Maun
Cavendish Wood
BUILDINGS DRIVE
DRIVE
146
WATERWORKS DR.
ROAD
4
Waterfield Farm
Chestnut Screed
Mast
Intake Wood
Kings Clipstone
64
High Rocks
EMMER
ROCKLEY CL.
MIDDLETON
BROUGHTON CL.
WARD RD.
HILCOTE DR.
NOS
DRIVE
DODSLEY WY.
WATERFIELD WY.
Badger Hill
HIGHFIELD RD.
WOODLAND CL.
B6030
CLIPSTONE WORKSHOP UNITS
5
NG21
PORTLAND WY.
CARDINAL WY.
HIGHFIELD ROAD
HIGHFIELD M.
DAVIS CL.
KING JOHN'S RD.
BAULKER LANE
Baulker Farm
Vicar Water
Cemetery
INTAKE ROAD
GREENDALE CR.
SHERWOOD PL.
Newlands Junior School
Play. Fld.
Playing Field
Lib.
GORSEWAY
THE CIRCLE
Works
FIRST
THIRD
Sch.
Play. Fld.
NTH. CRES.
STH. CRES.
Clipstone Colliery
CLIPSTONE
STONE
BRAEMAR
GREENWAY
PARKWAY
KELVIN CL.
CARLTON CL.
MOUNT
John T. Rice Inf. Sch.
FOURTH AV.
FIFTH
FOREST ROAD
SECOND AV.
AVENUE
6
Slurry Pond
CHURCH RD.
CHURCH AV.
HAVEN CL.
Play. Fld.
Pav.
MANSFIELD ROAD
THE CT.
COPPICE
QUEEN'S CT.
PELHAM WAY
BIRCH TREE CL.
SEVENTH
SIXTH
CHURCH
AMBERLEY CT.
Sports Ground
Pav.
154
OSBERNE WY.
ZERS DR.
Vicar Water Country Park
63
GLEBE CT.
NEWLANDS DRIVE
GARIBALDI RD.
LILAC GRO.
WALNUT TREE CRES.
FIR TREE CL.
WILLOW TREE CL.
YEW TREE AV.
Garibaldi College Playing Field
Football Grd.
AVENUE
FAIRHOLME CL.
153
VICARS CT.
CENTRAL
EASTFIELD CT.
Vicar Pond
EAST MANSFIELD ROAD
B6030
EDMONTON RD.
STATION ROAD
DRIVE
Vicar Water Visitor Cen.
Water
7
Clipstone Colliery Junction
NEWLANDS
Newlands Farm
ROAD
NEWLANDS ROAD
Vicar
49
460

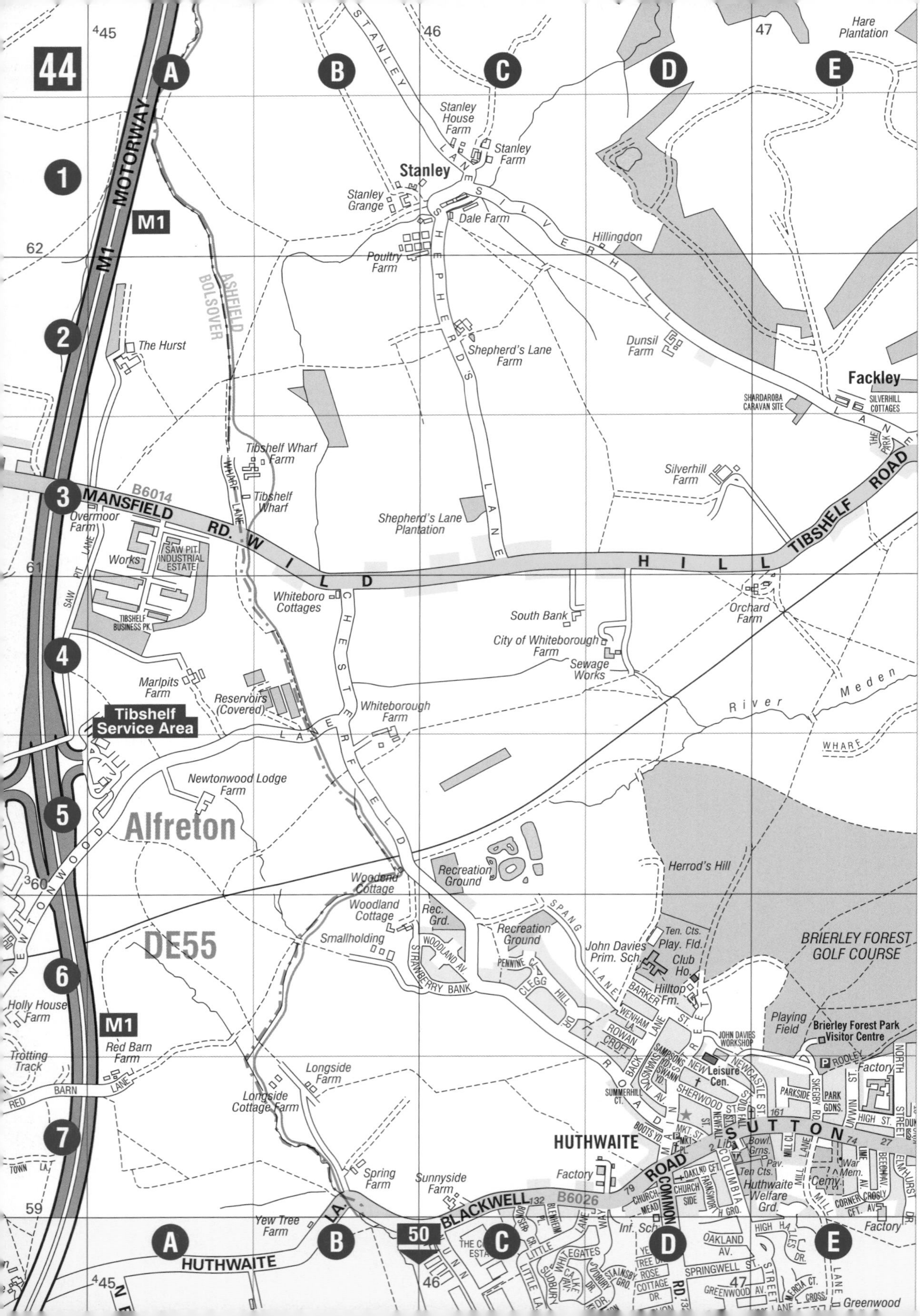

445
46
47
A
B
C
D
E
1
2
3
4
5
6
7
62
61
360
59
M1 MOTORWAY
M1
Hare Plantation
STANLEY LANE
Stanley House Farm
Stanley Farm
Stanley
Stanley Grange
Dale Farm
SILVERHILL LANE
Hillingdon
Poultry Farm
SHEPHERD'S LANE
ASHFIELD
BOLSOVER
The Hurst
Shepherd's Lane Farm
Dunsil Farm
Fackley
SHARDAROBA CARAVAN SITE
SILVERHILL COTTAGES
THE PARK
Tibshelf Wharf Farm
Silverhill Farm
B6014
MANSFIELD RD.
WILD HILL
TIBSHELF ROAD
WHARF LANE
Tibshelf Wharf
Overmoor Farm
Shepherd's Lane Plantation
SAW PIT LANE
Works
SAW PIT INDUSTRIAL ESTATE
TIBSHELF BUSINESS PK.
Whiteboro Cottages
CHESTERFIELD LANE
South Bank
Orchard Farm
City of Whiteborough Farm
Sewage Works
Marlpits Farm
Reservoirs (Covered)
Whiteborough Farm
River Meden
Tibshelf Service Area
WHARF
Newtonwood Lodge Farm
Alfreton
NEWTONWOOD LANE
Recreation Ground
Herrod's Hill
Woodend Cottage
Woodland Cottage
Rec. Grd.
SPANG LANE
DE55
Smallholding
WOODLAND AV.
STRAWBERRY BANK
Recreation Ground
PENNINE CL.
CLEGG HILL DR.
Ten. Cts.
Play. Fld.
John Davies Prim. Sch.
Club Ho.
BRIERLEY FOREST GOLF COURSE
Holly House Farm
Hilltop Fm.
BARKER ST.
WENHAM LA.
ROWAN CROFT
Playing Field
Brierley Forest Park Visitor Centre
Red Barn Farm
Trotting Track
Longside Farm
JOHN DAVIES WORKSHOP
ROWLEY
Factory
NORTH ST.
RED BARN LANE
Longside Cottage Farm
SUMMERHILL CT.
Leisure Cen.
NEWCASTLE ST.
PARKSIDE
SKEGBY RD.
PARK GDNS.
HIGH ST.
SHERWOOD ST.
Huthwaite
SUTTON ROAD
BOOTS YD.
MKT. ST.
MKT. PL.
Lib.
Bowl. Grns.
Pav.
Ten Cts.
War Mem.
Cemy.
TOWN LA.
Spring Farm
Sunnyside Farm
Factory
Huthwaite Welfare Grd.
COLUMBIA
MILL LANE
Yew Tree Farm
BLACKWELL ROAD
B6026
CHURCH SIDE
COMMON RD.
CORNER CFT.
Factory
HUTHWAITE LANE
50
THE C... ESTA...
LITTLE LANE
WHITEGATES
Inf. Sch.
OAKLAND AV.
HIGH PAVEMENT
SPRINGWELL ST.
GREENWOOD AV.
MERCIA CT.
CROSS
Greenwood

NG19
Hill Farm
River Meden
Little Dawgates Wood
DAWGATES LANE
GREEN
Ladywell
PEARTREE
PLEASLEY ROAD
Cemetery
Rec. Grd.
Teversal Farm
The Grange
BUTTERY
GRANGE CL.
MANOR CL.
Teversal Manor
Manor Farm
Teversal
Howlish
Sutton in Ashfield
Coppy Wood
Dawgates Wood
Dawgates Farm
Sewage Works
Dawgates
Station Farm
Pav.
Bowl. Grn.
Ten. Cts.
Spts. Grd.
Visitors Cen.
Cricket Ground
NG17
Football Ground
Fackley Farm
FACKLEY ROAD
River Meden
Heald's Wood
Driving Range
River Bank Fm.
Molineux House Farm
Skegby Lodge
WOODHOUSE
Daneswood Jun. Sch.
DENE
OLD RD.
BACK LA.
LOW RD.
B6014
MANSFIELD ROAD
Healdswood Inf. Sch.
Rec. Grd.
Play Fld.
Comm. Cen.
Lib.
Vic. Hall
Hall
Manor Ho. (remains)
Prim. Sch.
Skegby Hall
Meden Bank
Spring Wood Farm
Spring Wood
HIGH ST.
STONEYFORD ROAD
Sports Ground
SKEGBY
Stanton Hill
Recreation Ground
Stubbinghill Farm
BRAND LANE
BRIERLEY FOREST PARK
ROOLEY LANE
Rooley Tops
Wildflower Meadows
Brierley Waters
SUTTON IN ASHFIELD
Playing Field
Ten. Cts.
Quarrydale School
Nurs. Home
B6028
Rec. Grd.
Carsic Prim. Sch.
Playgrd.
Prim. Sch.
Cycle Track
Cemetery
Rec. Grd.
Nurs. Home
New Cross
Superstore
Bus Sta.
Lib.
IDLEWELLS SHOP. CEN.
Factories
Sutton Forest Side
Ten. Cts.
THE LAWN PLEASURE GROUNDS
HUTHWAITE ROAD
B6026
Sports Grd.
Ware-house
PRIESTSIC ROAD
B6023
LAMMAS ROAD
War Mem.
Playing Field
Jubilee Gdns.
Coll.
Leis. Cen.
Prim. Sch.
Bowl. Grn.
Pav.
48
49
450
62
61
360
59
F
G
H
J
K
1
2
3
4
5
6
7
46
51

40
45
52
A
B
C
D
E
1
2
3
4
5
6
7
NG19
NG17
SUTTON IN ASHFIELD
Sutton in Ashfield
Dalestorth
Bull Farm
Crescent Primary School
Water Lane Farm
Penniment Lodge Farm
Penniment House Farm
Penniment Farm
Penniment Cottage
Reservoirs (Covered)
Road Safety Training Cen.
Fields Farm
Hill Top
Fishpond Hill
Ashland Farm
Ashlands House
Dalestorth House
Nursery
Dawgates
Skegby Lodge
Dene Farm
Ladybrook
Ladybrook Prim. Sch.
New Rose Primary Sch.
Playing Fields
Playing Field
Redgate Sch.
All Saints RC School
KING'S MILL HOSPITAL
Millbrook
Byron Ho.
Superstore
The Dukeries Cen.
Day Cen.
HOSPICE
KINGSMILL RESERVOIR
Viaduct
River Maun
STOKES TRADING ESTATE
Hamilton Hill
Hamilton Hill Farm
Recreation Ground
Rec. Grd.
Prim. School
Comm. Cen.
Nursing Home
Works
Factory
Sewage Works
Sports Ground
Hillocks Prim. Sch.
Sutton Forest Side
THE LAWN PLEASURE GROUND
Playground
Bowling Green
MAUN INDUSTRIAL PARK
Depot
A617
A6075
A38
B6014
B6023
SKEGBY ROAD
SKEGBY LANE
ABBOTT ROAD
BECK LANE
KINGS MILL ROAD EAST
MANSFIELD ROAD
SUTTON ROAD
NORTH ROAD
WESTFIELD LANE
PENNIMENT LANE
WATER LANE
RUSKIN ROAD
BRICK KILN LANE
LADYBROOK LANE
DALESTORTH ROAD
DAWGATES LANE
WOODHOUSE LANE
HERMITAGE LANE
KINGS LODGE DRIVE
HAMILTON ROAD
50
51
52
59
60
61
62

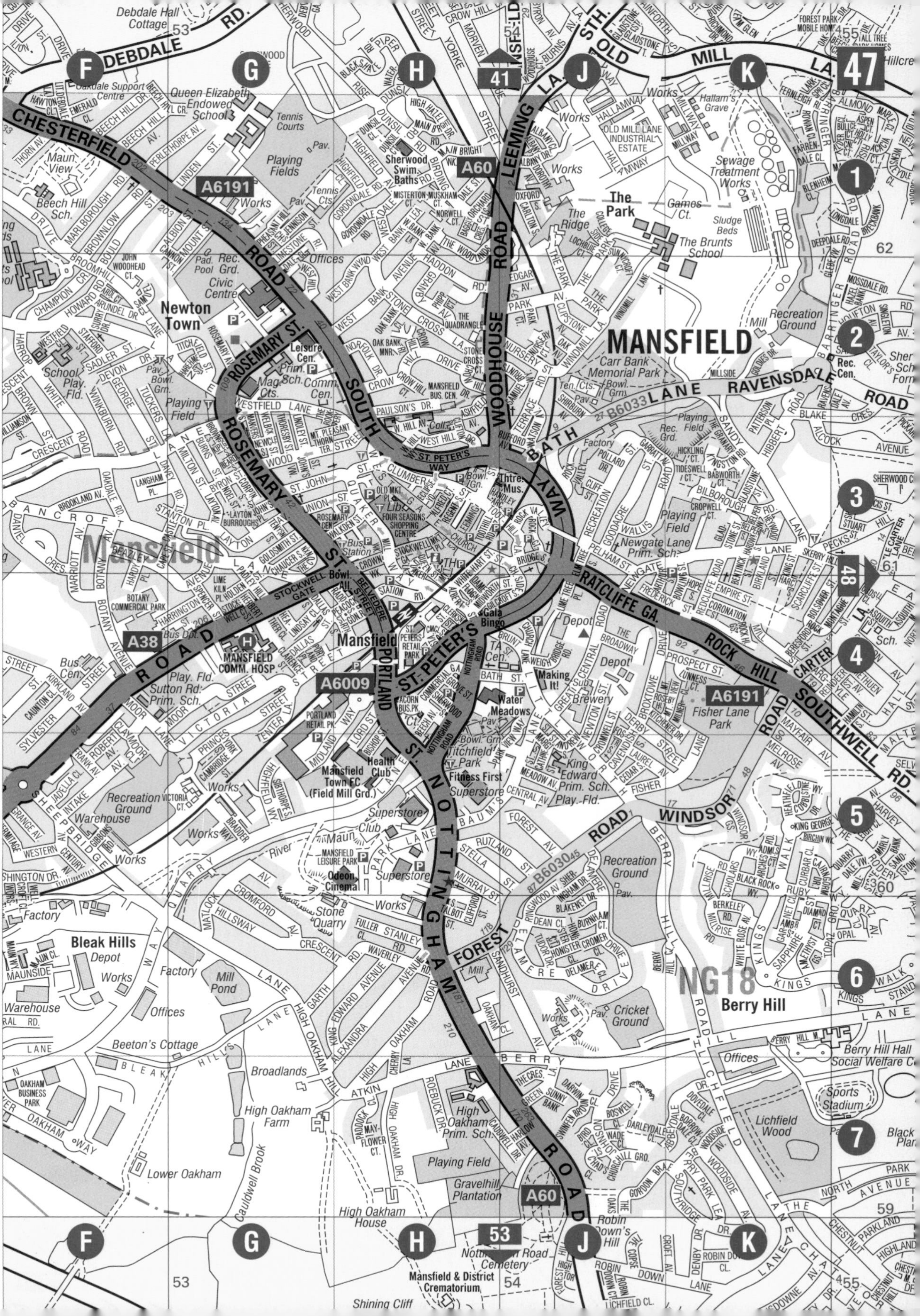
MANSFIELD
Mansfield
Newton Town
Berry Hill
NG18
CHESTERFIELD ROAD
DEBDALE RD.
OLD MILL LA.
LEEMING LA.
WOODHOUSE ROAD
ROSEMARY ST.
SOUTH
RAVENSDALE ROAD
SANDY LANE
BATH LANE
WAY
RATCLIFFE GA.
ROCK HILL
SOUTHWELL RD.
CARTER LA.
ST. PETER'S WAY
PORTLAND ST.
ST. PETER'S WAY
NOTTINGHAM ROAD
WINDSOR ROAD
FOREST ROAD
BERRY HILL LANE
LICHFIELD LANE
KINGS WALK
QUARRY LANE
BLEAK HILLS LANE
OAKHAM WAY
VICTORIA STREET
STOCKWELL GATE
ROAD
A6191
A60
A38
A6009
B6033
B6030
41
48
53
F
G
H
J
K
1
2
3
4
5
6
7
Debdale Hall Cottage
Oakdale Support Centre
Queen Elizabeth Endowed School
Tennis Courts
Playing Fields
Sherwood Swim. Baths
Maun View
Beech Hill Sch.
Civic Centre
Rec. Grd.
Pad. Pool
Offices
Works
Old Mill Lane Industrial Estate
Hallam's Grave
Sewage Treatment Works
Sludge Beds
The Park
Games Ct.
The Ridge
The Brunts School
Recreation Ground
Carr Bank Memorial Park
Rec. Cen.
Leisure Cen.
Mag. Cts.
Comm. Cen.
Playing Field
School Play. Fld.
Mansfield Bus. Cen.
Four Seasons Shopping Centre
Bus Station
Thtre. Mus.
Bowl. Gn.
Old Mkt. Pl.
Gala Bingo
Lib.
Botany Commercial Park
Mansfield Comm. Hosp.
Bus. Cen.
Play. Fld.
Sutton Rd. Prim. Sch.
Portland Retail Pk.
Peters Retail Park
TA Cen.
Making It!
Water Meadows
Depot
Brewery
Fisher Lane Park
Newgate Lane Prim. Sch.
Health Club
Mansfield Town FC (Field Mill Grd.)
Titchfield Park
Fitness First
Superstore
King Edward Prim. Sch.
Mansfield Leisure Park
Odeon Cinema
Club
Stone Quarry
Factory
Bleak Hills Depot
Mill Pond
Warehouse
Beeton's Cottage
Broadlands
Oakham Business Park
High Oakham Farm
Lower Oakham
Cauldwell Brook
High Oakham Prim. Sch.
Playing Field
Gravelhill Plantation
High Oakham House
Nottingham Road Cemetery
Mansfield & District Crematorium
Shining Cliff
Robin Down's Hill
Cricket Ground
Berry Hill Hall Social Welfare C
Sports Stadium
Lichfield Wood
River Maun
Forest Park Mobile Home Park

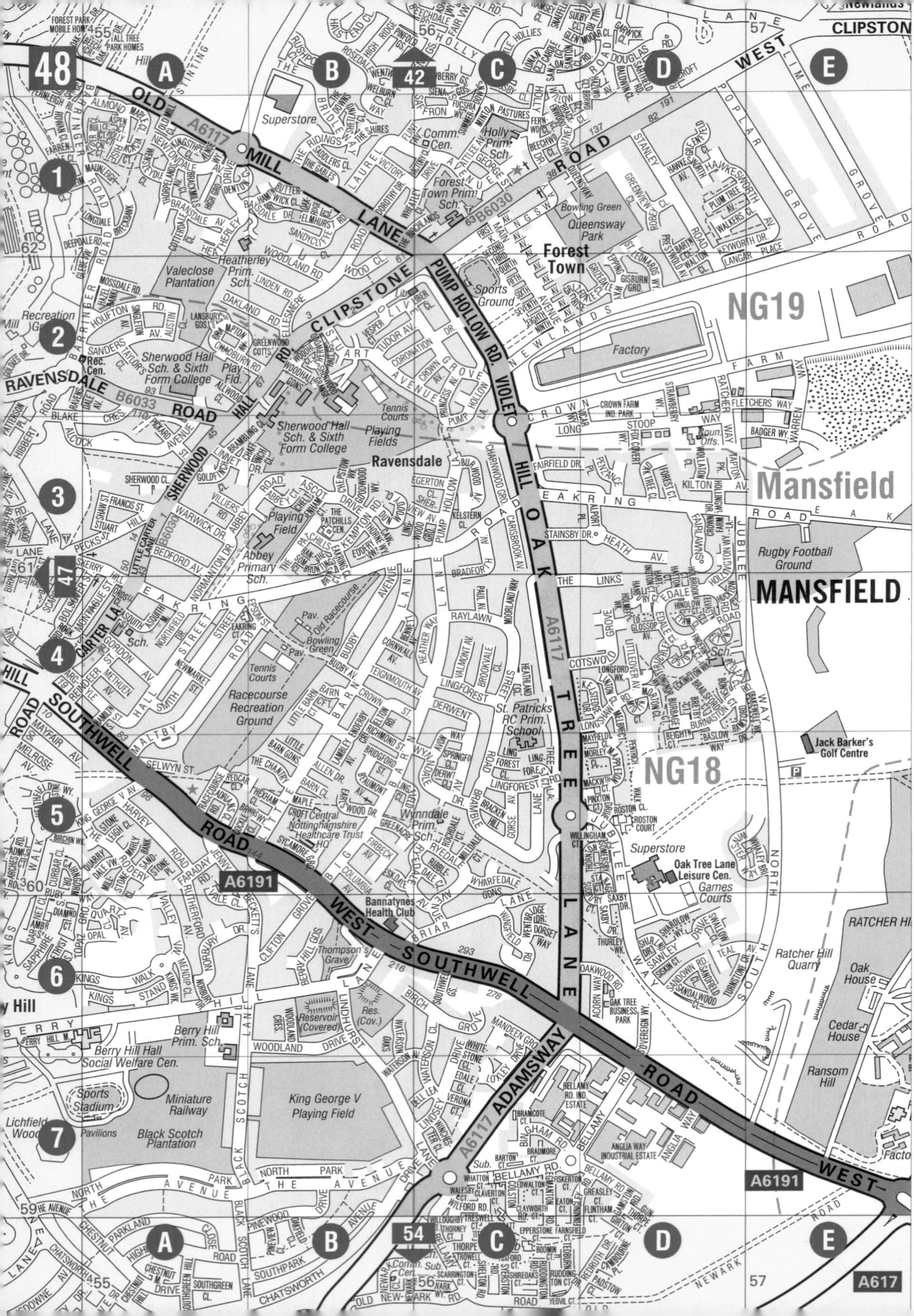

CLIPSTONE
WEST
ROAD
OLD MILL LANE
A6117
Superstore
Comm. Cen.
Holly Prim. Sch.
Forest Town Prim. Sch.
B6030
Bowling Green
Queensway Park
Forest Town
Valeclose Plantation
Heatherley Prim. Sch.
Sports Ground
NG19
Factory
NEWLANDS
FARM
CROWN FARM IND. PARK
FLETCHERS WAY
BADGER WY.
Coun. Offs.
Recreation Gd.
Rec. Cen.
RAVENSDALE ROAD
B6033
Sherwood Hall Sch. & Sixth Form College
Play Fld.
Tennis Courts
Playing Fields
Ravensdale
CLIPSTONE RD.
PUMP HOLLOW RD.
VIOLET HILL
OAK TREE LANE
SHERWOOD HALL RD.
Mansfield
EAKRING ROAD
KILTON AV.
Playing Field
Abbey Primary Sch.
Rugby Football Ground
MANSFIELD
THE LINKS
Old Racecourse
Pav.
Bowling Green
Tennis Courts
Racecourse Recreation Ground
Sch.
St. Patricks RC Prim. School
NG18
Jack Barker's Golf Centre
SOUTHWELL ROAD
WEST
Central Nottinghamshire Healthcare Trust HQ
Wynndale Prim. Sch.
Superstore
Oak Tree Lane Leisure Cen.
Games Courts
A6191
Bannatynes Health Club
Thompson's Grave
WEST SOUTHWELL ROAD
Ratcher Hill Quarry
Oak House
Cedar House
Ransom Hill
RATCHER HILL
OAK TREE BUSINESS PARK
Reservoir (Covered)
Res. (Cov.)
BERRY HILL
Berry Hill Prim. Sch.
Berry Hill Hall Social Welfare Cen.
Sports Stadium
Miniature Railway
Lichfield Wood
Pavilions
Black Scotch Plantation
King George V Playing Field
ADAMSWAY
BELLAMY RD. IND. ESTATE
ANGLIA WAY INDUSTRIAL ESTATE
NORTH PARK
THE AVENUE
BLACK SCOTCH LANE
CHATSWORTH
NEWARK
OLD NEWARK RD.
Comm. Cen.
Sub.
A617
A B C D E
1 2 3 4 5 6 7
42
47
54
55
56
57
59
60
61
62

49
ROAD
58
59
Playing Field
EDMONTON RD.
DRIVE
ROAD
Vicar Water
Visitor Cen.
Vicar Water
Clipstone Colliery Junction
43
F
G
H
J
K
NEWLANDS ROAD
Newlands Farm
NEWLANDS
Vicar Water
WAY
Long Plantation
1
2
3
4
5
6
7
62
61
60
59
146
SHERWOOD FOREST GOLF COURSE
MANSFIELD NEWARK and SHERWOOD
Club House
RING ROAD
NG21
CLIPSTONE FOREST
Strawberry Hill
Slurry Pond
Ransom Hall (North Nottingham Health HQ)
RANSOM WOOD BUSINESS PARK
Red Oaks Day Cen.
Dawn House School
A617
The Sherwood Village Settlement
Sports Pitch
Heathlands Prim. Sch.
RANSOM ROAD
ROAD
Works
RAINWORTH BY-PASS
Rainworth Nursery
Spring Hill
Filter Beds
Sewage Works
Water
Rainworth
B6020
SOUTHWELL ROAD EAST
HELMSLEY
THE CLOSE
Nursery Cott.
BIRCHWOOD PARK HOMES
PARK HOMES
LEEWAY CL.
LEEWAY RD.
FOURTH AV.
55
Three Thorn Hollow
58
59
460

50
44
58
A
B
C
D
E
1
2
3
4
5
6
7
45
46
47
59
58
57
56
HUTHWAITE
Spring Farm
Sunnyside Farm
Factory
Yew Tree Farm
BLACKWELL ROAD
SUTTON ROAD
Huthwaite Welfare Grd.
Inf. Sch.
Lib.
Bowl.
Ten Cts.
Pav.
War Mem.
Pipes Fm.
HUTHWAITE LANE
B6026
M1 MOTORWAY
M1
NEW LANE
B6406
Twinyards Farm
THE COUNTY ESTATE
NUNN BROOK ROAD
LITTLE LANE
WHITEGATES
OAKLAND AV.
SPRINGWELL ST.
GREENWOOD AV.
CARNARVON
CROSS
BAINBRIDGE
HIGH HALLES DR.
Greenwood Falls Farm
Commonside
Depot
ROBERTS AV.
THE PADDOCKS
THE GREEN
NEW HUCKNALL WAY
MILL LANE
PROSPECT CT.
NUNN CL.
Works
COMMON ROAD
B6027
Household Waste & Recycling Centre
Sewage Works
BROOKSIDE WAY
Nunn Brook
Recreation Ground
PASTURE LA.
HILCOTE LANE
FAIRFIELD
OAK TREE AV.
COKEFIELD TER.
STREET
Hilcote
Alfreton
Fish Farm
Normanton Brook
WATERLOO
BERRISTOW LANE
ASHFIELD
BOLSOVER
DE55
Sewage Works
HIGH VIEW ROAD
Works
Industrial Estate
Wincobank Farm
FULWOOD RD. NORTH
Factory
Wks.
FULWOOD INDUSTRIAL ESTATE
SOUTH ST.
ROOKERY LANE
FULWOOD DRIVE
FULWOOD ROAD
VENTURE AV.
EXPORT DRIVE
Depot
Freight Terminal
Cutting Farm
ALFRETON ROAD
Berristow Farm
BERRISTOW PL.
CARTWRIGHT LANE
NORMANTON BROOK RD.
Normanton Lodge
Factory
Grange Farm
EAST
VIEW
Weir
McARTHURGLEN DESIGNER OUTLET
Moat
Castle Wood
Range Farm
Crow Trees Farm
The Dumbles
BALL HILL
CARTER LANE
CARTER LANE EAST
WATER LA.
THORNHILL DR.
NEWLYN DR.
KENWACK CL.
KYNANCE CL.
PENDINE CL.
PENRYN CL.
TURNLEY
HARDWICK CT.
CORN CLOSE
CORONATION
HIGHFIELD DR.
LEAMINGTON DR.
HAZEL GRO.
CARTER LA. WEST
SOUTHFIELD DR.
MANSFIELD ROAD
A38
Hotel
PINXTON LANE
Terrace Wood
Brookhill Hall Farm
NG16
Junction 28
MANSFIELD RD.
PINXTON LA.
Frederick Gent School
Playing Field
PADDOCKS CL.
ALFRETON RD.
M1 MOTORWAY
BROOKHILL
Brookhill Hall
Halfmoon Pond
Weir
Kirkby Cliff Farm
Shire Carr Farm
STORTH LA.
NURSERY
FINLEY
BROOME ACRE
STORTH
GEORGE ST.
WEST END
TOWN STREET
B6019
BROOKHILL LA.
WOODFIELD
Maghole
Brook
CLIFF LANE COTTAGES
CLIFF LANE
Works
Cliff Farm
KIRKBY LANE
PINXTON GN.
HILLTOP
WESTLAND DR.
SACHEVERALL AV.
BILLINGSLEY AV.
LAMBCROFT RD.
KING ARTHUR'S ST.
VICTORIA RD.
SOUTHFIELDS AV.
King John's Workshop Mus.
Sch.
CHURCH
GLEBE
WEST
Kirkstead
ACER CL.
QUEEN ST.
Hall Farm

51
SUTTON IN ASHFIELD
Sutton in Ashfield
NG17
KIRKBY-IN-ASHFIELD
Kirkby-in-Ashfield
Nottingham
Fulwood
New Cross
Bentinck Town
Castle Hill
Mapplewells Prim. Sch.
Recreation Ground
Jubilee Gdns.
Playing Field
Ashfield Sch. & Technology College
Running Track
Birchwood Grange
Bloomer Wood
The Dumbles Bungalow
Mowlands Farm
Franderground Farm
Springfield Cottage
Tichfield Park
Greenwood Prim. Sch.
Leamington Prim. Sch.
Orchard Prim. Sch.
Jeffries Sch.
THE LAWN PLEASURE GROUNDS
Studfold Farm
Studfold Wood
River Erewash
Boar Hill
Fish Ponds
Cemetery
Works
Factories
KINGS MILL ROAD
A38
B6023
B6026
B6021
B6018
B6019
B6020
PINXTON LANE
ALFRETON ROAD
HUTHWAITE ROAD
LAMMAS RD.
PRIESTSIC RD.
CHURCH ST.
CHAPEL ST.
THE HILL
VICTORIA ROAD
SUTTON ROAD
KIRKBY ROAD
STATION ROAD
EAST
ODDICROFT LANE
COW PASTURE LANE
WENTWORTH ROAD
45
52
59
F
G
H
J
K
1
2
3
4
5
6
7
48
49
450

52
A
B
C
D
E
46
60
51
1
2
3
4
5
6
7
SUTTON IN ASHFIELD
Sutton Forest Side
THE LAWN PLEASURE GROUNDS
MILL ROAD
A38
EAST
COXMOOR ROAD
A617
Hamilton Hill
Hamilton Hill Farm
CAULDWELL ROAD
Nursery
Sutton in Ashfield
NG17
STATION ROAD
B6022
NEWARK ROAD
MAUN VALLEY INDUSTRIAL PARK
Willow Wood Cen.
KIRKBY FOLLY RD.
Round Hill
Roundhill Farm
Redhouse Farm
B6139
Fairway
Bellever
The Cedars
Sherwood Observatory
Hacienda
High Close
La Vista
Windmill Hill
KINGS MILL ROAD
ODDICROFT LANE
B6021
Sutton Parkway
Kirkby Hardwick
LOWMOOR ROAD
LOWMOOR BUSINESS PARK
BYRON AVENUE
Nottingham
NG17
KIRKBY-IN-ASHFIELD
PORTLAND INDUSTRIAL ESTATE
SOUTHWELL LANE IND. ESTATE
SOUTHWELL LANE
Nursing Home
Coxmoor Lodge
Coxmoor Plantation
Coxmoor Farm
Coxmoor House
Cox Moor
Football Ground
ASHFIELD COMMUNITY HOSPITAL
Kirkby-in-Ashfield
Council Offs.
VICTORIA ROAD
URBAN RD.
STATION ST.
DIAMOND AVENUE
B6020
BLIDWORTH
KINGSWAY
Coxmoor Prim. Sch.
Bracken Hill Sch.
Heaths Cottages
Forest
A611
DERBY ROAD
Reservoirs (covered)
Kingsway Park
Studfold Farm
Studfold Wood
Cemetery
Pearl Farm
Kingsway Prim. Sch.
Vernon Farm

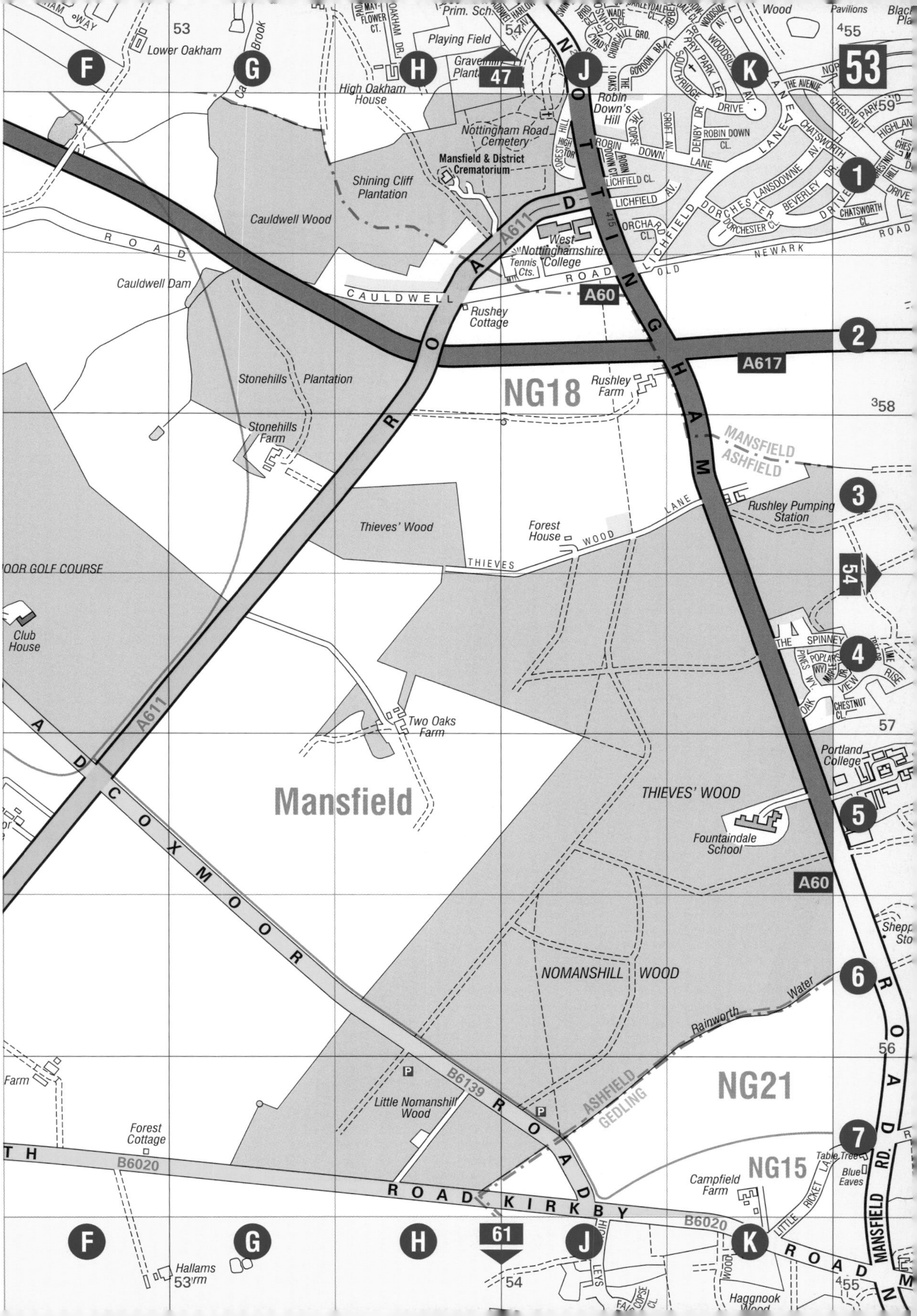
Lower Oakham
Prim. Sch.
Playing Field
High Oakham House
Robin Down's Hill
Nottingham Road Cemetery
Mansfield & District Crematorium
Shining Cliff Plantation
Cauldwell Wood
Cauldwell Dam
West Nottinghamshire College
Tennis Cts.
CAULDWELL ROAD
NEWARK ROAD
OLD
A60
A611
A617
Rushey Cottage
Stonehills Plantation
NG18
Rushley Farm
Stonehills Farm
MANSFIELD
ASHFIELD
Rushley Pumping Station
Thieves' Wood
Forest House
THIEVES WOOD LANE
NOTTINGHAM ROAD
MOOR GOLF COURSE
Club House
THE SPINNEY
Two Oaks Farm
Portland College
Mansfield
THIEVES' WOOD
Fountaindale School
COXMOOR ROAD
NOMANSHILL WOOD
Rainworth Water
NG21
B6139
Little Nomanshill Wood
ASHFIELD
GEDLING
Forest Cottage
B6020
KIRKBY ROAD
NG15
Campfield Farm
Table Tree
Blue Eaves
LITTLE RICKET LA.
MANSFIELD RD.
Hallams Farm
Haggnook Wood
Pavilions
Wood
47
54
61
F
G
H
J
K
1
2
3
4
5
6
7
53
54
455
359
358
57
56
455

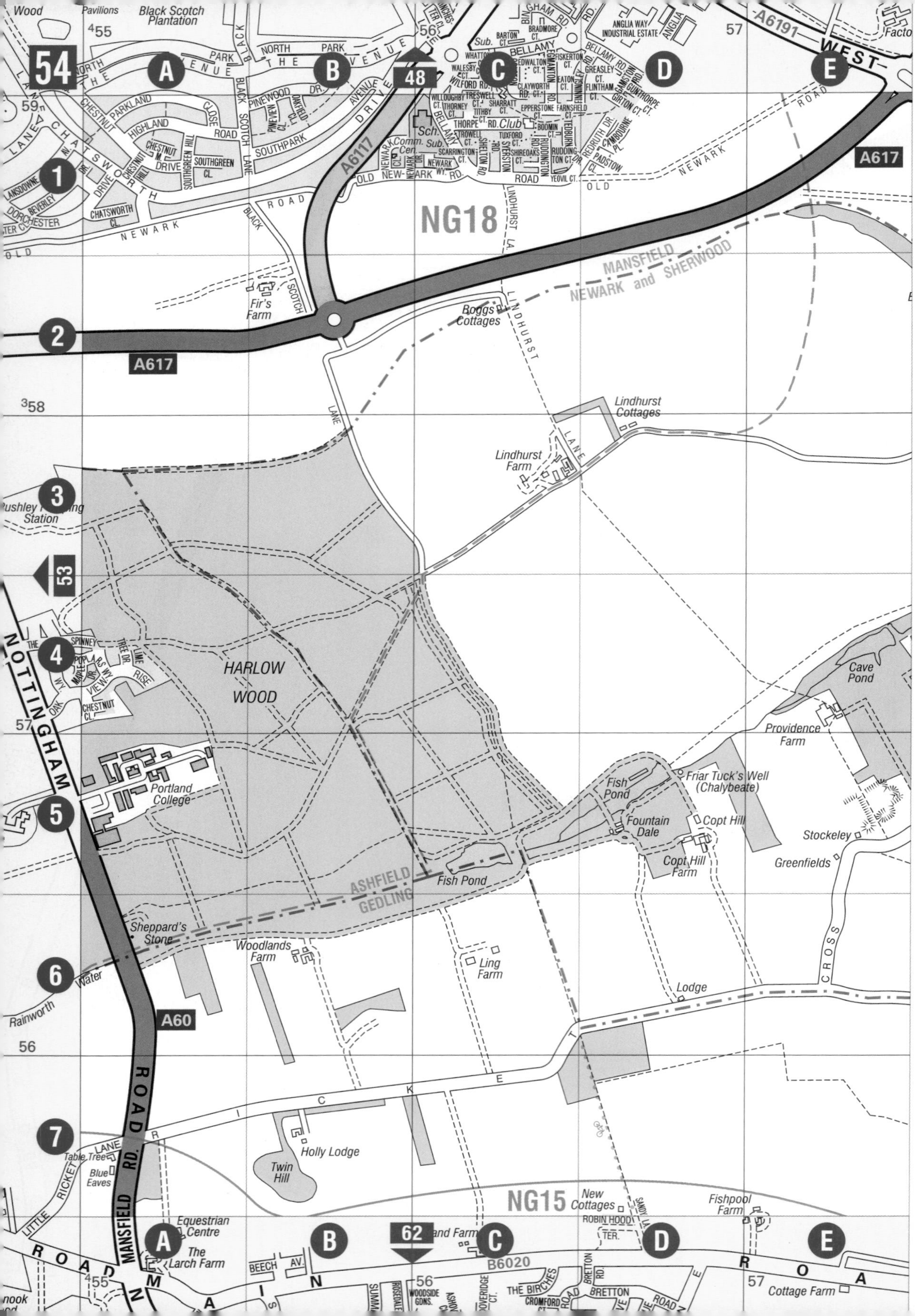

54
48
53
62
A
B
C
D
E
1
2
3
4
5
6
7
455
456
457
358
59
57
56
NG18
NG15
A617
A6117
A6191
A60
B6020
Black Scotch Plantation
Pavilions
Wood
NORTH PARK
THE AVENUE
CHESTNUT
PARKLAND
HIGHLAND
CLOSE
ROAD
BLACK SCOTCH LANE
PINEWOOD DR.
SOUTHPARK
SOUTHGREEN HILL
SOUTHGREEN CL.
CHATSWORTH DRIVE
CHATSWORTH CL.
LANSDOWNE
BEVERLEY
DORCHESTER
OLD NEWARK ROAD
ANGLIA WAY INDUSTRIAL ESTATE
BINGHAM RD.
BRADMORE CT.
BARTON CT.
BELLAMY
BELLAMY RD.
Sch.
Sub.
Comm. Cen.
Club
Fir's Farm
Boggs Cottages
LINDHURST LA.
LINDHURST LANE
Lindhurst Cottages
Lindhurst Farm
MANSFIELD
NEWARK and SHERWOOD
ASHFIELD
GEDLING
Station
HARLOW WOOD
THE SPINNEY
LIME TREE DR.
RISE
CHESTNUT CL.
NOTTINGHAM ROAD
Portland College
Fish Pond
Fish Pond
Friar Tuck's Well (Chalybeate)
Fountain Dale
Copt Hill
Copt Hill Farm
Providence Farm
Cave Pond
Stockeley
Greenfields
CROSS
Sheppard's Stone
Woodlands Farm
Ling Farm
Lodge
Rainworth Water
RICKET LANE
LITTLE RICKET
Table Tree
Blue Eaves
Holly Lodge
Twin Hill
New Cottages
ROBIN HOOD TER.
SANDY LA.
Fishpool Farm
Equestrian Centre
The Larch Farm
MANSFIELD RD.
MANSFIELD ROAD
ROAD
MAIN
BEECH AV.
ROSEDALE
WOODSIDE GDNS.
THE BIRCHES
BRETTON RD.
BRETTON
CROMFORD
Cottage Farm

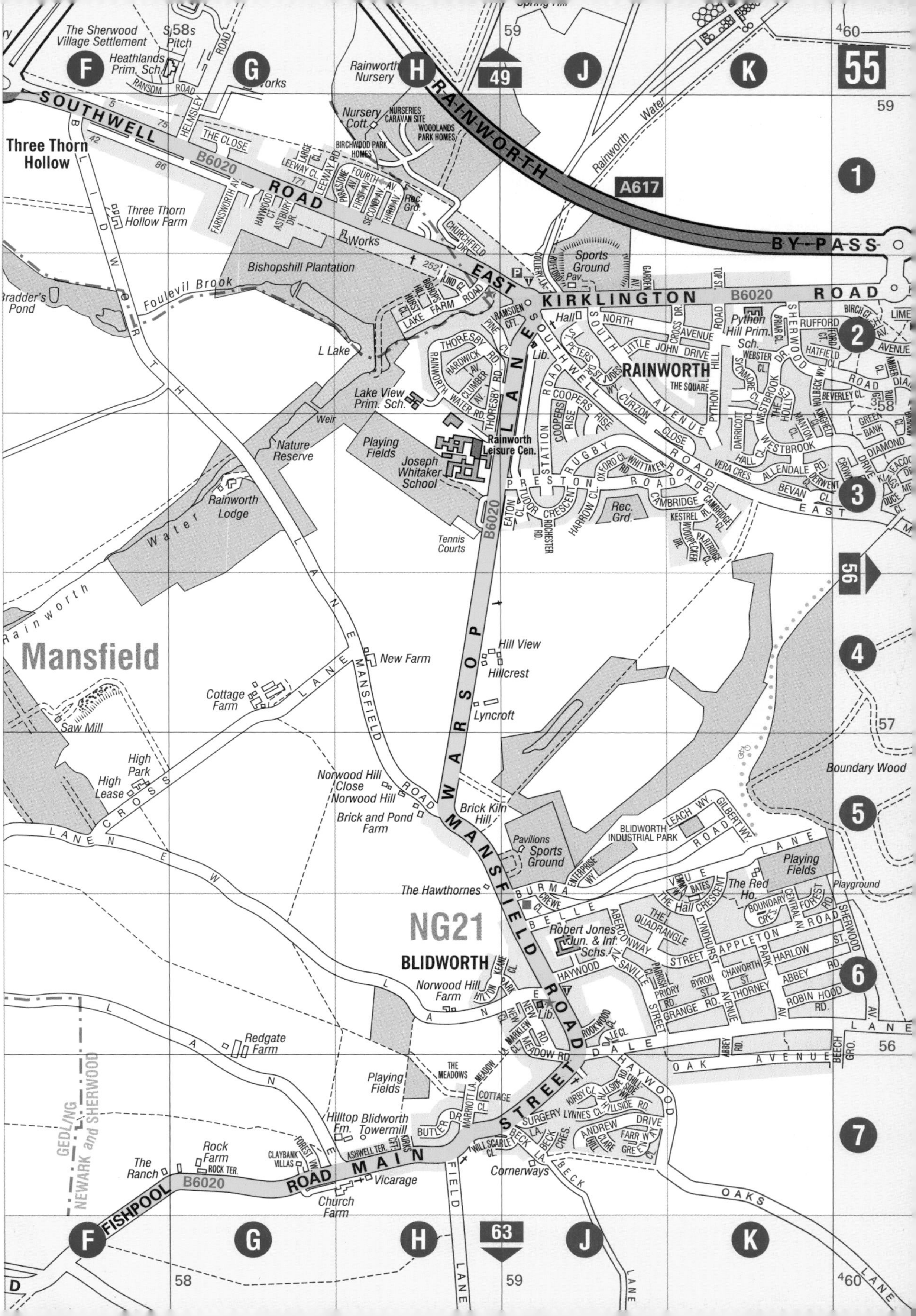
55
49
56
63
F
G
H
J
K
1
2
3
4
5
6
7
58
59
460
57
56
The Sherwood Village Settlement
58s Pitch
Heathlands Prim. Sch.
Works
RANSOM ROAD
HELMSLEY
SOUTHWELL ROAD
B6020
THE CLOSE
Three Thorn Hollow
Three Thorn Hollow Farm
BLIDWORTH LANE
FARNSWORTH AV.
HAYWOOD CT.
ASTBURY DR.
LEEWAY CL.
LEEWAY RD.
LARGE CL.
PARKSTONE AV.
FIRST AV.
FOURTH AV.
SECOND AV.
THIRD AV.
Rec. Grd.
Rainworth Nursery
Nursery Cott.
NURSERIES CARAVAN SITE
WOODLANDS PARK HOMES
BIRCHWOOD PARK HOMES
RAINWORTH BY-PASS
A617
Rainworth Water
CHURCHFIELD DR.
Bishopshill Plantation
Foulevil Brook
Bradder's Pond
EAST
BISHOPS HILL
HURST CL.
LIND CL.
LAKE FARM ROAD
LAKE CL.
L Lake
COLLERY LA.
RUFFORD
Sports Ground
Pav.
KIRKLINGTON ROAD
GARDEN AV.
TOP ST.
NORTH
Hall
RAMSDEN CFT.
PINE CL.
THORESBY RD.
HARDWICK AV.
CLIMBER AV.
RAINWORTH WATER RD.
Lib.
SOUTHWELL WY.
ST. PETERS
ST. JUDES
LITTLE JOHN DRIVE
CROSS DR.
AVENUE
Python Hill Prim. Sch.
PYTHON HILL
RAINWORTH
THE SQUARE
SOUTH AVENUE
CURZON
CLOSE
WEBSTER CL.
SYCAMORE CL.
WESTBROOK DR.
SHERWOOD
RUFFORD CT.
FORD
HATFIELD CL.
BIRCH CL.
LIME
AVENUE
BEVERLEY CL.
HOLBECK WY.
KINGFIELD
Lake View Prim. Sch.
Weir
Nature Reserve
Playing Fields
Joseph Whitaker School
Rainworth Leisure Cen.
COOPERS RISE
STATION ROAD
RUGBY
OXFORD CL.
WHITTAKER RD.
PRESTON ROAD
EATON CL.
TUDOR CRESCENT
HARROW CL.
ROCHESTER RD.
Rec. Grd.
CAMBRIDGE
KESTREL RI.
WOODPECKER DR.
PARTRIDGE CL.
DARRICOTT CL.
HALL
VERA CRES.
ALLENDALE RD.
WESTBROOK
GREEN BANK
DIAMOND
BEVAN CL.
DERWENT
EAST
Rainworth Lodge
Water
Tennis Courts
B6020
Rainworth
Mansfield
WARSOP LANE
Hill View
Hillcrest
Lyncroft
New Farm
MANSFIELD LANE
Cottage Farm
Saw Mill
High Park
High Lease
CROSS LANE
NEW LANE
Norwood Hill Close
Norwood Hill
Brick and Pond Farm
Brick Kiln Hill
MANSFIELD ROAD
Pavilions
Sports Ground
BLIDWORTH INDUSTRIAL PARK
LEACH WY.
GILBERT WY.
ROAD
LANE
Boundary Wood
Playing Fields
Playground
The Red Ho.
ENTERPRISE WY.
BURMA
BELLE VUE
CREWE CL.
BATES
The Hall
CRESCENT
THE QUADRANGLE
ABERCONWAY
LYNDHURST
BOUNDARY CRES.
CENTRAL AV.
FOREST RD.
SHERWOOD
The Hawthornes
NG21
BLIDWORTH
Robert Jones Jun. & Inf. Schs.
STREET
APPLETON
HARLOW
PARK
HAYWOOD
SAVILLE
PARRISH CL.
CHAWORTH ST.
THORNEY
ABBEY RD.
ROBIN HOOD RD.
PRIORY RD.
BYRON ST.
GRANGE RD.
AVENUE
KEANE CL.
PARK
HILTON
Norwood Hill Farm
NEW LA.
Lib.
ROOKWOOD CL.
DALE CL.
LANE
DALE
OAK AVENUE
ABBEY RD.
BEECH GRO.
MARKLEW
MEADOW RD.
Redgate Farm
GEDLING
NEWARK and SHERWOOD
Playing Fields
THE MEADOWS
MEADOW
MARRIOTT LA.
COTTAGE CL.
BUTLER DR.
HAYWOOD
KIRBY CL.
HILLSIDE RD.
LYNNES CL.
SURGERY
ANDREW DRIVE
FARR WY.
CLARE HILL
GREEN CL.
BECK LA.
BECK CRES.
WILL SCARLET CL.
Hilltop Fm.
Blidworth Towermill
KIRKS CFT.
ASHWELL TER.
FOREST VW.
CLAYBANK VILLAS
The Ranch
Rock Farm
ROCK TER.
FISHPOOL ROAD
B6020
MAIN STREET
Vicarage
Church Farm
FIELD LANE
Cornerways
BECK LANE
OAKS LANE
D

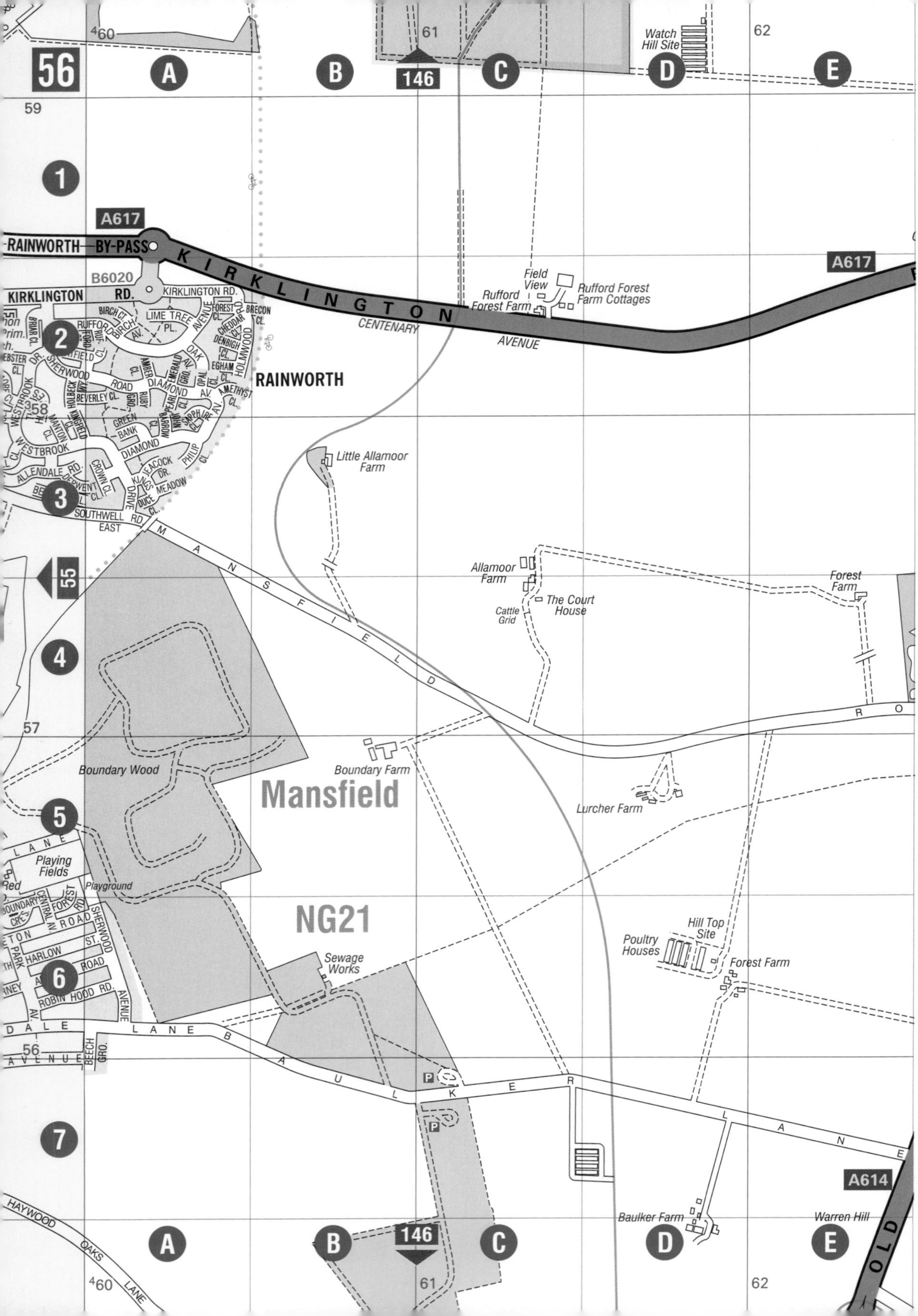
A
B
C
D
E
1
2
3
4
5
6
7
146
55
59
58
57
56
460
61
62
A617
RAINWORTH BY-PASS
B6020
KIRKLINGTON RD.
KIRKLINGTON
RAINWORTH
CENTENARY
AVENUE
Field View
Rufford Forest Farm
Rufford Forest Farm Cottages
Watch Hill Site
Little Allamoor Farm
Allamoor Farm
The Court House
Cattle Grid
Forest Farm
MANSFIELD
ROAD
Boundary Wood
Boundary Farm
Mansfield
Lurcher Farm
Playing Fields
Playground
NG21
Sewage Works
Hill Top Site
Poultry Houses
Forest Farm
LANE
BAULKER LANE
A614
Baulker Farm
Warren Hill
OLD
HAYWOOD OAKS LANE
SOUTHWELL RD. EAST
SHERWOOD
DIAMOND AV.
WESTBROOK
ALLENDALE RD.
ROBIN HOOD RD.
HARLOW ST.
BEECH GRO.
AVENUE

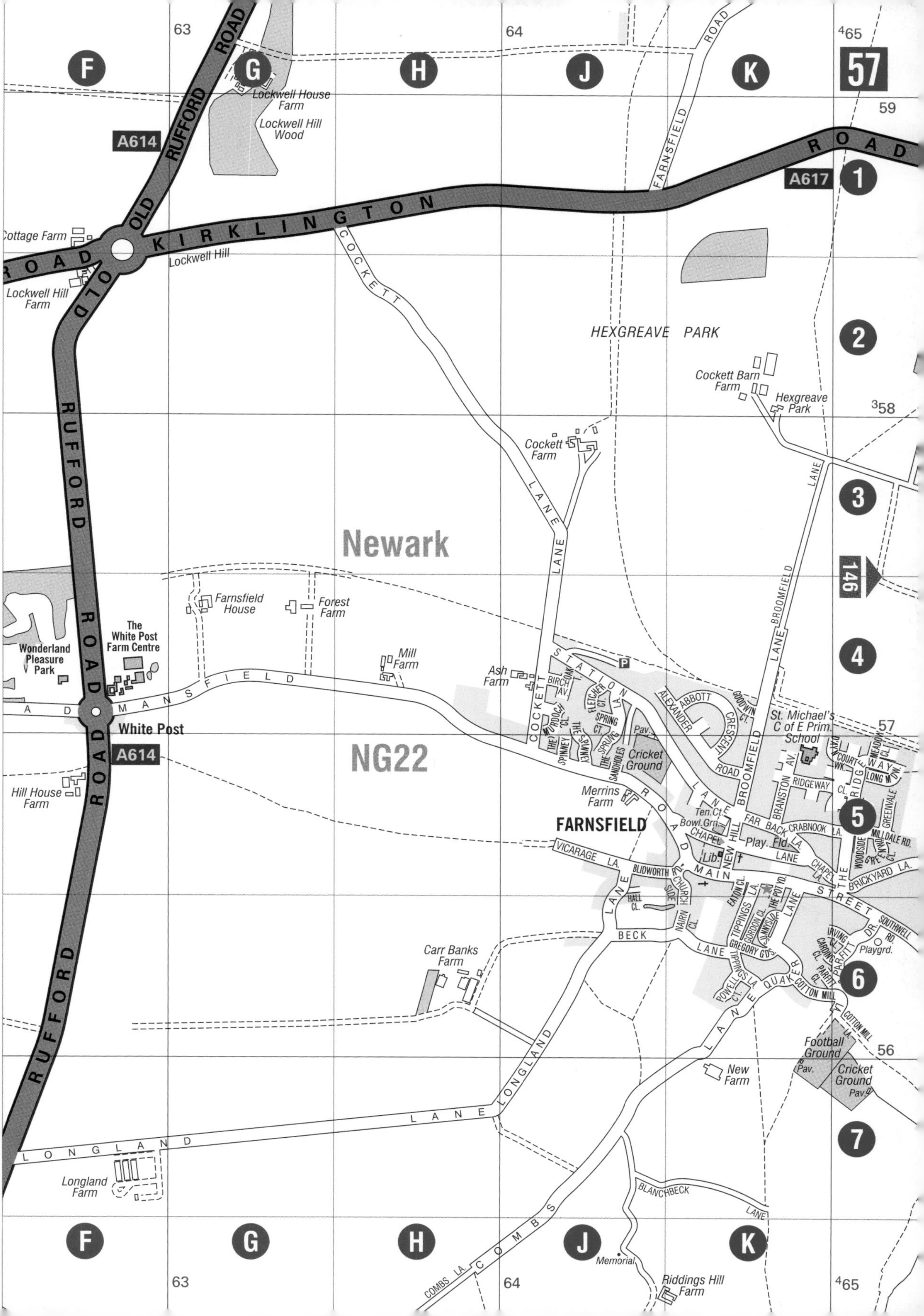
63
64
465
F
G
H
J
K
59
Lockwell House Farm
Lockwell Hill Wood
A614
OLD RUFFORD ROAD
FARNSFIELD
ROAD
KIRKLINGTON ROAD
A617
1
Cottage Farm
Lockwell Hill
Lockwell Hill Farm
COCKETT LANE
HEXGREAVE PARK
2
Cockett Barn Farm
Hexgreave Park
358
Cockett Farm
3
Newark
146
BROOMFIELD LANE
Farnsfield House
Forest Farm
The White Post Farm Centre
Wonderland Pleasure Park
Mill Farm
MANSFIELD ROAD
Ash Farm
STATION LANE
4
White Post
A614
NG22
St. Michael's C of E Prim. School
57
Cricket Ground
Pav.
Hill House Farm
Merrins Farm
FARNSFIELD
5
Ten.Ct.
Bowl.Grn.
Play. Fld.
Lib.
VICARAGE LA.
BLIDWORTH RD.
MAIN STREET
BRICKYARD LA.
BECK LANE
Carr Banks Farm
Playgrd.
6
QUAKER LANE
COTTON MILL LA.
Football Ground
Cricket Ground
56
New Farm
LONGLAND LANE
7
Longland Farm
BLANCHBECK LANE
COMBS LA.
COMBS LANE
Memorial
Riddings Hill Farm
F
G
H
J
K
63
64
465

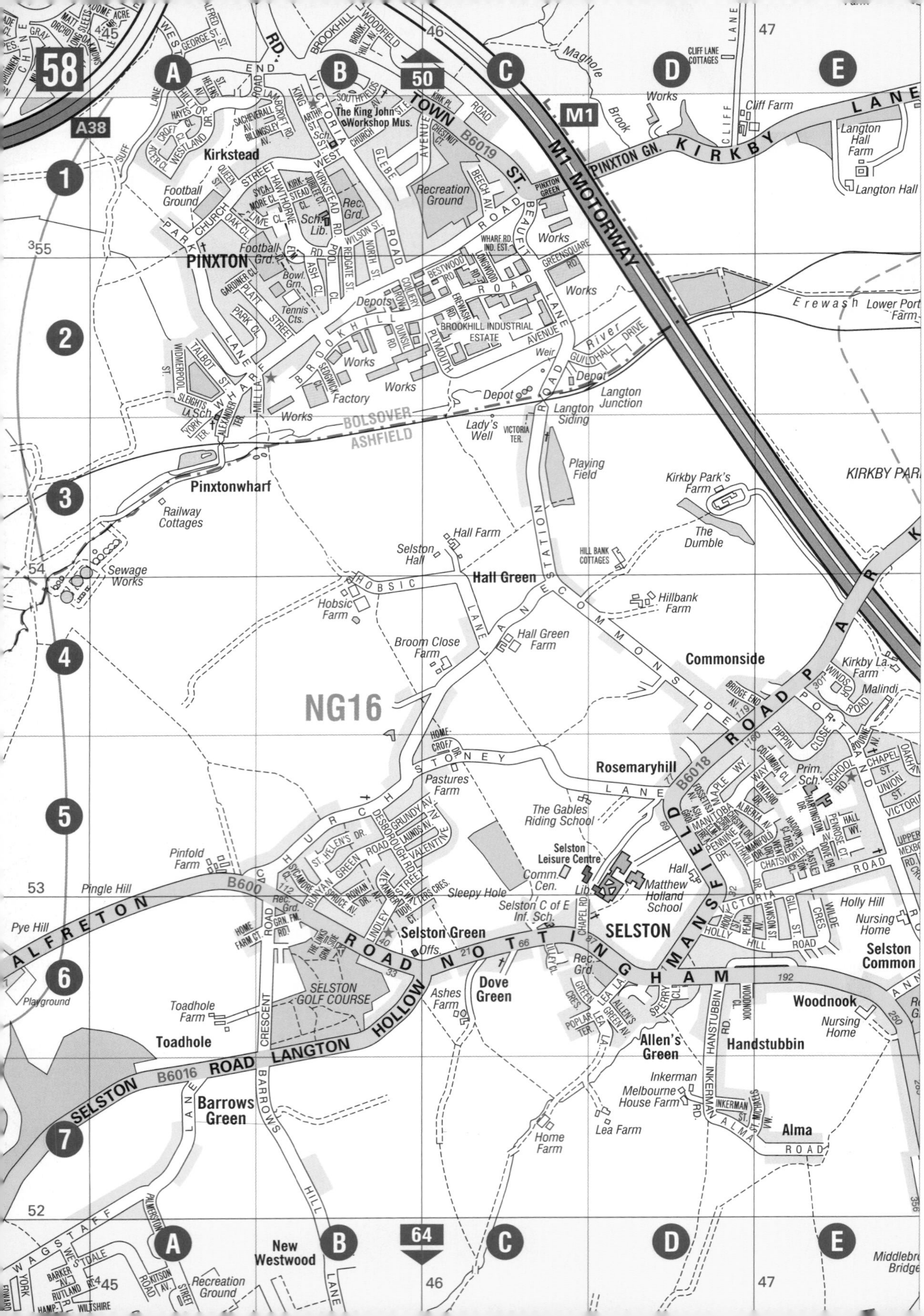

58
50
64
A
B
C
D
E
1
2
3
4
5
6
7
45
46
47
52
53
54
55
A38
M1
M1 MOTORWAY
B6019
B6018
B600
B6016
NG16
PINXTON
Kirkstead
Pinxtonwharf
Railway Cottages
Sewage Works
Football Ground
Football Grd.
Bowl. Grn.
Tennis Cts.
Rec. Grd.
Recreation Ground
The King John Workshop Mus.
TOWN END
Depots
Works
Factory
Depot
BROOKHILL INDUSTRIAL ESTATE
WHARF RD. IND. EST.
BOLSOVER
ASHFIELD
Langton Junction
Langton Siding
Lady's Well
VICTORIA TER.
Weir
River Erewash
Erewash
Lower Portland Farm
Playing Field
Kirkby Park's Farm
The Dumble
KIRKBY PARK
Cliff Farm
CLIFF LANE COTTAGES
Langton Hall Farm
Langton Hall
Maghole Brook
PINXTON GN.
KIRKBY LANE
Selston Hall
Hall Farm
Hall Green
HILL BANK COTTAGES
Hillbank Farm
Hobsic Farm
Hall Green Farm
Broom Close Farm
Commonside
Kirkby La. Farm
Malindi
Rosemaryhill
Pastures Farm
The Gables Riding School
Selston Leisure Centre
Comm. Cen.
Lib.
Hall
Matthew Holland School
Selston C of E Inf. Sch.
Prim. Sch.
Pinfold Farm
Pingle Hill
Pye Hill
Playground
Selston Green
Offs.
Sleepy Hole
SELSTON
Holly Hill
Nursing Home
Selston Common
Woodnook
Dove Green
Ashes Farm
SELSTON GOLF COURSE
Toadhole Farm
Toadhole
Barrows Green
Allen's Green
Handstubbin
Inkerman
Melbourne House Farm
Lea Farm
Home Farm
Alma
New Westwood
Recreation Ground
Middlebrook Bridge
ALFRETON ROAD
NOTTINGHAM ROAD
MANSFIELD ROAD
PARK LANE
COMMONSIDE
STATION ROAD
HOBSIC LANE
CHURCH LANE
STONEY LANE
SELSTON ROAD
LANGTON HOLLOW
BARROWS HILL
BROOKHILL
VICTORIA ROAD
ALMA ROAD
WAGSTAFF

Springfield Cottage
Hill
Fish Ponds
Depot
Cemetery
Pinxton Lane
Pinxton Rd.
Lane End Rd.
Church Hill
Bentinck Town
B6019
Rec. Grd.
Works
Mayfield St.
Princess
Laburnum Av.
Springmeadow
Meadow Farm
Sewage Works
Portland Fields House
Wks.
Works
B6018
The Hollies
High Cliff
River Erewash
Studfold Wood
Portland Park
Grives Wood
The Bungalow
Portland Park Visitors Cen.
Weir
Old Mill Pond
The Nook
Grives Farm
NG17
Kirkby Woodhouse
Prospect Fm.
Southfields
Hardstaff Cl.
Sherwood Cl.
Wharf Yard
Arthur Green Av.
Skegby Lane
Larkfield Av.
Prim. Sch.
Play. Fld.
Main Rd.
Rise Hill
Cricket Ground
Mount Pleasant
Nuncar Ct.
Nuncargate Road
Edison St.
Bentinck Cl.
Cricket Cl.
Thornham Cres.
Greenhill
Kendal Cl.
Rise
Glebe Street
Main Street
Rec. Grd.
Felley Av.
Beauvale Gdns.
The Gables
Croft Cottage
Cemetery
Vicarage Way
Church Vw.
Northrowe
Bleak Hall Farm
Nuncargate
Sycamore Farm
Lib.
Lawns Rd.
The Dell
Wesley St.
Astley Cl.
Reservoir (covered)
Salmon Farm
Salmon House
Forest Road
Southfields Farm
Bryngwyn
Salmon Lane
Kirkby Park's Farm
Sub.
Butler Wood
Nottingham
Suvla Bay
Middleton Cl.
Royal Oak Dr.
Newstead Cl.
Willow Cl.
Forest Cl.
Sherwood
Nightingale
Annesley Lane End
Toll Bar Farm
Two Dale Farm
Damstead
Works
Little Oak Drive
Sherwood Park
Lake View Drive
Willow Drive
Davis's Bottom
Fish Ponds
Works
Skegness
Melbourne St.
Recreation St.
M1 Motorway
M1
NG15
Old Park H
Frank's Plantation
Icehouse Wood
Middlebrook Farm
Brook
Millington Springs
Middle
Depot
Junction 27
Mansfield Road
A608
Home Farm
B600 Road
Mansfield Rd.
William Wood Spinney
60
51
65
F G H J K
1 2 3 4 5 6 7
48 49 450 355 54 53 52

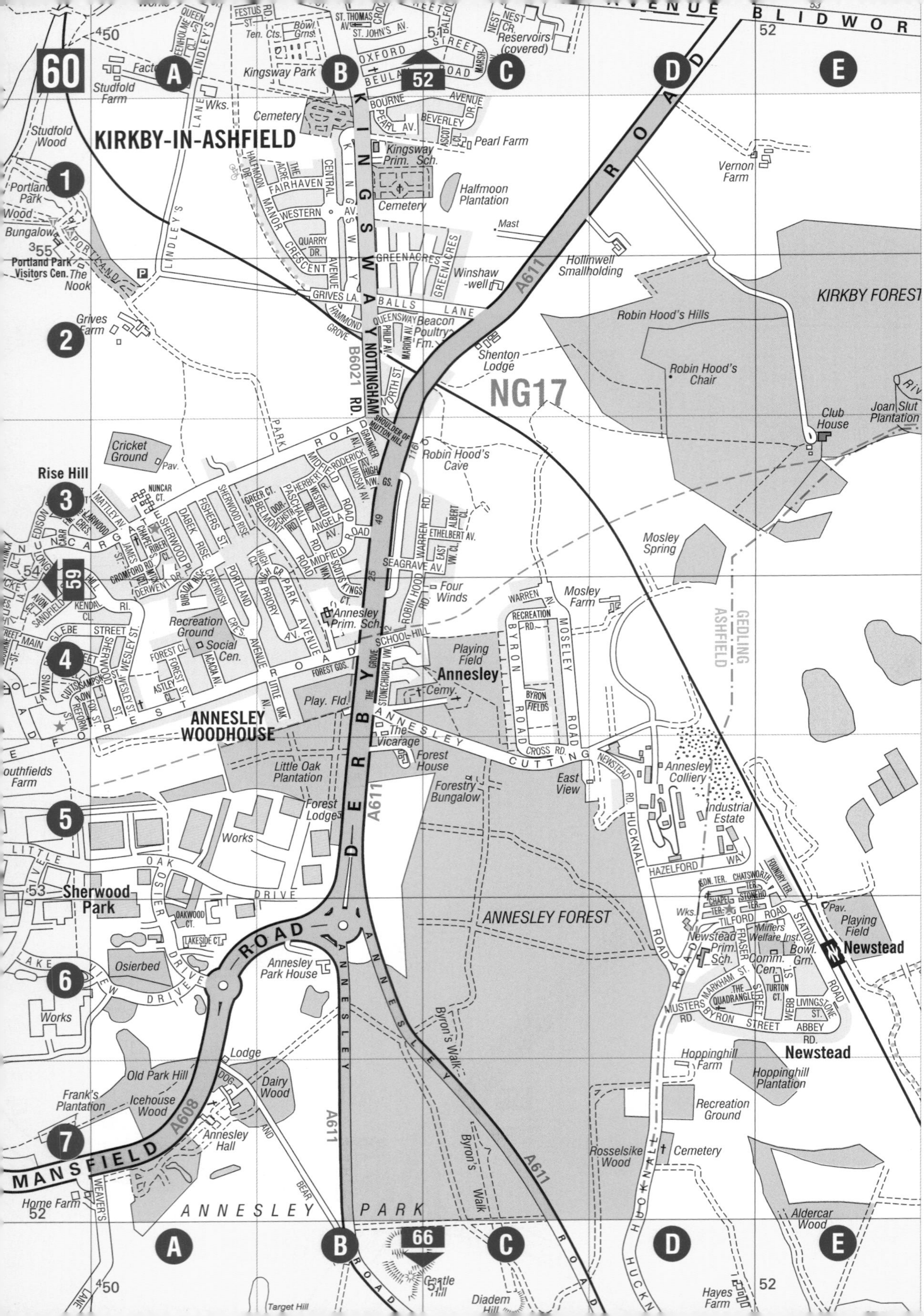
60
52
59
66
A
B
C
D
E
1
2
3
4
5
6
7
450
452
52
53
54
355
KIRKBY-IN-ASHFIELD
Studfold Farm
Studfold Wood
Portland Park Wood
Bungalow
Portland Park Visitors Cen.
The Nook
Grives Farm
Factory
Wks.
Kingsway Park
Cemetery
Kingsway Prim. Sch.
Halfmoon Plantation
Pearl Farm
Vernon Farm
Reservoirs (covered)
Bowl. Grns.
Ten. Cts.
Winshaw-well
Hollinwell Smallholding
Mast
Beacon Poultry Fm.
Shenton Lodge
Robin Hood's Hills
Robin Hood's Chair
KIRKBY FOREST
Club House
Joan Slut Plantation
NG17
Robin Hood's Cave
Cricket Ground
Pav.
Rise Hill
Mosley Spring
Mosley Farm
Four Winds
Annesley Prim. Sch.
Recreation Ground
Social Cen.
Playing Field
Annesley
Cemy.
Play. Fld.
ANNESLEY WOODHOUSE
The Vicarage
Forest House
Forestry Bungalow
Little Oak Plantation
Forest Lodge
East View
Annesley Colliery
Industrial Estate
GEDLING
ASHFIELD
Southfields Farm
Works
Sherwood Park
Osierbed
ANNESLEY FOREST
Annesley Park House
Newstead Prim. Sch.
Miners Welfare Inst.
Comm. Cen.
Bowl. Grn.
Playing Field
Newstead
Hoppinghill Farm
Hoppinghill Plantation
Recreation Ground
Cemetery
Rosselsike Wood
Aldercar Wood
Hayes Farm
Lodge
Old Park Hill
Dairy Wood
Frank's Plantation
Icehouse Wood
Annesley Hall
Home Farm
ANNESLEY PARK
Byron's Walk
Castle Hill
Diadem Hill
Target Hill
KINGSWAY
NOTTINGHAM RD.
B6021
DERBY ROAD
A611
A608
MANSFIELD ROAD
ROAD
BLIDWORTH
AVENUE
OXFORD STREET
BEULAH ROAD
BOURNE AVENUE
PEARL AV.
BEVERLEY DR.
ASCOT CL.
ST. THOMAS AV.
ST. JOHN'S AV.
BALFOUR
FESTUS ST.
QUEEN ST.
LINDLEY'S LANE
NEST CR.
MARSH
HALFMOON DR.
THE ACRE
FAIRHAVEN
CENTRAL AV.
WESTERN AV.
MANOR CRESCENT
QUARRY DR.
GREENACRES
GRIVES LA.
BALLS LANE
HAMMOND GROVE
QUEENSWAY
PHILIP AV.
MARION AV.
NORTH ST.
SHOULDER OF MUTTON HILL
PARK ROAD
GRAINGER AV.
RODERICK ST.
LINDSAY AV.
HIGH VW. GS.
MIDFIELD RD.
HERBERT RD.
WESTFIELD RD.
ANGELA AV.
PASCHALL RD.
DORCHESTER RD.
BELMONT RD.
GREER CT.
SHERWOOD RISE
FISHERS ST.
DABEK RISE
NUNCAR CT.
MATTLEY AV.
LARWOOD
CARGATE
CHAPEL ST.
JAMES ST.
SHERWOOD PL.
BURTON RISE
CAVENDISH CRES.
PORTLAND AVENUE
PRIORY AV.
PARK AVENUE
HIGH CR.
HIGH ST.
CROMFORD RD.
DERWENT DR.
KENDAL CL.
GLEBE STREET
MAIN
FOREST CL.
FOREST ST.
ACACIA AV.
ASTLEY CL.
FOREST GDS.
FOREST ROAD
LITTLE OAK AV.
WESLEY ST.
WESLEY PL.
CUTTS ST.
SAMPSON ST.
REFORM ST.
ROW
FOX ST.
LAWNS
SANDFIELD
AVON
EDISON
SCOTTS WAY
KINGS CT.
SEAGRAVE AV.
WARREN RD.
ROBIN HOOD RD.
ALBERT CL.
ETHELBERT AV.
EAST VW. CL.
SCHOOL HILL
THE GROVE
STONECHURCH VW.
ANNESLEY CUTTING
WARREN
RECREATION RD.
BYRON ROAD
MOSELEY ROAD
BYRON FIELDS
CROSS RD.
NEWSTEAD RD.
HUCKNALL ROAD
HAZELFORD WAY
LITTLE OAK DRIVE
OSIER DRIVE
OAKWOOD CT.
LAKESIDE CT.
LAKE VIEW DRIVE
ANNESLEY
DOG AND BEAR LANE
WEAVER'S LANE
GDN. TER.
CHATSWORTH TER.
FOUNDRY TER.
CHAPEL TER.
STONEHO. TER.
TILFORD ROAD
STATION ROAD
FRASER ST.
MARKHAM ST.
THE QUADRANGLE
TURTON CT.
WEBB ST.
LIVINGSTONE ST.
MUSTERS RD.
BYRON STREET
ABBEY RD.
Wks.

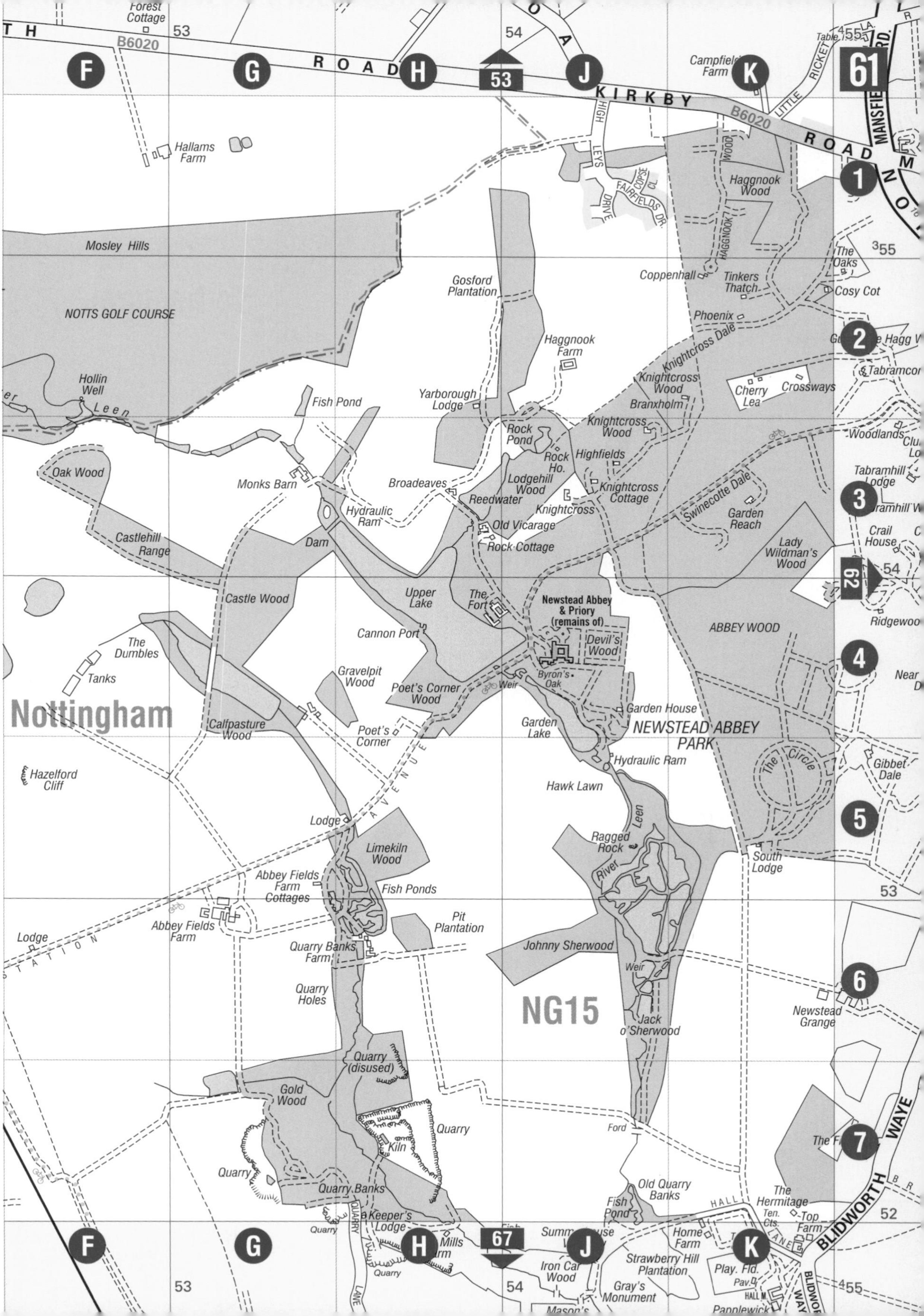
61
Forest Cottage
53
54
B6020
ROAD
KIRKBY
F
G
H
J
K
53
Campfield Farm
Table
LITTLE RICKETT LA.
MANSFIELD RD.
B6020
ROAD
HIGH
LEYS
WOOD
COPSE CL.
FAIRFIELDS DR.
DRIVE
Hallams Farm
Haggnook Wood
HAGGNOOK
1
Mosley Hills
NOTTS GOLF COURSE
The Oaks
355
Gosford Plantation
Coppenhall
Tinkers Thatch
Cosy Cot
Phoenix
Haggnook Farm
Knightcross Dale
2
Hollin Well
Leen
Fish Pond
Yarborough Lodge
Knightcross Wood
Branxholm
Cherry Lea
Crossways
Rock Pond
Knightcross Wood
Woodlands
Oak Wood
Rock Ho.
Highfields
Tabramhill Lodge
Monks Barn
Broadeaves
Lodgehill Wood
Knightcross Cottage
Swinecotte Dale
Reedwater
Knightcross
Garden Reach
3
Hydraulic Ram
Old Vicarage
Crail House
Castlehill Range
Dam
Rock Cottage
Lady Wildman's Wood
62
54
Castle Wood
Upper Lake
The Fort
Newstead Abbey & Priory (remains of)
ABBEY WOOD
Ridgewood
Cannon Port
Devil's Wood
The Dumbles
4
Tanks
Gravelpit Wood
Byron's Oak
Poet's Corner Wood
Weir
Nottingham
Garden House
Calfpasture Wood
Poet's Corner
Garden Lake
NEWSTEAD ABBEY PARK
AVENUE
The Circle
Gibbet Dale
Hazelford Cliff
Hydraulic Ram
Hawk Lawn
5
Lodge
Leen
Limekiln Wood
Ragged Rock
River
South Lodge
Abbey Fields Farm Cottages
Fish Ponds
53
Pit Plantation
Abbey Fields Farm
Lodge
STATION
Quarry Banks Farm
Johnny Sherwood
Weir
6
Quarry Holes
NG15
Newstead Grange
Jack o'Sherwood
Quarry (disused)
Gold Wood
Quarry
Ford
Kiln
The
7
Quarry
Old Quarry Banks
WAYE
Quarry Banks
Fish Pond
The Hermitage
HALL
Keeper's Lodge
Ten. Cts.
Top Farm
BLIDWORTH
52
QUARRY
LANE
Quarry
Mills Farm
67
Summer House
Home Farm
LANE
F
G
H
J
K
Quarry
Iron Car Wood
Strawberry Hill Plantation
Play. Fld.
Pav.
HALL
53
54
Gray's Monument
455
Mason's
Papplewick
BLIDWORTH WAY

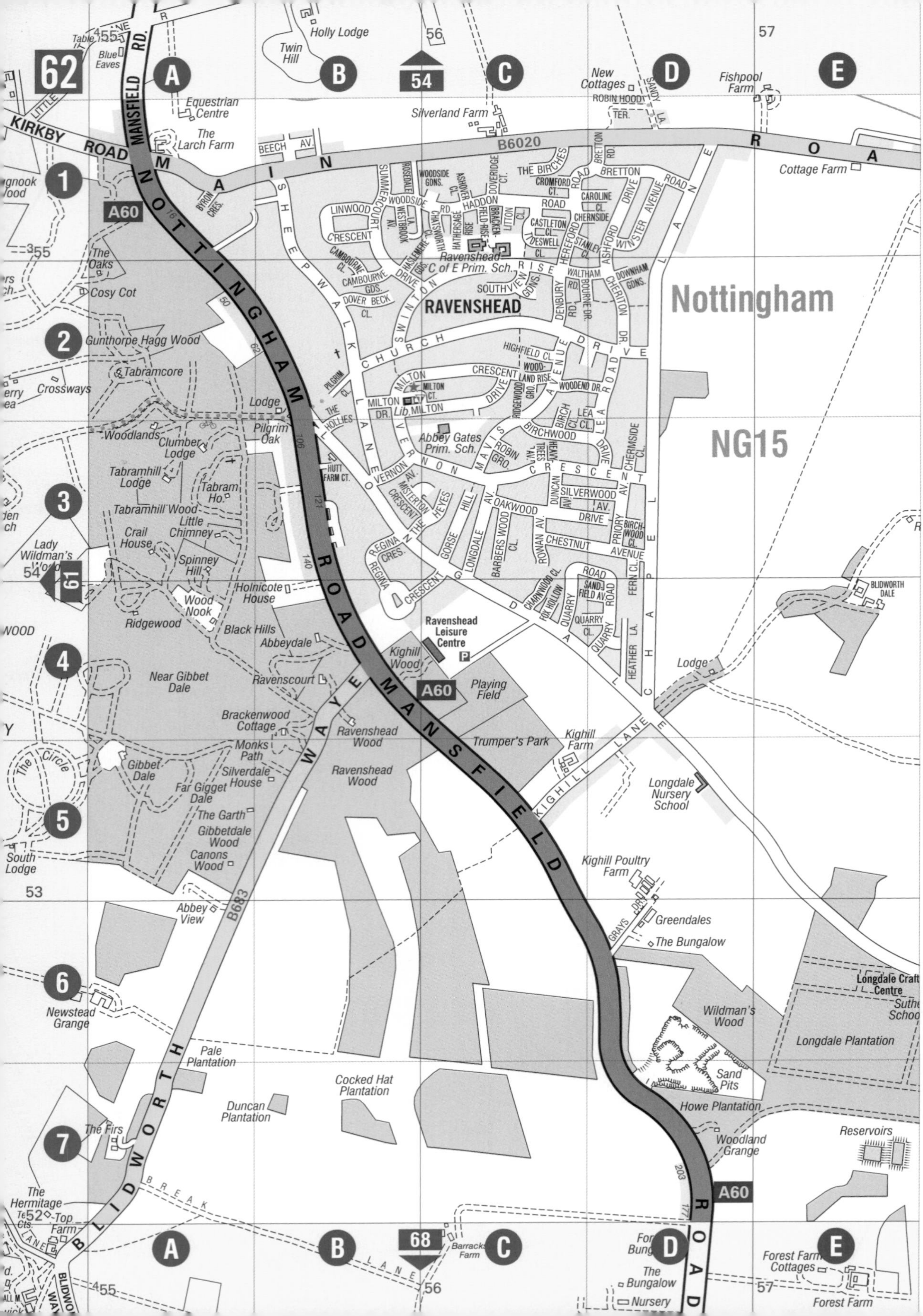
62
A
B
C
D
E
54
56
57
1
2
3
4
5
6
7
Holly Lodge
Twin Hill
New Cottages
Robin Hood Ter.
Sandy La.
Fishpool Farm
Blue Eaves
Table
Equestrian Centre
The Larch Farm
Silverland Farm
Kirkby Road
Little
Mansfield Rd.
Main Road
B6020
Cottage Farm
A60
Nottingham Road
Byron Cres.
Beech Av.
Sheepwalk Lane
Linwood Crescent
Summercourt
Rosedale
Woodside
Woodside Gdns.
Ashover Cl.
Doveridge Ct.
The Birches
Bretton Rd.
Bretton Road
Cromford Ct.
Caroline Cl.
Chernside
Haddon
Castleton Cl.
Eswell Cl.
Stanley Cl.
Hereford Drive
Ashford
Winster Avenue
Chapel Lane
Westbrook Av.
Chatsworth Cl.
Hathersage Rise
Bracken Cl.
Litton Cl.
Ravenshead C of E Prim. Sch.
Cambourne Cl.
Cambourne Gdns.
Haslemere Drive
Swinton Rise
Southview Gdns.
Waltham Rd.
Denbury Rd.
Bourne Dr.
Cheriton Dr.
Downham Gdns.
Dover Beck Cl.
RAVENSHEAD
Nottingham
Church Drive
Highfield Cl.
Woodland Rise
Woodend Dr.
Pilgrim Cl.
Milton Crescent
Milton Ct.
Milton Dr.
Lib.
The Hollies
Ridgewood Gro.
Birch Cl.
Lea Cl.
Lea Drive
Chermside Cl.
NG15
Abbey Gates Prim. Sch.
Mavis Av.
Birchwood Road
Robin Gro.
Trees Av.
Heavy Cl.
Vernon Crescent
Hutt Farm Ct.
Vernon Av.
Misterton Crescent
The Heyes
Gorse Hill
Longdale Av.
Barbers Wood Cl.
Duncan Av.
Silverwood Av.
Oakwood Drive
Priory Av.
Birchwood Cl.
Rowan Av.
Chestnut Avenue
Regina Cres.
Regina Crescent
Longdale Lane
Charnwood Cl.
Fox Hollow
Sandfield Av.
Sandfield Road
Quarry Road
Quarry Cl.
Fern Cl.
Heather La.
Bldworth Dale
Ravenshead Leisure Centre
Kighill Wood
Playing Field
Trumper's Park
Kighill Farm
Kighill Lane
Lodge
Longdale Nursery School
Waye
Mansfield Road
Kighill Poultry Farm
Grays Dr.
Greendales
The Bungalow
Longdale Craft Centre
Wildman's Wood
Sand Pits
Longdale Plantation
Howe Plantation
Woodland Grange
Reservoirs
Gagnook Wood
The Oaks
Cosy Cot
Gunthorpe Hagg Wood
Tabramcore
Crossways
Lodge
Pilgrim Oak
Woodlands
Clumber Lodge
Tabramhill Lodge
Tabram Ho.
Tabramhill Wood
Little Chimney
Crail House
Lady Wildman's Wood
Spinney Hill
61
Holnicote House
Wood Nook
Ridgewood
Black Hills
Abbeydale
Near Gibbet Dale
Ravenscourt
Brackenwood Cottage
Ravenshead Wood
The Circle
Gibbet Dale
Monks Path
Silverdale House
Far Gigget Dale
The Garth
Gibbetdale Wood
Canons Wood
South Lodge
Abbey View
B683
Newstead Grange
Pale Plantation
Cocked Hat Plantation
Duncan Plantation
The Firs
The Hermitage
Top Farm
Blidworth Road
Break Lane
68
Barracks Farm
Forest Farm Cottages
Forest Farm
The Bungalow
Nursery
Road

F
G
H
J
K
1
2
3
4
5
6
7
55
69
146
54
53
52
58
59
460
The Ranch
Rock Farm
ROCK TER.
CLAYBANK VILLAS
FOREST VW.
ASHWELL TER.
KIRKS CFT.
Towermill
BUTLER
Vicarage
Church Farm
MAIN RD.
B6020
FISHPOOL RD.
WILL SCARLET CL.
BECK LA.
BECK CRES.
ANDREW HILL
CLARE
FARR WAY
HAYWOOD
Cornerways
HAYWOOD OAKS LANE
Haywood Oaks
355
BECK LANE
FIELD LANE
Bottom Farm
NEWARK and SHERWOOD
GEDLING
Jackson's Hill
Blidworth Bottoms
CALVERTON RD.
TOP RD.
Rose Cottage Farm
BLIDWORTH LANE
Kirkfield
Green Park
Mansfield
NG21
Rose Cottage
Sykebreck Farm
GORSE COVERT
Appleton Dale House
Appleton Dale
Forestry Tower
RIGG LANE
Blidworth Lodge
GORSE COVERT
Long Dale
Sand Holes
Forestry Bungalows
LONGDALE LANE
Big Tithe Farm
OLD RUFFORD RD.
WHINBUSH LA.
A614
NG14
Papplewick Pumping Station
Forestry Houses
Pea Plantation
LANE

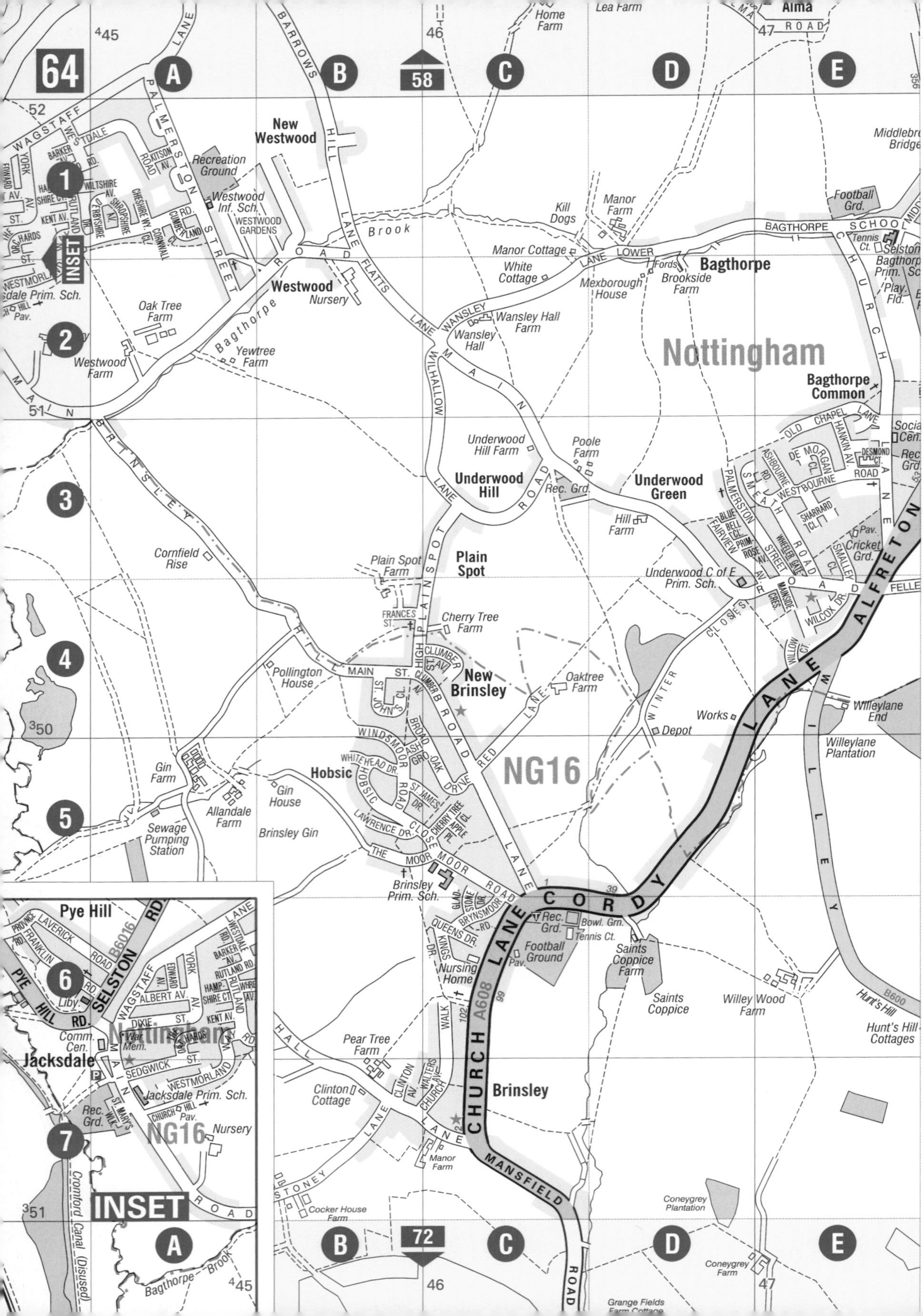
64
58
72
A
B
C
D
E
1
2
3
4
5
6
7
Nottingham
NG16
New Westwood
Westwood
Bagthorpe
Bagthorpe Common
Underwood Hill
Underwood Green
Plain Spot
New Brinsley
Hobsic
Brinsley
Recreation Ground
Westwood Inf. Sch.
Oak Tree Farm
Westwood Farm
Yewtree Farm
Westwood Nursery
Kill Dogs
Manor Farm
Manor Cottage
White Cottage
Mexborough House
Brookside Farm
Wansley Hall Farm
Wansley Hall
Underwood Hill Farm
Poole Farm
Rec. Grd.
Hill Farm
Cornfield Rise
Plain Spot Farm
Cherry Tree Farm
Underwood C of E Prim. Sch.
Pollington House
Oaktree Farm
Works
Depot
Willeylane End
Willeylane Plantation
Gin Farm
Gin House
Allandale Farm
Sewage Pumping Station
Brinsley Gin
Brinsley Prim. Sch.
Bowl. Grn.
Tennis Ct.
Football Ground
Saints Coppice Farm
Saints Coppice
Willey Wood Farm
Hunt's Hill Cottages
Nursing Home
Pear Tree Farm
Clinton Cottage
Manor Farm
Cocker House Farm
Coneygrey Plantation
Coneygrey Farm
Grange Fields Farm Cottage
Home Farm
Lea Farm
Alma
Middlebrook Bridge
Football Grd.
Selston Bagthorpe Prim. Sch.
Play. Fld.
Social Cen.
Cricket Grd.
Pav.
Brook
Bagthorpe
MAIN ROAD
LOWER BAGTHORPE
SCHOOL ROAD
CHURCH LANE
ALFRETON ROAD
CORDY LANE
CHURCH LANE A608
MANSFIELD ROAD
WILLEY LANE
B600
Hunt's Hill
BRINSLEY HILL
MAIN ST.
HIGH ST.
PLAIN SPOT ROAD
WILHALLOW LANE
RED LANE
WINTER CLOSES
MOOR ROAD
THE MOOR
HALL LANE
STONEY LANE
PALMERSTON STREET
WAGSTAFF LANE
FLATTS LANE
BARROWS HILL LANE
WANSLEY LANE
Pye Hill
Jacksdale
Comm. Cen.
War Mem.
Liby.
Jacksdale Prim. Sch.
Nursery
INSET
Cromford Canal (Disused)
Bagthorpe Brook
PYE HILL RD.
SELSTON RD.
B6016
445
46
47
350
351
356
52
51

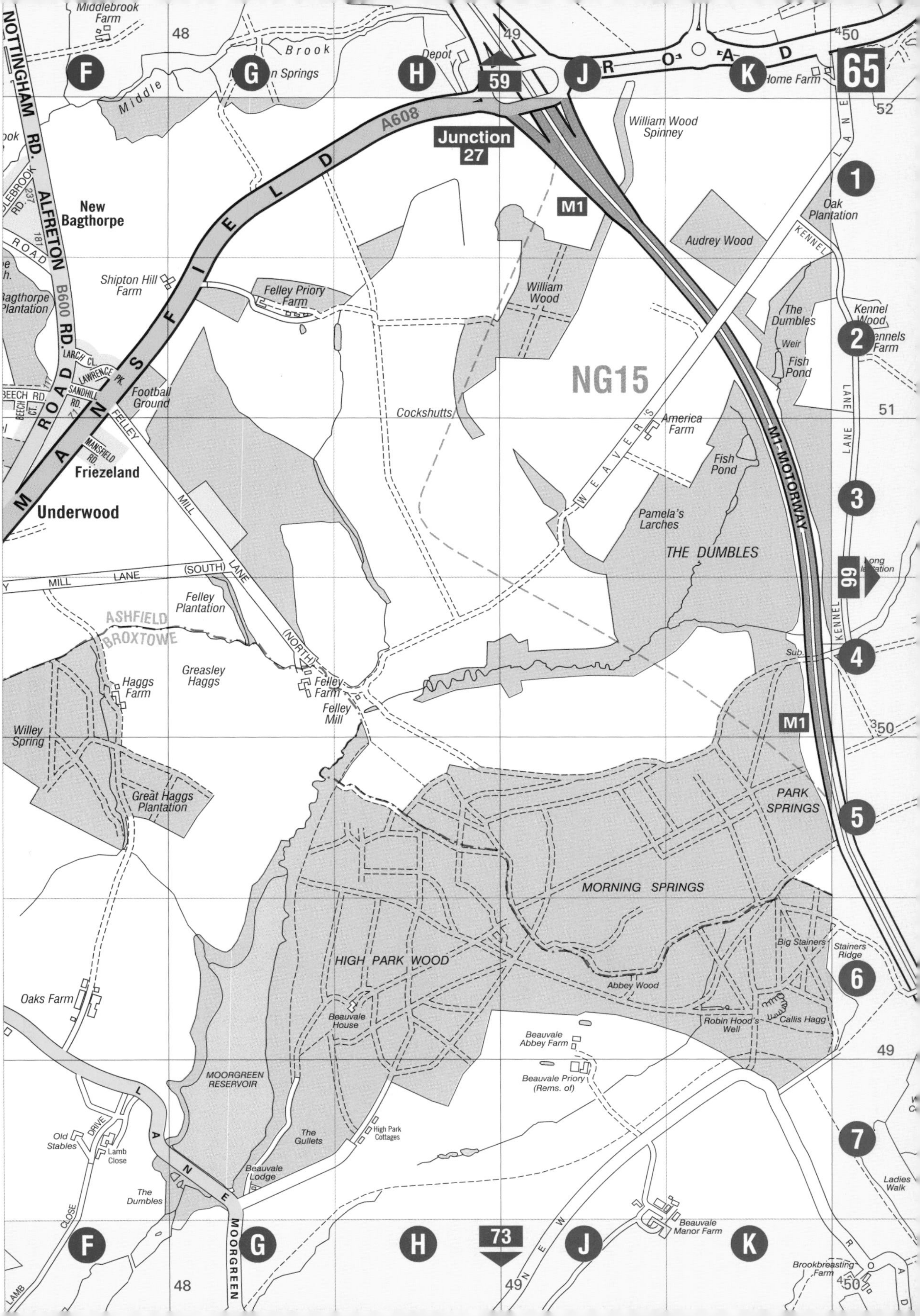

65
59
Junction 27
66
73
F
G
H
J
K
1
2
3
4
5
6
7
48
49
50
51
52
NG15
Middlebrook Farm
Brook
Middle
Depot
ROAD
Home Farm
A608
MANSFIELD ROAD
NOTTINGHAM RD.
ALFRETON RD.
B600 RD.
New Bagthorpe
Bagthorpe Plantation
Shipton Hill Farm
Felley Priory Farm
William Wood Spinney
M1
Oak Plantation
Audrey Wood
William Wood
KENNEL LANE
The Dumbles
Kennel Wood
Kennels Farm
Weir
Fish Pond
LANE
LARCH CL.
LAWRENCE PK.
SANDHILL RD.
BEECH RD.
BEECH CT.
MANSFIELD RD.
Football Ground
Friezeland
Underwood
FELLEY MILL LANE
Cockshutts
WEAVERS
America Farm
Fish Pond
M1-MOTORWAY
Pamela's Larches
THE DUMBLES
MILL LANE (SOUTH)
(NORTH)
Felley Plantation
ASHFIELD
BROXTOWE
Greasley Haggs
Haggs Farm
Felley Farm
Felley Mill
Sub.
Willey Spring
Great Haggs Plantation
PARK SPRINGS
MORNING SPRINGS
HIGH PARK WOOD
Big Stainers
Stainers Ridge
Abbey Wood
Oaks Farm
Beauvale House
Robin Hood's Well
Callis Hagg
Beauvale Abbey Farm
Beauvale Priory (Rems. of)
MOORGREEN RESERVOIR
Old Stables
DRIVE
Lamb Close
The Gullets
High Park Cottages
Beauvale Lodge
The Dumbles
CLOSE
LAMB
MOORGREEN
NEW
Beauvale Manor Farm
Ladies Walk
Brookbreasting Farm
ROAD

66
60
65
74
M1
A
B
C
D
E
1
2
3
4
5
6
7
450
51
52
350
49
ANNESLEY PARK
Annesley Hall
Byron's Walk
Rosselsike Wood
Cemetery
Aldercar Wood
Castle Hill
Diadem Hill
Target Hill
Hayes Farm
Oak Plantation
Heatherdale Pond
Joe's Wood
Big Pond
The Dumbles
Fish Pond
Kennel Wood
Kennels Farm
Top Wighay Farm
Wighay Wood
Balaklava Wood
PARK FOREST
Long Plantation
Thurland Hall Farm
NOTTINGHAM INT. CLOTHING CEN.
New Farm
Whyburn House
Nottingham
Whyburn Cottages
PARK SPRI
MISK HILL
Big Stainers
Stainers Ridge
Misk Farm
Reservoir (covered)
Silo Farm
Reservoirs (covered)
Nursery
Poultry Farm
Callis Hagg
Fox Covert
Brier Plantation
Long Hill
Beacon Hill
Beacon Hill Farm
Beacon Hill House
Leiver's Hill
Beauvale
NG16
Watnall Coppice
Bottom Plantation
ASHFIELD
BROXTOWE
GEDLING
Ladies Walk
Coppice Farm
Running Track
Playing Field
The Holgate Comprehensive School
Brookbreasting Farm
Ruffs
ANNESLEY ROAD
A611
HUCKNALL ROAD
HUCKNALL BY-PASS
M1 MOTORWAY
WHYBURN LANE
WOOD LANE
KENNEL LANE
WEAVER'S
BEAR LANE
WASHDYKE LANE
LONG ACRE
BEAUVALE ROAD
BEAUVALE DRIVE
ROCKWOOD
SPRINGFIELD RD.
HILLCREST
LAXTON DR.
ABBOTS CRES.
CRESCENT
THE COMMON
NABBS LANE
DAWLISH CL.
CASTLETON CL.
EDALE CL.
BRAUNTON CL.
BABBACOMBE WAY
TENNYSON CT.
TOTNES CL.
KEATS DR.
SHELLEY CL.
HARTINGTON AV.
STAINSBOROUGH RD.
ROCKLEY CL.
BADGER CL.
BLUEBELL CL.
HAZELWOOD
BOLINGEY WAY
PINEHURST AV.
DALEBROOK
DALE CL.
EDEN CL.
ASH CL.
CYPRESS CT.
WHYSTON CT.
BODMIN AV.
CHILTON DR.
WORDSWORTH AV.
ROLLESTON DR.
NIXON
POLPERRO WAY
BEACON HILL
MILTON CL.
NORFOLK CL.
HOLLYTHORN
BRIXHAM RD.
TAVISTOCK CL.
PRIVATE RD.
PRIORY RD.
FOREST VIEW DR.
CHARNWOOD GRO.
MAPLE DR.
ELM AVENUE
SALTERFORD
JUBILEE CT.
Holgate Wk.
Abbots Wk.
Beauvale Ct.
Whyb Prim.

67
61
75
68
53
54
55
52
51
50
49
F
G
H
J
K
1
2
3
4
5
6
7
Quarry
Kiln
Quarry Banks
Keeper's Lodge
Weir Mills Farm
Fish Pond
Summerhouse Wood
Old Quarry Banks
The Hermitage
Top Farm
Home Farm
Ten. Cts.
Strawberry Hill Plantation
Play. Fld.
Pav.
Iron Car Wood
Gray's Monument
Mason's Monument
Weirs
Weir
River
Papplewick Hall
HALL
BLIDWORTH WAYE
QUARRY LANE
The Lodge
Mill Pond Plantation
Mortons Farm
Church Plantation
Linby-cum-Papplewick C of E Prim. Sch.
School Plantation
Sherwood House
West View Court
West View Farm
B683
Hall Farm
LINBY LANE
B6011
MAIN ST.
Papplewick
FOREST LANE
MAIN STREET
MOOR ROAD
The Poplars
BLACKSMITHS CT.
Leen
Colliery Farm
Linby
Linby House
Castle Mill Farm
Dam Banks
Playgrd.
ROAD
CHURCH LANE
Cricket Ground
HAYDEN LANE
WATERLOO
Station House
Pump House
Moor Pond Wood
NG15
Wighay
WIGHAY
ANNESLEY ROAD
The Mill House
Papplewick Moor
Victoria Gro.
SHERWOOD WALK
ROBEY CL.
Great Northern Cotts.
THE DRIFT
BERNARD AV.
DOROTHY AV.
HAYDEN LANE
Grange Cottages
The National School
Nursing Home
Grange Farm
Papplewick Grange
GRANGE-MOOR
Congel Hill
PAPPLEWICK LANE
LYNMOOR CT.
VAUGHAN
ROSSLYN DR.
Prim. Sch.
Leen Mills Prim. Sch.
BALMORAL GRO.
Recreation Ground
ST. MARYS WAY
Ten. Cts.
Jun. & Inf. Schs.
Hucknall Leis. Cen.
Rec. Grd.
BUCKINGHAM
Playing Field
LEEN VALLEY GOLF COURSE
Dobpark
CONISTON
RYDAL DR.
OGLE STREET
The Byron Cen
Mill Yard
Lib.
HIGH STREET
Hucknall
WIGWAM
BATHS LA.
ASHGATE
Superstore
Byron Bingo
Club House
DERBYSHIRE LANE
Beardall St. Prim. Sch.
Superstore
Bus Sta.
Nurs. Home
Works
HUCKNALL
LONG HILL RISE
Playing Field
Annie Holgate Jun. & Inf. Schs.
IMEX ENTERPRISE PARK
Nursing Home
Bowl. Grn.
War Mem.
Tennis Cts.
Titchfield Park
Butler's Hill
Household Waste Cen.
BESTWOOD
LEEN VALLEY COUNTRY PARK
Nursing Home
Cemetery
Rec. Ground
Pav.
Football Ground
A611
BY-PASS
WATNALL ROAD

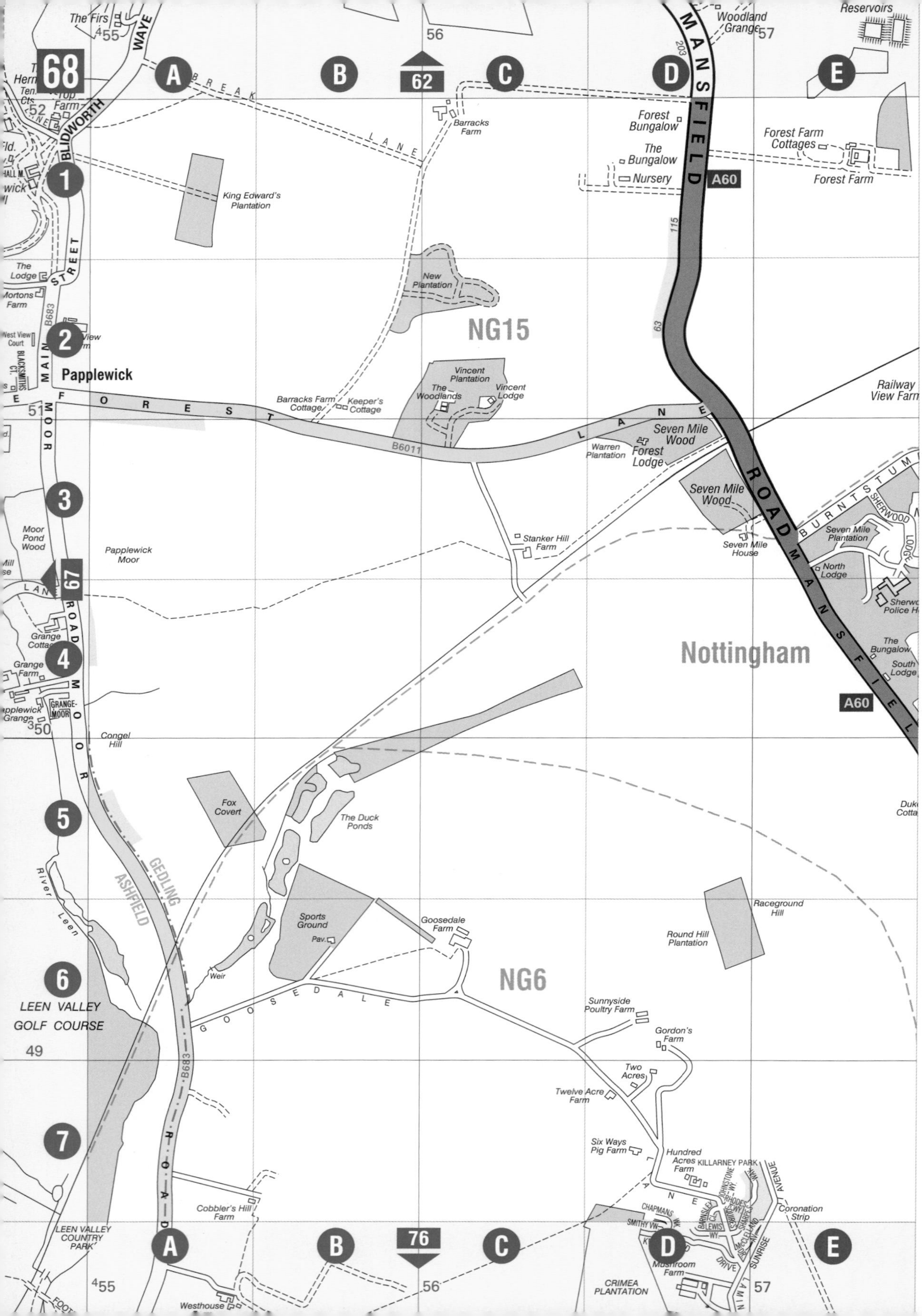

68
62
76
67
A
B
C
D
E
1
2
3
4
5
6
7
56
57
51
50
49
455
The Firs
WAYE
BLIDWORTH
BREAK LANE
Barracks Farm
Woodland Grange
Reservoirs
MANSFIELD ROAD
A60
Forest Bungalow
The Bungalow
Nursery
Forest Farm Cottages
Forest Farm
King Edward's Plantation
The Lodge
Mortons Farm
MAIN STREET
B683
Papplewick
New Plantation
NG15
Vincent Plantation
The Woodlands
Vincent Lodge
Barracks Farm Cottage
Keeper's Cottage
FOREST LANE
B6011
Seven Mile Wood
Warren Plantation
Forest Lodge
Railway View Farm
Seven Mile House
BURNTSTUMP
SHERWOOD
Seven Mile Plantation
North Lodge
MOOR ROAD
Moor Pond Wood
Papplewick Moor
Stanker Hill Farm
Nottingham
Grange Farm
GRANGE-MOOR
Papplewick Grange
Congel Hill
The Bungalow
South Lodge
Fox Covert
The Duck Ponds
GEDLING
ASHFIELD
River Leen
Sports Ground
Pav.
Goosedale Farm
Raceground Hill
Round Hill Plantation
Weir
GOOSEDALE LANE
NG6
LEEN VALLEY GOLF COURSE
Sunnyside Poultry Farm
Gordon's Farm
Two Acres
Twelve Acre Farm
Six Ways Pig Farm
Hundred Acres Farm
KILLARNEY PARK
AVENUE
Coronation Strip
Cobbler's Hill Farm
CHAPMANS WK.
SMITHY VW.
LEWIS
SUNRISE
LEEN VALLEY COUNTRY PARK
Mushroom Farm
CRIMEA PLANTATION
Westhouse

58
59
460
Papplewick Pumping Station
Forestry Houses
F
G
H
63
J
K
Pea Plantation
A614
52
SANSOM WOOD
RUFFORD
OLD
ROAD
1
Sansom Wood Farm
Sansom Wood Gorse
LANE
Great Burntstump Plantation
Sawpit Plantation
Watchwood Plantation
Richmond's Farm
2
51
ASH
LANE
Oak Wood
Burntstump Plantation
The Nursery
Beech Wood
Spts. Gd.
Ckt. Grd.
Burntstump Country Park
Nursery
BMI THE PARK HOSPITAL
DRIVE
Burnstump Country Park Woodland Walks
Seely C of E Prim. Sch.
HILL
Foxcovert Plantation
3
GRAVELLY
70
NG14
Cockliff Wood
Sports Ground
Cockliffe Hill Farm
Cockliffe House
A614
OLLERTON
HOLLOW
4
Dairy Farm
The Warren
The Knoll
Round Plantation
ROAD
350
Sports Ground
Cottage Wood
NG5
Turnpike Plantation
Patchings Farm Art Centre
MAIN
STREET
5
RAMSDALE PARK GOLF CENTRE
B6386
LANE
Jubilee Plantation
Ramsdale Cottages
Robin Hood Farm
The Rowans
Club House
East Hill Plantation
6
OXTON
Greenwood Bonsai Studio
Ramsdale House
RAMSDALE PARK GOLF CENTRE
HOLLINWOOD
Hollinwood House
Ramper Covert
49
Fox Covert
Forest Farm
Bottomhouse Farm
Leila's Plantation
A614
7
RAMSDALE PARK
North Peacock
The Belt
Ramsdale Park
Ramsdale Hill
A60
ROAD
F
G
H
77
J
K
GEORGE
ROAD
58
59
460
Reservoirs

A614
A6097
B6386
146
69
78
Salterford Cottages
OLD RUFFORD ROAD
WHINBUSH LANE
SALTERFORD LANE
Gorse Covert
OXTON BOGS
Beanford Farm
BEANFORD LANE
Foulds Plantation
Settling Pond
OXTON ROAD
Lodge Farm
FLATTS LANE
Thorndale Plantation
Whitehaven Farm
Nottingham
NG14
MANSFIELD LANE
Recreation Ground
Tennis Court
Bowling Green
Pav.
Sports Ground
HILL CREST PK. IND. EST.
Works
Broom House
CARRINGTON LANE
Carrington Farm
NORTH GRN.
COLLYER ROAD
PARK ROAD
MAIN STREET
HOLLINWOOD LANE
RAMSDALE PARK GOLF CENTRE
Calverton Leisure Centre
Cemy.
Sir John Sherbrooke Jun. Sch.
School
Manor Park Inf. School
Rec. Grd.
Rec. Ground
Redgates
CALVERTON
Nabarro Ct.
CROOKDOLE LANE
St. Wilfrid's Square
Lib.
James Seely Play. Fld.
Springwater Lodge
Cricket Ground
Riding Sch.
St. Wilfrid's C of E Prim. Sch.
BONNER LANE
Windles Square
Plumtree Gdns.
CHURCH MDW.
SPINDLE VW.
Borrowside Farm
Hollinwood House
Fox Covert
Spring Cottages
Lamp Wood
DARK LANE
Bonner Hill
BONNER LANE
FOXWOOD LANE
SPINDLE LANE
GEORGE'S LANE
Fox Wood
High Trees
Foxwood House
A B C D E
1 2 3 4 5 6 7
460 61 62
52 51 50 49

71
146
148
79
Oxton
Southwell
NG25
Epperstone
EPPERSTONE PARK
NETHER FIELD
A6097
B6386
OXTON ROAD
SOUTHWELL ROAD
EPPERSTONE ROAD
EPPERSTONE BY-PASS
HILL SOUTHWELL RD.
Oxton Dumble
MAIN STREET
MOOR LANE
ROE HILL
SHELT HILL
SPRINGWATER GOLF COURSE
Windmill Hill
Far Leys
Oxton Hill Farm
Marsett House
Deer Leap
Birkhouse
Ridge House
Reservoirs (covered)
Birkhouse Wood
Cricket Ground
Sports Ground
Fish Pond
Holly Lodge
Rossellewood Farm
Rosselle Wood
Norwood Farm
Meadow View
Park Farm
Mill Farm
Crifton Mill
CRIFTON ENTERPRISE CENTRE
NEWARK and SHERWOOD
GEDLING
Slaughter House
Kennels
Cottage Farm
Greenacres
Hill House
Spring Hill Farm
Works
Moor Farm Holiday & Home Park
Club House
Experimental Fish Farm
Grimesmoor
Grimesmoor Dyke
Epperstone Manor (Notts. Constabulary HQ)
Shelt Hill Farm
Fox Covert
Cemetery
Sports Ground
CHURCH LA.
CHAPEL LANE
BLAND LA.
TOAD LA.
PARK LA.
NOTTINGHAM RD.
WATER
SCHOOL GDNS.
ELMCROFT
NEW RD.
SANDY LA.
MANOR CL.
CHURCH VW.
BLIND LA.
HONEYKNAB
WINDMILL HILL
CHAPEL LA.
THE ORCHARDS
ORCHARD CT.
FOREST ROAD
Dover Beck
Order Beck
Grimestone Dyke
F G H J K
1 2 3 4 5 6 7
63 64 465 52 51 350 49

64
A
B
C
D
E
1
2
3
4
5
6
7
Stoney Paddock
STONEY LANE
Cockerhouse Farm
MANSFIELD ROAD
A608
A610
LANGLEY MILL BY-PASS
Coneygrey Farm
Grange Fields Farm Cottage
Weir
Brinsley Brook
Hall Farm
Lodge
COCKERHOUSE RD.
Nether Green
EASTWOOD HALL
THORPE RD.
CRESCENT
THORN TREE GDNS.
MEADOW CL.
COACH DRIVE
ROBEY DRIVE
Cricket Ground
Beauvale Brook
LOWER BEAUVALE
LAMB CLOSE
Nether Green Hall Pk.
Pavilion
Durban Ho. Heritage Cen.
Playing Fields
GREENHILLS ROAD
Rec. Ground
MOORFIELDS AV.
GARDEN RD.
D H Lawrence 'Sons & Lovers' Cottage
The Breach
Lynncroft Prim. Sch.
Playing Field
Tennis Cts.
LYNNCROFT
KIRBY ROAD
Eastwood Comm. Sports Centre
Eastwood Comp. Sch.
Superstore
GRANGE VIEW
Charlotte Ct.
KELHAM WY.
Mus.
NOTTINGHAM ROAD
DERBY ROAD
OLD DERBY RD.
Eastwood Jun. & Inf. Sch.
DEVONSHIRE DR.
The Rectory
IVY LANE
Tennis Courts
RATCLIFFE ST.
HOGGS FLD.
CHURCH STREET
QUEENS SQ.
Offs.
Bowl. Grn.
Football Ground
Coronation Park
Brookhill Leys Prim. Sch.
Community College
EDWARD ROAD
WALKER ST.
THREE TUNS ROAD
PERCY STREET
THE NURSERIES
CROMFORD ROAD
Caravan Park
HALL ROAD
CROMFORD ROAD IND. EST.
Foundry
LANGLEY PARK
Playgrd.
Rec. Grd.
QUEEN ST.
DEAN STREET
BRIDGE ST.
VICTORIA ST.
Works
Langley Mill
WESLEY ST.
STATION
Tom Norman Mem. Gdns.
ACORN CEN.
LANGLEY BUS. PK.
Bowling Green
MILNHAY
ACCESS 26 BUS. PK.
ENTERPRISE WY.
Depot
River Erewash
Mushroom Farm Ct.
MEADOWBANK WAY
CHRYSALIS WAY
Langley Bri.
BOUNDARY LA.
TOWSON AV.
BROOK VALE RD.
Brook Ct.
AMBER DR.
Bailey Grove
BAILEY GROVE ROAD
Sewage Works
EASTWOOD
A610
Playing Field
Pavilion
Works
FARRINGTON WAY
SOUTH ST.
MIDLAND RD.
PLUMPTRE WAY
The Island
SHERWOOD ROAD
Cemetery
Cemy.
QUEENS ROAD STH.
CHURCH ROAD
TINSLEY ROAD
BROOKHILL LEYS RD.
HEWTON
CRESCENT
ROCKLEY AV.
PHILIP AV.
CHEWTON AV.
RAGLAN
DAWSON CLOSE
NEWTHORPE COMMONS
LODGE
HALLS LANE
Cockfield Fm.
New Eastwood
Factory
NEWMANLEYS ROAD (STH.)
Works
KIMBERLEY EASTWOOD BY-PASS
KIRKSTONE AV.
BROOKFIELD
Langley
LACEYFIELDS RD.
KEW CR.
Playground
Lacey Fields Farm
Heanor
DE75
Nottingham Canal
Swing-Bridge
Eastwood Lock
(Disused)
AMBER VALLEY
BROXTOWE
Shipley Lock
Shipley Gate
Weir
Boat Inn Farm
LONG LANE
Sports Ground
Pavilion
HASSOCK LANE NTH.
A6007
THE FIELD
Shipley
Algrave Hall Farm
Bentley's Plantation
Purdy House Farm
AMBER VALLEY
EREWASH
Poplars Farm
The Bungalow
Cotmanhay Wood
DE7
CANAL
445
45
46
47
48

F
G
H
J
K
48
49
450
65
74
82
1
2
3
4
5
6
7
48
47
46
45
Old Stables
Lamb Close
The Gullets
High Park Cottages
Beauvale Lodge
The Dumbles
Beauvale Manor Farm
Ladies Walk
Brookbreasting Farm
Sluice
Overflow
MOORGREEN IND. PARK
Depot
Colliers Wood
Works
High Hazels Ct.
Nursery
Water Tower
Nottingham
Lower Beauvale
Manor House
Moorgreen
Crowhill Farm
NG16
Greasley House
Cemetery
Hall
Greasley
Beauvale
GREASLEY CASTLE (Rems.of)
Greasley Castle Fm.
Sledder Wood
Poplar Farm
Greasley Beauvale D H Lawrence Infants Sch.
Greasley Beauvale Jun. Sch.
Greasley Sports & Comm. Cen.
Rec. Grd.
Hill Top
Quarry Wood
Bogend
Newthorpe
Wood Villa
Opencast Workings
Hall Farm
Depot
WATNALL WOOD
Watnall Chaworth
Reckoning House Farm
Giltbrook
Newthorpe Common
Watnall Cantelupe
GILTBROOK IND. EST.
Works
Subway
Superstores
Gilt Hill Farm
Playing Field
Gilthill Prim. Sch.
Recycling Centre
Football Grd.
Hollywell Prim. Sch.
Edinboro Rw.
Brewery
Recreation Ground
A610
BY-PASS
KIMBERLEY
Sewage Works
Gilt Briggs Farm
The Fives
Church Hill Centre
Railway Cotts
Pav.
Cricket Grd.
Liby.
MOORGREEN
CHURCH ROAD
B600
MOORGREEN
BEAUVALE ROAD
DOVECOTE ROAD
B6010
NOTTINGHAM ROAD
EAST NOTTINGHAM ROAD
NEW ROAD
MAIN ROAD
NARROW LANE
KIMBERLEY ROAD
IKEA WAY
GILTWAY

Plantation
Watnall Coppice
66
Ladies Wood
Coppice Farm
Brookbreasting Farm
New Road
Long Lane
M1
M1 Motorway
Crowhill Farm
Hollybush Farm
Watson's Wood
Starthwood Farm
Starth Wood
Stubbing Wood Farm
Eelhole Wood
Leisure Cen.
Lib.
Sch.
Ruffs
Westville
The Holgate Comprehensive School
Running Track
Recreation Ground
Sports Ground
Works
HUCKNALL
Beauvale Ct.
Christchurch Rd.
Polperro Way
Bolingey Way
Babbacombe Way
Edgewood Dr.
Ruffs Dr.
Salterford Rd.
Watnall Rd.
B6009
73
Sledder Wood
Eel Hole Farm
Watnall Lane
Littlefields Farm
Long Lane
HUCKNALL AERODROME
Bullwell Woodhall Farm
Fish Pond
Blenheim
BULWELL WOOD
Quarry Wood
Hall Farm
Watnall Chaworth
NG16
Common Farm
New Farm Cottage
New Farm
Broxtowe
Dabell
Centurion Business Park
WATNALL
Meteorological Station
Works
Common La.
Main Road
B600
Holly Rd.
Bakery
New Farm Wood
Seller's Wood Nature Reserve
Redfield House Farm
Cemy
New Farm Lane
New Nuthall
83
Kimberley Comp. Sch.
Kimberley Leisure Centre
Playing Field
Cricket Grd.
Graphic Ho.
Railway Cotts
Springfield Paddocks
High Wood
Chilton Drive
Newdigate St.
Nottingham Rd.
Spinney
Liby.

75
NG15
NG6
Nottingham
Butler's Hill
Broomhill
Hazelgrove
Farleys
Blenheim
BULWELL
Bulwell Forest
Moor Bridge
LEEN VALLEY COUNTRY PARK
MILL LAKES
MILL LAKES COUNTRY PARK
HUCKNALL INDUSTRIAL PARK
NOTTINGHAM CITY GOLF COURSE
BULWELL FOREST GOLF COURSE
Bulwell Hall Park
The Screen
Home Wood
Allcock's Wood
Barker's Wood
Fish Ponds
Cricket Ground
Titchfield Park
Cemetery
NORTHERN CEMETERY
VISION BUSINESS CENTRE
BLENHEIM INDUSTRIAL ESTATE
SPRINGFIELD RETAIL PARK
Ken Martin Swim. Pool
Springfield Prim. Sch.
Broomhill Junior & Butler's Hill Infant Schools
Annie Holgate Jun. & Inf. Schs.
Stanstead Primary School
Cantrell Prim. Sch.
Snape Wood Prim. Sch.
Forge Mills
Broomhill Farm
BESTWOOD BUSINESS PARK
HUCKNALL BY-PASS
A611
A6002
B6009
B682
B683
SANDHURST ROAD
CAMBERLEY ROAD
HUCKNALL LANE
HUCKNALL ROAD
BESTWOOD ROAD
MOOR RD.
WATNALL ROAD
NOTTINGHAM ROAD
HIGHBURY RD.
MAIN ST.
67
76
84
53
54
455
48
47
46
45
1
2
3
4
5
6
7
F
G
H
J
K

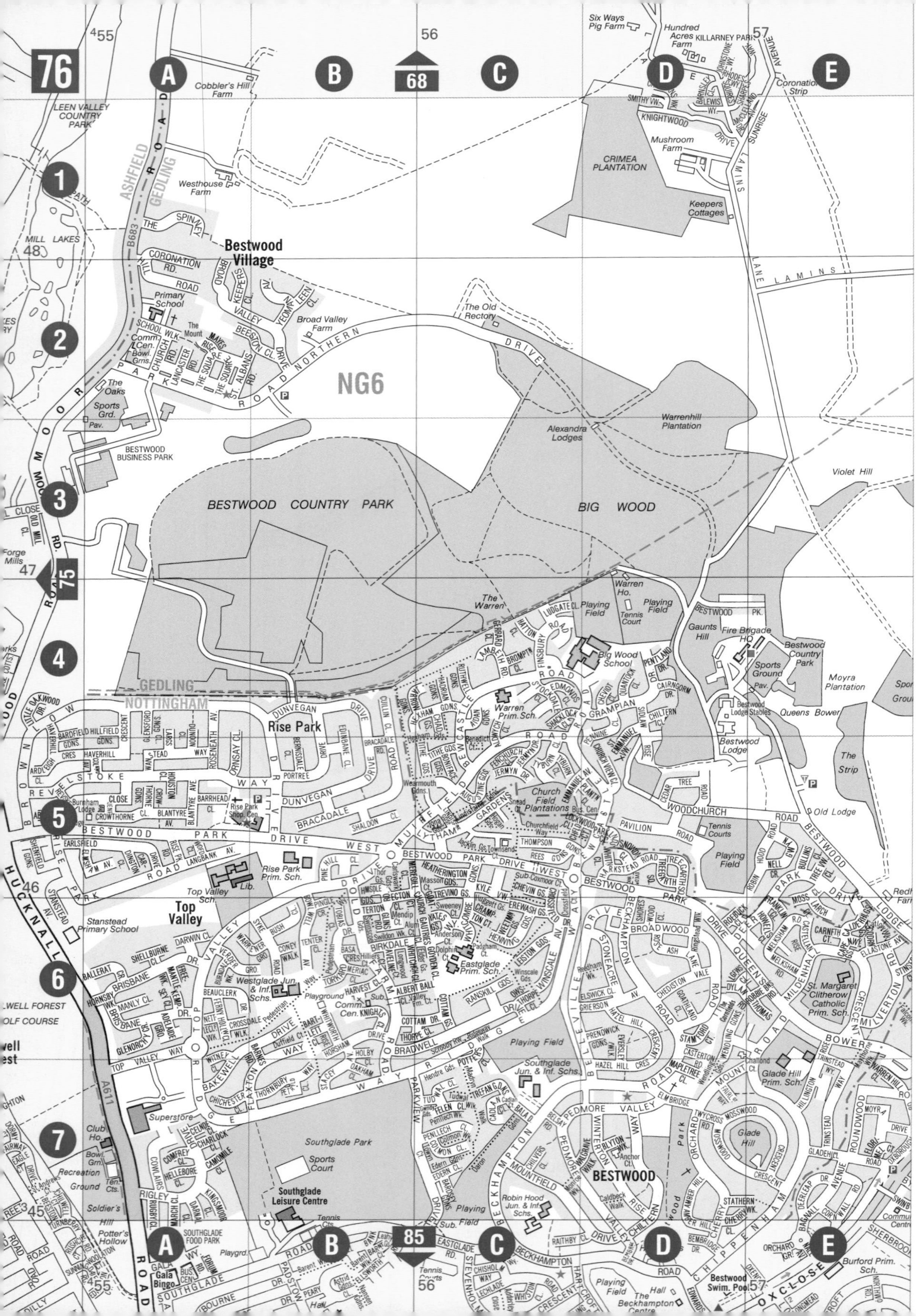
68
85
75
NG6
Bestwood Village
BESTWOOD COUNTRY PARK
BIG WOOD
Rise Park
Top Valley
BESTWOOD
GEDLING
NOTTINGHAM
LEEN VALLEY COUNTRY PARK
MILL LAKES
Cobbler's Hill Farm
Westhouse Farm
Six Ways Pig Farm
Hundred Acres Farm
Mushroom Farm
CRIMEA PLANTATION
Keepers Cottages
Coronation Strip
The Old Rectory
Broad Valley Farm
Alexandra Lodges
Warrenhill Plantation
Violet Hill
Forge Mills
The Warren
Warren Ho.
Playing Field
Tennis Court
Big Wood School
Gaunts Hill
Fire Brigade HQ
Bestwood Country Park
Sports Ground
Moyra Plantation
Queens Bower
Bestwood Lodge
The Strip
Old Lodge
Primary School
The Mount
Comm. Cen.
Bowl. Grns.
The Oaks
Sports Grd.
BESTWOOD BUSINESS PARK
Warren Prim. Sch.
Church Field Plantations
Rise Park Shop. Cen.
Rise Park Prim. Sch.
Top Valley Sch.
Lib.
Stanstead Primary School
Westglade Jun. & Inf. Schs.
Eastglade Prim. Sch.
Comm. Cen.
Southglade Jun. & Inf. Schs.
Playing Field
St. Margaret Clitherow Catholic Prim. Sch.
Glade Hill Prim. Sch.
Glade Hill
Superstore
Southglade Park
Sports Court
Southglade Leisure Centre
SOUTHGLADE FOOD PARK
Gala Bingo
Robin Hood Jun. & Inf. Schs.
Bestwood Swim. Pool
Burford Prim. Sch.
Recreation Ground
Soldier's Hill
Potter's Hollow
Club Ho.
GEDLING ROAD
ASHFIELD ROAD
MOOR ROAD
NORTHERN DRIVE
LAMINS LANE
BESTWOOD PARK DRIVE WEST
BESTWOOD PARK DRIVE
BESTWOOD LODGE DRIVE
WOODCHURCH ROAD
QUEENS BOWER ROAD
RIDGE WAY
BEESTON LANE
BECKHAMPTON ROAD
DUNVEGAN DRIVE
BROWNLOW DRIVE
REVELSTOKE WAY
HUCKNALL ROAD
TOP VALLEY WAY
TOP VALLEY DRIVE
OXCLOSE LANE
CHIPPENHAM ROAD
MILVERTON ROAD
MOUNT ROAD
BELLEVILLE DRIVE
BRADWELL ROAD
KNIGHTWOOD DRIVE
PEDMORE VALLEY
A611
B683

F
G
H
J
K
69
86
78
RAMSDALE PARK
North Peacock
South Peacock
The Belt
Ramsdale Hill
Reservoirs (covered)
GEORGE'S LANE
A60
A614
MANSFIELD ROAD
OLLERTON ROAD
LIME LANE
LITTLE LIME LA.
LAMINS LANE
Woodlands
Tophouse Farm
Limelane House
Leapool
ARCH HILL
Red Hill
Stockings Farm
Japanese Plantations
Ten Court
Cherry Holt
Reservoir (Covered)
New Farm
Works
B684
WOODBOROUGH LANE
Dorket Head Farm
Brick Works
Dorket Head
CALVERTON ROAD
Wood Farm
NG14
NG5
Nottingham
KILLISICK LANE
Redhill
Redhill School
Leisure Centre
Tennis Courts
Playing Field
Recreation Ground
Play-ground
Family Cen.
Comm. Centre
Derrymount Sch.
Richard Bonington Prim. Sch.
Pinewood Inf. Sch.
Killisick Jun. Sch.
Cemetery
Play. Field
COPPICE ROAD
Ground
Leis. Cen.
Shop. Cen.
Nurs. Home
Robert Mellors Prim. Sch.
Arnbrook Prim. Sch.
Church Drive Prim. Sch.
Coppice Farm Prim. Sch.
Christ The King Catholic School
ARNOLD
Arnold View Prim. Sch.
BYRON IND. EST.
NEWSTEAD IND. EST.
Superstore
Rec. Grd.
Daybrook
DAYBROOK BUS. CEN.
Depots
Fish Pond
Arnold Hill Sch.
Tennis Courts
B6004
A60
58
59
60
48
47
46
45
1
2
3
4
5
6
7

78
70
87
77
A
B
C
D
E
1
2
3
4
5
6
7
460
61
62
48
47
46
45
Lamp Wood
GEORGE'S
SPINDLE LANE
BONNER LANE
Bonner Hill
FOXWOOD LANE
Fox Wood
High Trees
Foxwood House
NG14
Thorne
Woodborough Park
Wynhill
Wood Farm
WESTFIELD LA.
Southwood
Bank Farm
Bank Hill Cottage
The Bank
WOODBOROUGH LANE
B684
Arnold Lodge
NG3
BANK ROAD
NOTTINGHAM
Wood Barn Farm
Lambley House
Nottingham
HUNGERHILL LANE
PLAINS
Barn Farm
Howbeck Clo.
Mellish Rugby Football Club
Fox Covert
NG5
CATFOOT LANE
Foxhill Farm
Cottage Farm
Nursery
Play Area
Coppice Farm
Mapperley Plains
NG4
Highclere House
Middlebeck Farm
Coppice Farm Prim. Sch.
MAPPERLEY
ORCHARD ROAD
MAPPERLEY DRIVE
COPPICE
HOWBECK
MIDDLEBECK
CRAWFORD
CROMDALE CL.
HAMILTON CL.
GLENEAGLES
Lambley Dumble
Springlane Farm
Chicken Farm
CORNCRAKE DR.
NEWCOMBE
EASTHAM ROAD
RAMSEY
ARMFIELD RD
OKEHAMPTON
SANDERSON DR.

SPRINGWATER GOLF COURSE
Dyke
Fish Farm
Chapel Farm
63
64
465
F
G
H
J
K
71
88
80
Grimesmoor
ROE HILL
HILL
MAIN
EPPERSTONE BY-PASS
A6097
Epperstone Manor (Notts. Constabulary HQ)
Pav.
Sports Ground
PARK LA.
BLAND LA.
TOAD LA.
LANE
Epper
1
2
3
4
5
6
7
48
47
46
345
Cemetery
Shelt Hill Farm
Fox Covert
Daybreak
PRIVATE ROAD
ASH GRO.
BIRCH RISE
ASH CL.
FIELD LA.
NEW ROW
BROAD CL.
WHITES CROFT
THE MEADOWS
TAYLORS CFT.
ROE LANE
SUNNINGDALE DRIVE
DOVERBECK DR.
ALDENE WAY
OLDACRES
PLOUGHMAN AV.
HAWTHORN CL.
STREET
LOWDHAM LANE
Woodborough Hall
PARK AV.
Rec. Grd.
Vic.
CHURCH WK.
PINFOLD CL.
PINFOLD CR.
BUCKLAND DR.
CROFT
HOLME CL.
SMALL'S CROFT
CHARNWOOD WY.
OLD MANOR CL.
Wood's Foundation Primary School
WOODBOROUGH
Play. Field
Fox Covert
Nursery
Woodlands
Lowdham Grange
GRANGE FM. COTTS.
PLOUGHMAN WOOD
HMP LOWDHAM GRANGE
THE GREEN
LONG MEADOW
HILL
HILL SYKE
ROCKLEY VIEW
LINGWOOD LANE
Well Cottage
GREEN
Hunters Hill
Jericho Farm
Lil-Yan Poultry Farm
NEWARK and SHERWOOD
GEDLING
Lowinds Farm
Hywinds Farm
LAMBLEY ROAD
Park Lane Nurseries
Bateman House
Harlow Wood Farm
LANE
The Poplars
DUMBLES
THE
CHURCH
LAMBLEY
ORCHARD
STEELES WY.
Cocker Beck
COCKER BECK
Works
MILL LA.
CHAPEL LA.
TRINITY CR.
WILLOW CR.
RISE
STREET
PARK
ROSS LA.
GRANGE CL.
Lambley Prim. Sch.
Rec. Grd.
MAIN
Cemetery
Cornwall's Hill
Broughton Park
Bulcote Wood
NG14
FLAMSTEAD AV.
Works
CROMWELL CRES.
NEGUS CT.
Stockhill Farm
SPRING
Road
Stockhill
LAMBLEY ROAD
Bulcote Lodge Fram

80
148
89
79
66
67
465
345
48
47
46
A
B
C
D
E
1
2
3
4
5
6
7
Chapel Farm
CHAPEL
NEEPS CFT.
CHURCH LA.
MAIN STREET
PADDOCK
FARM COTTS.
Epperstone Manor (Constabulary HQ)
Pav.
Sports Ground
BLAND LA.
TOAD LA.
PARK LA.
Epperstone
The Old House
HAGG LANE
Elm Park
Rifle Range
Bentley Wood
Netherfield Farm
Beck
Order
LOWDHAM ROAD
GONALSTON LANE
Village Hall
Pav.
Epperstone Playing Field
Dover Beck
EPPERSTONE BY-PASS
Wash Bridge
A6097
Netherfield Farm House
LOWDHAM LA.
Nursery
The Old Mill House
Car Holt Farm
Woodlands
OLD EPPERSTONE ROAD
Furleys Cotts.
Nurseries
Eliment Hill Farm
West End Villas
Weir
Lowdham Mill
Vicarage
Car Holt
Nottingham
GRANGE FM. COTTS.
The Hut
Orchard Nurseries
Brookfield
NG14
THE LEYS
MOUNT PLEASANT
Cemetery
C of E Sch.
NURSERY GS.
RIDGE HILL
Barker Hill
Hill House
THE GREEN
LONG MEADOW HILL
HILL SYKE
ROCKLEYS VIEW
CHURCH LA.
Grove Farm
Greenacres
The Old Hall
THE PRIORS
FRANCKLIN RD.
St. Mary's Cl.
Lib.
BARKER HILL
ROGERS AV.
BLACKTHORN DR.
THE FORGE
The Beck House
Nursery
STONEY BANK
PLOUGH LA.
MANOR HOUSE CL.
Hall Rec. Grd.
CRANLEIGH DR.
NEIGHBOURS LANE
LOWDHAM
SOUTHWELL ROAD
Elm Tree Farm
BROOKSIDE
PROSPECT VS.
MORLEY'S CL.
MAGNA CL.
Charta Mews
OLD TANNERY DRIVE
Rec. Grd.
THE CORNER
Pav.
War Mem.
WILLOW HO.
MERE CL.
VALE CL.
NEWTON CL.
Worlds End
Low Meadow
Hunters Hill
NOTT'GHM RD.
STATION RD.
LIME TREE GDS.
WORCESTER CL.
RUSSET CL.
VICTORIA AV.
BLENHEIM CL.
ROSS CL.
BECKSIDE
STOCKINGS
LONGMOOR AV.
THE ORCH.
Lowdham
CAYTHORPE ROAD
Cocker Beck
LAMBLEY LANE
Lowinds Farm
Hywinds Farm
SKITHORNE RISE
Brakes Farm
GUNTHORPE RD.
PAVILION CT.
Lowdham Lodge
Marlock Bridge
LOWDHAM ROAD
A612
COTTAGE PASTURE LA.
Little Marlock
NOTTINGHAM ROAD
Slurry Pond
Sunny Bank
Sibthorpe House
Beecroft Farm
Mumby House
Hill Farm
Hall Trees Nurseries
The Manor House
OLD

68
69
470
F
G
H
J
K
138
1
2
3
4
5
6
7
48
47
46
345
149
90
Thurgarton
Works
STATION
STATION ROAD
ROAD
HOVERINGHAM
LANE
THURGARTON
NOTTINGHAM ROAD
A612
The Dumble
Dumble
Spitalwood
Spital Wood
Wood Barn
Springfield House
The Gorse
Spital Farm
New Farm
Glebe Farm
The Hall
LANE
The Old Rectory
The Old Kennels
Holme Farm
The Almshouses
GONALSTON LANE
Gonalston
Rose Cottage
Four Winds
BROOKFIELD DR.
STREET
Hall Farm
Flora Farm
HOMELEIGH LA.
POST OFFICE YD.
Lindum Cotts.
Kneeton View
Pav.
Cricket Grd.
Hoveringham
West Farm
Manor Farm
MAIN
BOAT LANE
BRADLEY'S LANE
St. Michael's Farm
Church Farm
Dyke
Causeway
LANE
The Hermitage
Cliff Mill
Cliff Mill Farm
GONALSTON
Gonalston Crossing
Norrisdene
ELL ROAD
A612
Ford
Hoveringham Mill
Westfield House
Lansic House
LANSIC LANE
AVENUE
Lowdham Farm
THORPE
Springfield
Playing Field
Pav.
Car
Kennels
Caythorpe
ROAD
MAIN STREET
HOVERINGHAM
Hillcrest
Brackenhill
Clayton's Cottage
Fernhill House
Caythorpe House
Dyke
RIVER TRENT
ROAD
Watson's Piece
NG13
LANE
TRENT HILLS
HILL
OLD
Marlock Cottages
Marlock House Farm
A6097
Holly Farm
ROAD
THE AVENUE
The Parklands

73
92
A610
A6096
KIMBERLEY
AWSWORTH
NG16
Nottingham
Babbington
Cossall Marsh
Cossall
KIMBERLEY EASTWOOD BY-PASS
GIN CLOSE WAY
AWSWORTH & COSSALL BY-PASS
CORONATION RD.
CORONATION ROAD
NEWTON'S LANE
WESTBY LANE
AWSWORTH LANE
CHURCH LANE
ROBINETTES LANE
MILL LANE
DEAD LANE
COSSALL ROAD
MAIN STREET
STATION ROAD
AWSWORTH RD.
BABBINGTON
SPRING HILL
Nottingham Canal (Disused)
River Erewash
Robbinetts Arm (Disused)
Gilt Brook
Sewage Works
Works
Depot
Depots
Superstores
IKEA WAY
Subway
Pavilion
Gilt Hill Farm
Playing Field
Gilthill Prim. Sch.
Hollywell Prim. Sch.
Recreation Ground
Brewery
Church Hill Centre (Broxtowe Coll.)
The Fives
Gilt Briggs Farm
Crabcroft Farm
Whisgills
Grasscroft Farm
Reservoir (Covered)
Babbington Hall
Babbington House Farm
Strelley Park Farm
Holly Copse Nature Reserve
SPRING WOOD
Turkey Fields Farm
Moss Cottage
Robbinetts Cottage
Oldmoor Farmhouse
Brickyard Plantation Nature Reserve
OLDMOOR WOOD NATURE RESERVE
Oldmoor Pond
Weir
Manor Farm
Almshouses
Cedar Farm
The Hollies
Grange Farm
Glasshouse Yard
Barlows Cotts.
Comm. Cen.
Awsworth Prim. Sch.
Play. Fld.
Bowl. Grn.
Bungalow Farm
White House Fm.
The View
Bridge Farm
Newton's Bri.
Cossall Common
Nursery
Common Farm
Foundry House
Gin Stables
Factory
(Prop)
COSSALL INDUSTRIAL ESTATE
SOLOMAN RD.
Bakers Brothers Mobile Home Cvn. Site
Larklands Inf. Sch.
Small Holding
EREWASH
BROXTOWE
HEATHFIELD
GREEN LANE
A B C D E
1 2 3 4 5 6 7
345 44 43 42 48 49

New Nuthall
Larkfields
NUTHALL
Swingate
STRELLEY
NG6
NG8
Junction 26
M1 MOTORWAY
A610
A6002
B600
B6004
KIMBERLEY BY-PASS
EASTWOOD WAY
WATNALL ROAD
NOTTINGHAM ROAD
KIMBERLEY ROAD
WOODHOUSE ROAD
STRELLEY ROAD
MAIN ROAD
MAIN STREET
BILBOROUGH ROAD
BROXTOWE COUNTRY PARK
NOTTINGHAM BUSINESS PARK
THE LAKE
Verge Wood
Broad Oak Plantation
Stonepit Plantation
Windmill Plantation
Chilwell Dam Plantation
Windmill Farm
Swingate Farm
Bridlepath Cottage
Lodge
Home Farm
Quarry House
Fish Pond
Strelley Hall
Old Rectory Farm
Moat
Broad Oak Farm
Catstone Hill
Reservoir (covered)
Redfield House Farm
Bakery
Springfield Paddocks
High Wood
Low Wood
Hempshill Hall
Kimberley Comp. Sch.
Kimberley Leisure Centre
Playing Field
Cricket Grd.
Graphic Ho.
Superstore
Cemetery
The Coppice
Knowle Wood
Brackenhurst
Kimberley Prim. Sch.
THE NOOK
Knowlepark Farm
Larkfields Jun. & Inf. Schs.
Playing Fields
Bowling Green
Nursery
Community Centre
Horsendale Prim. Sch.
Prim. Sch.
Seagrave Prim. Sch.
Rec. Grd.
Comm. Cen.
Jubilee Ct.
Westbury School
Brocklewood Jun. & Inf. Schs.
Melbury Prim. Sch.
Bilborough Coll.
Harvey Hadden Sports Complex
Harvey Hadden Stadium
Bilborough Park
Tennis Courts
Glenbrook
Subway
74
84
93
450
51
52
345
44
43
42
F
G
H
J
K
1
2
3
4
5
6
7

BULWELL
75
NORTHERN CEMETERY
High Wood
Low Wood
Hempshill Vale
Hempshill Hall
Hempshill Hall Prim. Sch.
NG6
NG16
NG8
EASTWOOD BY-PASS
A610
A6002
LOW WOOD ROAD
Phoenix Park
MILLENNIUM WAY WEST
MILLENNIUM WAY EAST
Cinderhill
CINDERHILL ROAD
HIGHBURY ROAD
Highbury Vale
HIGHBURY HOSPITAL
Henry Mellish Comp. Sch.
Mill Street Playing Field
Football Pitch
Open Space
VERNON ROAD
B682
NOTTINGHAM ROAD
83
BROXTOWE NOTTINGHAM
BROXTOWE WOOD
BROXTOWE COUNTRY PARK
Broxtowe
AMESBURY CIRCUS
Rosslyn Park Prim. Sch.
Quarry Holes Plantation
Basford Hall Coll.
NUTHALL ROAD
B6004
STOCKHILL LANE
Old Basford Prim. Sch.
Ellis Guilford Sch. & Sports College
BAR LANE INDUSTRIAL PARK
BELLS LANE
B6008
BROXTOWE LANE
Minver Cres. Sports Centre
Aspley Comm. & Training Centre
Ambleside Jun. & Inf. Sch.
ALLENDALE ROAD
ASPLEY LANE
B690
STRELLEY ROAD
Superstore
The Aspley Centre
Recreation Ground
Aspley
WESTERN BOULEVARD
A6514
The Nottingham Bluecoat Sch. & Technology Coll.
Brocklewood Jun. & Inf. Schs.
King George V Playing Flds.
St. Teresa's Catholic Prim. Sch.
The Trinity Sch. (Lower)
The Trinity Sch. (Upper)
Beechdale Ho. (Nursing Home)
Harvey Hadden Sports Complex
94
Manning Comp. School
Whitemoor Prim. Sch.
42
43
44
45
53
54
A
B
C
D
E
1
2
3
4
5
6
7

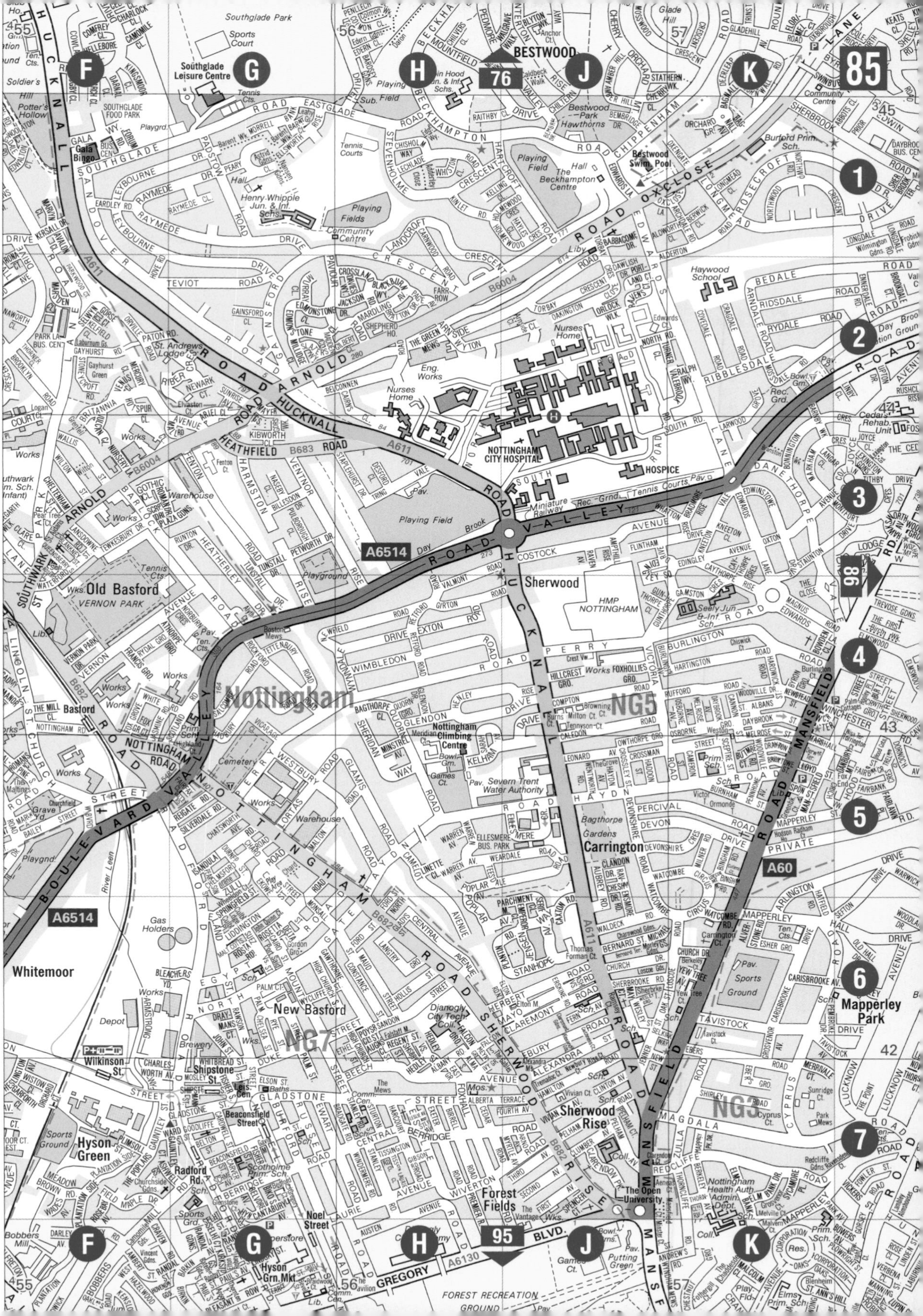
Southglade Park
Sports Court
Southglade Leisure Centre
BESTWOOD
76
Bestwood Park Hawthorns
The Beckhampton Centre
Bestwood Swim. Pool
Burford Prim. Sch.
Henry Whipple Jun. & Inf. Schs.
Playing Fields
Community Centre
Haywood School
Gala Bingo
SOUTHGLADE FOOD PARK
Nurses Home
Eng. Works
NOTTINGHAM CITY HOSPITAL
HOSPICE
Miniature Railway
Playing Field
A6514
A611
B6004
B683
B682
A60
A6130
Old Basford
VERNON PARK
Sherwood
HMP NOTTINGHAM
Nottingham
NG5
NG7
NG3
Basford
Nottingham Climbing Centre
Severn Trent Water Authority
Bagthorpe Gardens
Carrington
Cemetery
Gas Holders
Whitemoor
New Basford
Djanogly City Tech. Coll.
Mapperley Park
Sports Ground
Hyson Green
Radford Rd.
Shipstone St.
Wilkinson St.
Beaconsfield Street
Sherwood Rise
Forest Fields
The Open University
Nottingham Health Auth. Admin. Dept.
Noel Street
Hyson Grn. Mkt.
95
FOREST RECREATION GROUND
Putting Green
HUCKNALL ROAD
ARNOLD ROAD
VALLEY ROAD
NOTTINGHAM ROAD
BOULEVARD
SHERWOOD RISE
MANSFIELD ROAD
GREGORY BLVD.
OXCLOSE ROAD
PERRY ROAD
86
F G H J K
1 2 3 4 5 6 7
55 56 57
42 43 44 45

Daybrook
Daybrook Square
NG5
Woodthorpe
ARNOLD
MAPPERLEY
Nottingham
Mapperley
Porchester
NG3
Mapperley Park
Thorneywood
Alexandra Park
Hungerhill Gardens
A60
A6514
A6211
B684
ARNO VALE ROAD
GEDLING ROAD
THACKERAY'S LANE
MANSFIELD ROAD
WOODTHORPE DRIVE
PLAINS ROAD
WOODBOROUGH ROAD
PORCHESTER ROAD
HUNGERHILL ROAD
MAPPERLEY PLAINS
WELLS ROAD
THE NOTTINGHAM NUFFIELD HOSP.
Borough Council Offs.
Arnold Hill Sch.
Ernehale Jun. & Inf. Sch.
Woodthorpe Grange
Grange Park
Recreation Ground
Elliot Durham Comp. Sch.
Elliott Durham Swimming Pool
Duncan Macmillan House
Walter Halls Prim. Sch.
St. Ann's Well Jun. Sch.
Hine Hall
Stonepit Coppice Gardens
Hospice
Thorneywood Unit
Club House
Cricket Ground
Football Ground
Playing Field
Mapperley Plains Prim. Sch.
Arno Vale Jun. Sch.
Woodthorpe Inf. Sch.
The Good Shepherd RC Prim. Sch.
Burford Prim. Sch.
Day Brook Rec. Grd.
Miniature Golf Course
Hogarth Prim. Sch.
Standhill Inf. Sch.
A B C D E
1 2 3 4 5 6 7
77
85
96
58 59
42 43 44 45

78
88
97
F
G
H
J
K
1
2
3
4
5
6
7
60
61
62
345
44
43
42
NG4
Gedling
CARLTON
Carlton
ARNOLD LANE
A6211
B684
PLAINS
SPRING LANE
LAMBLEY LANE
MAIN RD.
SHEARING HILL
BURTON ROAD
COLWICK LOOP ROAD
A612
B686
CAVENDISH ROAD
CENTRAL AVENUE
WESTDALE LANE
PORCHESTER ROAD
PHOENIX AV.
GEDLING RD.
ORLANDO DRIVE
STATION ROAD
Springlane Farm
Chicken Farm
Crimea Farm
Wicketwood Hill
Grass Road
Wood Farm
Hill Top Nursery
Chase Farm
GOLF COURSE
Glebe Farm
Scotgrave Farm
Household Waste and Recycling Centre
Gedling Wharf
Playing Field
Pavilion
Rec. Ground
Harvey's Plantation
Kennels
Gedling Wood
Gedling Farm
Lambley Dumble
Lambley Prim. Sch.
Rec. Grd.
Stanhope Prim. Sch.
Carlton Digby Sch.
St. Andrews House
Westdale Jun. & Inf. Sch.
The Gedling School
Comm. Cen.
Lib.
Cemetery
Hardstaff Almshouses
Marion Murdoch Ct.
Willow Farm Prim. Sch.
Carlton le Willows Sch. & Technology College
Gedling Manor
Youth Cen.
Recreation Ground
Haddon Prim. Sch.
The Wheldon Comp. Sch.
Carlton Forum Leisure Centre
Phoenix Inf. Sch.
Priory Jun. Sch.
All Hallows Prim. Sch.
Bramble Ct.
Braywood Gardens
Football Pitch
Carlton Cemetery
TA Cen.
Council Offices
Central Inf. Sch.
Central Jun. Sch.
CARLTON BUSINESS CENTRE
Sacred Heart
Carlton Grange
Brooks Cotts.
Nethergate
Bowls Grn. Rec. Ground
The Chestnuts
Football Ground

79
87
98
A
B
C
D
E
1
2
3
4
5
6
7
63
64
45
44
43
42
BURTON JOYCE
Nottingham
NG4
GEDLING
RUSHCLIFFE
Broughton Park
Bulcote Wood
Cemetery
Cornwall's Hill
Stock Farm
Bulcote Lodge Fram
The Mount
Fox Hill
Stockhill Farm
Lodge Farm
Wicketwood Hill
Wood Farm
Hill Top Nursery
Burtonwood Farm
Crock Dumble
Barron's Plantation
Gedling Wood
Gedling Wood Farm
White Gates
Glebe Farm
Tennis Courts
New Plantation
Poultry Farm
Gedling House
Playing Field
Running Track
Carlton le Willows Sch. & Technology College
Gedling Manor
Youth Cen.
Recreation Ground
Burton Joyce
Bowl. Grn.
The Poplar Sports Ground
Sports Ground
Sewage Disposal Works
New Works Cotts.
Pav. Play. Fld.
Works
Stoke Farm
Stoke Bardolph
Cricket Field
Top Row
Football Ground
Pavilion
Burton Joyce Brookside Prim. Sch.
Lib.
Rec. Grd.
Lambley Prim. Sch.
Rec. Grd.
SPRING LA.
SPRING
LAMBLEY LANE
LAMBLEY BRIDLE ROAD
BRIDLE ROAD
GLEN RD.
FOXHILL
PADLEYS LANE
LAMBLEY LANE
COPSE CL.
COVERT CL.
MAIN ST.
CHURCH ROAD
NOTTINGHAM ROAD
BURTON ROAD
A612
STATION RD.
ST. HELEN'S GRO.
ST. HELEN'S CRES.
CHESTNUT GRO.
MEADOW LA.
WINIFRED CR.
CRAGMOOR RD.
CROW PARK DR.
MASSEY CL.
MILLFIELD CL.
TRENTHAM GDNS.
GLEBE DR.
BULCOTE DRIVE
WOODSIDE RD.
MARIS DR.
LOXLEY MDW.
PARK AV.
VICARAGE DR.
STOKE LANE
ST. LUKES WY.
STANHOPE CR.
Riverside
WHITWORTH DRIVE
LINDEN GROVE
LINDEN GRO.
CONWAY GRO.
HARRINGTON CL.
EMERYS ROAD
AMBLESIDE WAY
WILLIAM CL.
SHAW GS.
LOOP ROAD
COLWICK
A6211 HILL
BURTON
WOOD LANE
YEW TREE LANE
BLACKTHORN
TAMARIX CL.
Under Construction (Estimated Completion February 2007)

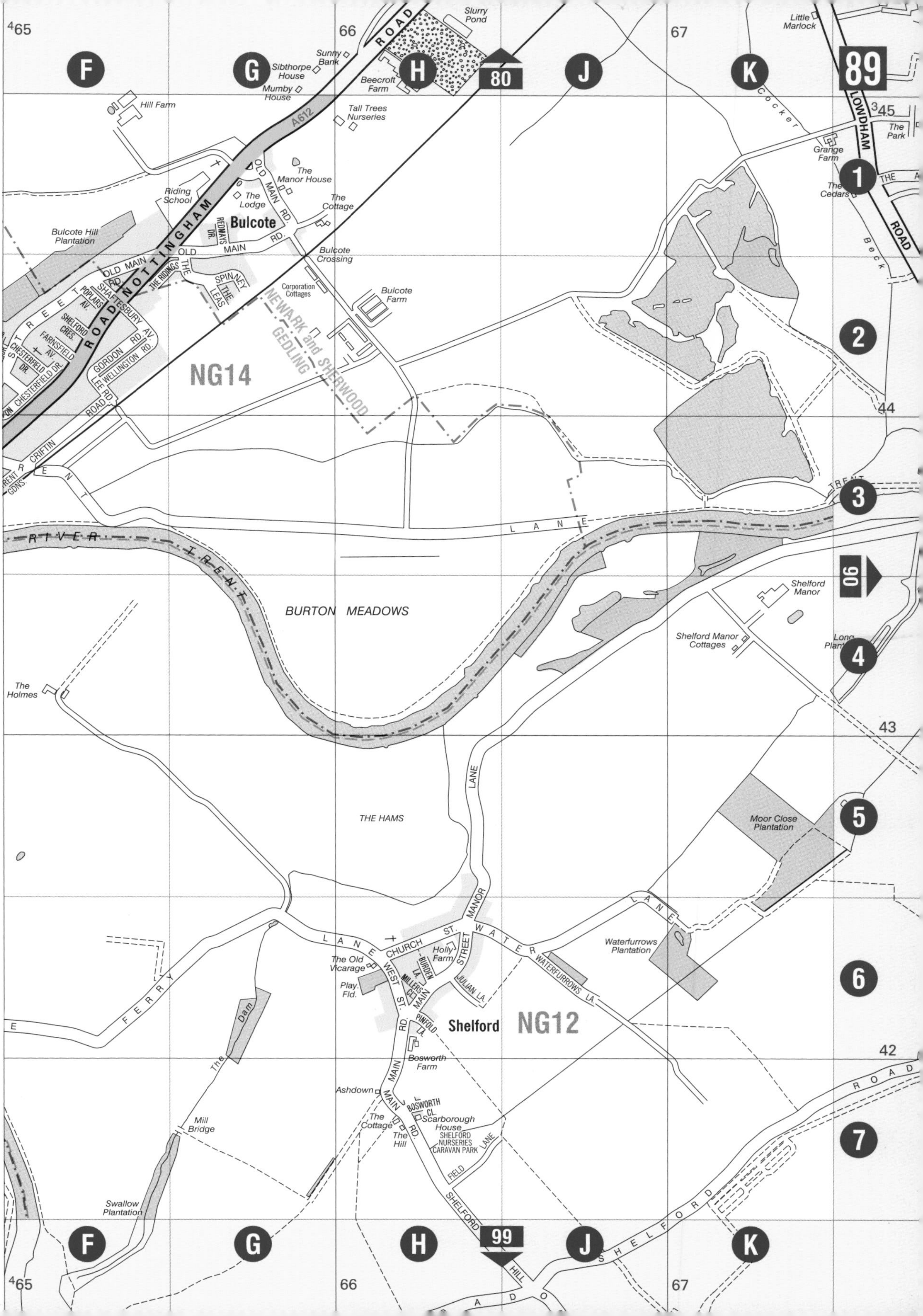
89
80
90
99
F
G
H
J
K
1
2
3
4
5
6
7
465
66
67
345
44
43
42
Slurry Pond
Little Marlock
Sunny Bank
Sibthorpe House
Mumby House
Beecroft Farm
Hill Farm
Tall Trees Nurseries
ROAD
A612
Cocker Beck
LOWDHAM ROAD
The Park
Grange Farm
The Cedars
THE
The Manor House
OLD MAIN RD.
Riding School
The Lodge
The Cottage
NOTTINGHAM ROAD
Bulcote
REDMAYS DR.
MAIN RD.
Bulcote Hill Plantation
OLD
Bulcote Crossing
OLD MAIN RD.
THE RIDINGS
THE
SPINNEY
THE LEAS
Corporation Cottages
Bulcote Farm
STREET
POPLARS AV.
SHAFTESBURY AV.
SHELFORD CRES.
FARNSFIELD AV.
CHESTERFIELD DR.
GORDON RD.
WELLINGTON RD.
LEE RD.
NEWARK and SHERWOOD
GEDLING
NG14
ROAD
CRIFTIN
TRENT GDNS.
TRENT LANE
RIVER TRENT
BURTON MEADOWS
Shelford Manor
Shelford Manor Cottages
Long Plant
The Holmes
LANE
THE HAMS
Moor Close Plantation
MANOR
LANE
CHURCH ST.
STREET
WATER
Holly Farm
BURDEN LA.
The Old Vicarage
WEST ST.
MILLERS CT.
MAIN
JULIAN LA.
WATERFURROWS LA.
Waterfurrows Plantation
Play. Fld.
PINFOLD LA.
RD.
Shelford
NG12
FERRY
E
The Dam
Bosworth Farm
Ashdown
MAIN
BOSWORTH CL.
Scarborough House
SHELFORD NURSERIES CARAVAN PARK
The Cottage
The Hill
MAIN RD.
FIELD LANE
Mill Bridge
Swallow Plantation
SHELFORD HILL
SHELFORD ROAD
ADO

Little Marlock
LOWDHAM ROAD BY-PASS
Holly Farm
68
69
A
B
C
D
E
81
TRENT HILLS
LANE
45
The Park
Parklands
Grange Farm
A6097
THE AVENUE
The Cedars
Lodge Farm
LANE
Glebe Farm
HILL
1
2
3
4
5
6
7
Caravan Site
FEARON CL.
Gunthorpe
MAIN
BRAMLEY CL.
HAZELAS DR.
PECK
LANE
NG14
HOBSON'S ACRE
THORPE LEA
RIVERLANDS CL.
INHAM FLDS. CL.
Hall
Playing Field
Pav.
DAVIDS LA.
Gunthorpe C of E Prim. Sch.
ORCHARD CL.
BROOK-LAND CL.
PASTURE
PEACOCK CL.
STREET
Cocker Beck
NEWARK and SHERWOOD
RUSHCLIFFE
TRENT
OLD
OLD HILL
44
Riverdale Park
Lock House
Warehouse
TRENT LANE
MAIN ST.
TRENTSIDE
ROAD
R I V E R
Gunthorpe Bridge
Weir
Gunthorpe Lock
Manor Farm
R
TRENT
The Moorings
BRIDGEFORD COURT CARAVAN PARK
MANOR RI.
CHERRYHOLT
LAMMAS GDS.
LAMMAS
LANE
89
NG12
Water Reclamation Works
CROFT RI.
FARM WK.
ORCHARD CL.
DOVECOTE CL.
BROWN'S LA.
BROWN'S LA.
MOSS CL.
STREET
MILL HEYES
LANE
CLOSES
SIDE
HACKERS CL.
KNEETON
Long Plantation
CUTTLE HILL GDS.
Cuttle Hill
LANE
STABLE CL.
LANE
A6097
School
Butt Close Playing Field
Pav.
STRAW'S CFT.
MAGDALE DR.
HOLLOWAY CL.
East Bridgford Hill
Meml.
HILL
MAIN
COLLEGE
STRAWS
CROSSWAYS DR.
43
MALTHOUSE CL.
MILL GA.
FARM CL.
BLENHEIM GS.
BROOKS CL.
CROSS
BRIDLE WAYS
Hill Farm
KIRK
STREET
BUTT
THE LYNGS
BRICKYARD LA.
LUDGATE DR.
KIRK HILL
WALNUT GRO.
WALNUT TREE LA.
BURNHAM CL.
Foxhills Farm
EAST BRIDGFORD
SPRINGDALE
LANE
Moor Close Plantation
ROAD
BRIDGFORD
Sewage Pump. Station
STREET
BRUNT'S
Newton Fields
BRIDGEFORD
42
Mill Farm
ROAD
EAST
Glebe Farm
Newton
Newton House Farm
MAIN
Hall
SHELFORD
Yew Tree Farm
White House
Nursery
FRIAR WLK.
A6097
FAIRWAY CRES.
CLOSE
CLOSE
Newton Spring
NEWTON AIRFIELD
Playgrd.
TRENCHARD
TRENCHARD
STREET
100
A46
ROAD
Tennis Cts.
68
69

91
F
G
H
J
K
70
71
72
Topfield Farm
Old Hill Farm
Bungalow Farm
Barbara's Wood
Newfield
345
A46
Stoneydale Plantation
Glebe Farm
Fosse Farm
KNEETON ROAD
RED LODGE LANE
LODGE LANE
Shacker Dale
Shackerdale Wood
OCCUPATION LANE
Cape Farm
Lammas Farm
Shackerdale Farm
Fosse Poultry Farm
44
Fosse Fields Farm
FOSSE ROAD
Fosse Way (ROMAN ROAD)
The Shacker
NEW LANE
149
Blagg's Covert
Nottingham
Sandfield House
Brunsell Hall
Little Green
Old Hall
BEDEHAM LA.
Wilmot Cl.
Hall
CHURCH LA.
Hall Farm
43
Arborfield
Car Colston
TENMAN LANE
The Hall
Beech Close Farm
CAR LA.
Ashclose Poultry Farm
Moorfield Cottage
Pav.
Cricket Ground
Nursery
NG13
Toll Bar Farm
Manor Farm
Field House Farm
Woodside Farm
Parrots Nest
Bulwell House
LANE
42
Burrowsmoor Holt
Thoroughfare Holt
MICKLEMOOR
Burrow Fields
Castle Hill
101
Bottom Plantation
High Westing Farm
1
2
3
4
5
6
7

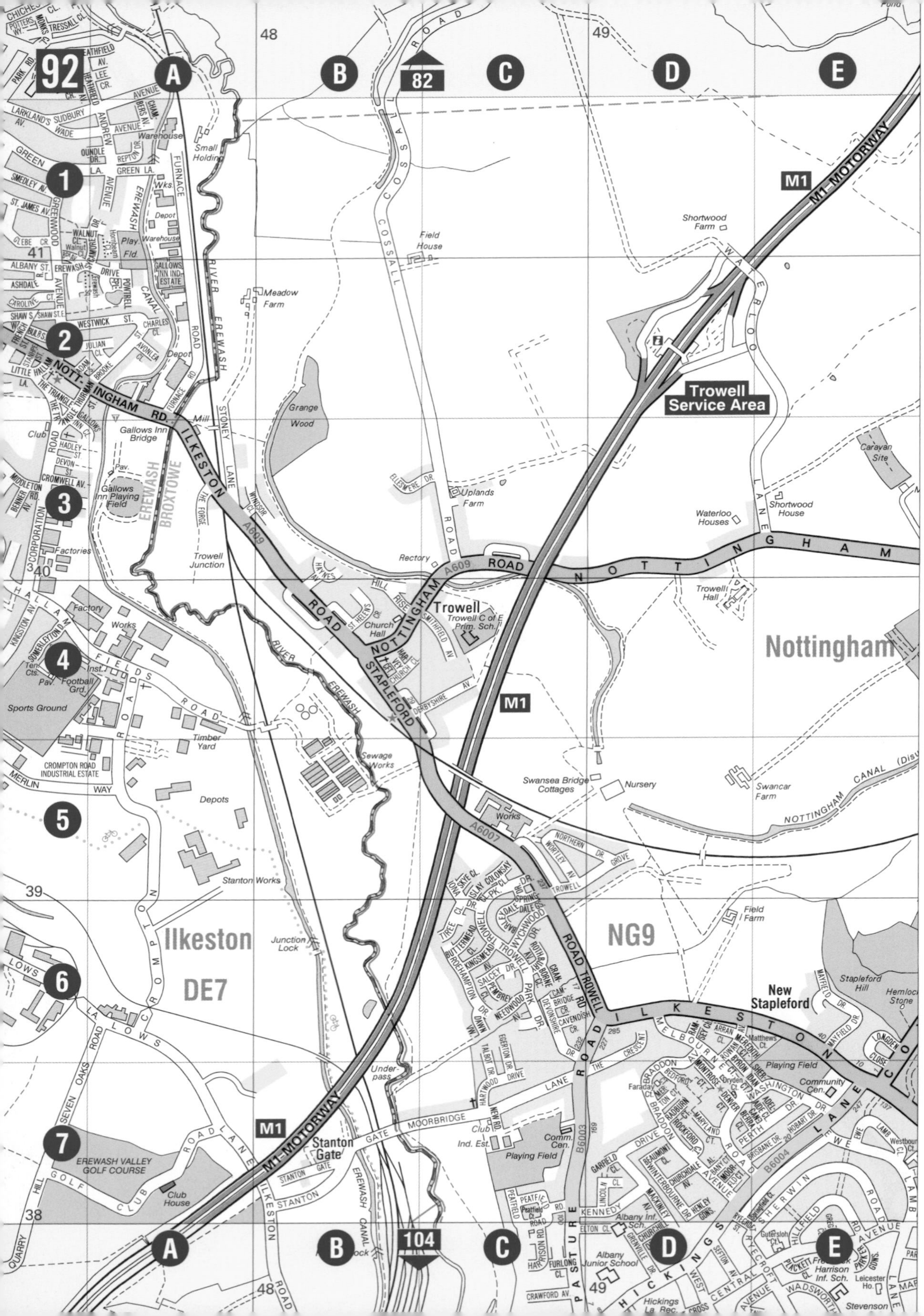

92
A
B
C
D
E
48
49
82
104
1
2
3
4
5
6
7
41
40
39
38
M1
M1 MOTORWAY
Trowell Service Area
Shortwood Farm
Waterloo Lane
Field House
Meadow Farm
Small Holding
Warehouse
Grange Wood
Cossall Road
Stoney Lane
Uplands Farm
Rectory
Nottingham Road
A609
Ilkeston Road
Trowell
Trowell C of E Prim. Sch.
Church Hall
Stapleford Road
Derbyshire Av.
Waterloo Houses
Shortwood House
Caravan Site
Trowell Hall
Nottingham
Swancar Farm
Nottingham Canal
Swansea Bridge Cottages
Nursery
Works
A6007
Sewage Works
River Erewash
Erewash Canal
Gallows Inn Bridge
Gallows Inn Playing Field
Gallows Inn Ind. Estate
Erewash
Broxtowe
Trowell Junction
The Forge
Factories
Factory
Hallam Fields Road
Sports Ground
Football Grd.
Crompton Road Industrial Estate
Merlin Way
Timber Yard
Depots
Stanton Works
Ilkeston
DE7
Junction Lock
Crompton Road
Lows Lane
Seven Oaks Road
Erewash Valley Golf Course
Golf Club Road
Club House
Quarry Hill
Stanton Gate
Moorbridge Lane
Ind. Est.
Club
Comm. Cen.
Playing Field
Underpass
NG9
Field Farm
Trowell Road
New Stapleford
Stapleford Hill
Hemlock Stone
Ilkeston Road
Community Cen.
Washington Dr.
Braddon Av.
Pasture Road
B6003
B6004
Hickings Lane
Albany Inf. Sch.
Albany Junior School
Hickings La. Rec.
Central Avenue
Wadsworth
Frederick Harrison Inf. Sch.
Leicester Ho.
Stevenson
Nott-ingham Rd.
Little Hallam La.
Westwick St.
Furnace Road
Green La.
Greenwood Avenue
Erewash Drive
Corporation Road
Cromwell Av.
Middleton Rd.
Benner Rd.
Kingston Av.
Larklands Av.
Sudbury Avenue
Heathfield Av.
Park Rd.

STRELLEY
83
94
105
Bilborough
Trowell Moor
NG8
WOLLATON
Bramcote Hills
Catstone Hill
Reservoir (covered)
Shaw's Plantation
Spring Farm
Moor Farm
Moor Cottages
Gables Farm
The Woodards
The Spinney
Bilborough Coll.
Bilborough Coll. Sports Centre
Playing Fields
William Sharp Comp. Sch.
Tennis Courts
Playground
Library
Melbury Prim. Sch.
Westbury School
Highwood Player Jun. & Inf. Sch.
Harvey Hadden Sports Complex
Harvey Hadden Stadium
Miniature Golf Course
Bilborough Park Pav.
Portland Prim. Sch.
Comm. Cen.
Bolsover Road Rec. Grd.
Glaisdale Park Industrial Estate
Works
Depots
Old Park Farm Gardens
Martin's Pond Nature Reserve
Martin's Pond
Superstore
Balloon Wood Industrial Estate
Balloon Wood
Firbeck Prim. Sch.
Potter's Plantation
Birchwood Nurseries
Fernwood Comp. Sch.
Fernwood Jun. & Inf. Schs.
Playing Field
Sports Ground
Coventry Lane Bridge
Hulks Farm
Bramcote Moor
Pavilion
Bramcote Crematorium
Moor Cott.
Sand Pit
Bramcote Hills Golf Course
Deddington Plantation
Bramcote Hills Sports and Comm. College
Bramcote Hills Prim. Sch.
Bramcote Park Business and Enterprise School
Bramcote Hills Park
Foxwood Foundation School and Technology College
Running Track
Crow Hill
Bramcote Leisure Centre
Open Space
Tottle Brook
Thompson's Wood
Recreation Ground
Cemetery
Beeston Fields Primary School
A609 TROWELL ROAD
A6002 BILBOROUGH ROAD
A6002 COVENTRY LANE
A52 DERBY ROAD (BRIAN CLOUGH WAY)
A6007
B6006 WOLLATON RD.
BROXTOWE
NOTTINGHAM
F G H J K
1 2 3 4 5 6 7
50 51 52
41 40 39 38

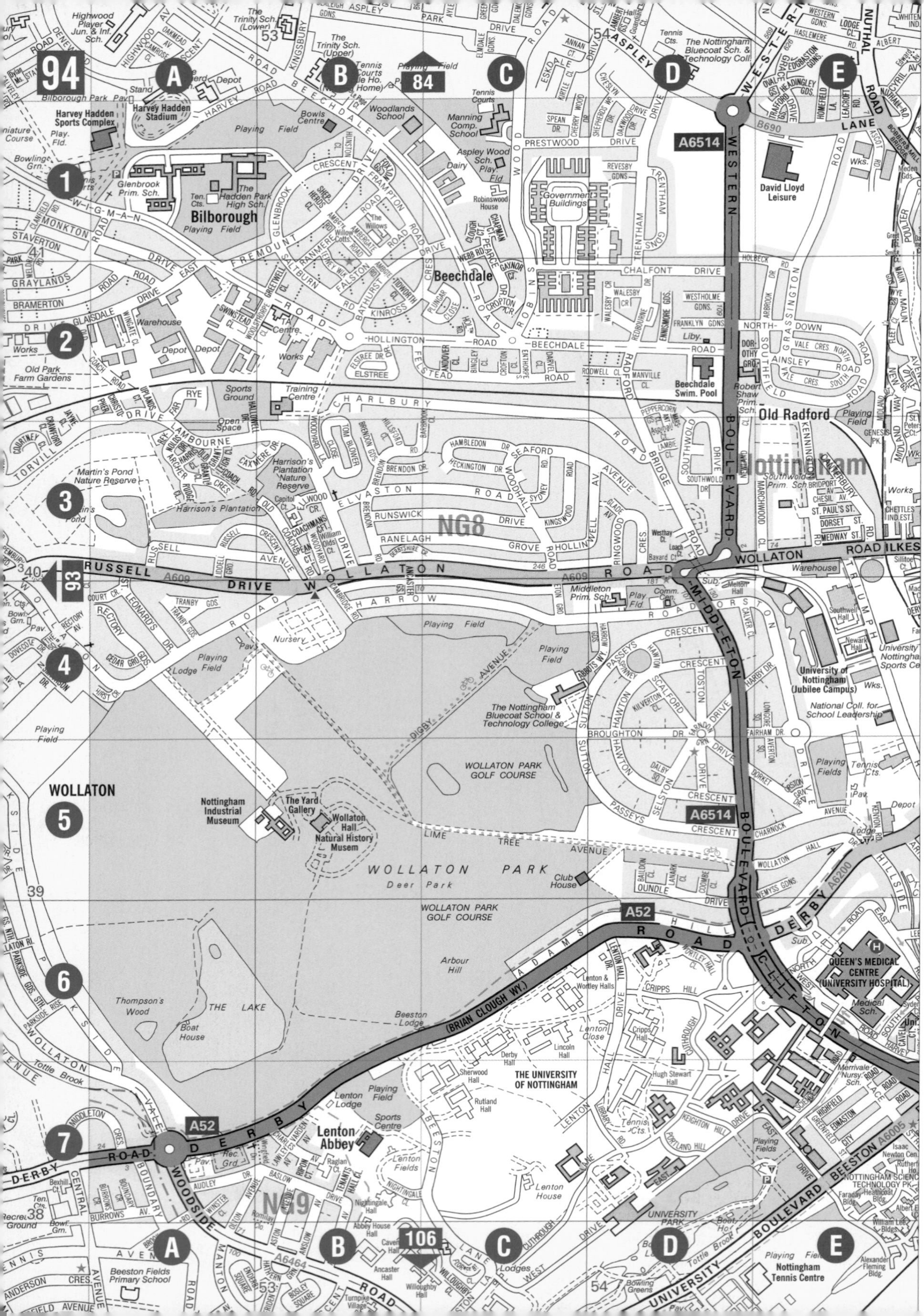
A
B
C
D
E
1
2
3
4
5
6
7
84
93
106
53
54
41
40
39
38
Highwood Player Jun. & Inf. Sch.
The Trinity Sch. (Lower)
The Trinity Sch. (Upper)
Tennis Courts
Playing Field
Bilborough Park
Harvey Hadden Sports Complex
Harvey Hadden Stadium
Depot
Bowls Centre
Woodlands School
Manning Comp. School
Tennis Courts
Aspley Wood Sch.
Dairy
Robinswood House
The Nottingham Bluecoat Sch. & Technology Coll.
Tennis Cts.
ASPLEY
WESTERN
A6514
B690
LANE
David Lloyd Leisure
Wks.
Glenbrook Prim. Sch.
The Hadden Park High Sch.
Bilborough
Playing Field
Bowling Grn.
Miniature Course
Play. Fld.
WIGMAN
MONKTON
STAVERTON
GRAYLANDS
BRAMERTON
GLAISDALE
DRIVE
FREMOUNT
SALTBURN
GLENBROOK
CRESCENT
FRAMPTON
PRESTWOOD DRIVE
Government Buildings
TRENTHAM
Beechdale
CHALFONT DRIVE
HOLBECK
GRASSINGTON
NORTH DOWN
VALE CRES NORTH
AINSLEY ROAD
SOUTHFIELD
Old Radford
Playing Field
Warehouse
Depot
Works
TA Centre
Old Park Farm Gardens
HOLLINGTON ROAD
BEECHDALE ROAD
ELSTREE
FELSTEAD
ROAD
MANVILLE CL.
Beechdale Swim. Pool
Robert Shaw Prim. Sch.
Liby.
FRANKLYN GDNS
WESTHOLME GDNS.
Sports Ground
Training Centre
CHARLBURY
RYE
Open Space
LAMBOURNE
Martin's Pond Nature Reserve
Harrison's Plantation Nature Reserve
Harrison's Plantation
HAMBLEDON DR
SEAFORD
HECKINGTON DR.
BRENDON DR.
ELVASTON ROAD
RUNSWICK DRIVE
RANELAGH GROVE
NG8
HOLLINWELL
RINGWOOD
KINGSWOOD
RADFORD BRIDGE ROAD
SOUTHWOLD
Nottingham
Southwold Prim. Sch.
MARCHWOOD
KENNINGTON
CANTERBURY
ST. PAUL'S ST.
DORSET ST.
MEDWAY ST.
CHETTLES IND. EST.
Works
RUSSELL DRIVE
A609
WOLLATON ROAD
RUSSELL AVENUE
WOLLATON ROAD
ILKESTON
Warehouse
Middleton Prim. Sch.
Play Fld.
Comm. Ctr.
Melton Hall
HARROW ROAD
ORSTON ROAD
MIDDLETON
Southwell Hall
Newark Hall
University of Nottingham Sports Ce
TRIUMPH
University of Nottingham (Jubilee Campus)
Wks.
National Coll. for School Leadership
RECTORY AV.
TRANBY GDS.
CEDAR GRO.
Lodge
Playing Field
Nursery
Playing Field
DIGBY AVENUE
The Nottingham Bluecoat School & Technology College
PASSEYS CRESCENT
TOSTON CRESCENT
HAWTON
SUTTON
BROUGHTON DR.
SCALFORD DRIVE
SELSTON DRIVE
CRESCENT
WOLLATON PARK GOLF COURSE
Playing Fields
Tennis Cts.
Pav.
Depot
WOLLATON
Nottingham Industrial Museum
The Yard Gallery
Wollaton Hall Natural History Museum
LIME TREE AVENUE
WOLLATON PARK
Deer Park
Club House
CHARNOCK AVENUE
WOLLATON HALL DRIVE
BOULEVARD
WOLLATON PARK GOLF COURSE
A52
ADAMS HILL
DERBY ROAD
A6200
HILLSIDE
QUEEN'S MEDICAL CENTRE (UNIVERSITY HOSPITAL)
Medical Sch.
CLIFTON
Arbour Hill
Lenton & Wortley Halls
CRIPPS HILL
(BRIAN CLOUGH WY.)
Beeston Lodge
Thompson's Wood
THE LAKE
Boat House
Derby Hall
Lincoln Hall
Sherwood Hall
Rutland Hall
THE UNIVERSITY OF NOTTINGHAM
Hugh Stewart Hall
Lenton Close
Merrivale Nursy. Sch.
Tottle Brook
WOLLATON VALE
Lenton Lodge
Playing Field
Sports Centre
Lenton Abbey
Lenton Fields
Lenton House
KEIGHTON HILL
PORTLAND HILL
Tennis Cts.
East Playing Fields
A6005
BEESTON
UNIVERSITY BOULEVARD
Isaac Newton Cen.
NOTTINGHAM SCIENCE TECHNOLOGY PK.
UNIVERSITY PARK
Boat Ho.
DERBY ROAD
WOODSIDE
BOUNDARY
CENTRAL
Rec. Grd.
AUDLEY
BURROWS AV.
Recre. Ground
Bowl. Grn.
NG9
Nightingale Hall
Abbey House Hall
Cavendish Hall
Ancaster Hall
Willoughby Hall
Lodges
WEST
A6464
ROAD
Beeston Fields Primary School
ANDERSON CRES.
FIELD AVENUE
Bowling Greens
Playing Fields
Nottingham Tennis Centre
Alexander Fleming Bldg.
University

Hyson Green
Radford Rd.
Noel Street
The Open University
Djanogly City Academy
Bobbers Mill
Hyson Grn. Mkt.
The Forest
FOREST RECREATION GROUND
Site of Goose Fair
Church Cemetery
BOULEVARD
A6130
A60
A610
ALFRETON
GREGORY
RADFORD
Castle Retail Park
Gala Bingo
Arboretum
Arboretum Nursery School
Nottingham Trent Uni.
Radford
General Cemetery
University
Nottingham Trent Uni.
Trent Uni.
Victoria Centre
Royal Cen.
ILKESTON
ROAD
A609
LENTON BOULEVARD
Recreation Ground
NG7
NG1
NG2
NG3
The Park
Albert Hall
Playho.
Old Mkt Sq.
Lace Mkt
Shire Hall
Standard Hill
Nottingham Castle Mus.
BROAD MARSH SHOP. CEN.
New Lenton
Halls of Residence
Lenton Recreation Ground
Old Lenton
DERBY ROAD
CASTLE BLVD.
A6005
ABBEY BRIDGE
Castle Marina Park
Castle Meadow Retail Park
NOTTINGHAM
County Archives
Magistrates Ct.
Station
Castle Marina Wharf
Clayton's Bridge
Castlebridge Office Village
Lenton North Junction
Superstore
Meadows
NET Extension (Proposed)
Enterprise Wy.
Dunkirk
East Midlands Television Centre
Riverside Prim. Sch.
Portland Leisure Cen.
Greenfields Prim. Sch.
Wilford Bridge
RIVER TRENT
Megabowl
Showcase Cinema
A52
VICTORIA EMBANKMENT
QUEEN'S DRIVE
Recreation Ground
Tennis Courts
85
96
107
6
F
G
H
J
K
1
2
3
4
5
6
7
55
56
57

86
95
108
7
A
B
C
D
E
1
2
3
4
5
6
7
Alexandra Park
Hungerhill Gardens
St. Ann's
NG3
NG1
NG2
Nottingham
NOTTINGHAM
Sneinton
Lace Mkt
Meadows
Blue Bell Hill Prim. School
Rosehill Sch.
Stonebridge City Farm
Victoria Park
Victoria Leis. Cen.
St Mary's Rest Garden
Gala Bingo
Shire Hall
Broad Marsh Shop. Cen.
The People's College Nottingham
Thornfield Ind. Est.
Playing Field
Greenwood Inf. Sch.
Iona School
Jesse Boot Prim. Sch.
Jesse Boot Wildcats Arena
Recreation Ground
Colwick Wood
Greenwood Junior School
Greenwood Dale School
Roughill Wood
Nottingham Greyhound Stadium
Daleside Road East
Grandstand
Sports Ground
Storage Tanks
Tennis Court Industrial Estate
White City Trading Estate
Trent South Ind. Pk.
British Waterways Board
Timber Yard Depot
Meadow Trading Estate
Cattle Market
Notts County FC (Meadow Lane)
Nottingham Forest FC (City Ground)
Nottinghamshire Co. Cricket Club (Trent Bridge)
County Hall
Trent Fields
Football Ground
Turners Quay
Portland Leisure Cen.
Greenfields Prim. Sch.
BBC East Midlands
Nottingham Bus. Pk.
Waterfront Plaza
Station St.
Hogarth Prim. Sch.
Thorneywood Unit
St. Ann's Well Jun.
Sycamore Jun. & Inf. Sch.
St. Ann's Well Inf. Sch.
Standhill Inf. Sch.
Adbolton
Carlight Gdns. Park Homes
Recreation Ground
Victoria Embankment
A60
A612
A6011
A6019
A6520
B684
B686
Carlton Road
London Road
Manvers Street
Daleside Road
Trent Bridge
Radcliffe Road
Lady Bay Bridge
Meadow Lane
Huntingdon Street
Woodborough Road
Sneinton Dale
Oakdale Road
Trent Boulevard
Holme Road
Nottingham
Rushcliffe
River Trent
38
39
40
41
58
59

CARLTON
Carlton
Netherfield
Colwick Vale
COLWICK
Bakers Fields
NG4
NG12
COLWICK PARK
Nottingham Race Course
COLWICK COUNTRY PARK
COLWICK LAKE
West Lake
Colwick Hall (Hotel)
HOLME PIERREPONT
HOLME PIERREPONT COUNTRY PARK
Holme Pierrepont Hall
National Water Sports Centre
Nottingham Sailing Club
Adbolton Hall
Skylarks
Holme Grange
Rowing Course
Canoe Slalom Course
Holme Sluices
Holme Lock
Holme Cut
Colwick Marina
Water Ski Lagoon
Polser Brook
Polser Bridge
Holme Lane
Sports Ground
Recreation Ground
Playing Field
Three Hills
Bowling Green
COLWICK INDUSTRIAL ESTATE
COLWICK QUAYS BUS. PK.
COLWICK BUSINESS PARK
CHURCHILL PARK
CARLTON BUSINESS CENTRE
NATIONAL WATER SPORTS CENTRE HOLME PIERREPONT CARAVAN & CAMPING PARK
GREENACRES PARK
Carlton Cemetery
Council Offices
CARLTON HILL
BURTON ROAD
COLWICK LOOP ROAD
COLWICK ROAD
MILE END RD.
ADBOLTON LANE
RADCLIFFE ROAD
REGATTA WAY
SOUTHDALE ROAD
OAKDALE ROAD
CLIFF ROAD
GREENWOOD ROAD
ST. MARY'S AVENUE
VICTORIA ROAD
CONWAY ROAD
MANOR ROAD
STATION ROAD
SANDY LANE
RIVER TRENT
GEDLING
NOTTINGHAM
RUSHCLIFFE
A612
A52
B686
F G H J K
1 2 3 4 5 6 7
460 61 62
340 39 38 41
87
86
109

98
A
B
C
D
E
1
2
3
4
5
6
7
63
64
88
110
97
340
39
38
Stoke Bardolph
NG14
NG4
Nottingham
Cricket Field
Works
Farm
Top Row
ST. LUKE'S WY.
STOKE LANE
STANHOPE CR.
COLWICK LOOP ROAD
Under Construction (Estimated Completion Feb. 2007)
Football Ground
Pavilion
Play. Fld.
Youth Cen.
Playgrd.
A612
VICTORIA BUSINESS PARK
PINTAIL
PARK WAY
MALLARD RD.
DRAKE RD.
CLOSE
TEAL CLOSE
Depot
PRIVATE ROAD 3
PRIVATE ROAD 5
PRIVATE ROAD 4
COLWICK INDUSTRIAL ESTATE
Ouse Dyke
Stoke Lock
Hallow Well
RIVER TRENT
GEDLING
RUSHCLIFFE
Viaduct
Water Ski Lagoon
HOLME PIERREPONT COUNTRY PARK
Brook
Polser
Holme Pierrepont Hall
The Firs
HOLME PIERREPONT
HOLME LANE
ADBOLTON LA.
Home Farm
SANDY LANE
The Rectory
Recreation Grd.
RADCLIFFE ON TRENT
The Chestnuts
Manor Ho.
Radcliffe Lodge
Radcliffe
ISLAND LANE
WHARF LANE
CLIFF RD.
FERNWOOD DR.
GRANDFIELD AV.
GRANDFIELD CRES.
HAMILTON DR.
OAK TREE DR.
ROCKLEY AV.
CLIFF CRES.
PARK
THE AVENUE
SHELFORD RD.
MAIN RD.
NEW RD.
LORNE GRO.
BINGHAM ROAD
BROOKFIELD
Comm. Cen.
Lib.
Station Ter.
Radcliffe-on-Trent Junior Sch.
Cemetery
THE GREEN
GREEN WAY
THE WOODLANDS
SHADWELL GRO.
WATER LANE
ORFORD AV.
WHITWORTH
VANCOUVER
BAILEY LA.
PADDOCK CL.
Bailey Ct.
EDWARD CRES.
PRINCE
ST. LAWRENCE BOULEVARD
KINGS WAY
WILLOW
SYCAMORE
MAPLE CL.
BEECH CL.
CHERRYTREE CL.
DRIVE
RSPCA Animal Shelter
NOTTINGHAM
GRANTHAM ROAD
A52
LEES BARN ROAD
Lees Barn
Pav.
Sports Ground
Lamcote Field
Works
Holme House
STRAGGLETHORPE LANE
RADCLIFFE ROAD
Polser Bridge
Thorntons Holt

F
G
H
J
K
465
66
67
89
1
2
3
4
5
6
7
41
340
39
38
100
A52
NG12
RIVER TRENT
Swallow Plantation
The Hill
SHELFORD NURSERIES CARAVAN PARK
FIELD LANE
SHELFORD HILL
SHELFORD ROAD
ROAD
OATFIELD LANE
No Joke Plantation
Malkin Hill
Gibbet Hill
Shelford Lodge Farm
Lawson's Barn Farm
Jubilee Plantation
Slack Hollow
CLIFFS
RIDGE LA.
VALLEY RD.
Crown Cottages
TRENT VW. GDS.
CLIFF DRIVE
HOPEWELL CL.
Shelford Road Farm
Spellow Hill
Depot
Spellow Farm
Hill Farm
CLUMBER
Westcliffe Ct.
WEST-CLIFFE AV.
WAKEFIELD
CHATSWORTH
HADDON WY.
BIRKIN AV.
BUTLER AV.
PENRITH
SHELFORD CL.
FRANCIS CL.
MALKIN AV.
NEWTON AV.
Craig Moray
ROAD
HUDSON WY.
DOWSON CL.
Playing Field
Addington Ct.
Mill
Works
OAKFIELD
Pav.
Oakfield Ct.
HARLEQUIN M.
Fenimore Ct.
SOUTH
THOMAS AV.
NORTHFIELD AV.
MORTON CL.
MORTON GDS.
MEADOW END
SAXONDALE
Brickyard Plantation
HOME FARM LA.
CARNABY CL.
HENSON LANE
PIMLICO CL.
CLOSE
PALIN GDS.
THE CRES.
GOLF ROAD
HAREWOOD CL.
NURSERY CL.
WOODSIDE AV.
WOODSIDE RD.
BRICKYARD LA.
CARTER AV.
DORMY CL.
COVERT CRES.
BLAKENEY RD.
MARL RD.
WOODLAND CL.
GATCOMBE CL.
EASTWOOD
Radcliffe-on-Trent Infant School
Tennis Cts.
Dayncourt Sch. Specialist Sports Coll.
Bowl. Grn.
CROPWELL GDS.
HILLSIDE RD.
ST JOHNS
Harlequin
New House
Parr's Barn Farm
GROSVENOR CL.
BERKELEY CR.
WESTMINSTER
SHAFTESBURY AV.
DRIVE
BLOOMSBURY M.
COVENT GDS.
MAYFAIR
CHELSEA M.
WHITEHALL CT.
HAMMERSMITH CL.
WESTMINSTER DR.
BUCKINGHAM
QUEEN MARYS CL.
SERPENTINE CL.
Cropwell Lings
Lings Cottage
Saxton's Lings
Dewberry Hill
RADCLIFFE ON TRENT GOLF COURSE
DEWBERRY LA.
Club House
WELL
Sunpit Plantation
The Fields
Radcliffe Barn Farm
Hall Farm
ROAD
New Barn Farm
Cropwell Court
Lodge
111

90
112
99
NEWTON
AIRFIELD
Newton Spring
MAIN STREET
AIRWAY CRES.
FRIAR WLK.
CLOSE
Playgrd
TRENCHARD
Tennis Cts.
Sewage Works
Ash Holt
NEWTON GARDENS
Dawson's Plantation
Jubilee Plantation
Foss Road Farm
A46
Foss Way
(Roman Road)
FOSSE ROAD
CHAPEL LANE
Nottingham
Saxondale
Sycamore Farmhouse
Lodge Farm
Manor Farm
Mount Pleasant
Manor Farm Cottages
Saxondale Island
A52
NOTTINGHAM
BINGHAM
Playing Field
Pav.
WESTERN AV.
EDINBURGH DR.
HILL
BISHOPS RD.
MARGARET PL.
QUEEN'S CT.
CARNARVON
PLACE
GRANBY CT.
HARVEST CL.
GARDEN RD.
ORCHARD AV.
Play Fld.
FOREST
FOREST RD.
ROTHBURY GRO.
BRENDON
COPELAND
ARDEN GRO.
WYNHILL CT.
HARDWICK RD.
MILBURN GRO.
RINGWOOD RD.
KIELDER
Harrison Ct.
GRIZEDALE GRO.
BOWLAND
LANGDALE GRO.
BALMORAL RD.
GLENDOE
ROCKINGHAM
THORESBY
MEADOWSWEET
CAMPION
PRIMROSE BANK
PORCHESTER
MUSTERS
RUPERT RD.
CHAWORTH RD.
Linear Park
THE FOXGLOVES
HONEYSUCKLE GRO.
BLUEBELL BANK
MILL HILL
HAREBELL GDS.
ANGELICA CT.
COLTSFOOT CL.
MALLOW WAY
VALERIAN WY.
VALERIAN
COWSLIP
BETONY CL.
HOLLYHOCK CL.
THE TEASELS
TANSY WY.
TREFOIL CL.
WAY
Foss Farm
Lings Farm
TOOT HILL
Cropwell Lings
Lings Cottage
HENSON LANE
NG12
High Thorpe
Top Brackendale Farm
Cropwell Grove Farm
New Banks Farm
Lodge
HARDIGATE RD.
Cropwell Court
Newlands
68
69
41
340
39
38
A
B
C
D
E
1
2
3
4
5
6
7

F
G
H
J
K
91
113
102
1
2
3
4
5
6
7
470
71
72
41
40
39
38
NG13
High Westing Farm
Bottom Plantation
Car Dyke
Holme Farm
Moor Bridge
Parson's Hill
Sewage Works
MOOR
MICKLEMOOR LA.
CHAPEL LANE
MOORBRIDGE
MOORBRIDGE RD.
BINGHAM INDUSTRIAL PARK
Tennis Ct.
Bingham
Playing Field
Pav.
CARNARVON CL.
PLACE
KIRKHILL
GILLOTTS CL.
MOOR LA.
Old Mill Ct.
LANGTRY GDS.
ST. MARYS
CHURCH CL.
RUTLAND RD.
GROVE
RD.
BUTT RD.
PRIORS CL.
BROWNES RD.
VICTORIA RD.
NURSERY RD.
CARR RD.
DOUGLAS RD.
BANES RD.
ABBEY ROAD
Playgrd.
Carnarvon Primary School
Robert Miles Jun. Sch.
Sch.
SCHOOL LA.
NEWGATE ST.
MARKET PL.
CHURCH ST.
Lib.
Eaton Place
UNION ST.
EAST ST.
HOLME
MANOR RD.
CROW CT.
COGLEY LANE
FAIRFIELD ST.
NEEDHAM ST.
HASSALL CT.
CHERRY ST.
FOSTERS LA.
EAST GRO.
CHESTERFIELD DRIVE
CARNARVON AV.
CHESTNUT AV.
BREWSTERS CL.
LONG ACRE
WALKERS CL.
THE CROFTS
MELVYN DR.
BANKS CRES.
THE PADDOCK
FISHER LA.
BANKS PADDOCK
BEETHAM CL.
JEBB'S LA.
PINFOLD
PERRY GRO.
DARK LA.
LONG ACRE EAST
RAYMOND DR.
ROWAN CL.
LARCH CL.
POPLAR CL.
OAK AV.
Oak Lodge
Beech Lodge
ASPEN CL.
HOLLY CL.
JUNIPER
HAZEL CL.
BLACKTHORN CL.
WILLOW RD.
ASH CL.
CEDAR CL.
MAPLE CL.
BEECH AV.
SYCAMORE CL.
ELM AV.
GDS.
DERRY LA.
Stanhope Wy.
THE BANKS
GRANTHAM ROAD
Bingham Leisure Centre
Cemy.
Toot Hill School
Playing Field
Tennis Courts
Games Court
Sports Arena
Play. Fld.
BINGHAM
LANGAR RD.
TITHBY ROAD
WOODPECKER DR.
MALLARD CL.
WADES WY.
GOLDCREST
NIGHTINGALE WAY
AVOCET CL.
DOVE CL.
OSPREY CL.
KESTREL
SANDPIPER CL.
SWALLOW
SKYLARK CL.
GRANTHAM BY-PASS
A52
Sub.
GRANTHAM ROAD
Reservoir
Starnhill Cottages
Starnhill Farm
Starnhill Plantation
Spring Farm
Spring Farm Cotts.
Whitefield Farm
Tithby Grange Cottages
Tithby Grange
SMITE

73
74
A
B
C
D
E
1
2
3
4
5
6
7
41
40
39
38
149
101
Scarrington
Hall
Gables Farm
HAWKSWORTH RD.
STREET
THE SAUCERS
Manor Farm
MAIN
LANE
MILL
LONGMOOR
Gutter
The
CLIFF HILL
Hill Farm
Cliff Holme
Mill Field
Cemetery
Sewage Works
MOOR
LANE
ABBEY
NEW
Malthouse
Corner Farm
CHAPEL LA.
NEW ROW
THE STACKYARD
The Fields
STREET
Spinney Corner
MEADOW CL.
Holme View
The Abbey
FIELDS DR.
ABBEY CL.
WALNUT
Sch.
NOBLE LA.
SCH. LA.
ST. THOMAS DR.
DAWN'S LA.
Saucer Farm
ASLOCKTON
THE CAPES
THE SIDINGS
VALE CL.
Aslockton
Crossing House
Aslockton Hall
Brocker Farm
BEVERLEY'S
MT. BERYL
COTTAGE
SMITE CL.
GREEN WLK.
AV.
AVENUE
DARK
LANE
Rec. Grd.
Pav.
Fish Pond
AZIMGHUR RD.
RIVER
SMITE
CHURCH WLK.
RIVERSIDE
CHAPEL WLK.
The Grange
STREET
BURTON
SUNBEAM ST.
Manor Farm
The Gables
SCHOOL LA.
CHURCH
MAIN
STREET
Whipling Farm
Hollies Farm
OLD
GRANTHAM
LANE
Whatton Bridge
Whatton
THE LAWNS
CONERY GARDENS
IVY ROW
GRIFFINS END
ORSTON
ROAD
HM Young Offender Institution
BELVOIR CL.
CROMWELL RD.
CRANMER
AVENUE
GRANTHAM
A52
Aslockton Grange
GRANBY
CONERY
LANE
Greenacres
Whatton Lodge Farm
Long Meadow
Butlers Cottage
Starnhill Cottages
Thorough Bridge
Starnhill Plantation
RIVER SMITE
Keeper's Cottage
Whatton Barn
Playhouse Plantation
Lane Plantations
Vicars Croft
Whatton Manor
Pond Plantation
Whatton Fields
Front Plantation
Middle Covert
River
New Covert
Manor Lodge
HALL

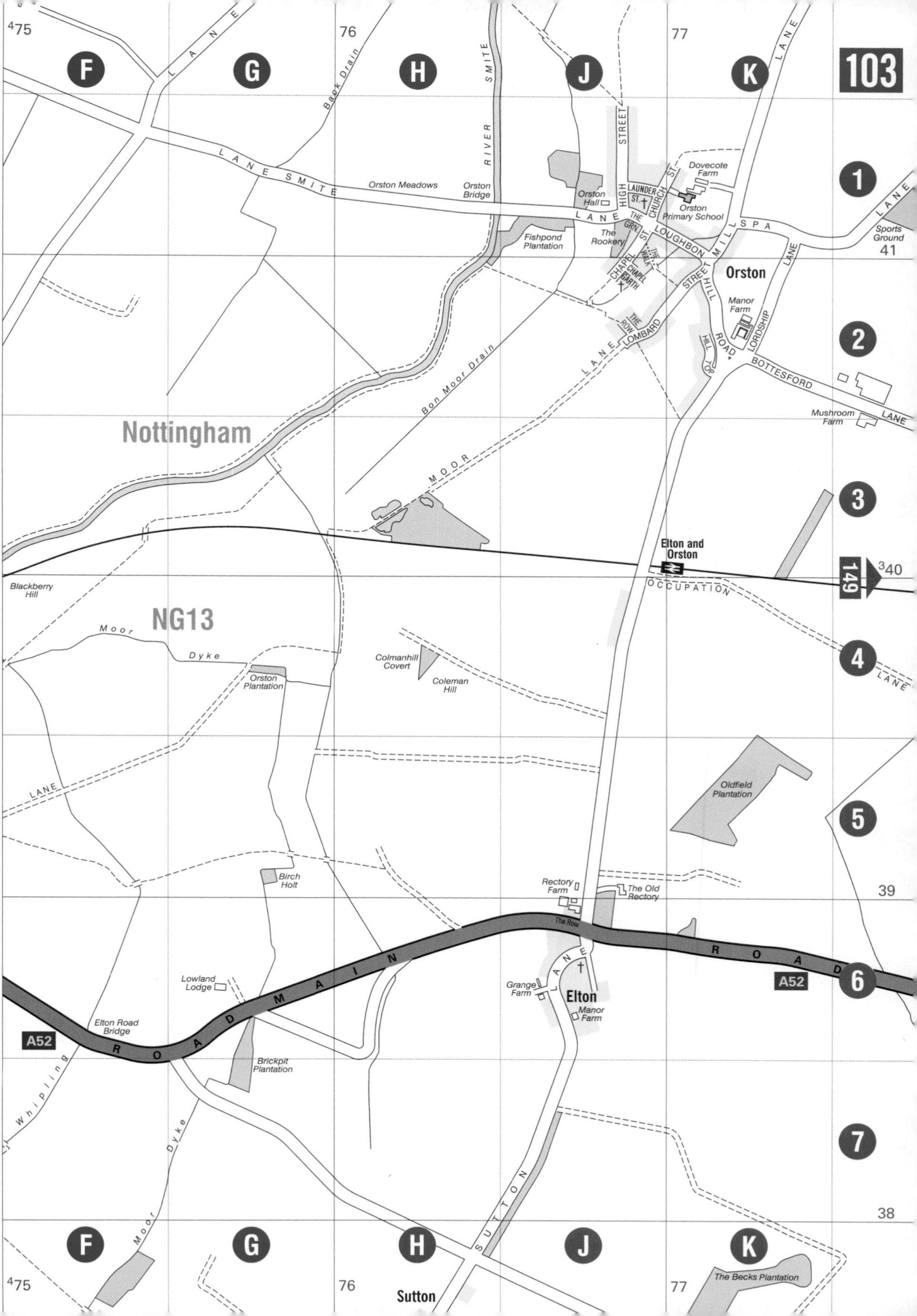

475
76
77
F
G
H
J
K
Back Drain
RIVER SMITE
STREET
LANE
Dovecote Farm
LANE SMITE
Orston Meadows
Orston Bridge
Orston Hall
HIGH
LAUNDER
ST.
CHURCH
ST.
Orston Primary School
LANE
THE GRN.
SPA
MILL
Sports Ground
41
Fishpond Plantation
The Rookery
ST.
LOUGHBON
THE WALK
CHAPEL
CHAPEL GARTH
STREET
HILL
Orston
Manor Farm
LANE
THE ROW
LOMBARD
HILL TOP
ROAD
LORDSHIP
BOTTESFORD
LANE
Bon Moor Drain
Mushroom Farm
LANE
Nottingham
MOOR
Elton and Orston
149
340
Blackberry Hill
OCCUPATION
NG13
Moor
Dyke
Colmanhill Covert
Coleman Hill
Orston Plantation
LANE
LANE
Oldfield Plantation
Birch Holt
Rectory Farm
The Old Rectory
39
The Row
ROAD
MAIN
ROAD
A52
LANE
Lowland Lodge
Grange Farm
Elton
Manor Farm
Elton Road Bridge
A52
Brickpit Plantation
Whipling
Dyke
SUTTON
Moor
38
The Becks Plantation
Sutton
1
2
3
4
5
6
7

A
B
C
D
E
1
2
3
4
5
6
7
48
49
38
37
36
35
92
Stanton Gate
Ilkeston
DE7
ERWASH VALLEY GOLF COURSE
M1 MOTORWAY
M1
Stony Clouds Local Nature Reserve
Cloudside
Cloud House
Church Farm
St. Giles Park
Mill
Halls
Pasture Lock
Stanton Gate New Sidings
Ind. Est.
Playing Field
Albany Inf. Sch.
Albany Junior School
Hickings La. Rec. Grd.
Frederick Harrison Inf. Sch.
Stevenson Jun. Sch.
St. John's C of E Primary School
Tennis Courts
STAPLEFORD
Cemetery
Windmill Hill
Hill Top Farm
Fairfield Prim. Sch.
Queen Elizabeth Park
Playing Field
SANDIACRE
Cloudside Jun. Sch.
Recreation Ground
Lib.
Cricket Grd.
Sports Ground
Warehouses
Cricket Ground
Rec. Ground
Archers Field Recreation Ground
George Spencer Sch. & Tech. Coll.
George Spencer Sch. & Tech. Coll. (Lower Site)
Sewage Works
Bessell Lane Farm
Nursery
A52
(BRIAN CLOUGH WAY)
STAPLEFORD BY-PASS
B5010
B6003
B6002
B6004
EREWASH
BROXTOWE
NG10
Junc. 25
Sandiacre Lock
Weir
Springfield Park
Longmoor Prim. Sch.
Sports Ground
Depot
Toton Sidings
Dockholm Lock
Bispham Dr. Jun. Sch.
Banks Rd. Inf. Sch.
Works
Mills
Training Cen.
English Martyrs Sch.
Wilsthorpe School
Erewash Canal
River Erewash
By-Pass Channel
STATION RD.
DERBY RD.
TOTON LANE
CHURCH STREET
PASTURE ROAD
HICKINGS LANE
LONGMOOR ROAD
STAPLEFORD ROAD

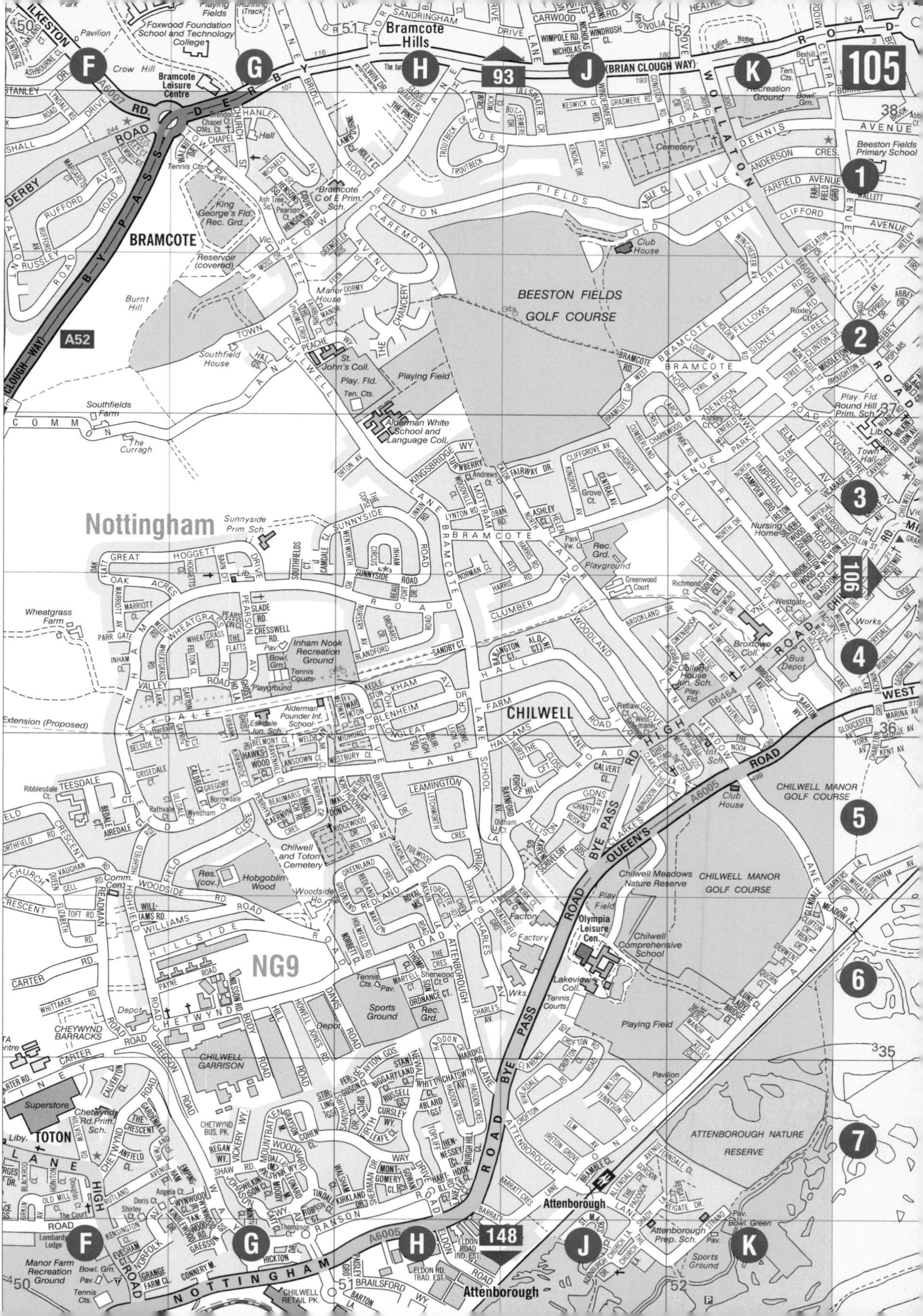
Bramcote Hills
Foxwood Foundation School and Technology College
Bramcote Leisure Centre
Crow Hill
Pavilion
ILKESTON ROAD
DERBY ROAD
A6007
(BRIAN CLOUGH WAY)
93
WOLLATON ROAD
Beeston Fields Primary School
Cemetery
Recreation Ground
DENNIS AVENUE
ANDERSON CRES.
FARFIELD AVENUE
CLIFFORD AVENUE
BRAMCOTE
BY PASS
A52
CLOUGH WAY
King George's Fld. Rec. Grd.
Reservoir (covered)
Burnt Hill
Southfield House
Southfields Farm
COMMON LANE
The Curragh
Bramcote C of E Prim. Sch.
BEESTON FIELDS
Club House
BEESTON FIELDS GOLF COURSE
St. John's Coll.
Play. Fld.
Ten. Cts.
Playing Field
Alderman White School and Language Coll.
THE CHANCERY
Manor House
TOWN STREET
CHILWELL LANE
BRAMCOTE LANE
BRAMCOTE DR. WEST
BRAMCOTE RD.
B6006
Play. Fld. Round Hill Prim. Sch.
Town Hall
Lib.
Nursing Home
Nottingham
Sunnyside Prim. Sch.
GREAT HOGGETT DRIVE
OAK ACRES
Wheatgrass Farm
Inham Nook Recreation Ground
Bowl. Grn.
Tennis Courts
Playground
Alderman Pounder Inf. School
Eskdale Jun. Sch.
Extension (Proposed)
ESKDALE DRIVE
CHILWELL
HALLAMS LANE
Rec. Grd.
Playground
Greenwood Court
Richmond Ct.
Broxtowe Coll.
Bus Depot
Westgate Ct.
Works
College House Jun. Sch.
B6464
HIGH ROAD
106
WEST
CHILWELL MANOR GOLF COURSE
Club House
QUEEN'S ROAD
A6005
BYE PASS
Chilwell Meadows Nature Reserve
Play Field
Olympia Leisure Cen.
Chilwell Comprehensive School
Lakeview Coll.
Tennis Courts
Playing Field
Factory
Wks.
Chilwell and Toton Cemetery
Hobgoblin Wood
Res. (cov.)
Woodside Ho.
NG9
Sports Ground
Rec. Grd.
Depot
CHILWELL GARRISON
CHEYWYND BARRACKS
Superstore
Chetwynd Rd. Prim. Sch.
CHETWYND BUS. PK.
TOTON
Liby.
HIGH ROAD
TOTON LANE
Lombardy Lodge
Manor Farm Recreation Ground
Bowl. Grn.
Pav.
Tennis Cts.
NOTTINGHAM ROAD
CHILWELL RETAIL PK.
ELDON ROAD IND. EST.
ELDON RD. TRAD. EST.
148
Attenborough
Attenborough Prep. Sch.
Pav. Bowl. Green
Sports Ground
Pavilion
ATTENBOROUGH NATURE RESERVE
ATTENBOROUGH LANE
F
G
H
J
K
1
2
3
4
5
6
7
450
51
52
38
37
36
35

106
94
105
114
53
54
35
36
37
38
A
B
C
D
E
1
2
3
4
5
6
7
Lenton Abbey
THE UNIVERSITY OF NOTTINGHAM
UNIVERSITY PARK
Nottingham Tennis Centre
NOTTINGHAM SCIENCE TECHNOLOGY PK.
Beeston Fields Primary School
BEESTON
Nottingham
NG7
NG9
Rylands
Beeston
CHILWELL MANOR GOLF COURSE
ATTENBOROUGH NATURE RESERVE
Beeston Sailing Club
Holme Pit (Fish Pond)
Clifton Wood
Playing Field
Nottingham Trent University
Nottingham Trent Uni. Sports Hall
Glapton Prim. Sch.
A453
A6005
A6464
B6006
B6464
WOODSIDE ROAD
UNIVERSITY BOULEVARD
QUEEN'S RD. EAST
QUEEN'S ROAD WEST
BROADGATE
HIGH RD.
STATION ROAD
MIDDLE STREET
CHILWELL ROAD
BEESTON CANAL
CANAL SIDE
CLIFTON LANE
BROXTOWE
NOTTINGHAM
Sports Ground
Cricket Ground
Boulevard Ind. Pk
Chemical & Pharmaceutical Works
Sewage Works
Refuse Tip
Rugby Ground
Weir Field Recreation Ground
SGCS Business Park
Trent Vale Inf. Sch.
Rylands Jun. Sch.
John Clifford Prim. Sch.
Round Hill Prim. Sch.
Superstore
Factory
Castle Vw. Cotts.
Padge Bri.
Boating Lake
Florence Boot Hall
Lenton House
Lenton Fields
Home Farm
Halls of Residence
Rugby Football Ground

F
G
H
J
K
95
107
Megabowl
Showcase Cin.
A52
CLIFTON
BOULEVARD
NG2
QUEEN'S DRIVE
A453
Riverside Prim. Sch.
Wilford Bridge
VICTORIA
EMBANKMENT
Recreation Ground
Bowling Grn.
Paddling Pool
Warehouse
Warehouses
Works
TOTTLE ROAD
RIVERSIDE RETAIL PARK
LENTON IND. EST. WEST
LENTON IND. EST. EAST
CENTURION WY.
ELECTRIC AVENUE
HOGG ROAD
FINCH CLOSE
PHOENIX CT.
ABBEYFIELD ROAD
REDFIELD WAY
BULL CLOSE ROAD
LENTON LANE
TONNELIER RD.
BARRIQUE RD.
Club
Factory
Queen's Drive
CORONATION AV.
St. Patrick's Catholic Prim. Sch.
Nottingham Emmanuel School
The Dorothy Boot Homes
Playing Field
Playing Fields
Gresham Playing Fields
Sports Ground
Pavilion
NET Extension (Proposed)
GRESHAM GDNS.
Notting Footba
Gas Valve Compound
RIVERSIDE GOLF COURSE
Powerleague Soccer Centre
Driving Range
Riverside Golf Centre
Cricket Ground
Grove Farm
Grove Farm Cotts
THANE ROAD
TRENT LANE
Clifton Bridge
WILFORD LANE
Wilford House
Lib.
B679
RUDDINGTON
Wilford
ST. AUSTELL
NG2
Household Waste Recycling Centre
Rushcliffe Arena
108
Lloyd Leisure
RIVER
A453
CLIFTON LANE
The Becket Sch.
B680
Compton Acres Shop. Cen.
RUGBY
COMPTON ACRES
NOTTINGHAM SOUTH & WILFORD IND. EST.
Clifton Spinney
NG11
Silverdale
Fairham Brook
MONKSWAY
BROOKTHORPE
THE DOWNS
Community Centre
Dovecote Prim. Sch.
Youth Club
Comm. Cen.
Play grd.
NET Extension (Proposed)
Farnborough Sch. Technology Coll.
Playing Field
Clifton Playing Fields
RUSHCLIFFE
NOTTINGHAM
WILFORD LANE
Willwell Bungalow
BOULEVARD
A52
Hotel
LOUGHBOROUGH ROAD
A60
RUDDINGTON GRANGE GOLF COURSE
Club House
Tennis Courts
Bowling Green
Clifton Leis. Cen.
CLIFTON
Nethergate School
115
Lodge Farm
Long Plantation
Sun Valley Leisure Cen.
Fairham House
RIVERGREEN
GREENCROFT
FARNBOROUGH ROAD
SOUTHCHURCH DRIVE
SWANSDOWNE DRIVE
COLLEYMOOR LEYS LA
ROAD
1
2
3
4
5
6
7
55
56
57
38
37
36
35

A
B
C
D
E
1
2
3
4
5
6
7
96
107
116
A52
NG2
NG11
Nottingham
WEST BRIDGFORD
Wilford Hill
Nottinghamshire Co. Cricket Club (Trent Bridge)
County Hall
Recreation Ground
Tennis Courts
Meml. Gdns.
Bandstand
Paddling Pool
Playing Field
Nottingham Forest Football Academy
West Park
David Lloyd Leisure
Rushcliffe Arena
Supermarket
South Nottingham College
West Bridgford School
Heymann Prim. Sch.
Greythorn Prim. Sch.
Jesse Gray Primary Sch.
Grosvenor Sch.
Rushcliffe Comp. Sch.
Rushcliffe Leisure Centre
Abbey Road Prim. Sch.
St. Edmund Campion Catholic Prim. Sch.
Public Open Space
War Memorial Playing Fields
Depot
Southern Cemetery
Wilford Hill Crematorium
Garden of Remembrance
Reservoir (covered)
Jewish Cemetery
Sharphill Wood
Sharp Hill
Spinney Hill
Nursery
Lodge Farm
Sunny Crest
Westwoods
Hill Farm House
Landmere Farm
Mickleborough Hill
Garden Centre
Toll Bar House
Club House
Ruddington Grange Golf Course
Grantham Canal (Dis.)
Gamston Bridge
Carlight Gdns. Park Homes
The Park
Trent Bridge
Loughborough Road
Melton Road
Radcliffe Road
Victoria Embankment
Wilford Lane
Clifton Boulevard
Landmere Lane
A60
A606
B679

109
97
110
117
F
G
H
J
K
1
2
3
4
5
6
7
460
61
62
38
37
36
335
A6011
A52
RADCLIFFE ROAD
REGATTA WAY
Council Yard
Gamston
BEL-AIR RESIDENTIAL HOMES
Superstore
GAMSTON DISTRICT CEN.
Comm. Cen.
Prim. Sch.
LINGS BAR HOSP.
Holme Lane
BASSINGFIELD LANE
NATHANS LANE
Holly Farm
Lea Farm
Manor Farm
The Elms Farm
Bassingfield
Cherry Tree Cottage
Smallholding
Grantham Canal (Disused)
Landfill Waste Site
Polser Brook
TOLLERTON ROAD
Tollerton Bridge
TOLLERTON PARK CARAVAN PARK
Hill Farm
NOTTINGHAM AIRPORT
Hangar
Control Tower
NG12
Meadow Covert
Edwalton Primary Sch.
Edwalton
MUNICIPAL GOLF COURSE
Club Ho.
LITTLE LANE
Homestead Farm
Jubilee Plantation
CHESTNUT M.
COTGRAVE LANE
Bassingfield House
Manor Farm
Glebe Farm
The Lake
Nursery
Tollerton Nurseries
TOLLERTON
Sewage Works
MEDINA DRIVE
SUNNINDALE DR.
Hall Farm
The Decoy
Tollerton Wood
Tollerton Prim. Sch.
BURNSIDE
Thurlbeck

110
RADCLIFFE ROAD
A
B
C
D
E
98
Holme House
Lamcote Field
Works
STRAGGLETHORPE
Landfill Waste Site
Thorntons Holt Camping Park
Shepherd's Houses
Cockedhat Plantation
North Farm
Polser Brook
MAIN ROAD
Cotgrave Place
Club House
COTGRAVE PLACE
GOLF & COUNTRY CLUB
COTGRAVE
COUNTRY PARK
Cotgrave Bridge
Grantham Canal (Disused)
Lock House
109
LANE
PEASHILL
Peashill Farm
Brown's Bridge
Weirs
Homefields
Gozen Lodge
Windmill Hill
Thurlbeck Dyke
WOODGATE
Sewage Works
COTGRAVE
MILL LA.
BLACKSMITH CT.
MORKINSHIRE CRES.
MORKINSHIRE LA.
VINE FARM CL.
THURMAN DR.
BINGHAM RD.
THE CHURCH CROSS LA.
Prim. Sch.
Church Cl.
CANDLEBY LA.
LAWRENCE CL.
COTGRAVE SHOP. CEN.
Scotland Bank
Library
HALES CL.
MILLER HIVES CL.
RECTORY ROAD
Rectory
Cemy.
SCRIMSHIRE LA.
CHERRY ORCHARD
WALNUT GRO.
RISEGATE
CANDLEBY CL.
Infant & Nursery School
Cotgrave Manvers Jun. Sch.
Bowl. Grns.
Cotgrave Highfield Prim. & Nursy. Sch.
Playing Field
Ash Lea Sch.
WOODGATE LA.
BAKER'S HOLLOW
MENSING AV.
GREEN PLATT
BROADMEER
GOOSE GATE
LAMPLDS
FOREST CL.
FURROWS
WHITE AV.
DAISY CL.
FERN AV.
GREEN LA.
FLDS. DR.
HAWTHORNE
ASH LEA CL.
SANDSIDE
FLAGHOLME
CARTBRIDGE
RINGS
MANNS LEYS
TOFT CL.
CORN CL.
MILLERS BRI.
BONNYMEAD
THE DIAL
FOXHILL
SPINNEY CL.
WOODLAND
WESTWAY
MANOR WD.
THE RD.
RUNCIE CL.
Play. Fld.
GRIPPS
PLUMTREE ROAD
COTGRAVE LANE
COTGRAVE
148
Boot Pit
MILL LANE
GILLIVER LA.
Manor Farm
Clipston
The Brickyard
Brickyard Plantation
Scotton's Hill
SAXON
KINGS
WARWICK GDS.
ROAD
63
64
38
37
36
35
1
2
3
4
5
6
7

465
66
67
Radcliffe Barn Farm
The Fields
F
G
H
J
K
99
Hall Farm
CROPWELL ROAD
Lodge
38
New Barn Farm
Cropwell Court
Lodge
1
RADCLIFFE RD.
A46
Stragglethorpe
The Limes
2
Paddock Cottages
37
Foss Bridge
Berry Hill
3
Brown's Cotts.
LANE
Sports Ground
Pav.
Hollygate Farm
COLLIERS WAY
COLLIERS BUSINESS PARK
112
4
Mann's Bridge
Nottingham
36
NOTTINGHAM ROAD
Grantham Canal (Disused)
HOLLYGATE IND. PARK
Hollygate Bridge
NG12
HOLLYGATE
Hollygate House
5
Works
The Bungalow
6
Play. Fld.
TROUT BECK
GLENBROOK
AVONDALE
DEANS CT.
GRASSMERE
WILLOWDENE
FIRDALE
SPRING MEADOW
CROSSHILL
Cotgrave Leisure Centre
Playing Fld.
Foss House
335
Foss Cottages
Reservoir (covered)
HILL
SKYLARK
7
LITTLE MDW
WHITE LANDS
PRIORIDGE
WOODHAMS
Smith's Round Hill
BURHILL
CLOVERDALE
FLAX
ENDALE
EASTWOLD
BRIAR GATE
MARLWOOD
A46
THE FOSSE
Long Plantation
Groundwells Farm
Cropwell Wolds Farm
Three Corner Plantation
Cotgrave Copse
EDGINGTON CL.
THURLBECK
WEST FURLONG
148
CROPWELL WOLDS
Firdale Holt
Stone Pit Plantation

68
69
A
B
C
D
E
100
38
37
36
35
1
2
3
4
5
6
7
111
148
141
Lodge
A46
HARDIGATE
Newlands
The Grove
ROAD
RADCLIFFE
The Limes
Barnsfield Farm
Cropwell Grange
Works
GRANGE PK.
ROAD
MAIN
BACK
The Court
OLD SCHOOL HOUSE CL.
Cropwell Butler
Meadow Court
CARPENTERS CL.
CARPENTERS CL.
ROOKERY FM.
THE POSTS
LANE
STREET
TITHBY
Cemetery
LANE
CLOSE
BUTLER
Lych Gate
Rookery Cottages
Millfield Cottage
Millfield House
Lower Brackendale Farm
New Banks Farm
Tithby
Manor Farm
TITHBY
ROAD
DOVECOTE LA.
Holly Tree Farm
MEADOW
LANE
Stratford House
ROAD
BISHOP
HOE
Hoe Hill
NG12
CROPWELL
RD.
Grantham
Canal
(disused)
HOE
VIEW
ROAD
PARKIN CL.
SALVIN CL.
RD.
COOPER CL.
COOPER CL.
NEW-BERRY CL.
KENDAL
HALL DR.
THURLBY CL.
SQUIRES CL.
THE MALTINGS
CROPWELL
HARDYS CL.
ETHELDENE
BUTLER
Sewage Works
Cropwell Bishop
Spring Hill
BROWNHILL CL.
ST. GILES WY.
Rawlings Ct.
SPRINGFIELD
SPRING VW.
Cropwell Bishop Primary School
MARSHALL RD.
SMITHS CL.
MILL LA.
CHURCH
STOCKWELL LA.
DOBBIN CL.
MERCIA AV.
CLARKE CL.
OLD LENTON
HOE
NOOK
FIELD LA.
BARRATT CL.
Playing Field
Hall
NOTTINGHAM
Works
Cropwell Bridge
ROAD
FERN
RICHARDS CL.
Home Farm
CROPWELL MANOR CT.
PASTURE
Mill Hill
Fern Hill
Fern Hill Cottage
Fern Hill Farm Cottages
Fern Hill Farm
ROAD
Ash Holt
HILL
SKYLARK
KNOULTON
CANALSIDE INDUSTRIAL UNITS
LANE
Groundwel Farm
COLSTON
ROAD
SWAB'S LA.
Blue Hill
Old Brickyard Plantation
Reecy Plantation
Home Farm Cottages
NEW

F
G
H
101
J
K
70
71
72
38
37
36
35
1
2
3
4
5
6
7
149
141
Whitefield Farm
Farm Cotts.
Tithby Grange Cottages
Tithby Grange
TITHBY ROAD
BINGHAM ROAD
ROAD
Crane's Covert
RIVER SMITE
Smite Hill Covert
Wiverton Hall Farm
Moat Covert
Nottingham
Wiverton Hall
New Plantation
Smite Hill Farm
Northfield Farm
Wiverton Smite Bridge
Langar Lane Covert
The Ferns
Covert Farm
LANGAR LANE
ROAD
Langar Lane Bridge
ROAD
BARNSTONE ROAD
Works
NG13
Langar C of E Primary School
Langar Ho.
MUSTERS RD.
BARNSTONE
BUTLERS FIELD
CHURCH LA.
MAIN
HOWE
BELVOIR CRES.
WILLOW LA.
ROAD
HARBY RD.
ST.
Langar C of E Primary School
Tennis Court
The Limes Farm
Langar
CROPWELL ROAD
LANGAR LA.
Edmondthorpe Lodge
Winifred Wood

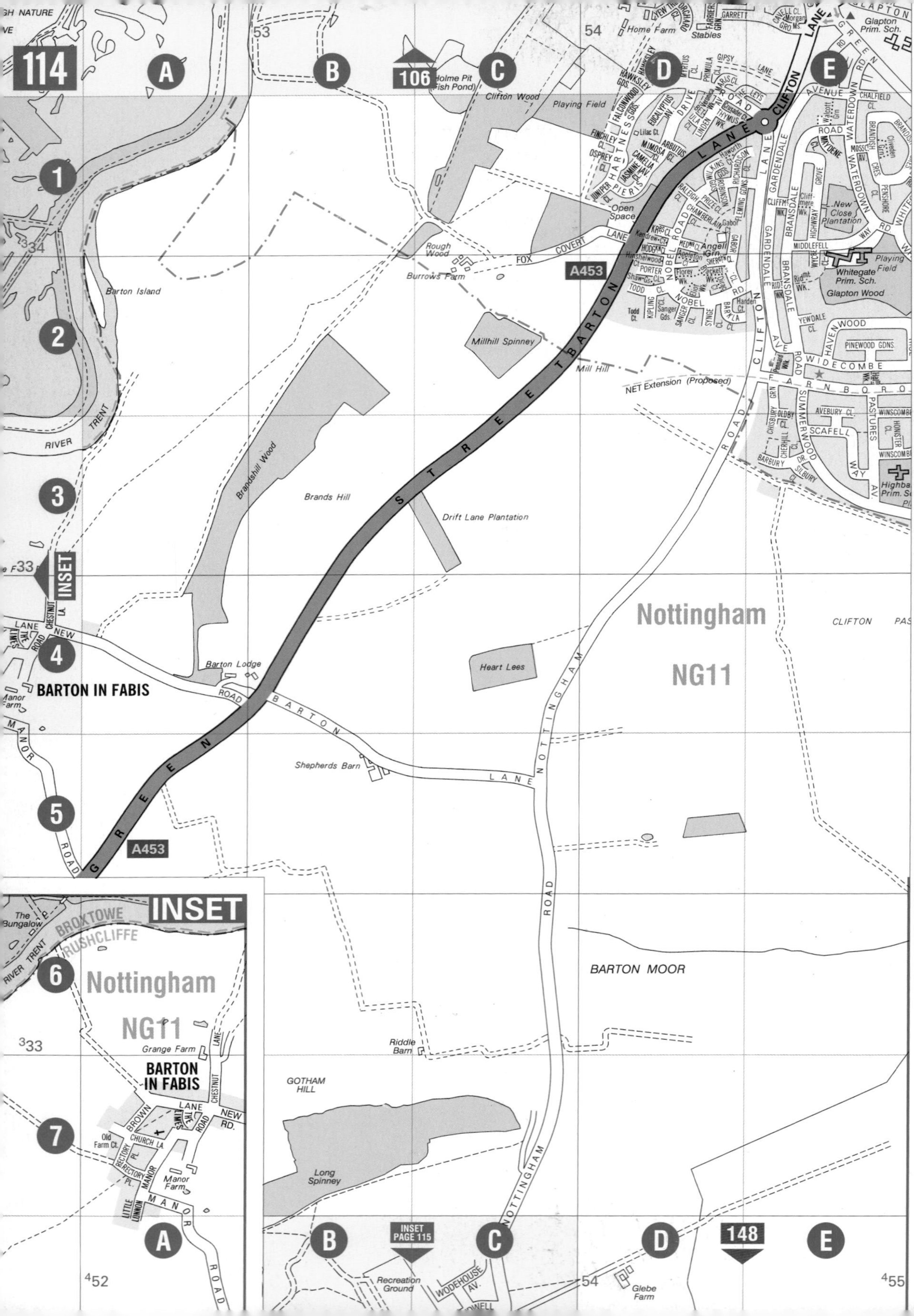
114
A
B
C
D
E
106
Holme Pit (Fish Pond)
Clifton Wood
Playing Field
Home Farm
Stables
Glapton Prim. Sch.
CLIFTON LANE
AVENUE
WATERDOWN
CHALFIELD CL.
FALCONWOOD GDS.
HAWKSLEY GDS.
FINCHLEY CL.
OSPREY CL.
JUNIPER CL.
HARTNESS RD.
PIERIS DR.
EUCALYPTUS AV.
MIMOSA CL.
ARBUTUS CL.
CAMELIA AV.
JASMINE CL.
Lilac Ct.
Open Space
FOX COVERT LANE
Rough Wood
Burrows Farm
A453
CHAMBERLAIN
NOBEL ROAD
Angell Grn.
GABOR CL.
PORTER CL.
TODD CL.
Todd Ct.
KIPLING CL.
SANGER CL.
Sanger Gds
SYNGE CL.
Harden Ct.
GARDENDALE
BRANSDALE
New Close Plantation
MIDDLEFELL WAY
Playing Field
Whitegate Prim. Sch.
Glapton Wood
YEWDALE CL.
HAVENWOOD
PINEWOOD GDNS.
WIDECOMBE
Millhill Spinney
Mill Hill
NET Extension (Proposed)
FARNBOROUGH RD
AVEBURY CL.
SCAFELL
SUMMERWOOD
PASTURES AV.
WINSCOMBE
CHISBURY GRN
OLDBY CL.
CHERHILL CL.
BARBURY CL.
SILBURY CL.
Highbank Prim. Sch.
RIVER TRENT
Barton Island
Brandshill Wood
Brands Hill
BARTON STREET GREEN
Drift Lane Plantation
Nottingham
NG11
CLIFTON PASTURES
INSET
Heart Lees
Barton Lodge
BARTON IN FABIS
NEW ROAD
BARTON LANE
Shepherds Barn
NOTTINGHAM ROAD
MANOR ROAD
Manor Farm
BARTON MOOR
Riddle Barn
GOTHAM HILL
Long Spinney
INSET PAGE 115
148
Recreation Ground
WODEHOUSE AV.
Glebe Farm
The Bungalow
BROXTOWE
RUSHCLIFFE
Grange Farm
CHESTNUT LANE
BROWN LANE
THE LIMES
CHURCH LA.
Old Farm Ct.
RECTORY PL.
LITTLE LUNNON
1
2
3
4
5
6
7
33
34
452
53
54
455

107
116
148
INSET
CLIFTON
Clifton Leisure Centre
CLIFTON PARK
Nethergate School
Sun Valley Leisure Cen.
Fairham House
Playing Field
Tennis Courts
South Notts. Coll. (Charnwood Centre)
Football Ground
Fairham Bridge
Fairham Brook Nature Reserve
Milford Prim. Sch.
Brook Hill
Fairham Community College
Brecks Plantation
NOTTINGHAM
RUSHCLIFFE
Long Plantation
Lodge Farm
Willwell Bungalow
RUDDINGTON GRANGE GOLF COURSE
Club House
St. Peter's C of E Junior Sch.
Rec. Grnd.
Depot
Works
Tall Trees Farm
Printing Works
James Peacock Infant School
Ruddington Village Museum
Cemetery
Youth & Comm. Cen.
RUDDINGTON
Leys Farm
Nottingham Transport Heritage Centre
Ruddington Station
Great Central Railway (Nottingham)
West End
Ruddington Fields Farm
Fields Farm Cottages
RUSHCLIFFE COUNTRY PARK
Moorend Farm Cottages
Moorend Farm
Moor Farm
RUDDINGTON MOOR
BRADMORE MOOR
WILFORD ROAD
HIGH ST.
KIRK LA.
BARLEY LANDS
ASHER LANE
CLIFTON LANE
PASTURE LANE
SOUTHCHURCH DRIVE
FARNBOROUGH ROAD
B680
Long Spinney
Round Spinney
Recreation Ground
Nottingham
NG11
GOTHAM
Gotham Prim. Sch.
Home Farm
Playing Fld.
Factory
Liby. & Hall
KEGWORTH ROAD
GYPSUM WAY
NOTTINGHAM ROAD
LEAKE ROAD
MOOR LANE
The Rectory
Depot
Nursery
F
G
H
J
K
1
2
3
4
5
6
7
455
56
57
53
454
33
32
31
30

A B C D E
1 2 3 4 5 6 7
58 59
334 33 32 31
108
115
118
Nursery
Sharp Hill
Hill Farm House
LANDMERE
Landmere Farm
Home Farm
Hall Farm
WAYTE CT.
LANE
Landmere
Mickleborough Hill
OLD ROAD
Roberts Farm
Garden Centre
LANDMERE
LANE
Toll Bar House
MELTON ROAD
A606
A52
MELTON
A606
A52
RUDDINGTON GRANGE GOLF COURSE
LOUGHBOROUGH
A60
Ruddington Hall
Lodge
Olgalans Lodge
St. Peter's C of E Junior School
Playing Field
ASHWORTH
DEVON DR.
AVENUE
LWR. CANAAN
PACKMAN DR.
ABINGDON DR.
ROAD
SALCOMBE CRES.
UPPER CANAAN
PAGET CRES.
WILFORD CRES.
SAVAGES RD.
ST. JOHNS RD.
ST. MARY'S
Wilsons Cl.
WOODLEY ST.
CRES.
RUFFORD
STREET
Easthorpe Farm
Works
Nottingham
Shire Farm
Flawforth Lodge
Hillcrest
The Orchard
FLAWFORTH
Flawford House Farm
Nursery
ROAD
HIGH
EASTHORPE
Easthorpe Cotts.
SAXBY CT.
KIRK
B680
LANE
FLAWFORTH AV.
ELMS
CLOSE
Crockhill Wood
THE GREEN
ELMS GDNS.
Youth & Comm. Cen.
RUDDINGTON
LEYS
Bowl. Grn.
Pav.
WESLEY WY.
GREENWOOD GDS.
Pav.
Elms Park (Rec. Grd.)
MOOR
LANE
SHEPPFOLD
SHRIMPTON CT.
DICKSON DR.
STEVENSON GDS.
SELLARS AV.
LEYLANDS
FIELDS AV.
WHEATLEY
FOLD
MEADOW
MAC-LAREN GDS.
HARVEY
RUDDINGTON FLDS. BUSINESS PARK
Works
THE AVENUE
WAY
NG11
ROAD
Barn Farm
LANE
Nottingham Transport Heritage Centre
Ruddington Station
MERE
WAY
RUDDINGTON FIELDS BUSINESS PARK
MERE
MILL
Long Farm
FARMER
MANOR FM. CL.
BLACKCLIFFE FARM M.
Nursery
DONKEY LA.
STREET
MAIN
STREET
LITTLEMOOR LA.
FAR
Bradmore
LANE
MOOR
ROAD
POCK
Nursery
BRADMORE MOOR
Rancliffe Wood

TOLLERTON
Plumtree
Normanton-on-the-Wolds
Plumtree Park
KEYWORTH
NG12
ROAD MELTON
A606
COTGRAVE ROAD
BRADMORE LANE
MAIN ROAD
STATION ROAD
PLATT LANE
NICKER HILL
STANTON HILL
BUNNY LANE
NOTTINGHAM ROAD
CLIPSTON LANE
WOLDS LANE
Sewage Works
Play. Field
Tollerton Prim. Sch.
Hall Farm
The Decoy
Tollerton Wood
The Lake
Tollerton Nurseries
Nursery
Ranch House
Hoehill Farm
Hoe Hill
Hoe Hill Cottages
Weir
Town End Cottages
Manor Farm
Flawford House
Chapel Yard
The Lawns
Manor House
Normanton House
Avenue Farm
Cricket Grd.
Pav.
Plumtree Sch.
Chestnut Farm
Playing Field
Blackcliffe Hill
Sheltons Houses
British Geological Survey
NORMANTON WOLDS
Crossdale Drive Prim. Sch.
Cotton's Plantation
Firs Farm
Stanwolds Kennels
Keyworth Prim. Sch.
Recreation Grd.
South Wolds Comm. Sch.
Keyworth Leis. Cen.
Woodfields
Debdale Ho.
Walton Ct.

109
148
119

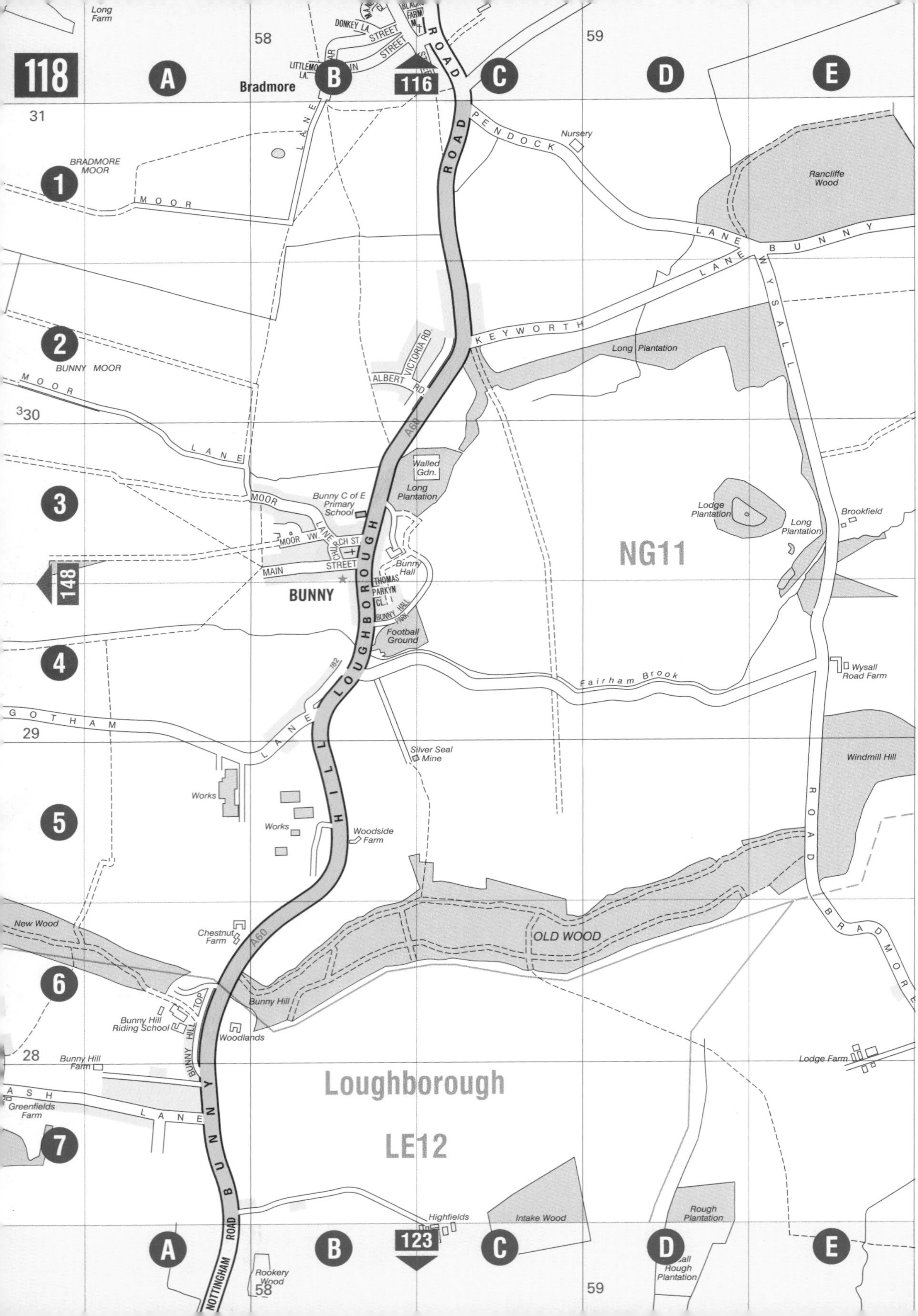
Long Farm
58
59
A
B
C
D
E
Bradmore
116
123
148
DONKEY LA.
STREET
LITTLEMOOR LA.
ROAD
PENDOCK
Nursery
LANE
31
BRADMORE MOOR
MOOR
1
Rancliffe Wood
LANE
BUNNY
WYSALL
KEYWORTH
Long Plantation
2
BUNNY MOOR
MOOR
VICTORIA RD.
ALBERT RD.
A60
330
LANE
Walled Gdn.
Long Plantation
3
MOOR
Bunny C of E Primary School
Lodge Plantation
Long Plantation
Brookfield
MOOR VW.
LANE
CH ST.
CHURCH
Bunny Hall
NG11
MAIN STREET
THOMAS PARKYN CL.
BUNNY
LOUGHBOROUGH
BUNNY HALL PARK
Football Ground
4
Wysall Road Farm
Fairham Brook
GOTHAM
LANE
29
Silver Seal Mine
Windmill Hill
Works
HILL
5
Works
Woodside Farm
ROAD
New Wood
Chestnut Farm
OLD WOOD
BRADMORE
6
Bunny Hill
BUNNY HILL TOP
Bunny Hill Riding School
Woodlands
28
Bunny Hill Farm
Lodge Farm
Loughborough
ASH
Greenfields Farm
LANE
7
LE12
BUNNY
Highfields
Intake Wood
Rough Plantation
NOTTINGHAM ROAD
Rookery Wood
Rough Plantation
58
59

119
117
148
INSET
INSET Page 123
F
G
H
J
K
1
2
3
4
5
6
7
460
61
62
63
31
330
29
28
KEYWORTH
Nottingham
NG12
Plantation
Plantation Rd.
Intake Rd.
Fairham Rd.
Manor Rd.
Rose Hill
Barnt Ct.
Ashley
Church
Walton
Rannock Gds.
Crantock Gds.
Walton Ct.
Cherry Hill
Mount
High View
Nicker Dr.
Meadow
The Ridings
Pleasant
Croft
Park Av. West
Park Av. East
Keyworth Prim. Sch.
Recreation Grd.
Hall
South Wolds Comm. Sch.
Keyworth Leis. Cen.
Playing Fld.
Beech
Larch Wy.
Labur-num Av.
Alder Wy.
Rowan Dr.
Maple Cl.
Stanton Lane
Hill
Brook
Firs Farm
Greenhays Farm
Avenue
Wood Av.
Charn-wood Av.
West Cl.
East Cl.
Leigh Cl.
Wood-
Nottingham Road
Elm Av.
Elm Cl.
Windmill Ct.
Wolds
Laurel Av.
Limetree Cl.
Ash Gro.
Avenue
Lilac Cl.
Willow Brook
Willow Brook Prim. Sch.
Woodfields
Wheatcroft Farm
Lynwood
Roseland Cl.
Hawthorn Cl.
Wrights Orchard
Commercial Rd.
The Sq.
Blind La.
Holm
Barrow Slade
Fairfield Drive
Pastures Cl.
Brook Vw. Ct.
Cedar Dr.
Selby Lane
Brook View
Main Street
Holly Farm Cotts.
Burial Grd.
Lane
Holmcroft
Widmerpool Lane
High View
Fairfield House
The Pastures
Sewage Works
The Bungalow
Twyn-Bays
Lings Lane
Wolds Lane
Wembley Lodge
Keyworth Wolds
Fairham Brook
Wembley Farm
Wysall Road
Wolds Barn
Wolds Farm
North Lodge House
North Lodge
Roehoe Brook
Longcliffe Farm
Lorne House
The Old Vicarage
Keyworth Road
Little London La.
Tuckwood Ct.
Laurel Cl.
Main
Manor
Wysall
Widmerpool Road
Cricket Field Farm
Widmerpool Hall (Training School)
Keyworth Road
Station Road
Hall Dr.
Old
Widmerpool
The Grange
Church La.
Brooklands
Main Street
Ford
Field Lane
Penn Lane
Willoughby Lane
Pav.
Sports Ground
Oak Farm Nurseries
Wysall Lane
Green Hill
Greenhill Plantation

Kingston on Soar
Nottingham
NG11
Loughborough
LE12
KINGSTON PARK
Weir
The Pool
Boat House
Sluice
148
Hall
KEGWORTH RD.
THE GRN.
GOTHAM RD.
ST. WINIFRED'S CL.
MANOR FARM CT.
LONG ROW
STATION ROAD
WEST LEAKE LANE
WOSS
Station Plantation
Woodside
Dairy Centre
Scotland Farm
Scotland Plantation
Moulter Hill
Kingston Brook
STATION ROAD
OLD BULL FARM CL.
CHESTNUTS CL.
MELTON ROAD
COLLEGE ROAD
Halls of Residence
Black Pool
Sewage Works
Playing Field
Nursery
Sports Centre
Veterinary Laboratories Agency
University of Nottingham School of Agriculture
Halls of Residence
Playing Field
Tennis Courts
Froghole Farm
Domleo's Spinney
Meteorological Station
LANDCROFT LANE
Glebe Farm
Works
PITHOUSE LANE
Gold Hill Farm
SOAR LANE
Cemetery
Valley Farm
MARLE PIT HILL
Tennis Courts
Bowl Grn.
ST. MICHAELS
Hall Farm Cottages
Hall Farm
BOLLARD'S LA.
BUCK'S LA.
The Hall
MAIN STREET
St.Anne's Manor
Lodge
LANE
TROWELL LANE
RECTORY
ST. ANNE'S LA.
SWAN CT.
THE PADDOCKS
Lib.
HUNGARY LANE
SUTTON BONINGTON
GABLE'S LEA
BARRINGTON CT.
Sutton Bonington Primary School
Park Lane Farm
PARK LANE
PASTURE LANE
Devil's Elbow
RIVER SOAR
ORCHARD CL.
WILLOW
POOLE LA.
SHEPHERD'S CL.
CHARNWOOD AV.
CHARNWOOD FIELDS
SUTTON CL.
HATHERNWARE INDUSTRIAL ESTATE
County Council Depot
A6006
INSET
A
B
C
D
E
1
2
3
4
5
6
7
450
51
52
27
26
25
24

121
122
148
148
INSET
F
G
H
J
K
1
2
3
4
5
6
7
53
54
455
427
326
325
24
455
51
52
54
West Leake
EAST LEAKE
Loughborough
LE12
Normanton on Soar
Rushcliffe Halt
Club Ho.
Rushcliffe Lodge
STOCKING LANE
GOTHAM ROAD
The Cottage
Crow Wood
Ash Spinney
Fir Dale Plantation
Fox Hill
Foxhill Wood
Reservoir (covered)
Fox Hill Farm
Kingston Brook
Hall
West Leake Manor
Churchside Farm
Old Rectory
MAIN STREET
VILLAGE FARM CL.
Sewage Works
WEST LEAKE ROAD
STATION ROAD
FIELD END CL.
Hall
BIRCH LEA
ROPEWALK
BATEMAN
EXETER CL.
BATEMAN RD.
YORK CL.
TRURO CL.
SOUTHWELL CL.
WIN-IMANOR
FARM
Arley House PNEU Sch.
THISTLE BANK
HEAVENSIDE
HOLLIS
NORTHFIELD
BROOKFIELDS
THE ARCHES
BROOK END
THE BURROWS
SPRUCE CL.
LANDS DR.
TWENTYLANDS
East Leake Hall
LEIVERS CLOSE
SYCAMORE
MAPLE CL.
ASH WK.
WILLOW
POPLAR AV.
BEECH AV.
OAK CR.
BROOKSIDE AV.
PINE CL.
YEW CL.
ORCHARD CL.
CEDAR AV.
BROOKSIDE ROAD
AVENUE
BURTON
BRICKYARD LANE
Manor Farm
Calke Hall Farm
California Farm
California Plantation
New Plantation
Cold Harbour Plantation
Hills Farm
TRAVELL'S HILL WOODGATE
Emsway
Brickyard Plantation
REMPSTONE ROAD
KIRK LEY ROAD
Woodgate Farm
The Gorse
Gould's Barn
Stackyard Spinney
Pit Hole
Whitehills Farm
Devil's Garden
Limekiln Farm
Limekiln Cotts.
REMPSTONE ROAD A6006 MELTON ROAD
Stanford Hills Farm
Trafalgar Wood
Shaw's Park Farm
The Plains
The Evergreens
Stanford Hills
The Belt
Kingsbrook Ct.
LEAKE LANE
PARK LANE
A6006
MOOR LANE
Playing Field
FAR LANE
MAIN STREET
Normanton House
Normanton on Soar Prim. Sch.
RUSHCLIFFE
CHARNWOOD
STONEHURST LA.
BUTT LANE
SOAR LA.
VILLAGE RD.
PASTURE LANE
Foot Ferry

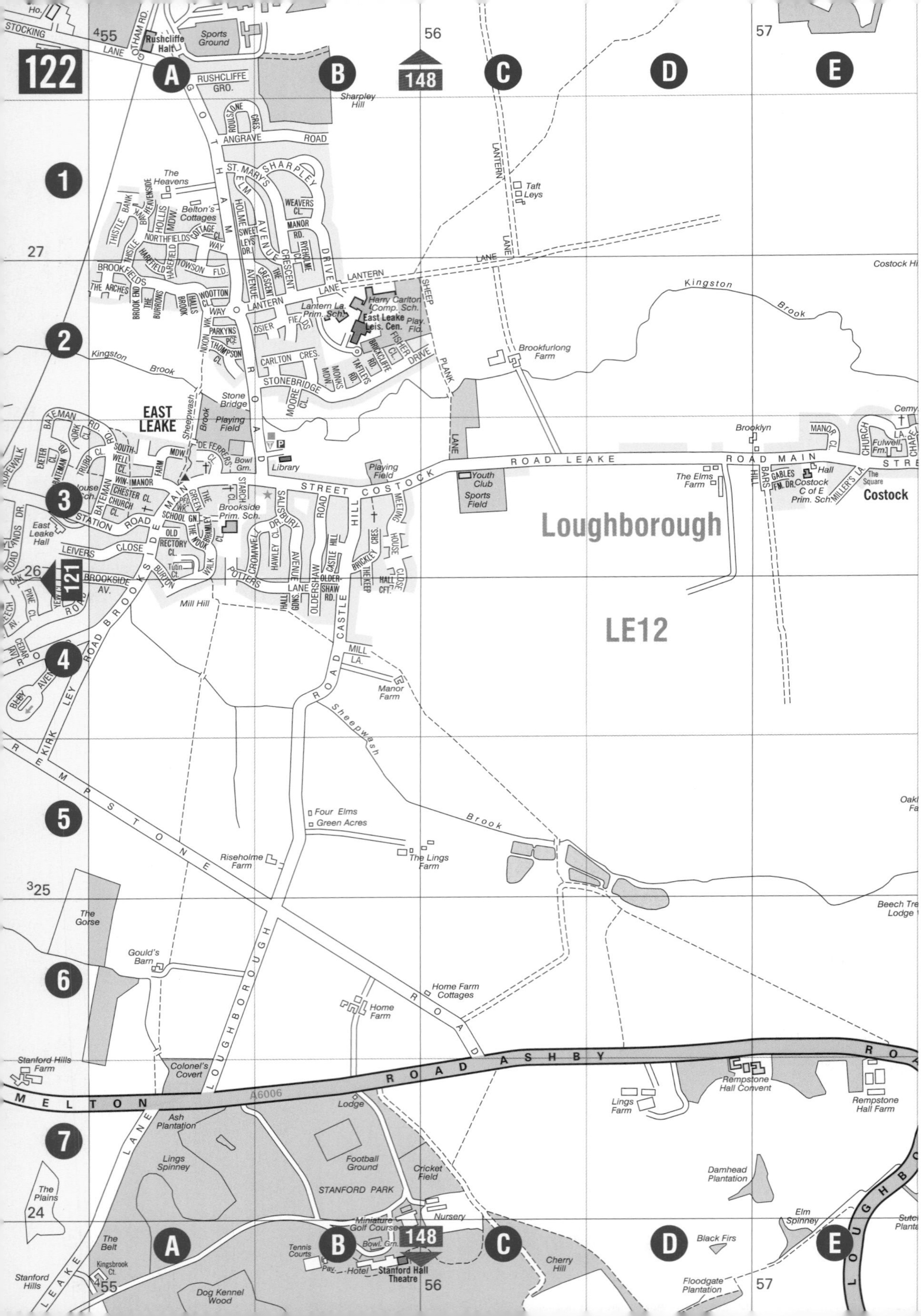

EAST LEAKE
Loughborough
LE12
Costock
A B C D E
1 2 3 4 5 6 7
148
121
55
56
57
27
26
25
24
STOCKING LANE
Rushcliffe Halt
Sports Ground
GOTHAM RD.
RUSHCLIFFE GRO.
Sharpley Hill
ROULSTONE CRES.
ANGRAVE ROAD
ST. MARY'S
SHARPLEY DRIVE
The Heavens
THISTLE BANK
HOLLIS MDW.
Belton's Cottages
NORTHFIELDS
COTTAGE CL.
WEAVERS CL.
MANOR RD.
RYEHOLME
HOLME AVENUE
SWEET LEYS DR.
THE CRESCENT
WAY
BROOKFIELDS
HAREFIELD
TOWSON FLD.
THE ARCHES
BROOK END
THE BURROWS
HALLS BROOK
WOOTTON CL.
LANTERN LANE
LANTERN WAY
Lantern La. Prim. Sch.
Harry Carlton Comp. Sch.
East Leake Leis. Cen.
Play. Fld.
SHEEP PLANK LANE
LANTERN LANE
Taft Leys
Costock Hill
Kingston Brook
Brookfurlong Farm
PARKYNS PCE.
THOMPSON CL.
NIXON WK.
OSIER
CARLTON CRES.
STONEBRIDGE
MONKS MDW.
TAFTLEYS RD.
BRICKCLIFFE RD.
FISHER CL.
DRIVE
MOORE CL.
Stone Bridge
Sheepwash Brook
Playing Field
BATEMAN RD.
YORK CL.
EXETER CL.
TRURO CL.
SOUTHWELL CL.
DE FERRERS CL.
Bowl Grn.
Library
FARM MDW.
WINDMILL
MANOR CL.
CHESTER CL.
CHURCH CL.
STATION ROAD
MAIN STREET
SCHOOL GN.
THE GREEN
THE NOOK
OLD RECTORY CL.
STARCH CL.
Brookside Prim. Sch.
East Leake Hall
LEIVERS CLOSE
BROOKSIDE AV.
BROOKSIDE ROAD
BURTON WALK
Tutin Ct.
POTTERS
CROMWELL
HAWLEY CL.
SALISBURY DR.
AVENUE
OLDERSHAW ROAD
OLDERSHAW RD.
CASTLE HILL
HALL GDNS.
LANE
BRICKLEY CRES.
THE KEEP
HALL CFT.
CLOSE
MEETING HOUSE
COSTOCK ROAD
LEAKE ROAD
Playing Field
Youth Club
Sports Field
Brooklyn
The Elms Farm
MANOR CL.
CHURCH LA.
Fulwell Fm.
Cemy.
MAIN ROAD
HILL
BARS
GABLES FM. DR.
Hall
Costock C of E Prim. Sch.
MILLER'S LA.
The Square
CHAPEL STREET
Mill Hill
OAK
PINE CL.
YEW
CEDAR AV.
KIRK LEY ROAD
MILL LA.
CASTLE ROAD
Manor Farm
Sheepwash Brook
REMPSTONE ROAD
Four Elms
Green Acres
Riseholme Farm
The Lings Farm
The Gorse
Oakl Fa
Beech Tre Lodge
Gould's Barn
LOUGHBOROUGH ROAD
Home Farm Cottages
Home Farm
Stanford Hills Farm
Colonel's Covert
ASHBY ROAD
MELTON ROAD
A6006
Lodge
Rempstone Hall Convent
Rempstone Hall Farm
Lings Farm
Ash Plantation
Lings Spinney
LANE
Football Ground
Cricket Field
STANFORD PARK
Damhead Plantation
The Plains
Miniature Golf Course
Nursery
Elm Spinney
Sutc Planta
The Belt
Tennis Courts
Bowl. Grn.
Pav.
Hotel
Stanford Hall Theatre
Black Firs
Cherry Hill
Kingsbrook Ct.
Stanford Hills
LEAKE
Dog Kennel Wood
Floodgate Plantation
LOUGHBOROUGH

F
G
H
J
K
58
59
460
118
Intake Wood
Rough Plantation
Highfields
Rookery Wood
Wysall Rough Plantation
Lough Rough Plantation
BUNNY HILL
NOTTINGHAM ROAD
A60
Grange Farm
Nottingham
NG12
INSET
27
Field Farm
Hall Farm
COSTOCK ROAD
Scotland Hill Farm
WYSALL LANE
OLD MAIN ROAD
Nouvelle Farm
Glebe Farm
THORPE LANE
148
26
Nursery
REMPSTONE LANE
Wolds Farm
Canaan Farm
Hill Farm
Sheepwash Brook
Burial Ground
Rempstone
Grange Farm
Playing Field
Pav.
KINGS BROOK CL.
SCHOOL LA.
ELMS CL.
MAIN
STREET
WYSALL
WYMESWOLD ROAD
A6006
DALES CL.
WOLDS CL.
THE OLD ENGINE YARD
Sutcliffe Hill
1
2
3
4
5
6
7
LITTLE LONDON LA.
KEYWORTH RD.
LAUREL CL.
TUCKWOOD CT.
WIDMERPOOL ROAD
MAIN STREET
MANOR HOUSE DR.
Wysall
Bowl. Green
Tennis Court
Cricket Field Farm
WYMESWOLD ROAD
LITTLE LINCOLN
COSTOCK
Kingston Brook
Brooklea Farm
Windyridge Farm
Thorpe in the Glebe
61

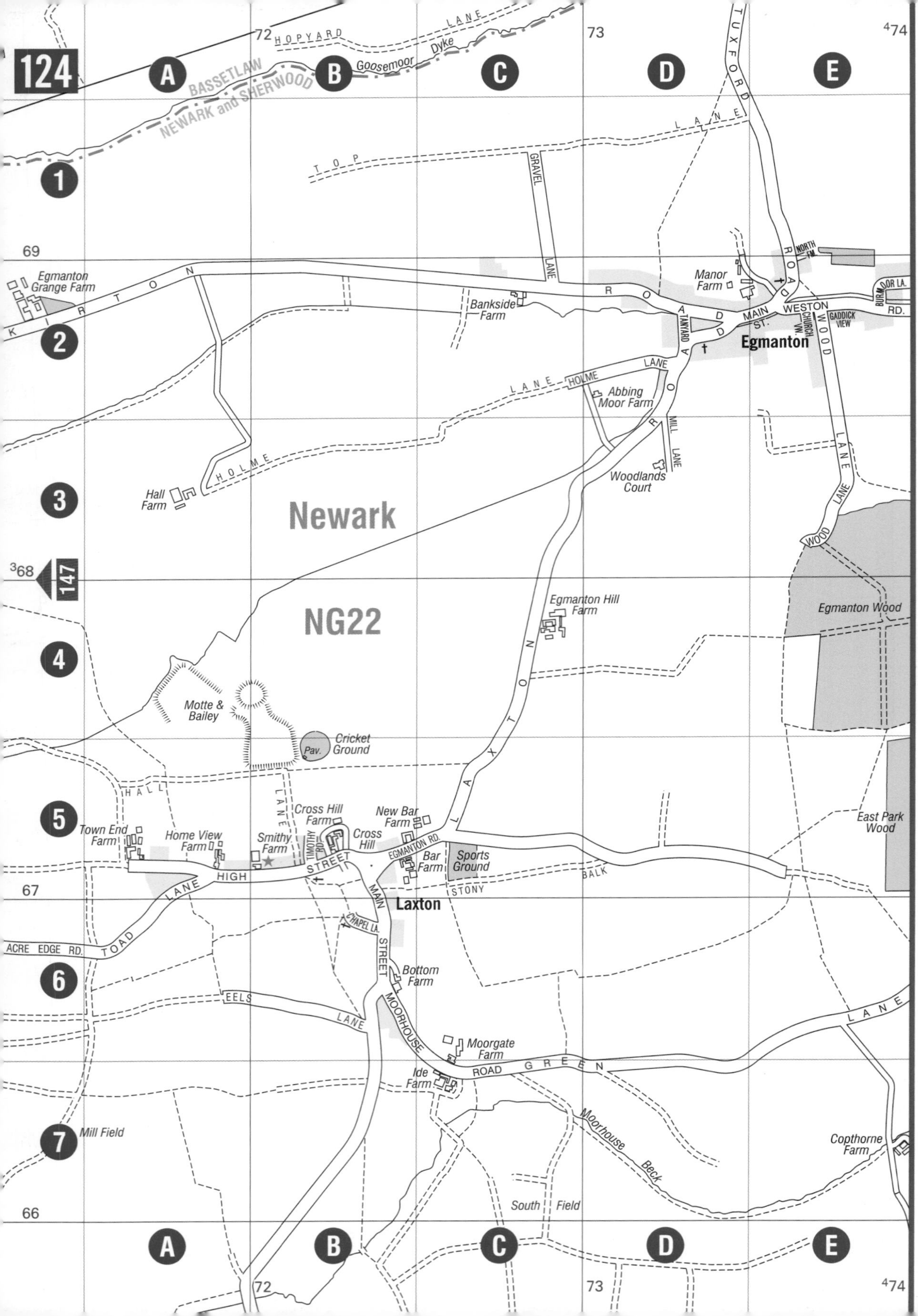

HOPYARD LANE
Goosemoor Dyke
BASSETLAW
NEWARK and SHERWOOD
TUXFORD ROAD
TOP LANE
GRAVEL LANE
Egmanton Grange Farm
KIRTON ROAD
Bankside Farm
Manor Farm
NORTH FM.
WESTON RD.
MAIN ST.
TANYARD
CHURCH VW.
GADDICK VIEW
BURMOOR LA.
Egmanton
HOLME LANE
Abbing Moor Farm
MILL LANE
WOOD LANE
Woodlands Court
Hall Farm
HOLME
Newark
NG22
Egmanton Hill Farm
Egmanton Wood
LAXTON ROAD
Motte & Bailey
Cricket Ground
Pav.
HALL LANE
Cross Hill Farm
New Bar Farm
Town End Farm
Home View Farm
Smithy Farm
TIMOTHY RD.
Cross Hill
EGMANTON RD.
Bar Farm
Sports Ground
East Park Wood
HIGH STREET
STONY BALK
Laxton
MAIN STREET
CHAPEL LA.
TOAD LANE
ACRE EDGE RD.
Bottom Farm
EELS LANE
MOORHOUSE ROAD
Moorgate Farm
GREEN LANE
Ide Farm
Moorhouse Beck
Copthorne Farm
Mill Field
South Field
A B C D E
1 2 3 4 5 6 7
72 73 474
69 368 67 66
147

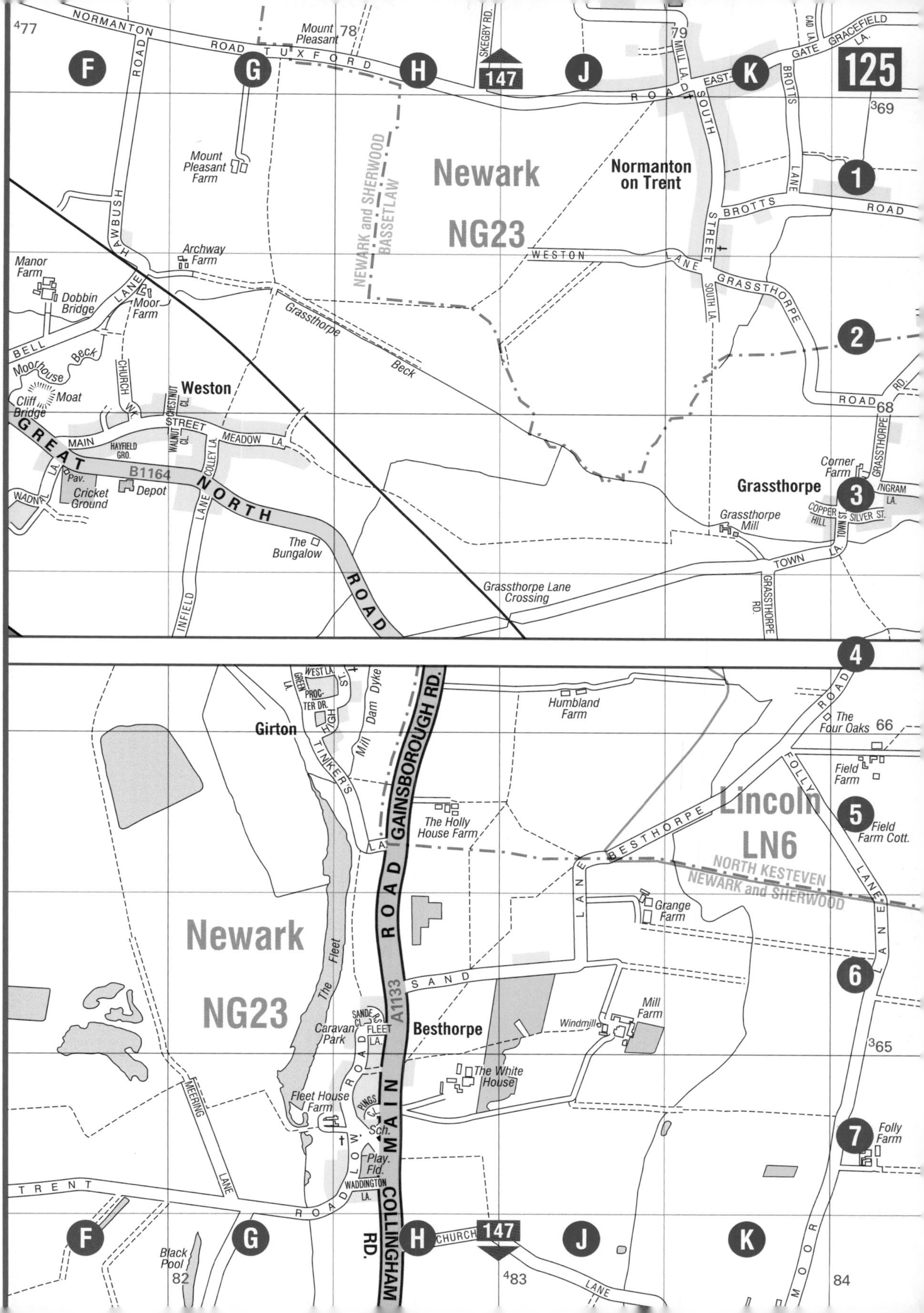
NORMANTON ROAD
TUXFORD ROAD
Mount Pleasant
78
SKEGBY RD.
79
MILL LA.
CAD LA.
GRACEFIELD LA.
GATE
EAST
ROAD
SOUTH STREET
BROTTS LANE
F
G
H
147
J
K
369
Mount Pleasant Farm
NEWARK and SHERWOOD
BASSETLAW
Newark
NG23
Normanton on Trent
1
BROTTS ROAD
HAWBUSH ROAD
Archway Farm
WESTON LANE
GRASSTHORPE ROAD
SOUTH LA.
Manor Farm
Dobbin Bridge
Moor Farm
LANE
BELL
Moorhouse Beck
Grassthorpe Beck
2
CHURCH W.
Weston
CHESTNUT CL.
Moat
Cliff Bridge
STREET
MAIN
HAYFIELD GRO.
WALNUT CL.
COLLEY LA.
MEADOW LA.
ROAD
68
RD.
GREAT NORTH ROAD
B1164
LA.
Pav.
WADNAL
Cricket Ground
Depot
LANE
Corner Farm
GRASSTHORPE
Grassthorpe
3
INGRAM LA.
COPPER HILL
SILVER ST.
TOWN ST.
Grassthorpe Mill
The Bungalow
TOWN LA.
Grassthorpe Lane Crossing
GRASSTHORPE RD.
INFIELD
4
WEST LA.
GREEN LA.
PROCTER DR.
HIGH ST.
Mill Dam Dyke
GAINSBOROUGH RD.
Humbland Farm
ROAD
The Four Oaks
66
Girton
TINKER'S LA.
Field Farm
FOLLY LANE
The Holly House Farm
BESTHORPE LANE
Lincoln
LN6
5
Field Farm Cott.
NORTH KESTEVEN
NEWARK and SHERWOOD
Grange Farm
MAIN ROAD
Newark
NG23
The Fleet
6
SAND LANE
A1133
SANDE CL.
FLEET LA.
Caravan Park
Besthorpe
Windmill
Mill Farm
365
The White House
Fleet House Farm
RINGS CL.
Sch.
LOW ROAD
Play. Fld.
MEERING LANE
7
Folly Farm
TRENT ROAD
WADDINGTON LA.
COLLINGHAM RD.
F
G
H
CHURCH LANE
147
J
K
MOOR
Black Pool
82
483
84
477

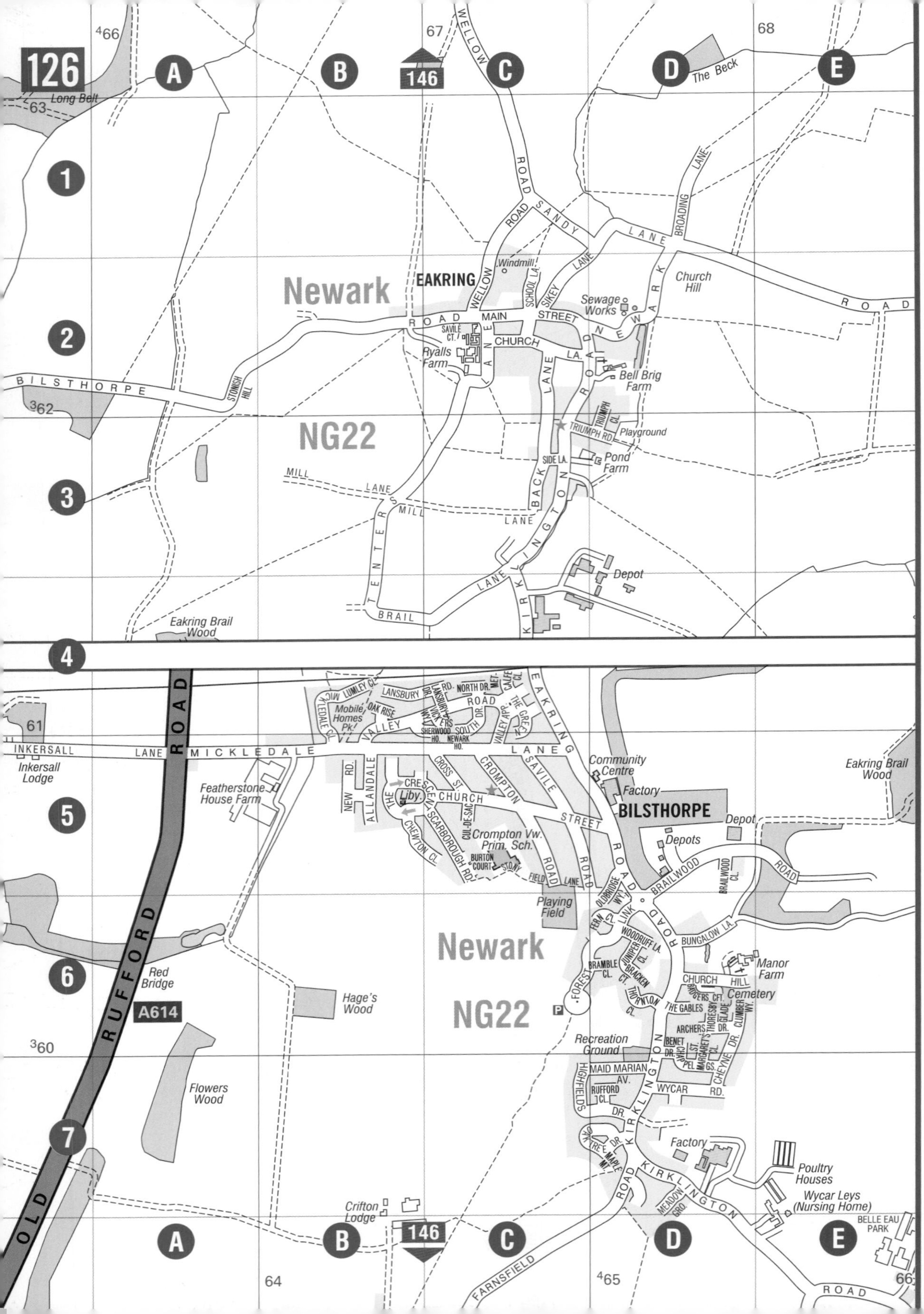
Long Belt
146
The Beck
WELLOW ROAD
SANDY LANE
BROADING LANE
Windmill
EAKRING
Newark
Church Hill
SCHOOL LA.
SIKEY LANE
Sewage Works
ROAD
MAIN STREET
SAVILE CT.
CHURCH LA.
NEWARK ROAD
Ryalls Farm
Bell Brig Farm
BILSTHORPE
STONISH HILL
NG22
TRIUMPH CL.
TRIUMPH RD.
Playground
SIDE LA.
Pond Farm
MILL LANE
BACK LANE
TENTERS LANE
KIRKLINGTON
Depot
BRAIL LANE
Eakring Brail Wood
LUMLEY CL.
LANSBURY RD.
NORTH DR.
METCALFE CL.
Mobile Homes Pk.
OAK RISE
VALLEY ROAD
SOUTH DR.
SHERWOOD HO.
NEWARK HO.
VALLEY APP.
THE GREEN
EAKRING ROAD
INKERSALL LANE
MICKLEDALE LANE
Inkersall Lodge
OLD RUFFORD ROAD
Featherstone House Farm
NEW RD.
ALLANDALE
THE CRESCENT
CROSS ST.
CROMPTON STREET
SAVILE STREET
Community Centre
Factory
BILSTHORPE
Liby.
CHURCH STREET
Depot
CHEWTON CL.
SCARBOROUGH RD.
CUL-DE-SAC
Crompton Vw. Prim. Sch.
BURTON COURT
STONY FIELD LANE
ROAD
Depots
BRAILWOOD ROAD
BRAILWOOD CL.
OLDBRIDGE WY.
LINK
FERN CL.
Playing Field
WOODRUFF LA.
JUNIPER CL.
BRACKEN CL.
BUNGALOW LA.
Manor Farm
Newark
Red Bridge
A614
BRAMBLE CL.
FOREST
THORNTON CL.
CHURCH HILL
Cemetery
ROGERS CFT.
THE GABLES
Hage's Wood
NG22
ARCHERS
THORESBY DR.
GLADE
CLUMBER WY.
Recreation Ground
BENET DR.
ST. MARGARET'S CL.
CHAPEL GS.
CHEYNE DR.
Flowers Wood
HIGHFIELDS DR.
MAID MARIAN AV.
RUFFORD CL.
WYCAR RD.
OAK TREE DR.
MAPLE WY.
Factory
Poultry Houses
Wycar Leys (Nursing Home)
Crifton Lodge
MEADOW GRO.
BELLE EAU PARK
FARNSFIELD ROAD
KIRKLINGTON ROAD
ROAD

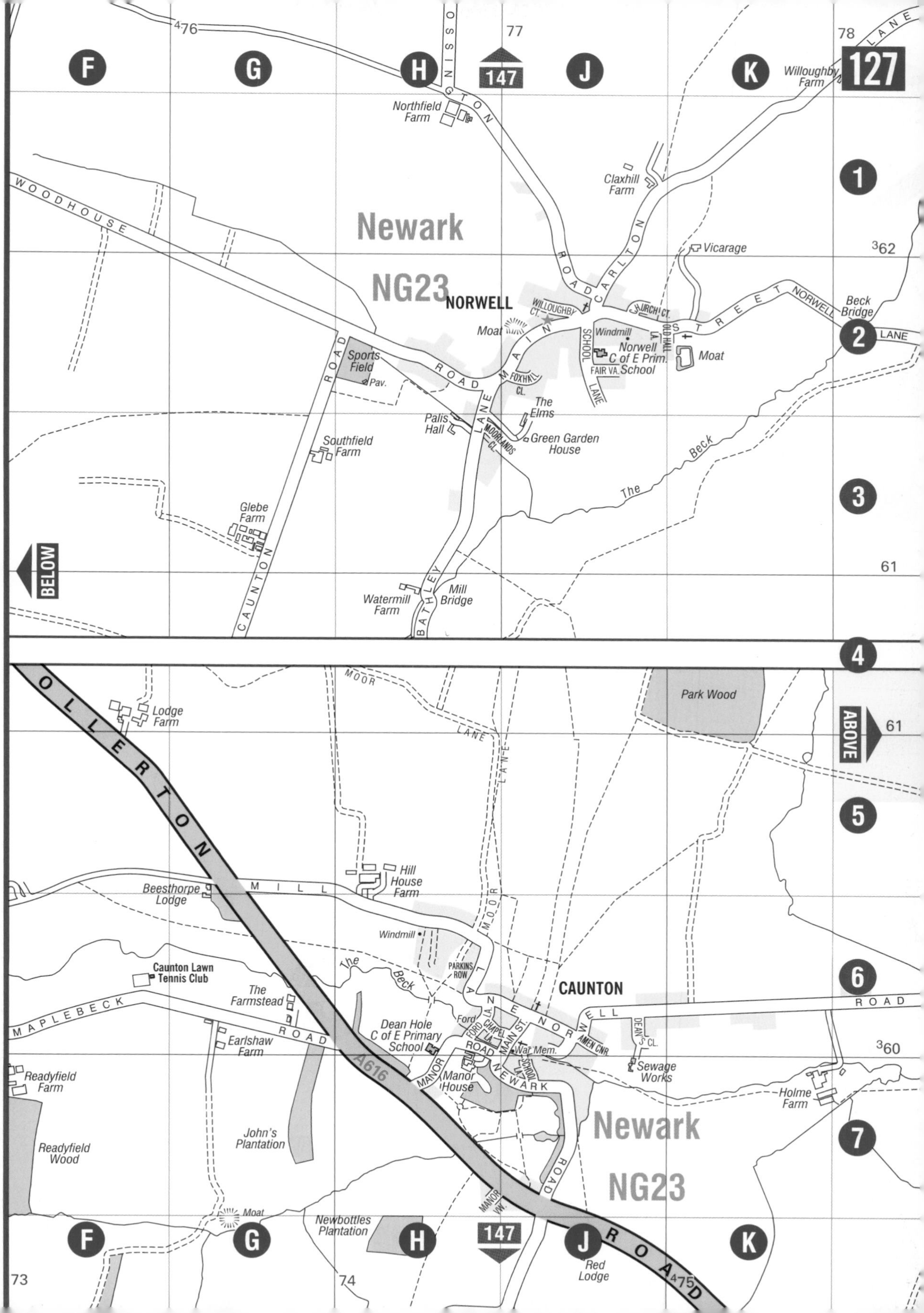

F
G
H
J
K
147
76
77
78
Willoughby Farm
Northfield Farm
Claxhill Farm
Vicarage
362
Newark
NG23
NORWELL
WOODHOUSE ROAD
CARLTON LANE
WILLOUGHBY CT.
CHURCH CT.
NORWELL LANE
STREET
Beck Bridge
Moat
Windmill
Norwell C of E Prim. School
OLD HALL LA.
FAIR VA.
SCHOOL LANE
FOXHALL CL.
Sports Field
Pav.
MAIN
The Elms
Palis Hall
MOORLANDS CL.
Green Garden House
Southfield Farm
The Beck
Glebe Farm
CAUNTON ROAD
BATHLEY LANE
Watermill Farm
Mill Bridge
61
BELOW
ABOVE
1
2
3
4
5
6
7
MOOR LANE
Park Wood
Lodge Farm
OLLERTON
Hill House Farm
Beesthorpe Lodge
MILL
Windmill
MOOR LANE
Caunton Lawn Tennis Club
PARKINS ROW
The Beck
CAUNTON
NORWELL ROAD
The Farmstead
MAPLEBECK ROAD
Ford
FORD LA.
CHAPEL LA.
MAIN ST.
SCHOOL LA.
AMEN CNR
DEAN'S CL.
Dean Hole C of E Primary School
Earlshaw Farm
War Mem.
Sewage Works
360
Readyfield Farm
A616
MANOR ROAD
Manor House
NEWARK ROAD
Holme Farm
John's Plantation
Readyfield Wood
Newark
NG23
MANOR VW.
Moat
Newbottles Plantation
Red Lodge
ROAD
73
74
75

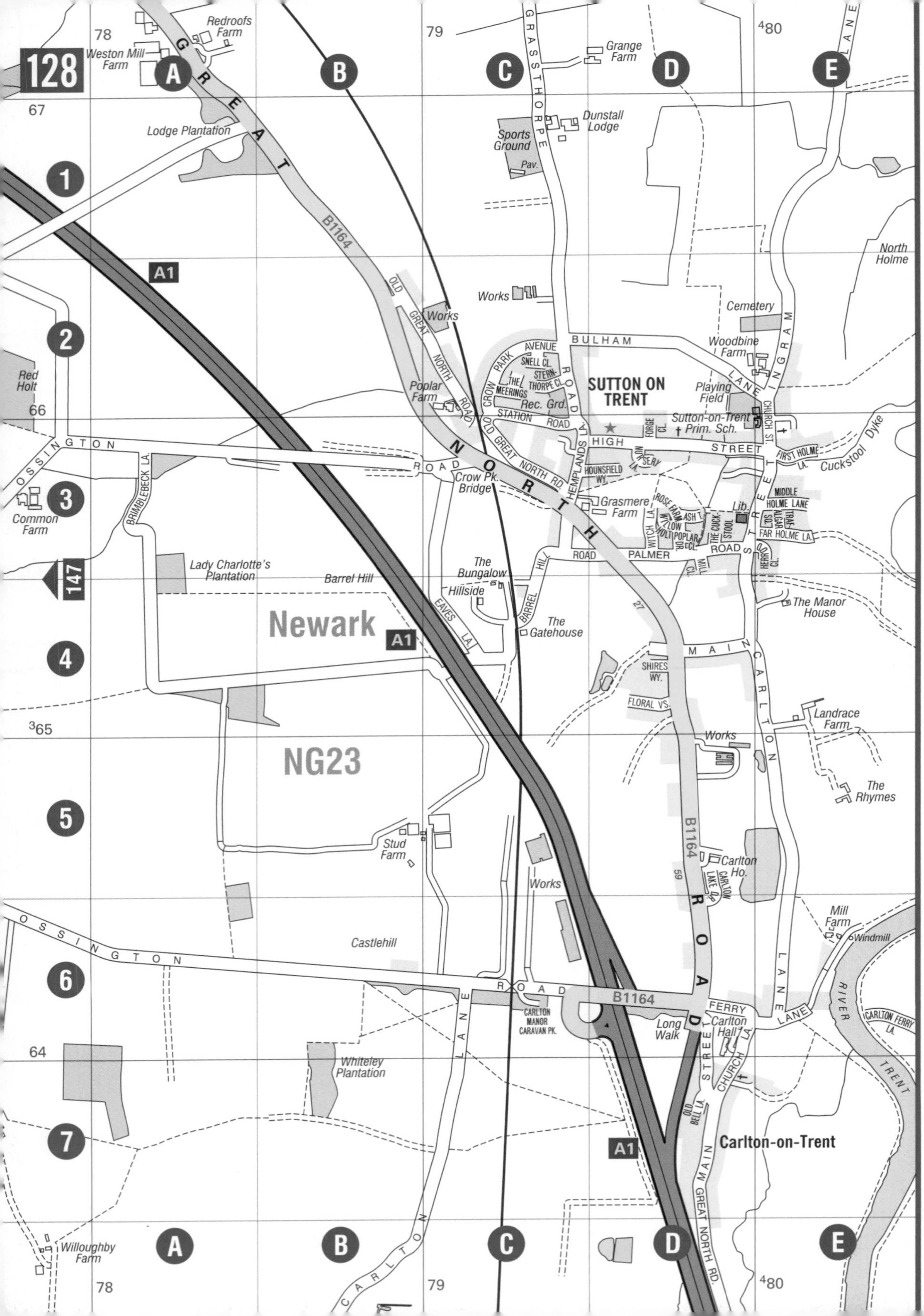

Redroofs Farm
Weston Mill Farm
78
79
480
A
B
C
D
E
67
66
365
64
1
2
3
4
5
6
7
GREAT NORTH ROAD
Lodge Plantation
GRASSTHORPE
Grange Farm
Dunstall Lodge
Sports Ground
Pav.
B1164
A1
North Holme
Works
OLD GREAT NORTH ROAD
Cemetery
Red Holt
BULHAM LANE
AVENUE
CROW PARK
SNELL CL.
STERNTHORPE CL.
THE MEERINGS
Rec. Grd.
SUTTON ON TRENT
Woodbine Farm
Playing Field
INGRAM LANE
Poplar Farm
STATION ROAD
Sutton-on-Trent Prim. Sch.
FORGE CL.
CHURCH ST.
HIGH STREET
OSSINGTON ROAD
BRIMBLEBECK LA.
Crow Pk. Bridge
OLD GREAT NORTH RD.
HEMPLANDS LA.
HOUNSFIELD WY.
NURSERY LA.
FIRST HOLME LA.
Cuckstool Dyke
Common Farm
Grasmere Farm
ROSE FARM
MIDDLE HOLME LANE
ASH T.
Lib.
ALGAR SQ.
TRAFALGAR
WITCH LA.
LOW HOLT
POPLAR DR.
POPLAR CL.
THE CUCKSTOOL
FAR HOLME LA.
HILL ROAD
PALMER ROAD
MILL CL.
HERON CL.
Lady Charlotte's Plantation
Barrel Hill
The Bungalow
Hillside
EAVES LA.
BARREL HILL
The Manor House
Newark
The Gatehouse
MAIN STREET
27
SHIRES WY.
FLORAL VS.
CARLTON LANE
Landrace Farm
NG23
Works
The Rhymes
Stud Farm
Carlton Ho.
CARLTON LAKE DR.
59
Castlehill
Mill Farm
Windmill
OSSINGTON ROAD
RIVER TRENT
CARLTON FERRY LA.
B1164
FERRY LANE
Long Walk
Carlton Hall
CARLTON MANOR CARAVAN PK.
CARLTON LANE
Whiteley Plantation
CHURCH LA.
MAIN STREET
OLD BELL LA.
Carlton-on-Trent
GREAT NORTH RD.
Willoughby Farm

147

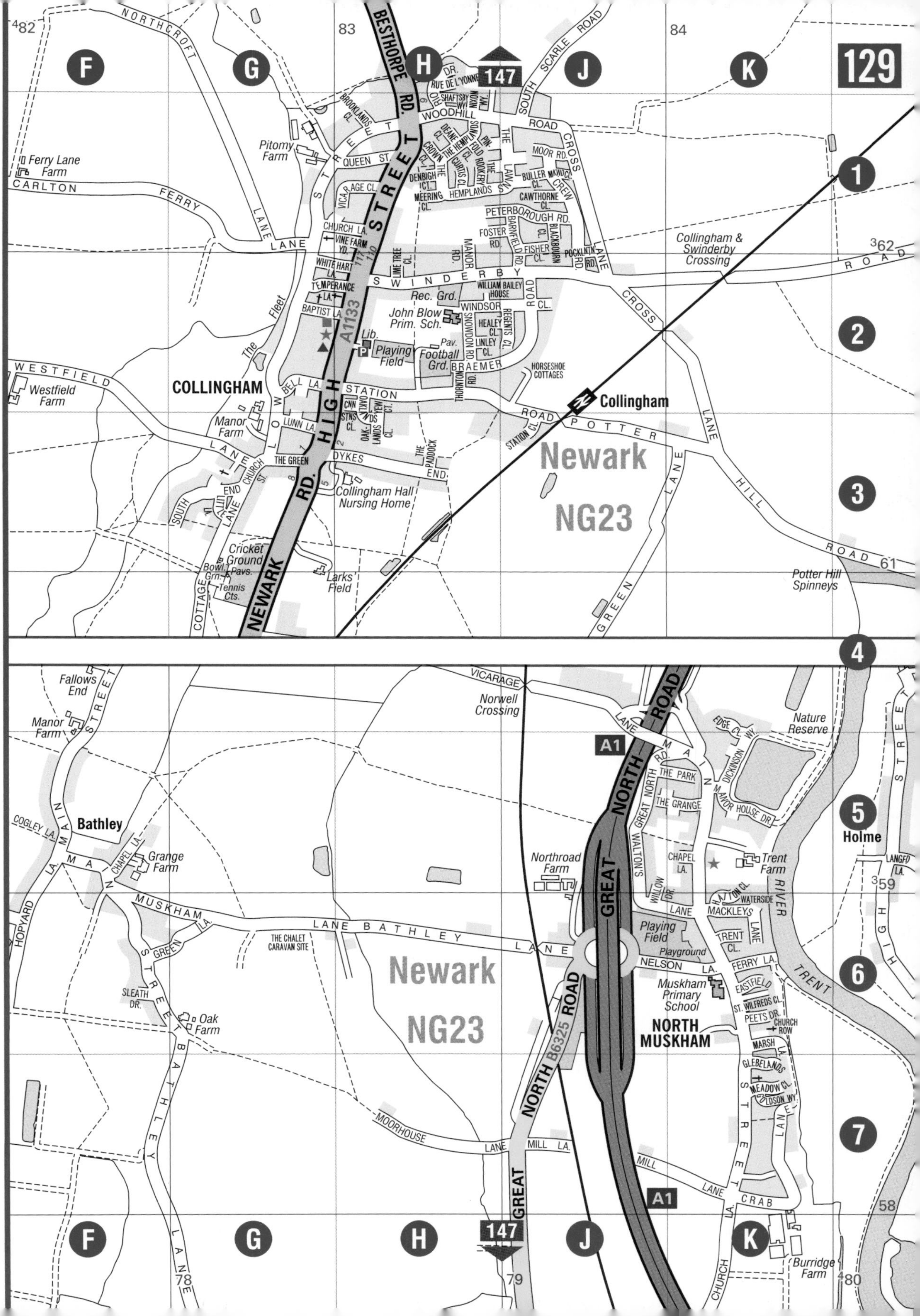
147
COLLINGHAM
Collingham
Newark
NG23
Collingham & Swinderby Crossing
Pitomy Farm
Ferry Lane Farm
Westfield Farm
Manor Farm
John Blow Prim. Sch.
Rec. Grd.
Playing Field
Football Grd.
Collingham Hall Nursing Home
Cricket Ground
Larks Field
Potter Hill Spinneys
BESTHORPE RD.
HIGH STREET
NEWARK RD.
A1133
NORTHCROFT
CARLTON FERRY LANE
SOUTH SCARLE ROAD
WOODHILL ROAD
CROSS LANE
SWINDERBY ROAD
STATION ROAD
POTTER HILL ROAD
GREEN LANE
WESTFIELD LANE
DYKES END
THE GREEN
COTTAGE LANE
SOUTH END
CHURCH ST.
LOW STREET
Fallows End
Manor Farm
Bathley
Grange Farm
Northroad Farm
Norwell Crossing
Trent Farm
Nature Reserve
Holme
NORTH MUSKHAM
Muskham Primary School
THE CHALET CARAVAN SITE
Oak Farm
Burridge Farm
A1
GREAT NORTH ROAD
B6325
BATHLEY LANE
MUSKHAM LANE
MAIN STREET
BATHLEY LANE
MOORHOUSE LANE
MILL LANE
CRAB LANE
CHURCH LA.
VICARAGE LANE
NELSON LA.
RIVER TRENT
HIGH STREET
Newark
NG23
F G H J K
1 2 3 4 5 6 7
82 83 84 78 79 80
362 61 359 58

67
68
A
B
C
D
E
1
2
3
4
5
6
7
56
355
54
53
Station House
132
146
Cotton Mill Dyke
Edingley Beck
STATION ROAD
HOLME LANE
MAIN STREET
BELFIELDS YD.
CHAPEL CT.
Moat
STATION
Highfields Nursing Home
Edingley
EDINGLEY HILL
MANSFIELD ROAD
Newark
NG22
LANE
Diamond Cottage Farm
GREAVES
LITTLE LA.
LANE
Grange Farm
St. Helens Croft
NEWHALL
GRAY
Goldhill Farm
Halam Beck
Halam Osier Beds Wood
Mill Farm
Halam Mill
Ford
LANE
SAINT HELEN'S
Strickland Farm
THE TURNPIKE
Halam
Halam C of E Prim. Sch.
SCHOOL LANE
LOW
NORWOOD PARK GOLF COURSE
Club House
NORWOOD PARK
New Plantation
The Temple Wood
GRAY LANE
Middlebeck Farm
BACK LANE
RADLEY R.
RADLEY TER.
HALAM
ST. MICHAEL'S CL
LANE
CHURCH LANE
Machin's Farm
MANOR FLDS.
ROAD
Farm Plantation
Norwood Park Farm
HALAM HILL
SAVERSICK LANE
COOKS LA.
OXTON ROAD
Cricket Ground
Pav.
Halam Beck
Lowbank Farm
CUTLERSFORTH
Cutlersforth Farm
THE PUMPING STATION
LEACHCROFT HILL
Westhorpe Hall
WESTHORPE
Westhorpe
LANE
THE HOLME
CUNDY HILL
B6386
BATH
RADLEY
OXTON
Thorney Abbey Farm
New Radley Farm

Southwell
NG25
SOUTHWELL
Normanton
Hockerton
KIRKLINGTON RD.
A617
A612
B6386
Meadow Farm
Far Corkhill Farm
Cork Hill
Middle Corkhill Farm
Little Corkhill Farm
Hockerton Grange
Manor Farm
Hockerton Dumble
MAYTHORNE INDUSTRIAL ESTATE
THE OLD SILK MILL
Driving Range
Crow Wood
Lodge Plantation
Recreation Ground
RIVER GREET
Chestnut Farm
Ornamental Water Gardens
MILL PARK INDUSTRIAL ESTATE
Rifle Range
Upton Field
UPTON ROAD
The Workhouse
Greet Bri.
Depot
War Mem.
Lib
Southwell Minster
The Minster School
Lowe's Wong Jun. & Inf. Sch.
Tanyard Farm
Westhorpe Dumble
Bowl. Grn. Ten. Cts.
War Mem. Rec. Grd.
Squire's Pond
Cemetery
Mon.
Potwell Dyke
CREW LANE INDUSTRIAL ESTATE
Dale Farm
Brandreth
Park Farm
Smithfield Farm
Southwell Leisure Cen.
Rugby Football Ground
Wilderness
Bracken Lodge
Brinkley Hall Farm
Brinkley Hill Farm
NOTTINGHAM ROAD
WESTGATE
CHURCH STREET
EASTHORPE
UPTON ROAD
KIRKLINGTON ROAD
HOCKERTON ROAD
NORMANTON ROAD
STATION RD.
NEWARK ROAD
LANE
FISKERTON RD.
FISKERTON
SPRING HILL
CRINK LANE
POLLARD'S LANE
GALLEY HILL ROAD
BURGAGE
QUEEN ST.
KING ST.
MARKET PLACE
ROPEWALK
RIDGEWAY
SPRINGFIELD
NORWOOD GDNS.
NORWOOD GARDENS
SILVEY AVENUE
LEEWAY ROAD
HOPKILN LANE
ALLENBY ROAD
VICARAGE RD.
LOWES WONG
HALLOUGHTON
BRACKEN-HURST LA.
LANE
69
470
71
56
55
54
53
F
G
H
J
K
1
2
3
4
5
6
7
147

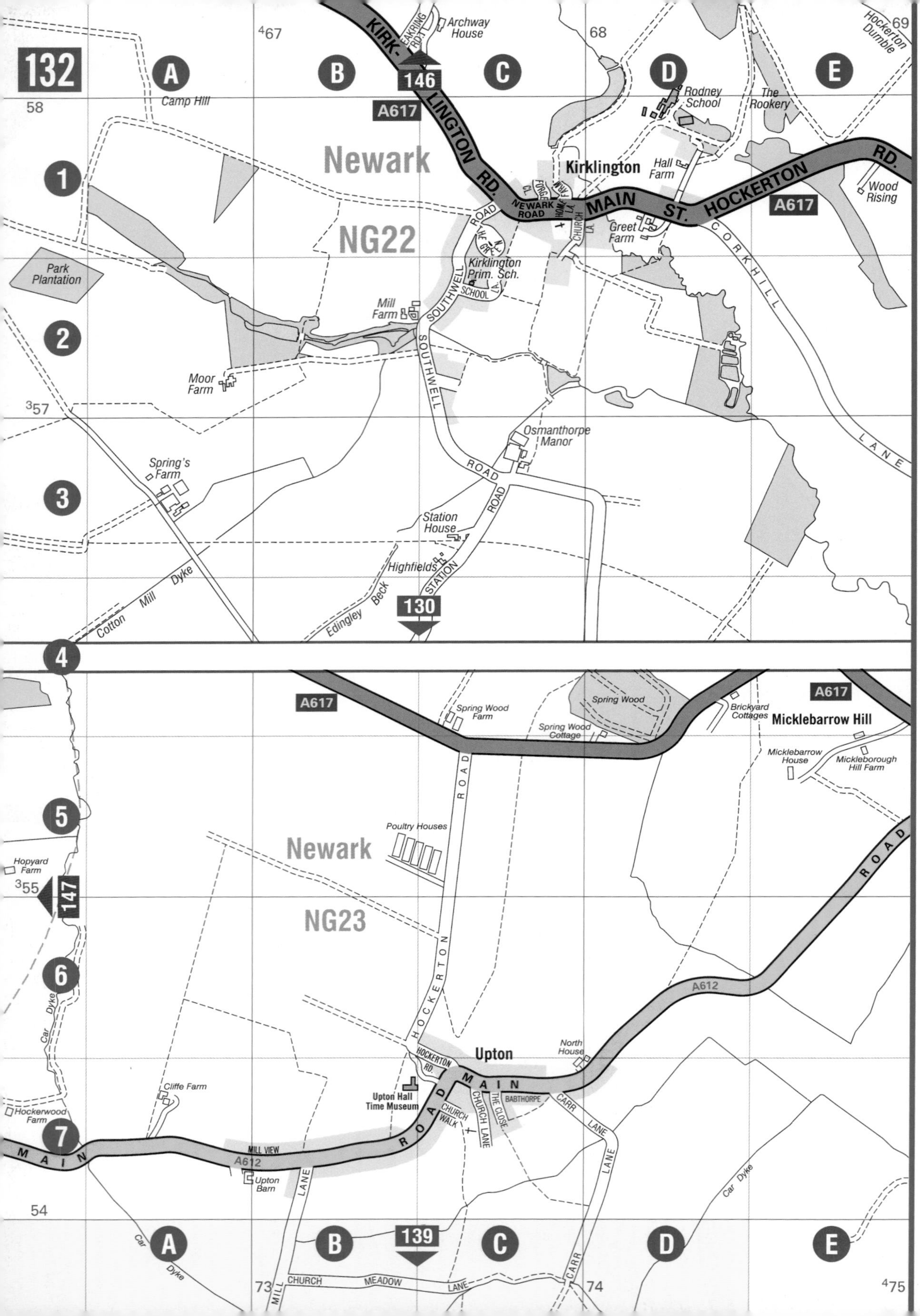
A
B
C
D
E
1
2
3
4
5
6
7
467
68
Hockerton Dumble
69
58
146
Archway House
EAKRING RD.
Camp Hill
A617
KIRK-LINGTON RD.
Rodney School
The Rookery
Newark
Kirklington
Hall Farm
FORGE CL.
NEWARK ROAD
HOME FARM LA.
MAIN ST.
HOCKERTON RD.
Wood Rising
A617
CHURCH LA.
Greet Farm
NG22
Park Plantation
THE GREEN
Kirklington Prim. Sch.
SCHOOL LA.
CORKHILL LANE
Mill Farm
SOUTHWELL ROAD
Moor Farm
357
Osmanthorpe Manor
Spring's Farm
ROAD
STATION ROAD
Station House
Highfields
Cotton Mill Dyke
Edingley Beck
130
A617
Spring Wood Farm
Spring Wood
Spring Wood Cottage
Brickyard Cottages
A617
Micklebarrow Hill
Micklebarrow House
Mickleborough Hill Farm
Poultry Houses
Newark
Hopyard Farm
355
147
NG23
HOCKERTON ROAD
A612
ROAD
Car Dyke
North House
Upton
HOCKERTON RD.
Upton Hall Time Museum
MAIN ROAD
CHURCH WALK
CHURCH LANE
THE CLOSE
BATHTHORPE
CARR LANE
Cliffe Farm
Hockerwood Farm
MAIN
MILL VIEW
A612
Upton Barn
LANE
Car Dyke
54
Car Dyke
139
73
CHURCH MEADOW LANE
MILL LANE
CARR
74
475

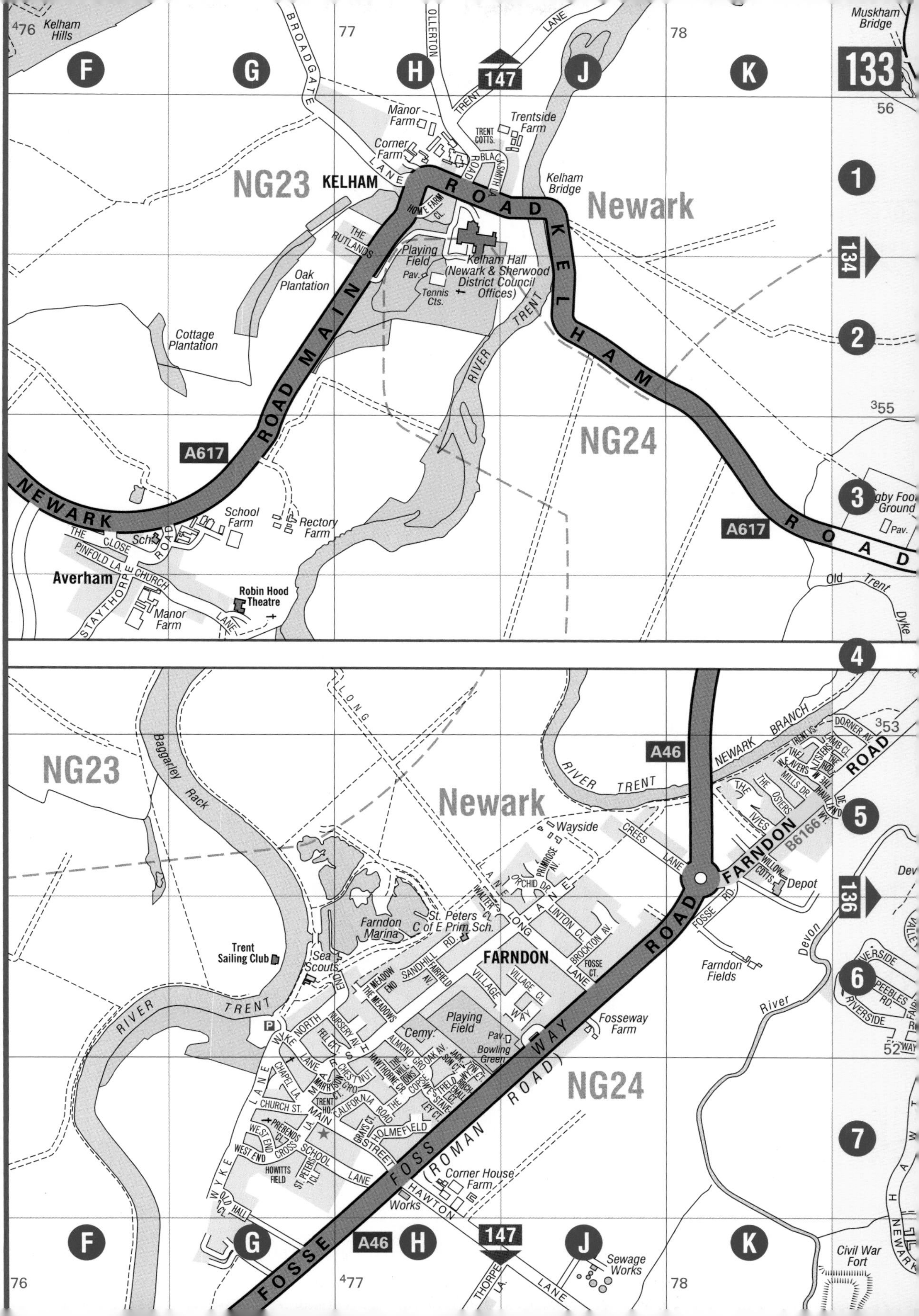

Kelham Hills
Muskham Bridge
BROADGATE
OLLERTON
TRENT LANE
147
Manor Farm
Trentside Farm
TRENT COTTS.
Corner Farm
LANE
BLACKSMITH LA.
Kelham Bridge
NG23
KELHAM
ROAD
Newark
HOME FARM CL.
THE RUTLANDS
Playing Field
Pav.
Kelham Hall (Newark & Sherwood District Council Offices)
Tennis Cts.
Oak Plantation
134
KELHAM
Cottage Plantation
MAIN ROAD
RIVER TRENT
NG24
A617
NEWARK ROAD
School Farm
Rectory Farm
THE CLOSE
Sch.
PINFOLD LA.
CHURCH
Averham
STAYTHORPE
Manor Farm
Robin Hood Theatre
LANE
Rugby Football Ground
Pav.
Old Trent Dyke
LONG
A46
NG23
Baggarley Rack
RIVER TRENT
NEWARK BRANCH
DORNER AV.
TRENT VS.
LAMB CL.
THE WEAVERS
MILLS DR.
THE OSIERS
THE IVIES
FARNDON
B6166
Newark
Wayside
CREES LANE
PRIMROSE AV.
ORCHID DR.
LONG LANE
WALTERS CL.
WILLOW COTTS.
Depot
136
FOSSE RD.
St. Peters C of E Prim.Sch.
Farndon Marina
LINTON CL.
BROCKTON AV.
FOSSE CT.
Trent Sailing Club
Sea Scouts
FARNDON
SANDHILL RD.
FAIRFIELD AV.
MEADOW END
THE MEADOWS
VILLAGE CL.
VILLAGE WAY
Farndon Fields
Devon
River
RIVERSIDE
PEEBLES RD.
RIVER TRENT
P
NORTH END
NURSERY AV.
FELL CT.
Playing Field
Cemy.
Pav.
Bowling Green
Fosseway Farm
WYKE LANE
CHAPEL LA.
MAIN ST.
CHESTNUT GRO.
HAWTHORNE CR.
ALMOND GRO.
OAK AV.
THE COPSE
NG24
ROAD
FOSSE WAY
CHURCH ST.
CALIFORNIA ROAD
HOLMEFIELD
PREBENDS CL.
WEST END
CROSS
SCHOOL LANE
STREET
ROMAN
HOWITTS FIELD
ST. PETERS CL.
Corner House Farm
Works
HAWTON
OLD HALL
FOSSE
A46
Sewage Works
THORPE LA.
LANE
Civil War Fort
NEWARK
F
G
H
J
K
1
2
3
4
5
6
7
76
77
78
56
355
353
52

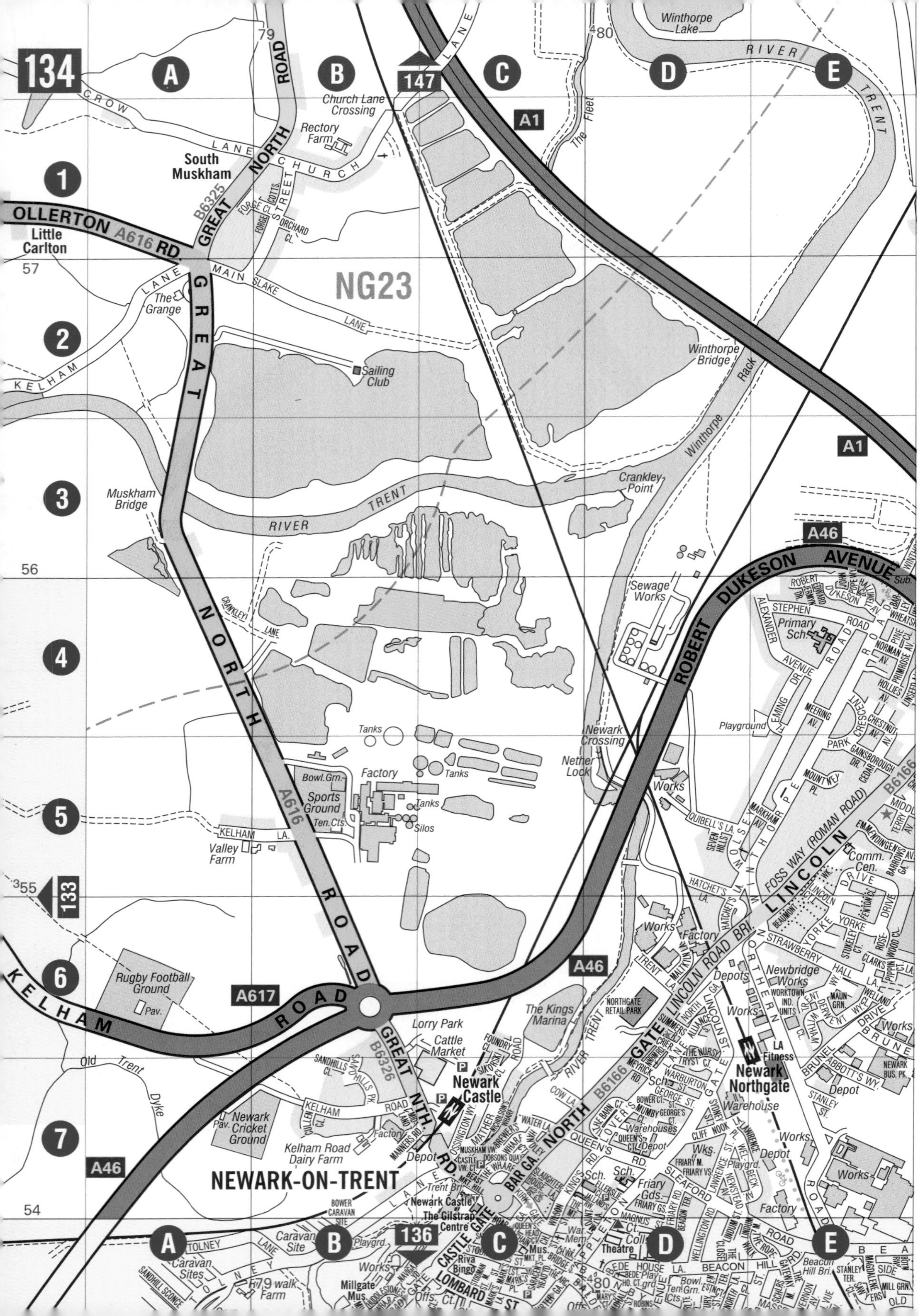

134
147
133
136
A
B
C
D
E
1
2
3
4
5
6
7
79
80
57
56
55
54
NG23
South Muskham
Little Carlton
OLLERTON A616 RD.
GREAT NORTH ROAD
B6325
CROW LANE
CHURCH LANE
Church Lane Crossing
Rectory Farm
FORGE CL.
FORGE COTTS.
STREET
ORCHARD CL.
MAIN SLAKE LANE
LANE
The Grange
KELHAM
A1
The Fleet
Winthorpe Lake
RIVER TRENT
Winthorpe Bridge
Winthorpe Rack
Sailing Club
Muskham Bridge
Crankley Point
Sewage Works
CRANKLEY LANE
A616
Tanks
Factory
Bowl.Grn.
Sports Ground
Ten.Cts.
Silos
KELHAM LA.
Valley Farm
Newark Crossing
Nether Lock
Works
A46
ROBERT DUKESON AVENUE
Playground
Primary Sch.
STEPHEN ROAD
ALEXANDER AVENUE
FLEMING DR.
MEERING AV.
PARK CRESCENT
GAINSBOROUGH DR.
MOUNT VIEW PL.
MARKHAM AV.
SEVEN HILLS
QUIBELL'S LA.
HATCHET'S LA.
FOSS WAY (ROMAN ROAD)
LINCOLN ROAD BRI.
B6166
Comm. Cen.
YORKE DRIVE
STRAWBERRY HALL LA.
Newbridge Works
Depots
Factory
Rugby Football Ground
Pav.
A617
KELHAM ROAD
Lorry Park
Cattle Market
The Kings Marina
NORTHGATE RETAIL PARK
GREAT NTH. RD.
B6326
SANDHILLS CL.
Old Trent Dyke
Newark Cricket Ground
Kelham Road Dairy Farm
Newark Castle
NORTH GATE
RIVER TRENT
Warehouses
Warehouse
Newark Northgate
LA Fitness
Depot
NEWARK-ON-TRENT
Trent Bri.
The Gilstrap Centre
BOWER CARAVAN SITE
Caravan Site
Caravan Sites
TOLNEY LANE
Playgrd.
Millgate Mus.
Riva Bingo
CASTLE GATE
LOMBARD ST
Friary Gds.
SLEAFORD RD.
Theatre
Wks.
BEACON HILL RD.
Beacon Hill Bri.
Bowl. Grn.
Ten. Cts.
STANLEY ST.
BRUNEL DRIVE
ABBOTT'S WY.
NEWARK BUS. PK.
Works

81
82
83
F
G
H
J
K
1
2
3
4
5
6
7
57
56
55
54
147
137
A46
A1133
A17
A1
DANETHORPE
LANE
The Fleet
Hall Farm
Langford Hall
Winthorpe Crossing
HOLME
Pav.
Cricket Ground
ROAD
THOROUGHFARE LA.
Winthorpe Prim. Sch.
High Wood
WOODLANDS
Comm. Cen.
CHAPEL LA.
OLD RTRY CL.
GAINSBOROUGH
POCKLINGTON
CRESCENT
BRAYSTON CL.
HARGON
LANE
Airfield (disused)
Quarry Plantation
THE DRIVE
LANE
Winthorpe
Newark
Nursing Home
SPEIGHT CL.
THE SPINNEY
GAINSBOROUGH
DROVE
Lingspot Farm
FOSS WAY
ROAD
ROMAN
Newark & Nottingham Agricultural Society's Showground
Newark Golf Centre (Driving Range)
Bowling Green
Service Area
Service Area
Newark & Notts Gliding Club
Newark Air Museum
Airfield (disused)
LONG HOLLOW WY.
WHEATSHEAF AV.
HARVEST DR.
ROAD
BRUNEL
BRUNEL DR. WORKSHOPS
ENTERPRISE PARK
STANHOPE AV.
PEMBROKE
CLIFTON
Depot
Drove Cottage Farm
LANE
The Bungalow
STEPHENSON
WAY
TELFORD
Depot
Depot
Works
TELFORD CT.
DRIVE
Works
DRIVE
DROVE
Playing Field
Beaconfield Farm
Depot
Factory
SANIGAR CT.
WHITTLE CL.
DRIVE
BRUNEL CT.
NG24
YEW TREE WY.
BEACONSFIELD
ORDOYNO GRO.
ORCHARD PK.
DR.
THE COURT YARD
WELL GRN. HO.
THE GRN.
LANE
FARRAR CL.
YOUNGS CL.
THOMPSON CL.
BRYANS HAMP.
DENS CL.
STIRLING
ARICOTES
LANCASTER
Play. Fld.
BEACONSFIELD DR.
PARKLANDS CL.
MORGANS CL.
PARKES CL.
MAIN ST.
HALL FM. CT.
VICARAGE CT.
Coddington
Depot
Works
MARLES CL.
WAY
HENTON CL.
PENSWICK GRO.
OLD HALL GDNS.
ROAD
ROAD
JESSOP
JESSOP CL.
Depot
Depot
DR.
BRISTOL CL.
RD.
NEWARK
Black's Farm
BROWNLOW'S HILL
VALLEY VW.
CHAPEL LA.
STREET
MAIN
Sunnyside Farm
Cotswold
NEWARK RD.
Coddington C of E Primary School
LANE
Coddington House
Vale Farm
BLACKBROOK RD.
BROOK CL.
AUTUMN CROFT RD.
WINTERDALE CL.
NORMANTON RD.
SWINDERBY CL.
CRANWELL CL.
SYERSTON
WAY
CANNON CL.
GREEN FIELD CL.
BECKINGHAM
ROAD
NEWBURY
Moat
PHILLIPOTTS CL.
HILL
CONEY
HEIGHTS
WAY
RANSOME CL.
HINE
HOUNSFIELD CL.
LILBURNE CL.
Ark Fm.
SHELDRAKE RD.
GOODWIN CL.
HEATON APP.
GILSTRAP CL.
LEBY
ASHWORTH
HUTCHINSON RD.
PRESTON RD.
EVELLERS WY.
IRETON
ROAD
BALDERTON
Reservoir (covered)
BEACON

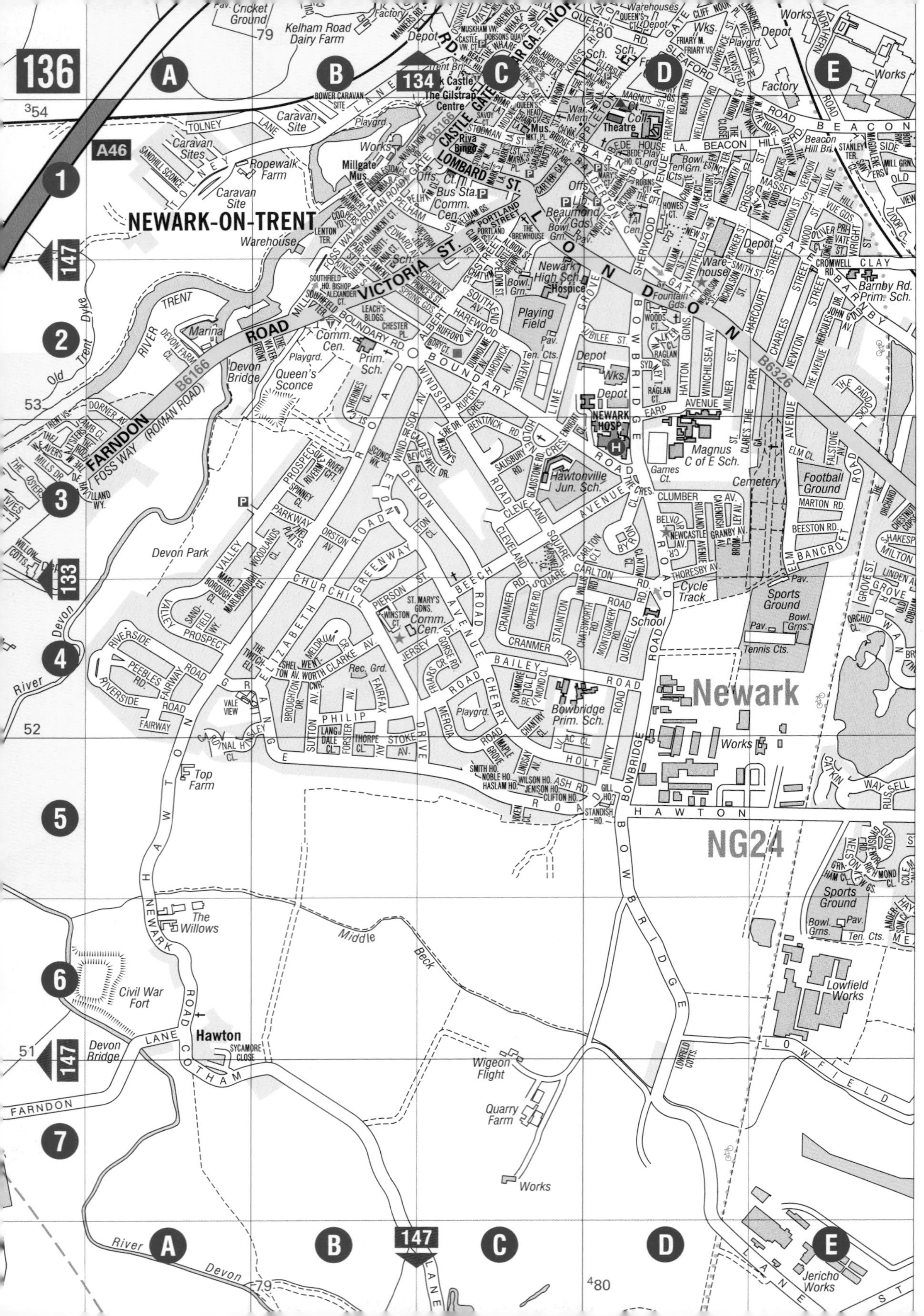
NEWARK-ON-TRENT
Newark
NG24
A B C D E
1 2 3 4 5 6 7
134
147
133
147
147
A46
B6166
B6326
354
53
52
51
79
480
Cricket Ground
Kelham Road Dairy Farm
Depot
Factory
Caravan Site
Caravan Sites
Ropewalk Farm
Caravan Site
Bower Caravan Site
TOLNEY LANE
Playgrd.
Works
Millgate Mus.
The Gilstrap Centre
Castle
Riva Bingo
Mus.
War Mem.
Theatre
Coll.
Bus Sta.
Comm. Cen.
Offs.
Beaumond Gds.
Warehouse
VICTORIA ST.
LOMBARD ST.
CASTLE GATE
LONDON ROAD
BEACON HILL RD.
BEACON LA.
SLEAFORD RD.
Beacon Hill Bri.
Barnby Rd. Prim. Sch.
CROMWELL CLAY
Newark High Sch.
Hospice
Playing Field
Fountain Gds.
Ware house
Depot
Wks.
Depot
NEWARK HOSP.
Magnus C of E Sch.
Games Ct.
Cemetery
Football Ground
Hawtonville Jun. Sch.
RIVER TRENT
Old Trent Dyke
Marina
Devon Bridge
Queen's Sconce
Comm. Cen.
Prim. Sch.
FARNDON ROAD
FOSS WAY (ROMAN ROAD)
BOUNDARY RD.
Devon Park
CHURCHILL
Cycle Track
Sports Ground
Pav.
Bowl. Grns.
Tennis Cts.
School
Comm. Cen.
Rec. Grd.
Bowbridge Prim. Sch.
Playgrd.
Works
Top Farm
HAWTON
BOWBRIDGE
HAWTON ROAD
The Willows
Middle Beck
Civil War Fort
Hawton
Devon Bridge
FARNDON
COTHAM LANE
Wigeon Flight
Quarry Farm
Works
Lowfield Works
LOWFIELD
Sports Ground
Jericho Works
River Devon
River Devon

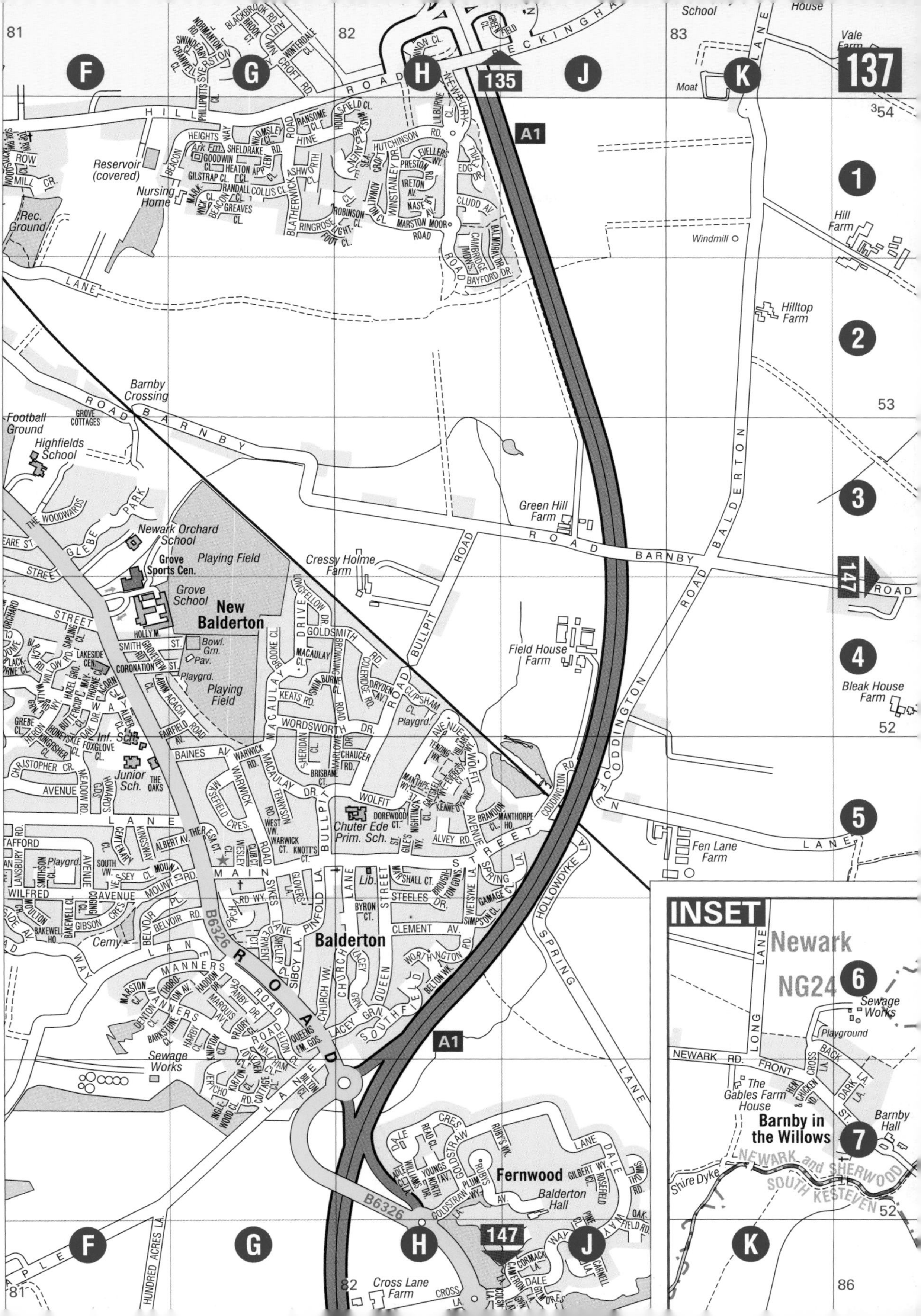

81
82
83
F
G
H
J
K
135
A1
354
53
52
1
2
3
4
5
6
7
HILL ROAD
School
House
Vale Farm
Moat
Reservoir (covered)
Nursing Home
Rec. Ground
Ark Fm.
HEIGHTS
SHELDRAKE RD.
GOODWIN CL.
HEATON
GILSTRAP CL.
RANDALL CL.
COLLIS CL.
GREAVES CL.
BEACON
ASHWORTH
BLATHERWICK RD.
RINGROSE CL.
LIGHTFOOT CL.
ROBINSON CL.
HUTCHINSON RD.
PRESTON
IRETON AV.
MARSTON MOOR ROAD
CLUDD AV.
BALMORAL DR.
CAMBRIDGE MDWS.
BAYFORD DR.
RANSOME CL.
HOUNSFIELD CL.
LILBURNE CL.
NEWBURY
LANE
Hill Farm
Windmill
Hilltop Farm
Barnby Crossing
BARNBY ROAD
Football Ground
GROVE COTTAGES
Highfields School
THE WOODWARDS
PARK
GLEBE
Newark Orchard School
Grove Sports Cen.
Playing Field
Grove School
New Balderton
Green Hill Farm
Cressy Holme Farm
BULLPIT ROAD
BALDERTON LANE
147
ROAD
Field House Farm
CODDINGTON ROAD
FEN LANE
Bleak House Farm
LONGFELLOW DR.
GOLDSMITH DR.
MACAULAY DR.
BROWNING ROAD
COLERIDGE RD.
DRYDEN AV.
CLIPSHAM CL.
KEATS RD.
SWINBURNE CL.
WORDSWORTH DR.
SHERIDAN CL.
MARLOWE DR.
CHAUCER RD.
BRISBANE CT.
BAINES AV.
WARWICK RD.
TENNYSON
WOLFIT AV.
Playgrd.
Bowl. Grn.
Pav.
Playing Field
STREET
HOLLY M.
SMITH ST.
CORONATION ST.
ACACIA
FAIRFIELD ROAD
Inf. Sch.
FOXGLOVE CL.
Junior Sch.
THE OAKS
CHRISTOPHER CR.
AVENUE
MEADOW RD.
LANE
CENTENARY
KINGSWAY
ALBERT AV.
THERESA CL.
WESLEY
ROAD
WEST VW.
WARWICK CT.
KNOTT'S CT.
Chuter Ede Prim. Sch.
DOREWOOD CT.
ALVEY RD.
BRANDON CL.
MANTHORPE HO.
STAFFORD
LANSBURY
Playgrd.
SOUTH VW.
MAIN STREET
Lib.
MARSHALL CT.
SPRING LA.
WILFRED AVENUE
MOUNT RD.
STEELES DR.
BYRON CT.
PINFOLD LA.
GLOVERS LA.
HOLLOWDYKE LA.
SPRING LANE
BAKEWELL CL.
GIBSON CRES.
Cemy.
BELVOIR RD.
B6326 ROAD
Balderton
CLEMENT AV.
SIBCY LA.
CHURCH VW.
QUEEN
WORTHINGTON RD.
BELTON WK.
SOUTHFIELD
LACEY GRN.
MANNERS
MARSTON CL.
HADDON DR.
MARQUIS AV.
PRIORY CL.
QUEENS FM. GDS.
A1
Sewage Works
LANE
Fernwood
CRES
RUBY'S WK.
GOLDSTRAW
GILBERT WY.
ROSEFIELD
DALE
Balderton Hall
WAY
B6326
F
G
H
147
J
K
HUNDRED ACRES LA.
Cross Lane Farm
CROSS
81
82
Fen Lane Farm
LANE
INSET
Newark
NG24
LONG LANE
Sewage Works
Playground
NEWARK RD.
FRONT
BACK LA.
CROSS LA.
DARK LA.
The Gables Farm House
Barnby in the Willows
Barnby Hall
Shire Dyke
NEWARK and SHERWOOD
SOUTH KESTEVEN
52
86

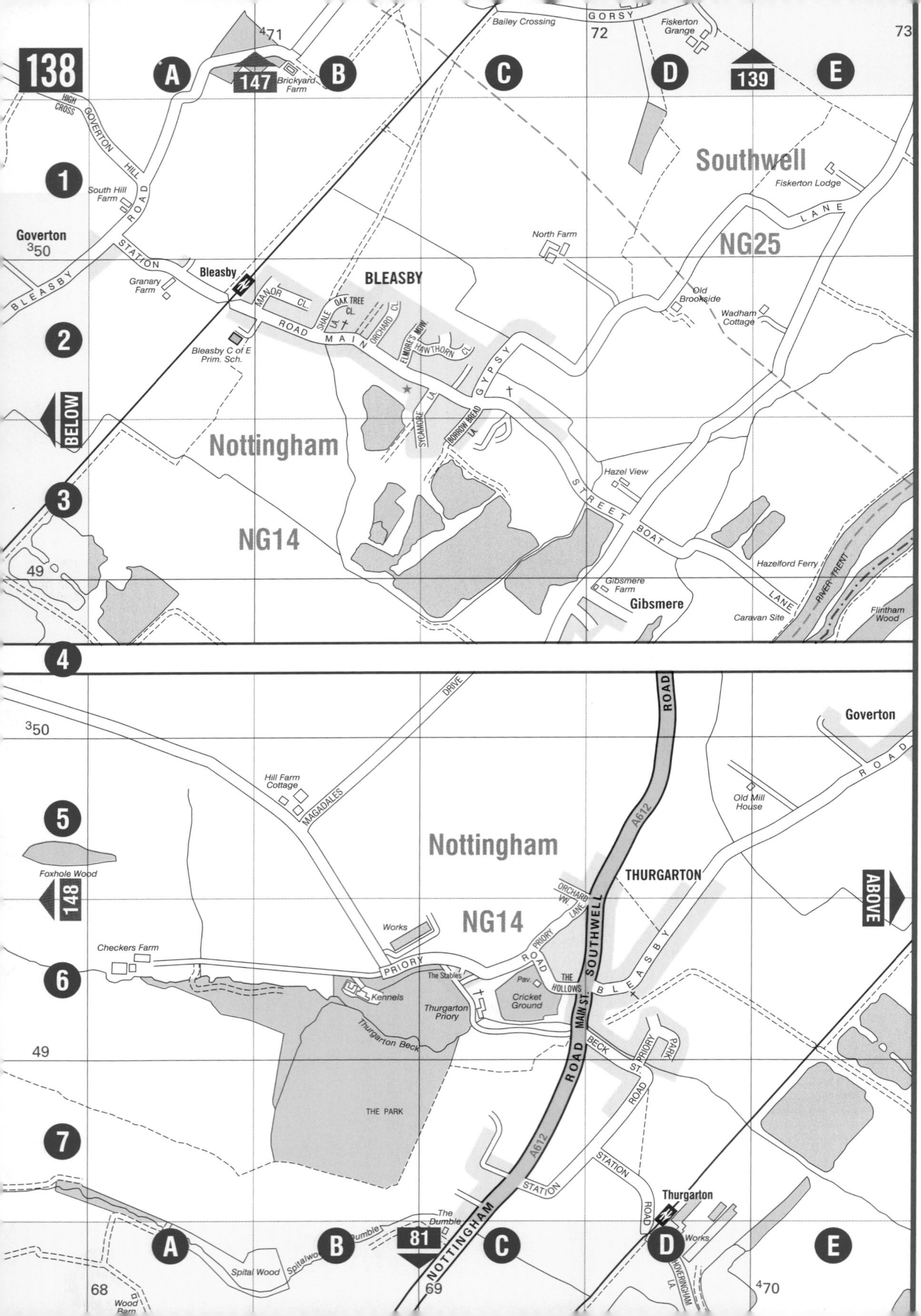
A
B
C
D
E
147
139
471
72
73
Bailey Crossing
GORSY
Fiskerton Grange
Brickyard Farm
HIGH CROSS
GOVERTON HILL
ROAD
1
South Hill Farm
Goverton
350
Southwell
Fiskerton Lodge
LANE
NG25
North Farm
STATION
Bleasby
BLEASBY
BLEASBY
Granary Farm
MANOR CL.
OAK TREE CL.
SHALE LA.
ORCHARD CL.
ELMORE'S MDW.
HAWTHORN CL.
Old Brookside
Wadham Cottage
2
ROAD
MAIN
GYPSY
Bleasby C of E Prim. Sch.
BELOW
SYCAMORE LA.
BORROW BREAD LA.
Nottingham
Hazel View
STREET
3
BOAT
NG14
Hazelford Ferry
49
Gibsmere Farm
Gibsmere
LANE
RIVER TRENT
Caravan Site
Flintham Wood
4
ROAD
DRIVE
350
Goverton
ROAD
Hill Farm Cottage
MAGADALES
Old Mill House
5
Nottingham
A612
Foxhole Wood
THURGARTON
148
ORCHARD VW.
LANE
ABOVE
Works
NG14
SOUTHWELL
PRIORY
Checkers Farm
ROAD
BLEASBY
6
PRIORY
The Stables
THE HOLLOWS
Kennels
Pav.
Cricket Ground
Thurgarton Priory
MAIN ST.
Thurgarton Beck
BECK
PRIORY
PARK
49
ST.
ROAD
ROAD
THE PARK
7
A612
STATION
STATION
Thurgarton
ROAD
The Dumble
Dumble
81
NOTTINGHAM
Works
A
B
C
D
E
Spital Wood
68
69
470
HOVERINGHAM LA.
Wood Barn

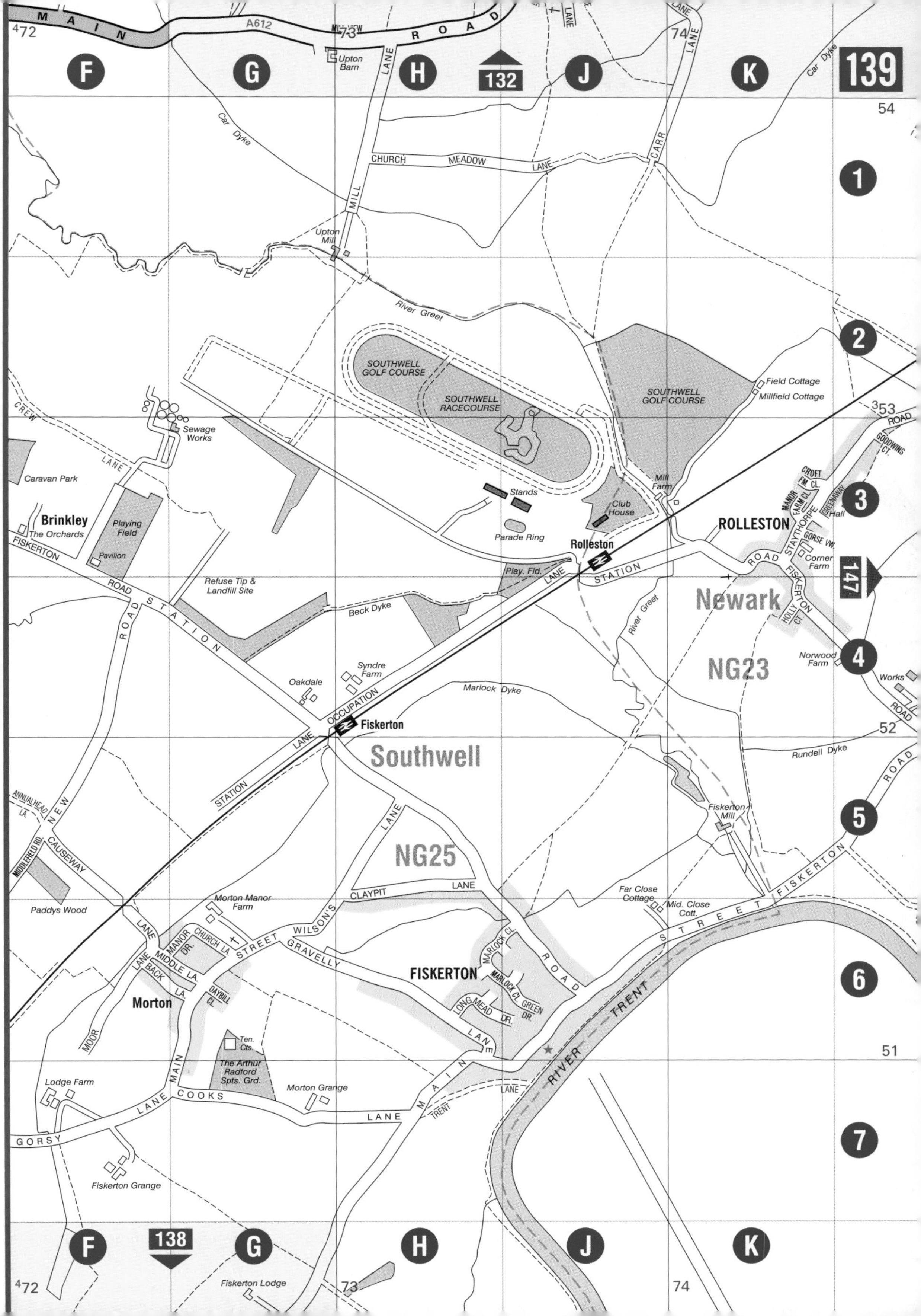
MAIN ROAD
A612
472
73
74
54
53
52
51
F
G
H
J
K
1
2
3
4
5
6
7
132
138
147
Upton Barn
MILL LANE
CARR LANE
Car Dyke
CHURCH MEADOW LANE
Upton Mill
River Greet
SOUTHWELL GOLF COURSE
SOUTHWELL RACECOURSE
Field Cottage
Millfield Cottage
CREW LANE
Sewage Works
Caravan Park
Stands
Mill Farm
Club House
Brinkley
The Orchards
Playing Field
Pavilion
Parade Ring
Rolleston
ROLLESTON
GOODWINS CT.
CROFT FM. CL.
MANOR FARM CL.
GREENAWAY
Hall
STAYTHORPE
GORSE VW.
Corner Farm
FISKERTON ROAD
HOLLY CT.
FISKERTON ROAD
STATION ROAD
STATION LANE
Play. Fld.
Refuse Tip & Landfill Site
Beck Dyke
Newark
NG23
Norwood Farm
Works
ROAD
Syndre Farm
Oakdale
OCCUPATION LANE
Marlock Dyke
Fiskerton
Southwell
Rundell Dyke
ANNUALHEAD LA.
NEW ROAD
MIDDLEFIELD RD.
CAUSEWAY
LANE
NG25
Fiskerton Mill
CLAYPIT LANE
Paddys Wood
Morton Manor Farm
Far Close Cottage
Mid. Close Cott.
FISKERTON STREET
WILSON'S STREET
MANOR DR.
CHURCH LA.
MIDDLE LA.
BACK LA.
GRAVELLY LANE
MARLOCK CL.
FISKERTON
ROAD
MARLOCK CL.
GREEN DR.
LONG MEAD DR.
DAYBILL CL.
Morton
MOOR LANE
MAIN
Ten. Cts.
The Arthur Radford Spts. Grd.
RIVER TRENT
Lodge Farm
COOKS LANE
Morton Grange
MAIN
TRENT LANE
GORSY LANE
Fiskerton Grange
Fiskerton Lodge

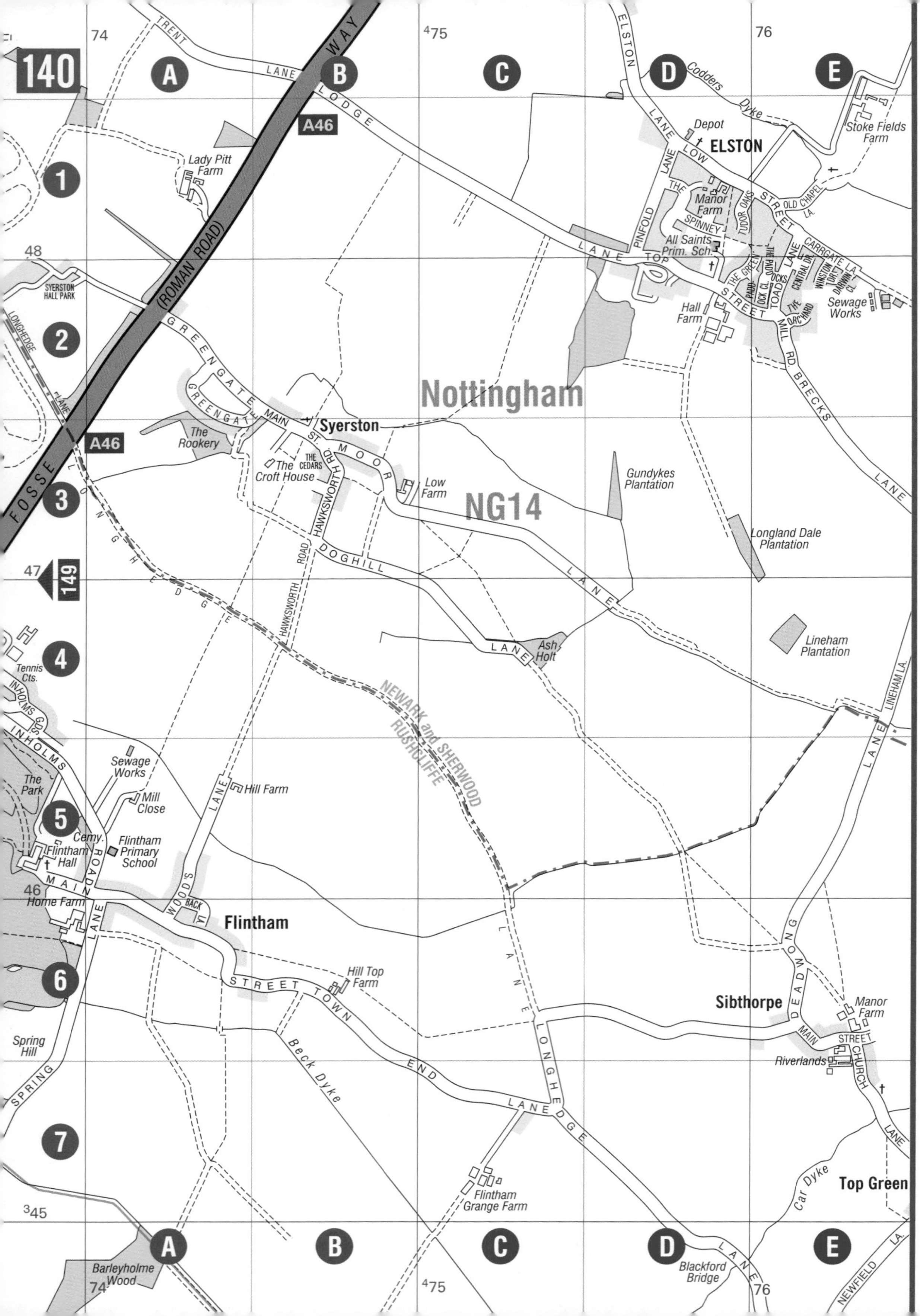

140
74
475
76
A
B
C
D
E
1
2
3
4
5
6
7
48
47
46
345
149
TRENT LANE
WAY
LODGE
A46
(ROMAN ROAD)
FOSSE
Lady Pitt Farm
SYERSTON HALL PARK
LONGHEDGE LANE
GREENGATE
The Rookery
MAIN ST.
Syerston
MOOR
The Croft House
THE CEDARS
HAWKSWORTH RD.
HAWKSWORTH ROAD
DOGHILL LANE
Low Farm
NG14
Nottingham
LONGHEDGE
ELSTON
Codders Dyke
Depot
ELSTON
LOW
PINFOLD LANE
THE SPINNEY
Manor Farm
TUDOR OAKS
STREET
OLD CHAPEL LA.
All Saints Prim. Sch.
TOP LANE
THE GREEN
THE PADDOCKS
PADDOCK CL.
TOAD LANE
CARRGATE LA.
CENTRAL DR.
WINSTON DR.
DARWIN CL.
THE ORCHARD
Hall Farm
Sewage Works
Stoke Fields Farm
MILL RD.
BRECKS LANE
Gundykes Plantation
Longland Dale Plantation
Lineham Plantation
LINEHAM LA.
LANE
Ash Holt
NEWARK and SHERWOOD
RUSHCLIFFE
Tennis Cts.
INHOLMS GDS.
INHOLMS
The Park
Sewage Works
Mill Close
Hill Farm
Cemy.
Flintham Hall
Flintham Primary School
MAIN ROAD
Home Farm
WOOD'S LANE
BACK LA.
Flintham
STREET
Hill Top Farm
TOWN END LANE
Beck Dyke
Spring Hill
SPRING
LONGHEDGE LANE
Flintham Grange Farm
DEADWONG LANE
Sibthorpe
Manor Farm
MAIN STREET
Riverlands
CHURCH LANE
Car Dyke
Top Green
Blackford Bridge
NEWFIELD LA.
Barleyholme Wood

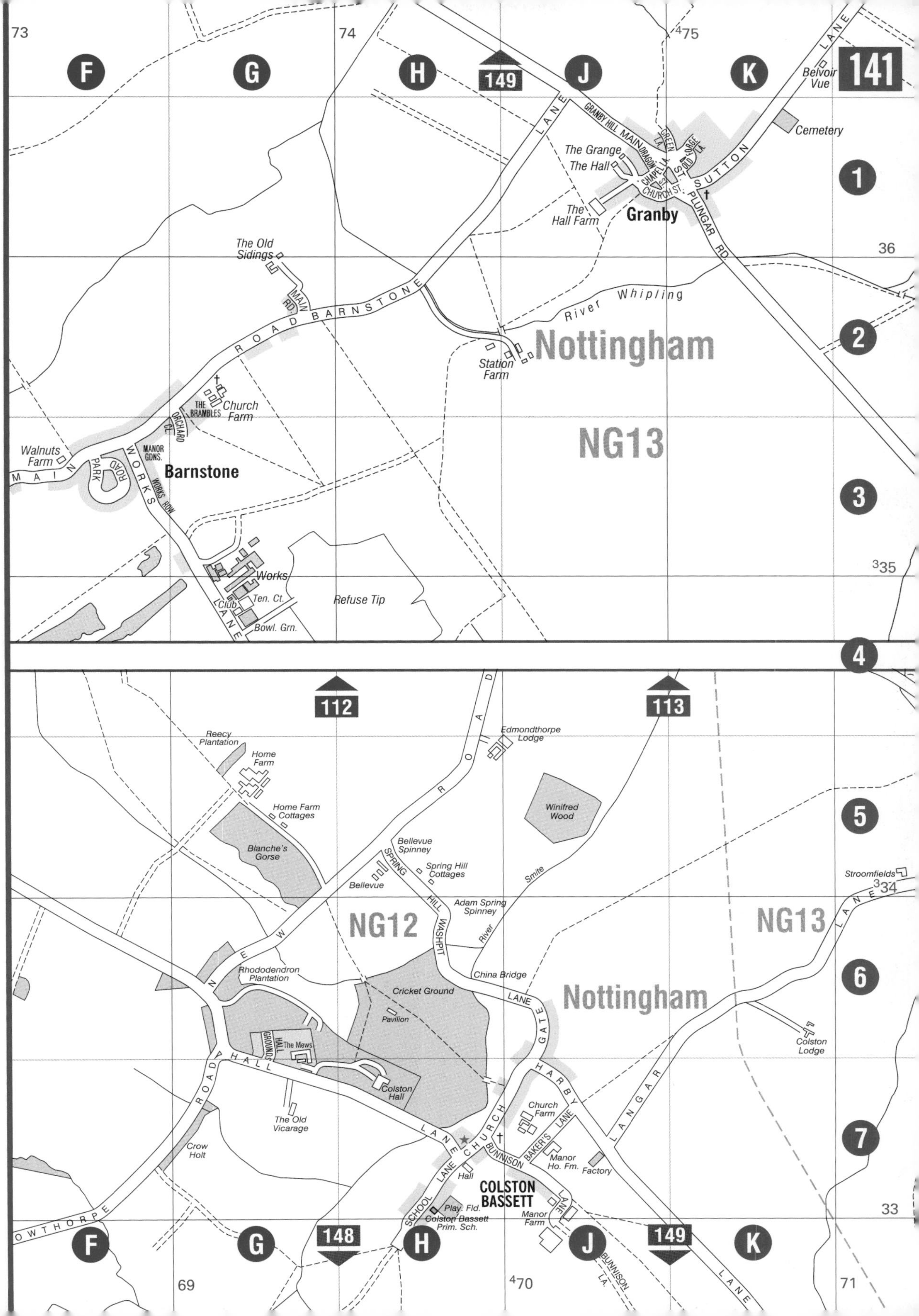
73
74
75
F
G
H
149
J
K
Belvoir Vue
Cemetery
LANE
GRANBY HILL
MAIN
DRAGON
GREEN LA.
ST.
OLD LA.
FORGE
The Grange
The Hall
CHAPEL LA.
CHURCH ST.
SUTTON
PLUNGAR RD.
The Hall Farm
Granby
1
36
The Old Sidings
MAIN RD.
BARNSTONE
ROAD
River Whipling
2
Nottingham
Station Farm
THE BRAMBLES
Church Farm
ORCHARD CL.
NG13
Walnuts Farm
MAIN
PARK ROAD
MANOR GDNS.
WORKS
Barnstone
WORKS ROW
3
Works
35
Club
Ten. Ct.
Refuse Tip
LANE
Bowl. Grn.
4
112
113
ROAD
Edmondthorpe Lodge
Reecy Plantation
Home Farm
Winifred Wood
Home Farm Cottages
5
Blanche's Gorse
Bellevue Spinney
SPRING
Spring Hill Cottages
Bellevue
Smite
Stroomfields
34
HILL
Adam Spring Spinney
NG12
WASHPIT
NEW
River
NG13
LANE
6
China Bridge
Rhododendron Plantation
Cricket Ground
LANE
Nottingham
Pavilion
GATE
GROUNDS
HALL
The Mews
Colston Lodge
HALL
ROAD
HARBY
Colston Hall
Church Farm
LANGAR
The Old Vicarage
LANE
CHURCH
BAKER'S LANE
7
Crow Holt
BUNNISON
Manor Ho. Fm.
Factory
Hall
SCHOOL LANE
COLSTON BASSETT
Play. Fld.
Colston Bassett Prim. Sch.
Manor Farm
LANE
33
OWTHORPE
F
148
G
H
J
149
K
BUNNISON LA.
LANE
69
70
71

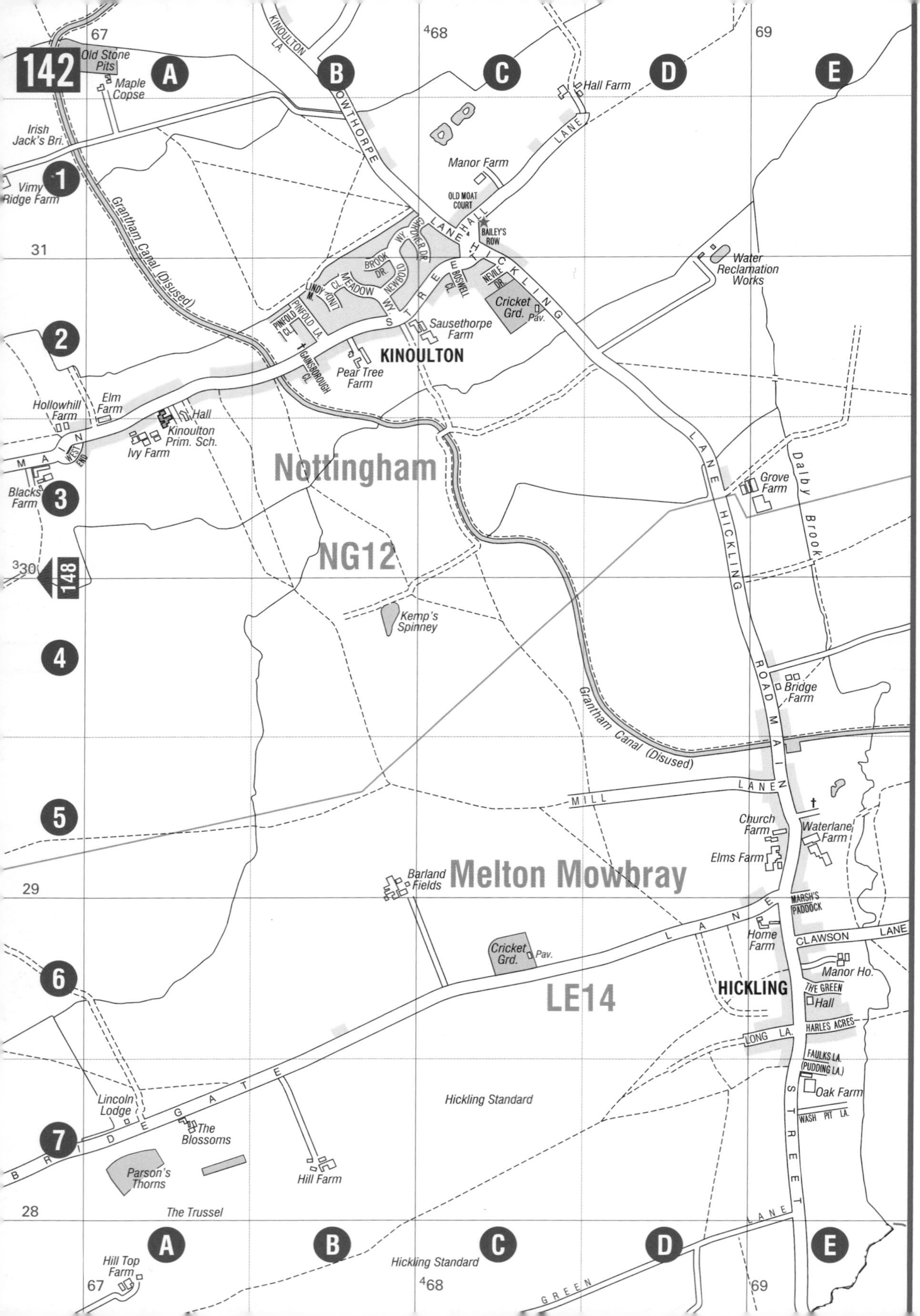

142
67
468
69
A
B
C
D
E
Old Stone Pits
Maple Copse
Irish Jack's Bri.
Vimy Ridge Farm
1
KINOULTON LA.
OWTHORPE
Hall Farm
LANE
Manor Farm
OLD MOAT COURT
BAILEY'S ROW
HALL LANE
31
Grantham Canal (Disused)
BROOK DR.
MEADOW CL.
NEWBOLD WY.
GARDNER DR.
LINDY M.
LINDEN CL.
PINFOLD LA.
PINFOLD CL.
W. STREET
BOSWELL CL.
NEVILE DR.
Cricket Grd.
Pav.
HICKLING
Water Reclamation Works
2
Sausethorpe Farm
KINOULTON
Pear Tree Farm
GAINSBOROUGH CL.
Hollowhill Farm
Elm Farm
Hall
Kinoulton Prim. Sch.
Ivy Farm
MAIN
WEST END
Nottingham
3
Blacks' Farm
LANE
Grove Farm
Dalby Brook
NG12
330
148
HICKLING
Kemp's Spinney
4
ROAD
Bridge Farm
MAIN
Grantham Canal (Disused)
MILL
LANE
5
Church Farm
Waterlane Farm
Elms Farm
29
Barland Fields
Melton Mowbray
MARSH'S PADDOCK
LANE
Home Farm
CLAWSON LANE
Cricket Grd.
Pav.
Manor Ho.
6
HICKLING
LE14
THE GREEN
Hall
HARLES ACRES
LONG LA.
FAULKS LA. (PUDDING LA.)
Oak Farm
Lincoln Lodge
BRIDEGATE
Hickling Standard
WASH PIT LA.
STREET
7
The Blossoms
Parson's Thorns
Hill Farm
28
The Trussel
LANE
Hill Top Farm
Hickling Standard
GREEN
67
468
69

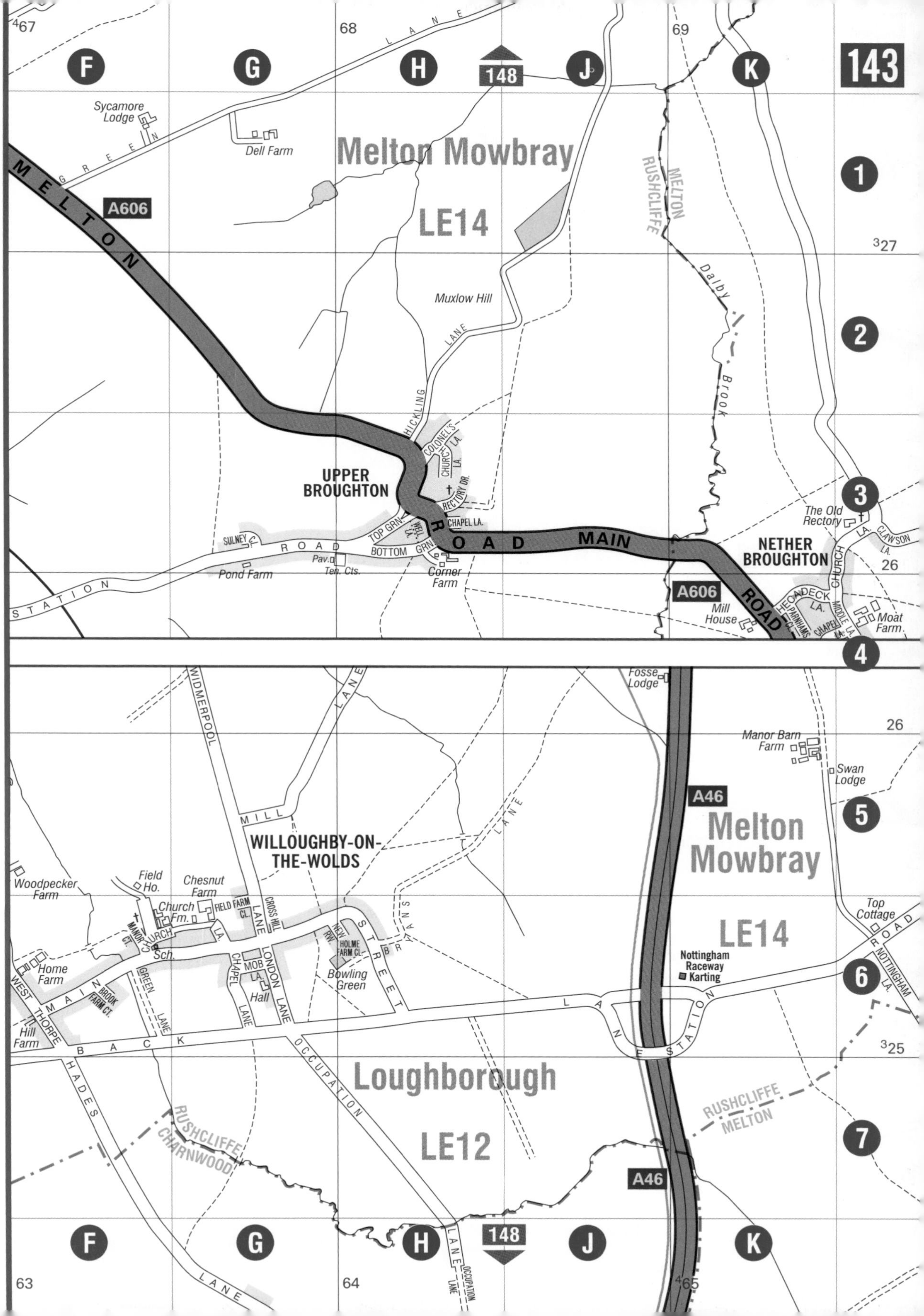
148
Sycamore Lodge
Dell Farm
Melton Mowbray
LE14
MELTON
A606
GREEN LANE
Muxlow Hill
HICKLING LANE
RUSHCLIFFE
MELTON
Dalby Brook
UPPER BROUGHTON
COLONEL'S LA.
CHURCH LA.
RECTORY DR.
CHAPEL LA.
TOP GRN.
WELL LA.
BOTTOM GRN.
SULNEY CL.
ROAD
Pav.
Ten. Cts.
Pond Farm
Corner Farm
STATION ROAD
MAIN ROAD
A606
Mill House
NETHER BROUGHTON
The Old Rectory
CLAWSON LA.
CHURCH LA.
HECADECK LA.
PARNHAMS CL.
CHAPEL LA.
MIDDLE LA.
Moat Farm
Fosse Lodge
WIDMERPOOL LANE
MILL LANE
LANE
Manor Barn Farm
Swan Lodge
A46
Melton Mowbray
WILLOUGHBY-ON-THE-WOLDS
Field Ho.
Chesnut Farm
Woodpecker Farm
Church Fm.
FIELD FARM CL.
CROSS HILL LANE
MANOR CT.
CHURCH LA.
Sch.
NEW RW.
HOLME FARM CL.
BRANS
STREET
Home Farm
GREEN LANE
CHAPEL LANE
MOB LA.
LONDON LANE
Hall
Bowling Green
WEST THORPE
MAIN
BROOK FARM CT.
Hill Farm
BACK LANE
STATION LANE
LE14
Top Cottage
ROAD
NOTTINGHAM LA.
Nottingham Raceway Karting
Loughborough
OCCUPATION
HADES LANE
RUSHCLIFFE
CHARNWOOD
LE12
RUSHCLIFFE
MELTON
A46
OCCUPATION LANE
148
F
G
H
J
K
1
2
3
4
5
6
7
467
68
69
327
26
26
325
63
64
465

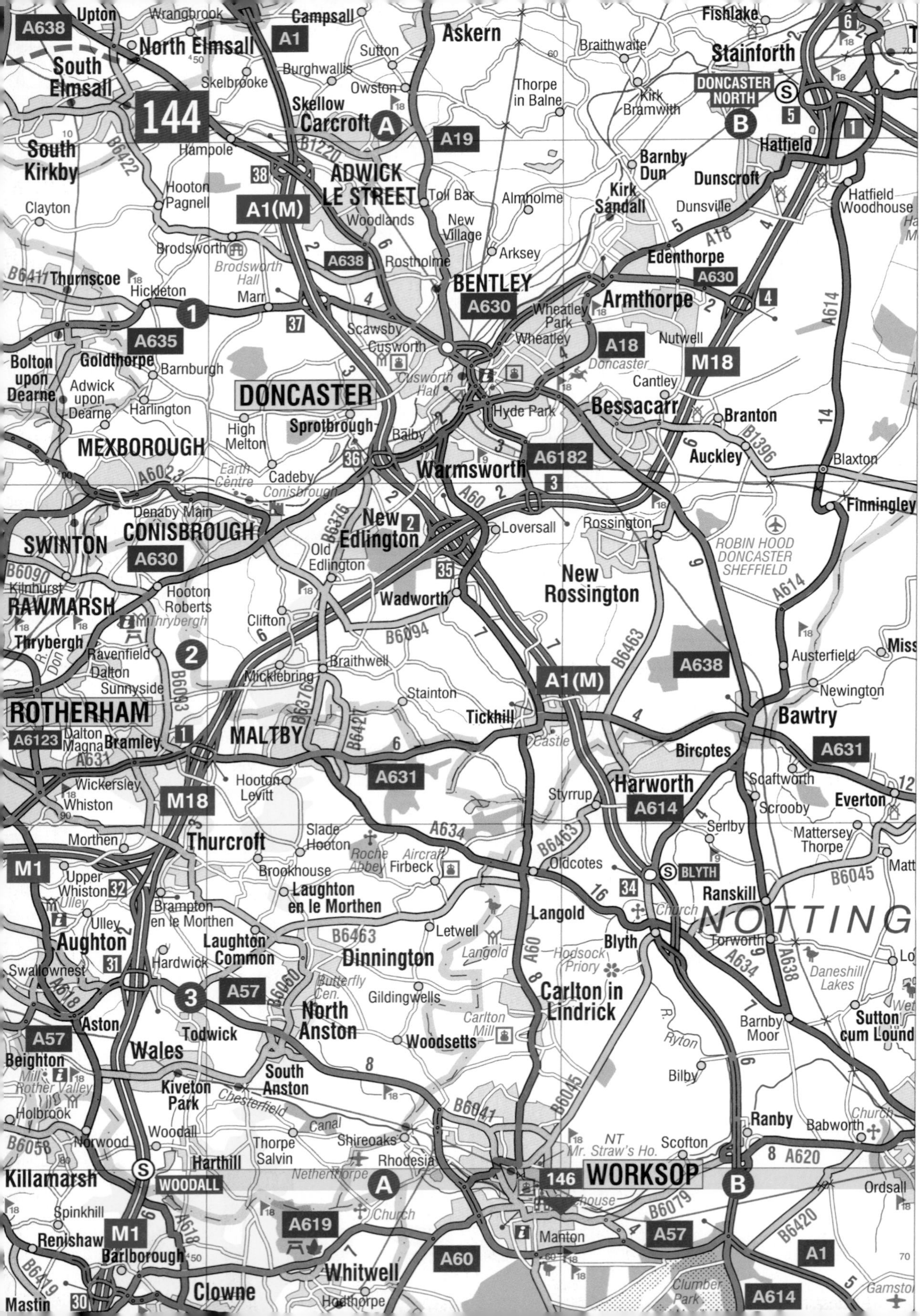
144
A638
Upton
Wrangbrook
Campsall
Askern
Fishlake
North Elmsall
A1
South Elmsall
Sutton
Braithwaite
Stainforth
Skelbrooke
Burghwallis
Owston
Thorpe in Balne
Kirk Bramwith
DONCASTER NORTH
Skellow
Carcroft
A19
Hatfield
South Kirkby
Hampole
B6422
B1220
ADWICK LE STREET
Barnby Dun
Dunscroft
Hooton Pagnell
A1(M)
Toll Bar
Almholme
Kirk Sandall
Dunsville
Hatfield Woodhouse
Clayton
Woodlands
New Village
Arksey
A18
Brodsworth
Brodsworth Hall
A638
Rostholme
Edenthorpe
B6411
Thurnscoe
Hickleton
Marr
BENTLEY
A630
Armthorpe
A630
Wheatley Park
Wheatley
A18
Nutwell
A614
A635
Goldthorpe
Scawsby
Cusworth
Cusworth Hall
Doncaster
M18
Bolton upon Dearne
Barnburgh
Adwick upon Dearne
Harlington
DONCASTER
Cantley
Hyde Park
Bessacarr
Branton
High Melton
Sprotbrough
Balby
MEXBOROUGH
Auckley
B1396
Blaxton
A6182
Warmsworth
Earth Centre
Cadeby
A6023
Conisbrough
A60
Finningley
Denaby Main
CONISBROUGH
B6376
New Edlington
Loversall
Rossington
SWINTON
A630
Old Edlington
ROBIN HOOD DONCASTER SHEFFIELD
B6090
Kilnhurst
Hooton Roberts
Wadworth
New Rossington
RAWMARSH
Thrybergh
Clifton
B6094
A614
Thrybergh
Ravenfield
B6463
Austerfield
Dalton
B6093
Braithwell
Micklebring
A638
Sunnyside
A1(M)
Newington
ROTHERHAM
Stainton
Tickhill
Bawtry
A6123
Dalton Magna
Bramley
MALTBY
B6427
Castle
Bircotes
A631
A631
A631
Scaftworth
Wickersley
Hooton Levitt
Harworth
Everton
Whiston
M18
Styrrup
A614
Scrooby
Serlby
Mattersey Thorpe
Morthen
Thurcroft
Slade Hooton
A634
B6463
M1
Upper Whiston
Roche Abbey
Aircraft
Brookhouse
Firbeck
Oldcotes
BLYTH
B6045
Laughton en le Morthen
Ranskill
Ulley
Brampton en le Morthen
Langold
Church
NOTTING
Letwell
Blyth
Torworth
Aughton
Laughton Common
B6463
Langold
Dinnington
A60
Hodsock Priory
A634
A638
Daneshill Lakes
Swallownest
Hardwick
A618
A57
B6060
Butterfly Cen.
Gildingwells
Carlton in Lindrick
Aston
North Anston
Barnby Moor
Sutton cum Lound
A57
Todwick
Carlton Mill
Woodsetts
Ryton
Beighton
Wales
South Anston
Rother Valley
Bilby
Kiveton Park
Chesterfield
Holbrook
B6041
B6045
Ranby
Babworth
Norwood
Woodall
Canal
Shireoaks
NT
Mr. Straw's Ho.
Scofton
B6058
Thorpe Salvin
A620
Harthill
Rhodesia
Killamarsh
WOODALL
Netherthorpe
146
WORKSOP
Ordsall
Spinkhill
A619
Church
B6079
B6420
Renishaw
M1
A618
Manton
A57
Barlborough
A60
A1
B6419
Whitwell
Clowne
Clumber Park
A614
Mastin
Hodthorpe
Gamston

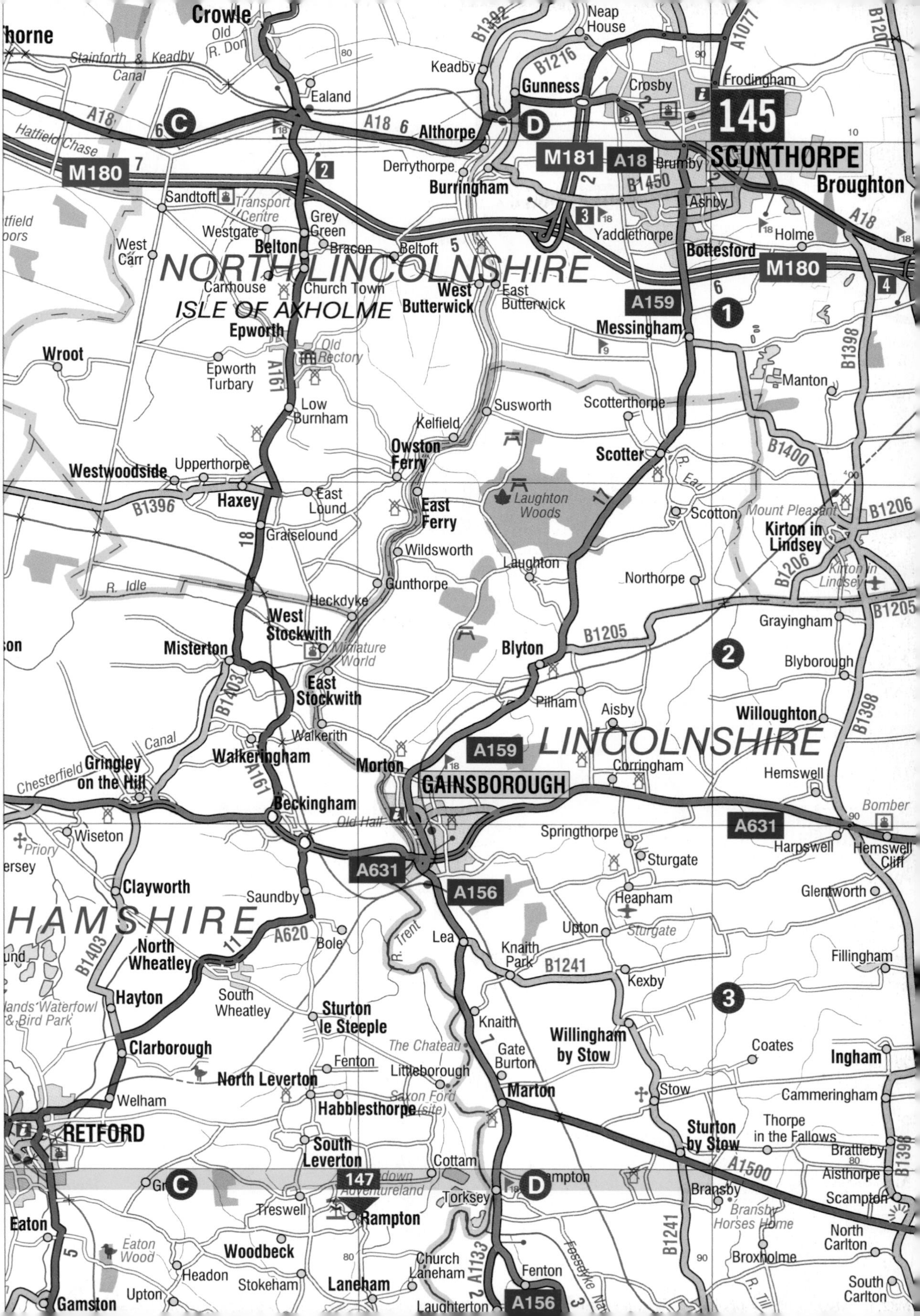

145
SCUNTHORPE
NORTH LINCOLNSHIRE
ISLE OF AXHOLME
LINCOLNSHIRE
HAMSHIRE
GAINSBOROUGH
RETFORD
147
Crowle
horne
Old R. Don
Stainforth & Keadby Canal
Hatfield Chase
Ealand
Keadby
Neap House
Gunness
Crosby
Frodingham
Althorpe
Derrythorpe
Burringham
Brumby
Broughton
Ashby
Yaddlethorpe
Bottesford
Holme
Sandtoft
Transport Centre
Westgate
Grey Green
Belton
Bracon
Beltoft
West Carr
tfield oors
Carrhouse
Church Town
West Butterwick
East Butterwick
Messingham
Epworth
Old Rectory
Wroot
Epworth Turbary
Manton
Susworth
Scotterthorpe
Low Burnham
Kelfield
Owston Ferry
Scotter
R. Eau
Westwoodside
Upperthorpe
Haxey
East Lound
East Ferry
Laughton Woods
Scotton
Mount Pleasant
Kirton in Lindsey
Graiseland
Wildsworth
Laughton
Northorpe
R. Idle
Gunthorpe
Heckdyke
West Stockwith
Miniature World
Misterton
Blyton
Grayingham
Blyborough
East Stockwith
Pilham
Aisby
Willoughton
Walkerith
Canal
Chesterfield
Gringley on the Hill
Walkeringham
Morton
Corringham
Hemswell
Beckingham
Old Hall
Bomber
Wiseton
Priory
Springthorpe
Sturgate
Harpswell
Hemswell Cliff
ersey
Clayworth
Saundby
Heapham
Glentworth
Bole
R. Trent
Lea
Upton
Knaith Park
North Wheatley
Kexby
Fillingham
und
Hayton
South Wheatley
Knaith
lands Waterfowl & Bird Park
Sturton le Steeple
The Chateau
Willingham by Stow
Coates
Ingham
Clarborough
Fenton
Gate Burton
Littleborough
North Leverton
Saxon Ford (site)
Marton
Stow
Cammeringham
Welham
Habblesthorpe
Sturton by Stow
Thorpe in the Fallows
Brattleby
South Leverton
Cottam
Aisthorpe
Adventureland
Torksey
Bransby
Scampton
Treswell
Rampton
Bransby Horses Home
Eaton
Eaton Wood
Woodbeck
North Carlton
Headon
Church Laneham
Broxholme
Fenton
Stokeham
Laneham
Upton
South Carlton
Gamston
Laughterton
Fossdyke Nav
R. Till
M180
M181
A18
A159
A161
A631
A156
A620
A1500
A1133
A1077
B1392
B1216
B1450
B1398
B1400
B1206
B1205
B1396
B1403
B1241
B1207

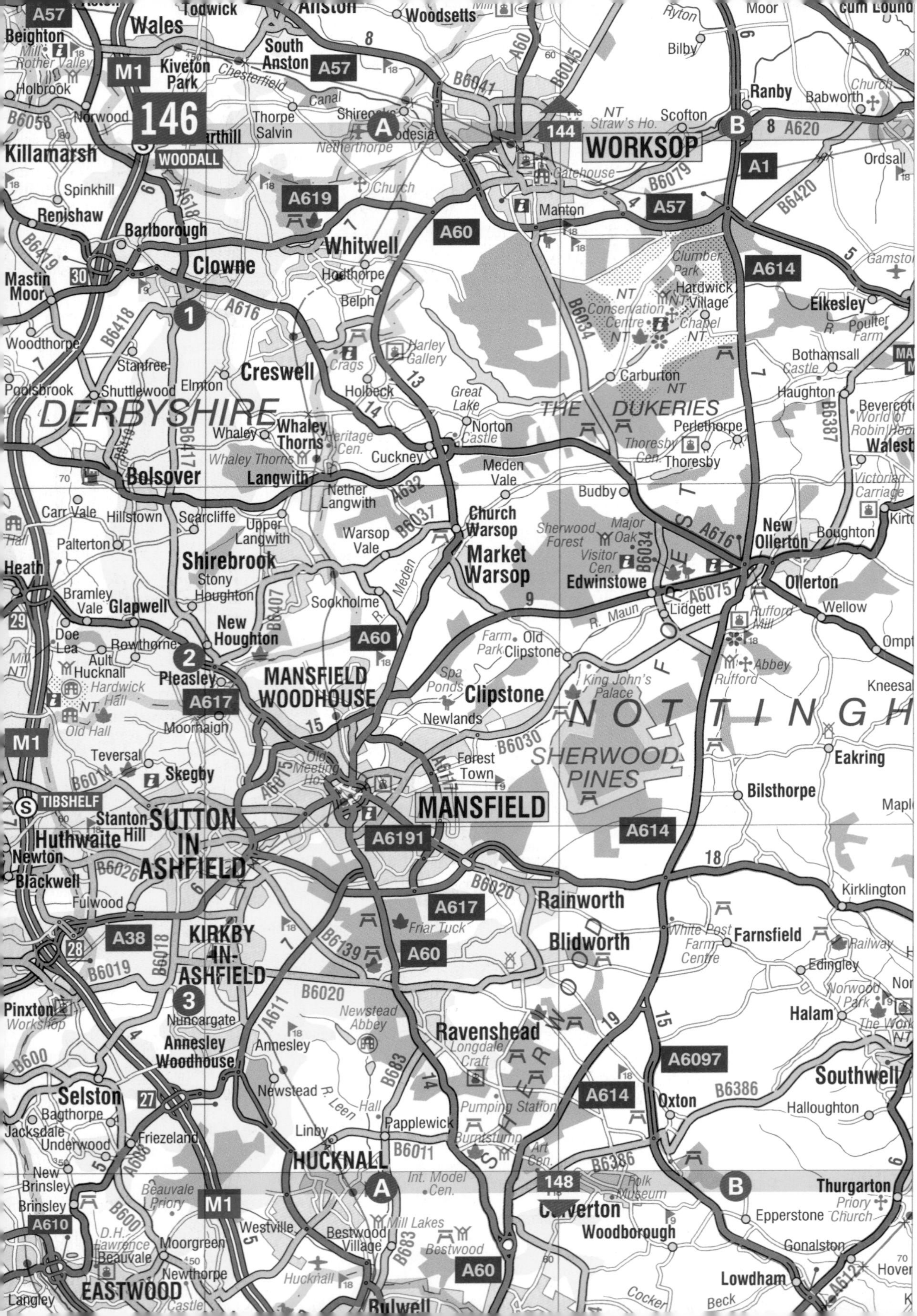

A57
Todwick
Anston
Woodsetts
Ryton
Moor
Cum Lound
Wales
Beighton
South Anston
A57
Bilby
M1
Kiveton Park
Rother Valley
Chesterfield Canal
B6041
B6045
A60
Holbrook
146
Norwood
Thorpe Salvin
Shireoaks
A
Rhodesia
Ranby
Babworth
Church
B6058
Harthill
NT Straw's Ho.
Scofton
B
A620
Killamarsh
WOODALL
Netherthorpe
144
WORKSOP
A1
Ordsall
Spinkhill
A619
Church
Gatehouse
B6079
Renishaw
A618
Manton
A57
B6420
Barlborough
A60
Whitwell
Mastin Moor
30
Clowne
Hodthorpe
Clumber Park
A614
Gamston
B6419
Belph
NT
Hardwick Village
Elkesley
1
A616
NT Conservation Centre
Chapel
R. Poulter
Woodthorpe
B6418
Crags
Harley Gallery
Farm
B6034
NT
Bothamsall
Stanfree
Creswell
Castle
Carburton
Poolsbrook
Shuttlewood
Elmton
Holbeck
13
NT
Haughton
Great Lake
THE DUKERIES
B6387
DERBYSHIRE
14
Bevercotes
World of Robin Hood
Whaley
Whaley Thorns
Heritage Cen.
Norton
Castle
Perlethorpe
B6417
Whaley Thorns
Cuckney
Thoresby Cen.
Thoresby
Walesby
Bolsover
Langwith
Meden Vale
Victorian Carriage
Nether Langwith
A632
Budby
Carr Vale
Hillstown
Scarcliffe
Upper Langwith
B6031
Church Warsop
Hall
Palterton
Warsop Vale
Sherwood Forest
Major Oak
New Ollerton
Boughton
Shirebrook
Market Warsop
Visitor Cen.
B6034
A616
Heath
Stony Houghton
Meden
Edwinstowe
Ollerton
Bramley Vale
Glapwell
B6407
Sookholme
R. Meden
9
A6075
29
R. Maun
Lidgett
Wellow
Doe Lea
New Houghton
A60
Rufford Mill
Rowthorne
Farm Park
Old Clipstone
Ompton
Mill NT
Ault Hucknall
2
Abbey
Pleasley
MANSFIELD WOODHOUSE
Spa Ponds
King John's Palace
Rufford
Hardwick Hall
Kneesall
NT
A617
Clipstone
NOTTINGH
Old Hall
Moorhaigh
15
Newlands
M1
B6030
Eakring
Teversal
Old Meeting Ho.
A6117
Forest Town
SHERWOOD PINES
Skegby
B6014
A6075
TIBSHELF
Stanton Hill
SUTTON IN ASHFIELD
MANSFIELD
Bilsthorpe
Maplebeck
Huthwaite
A6191
A614
Newton
Blackwell
18
B6026
B6020
Rainworth
Kirklington
Fulwood
A617
A38
KIRKBY IN ASHFIELD
Friar Tuck
White Post Farm Centre
Farnsfield
Railway
28
B6018
B6139
A60
Blidworth
B6019
Edingley
3
B6020
Norwood Park
Pinxton
Workshop
Nuncargate
Newstead Abbey
A611
Halam
Annesley Woodhouse
Annesley
Ravenshead
Longdale Craft
15
The Workhouse NT
A6097
B600
Southwell
Selston
27
Newstead
R. Leen
B683
A614
B6386
Oxton
Bagthorpe
Hall
Pumping Station
Halloughton
Jacksdale
Underwood
Friezeland
Linby
Papplewick
Burntstump
Art Cen.
New Brinsley
A608
HUCKNALL
B6011
B6386
Int. Model Cen.
148
Folk Museum
B
Thurgarton
Priory Church
Brinsley
Beauvale Priory
M1
B600
A
Calverton
Epperstone
A610
Westville
Mill Lakes
Bestwood Village
Woodborough
Gonalston
D.H. Lawrence
Moorgreen
Beauvale
B683
Bestwood
A60
Newthorpe
Hucknall
Lowdham
A612
Hoveringham
Langley
EASTWOOD
Castle
Bulwell
Cocker Beck

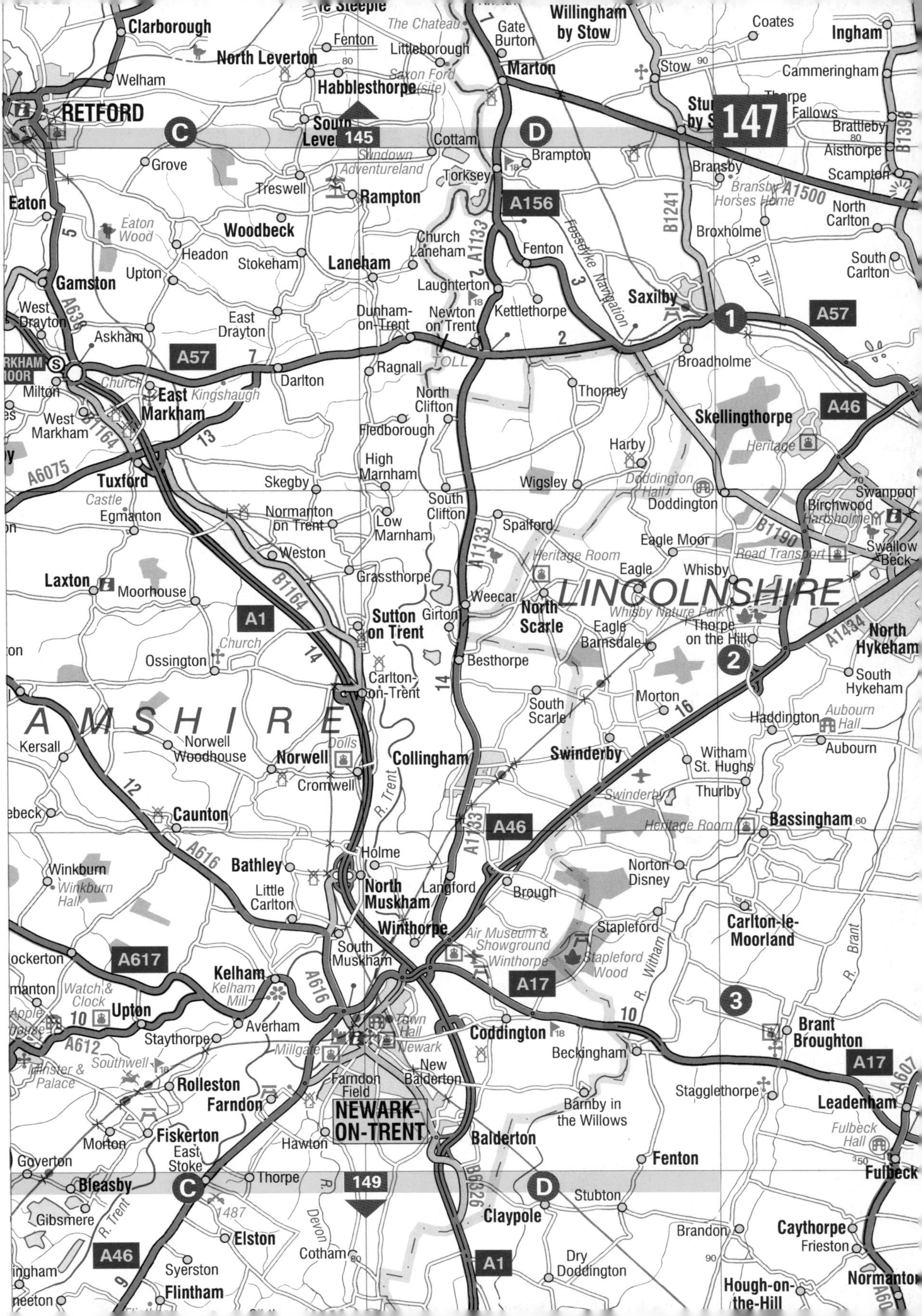

Clarborough
North Leverton
Fenton
Littleborough
The Chateau
Gate Burton
Willingham by Stow
Coates
Ingham
Welham
Habblesthorpe
Saxon Ford (site)
Marton
Stow
Cammeringham
RETFORD
South Leverton
145
147
Thorpe le Fallows
Brattleby
Aisthorpe
B1398
C
D
Cottam
Brampton
Grove
Sundown Adventureland
Torksey
Bransby
Scampton
Eaton
Treswell
Rampton
A156
Bransby Horses Home
A1500
North Carlton
Eaton Wood
Woodbeck
A1133
Fossdyke Navigation
B1241
Broxholme
Headon
Stokeham
Church Laneham
Laneham
Fenton
South Carlton
Gamston
Upton
Laughterton
R. Till
West Drayton
A638
East Drayton
Dunham-on-Trent
Newton on Trent
Kettlethorpe
Saxilby
A57
Askham
TOLL
Broadholme
MARKHAM MOOR
A57
Darlton
Ragnall
Milton
Church
East Markham
Kingshaugh
North Clifton
Thorney
A46
West Markham
B1164
Fledborough
Skellingthorpe
Heritage
Harby
A6075
Tuxford
High Marnham
Skegby
Wigsley
Doddington Hall
Swanpool
Castle
South Clifton
Doddington
Birchwood
Hartsholme
Egmanton
Normanton on Trent
Low Marnham
Spalford
B1190
Eagle Moor
Swallow Beck
Weston
Heritage Room
Road Transport
A1133
Eagle
Whisby
Laxton
Moorhouse
Grassthorpe
LINCOLNSHIRE
Weecar
North Scarle
Whisby Nature Park
B1164
A1
Sutton on Trent
Girton
Eagle Barnsdale
Thorpe on the Hill
A1434
North Hykeham
Church
Ossington
Besthorpe
Carlton-on-Trent
South Hykeham
Morton
South Scarle
AMSHIRE
Haddington
Aubourn Hall
Kersall
Norwell Woodhouse
Dolls
Norwell
Collingham
Swinderby
Witham St. Hughs
Aubourn
Cromwell
Swinderby
Thurlby
R. Trent
Caunton
Heritage Room
Bassingham
A46
A616
Bathley
Holme
Norton Disney
Winkburn
Winkburn Hall
Little Carlton
North Muskham
Langford
Brough
Carlton-le-Moorland
Winthorpe
Air Museum & Showground
Stapleford
South Muskham
Winthorpe
Stapleford Wood
R. Brant
Brant
A617
Kelham
Kelham Mill
A616
A17
R. Witham
Watch & Clock
Upton
Town Hall
Coddington
Brant Broughton
Averham
Staythorpe
Millgate
Newark
Beckingham
A612
Southwell
New Balderton
A17
Minster & Palace
Rolleston
Farndon Field
Stagglethorpe
Farndon
NEWARK-ON-TRENT
Barnby in the Willows
Leadenham
Fiskerton
Hawton
Balderton
Fulbeck Hall
Morton
East Stoke
Fenton
Goverton
Fulbeck
Bleasby
Thorpe
149
Stubton
R. Devon
B6326
Claypole
Gibsmere
R. Trent
Elston
Brandon
Caythorpe
Frieston
A46
Cotham
A1
Syerston
Dry Doddington
Flintham
Hough-on-the-Hill
Normanton
A607

Annesley Woodhouse
Annesley
Ravenshead
Longdale Craft
Southwell
B600
Selston
Newstead
R. Leen
Hall
B683
Pumping Station
A614
Oxton
A6097
B6386
Halloughton
Bagthorpe
Jacksdale
Underwood
148
27
Papplewick
Linby
Burntstump
A
B6011
146
B6386
B
New
Int. Model Cen.
Folk Museum
Thurgarton
Priory Church
Beauvale Priory
M1
Brinsley
A610
B600
HUCKNALL
Mill Lakes
Calverton
Epperstone
D.H. Lawrence
Westville
Bestwood Village
Woodborough
Gonalston
Aldercar
Moorgreen
Beauvale
B683
Bestwood
A60
Hover
Newthorpe
Hucknall
Lowdham
EASTWOOD
Castle
Cocker
Beck
Langley
Kimberley
Bulwell
ARNOLD
B684
A612
Shipley
Giltbrook
A6002
B6004
Lambley
Burton Joyce
Nuthall
A611
Woodthorpe
Bulcote
Gunthorpe
Cotmanhay
A6096
A610
Old Basford
A6211
Awsworth
Swingate
26
Sherwood
Mapperley
Gedling
A6097
American Adventure
Cossall
B682
Mapperley Park
Stoke Bardolph
Shelford
Strelley
B690
CARLTON
Newton
ILKESTON
TROWELL
Bilborough
A6514
A609
A6096
S
NOTTINGHAM
Radford
B686
Netherfield
Radcliffe on Trent
Newton
Saxondale
Hallam Fields
Colwick
Kirk Hallam
A609
Wollaton
New Lenton
Holme Pierrepont
Wollaton Hall
A612
Trowell
B6007
History & Indus.
Old Lenton
Nottingham
Harlequin
Stanton by Dale
Bramcote
Meadows
A6011
Hall
A52
STAPLEFORD
B6006
A6005
Wilford
A606
Gamston
Bassingfield
Stragglethorpe
Cropwell Butler
Sandiacre
B6003
Beeston Canal
B679
WEST BRIDGFORD
Nottingham
NOTTINGHA
Risley
BEESTON
Rylands
Cotgrave
Chilwell
Attenborough
A52
Edwalton
Cropwell Bishop
A52
25
Breaston
2
Toton
Clifton
Tollerton
Clipston
A6005
A6005
Canal
B680
Owthorpe
Barton in Fabis
Brook
Village
Plumtree
Normanton-on-the-Wolds
Church Wilne
LONG EATON
Ruddington
Framework Knitters'
Plumtree Park
Market Cross NT
Sawley
Transport Heritage Centre
A606
A46
Great Wilne
Trentlock
Thrumpton
A453
Fairham
Rushcliffe
Bradmore
Kinoulton
Cavendish Bridge
Gotham
Great Central Railway (Nottingham)
A60
Keyworth
Stanton-on-the-Wolds
Bunny
Hemington
24a
Ratcliffe on Soar
Lockington
Kingston on Soar
Widmerpool
Castle Donington
NOTTINGHAM EAST MIDLANDS
West Leake
Wysall
Kegworth
Kingston
Brook
24
Upper Broughton
River Soar
Willoughby-on-the-Wolds
Sutton Bonington
East Leake
Costock
Whatton
Diseworth
3
Rempstone
Old Dalby
DONINGTON PARK
23a
Long Whatton
A6006
A6006
Zouch
Wymeswold
LEICEST
Normanton on Soar
Dalby Wolds
Hathern
Stanford on Soar
Hoton
A42
Burton Wolds
A60
Prestwold
Grimston
M1
Belton
B5324
A6
Bell Foundry
Cotes
B676
Six Hills
A6006
Thorpe Acre
Burton on the Wolds
Shoby
Shepshed
Obelisk
Old Rectory
B676
Walton on the Wolds
A
B
Ragdale
Asfordby
A512
23
A512
LOUGHBOROUGH
Frisby on the Wreake
Ringing Hill
Shelthorpe
Seagrave
Hoby
Woodthorpe
Barrow upon Soar
Rotherby
Blackbrook Resr.
Nanpantan
Quorndon (Quorn)
Farm Park
A6
Sileby
A46
Thrussington
Brooksby
Abbey

Staythorpe
A612
Southwell
Minster & Palace
A46
Millgate
Newark
New Balderton
Farndon Field
Rolleston
Farndon
Coddington
Beckingham
NEWARK-ON-TRENT
Barnby in the Willows
Brant Broughton
A17
Stragglethorpe
Leadenham
A607
Morton
Fiskerton
Hawton
Balderton
Fenton
149
Fulbeck Hall
Fulbeck
Goverton
C
D
147
East Stoke
Thorpe
A1
B6326
Stubton
Bleasby
1487
Gibsmere
R. Trent
Claypole
Brandon
Caythorpe
Frieston
Elston
R. Devon
Cotham
Dry Doddington
Normanton
Syerston
Hough-on-the-Hill
Flintham
Flintham Hall
Sibthorpe
Shelton
Staunton in the Vale
Hougham
Carlton Scroop
Gelston
Long Bennington
Westborough
Screveton
Hawksworth
Flawborough
Kilvington
Marston
Marston Hall
River Witham
Honington
A153
Car Colston
Thoroton
Alverton
Foston
Foston Beck
Scarrington
Orston
LINCOLNSHIRE
Barkston
Syston
Bingham
Aslockton
Castle
Normanton
Allington
Whatton
Elton
Bottesford
Church
Easthorpe
GRANTHAM
B1174
Belton
Belton House NT
A52
Vale of Belvoir
Sutton
Muston
Sedgebrook
Great Gonerby
Manthorpe
Londonthorpe
Tithby
R. Smite
Gonerby Hill Foot
NT Grantham House
MSHIRE
Granby
Stenwith
Barrowby
Earlesfield
GRANTHAM
Barnstone
Redmile
Barkestone-le-Vale
Langar
Naturescape Wildflower Farm
Queen's Royal Lancers
Belvoir
Woolsthorpe
Colston Bassett
Plungar
Grantham Canal (dis.)
Belvoir Castle
Denton Resr.
Denton
Harlaxton
Harlaxton Manor
Woodnook
B6403
Little Ponton
Knipton
Harston
A607
Stroxton
Harby
Stathern
Knipton Resr.
Great Ponton
Hungerton
Wyville
Hose
Branston
Eastwell
Eaton
Croxton Kerrial
Water Spout Monument
Long Clawson
Stoke Rochford
Easton
Nether Broughton
Bescaby
Saltby
Skillington
Goadby Marwood
Clawson Hill
A606
Waltham on the Wolds
Woolsthorpe
NT Manor
Colsterworth
Scalford
Chadwell
Stonesby
Sproxton
A151
Holwell
ERSHIRE
Buckminster
Stainby
COLSTERWORTH
B676
Ab Kettleby
Potter Hill
Coston
Sewstern
Gunby
North Witham
Saxelby
Thorpe Arnold
Garthorpe
R. Eye
Asfordby Hill
A6006
Freeby
Saxby
South Witham
MELTON MOWBRAY
Wyfordby
Brentingby
Wymondham
Stapleford
Thistleton
R. Wreake
Kirby Bellars
A607
B6047
Burton Lazars
Edmondthorpe
Market Overton
RUTLAND
Teigh

INDEX

Including Streets, Places & Areas, Industrial Estates,
Flats & Walkways, Stations and Places of Interest.

HOW TO USE THIS INDEX

1. Each street name is followed by its Postcode District and then by its Locality abbreviation(s) and then by its map reference; e.g. **Abbeyfield Rd.** NG7: Lent . . . .1G **107** is in the NG7 Postcode District and the Lenton Locality and is to be found in square 1G on page **107**. The page number is shown in bold type.

2. A strict alphabetical order is followed in which Av., Rd., St., etc. (though abbreviated) are read in full and as part of the street name; e.g. **Ashcourt Gdns.** appears after **Ash Ct.** but before **Ash Cres.**

3. Streets and a selection of flats and walkways too small to be shown on street map pages **6-143**, appear in the index with the thoroughfare to which it is connected shown in brackets; e.g. **Albert Sq.** *NG7: Lent . . . . 5F **95** (off Church St.)*

4. Addresses that are in more than one part are referred to as not continuous.

5. Places and areas are shown in the index in **BLUE TYPE** and the map reference is to the actual map square in which the town centre or area is located and not to the place name shown on the map. Map references for entries that appear on street map pages **6-143** are shown first, with references to road map pages **144-149** shown in brackets; e.g. **ASPLEY 7C 84**

6. An example of a selected place of interest is D H Lawrence Birthplace Mus. 3D 72

7. An example of a station is **Aslockton Station (Rail) . . . . 4D 102.** Included are Rail **(Rail)**, Nottingham Express Transit **(NET)** and Park & Ride **(Park & Ride)**

8. Map references for entries that appear on large scale pages **6-7** are shown first, with small scale map references shown in brackets; e.g. **Abbotsford Dr.** NG3: Nott 2G **7** (2A **96**)

GENERAL ABBREVIATIONS

All. : Alley
App. : Approach
Arc. : Arcade
Av. : Avenue
Blvd. : Boulevard
Bri. : Bridge
Bldg. : Building
Bldgs. : Buildings
Bungs. : Bungalows
Bus. : Business
Cvn. : Caravan
C'way. : Causeway
Cen. : Centre
Chu. : Church
Circ. : Circle
Cir. : Circus
Cl. : Close
Comn. : Common
Cnr. : Corner
Cott. : Cottage
Cotts. : Cottages
Ct. : Court
Cres. : Crescent
Cft. : Croft
Dr. : Drive
E. : East
Emb. : Embankment
Ent. : Enterprise
Est. : Estate
Fld. : Field
Flds. : Fields
Gdns. : Gardens
Gth. : Garth
Ga. : Gate
Gt. : Great
Grn. : Green
Gro. : Grove
Hgts. : Heights
Ho. : House
Ho's. : Houses
Ind. : Industrial
Info. : Information
La. : Lane
Lit. : Little
Lwr. : Lower
Mnr. : Manor
Mkt. : Market
Mdw. : Meadow
Mdws. : Meadows
M. : Mews
Mt. : Mount
Mus. : Museum
Nth. : North
Pde. : Parade
Pk. : Park
Pas. : Passage
Pl. : Place
Pct. : Precinct
Prom. : Promenade
Ri. : Rise
Rd. : Road
Shop. : Shopping
Sth. : South
Sq. : Square
Sta. : Station
St. : Street
Ter. : Terrace
Trad. : Trading
Up. : Upper
Va. : Vale
Vw. : View
Vs. : Villas
Vis. : Visitors
Wlk. : Walk
W. : West
Yd. : Yard

LOCALITY ABBREVIATIONS

Ann : **Annesley**
Ann W : **Annesley Woodhouse**
Arn : **Arnold**
Aslo : **Aslockton**
Aspl : **Aspley**
Atten : **Attenborough**
Aver : **Averham**
Aws : **Awsworth**
Babb : **Babbington**
Babw : **Babworth**
Bagt : **Bagthorpe**
Bald : **Balderton**
Barn W : **Barnby in the Willows**
Barn M : **Barnby Moor**
Barns : **Barnstone**
Bart F : **Barton in Fabis**
Basf : **Basford**
Bath : **Bathley**
Bawt : **Bawtry**
Beck : **Beckingham**
Bee : **Beeston**
Best : **Besthorpe**
Bestw : **Bestwood**
Bestw V : **Bestwood Village**
Bilb : **Bilborough**
Bils : **Bilsthorpe**
Bing : **Bingham**
Birc : **Bircotes**
Blac : **Blackwell**
Blea : **Bleasby**
Blid : **Blidworth**
Blyth : **Blyth**
Bol : **Bolham**
Bou : **Boughton**
Bram : **Bramcote**
Brink : **Brinkley**
Brins : **Brinsley**
Brox : **Broxtowe**
Bud : **Budby**
Bulc : **Bulcote**
Bulw : **Bulwell**
Bunny : **Bunny**
Bur J : **Burton Joyce**
Calv : **Calverton**
Carb : **Carburton**
Car C : **Car Colston**
Carl : **Carlton**
Carl L : **Carlton in Lindrick**
Carl T : **Carlton-on-Trent**
Caus : **Causton**
Cayt : **Caythorpe**
Chil : **Chilwell**
Chu L : **Church Laneham**
Chu W : **Church Warsop**
Cin : **Cinderhill**
Clar : **Clarborough**
Clay : **Clayworth**
Clif : **Clifton**
C'ton : **Clipston**
C'tone : **Clipstone**
Codd : **Coddington**
Coll : **Collingham**
Cols B : **Colston Bassett**
Colw : **Colwick**
Coss : **Cossall**
Costh : **Costhorpe**
Costo : **Costock**
Cotg : **Cotgrave**
Cott : **Cottam**
Crom : **Cromwell**
Crop Bi : **Cropwell Bishop**
Crop Bu : **Cropwell Butler**
Cuck : **Cuckney**
Dane : **Danethorpe**
Darf : **Darfoulds**
Darl : **Darlton**
Drake : **Drakeholes**
Dri N : **Drisney Nook**
Dun T : **Dunham-on-Trent**
Eakr : **Eakring**
East B : **East Bridgford**
East L : **East Leake**
East M : **East Markham**
East S : **East Stoke**
Eastw : **Eastwood**
Eaton : **Eaton**
Edin : **Edingley**
Edwal : **Edwalton**
Edwin : **Edwinstowe**
Egma : **Egmanton**
Elk : **Elkesley**
Elston : **Elston**
Elton : **Elton**
Epp : **Epperstone**
Eve : **Everton**
Farnd : **Farndon**
Farns : **Farnsfield**
Fen : **Fenton**
Fir : **Firbeck**
Fis : **Fiskerton**
Flin : **Flintham**
Gam : **Gamston**
Gate : **Gateford**
Ged : **Gedling**
Gilt : **Giltbrook**
Girt : **Girton**
Gon : **Gonalston**
Goth : **Gotham**
Gran : **Granby**
Grass : **Grassthorpe**
Grea : **Greasley**
Gri H : **Gringley on the Hill**
Grove : **Grove**
Gun : **Gunthorpe**
Habb : **Habblesthorpe**
Halam : **Halam**
Harby : **Harby**

Harwe : **Harwell**
Harwo : **Harworth**
Hath : **Hathern**
Haw : **Hawton**
Hay : **Hayton**
Hea : **Heanor**
Hick : **Hickling**
Hick P : **Hickling Pastures**
High M : **High Marnham**
Hilc : **Hilcote**
Hock : **Hockerton**
Hods : **Hodsock**
Holb : **Holbeck**
Holb W : **Holbeck Woodhouse**
Hol : **Holme**
Hol P : **Holme Pierrepont**
Hove : **Hoveringham**
Huck : **Hucknall**
Huth : **Huthwaite**
Hyson G : **Hyson Green**
Ilk : **Ilkeston**
Jack : **Jacksdale**
Kel : **Kelham**
Kett : **Kettlethorpe**
Key : **Keyworth**
Kimb : **Kimberley**
King : **Kingston on Soar**
Kin : **Kinoulton**
Kirk A : **Kirkby-in-Ashfield**
Kirk : **Kirklington**
Kirt : **Kirton**
Knee : **Kneeton**
Lamb : **Lambley**
Lane : **Laneham**
Lang : **Langar**
Lang M : **Langley Mill**
Lango : **Langold**
Langw : **Langwith**
Lax : **Laxton**
Lent : **Lenton**
Lent A : **Lenton Abbey**
Lin : **Linby**
Lit C : **Little Carlton**
Long E : **Long Eaton**
Lound : **Lound**
Lowd : **Lowdham**
Mans : **Mansfield**
Mans W : **Mansfield Woodhouse**
Mapp : **Mapperley**
Mapp P : **Mapperley Park**
Mkt W : **Market Warsop**
Matt : **Mattersey**
Matt T : **Mattersey Thorpe**
Mayt : **Maythorne**
Mede V : **Meden Vale**
Miss : **Misson**
Mist : **Misterton**
Moor : **Moorhouse**
Mort : **Morton**
Neth B : **Nether Broughton**
Neth : **Netherfield**
Neth L : **Nether Langwith**
New T : **Newark-on-Trent**
New B : **New Balderton**
New H : **New Houghton**
Newi : **Newington**
New O : **New Ollerton**
News : **Newstead**
Newth : **Newthorpe**
Newton : **Newton**
Newt T : **Newton on Trent**
Norm : **Normanton**
Norm S : **Normanton on Soar**
Norm W : **Normanton-on-the-Wolds**
Norm T : **Normanton on Trent**
Nth C : **North Clifton**
Nth L : **North Leverton**
Nth M : **North Muskham**
Nth S : **North Scarle**
Nth W : **North Wheatley**
Nort : **Norton**
Norw : **Norwell**
Norw W : **Norwell Woodhouse**
Nott : **Nottingham**
Nuth : **Nuthall**
Old C : **Old Clipstone**
Oldc : **Oldcotes**
Oll : **Ollerton**
Omp : **Ompton**
Ord : **Ordsall**
Ors : **Orston**
Owt : **Owthorpe**
Oxt : **Oxton**
Pap : **Papplewick**
Perl : **Perlethorpe**
Pinx : **Pinxton**
Plea : **Pleasley**
Plum : **Plumtree**
Pye B : **Pye Bridge**
Rad T : **Radcliffe on Trent**
Radf : **Radford**
Ragn : **Ragnall**
Rain : **Rainworth**
Ramp : **Rampton**
Rans : **Ranskill**
Rave : **Ravenshead**
Redh : **Redhill**
Remp : **Rempstone**
Retf : **Retford**
Rhod : **Rhodesia**
Rock : **Rockley**
Roll : **Rolleston**
Rudd : **Ruddington**
Ruff : **Rufford**
Sand : **Sandiacre**
Saun : **Saundby**
Sax : **Saxilby**
Saxon : **Saxondale**
Scaf : **Scaftworth**
Scar : **Scarrington**
Scre : **Screveton**
Scro : **Scrooby**
Sels : **Selston**
Serl : **Serlby**
Shel : **Shelford**
Sher : **Sherwood**
Ship : **Shipley**
Shire : **Shireoaks**
Sibt : **Sibthorpe**
Skeg : **Skegby**
Sook : **Sookholme**
Sth C : **South Clifton**
Sth L : **South Leverton**
Sth M : **South Muskham**
Sth N : **South Normanton**
Sth S : **South Scarle**
Sout : **Southwell**
Sth W : **South Wheatley**
Stan : **Stanford on Soar**
Stan D : **Stanton-by-Dale**
Stan H : **Stanton Hill**
Stan W : **Stanton-on-the-Wolds**
Stap : **Stapleford**
Sto B : **Stoke Bardolph**
Sto H : **Stony Houghton**
Stre : **Strelley**
Stu S : **Sturton le Steeple**
Sty : **Styrrup**
Sut B : **Sutton Bonington**
Sut L : **Sutton cum Lound**
Sut A : **Sutton in Ashfield**
Sut T : **Sutton-on-Trent**
Swin : **Swinethorpe**
Syer : **Syerston**
Teve : **Teversal**
Thor : **Thorney**
Thru : **Thrumpton**
Thur : **Thurgarton**
Tibs : **Tibshelf**
Tick : **Tickhill**
Tith : **Tithby**
Toll : **Tollerton**
Top V : **Top Valley**
Torw : **Torworth**
Toton : **Toton**
Tres : **Treswell**
Trow : **Trowell**
Tuxf : **Tuxford**
Unde : **Underwood**
Upp B : **Upper Broughton**
Upton : **Upton**
Wale : **Walesby**
Walk : **Walkeringham**
Wall : **Wallingwells**
Wars : **Warsop Vale**
Want : **Watnall**
Welb : **Welbeck**
Welh : **Welham**
Well : **Wellow**
West Br : **West Bridgford**
West Bu : **West Burton**
West D : **West Drayton**
West L : **West Leake**
West M : **West Markham**
West S : **West Stockwith**
Weston : **Weston**
Westw : **Westwood**
Whal T : **Whaley Thorns**
What : **Whatton**
Widm : **Widmerpool**
Wigs : **Wigsley**
Wigt : **Wigthorpe**
Wil : **Wilford**
Will W : **Willoughby on the Wolds**
Wint : **Winthorpe**
Wise : **Wiseton**
Woll : **Wollaton**
Woodbe : **Woodbeck**
Woodbo : **Woodborough**
Woods : **Woodsetts**
Woodt : **Woodthorpe**
Work : **Worksop**
Wym : **Wymeswold**
Wys : **Wysall**

A

Aaron Cl. NG11: Wil 2J **107**
Abba Cl. NG16: Kimb 7K **73**
Abbey Bri. NG7: Lent 6F **95**
Abbey Cir. NG2: West Br 2D **108**
Abbey Cl. NG13: Aslo 3C **102**
NG15: Huck 6E **66**
Abbey Ct. NG7: Lent 4G **95**
NG9: Bee 1A **106**
NG18: Mans 3B **48**
Abbeydale Dr. NG18: Mans 7K **47**
Abbey Dr. NG9: Bee 2A **106**
Abbeyfield Rd. NG7: Lent 1G **107**
Abbey Gro. NG3: Nott 1C **96**
Abbey Ho. Hall NG7: Nott 1B **106**
Abbey La. NG13: Aslo 3B **102**
Abbey M. DN10: Matt 2H **15**
Abbey Rd. DN10: Matt 2J **15**
NG2: West Br 2D **108**
NG9: Bee 1A **106**
NG13: Bing 3H **101**
NG15: News 6E **60**
NG16: Eastw 4F **73**
NG17: Kirk A 6C **52**
NG18: Mans 3A **48**
NG21: Blid 6K **55**
NG21: Edwin 7F **37**
Abbey St. NG7: Lent 6F **95**
S80: Work 3G **21**
Abbot Cl. NG12: Key 6H **117**
Abbotsbury Cl. NG5: Top V 5K **75**
Abbots Cl. NG5: Arn 1A **86**
Abbots Dr. NG15: Huck 7E **66**
Abbotsford Dr. NG3: Nott 2G **7** (2A **96**)
Abbots Rd. NG15: Huck 7E **66**
Abbot St. NG16: Aws 3B **82**
Abbots Wlk. NG15: Huck 7E **66**
Abbots Way NG8: Woll 4C **94**
Abbott Cres. NG22: Farns 4K **57**
Abbott Lea NG19: Mans 2D **46**
Abbott Rd. NG19: Mans 3C **46**
Abbotts Cft. NG19: Mans 1E **46**
Abbott's Way NG24: New T 7E **134**
Abercarn Cl. NG6: Bulw 7H **75**
Abercarn M. NG6: Bulw 7H **75**
Aberconway St. NG21: Blid 6J **55**
Aberdeen St. NG3: Nott 4J **7** (3B **96**)
Aberford Av. NG8: Basf 7E **84**
Abingdon Dr. NG11: Rudd 2A **116**
Abingdon Gdns. NG5: Woodt 2D **86**
NG9: Chil 5J **105**
Abingdon Rd. NG2: West Br 2D **108**
Abingdon Sq. NG8: Aspl 6C **84**
Abingdon Vw. S81: Gate 4D **18**
Abington Av. NG17: Skeg 5K **45**
AB KETTLEBY **3C 149**
Ablard Gdns. NG9: Chil 7H **105**
Acacia Av. NG17: Ann W 4A **60**
Acacia Cl. NG15: Huck 1H **75**
S80: Work 3D **20**
Acacia Ct. NG3: Nott 1H **7** (2A **96**)
NG19: Mans W 1A **48**
Acacia Cres. NG4: Carl 7J **87**
Acacia Gdns. NG16: Want 6K **73**
Acacia Rd. NG24: New B 4G **137**
Acacia Wlk. NG9: Bee 3A **106**
Academy Cl. NG6: Basf 4E **84**
Acaster Cl. NG9: Bee 5C **106**
Access 26 Bus. Pk. NG16: Lang M 3A **72**
Acer Cl. NG16: Pinx 1A **58**
Ackford Dr. S80: Work 2E **20**
Acle Gdns. NG6: Bulw 5H **75**
Acorn Av. NG16: Gilt 6F **73**
(not continuous)
Acorn Bank NG2: West Br 5J **107**
Acorn Bus. Pk. NG18: Mans 4H **47**
Acorn Cen. NG16: Lang M 3A **72**
Acorn Cl. NG24: New B 4F **137**
Acorn Dr. NG4: Ged 4K **87**
Acorn Pk. NG7: Lent 1F **107**
Acorn Vw. NG17: Kirk A 5C **52**
Acorn Way NG18: Mans 6D **48**
A'court St. NG7: Hyson G 2G **95**
Acre, The NG17: Kirk A 1B **60**
Acre Cl. NG2: West Br 7F **97**

Angletarn Cl. NG2: West Br 3F 109
Anglia Way NG18: Mans 7D 48
Anglia Way Ind. Est. NG18: Mans 7D 48
Angrave Cl. NG3: Nott 1K 7 (1B 96)
Angrave Rd. LE12: East L 1A 122
Angus Cl. NG5: Arn 5K 77
NG16: Kimb 2F 83
Anmer Cl. NG2: Nott 7J 95
Annan Ct. NG8: Aspl 7C 84
Anne's Cl. NG3: Mapp 5D 86
ANNESLEY 4B 60 (3A 146)
Annesley Cutting NG15: Ann 4B 60
Annesley Gro. NG1: Nott 1D 6 (2J 95)
Annesley La. NG16: Sels 6E 58
ANNESLEY LANE END 5F 59
Annesley Rd. NG2: West Br 2C 108
NG15: Ann 6B 60
(not continuous)
NG15: Huck 2D 66
Annesley Way NG19: Mans 4D 46
ANNESLEY WOODHOUSE 4K 59 (3A 146)
Annies Cl. NG15: Huck 1F 75
Annual Head La. NG25: Mort 5F 139
Anslow Av. NG9: Lent A 1B 106
NG17: Skeg 5K 45
Anson Cl. S81: Work 4F 19
Anson Ter. NG7: Hyson G 1G 95
Anstey Ri. NG3: Nott 3C 96
Anston Av. S81: Work 7F 19
Anthony Wharton Ct. NG11: Clif 6F 107
Antill St. NG9: Stap 3C 104
Apollo Dr. NG6: Bulw 2A 84
Appin Rd. NG19: Mans 5D 46
Appleby Cl. NG24: New T 1G 137
Appleby Ct. S81: Work 4G 19
Appleby Rd. NG19: New H 3A 40
Appledore Av. NG8: Woll 6J 93
Appledorne Way NG5: Arn 5G 77
Appleton Cl. NG11: Clif 2D 114
Appleton Ct. NG9: Bee 5C 106
Appleton Gdns. NG3: Mapp 2E 86
Appleton Ga. NG24: New T 1D 136
Appleton Rd. NG9: Bee 5C 106
NG21: Blid 6K 55
Appleton St. NG20: Mkt W 4D 34
Apple Tree Cl. NG12: Edwal 5D 108
Appletree Cl. NG25: Sout 5H 131
Apple Tree La. NG4: Ged 5J 87
Apple Wlk. NG3: Nott 7D 86
Applewood Cl. S81: Gate 4E 18
Applewood Gro. NG5: Sher 4A 86
Arboretum St. NG1: Nott 1C 6 (2J 95)
Arbrook Dr. NG8: Aspl 2E 94
Arbutus Cl. NG11: Clif 1D 114
Arcade, The NG24: New T 1C 136
S81: Carl L 6C 12
Archdale Rd. NG5: Bestw 1K 85
Archer Cres. NG8: Woll 3A 94
Archer Rd. NG9: Stap 4D 104
Archers Dr. NG22: Bils 6D 126
Archers Fld. NG25: Sout 5H 131
Arches, The LE12: East L 2A 122
Arches Rd. NG18: Mans 5K 47
Arch Hill NG5: Redh 3G 77
Archway Cotts. NG25: Sout 6G 131
Archway Ct. NG7: Radf 2A 6
Arden Cl. NG9: Lent A 1B 106
NG15: Huck 1J 75
Arden Gro. NG13: Bing 3D 100
Ardleigh Cl. NG5: Top V 5K 75
Ardmore Cl. NG2: Nott 7K 7 (5C 96)
Arena, The NG1: Nott 6D 6 (4J 95)
Argyle Cl. NG20: Mkt W 3B 34
Argyle Ct. NG7: Radf 3G 95
Argyle M. NG16: Eastw 4D 72
Argyle St. NG7: Radf 3A 6 (3G 95)
NG16: Lang M 2A 72
NG18: Mans 4K 47
Ariel Cl. NG6: Basf 2G 85
Arkers Cl. NG6: Basf 4E 84
Arklow Cl. NG8: Aspl 5B 84
ARKSEY 1A 144
Arkwright St. NG2: Nott 7A 96
Arkwright St. Nth. NG2: Nott 5K 95
Arkwright St. Sth. NG2: Nott 7A 96
Arkwright Wlk. NG2: Nott 6K 95
(not continuous)
Arleston Dr. NG8: Woll 5J 93
Arlington Av. NG19: Mans W 6A 42
Arlington Cl. NG15: Huck 2G 75
Arlington Dr. NG3: Mapp P 6K 85
Arlington Way DN22: Retf 3F 23
Armadale Cl. NG5: Arn 6A 78
Armfield Rd. NG5: Arn 1F 87
Armstrong Rd. DN22: Retf 3F 23
NG6: Bulw 2A 84
NG19: Mans 3D 46
Armstrong Way NG7: Basf 6F 85
ARMTHORPE 1B 144
Arncliff Cl. NG8: Woll 4H 93
Arndale Rd. NG5: Sher 2K 85
Arne Ct. NG2: Nott 7K 95
Arnesby Rd. NG7: Lent 5E 94
Arno Av. NG7: Hyson G 7J 85
ARNOLD 1F 87 (1A 148)
Arnold Av. DN22: Retf 7H 23
NG25: Sout 5H 131
Arnold La. NG3: Mapp 2E 86
NG4: Ged 4H 87
Arnold Rd. NG5: Bestw 2G 85
NG6: Basf, Bestw 3F 85
Arnold Sports & Leisure Cen. 6H 77
Arnos Gro. NG16: Nuth 4J 83
Arnot Hill Pk. 1B 86
Arnot Hill Rd. NG5: Arn 7G 77
Arnot Ho. *NG4: Carl* *7H 87*
(off Foxhill Rd. E.)
Arno Va. Gdns. NG5: Woodt 2C 86
Arno Va. Rd. NG5: Woodt 2B 86
Arnside NG9: Stap 4D 104
Arnside Cl. NG5: Bestw 2J 85
Arnside Rd. NG5: Bestw 2H 85
A Road NG7: Nott 3D 106
Arran Cl. NG9: Stap 6D 92
Arran Sq. NG19: Mans 5D 46
Arthur Av. NG7: Lent 4G 95
NG9: Stap 1E 104
Arthur Cres. NG4: Carl 1F 97
Arthur Grn. Av. NG17: Ann W 3J 59
Arthur Mee Rd. NG9: Stap 4D 104
Arthur St. NG4: Neth 2K 97
NG7: Radf 1B 6 (2H 95)
NG16: Pinx 1B 58
NG18: Mans 4J 47
Artic Way NG16: Kimb 7H 73
Artillery Ter. DN22: Retf 4E 22
Arum Cft. DN22: Ord 6D 22
Arun Dale NG19: Mans W 6K 41
Arundel Cl. NG10: Sand 5A 104
Arundel Ct. NG19: Mans 2F 47
Arundel Dr. DN22: Rans 1J 13
NG9: Bram 6G 93
NG19: Mans 2F 47
S81: Carl L 6C 12
Arundel St. NG7: Lent 4A 6 (3H 95)
Arundel Wlk. DN11: Birc 1E 8
Arundel Way DN22: Retf 2C 22
Ascot Av. NG16: Kimb 7J 73
Ascot Cl. NG17: Kirk A 1C 60
Ascot Dr. NG5: Redh 6F 77
NG15: Huck 1D 74
NG18: Mans 3B 48
Ascot Pk. Est. NG10: Sand 2B 104
Ascot Rd. NG8: Aspl 1E 94
Ascott Gdns. NG2: West Br 4J 107
ASFORDBY 3C 149
ASFORDBY HILL 3C 149
Ashbourne Cl. NG9: Bram 7F 93
Ashbourne Ct. NG6: Bulw 1A 84
Ashbourne Rd. NG16: Unde 3E 64
Ashbourne St. NG7: Lent 4A 6 (3H 95)
Ashburnham Av. NG7: Lent 4G 95
ASHBY 1D 145
Ashby Av. NG19: Mans W 4K 41
Ashby Rd. LE12: Remp 6C 122
Ashchurch Dr. NG8: Woll 6J 93
Ash Cl. NG13: Bing 4H 101
NG14: Bur J 3D 88
NG14: Woodbo 2G 79
NG15: Huck 1C 74
NG16: Pinx 2B 58
S80: Work 4F 21
Ash Ct. NG4: Carl 1G 97
Ashcourt Gdns. NG17: Sut A 6B 46
Ash Cres. NG16: Nuth 1G 83
NG17: Kirk A 5H 51
NG19: Mans W 7A 42
Ashcroft DN22: Ord 6D 22
Ashdale Av. NG15: Huck 1G 75
Ashdale Rd. DE7: Ilk 2A 92
NG3: Nott 2E 96
NG5: Arn 6J 77
Ashdown Cl. NG11: Wil 3J 107
Ashdown Gro. NG13: Bing 4E 100
Ashdown Way DN10: Mist 2G 11
Ashe Cl. NG5: Arn 7K 77
Asher La. NG11: Rudd 4K 115
Ashes Pk. Av. S81: Gate, Work 4E 18
Ashfield Av. NG9: Bee 4C 106
NG18: Mans 2H 47
Ashfield Dr. NG17: Kirk A 6K 51
Ashfield Mobile Home Pk. NG17: Skeg 5K 45
Ashfield Pct. NG17: Kirk A 6B 52
Ashfield Rd. NG2: Nott 4C 96
NG17: Huth 7F 45
Ashfield St. NG17: Skeg 5K 45
Ashford Ct. DN22: Ord 6D 22
Ashford Dr. NG15: Rave 1D 62
Ashford Ri. NG8: Woll 6J 93
NG17: Sut A 6J 45
Ashforth Bus. Cen. NG3: Nott 1G 7
Ashforth St. NG3: Nott 1G 7 (2A 96)
Ashgate NG17: Sut A 7H 45
Ashgate Rd. NG15: Huck 6H 67
Ash Gro. NG9: Stap 3C 104
NG10: Sand 2A 104
NG12: Key 1J 119
NG14: Woodbo 1G 79
NG16: Brins 5B 64
NG16: Sels 5D 58
NG17: Skeg 3H 45
Ash Holt Dr. S81: Work 4G 19
Ashiana NG2: Nott 5J 7 (4B 96)
Ashington Dr. NG5: Arn 4J 77
Ashland Rd. NG17: Sut A 7G 45
Ashland Rd. W. NG17: Sut A 7F 45
Ashlands Cl. NG17: Sut A 7F 45
Ash La. DN22: Rans 3H 13
LE12: Costo 7A 118
NG15: Pap 3F 69
Ashlea DN10: Mist 2G 11
Ash Lea Cl. NG12: Cotg 7E 110
Ashleigh Av. NG17: Sut A 1H 51
Ashleigh Way NG19: Mans W 7C 42
Ashley Cl. NG9: Chil 3J 105
Ashley Ct. NG9: Bee 3K 105
S81: Work 7G 19
Ashley Cres. NG12: Key 7J 117
Ashley Gro. NG15: Huck 6E 66
Ashley La. DN22: Tres 5F 25
Ashley Rd. NG12: Key 7H 117
S81: Work 6F 19
Ashley St. NG3: Nott 4J 7 (3B 96)
Ashley Ter. S80: Work 1G 21
Ashling Ct. NG2: Nott 6B 96
Ashling St. NG2: Nott 6A 96
Ashmore Av. NG17: Sut A 1G 51
Ashness Cl. NG2: Gam 3F 109
Ashover Cl. NG3: Nott 7B 86
NG15: Rave 1C 62
Ashridge Way NG12: Edwal 5F 109
Ash Rd. NG24: New T 5C 136
Ashton Av. NG5: Arn 4H 77
Ashton Ct. NG17: Skeg 5A 46
Ash Tree Av. NG19: Mans W 4J 41
Ash Tree Cl. NG25: Sout 6G 131
Ash Tree Sq. NG9: Bram 1G 105
Ashurst Gro. NG15: Huck 2E 74
Ash Vale NG22: Wale 5G 27
Ashvale NG22: Tuxf 7D 28
Ashvale Rd. NG22: Tuxf 6C 28
Ash Vw. NG7: Radf 2G 95
Ash Vs. NG5: Sher 6J 85
Ashville Cl. NG2: Nott 7H 95
Ash Wlk. LE12: East L 4K 121
Ashwater Dr. NG3: Mapp 1G 87
Ashwell Av. NG19: Mans W 4A 42
Ashwell Ct. NG5: Woodt 3B 86
Ashwell Gdns. NG7: Hyson G 7F 85
Ashwell St. NG4: Neth 2J 97
Ashwell Ter. NG21: Blid 7H 55
Ashwick Cl. NG11: Wil 4H 107
Ashwood Av. NG17: Kirk A 5C 52
Ashwood Cl. NG17: Sut A 2J 51
NG19: Mans W 4A 42
Ashwood Gro. NG17: Sut A 2J 51
Ashwood Rd. S80: Work 3C 20
Ashworth Av. NG11: Rudd 2K 115
Ashworth Cl. NG3: Nott 3F 97
NG24: New T 1G 137
Ashworth Cres. DN22: Nth L 6B 24
NG3: Mapp 5E 86
Ashworth Dr. NG19: Mans W 5A 42
Askeby Dr. NG8: Stre 6J 83
ASKERN 1A 144
Askew La. NG20: Mkt W 5C 34
ASKHAM 1C 147
Askham Rd. NG22: East M 2C 28
ASLOCKTON 3D 102 (1C 149)
Aslockton Dr. NG8: Aspl 5E 84
Aslockton Station (Rail) 4D 102
Aspen Cl. NG13: Bing 4H 101
NG22: Tuxf 7D 28
NG22: Wale 5G 27
Aspen Ct. NG19: Mans W 1A 48
NG22: Tuxf 7D 28
Aspen Rd. NG6: Bulw 1A 84
Asper St. NG4: Neth 1K 97
Aspinall Ct. NG8: Woll 3D 94
ASPLEY 7C 84
Aspley La. NG8: Aspl, Bilb 6A 84
Aspley Pk. Dr. NG8: Bilb 7B 84
Aspley Pl. NG7: Radf 2G 95
Aspley Rd. NG17: Sut A 7H 45
Asquith M. NG18: Mans 4A 48
Asquith St. NG18: Mans 4A 48
Assarts Rd. NG16: Nuth 3K 83
Astbury Dr. NG21: Rain 1G 55
Aster Rd. NG3: Nott 1J 7 (1A 96)
Astle Ct. NG5: Arn 1F 87

Astley Cl. NG17: Ann W 4A 60
Astley Dr. NG3: Nott 6C 86
ASTON 3A 144
Aston Av. NG9: Lent A 1B 106
Aston Ct. NG7: Lent 7F 95
Aston Dr. NG6: Bulw 4J 75
Aston Grn. NG9: Toton 6D 104
Astral Dr. NG15: Huck 2E 74
Astral Gro. NG15: Huck 2D 74
(not continuous)
Astrid Gdns. NG5: Bestw 1G 85
Astron Ct. NG15: Huck 2E 74
Astwood Cl. NG8: Bilb 1K 93
Athelstan Rd. S80: Work 4G 21
Atherfield Gdns. NG16: Eastw 3D 72
Atherton Ri. NG8: Cin 4C 84
Athorpe Gro. NG6: Basf 4F 85
Atkin La. NG18: Mans 7H 47
ATTENBOROUGH 7J 105 (2A 148)
Attenborough La. NG9: Chil 6H 105
(not continuous)
Attenborough Station (Rail) 7J 105
Attercliffe Ter. NG2: Nott 7K 95
Attewell Rd. NG16: Aws 2A 82
Attlee Av. NG19: Mans W 1C 48
AUBOURN 2D 147
Aubrey Av. NG2: Nott 6K 7 (4B 96)
Aubrey Rd. NG5: Sher 5J 85
Auckland Cl. NG7: Radf 3F 95
Auckland Rd. DN22: Retf 2C 22
NG15: Huck 1D 74
AUCKLEY 1B 144
Audley Dr. NG9: Lent A 7A 94
Audon Av. NG9: Chil 4K 105
Audrey Cres. NG19: Mans W 4H 41
AUGHTON 3A 144
Augustine Gdns. NG5: Top V 5C 76
AULT HUCKNALL 2A 146
Aurillac Way DN22: Retf 1D 22
Austen Av. NG7: Hyson G 1H 95
AUSTERFIELD 2B 144
Austin Cl. NG18: Mans 2A 48
Austins Dr. NG10: Sand 5A 104
Austin St. NG6: Bulw 7J 75
Austrey Av. NG9: Lent A 1B 106
Autumn Ct. NG15: Huck 7G 67
Autumn Cft. Rd.
NG24: New T 7G 135
Avalon Cl. NG6: Bulw 1F 85
Avebury Cl. NG11: Clif 2E 114
Aveline Cl. NG5: Top V 6B 76
Avenue, The NG11: Rudd 5A 116
NG12: Rad T 4E 98
NG14: Calv 6D 70
NG14: Gun 1A 90
NG17: Sut A 2H 51
NG18: Mans 7K 47
NG24: New T 2E 136
Avenue A NG1: Nott 5H 7 (4A 96)
Avenue B NG1: Nott 5H 7 (4A 96)
Avenue C NG1: Nott 5J 7 (4B 96)
Avenue D NG1: Nott 5J 7 (4B 96)
Avenue E NG1: Nott 4J 7 (3B 96)
Avenue Rd. DN22: Retf 5F 23
AVERHAM 4F 133 (3C 147)
Averham Cl. NG19: Mans 4D 46
Averton Sq. NG8: Woll 5E 94
Aviemore Cl. NG5: Arn 5K 77
Avocet Cl. NG13: Bing 5H 101
NG15: Huck 4H 67
Avocet Gro. S81: Gate 6D 18
Avocet Wharf NG7: Lent 6H 95
Avon Av. NG15: Huck 3E 74
Avonbridge Cl. NG5: Arn 5A 78
Avon Cl. NG17: Ann W 4K 59
Avondale NG12: Cotg 6F 111
Avondale Rd. NG4: Carl 2G 97
Avon Gdns. NG2: West Br 2C 108
Avonlea Cl. DE7: Ilk 2A 92
Avon Pl. NG9: Bee 2B 106
Avon Ri. DN22: Retf 3G 23
Avon Rd. NG3: Nott 3E 96
NG4: Ged 5J 87
Avon Way NG18: Mans 5C 48
S81: Work 5F 19
AWSWORTH 2B 82 (1A 148)
Awsworth & Cossall By-Pass
NG16: Aws, Coss 3A 82
Awsworth La. NG16: Coss 5B 82
NG16: Kimb 2C 82
Awsworth Rd. DE7: Ilk 4A 82
Axford Cl. NG4: Ged 5J 87
Aylesham Av. NG5: Arn 1C 86
Aylestone Dr. NG8: Bilb 7C 84
Ayr St. NG7: Radf 2A 6 (2H 95)
Ayscough Av. NG16: Nuth 1H 83
Ayton Cl. NG2: Nott 6J 95
Ayton Gdns. NG9: Chil 7H 105
Azalea Ct. NG16: Gilt 6G 73
Azimghur Rd. NG13: What 4D 102

B

Babbacombe Dr. NG5: Bestw 1J 85
Babbacombe Way NG15: Huck 7D 66
Babbage Way S80: Work 1F 21
BABBINGTON 4D 82
Babbington Cres. NG4: Ged 5H 87
Babbington Dr. NG6: Cin 3C 84
Babbington La. NG16: Kimb 3E 82
Babington Ct. NG9: Chil 4H 105
Babthorpe NG23: Upton 7C 132
BABWORTH 4A 22 (3B 144)
Babworth Ct. NG18: Mans 3K 47
Babworth Cres. DN22: Retf 4C 22
Babworth Rd. DN22: Babw, Retf 4A 22
Back La. DN10: Miss 3C 10
DN22: Rans 2H 13
LE12: Will W 6F 143
NG12: Crop Bu 2B 112
NG12: Norm W 4K 117
NG16: Nuth 1J 83
NG17: Huth 7D 44
NG17: Skeg 4K 45
NG22: Eakr 3C 126
NG22: East M 2D 28
(not continuous)
NG22: Halam 5C 130
NG22: Oll 5B 38
NG23: Flin 6A 140
NG23: Nth C 3D 30
NG24: Barn W 6K 137
NG25: Mort 6F 139
Back Pk. Pl. S80: Work 3G 21
Back St. NG23: Sth C 7D 30
Back Ter. DN22: Retf 2F 23
Bacon Cl. NG16: Gilt 6E 72
Bacton Av. NG6: Bulw 6H 75
Bacton Gdns. NG6: Bulw 6H 75
Baden Powell Rd. NG2: Nott 4D 96
Bader Cl. DN10: Matt T 1G 15
Bader Ri. DN10: Matt T 1G 15
Bader Rd. NG11: Wil 2J 107
Bader Vw. DN10: Matt T 1G 15
Badger Cl. NG4: Carl 7H 87
NG15: Huck 7C 66
Badgers Chase DN22: Retf 1F 23
Badgers Cft. NG22: Bils 6D 126
Badger Way NG19: Mans W 3E 48
Baggaley Cres. NG19: Mans 1H 47
Bagnall Av. NG5: Arn 1K 85
Bagnall Cotts. NG6: Bulw 2C 84
Bagnall Rd. NG6: Basf, Cin 3C 84
Bagshaw St. NG19: Plea 4B 40
BAGTHORPE 1D 64 (3A 146)
Bagthorpe Cl. NG5: Sher 4H 85
BAGTHORPE COMMON 2F 65
Baildon Cl. NG8: Woll 5D 94
Bailey Cl. NG5: Arn 7F 77
Bailey Ct. NG4: Neth 1K 97
NG12: Rad T 6D 98
Bailey Cres. NG19: Mans 3E 46
BAILEY GROVE 4B 72
Bailey Gro. Rd. NG16: Eastw 4B 72
Bailey La. NG12: Rad T 6D 98
Bailey Rd. NG24: New T 4C 136
Bailey's Row NG12: Kin 1C 142
Bailey St. NG4: Neth 1K 97
NG6: Basf 5F 85
NG9: Stap 3B 104
Bainbridge, The NG14: Calv 6E 70
Bainbridge Rd. NG20: Mkt W 4D 34
Bainbridge Ter. NG17: Huth 1D 50
NG17: Stan H 4H 45
Baines Av. NG24: New B 5G 137
Bainton Gro. NG11: Clif 1G 115
Baker Av. NG5: Arn 5J 77
Baker Brook Cl. NG15: Huck 7K 67
Baker Cl. S81: Work 7E 18
Bakerdale Rd. NG3: Nott 2E 96
Baker La. NG20: Cuck 4C 32
Baker Rd. NG16: Gilt, Newth 6G 73
NG19: Mans W 3J 41
Bakers Cl. NG7: Radf 2F 95
BAKERS FIELDS 2E 96
Baker's Hollow NG12: Cotg 6D 110
Baker's La. NG12: Cols B 7J 141
Baker St. NG1: Nott 1D 6 (1J 95)
NG15: Huck 6G 67
Bakewell Av. NG4: Carl 6H 87
Bakewell Cl. NG24: New B 6F 137
Bakewell Dr. NG5: Top V 7A 76
Bakewell Ho. NG24: Bald 6F 137
Bakewell Wlk. NG18: Mans 4E 48
Bala Dr. NG5: Bestw 7C 76
BALBY 1A 144
BALDERTON 6G 137 (3D 147)
Balderton Ct. NG19: Mans 3E 46
Balderton Ga. NG24: New T 1D 136
Baldwin Cl. NG19: Mans W 7D 42
Baldwin Ct. NG7: Radf 4A 6 (3G 95)
Baldwin St. NG7: Radf 3A 6 (3H 95)
NG16: Newth 5G 73
Balerton La. NG24: Codd 3K 137
Balfour Rd. NG7: Lent, Radf 4A 6 (3G 95)
NG9: Stap 3C 104
Balfour St. NG17: Kirk A 7C 52
Balfron Gdns. NG2: Nott 6J 95
BALK FIELD 3F 23
Ballantrae Cl. NG5: Arn 6K 77
Ballater Cl. NG19: Mans 7E 40
Ballerat Cres. NG5: Top V 6A 76
Ball Hill DE55: Sth N 5A 50
Balloon Wood Ind. Est. NG9: Bram 4F 93
Balls La. NG17: Kirk A 2B 60
Ball St. NG3: Nott 1C 96
Balmoral Av. NG2: West Br 1B 108
Balmoral Cl. NG10: Sand 6A 104
NG19: Mans W 4A 42
S81: Carl L 6C 12
Balmoral Ct. *DN11: Birc* 1E 8
(off Bawtry Rd.)
Balmoral Cres. NG8: Woll 3H 93
Balmoral Dr. NG9: Bram 6G 93
NG19: Mans 7E 40
NG24: New T 1H 137
Balmoral Gro. NG4: Colw 2J 97
NG15: Huck 5H 67
Balmoral Ho. NG5: Woodt 3A 86
Balmoral Lodge NG19: Mans 7E 40
Balmoral Rd. NG1: Nott 1C 6 (2J 95)
NG4: Colw 2J 97
NG13: Bing 4D 100
Balshaw Way NG9: Chil 7G 105
Bamburgh Cl. NG17: Kirk A 4J 51
Bamford Dr. NG18: Mans 4D 48
Bamkin Cl. NG15: Huck 7H 67
Bampton Ct. NG2: Gam 2F 109
Banbury Av. NG9: Toton 6E 104
Banchory Cl. NG19: Mans 7E 40
Bancroft Ho. *NG18: Mans* 3G 47
(off The Connexion)
Bancroft La. NG18: Mans 3F 47
Bancroft Rd. NG24: New T 3E 136
Bancroft St. NG6: Bulw 7J 75
Bandstand Yard 7D 6
Banes Rd. NG13: Bing 4J 101
Bangor Wlk. NG3: Nott 1F 7 (1K 95)
Bank Av. NG17: Sut A 2J 51
Bankfield Dr. NG9: Bram 7H 93
Bank Hill NG14: Woodbo 3D 78
Bank Pl. NG1: Nott 5F 7 (4K 95)
Banks, The NG13: Bing 4F 101
Banks Av. NG17: Kirk A 5J 51
Banks Cl. NG5: Arn 1E 86
Banks Cres. NG13: Bing 4F 101
Bank Side DN22: Ord 7F 23
Banksman Cl. NG3: Nott 1C 96
Banks Paddock NG13: Bing 4G 101
Banks Rd. NG9: Toton 6D 104
Bank St. NG16: Lang M 2A 72
Banks Yd. *NG6: Bulw* 7H 75
(off Main St.)
Bankwood Cl. NG8: Aspl 6B 84
Bannatynes Health Club 6B 48
Bannerman Rd. NG6: Bulw 1D 84
NG17: Kirk A 6K 51
Baptist La. NG23: Coll 2G 129
Barbara Sq. NG15: Huck 4F 67
Barber St. NG16: Eastw 4E 72
Barbers Wood Cl. NG15: Rave 3C 62
Barbrook Cl. NG8: Woll 3C 94
Barbury Dr. NG11: Clif 3E 114
Barcroft La. DN22: Clar 7H 17
Barden Rd. NG3: Mapp 2D 86
Bardfield Gdns. NG5: Top V 4K 75
Bardney Dr. NG6: Bulw 6G 75
Bardsey Gdns. NG5: Bestw 7C 76
Barent Cl. NG5: Bestw 1G 85
Barent Wlk. NG5: Bestw 1G 85
Bar Ga. NG24: New T 7C 134
Barker Av. NG16: Jack 6A 64
NG17: Skeg 4H 45
Barker Av. E. NG10: Sand 3A 104
Barker Av. Nth. NG10: Sand 3A 104
Barker Ga. NG1: Nott 5G 7 (4A 96)
NG15: Huck 6F 67
Barker Hill NG14: Lowd 4D 80
Barker's La. NG9: Chil 5A 106
Barker St. NG17: Huth 6D 44
BARKESTONE-LE-VALE 2C 149
Barkla Cl. NG11: Clif 2D 114
BARKSTON 1D 149
Barkstone Cl. NG24: Bald 6F 137
Bar La. NG6: Basf 5D 84
Bar La. Ind. Pk. NG6: Basf 5E 84
BARLBOROUGH 1A 146
Barley Cft. NG2: West Br 5K 107
Barleydale Dr. NG9: Trow 6C 92
Barleylands NG11: Rudd 4K 115

Barley M. NG19: Mans W 3A **42**
Barley Way NG24: New T 4E **134**
Barlock Rd. NG6: Basf 3F **85**
Barlow Dr. Nth. NG16: Aws 3A **82**
Barlow Dr. Sth. NG16: Aws 3A **82**
Barlows Cotts. NG16: Aws 2B **82**
Barlows Cotts. La. NG16: Aws 2B **82**
BARNBURGH 1A **144**
BARNBY DUN 1B **144**
Barnby Ga. NG24: New T 1D **136**
BARNBY IN THE WILLOWS 7K **137** (3D **147**)
BARNBY MOOR 3B **144**
Barnby Rd. NG24: Bald, Barn W, New T 2E **136**
Barnby Wlk. NG5: Sher 2K **85**
Barn Cl. NG6: Bulw 2A **84**
NG12: Cotg 7D **110**
NG18: Mans 5B **48**
S81: Work 5H **19**
Barn Cft. NG9: Chil 3G **105**
NG18: Mans 4B **48**
Barndale Cl. NG2: West Br 6K **107**
Barnes Ct. DN22: Retf 1D **22**
Barnes Cres. NG17: Sut A 3J **51**
Barnes Rd. NG5: Top V 6B **76**
Barnet Rd. NG3: Nott 1E **96**
Barnett Ct. NG12: Key 7H **117**
Barnfield NG11: Wil 5J **107**
Barnfield Rd. NG23: Coll 1J **129**
Barn Owl Cl. NG20: Chu W 2E **34**
Barnsley Cl. NG6: Bestw V 7D **68**
Barnsley Ter. NG2: Nott 7K **95**
BARNSTONE 3F **141** (2C **149**)
Barnstone La. NG13: Barns, Gran 2H **141**
Barnstone Rd. NG13: Barns 7K **113**
NG13: Lang 7K **113**
Barnston Rd. NG2: Nott 3C **96**
Barnum Cl. NG8: Woll 3K **93**
Barons Cl. NG4: Ged 6H **87**
Barons Dr. NG22: Bou 2F **39**
Barrack La. NG7: Nott 5A **6** (4G **95**)
Barra M. NG2: Nott 6J **95**
Barratt Cl. NG9: Atten 7J **105**
NG12: Crop Bi 5B **112**
Barratt Cres. NG9: Atten 7J **105**
Barratt La. NG9: Atten 7H **105**
Barrel Hill Rd. NG23: Sut T 4C **128**
Barrhead Cl. NG5: Top V 5A **76**
Barringer Rd. NG18: Mans 2K **47**
NG19: Mans W 7A **42**
Barrington Cl. NG12: Rad T 6D **98**
Barrington Ct. LE12: Sut B 6B **120**
Barrique Rd. NG7: Lent 7F **95**
Bar Rd. DN10: Beck, Saun 7D **16**
DN22: Saun 7D **16**
Bar Rd. Nth. DN10: Beck 7D **16**
Bar Rd. Sth. DN10: Beck 7D **16**
BARROWBY 2D **149**
Barrowhill Wlk. *NG18: Mans* *4D 48*
(off Beeley Cl.)
Barrows Ga. NG24: New T 5E **134**
BARROWS GREEN 7B **58**
Barrows Hill La. NG16: Westw 7B **58**
Barrow Slade NG12: Key 1H **119**
BARROW UPON SOAR 3A **148**
Barrydale Av. NG9: Bee 4A **106**
Barry St. NG6: Bulw 7H **75**
Bars Hill LE12: Costo 3E **122**
Bartlow Rd. NG8: Bilb 1J **93**
Barton Cl. NG11: Rudd 4J **115**
NG19: Mans W 1D **48**
Barton Ct. NG18: Mans 7C **48**
BARTON IN FABIS 7A **114** (2A **148**)
Barton La. NG9: Atten 7H **105**
NG11: Bart F 4B **114**
NG11: Clif 2D **114**
Bartons Cl. NG16: Newth 4G **73**
Barton St. NG9: Bee 4B **106**
Barton Way NG9: Chil 4K **105**
Barwell Dr. NG8: Stre 6J **83**
Basa Cres. NG5: Top V 6B **76**
Basford Rd. NG6: Basf 6E **84**
Basford Stop (NET) 4F **85**
Baskin La. NG9: Chil 5H **105**
Baslow Av. NG4: Carl 6G **87**
Baslow Dr. NG9: Lent A 7B **94**
Baslow Way NG18: Mans 5D **48**
Bassetlaw Leisure Cen. 1H **21**
Bassett Cl. NG16: Kimb 7J **73**
BASSINGFIELD 2J **109** (2B **148**)
Bassingfield La. NG2: Gam 2G **109**
(not continuous)
NG12: Rad T 1J **109**
BASSINGHAM 3D **147**
Bastion St. NG7: Radf 3F **95**
Bateman Gdns. NG7: Hyson G 1G **95**
Bateman Rd. LE12: East L 3K **121**
Bateman's Yd. NG17: Kirk A 7H **51**
Bath La. NG18: Mans 3J **47**
NG25: Sout 7E **130**
BATHLEY 5F **129** (3C **147**)
Bathley La. NG23: Bath 7G **129**
NG23: Norw 4H **127**
NG23: Nth M 6H **129**
Bathley St. NG2: Nott 7K **95**
Baths La. NG15: Huck 6H **67**
Bath St. NG1: Nott 3G **7** (3A **96**)
NG17: Sut A 6K **45**
NG18: Mans 4H **47**
Bathurst Dr. NG8: Bilb 2B **94**
Bathurst Ter. NG20: Whal T 5A **26**
Bathwood Dr. NG17: Sut A 1A **52**
NG18: Mans 5E **46**
Battery La. DN22: Elk 3G **27**
Baulk, The S81: Work 7G **19**
Baulker La. NG21: Blid 7B **56**
NG21: C'tone 5K **43**
NG22: Farns 7B **56**
Baulk La. DN11: Harwo 1C **8**
DN22: Torw 4H **13**
NG9: Stap 1E **104**
S81: Work 7F **19**
(not continuous)
Baum's La. NG18: Mans 5H **47**
BAWTRY 2B **144**
Bawtry Cl. DN11: Harwo 2C **8**
Bawtry Rd. DN10: Eve, Scaf 6A **10**
DN10: Miss 2C **10**
DN10: Miss, Newi 4A **10**
DN10: Serl 7E **8**
DN11: Birc, Harwo 2C **8**
DN11: Harwo, Tick 1D **8**
S81: Blyth 4G **13**
Bawtry Wlk. NG3: Nott 2C **96**
Bayard Ct. NG8: Woll 3D **94**
Bayford Dr. NG24: New T 2H **137**
Bayliss Rd. NG4: Ged 4G **87**
Baysdale Dr. NG19: Mans W 1B **48**
Bayswater Rd. NG16: Kimb 7K **73**
Baythorn Rd. NG8: Bilb 2J **93**
Beacon Ct. NG22: New O 5D **38**
Beacon Dr. NG17: Kirk A 5C **52**
Beacon Flatts NG9: Bee 3C **106**
Beacon Hgts. NG24: New T 1G **137**
Beacon Hill Dr. NG15: Huck 1C **74**
Beacon Hill Ri. NG3: Nott 3J **7** (3B **96**)
Beacon Hill Rd. DN10: Gri H 3C **16**
NG24: New T 1D **136**
Beacon Rd. NG9: Bee 3C **106**
Beaconsfield Dr. NG24: Codd 6J **135**
Beaconsfield St. NG7: Hyson G 7G **85**
Beaconsfield Street Stop (NET) 7G **85**
Beacon Ter. NG24: New T 1D **136**
Beacon Wlk. DN10: Gri H 3C **16**
Beacon Way NG24: New T 1G **137**
Bean Av. S80: Work 2J **21**
Bean Cl. NG6: Bulw 2A **84**
Beanford La. NG14: Calv 2C **70**
NG25: Oxt 2C **70**
Beardall St. NG15: Huck 6H **67**
NG18: Mans 3G **47**
Beardsall's Row DN22: Retf 3F **23**
Beardsley Gdns. NG2: Nott 6J **95**
(not continuous)
Beardsley Rd. NG21: Edwin 7G **37**
(not continuous)
Beardsmore Gro. NG15: Huck 4F **67**
Beast Mkt. Hill NG24: New T 7C **134**
Beastmarket Hill NG1: Nott 5E **6** (4K **95**)
Beauclerk Dr. NG5: Top V 6A **76**
Beaufit La. NG16: Pinx 1C **58**
Beaufort Ct. NG2: West Br 6K **107**
Beaufort Dr. NG9: Chil 4H **105**
Beaufort Way S81: Work 4F **19**
Beaulieu Gdns. NG2: West Br 4K **107**
Beauly Dr. NG19: Mans 5D **46**
Beaumaris Dr. NG4: Ged 6A **88**
NG9: Chil 5G **105**
Beaumont Av. NG18: Mans 5B **48**
NG25: Sout 6F **131**
Beaumont Cl. NG9: Stap 7D **92**
NG12: Key 6H **117**
Beaumont Gdns. NG2: West Br 5A **108**
Beaumont Ri. S80: Work 2E **20**
Beaumont St. NG2: Nott 6K **7** (4B **96**)
Beaumont Wlk. NG24: New T 6E **134**
BEAUVALE
NG15 . . . . . 7D **66**
NG16 . . . . . 3F **73** (1A **148**)
Beauvale NG16: Newth 4F **73**
Beauvale Ct. NG15: Huck 7E **66**
Beauvale Cres. NG15: Huck 7D **66**
Beauvale Gdns. NG17: Ann W 4J **59**
Beauvale Ri. NG16: Eastw 3F **73**
Beauvale Rd. NG2: Nott 7K **95**
NG15: Huck 7D **66**
NG17: Ann W 4J **59**
Beaver Grn. NG2: West Br 2A **108**
Beaver Pl. S80: Work 2G **21**
Beazley Av. NG18: Mans 3F **47**
Beck Av. NG14: Calv 5D **70**
Beck Cres. NG19: Mans 3E **46**
NG21: Blid 7J **55**
Beckenham Rd. NG7: Radf 2G **95**
Beckett Av. NG19: Mans 1E **46**
S81: Carl L 5C **12**
Beckett Ct. NG4: Ged 4G **87**
Beckford Rd. NG2: Nott 5C **96**
Beckhampton Rd. NG5: Bestw 6D **76**
BECKINGHAM
Gainsborough 6C **16** (2C **145**)
Newark-on-Trent 3D **147**
Beckingham Ct. *NG18: Mans* *3E 46*
(off Kelham Rd.)
Beckingham La. DN22: Sth L 4G **25**
Beckingham Rd. DN10: Beck, Walk . . . . . 7J **11** & 6C **16**
NG24: Codd 7J **135**
Beckland Hill NG22: East M 3C **28**
Beck La. DN22: Clay 7J **15**
NG17: Skeg 4B **46**
NG21: Blid 7J **55**
NG22: Farns 6J **57**
Beckley Rd. NG8: Brox 5A **84**
Beckside NG2: West Br 5F **109**
NG14: Lowd 5E **80**
Beck St. NG1: Nott 4G **7** (3A **96**)
NG4: Carl 7G **87**
NG14: Thur 6D **138**
Bedale S81: Work 4H **19**
Bedale Ct. NG9: Chil 5F **105**
Bedale Rd. NG5: Sher 2K **85**
Bedarra Gro. NG7: Lent 4F **95**
Bedeham La. NG13: Car C 4K **91**
Bede Ho. Ct. NG24: New T 1D **136**
Bede Ho. La. NG24: New T 1D **136**
Bede Ling NG2: West Br 3K **107**
Bedford Av. NG18: Mans 3A **48**
Bedford Ct. NG7: Hyson G 7G **85**
NG9: Stap 7D **92**
Bedford Gro. NG6: Bulw 2E **84**
Bedford Row NG1: Nott 4H **7** (3A **96**)
Bedlington Gdns. NG3: Mapp 5B **86**
Beecham Av. NG3: Nott 2C **96**
Beech Av. LE12: East L 4K **121**
NG3: Mapp 3C **86**
NG4: Neth 2J **97**
NG7: Basf 7H **85**
NG9: Bee 4C **106**
NG10: Sand 2A **104**
NG12: Key 1J **119**
NG13: Bing 4H **101**
NG15: Huck 6G **67**
NG15: Rave 1B **62**
NG16: Nuth 1G **83**
NG16: Pinx 1C **58**
NG17: Huth 7E **44**
NG17: Kirk A 6J **51**
NG18: Mans 4H **47**
NG22: New O 4C **38**
NG22: Oll 3K **37**
NG24: New T 4C **136**
S81: Work 6G **19**
Beech Cl. DN10: Gri H 3B **16**
NG2: West Br 7G **97**
NG6: Cin 3D **84**
NG12: Edwal 5E **108**
NG12: Rad T 6E **98**
Beech Ct. NG3: Mapp 3D **86**
NG16: Unde 2F **65**
NG19: Mans 4D **46**
NG19: Mans W 4H **41**
Beech Cres. NG19: Mans W 7A **42**
Beechcroft S81: Work 6H **19**
BEECHDALE 2B **94**
Beechdale Av. NG17: Sut A 6K **45**
Beechdale Cres. NG17: Sut A 6K **45**
Beechdale Rd. NG8: Aspl, Bilb 7A **84**
NG19: Mans W 7C **42**
Beecher La. DN10: Beck 6C **16**
Beeches, The NG3: Nott 7D **86**
NG17: Skeg 3H **45**
NG22: Tuxf 7C **28**
Beeches Wlk. NG25: Sout 6H **131**
Beech Gro. NG21: Blid 6A **56**
S81: Carl L 5B **12**
Beech Hill Av. NG19: Mans 1F **47**
Beech Hill Cres. NG19: Mans 7F **41**
Beech Hill Dr. NG19: Mans 1F **47**
Beech Lodge NG13: Bing 4H **101**
Beech Rd. DN11: Harwo 1D **8**
NG16: Unde 2F **65**
Beech St. NG17: Skeg 3H **45**
Beech Tree Av. NG19: Mans W 4H **41**
Beech Wlk. DN22: Elk 2G **27**
Beechways DN22: Ord 6D **22**
Beechwood Cl. NG17: Skeg 5A **46**
NG19: Mans W 1C **48**
Beechwood Ct. NG17: Skeg 5A **46**
Beechwood Gro. NG17: Skeg 5A **46**
Beechwood Rd. NG5: Arn 6J **77**
NG17: Kirk A 4K **51**

Beehive St. DN22: Retf 4F **23**
Beeley Av. NG17: Sut A 2J **51**
Beeley Cl. NG18: Mans 4D **48**
BEESTON 2B **106** (2A **148**)
Beeston Cl. NG6: Bestw V 2A **76**
Beeston Ct. NG6: Bulw 7K **75**
Beeston Flds. Dr. NG9: Bee, Bram 1H **105**
Beeston La. NG7: Nott 1C **106**
Beeston Rd. NG7: Nott 7E **94**
NG24: New T 3E **136**
Beeston Sailing Club 7B 106
Beeston Station (Rail) 4B **106**
Beetham Cl. NG13: Bing 4G **101**
Beggarlee Pk. NG16: Newth 2F **73**
BEIGHTON 3A **144**
Beighton Ct. NG18: Mans 5D **48**
Beighton St. NG17: Sut A 7K **45**
Bel-air Residential Homes
NG2: Gam 2G **109**
Belconnen Rd. NG5: Bestw 2G **85**
Belfields Yd. NG22: Edin 2A **130**
Belford Cl. NG6: Bulw 6F **75**
Belfry Cl. NG17: Kirk A 4J **51**
Belfry Way NG12: Edwal 5F **109**
Belgrave M. NG2: West Br 6K **107**
Belgrave Rd. NG6: Bulw 7G **75**
Belgrave Sq. NG1: Nott 4D **6** (3J **95**)
Bellamy Rd. NG18: Mans 7C **48**
(not continuous)
Bellamy Rd. Ind. Est. NG18: Mans 7C **48**
Bellar Ga. NG1: Nott 5H **7** (4A **96**)
Belle Eau Pk. NG22: Bils 7E **126**
Belle Isle Rd. NG15: Huck 7G **67**
Belleville Dr. NG5: Bestw 7D **76**
Bellevue Ct. NG3: Nott 1J **7** (2B **96**)
Belle Vue La. NG21: Blid 6J **55**
Bell Ho. NG7: Nott 1F **107**
Bell La. NG11: Wil 2J **107**
NG23: Coll 2G **129**
NG23: Weston 2F **125**
Bellmond Cl. NG24: New T 4C **136**
Bellmore Gdns. NG8: Bilb 3J **93**
Bells Ct. DN10: Beck 7C **16**
Bells La. NG8: Cin 5B **84**
Bell St. NG4: Carl 7G **87**
Belmont Av. NG6: Bulw 7J **75**
Belmont Cl. NG9: Chil 5G **105**
NG15: Huck 2G **75**
NG19: Mans W 7C **42**
Belmont Rd. NG17: Ann W 3B **60**
Belper Av. NG4: Carl 6G **87**
Belper Cres. NG4: Carl 6G **87**
Belper Rd. NG7: Hyson G 1A **6** (1G **95**)
Belper St. NG18: Mans 3K **47**
Belper Way NG18: Mans 3K **47**
BELPH 1A **146**
Belsay Rd. NG5: Bestw 7C **76**
Belsford Ct. NG16: Want 6A **74**
BELTOFT 1D **145**
BELTON
Crowle 1C **145**
Grantham 2D **149**
Shepshed 3A **148**
Belton Cl. NG10: Sand 5A **104**
Belton Dr. NG2: West Br 5J **107**
Belton St. NG7: Hyson G 7G **85**
Belvedere Av. NG7: Hyson G 7G **85**
Belvedere Cl. NG12: Key 6H **117**
Belvedere Ho. *NG18: Mans* *3G 47*
(off The Connexion)
Belvedere St. NG18: Mans 4H **47**
BELVOIR 2D **149**
Belvoir Cl. NG13: What 5B **102**
Belvoir Cres. NG13: Lang 7K **113**
NG24: New T 3D **136**
Belvoir Hill NG2: Nott 6K **7** (4C **96**)
Belvoir Lodge NG4: Carl 2H **97**
Belvoir Pl. NG24: Bald 6F **137**
Belvoir Rd. NG2: West Br 7D **96**
NG4: Neth 1K **97**
NG24: Bald 6F **137**
Belvoir St. NG3: Mapp 5C **86**
NG15: Huck 5F **67**
Belvoir Ter. NG2: Nott 6K **7** (4C **96**)
Belward St. NG1: Nott 5H **7** (4A **96**)
Belwood Cl. NG11: Clif 7G **107**
Bembridge S81: Work 6J **19**
Bembridge Ct. NG9: Bram 1F **105**
Bembridge Dr. NG5: Bestw 1J **85**
(not continuous)
Bendigo La. NG2: Nott 5D **96**
Benedict Ct. NG5: Top V 5C **76**
Benet Dr. NG22: Bils 6D **126**
Benington Dr. NG8: Woll 5H **93**
Ben Mayo Ct. NG7: Radf 2G **95**
Benner Av. DE7: Ilk 3A **92**
Bennerley Ct. NG6: Bulw 6F **75**
Bennerley Rd. NG6: Bulw 6F **75**
Bennett Av. NG18: Mans 4B **48**
Bennett Rd. NG3: Mapp 4D **86**
Bennett St. NG3: Mapp 5C **86**
NG10: Long E 6B **104**
NG10: Sand 4A **104**
Benneworth Cl. NG15: Huck 1F **75**
Bennington Wlk. NG19: Mans W 5A **42**
Ben St. NG7: Radf 2G **95**
Bentinck Av. NG12: Toll 1G **117**
Bentinck Cl. NG17: Ann W 3K **59**
NG22: Bou 2E **38**
Bentinck Ct. NG2: Nott 4B **96**
S80: Work 5G **21**
Bentinck Rd. NG4: Carl 5F **87**
NG7: Hyson G, Radf 1A **6** (2G **95**)
NG24: New T 3C **136**
Bentinck St. NG15: Huck 5F **67**
NG17: Ann W 4K **59**
NG17: Sut A 7K **45**
NG18: Mans 4K **47**
Bentinck Ter. NG20: Mkt W 5D **34**
BENTINCK TOWN 7H **51**
BENTLEY 1A **144**
Bentley Av. NG3: Nott 2D **96**
Bentwell Av. NG5: Arn 7J **77**
Beresford Rd. NG19: Mans W 3J **41**
Beresford St. NG7: Radf 3F **95**
NG18: Mans 4K **47**
Berkeley Av. NG3: Mapp P 7K **85**
Berkeley Ct. NG5: Sher 6K **85**
Berkeley Cres. NG12: Rad T 5J **99**
Berkeley Rd. NG18: Mans 6K **47**
Bernard Av. NG15: Huck 4H **67**
NG19: Mans W 4H **41**
Bernard Rd. NG19: Mans 2D **46**
Bernard St. NG5: Sher 6J **85**
Bernard Ter. NG5: Sher 6J **85**
Bernisdale Cl. NG5: Top V 5B **76**
Berridge Rd. NG7: Hyson G 7H **85**
Berridge Rd. Central NG7: Hyson G 7G **85**
Berridge Rd. W. NG7: Hyson G 1F **95**
Berriedale Cl. NG5: Arn 5K **77**
Berristow Grange NG17: Sut A 2G **51**
Berristow La. DE55: Sth N 3A **50**
Berristow Pl. DE55: Sth N 4C **50**
Berry Av. NG17: Kirk A 5J **51**
Berrydown Cl. NG8: Aspl 6D **84**
BERRY HILL 5A **48**
Berry Hill Cl. NG18: Mans 6J **47**
Berry Hill Gdns. NG18: Mans 6B **48**
Berry Hill Gro. NG4: Ged 5H **87**
Berry Hill La. NG18: Mans 7J **47**
Berry Hill M. NG18: Mans 6K **47**
Berry Hill Rd. NG18: Mans 5J **47**
Berry Pk. Lea NG18: Mans 7K **47**
Berwick Av. NG19: Mans 2D **46**
Berwick Cl. NG5: Bestw 1K **85**
Berwin Cl. NG10: Long E 7A **104**
Beryldene Av. NG16: Want 7A **74**
BESCABY 3D **149**
Bescar La. NG22: Oll 5A **38**
Bescoby St. DN22: Retf 4F **23**
Besecar Av. NG4: Ged 5H **87**
Besecar Cl. NG4: Ged 5H **87**
BESSACARR 1B **144**
Bessell La. NG9: Stap 4B **104**
BESTHORPE 6H **125** (2D **147**)
Besthorpe Ct. NG18: Mans 3E **46**
Besthorpe Rd. LN6: Nth S 5J **125**
NG23: Coll 1H **129**
BESTWOOD 7D **76**
Bestwood Av. NG5: Arn 6G **77**
Bestwood Bus. Pk. NG6: Bestw V 3A **76**
Bestwood Cl. NG5: Arn 6G **77**
Bestwood Country Pk. 3A 76
Bestwood Footpath NG15: Huck 1K **75**
Bestwood Lodge Dr. NG5: Arn 5E **76**
Bestwood Lodge Stables
NG5: Arn 4D **76**
Bestwood Pk. NG5: Arn 4D **76**
Bestwood Pk. Dr. NG5: Top V 5D **76**
Bestwood Pk. Dr. W. NG5: Top V 5K **75**
Bestwood Pk. Vw. NG5: Arn 5G **77**
Bestwood Rd. NG6: Bulw 6J **75**
NG15: Huck 1J **75**
NG16: Pinx 2C **58**
Bestwood Swimming Pool 1J 85
Bestwood Ter. NG6: Bulw 6K **75**
BESTWOOD VILLAGE 2A **76** (1A **148**)
Bethel Ct. NG19: Mans W 5J **41**
Bethel Gdns. NG15: Huck 1C **74**
Bethnal Wlk. NG6: Bulw 7H **75**
Betony Cl. NG13: Bing 5D **100**
Betula Cl. NG11: Clif 1D **114**
Beulah Rd. NG17: Kirk A 7B **52**
Bevan Cl. NG21: Rain 3K **55**
Bevel St. NG7: Hyson G 1G **95**
BEVERCOTES 1C **147**
Bevercotes Cl. NG24: New T 3B **136**
Bevercotes La. NG22: Tuxf 6A **28**
Beverley Cl. NG8: Woll 4G **93**
NG21: Rain 2K **55**
Beverley Dr. NG16: Kimb 7J **73**
NG17: Kirk A 1C **60**
NG18: Mans 1K **53**
Beverley Gdns. NG4: Ged 6J **87**
Beverley Rd. DN11: Harwo 2D **8**
Beverley's Av. NG13: What 4C **102**
Beverley Sq. NG3: Nott 1J **7** (1B **96**)
Beverley Wlk. S81: Carl L 5B **12**
Bewcastle Rd. NG5: Arn, Top V 5C **76**
Bewick Dr. NG3: Nott 3F **97**
Bexhill Ct. NG9: Bee 7K **93**
Bexleigh Gdns. NG8: Bilb 7B **84**
Bexon Ct. NG4: Carl 1H **97**
Bexwell Cl. NG11: Clif 2F **115**
Biant Cl. NG8: Cin 4C **84**
Bible Wlk. NG1: Nott 3D **6** (3J **95**)
Bidford Rd. NG8: Brox 6A **84**
Bidwell Cres. NG11: Goth 6G **115**
Big Barn La. NG18: Mans 5B **48**
Biggart Cl. NG9: Chil 7H **105**
Big La. DN22: Clar 7H **17**
Bigsby Rd. DN22: Retf 2G **23**
Biko Sq. NG7: Hyson G 7G **85**
Bilberry Wlk. NG3: Nott 1K **7** (2B **96**)
BILBOROUGH 1J **93** (1A **148**)
Bilborough College Sports Cen. 1H 93
Bilborough Rd. NG8: Stre 3G **93**
NG18: Mans 3K **47**
BILBY 3B **144**
Bilby Gdns. NG3: Nott 3C **96**
Billesdon Dr. NG5: Sher 3G **85**
Billingsley Av. NG16: Pinx 1B **58**
BILSTHORPE 5C **126** (2B **146**)
Bilsthorpe Rd. NG22: Eakr 2A **126**
Bilton Cl. NG24: Bald 7G **137**
Binbrook Ct. DN10: Bawt 1J **9**
BINGHAM 4F **101** (1C **149**)
Bingham Av. NG17: Skeg 5A **46**
Bingham By-Pass NG13: Bing 4C **100**
Bingham Ind. Pk. NG13: Bing 3F **101**
Bingham Leisure Cen. 4G 101
Bingham Rd. NG5: Sher 5K **85**
NG12: Cotg 6E **110**
(not continuous)
NG12: Rad T 5E **98**
NG13: Lang, Tith 2G **113**
NG18: Mans 7C **48**
Bingham Station (Rail) 3G **101**
Bingley Cl. NG8: Bilb 2C **94**
Birch Av. DE7: Ilk 1A **92**
NG4: Carl 1G **97**
NG9: Bee 5C **106**
NG16: Nuth 1G **83**
NG21: Rain 2A **56**
NG22: Farns 4J **57**
Birch Cl. DN22: Ramp 6K **25**
NG15: Rave 3C **62**
NG16: Nuth 1G **83**
Birch Ct. NG21: Rain 2A **56**
NG22: Tuxf 7C **28**
Birch Cft. Dr. NG19: Mans W 7C **42**
Birchcroft Rd. DN22: Retf 2E **22**
Birchdale Av. NG15: Huck 1G **75**
Birchenall Ct. NG24: Farnd 7H **133**
Birches, The NG15: Rave 1C **62**
Birchfield Dr. S80: Work 3C **20**
Birchfield Rd. NG5: Arn 6J **77**
Birch Gro. NG18: Mans 6B **48**
Birchin Wlk. NG18: Mans 5K **47**
Birchlands, The NG19: Mans W 1B **48**
Birch Lea LE12: East L 3K **121**
NG5: Redh 6F **77**
Birchover Rd. NG8: Bilb 3H **93**
Birch Pas. NG7: Radf 3A **6** (3H **95**)
Birch Ri. NG14: Woodbo 1G **79**
Birch Rd. NG22: New O 4C **38**
NG24: New B 4F **137**
Birch St. NG20: Chu W 2B **34**
Birch Tree Cl. NG19: Mans W 6F **43**
Birch Tree Cres. NG17: Kirk A 7K **51**
Birch Wlk. NG5: Sher 4A **86**
BIRCHWOOD 2D **147**
Birchwood Cl. NG15: Rave 3D **62**
NG17: Skeg 4J **45**
NG25: Sout 5G **131**
S81: Lango 1C **12**
Birchwood Dr. NG15: Rave 3C **62**
NG17: Skeg 4H **45**
Birchwood Pk. NG19: Mans W 6E **42**
Birchwood Pk. Homes NG21: Rain 1H **55**
Birchwood Rd. NG8: Woll 4H **93**
BIRCOTES 2G **9** (2B **144**)
Bircotes Leisure Cen. 1E 8
Bird Cl. NG18: Mans 7J **47**
Birdcroft La. DN10: Walk 7J **11**
Birding St. NG19: Mans 1H **47**
Birdsall Av. NG8: Woll 4K **93**
Bird's La. NG17: Ann W 3J **59**
Birkdale S81: Work 6J **19**
Birkdale Av. NG22: New O 2D **38**

Bourne St. NG4: Neth 2K 97
Bournmoor Av. NG11: Clif 1F 115
Bovill St. NG7: Radf 2G 95
Bovington Ct. DN22: Retf 1E 22
Bowbridge La. NG24: New B 5D 136
Bowbridge Rd. NG24: New T 2D 136
Bowden Cl. NG5: Sher 4K 85
Bowden Dr. NG9: Bee 3C 106
Bower Cvn. Site NG24: New T 7B 134
Bower Ct. NG24: New T 7D 134
Bowers Av. NG3: Mapp P 1A 96
Bowland Cl. NG3: Nott 1D 96
Bowland Rd. NG13: Bing 4D 100
Bowling St. NG18: Mans 4K 47
Bowlwell Av. NG5: Top V 6B 76
Bowman Pl. NG22: Well 7D 38
Bowness Av. NG6: Basf 5D 84
Bowness Cl. NG2: Gam 2F 109
Bowne St. NG17: Sut A 7K 45
Bowscale Cl. NG2: West Br 4F 109
Bow St. NG19: Mans W 5A 42
Box Cres. NG17: Kirk A 5K 51
Boxley Dr. NG2: West Br 5K 107
Boyce Gdns. NG3: Mapp 6C 86
Boycroft Av. NG3: Nott 7C 86
Boyd Cl. NG5: Arn 5K 77
Boy La. NG21: Edwin 7F 37
Boynton Dr. NG3: Mapp 6C 86
Bracadale Rd. NG5: Top V 5B 76
BRACEBRIDGE 3H 21
Bracebridge S80: Work 3H 21
(not continuous)
Bracebridge Av. S80: Work 2J 21
Bracebridge Ct. S80: Work 3H 21
Bracebridge Dr. NG8: Bilb 2J 93
Bracey Ri. NG2: West Br 6B 108
Bracken Av. NG22: New O 2E 38
Bracken Cl. NG4: Carl 5G 87
NG8: Bilb 6A 84
NG10: Long E 7A 104
NG17: Kirk A 5K 51
NG20: Mkt W 5E 34
Bracken Ct. DN11: Harwo 2B 8
NG22: Bils 6D 126
Brackendale Av. NG5: Arn 6H 77
Brackendale Dr. NG22: Wale 5G 27
Brackenfield Av. NG19: Mans W 5A 42
Brackenfield Dr. NG16: Gilt 6F 73
Brackenfield Ri. NG15: Rave 1C 62
Bracken Hill NG18: Mans 5C 48
Brackenhill NG14: Cayt 6J 81
Bracken Hill La. DN10: Miss 1B 10
Brackenhurst La. NG25: Sout 7G 131
Bracken La. DN22: Retf 5G 23
Bracken Rd. NG10: Long E 7A 104
Bracken Way DN11: Harwo 2A 8
Brackenwood Cl. NG19: Mans W 1C 48
Brackmills Cl. NG19: Mans W 1A 48
Bracknell Cres. NG8: Basf 6E 84
BRACON 1C 145
Bracton Dr. NG3: Nott 2C 96
Bradbourne Av. NG11: Wil 4H 107
Bradbury Gdns. NG11: Rudd 3J 115
Bradbury/Midway Ind. Est. NG7: Lent 1F 107
Bradbury St. NG2: Nott 4D 96
Bradder Way NG18: Mans 5G 47
Braddock Cl. NG7: Lent 4F 95
Braddon Av. NG9: Stap 7D 92
Bradfield Rd. NG8: Brox 6A 84
Bradford Ct. NG6: Bulw 1B 84
Bradforth Av. NG18: Mans 3C 48
Bradgate Cl. NG10: Sand 5A 104
Bradgate Rd. NG7: Hyson G 7H 85
Bradley Ct. NG9: Bee 3B 106
Bradleys La. NG14: Hove 4J 81
Bradley St. NG10: Sand 4B 104
Bradleys Yd. NG12: Plum 3H 117
NG20: Mkt W 4D 34
Bradley Wlk. NG11: Clif 2G 115
Bradman Gdns. NG5: Arn 1E 86
BRADMORE 7B 116 (2A 148)
Bradmore Av. NG11: Rudd 2K 115
Bradmore Ct. NG18: Mans 7C 48
Bradmore La. NG12: Plum 6F 117
Bradmore Ri. NG5: Sher 3K 85
Bradmore Rd. NG12: Wys 6E 118
Bradwell Cl. NG16: Gilt 6G 73
Bradwell Dr. NG5: Top V 6B 76
Braefell Cl. NG2: West Br 4G 109
Braemar Av. NG16: Eastw 6D 72
Braemar Dr. NG4: Ged 6A 88
Braemar Rd. NG6: Bulw 7J 75
NG19: Mans W 6F 43
Braemer Rd. NG23: Coll 2H 129
Braidwood Ct. NG7: Hyson G 1G 95
Brail La. NG22: Eakr 4B 126
Brailsford Ct. NG18: Mans 4D 48
Brailsford Rd. NG7: Lent 7F 95
Brailsford Way NG9: Chil 7H 105
Brailwood Cl. NG22: Bils 5D 126
Brailwood Rd. NG22: Bils 5D 126
BRAITHWAITE 1B 144
BRAITHWELL 2A 144
Brake La. NG22: Wale 1D 38 & 7F 27
Brake Rd. NG22: Wale 6F 27
Brake Vw. NG22: New O 2E 38
Bramber Gro. NG11: Clif 3F 115
Bramble Cl. DN22: Nth L 7C 24
NG6: Basf 4E 84
NG9: Atten 7J 105
NG10: Long E 7A 104
NG22: Bils 6D 126
NG22: New O 2D 38
Bramble Ct. NG4: Ged 6J 87
Bramble Cft. NG17: Sut A 2G 51
Bramble Dr. NG3: Nott 1D 96
Bramble Gdns. NG8: Bilb 7B 84
Bramble La. NG18: Mans 5C 48
Bramble Rd. DN22: Retf 6H 23
Brambles, The NG13: Barns 2G 141
NG22: Wale 5G 27
Bramble Way DN11: Harwo 2B 8
NG12: Cotg 7F 111
Brambling Cl. NG18: Mans 3A 48
Bramblings, The S81: Gate 5D 18
BRAMCOTE 1F 105 (2A 148)
Bramcote Av. NG9: Chil 3H 105
Bramcote Ct. NG18: Mans 7C 48
Bramcote Crematorium NG9: Bram 5F 93
Bramcote Dr. DN22: Retf 5D 22
NG8: Woll 5J 93
NG9: Bee 2K 105
Bramcote Dr. W. NG9: Bee 3J 105
BRAMCOTE HILLS 7H 93
Bramcote La. NG8: Woll 6J 93
NG9: Chil 3H 105
Bramcote Rd. NG9: Bee 2J 105
Bramcote St. NG7: Radf 3F 95
Bramcote Wlk. NG7: Radf 3F 95
Bramerton Rd. NG8: Bilb 2H 93
Bramhall Rd. NG8: Bilb 2H 93
BRAMLEY 2A 144
Bramley Cl. NG14: Gun 2B 90
NG25: Sout 6J 131
Bramley Ct. LE12: East L 3A 122
NG16: Kimb 1E 82
NG17: Sut A 7K 45
Bramley Grn. NG8: Brox 6K 83
Bramley Rd. NG8: Brox 6K 83
BRAMLEY VALE 2A 146
Bramley Wlk. NG19: Mans 3D 46
Bramley Way DN10: Mist 4K 11
BRAMPTON 1D 147
Brampton Dr. NG9: Stap 4E 104
BRAMPTON EN LE MORTHEN 3A 144
Brancaster Cl. NG6: Cin 3C 84
Brancliffe La. S81: Shire 4A 18
Brand Ct. NG17: Stan H 4G 45
Brandish Cres. NG11: Clif 1E 114
Brand La. NG17: Stan H 5G 45
BRANDON 1D 149
Brandon Cl. NG24: Bald 5H 137
Brandon Wlk. NG17: Sut A 3H 51
Brandreth Av. NG3: Nott 7C 86
NG17: Sut A 6H 45
Brandreth Dr. NG16: Gilt 6E 72
Brand St. NG2: Nott 6C 96
Branklene Cl. NG16: Kimb 7J 73
Branksome Wlk. NG2: Nott 6K 95
BRANSBY 1D 147
Bransdale S81: Work 4H 19
Bransdale Av. NG19: Mans W 1A 48
Bransdale Rd. NG11: Clif 1E 114
BRANSTON 3D 149
Branston Av. NG22: Farns 5K 57
Branston Cl. NG24: Wint 2G 135
Branston Gdns. NG2: West Br 5A 108
Branston Wlk. NG5: Sher 3K 85
BRANT BROUGHTON 3D 147
Brantford Av. NG11: Clif 1G 115
BRANTON 1B 144
Brassington Cl. NG16: Gilt 7F 73
Brassington Ct. NG19: Mans W 5A 42
BRATTLEBY 3D 145
Bratton Dr. NG5: Bestw 2H 85
Braunton Cl. NG15: Huck 7D 66
Brayton Cres. NG6: Bulw 2E 84
Break La. NG15: Pap 7A 62
BREASTON 2A 148
Breaston Ct. *NG5: Top V 6C 76*
(off Erewash Gdns.)
Brechin S81: Work 7J 19
Brechin Cl. NG5: Arn 5K 77
Brechin Ct. NG19: Mans W 3H 41
Breck Bank NG22: New O 3C 38
Breckbank NG19: Mans W 1A 48
Breck Bank Cres. NG22: New O 3C 38
Breckhill Rd. NG3: Mapp 2B 86
NG5: Woodt 2B 86
Breck La. DN10: Matt, Matt T 3F 15
Brecks La. DN22: Tres 4K 25
NG23: Elston 2E 140
Brecks Rd. DN22: Ord 7D 22
Breckswood Dr. NG11: Clif 3F 115
Brecon Cl. NG8: Cin 4B 84
NG21: Rain 2B 56
Breedon St. NG10: Long E 6A 104
Brendon Ct. NG9: Bram 1G 105
Brendon Dr. NG8: Woll 3B 94
NG16: Kimb 7K 73
Brendon Gdns. NG8: Woll 3B 94
Brendon Gro. NG13: Bing 3D 100
Brendon Rd. NG8: Woll 3B 94
Brendon Way NG10: Long E 7A 104
Brentcliffe Av. NG3: Nott 1D 96
BRENTINGBY 3C 149
Brentnall Ct. NG9: Chil 6J 105
Bressingham Dr. NG2: West Br 6K 107
Bretby Ct. NG18: Mans 4D 48
Brett Cl. NG15: Huck 1E 74
Bretton Rd. NG15: Rave 1D 62
Brettsil Dr. NG11: Rudd 3J 115
Brewers Way NG18: Mans 5B 48
Brewer's Wharf NG24: New T 7C 134
Brewery La. DN10: Eve 6B 10
DN22: Retf 4F 23
Brewery St. NG16: Kimb 1E 82
Brewhouse, The NG24: New T 1C 136
Brewhouse Mus. 7D 6
Brewhouse Yd. NG1: Nott 7D 6 (5J 95)
Brewsters Cl. NG13: Bing 4F 101
Brewsters Rd. NG3: Nott 7B 86
Brewsters Way DN22: Retf 1C 22
Brian Clough Way NG7: Lent, Nott 5A 6 (6C 94)
NG9: Bram, Stap 3E 104
Briar Av. NG10: Sand 6A 104
Briarbank Av. NG3: Nott 7D 86
Briarbank Wlk. NG3: Nott 1D 96
Briar Cl. NG9: Bram 7K 93
NG12: Key 6J 117
NG15: Huck 1D 74
NG17: Stan H 4G 45
NG21: Rain 2K 55
S80: Work 3D 20
Briar Ct. DN11: Harwo 2B 8
NG2: Nott 7J 95
NG22: New O 3C 38
Briar Gdns. NG14: Calv 5A 70
Briar Ga. NG10: Long E 7A 104
NG12: Cotg 7F 111
Briar Gro. DN11: Harwo 2B 8
Briar La. NG18: Mans 6C 48
Briar Lea DN22: Ord 6D 22
S80: Work 3D 20
Briar Rd. NG16: Newth 6F 73
NG22: New O 3C 38
Briars, The DN10: Miss 2D 10
Briarwood Av. NG3: Nott 1D 96
Briarwood Cl. NG19: Mans W 1D 48
Briarwood Ct. NG5: Sher 4B 86
Briber Hill S81: Blyth 7G 13
Briber Rd. S81: Blyth 7G 13
Brickcliffe Rd. LE12: East L 2B 122
Brickenell Rd. NG14: Calv 7D 70
Brickenhole La. DN10: Walk 7H 11
Brickings La. DN22: Sth L 2H 25
Brickings Way DN22: Stu S 2C 24
Brick Kiln La. NG18: Mans 3C 46
NG19: Mans 3C 46
Brickley Cres. LE12: East L 3B 122
Brickyard NG15: Huck 7J 67
Brickyard Dr. NG15: Huck 1J 75
Brickyard La. DN10: Miss 1E 10
LE12: West L 3F 121
NG12: Rad T 5G 99
NG13: East B 5E 90
NG20: Cuck 2B 32
NG22: Farns 5K 57
Brickyard Plantation Nature Reserve 7D 82
Brick Yard Rd. DN22: Gam 1G 27
Bridegate La. LE14: Hick, Hick P 7A 142
Bridge Av. NG9: Chil 4K 105
Bridge Ct. NG9: Bee 2C 106
NG15: Huck 7G 67
Bri. End Av. NG16: Sels 4D 58
Bri. Farm La. NG11: Clif 7F 107
Bridgeford Ct. Cvn. Pk. NG13: East B 4C 90
Bridgegate DN22: Retf 3E 22
Bridgegate Cen. DN22: Retf 3E 22
Bridge Grn. NG8: Brox 6K 83
Bridge Grn. Wlk. NG8: Brox 6K 83
Bridge Gro. NG2: West Br 1B 108
Bridge Ho. Ct. S81: Carl L 7D 12
Bridgend Cl. NG9: Stap 4C 104
Bridge Pl. S80: Work 2G 21
Bridge Rd. NG8: Woll 3J 93
Bridge Row S81: Carl L 6D 12
Bridge St. NG10: Long E 7C 104
NG10: Sand 4B 104
NG16: Lang M 3A 72

BUDBY 2B 146
Budby Av. NG18: Mans 4B 48
Budby Cres. NG20: Mede V 6G 33
Budby Dr. NG20: Mede V 4K 33
Budby Ri. NG15: Huck 6H 67
Budby Rd. NG20: Cuck 4D 32
BULCOTE 1G 89 (1B 148)
Bulcote Dr. NG14: Bur J 4C 88
Bulcote Rd. NG11: Clif 6G 107
Bulham La. NG23: Sut T 2C 128
Bullace Ct. NG19: Mans W 1A 48
Bullace Rd. NG3: Nott 1K 7 (1C 96)
Bull Cl. Rd. NG7: Lent 1F 107
Bulldole La. DN22: Clay 7H 15
Buller Cl. NG23: Coll 1J 129
Buller St. DE7: Ilk 2A 92
Buller Ter. NG5: Sher 4A 86
BULL FARM 7E 40
Bullfinch Rd. NG6: Basf 3E 84
Bullins Cl. NG5: Arn 5E 76
Bullivant St. NG3: Nott 1G 7 (2A 96)
Bullock Cl. NG19: Mans W 4H 41
Bullpit Rd. NG24: Bald 5G 137
Bull Yd. NG25: Sout 5H 131
S80: Work 3F 21
Bully La. NG19: Sook 5A 34
BULWELL 7H 75 (1A 148)
Bulwell Bus. Cen. NG6: Bulw 7G 75
BULWELL FOREST 6J 75
Bulwell Forest Stop (NET) 6J 75
Bulwell Hall Pk. 4H 75
Bulwell High Rd.
NG6: Bulw 1C 84
Bulwell La. NG6: Basf 3E 84
Bulwell Station (Rail) 1D 84
Bulwell Stop (NET) 1D 84
Bulwer Rd. NG7: Radf 3G 95
NG17: Kirk A 6K 51
Bunbury St. NG2: Nott 7A 96
Bungalow La. NG22: Bils 6D 126
Bungalows, The DN11: Birc 2F 9
(off Whitehouse Rd.)
NG22: Wale 5G 27
Bunnison La. NG12: Cols B 7H 141
BUNNY 3B 118 (3A 148)
Bunny Hall Pk. NG11: Bunny 4B 118
Bunny Hill LE12: Bunny, Costo 7A 118
NG11: Bunny 7A 118
Bunny Hill Top LE12: Costo 6A 118
Bunny La. NG11: Bunny 1E 118
NG12: Key 1E 118
Buntings La. NG4: Carl 1F 97
Bunting St. NG7: Lent 7F 95
Bunyan Grn. Rd. NG16: Sels 6B 58
Burbage Ct. NG18: Mans 4D 48
Burberry Av. NG15: Huck 2J 75
Burden Cres. DN22: Woodbe 7G 25
Burden La. NG12: Shel 6H 89
Burford Rd. NG7: Hyson G 7G 85
Burford St. NG5: Arn 6G 77
Burgage NG25: Sout 5H 131
Burgage Cl. NG25: Sout 5H 131
Burgage La. NG25: Sout 5H 131
Burgass Rd. NG3: Nott 1D 96
Burge Cl. NG2: Nott 6K 95
Burgh Hall Cl. NG9: Chil 7H 105
BURGHWALLIS 1A 144
Burhill NG12: Cotg 7F 111
Burke St. NG7: Radf 3A 6 (3H 95)
Burleigh Cl. NG4: Carl 1J 97
Burleigh Ct. NG22: Tuxf 6C 28
Burleigh Ri. NG22: Tuxf 6C 28
Burleigh Rd. NG2: West Br 3C 108
Burleigh Sq. NG9: Chil 5H 105
Burley Ct. DN10: Walk 6G 11
Burlington Av. NG5: Sher 4J 85
Burlington Ct. NG5: Sher 4K 85
Burlington Dr. NG19: Mans 7E 40
Burlington Rd. NG4: Carl 7H 87
NG5: Sher 4K 85
Burma Rd. NG21: Blid 5J 55
Burnaby St. NG6: Basf 3E 84
Burnaston Ct. NG19: Mans W 5A 42
Burnaston Rd. NG18: Mans 4D 48
Burnbank Cl. NG2: West Br 4G 109
Burnbreck Gdns. NG8: Woll 4K 93
Burndale Wlk. NG5: Top V 6A 76
Burneham Cl. NG13: East B 5D 90
Burnham Av. NG9: Chil 5A 106
Burnham Ct. NG18: Mans 6J 47
Burnham Lodge NG5: Top V 5K 75
Burnham St. NG5: Sher 5K 85
Burnham Way NG2: Nott 5K 95
Burnmoor La. NG22: Egma 2E 124
Burnor Pool NG14: Calv 6D 70
Burns, The NG20: Mkt W 3E 34
Burns Av. NG7: Radf 2B 6 (2H 95)
NG19: Mans W 7J 41
Burns Ct. NG5: Sher 4J 85
Burnside Cl. NG17: Kirk A 4K 51
Burnside Dr. NG9: Bram 6H 93
NG19: Mans 7E 40
Burnside Grn. NG8: Bilb 2J 93
Burnside Gro. NG12: Toll 1F 117
Burnside Rd. NG2: West Br 4B 108
NG8: Bilb 2J 93
Burns La. NG20: Chu W, Mkt W 3D 34
Burns Rd. S81: Work 7J 19
Burns St. NG7: Radf 2A 6 (2H 95)
NG18: Mans 3G 47
Burn St. NG17: Sut A 7A 46
Burnt Oak Cl. NG16: Nuth 4J 83
Burnt Oaks Cl. NG19: Mans W 6K 41
Burntstump Country Pk. 3F 69
Burntstump Hill NG5: Arn 3E 68
Burnwood Dr. NG8: Woll 3J 93
BURRINGHAM 1D 145
Burrows, The LE12: East L 2A 122
Burrows Av. NG9: Bee 7A 94
Burrows Ct. NG3: Nott 3C 96
Burrows Cres. NG9: Bee 7A 94
Burrow Wlk. NG17: Kirk A 7J 51
Bursar Way NG10: Long E 6B 104
Burtness Rd. NG11: Clif 1F 115
Burton Av. NG4: Carl 7E 86
Burton Cl. NG4: Carl 6K 87
NG17: Sut A 7G 45
Burton Ct. NG22: Bils 5C 126
Burton Dr. NG9: Chil 5H 105
BURTON JOYCE 3E 88 (1B 148)
Burton Joyce Station (Rail) 4D 88
Burton La. DN22: Sth W 3K 17
NG13: What 4E 102
BURTON LAZARS 3C 149
Burton Manderfield Ct.
NG2: Nott 6K 95
BURTON ON THE WOLDS 3A 148
Burton Ri. NG17: Ann W 4A 60
NG22: Wale 5G 27
Burton Rd. NG4: Carl, Ged 7J 87
NG17: Sut A 7G 45
Burton St. NG1: Nott 4E 6 (3K 95)
Burton Wlk. LE12: East L 3A 122
BURTON WOLDS 3B 148
Burwell Ct. NG19: Mans W 5A 42
Burwell St. NG7: Hyson G 2G 95
Burwood Av. NG18: Mans 3C 48
Bush Cl. NG5: Top V 6B 76
Bushmead M. S80: Work 3G 21
(off Pilgrim Way)
Bushstocks La. DN22: Tres 5G 25
Buskeyfield La. NG20: Cuck 3A 32
Bute Av. NG7: Lent 4G 95
Butler Av. NG12: Rad T 4F 99
Butler Cl. NG12: Crop Bu 3B 112
Butler Cres. NG19: Mans 7D 40
Butler Dr. NG21: Blid 7H 55
Butlers Cl. NG15: Huck 1J 75
Butlers Fld. NG13: Lang 7K 113
BUTLER'S HILL 7J 67
Butlers Hill Station (Rail) 1K 75
Butlerwood Cl. NG17: Ann W 3J 59
Buton Rd. NG14: Bur J 5B 88
Buttercup Cl. NG24: New B 4F 137
Butterfield Ct. NG16: Want 7A 74
Buttergate, The NG24: New T 1C 136
(off Market Pl.)
Buttermead Cl. NG9: Trow 6C 92
Buttermere Cl. NG2: Gam 2G 109
NG10: Long E 7A 104
Buttermere Ct. NG5: Sher 5K 85
NG19: Mans W 6K 41
Buttermere Dr. NG9: Bram 1J 105
Butterwick Cl. NG19: Mans W 1B 48
Buttery Gdns. NG11: Rudd 4K 115
Buttery La. NG17: Skeg, Teve 2G 45
Butt Ho's. NG7: Lent 4F 95
Butt La. LE12: Norm S 7G 121
NG13: East B 5E 90
NG19: Mans W 7J 41
Butt Rd. NG13: Bing 4H 101
Butt St. NG10: Sand 4A 104
Buxton Av. NG4: Carl 6G 87
Buxton Rd. NG19: Mans 1D 46
Byard La. NG1: Nott 6F 7 (4K 95)
Bye Pass Rd. NG9: Chil 7J 105
Bye Path Rd. DN22: Retf 2F 23
Byfield Cl. NG7: Radf 2G 95
Byford Cl. NG3: Mapp 5B 86
Byley Rd. NG8: Bilb 3G 93
By-Pass Rd. NG14: Gun 2A 90
Byrne Ct. NG5: Arn 2E 86
Byron Av. NG10: Long E 6A 104
NG17: Kirk A 4B 52
NG17: Sut A 6B 46
NG19: Mans W 7J 41
Byron Bingo 6H 67
Byron Cen., The
NG15: Huck 6G 67
Byron Cl. NG24: New T 3D 136
Byron Ct. NG2: Nott 5J 7 (4B 96)
NG9: Stap 7D 92
NG24: Bald 6H 137
Byron Cres. NG15: Rave 1A 62
NG16: Aws 3B 82
Byron Flds. NG15: Ann 4C 60
Byron Gdns. NG25: Sout 5H 131
Byron Gro. NG5: Sher 4K 85
Byron Ind. Est. NG5: Arn 7J 77
Byron Pl. NG7: Lent 3F 95
(off Wragby Rd.)
Byron Rd. NG2: West Br 2C 108
NG15: Ann 4C 60
Byron Sq. NG15: Huck 6G 67
(off Baker St.)
Byron St. NG5: Arn 7F 77
NG15: Huck 7G 67
NG15: News 6D 60
NG18: Mans 3G 47
NG21: Blid 6K 55
Byron Way S81: Work 1J 21
Bythorn Cl. NG17: Skeg 5B 46

C

Caddaw Av. NG15: Huck 7G 67
CADEBY 1A 144
Cadlan Cl. NG5: Bestw 7C 76
Cadlan Ct. NG5: Bestw 7C 76
Cad La. NG23: Norm T 1K 125
Caernarvon Pl. NG9: Chil 5G 105
Caincross Rd. NG8: Bilb 1J 93
Cairngorm Dr. NG5: Arn 4D 76
NG18: Mans 5K 47
Cairns Cl. NG5: Bestw 2H 85
Cairns St. NG1: Nott 3F 7 (3K 95)
Cairo St. NG7: Basf 6G 85
Caister Rd. NG11: Clif 2F 115
Caithness Ct. NG5: Sher 6J 85
Calcroft Cl. NG8: Aspl 5D 84
Caldbeck Cl. NG2: Gam 2F 109
Caldbeck Ct. NG9: Chil 5G 105
Caldbeck Wlk. NG5: Bestw 7D 76
Calderdale NG8: Woll 5G 93
Calderhall Gdns. NG5: Bestw 6E 76
Calder Wlk. NG6: Bulw 7H 75
Caldon Grn. NG6: Bulw 4J 75
Caledonian Rd. DN22: Retf 5G 23
Caledon Rd. NG5: Sher 4J 85
California Rd. NG24: Farnd 7H 133
Calke Av. NG17: Huth 1C 50
Calladine Cl. NG17: Sut A 2H 51
Calladine Ct. NG6: Bulw 1B 84
Calladine Gro. NG17: Sut A 2H 51
Calladine La. NG17: Sut A 3G 51
Callaway Cl. NG8: Woll 3K 93
Calstock Rd. NG5: Woodt 2B 86
Calveley Rd. NG8: Bilb 7K 83
Calver Cl. NG8: Woll 4D 94
Calver St. NG19: Mans W 6A 42
Calvert Cl. NG9: Chil 5J 105
CALVERTON 6D 70 (1B 148)
Calverton Av. NG4: Carl 6E 86
Calverton Cl. NG9: Toton 7F 105
Calverton Dr. NG8: Stre 5J 83
Calverton Rd. NG5: Arn 5H 77
NG21: Blid 2J 63
Calverton Sports & Leisure Cen. 5C 70
Camberley Ct. NG6: Bulw 6G 75
Camberley Rd. NG6: Bulw 6G 75
Camborne Cl. DN22: Retf 2E 22
Camborne Cres. DN22: Retf 1E 22
Camborne Dr. NG8: Aspl 5D 84
Camborne M. DN22: Retf 1D 22
Cambourne Gdns. NG15: Rave 2B 62
Cambourne Pl. NG18: Mans 1D 54
Cambria M. NG3: Nott 1K 95
Cambria Rd. NG19: Plea 5C 40
Cambria Ter. S80: Work 1F 21
Cambridge Cl. NG21: Rain 3K 55
Cambridge Ct. NG2: West Br 1B 108
NG7: Radf 2G 95
Cambridge Cres. NG9: Stap 6C 92
Cambridge Gdns. NG5: Woodt 2E 86
Cambridge Mdws. NG24: New T 1H 137
Cambridge Rd. DN11: Harwo 2C 8
NG2: West Br 2D 108
NG8: Woll 4B 94
NG21: Rain 3J 55
Cambridge St. NG4: Carl 6H 87
NG18: Mans 5G 47
Camb's La. DN22: Nth W 2J 17
Camdale Cl. NG9: Chil 3G 105
Camden Cl. NG2: Nott 5K 7 (4B 96)
Camelia Av. NG11: Clif 1D 114
Camelot Av. NG5: Sher 5H 85
Camelot Cres. NG11: Rudd 2J 115
Camelot St. NG11: Rudd 2J 115
Cameo Cl. NG4: Colw 2J 97

Cameron La. NG24: Bald 7J 137
Camerons, The NG19: Mans 5D 46
Cameron St. NG5: Sher 5K 85
CAMMERINGHAM 3D 145
Camomile Cl. NG5: Top V 7A 76
Camomile Gdns. NG7: Hyson G 1F 95
Campbell Cl. NG8: Brox 6B 84
S81: Work 4G 19
Campbell Dr. NG4: Carl 7F 87
Campbell Gdns. NG5: Arn 5A 78
Campbell Gro. NG3: Nott 3H 7 (3A 96)
Campbell St. NG3: Nott 3J 7 (3B 96)
NG16: Lang M 2A 72
Campden Grn. NG11: Clif 7F 107
Campion St. NG5: Arn 6G 77
Campion Way NG13: Bing 4E 100
CAMPSALL 1A 144
Camrose Cl. NG8: Bilb 7A 84
Canal Rd. S80: Work 2G 21
Canal Side NG9: Bee 6C 106
Canalside NG1: Nott 7F 7 (5K 95)
Canalside Ind. Units NG12: Crop Bi 7B 112
Canalside M. S80: Work 2F 21
Canalside Wlk. NG1: Nott 7C 6 (5K 95)
Canalside Workshops DN22: Retf 3G 23
Canal St. DN22: Retf 4F 23
NG1: Nott 7E 6 (5K 95)
NG10: Long E 7B 104
NG10: Sand 4A 104
Canal Ter. S80: Work 2H 21
Canberra Cl. NG9: Stap 7D 92
Canberra Cres. NG2: West Br 5A 108
Canberra Gdns. NG2: West Br 6A 108
Candleby Cl. NG12: Cotg 6E 110
Candleby Ct. NG12: Cotg 6E 110
Candleby La. NG12: Cotg 6E 110
Candlemass Ct. NG19: Mans W 7K 41
Candle Mdw. NG2: Colw 4G 97
Canning Cir. NG7: Nott 4B 6 (3H 95)
Canning Ter. NG7: Nott 4B 6 (3H 95)
Cannon Cl. NG24: New T 7H 135
Cannon M. DN22: Retf 3F 23
Cannon Sq. *DN22: Retf 3F 23*
(off Churchgate)
Cannon Stevens Cl. NG23: Coll 2H 129
Cannon St. NG5: Sher 4K 85
NG19: Mans 1F 47
Canonbie Cl. NG5: Arn 5K 77
Canon's Cl. NG25: Sout 5J 131
Cantabury Av. NG7: Hyson G 7G 85
Cantelupe Gdns. NG16: Gilt 6G 73
Canterbury Cl. NG16: Nuth 3J 83
NG19: Mans W 4J 41
S81: Work 5H 19
Canterbury Ct. NG1: Nott 2D 6 (2J 95)
Canterbury Rd. NG8: Radf 3E 94
Canterbury Wlk. *S81: Carl L 5B 12*
(off Beverley Wlk.)
CANTLEY 1B 144
Cantley Av. NG4: Ged 5H 87
Cantrell Rd. NG6: Bulw 1D 84
Canver Cl. NG8: Bilb 2H 93
Canwick Cl. NG8: Bilb 3H 93
Capenwray Gdns. NG5: Bestw 6E 76
Capes, The NG13: Aslo 4C 102
Cape St. NG18: Mans 3F 47
Capitol Ct. NG8: Woll 3B 94
Caporn Cl. NG6: Bulw 2D 84
Capps Pl. NG22: Tuxf 7D 28
CARBURTON 1B 146
Carburton Av. NG20: Mede V 7F 33
Carburton La. NG20: Nort 3E 32
Carburton Way NG17: Kirk A 5D 52
CAR COLSTON 4K 91 (1C 149)
CARCROFT 1A 144
Cardale Rd. NG3: Nott 2D 96
NG19: Plea 5C 40
Cardiff St. NG3: Nott 3K 7 (3C 96)
Cardinal Cl. NG3: Nott 1K 7 (2B 96)
Cardinal Ct. NG17: Sut A 2C 52
Cardinal Hinsley Cl. NG24: New T 5A 136
Cardinal Way NG21: C'tone 5J 43
Carding Cl. NG22: Farns 6K 57
Cardington Cl. NG5: Top V 5A 76
Cardle Cl. NG19: Mans W 7C 42
Cardwell St. NG7: Hyson G 7G 85
Carew Rd. NG11: Clif 7F 107
Carey Rd. NG6: Bulw 6J 75
Carisbrook Av. NG18: Mans 3C 48
Carisbrooke Av. NG3: Mapp P 6K 85
NG4: Ged 6A 88
NG9: Bee 1B 106
Carisbrooke Cl. NG17: Kirk A 7C 52
Carisbrooke Dr. NG3: Mapp P 6K 85
Carisbrook Rd. S81: Carl L 6B 12
Car La. NG13: Car C 5K 91
Carlight Gdns. Pk. Homes NG2: West Br 7E 96
Carlile Rd. NG4: Carl 7H 87
Carling Av. S80: Work 3E 20
Carlingford Rd. NG15: Huck 5G 67
Carlin St. NG6: Bulw 7H 75
Carlisle Av. NG6: Bulw 7J 75
Carlswark Gdns. NG5: Top V 5B 76
CARLTON 1J 97 (1B 148)
Carlton Av. S81: Work 6F 19
Carlton Bus. Cen. NG4: Carl 1J 97
Carlton Cl. NG19: Mans W 6F 43
NG24: New T 3D 136
S81: Work 5F 19
Carlton Ct. S81: Work 5G 19
Carlton Cres. LE12: East L 2B 122
Carlton Ferry La. NG23: Coll 6E 128 & 1F 129
Carlton Fold NG2: Nott 5C 96
Carlton Forum Leisure Cen. 6F 87
Carlton Grange NG4: Carl 1F 97
Carlton Hall La. S81: Carl L 7B 12
Carlton Hgts. NG4: Carl 1F 97
Carlton Hill NG4: Carl 1E 96
CARLTON IN LINDRICK 7D 12 (3A 144)
Carlton Lake Dr. NG23: Carl T 5D 128
Carlton La. NG23: Carl T 7B 128
NG23: Carl T, Sut T 4E 128
NG23: Norw 2J 127
CARLTON-LE-MOORLAND 3D 147
Carlton Mnr. Cvn. Pk. NG23: Carl T 6C 128
Carlton M. NG4: Carl 1F 97
CARLTON-ON-TRENT 7D 128 (2D 147)
Carlton Phoenix Ind. Est. S81: Work 1H 21
Carlton Rd. NG3: Nott 5J 7 (4B 96)
NG24: New T 3C 136
S80: Work 2G 21
S81: Work 4G 19
CARLTON SCROOP 1D 149
Carlton Sq. NG4: Carl 1H 97
Carlton Station (Rail) 1J 97
Carlton St. NG1: Nott 5G 7 (4A 96)
NG18: Mans 1J 47
Carlton Va. Cl. NG4: Carl 6G 87
Carlyle Rd. NG2: West Br 2B 108
Carman Cl. NG16: Want 6A 74
Carmel Gdns. NG5: Arn 1C 86
Carnaby Cl. NG12: Rad T 5K 99
Carnarvon Cl. NG13: Bing 3F 101
Carnarvon Dr. NG14: Bur J 2E 88
Carnarvon Gro. NG4: Carl 7G 87
NG4: Ged 6J 87
NG17: Sut A 7F 45
Carnarvon Pl. NG13: Bing 4E 100
Carnarvon Rd. NG2: West Br 3C 108
NG17: Huth 1D 50
Carnarvon St. NG4: Neth 2K 97
NG17: Teve 3F 45
Carnell La. NG24: Bald 7J 137
Carnforth Cl. NG9: Stap 4C 104
Carnforth Ct. NG5: Bestw 6E 76
Carnoustie S81: Work 7J 19
Carnoustie Cl. NG17: Kirk A 4J 51
Carnwood Rd. NG5: Bestw 1H 85
Carolgate DN22: Retf 3F 23
Caroline Cl. NG15: Rave 1D 62
Caroline Ct. DE7: Ilk 2A 92
Caroline Wlk. NG3: Nott 1G 7 (2A 96)
Carpenter Av. NG19: Mans 7D 40
Carpenters Cl. NG12: Crop Bu 3C 112
(not continuous)
Carr, The DN22: Retf 4E 22
Carradale Cl. NG5: Arn 6A 78
Carr Farm Rd. NG17: Ann W 3K 59
Carrfield Av. NG9: Toton 7E 104
Carrfield Cl. NG17: Sut A 7H 45
Carrgate La. NG23: Elston 1E 140
Carr Gro. NG17: Kirk A 6J 51
Carr Hill Way DN22: Retf 1F 23
CARRHOUSE 1C 145
CARRINGTON 5J 85
Carrington Ct. NG5: Sher 6K 85
Carrington La. NG14: Calv 4D 70
Carrington St. NG1: Nott 7F 7 (5K 95)
Carrion Vw. S81: Gate 6E 18
Carr La. DN10: Mist 2G 11
NG20: Mkt W 4C 34
NG23: Upton 7C 132
Carroll Gdns. NG2: Nott 7K 95
Carr Rd. DN10: Gri H 1A 16
DN10: Matt 4J 15
DN22: Retf 4E 22
NG13: Bing 3J 101
CARR VALE 2A 146
Carr Vw. DN10: Eve 6B 10
Carsic La. NG17: Sut A 7J 45
Carsic Rd. NG17: Sut A 5H 45
Carsington Ct. NG19: Mans W 6A 42
Carswell Cl. NG24: New T 3C 136
Cartbridge NG12: Cotg 7E 110
Carter Av. NG11: Rudd 4K 115
NG12: Rad T 5G 99
Carter Ga. NG1: Nott 6H 7 (4A 96)
NG24: New T 1C 136
Carter La. NG18: Mans 4K 47
NG20: Chu W, Wars 4A 34
Carter La. E. DE55: Sth N 5A 50
Carter La. W. DE55: Sth N 6A 50
Carter Rd. NG9: Chil 6F 105
(Readman Rd.)
NG9: Chil 7F 105
(Swiney Way, not continuous)
Carterswood Dr. NG16: Nuth 4A 84
Cartwright Cl. NG22: Dun T 5G 29
Cartwright La. DE55: Sth N 4C 50
Cartwright St. S81: Shire 5A 18
Carver Cl. NG21: Edwin 7F 37
Carver St. NG7: Hyson G 7G 85
Carwood Rd. NG9: Bram 7J 93
Casper Ct. *NG5: Top V 6C 76*
(off Birkdale Way)
Castellan Ri. NG5: Bestw 6E 76
Casterton Rd. NG5: Bestw 6D 76
Castle Blvd. NG7: Lent, Nott 7A 6 (5G 95)
Castle Brewery Ct. NG24: New T 1C 136
Castlebridge Office Village
NG7: Lent 6H 95
Castle Bri. Rd. NG7: Lent 5H 95
Castle Cl. NG14: Calv 6B 70
Castle Ct. NG7: Nott 7D 6 (5J 95)
CASTLE DONINGTON 3A 148
Castle Exchange NG1: Nott 4G 7
Castle Farm La. S80: Work 6D 20
Castlefields NG2: Nott 6K 95
Castle Gdns. NG7: Lent 5G 95
Castle Ga. NG1: Nott 6E 6 (4K 95)
(not continuous)
NG24: New T 1C 136
Castle Gro. NG7: Nott 6D 6 (4J 95)
CASTLE HILL 7J 51
Castle Hill LE12: East L 4B 122
Castle Hill Cl. NG17: Kirk A 6J 51
Castle Hill Sq. *S80: Work 3F 21*
(off West St.)
Castle Ind. Pk. NG15: Huck 1F 75
Castle Marina Pk. NG7: Lent 5H 95
Castle Marina Rd. NG7: Lent 6H 95
Castle Mdw. Retail Pk.
NG7: Lent 7C 6 (5J 95)
Castle Mdw. Rd. NG2: Nott 7E 6 (5J 95)
Castle M. NG7: Lent 7A 6 (5H 95)
NG19: Mans W 6H 41
Castle Mus. & Art Gallery 6D 6 (5J 95)
Castle Pk. Ind. Est. NG2: Nott 6J 95
Castle Pl. NG1: Nott 6D 6 (4J 95)
Castle Quay NG7: Nott 7C 6 (5J 95)
Castle Quay Cl. NG7: Lent 5H 95
Castle Retail Pk. NG7: Radf 2F 95
Castlerigg Cl. NG2: West Br 4F 109
Castle Rising *NG24: New T 1C 136*
(off Lombard St.)
Castle Rd. NG1: Nott 6D 6 (4J 95)
Castle Rock NG7: Nott 7D 6 (5J 95)
Castle St. NG2: Nott 4C 96
NG16: Eastw 5E 72
NG18: Mans 3G 47
NG19: Mans W 6H 41
S80: Work 3F 21
Castleton Av. NG4: Carl 6H 87
NG5: Arn 7H 77
Castleton Cl. NG2: Nott 6J 95
NG15: Huck 7D 66
NG15: Rave 1C 62
NG16: Sels 5E 58
NG19: Mans W 5J 41
Castleton Ct. NG6: Bulw 1A 84
Castle Vw. NG2: West Br 3A 108
Castle Vw. Cotts. NG9: Bee 3D 106
Castle Vw. Ct. NG24: New T 7C 134
Castle Vs. NG2: Nott 6K 7 (4C 96)
Castle Wlk. NG7: Hyson G 1G 95
Castle Wharf NG1: Nott 5K 95
Castlewood Gro. NG17: Sut A 2H 51
Caterham Cl. NG8: Bilb 1J 93
Catfoot La. NG4: Lamb 6B 78
Catherine Av. NG19: Mans W 6J 41
Catherine Cl. NG6: Bulw 7G 75
NG17: Kirk A 4K 51
Catherine St. NG6: Bulw 7G 75
Catkin Dr. NG16: Gilt 6G 73
Catkin Way NG24: New B 5E 136
Catlow Wlk. NG5: Bestw 6E 76
Caton Cl. NG17: Sut A 7H 45
Cator Cl. NG4: Ged 4G 87
Cator La. NG9: Chil 3J 105
Cator La. Nth. NG9: Chil 3J 105
Cator Rd. NG19: Plea 6C 40
Catriona Cres. NG5: Arn 4J 77
Catt Cl. NG9: Chil 7G 105
Catterley Hill Rd. NG3: Nott 1D 96
Cattle Mkt. Rd. NG2: Nott 6A 96
Cattle Rd. DN10: Mist 2F 11
Catton Rd. NG5: Arn 6J 77
Caudale Ct. NG2: Gam 2F 109
Caudwell Cl. NG25: Sout 4H 131
Caudwell Dr. NG18: Mans 7H 47

Cauldwell Rd. NG17: Sut A 1D **52**
(not continuous)
NG18: Mans 2H **53**
Caulton St. NG7: Hyson G 2G **95**
(not continuous)
CAUNTON 7J **127** (2C **147**)
Caunton Av. NG3: Nott 6B **86**
Caunton Cl. NG18: Mans 4F **47**
NG20: Mede V 1F **35**
Caunton Lawn Tennis Club 6F **127**
Caunton Rd. NG23: Norw 4G **127**
NG25: Hock 1K **131**
Caunt's Cres. NG17: Sut A 7H **45**
Causeway La. NG25: Mort 5F **139**
Causeway M. NG2: Nott 6J **95**
Cavan Ct. NG2: Nott 7K **95**
Cavell Cl. DN22: Woodbe 7G **25**
NG11: Clif 7E **106**
Cavell Ct. NG7: Nott 6E **94**
Cavendish Av. NG4: Ged 5G **87**
NG5: Sher 4A **86**
NG17: Sut A 7J **45**
NG21: Edwin 6D **36**
NG24: New T 3D **136**
CAVENDISH BRIDGE 2A **148**
Cavendish Cl. NG15: Huck 7J **67**
Cavendish Ct. NG3: Mapp 4C **86**
NG7: Nott 5B **6** (4H **95**)
Cavendish Cres. NG4: Carl 5F **87**
NG9: Stap 6C **92**
NG17: Ann W 3A **60**
Cavendish Cres. Nth. NG7: Nott 6A **6** (4H **95**)
Cavendish Cres. Sth. NG7: Nott 7A **6** (5H **95**)
Cavendish Dr. NG4: Carl 7H **87**
Cavendish Hall NG7: Nott 1B **106**
Cavendish Ho. *NG4: Carl* *7H **87***
(off Foxhill Rd. E.)
Cavendish M. NG7: Nott 5B **6** (4H **95**)
Cavendish Pl. NG7: Nott 7A **6** (5H **95**)
NG9: Bee 3A **106**
Cavendish Rd. DN22: Retf 6H **23**
NG4: Carl 5F **87**
NG10: Long E 7B **104**
S80: Work 5H **21**
Cavendish Rd. E. NG7: Nott 5B **6** (4H **95**)
Cavendish Rd. W. NG7: Nott 6A **6** (4H **95**)
Cavendish St. NG5: Arn 6G **77**
NG7: Lent 7F **95**
NG17: Sut A 6A **46**
NG18: Mans 5J **47**
NG19: Mans W 6G **41**
NG20: Langw 7A **26**
Cavendish Va. NG5: Sher 4A **86**
Cave's La. DN10: Walk 6F **11**
Cawdron Wlk. NG11: Clif 7F **107**
Cawston Gdns. NG6: Bulw 6H **75**
Cawthorne Cl. NG23: Coll 1J **129**
Cawthorne Way NG18: Mans 3B **48**
Caxmere Dr. NG8: Woll 3A **94**
Caxton Cl. NG4: Neth 1K **97**
Caxton Rd. NG5: Sher 6J **85**
CAYTHORPE
East Bridgford 6G **81** (1B **148**)
Normanton 1D **149**
Caythorpe Ct. *NG19: Mans W* *6A **42***
(off Sedgebrook St.)
Caythorpe Cres. NG5: Sher 3K **85**
Caythorpe Ri. NG5: Sher 3K **85**
Caythorpe Rd. NG14: Cayt, Lowd 6E **80**
Cecil Cl. S80: Rhod 1B **20**
Cecil St. NG7: Lent 5G **95**
Cedar Av. LE12: East L 4K **121**
NG9: Bee 2B **106**
NG16: Nuth 3A **84**
NG17: Kirk A 7K **51**
NG19: Mans W 4H **41**
NG24: New T 5E **134**
Cedar Cl. NG10: Sand 2A **104**
NG13: Bing 4H **101**
NG17: Skeg 3H **45**
S81: Carl L 5B **12**
Cedar Ct. NG9: Bee 2B **106**
Cedar Dr. NG12: Key 1H **119**
NG16: Sels 5D **58**
Cedar Gro. NG5: Arn 6K **77**
NG8: Woll 4A **94**
NG15: Huck 1H **75**
Cedarland Cres. NG16: Nuth 3A **84**
Cedar La. NG22: New O 2C **38**
Cedar Lodge NG7: Nott 5B **6** (4H **95**)
Cedar Rd. NG7: Hyson G 7H **85**
NG9: Chil 4K **105**
Cedars, The NG5: Sher 3A **86**
NG23: Syer 3B **140**
Cedar St. NG18: Mans 5J **47**
Cedar Tree Rd. NG5: Arn 5D **76**
Cedar Tree Vw. DN22: Elk 3F **27**
Celandine Cl. NG5: Top V 7A **76**
Celandine Gdns. NG13: Bing 4D **100**
Celery Mdws. DN22: Clar 7H **17**
Celia Dr. NG4: Carl 1G **97**
Celtic Flds. S81: Work 5E **18**
Celtic Point S81: Work 5E **18**
Cemetery Rd. NG9: Stap 2D **104**
S80: Work 3H **21**
Centenary Cl. NG24: New B 5F **137**
Central Av. NG2: West Br 1C **108**
NG3: Mapp 3E **86**
NG5: Arn 7H **77**
NG7: Basf 6H **85**
NG9: Bee 7K **93**
NG9: Chil 3J **105**
NG9: Stap 1D **104**
NG10: Sand 3A **104**
NG15: Huck 7G **67**
NG17: Kirk A 1B **60**
NG18: Mans 5J **47**
NG21: Blid 6K **55**
NG22: Wale 5G **27**
S80: Work 3E **20**
Central Av. Sth. NG5: Arn 7H **77**
Central Ct. NG7: Lent 7G **95**
Central Dr. NG21: C'tone 7H **43**
NG23: Elston 2E **140**
Central St. NG3: Nott 1K **7** (2B **96**)
Central Wlk. NG15: Huck 6G **67**
Centre Way NG12: Rad T 4D **98**
Centurion Bus. Pk. NG6: Bulw 5E **74**
Centurion Way NG2: Nott 1H **107**
Century Av. NG18: Mans 5F **47**
Century Ct. NG1: Nott 1D **6**
Century Rd. DN22: Ord 5E **22**
Century St. NG24: New T 1D **136**
Cernan Ct. NG6: Bulw 2A **84**
Cerne Cl. NG11: Clif 2G **115**
Chaceley Way NG11: Wil 6H **107**
Chadborn Av. NG11: Goth 7G **115**
Chadburn Rd. NG18: Mans 2A **48**
Chaddesden, The NG3: Mapp P 1K **95**
Chad Gdns. NG5: Top V 4C **76**
CHADWELL 3C **149**
Chadwick Rd. NG7: Hyson G 1F **95**
Chadwick Wlk. DN22: Woodbe 7G **25**
Chaffinch Cl. NG18: Mans 3B **48**
Chaffinch M. S81: Gate 5D **18**
Chainbridge La. DN22: Lound 4D **14**
Chainbridge Rd. DN22: Lound 4D **14**
Chain La. NG7: Lent 7F **95**
NG24: New T 1C **136**
Chalet Cvn. Site, The NG23: Bath 6G **129**
Chalfield Cl. NG11: Clif 1E **114**
Chalfont Dr. NG8: Aspl 2D **94**
Challond Ct. NG5: Bestw 7E **76**
Chamberlain Cl. NG11: Clif 1D **114**
Chambers Av. DE7: Ilk 1A **92**
Chamber's Gdns. DN22: Clay 6H **15**
Champion Cres. NG19: Mans 2F **47**
Chancery, The NG9: Bram 2H **105**
Chancery Cl. NG17: Skeg 4A **46**
Chancery Ct. DN22: Retf 4E **22**
NG11: Wil 3H **107**
Chancery La. DN22: Retf 4E **22**
Chandos Av. NG4: Neth 7K **87**
Chandos St. NG3: Nott 1B **96**
NG4: Neth 1K **97**
Chantrey Rd. NG2: West Br 2B **108**
Chantry, The NG18: Mans 5B **48**
Chantry Cl. NG9: Chil 5J **105**
NG16: Kimb 2F **83**
NG24: New T 4C **136**
Chantry Wlk. *NG22: Tuxf* *6C **28***
(off Market Pl.)
Chapel Bar NG1: Nott 5D **6** (4J **95**)
Chapel Cl. DN10: Mist 2H **11**
DN22: Clar 7J **17**
NG22: Wale 5G **27**
Chapel Ct. NG11: Goth 7G **115**
NG21: Edwin 7F **37**
NG22: Edin 2A **130**
Chapel Gth. NG13: Ors 2J **103**
Chapel Ga. S81: Carl L 7D **12**
Chapelgate DN22: Retf 3F **23**
Chapel La. DN10: Eve 6B **10**
DN10: Mist 2H **11**
DN10: Scro 4K **9**
LE12: Costo 3E **122**
LE12: Will W 6G **143**
LE14: Neth B 4K **143**
LE14: Upp B 3H **143**
NG4: Lamb 7F **79**
NG5: Arn 6G **77**
NG12: Cotg 6E **110**
NG13: Aslo 3D **102**
NG13: Bing 1E **100**
NG13: Gran 1J **141**
NG14: Epp 7K **71**
NG15: Rave 4D **62**
NG22: Farns 5K **57**
NG22: Lax 6B **124**
NG22: Wale 5G **27**
Chapel La. NG23: Bath 5F **129**
NG23: Caus 6H **127**
NG23: Nth M 5K **129**
NG24: Codd 7K **135**
NG24: Farnd 7G **133**
NG24: Wint 2F **135**
NG25: Oxt 1F **71**
Chapel M. Ct. NG9: Bram 1G **105**
Chapel Pl. NG16: Kimb 1E **82**
Chapel Quarter NG1: Nott 5D **6**
Chapel Rd. NG16: Sels 6C **58**
Chapel St. NG7: Radf 3A **6** (3H **95**)
NG9: Bram 1G **105**
NG11: Rudd 4K **115**
NG13: Ors 2J **103**
NG15: Huck 6G **67**
NG16: Eastw 5D **72**
NG16: Kimb 1E **82**
NG16: Sels 5E **58**
NG17: Ann W 3A **60**
NG17: Kirk A 6J **51**
NG19: New H 2A **40**
NG20: Whal T 4B **26**
Chapel Ter. NG15: News 6D **60**
Chapel Wlk. NG13: What 4E **102**
S80: Work 3F **21**
Chapel Yd. NG12: Norm W 3K **117**
Chapman Ct. NG8: Bilb 1C **94**
Chapmans Wlk. NG6: Bestw V 7D **68**
Chappel Gdns. NG22: Bils 7D **126**
Chapter Dr. NG16: Kimb 2F **83**
Chardlace Wlk. *NG1: Nott* *4A **96***
(off Hollowstone)
Chard St. NG7: Basf 5G **85**
Chard Ter. NG7: Basf 5G **85**
Charlbury Ct. NG9: Bram 4G **93**
Charlbury Rd. NG8: Woll 2B **94**
Charlecote Dr. NG8: Woll 5H **93**
Charlecote Pk. Dr. NG2: West Br 5K **107**
Charles Av. NG9: Chil 6H **105**
NG9: Lent A 7B **94**
NG9: Stap 1E **104**
NG10: Sand 3A **104**
NG16: Eastw 4F **73**
Charles Cl. DE7: Ilk 2A **92**
NG4: Ged 5J **87**
Charles Ct. NG15: Huck 6G **67**
Charles St. NG5: Arn 7G **77**
NG11: Rudd 3K **115**
NG15: Huck 6G **67**
NG17: Sut A 7A **46**
NG19: Mans 1G **47**
NG19: Mans W 5J **41**
NG24: New T 2E **136**
Charleston Ho. NG1: Nott 2J **95**
Charles Way NG6: Bulw 2C **84**
Charles Way Bus. Pk. NG6: Bulw 2D **84**
Charlesworth Av. NG7: Basf 7F **85**
Charlesworth Ct. *NG19: Mans W* *6A **42***
(off Sedgebrook St.)
Charlock Cl. NG5: Top V 7A **76**
Charlock Gdns. NG13: Bing 5E **100**
Charlotte Cl. NG5: Arn 4G **77**
NG22: Kirt 2H **39**
NG24: New T 1D **136**
Charlotte Ct. NG16: Eastw 3D **72**
Charlotte Gro. NG9: Bram 7J **93**
Charlton Gro. NG9: Chil 5A **106**
Charnock Av. NG8: Woll 5E **94**
Charnwood Av. LE12: Sut B 7C **120**
NG9: Bee 3J **105**
NG10: Sand 5A **104**
NG12: Key 1H **119**
Charnwood Cl. NG15: Rave 4C **62**
Charnwood Gdns. NG5: Sher 6J **85**
Charnwood Gro. NG2: West Br 2B **108**
NG13: Bing 4E **100**
NG15: Huck 6E **66**
NG18: Mans 3C **48**
NG19: Mans W 4H **41**
Charnwood La. NG5: Arn 1D **86**
Charnwood St. NG17: Sut A 1F **51**
Charnwood Way NG14: Woodbo 2H **79**
Charta M. NG14: Lowd 5E **80**
Charter Pl. NG22: Tuxf 6D **28**
Charters Cl. NG17: Kirk A 4K **51**
Chartwell Av. NG11: Rudd 3J **115**
Chartwell Gro. NG3: Mapp 2F **87**
Chartwell Rd. NG17: Kirk A 6C **52**
Charwood Flds. LE12: Sut B 7C **120**
Chase Pk. NG2: Nott 5D **96**
Chatham Ct. NG6: Bulw 1D **84**
NG24: New T 2C **136**
Chatham St. NG1: Nott 1E **6** (2K **95**)
NG25: Sout 5J **131**
Chatsworth Av. NG4: Carl 7H **87**
NG7: Basf 5G **85**
NG9: Chil 7H **105**
NG12: Rad T 4F **99**
NG16: Sels 5E **58**

Church La. NG18: Mans .4J **47**
NG19: Plea .4A **40**
(not continuous)
NG22: Bou .3F **39**
NG22: Eakr .2C **126**
NG22: Halam .5C **130**
NG22: Kirk .1C **132**
NG23: Aver .4F **133**
NG23: Best .7H **125**
NG23: Carl T .7D **128**
NG23: Coll .1H **129**
NG23: Nth C, Sth C .5C **30**
NG23: Nth M, Sth M .1B **134** & 7K **129**
NG23: Sibt .6E **140**
NG23: Sth C .7D **30**
NG23: Upton .7C **132**
NG24: Bald .6H **137**
NG25: Mort .6G **139**
S81: Carl L .7C **12** & 1G **19**
CHURCH LANEHAM .1J **29** (1D **147**)
Churchmead NG17: Huth .7D **44**
Church Mdw. NG14: Calv .7D **70**
Church Mdw. La. NG23: Upton .1H **139**
(not continuous)
Church M. NG2: Nott .7A **96**
NG17: Kirk A .7J **51**
NG17: Sut A .1J **51**
Churchmoor Ct. NG5: Arn .5G **77**
Churchmoor La. NG5: Arn .5G **77**
Church Rd. DN11: Birc .2F **9**
LN6: Swin .7K **31**
NG3: Nott .1H **7** (1A **96**)
NG6: Bestw V .2A **76**
NG14: Bur J .3E **88**
NG16: Grea, Want .3H **73**
NG20: Chu W, Mkt W .2D **34**
NG21: C'tone .6G **43**
NG22: Bou .2F **39**
NG23: Harby .7K **31**
Church Row NG23: Nth M .6K **129**
Church Side NG17: Huth .7D **44**
NG18: Mans .3J **47**
NG22: Farns .5K **57**
Churchside Gdns. NG7: Hyson G .7F **85**
Church Sq. NG7: Lent .5G **95**
Church St. DN10: Bawt .1K **9**
(not continuous)
DN10: Beck .6C **16**
DN10: Eve .6B **10**
DN10: Mist .2G **11**
DN22: Nth W .2J **17**
DN22: Sth L .1G **25**
DN22: Stu S .3C **24**
NG4: Carl .1H **97**
NG4: Lamb .6G **79**
NG5: Arn .6H **77**
NG6: Basf .5F **85**
NG7: Lent .5F **95**
NG9: Bee .3A **106**
NG9: Bram .1G **105**
NG9: Stap .2C **104**
NG10: Sand .2A **104**
NG11: Bunny .3B **118**
NG11: Goth .7G **115**
NG11: Rudd .3K **115**
NG12: Crop Bi .5B **112**
NG12: Shel .6H **89**
NG13: Bing .4G **101**
NG13: Gran .1J **141**
NG13: Ors .1J **103**
NG13: What .5E **102**
NG16: Eastw .5C **72**
NG17: Kirk A .6H **51**
NG17: Sut A .1H **51**
NG18: Mans .3H **47**
NG19: Mans W .6J **41**
NG19: Plea .4B **40**
NG20: Mkt W .4D **34**
NG20: Whal T .5B **26**
NG21: Edwin .5F **37**
NG22: Bils .5C **126**
NG22: East M .3D **28**
NG22: Oll .5A **38**
NG23: Coll .3G **129**
NG23: Sut T .2E **128**
NG24: New T .1C **136**
NG25: Sout .6H **131**
S81: Lango .2B **12**
Church St. E. NG16: Pinx .1B **58**
Church St. W. NG16: Pinx .1A **58**
CHURCH TOWN .1C **145**
Church Vw. DN10: Beck .6C **16**
DN10: Scro .4K **9**
NG4: Ged .6J **87**
NG17: Stan H .4H **45**
NG19: New H .2A **40**
NG22: Egma .2E **124**
NG22: Oll .5A **38**
NG24: Bald .6G **137**
NG25: Oxt .2F **71**
Church Vw. Cl. NG5: Arn .5D **76**
Church Vw. Gdns. NG17: Ann W .4J **59**
Church Wlk. DN11: Harwo .2B **8**
NG4: Carl .1H **97**
NG9: Stap .2C **104**
NG13: What .4D **102**
NG14: Woodbo .2G **79**
NG16: Brins .7C **64**
NG16: Eastw .4D **72**
NG22: Dun T .6J **29**
NG23: Upton .7C **132**
NG23: Weston .2F **125**
NG24: New T .1C **136**
S80: Work .2G **21**
CHURCH WARSOP .1C **34** (2A **146**)
Church Way DN22: Sut L .6B **14**
CHURCH WILNE .2A **148**
Churnet Cl. NG11: Clif .5F **107**
Churston Ct. NG9: Bee .3B **106**
Cigar Factory, The *NG7: Nott* .*4B* ***6***
(off Derby Rd.)
CINDERHILL .3C **84**
Cinderhill Footway NG6: Bulw .3E **84**
Cinderhill Gro. NG4: Ged .5H **87**
Cinderhill Rd. NG6: Bulw, Cin .3C **84**
Cinderhill Stop (NET) .3C **84**
Cinderhill Wlk. NG6: Bulw .1C **84**
Cinder La. NG22: Oll .6B **38**
Circle, The NG19: Mans W .5H **41**
NG21: C'tone .6J **43**
Cirrus Dr. NG16: Want .7A **74**
Citadel St. NG7: Radf .3F **95**
City, The NG9: Bee .3B **106**
(not continuous)
City Ground .7B **96**
City Link NG2: Nott .7H **7** (5A **96**)
City of Caves .6F **7**
City Point NG1: Nott .6D **6** (4J **95**)
City Rd. NG7: Nott .7E **94**
NG9: Bee .2B **106**
City Vw. NG3: Mapp .5C **86**
Clandon Dr. NG5: Sher .5J **85**
Clanfield Rd. NG8: Bilb .1K **93**
Clapham St. NG7: Radf .3F **95**
CLARBOROUGH .7J **17** (3C **145**)
Clarborough Dr. NG5: Arn .1D **86**
Clarborough Hill DN22: Clar .7J **17**
Clare Cl. NG6: Basf .3F **85**
Clarehaven NG9: Stap .4D **104**
Clare Hill NG21: Blid .7J **55**
Claremont Av. NG9: Bram .1H **105**
NG15: Huck .1G **75**
Claremont Cl. NG19: Mans W .5A **42**
Claremont Dr. NG2: West Br .6K **107**
Claremont Gdns. NG5: Sher .6J **85**
Claremont Rd. NG5: Sher .6J **85**
Clarence Ct. NG3: Nott .4K **7** (3B **96**)
NG17: Sut A .7F **45**
Clarence Rd. NG9: Chil .7J **105**
S80: Work .1F **21**
Clarence St. NG3: Nott .3K **7** (3B **96**)
NG18: Mans .4G **47**
NG19: Plea .6C **40**
Clarendon Chambers NG1: Nott .3D **6** (3J **95**)
Clarendon Ct. NG5: Sher .7J **85**
Clarendon Dr. S81: Work .6E **18**
Clarendon Pk. NG5: Sher .7J **85**
Clarendon Rd. NG19: Mans .2E **46**
Clarendon St. NG1: Nott .3C **6** (3J **95**)
Clare Rd. NG17: Sut A .3K **51**
Clare St. NG1: Nott .4F **7** (3K **95**)
Clare Valley NG7: Nott .6C **6** (4J **95**)
Clarewood Gro. NG11: Clif .3F **115**
Clarges St. NG6: Bulw .1D **84**
Claricoates Dr. NG24: Codd .6H **135**
Clarke Av. NG5: Arn .6H **77**
NG24: New T .4B **136**
Clarke Cl. NG12: Crop Bi .5B **112**
Clarke Rd. NG2: Nott .6B **96**
Clarke's La. NG9: Chil .5J **105**
Clark La. NG22: Tuxf .7C **28**
Clarks La. NG24: New T .6E **134**
Clarkson Dr. NG9: Bee .3C **106**
Clarkwoods Cl. NG22: Bou .4D **38**
Clater's Cl. DN22: Retf .3G **23**
Claude St. NG7: Lent .7F **95**
Claverton Ct. NG18: Mans .7C **48**
CLAWSON HILL .3C **149**
Clawson La. LE14: Hick .6E **142**
LE14: Neth B .3K **143**
Clay Av. NG3: Mapp .4D **86**
Claybank Vs. NG21: Blid .7G **55**
Clayfield Cl. NG6: Bulw .1B **84**
Claygate NG3: Nott .1D **96**
Clayhough La. DN22: Chu L .1J **29**
Claylands Av. S81: Work .5C **18**
Claylands Cl. S81: Work .6E **18**
Claylands La. S81: Work .7E **18**
Clay La. NG23: Harby .6K **31**
NG24: New T .2E **136**
Claymoor Cl. NG18: Mans .4F **47**
Claypit La. NG25: Fis .5H **139**
CLAYPOLE .1D **149**
Claypole Rd. NG7: Hyson G .1G **95**
CLAYTON .1A **144**
Clayton Cl. NG24: New T .3D **136**
Clayton Ct. NG7: Radf .3G **95**
NG9: Bee .4B **106**
Claytons Dr. NG7: Lent .6F **95**
Claytons Wharf NG7: Lent .6F **95**
CLAYWORTH .7J **15** (3C **145**)
Clayworth Comn. DN22: Clay .7J **15**
Clayworth Ct. NG18: Mans .7C **48**
Clayworth Rd. DN10: Gri H .4B **16**
Clegg Hill Dr. NG17: Huth .6C **44**
Clement Av. NG24: Bald .6H **137**
Clerkson's All. *NG18: Mans* .*3H* ***47***
(off Leeming St.)
Clerkson St. NG18: Mans .4H **47**
Clether Rd. NG8: Bilb .2J **93**
Cleve Av. NG9: Toton .6D **104**
Clevedon Dr. NG5: Arn .5A **78**
Cleveland Cl. NG7: Radf .3F **95**
S81: Carl L .5B **12**
Cleveland Hill NG22: West M .2A **28**
Cleveland Sq. NG24: New T .3C **136**
Cleveley's Rd. NG9: Toton .6D **104**
Clevely Way NG11: Clif .6F **107**
Cliff, The NG6: Bulw .3C **84**
Cliff Blvd. NG16: Kimb .7K **73**
(not continuous)
Cliff Cres. NG12: Rad T .4E **98**
Cliff Dr. NG12: Rad T .3F **99**
Cliffe Hill Av. NG9: Stap .2C **104**
Cliff Ga. DN22: Rock .1A **28**
Cliffgrove Av. NG9: Chil .3J **105**
Cliffhill La. NG13: Aslo .3D **102**
Cliff La. NG16: Pinx .1D **58**
Cliff La. Cotts. NG16: Pinx .7D **50**
Cliffmere Wlk. NG11: Clif .1E **114**
(not continuous)
Cliff Nook DE55: Sth N .7A **50**
Cliff Nook La. NG24: New T .7D **134**
Clifford Av. NG9: Bee .1K **105**
Clifford Cl. NG12: Key .6J **117**
Clifford Ct. NG7: Radf .3A **6** (3G **95**)
Clifford St. NG7: Radf .2A **6** (2G **95**)
NG18: Mans .6H **47**
Cliff Rd. NG1: Nott .6G **7** (4A **96**)
NG4: Carl .2G **97**
NG12: Rad T .4D **98**
Cliffs, The NG12: Rad T .3F **99**
Cliff St. NG18: Mans .3J **47**
Cliff Way NG12: Rad T .4E **98**
CLIFTON
Maltby .2A **144**
West Bridgford .1G **115** (2A **148**)
Clifton Av. NG11: Rudd .2K **115**
Clifton Blvd. NG7: Lent, Nott .6E **94**
NG11: Rudd, Wil .4H **107**
Clifton Cres. NG9: Atten .6K **105**
NG24: New T .5F **135**
Clifton Grn. NG11: Clif .7E **106**
Clifton Gro. NG4: Ged .5H **87**
NG18: Mans .6B **48**
Clifton Ho. NG24: New T .5C **136**
Clifton La. NG11: Clif, Wil .2E **114**
NG11: Rudd .2H **115**
Clifton Leisure Cen. .1G **115**
Clifton M. NG7: Nott .5A **6** (4H **95**)
Clifton Pl. NG18: Mans .3H **47**
Clifton Rd. NG11: Rudd .3J **115**
Clifton St. NG9: Bee .3B **106**
Clifton Ter. NG7: Nott .7B **6** (5H **95**)
Clifton Way DN22: Retf .2C **22**
Clinton Arms Ct. *NG24: New T* .*1C* ***136***
(off St Mark's Pl.)
Clinton Av. NG5: Sher .7J **85**
NG16: Brins .7B **64**
Clinton Ct. NG1: Nott .3E **6** (3K **95**)
Clinton Ri. DN22: Gam .1K **27**
Clinton St. NG5: Arn .7G **77**
NG9: Bee .2K **105**
NG24: New T .1C **136**
S80: Work .4H **21**
Clinton St. E. NG1: Nott .4F **7** (3K **95**)
Clinton St. W. NG1: Nott .4F **7** (3K **95**)
Clinton Ter. NG7: Nott .4A **6** (3H **95**)
Clipsham Cl. NG24: Bald .4H **137**
CLIPSTON .7B **110** (2B **148**)
CLIPSTONE .6G **43** (2A **146**)
Clipstone Av. NG1: Nott .1D **6** (2J **95**)
NG3: Mapp .3D **86**
NG17: Sut A .6A **46**
NG18: Mans .2J **47**
Clipstone Cl. NG8: Stre .5J **83**
Clipstone Dr. NG19: Mans W .7E **42**
NG21: Edwin .7H **35**
Clipstone Rd. NG21: Edwin .7H **37**
Clipstone Rd. E. NG19: Mans W .7E **42**

D

EAST FERRY 2D 145
Eastfield DN22: Nth W 2J 17
NG23: Nth M 6K 129
Eastfield Cl. NG21: C'tone 7H 43
Eastfield Ct. NG25: Sout 6F 131
Eastfield Pk. NG22: Tuxf 5E 28
Eastfield Side NG17: Sut A 6A 46
Eastgate S80: Work 2G 21
Eastglade Rd. NG5: Bestw 1G 85
East Gro. NG7: Basf 7H 85
NG13: Bing 4G 101
Eastham Cl. NG3: Nott 2J 7 (2B 96)
Eastham Rd. NG5: Arn 1E 86
EASTHORPE 2D 149
Easthorpe NG25: Sout 6J 131
Easthorpe Cotts.
NG11: Rudd 3A 116
Easthorpe St. NG11: Rudd 3K 115
Eastlands La. NG20: Chu W 2D 34
Eastland Ter. NG20: Mede V 7G 33
East La. NG21: Edwin 6F 37
EAST LEAKE 3B 122 (3A 148)
East Leake Leisure Cen. 2B 122
Eastleigh Dr. NG19: Mans W 3H 41
EAST LOUND 2C 145
EAST MARKHAM 2C 28 (1C 147)
East Moor NG12: Cotg 7F 111
Eastmoor Cft. NG2: Colw 3G 97
Eastmoor Dr. NG4: Carl 7J 87
EASTON 3D 149
East Rd. NG7: Nott 6E 94
EAST STOCKWITH 2C 145
EAST STOKE 1C 149
East St. DN11: Harwo 1D 8
DN22: Retf 4F 23
NG1: Nott 4G 7 (3A 96)
NG11: Goth 7G 115
NG13: Bing 4G 101
NG17: Sut A 7A 46
East Vw. NG2: West Br 3A 108
NG22: East M 3C 28
East Vw. Cl. NG17: Ann W 3C 60
Eastview Ter. NG16: Lang M 3A 72
East Wlk. DN22: Retf 2C 22
EASTWELL 3C 149
Eastwell Ct. NG15: Huck 5G 67
Eastwell St. NG15: Huck 5G 67
Eastwold NG12: Cotg 7F 111
EASTWOOD 4D 72 (1A 148)
Eastwood Av. NG20: Mkt W 3D 34
Eastwood Cl. NG15: Huck 2E 74
Eastwood Community Sports Cen. 3C 72
Eastwood Ct. S81: Work 3G 19
Eastwood La. DN10: Miss 2E 10
Eastwood Rd. NG12: Rad T 5F 99
NG16: Kimb 7H 73
Eastwood St. NG6: Bulw 2D 84
Eather Av. NG19: Mans W 5J 41
EATON
Melton Mowbray 3C 149
Retford 1C 147
Eaton Av. NG5: Arn 7J 77
Eaton Cl. NG9: Bee 3C 106
NG21: Rain 3J 55
NG22: Farns 5K 57
Eaton Ct. NG18: Mans 7C 48
Eaton Pl. NG13: Bing 4F 101
Eatons Rd. NG9: Stap 3C 104
Eaton St. NG3: Mapp 4C 86
Eaton Ter. NG3: Mapp 5C 86
Eaves La. NG23: Sut T 4C 128
Ebenezer St. NG16: Lang M 3A 72
Ebers Gro. NG3: Mapp P 7K 85
Ebers Rd. NG3: Mapp P 6K 85
Ebony Wlk. NG3: Nott 7E 86
Ebury Rd. NG5: Sher 6J 85
Eccleston's Yd. *NG24: New T* *1C 136*
(off Market Pl.)
Eccles Way NG3: Nott 1C 96
Eckford Ct. *NG18: Mans* *1C 54*
(off Bellamy Rd.)
Eckington Ter. NG2: Nott 7K 95
Eckington Wlk. NG18: Mans 4D 48
(not continuous)
Eclipse Yd. *NG18: Mans* *3H 47*
(off Clumber St.)
Ecton Cl. NG5: Top V 5B 76
Edale Cl. NG15: Huck 7C 66
NG18: Mans 7C 48
Edale Ct. NG17: Sut A 6J 45
Edale Ri. NG9: Toton 6D 104
Edale Rd. NG2: Nott 3D 96
NG18: Mans 4D 48
Eddery Vw. NG18: Mans 3B 48
Eddison Cl. S81: Work 5H 19
Eddlestone Dr. NG11: Clif 1G 115
Edenbridge Ct. NG8: Woll 6J 93
Eden Cl. NG5: Arn 1C 86
NG15: Huck 7C 66
Eden Ct. DN22: Ord 7E 22
Edenhall Gdns. NG11: Clif 7G 107
Eden Low NG19: Mans W 6K 41
EDENTHORPE 1B 144
Edern Cl. NG5: Bestw 7C 76
Edern Gdns. NG5: Bestw 7C 76
Edgar Av. NG18: Mans 2J 47
Edgbaston Gdns. NG8: Aspl 7E 84
Edge Cl. NG23: Nth M 4K 129
Edgecote Way NG5: Bestw 1H 85
Edgehill Dr. NG24: New T 1H 137
Edgehill Gro. NG19: Mans W 7J 41
Edgeway NG8: Stre 6J 83
Edgewood Dr. NG15: Huck 1D 74
Edgewood Leisure Cen. 2D 74
Edgington Cl. NG12: Cotg 7F 111
Edginton St. NG3: Nott 1C 96
Edginton Ter. NG3: Nott 1C 96
Edgware Rd. NG6: Bulw 7K 75
Edgwood Rd. NG16: Kimb 1E 82
Edinbane Cl. NG5: Top V 4B 76
Edinboro Row NG16: Kimb 7J 73
Edinburgh Dr. NG13: Bing 3E 100
Edinburgh Rd. S80: Work 5J 21
Edinburgh Wlk. S80: Work 5J 21
Edingale Ct. NG9: Bram 4G 93
EDINGLEY 2A 130 (3B 146)
Edingley Av. NG5: Sher 3K 85
NG19: Mans 3D 46
Edingley Hill NG22: Edin 2A 130
Edingley Sq. NG5: Sher 3J 85
Edison Ri. NG22: New O 4C 38
Edison St. NG17: Ann W 3K 59
Edison Village NG7: Nott 7F 95
Edison Way NG5: Arn 7A 78
Edith Ter. *NG7: Radf* *2F 95*
(off Hartley Rd.)
Edlington Dr. NG8: Woll 5H 93
Edmond Gro. NG15: Huck 5J 67
Edmonds Cl. NG5: Arn 4C 76
EDMONDTHORPE 3D 149
Edmonstone Cl. NG5: Bestw 2G 85
Edmonton Ct. NG2: West Br 3A 108
Edmonton Rd. NG21: C'tone 7G 43
Ednaston Rd. NG7: Nott 7E 94
Edwald Rd. NG12: Edwal 6E 108
EDWALTON 6E 108 (2B 148)
Edwalton Av. NG2: West Br 2C 108
Edwalton Cl. NG12: Edwal 6E 108
Edwalton Ct. NG6: Bulw 1F 85
NG18: Mans 7C 48
Edwalton Hall NG12: Edwal 6D 108
Edwalton Lodge Cl. NG12: Edwal 6D 108
Edward Av. NG8: Aspl 7E 84
NG16: Jack 6A 64
NG17: Sut A 6K 45
NG24: New T 1B 136
Edward Cl. NG15: Huck 2D 74
Edward Ct. NG2: West Br 7C 96
Edward Jermyn Dr. NG24: New T 4E 134
Edward Rd. NG2: West Br 7C 96
NG16: Eastw 4E 72
NG16: Nuth 2H 83
Edwards Ct. NG5: Sher 2J 85
S80: Work 2E 20
Edwards La. NG5: Bestw, Sher 1J 85
Edward St. NG9: Stap 2C 104
NG16: Lang M 2A 72
NG17: Kirk A 5B 52
NG20: Mkt W 3C 34
S80: Work 2G 21
EDWINSTOWE 6F 37 (2B 146)
Edwinstowe Av. NG2: West Br 2C 108
Edwinstowe Dr. NG5: Sher 3K 85
NG16: Sels 5F 59
Edwin St. NG5: Arn 1A 86
NG17: Sut A 7J 45
Eeatgate NG23: Norm T 1K 125
Eel Pool Rd. DN10: Drake, Eve 1J 15 & 7D 10
Eels La. NG22: Lax 6A 124
Eelwood Rd. NG15: Huck 2D 74
Egerton Cl. NG18: Mans 3C 48
Egerton Dr. NG9: Stap 6C 92
Egerton Rd. NG5: Woodt 3A 86
Egerton St. NG3: Nott 1E 6 (1K 95)
Egerton Wlk. NG3: Nott 1F 7 (1K 95)
Egham Cl. NG21: Rain 2A 56
Egling Cft. NG4: Colw 4J 97
EGMANTON 2E 124 (2C 147)
Egmanton Rd. NG18: Mans 7C 48
NG20: Mede V 7F 33
NG22: Lax 5B 124
NG22: Tuxf 7B 28
Egmont Ct. NG2: Nott 6K 95
Egypt Rd. NG7: Basf 6G 85
(not continuous)
Eighth Av. NG7: Nott 4D 106
NG19: Mans W 2C 48
Eileen Rd. NG9: Bee 6B 106
Eisele Cl. NG6: Bulw 1A 84
Ekowe St. NG7: Basf 5G 85
Eland St. NG7: Basf 6G 85
Elder Cl. NG5: Arn 5J 77
Elder Gdns. NG5: Top V 6C 76
Elder Gro. NG15: Huck 2H 75
Elder St. NG17: Kirk A 5J 51
NG17: Skeg 3H 45
Eldon Chambers NG1: Nott 5E 6 (4K 95)
Eldon Grn. NG22: Tuxf 6C 28
Eldon Rd. NG9: Atten 7H 105
Eldon Rd. Ind. Est. NG9: Atten 7H 105
Eldon Rd. Trad. Est. NG9: Chil 7H 105
Eldon St. NG22: Tuxf 6B 28
NG24: New T 2C 136
Eleanor Cres. NG9: Stap 2E 104
Electric Av. NG2: Nott 2H 107
Elford Ri. NG3: Nott 5K 7 (4C 96)
Elgar Gdns. NG3: Nott 2C 96
Eliot Wlk. NG11: Clif 2D 114
Elizabeth Cl. NG15: Huck 1E 74
Elizabeth Gro. NG4: Ged 5H 87
Elizabeth Rd. NG24: New T 4B 136
ELKESLEY 2G 27 (1B 146)
Elkesley Pk. DN22: Gam 2H 27
Elkesley Pl. NG20: Mede V 6G 33
Elkesley Rd. NG20: Mede V 6G 33
Ella Rd. NG2: West Br 7C 96
Ellastone Av. NG5: Bestw 6E 76
Ellerby Av. NG11: Clif 7F 107
Ellerslie Cl. NG24: New T 7D 134
Ellerslie Gro. NG10: Sand 4A 104
Ellesmere Bus. Pk. NG5: Sher 5H 85
Ellesmere Cl. NG5: Arn 7K 77
Ellesmere Cres. NG5: Sher 5J 85
Ellesmere Dr. NG9: Trow 3B 92
Ellesmere Rd. NG2: West Br 5C 108
NG19: Mans W 2B 48
Ellington Rd. NG5: Arn 4J 77
Elliot St. NG7: Nott 4B 6 (3H 95)
Elliott Durham Swimming Pool 6B 86
Ellis Av. NG15: Huck 7H 67
Ellis Ct. NG3: Nott 1G 7 (2A 96)
Ellis Gro. NG9: Bee 4A 106
Ellis St. NG17: Kirk A 6B 52
Ellsworth Ri. NG5: Bestw 1G 85
Ellwood Cres. NG8: Woll 3B 94
Elma La. NG20: Holb, Holb W 1A 32
S80: Holb 4B 26
Elm Av. LE12: East L 1A 122
NG3: Nott 1E 6 (1K 95)
NG4: Carl 1J 97
NG9: Atten 7J 105
NG9: Bee 3K 105
NG10: Sand 2A 104
NG12: Key 1J 119
NG13: Bing 4H 101
NG15: Huck 1E 74
NG16: Nuth 1G 83
NG24: New T 3E 136
Elm Bank NG3: Mapp P 7K 85
Elm Bank Dr. NG3: Mapp P 7K 85
Elmbridge NG5: Bestw 7D 76
Elm Cl. NG3: Mapp P 1K 95
NG12: Key 1J 119
NG16: Pinx 1B 58
NG24: New T 3E 136
Elmcroft NG25: Oxt 2F 71
Elmdale Gdns. NG8: Bilb 7C 84
Elm Dr. NG4: Carl 1J 97
Elmfield NG20: Mkt W 5C 34
Elm Gro. NG5: Arn 5J 77
NG20: Chu W 2C 34
Elmhurst Av. NG3: Mapp 5F 87
Elmhurst Dr. NG17: Huth 7E 44
Elmhurst Rd. NG19: Mans W 1B 48
Elmore Ct. NG7: Radf 2A 6 (2H 95)
Elmore's Mdw. NG14: Blea 2B 138
Elms, The NG4: Colw 2J 97
NG16: Want 7K 73
Elms Cl. LE12: Remp 7F 123
NG11: Rudd 4A 116
Elmsdale Gdns. NG14: Bur J 3E 88
Elms Gdns. NG11: Rudd 4K 115
Elmsham Av. NG5: Top V 5A 76
Elmsmere Dr. S81: Oldc 6B 8
Elms Pk. NG11: Rudd 4A 116
Elms Rd. S80: Work 1F 21
Elmsthorpe Av. NG7: Lent 4F 95
Elmswood Gdns. NG5: Sher 4A 86
ELMTON 1A 146
Elm Tree Av. NG2: West Br 2A 108
NG19: Mans W 5G 41
Elmtree Av. NG16: Sels 5D 58
Elmtree Cl. S81: Shire 5A 18
Elm Tree Ct. S80: Work 3G 21
Elm Tree Pl. DN22: Elk 2G 27
Elm Tree Rd. NG17: Kirk A 5K 51
Elmtree Rd. NG14: Calv 6B 70
Elm Tree St. NG18: Mans 3J 47
Elm Vw. NG7: Radf 2G 95
Elm Wlk. DN22: Retf 5G 23

Goldcrest Cl. NG13: Bing 5H **101**
Goldcrest Ri. S81: Gate 5D **18**
Goldcrest Rd. NG6: Cin 4C **84**
Golden Hill La. NG22: Kirt 2K **39**
Goldenholme La. DN22: Ramp 7K **25**
Goldfinch Cl. NG18: Mans 3A **48**
Goldham Rd. NG8: Stre 7J **83**
Goldies Dr. NG18: Mans 2K **47**
Goldsmith Ct. NG1: Nott 3D **6**
Goldsmith Ho. *NG18: Mans 3G 47*
(off The Connexion)
Goldsmith Rd. NG24: Bald 4G **137**
S81: Work 7J **19**
Goldsmith St. NG1: Nott 3D **6** (3J **95**)
NG18: Mans 3G **47**
Goldson Way NG23: Nth M 7K **129**
Goldstraw La. NG24: Bald 7H **137**
Goldswong Ter. NG3: Nott 1K **95**
GOLDTHORPE **1A 144**
Goldthorpe Av. S81: Lango 1C **12**
Goldthorpe Cl. S81: Lango 1C **12**
Golf Club Rd. DE7: Stan D 7A **92**
Golf Rd. NG12: Rad T 5F **99**
Gomersall Cl. DN22: Retf 4G **23**
GONALSTON **3F 81 (1B 148)**
Gonalston La.
NG14: Epp, Hove, Gon 1B **80**
GONERBY HILL FOOT **2D 149**
Goodacre St. NG18: Mans 3J **47**
Goodall Cres. NG15: Huck 7J **67**
Goodall St. NG7: Hyson G 1G **95**
Goodhand Cres. NG18: Mans 4E **46**
Goodliffe St. NG7: Hyson G 7G **85**
Goodman Cl. NG16: Gilt 6G **73**
Goodwin Cl. NG24: New T 1G **137**
Goodwin Ct. NG22: Farns 4K **57**
Goodwin Dr. NG16: Kimb 1D **82**
Goodwin La. NG24: Bald 7J **137**
Goodwins Ct. NG23: Roll 3K **139**
Goodwin St. NG7: Radf 2B **6** (2H **95**)
Goodwood Av. NG5: Arn 6G **77**
Goodwood Dr. NG9: Toton 7E **104**
Goodwood Rd. NG8: Woll 4J **93**
Goodwood Way NG18: Mans 3B **48**
Goosedale La. NG6: Bestw V 6A **68**
Goose Ga. NG1: Nott 5G **7** (4A **96**)
Goosegate NG12: Cotg 6D **110**
Goosemoor La. DN22: Retf 6F **23**
Gopher Rd. NG24: New T 4C **136**
Gordon Av. NG18: Mans 4A **48**
Gordon Brae NG18: Mans 7J **47**
Gordon Cl. NG9: Atten 7J **105**
NG22: Farns 6K **57**
S80: Work 2J **21**
Gordondale Rd. NG19: Mans 1H **47**
Gordon Gro. NG7: Basf 6G **85**
Gordon Ri. NG3: Mapp 5B **86**
Gordon Rd. NG2: West Br 2C **108**
NG3: Nott 2K **7** (2B **96**)
NG14: Bur J 2F **89**
Gordon Sq. NG2: West Br 2C **108**
Gordon St. NG6: Basf 3E **84**
Gorman Ct. NG5: Arn 7K **77**
Gorse Av. NG18: Mans 5C **48**
Gorse Cl. NG10: Long E 7A **104**
NG14: Calv 6B **70**
NG16: Newth 5F **73**
Gorse Ct. NG6: Bulw 2F **85**
Gorse Hill NG15: Rave 3C **62**
Gorselands Av. S80: Work 4K **21**
Gorse Rd. NG12: Key 7G **117**
NG24: New T 4C **136**
Gorsethorpe Cotts. NG21: Edwin 1J **43**
Gorsethorpe La. NG21: Edwin, Old C 7H **35**
Gorse Vw. NG23: Roll 3K **139**
Gorse Wlk. NG3: Nott 1E **96**
Gorseway NG21: C'tone 6J **43**
Gorsey Rd. NG3: Mapp P 1A **96**
Gorsy La. NG25: Fis 7F **139**
Gosforth Ct. NG2: Nott 7A **96**
GOTHAM **7G 115 (2A 148)**
Gotham La. NG11: Bunny 4A **118**
Gotham Rd. LE12: East L 1A **122**
NG11: King 1A **120**
Gothic Cl. NG6: Basf 3F **85**
GOVERTON **4E 138 (1C 149)**
Goverton Hill NG14: Blea 1A **138**
Goverton Sq. NG6: Bulw 2E **84**
Gowan Cl. NG9: Chil 7H **105**
Goyden Cl. NG5: Top V 6C **76**
GPT Bus. Pk. NG9: Bee 4B **106**
Grace Av. NG9: Bee 4C **106**
Grace Dr. NG8: Aspl 7E **84**
Gracefield La. NG23: Norm T 1K **125**
Grafton Av. NG5: Woodt 2B **86**
Grafton Cl. NG17: Skeg 5B **46**
Grafton Ct. NG7: Radf 4A **6** (3H **95**)
Grafton St. S80: Work 1F **21**
Graham Cl. NG24: New B 5E **136**
Graham St. NG7: Radf 3G **95**
Grainger Av. NG2: West Br 6B **108**
NG17: Ann W 3B **60**
Graingers Ter. NG15: Huck 7H **67**
Grainger St. NG2: Nott 6B **96**
GRAISELOUND **2C 145**
Grampian Dr. NG5: Arn 4D **76**
Granary, The NG18: Mans 3K **47**
Granary Ct. S81: Carl L 6D **12**
GRANBY **1J 141 (2C 149)**
Granby Av. NG19: Mans 2H **47**
NG24: New T 3D **136**
Granby Ct. NG13: Bing 4E **100**
Granby Dr. NG24: Bald 6G **137**
Granby Hill NG13: Gran 1J **141**
Granby La. NG13: Bing, What 5A **102**
Granby Vs. NG2: Nott 4C **96**
Grandfield Av. NG12: Rad T 4E **98**
Grandfield Cres. NG12: Rad T 4E **98**
Grange, The DN22: Ord 7E **22**
NG23: Nth M 5J **129**
Grange Av. DN10: Mist 4J **11**
NG9: Bee 3A **106**
NG11: Rudd 2J **115**
NG18: Mans 5F **47**
NG22: Oll 5B **38**
S81: Woods 1A **18**
Grange Cl. DN10: Mist 3J **11**
NG4: Lamb 7G **79**
NG11: Wil 1J **107**
NG17: Teve 2G **45**
S81: Carl L 6D **12**
Grange Ct. NG11: Rudd 7K **107**
NG17: Kirk A 6D **52**
Grange Cres. NG4: Ged 4J **87**
Grange Dr. DN10: Mist 4J **11**
DN11: Harwo 1D **8**
Grange Farm NG2: Gam 2F **109**
Grange Farm Cl. NG9: Toton 7F **105**
NG17: Sut A 3G **51**
Grange Farm Cotts. NG14: Lowd 3K **79**
Grangelea Gdns. NG9: Bram 1G **105**
Grangemoor NG15: Pap 4K **67**
Grange Pk. NG2: West Br 4E **108**
NG12: Crop Bu 2B **112**
Grange Rd. DN22: Ord 7E **22**
NG5: Woodt 3B **86**
NG6: Basf 4E **84**
NG12: Edwal 5D **108**
NG21: Blid 6K **55**
NG24: New T 4A **136**
Grange Vw. DN11: Harwo 1D **8**
NG16: Eastw 3D **72**
Grange Vw. Rd. NG4: Ged 5J **87**
Grange Wlk. DN10: Mist 3J **11**
Grangewood Ct. NG8: Woll 5H **93**
Grangewood Rd. NG8: Woll 5H **93**
NG17: Kirk A 4K **51**
Grannis Dr. NG8: Bilb 7B **84**
GRANTHAM **2D 149**
Grantham Cl. NG16: Gilt 7G **73**
Grantham Rd. NG12: Rad T 6C **98**
NG13: Aslo, Bing, What 5J **101**
NG13: Bing 4G **101**
Grantleigh Cl. NG8: Woll 3A **94**
(not continuous)
Granton Av. NG11: Clif 2G **115**
Granton Ri. NG19: Mans 5D **46**
Grant St. NG7: Radf 3A **6** (3G **95**)
Granville Av. NG10: Long E 7C **104**
Granville Ct. NG3: Nott 3C **96**
Granville Cres. NG12: Rad T 6D **98**
Granville Gro. NG3: Nott 3C **96**
Grasby Wlk. NG11: Clif 7E **106**
Grasmere Av. NG8: Aspl 5D **84**
Grasmere Cl. NG15: Huck 5F **67**
Grasmere Ct. NG10: Long E 7A **104**
NG18: Mans 3G 47
(off Layton Av.)
Grasmere Gdns. NG11: Goth 6G **115**
Grasmere Rd. NG9: Bram 1J **105**
NG10: Long E 7A **104**
S81: Work 5G **19**
Grasmere St. NG10: Sand 4A **104**
Grasmoor Cl. NG3: Nott 7C **86**
Grassingdale Cl. NG4: Carl 5G **87**
Grassington Rd. NG8: Aspl 2E **94**
Grassmere NG12: Cotg 6F **111**
GRASSTHORPE **3K 125 (2C 147)**
Grassthorpe Rd. NG23: Grass 3K **125**
NG23: Norm T 2K **125**
NG23: Sut T 4K **125** & 1C **128**
Grassy La. NG9: Bee 4B **106**
Gratton Ct. NG17: Kirk A 4J **51**
Gravelholes La. DN10: Mist 3G **11**
Gravel La. NG22: Egma 1C **124**
Gravelly Hollow NG14: Calv 3H **69**
Gravelly La. NG25: Fis 6G **139**
Graveney Gdns. NG5: Arn 1E **86**
Graves Moor La. S81: Blyth 7K **13**
Gravia Ct. S81: Work 5G **19**
Gray Fallow DE55: Sth N 7A **50**
GRAYINGHAM **2D 145**
Graylands Rd. NG8: Bilb 1J **93**
Gray La. NG22: Edin, Halam 4A **130**
Grays Ct. NG24: Farnd 7H **133**
Grays Dr. NG15: Rave 6D **62**
Grayson M. NG9: Chil 7G **105**
Graystones Cl. NG2: West Br 4F **109**
Grazingfield NG11: Wil 5H **107**
GREASLEY **3J 73**
Greasley Av. NG16: Newth 4G **73**
Greasley Ct. NG18: Mans 7D **48**
Greasley Sports & Community Cen. 4F **73**
Greasley St. NG6: Bulw 7H **75**
Gt. Black La. DN11: Tick 1A **8**
Great Central Railway (Nottingham)
Ruddington Station 5A **116**
Rushcliffe Halt Station 1A **122**
Gt. Central Rd. NG18: Mans 4J **47**
Gt. Freeman St. NG3: Nott 2F **7** (2K **95**)
GREAT GONERBY **2D 149**
Gt. Hoggett Dr. NG9: Chil 3F **105**
Great La. NG22: East M 2B **28**
Gt. Northern Cl., The NG2: Nott 7H **7** (5A **96**)
Gt. Northern Cotts. NG15: Huck 4H **67**
NG19: Plea 4A 40
(off Pit Hill)
Gt. Northern Rd. NG16: Eastw 4B **72**
Gt. Northern Way NG4: Neth 2A **98**
Great Nth. Rd. DN10: Bawt, Scro 1J **9**
DN22: Rans, Torw 1H **13**
NG22: Tuxf 7D **28**
NG22: West M 3A **28**
NG23: Carl T, Weston, Sut T 3F **125** & 1A **128**
(not continuous)
NG23: New T, Nth M, Sth M 1A **134** & 7J **129**
NG23: Nth M 5J **129**
NG24: New T 6B **134**
GREAT PONTON **2D 149**
GREAT WILNE **2A 148**
Greaves Cl. NG5: Arn 2E **86**
NG8: Stre 6J **83**
NG24: New T 1G **137**
Greaves La. NG22: Edin 3A **130**
Grebe Cl. NG24: New B 4F **137**
Greek St. NG7: Radf 4A **6** (3H **95**)
Green, The DN10: Beck 7D **16**
DN11: Harwo 3B **8**
DN22: Ramp 6K **25**
LE12: East L 3A **122**
LE14: Hick 6E **142**
NG4: Carl 7F **87**
NG9: Chil 5K **105**
NG11: King 1A **120**
NG11: Rudd 4K **115**
NG12: Rad T 5D **98**
NG13: Ors 1J **103**
NG14: Lowd 4K **79**
NG17: Huth 1E **50**
NG19: Mans W 4G **41**
NG22: Bils 4C **126**
NG22: Dun T 6J **29**
NG22: Kirk 1C **132**
NG23: Coll 3G **129**
NG23: Elston 2D **140**
NG24: Codd 6K **135**
S81: Carl L 6D **12**
Green Acre NG8: Woll 3G **93**
Greenacre NG12: Edwal 5E **108**
NG14: Bur J 2D **88**
NG17: Stan H 5G **45**
NG18: Mans 5B **48**
Greenacre Rd. S81: Work 6H **19**
Greenacres NG17: Kirk A 2B **60**
Greenacres Cvn. Pk.
NG22: Tuxf 5E **28**
Greenacres Cl. NG16: Newth 4G **73**
Greenacres Pk. NG2: West Br 7G **97**
Green App. NG4: Carl 7F **87**
Green Av. NG4: Neth 1K **97**
Greenaway NG23: Roll 3K **139**
Green Bank NG21: Rain 3A **56**
Greenbank NG4: Carl 2G **97**
Greenbank Ct. NG5: Sher 5K **85**
Greenbank Dr. NG17: Sut A 6J **45**
Greenbanks NG5: Woodt 3B **86**
Greenburn Cl. NG2: Gam 3G **109**
Green Cl. NG12: Key 6J **117**
NG15: Huck 1J **75**
NG21: Blid 7J **55**
Green Ct. NG13: Bing 3F **101**
Green Cres. NG16: Sels 6C **58**
Greencroft NG11: Clif 7G **107**
Greendale Av. NG21: Edwin 5D **36**
Greendale Cl. NG17: Stan H 4G **45**
NG20: Mkt W 4C **34**
Greendale Cres. NG21: C'tone 5K **43**
Greendale Gdns. NG8: Bilb 7C **84**
Greendale Rd. NG3: Nott 2F **97**
NG5: Arn 1C **86**

Green Dr. NG21: Edwin . . . 5K **35**
NG25: Fis . . . 6J **139**
Grn. Farm Ct. S81: Carl L . . . 6D **12**
Grn. Farm Rd. NG16: Sels . . . 6B **58**
Greenfield Cl. NG19: Mans W . . . 1D **48**
NG21: Edwin . . . 7H **37**
NG24: Codd . . . 7H **135**
Greenfield Gro. NG4: Carl . . . 7E **86**
Greenfields Cres. NG22: New O . . . 4C **38**
Greenfields Dr. NG12: Cotg . . . 7E **110**
Greenfield St. NG7: Nott . . . 7E **94**
Greenfields Way S81: Carl L . . . 5C **12**
Greenfinch Dale S81: Gate . . . 5D **18**
Greenford Cl. NG16: Nuth . . . 4K **83**
Greengate NG23: Syer . . . 2A **140**
Greengates Av. NG3: Mapp . . . 4C **86**
Greenhill Cres. NG4: Carl . . . 2H **97**
Greenhill La. NG17: Ann W . . . 4K **59**
Greenhill Ri. NG4: Carl . . . 1H **97**
Greenhill Rd. NG4: Carl . . . 2H **97**
Greenhills Av. NG16: Eastw . . . 3E **72**
Greenhills Rd. NG16: Eastw . . . 3D **72**
Greenholme Cl. NG17: Kirk A . . . 7A **52**
Greenholme Pk. NG19: Mans W . . . 3A **42**
Greenland Cres. NG9: Chil . . . 5H **105**
Greenland Rd. NG17: Skeg . . . 3J **45**
Green La. DE7: Ilk . . . 1A **92**
DN10: Scro . . . 7H **9**
DN22: Sth L . . . 2H **25**
DN22: Tres . . . 5H **25**
LE12: Will W . . . 6F **143**
LE14: Hick, Hick P . . . 1F **143** & 7D **142**
NG4: Lamb . . . 5F **79**
NG11: Clif . . . 7E **106**
NG13: Gran . . . 1K **141**
NG18: Mans . . . 7J **47**
NG19: Mans W . . . 4B **42**
NG19: Plea . . . 1K **45**
NG22: Dun T . . . 6K **29**
NG22: Lax, Moor . . . 7C **124**
NG22: Wale . . . 4G **27**
NG23: Bath . . . 6F **129**
NG23: Coll . . . 4J **129**
NG23: Girt . . . 4G **125**
S81: Carl L . . . 6A **12**
Green Leys NG2: West Br . . . 5K **107**
Green M., The NG5: Bestw . . . 2H **85**
Grn. Mile La. DN22: Babw . . . 4A **22**
Green Platt NG12: Cotg . . . 6D **110**
Green Rd. DN10: Gri H . . . 3C **16**
Greens Farm La. NG4: Ged . . . 5K **87**
Greensfields NG17: Skeg . . . 5A **46**
Green Side NG16: Sels . . . 6B **58**
Greenside Av. DN22: Ramp . . . 6K **25**
Greenside Wlk. NG3: Nott . . . 2F **97**
Greens La. NG16: Kimb . . . 1E **82**
Green Sq. Rd. NG16: Pinx . . . 2C **58**
Greensquare Rd. NG16: Pinx . . . 2C **58**
Green St. NG2: Nott . . . 7A **96**
NG11: Bart F, Thru . . . 5A **114**
Green's Windmill . . . 5K **7** (4C **96**)
Greentrees Ct. NG17: Sut A . . . 2H **51**
Greenvale NG22: Farns . . . 5K **57**
Green Vw. Bungs. S81: Blyth . . . 6G **13**
Greenview Cl. NG19: Mans W . . . 1D **48**
Green Wlk. NG13: What . . . 4D **102**
Greenway DN22: Ord . . . 7D **22**
NG19: Mans W . . . 6F **43**
NG24: New T . . . 4B **136**
S81: Carl L . . . 6D **12**
Greenway, The NG10: Sand . . . 3A **104**
Greenway Cl. NG12: Rad T . . . 5D **98**
Greenwich Av. NG6: Basf . . . 3D **84**
Greenwich Pk. Cl. NG2: West Br . . . 4K **107**
Greenwood Av. DE7: Ilk . . . 1A **92**
DN11: Harwo . . . 1C **8**
NG3: Nott . . . 3G **97**
NG15: Huck . . . 5F **67**
NG17: Huth . . . 1D **50**
NG19: Mans W . . . 5H **41**
NG21: Edwin . . . 6F **37**
Greenwood Cl. NG22: Farns . . . 5K **57**
S81: Gate . . . 3E **18**
Greenwood Cotts. NG18: Mans . . . 2B **48**
Greenwood Ct. NG9: Chil . . . 4J **105**
Greenwood Cres. NG4: Carl . . . 2H **97**
NG22: Bou . . . 3E **38**
Greenwood Dr. NG17: Kirk A . . . 6J **51**
Greenwood Gdns. NG11: Rudd . . . 4A **116**
Greenwood Rd. NG3: Nott . . . 3D **96**
NG4: Carl . . . 3F **97**
Greenwood Va. NG15: Huck . . . 5E **66**
Greet Ct. NG7: Radf . . . 1E **94**
Greet Lily Mill *NG25: Sout . . . 5J 131*
(off Mill Pk.)
Greet Pk. Cl. NG25: Sout . . . 5J **131**
Greetwell Cl. NG8: Bilb . . . 2B **94**
Gregory Av. NG3: Mapp . . . 5D **86**
NG7: Lent . . . 5G **95**
Gregory Blvd. NG7: Hyson G . . . 1F **95**
Gregory Cl. NG9: Stap . . . 1E **104**
Gregory Ct. NG7: Hyson G . . . 7G **85**
NG7: Lent . . . 5F **95**
NG9: Chil . . . 5G **105**
Gregory Cres. DN11: Harwo . . . 2B **8**
Gregory Gdns. NG22: Farns . . . 6K **57**
Gregory St. NG7: Lent . . . 5F **95**
Gregson Gdns. NG9: Toton . . . 7G **105**
Gregson Rd. NG9: Chil . . . 6F **105**
Grenay Ct. NG11: Rudd . . . 2J **115**
(not continuous)
Grendon Way NG17: Skeg . . . 5B **46**
Grenfell Ter. NG6: Basf . . . 3F **85**
Grenville Dr. NG9: Stap . . . 1D **104**
Grenville Ri. NG5: Arn . . . 5H **77**
Grenville Rd. NG9: Bee . . . 5C **106**
Gresham Cl. NG2: West Br . . . 2K **107**
NG24: New T . . . 1H **137**
Gresham Gdns. NG2: West Br . . . 2A **108**
NG5: Woodt . . . 2D **86**
Gresley Dr. NG2: Nott . . . 7K **7** (5C **96**)
Gresley Rd. DN22: Retf . . . 5D **22**
Gretton Rd. NG3: Mapp . . . 3D **86**
Greyfriar Ga. NG1: Nott . . . 7E **6** (5K **95**)
GREY GREEN . . . 1C **145**
Greyhound St. NG1: Nott . . . 4F **7** (4K **95**)
Greys Rd. NG5: Woodt . . . 3C **86**
Greystoke Dr. NG8: Bilb . . . 1H **93**
Grey St. NG16: Newth . . . 5E **72**
NG17: Kirk A . . . 6H **51**
Greythorn Dr. NG2: West Br . . . 5A **108**
Griceson Cl. NG22: Oll . . . 6B **38**
Grierson Av. NG5: Bestw . . . 6D **76**
Grieves Cl. DN22: Retf . . . 5F **23**
Griffins End NG13: What . . . 5E **102**
Griffiths Way NG15: Huck . . . 7H **67**
Griffs Hollow NG4: Carl . . . 1H **97**
Grimesmoor Rd. NG14: Calv . . . 5E **70**
Grimsby Ter. NG3: Nott . . . 2F **7** (2K **95**)
GRIMSTON . . . 3B **148**
Grimston Rd. NG7: Radf . . . 2F **95**
Grindley Ct. DN10: Gri H . . . 3A **16**
Grindon Cres. NG6: Bulw . . . 4J **75**
GRINGLEY ON THE HILL . . . 3B **16** (2C **145**)
Gringley Rd. DN10: Beck . . . 6A **16**
DN10: Mist . . . 4F **11**
DN10: Walk . . . 7F **11**
DN22: Clay . . . 6J **15**
Grinsbrook NG7: Lent . . . 4F **95**
Gripps, The *NG12: Cotg . . . 7E 110*
(off Owthorpe Rd.)
Gripps Comn. NG12: Cotg . . . 7E **110**
Grisedale Ct. NG9: Chil . . . 5F **105**
Gritley M. NG2: Nott . . . 6J **95**
Grives La. NG17: Kirk A . . . 2B **60**
Grizedale Cl. NG19: Mans W . . . 2D **48**
Grizedale Gro. NG13: Bing . . . 4C **100**
Grizedale Ri. NG19: Mans W . . . 2C **48**
Grosvenor Av. NG3: Mapp P . . . 6K **85**
NG17: Sut A . . . 1H **51**
Grosvenor Cl. DN22: Retf . . . 6G **23**
NG12: Rad T . . . 5J **99**
Grosvenor Ct. NG3: Mapp P . . . 7K **85**
Grosvenor Pl. *NG17: Sut A . . . 1H 51*
(off Grosvenor Av.)
Grosvenor Rd. DN11: Birc . . . 2E **8**
NG16: Eastw . . . 3D **72**
NG24: New B . . . 5E **136**
Grouville Dr. NG5: Woodt . . . 2D **86**
GROVE . . . 1C **147**
Grove, The DN10: Beck . . . 6C **16**
NG5: Sher . . . 5J **85**
NG7: Radf . . . 1A **6** (2G **95**)
NG14: Calv . . . 6E **70**
NG15: Ann . . . 4B **60**
S81: Work . . . 5G **19**
Grove Av. NG7: Radf . . . 1A **6** (2H **95**)
NG9: Chil . . . 3K **105**
Grove Cl. NG14: Bur J . . . 2E **88**
Gro. Coach Rd. DN22: Retf . . . 6G **23**
(not continuous)
Grove Cotts. NG19: Plea . . . 4B **40**
NG24: New T . . . 3F **137**
Grove Ct. NG9: Chil . . . 3J **105**
Grove Dr. DN22: Grove . . . 6K **23**
Grove La. DN22: Retf . . . 3G **23**
Grove M. NG16: Eastw . . . 5C **72**
Grove Pk. DN10: Mist . . . 3H **11**
Grover Av. NG3: Mapp . . . 4D **86**
Grove Rd. DN22: Grove, Retf . . . 7G **23**
NG7: Lent . . . 5G **95**
NG13: Bing . . . 3G **101**
NG17: Sut A . . . 7B **46**
NG20: Chu W . . . 2C **34**
Groveside Cres. NG11: Clif . . . 6D **106**
Grove Sports Cen. . . . 3F **137**
Grove St. DN22: Retf . . . 3F **23**
NG9: Bee . . . 4B **106**
NG18: Mans . . . 4H **47**
NG19: Mans W . . . 6H **41**
Grove St. NG24: New B . . . 4E **136**
Groveview Rd. NG24: New B . . . 4F **137**
Grove Way NG19: Mans W . . . 6H **41**
Grove Wood Rd. DN10: Mist . . . 3H **11**
Grovewood Ter. DN10: Mist . . . 3H **11**
Grundy Av. NG16: Sels . . . 5B **58**
Grundy St. NG7: Hyson G . . . 1F **95**
Guardian Ct. NG8: Aspl . . . 7D **84**
Guildford Av. NG19: Mans W . . . 3J **41**
Guildhall Dr. NG16: Sels . . . 2C **58**
Guildhall St. NG24: New T . . . 1D **136**
GUNBY . . . 3D **149**
Gunn Cl. NG6: Bulw . . . 7G **75**
Gunnersbury Way NG16: Nuth . . . 4J **83**
GUNNESS . . . 1D **145**
GUNTHORPE
East Bridgford . . . 2B **90** (1B **148**)
Gainsborough . . . 2D **145**
Gunthorpe Cl. NG5: Sher . . . 4J **85**
Gunthorpe Ct. NG18: Mans . . . 7D **48**
Gunthorpe Dr. NG5: Sher . . . 4J **85**
Gunthorpe Rd. NG4: Ged . . . 4F **87**
NG14: Lowd . . . 6E **80**
Gutersloh Ct. NG9: Stap . . . 1E **104**
Guy Cl. NG9: Stap . . . 3D **104**
Guylers Hill Dr. NG21: C'tone . . . 7H **43**
Gwenbrook Av. NG9: Chil . . . 4K **105**
Gwenbrook Rd. NG9: Chil . . . 4K **105**
Gwndy Gdns. NG5: Bestw . . . 7C **76**
Gypsum La. NG11: Goth . . . 7F **115**
Gypsy La. NG14: Blea . . . 2C **138**
NG25: Fis . . . 2C **138**

H

HABBLESTHORPE . . . 6D **24** (3C **145**)
Habblesthorpe Cl. DN22: Habb . . . 6D **24**
Habblesthorpe Rd. DN22: Habb . . . 6D **24**
Habitat, The NG1: Nott . . . 5G **7**
Hackers Cl. NG13: East B . . . 4D **90**
Hack La. NG17: Sut A . . . 1J **51**
Hackworth Cl. NG16: Newth . . . 3F **73**
Hadbury Rd. NG5: Sher . . . 4G **85**
Hadden Ct. NG8: Bilb . . . 3J **93**
HADDINGTON . . . 2D **147**
Haddon Cl. NG4: Carl . . . 5G **87**
NG15: Huck . . . 7G **67**
NG16: Sels . . . 5E **58**
Haddon Cres. NG9: Chil . . . 6H **105**
Haddon Dr. NG24: Bald . . . 6G **137**
Haddon Rd. DN22: Retf . . . 6H **23**
NG2: West Br . . . 3C **108**
NG15: Rave . . . 1C **62**
NG19: Mans . . . 2H **47**
Haddon St. NG5: Sher . . . 5J **85**
NG17: Sut A . . . 6J **45**
Haddon Way NG12: Rad T . . . 4F **99**
Hades La. LE12: Will W, Wym . . . 7F **143**
Hadfield Wlk. *NG18: Mans . . . 4D 48*
(off Edale Rd.)
Hadleigh Cl. NG9: Toton . . . 7D **104**
Hadley St. DE7: Ilk . . . 3A **92**
Hadrian Gdns. NG5: Top V . . . 4C **76**
Hadstock Cl. NG10: Sand . . . 5A **104**
Hagg La. NG14: Epp . . . 1B **80**
Haggnook Wood NG15: Rave . . . 1K **61**
Haggonfields S80: Rhod . . . 1B **20**
Hagley Cl. NG3: Nott . . . 2D **96**
Haileybury Cres. NG2: West Br . . . 4C **108**
Haileybury Rd. NG2: West Br . . . 4C **108**
Haise Ct. NG6: Bulw . . . 2A **84**
HALAM . . . 4C **130** (3B **146**)
Halam Cl. NG19: Mans . . . 3D **46**
Halam Hill NG22: Halam . . . 5C **130**
NG25: Sout . . . 5C **130**
Halam Rd. NG25: Sout . . . 5D **130**
Halberton Dr. NG2: West Br . . . 5A **108**
Haldon Way S81: Gate . . . 4D **18**
Hales Cl. NG12: Cotg . . . 6D **110**
Halfmoon Dr. NG17: Kirk A . . . 1A **60**
Halifax Av. NG20: Chu W . . . 1D **34**
Halifax Ct. NG8: Stre . . . 5J **83**
Halifax Dr. S81: Work . . . 4F **19**
Halifax Pl. NG1: Nott . . . 6G **7** (4A **96**)
Halina Ct. NG9: Bee . . . 2A **106**
HALLAM FIELDS . . . 1A **148**
Hallam Flds. Rd. DE7: Ilk . . . 4A **92**
Hallam Rd. NG3: Mapp . . . 5D **86**
NG9: Bee . . . 3A **106**
NG22: New O . . . 2D **38**
Hallams La. NG5: Arn . . . 7H **77**
NG9: Chil . . . 5H **105**
Hallam Way NG16: Lang M . . . 3A **72**
Hallamway NG19: Mans W . . . 1J **47**
Hall Barn La. NG19: Mans . . . 2D **46**
Hall Cl. NG12: Rad T . . . 5D **98**
NG21: Rain . . . 3K **55**
NG22: Farns . . . 6J **57**
Hall Cl., The NG22: East M . . . 2D **28**

Hatchet's La. NG24: New T 5D 134
HATFIELD 1B 144
Hatfield Av. NG10: Sand 5A 104
NG20: Mede V 7H 33
Hatfield Cl. NG21: Rain 2K 55
Hatfield Dr. NG2: West Br 5K 107
Hatfield La. NG25: Oxt 1E 70
Hatfield Rd. NG3: Mapp P 6K 85
Hatfield St. DN22: Retf 4G 23
HATFIELD WOODHOUSE 1B 144
Hatherleigh Cl. NG3: Mapp 1F 87
HATHERN 3A 148
Hathern Grn. NG9: Lent A 1B 106
Hathernware Ind. Est.
LE12: Norm S 7C 120
Hathersage Ri. NG15: Rave 1C 62
Hathersage Wlk. *NG18: Mans 4D 48*
(off Edale Rd.)
Hathersage Way NG17: Sut A 6J 45
Hatley Cl. NG2: Nott 7J 95
Hatton Cl. NG5: Arn 4C 76
NG23: Nth M 6K 129
Hatton Ct. NG18: Mans 4D 48
Hatton Gdns. NG16: Nuth 4K 83
NG24: New T 2D 136
Haughgate Hill DN22: Nth W 1F 17
HAUGHTON 1B 146
Haughton Pk. Farm 1B 146
Havelock Gdns. NG3: Nott 2H 7 (2A 96)
Haven, The NG22: Kirt 7J 27
Haven Cl. NG2: West Br 4A 108
NG17: Sut A 7H 45
NG21: C'tone 6H 43
Havenwood Ri. NG11: Clif 2E 114
Haverhill Cres. NG5: Top V 4K 75
Haversham Cl. NG6: Basf 5E 84
Hawarden Ter. NG7: Hyson G 1G 95
Hawbush Rd. NG23: Weston 1F 125
Hawkesworth Av. NG19: Mans W 1D 48
Hawkhill Cl. NG22: Oll 6A 38
Hawkhurst Dr. NG8: Woll 6J 93
Hawkins Cl. DN11: Harwo 1D 8
Hawkridge Gdns. NG3: Nott 3J 7 (3B 96)
Hawkshead Cl. NG2: West Br 4G 109
Hawksley Gdns. NG11: Clif 7D 106
Hawksley Rd. NG7: Hyson G 1G 95
Hawk's Nest Owl Sanctuary 1J 9
Hawkswood Cl. NG9: Chil 5G 105
HAWKSWORTH 1C 149
Hawksworth Av. NG5: Sher 3A 86
Hawksworth Rd. NG2: West Br 7C 96
NG13: Scar 1C 102
NG23: Syer 4B 140
Hawksworth St. NG3: Nott 4K 7 (3B 96)
Hawley Cl. LE12: East L 3B 122
Hawley Mt. NG5: Sher 4C 86
Haworth Ct. NG11: Clif 1D 114
Hawson Way S81: Gate 5D 18
Hawthorn Av. NG15: Huck 6F 67
Hawthorn Cl. DN10: Beck 7C 16
NG2: Nott 7J 95
NG12: Edwal 5E 108
NG12: Key 1H 119
NG14: Blea 2C 138
NG14: Woodbo 2G 79
NG19: Mans W 4A 42
NG22: New O 3D 38
Hawthorn Cres. NG5: Arn 5J 77
NG17: Kirk A 5A 52
Hawthorn Dr. NG22: New O 3D 38
Hawthorne Av. NG9: Stap 3C 104
NG12: Cotg 7E 110
Hawthorne Cl. DN22: Nth L 7C 24
NG17: Stan H 4G 45
Hawthorne Ct. DN22: Ord 6E 22
Hawthorne Cres. NG24: Farnd 7H 133
Hawthorne Gro. NG9: Bee 3C 106
Hawthorne Lodge NG2: West Br 7E 96
Hawthorne Ri. NG16: Aws 3A 82
Hawthorne Rd. NG16: Pinx 1B 58
Hawthorne Way NG21: Edwin 7H 37
Hawthorns, The NG17: Kirk A 5K 51
NG20: Mkt W 4C 34
NG22: Dun T 6J 29
NG22: Wale 5G 27
Hawthorn Vw. NG2: Nott 6J 95
(not continuous)
Hawthorn Wlk. NG3: Nott 1E 96
Hawthorn Way S81: Carl L 5B 12
HAWTON 6A 136 (3C 147)
Hawton Cl. NG19: Mans 1F 47
Hawton Cres. NG8: Woll 4D 94
Hawton La. NG24: Farnd 7H 133
NG24: New B 5D 136
Hawton Rd. NG24: New T 5A 136
Hawton Spinney NG8: Woll 4D 94
HAXEY 2C 145
Haxey Rd. DN10: Mist 2H 11
Haycroft Cl. NG19: Mans W 4K 41
Haycroft Way NG13: East B 4D 90
Hayden La. NG15: Lin 3H 67
(not continuous)
Haydn Av. NG5: Sher 5J 85
Haydn Rd. NG5: Sher 5H 85
Haydock Cl. NG16: Kimb 7J 73
Hayes Cl. NG16: Pinx 1A 58
Hayes Ct. DN22: Rans 2J 13
Hayes Rd. NG12: Key 7G 117
Hayfield Gro. NG23: Weston 3F 125
Hayles Cl. NG5: Bestw 1J 85
Hayley Cl. NG16: Kimb 1C 82
Hayling Dr. NG8: Basf 6E 84
Haynes Av. NG9: Trow 3B 92
Haynes Cl. NG11: Clif 6G 107
NG22: Tuxf 6D 28
Hayside Av. NG24: Bald 6E 136
HAYTON 6H 17 (3C 145)
Haywood Av. NG21: Blid 6J 55
Haywood Ct. NG2: Nott 5J 7 (4B 96)
NG21: Rain 1G 55
Haywood Oaks La. NG21: Blid 7J 55
Haywood Rd. NG3: Mapp 5C 86
Haywood St. NG2: Nott 5J 7 (4B 96)
Hayworth Rd. NG10: Sand 4A 104
Hazelas Dr. NG14: Gun 2B 90
Hazel Bank NG19: Mans W 2A 48
Hazelbank Av. NG3: Nott 6C 86
Hazel Cl. NG2: West Br 7F 97
NG13: Bing 4H 101
Hazel Dr. NG16: Nuth 1G 83
Hazelford Way NG15: News 5D 60
HAZELGROVE 1G 75
Hazel Gro. DE55: Sth N 6A 50
NG3: Mapp 3D 86
NG15: Huck 1G 75
NG17: Kirk A 6C 52
NG19: Mans W 4H 41
NG21: Edwin 7E 36
NG24: New B 4F 137
Hazel Hill Cres. NG5: Bestw 6D 76
Hazelhurst Gdns. NG6: Bulw 7H 75
Hazel Mdws. NG15: Huck 1G 75
Hazelmere Gro. NG7: Lent 4F 95
Hazel Rd. NG22: New O 3D 38
Hazel St. NG6: Bulw 6H 75
(not continuous)
NG17: Skeg 3H 45
Hazel Way NG15: Lin 3H 67
Hazelwood NG12: Cotg 6F 111
Hazelwood Cl. NG16: Newth 4F 73
NG19: Mans W 7D 42
Hazelwood Dr. NG15: Huck 7C 66
Hazelwood Gro. S80: Work 3C 20
Hazelwood Rd. NG7: Hyson G 1F 95
Headingley Gdns. NG8: Aspl 7E 84
Headland Av. DN22: Elk 2F 27
Headland La. DN22: Rans 3J 13
HEADON 1C 147
Headstocks, The NG17: Huth 1E 50
Healdswood St. NG17: Skeg 3H 45
Healey Cl. NG2: Nott 6K 95
NG23: Coll 2H 129
Heanor Wlk. *NG18: Mans 4D 48*
(off Edale Rd.)
HEAPHAM 3D 145
Heard Cres. NG9: Bee 1A 106
HEATH 2A 146
Heath, The NG16: Gilt 6E 72
Heath Av. NG18: Mans 3D 48
Heathcoat Bldg. NG7: Nott 7E 94
Heathcoat St. NG1: Nott 5G 7 (4A 96)
Heathcote Ct. NG17: Sut A 2J 51
Heathcote Pl. NG17: Sut A 1A 52
Heather Cl. NG3: Nott 1A 96
NG16: Newth 5F 73
NG17: Kirk A 4K 51
NG18: Mans 4G 47
Heather Ct. DE75: Hea 5A 72
Heather Cft. NG2: West Br 5K 107
Heatherington Gdns. NG5: Top V 5C 76
Heather La. NG15: Rave 4D 62
Heatherley Dr. NG6: Basf 3G 85
NG19: Mans W 1A 48
Heather Ri. NG9: Bram 7K 93
Heather Rd. NG4: Carl 6G 87
Heathers, The NG22: Bou 3E 38
Heathervale NG2: West Br 3J 107
Heather Way NG18: Mans 4C 48
Heathfield Av. DE7: Ilk 7A 82
Heathfield Ct. NG17: Kirk A 4J 51
Heathfield Gdns. DN22: Retf 2E 22
Heathfield Gro. NG9: Chil 6H 105
Heathfield Rd. NG5: Sher 3G 85
Heathfield Way NG18: Mans 5K 47
Heathland Cl. NG18: Mans 4C 48
Heaton Cl. NG3: Nott 6C 86
NG24: New T 1G 137
Heavenside LE12: East L 1A 122
Heavytrees Av. NG15: Rave 3C 62
Hecadeck La. LE14: Neth B 4K 143
HECKDYKE 2C 145
Heckington Dr. NG8: Woll 3C 94
Hedderley Wlk. NG3: Nott 2G 7 (2A 96)
Heddington Gdns. NG5: Arn 6F 77
Heddon Bar NG19: Mans W 6A 42
Hedgerow Cl. NG17: Sut A 2G 51
Hedley St. NG7: Basf 7H 85
Hedley Vs. NG7: Basf 6H 85
Helen Cl. NG9: Chil 3J 105
Hellebore Cl. NG5: Top V 7A 76
Helm Cl. NG6: Bulw 7F 75
Helmsdale Cl. NG5: Arn 5K 77
NG19: Mans 5E 46
Helmsdale Gdns. NG5: Top V 5B 76
Helmsley Dr. NG16: Eastw 3B 72
Helmsley Rd. NG21: Rain 1G 55
Helston Dr. NG8: Stre 5J 83
Helvellyn Cl. NG2: Nott 6K 95
Helvellyn Way NG10: Long E 7A 104
HEMINGTON 3A 148
Hemingway Cl. NG4: Carl 1F 97
NG16: Newth 5G 73
Hemlock Av. NG9: Stap 1D 104
NG10: Long E 7C 104
Hemlock Gdns. NG6: Bulw 1A 84
Hemmingfield Cl. S81: Work 4G 19
Hemmingfield Cres. S81: Work 4G 19
Hemmingfield Ri. S81: Work 4G 19
Hemmingfield Rd. S81: Work 5G 19
Hemmingfield Way S81: Work 4H 19
Hemplands, The NG23: Coll 1H 129
Hemplands La. NG23: Sut T 3C 128
Hempshill La. NG6: Bulw 1A 84
(Low Wood Rd.)
NG6: Bulw 1C 84
(Sellers Wood Dr.)
HEMPSHILL VALE 2A 84
Hemsby Gdns. NG6: Bulw 6H 75
(not continuous)
Hemscott Cl. NG6: Bulw 6F 75
HEMSWELL 2D 145
HEMSWELL CLIFF 3D 145
Hemswell Cl. NG3: Nott 3D 96
Hen & Chicken Yd. NG24: Barn W 7K 137
Hendon Ct. NG3: Nott 7C 86
Hendon Ri. NG3: Nott 7C 86
Hendre Gdns. NG5: Top V 7C 76
Henley Cl. NG4: Neth 2K 97
Henley Gdns. NG9: Stap 7D 92
Henley Ri. NG5: Sher 4H 85
Hennessey Cl. NG9: Chil 7H 105
Henning Gdns. NG5: Top V 6C 76
Henning La. NG17: Sut A 2F 51
Henrietta St. NG6: Bulw 1D 84
Henry Av. NG19: Mans W 4H 41
Henry Ct. NG2: Nott 6K 95
Henry Rd. NG2: West Br 1B 108
NG7: Lent 5G 95
NG9: Bee 3B 106
Henry St. NG2: Nott 5K 7 (4B 96)
NG5: Redh 4G 77
NG15: Huck 7H 67
NG17: Sut A 2K 51
Henson Cl. NG12: Rad T 5K 99
Henson La. NG12: Crop Bu, Rad T 4K 99
Hensons Row NG6: Basf 5E 84
Hensons Sq. NG9: Bram 1G 105
(not continuous)
Henton Cl. NG24: Codd 6H 135
Henton Rd. NG21: Edwin 7F 37
Hepple Dr. NG6: Bulw 7F 75
Herald Cl. NG9: Bee 2C 106
Herbert Buzzard Ct. *NG15: Huck 7J 67*
(off Hankin St.)
Herbert Rd. NG5: Sher 6J 85
NG17: Ann W 3B 60
Herbert St. NG18: Mans 4G 47
Hercules Dr. NG24: New T 2E 136
Hereford Av. NG19: Mans W 4J 41
NG22: Oll 4B 38
Hereford Cl. S81: Work 6H 19
Hereford Rd. NG3: Nott 3E 96
NG4: Ged 4J 87
NG5: Woodt 2B 86
NG15: Rave 1C 62
Hermitage, The NG18: Mans 6E 46
Hermitage Av. NG18: Mans 5F 47
Hermitage La. NG18: Mans 6E 46
Hermitage Sq. NG2: Nott 4C 96
Hermitage Wlk. NG7: Nott 7B 6 (5H 95)
Hermitage Way NG18: Mans 6E 46
Hermon St. NG7: Nott 4A 6 (3H 95)
Herne St. NG17: Sut A 6A 46
Heron Dr. NG7: Lent 4F 95
Heron Glade S81: Gate 5D 18
Herons Ct. NG2: West Br 5F 109
Heron Way NG19: Mans 1C 46
NG24: New B 4F 137
Heron Wharf NG7: Lent 6G 95
Herrick Dr. S81: Work 1K 21

M

Maid Marion Dr. NG21: Edwin .6G 37
Maid Marion Ri. NG20: Mkt W .4D 34
Maid Marion Way NG22: New O .2D 38
Maidstone Dr. NG8: Woll .6J 93
Main Av. NG19: Mans W .1C 48
Main Bright Rd. NG19: Mans W .1H 47
Main Bright Wlk. NG19: Mans W .1H 47
Main Rd. LE14: Neth B, Upp B .3J 143
NG4: Ged .6J 87
NG7: Nott .3D 106
NG11: Wil .3J 107
NG12: Cotg, Rad T .2C 110
NG12: Plum .2H 117
NG12: Rad T .5D 98
NG12: Shel .7H 89
NG13: Barns .3F 141
NG13: Elton .6G 103
NG15: Rave .1A 62
NG16: Jack .7A 64
NG16: Unde .2C 64
NG16: Want .5K 73
NG17: Ann W .3J 59
NG20: Langw, Neth L .6A 26
NG22: Bou .3E 38
NG23: Aver, Upton .1F 139
NG23: Best .7H 125
NG23: Kel .2G 133
NG23: Nth C .2E 30
Mainside Cres. NG16: Unde .4E 64
Main St. DN10: Matt .2H 15
DN11: Harwo .2B 8
DN11: Sty .5A 8
DN22: Clar, Hay .4H 17
DN22: Lane .2G 29
DN22: Nth L .7A 24
LE12: Costo .3E 122
LE12: East L .3A 122
LE12: Norm S .7G 121
LE12: Remp .7F 123
LE12: Sut B .4A 120
LE12: West L .3F 121
LE12: Will W .6F 143
LE14: Hick .5E 142
NG2: Gam .2F 109
NG4: Lamb .7F 79
NG6: Bulw .1C 84
NG8: Stre .5G 83
NG11: Bunny .3B 118
NG11: Rudd .7B 116
NG12: Crop Bu .2B 112
NG12: Key .2H 119
NG12: Kin .3A 142
NG12: Shel .6H 89
NG12: Widm .6K 119
NG12: Wys .6J 123
NG13: Aslo .4D 102
NG13: East B .4D 90
NG13: Gran .1J 141
NG13: Lang .7K 113
NG13: Newton .7C 90
NG13: Scar .1B 102
NG13: What .5E 102
NG14: Blea .2B 138
NG14: Bur J .3E 88
NG14: Calv .5K 69
NG14: Cayt .6H 81
NG14: Epp .7J 71
NG14: Gun .2A 90
NG14: Hove .4K 81
NG14: Lowd .4D 80
NG14: Thur .6C 138
NG14: Woodbo .2F 79
NG15: Lin .2G 67
NG15: Pap .2K 67
NG16: Aws .2B 82
NG16: Brins .4B 64
NG16: Eastw .5D 72
NG16: Kimb .1E 82
NG16: Newth .4G 73
NG17: Ann W .4K 59
(not continuous)
NG17: Huth .7D 44
NG20: Nort .3E 32
NG20: Whal T .5B 26
NG21: Blid .7H 55
NG22: Dun T .5J 29
NG22: Eakr .2C 126
NG22: Edin .2A 130
NG22: Egma .2E 124
NG22: Farns .5K 57
NG22: Kirk .1D 132
NG22: Kirt .3H 39
NG22: Lax .5B 124
NG22: Oll .5A 38
NG22: Wale .5G 27
NG22: West M .4A 28
NG23: Bath .5F 129
NG23: Carl T .7D 128
NG23: Caus .6J 127
NG23: Flin .5A 140
Main St. NG23: Norw .2J 127
NG23: Nth M .5K 129
NG23: Sibt .6E 140
NG23: Sth M .2A 134
NG23: Sut T .4D 128
NG23: Syer .2B 140
NG23: Thor .2G 31
NG23: Weston .3F 125
NG24: Bald .5G 137
NG24: Codd .6K 135
NG24: Farnd .7G 133
NG25: Mort .7G 139
NG25: Fis .7H 139
NG25: Oxt .2F 71
S81: Oldc .6A 8
Maitland Av. NG5: Woodt .3C 86
Maitland Rd. NG5: Woodt .3C 86
Majestic Theatre .3E 22
Major St. NG1: Nott .2E 6 (3K 95)
Making It! Discovery Cen. .4J 47
Malbon Cl. NG3: Nott .7C 86
Malcolm Cl. NG3: Mapp P .1K 95
Maldon Cl. NG9: Chil .5H 105
Malin Cl. NG5: Arn .6K 77
Malin Hill NG1: Nott .6G 7 (4A 96)
Malkin Av. NG12: Rad T .4F 99
Mallard Cl. NG6: Basf .3G 85
NG13: Bing .5H 101
Mallard Ct. NG9: Bee .4B 106
NG19: Mans W .7G 41
Mallard Grn. NG24: New B .4F 137
Mallard Rd. NG4: Neth .2A 98
Mallards, The S81: Gate .5D 18
Mallatratt Pl. NG19: Mans W .5H 41
Mallory Dr. S80: Work .3D 20
Mallow Way NG13: Bing .4D 100
(not continuous)
Malmesbury Rd. NG3: Mapp .3D 86
MALTBY .2A 144
Maltby Cl. NG8: Aspl .5C 84
Maltby Rd. NG3: Mapp .3D 86
NG18: Mans .5A 48
S81: Oldc .6A 8
Malt Cotts. NG7: Basf .6G 85
Malt Cross Music Hall, The .5E 6
Malthouse Cl. NG16: Eastw .5D 72
Malthouse Ct. NG13: East B .4D 90
Malting Cl. NG11: Rudd .4K 115
Maltings, The NG3: Nott .1C 96
NG6: Basf .5F 85
NG12: Crop Bi .5B 112
S81: Blyth .6H 13
Malt Kiln Cl. NG22: Oll .6B 38
Maltkiln La. NG24: New T .6D 134
Maltkiln Row NG20: Cuck .4C 32
Maltkins, The DN22: Nth L .7B 24
Maltmill La. NG1: Nott .6F 7 (4A 96)
Malton Rd. NG5: Sher .5G 85
Maltsters, The NG24: New T .5K 133
Malt St. NG11: Goth .7G 115
Malvern Cl. NG3: Nott .6B 86
Malvern Ct. NG3: Mapp P .1K 95
NG9: Bee .3C 106
Malvern Cres. NG2: West Br .4C 108
Malvern Rd. NG2: West Br .4B 108
NG3: Nott .6B 86
Manby Ct. NG20: Mede V .7F 33
Mandalay St. NG6: Basf .3E 84
Mandeen Gro. NG18: Mans .6C 48
Manesty Cres. NG11: Clif .3F 115
Manifold Dr. NG16: Sels .5E 58
Manifold Gdns. NG2: Nott .6K 95
Manitoba Way NG16: Sels .5D 58
Manly Cl. NG5: Top V .6A 76
Manners Rd. NG24: Bald .6F 137
NG24: New T .7B 134
Manning St. NG3: Nott .1A 96
Manns Leys NG12: Cotg .7D 110
Mann St. NG7: Basf .7G 85
Manor Av. NG2: Nott .6K 7 (4B 96)
NG9: Atten .6K 105
NG9: Bee .3A 106
NG9: Stap .1C 104
Manor Cl. DN10: Miss .2D 10
LE12: Costo .3E 122
NG12: Edwal .6E 108
NG14: Blea .2B 138
NG17: Teve .2G 45
NG22: Bou .2F 39
NG22: Wale .5G 27
NG25: Oxt .2F 71
NG25: Sout .5H 131
S80: Work .3D 20
Manor Ct. LE12: Will W .6F 143
NG4: Carl .1J 97
NG9: Bram .2G 105
NG20: Chu W .2E 34
Manor Cres. NG4: Carl .7J 87
NG17: Kirk A .1B 60
Manor Cft. NG6: Basf .4F 85
Manor Dr. NG25: Mort .6G 139
Mnr. Farm Cl. NG11: Rudd .7B 116
NG23: Roll .3K 139
Mnr. Farm Ct. NG11: King .1A 120
Mnr. Farm La. NG11: Clif .7F 107
Mnr. Farm Mdw. LE12: East L .3A 122
Mnr. Farm Ri. DN22: Nth L .6B 24
Mnr. Farm Ri. *NG22: Well .7E 38*
(off Newark Rd.)
Manor Flds. NG22: Halam .5B 130
Manor Gdns. NG13: Barns .3F 141
Manor Grn. NG4: Carl .7J 87
Mnr. Green Wlk. NG4: Carl .7J 87
Manor Gro. DN22: Nth L .6B 24
S80: Work .3D 20
Manor Ho. NG19: Mans W .6H 41
Manor Ho. Cvn. Pk. DN22: Chu L .1J 29
Manor Ho. Cl. NG11: Wil .1J 107
NG14: Lowd .4D 80
Manor Ho. Ct. NG17: Kirk A .7H 51
Manor Ho. Dr. NG12: Wys .6K 123
NG23: Nth M .5K 129
Manor La. NG12: Shel .6H 89
Manor Pk. NG11: Rudd .3J 115
Manor Pk. Sports Complex .4K 41
Manor Ri. NG13: East B .3D 90
Manor Rd. DN10: Scro .4K 9
LE12: East L .1B 122
NG4: Carl .7J 87
NG11: Bart F .7A 114
NG12: Key .7H 117
NG13: Bing .4G 101
NG14: Calv .6C 70
NG16: Eastw .5D 72
NG17: Skeg .3J 45
NG19: Mans W .5G 41
NG20: Chu W .2E 34
NG23: Caus .7H 127
NG23: Coll .1H 129
Manor St. NG2: Nott .7K 7 (4B 96)
NG17: Sut A .1J 51
Manor Vw. NG23: Caus .7H 127
Manorwood Rd. NG12: Cotg .7E 110
Mansell Cl. NG16: Eastw .5F 73
MANSFIELD .3H 47 (2A 146)
Mansfield & District Crematorium NG18: Mans .1H 53
Mansfield Bus. Cen. NG19: Mans .2H 47
Mansfield Ct. NG5: Sher .7J 85
Mansfield Gro. NG1: Nott .2D 6 (2J 95)
Mansfield La. NG14: Calv .4D 70
NG17: Skeg .4A 46
Mansfield Leisure Cen. .2G 47
Mansfield Leisure Pk. .5G 47
Mansfield Mus. .3J 47
Mansfield Rd. DE55: Sth N .6A 50
DE55: Tibs .3A 44
DN22: Babw, Retf .5A 22
NG1: Nott .1E 6 (1J 95)
NG5: Arn, Redh, Sher .4E 68
NG5: Sher .7J 85
NG15: Ann .3F 65
NG15: Pap, Rave .4B 62
NG15: Rave .1A 62
NG16: Brins, Eastw .7C 64
NG16: Sels .6D 58
NG16: Unde .3F 65
NG17: Skeg .4H 45
NG17: Sut A .6K 45
NG19: Mans W .7J 41
NG20: Cuck .4D 32
NG20: Mkt W .7B 34
NG21: Blid .4H 55
NG21: C'tone, Old C .7H 43
NG21: Edwin .7B 36
NG21: Rain .3A 56
NG22: Edin, Halam .2A 130
NG22: Farns .3A 56
NG22: Oll .5K 37
S80: Work .7A 20
Mansfield Station (Rail) .4H 47
Mansfield St. NG5: Sher .5K 85
Mansfield Superbowl .4H 47
Mansfield Town FC .5G 47
MANSFIELD WOODHOUSE .6H 41 (2A 146)
Mansfield Woodhouse Station (Rail) .6G 41
Manston M. NG7: Radf .2G 95
Manston Way S81: Gate .4D 18
MANTHORPE .2D 149
Manthorpe Cres. NG5: Sher .4C 86
Manthorpe Ho. NG24: Bald .5J 137
Manthorpe Way NG24: Bald .5H 137
MANTON
Scunthorpe .1D 145
Worksop .4J 21 (1A 146)
Manton Cl. NG21: Rain .3K 55
Manton Cres. NG9: Lent A .1A 106
S80: Work .4J 21
Manton Dale S80: Work .4J 21
Manton Vs. S80: Work .3K 21
Manvers Bus. Pk. NG12: Cotg .5F 111

Millennium Bus. Pk. NG19: Mans 7D **40**
Millennium Ct. NG6: Bulw 2E **84**
NG19: Mans 7E **40**
Millennium Way NG8: Cin 3B **84**
Millennium Way E. NG8: Cin 3B **84**
Millennium Way W. NG8: Cin 3B **84**
Miller Hives Cl. NG12: Cotg 6D **110**
Millers Bri. NG12: Cotg 7D **110**
Millers Cl. NG12: Shel 6H **89**
Millers Ct. DN22: Clar 7J **17**
NG7: Radf 2F **95**
Millersdale Av. NG18: Mans 6D **46**
Millers Grn. NG2: Nott 4D **96**
Miller's La. LE12: Costo 3E **122**
Millers Way DN22: Retf 1C **22**
NG17: Kirk A 6A **52**
NG17: Sut A 5D **46**
Mill Fld. Cl. NG14: Bur J 4D **88**
NG23: Harby 6K **31**
Millfield Cl. DN22: Ord 7E **22**
Millfield Rd. NG16: Kimb 7J **73**
Millfield Vw. S80: Work 3D **20**
Mill Gdns. S80: Work 3D **20**
Mill Ga. NG13: East B 5D **90**
NG24: New T 2B **136**
Millgate Mus. 1B **136**
Mill Grn. NG24: New T 1E **136**
Mill Heyes NG13: East B 4E **90**
Mill Hill Rd. NG13: Bing 5E **100**
Mill Holme DE55: Sth N 7A **50**
Mill Ho. *NG1: Nott 6G 7*
(off Stoney St.)
Mill Ho. Pk. S80: Work 3E **20**
Millicent Gro. NG2: West Br 1C **108**
Millicent Rd. NG2: West Br 1B **108**
Millidge Cl. NG5: Bestw 2G **85**
Mill Lakes Country Pk. 2K **75**
Mill La. DN10: Bawt, Scro 2J **9**
DN10: Eve 7B **10**
DN10: Walk 7H **11**
DN22: Clay 7J **15**
DN22: Nth L 7A **24**
DN22: Sth L 1H **25**
LE12: East L 4B **122**
LE12: Will W 5G **143**
LE14: Hick 5C **142**
NG4: Lamb 7F **79**
NG5: Arn 6G **77**
NG10: Sand 3B **104**
NG11: Rudd 6C **116**
NG12: Cotg 5D **110**
NG12: Crop Bi 5B **112**
NG12: C'ton, Cotg 7C **110**
NG13: Aslo, Scar 1C **102**
NG13: Ors 1K **103**
NG16: Coss 7A **82**
NG16: Pinx 2B **58**
NG17: Huth 7E **44**
(not continuous)
NG17: Kirk A 7H **51**
(not continuous)
NG17: Sut A 6D **46**
NG21: Edwin 7E **36**
NG22: Eakr 3B **126**
NG22: Egma 3D **124**
NG22: Wale 5F **27**
NG23: Caus 5G **127**
NG23: Norm T 1K **125**
NG23: Nth C 3D **30**
NG23: Nth M, Sth M 7J **129**
(not continuous)
NG23: Thor 3G **31**
NG23: Upton 1H **139**
NG23: Wigs 7F **31**
NG24: New T 1B **136**
Millman Way DN22: Retf 1C **22**
Mill Mdw. Vw. S81: Blyth 6H **13**
Mill Pk. NG25: Sout 4J **131**
Mill Pk. Ind. Est. NG25: Sout 4J **131**
Mill Pond Cl. NG17: Ann W 3J **59**
Millrise Rd. NG18: Mans 5K **47**
Mill Rd. DN10: Gri H 3A **16**
NG9: Stap 1C **104**
NG16: Newth 3E **72**
NG23: Elston 2E **140**
Mills Bldg. NG1: Nott 6H **7**
Mills Dr. NG24: New T 5K **133**
Millside NG18: Mans 2K **47**
Millstone Cl. NG18: Mans 5A **48**
Mill St. DN22: Retf 4F **23**
NG6: Basf 4E **84**
NG17: Sut A 1J **51**
NG18: Mans 4K **47**
S80: Work 1F **21**
Mill Vw. NG23: Upton 7B **132**
Mill Vw. Cl. NG2: Nott 4C **96**
Millview Ct. NG2: Nott 6K **7** (4B **96**)
Mill Wlk. *NG18: Mans 3H 47*
(off Quaker Way)
Millway NG19: Mans W 1K **47**
Mill Yd. NG15: Huck 6G **67**
Milne Av. DN11: Birc 2F **9**
Milne Dr. DN11: Birc 2G **9**
Milne Gro. DN11: Birc 2F **9**
Milnercroft DN22: Retf 1D **22**
(not continuous)
Milnercroft Grn. *DN22: Retf 1D 22*
(off Milnercroft)
Milne Rd. DN11: Birc 2F **9**
Milner Rd. NG5: Sher 5K **85**
Milner St. NG17: Skeg 4A **46**
NG24: New T 2D **136**
Milnhay Rd. DE75: Hea 5A **72**
NG16: Lang M 4A **72**
MILTON 1C **147**
Milton Cl. NG17: Sut A 6B **46**
Milton Ct. NG5: Arn 7K **77**
NG5: Sher 4J **85**
NG15: Rave 2C **62**
Milton Cres. NG9: Atten 7J **105**
NG15: Rave 2B **62**
Milton Dr. NG15: Rave 2B **62**
S81: Work 1J **21**
Milton Ri. NG15: Huck 1D **74**
Milton St. NG1: Nott 3F **7** (3K **95**)
NG17: Kirk A 6B **52**
NG18: Mans 3G **47**
NG24: New B 3E **136**
Milton Wlk. S81: Work 1J **21**
Milverton Rd. NG5: Bestw 6E **76**
Mimosa Cl. NG11: Clif 1D **114**
Minerva St. NG6: Bulw 6H **75**
(not continuous)
Miniature World Mus. 2C **145**
Minkley Dr. NG16: Lang M 2A **72**
Minster Cl. NG15: Huck 5H **67**
NG17: Kirk A 5K **51**
Minster Ct. NG5: Sher 1J **95**
Minster Gdns. NG16: Newth 5F **73**
Minster Rd. DN10: Mist 2G **11**
Minstrel Av. NG5: Sher 5H **85**
Minstrel Cl. NG15: Huck 1G **75**
Minton Cl. NG9: Chil 7G **105**
Minton Pastures NG19: Mans W 1C **48**
Minver Cres. NG8: Aspl 6B **84**
Minver Crescent Sports Cen. 6C **84**
Mirberry M. NG7: Lent 5F **95**
Mire La. DN22: Sut L 6A **14**
Miriam Ct. NG2: West Br 2B **108**
Misk Hollows NG15: Huck 5F **67**
Misk Vw. NG16: Eastw 4F **73**
Mission St. NG3: Mapp 5B **86**
MISSON 3C **10** (2B **144**)
MISTERTON 2H **11** (2C **145**)
Misterton Ct. NG19: Mans 1H **47**
Misterton Cres. NG15: Rave 3B **62**
Mitchell Cl. NG6: Bulw 1B **84**
S81: Work 4F **19**
Mob La. LE12: Will W 6G **143**
Moffat Cl. NG3: Nott 1K **7** (1C **96**)
Mollington Sq. NG6: Cin 3C **84**
Mona Rd. NG2: West Br 7D **96**
Mona St. NG9: Bee 3B **106**
Monckton Dr. NG25: Sout 5H **131**
Monckton Rd. DN11: Birc 2F **9**
DN22: Retf 2C **22**
Monks Cl. DE7: Ilk 7A **82**
Monk's La. NG11: Goth 7G **115**
Monks Mdw. LE12: East L 2B **122**
Monks Way S81: Shire 5A **18**
Monksway NG11: Wil 5H **107**
Monkton Dr. NG8: Bilb 1K **93**
Monkwood Cl. NG23: Coll 1J **129**
Monmouth Cl. NG8: Woll 4G **93**
Monmouth Rd. S81: Work 6H **19**
Monroe Wlk. NG5: Bestw 7C **76**
Monsall St. NG7: Basf 6G **85**
Monsell Dr. NG5: Redh 5G **77**
Montague Rd. NG15: Huck 5G **67**
Montague St. NG6: Bulw 7J **75**
NG9: Bee 2K **105**
NG18: Mans 4A **48**
Montford Rd. S81: Gate 4D **18**
Montfort Cres. NG5: Sher 3A **86**
Montfort St. NG7: Radf 4A **6** (3H **95**)
Montgomery Cl. NG9: Chil 7H **105**
Montgomery Rd. NG24: New T 4D **136**
Montgomery St. NG7: Radf 2B **6** (2H **95**)
Montpelier Rd. NG7: Lent 7F **95**
Montrose S81: Work 7J **19**
Montrose Ct. NG9: Stap 7D **92**
Montrose Sq. NG19: Mans W 3H **41**
Montys Mdw. S81: Gate 5E **18**
Moody Cl. NG9: Chil 7G **105**
Moor, The NG9: Trow 2F **93**
NG16: Brins 5B **64**
Moorbridge Cotts. NG6: Bulw 4K **75**
Moorbridge Ct. NG13: Bing 3F **101**
Moorbridge La. NG9: Stap 7C **92**
Moorbridge Rd. NG13: Bing 3F **101**
Moorbridge Rd. E. NG13: Bing 3F **101**
Moor Bridge Stop (NET) 4K **75**
Moore Cl. LE12: East L 2B **122**
NG2: West Br 7E **96**
Moore Ga. NG9: Bee 3A **106**
Moore Rd. NG3: Mapp 5D **86**
Moores Av. NG10: Sand 2B **104**
Moore St. NG6: Bulw 2D **84**
Moor Farm Holiday & Home Pk. NG14: Calv 7G **71**
Moor Farm Inn La. NG9: Bram 6F **93**
Moorfield Ct. NG9: Stap 7D **92**
NG25: Sout 7G **131**
Moorfield Cres. NG10: Sand 4A **104**
Moorfield Pl. NG20: Mkt W 3E **34**
Moorfields Av. NG16: Eastw 3D **72**
Moorgate DN22: Retf 2F **23**
Moorgate Pk. DN22: Retf 2F **23**
Moorgate St. NG7: Radf 3A **6** (3H **95**)
MOORGREEN 3H **73** (1A **148**)
Moorgreen NG16: Newth 1G **73**
Moorgreen Dr. NG8: Stre 5J **83**
Moorgreen Ind. Pk. NG16: Newth 1F **73**
Moorhades La. DN22: Ramp 7K **25**
MOORHAIGH 2A **146**
Moorhaigh La. NG19: Plea 6A **40**
MOORHOUSE 2C **147**
Moorhouse La. NG23: Sth M 7H **129**
Moorhouse Rd. NG8: Bilb 2K **93**
NG22: Lax 6B **124**
Moorings, The NG7: Lent 6G **95**
Moorland Av. DN10: Walk 6H **11**
NG9: Stap 3C **104**
Moorland Cl. DN10: Walk 6H **11**
NG17: Skeg 4A **46**
Moorlands Cl. NG10: Long E 7A **104**
NG23: Norw 3H **127**
Moorland Wlk. *DN10: Walk 6H 11*
(off Moorland Av.)
Moorland Way NG18: Mans 4C **48**
Moor La. DN22: Chu L 2H **29**
DN22: Ramp 7K **25**
LE12: Norm S 6F **121**
NG9: Bram 6G **93**
NG11: Bunny 2A **118**
NG11: Goth, Rudd 7G **115**
NG11: Rudd 1A **118**
(Bradmore)
NG11: Rudd 4K **115**
(Ruddington)
NG13: Bing 3F **101**
NG13: Ors 3H **103**
NG13: Scar 3A **102**
NG14: Calv 7G **71**
NG18: Mans 1F **47**
NG23: Caus 4H **127**
NG23: Nth C 4E **30**
NG23: Sth C 7D **30**
NG23: Sth S 7K **125**
NG23: Syer 3B **140**
NG23: Thor 4F **31**
NG25: Mort 6F **139**
S81: Blyth 7K **13**
Moor Rd. NG6: Bestw V 3K **75**
NG8: Stre 6J **83**
NG14: Calv 6E **70**
NG15: Pap 3K **67**
NG16: Brins 5C **64**
NG23: Coll 1J **129**
Moorsholm Dr. NG8: Woll 4H **93**
Moor St. NG4: Neth 1J **97**
NG18: Mans 4G **47**
Moor Top Rd. DN11: Harwo 1C **8**
Moor Vw. NG11: Bunny 3B **118**
Moray Ct. NG16: Kimb 7K **73**
Moray Sq. NG19: Mans 5D **46**
Morden Cl. NG8: Bilb 7J **83**
Morden Rd. NG16: Gilt 6G **73**
Moreland Ct. NG2: Nott 5C **96**
NG4: Carl 1F **97**
Moreland Pl. NG2: Nott 5C **96**
Moreland St. NG2: Nott 5C **96**
Morello Av. NG4: Carl 1J **97**
Moreton Rd. NG11: Clif 3F **115**
Morgan M. NG11: Clif 7E **106**
Morgans Cl. NG24: Codd 6K **135**
Morkinshire Cres. NG12: Cotg 5E **110**
Morkinshire La. NG12: Cotg 5D **110**
Morley Av. DN22: Retf 1C **22**
NG3: Mapp 5B **86**
Morley Cl. NG18: Mans 5D **48**
Morley Ct. NG2: Nott 4J **7** (4B **96**)
Morley Gdns. NG5: Sher 6J **85**
Morley Rd. NG3: Nott 6D **86**
Morleys Cl. NG14: Lowd 5E **80**
Morley St. NG5: Arn 1A **86**
NG17: Kirk A 7B **52**
NG17: Stan H 4G **45**
NG17: Sut A 7K **45**
Mornington Cl. NG10: Sand 3B **104**
Mornington Cres. NG16: Nuth 4J **83**

Morrell Bank NG5: Bestw .1G **85**
Morris Rd. NG8: Stre .6J **83**
Morris St. NG4: Neth .1K **97**
MORTHEN .3A **144**
Mortimer's Hole Cave .7D **6**
MORTON
Fiskerton .6F **139** (3C **147**)
Gainsborough .2D **145**
Swinderby .2D **147**
Morton Cl. NG12: Rad T .5H **99**
NG18: Mans .4D **48**
Morton Gdns. NG12: Rad T .5H **99**
Morton Gro. S81: Work .4F **19**
Morton St. NG19: Mans .1E **46**
Morval Rd. NG8: Bilb .1K **93**
Morven Av. NG15: Huck .7H **67**
NG17: Sut A .1J **51**
NG19: Mans W .7H **41**
Morven Ho. S80: Work .4H **21**
Morven Rd. NG17: Kirk A .6B **52**
Morven Ter. NG20: Mkt W .5D **34**
Mosborough Rd. NG17: Huth .2E **50**
Moseley Rd. NG15: Ann .4C **60**
Moses Vw. S81: Shire .4A **18**
Mosgrove Cl. S81: Gate .5D **18**
Mosley St. NG7: Basf .7G **85**
NG15: Huck .7G **67**
Mosscar Cl. NG20: Mkt W .7B **34**
Mosscar La. NG20: Mkt W .6A **34**
Moss Cl. NG5: Arn .6E **76**
NG13: East B .4E **90**
Mosscroft Av. NG11: Clif .1E **114**
Mossdale S81: Work .4H **19**
Mossdale Rd. NG5: Sher .2K **85**
NG19: Mans W .2A **48**
Moss Dr. NG9: Bram .2G **105**
Moss Ri. NG3: Mapp .5E **86**
Moss Rd. NG15: Huck .6F **67**
Moss Side NG11: Wil .6H **107**
Mosswood Cres. NG5: Bestw .7D **76**
Mottram Rd. NG9: Chil .3H **105**
Moulton Cres. NG24: New B .6F **137**
Mount, The NG3: Mapp .5F **87**
NG5: Redh .5F **77**
NG6: Bestw V .2A **76**
NG8: Stre .6K **83**
NG9: Stap .3C **104**
NG19: Mans W .6F **43**
NG24: New T .7C **134**
Mount Av. S81: Work .7F **19**
Mountbatten Gro. NG4: Ged .5H **87**
Mountbatten Way NG9: Chil .7G **105**
Mount Cl. DN11: Harwo .1C **8**
Mount Ct. NG24: Bald .5F **137**
NG24: New T .7C 134
(off Mount La.)
Mount Cres. NG20: Mkt W .5E **34**
Mountfield Av. NG10: Sand .5A **104**
Mountfield Dr. NG5: Bestw .7C **76**
Mt. Hooton NG1: Nott .1B **6** (2H **95**)
Mt. Hooton Rd. NG7: Radf .1A **6** (1H **95**)
Mount La. NG24: New T .1D **136**
Mount Milner NG18: Mans .4K **47**
Mountney Pl. NG24: New T .5E **134**
MOUNT PLEASANT .5E **34**
Mt. Pleasant DN22: Retf .3F **23**
NG4: Carl .1H **97**
NG6: Basf .5E **84**
NG12: Key .7J **117**
NG12: Rad T .5D **98**
NG14: Lowd .4D **80**
NG17: Ann W .3K **59**
NG17: Sut A .6K **45**
NG18: Mans .3G **47**
Mt. Prospect DN10: Eve .5B **10**
Mount Rd. NG24: Bald .5F **137**
Mountsorrel Dr. NG2: West Br .3E **108**
Mount St. NG1: Nott .5D **6** (4J **95**)
(not continuous)
NG7: Basf .6G **85**
NG9: Stap .2D **104**
NG19: Mans .1G **47**
Mount St. Arc. NG1: Nott .5D **6**
Mt. Vernon Pk. DN22: Retf .6G **23**
Mount Vw. Cl. NG18: Mans .4K **47**
Mowbray Ct. NG3: Nott .3H **7** (3A **96**)
Mowbray Gdns. NG2: West Br .4C **108**
Mowbray Ri. NG5: Arn .5H **77**
Mowcrofts La. NG22: Ragn .7G **29**
Mowlands Cl. NG17: Sut A .1B **52**
Moyra Dr. NG5: Arn .7E **76**
Moyra Ho. NG5: Arn .7G **77**
Mozart Cl. NG7: Radf .3F **95**
Mudpie La. NG2: West Br .7E **96**
Muir Av. NG12: Toll .2G **117**
Muirfield S81: Work .6J **19**
Muirfield Cl. NG17: Kirk A .4J **51**
Muirfield Rd. NG5: Top V .5B **76**
Muirfield Way NG19: Mans W .3A **42**
Mulberry Cl. NG2: West Br .4J **107**
Mulberry Ct. DN10: Miss .3C **10**
Mulberry Cres. S81: Carl L .5C **12**
Mulberry Gdns. NG6: Bulw .6G **75**
Mulberry Gro. NG15: Huck .2H **75**
Mulberry Way DN11: Harwo .2C **8**
Mumby Cl. NG24: New T .7D **134**
Mundella Rd. NG2: Nott .7A **96**
Munford Cir. NG8: Cin .4B **84**
Munks Av. NG15: Huck .6F **67**
Murby Cres. NG6: Bulw .6H **75**
Murden Way NG9: Bee .3C **106**
Murdoch Cl. NG22: Farns .4J **57**
Muriel Rd. NG9: Bee .2A **106**
Muriel St. NG6: Bulw .7H **75**
Murray Cl. NG5: Bestw .2G **85**
Murray St. NG18: Mans .5H **47**
Muschamp Ter. NG20: Mkt W .5D **34**
Mus. of Law
Shire Hall .6G **7** (4A **96**)
Mushroom Farm Ct. NG16: Eastw .3B **72**
Muskham Ct. NG19: Mans .1H **47**
Muskham La. NG23: Bath .6F **129**
Muskham St. NG2: Nott .7A **96**
Muskham Vw. NG24: New T .7C **134**
Muspitts La. DN22: Sth W .4H **17**
Musters Ct. NG2: West Br .1B **108**
NG15: Huck .7J **67**
Musters Cres. NG2: West Br .4C **108**
Musters Cft. NG4: Colw .5J **97**
Musters Rd. NG2: West Br .1B **108**
NG11: Rudd .4J **115**
NG13: Bing .4E **100**
NG13: Lang .7K **113**
NG15: News .6D **60**
Musters Wlk. NG6: Bulw .7G **75**
MUSTON .2D **149**
Muston Cl. NG3: Mapp .6C **86**
Mutton La. DN10: Beck .6A **16**
Muttonshire Hill DN22: Gam .1K **27**
Mynd, The NG19: Mans W .4A **42**
Myrtle Av. NG7: Hyson G .7J **85**
NG9: Stap .3D **104**
Myrtle Gro. NG9: Bee .2B **106**
Myrtle Rd. NG4: Carl .7F **87**
Myrtle St. DN22: Retf .4D **22**
Myrtus Cl. NG11: Clif .7D **106**
Mytholme Cl. NG10: Long E .7B **104**

N

Nabarro Ct. NG14: Calv .6C **70**
Nabbs La. NG15: Huck .7D **66**
Naburn Ct. NG8: Basf .6E **84**
Nairn Cl. NG5: Arn .5K **77**
NG22: Farns .6K **57**
Nairn M. NG4: Carl .1H **97**
NANPANTAN .3A **148**
Nansen Gdns. NG5: Bestw .1G **85**
Nansen St. NG6: Bulw .1D **84**
Naomi Ct. NG6: Bulw .5J **75**
Naomi Cres. NG6: Bulw .5J **75**
Naranjan M. NG7: Radf .1B **6** (2H **95**)
Narrow La. NG16: Want .5K **73**
Naseby Av. NG24: New T .1H **137**
Naseby Cl. NG5: Sher .3G **85**
Nash Cl. S81: Work .1K **21**
Nathans La. NG12: Rad T .2K **109**
National Ice Cen., The .5H **7** (4A **96**)
National Water Sports Cen. .6H **97**
Natural History Mus. .5B **94**
Naturescape Wildflower Farm .2C **149**
Navdeep Ct. NG2: West Br .2B **108**
Navenby Wlk. NG11: Clif .7F **107**
Navigation Yd. NG24: New T .1B **136**
Naworth Cl. NG6: Bulw .2F **85**
Naylor Av. NG11: Goth .7G **115**
Naylor Ho. *NG5: Arn .1D 86*
(off Derwent Cres.)
Nazareth Ct. NG7: Lent .6F **95**
Nazareth Rd. NG7: Lent .6F **95**
NEAP HOUSE .1D **145**
Nearsby Dr. NG2: West Br .3E **108**
Neatholme Rd. DN22: Lound .3D **14**
Needham Rd. NG5: Arn .6J **77**
Needham St. NG13: Bing .4F **101**
Needwood Av. NG9: Trow .6C **92**
Neeps Cft. NG14: Epp .1A **80**
Negus Ct. NG4: Lamb .7F **79**
Neighbours La. NG14: Lowd .5E **80**
Neighwood Cl. NG9: Toton .7D **104**
Nell Gwyn Cres. NG5: Arn .5E **76**
Nelson Cl. NG19: Mans .3E **46**
Nelson La. NG23: Nth M .6J **129**
Nelson Rd. NG5: Arn .7G **77**
NG6: Bulw .7J **75**
NG9: Bee .5B **106**
NG24: New B .5E **136**
Nelson St. DN22: Retf .4G **23**
NG1: Nott .5H **7** (4A **96**)
Nene Cl. NG15: Huck .3E **74**
Nene Wlk. S81: Work .5F **19**
Nesbitt St. NG17: Sut A .2K **51**
Nest Av. NG17: Kirk A .7C **52**
Nest Cres. NG17: Kirk A .7C **52**
Neston Dr. NG6: Cin .3C **84**
NETHER BROUGHTON .3K **143** (3B **148**)
Nether Cl. NG3: Nott .2D **96**
NG16: Eastw .2D **72**
Nethercross Dr. NG20: Mkt W .3E **34**
NETHERFIELD .2J **97** (1B **148**)
Netherfield Cl. NG20: Mede V .1F **35**
Netherfield Grange NG17: Sut A .2H **51**
Netherfield La. NG20: Chu W, Mede V .1E **34**
Netherfield Rd. NG10: Sand .4A **104**
Netherfield Station (Rail) .2J **97**
Nethergate NG11: Clif .7D **106**
NETHER GREEN .2D **72**
Nether Grn. NG16: Eastw .3D **72**
NETHER LANGWITH .5B **26** (1A **146**)
Nether Pasture NG4: Neth .2K **97**
Nether St. NG9: Bee .3B **106**
Netherton Pl. S80: Work .4H **21**
Netherton Rd. S80: Work .4H **21**
Nettlecliff Wlk. NG5: Top V .6A **76**
Nevile Dr. NG12: Kin .2C **142**
Neville Rd. NG14: Calv .7D **70**
Neville Sadler Ct. NG9: Bee .2B **106**
New Alexandra Ct., The NG3: Nott .7A **86**
Newall Dr. DN10: Matt T .1G **15**
NG9: Chil .7H **105**
Newark Agricultural Society's Showground .3J **135**
Newark Air Mus. .3K **135**
Newark & Notts Gliding Club .3J **135**
Newark Av. NG2: Nott .6K **7** (4B **96**)
Newark Bus. Pk. NG24: New T .7E **134**
Newark Castle .7C **134**
Newark Castle Station (Rail) .7C **134**
Newark Cl. NG18: Mans .1B **54**
Newark Ct. NG5: Bestw .2G **85**
Newark Cres. NG2: Nott .6K **7** (4B **96**)
Newark Dr. NG18: Mans .1B **54**
Newark Golf Cen. .3H **135**
Newark Hall NG8: Woll .4E **94**
Newark Ho. NG22: Bils .5C **126**
Newark Northgate Station (Rail) .6E **134**
NEWARK-ON-TRENT .7C **134** (3C **147**)
Newark Rd. NG17: Sut A .2C **52**
NG22: Eakr .2D **126**
NG22: Kirk .1C **132**
NG22: New O, Well .6D **38**
NG22: Oll .5A **38**
NG22: Tuxf .7C **28**
NG23: Aver .3F **133**
NG23: Caus .7J **127**
NG23: Coll .4G **129**
NG24: Barn W .6K **137**
NG24: Codd .7H **135**
NG24: Haw .6A **136**
NG25: Sout .5J **131**
Newark St. NG2: Nott .6J **7** (4B **96**)
Newark Way NG18: Mans .1C **54**
NEW BAGTHORPE .1F **65**
NEW BALDERTON .5G **137** (3D **147**)
NEW BASFORD .6G **85**
New Basford Bus. Area *NG7: Basf .6G 85*
(off Palm St.)
Newberry Cl. NG12: Crop Bi .5B **112**
Newbery Cl. NG21: Edwin .6E **36**
Newbold Way NG12: Kin .2B **142**
Newboundmill La. NG19: Plea .6A **40**
NEW BRINSLEY .4C **64** (3A **146**)
New Bldgs. Dr. NG20: Mans W .2E **42**
Newbury Cl. NG3: Mapp .3D **86**
Newbury Ct. NG5: Sher .7J **85**
Newbury Dr. NG16: Nuth .4J **83**
Newbury M. S80: Work .3G **21**
Newbury Rd. NG24: New T .7H **135**
Newcastle Av. NG4: Ged .6H **87**
NG9: Bee .3A **106**
NG24: New T .3D **136**
S80: Work .3E **20**
Newcastle Chambers NG1: Nott .5E **6** (4K **95**)
Newcastle Cir. NG7: Nott .6A **6** (4H **95**)
Newcastle Ct. NG7: Nott .6A **6** (4H **95**)
NG22: Tuxf .7C **28**
Newcastle Dr. NG7: Nott .5A **6** (4H **95**)
Newcastle Farm Dr. NG8: Aspl .6D **84**
Newcastle St. NG6: Bulw .6J **75**
NG17: Huth .7D **44**
NG18: Mans .3G **47**
NG19: Mans W .6H **41**
NG20: Mkt W .4D **34**
NG22: Tuxf .7B **28**
S80: Work .3G **21**
Newcastle Ter. NG7: Nott .4B **6** (3H **95**)
NG8: Aspl .6E **84**
New Cl. NG17: Kirk A .6A **52**
NG21: Blid .6J **55**
Newcombe Dr. NG5: Arn .7A **78**

O

P

Q

R

River Rd. NG4: Colw 4H 97
Riverside NG13: What 4E 102
NG14: Sto B 7E 88
NG25: Sout 5J 131
Riverside Cvn. Pk. S80: Work 2F 21
Riverside Cl. NG9: Bee 6C 106
NG20: Cuck 4C 32
Riverside Point NG7: Lent 5F 95
Riverside Retail Pk. NG2: Nott 1H 107
Riverside Rd. NG9: Bee 6B 106
NG24: New T 4A 136
Riverside Wlk. DN22: Retf 3E 22
Riverside Way NG2: Nott 7J 95
NG19: Mans W 4K 41
River Vw. DN22: Ord 7E 22
NG2: Nott 7A 96
NG20: Mkt W 3D 34
Riverway Gdns. NG2: Nott 6A 96
Rivington Rd. NG9: Toton 7D 104
Roadways, The S80: Work 2F 21
Roadwood La. NG23: Thor 1F 31
Robbie Burns Rd. NG5: Bestw 6E 76
Robert Av. NG18: Mans 5F 47
Robert Dukeson Av. NG24: New T 4D 134
(not continuous)
Roberts Av. NG17: Huth 1D 50
Roberts Cl. NG22: Ragn 7G 29
Roberts La. NG15: Huck 6F 67
Roberts St. DE7: Ilk 2A 92
NG2: Nott 5K 7 (4B 96)
Roberts Yd. NG9: Bee 2B 106
Robey Cl. NG15: Lin 4H 67
NG19: Mans W 1D 48
Robey Dr. NG16: Eastw 2D 72
Robey Ter. NG7: Hyson G 1G 95
Robina Dr. NG16: Gilt 6G 73
Robin Bailey Way NG15: Huck 7J 67
Robin Down Cl. NG18: Mans 1K 53
Robin Down Ct. NG18: Mans 1J 53
Robin Down La. NG18: Mans 1J 53
Robinet Rd. NG9: Bee 4A 106
Robinettes La. NG16: Coss 6C 82
Robin Gro. NG15: Rave 3C 62
ROBIN HOOD AIRPORT DONCASTER SHEFFIELD 2B 144
Robin Hood Av. NG20: Mkt W 6D 34
NG21: Edwin 7J 37
Robin Hood Chase NG3: Nott 1H 7 (1A 96)
Robin Hood Cl. NG16: Eastw 5D 72
Robin Hood Dr. NG15: Huck 2E 74
Robin Hood Ind. Est. NG3: Nott 3J 7 (3B 96)
Robin Hood Rd. NG5: Arn 5E 76
NG17: Ann W 4B 60
NG21: Blid 6K 55
Robin Hood Statue 6D 6
Robin Hood St. NG3: Nott 4J 7 (3B 96)
Robin Hood Ter. NG3: Nott 3H 7 (3A 96)
NG15: Rave 1D 62
Robin Hood Theatre 4G 133
Robin Hood Way NG2: Nott 7J 95
Robinia Ct. NG2: West Br 4D 108
Robins Ct. NG24: New T 1D 136
Robinson Cl. *DN22: Elk 2G 27*
(off High St.)
NG24: New T 1H 137
Robinson Ct. NG9: Chil 7G 105
Robinson Dr. S80: Work 4F 21
Robinson Gdns. NG11: Clif 1D 114
Robinson Rd. NG3: Mapp 4C 86
Robinsons Hill NG6: Bulw 7H 75
Robinswood Ho. NG8: Bilb 1C 94
Robins Wood Rd. NG8: Aspl 2C 94
Rob Roy Av. NG7: Lent 5G 95
Rochdale Ct. NG18: Mans 5C 48
Roche Cl. NG5: Arn 7A 78
Rochester Av. NG4: Neth 1K 97
Rochester Cl. S81: Work 5H 19
Rochester Ct. NG6: Bulw 1A 84
Rochester Rd. NG21: Rain 3J 55
Rochester Wlk. NG11: Clif 1G 115
Rochford Ct. NG12: Edwal 6F 109
Rock Ct. NG6: Basf 4E 84
NG18: Mans 3J 47
Rock Dr. NG7: Nott 7B 6 (5H 95)
Rocket Cl. NG16: Want 7A 74
Rockfield Dr. S81: Woods 1A 18
Rockford Ct. NG9: Stap 7D 92
Rockford Rd. NG5: Sher 4G 85
Rock Hill NG18: Mans 4K 47
Rock Hill Gdns. NG18: Mans 4K 47
Rockingham Gro. NG13: Bing 4D 100
Rock La. DN10: Eve 7C 10
Rockley Av. NG12: Rad T 4E 98
NG16: Newth 5E 72
Rockley Cl. NG15: Huck 7C 66
NG21: C'tone 5H 43
Rockleys Vw. NG14: Lowd 4A 80
Rock Side *NG16: Kimb 1E 82*
(off The Sidings)
Rockside Gdns. NG15: Huck 6E 66
Rock St. NG6: Bulw 6G 75
NG18: Mans 4K 47
Rock Ter. NG21: Blid 7G 55
Rock Valley NG18: Mans 3J 47
(not continuous)
Rockwell Ct. NG9: Stap 2D 104
Rockwood Cres. NG15: Huck 7D 66
Rockwood Wlk. NG15: Huck 7E 66
Rodel Ct. NG3: Nott 2G 7 (2A 96)
Roden St. NG3: Nott 4J 7 (3B 96)
Roderick Av. NG17: Ann W 3B 60
Roderick St. NG6: Basf 3E 84
Rodery, The NG18: Mans 5A 48
Rodice Ct. NG7: Lent 3F 95
Rodney Rd. NG2: West Br 3D 108
Rodwell Cl. NG8: Aspl 2D 94
Roebuck Cl. NG5: Arn 6D 76
Roebuck Dr. NG18: Mans 7H 47
Roecliffe NG2: West Br 5B 108
Roe Gdns. NG11: Rudd 3J 115
Roehampton Dr. NG9: Trow 6C 92
Roe Hill NG14: Woodbo 7G 71
(not continuous)
Roe La. DN10: Eve 6B 10
NG14: Woodbo 2G 79
Roes La. NG14: Calv 6E 70
Roewood Cl. NG17: Kirk A 4K 51
Roger Cl. NG17: Skeg 5K 45
Roker Cl. NG8: Aspl 6B 84
Rolaine Cl. NG19: Mans W 5J 41
Roland Av. NG11: Wil 2J 107
NG16: Nuth 3K 83
ROLLESTON 3K 139 (3C 147)
Rolleston Cl. NG15: Huck 1D 74
Rolleston Cres. NG16: Want 5K 73
Rolleston Dr. NG5: Arn 7J 77
NG7: Lent 7A 6 (4G 95)
NG16: Newth 6E 72
Rolleston Station (Rail) 3J 139
Roman Bank NG19: Mans W 6K 41
Roman Bank La. DN10: Serl 7H 9
DN22: Rans 6K 13
S81: Blyth 6K 13
Roman Dr. NG6: Basf 3F 85
Roman Rd. S81: Gate, Work 5E 18
Romans Ct. NG6: Basf 5F 85
Romilay Cl. NG9: Lent A 7B 94
Romney Av. NG8: Woll 6J 93
Romsey Pl. NG19: Mans 4D 46
Rona Cl. NG19: Mans 5E 46
Rona Ct. NG6: Bulw 2F 85
Ronald St. NG7: Radf 4A 6 (3G 95)
Roods Cl. NG17: Sut A 3H 51
Rookery, The NG18: Mans 2G 47
NG23: Coll 1H 129
Rookery Farm NG12: Crop Bu 3C 112
Rookery Gdns. NG5: Arn 6H 77
Rookery La. NG17: Sut A 3E 50
Rook's La. DN10: Mist 1G 11
Rookwood Cl. NG9: Bee 3K 105
NG21: Blid 6J 55
Rooley Av. NG17: Sut A 7G 45
Rooley Dr. NG17: Sut A 7G 45
Rooley La. NG17: Huth, Sut A 7E 44
Roosa Cl. NG6: Bulw 2A 84
Roosevelt Rd. NG17: Sut A 6B 46
Rooth St. NG18: Mans 4H 47
Ropewalk LE12: East L 3K 121
Ropewalk, The NG1: Nott 4B 6 (3H 95)
NG24: New T 1E 136
NG25: Sout 5G 131
Ropewalk Ct. NG1: Nott 3H 95
Ropeway, The NG17: Kirk A 6J 51
Ropsley Cres. NG2: West Br 7D 96
Roscoe Av. NG5: Redh 4G 77
Roseacre NG9: Bee 4B 106
Rose Ash La. NG5: Bestw 6D 76
Rose Av. DN22: Retf 6G 23
Rosebank Dr. NG5: Arn 5K 77
Rosebay Av. NG7: Hyson G 7F 85
Roseberry Gdns. NG15: Huck 7J 67
Roseberry St. NG17: Kirk A 7B 52
Rosebery Av. NG2: West Br 7B 96
Rosebery Hill NG18: Mans 4J 47
Rosebery St. NG6: Basf 3F 85
Rose Cl. NG3: Nott 1A 96
Rose Cott. Dr. NG17: Huth 1D 50
Rose Cotts. NG14: Bur J 2D 88
Rosecroft Dr. NG5: Bestw 1K 85
Rosedale S81: Work 4H 19
Rosedale Dr. NG8: Woll 4G 93
Rosedale Gdns. NG17: Sut A 3H 51
Rosedale La. NG15: Rave 1B 62
Rosedale Rd. NG3: Nott 2F 97
Rosedale Way NG19: Mans W 7B 42
Rose Farm Dr. NG23: Sut T 3D 128
Rosefield Cl. NG24: Bald 7J 137
Rose Flower Gro. NG15: Huck 2J 75
Rose Gdns. DN22: Retf 2D 22
S80: Work 3F 21
Rosegarth Wlk. NG6: Basf 3E 84
Rose Gro. NG9: Bee 4C 106
NG12: Key 6J 117
Rosegrove Av. NG5: Arn 5H 77
Rose Hill NG12: Key 7H 117
Roseland Cl. NG12: Key 1H 119
Rose La. NG19: Mans W 5J 41
Rose Lea DN22: Ord 6D 22
Roseleigh Av. NG3: Mapp 5E 86
Rosemary Av. NG19: Mans 2G 47
Rosemary Cen. NG18: Mans 3G 47
Rosemary Cl. NG8: Brox 6K 83
ROSEMARYHILL 5D 58
Rosemary St. NG18: Mans 3G 47
NG19: Mans 2G 47
Rosemont Cl. NG17: Skeg 4K 45
Roseneath Av. NG5: Top V 5A 76
Rosetta Rd. NG7: Basf 6G 85
(not continuous)
Rosewall Ct. NG5: Arn 7K 77
Rosewood Cl. NG24: New T 6E 134
S81: Gate 3E 18
Rosewood Ct. NG17: Kirk A 5C 52
Rosewood Dr. NG17: Kirk A 5C 52
Rosewood Gdns. NG2: West Br 6K 107
NG6: Bulw 7F 75
Rosings Ct. NG17: Sut A 2J 51
Roslyn Av. NG4: Ged 5H 87
Roslyn Ct. NG14: Bur J 2E 88
Ross Cl. NG14: Lowd 5E 80
Rossell Dr. NG9: Stap 4C 104
Rossett Cl. NG2: Gam 3G 109
Rossetti Gdns. S81: Work 2K 21
ROSSINGTON 2B 144
Rossington Rd. NG2: Nott 3C 96
Ross La. NG4: Lamb 7G 79
Rosslyn Dr. NG8: Aspl 5B 84
NG15: Huck 5J 67
ROSTHOLME 1A 144
Rosthwaite Cl. NG2: West Br 4F 109
Roston Cl. NG18: Mans 5D 48
Roston Ct. NG18: Mans 5D 48
Rothbury Av. NG9: Trow 6C 92
Rothbury Gro. NG13: Bing 3D 100
ROTHERBY 3B 148
ROTHERHAM 2A 144
Rotherham Baulk S81: Carl L 5A 12
Rotherham Rd. NG19: New H, Sto H 1A 40
Rothesay Av. NG7: Lent 3G 95
Rothley Av. NG3: Nott 3C 96
Rothwell Cl. NG11: Wil 5H 107
Roughs Wood La. NG15: Huck 2D 74
Roulstone Cres. LE12: East L 1A 122
ROUND HILL 2C 52
Roundhill Cl. NG17: Sut A 2C 52
Roundhouse Cres. S81: Work 5E 18
Roundwood Rd. NG5: Arn 7E 76
Row, The NG13: Elton 6J 103
NG13: Ors 2J 103
Rowan Av. NG9: Stap 6D 92
NG15: Rave 3C 62
Rowan Cl. NG13: Bing 4H 101
NG14: Calv 6B 70
NG17: Kirk A 6J 51
NG19: Mans W 1K 47
Rowan Ct. NG16: Nuth 1G 83
Rowan Cres. NG6: Cin 3C 84
S80: Work 4F 21
Rowan Cft. NG17: Huth 6D 44
Rowan Dr. NG11: Wil 5H 107
NG12: Key 1K 119
NG16: Sels 5B 58
NG17: Kirk A 5K 51
Rowan Gdns. NG6: Bulw 7F 75
Rowan Wlk. NG3: Nott 7D 86
Rowan Way NG24: New B 4E 136
Rowe Gdns. NG6: Bulw 1E 84
Rowland Av. NG3: Mapp 5D 86
Rowland M. NG3: Nott 1B 96
Rowsley Ct. NG17: Sut A 2F 51
ROWTHORNE 2A 146
Roxby Ho. NG5: Arn 1D 86
Roxley Ct. NG9: Bee 2K 105
Roxton Ct. NG16: Kimb 7K 73
Royal Albert Ct. NG7: Radf 2A 6
Royal Av. NG10: Long E 7C 104
Royal Cen. NG1: Nott 4E 6
Royal Centre Stop (NET) 4E 6 (3J 95)
Royal Concert Hall 4E 6 (3K 95)
Royal Ct. *NG5: Sher 5K 85*
(off Haydn Rd.)
S80: Work 3G 21
(off Newcastle St.)
Royal Cres. S81: Work 6F 19
Royal Exchange Shop. Cen. *NG24: New T 1C 136*
(off Middle Ga.)
Royal M. NG9: Chil 6H 105
Royal Oak Ct. NG21: Edwin 6F 37
Royal Oak Dr. NG16: Sels 5F 59
Royal Standard Ho. NG1: Nott 6D 6 (4J 95)

Royal Standard Pl. NG1: Nott 6D **6**
Royal Victoria Ct. NG7: Radf 2A **6** (2H **95**)
Roy Av. NG9: Bee 5C **106**
Royce Av. NG15: Huck 2E **74**
Royds Cres. S80: Rhod 7B **18**
Royston Cl. NG2: Nott 7J **95**
Ruby Gdns. NG17: Kirk A 7D **52**
Ruby Gro. NG21: Rain 2A **56**
Ruby Paddocks NG16: Kimb 2E **82**
Rubys Av. NG24: Bald 7H **137**
Ruby's Wlk. NG24: Bald 7H **137**
Ruby Way NG18: Mans 5K **47**
RUDDINGTON 3K **115** (2A **148**)
Ruddington Ct. NG18: Mans 1C **54**
Ruddington Flds. Bus. Pk. NG11: Rudd 5A **116**
Ruddington Framework Knitters Mus. 4K **115**
Ruddington La. NG11: Wil 3J **107**
Ruddington Rd. NG18: Mans 1C **54**
Ruddington Village Mus. 3K **115**
Ruddington Station
Great Central Railway (Nottingham) 5A **116**
Rudge Cl. NG8: Woll 3A **94**
Rue De L'Yonne NG23: Coll 1H **129**
Ruffles Av. NG5: Arn 2E **86**
Rufford Abbey (remains of) 2B **146**
Rufford Av. DN22: Ord 7D **22**
NG4: Ged 5G **87**
NG9: Bram 1F **105**
NG18: Mans 3J **47**
NG20: Mede V 6G **33**
NG21: Rain 2K **55**
NG22: New O 4C **38**
NG24: New T 2C **136**
Rufford Cl. NG15: Huck 7J **67**
NG17: Skeg 5K **45**
NG22: Bils 7D **126**
Rufford Colliery La. NG21: Rain 2J **55**
Rufford Country Pk. 2B **146**
Rufford Country Pk. Formal Gdns. 2B **146**
Rufford Ct. NG21: Rain 2A **56**
Rufford Dr. NG19: Mans W 6A **42**
Rufford Gro. NG13: Bing 4E **100**
Rufford La. NG22: Ruff, Well 7A **38**
Rufford Rd. NG5: Sher 4K **85**
NG11: Rudd 3A **116**
NG21: Edwin 7F **37**
Rufford St. S80: Work 5J **21**
Rufford Wlk. NG6: Bulw 7H **75**
Rufford Way NG2: West Br 3E **108**
RUFFS 1E **74**
Ruffs Dr. NG15: Huck 1D **74**
Rugby Cl. NG5: Top V 7A **76**
Rugby Ct. NG2: West Br 4B **108**
Rugby Rd. NG2: West Br 4K **107**
NG21: Rain 3J **55**
Rugby Ter. NG7: Hyson G 1G **95**
Rugged Butts La. DN10: Miss 1B **10**
Ruislip Cl. NG16: Kimb 7J **73**
Runcie Cl. NG12: Cotg 7E **110**
Runnymede Ct. NG7: Radf 3B **6** (3H **95**)
*NG9: Bee 4B **106***
(off Grove St.)
Runswick Dr. NG5: Arn 6H **77**
NG8: Woll 3B **94**
Runton Dr. NG6: Basf 3G **85**
Rupert Cres. NG24: New T 2C **136**
Rupert Rd. NG13: Bing 4E **100**
Ruscombe Pl. NG3: Nott 1H **7** (2A **96**)
Rushcliffe Arena 3K **107**
Rushcliffe Av. NG4: Carl 7G **87**
NG12: Rad T 5E **98**
Rushcliffe Country Pk. 5K **115**
Rushcliffe Ct. NG6: Bulw 1E **84**
Rushcliffe Gro. LE12: East L 1A **122**
Rushcliffe Halt Station
Great Central Railway (Nottingham) 1A **122**
Rushcliffe Leisure Cen. 5C **108**
Rushcliffe Ri. NG5: Sher 2A **86**
Rushcliffe Rd. NG15: Huck 1E **74**
Rushes, The NG11: Goth 7G **115**
NG19: Mans W 4K **41**
Rushey Cl. S80: Work 3J **21**
Rushford Dr. NG8: Woll 4H **93**
Rushley Vw. NG17: Sut A 2G **51**
Rushmere Wlk. NG5: Woodt 2C **86**
Rushpool Av. NG19: Mans W 5K **41**
Rushpool Cl. NG19: Mans W 7B **42**
Rushton Gdns. NG3: Nott 1K **7** (1B **96**)
Rushworth Av. NG2: West Br 1B **108**
Rushworth Cl. NG3: Nott 1J **7** (1B **96**)
Rushworth Ct. NG2: West Br 1B **108**
Rushy Cl. NG8: Bilb 3J **93**
Ruskin Av. NG9: Chil 5J **105**
Ruskin Cl. NG5: Arn 7F **77**
Ruskin Rd. NG19: Mans 7D **40**
Russell Av. DN11: Harwo 2C **8**
NG8: Woll 3A **94**
NG24: New B 5E **136**
Russell Cres. NG8: Woll 3A **94**
Russell Dr. NG8: Woll 3K **93**
Russell Gdns. NG9: Chil 7H **105**
Russell Pl. NG1: Nott 4D **6** (3J **95**)
Russell Rd. NG7: Hyson G 7G **85**
Russell St. NG7: Radf 2B **6** (2H **95**)
NG17: Sut A 7K **45**
Russet Av. NG4: Carl 1H **97**
Russet Cl. NG14: Lowd 5E **80**
Russley Rd. NG9: Bram 1F **105**
Ruth Dr. NG5: Arn 5J **77**
Rutherford Av. NG18: Mans 5A **48**
Rutherford Ho. NG7: Nott 7E **94**
Ruthwell Gdns. NG5: Top V 4C **76**
Rutland NG17: Kirk A 5D **52**
Rutland Av. NG9: Toton 7F **105**
NG24: New T 3D **136**
Rutland Cl. NG20: Mkt W 4C **34**
Rutland Cres. DN11: Harwo 1C **8**
Rutland Dr. DN11: Harwo 1C **8**
Rutland Gro. NG10: Sand 4B **104**
Rutland Hall NG7: Nott 7C **94**
Rutland Rd. DN22: Retf 6H **23**
NG2: West Br 7C **96**
NG4: Ged 4G **87**
NG13: Bing 4G **101**
NG16: Westw 6A **64**
Rutlands, The NG23: Kel 1H **133**
Rutland St. NG1: Nott 6D **6** (4J **95**)
NG18: Mans 5H **47**
Rutland Ter. NG16: Kimb 2F **83**
Rutland Vs. NG2: Nott 4C **96**
Ryan Way NG9: Bee 6B **106**
Rydal Av. NG10: Long E 7A **104**
Rydal Dr. NG9: Bram 1J **105**
NG15: Huck 5F **67**
S81: Work 4F **19**
Rydale Rd. NG5: Sher 2K **85**
Rydal Gdns. NG2: West Br 4D **108**
Rydal Gro. NG6: Basf 4F **85**
Ryder St. NG6: Basf 3E **84**
Ryecroft NG19: Mans W 7D **42**
Ryecroft St. NG9: Stap 7D **92**
Ryedale Av. NG18: Mans 5C **48**
Ryehill Cl. NG2: Nott 6A **96**
Ryehill St. NG2: Nott 6A **96**
Ryeholme Cl. LE12: East L 1B **122**
Ryeland Gdns. NG2: Nott 6K **95**
Ryemere Cl. NG16: Eastw 4C **72**
Ryemere Ct. *NG16: Eastw 4C **72***
(off Ryemere Cl.)
Rye St. NG7: Basf 6G **85**
RYLANDS 4C **106** (2A **148**)
Rylands Cl. NG9: Bee 5C **106**
Rylands Ct. NG9: Bee 4B **106**
Ryton Cl. S81: Blyth 7H **13**
Ryton Ct. NG2: Nott 7A **96**
Ryton Flds. S81: Blyth 7H **13**
Ryton Pl. S80: Work 2G **21**
Ryton Sq. NG8: Aspl 6C **84**
Ryton St. S80: Work 2G **21**

S

Sacheverall Av. NG16: Pinx 1A **58**
Saddlers Cl. NG19: Mans W 1B **48**
Saddlers Yd. NG12: Plum 3H **117**
Saddleworth Ct. NG3: Nott 1F **7** (2K **95**)
Sadler St. NG19: Mans 2F **47**
Saffron Gdns. NG2: Nott 6J **95**
Safron St. NG19: Mans W 1C **48**
St Agnes Cl. NG8: Bilb 7J **83**
St Aidans Ct. NG6: Basf 3F **85**
St Albans M. NG6: Bulw 1E **84**
St Albans Rd. NG5: Arn 7F **77**
NG6: Bestw V 2A **76**
NG6: Bulw 6J **75**
St Albans St. NG5: Sher 4K **85**
St Andrew Cl. NG11: Goth 7G **115**
St Andrews Cl. NG6: Bulw 7J **75**
NG15: Huck 5G **67**
St Andrews Ct. NG6: Bulw 7K **75**
St Andrews Cres. NG17: Skeg 4K **45**
St Andrews Ho. NG3: Mapp 4F **87**
St Andrew's Rd. NG3: Mapp P 1J **95**
St Andrews St. NG17: Kirk A 5B **52**
NG17: Skeg 4J **45**
St Andrew St. NG18: Mans 5J **47**
St Andrews Way DN22: Ord 7E **22**
St Annes Cl. S80: Work 2D **20**
St Annes Dr. S80: Work 3C **20**
St Anne's La. LE12: Sut B 6B **120**
St Annes M. *S80: Work 2D **20***
(off St Annes Way)
St Annes Vw. S80: Work 2D **20**
St Annes Way S80: Work 2D **20**
ST ANN'S 1J **7** (2A **96**)
St Ann's Gdns. NG3: Nott 1B **96**
St Ann's Hill NG3: Nott 1K **95**
St Ann's Hill Rd. NG3: Nott 1E **6** (1K **95**)
St Ann's St. NG1: Nott 3F **7** (3K **95**)
St Ann's Valley NG3: Nott 1J **7** (2B **96**)
St Ann's Way NG3: Nott 1E **6** (2K **95**)
St Ann's Well Rd. NG3: Nott 3G **7** (3A **96**)
St Anthony Ct. NG7: Lent 6F **95**
St Augustines Cl. NG7: Basf 6H **85**
*NG24: New T 2E **136***
(off Newton St.)
St Austell Dr. NG11: Wil 4J **107**
St Austins Ct. NG4: Carl 7J **87**
St Austins Dr. NG4: Carl 7J **87**
St Barnabas' RC Cathedral 4C **6** (4J **95**)
St Bartholomews Ct.
DN22: Sut L 6B **14**
St Bartholomew's Rd. NG3: Nott 1C **96**
St Catherines Cl. NG24: New T 2B **136**
St Catherines St. NG12: Rad T 6D **98**
St Catherine St. NG18: Mans 5J **47**
St Cecilia Gdns. NG3: Nott 1G **7** (2A **96**)
St Chads NG4: Carl 1J **97**
St Chads Cl. NG18: Mans 7J **47**
St Chad's Rd. NG3: Nott 4K **7** (3B **96**)
St Christopher St. NG2: Nott 4C **96**
St Clare's Ga. NG24: New T 3D **136**
St Cuthbert's Rd. NG3: Nott 3K **7** (3B **96**)
St Cuthbert St. S80: Work 3G **21**
St David's Cl. S81: Work 6H **19**
St Edmund's Av. NG19: Mans W 6J **41**
St Edwin's Dr. NG21: Edwin 6E **36**
St Emmanuel Vw. NG5: Arn 5D **76**
St Ervan Rd. NG11: Wil 3J **107**
St Georges Ct. NG15: Huck 5G **67**
NG24: New T 7D **134**
St Georges Dr. NG2: Nott 6K **95**
NG9: Toton 7E **104**
St Giles Way NG12: Crop Bi 5B **112**
NG24: Bald 5H **137**
St Helens Av. NG16: Pinx 7A **50**
St Helens Cres. NG9: Trow 4B **92**
NG14: Bur J 3E **88**
St Helen's Dr. NG16: Sels 5B **58**
St Helen's Gro. NG14: Bur J 4D **88**
St Helen's La. NG22: Halam 4B **130**
St Helens Ri. DN22: Sth W 2K **17**
St Helens Rd. DN22: Retf 6H **23**
NG2: West Br 3C **108**
St Helen's St. NG7: Nott 4B **6** (3H **95**)
St Helier NG7: Nott 6B **6** (4H **95**)
St James Av. DE7: Ilk 1A **92**
St James Ct. NG3: Mapp 5E **86**
NG10: Sand 6A **104**
NG15: Huck 5G **67**
St James Dr. NG16: Brins 5B **64**
St James's St. NG1: Nott 6D **6** (4J **95**)
(not continuous)
St James's Ter. NG1: Nott 6D **6** (4J **95**)
St James St. NG9: Stap 3B **104**
St James Ter. NG9: Stap 3B **104**
St John M. *DN22: Retf 3F **23***
(off St John St.)
St Johns S81: Blyth 7H **13**
St John's Av. NG17: Kirk A 7B **52**
St John's Cl. NG16: Brins 4B **64**
St John's Ct. NG4: Carl 1G **97**
S80: Work 2G **21**
St John's Cres. NG15: Huck 1J **75**
St John's Dr. DN22: Clar 7H **17**
St John's Pl. NG18: Mans 3G **47**
St John's Rd. NG11: Rudd 3K **115**
St John St. DN22: Retf 3F **23**
NG18: Mans 3G **47**
St John's Vw. NG18: Mans 3G **47**
St Jude's Av. NG3: Mapp 5A **86**
St Judes Way NG21: Rain 2J **55**
St Lawrence Blvd. NG12: Rad T 6C **98**
St Leonard's Ct. *NG24: New T 7C **134***
(off Kirk Ga.)
St Leonards Dr. NG8: Woll 4A **94**
St Leonards Way NG19: Mans W 1D **48**
St Leven Cl. NG8: Bilb 7J **83**
St Lukes Cl. NG2: West Br 4E **108**
St Luke's St. NG3: Nott 4J **7** (3B **96**)
St Lukes Vw. S81: Shire 5A **18**
St Lukes Way DN22: Woodbe 7F **25**
NG14: Sto B 7E **88**
St Margaret's Av. NG8: Aspl 7D **84**
St Margaret's Cl. NG22: Bils 7D **126**
St Margaret St. NG18: Mans 5J **47**
St Mark's Cl. S81: Gate 4E **18**
St Marks Ct. NG17: Sut A 3F **51**
St Mark's La. NG24: New T 1C **136**
(not continuous)
St Mark's Pl. NG24: New T 1C **136**
St Mark's St. NG3: Nott 3G **7** (3A **96**)
St Martins Cl. DN22: Nth L 6B **24**
NG8: Stre 7K **83**
S81: Blyth 7H **13**
St Martin's Gdns. NG8: Stre 7J **83**
St Martins Rd. DN22: Nth L 6B **24**
NG8: Stre 7K **83**
St Mary's Av. NG4: Ged 5H **87**

T

U

V

W

Y

Z

HOSPITALS and HOSPICES covered by this atlas.

N.B. Where Hospitals and Hospices are not named on the map, the reference given is for the road in which they are situated.

ASHFIELD COMMUNITY HOSPITAL 6A **52**
Portland Street
Kirkby-in-Ashfield
NOTTINGHAM
NG17 7AE
Tel: 01623 785050

BASSETLAW HOSPICE 3D **22**
Cedar House
North Road
RETFORD
DN22 7XF
Tel: 01777 869239

BASSETLAW HOSPITAL 7H **19**
Kilton Hill
WORKSOP
S81 0BD
Tel: 01909 500990

BEAUMOND HOUSE COMMUNITY HOSPICE 1C **136**
32 London Road
NEWARK
NG24 1TW
Tel: 01636 610556

HAYWOOD HOUSE MACMILLAN SPECIALIST PALLIATIVE CARE UNIT 3J **85**
Nottingham City Hospital
Hucknall Road
NOTTINGHAM
NG5 1PB
Tel: 0115 962 7619

HIGHBURY HOSPITAL 2D **84**
Highbury Road
Bulwell
NOTTINGHAM
NG6 9DR
Tel: 0115 9770000

HOSPITAL PALLIATIVE CARE TEAM (UNIVERSITY HOSPITAL) 6E **94**
E Floor East Block
Queen's Medical Centre)
NOTTINGHAM
NG7 2UH
Tel: 0115 919 4402

JOHN EASTWOOD HOSPICE 6C **46**
John Eastwood House
Mansfield Road
SUTTON-IN-ASHFIELD
NG17 4HJ
Tel: 01623 622626

KING'S MILL HOSPITAL 5C **46**
Mansfield Road
SUTTON-IN-ASHFIELD
NG17 4JL
Tel: 01623 622515

LINGS BAR HOSPITAL 3G **109**
Beckside
Gamston
NOTTINGHAM
NG2 6PR
Tel: 0115 945 5577

MANSFIELD COMMUNITY HOSPITAL 4G **47**
Stockwell Gate
MANSFIELD
NG18 5QJ
Tel: 01623 785050

MEADOWBANK DAY HOSPITAL 7J **95**
Queen's Walk
NOTTINGHAM
NG2 1JT
Tel: 0115 9860883

NEWARK HOSPITAL 3D **136**
Boundary Road
NEWARK
NG24 4DE
Tel: 01636 681681

NOTTINGHAM CITY HOSPITAL (TRUST) 2J **85**
Hucknall Road
NOTTINGHAM
NG5 1PB
Tel: 0115 969 1169

NOTTINGHAM NUFFIELD HOSPITAL, THE 2A **86**
748 Mansfield Road
Woodthorpe
NOTTINGHAM
NG5 3FZ
Tel: 0115 9209209

NOTTINGHAMSHIRE HOSPICE 7A **86**
384 Woodborough Rd
NOTTINGHAM
NG3 4JF
Tel: 0115 910 1008

PARK BMI HOSPITAL, THE 3F **69**
Sherwood Lodge Drive
Burntstump Country Park
Arnold
NOTTINGHAM
NG5 8RX
Tel: 0115 9670670

QUEEN'S MEDICAL CENTRE (UNIVERSITY HOSPITAL, NOTTINGHAM) 6E **94**
Derby Rd.,
NOTTINGHAM
NG7 2UH
Tel: 0115 9249924

RAMPTON HOSPITAL 7G **25**
Rampton Hospital
RETFORD
DN22 0PD
Tel: 01777 248 321

RETFORD HOSPITAL 2D **22**
North Road
RETFORD
DN22 7XF
Tel: 01777 274 400

Perform
Poen

Edited by
Brian Moses

with additional material by
Terence Copley

SOUTHGATE

First published 1996 by Southgate Publishers Ltd

Southgate Publishers Ltd
15 Barnfield Avenue, Exmouth,
Devon EX8 2QE

Illustrator: Jed Pascoe, Sandy, Bedfordshire.

Printed and bound in Great Britain by Short Run Press, Exeter, Devon.

British Library Cataloguing in Publication Data
A CIP catalogue record for this book is available from the British Library.

ISBN 1–85741–087–4

Acknowledgements, see page 79

Contents

Introduction

BRIAN MOSES

The oral performance of poetry, where language is used to communicate meaning, is a very valuable one, and this book aims to provide teachers with a number of poems on a variety of themes, along with advice as to how the poems might be presented. The poems are a mixed-bag of styles and language from the richness of traditional verse to the immediacy of modern writing. Each poem is accompanied by notes on the themes in the poem and suggestions as to how it might be used and presented both in English class work and collective worship.

Throughout the school year there are many occasions where poems can be presented – an alfresco performance to peers in the classroom, a reading to younger children, a school assembly, a taped performance for broadcasting on the school radio network, a function for parents, or as part of a larger endeavour involving music and drama. Whatever the occasion, it should be remembered that poetry is written to be heard, and the way in which a poem is presented is of the greatest importance. It will take time and effort to prepare a poem for reading aloud – tone of voice, clarity of diction, emphasis, speed of reading – if these are right, then the audience's enjoyment of a poem will be increased.

Children will have their own ideas about how the poems can best be presented and these should obviously be discussed and incorporated, if considered feasible. Performances may well involve acting, lighting and sound effects and it may be useful here for children to learn their parts of the poem by heart. Alternatively there may be two separate groups, one performing the poem and another acting it out.

Initially, any poem chosen for performance will need to be read and discussed. Any parts of the poem which are unclear will need talking over and children will need to know that they can feel reasonably happy with the poem before they think about performing it. There are a number of questions that need to be asked at this stage: a) Where should the poem be divided up for different voices or for choral speaking? b) How should the different parts be read? c) Which parts need to be spoken more loudly or more quietly than others? d) Are there appropriate actions or sound effects which would add something to the performance?

Once these considerations have been taken into account and the poem has been practised, it may well be useful to read the poem into a tape recorder so that the readers can listen to it and be critical of their own efforts. Listen particularly to see who is reading too quickly or too quietly at this stage. Finally, when children really feel confident, they can perform the poem to their intended audience. After the performance, of course, it would be extremely useful to seek out audience opinion as to what worked and what did not.

Performances of poetry at whatever level allow children to hear different kinds of rhythms and to understand that poetry does not and should not just sit on the page, rather it should be brought to life using a variety of techniques. This 'bringing to life' will also encourage other children to seek out their favourite poems for presentation and help to raise the profile of poetry within school.

Terence Copley contributed the 'Thoughtful Moments' and 'Related Religious Material'.

The Most Important Rap

Roger Stevens

I am an astronaut
I circle the stars
I walk on the Moon
I travel to Mars
I'm brave and tall
There is nothing I fear
And I am the most important person here.

I am a teacher
I taught you it all
I taught you why your
spaceship doesn't fall
If you couldn't read or write
Where would you be?
The most important person here is me.

Who are you kidding?
Are you taking the mick?
Who makes you better
when you're feeling sick?
I am a doctor
and I'm always on call
and I am more important than you all.

But I'm your mother
Don't forget me
If it wasn't for your mother
where would you be?
I washed your nappies
and changed your vest
I'm the most important
and Mummy knows best.

I am a child
and the future I see

and there'd be no future
if it wasn't for me
I hold the safety
of the planet in my hand
I'm the most important
and you'd better understand.

Now just hold on
I've a message for you all
Together we stand
and divided we fall
So let's make a circle
and all remember this
Who's the most important?

EVERYBODY IS

DEVELOPING THEMES

Working together: Co-operating with others to make something succeed.

Interdependence: A community is made up of people with different skills and talents who perform essential services. Day to day life can only run smoothly if everyone is playing their part.

Attitudes: Despite everything, there are always people who think that they are better than others, or that they are always right.

PRESENTING THE POEM

This poem helps to reinforce the notion of equality, with everyone having an important part to play in life.

It is probably best to have individual readers for each section of the poem, with everyone joining in on 'Everybody is'. Readers could either dress up or hold something appropriate to indicate their rôle in life – the astronaut could hold a model rocket, the teacher a book, and so on.

Children could stand in a line for the performance of the poem and step forward when it is their turn to read. The last person to read is the narrator. Further verses about different jobs could be written by the children and included in the performance.

Experiment with performing the poem to an accompaniment of handclaps. Try two claps for each line in each verse apart from the last one which may need four claps. Try using a drum to keep the beat. Movement could also be added if required, with children miming appropriate actions and activities for each verse.

ENGLISH LINKS

Working together: List occasions when working together is fun, such as team games, sport, quiz teams and so on. List other occasions when teamwork is vital, such as building a house, running a school or hospital, playing in an orchestra. Suggest that groups of children take one of the items on this list and try to list all of the types of jobs involved. All sorts of people are involved in building a house – architects, surveyors, site managers, plumbers, electricians, and so on. Consider also great feats of courage and endeavour throughout history that were successful through teamwork – the defeat of the Armada, the building of Stonehenge, the D-Day Invasion of Europe.

Pig-headed/big-headed: We often describe people who refuse to see another point of view as 'pig-headed' and those who are always right and like to boast about the fact as 'big-headed'. Suggest that children draw cartoon characters to show both types of people and then think of situations where these characteristics might be encountered. This could lead to the development of storyboards by the children and to interpretation through drama.

Uniqueness: Although working together is important, we all like to feel that we are different at some time. Ask children to think of ways in which they like to express their individuality. Our fingerprints, too, mark us out as individuals and children might like to take their own fingerprints using ink pads and then compare them.

RELATED RESOURCES

The Best of Aesop's Fables retold by Margaret Clark (Walker Books, 1990). Search out tales of creatures who help each other for mutual benefit.

Music – 'Colonel Bogey March' from *Bridge Over the River Kwai* (the bridge built by the teamwork of British POWs). Theme from *The Dambusters.*

THOUGHTFUL MOMENT

Dear God,
Teach us just how big and small we really are.
Then help us to live together as we really ought.
Amen.

RELATED RELIGIOUS MATERIAL

This is part of an ancient Jewish poem:

When I look at the heavens, the work of your fingers,
The moon and the stars that you have established,
What are human beings that you are mindful of them,
What are people that you care for them?
Yet you have made them a little lower than the angels,
and crowned them with glory and honour ...
O Lord our King.
How majestic is your name in all the earth.
(from *Psalm 8*)

Morning Has Decorated the Park

ROBIN MELLOR

Overnight frost has sprinkled the branches,
like sugar icing on a cake;
small squirrels pass
through tinsel grass,
and the sun puts sequins on the lake.

The web of the wild hedgerow spider
is gleaming with neon lights,
and jewels abound
all over the ground,
like the pattern on a new pair of tights.

Over the long lines of beeches
the leaves have been spilt from a can,
just as red finger tips
colour the lips,
on the face of aboriginal man.

At the lake-side the mallards are standing;
in the dark water, patterns play,
the ripples whirl
like the necklace of pearls
a bride wears on her wedding day.

The playground is lying deserted,
and empty the putting green holes,
but the grass was adorned
some time before dawn,
by the efforts of scurrilous moles.

The path-side meadow is glistening
with a hundred thousand sparks
of shimmering stalks
where the sparrow walks,
in a trail of wriggling marks.

When the people come here later
they'll frighten the blackbird and lark
and, unlike me,
they won't even see
Where morning has decorated the park.

DEVELOPING THEMES

A love of nature: Are we always aware? Do we miss lots of things through not seeing them? The poem is written from Robin Mellor's own experience. As a child he enjoyed exploring a nearby park when nobody else was about. Have the children ever done anything similar? Perhaps on holiday, setting off early on a long drive.
The enjoyment of being alone: We often deliberately seek out quiet places where we can be alone, perhaps to think about a problem that needs solving or just to escape from 'the crowds'.
Patterns and decorations: Investigate the poem to discover examples, such as ripples on the lake, frost on the ground like jewels. Look at the pattern of the poem itself. What do children notice about each verse?

PRESENTING THE POEM

Children can decide on which parts of the poem they think might be interpreted musically; for example:

Overnight *frost has sprinkled the branches*
like sugar icing on a cake;
small squirrels pass
through tinsel grass
and *the sun puts sequins on the lake.*

Groups of children can then look at different verses and decide which musical sounds might represent the parts they have picked out.

'... *frost has sprinkled the branches*' might be the high notes of a xylophone.
'*small squirrels pass/through tinsel grass*' might be a drum being brushed.
'... *the sun puts sequins on the lake*' might be bells or a sequence of notes that increase in pitch as sunlight takes over from shade.

The poem could be read by one child or by a group of children who should practise speaking it clearly and in an unhurried manner so that in the final performance those who are working with instruments have time to make their contributions.

ENGLISH LINKS

Different days: Think about early morning at different times of the year – a snowy day, misty conditions at the start of a very warm summer's day. Children could write about what might be observed, as a poem:

On a snowy morning I found
a line of tracks like stitches
on a sheet of white,
I found ...

Being alone: When and why do children like to be alone? Have they got favourite places where they choose to go and be alone? Compare the differences between being alone and being lonely.

Patterns in poems: Discover more poems with patterns to them. Children could copy out and illustrate a favourite poem and then be prepared to talk about its pattern and the reason why they like the poem. Listen to music that has a 'pattern' to it, e.g. Ravel's 'Bolero'.

RELATED RESOURCES

'Quite Early One Morning' by Dylan Thomas: 'The town was not yet awake and I walked through the streets like a stranger come out of the sea ...'

'Snowy Morning' by Lilian Moore, from *Another Second Poetry Book*, edited by John Foster (OUP).

'Empty House' by Gareth Owen, from *Salford Road and Other Poems* (Young Lions). (Can lead to much discussion about being alone.)

Poems with different patterns and shapes may be found in *Madtail, Miniwhale and Other Shape Poems*, edited by Wes Magee (Viking/Puffin) and *My First Has Gone Bonkers: Poems to Puzzle Over*, edited by Brian Moses (Blackie/Puffin).

Music – *Peer Gynt Suite No.1. Op.46*, 'Morning' by Edvard Grieg. (This piece of music could provide a suitable assembly introduction.)

THOUGHTFUL MOMENT

Dear God,
Thank you for untrodden snow and sparkling frost and summer's warm, wet sand.
Help us tread carefully, not trample through beautiful places.
Help us to see beauty in places we might take for granted, like playground, path and garden.
Amen.

RELATED RELIGIOUS MATERIAL

And it is He (Allah, God) who spread out the earth,
And set on it the mountains standing firm,
And flowing rivers, and fruit of every kind ...
In these things there are signs for those who consider.
(*Quran, Sura 13.3*)

Make Friends With a Tree

Brian Moses

Give a tree a squeeze,
give a tree a hug,
join in celebration
with every bird and bug,

with every bat and badger,
with beetles and with bees
a new year's resolution,
show kindness to the trees.

Make friends with a tree,
make friends with a tree,
hug a tree, go on show it
you really care, let a tree know it.
Make friends with a tree,
make friends with a tree.

Trees are always homes
to every sort of creature.
In a flat and empty landscape
a tree is a special feature.

Trees can be deciduous,
pine trees are coniferous,
but trees will never hurt you
no tree is carnivorous!

So treat a tree politely,
show it you're sincere.
Long after we have disappeared,
trees will still be here.

Make friends with a tree,
make friends with a tree,

hug a tree, go on show it
you really care, let a tree know it.
Make friends with a tree,
make friends with a tree.

Snuggle up to a sycamore,
cuddle up to a pine,
wrap your arms around an oak,
enjoy a joke with a lime.

A tree will always listen,
tell your troubles to a tree.
To the mystery of life
an ash may hold the key.

So don't be abrupt with a birch,
don't try to needle a pine.
Don't interrupt a horse chestnut,
don't give a tree a hard time.

Make friends with a tree,
make friends with a tree,
hug a tree, go on show it
you really care, let a tree know it.
Make friends with a tree,
make friends with a tree.

A tree is a living thing,
it's not just a lump of wood.
Trees in Sherwood Forest
know all about Robin Hood.

A tree can tell us stories,
a tree knows history,
so in this world of fake and sham
let's celebrate truth in a tree.

Make friends with a tree,
make friends with a tree,
hug a tree, go on show it
you really care, let a tree know it.
Make friends with a tree,
make friends with a tree.

DEVELOPING THEMES

Friendship: Can we be friends with inanimate objects or with other living things? Consider examples – pets, plants, comfort objects – the young child's cuddly toy, imaginary friends and so on. How valuable is such a friendship?

Interdependence: Consider how a tree becomes a good friend to all the creatures living on or in the tree.

Time and human mortality: Trees have very long lives in comparison with humans. There are ancient oaks in Sherwood forest that would have been growing at the time of Robin Hood. Is there a really old tree close by the school?

PRESENTING THE POEM

'Make Friends With a Tree' is a poem that mixes humour with a serious message – trees really do need all the friends they can get. It should be read with feeling and with great gusto, particularly on the chorus. The verses can be taken by different children either individually or in pairs but the chorus should involve everyone. I describe it as my 'environmental, evangelical poem' and the chorus really does need to be belted out in the sort of way that you might hear a congregation responding at a revivalist church meeting.

Some children might like to try keeping a beat to this poem either by hand clapping or by tapping a tambourine against the thigh.

ENGLISH LINKS

'The tree which moves some to tears of joy is, in the eyes of others, only a green thing which stands in the way.' (William Blake)

Hugging trees: *The People Who Hugged the Trees*, adapted by Deborah Lee Rose (Roberts Rheinhart, 1990), is a retelling of a classic Indian folktale. It tells of the first Chipko ('Hug-the-Tree') people who understood how vital trees were in their desert environment. The trees offered shade from the sun, indicated the presence of water, and helped to stop sand shifting during sandstorms. When a Maharajah decided to have the trees cut down so that he could build a fortress, the people hugged the trees and prevented the axe-men from cutting them down.

This is a wonderful story for children to retell themselves or to act out as part of an assembly which focuses on the importance of trees. It shows how individual actions can make a difference and has a relevance for today's world and its environmental concerns. Look out for 'Hug-a-Tree' events in this country. They are often featured as part of National Tree Week.

Shape poems: Write a poem about a tree in the shape of a tree. One viewpoint could be for children to imagine themselves as trees and to think of all the different things they would see/hear/feel/smell/do as a tree and of all the creatures who live in the tree and around its roots and rely on it for their own existence.

Friends: What makes a good friend? List the qualities required. Write an advertisement for a friend. Trees really do need all the friends they can get these days. Why?

RELATED RESOURCES

The Forgotten Forest by Laurence Anholt (Frances Lincoln, 1992). A picture book that tells about a city where all trees have disappeared apart from one small forest. When builders arrive to chop down the trees, all that they can hear is the sound of children crying for their trees. (Another good story for acting out.)

Where the Forest Meets the Sea by Jeannie Baker (Walker Books, 1988). A picture book which shows a young boy and his father exploring a prehistoric rainforest. They wonder how much longer the forest will survive. The illustrations are relief collages made from a variety of materials including preserved natural materials.

Poetry – A selection of poetry about trees may be found in *Earthways, Earthwise – Poems on Conservation*, selected by Judith Nicholls (OUP, 1993), and *The Last Rabbit*, a collection of Green Poems selected by Jennifer Curry (Methuen/Mammoth 1990).

'Chipko Andolan', a poem about hugging trees by Cath Staincliffe; 'For Forest' by Grace Nichols; 'Tree-kill' by Spike Milligan; and 'Requiem for a Rainforest' by Cecil Rajendra can all be found in *Can You Hear?,* poems for Oxfam, edited by John Foster (Macmillan, 1992).

Music – *Dumbarton Oaks* by Stravinsky, *Finlandia* by Sibelius. Folk song – *The Oak and the Ash and the Bonny Ivy Tree.*

THOUGHTFUL MOMENT

Dear God,
Help us always to remember the real value of trees,
To treat them as friends,
To help them to grow.
Amen.

RELATED RELIGIOUS MATERIAL

Although you may take food from them, you must not cut trees down. Are trees in the country enemies that they should come under siege from you?
(*Deuteronomy 20.19*)

Voices of Water

TONY MITTON

The water in the rain says	TICK TICK TACK
The water in the sleet says	SLUSH
The water in the ice says	CRICK CRICK CRACK
The water in the snow says	HUSH
The water in the sink says	SLOSH SLOSH
The water in the tap says	DRIP
The water in the bath says	WASH WASH
The water in the cup says	SIP
The water in the pool says	SPLISH SPLASH
The water in the stream says	TRILL
The water in the sea says	CRISH CRASH
The water in the pond (pause)	stays still
The water in the soil says	sow, sow
The water in the cloud says	give
The water in the plant says	grow, grow
The water in the world says	live.

DEVELOPING THEMES

The value of water: Where does water come from and why is it so valuable? Consider the effects of drought and flood. How does a lack of water affect the lives of people living in that country? How can these countries be helped? Consider the symbolic value of water.
The uses of water: Water is used for everything, from teeth cleaning to car washing, water pistols to hydro-electric power. Consider the versatility of water.

PRESENTING THE POEM

At its simplest, 'Voices of Water' is a 'call and response' poem, with the leading 'caller' reading the first section of each line and the rest of the group or class chanting the onomatopoeic response words. Alternatively the assembly audience could chant the response words in chorus, providing these were written out on calling cards and held up at appropriate moments.
The poem can also be divided up into parts and children encouraged to develop mimes or dances which in turn may be accompanied by musical instruments such as shakers or rain sticks, or sound effects which can help to convey the idea of moving water.
Perhaps the poem could also be attempted as a spoken round, with one group beginning and a second starting off when the first group reach their third line. Will it work if other groups are added every third line?

ENGLISH LINKS

Using the poem as a model for children's own writing: Children may enjoy writing their own versions of the poem, featuring such subjects as rain, snow, wind or fire.

The fire in the grate says	CRACKLE, CRACKLE
The fire in the oven says	ROAST
The fire in the forest says	BURN BURN
The fire in the grill says	TOAST.

Water festivals: In the distant past, people often believed that streams and rivers were the homes of water spirits who needed to be pleased if their supply of water was to continue. An old rhyme about the River Dart shows how people believed that rivers needed sacrifices.

Dart, Dart, cruel dart,
Every year thou claim'st a heart.

Encourage children to write as if they are a river god or goddess. What revenge will be taken if people fail to satisfy the river's demands?

RELATED RESOURCES

Rain for Christmas by Richard Tulloch (Cambridge University Press,

1989). Picture book about Christmas in the drought-stricken outback of Australia. Excellent story for Years 3 and 4.

Shaker Lane by Alice and Martin Provensen (Julia MacRae, 1988). This picture book for older readers charts the growth of a small community in the USA and the subsequent destruction of that community with the excavation of a reservoir. Thoughtful material on the good and bad sides to such development.

Water by Gabrielle Woolfitt (Wayland: The Elements Series, 1992). Explores the many facets of water – in the home, in religion, the water cycle, water myths, sports, dirty water, etc. Sound reference book for lower juniors.

Poetry – *You'll Love This Stuff*, Poems from Many Cultures, selected by Morag Styles (C.U.P. 1986). This contains a section, 'Water, Water Everywhere', which includes poems about rain, storms, the monsoon, etc.

Words on Water, an anthology of poems entered for the Young Observer National Children's Poetry Competition (Viking Kestrel, 1987). Poems to inspire and promote writing in the classroom. Well worth searching out.

Music – *The Water Music* by Handel, *Singing in the Rain* – Gene Kelly. *Mammumia* by Paul McCartney & Wings (*Band on the Run* CD).

THOUGHTFUL MOMENT

The water in the world says, 'Live!'
Thank you, Lord, for life-giving water.
Amen.

RELATED RELIGIOUS MATERIAL

He (God) leads me beside still waters,
He restores my soul.
(from *Psalm 23*)

Listen to Machines!

IAN SOUTER

Munch, crunch, clickety, clackety,
whirr, gurr, bong, bang.
Grrr, whishity, zip-zap,
listen to machines, listen to them rap!

(All together)
Machines, machines, machines, machines,
everywhere, everywhere, even in dreams.

Clanging, banging, whirring and gurring,
crashing, thrashing, cracking and whacking.
On roadways and railways,
on seaways and airways.

(All together)
All we can hear are machines, machines,
the world is metal and plastic it seems.

Munch, crunch, clickety, clackety,
whirr, gurr, bong, bang.
Grrr, whishity, zip-zap,
listen to machines, listen to them rap!

(All together)
Machine, machine, machine, machine,
everyone uses one, even the Queen.

Washing, cooking, cleaning and preening,
digging, jigging, repairing and blaring.
Pumping, thumping, sprawling, stalling,
thunderous, blunderous, furious, curious.

(All together)
Stereo, washing machine, car, bus,
soon there'll be no need for any of US!

(All together)
Munch, crunch, clickety, clackety,
whirr, gurr, bong, bang.
Grrr, whishity, zip-zap,
listen to machines, listen to them RAP!

DEVELOPING THEMES

Could we live without machines? Machines are so much a part of our lives it is difficult to imagine us ever living without them. Would we ever want to? Should we want to? Is there anything we can do that machines can't?
Good versus evil: Think in terms of a balance sheet that might show, on one side, all the good that has resulted from the development of machinery and, on the other, how machines have been harnessed for evil ends, such as machines of war.
Scientists and inventors: How much of a debt do we owe to those people whose vision and skill have provided us with all kinds of machines? Using reference books, children could find out about the lives of inventors and scientists.

PRESENTING THE POEM

Once they are familiar with the poem, then children may like to think how it might be interpreted through drama. In groups of seven or eight, children can devise a sequence of movements for an imaginary machine and then present these to the other groups for comment and criticism. Alternatively there might be one huge class machine with the poem being split into four machine parts and then everyone joining in.
The poem should be read in a spirited manner with machinery parts keeping pace with the words. It should build up to a crescendo at the conclusion of the poem.
If children are not involved in the dramatic presentation of the piece, it may well be effective to accompany the words and actions with instruments such as tambourines. Try four beats to each line initially, although shorter lines such as 'on roadways and railways' might only need two beats.
Experiment with other instruments – a drum of some kind could provide a strong beat to underpin the words. Finding a comfortable beat will really be a matter of experimentation.

ENGLISH LINKS

Write another machine poem: Use real words and/or invented words to express one of the following:

a) a factory making cars,
b) a house being built,
c) a busy day in a space station,
d) a washing machine going wrong.

Encourage children to use their voices to make the sounds of the machines and then to try and write down these sounds in some sort of pattern. Once they have their poems, they can practise speaking them aloud and if possible add instruments.
Invent: Suggest that children describe a machine of their own which will perform some tiresome task that they dislike being asked to do. It could be a bed-making machine, or a room-tidying machine, or a

dog-walking machine. If they go on to draw a design, it should be clearly labelled so that the reader can see just what materials will be needed to build the machine. Children might like to make models of their machines.

RELATED RESOURCES

The Incredible Adventures of Professor Branestawm by Norman Hunter (Puffin). The Professor's instant solution to any problem is to invent another of his incredible machines.

Charlie and the Chocolate Factory by Roald Dahl (Puffin). Lots of good descriptions of machines, particularly in Chapter 19, 'The Inventing Room', and in Chapter 20, 'The Great Gum Machine'.

Poetry – *Machine Poems*, collected by Jill Bennett, illustrated by Nick Sharratt (OUP, 1991). Good for years 3 and 4. 'The Secret of the Machines' by Rudyard Kipling (*Selected Verse*, Penguin).

THOUGHTFUL MOMENT

Dear God,
Thank you for machines that save us time and effort.
Teach us to enjoy the time they make for us with thanks.
Amen.

RELATED RELIGIOUS MATERIAL

(For discussion)

Try to live simply. A simple lifestyle ... is a source of strength. Do not be persuaded into buying what you do not need or cannot afford.
(*Quaker Advices, 1995*)

Sounds Familiar ...

Trevor Harvey

What I am about to tell you
Happened long ago,
When I was younger
Than I am now
And older than
Any of you.
There was a blackout
One evening
And we had only
The stars to guide us,
When suddenly –

The cat miaowed
The dog howled
Footsteps grew louder
The door creaked
My heart thumped
The doorbell rang
The wind whistled
The windows rattled
The traffic roared
And the football crowd chanted

– **BUT** *all at the same time*!

It was **SO** noisy, Mum said,
'Right! That does it!
We're moving to the country.
I've had enough of living in the town.'

So – a few months later,

We loaded all our goods
Into the removal van.

And the cat miaowed
The dog still howled
The saucepans clattered
The china smashed
The furniture bumped
And the engine roared

– **YES**, *all at the same time*!

It was **SO** noisy, Mum said,
'It'll be worth it!
When we reach the country
We'll have peace and quiet.'

So – a few weeks later,
We had settled in
At our country cottage
Miles from the town.

And the fieldmice squeaked
The cat miaowed
The doorbell rang
The dog still howled
The floorboards creaked
The windows rattled
The sheep went baa
The cows went moo
The tractors chugged
The wind still whistled
And the rain **POURED** down.

It was **SO** noisy, Mum said,
'Country sounds! They're
DIFFERENT somehow ...
This is the life!
Even if we do hear them
ALL AT THE SAME TIME!'

I wish we'd move back to the town –
These country noises are *getting me down*!

DEVELOPING THEMES

Appreciation of noises/sounds: When do we like noise? Such as turning the television on for company when you're alone in the house, hearing birdsong, music, trains in the distance.

Appreciation of our sense of hearing: Without a sense of hearing we could not appreciate pleasant sounds. Examples of famous people who overcame this handicap, such as Beethoven, who couldn't hear the music that he was creating.

Noise pollution: When does noise become intrusive? Think of examples – traffic noise, noisy neighbours, blaring radios, road drills.

PRESENTING THE POEM

This poem might be best performed with a main speaker, a second voice for the words that Mum actually says, and everyone else ready with appropriate sound effects. These could be devised by the children. In groups they might like to experiment with different sounds. Children can then vote on the one that works best with each line. Suggestions for the first set of sounds might be as follows:

The cat miaowed	(loud miaow)
The dog howled	(loud howl)
Footsteps grew louder	(tapping on tambour)
The door creaked	(stick on scraper)
My heart thumped	(beats on a drum)
The doorbell rang	(chime bars)
The wind whistled	(blow between teeth, or instrument)
The windows rattled	(shake tambourine)
The traffic roared	('rrrmmmm' sound)
And the football crowd chanted	('We are the champions!')
– BUT all at the same time!	(All make their sounds together)

ENGLISH LINKS

A noisy story: Take a subject such as a storm, a fairground ride or a journey through a noisy city, and write a noisy story that makes use of all kinds of sound effects to help tell the story. For example:

I was lying in bed on a *windy night*, my bedroom door was *creaking* and downstairs a window was *rattling*. I heard the dog begin to bark and our next door neighbour's *car backed into the driveway. The wind was increasing in strength*, it was *swooshing* against my bedroom window and *rolling empty flower pots around the garden.* Suddenly there was a *tremendous gust of wind* followed by the *sound of breaking glass ...*

(Sound effects can be added to the parts of the story that are shown in italics.)

Pleasant and unpleasant sounds: Suggest that children compile individual lists of pleasant and unpleasant sounds. If possible, read John Clare's poem 'Pleasant Sounds' (see below) as this spotlights the small details that make up the sounds that the poet enjoys.

Once the lists have been compiled it would be interesting to compare lists. Are there sounds that appear on both lists? i.e. some children might enjoy the noise of aeroplanes while others might dislike their racket.

Noise pollution: Children might like to produce posters that encourage others to think carefully about the levels of noise that will be tolerated.

RELATED RESOURCES

Poetry – 'Pleasant Sounds' by John Clare may be found in *I Like That Poem,* edited by Kaye Webb (Puffin), or in *This Poem Doesn't Rhyme*, edited by Gerard Benson (Puffin).

'The Sound Collector' by Roger McGough, from *Pillow Talk* (Puffin). A stranger calls one morning, puts every sound into a bag and carries them away. Good for discussion – what would life be like without noise?

Music – Tchaikovsky *1812 Overture* (the final section). Haydn *Clock Symphony*, *Surprise Symphony*.

THOUGHTFUL MOMENT

Dear God,

Thank you for the familiar noises we enjoy, like ... (*Collect a list before the prayer is read*).

Thank you, too, for silence and space to find ourselves.

Amen.

RELATED RELIGIOUS MATERIAL

Make a joyful noise to God, all the earth!

(*Psalm 66*)

The Green Unicorn

MIKE JUBB

He came with the storm.

On Monday,
he evaporated all weapons
as though they had never been invented.

On Tuesday,
he turned all the cars and lorries
into bicycles and milk floats.

On Wednesday,
he destroyed all polluting factories
and he refreshed the air.

On Thursday,
he cleansed the lakes and the seas
and he breathed life into dead rivers.

On Friday,
he freed all zoo animals
and returned them to renewed homelands.

On Saturday,
he took a little from those that had much
and gave much to those that had little.

On Sunday,
he tried to share his love with every heart;
but he was weary
and couldn't be sure that he had reached them all.

He left with the wind,
and he whispered to the world,
'Now have another try.'

DEVELOPING THEMES

Creation and re-creation: God took seven days to create the world and in this poem the world is re-created in the same amount of time. How do children feel about the idea of re-creating the world? Have they any ideas of their own as to how they would tackle the problem?
Too simple an idea? Does the idea of a green unicorn represent too simple a solution to the world's problems?
Environmental damage: Consider the major environmental issues that beset our planet. Try to agree an order of priority.

PRESENTING THE POEM

If the poem is to be performed, consider using it as part of a news broadcast:

'Now for our review of this week's environmental news. And what a truly remarkable seven days these have been ...'

'The last seven days have completely turned the world around, so let's look back on the progress of the green unicorn's sweeping reforms to the lifestyle of our planet.'

(*Read the poem*)
He came with the storm ...

Perhaps using a different voice for each day of the week might be the best way to approach a reading of the poem. Between each verse there might also be a musical sound effect – scraping a beater along a xylophone, ringing a bell, playing a sequence of notes on a keyboard or a recorder. Children can write their own summing up (or looking ahead) features for the news broadcast. They may also wish to use their own words to introduce the programme.

ENGLISH LINKS

Write a 'Days of the Week' poem: How would children help the world if they suddenly found themselves with unlimited supplies of money. Suggest that they think of a fantastic idea as to where the money came from and then work from the premise that there is nothing that money can't buy.

On Saturday I discovered that money does grow on trees.
I picked and picked and picked till every bucket and saucepan was overflowing.
On Sunday I thought what I could do with it all.
On Monday I bought a cure for cancer.
On Tuesday I purchased homes for the city's homeless.
On Wednesday ...

Other days-of-the-week poems might concentrate on the measures that could be taken to clean up the local environment.
Prepare a campaign kit: Ask children to pick an environmental

issue and to research it in reference books. When they feel that they have some background information, they should begin to prepare a campaign kit – a poster which makes others aware of the issue, a fact sheet, car stickers and badges which should feature a slogan that children have thought up. Campaign kits can then be displayed and discussed as to their effectiveness.

RELATED RESOURCES

Adam's Ark by Paul Stewart (Puffin). Adam's autism is confirmed at an early age and he remains locked in his silent world until he is given a cat as a companion. He discovers that he can 'Think-talk' with the cat and subsequently with other mammals, all with sad tales to tell of how their species has suffered at the hands of mankind.

Save the Humans by Tony Husband and David Wood (Antelope Books, Hamish Hamilton). Animals are in charge of the world and some keep humans as pets. An interesting and entertaining turn-around.

Poetry – *Earthways, Earthwise*, Poems on Conservation, edited by Judith Nicholls (OUP, 1992); *The Last Rabbit*, a Collection of Green Poems, edited by Jennifer Curry (Mammoth); and *What on Earth ...?*, Poems with a Conservation Theme, edited by Judith Nicholls (Faber).

Music – 'Big Yellow Taxi' by Joni Mitchell; 'Whose Garden Was This?' by Tom Paxton.

THOUGHTFUL MOMENT

For the message of the unicorn
And the whispers of angels,
Thank you God.

RELATED RELIGIOUS MATERIAL

There are two accounts of Creation in the Hebrew Bible: *Genesis 1.1 to 2.4* and *Genesis 2.5 to 2.23*. Read them like poetry.

The Listeners

WALTER DE LA MARE

"Is there anybody there?" said the Traveller,
Knocking on the moonlit door;
And his horse in the silence champed the grasses
Of the forest's ferny floor:
And a bird flew up out of the turret,
Above the Traveller's head:
And he smote upon the door again a second time;
"Is there anybody there?" he said,
But no one descended to the Traveller;
No head from the leaf-fringed sill
Leaned over and looked into his grey eyes,
Where he stood perplexed and still.
But only a host of phantom listeners
That dwelt in the lone house then
Stood listening in the quiet of the moonlight
To that voice from the world of men:
Stood thronging the faint moonbeams on the dark stair,
That goes down to the empty hall,
Hearkening in an air stirred and shaken
By the lonely Traveller's call.
And he felt in his heart their strangeness,
Their stillness answering his cry,
While his horse moved, cropping the dark turf,
'Neath the starred and leafy sky;
For he suddenly smote on the door, even
Louder, and lifted his head:
"Tell them I came, and no one answered,
That I kept my word," he said.
Never the least stir made the listeners,
Though every word he spake
Fell echoing through the shadowiness of the still house
From the one man left awake:
Ay, they heard his foot upon the stirrup,
And the sound of iron on stone,
And how the silence surged softly backward,
When the plunging hoofs were gone.

DEVELOPING THEMES

A sense of mystery: Not everything is clear cut. Stories and poems are open to interpretation. Often, letting the imagination play with meaning is just as important, if not more important, than finding out what actually happened.

Strangers/Travellers: How do we feel when we are travelling in strange places? How do we feel about strangers visiting us for the first time? What differences do we notice between these feelings? Does our imagination sometimes make things stranger than they really are?

PRESENTING THE POEM

Any presentation of this poem should strive to underline its mystery by means of atmospheric music and/or sound effects. A strong voice is required for the words spoken by the traveller, while the general reader will need to tell the tale in a softer voice as if imparting a secret to the audience. Encourage children to experiment with background music – recorders, keyboards, xylophones – and to test out possible sound effects for lines such as, 'And a bird flew up out of the turret', and, 'Ay, and they heard his foot upon the stirrup'. The knocking on the door should be strong and clear, while the poem might finish with the sound of a horse's hoofbeats fading into the distance.

Sensitive lighting could help to heighten the atmosphere of the poem and art work could be displayed featuring black paper and silver foil to create the effects of an eerie forest by moonlight.

ENGLISH LINKS

Title: Prior to any reading of this poem, offer children the first two lines and ask them to predict what the poem will be about. Alternatively, photocopy and hand round copies of the poem with the title omitted. Children can read the poem and suggest possible titles. Who comes up with the best title? Whose title is closest to the poet's choice?

Thinking about the mystery: Why was the traveller 'knocking on the moonlit door'? What was his errand? Where had he come from? Who sent him on his fruitless mission? Suggest that children give a reasoned reply as to what has led up to the actions that we read about in the poem. Alternatively, children may like to write the traveller's report on the incident as he explains what came about to those who sent him on his errand.

Picture in your mind: A good poem conjures up all kinds of pictures in our minds. Talk about the pictures that this poem presents. Children may like to draw a response to the poem, looking for clues in the text – moonlight, a traveller, forest, door, turret and so on. Some may wish to pay particular attention to one line of the poem and to sketch this.

A class anthology of mystery poems: Collect and copy out other mystery poems. Talk about what makes them effective. The following may be worth tracking down: 'The Sands of Dee', Charles Kingsley; 'What Has Happened to Lulu', Charles Causley; 'The Tide Rises, the

Tide Falls', Henry W. Longfellow; 'Mary Celeste', Judith Nicholls; 'The Frozen Man', Kit Wright.

RELATED RESOURCES

Poetry – The following books may well be a useful source of mystery poems: *I Like That Poem*, edited by Kaye Webb (Puffin); *Every Poem Tells a Story*, a Collection of Stories in Verse, chosen by Raymond Wilson (Puffin); *The Young Dragon Book of Verse* and *The Oxford Book of Story Poems*, both edited by Michael Harrison and Christopher Stuart-Clark (OUP).

THOUGHTFUL MOMENT

God is not often proved, but felt.
God is not often seen, but heard. (*Pause*)
'The silence surged softly backward,
When the plunging hooves were gone'. (*Pause again*)

RELATED RELIGIOUS MATERIAL

God moves in a mysterious way
His wonders to perform;
He plants his footsteps in the sea
And rides upon the storm.

Deep in unfathomable mines
Of never-failing skill
He treasures up his bright designs
And works his sovereign will.
(*William Cowper, 1731–1800*)

Camping Out

JUDITH NICHOLLS

Can we sleep out in the tent, Dad?
Go on, just him and me!
It's a full moon,
not a cloud in sight!
We'll be quiet as
mice when the cat's about –
oh, *please* let us stay the night?

You can pitch your tent down the garden
by the lilac, or just behind;
but mind you're in by midnight
if you're going to change your mind.
The key will be out till twelve,
but not a second more.
I don't want prowlers after that –
at twelve I lock the door!

Great, Dad!
We'll be out till morning –
you've never let us before!
We'll fetch all we need
before it's dark
then you can lock your door.

The key will be out till twelve,
I said, but not a second more!

Now, what do we need?
Water, jug,
toothpaste, mug,
towel, rug,
toothbrush ...

Since when were you so keen
on keeping clean?

You can't camp out down the Amazon
without the proper gear.
We could be here a *year*,
exploring dark Brazil
until – who knows?

All right, a torch then,
I suppose. Sleeping bags.
Pillows?

There's no room.
Mosquito nets come first,
and books to read
by torch or moon.
Pencils, notebooks.
Sweaters – two at least.
And don't forget the midnight feast!

What do explorers eat?
Will crisps and apples do,
with peanut-butter sandwiches,
bananas, orange juice,
and baked beans for the stew?

They'll do!

I wish we'd brought a pillow.
It's really dark.
I thought you said no cloud?
Should we close the flap –
to keep mosquitoes out, I mean?

Or Leopards!

... and to keep us warm.
There goes that flash again.
The air feels heavy.
P'rhaps a jungle storm?

Listen!
Can you hear – a breeze?
Something's rustling,
quickly, *freeze!*

Could it be
some deadly snake,
uncoiling for ...

For goodness sake,
it's only trees!

Oh, look!
What IS that shadow up above?
I'm sure I saw it move!

It's nothing,
just the lilac.
Or some bat or owl
out on the prowl
for supper too.

TOOWHIT, TOOWHOO!

No need to jump,
it's nearer me than you!

I didn't jump!
What time is it,
only five to midnight?
Just wondered.
Thought it might be more.

I DON'T WANT PROWLERS AFTER THAT,
AT TWELVE I LOCK THE DOOR ...!

Aren't you cold?
I wish we'd brought more blankets,
the jungle's not so hot
when sun's gone down;
we didn't think of that.

Not cold, just hungry.
It's great out here,
but as for food –
we should have brought much more.
Explorers need their sustenance.
Another time, we'll plan it better ...

But meantime,

Race you to the door!/**Race you to the door!**

DEVELOPING THEMES

Conquering fear: We all have different things that we are afraid of – the dark, trips to the dentist, injections, heights, and so on. How can these fears be confronted and conquered? Should we admit to our fears and try to face up to them or should we hide them away and hope that they disappear?

Being brave: Think of occasions where we simply have to be brave and do things on the spur of the moment which, if we had time to think them through, we probably would not do.

The bravery of explorers: Exploration in space or under the sea; early explorers who sailed 'to the edge of the world'.

PRESENTING THE POEM

This is essentially a poem for three voices – Dad and two children. Different voices are indicated by changes in type style.

At the start of the poem the first child's voice should be pleading, then excited. Dad's voice is stern, authoritative. With the children, excitement turns to worry as the second child adds to the first child's fears. Towards the end of the piece there is panic in their voices.

Sound effects will help with the atmosphere of the piece – general night noises perhaps with more specific effects for 'Something's rustling ...', a snake hissing, the owl, and so on.

If the poem is to be staged, an actual tent might well be erected in the performance area and lighting gradually reduced as the poem is read. The two children can then act out the last half of the play from the tent doorway.

ENGLISH LINKS

Camping: Most children will have tried camping, either in the back garden or on holiday. Encourage the sharing of camping anecdotes.

Your own fears: Children in groups can discuss the things that they are afraid of. Make lists and bring them to a class discussion. Are there common fears? Do your fears change as you grow older? What are adults afraid of? What can be done to conquer fears? Suggest that children use their lists to compose poems about their fears. No need to worry about rhyme, simply use the same start to each line and this will help to promote a rhythm and give the poem a structure:

When foes hold out hard knuckles,
when Mum comes in with hair scissors,
when a stern look comes over my teachers,
these are my fears.

Or perhaps the fears are linked together to tell a story:

When my cat is out all night,
when her sleeping place is empty,
when her food is still there,
these are my fears.

Being brave: Ask children to write about the bravest thing that they have ever done. Set the scene first – when, where, how, why – then explore how they felt before the event and again after it had happened.

RELATED RESOURCES

The Midnight Fox by Betsy Byars (Puffin). A thought-provoking book but full of lighter moments, too. Tom's fear of all things outdoors is conquered during a summer on his uncle's farm where he discovers a black fox and then has to try to save her from his uncle's gun.

Nothing To Be Afraid Of by Jan Mark (Puffin). Short stories set in the 1950s. Title story is a gem and guaranteed to succeed when read aloud.

Can't You Sleep Little Bear? by Martin Waddell and Barbara Firth (Walker Books). For younger children. 'A book that evaporates and dispels all fear of the dark.' *(Sunday Times Review).*

Poetry – *Shadow Dance*, collected by Adrian Rumble. Poems that celebrate night and darkness. 'Posting Letters' by Gregory Harrison is in this book or in *A Calendar of Poems*, edited by Wes Magee (Bell & Hyman) – a poem about taking letters to the postbox in the unlit village.

Music – *A Night on the Bare Mountain*; *Fantasia*, by Moussorgsky.

THOUGHTFUL MOMENT

Dear God,
Help us enjoy adventure and exploring;
Remind us to remember caution and care;
Our world is exciting, but also has danger.
We need you there.
Amen.

RELATED RELIGIOUS MATERIAL

For everything there is a season ...
a time to seek, and a time to lose,
a time to keep, and a time to throw away,
a time to tear up, and a time to sow,
a time to keep silence, and a time to speak,
a time to leave home, and a time to return.
(freely adapted from *Ecclesiastes Chapter 3*)

The Hairy Toe

Traditional

Once there was a woman went out to pick beans,
and she found a Hairy Toe.
She took the Hairy Toe home with her,
and that night, when she went to bed,
the wind began to moan and groan.
Away off in the distance
she seemed to hear a voice crying.
'Where's my Hair-r-ry To-o-oe?
Who's got my Hair-r-ry To-o-oe?'

The woman scrooched down,
way under the covers,
and about that time
the wind appeared to hit the house,

smoosh,

and the old house creaked and cracked
like something was trying to get in.
The voice had come nearer,
almost at the door now,
and it said,
'Where's my Hair-r-ry To-o-oe?
Who's got my Hair-r-ry To-o-oe?'

The woman scrooched further down
under the covers
and pulled them tight around her head.

The wind growled around the house
like some big animal
and r-r-rumbled
over the chimbley.
All at once she heard the door cr-r-a-ck

and Something slipped in
and began to creep over the floor.

The floor went
cre-e-eak, cre-e-eak,
at every step that thing took towards her bed.
The woman could almost feel
it bending over her bed.
There in an awful voice it said:
'Where's my Hair-r-ry To-o-oe?
Who's got my Hair-r-ry To-o-oe?
You've got it!'

DEVELOPING THEMES

Taking something which isn't yours: For all of us there have been times when we have been tempted to take what isn't ours. Give examples of these occasions. Do we always react in the way that we should?

Fear of the unknown: Bedrooms at night can be very scary places for children. Ask children if anyone follows a routine before getting into bed at night – peeping round the door to check out the room, looking under the bed, behind the curtains, and so on. How do we combat such irrational fears?

PRESENTING THE POEM

This is a scary poem and children will need to bear this in mind once they start to consider how best to present the piece. It needs to be spoken in a low menacing manner. It should be taken slowly, with every line savoured as to the effect that it is having on the listeners. Better still if children can learn the poem by heart.

There are plenty of opportunities within the poem for spooky sound effects – 'the wind began to moan and groan', 'The wind growled around the house ...', 'The floor went/cre-e-eak, cre-e-eak'. It may well be appropriate to keep the sound of the wind as a background noise throughout the poem, allowing it to rise and fall in volume as the poem indicates. Children can experiment to see who can make the most realistic effects.

It would add to the atmosphere of the poem if 'Where's my Hair-r-ry To-o-oe' was distanced on the first two occasions. Perhaps it could come from offstage or outside a door. The final 'Where's my ...' should be spoken in a really awful voice and a good effect may be achieved if, at the moment that 'You've got it!' is spoken, the reader should slam a fist down on a table causing as many people as possible to 'jump out of their skins'.

ENGLISH LINKS

Word bank: Make a collection of words and phrases that are used to denote fear and being frightened, such as: shaking like a leaf, frightened to death, white as a sheet, in a cold sweat, horror-struck, scared out of your wits, quake in your shoes, feel your blood run cold, change colour, scare the living daylights out of, make your hair stand on end, make your knees knock. Suggest that children take one of these phrases and illustrate it in a cartoon style.

Alone in the house: How do children feel about being left alone in the house? Are there routines to follow which provide comfort or security – switching on the TV for company, looking under beds just to make sure, cuddling up to the cat? Some children might like to write their own poems about how they feel in such a situation:

Coming home from school,
I slot my key into the keyhole,
an empty feeling reaches out
and pulls me in ...

Spooky anthology: Search out other spooky poems for a class anthology. Look in particular for those poems that are good for reading aloud. Children in groups should then choose a poem to prepare and present to the rest of the class. Suggest that they really think about how to dramatise the piece to achieve maximum impact. (Some suggestions for poems that could prove useful are given below.)

RELATED RESOURCES

Room 13 by Robert Swindells (Doubleday). Children on a residential visit to Whitby discover its links with the Dracula legend. A wonderful story that can't fail as a read aloud. Funny and frightening.

The Puffin Book of Horror Stories. Good examples of the genre from skilled practitioners such as Robert Westall, Roald Dahl, Stephen King, plus an excerpt from Bram Stoker's 'Dracula'.

Poetry – *Never Say Boo to a Ghost*, edited by John Foster with illustrations by Korky Paul (OUP); particularly 'The Cupboard on the Landing' by John Coldwell.

Dracula's Auntie Ruthless, chosen by David Orme (Macmillan). Try 'Is There a Ghost in this Classroom?' by Dave Calder and 'My Gran's Box' by Janis Priestley.

Salford Road by Gareth Owen (Lions) contains 'Empty House' which may be useful for the above activity; and *Morning Break* by Wes Magee (Cambridge) features 'The House on the Hill'.

Music – 'Fossils' by Saint-Saens.

THOUGHTFUL MOMENT

Dear God,
We know
That toe
Was odd.
But when
Real fear
Is near
It's then
We want
You here.
Amen.

RELATED RELIGIOUS MATERIAL

(for discussion)

People are like camels; there is hardly one in a hundred that you would trust with your life.
(saying of Prophet Muhammad)

Are you honest and truthful in all you say and do?
(*Quaker Advices, 1995*)

Monster Crazy

BRIAN MOSES

Everyone here has gone Monster Crazy,
even those who are normally lazy,
binoculars raised, though the view may be hazy,
everyone here has gone Monster Crazy.

So come on Nessie, give us a wave,
don't stay hidden in your underwater cave.
You're the talk of the town, the darling of the Press,
it wouldn't be summer without you in Loch Ness.

Just come on up and prove that you're there,
sometime or other you must surface for air,
somebody's camera will photograph you,
proving, at last, if you're one hump or two!

Everyone here has gone Monster Crazy,
even those who are normally lazy,
binoculars raised, though the view may be hazy,
everyone here has gone Monster Crazy.

Just waggle your flipper or flip your tail,
make some fisherman's face turn pale
as you lift your head to look at the view,
there are hundreds waiting to interview you.

Just one word Nessie, go on, be a pet,
can't you stop playing hard to get?
You could be on TV, you'd have lots of money,
with American tourists calling you 'Honey!'

Everyone here has gone Monster Crazy,
even those who are normally lazy,
binoculars raised, though the view may be hazy,
everyone here has gone MONSTER CRAZY!

DEVELOPING THEMES

Mysteries/The unknown: Even now, with so much modern technology at our fingertips, it is impossible for us to know everything about our world. What are the areas that we still need to find out about?

Because it's there: Explorers sometimes give this as the answer to the question, why did you need to go there? Mountaineers give the same answer to the question, why did you need to climb it? Are we ever content to leave anything alone, or unexplored, or unclimbed? Will scientists ever stop searching for 'Nessie'?

Disappearing species: There are examples of species that were thought to be extinct, being discovered again. A fish called a Coelacanth was discovered off the coast of South Africa in 1938, some seventy million years after it was thought to have become extinct. There are other examples of survival stories to be found in *Noah's Choice* (see below).

PRESENTING THE POEM

This is a fun poem and needs to be presented in a lively manner. Children will have their own ideas as to how this can best be achieved and they should consider how the poem should be read, what actions are appropriate to accompany the reading and what instruments might be used to emphasise the rhythm.

Essentially a number of voices will be needed for the chorus with individual or paired voices on the verses. Other children can provide appropriate actions for different lines; for example in verse one – waving, hiding, holding newspapers and pointing out Loch Ness stories to others. Again, children will come up with ideas. Try splitting the class into groups of four or five and then allowing each group to consider the poem and then perform it to others. Consider which instruments might be used to emphasise the rhythm of the poem. Claves are excellent for keeping the beat but children could also try finger-clicking (four beats to a line).

In the final chorus, the last 'MONSTER CRAZY' should be shouted out.

ENGLISH LINKS

Report a sighting: Suggest that children prepare a newspaper report concerning a sighting of the Loch Ness Monster. Begin by examining road atlases to find names of places around the Loch. These will add authenticity to the reports. Decide where the sighting has taken place and at what time of day. Is there photographic evidence – a still photograph or an amateur video? Who else witnessed the sighting? Children will need to interview witnesses and add their views to the report. Try to find out something about previous sightings at the Loch; these could be added to the report so that the most recent sighting can be put into historical perspective.

Investigate other strange phenomena: Bigfoot, the Abominable Snowman, UFOs, the Bermuda Triangle. Prepare a factsheet detailing what is known about the phenomenon.

A monster publicity campaign: Design a poster advertising the delights of Scotland. The Loch Ness Monster should feature as part of the poster. Perhaps the creature will be giving a message to potential visitors. What would the message say? Badges, Car stickers and T-shirts could also be designed featuring a monster logo.

RELATED RESOURCES

The Water Horse by Dick King-Smith (Puffin). Great fun! An explanation for the origin of the Loch Ness Monster.
Nessie the Mannerless Monster by Ted Hughes (Faber). A story in verse. Nessie is tired of hearing that she doesn't exist and sets out on the road to London, hoping for an audience with the Queen.
Noah's Choice: True Stories of Extinction and Survival by David Day. (Viking/Puffin).
Poetry – 'The Loch Ness Monster's Song' by Edwin Morgan. This can be found in *My First Has Gone Bonkers*, edited by Brian Moses (Puffin), and in *This Poem Doesn't Rhyme*, edited by Gerard Benson (Puffin).

THOUGHTFUL MOMENT

Dear God,
Teach us always to be open-minded,
Ready to listen to new evidence;
Teach us to be critical, too, so as not just to believe anything.
Amen.

RELATED RELIGIOUS MATERIAL

Can we tell the difference between blind belief and faith? Here's one Christian writer's view of faith:

'Now faith is confidence about things unseen ... By faith we understand that the world was created by the word of God, so that what we can see was made from things that are invisible ... By faith Abraham set out for a place he did not know and had not seen. By faith Moses was hidden by his parents when he was born ... People suffered because they had faith. Some were tortured, flogged, imprisoned, exiled, killed. Jesus by faith even endured crucifixion for the joy that was set before him ...'
(adapted from *Hebrews 11 and 12*)

The Museum of Mythical Beasts

BRIAN MOSES

Go right in, past a beam of light
that shoots from a Cyclops' eye,
then put on armour and pick up a sword,
test how much of a hero you are:
Only the bravest and best may steal the gold
from a griffin's nest.

Then try to resist a mermaid's song.
How long will you stay before you're forced
to block your ears and turn away.

Now braver souls have tangled with trolls,
they'll carry you off to be their slave.
Careful, don't trip, just a pile of old bones,
previous visitors, I suppose!

A date with Medusa! What a surprise!
Keep your head and don't look in her eyes.
Move forward once more till you reach a door.
The Minotaur is next on our list,
a horrible task, you'd be well advised
to go prepared when you visit his lair.

That terrible smell is the Gorgon of death;
run past, run fast, don't waste any time
in escaping the blast of its breath.

Beware the Roc that will snatch you away
as a plaything for one of her young
or the goblins already hung over their pans
or the two-headed ogre who can't decide
which mouth he should slide you in!

And now you head for the final test,
a dragon, so deadly, so dreadful, so strong.

Don't weaken at all when you hear her ROAR
as you score more points with Saint George.

Then at the exit, don't forget
to collect your certificate,
dated and signed to say you survived
the museum of mythical beasts.

DEVELOPING THEMES

Good versus evil: Myths and legends often explore the clash between good and evil. They help people distinguish good from evil, e.g. St George and the Dragon, the Knights of the Round Table, Beowulf.

Enjoying being scared: There is a difference between the 'edge of the seat' fear that we all enjoy occasionally and the real fears that we need to heed. How far does watching a scary film affect our behaviour?

PRESENTING THE POEM

Any presentation of this poem would greatly benefit from atmospheric lighting. Children should imagine they are inside a theme museum and are actively involved in finding their way around it. There is plenty of scope for actions and sound effects, or even a background of creepy music, either pre-recorded on tape or composed by the children and performed while the poem is being read.

Each line in the poem should be read for maximum effect. Children should consider where to pause so that dramatic tension is heightened. Some lines could be spoken out in a venomous way to highlight the implied threats – 'they'll carry you off to be their slaves', 'Keep your head and don't look in her eyes.' Others need to be read with panic in the voice – 'Run past, run fast, don't waste any time/in escaping the blast of its breath.'

In the last verse emphasise the 'you' in line 3.

ENGLISH LINKS

Likes, dislikes and patterns: Read the poem aloud to the class and ask them to tell you the parts they liked best. Hand out copies of the poem and ask children to underline the following in different colours: a) lines they like, b) lines they dislike, c) lines that puzzle them. Ask them to note down also any patterns that they notice. This isn't a rhyming poem (there are no clear rhymes at the ends of lines) but it does include a number of internal rhymes (rhymes within the lines) to help strengthen the rhythm of the poem. Suggest that children pick out and circle any of these words that they can find.

Prepare a dossier of mythical creatures: Begin by finding out about the creatures mentioned in the poem. Ask children to prepare a factsheet about a creature of their choice and submit this along with an illustration as to how the creature might look. These can then be included in a class book of beasts. Discuss which would be the creature that you'd most/least like to meet!

Telling a story: Ask children in pairs to familiarise themselves with one of the stories about Cyclops, or Medusa, or the Minotaur, or something else of their own choice. Some children might like to put the story into a storyboard sequence as this will help them fix the sequence of events. Children can then begin to tell their stories to each other, taking it in turns and helping each other out if they are stuck. After plenty of practice when they are fairly confident, link each pair with another pair. Each pair then takes it in turns to tell their story. Later on, as the children become more skilful, they can share their stories with children from other classes.

Instructions for an interactive computer game: Suggest that children think of 'The Museum of Mythical Beasts' as a set of instructions for a computer game. Can they develop something similar for a game of their own devising? Possible themes might include a journey through space, a fantasy island, a battle game, a trip through the jungle. If they wish they can begin as I have with 'Go right in ...'.

RELATED RESOURCES

Tales, Myths and Legends, compiled by Pie Corbett (Scholastic). A huge compendium of tales to be told aloud.

Myths and Legends, retold by Anthony Horowitz (Kingfisher). Retellings of most of the familiar stories concerning heroes such as Perseus, Hercules and Odysseus, along with those about fabulous beasts such as the Minotaur, the Gorgon, Cyclops and Grendel.

Greek Myths and Legends as Never Told Before, by Diane Redmond (Viking). Excellent retellings of the main Greek stories.

Myths and Legends, Focus Pack, by Anne Faundez and Brian Moses, (Junior Education, February 1995).

Poetry – *Amazing Monsters*, edited by Robert Fisher (Faber). Poems about Centaurs and the Minotaur.

RELATED RELIGIOUS MATERIAL

(for discussion)

It is a person's own mind, not their enemy or foe, that lures them into evil ways.

(The Teaching of the Buddha)

THOUGHTFUL MOMENT

It's worth reading this once, discussing its meaning with children and then reading it again.

Imagine life without 'imagine' –
How dull it would be.
'Imagine' fills us with fun and fear
Brings saints and monsters near,
Shows us how the world should be –
Lord, keep my imagination free.

Rat Rap
(The Hamelin Special!)

Brian Moses

We're the rats,
we're the rats.

We *strut* through the kitchen and we *sniff* for cheese,
we *turn* around and we *chase* our fleas.

We're the rats,
we're the rats.

We *take* the food right *out* of their hands,
we *eat* gorgonzola, it's the *best* in the land.

We're the rats,
we're the rats.

We *wake* the old men *from* their naps,
we *guzzle* the wine right *out* of the vats.

We're the rats,
we're the rats.

We *jump* into the *frying* pan,
we *grab* the food as *quick* as we can.

We're the rats,
we're the rats.

We've *kicked* the dogs right *out* of town,
they *thought* they were tops, but *we* knocked them down.

We're the rats,
we're the rats,
we're the rats,
and that's that!

(*Each 'We're the rats' is followed by two beats and then four beats on the tambour. Hit the tambour once on each italicised word in the verse.*)

DEVELOPING THEMES

Running with the pack: Rats often move around and hunt for food in packs. People sometimes act as a pack which is made up of separate people but united by some common emotion or desire. A crowd of people can be angry as at a protest meeting, or excited at a sporting event, or frightened during a disaster of some kind.

The image of the rat: Rats have a bad reputation but some people keep rats as pets and grow very fond of them. What other creatures inspire both revulsion and affection?

PRESENTING THE POEM

The 'Rat Rap' may be used in conjunction with the descriptive passage from Robert Browning's poem, 'The Pied Piper of Hamelin'.

Rats!
They fought the dogs and killed the cats,
And bit the babies in the cradles,
And ate the cheeses out of the vats,
And licked the soup from the cooks' own ladles,
Split open the kegs of salted sprats,
Made nests inside men's Sunday hats,
And even spoiled the women's chats
By drowning their speaking
With shrieking and squeaking
In fifty different sharps and flats.

A group of four or five children can be involved in performing the poem with one child taking the verses and the others filling in on the chorus. Another child, perhaps the lead voice, should be striking a tambour as follows:

We're the rats,
(followed by two beats, then four beats on the tambour)
We're the rats,
(again, two beats, then four beats.)

We *strut* through the kitchen and we *sniff* for cheese,
we *turn* around and we *chase* our fleas.
(Hit the tambour on each italicised word.)

We're the rats,
we're the rats.

As with all rap poems, the words are important and should not be obscured by accompanying music that is performed too vigorously! Children may care to consider (and practise) the movements of rats – leaping, crouching, scampering, zigzagging, dodging or pouncing. They should develop the idea of working as a pack and co-ordinating their movements. They can also make up sequences of movement and play follow my leader. They will produce their own imaginative ideas.

ENGLISH LINKS

The Pied Piper of Hamelin: Explore Browning's poem section by section, making sure that everyone understands what is happening. Focus on particular sections of the poem such as the description of the Pied Piper. Children could write their own descriptions:

His thin face was as pale as snow, fresh from the heavens.
His eyes shimmered like cool water on a hot summer day.
This mysterious man's laugh seemed to dance.
Like the far off call of a lark.

Children could write diary extracts about everyday life in Hamelin. Perhaps there are important events such as weddings or council meetings that are disrupted by the rats. These could be written up as newspaper reports. Children could also write about the 'joyous land' inside the mountain or make up a travel brochure encouraging others to visit.

Write an acrostic: An acrostic is a poem where the first letter of each line spells out a word. This technique means that children will need to think very carefully about the way that they write their poem as it is tied to a particular form but it will still need to read well:

R unning through the houses,
A nnoying everyone.
T errorising Hamelin,
S topping the children's fun.

Rat expressions: Make a list of rat expressions and their meanings, e.g. to smell a rat, caught like a rat in a trap, rat race, desert rat, ratline, a cornered rat, you dirty rat, water rat, rat catcher. Children could take one of these expressions and illustrate it in an amusing way.

RELATED RESOURCES:

'The Pied Piper of Hamelin' by Robert Browning. Various sources including *The Oxford Book of Story Poems*, edited by Michael Harrison and Christopher Stuart-Clark (OUP 1990), and *The New Dragon Book of Verse*, edited by Michael Harrison and Christopher Stuart-Clark (OUP 1989).

'Rat Trap' by Mick Gowar, from *Carnival of the Animals and Other Poems* (Puffin, 1994). A modern day re-telling. Discover what really happened to the rats and the people of Hamelin.

'Bishop Hatto' by Robert Southey, from *A World of Poetry*, selected by Michael Rosen (Kingfisher 1991). A Victorian ballad in which an army of rats bring judgement on Bishop Hatto for his selfishness and his greed.

The Journal of Watkin Stench by Meredith Hooper (Pan Macmillan). Journal of a ship's rat taking up a new life in Australia's first settlements.

Ratz by Simon Adorian (Upstagers series, Collins, 1991). This puts a new twist in an old tale.

THOUGHTFUL MOMENT:

Dear God,
If people turn to crowds,
If crowds turn to packs,
If packs start to bully –
Help us to stand fast,
Help us to speak out,
Help us to help the helpless.
Amen.

RELATED RELIGIOUS LINKS:

A warning about who you mix with: Whoever touches tar gets dirty and whoever pals up with a bighead gets like them. A rich person might exploit you if you can be of use, and finally might laugh at you. Take care not to be led astray and shown up when you are enjoying yourself. Every creature loves its like ... All living beings associate with their own kind.
(adapted from *Ecclesiasticus 13*)

Happy Dogday

PETER DIXON

Today –
Is our dog's birthday.

It's Happydogdayday.
Sixteen years of panting
And sixteen years of play.

Sixteen years of dogtime.
Sixteen years of barks
– eating smelly dog food
And making muddy marks.

It's a hundred years of our time.
It's a hundred human years
– of digging in the garden
and scratching itchy ears.
It's a hundred years of living rooms
(he never goes upstairs)
and dropping hairy whiskers
and being pushed off chairs ...

It's a hundred years of being with us
A hundred years of Dad,
and a hundred of my sister
(that must be really bad!)

So:
No wonder he looks really old
No wonder he is grey
And cannot hear
Or jump
Or catch
Or even run away ...
No wonder that he sleeps all day,
No wonder that he's fat

And only dreams of catching things
and chasing neighbours' cats ...

So fight your fights
In dogdream nights
Deep within your bed ...

today's your day
and we all say ...

HAPPY BIRTHDAY FRED

DEVELOPING THEMES

Friendship: Dogs are often spoken of as being 'Man's best friends'. Dogs are faithful, they are protective of the house and family. Do dogs ever let us down? What about human friends? *Greyfriars Bobby* is the ultimate tale of doggy devotion. Plenty of dog anecdotes will emerge from discussion on this theme.

Looking after a pet: Caring, and showing that you care. Right and wrong ways of treating animals. The work of the R.S.P.C.A.

Birthdays: The importance of birthdays; how birthdays are celebrated and how they mark the passing of time.

PRESENTING THE POEM

This could be a poem for two voices and then, later on, for several voices. The first voice should make the announcement in a news broadcast way. The second voice calls out in a bright and cheerful style, as if advertising a product, 'It's Happydogdayday'. Lines are then traded between the two voices until the part of the poem that begins 'So:'. Here it would be interesting to have a group of voices, one voice for each different line, all contributing to the whole section and giving it a 'gossipy' feel.

The final part of the poem could revert to the two original voices until the very last line, 'Happy Birthday Fred', which could be called out by everyone.

Any presentation of this poem could be aided visually by children holding balloons, banners with 'Happy Birthday Fred' written on them, and other birthday paraphernalia. If the poem is used in a pets' assembly then a well-behaved dog might form a focus for the poem. Alternatively use slides, pictures or sound effects of barking dogs.

ENGLISH LINKS

Telling anecdotes: Children in groups may enjoy telling each other about ways in which their own dogs behave, or other dogs that they know. They can be asked to think of examples of different ways in which their dogs behave – funny, mischievous, naughty, noisy, cowardly, quirky. For example, my dog used to jump on top of the dining-room table when he heard a clap of thunder, even if the table was laid for tea at the time!

Plan a dog's birthday party: What would you need for a really good birthday party for a dog? Would you hold the party at home, in the park, at the butcher's shop! Think of a whacky location and write an invitation. Who would be on the guest list? What will be needed for a doggy party? Make a list. Design the plates, napkins, crackers. Older children may care to compose advertisements for their doggy party package, either for inclusion in magazines or to be broadcast on radio or TV.

Birthday interviews: Interview different people around the school – pupils, teachers, cleaners, kitchen staff, etc., about how they celebrate their birthdays. Ask them about their biggest birthday surprises or about things they have done to surprise other people on their birthdays. Report back to the class.

RELATED RESOURCES

It's Raining Cats and Dogs, a collection of four-legged poems, edited by Pie Corbett (Blackie/Puffin).
Please Mrs Butler by Alan Ahlberg (Puffin) contains the wonderful 'Dog in the Playground'.
Greyfriars Bobby by Eleanor Atkinson (Puffin Classics).
A Dog Called Nelson by Bill Naughton (Puffin). Real-life story about a one-eyed mongrel.

THOUGHTFUL MOMENT

Dear God,
Thank you for the friendship dogs and other pets can give us. May we be friendly and considerate to them, and to all users of pavements who will walk along after we have walked our dog!

RELATED RELIGIOUS MATERIAL

There is not an animal that lives on the earth, nor a bird, but forms communities like you.
(*Quran Sura 6.38*)

When one of the prophets was bitten by an ant he had the ant hill burned. Then God revealed to him, 'Because of a single ant which bit you, you have burned an entire community that praised God.'
(sayings of Prophet Muhammad)

Tom Becomes Giant

Charles Thomson

'It isn't much fun,'
said Tom, 'being small.
Everyone's bigger
than me at school.

'I wish I was giant.'
Then he saw – guess who?
A fairy! who said,
'Your wish shall come true.'

Can fairies grant wishes?
Yes, – Tom has the proof:
next moment his head
shot straight through the roof.

'Oh great!' he exclaimed,
'this is really good fun,
and now I'm much taller
than everyone.'

By now Tom was feeling
both happy and proud,
as his head re-appeared
from the top of a cloud.

His head bumped the moon,
then whizzed on past Mars,
till his feet were on earth
and his head in the stars.

When he carried on growing
he started to worry:
'I didn't mean *so* giant
in *quite* such a hurry.

'I'm lonely and hungry –
there's nothing to eat.'
(By now he'd completely
lost sight of his feet.)

'Will I ever stop growing?
How can I turn back?'
(The stars were behind him;
in front it was black.)

He bit on his lip
and cried for a while,
then thought of his hamster
and gave a small smile.

'I thought being giant
would be really fantastic,
but it isn't much fun
being stretched like elastic.

'I wish I was back
to just little me.'
The fairy appeared
(just like that!) – 'I agree!'

And then, as if
an unseen hand
had let go of
a rubber band,

he whizzed back, much
to his surprise,
and found he was
his usual size.

He blinked. His teacher,
Mrs Biddy,
said, 'Tom, you do
look rather giddy.

'Sit down. Your face
has gone quite white.'
'Oh thanks,' said Tom,
'I'm quite alright.'

'I'm really glad,'
he thought, 'I'm small.
I don't want to
be giant at all.'

DEVELOPING THEMES

'The other man's grass is always greener.' How often do we envy someone else because of the way that they look, the way they behave or the things that they have? Should we be able to make the best of what we have? Older people often use the phrase, 'Count Your Blessings'. What does this mean?

King Midas: In this poem, Tom is a bit like King Midas, who wanted everything he touched to turn to gold. Then, when he achieved this, he found that he didn't want it after all. Children will remember times when they desperately wanted something – a toy, a trip somewhere – but the reality failed to match up to the anticipation.

Being short: Consider the advantages of being short – squeezing into small spaces during hide and seek, crawling under fences, being lifted up to look at things, and so on.

PRESENTING THE POEM

This is a poem for at least four voices – a narrator, Tom, a fairy, Tom's teacher. Children in groups should be asked to underline the various parts in different colours. The poem could then be acted out or recorded as a radio broadcast.

At the start of the poem, Tom is in a complaining mood and his voice should reflect this. As the poem progresses he is, by turn, excited, worried, upset, pleading and then happy to be back to normal.

If the poem is to be acted out, Tom could be standing on the floor to begin with. Then, if a curtain could be strung up or held up, Tom could move behind the curtain to stand on a chair and peep over the top. He could then move to two taller chairs or tables so that the audience receives the impression that he is growing taller. If chairs are used, make sure they are being held securely by one or two adults. The narrator should stand apart from the three actors.

If a radio play is being produced, then sound effects should be considered for the appearance of the fairy, for words such as 'bumped', 'whizzed', for when Tom cries, for 'being stretched like elastic', and for background classroom noise at the end of the poem.

ENGLISH LINKS

Storyboard: Try to rewrite the story of 'Tom Becomes Giant' using only eight sentences. Pick out the important points and these can then be illustrated as a storyboard. Children might like to work at this in pairs so that there is plenty of discussion about what to include and what to leave out. There should also be discussion about the nature of the illustrations.

Rewrite the poem as a newspaper account: Someone should first be chosen as Tom and children can prepare questions to ask him. Tom's teacher might also be questioned and both sets of answers used as a basis for writing a newspaper account of the event:

It was Sunday 9th September and Tom Baker, a pupil from St Mary's Primary School, had been complaining about being small. As he was talking, a fairy appeared (Tom's words) and told him that his wish would come true. Next minute he grew really tall and his head shot through the school roof ...

RELATED RESOURCES

'The Golden Touch', a Greek Myth about King Midas, may be found in *Realms of Gold – Myths and Legends from Around the World* by Anne Pilling (Kingfisher). What are the similarities between this ancient legend and Charles Thomson's modern story poem?
I wish I could Fly by Ron Maris (Picture Puffin) – for young children but older children may be inspired to write their own picture books.

THOUGHTFUL MOMENT

Thank you God, for accepting me just as I am. I hope that improvements will follow!
Amen.

RELATED RELIGIOUS MATERIAL

Then Peter began to speak to them.
'I understand fully that God has no favourites. In every nation anyone who fears him and does what is right is acceptable to him.'
(*Acts 10.34*)

Not the Dreaded Photo Album!

Paul Cookson

Parents! Huh!
Don't you just hate them?

You can guarantee that whenever we have visitors –
Uncle Fred, Auntie Ivy, Grandma Madge and Grandad Bill,
long lost Auntie Alice or cousin Sidney twice removed –
Mum and Dad will always, and I mean **ALWAYS**
get out the dreaded photo albums
and we have to sit through two and a half hours of
embarrassing snapshots of me ...

stark naked in the bath with bubbles in my ears

cuddling a four foot pink fluffy teddy bear

sitting on my potty with my finger up my nose
and my nappy on my head

wearing chocolate cake like a balaclava,
cherries all over my face like extra alien eyes

the first time I tried to dress myself
with my shorts over my eyes and socks on my hands

dressed as a page boy at my Auntie's wedding
in a blue and white sailor suit and silly hat with ribbons

holding hands and kissing my posh cousin Tabitha
who has pink ribbons and flowery dresses
but never wipes her nose

blinking on every school photograph where it looks like
Mum cut my fringe with the crimping scissors

in the clothes that Mum and Dad bought me

thinking they were really trendy but were two years behind
and cheap off the market so it was okay

wearing that lovely woolly jumper that Nanna knitted
as a Christmas present using left over wool
so that it had twenty-seven shades of green and brown
with a Thomas The Tank Engine motif
and the left arm was longer than the right
and it itched like crazy.

Everyone has a really good laugh
and I have to sit through it all tight lipped and red faced.
When I suggest that we look at last year's holiday snaps
where Mum won the knobbly knees contest
and Dad dressed up as an oven ready turkey for the fancy dress
they tell me it's time I went to bed
and that our visitors wouldn't be interested anyway.

Parents! Huh!
Don't you just hate them?

DEVELOPING THEMES

Looking back: Photographs are milestones along the route we have travelled to what we are now. They are valuable artefacts when we are seeking the person we once were and they contribute to a sense of 'belonging'.

Embarrassment: Photographs can be 'skeletons in the cupboard'. They are of great sentimental value to Mum and Dad but you would prefer to lose them. Why do we get embarrassed so easily? What other things cause embarrassment?

History of photography: Before photography we only had artists' impressions of people to help us find out what they looked like. When were cameras invented? What advantages might there be in being able to take 'instant' shots of people? Can paintings portray people in ways that photographs cannot?

PRESENTING THE POEM

Most children will immediately identify with this poem.

The first two lines – 'Parents! Huh!/Don't you just hate them?' – might well become a chant that is repeated four or five times at the beginning and the end of the poem.

The poem can then be divided into sections, with a narrator taking the section that begins, 'You can guarantee ...', and the penultimate section, 'Everyone has a really good laugh ...'. Each description of a photograph should then be read by a different voice. At the appropriate point, children should step forward and read their lines in a weary, resigned manner, whereas others might sound indignant, resentful, annoyed, or incredulous.

If the poem is to be used in assembly, consider the use of props such as photograph albums or large boards covered in suitable photographs of the children at school or brought in from home. Some children might like to dress for the parts or hold appropriate items – a fluffy teddy bear, a potty, Thomas The Tank Engine jumper, and so on.

ENGLISH LINKS

Embarrassing moments: Children can think of times when they were really embarrassed, when they wanted the ground to open up and swallow them. Some of these moments are pushed to the backs of our minds until we are asked to reflect upon them, and children might like to think about all the things that they wouldn't like to be reminded of if their whole lives were to flash before them:

If my whole life flashed before me
I wouldn't want to remember
the day I took hold of somebody's hand
in the supermarket, and it wasn't Mum's,
the moment my Dad took his trousers off in public
because a bee had got inside them,
the kiss from Great Aunt Mabel
when she forgot to put her teeth in,
the holiday ...

By starting each line with '*the* time, *the* moment, *the* journey, *the* meal,' etc., the poem develops a rhythm without resorting to rhyme, and will sound good when read aloud.

Write about a photograph: Find a photograph of someone that you don't know and try to think about what they might be like. Write a description of the person but concentrate less on physical details and more on the kind of things that you can only guess about – interests, temperament, hopes, fears.

Talk: About the person you were and the person that you have become. What did you used to do that was annoying, troublesome or sheer bad behaviour? Are there things that you did then that you wish you could do now?

RELATED RESOURCES

Uzma's Photo Album by A Morris & H Larson (A&C Black, 1989). A story about a family journey and about keeping memories in a photograph album.

For younger children, 'Grandma's Pictures' from *The Big Alfie and Annie Rose Storybook* by Shirley Hughes (Red Fox, 1990).

Poetry – 'Photographs' and 'The Family Book', both by Brian Moses, from *Hippopotamus Dancing* and *Knock Down Ginger* respectively (Cambridge University Press, 1994).

'Can't Wait' by John Kitching, from *A First Poetry Book*, edited by John Foster (OUP, 1979).

THOUGHTFUL MOMENT

Dear God,

Thank you for photographs of us and all the different memories they bring back that help us travel in time back to our past.

RELATED RELIGIOUS MATERIAL

Paintings sometimes try to emphasize the character of the person more than a photograph. Sometimes all they can do is to try to show character, as no picture of the person's real face survives. Look at some pictures of Jesus or Moses or Guru Nanak. What do you think they're trying to show about the person's character? Is it better, like Islam, not to try to draw the person at all (Muhammad's face is not depicted)?

Leisure Centre, Pleasure Centre

John Rice

You go through plate glass doors
  with giant red handles
into light that's as bright
  as a million candles.
The chlorine smells,
  the whole place steaming,
the kids are yelling
  and the kids are screaming.

Watch them
  wave jump
  dive thump
  cartwheel
  free wheel
  look cute
  slip chute
  toe stub
  nose rub
  in the leisure centre, pleasure centre.

Sporty people laugh and giggle,
  folk in swim suits give a wiggle.
Kids are in the café busy thinking
  if they can afford some fizzy drinking.
In the changing rooms
  wet folk shiver,
It's hard to get dressed
  when you shake and quiver.

And we go
  breast stroke
  back stroke
  two stroke
  big folk
  hair soak

little folk
eye poke
no joke
in the leisure centre, pleasure centre.

And now we're driving back home,
fish'n'chips in the car,
eyes are slowing closing
but it's not very far.
Snuggle wuggle up in fresh clean sheets,
a leisure centre trip
is the best of treats

because you can
keep fit
leap sit
eat crisps
do twists
belly flop
pit stop
fill up
with 7–Up
get going
blood flowing
look snappy
be happy
in the leisure centre, pleasure centre.

DEVELOPING THEMES

Why do we need to keep fit? Compare our bodies with machines that need looking after. What are the factors that promote fitness and good health?

Discipline: Have you got what it takes to be a champion athlete? Champions are dedicated and train regularly over a number of years.

Sports facilities: The importance of purpose-built centres where people can take exercise alongside other enthusiasts.

PRESENTING THE POEM

This poem needs an energetic reading to match the various activities that are being described. Children may find it easier to take alternate lines in any reading aloud with a number of voices joining in on the line '... in the leisure centre, pleasure centre'.

A presentation of this poem would be greatly enhanced by actions. Children who are involved might like to dress as swimmers with towels under arms or around necks. Some children may like to provide an exercise routine or a dance to accompany the poem. Experiment, too, with reading the poem against a pre-set dance or rap rhythm on keyboards.

ENGLISH LINKS

Leisure centres: Talk about leisure centres and the facilities they offer. What do children like about such centres? Are there aspects that they dislike? Suggest that children design their ideal leisure centre. List the facilities that it will contain and mark these on an annotated plan of the complex. Children could then prepare a poster advertising the complex and extolling its many attractions. Further work might well include an account of the opening ceremony. Who would they invite to perform the official opening?

Keeping fit: Ask children to list the different ways in which they exercise. What is their favourite form of activity? Ask children to produce a piece of writing that outlines the benefits and enjoyment to be gained from this activity and encourages others to try it out, too.

Drama: Suggest that children improvise scenes between keen fitness fanatics and 'couch potatoes'. A typical scene might involve a son and daughter trying to persuade Dad to go jogging with them, or a daughter trying to convince Mum that she ought to try aerobics.

RELATED RESOURCES

The Wacky World of Wesley Baker by Gene Kemp (Viking). Wesley Baker's family are all fitness freaks and his Dad puts him on an intensive bodybuilding programme for sports day. Lots to discuss.

A Bag of Sports Stories, edited by Tony Bradman (Transworld). A collection that highlights the fun and personal achievement of sporting activities. Includes stories from Jan Mark and Jean Ure.

Poetry – Sports Poems, compiled by John Foster (Jackdaws Poetry/ Oxford Reading Tree); 'Come on in the Water's Lovely' by Gareth Owen from *Song of the City* (Young Lions); 'Learning to Swim' by Brian Moses, from *Knock Down Ginger* (Cambridge University Press).

THOUGHTFUL MOMENT

For wave jump
dive thump
cartwheel
free wheel
and the swirling, whirling, twirling rest
Thank you God.

RELATED RELIGIOUS MATERIAL

Young adults were once invited to join something called 'Time for God'. They were asked to give up part of their life, some months or even a year, as Time for God. Some did this between leaving school and going to university. What do you think they were asked to do during their time? It wasn't to sing hymns or say prayers; it was to help homeless people and drug addicts and all sorts of people in need. Why do you think they called it 'Time for God'? Most of those who took part would have called it pleasure to be of help to others. What sort of things do we enjoy doing for other people?

The Whale

(Anon) Author Unknown

O, 'twas in the year of ninety-four,
And of June the second day,
That our gallant ship her anchor weighed
And from Stromness bore away, brave boys!
    And from Stromness bore away!

Now Speedicut was our captain's name,
And our ship the *Lion* bold,
And we were bound to far Greenland,
To the land of ice and cold – brave boys,
    To the land of ice and cold.

And when we came to far Greenland,
And to Greenland cold came we,
Where there's ice, and there's snow, and the whalefishes blow,
We found all open sea – brave boys,
    We found all open sea.

Then the mate he climbed to the crow's nest high,
With his spy-glass in his hand,
'There's a whale, there's a whale, there's a whalefish,' he cried,
'And she blows at every span' – brave boys,
    She blows at every span.

Our captain stood on his quarter-deck,
And a fine little man was he.
'Overhaul, overhaul, on your davit tackle fall,
And launch your boats to the sea' – brave boys,
    And launch your boats to the sea.

Now the boats were launched and the men a-board,
With the whalefish full in view;
Resol-ved were the whole boats' crews
To steer where the whalefish blew – brave boys,
    To steer where the whalefish blew.

And when we reached that whale, my boys,
He lashed out with his tail,
And we lost a boat, and seven good men,
And we never caught that whale – brave boys,
    And we never caught that whale.

Bad news, bad news, to our captain came,
That grieved him very sore.
But when he found that his cabin-boy was gone,
Why it grieved him ten times more – brave boys,
    It grieved him ten times more.

O, Greenland is an awful place,
Where the daylight's seldom seen,
Where there's ice, and there's snow, and the whalefishes blow,
Then *adieu* to cold Greenland – brave boys,
    Adieu to cold Greenland.

DEVELOPING THEMES

Whaling and conservation of whales: Importance of conserving whales as some breeds are very low in numbers. There are adequate substitutes for every product that is made from whales.

Courage of the whalers in the past: Whaling in the past was very much a contest between man and beast. Harpoons were primitive. Compare this with today's modern methods of catching whales where modern technology means that the whale has very little chance of escaping its pursuers.

The strength of the sea: Any sailors who put out to sea for whatever reason need to be courageous in order to face up to terrible weather conditions.

PRESENTING THE POEM

When the poem is performed it might be an idea for single voices to speak the first three lines of each verse with the last two lines being spoken by a chorus of voices. Consider how the poem should be presented visually. Children will probably suggest various actions that might accompany the reading – the mate peering from the crow's nest, the boat being launched, the crew rowing towards the whale. Children might also like to dress as if they are muffled up against the bitter cold. A performance of this poem may well benefit from background music and/or sound effects for the sea and wind. The lonesome sound of a harmonica or an accordian, as though it were drifting on the wind, might well add atmosphere to the piece.

ENGLISH LINKS

Making sense of the poem: Hand out copies of the poem; in groups children can underline any parts of the poem that they don't understand. Some of the nautical terms such as 'davit tackle fall', 'span' and 'crow's nest' may need some explanation (see below*). Also, try to fix the location – where is Stromness? Talk, too, about where this poem might have originated. It more than likely started life as a song that was written to record the whaling crew's adventures. Children could research whaling and whalers and prepare factsheets accompanied by talks to the class.

* *a) 'And she blows at every span' (the whale comes to the surface and spouts water at regular intervals).*
b) 'Overhaul' (catch up and overtake).
c) 'On your davit tackle fall' (lower the boats quickly – 'davit' = crane for lowering ship's boats; 'tackle' = system of ropes and blocks).

Write a poem: Look at the rhyming scheme that is featured in this poem. It is a less popular scheme than those that we usually find in rhyming poems. The second and the fifth lines rhyme in each verse, although the fifth line is an echo of the fourth, aside from the phrase 'brave boys' which is tacked on to it. Suggest that children attempt to write in a similar way using 'The Whale' as a model. Think of an event in school that could be celebrated and then write about it:

It was in the year of ninety-five
and on May the 7th day,
that our football team in their minibus
from school they drove away, brave lads/lasses,
from school they drove away.

Now Simpkins was their captain's name
and their team St Mary's best,
and they were bound for St Gregory's
to put their skills to the test, brave lads/lasses,
to put their skills to the test.

Whaling – for or against? Hold a class discussion about the ethics of whaling today. Suggest that children write letters to environmental organizations such as Greenpeace, Friends of the Earth, and the Whale and Dolphin Conservation Society to find out facts about whaling.

RELATED RESOURCES

Moby Dick or The Whale by Herman Melville. Extracts from this book can be used to accompany this poem.
My Friend Whale by Simon James (Walker Books). A small boy makes friends with a whale, swimming with him each night until one day the whale disappears. Sensitive introduction to the plight of whales.
The Whales' Song by Dyan Sheldon and Gary Blythe (Hutchinson). Lily longs to hear the singing of the whales as her grandmother once did. Wonderful paintings. A picture book for everyone.
Poetry – *Earthways, Earthwise*, Poems on Conservation, selected by Judith Nicholls, contains a section, 'Whale, I hear you calling ...', with several poems about whales, including 'The Song of the Whale' by Kit Wright which can also be found in his own book, *Hot Dog and Other Poems* (Puffin).
Whale Nation by Heathcote Williams (Jonathan Cape). Powerful poetry alongside quite stunning photography, plus a catalogue of quotes and opinions from the earliest times to the present day.

THOUGHTFUL MOMENT

Dear God,
When we have a whale of a time
may we always remember not to do it at the expense of other people, animals or the fragile environment.
Amen

RELATED RELIGIOUS MATERIAL

Don't do Jonah. Discuss instead this *Quaker Advice (1995)*:

'We do not own the world, and its riches are not ours to dispose of at will. Show a loving consideration for all creatures, and seek to maintain the beauty and variety of the world.'

What might this mean in practice?

Song of the Victorian Mine

SUE COWLING

Shut six men in a metal cage –
  Wind them down, wind them down.
Drop them in a dismal pit –
  Down in the mine,
  Deep in the mine,
  Dark in the mine all day.

Back the pony up to the cage –
  Wind him down, wind him down.
Trip him up and make him sit –
  Down in the mine,
  Deep in the mine,
  Dark in the mine all day.

Load the ore in the metal cage –
  Wind it down, wind it down.
Waterlogged and candlelit –
  Down in the mine,
  Deep in the mine,
  Dark in the mine all day.

Bring the canary in his cage –
  Wind him down, wind him down.
He'll die first if the air's not fit –
  Down in the mine,
  Deep in the mine,
  Dark in the mine all day.

Thirty thousand times in the cage –
  Wind me down, wind me down.
Fill my lungs with grime and grit –
  Down in the mine,
  Deep in the mine,
  Dark in the mine all day.

DEVELOPING THEMES

Danger: Men who work in the mines can often find themselves in danger despite the safety precautions that are taken. It requires a certain amount of courage to go down to the pit each day and to know that there is always the chance of a tunnel collapsing or a power failure. Are there other jobs that are equally as dangerous?

For the good of the nation: Pit workers were exempted from National Service during two world wars because the nation needed coal for fuel and their jobs were considered too valuable. Which jobs might be considered the most valuable to the nation today?

Cruelty to animals: Is it cruel to take animals such as ponies into the mines?

PRESENTING THE POEM

This is an excellent poem for reading aloud as it has a tight rhyming pattern which makes for a solid rhythm. It needs strong voices to emphasise the doom and gloom of its message. In each verse, one voice could take the first and third lines while a chorus of voices join in on the lines that are repeated. If the poem is being presented as part of an assembly then the audience might be encouraged to join in on the refrain.

Suggest that children experiment with a variety of percussion instruments which could serve to emphasise the rhythm. Claves, drums, tambours could be particularly effective. Aim for a slightly muted effect through the use of soft beaters. The poem could also be dramatised with actions and sound effects – six children standing as if in a cage, spotlighted if possible, while others mime the winding of the pit mechanism, sound effects of horses neighing, etc.

ENGLISH LINKS

Conversation in a cage: Suggest that children either script or improvise the kind of conversation that might take place each morning between six miners as they descend to the mine workings. Would they be talking about ordinary everyday events – last night's football on TV, the morning headlines, what they've got for lunch – or would they be cracking jokes to hide the slight nervousness that they feel each day, despite the familiarity of the situation? The scene might be extended if one of the miners loses his nerve. How would his companions react?

Research pit ponies: Why were they used? How were they used? Were there alternatives? From the information gathered, suggest that children write either a letter to the newspaper from the point of view of an animal rights supporter, highlighting the plight of the ponies, or a description of the ponies being brought to the surface and released into a field. With the second idea, children should try to capture the sense of freedom that the creatures feel after the confines of the mine.

Underground: Search out descriptions of what it is like to be underground – in mines, in cave systems, in tunnels, etc. Can children talk about an experience of their own. Talk in pairs initially, then join up with another pair and tell the stories again. Children should find that they add more detail during the second telling. Children can then write down their tales.

RELATED RESOURCES

Candle in the Dark by Robert Swindells (Knight Books, 1991). Jimmy Booth is sent to work as a pit-brat in the harsh and violent world of Rawdon Pit. Some excellent descriptions of life underground in Victorian times.
Twopence a Tub by Susan Price (Faber, 1975). This story contrasts the appalling conditions of the lives of the miners with the life enjoyed by the rich mine owner.
A Chance Child by Jill Paton Walsh (Puffin). A neglected child travels back in time to the 1840s where he joins other children who are working in the mines and factories.

THOUGHTFUL MOMENT

The teacher might light a candle first during a short time of silence and then say:

Lord, help us to turn darkness to light
In the lives of people.
or
An old proverb says: It is better to light a candle than to curse the darkness.

A few seconds of silence should follow.

RELATED RELIGIOUS MATERIAL

In early Bible times the Jews believed that after death, everybody went to a place of shadows, away from God's presence. They talked of it as dark and it was known as Sheol, or the Pit, a place far away from warmth and light and enjoyment of life, rather like the pits (as coal mines were known) that the Victorians later worked in. A Jewish hymn writer believed that however bad your situation, God was always near:

Where can I go from your spirit?
Or where can I run away from your presence?
If I climb to heaven, you are there;
If I have to live in the Pit, you are there ...
If I say, 'Surely the darkness will cover me
And the light around me become night',
Even the darkness is not dark to you,
The night is as bright as day,
For you can make darkness light.
(*from Psalm 139*)

Acknowledgements

Morning Has Decorated the Park by Robin Mellor, previously published in *Welsh Rhubarb*, Victoria Press, 1993.
Rat Rap, Make Friends With a Tree, Museum of Mythical Beasts, first published in *Croc City*, Victoria Press, 1993.
Monster Crazy by Brian Moses, previously published in *Rice, Pie & Moses*, Macmillan, 1995.
Camping Out by Judith Nicholls, previously published in *Dragonsfire*, Faber & Faber Ltd, 1990. Reprinted by permission of the author and the publishers.
Happy Dogday by Peter Dixon, previously published in *Matt, Wes & Pete*, Macmillan 1995.
Leisure Centre, Pleasure Centre by John Rice, previously published in *Rice, Pie & Moses*, Macmillan, 1995.
Song of the Victorian Mine by Sue Cowling, previously published in *What is a Kumquat?,* Faber & Faber Ltd. Reprinted by permission of the publishers.
The Listeners by Walter de la Mare, reproduced by kind permission of The Literary Trustees of Walter de la Mare, and The Society of Authors as their representative.
The Most Important Rap by Roger Stevens.

Voices of Water by Tony Mitton
Listen to Machines by Ian Souter
Sounds Familiar by Trevor Harvey
The Green Unicorn by Mike Jubb
Tom Becomes Giant by Charles Thomson
Not the Dreaded Photo Album by Paul Cookson
The preceding six poems © The author, 1996.

The Hairy Toe – Traditional
The Whale – Anon

Revolting Arithmetic
Ancient Egypt

Rowland Morgan

Revolting Arithmetic: Ancient Egypt

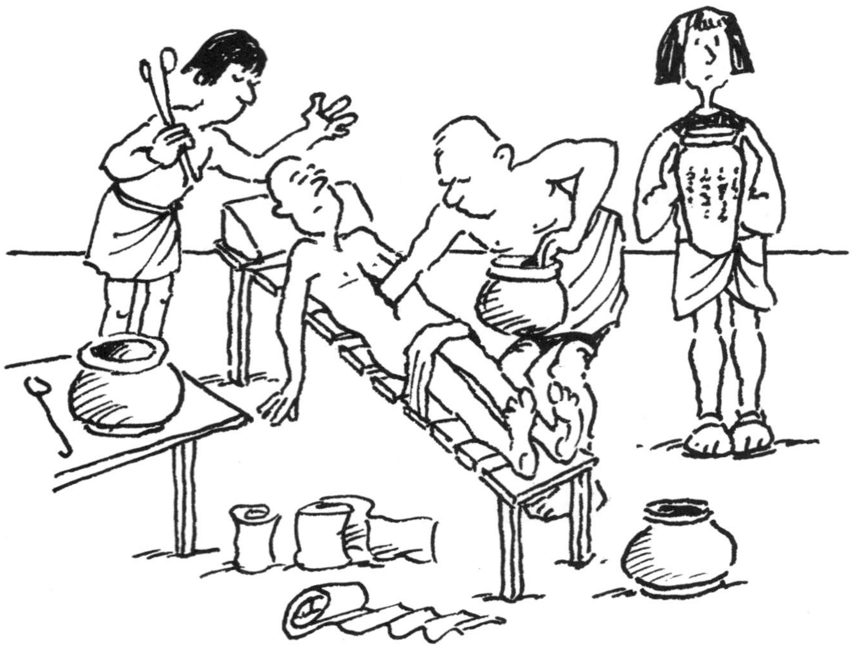

Embalming was a messy job, but somebody had to do it...

Editor: Terry Vittachi
Illustrations: Andrew Noble – Andrew Noble Design Team Ltd
Gary Clifford – The Drawing Room
Layout artist: Jane Conway
Cover image: Andrew Noble – Andrew Noble Design Team Ltd
Cover design: Ed Gallagher

First published 2000 by Belair Publications, Dunstable.

Belair Publications, Albert House, Apex Business Centre, Boscombe Road, Dunstable, LU5 4RL, England.

ISBN 1–84191–034–1

Printed in Singapore by Craft Print Pte Ltd.

Contents

Nefertiti Tot-Up

Choosing what to wear can be a real headache!

Introduction

Cross-curricular maths

Most people agree that there is a maths problem in Britain. Pupils tend not to like it much, teachers are in short supply and results could be better. Maths is not as popular as it could be. Sadly, that has been taken for granted.

Why has maths got a bad name when, of all the subjects in primary school, maths is the one where there is often a definite right answer or a wrong one? It is the subject in which you can learn an operation, perform it and get marks. It is quite straightforward.

People use maths all the time. In a game of darts, working out a knitting pattern, checking bank accounts – there are so many ways people enjoy their command of numbers, without thinking about it.

Revolting Arithmetic takes a shot at motivating children's enjoyment of maths by integrating parts of it with history. Children will just say: cross-curricular, here we come!

How to use this book

These activities are intended to help children practise their mathematics in the context of work on historical topics. They could be used for homework or for additional mathematical work outside the daily maths lesson. You may want children to write directly on the sheets, or they may be used as resource material, with pupils recording their answers elsewhere.

To give the flexibility to match the activities to work in different year groups or to children of differing ability, the copiable activity pages are laid out in three gradations of difficulty.

Level 1 uses mathematical operations (mostly arithmetic) at a level roughly equivalent to Year 3. This should suit most children in Years 3–4. Level 2 is more appropriate to Years 4–5. Level 3 is aimed at Years 5–6.

There is a self-checking function on each sheet in which we sometimes push the agenda a little, in the hope that self-marking will motivate some stretching. You may want some children to use a calculator for this. Answers and algorithms are provided at the back of the book.

Ancient Egypt

Three thousand years of civilisation...there's a number to write down! The mighty pyramids are perhaps the greatest symbols of maths in action the world has ever seen. Yet the ancient Egyptians did without cash, had few slaves and rarely used the wheel. Perhaps they did without maths lessons, too – we may never know.

Potty Pyramids

1 The three great pyramids near Cairo in Egypt are world-famous, but not many people know that there are at least eighty ancient pyramids along the river Nile. Write this number in figures.

PHARAOH'S FASCINATING FACT
To build the great pyramid of Giza, gangs of workers pulled sledges carrying stones weighing 2.5 tonnes – the weight of two family cars.

2 The bases of different pyramids are all square. How many sides do the bases have?

3 The great pyramids were built so that their sides faced north, south, east and west. Fill in the missing directions on the pyramid.
If N = 10 S = 20,
E = 30 and W = 40,
what do the directions add up to?

CHECK IT YOURSELF ✓

Your answer to 1 → ☐☐

Your answer to 2 → ☐

Your answer to 3 → ☐☐☐

Add them Result → ☐☐☐

Do you get **184**? *If not, check your answers and try again.*

Potty Pyramids

1 The three great pyramids near Cairo in Egypt are world-famous. It is less well known that more than 80 ancient pyramids stand along the west bank of the river Nile. Nine-tenths ($\frac{9}{10}$) of the total are now in ruins. Express that fraction as a decimal.

PHARAOH'S FASCINATING FACT
Workers took ten years to build the great pyramid of Giza. They placed one two-tonne stone every 38 seconds!

2 The sides of the first pyramid went up in steps. Another pyramid had bent sides. Still, the bases of these different pyramids are all square.

a) At what angle are the sides of the base to each other, in degrees?

b) What do the four angles of the base add up to?

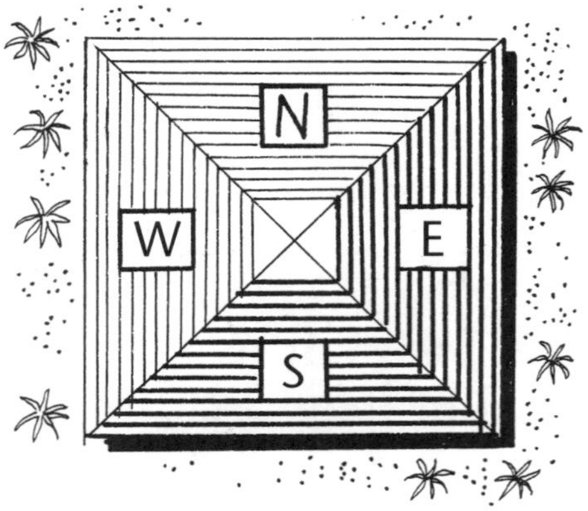

3 Using this chart, work out how many pyramids may have been built in:
a) the Old Kingdom **b)** the Middle Kingdom **c)** the New Kingdom

CHECK IT YOURSELF ✓

Your answer to 1 → ☐ . ☐

Your answer to 2a → ☐ ☐ . 0

Your answer to 2b → ☐ ☐ ☐ . 0

Your answer to 3b → ☐ ☐ . 0

Add them Result → ☐ ☐ ☐ . ☐

Do you get **460.9***? If not, check your answers and try again.*

Potty Pyramids

1 The three great pyramids near Cairo in Egypt are world-famous. It is less well known that 80 ancient pyramids stand along the west bank of the river Nile. Assuming that each pyramid took 35 years to build, how many years of building do the 80 pyramids represent?

PHARAOH'S FASCINATING FACT
To build the great pyramid of Giza, gangs of workers had to haul stones weighing about 2.5 tonnes. Two-and-a-half million such journeys were required, all uphill!

2 Some stone slabs in the temples of the great pyramids weigh 200 tonnes.
a) Nine extra-strong workers could haul one tonne. How many were needed to haul one of the slabs?
b) If four slabs were required, all at the same time, how many extra-strong workers were required?

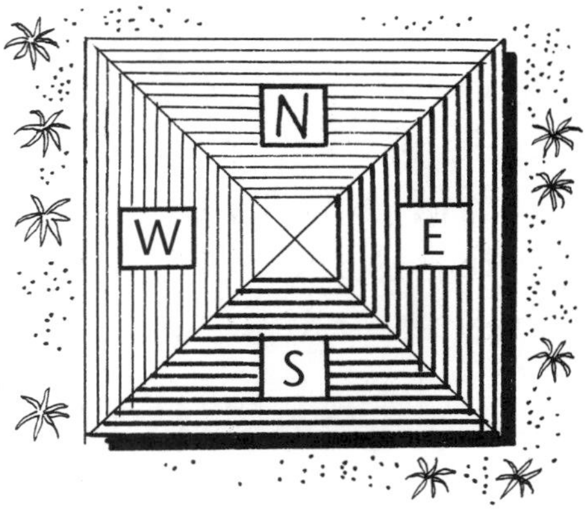

3 Not all pyramids look the same. King Zoser built the first pyramid in about 2680BC. Instead of sloping smoothly, the sides went up in steps. Another pyramid had bent sides. The famous great pyramids of Giza are true pyramids. Still, the bases of all these different pyramids face north, south, east and west.
a) If an architect made a mistake of 45 degrees to the east, in what direction would each of the sides face? Make a list of them. Using the key, turn the directions into a list of two-digit numbers (for example, NE = 28)
N = 2 E = 8 S = 9 W = 5
b) Now add them together.

CHECK IT YOURSELF ✓

Divide answer 1 by 10 and fill in → ☐☐☐
Divide answer 2a by 10 and fill in → ☐☐☐
Your answer to 2b → ☐☐☐☐
Your answer to 3b → ☐☐☐
Add them Result → ☐☐☐☐

Do you get ***7906****?*
If not, check your answers and try again.

Amazing Amenhotep

1 Although King Amenhotep III died over 3000 years ago, a thousand pictures and statues of him have survived. Write that number in figures.

PHARAOH'S FASCINATING FACT
The rock for Amenhotep's statues was transported by hand from a quarry over 600 kilometres away!

2 There are three statues of Amenhotep III. They are 21 metres high. If they stood on top of each other, how high would they be?

3 Amenhotep built a lake for his wife, Teye. It was $1\frac{1}{2}$ kilometres long and took 15 days to build. After five days, how many kilometres were built?

4 Amenhotep had 317 servants. Twenty-eight became ill. How many were left to serve the pharaoh?

CHECK IT YOURSELF ✓

Your answer to 1 → ☐ ☐ ☐ ☐

Your answer to 2 → ☐ ☐

Your answer to 3 → ☐

Your answer to 4 → ☐ ☐ ☐

Add them Result → ☐ ☐ ☐ ☐

Do you get **1357**? *If not, check your answers and try again.*

Amazing Amenhotep

1 Although King Amenhotep III died over 3000 years ago, 1000 pictures and statues of him have survived. He reigned from 1390 to 1352BC.

a) For how many years did he rule? (Remember, BC dates go down, not up!)

b) Complete the chart by filling in the date of each year. In which year were the most images made?

Year of reign	Date (BC)	Images made
1	1390	24
2		27
3		25
4		27
5		28
6		25

Year of reign	Date (BC)	Images made
7		24
8		26
9		29
10		26
11		27
12		28

Year of reign	Date (BC)	Images made
13		25
14		26
15		28
16		23
17		24
18		25

2 There are three statues of Amenhotep III, each 21 metres high. Imagine an office tower of that size beside them. Each storey is three metres high. How many storeys high is the tower?

3 The stone for Amenhotep's statues came from a quarry 630 kilometres away. The journey took seven months. (A month is 30 days.) How many miles was the stone dragged each day?

CHECK IT YOURSELF

Your answer to 1a → ☐☐

Your answer to 1b → ☐☐☐☐

Your answer to 2 → ☐

Add them Result → ☐☐☐☐

Your answer to 3 → ☐

Subtract it Result → ☐☐☐☐

Do you get **1424**? *If not, check your answers and try again.*

Amazing Amenhotep

3

1 King Amenhotep III built a lake for his wife, Teye. It was $1\frac{1}{2}$ kilometres long. His servants completed it in 15 days.

a) Write in decimals how many kilometres of the lake were built in five days.

b) What percentage of the lake is that (to the nearest one per cent)?

PHARAOH'S FASCINATING FACT

The rock for Amenhotep's statues was transported by hand from a quarry over 400 miles away!

2 Amenhotep had 317 servants.

a) If Queen Teye had twice as many, how many servants had they altogether?

b) If 12 servants left each year, how many would they have after three years?

3 King Amenhotep had 15 rival monarchs in Syria, Asia and Nubia. They each sent him a wife every year.

a) Amenhotep reigned from 1390 to 1352BC. How many wives was he sent between 1391 and 1380BC, including both these years? (Remember, BC dates go down, not up!)

b) Each of these had an average of 0.2 babies. How many is that altogether?

CHECK IT YOURSELF ✓

Your answer to 1a → ☐.☐

Your answer to 1b → ☐☐.0

Add them Result → ☐☐.☐

Do you get **33.5**? *If not, check your answers and try again.*

Your answer to 2a → ☐☐☐

Your answer to 2b → ☐☐☐

Add them Result → ☐☐☐☐

Do you get **1866**? *If not, check your answers and try again.*

Your answer to 3a → ☐☐☐

Your answer to 3b → ☐☐

Subtract it Result → ☐☐☐

Do you get **120**? *If not, check your answers and try again.*

Nefertiti Tot-Up

1 Nefertiti ruled Egypt after her husband died. Like all Egyptians, she shaved her head and wore wigs. She had many wigs, perhaps as many as a thousand. Write that number in figures.

2 Nefertiti wore a pad of incense on her head. The heat of her body made the incense melt slowly. When three-quarters of her incense pad had melted, what fraction was left?

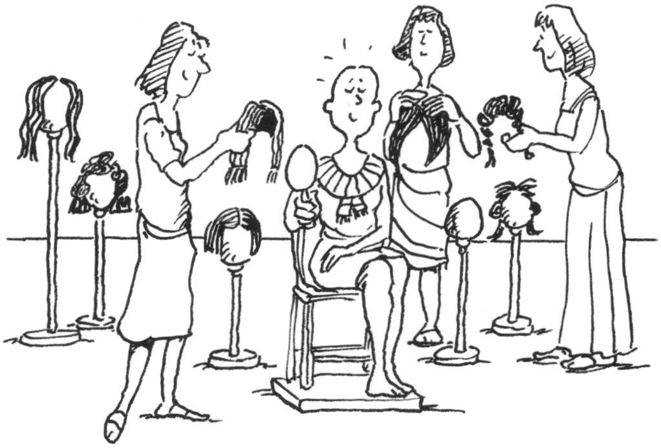

3 Nefertiti had a box for each type of jewellery. They were: necklaces, rings, bracelets, pendants, belts, anklets, armlets, collars and pectorals (worn over her chest). How many boxes were there?

4 Nefertiti may have had 42 pairs of sandals for the daytime and 53 pairs for the night-time. How many pairs is that altogether?

CHECK IT YOURSELF ✓

Your answer to 1 → ☐ ☐ ☐ ☐

Your answer to 2 → ☐ (fraction)

Find this fraction of your first answer → ☐ ☐ ☐

Do you get **250**? *If not, check your answers and try again.*

Your answer to 3 → ☐

Your answer to 4 → ☐ ☐

Add them Result → ☐ ☐ ☐

Do you get **104**? *If not, check your answers and try again.*

Nefertiti Tot-Up

1 Nefertiti was married to the pharaoh Akhenaten. She ruled Egypt after the pharaoh died. Like all Egyptians, she shaved her head and wore wigs. In the first three years of her reign, imagine she collected wigs as follows:
Year 1: 231   Year 2: 122   Year 3: 396
How many wigs did she collect in the three years?

2 Like all rich Egyptian women, Nefertiti went to parties wearing a pad of incense on her head. The heat of her body made the incense melt slowly, giving off a pleasant smell. When 0.75 of her incense pad had melted, how much of it was left?

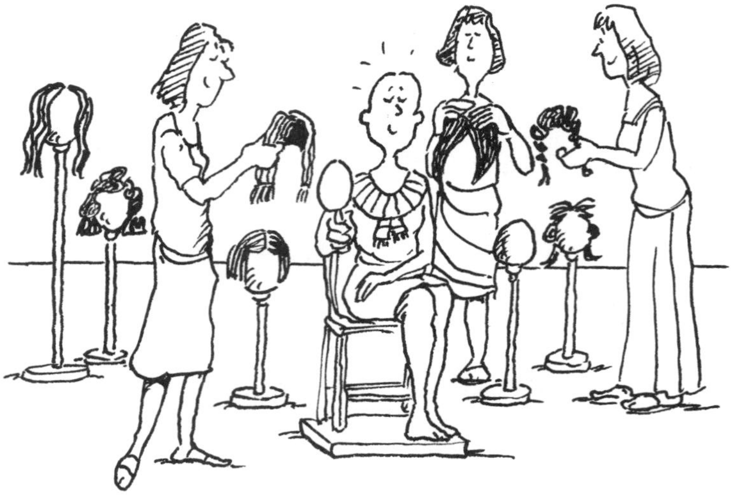

3 Nefertiti had lots of jewellery. She kept it in a set of boxes. Each box contained 85 examples of one type of jewellery. The different types were: necklaces, rings, bracelets, pendants, belts, anklets, armlets, collars and pectorals (worn over her chest). How many pieces of jewellery were there altogether?

4 Most Egyptians went barefoot, but Queen Nefertiti at one time had 22 pairs of sandals for the daytime and 32 pairs for the night-time. An Egyptian working week had nine days. If she wore different sandals each day of the week, how many pairs could she wear each day?

CHECK IT YOURSELF ✓

Your answer to 1 → ☐☐☐.0 0

Your answer to 2 → ☐.☐☐

Your answer to 3 → ☐☐☐.0 0

Your answer to 4 → ☐.0 0

Add them/Result → ☐☐☐☐.☐☐

Do you get **1520.25**? *If not, check your answers and try again.*

Nefertiti Tot-Up

1 Nefertiti was married to the pharaoh Akhenaten. After he died, she ruled Egypt. Like all Egyptians, she shaved her head and wore wigs. As Queen of Egypt, she had a fantastic number of wigs, which she shared with her handmaidens. In three years of her reign, imagine she collected wigs as follows:
Year 1: 983 Year 2: 1245 Year 3: 876
How many wigs did she collect in the three years?

2 Like all rich Egyptian women, Nefertiti went to parties wearing a pad of incense on her head. The heat of her body made the incense melt slowly, giving off a pleasant smell. When 32 per cent of her incense pad had melted, what percentage of it was left?

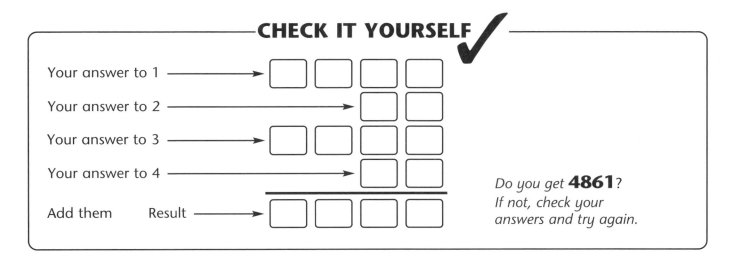

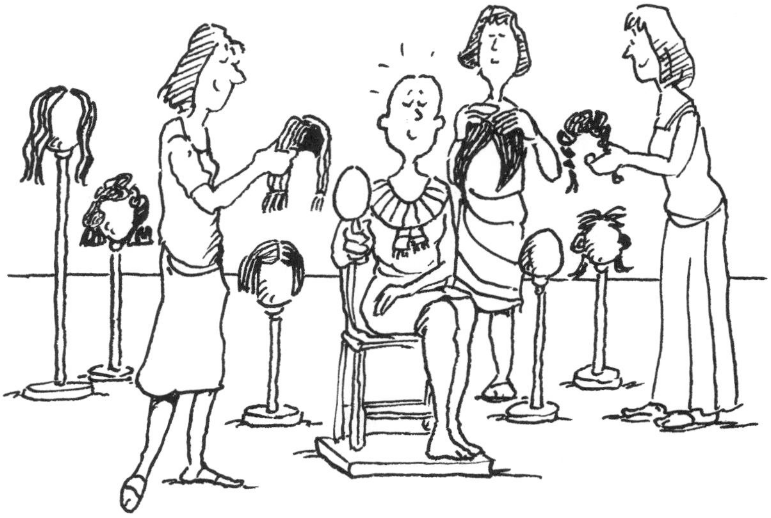

3 As wife of the pharaoh, Nefertiti had lots of jewellery. She kept her main pieces in a set of boxes which were guarded night and day. Each box contained 185 examples of one type of jewellery. The different types were: necklaces, rings, bracelets, pendants, belts, anklets, armlets, collars and pectorals (worn over her chest). How many pieces of jewellery were there altogether?

4 Most Egyptians went barefoot. Queen Nefertiti spent a lot of time in chilly temples. Her feet got cold on the stone floors. One year she had 86 pairs of sandals for the daytime and 132 pairs for the night-time. An Egyptian working week had nine days. If she wore different sandals each day of the week, how many pairs could she wear each day? (Round down to the nearest whole number.)

CHECK IT YOURSELF

Your answer to 1 → ☐☐☐☐

Your answer to 2 → ☐☐

Your answer to 3 → ☐☐☐☐

Your answer to 4 → ☐☐

Add them Result → ☐☐☐☐

Do you get **4861**?
If not, check your answers and try again.

Towering Triangles

1 The pyramids were built around five thousand years ago as homes for the kings' bodies. Write that number in figures.

2 The Great Pyramid was built for King Cheops. Look at the diagram of the passages inside it.

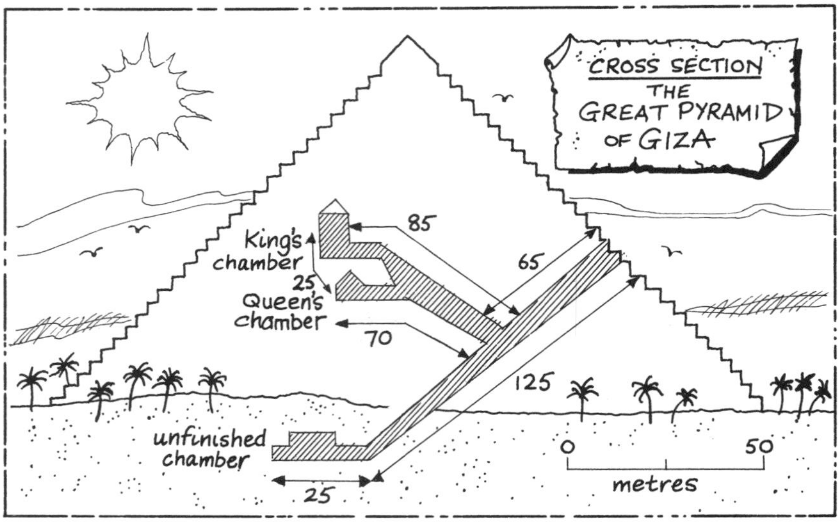

a) Pyramids were often robbed. How many metres would robbers have to travel to get to the king's chamber?

b) How many metres would robbers have to travel to get to the queen's chamber?

c) How many metres would robbers have to travel to get to the unfinished chamber?

3 When the robbers reached the turning to the royal chambers, how far were they from the unfinished chamber?

CHECK IT YOURSELF ✓

Your answer to 1 →				
Your answer to 2a →		1		
Your answer to 2b →		1		
Your answer to 2c →		1		
Your answer to 3 →			8	
Add them Result →	5			

Do you get **5520**?
If not, check your answers and try again.

Towering Triangles

1 The pyramids were built for the kings' bodies, between 4000 and 5000 years ago. Over a period of how many years were the pyramids built?

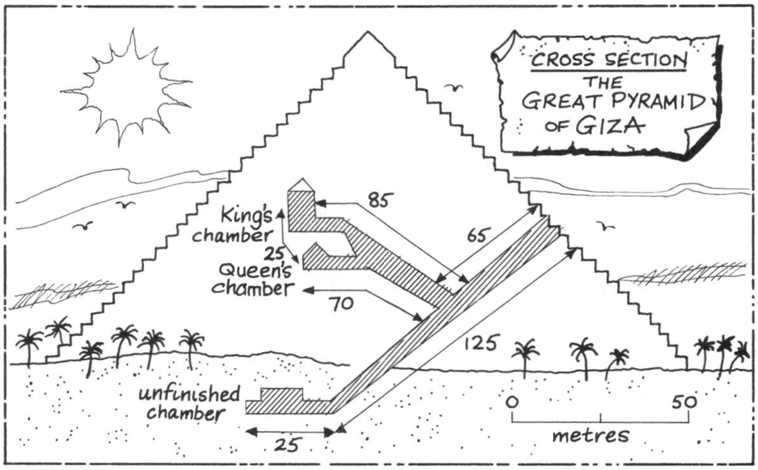

2 The Great Pyramid was the burial place of King Cheops. Look at the diagram of the passages inside it.

a) Pyramids were often robbed. How many metres would robbers have to travel to get to the king's chamber and back?

b) How many metres would robbers have to travel from the outside to get to the queen's chamber and back?

c) The robbers made **three** journeys to the unfinished chamber and back. How many metres did they travel altogether?

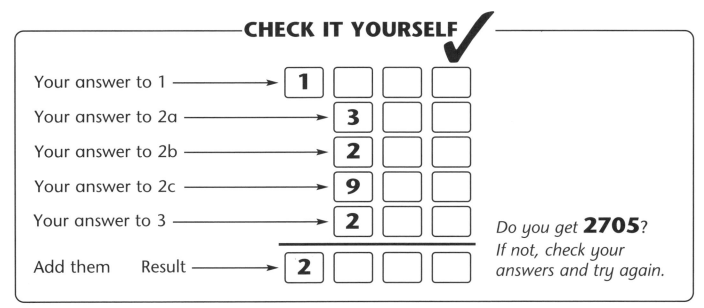

3 Grave-robbers reached the turn-off to the royal chambers. How many more metres was it altogether to the unfinished chamber and back to the outside?

CHECK IT YOURSELF ✓

Your answer to 1 →	1			
Your answer to 2a →		3		
Your answer to 2b →		2		
Your answer to 2c →		9		
Your answer to 3 →		2		
Add them Result →	2			

Do you get **2705**? *If not, check your answers and try again.*

Towering Triangles

1 The pyramids were built as enormous vaults for the kings' bodies. Sometimes thieves broke in. If it took three nights to rob a pyramid, working for nine hours a night, how many hours did robbers spend robbing 90 pyramids?

2 The Great Pyramid was the burial vault of King Cheops. Look at the diagram of the passages inside it.

a) How many metres did the robbers have to travel from the outside to fetch jewels from the king's chamber and back and then the queen's chamber and back?

b) A later gang of robbers went first to the king's chamber, then down 25 metres to the queen's, then on to the unfinished chamber before leaving. How many metres did they cover?

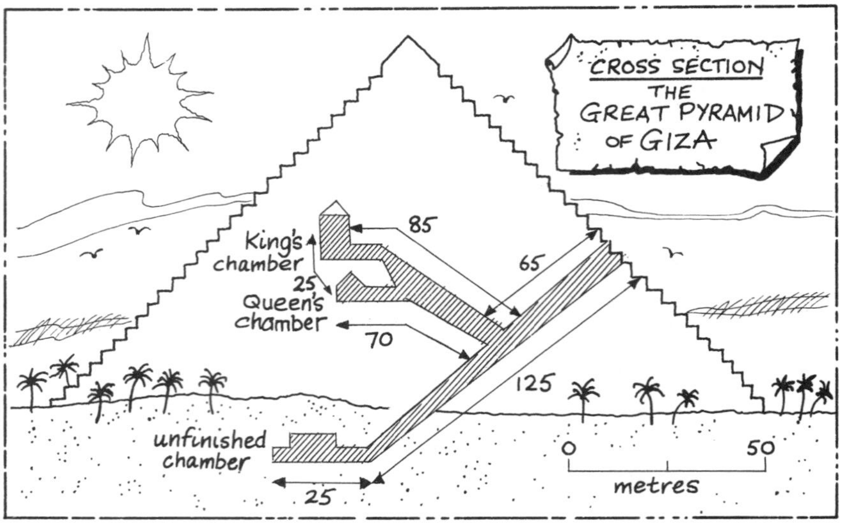

3 You are a grave-robber. Your boss has ordered you to steal the five golden thrones from the king's chamber. It took two of your men 12 minutes to steal the first throne. Your lookout signals that the king's guards will attack in 25 minutes. You have four men available. How many minutes will it take them to complete the job?

CHECK IT YOURSELF ✓

Your answer to 1 → □□□□

Your answer to 2a → □□□

Your answer to 2b → □□□

Your answer to 3 → □□

Add them Result → □□□□

Do you get **3504**? *If not, check your answers and try again.*

Nile Numbers

1 Egyptians used the Eye of Horus to write fractions, as in the picture. Write the fractions that are less than half.

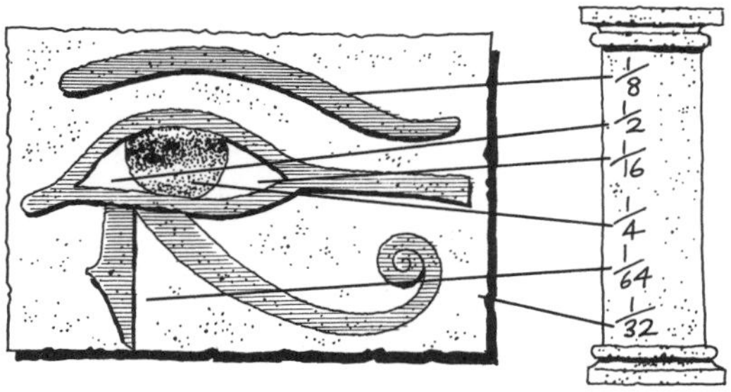

2 Another shorthand for fractions was a symbol meaning 'one part of': 

Underneath it, the fraction was given in tens and units, like this:

one ten   one unit

These jars have written on them the amount of litres they can hold. What fractions are they?

a   b   c   d

3 One jarful made a hekat. Sixteen hekats made a sackful. How many hekats were there in three sackfuls?

CHECK IT YOURSELF

Fill in the denominators from 1 →

Add them/Result →

Do you get **124**?
If not, check your answers and try again.

Fill in the denominators from 2 →

Add them/Result →

Your answer to 3 →

Add them/Result →

Do you get **72**?
If not, check your answers and try again.

Nile Numbers

1 Egyptians used the famous Eye of Horus as a way of writing fractions, as shown in the picture. How many sixteenths does the pupil represent?

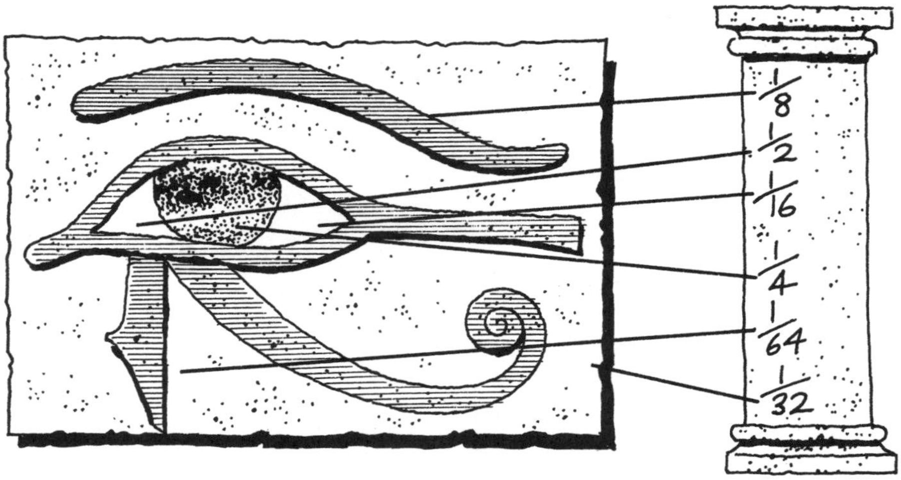

2 Ancient Egyptians wrote 100s, tens and units like this:

100 10 1

Do this Egyptian arithmetic:

a) ℓ∧II/II + ℓℓ∧∧I + ∧∧∧III

b) ℓ∧III − ∧∧∧I

c) ∧II ÷ /III

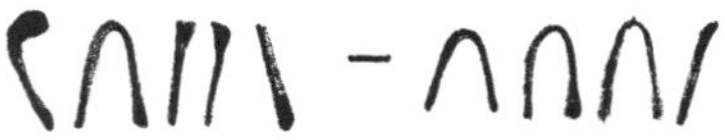

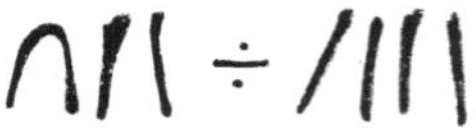

3 In ancient Egypt, a standard jar of liquid was 0.5 litres. How many litres would
a) two jars hold?
b) four jars hold?

CHECK IT YOURSELF ✔

The numerator from 1 ⟶ ☐

Your answer to 2a ⟶ ☐ ☐ ☐

Your answer to 2b ⟶ ☐ ☐

Your answer to 2c ⟶ ☐

Your answer to 3a ⟶ ☐

Your answer to 3b ⟶ ☐

Add them   Result ⟶ ☐ ☐ ☐

Do you get **460**?
If not, check your answers and try again.

Nile Numbers

1 Egyptians used the famous Eye of Horus as a way of writing fractions, as shown in the picture.

a) Express the left white of the eye and the pupil as decimals and add them.

b) Double the result.

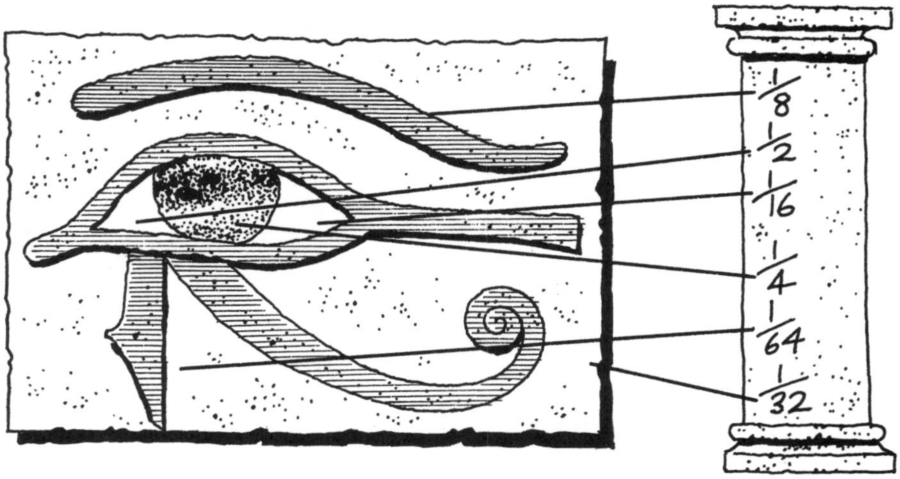

2 Ancient Egyptians wrote 100s, tens and units like this:

100 10 1

Do this Egyptian arithmetic:

a) 

b) 

c) 

3 In ancient Egypt, jars were used for storage. A one-hekat jar held 4.45 litres.

a) How many litres were contained in two hekats?

b) In four hekats?

c) Subtract the capacity of one hekat from your answer to b) to find out how many litres there are in three hekats.

CHECK IT YOURSELF ✓

Your answer to 1a → ☐.☐☐

Your answer to 1b → ☐.☐☐

Add them Result → ☐.☐☐

Do you get **2.25**? *If not, check your answers and try again.*

Your answer to 2a → ☐☐☐.0 0

Your answer to 2b → ☐☐☐☐.0 0

Your answer to 2c → ☐☐.0 0

Your answer to 3c → ☐☐.☐☐

Add them Result → ☐☐☐☐.☐☐

Do you get **2403.35**? *If not, check your answers and try again.*

Mummy Maths

1 Mummies are preserved bodies. After death, somebody removed the insides from the body. This took three days. Then the body was covered in salt for 40 days. Priests washed the body and stuffed it with linen. They wrapped the body in bandages and coated it with oils and resin. This took another 14 days. How many days did it all take?

2 Priests gave mummies artificial eyes that looked real. If they had to prepare 12 mummies, how many eyes did they need to order?

3 A mummy's internal organs were stored in four jars, each with the head of a god. For eight mummies, how many jars were needed?

4 One family tomb contained 103 mummies. Another contained 98. How many mummies were there altogether?

CHECK IT YOURSELF ✓

Your answer to 1 → ☐☐

Your answer to 2 → ☐☐

Your answer to 3 → ☐☐

Add them Result → ☐☐☐

Your answer to 4 → ☐☐☐

Add them Result → ☐☐☐

Do you get **314**? *If not, check your answers and try again.*

Mummy Maths

1 Mummies are preserved bodies. Ancient Egyptians believed that the spirits of the dead went into the underworld at night and they needed a body to return to. After death, somebody removed the insides from the body. This took three days. Then the body was covered in a kind of salt for 40 days. Priests washed the body and stuffed it with linen. They wrapped the body in bandages and coated it with oils and resin. This took another 14 days. How many days' work was involved in preparing **four** mummies?

2 Priests fitted mummies with artificial eyes that looked real. If they had to prepare 75 mummies, how many eyes did they need to order?

3 Priests used 324 square metres of linen to wrap a body. How many square metres of linen would they use on two bodies?

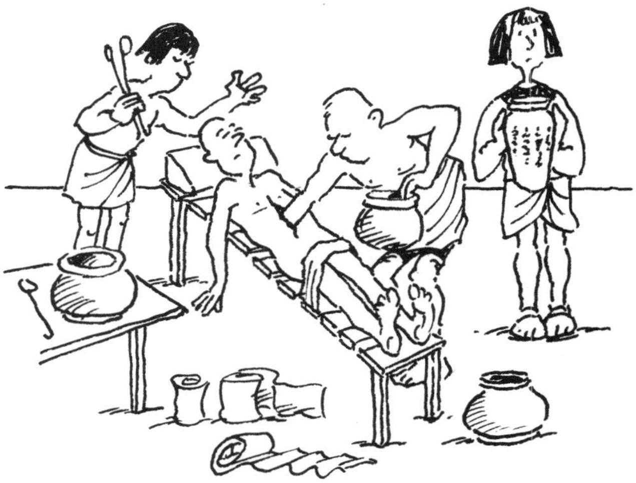

4 A mummy's internal organs were stored in four jars, each with the head of a god. For 28 mummies, how many jars were required?

5 The Osorkon family tomb contained 108 mummies. The Rahmen family tomb contained 234. How many more mummies did the Rahmen tomb contain than the Osorkon?

CHECK IT YOURSELF ✓

Your answer to 1 → ☐☐☐

Your answer to 2 → ☐☐☐

Your answer to 3 → ☐☐☐

Your answer to 4 → ☐☐☐

Your answer to 5 → ☐☐☐

Add them Result → ☐☐☐☐

Do you get **1264**? *If not, check your answers and try again.*

Mummy Maths

1 Mummies are preserved bodies. Ancient Egyptians believed that the spirits of the dead went into the underworld at night and they needed a recognisable body to return to. After death, the embalmer removed the insides from the body. This took three days. Then the body was covered in a kind of salt for 40 days, to dry it out. Priests washed the body and stuffed it with linen. They wrapped the body in bandages and coated it with oils and resin. This took another 14 days. How many days' work were involved in preparing 12 mummies?

2 Priests fitted mummies with artificial eyes that looked real. They also placed 20 precious stones in the linen. If they had to prepare 75 mummies, how many items did they need to obtain?

3 Priests used 324 square metres of linen to wrap a body. How many square metres of linen would they use on 36 bodies?

4 A mummy's internal organs were stored in four canopic jars, each with the head of a god. For 115 mummies, how many canopic jars were required?

5 In 1990 in the Valley of the Kings in Egypt, explorers found the biggest tomb ever discovered. It had contained the mummies of the 50 sons of Pharaoh Ramses III. The chambers were empty. All the mummies had been stolen. If it took the tomb raiders three hours to steal a mummy and strip its valuables, how many 12-hour nights did they have to spend emptying this tomb? (Round up to the nearest whole number.)

CHECK IT YOURSELF ✓

Your answer to 1 ⟶ ☐☐☐

Your answer to 2 ⟶ ☐☐☐☐

Your answer to 3 ⟶ ☐☐☐☐☐

Your answer to 4 ⟶ ☐☐☐

Your answer to 5 ⟶ ☐☐

Add them Result ⟶ ☐☐☐☐☐

Do you get **14 471***?*
If not, check your answers and try again

Cleopatra's Treasure

1 Queen Cleopatra VII invaded Armenia with the Roman general Mark Antony. She took home one thousand one hundred and twenty-two valuable gems. Write that number in figures.

2 There were 48 golden necklaces and 17 silver crowns in the treasure. Cleopatra boasted about them by rounding the numbers up to the nearest ten.

a) How many golden necklaces did she say she had?

b) How many silver crowns?

3 There were 13 pairs of golden slippers in the treasure. Cleopatra shared them with her three handmaidens. Of course, the queen had to have more than her servants.

a) What is the most she could give to each handmaiden?

b) How many pairs did she keep for herself?

CHECK IT YOURSELF ✓

Your answer to 1 → ☐ ☐ ☐ ☐

Your answer to 2a → ☐ ☐

Your answer to 2b → ☐ ☐

Your answer to 3a → ☐

Your answer to 3b → ☐

Add them/Result → 1 1 ☐ ☐

Do you get **1199**? *If not, check your answers and try again.*

Cleopatra's Treasure

1 Queen Cleopatra VII was the last Egyptian ruler. Together with the Roman general Mark Antony she invaded Armenia. Cleopatra took all the Armenian treasure back to her capital, Alexandria. In one box there were 135 diamonds, 129 sapphires and 102 emeralds. How many jewels did her treasurer list in the accounts?

2 The queen's treasurer listed some of the necklaces in the Armenian treasure:

Your Majesty,
The Armenian treasure contains 100 necklaces:
$\frac{1}{2}$ of them are made of gold
$\frac{1}{4}$ of them are made of silver
$\frac{1}{4}$ of them are made of electrum

a) How many necklaces were made of electrum?
b) How many were made of gold?

3 The Armenian treasure included 36 Persian cats. Cleopatra decided to share them out among nine favourite servants. How many cats did each servant receive?

4 The Armenian treasure contained the legendary Star of the East. It was a huge cut emerald, believed to be the biggest in the world. Using the diagram of the emerald, calculate its perimeter (shown by the bold lines).

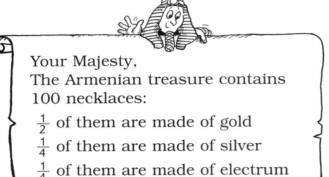

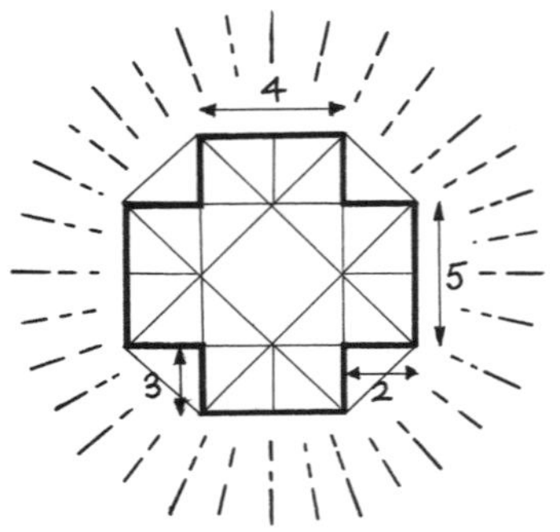

CHECK IT YOURSELF ✓

Your answer to 1 → ☐☐☐
Your answer to 2a → ☐☐
Your answer to 2b → ☐☐
Your answer to 3 → ☐
Your answer to 4 → ☐☐

Add them Result → ☐☐☐

Do you get **483**? *If not, check your answers and try again.*

Cleopatra's Treasure

1 Queen Cleopatra VII was the last Egyptian ruler. She tried to save her country from defeat by the Roman Empire. She made an alliance with the Roman general Mark Antony. Together they invaded Armenia. Cleopatra took all the Armenian treasure back to her capital, Alexandria. In the Armenian crown jewels there were 1235 diamonds and 3462 sapphires. Her treasurer listed them together in the royal accounts. How many jewels did he record?

2 The queen's treasurer loved to be exact. When she asked about the necklaces in the Armenian treasure, he wrote a list on papyrus and sent it to her. It said:

Your Majesty,
The Armenian treasure contains 200 necklaces:
50% of them are made of gold
25% of them are made of silver
25% of them are made of electrum

a) How many necklaces were made of electrum?
b) How many were made of gold?

3 Queen Cleopatra had nine favourite priests. They all loved cats. The Armenian treasure included 117 rare cats. She decided to share them out among the priests. How many rare cats did each priest receive?

4 The Armenian treasure contained the legendary Star of the East. It was a huge cut emerald, reputed to be the biggest in the world. Using the diagram of the emerald, calculate its perimeter (shown by the bold lines).

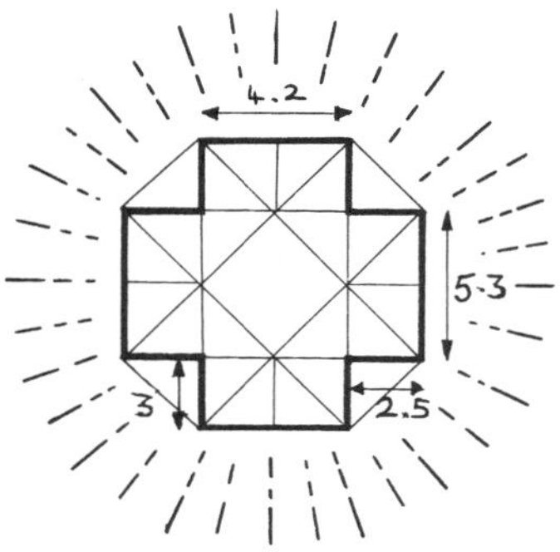

CHECK IT YOURSELF

Your answer to 1 → ☐☐☐☐
Your answer to 2a → ☐☐
Your answer to 2b → ☐☐☐
Your answer to 3 → ☐☐
Your answer to 4 → ☐☐

Add them Result → ☐☐☐☐

Do you get **4901**?
If not, check your answers and try again.

Battle Sums

1 Egypt's army was divided into four regiments. A regiment had 20 companies. The companies were divided into four units, with 50 men in each. How many men were there in a company?

2 Soldiers wore bands of leather around their chests and carried shields. Weapons included the javelin, axe, mace, sword, club and the bow-and-arrow.

a) If a soldier carried one weapon, how many pieces of equipment did he have in all?

b) How many different types of weapon were there altogether?

3 King Ramesses attacked the Hittites at Kadesh. There was a big battle and the Egyptians lost. The Hittites said Ramesses lost 1000 soldiers. Ramesses said he lost 500. What fraction of the Hittites' estimate was that?

4 The battle occurred in twelve eighty-five BC. Write that number in figures.

CHECK IT YOURSELF

Your answer to 1 → ☐☐☐

Your answer to 2a → ☐

Your answer to 2b → ☐

Add them/Result → ☐☐☐

Do you get **209**?

The numerator to 3 → ☐

The denominator to 3 → ☐

Your answer to 4 → ☐☐☐☐

Add them/Result → ☐☐☐☐

Do you get **1288**?

Battle Sums

1 Egypt's army was divided into four regiments. A regiment had 20 companies, each with its own standard. The companies were divided into four units, with 50 men in each. How many men were in a regiment?

2 The red standard company had the correct number of soldiers. The green standard company was six soldiers short. The yellow standard company had five men extra. How many soldiers altogether could the three companies put into battle?

3 At the battle of Kadesh, King Ramesses II attacked the capital of the Hittite people. He thought the Hittite king was away, but he was wrong. There was a big battle and the Egyptians were driven back. The Hittites said Ramesses had 330 soldiers killed and 470 injured.

a) How many casualties was that?

b) Ramesses said he had 60 men killed and 340 injured. How many casualties did he claim?

c) What fraction of the Hittites' estimate did Ramesses say he had lost?

4 The battle of Kadesh occurred in 1285BC. It started at 9am and lasted until 3pm.

a) How many hours is that?

b) How many minutes is that?

CHECK IT YOURSELF

Your answer to 1 → ☐☐☐☐

Your answer to 2 → ☐☐☐

Your answer to 3a → ☐☐☐

Your answer to 3b → ☐☐☐

The denominator to 3c → ☐

Your answer to 4a → ☐

Your answer to 4b → ☐☐☐

Add them Result → ☐☐☐☐

Do you get **6167**?
If not, check your answers and try again.

Battle Sums

1 The Egyptian army was divided into four regiments, each named after a god. A regiment had 20 companies. The companies were divided into four units, with 50 men in each. How many men were in the army?

2 Soldiers wore bands of leather around their chests and carried shields. Weapons included the javelin, axe, mace, sword, club and the bow-and-arrow. The soldiers in a company had weapons distributed in these proportions:

a) Javelins: 3 in 10 **b)** Maces: 1 in 4
c) Swords: 1 in 4 **d)** Clubs: 1 in 5

How many men carried each weapon?

3 King Ramesses II attacked the Hittites at the battle of Kadesh. The Egyptians were driven back. Some Hittites said Ramesses had 2200 soldiers killed and 1000 injured.

a) How many casualties was that?
b) Ramesses said he had 20 men killed and 300 injured. How many casualties did he claim?
c) What fraction of the Hittites' estimate did Ramesses say he had lost?

4 The battle of Kadesh occurred in 1285BC. The Second World War broke out in AD1939.

a) How many years apart were they?
b) How many centuries is that? (Round your answer to the nearest century.)

CHECK IT YOURSELF

Your answer to 1 →	☐☐☐☐☐
Your answer to 2a →	☐☐
Your answer to 2b →	☐☐
Your answer to 2c →	☐☐
Your answer to 2d →	☐☐
Your answer to 3a →	☐☐☐☐
Your answer to 3b →	☐☐☐
The denominator to 3c →	☐☐
Your answer to 4a →	☐☐☐☐
Your answer to 4b →	☐☐
Add them Result →	☐☐☐☐☐

Do you get **22 986**?
If not, check your answers and try again.

Kingdom Calculations

1 The great pyramid of Cheops is three hundred and twenty-five cubits wide. Write that width in figures.

2 Ancient Egyptians measured by hand. A hand was four digits (fingers) wide. Seven hands side by side made a cubit. A cubit was also the distance from elbow to fingertips.

a) How many digits could one person measure?

b) How many cubits?

3 How many hands was half a cubit?

4 An architect had to make a footpath of stones one cubit wide. The path went 150 cubits north and 75 west. How many stones did he need?

5 Pharaoh's ship had a mast 17 cubits high. He told his architect to build a new ship with a mast twice as high. How high was his new mast?

CHECK IT YOURSELF ✓

Your answer to 1 → ☐ ☐ ☐

Your answer to 2a → ☐

Your answer to 2b → ☐

Round up your answer to 3 and fill in → ☐

Add them Result → **3** ☐ ☐

Do you get **339**?
If not, check your answers and try again.

Your answer to 4 → ☐ ☐ ☐

Your answer to 5 → ☐ ☐

Add them Result → **2** ☐ ☐

Do you get **259**?
If not, check your answers and try again.

Kingdom Calculations

1 Ancient Egyptians measured by hand. A hand was four digits (fingers) wide. Seven hands side by side made a cubit. A cubit was also the distance from elbow to fingertips. The temple at Karnak is 96 cubits wide. How many people would be needed to measure half-way across it?

2 A stonemason needed a paving stone 84 digits wide. How many cubits was that?

4 The pharaoh's architect had to order stones for a wall near the pyramid. The wall was 98 cubits long and three cubits high. The stones were one cubit square. How many did he order?

5 Pharaoh's ship had a mast nine cubits high. He told his architect to build a new ship with a mast twice as high. The architect used a tree trunk 26 cubits long. He used the left-over wood to build himself a mast. How high was his mast?

3 Osorkon's ornamental pond was 20 cubits long by eight cubits wide. How many one cubit-square paving stones did he need to line the edge of it? Don't forget the corners!

CHECK IT YOURSELF ✓

Your answer to 1 → ☐☐

Your answer to 2 → ☐

Your answer to 3 → ☐☐

Your answer to 4 → ☐☐☐

Your answer to 5 → ☐

Add them   Result → ☐☐☐

Do you get **389**? *If not, check your answers and try again.*

Kingdom Calculations

1 For repairs to the temple at Karnak the pharaoh's architect required 2836 stones. In case there were breakages, he always rounded his order up to the next thousand. How many did he order?

2 Ancient Egyptians measured by hand. A hand was four digits (fingers) wide. Seven hands side by side made a cubit. A cubit was also the distance from elbow to fingertips. Seth the stonemason needed a stone 336 digits long. How many cubits was that?

3 Osorkon built a new ornamental pond for his wife. It was 220 cubits long by 120 cubits wide. When she saw it, she was disappointed. "My best friend's pond is 50 per cent longer and 30 per cent wider than this," she said.

a) What was the length of the pool after Osorkon had enlarged it to match her friend's?

b) What was the width?

4 The pharaoh's architect had to order stones for a wall near the pyramid. The wall was nine cubits long and 3.5 cubits high. The stones were one cubit square. How many did he order? (Round up to the nearest whole number.)

5 The young pharaoh visited the pyramid of his ancestor. "How high is it?" he asked his architect. "450 cubits, your majesty," the architect replied. The pharaoh visited the pyramid of his grandfather. The architect told him its height: 575 cubits. The pharaoh visited his father's pyramid. "How high is it?" he asked. "623 cubits," the architect replied. "My pyramid will be as high as all three put together," he said. How high did the architect build it?

CHECK IT YOURSELF ✓

Your answer to 1 → ☐☐☐☐

Your answer to 2 → ☐☐

Your answer to 3a → ☐☐☐

Your answer to 3b → ☐☐☐

Your answer to 4 → ☐☐

Your answer to 5 → ☐☐☐☐

Add them Result → ☐☐☐☐

Do you get ***5178****?*
If not, check your answers and try again.

Remarkable Ramesses

1 King Ramesses II built a temple at Abu-Simbel. Outside it was a statue of the hawk god and four statues of Ramesses. Inside there were three statues of gods and one of Ramesses. How many statues is that?

2 Here is a plan of the Abu-Simbel temple. Use it to work out the location of each statue. The first is done for you.

X = Amun-Re = B8
Y = Ptah
K = Re-Harakhti
M = Ramesses the god
O = Seated Ramesses
P = Seated Ramesses

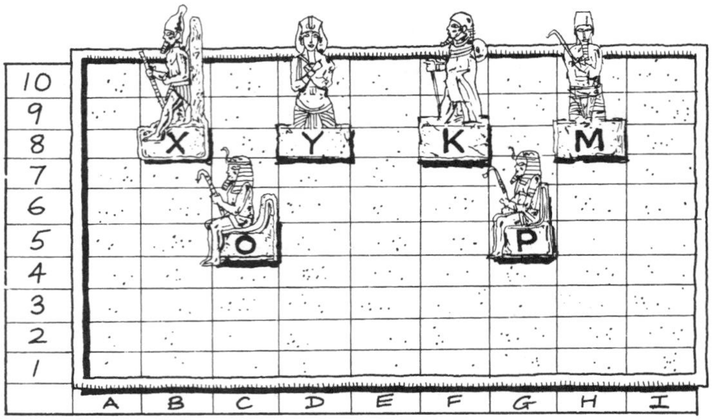

3 King Ramesses had 108 wives and 100 children. How many wives and children was that altogether?

4 King Ramesses was 90 years old when he died. For 60 years his reign was peaceful. What fraction of his life was that?

CHECK IT YOURSELF ✓

Your answer to 1 → ☐

Ptah's square from 2 → **D** ☐

Your answer to 3 → ☐ ☐ ☐

The numerator from 4 → ☐

The denominator from 4 → ☐

Add them Result → ☐ ☐ ☐

Do you get **230**? *If not, check your answer and try again.*

Remarkable Ramesses

1 King Ramesses II built a temple at Abu-Simbel, with many colossal statues. A statue of the hawk god faces the sunrise. Four statues of King Ramesses also face the sun. Inside are statues of the gods Amun-Re, Ptah, Re-Harakhti and Ramesses himself. What fraction of these statues are of King Ramesses?

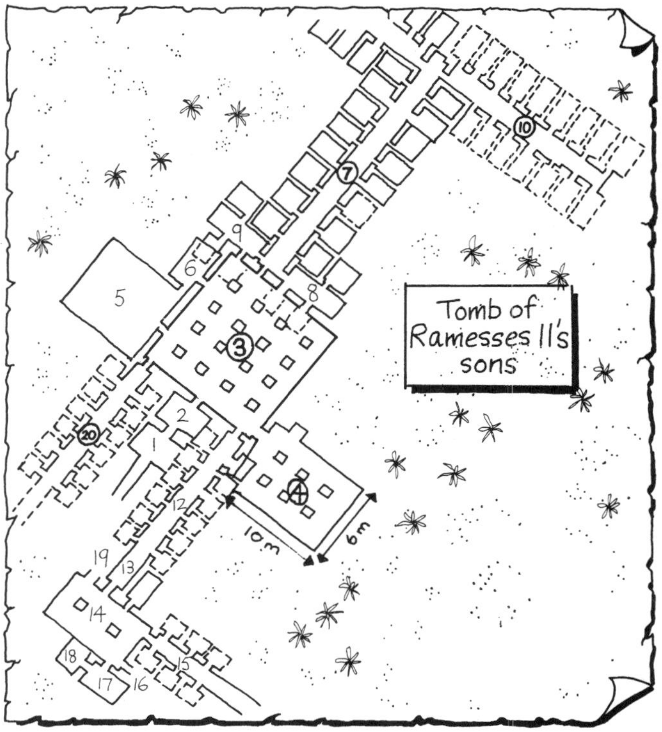

2 This is a plan of KV5, the tomb of about 50 sons of Ramesses the Great.

a) What is the area of chamber 4?

b) How many pillars are there in chamber 3?

c) How many small identical chambers are there in area 20?

d) Add c to the number of chambers drawn with dotted lines in area 10.

e) How many small chambers open directly off passage 7?

CHECK IT YOURSELF ✓

The numerator from 1 → ☐

The denominator from 1 → ☐

Your answer to 2a → ☐☐

Your answer to 2b → ☐☐

Your answer to 2c → ☐☐

Your answer to 2d → ☐☐

Your answer to 2e → ☐☐

Add them Result → ☐☐☐

Do you get **146**? *If not, check your answers and try again.*

Remarkable Ramesses

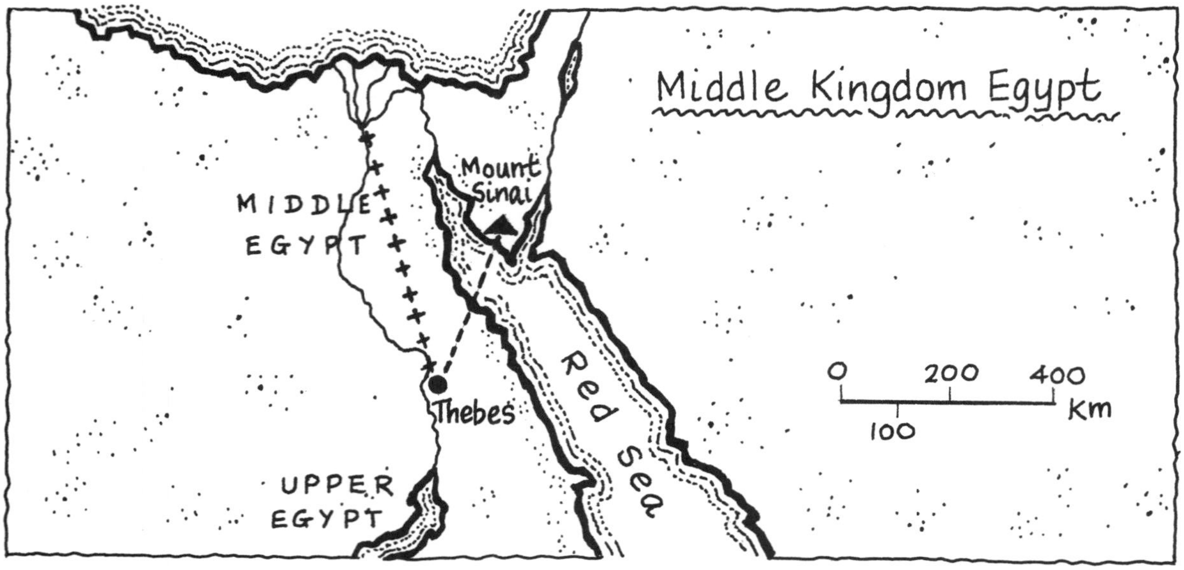

Here is a map of the Middle Kingdom.

1 The Bible says the Israelites were slaves in Egypt. Their leader, Moses, led them to freedom. Ramesses' army gave chase. When the Israelites reached the Red Sea, the water parted to let them through, then closed over the army. The Israelites settled at Mount Sinai.

a) How many kilometres did the Israelites travel from Thebes to Mount Sinai (to the nearest 100 km)?
b) If they fled at a rate of nine kilometres per day, how long did the journey take them? (Round to the nearest unit.)
c) What width (to the nearest 100 km) was the Red Sea where the Israelites crossed it?
d) Another of Ramesses' armies had to march from Thebes to the mouth of the Nile and back twice that year. The Nile was 900 kilometres away. How many kilometres did they march?

CHECK IT YOURSELF ✓

Your answer to a → ☐☐☐
Your answer to b → ☐☐
Add them Result → ☐☐☐
Your answer to c → ☐☐☐
Subtract it Result → ☐☐☐
Your answer to d → ☐☐☐☐
Add them Result → ☐☐☐☐

Do you get **3833**? *If not, check your answers and try again.*

Theban Games

1 We know from tomb paintings that people in ancient Egypt loved playing board games. Here is the game of Senet. How many pieces are there?

2 If two people played Senet and divided the pieces between them, how many would each player have?

3 This is the layout of the Senet board. How many rectangles are there?

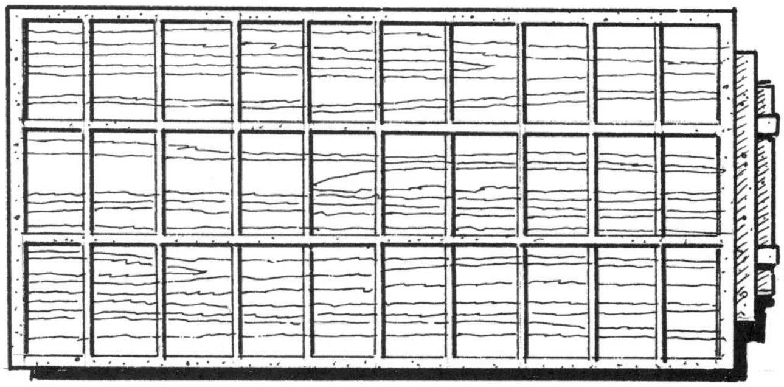

4 How many rectangles are there in each row?

5 If one player has three pieces on one row, two on another and two on another, how many pieces does the player have on the board?

CHECK IT YOURSELF ✓

Your answer to 1 → ☐☐

Your answer to 2 → ☐

Your answer to 3 → ☐☐

Your answer to 4 → ☐☐

Your answer to 5 → ☐

Add them Result → ☐☐

Do you get **68**?
If not, check your answers and try again.

Theban Games

1 We know from tomb paintings that people in ancient Egypt loved playing board games. Here is the game of Senet. Each player had 0.5 of the total number of pieces. How many pieces did each player have?

2 This is the layout of the Senet board. What fraction of the board is 20 rectangles?

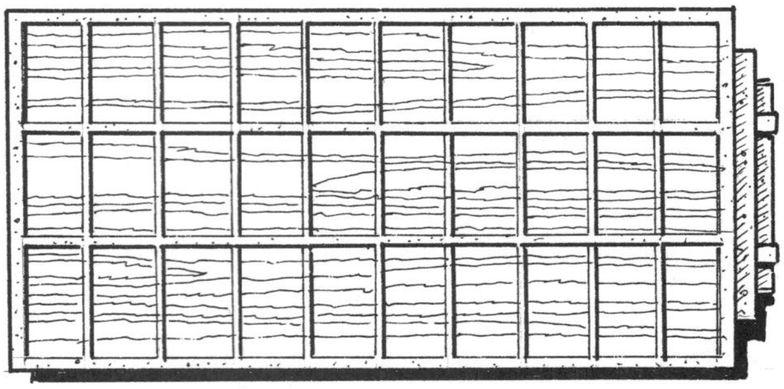

3 The purpose of the game is to get all your pieces off the board before your opponent, following an S in the direction of the arrows. Here is a game where each player has only one piece left.

a) If it took 22 moves to get each of your pieces off the board, how many moves would you make altogether?

b) If your opponent needed the same number, how many moves would you both play altogether?

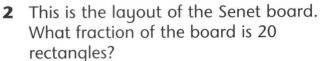

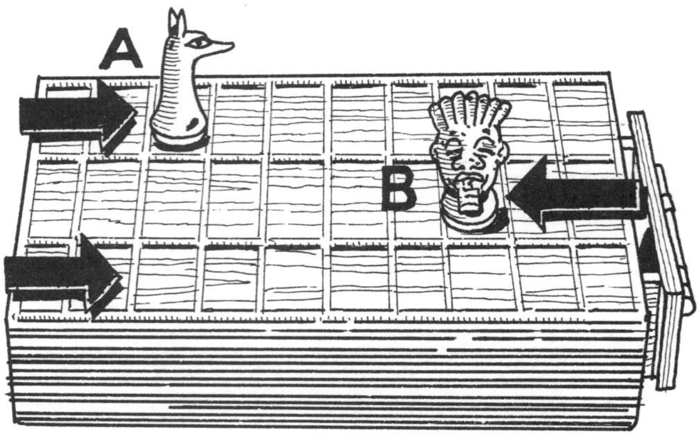

4 You make the pieces for Senet games. Pharoah orders eight sets of pieces from you. You can make four pieces per hour and you work a ten-hour day. How many days will the job take, to the nearest day?

CHECK IT YOURSELF

Your answer to 1 → ☐

Your answer to 2 → ☐ (fraction)

Your answer to 3b → ☐ ☐ ☐

Your answer to 4 → ☐

Add them Result → ☐ ☐ ☐ ☐

Do you get **$318\frac{2}{3}$**? *If not, check your answers and try again.*

Theban Games

1 We know from tomb paintings that people in ancient Egypt loved playing board games. Here is the game of Senet. Each player shared the total number of pieces in a ratio of 50 to 50. How many pieces did each player have?

2 This is the layout of the Senet board. What percentage of the board is ten rectangles?

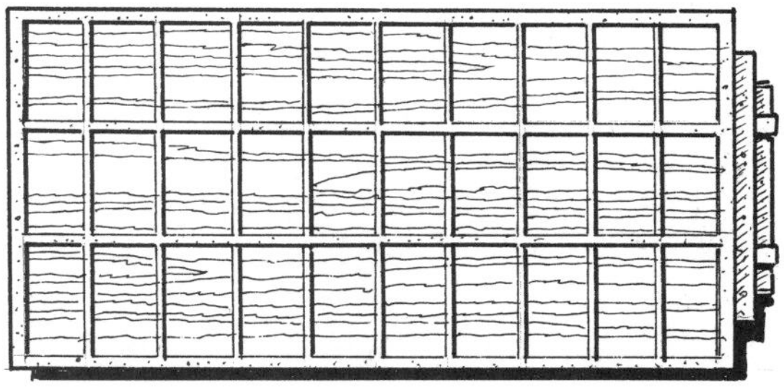

3 Pieces are placed alternately along the first 14 rectangles. The purpose of the game is to get all your pieces off the board before your opponent, following an S in the direction of the arrows. If a piece is blocked, it returns to the start. Here is a game where each player has only one piece left.

a) If it took 124 moves to get each of your pieces off the board, how many moves would you have to make altogether?

b) If your opponent needed the same number, how many moves would you both play altogether?

4 You are an artist, making ornate pieces for expensive Senet games. The pharaoh commands you to produce 36 sets of pieces for his next feast day. You are able to make them at a rate of four pieces per hour. You work a ten-hour day. How many days will the job take, to the nearest day?

CHECK IT YOURSELF ✓

Your answer to 1 →				☐	. 0
Your answer to 2 →			☐	☐	. ☐
Your answer to 3a →		☐	☐	☐	. 0
Your answer to 3b →	☐	☐	☐	☐	. 0
Add them Result →	☐	☐	☐	☐	. ☐
Your answer to 4 →			☐	☐	. 0
Subtract it Result →	☐	☐	☐	☐	. ☐

Do you get **2631.3**? *If not, check your answers and try again.*

King Tut

1 Tutankhamun became pharaoh at the age of eight, when the great pyramid was one thousand two hundred and fifty years old. Write that number in figures.

2 King Tut was only 18 when he died. For how many years did he reign?

3 King Tut was buried with a hoard of treasure. Robbers broke in and stole some of it. The chart shows how much they took.

a) What fraction of the treasure was stolen?

b) Out of every ten treasures, how many were stolen?

c) Out of every ten, how many remained?

4 It took archaeologists five years to find the tomb, eight to clear it and ten to record its treasures. How many years is that?

CHECK IT YOURSELF ✓

Your answer to 1 → ☐ ☐ ☐ ☐

Subtract 1000 → **1 0 0 0**

Result → ☐ ☐ ☐

Do you get **250**? *If not, check and try again.*

The numerator to 3a → ☐

The denominator to 3a → ☐ ☐

Add them Result → ☐ ☐

Do you get **16**? *If not, check and try again.*

Your answer to 2 → ☐ ☐

Your answer to 3b → ☐

Your answer to 3c → ☐

Your answer to 4 → ☐ ☐

Add them Result → ☐ ☐

Do you get **43**? *If not, check and try again.*

King Tut

1 Tutankhamun took the throne at the age of eight, when the great pyramid was already one thousand two hundred and fifty years old. Split the age of the great pyramid into thousands, hundreds, tens and units and write each separately.

2 When King Tut died he was only 18. If he had lived for 70 years, for how many years would he have reigned?

3 Like all pharaohs, King Tut was buried with a big hoard of treasure. Soon after the burial, grave-robbers broke into the underground chambers. The proportion of the treasure they stole is shown here.

a) What fraction of the treasure was stolen?

b) What fraction remained?

c) Add the two fractions together.

4 Howard Carter, an archaeologist, spent five years searching for King Tut's tomb before finding it. It took eight years to clear the tomb and ten to record all the treasures.

a) For how many months was he clearing King Tut's tomb?

b) For how many months was he recording the treasures?

CHECK IT YOURSELF ✓

Fill in the tens from 1 → ☐☐

Your answer to 2 → ☐☐

Your answer to 3c → ☐

Your answer to 4b → ☐☐☐

Add them Result → ☐☐☐

Do you get **233**? *If not, check your answers and try again.*

King Tut

1 King Tutankhamun's tomb was discovered in the year AD1922. King Tut died in 1327BC. How many years had passed between the king's death and the discovery of his tomb?

2 King Tut was probably murdered by a blow to the head from his guardian. He took the throne at the age of eight. When he died he was only 18.

a) How many years did he reign?

b) The warrior king Ramses III reigned from 1184BC to 1154BC. By what ratio does King Ramses' reign exceed King Tut's?

3 Like all pharaohs, King Tut was buried with a big hoard of treasure. One of the items was a baby's shawl made of linen so fine that experts estimate it took nine months to make. Egyptian workers had a nine-day week (resting every tenth day) and an 11-hour working day. How many hours' work did the shawl take? (Count a month as 30 days.)

PHARAOH'S FASCINATING FACT
King Tut was buried in three coffins, one inside the other. The smallest measured 1.88 metres and was made of gold!

4 An archaeologist called Howard Carter discovered King Tut's tomb in 1922. He had noticed a mention of Tutankhamun in a document 30 years earlier. He started working full-time on his search for the tomb five years before he found it. He spent eight years carefully clearing the tomb and another ten years writing up the 5000 remaining treasures. How many days did he spend working full-time on King Tut? (Assume he worked 280 days of each year.)

CHECK IT YOURSELF ✓

Your answer to 1 → ☐☐☐☐

Your answer to 3 → ☐☐☐☐

Subtract it Result → ☐☐☐

Your answer to 4 → ☐☐☐☐

The first part of your answer to 2b → ☐

Add them Result → ☐☐☐☐

Do you get ***7019****?*
If not, check your answers and try again.

Calendar Counting

1 The Egyptians had three calendars. The first was based on the stars, the second on the moon, the third on divisions of the year. A year had three hundred and sixty-five days. Write out that number in figures.

2 The year was divided as follows:
1 year = 3 seasons
1 season = 4 months
1 month = 3 weeks
1 week = 10 days
This only makes 360 days, which are not enough for a whole year. How many days did the Egyptians have to add on at the end to make a full year?

3 If there were three seasons of four months each, how many months were there in an ancient Egyptian year?

4 How many whole weeks were there in the Egyptian year?

CHECK IT YOURSELF

Your answer to 1 → ☐ ☐ ☐

Your answer to 2 → ☐

Your answer to 3 → ☐ ☐

Your answer to 4 → ☐ ☐

Add them Result → ☐ ☐ ☐

Do you get ***418****?*
If not, check your answers and try again.

Calendar Counting

1 The Egyptians had three calendars. The first was based on the stars, the second on the moon, the third on divisions of the year. The year was divided as follows:
1 year = 3 seasons 1 season = 4 months 1 month = 3 weeks 1 week = 10 days
a) How many days were there in this calendar?
b) How many had to be added at the end of each year in order to make a full year (the same as today's)?

2 The three Egyptian seasons were based on the cycle of the river Nile. In the first season, it flooded all the farms to a depth of a few centimetres, fertilising the soil. During this time Egyptian farmers did other work, such as building pyramids. In the second season of winter came ploughing and planting crops. The third season of summer was the harvest. How many days were there in each season?

3 A day was divided into 24 hours. How many hours had to be added at the end of each year?

4 The main feature of the Egyptians' star calendar was the movement of the star Sirius. Priests observed that it went below the horizon at the same time every year. When it reappeared 70 days later, the Nile started to rise. Work out for how many months Sirius was out of sight. Express the remainder as a fraction of a month.

CHECK IT YOURSELF ✓

Your answer to 1a → ☐ ☐ ☐

Your answer to 1b → ☐

Your answer to 2 → ☐ ☐ ☐

Your answer to 3 → ☐ ☐ ☐

The denominator of the remainder to 4 → ☐

Add them Result → ☐ ☐ ☐

Do you get **608**? *If not, check your answers and try again.*

Calendar Counting

1 The Egyptians had three calendars. The first was based on the stars, the second on the moon, the third on divisions of the year. The year was divided as follows:
1 year = 3 seasons 1 season = 4 months 1 month = 3 weeks 1 week = 10 days
extra days added at the end = 5
How many days does this make?

2 King Tut ruled for nine whole years.
How many days are there in nine years?

3 After many years, the priests realised their calendar had slipped behind. They were not adding an extra day every four years for the leap year. How many days would they lose each century?

4 The Egyptian seasons were based on the cycle of the river Nile. In the first season, it flooded all the farms to a depth of a few centimetres, fertilising the soil. During this time Egyptian farmers did other work, such as building pyramids. In the second season of winter came ploughing and planting crops. The third season of summer was the harvest.

a) How many days did farmers spend doing farm work?

b) For what percentage of the seasons (rounded to the nearest one) did they do other things?

CHECK IT YOURSELF

Your answer to 1 → ☐☐☐

Your answer to 2 → ☐☐☐☐

Your answer to 3 → ☐☐

Your answer to 4a → ☐☐☐

Your answer to 4b → ☐☐

Add them Result → ☐☐☐☐

Do you get **3948**? *If not, check your answers and try again.*

Answers

Potty Pyramids

Level 1
1 80
2 4
3 10 + 20 + 30 + 40 = 100

Level 2
1 0.9
2a 90
2b 90 + 90 + 90 + 90 = 360
3a 80
3b 10
3c 0

Level 3
1 80 x 35 = 2800 ÷ 10 = 280
2a 200 x 9 = 1800 ÷ 10 = 180
2b 4 x 1800 = 7200
3 NE = 28 SE = 98 SW = 95 NW = 25
28 + 98 + 95 + 25 = 246

Amazing Amenhotep

Level 1
1 1000
2 21 + 21 + 21 = 63
3 $\frac{1}{2}$ km
4 317 – 28 = 289

Level 2
1a 1390 – 1352 = 38
1b Year 9 = 1382BC
2 21 ÷ 3 = 7
3 7 x 30 = 210
630 ÷ 210 = 3

Level 3
1a 15 ÷ 5 = 3
1.5 ÷ 3 = 0.5 km
1b 100 x $\frac{1}{3}$ = 33$\frac{1}{3}$ = 33
2a 317 + 317 + 317 = 951
2b 12 x 3 = 36
951 – 36 = 915
3a 1391 – 1380 = 9 + 1 = 10 years
15 x 10 = 150
3b 150 x 0.2 = 30

Nefertiti Tot-Up

Level 1
1 1000
2 $1 - \frac{3}{4} = \frac{1}{4}$
1000 ÷ 4 = 250
3 9
4 42 + 53 = 95

Level 2
1 231 + 122 + 396 = 749
2 1 – 0.75 = 0.25
3 85 x 9 = 765
4 22 + 32 = 54 ÷ 9 = 6

Level 3
1 983 + 1245 + 876 = 3104
2 100 – 32 = 68
3 185 x 9 = 1665
4 86 + 132 = 218 ÷ 9 = 24.2 = 24

Answers

Towering Triangles

Level 1

1 5000
2a 65 + 85 = 150
2b 65 + 70 = 135
2c 125 + 25 = 150
3 125 + 25 = 150 – 65 = 85

Level 2

1 5000 – 4000 = 1000
2a 65 + 85 = 150 x 2 = 300
2b 65 + 70 = 135 x 2 = 270
2c 125 + 25 = 150 x 2 = 300 x 3 = 900
3 125 + 25 = 150 – 65 = 85 (to the unfinished chamber) 85 + 25 + 125 = 235

Level 3

1 3 x 9 = 27 x 90 = 2430
2a 65 + 85 = 150 x 2 = 300
65 + 70 = 135 x 2 = 270 + 300 = 570
2b 65 + 85 + 25 + 70 + (125 + 25 – 65 = 85) + 25 + 125 = 480
3 12 x 4 = 48 ÷ 2 = 24

Nile Numbers

Level 1

1 $\frac{1}{8}$ $\frac{1}{16}$ $\frac{1}{4}$ $\frac{1}{64}$ $\frac{1}{32}$
2a $\frac{1}{10}$
2b $\frac{1}{8}$
2c $\frac{1}{4}$
2d $\frac{1}{2}$
3 16 + 16 + 16 = 48

Level 2

1 $\frac{1}{4} = \frac{4}{16}$
2a 114 + 221 + 33 = 368
2b 113 – 31 = 82
2c 12 ÷ 4 = 3
3a 0.5 + 0.5 = $\frac{1}{2} + \frac{1}{2}$ = 1
3b 1 + 1 = 2

Level 3

1a $\frac{1}{4} + \frac{1}{2}$ = 0.25 + 0.5 = 0.75
1b 0.75 + 0.75 = 1.5
2a 122 x 8 = 976
2b 33 x 42 = 1386
2c 112 ÷ 4 = 28
3a 4.45 + 4.45 = 8.9
3b 8.9 + 8.9 = 17.8
3c 17.8 – 4.45 = 13.35

Mummy Maths

Level 1

1 3 + 40 + 14 = 57
2 2 x 12 = 24
3 8 x 4 = 32
4 103 + 98 = 201

Level 2

1 3 + 40 + 14 = 57 x 4 = 228
2 2 x 75 = 150
3 324 + 324 = 648
4 28 x 4 = 112
5 234 – 108 = 126

Level 3

1 3 + 40 + 14 = 57 x 12 = 684
2 2 + 20 = 22 x 75 = 1650
3 324 x 36 = 11 664
4 4 x 115 = 460
5 3 x 50 = 150 ÷ 12 = 12.5 = 13

Answers

Cleopatra's Treasure

Level 1

1 1122
2a 50
2b 20
3a 13 ÷ 4 = 3 (remainder 1)
3b 13 ÷ 4 = 3 + 1 = 4

Level 2

1 135 + 129 + 102 = 366
2a 100 ÷ 4 = 25
2b 100 ÷ 2 = 50
3 36 ÷ 9 = 4
4 5 x 2 = 10
4 x 2 = 8
3 x 4 = 12
2 x 4 = 8
10 + 8 + 12 + 8 = 38

Level 3

1 1235 + 3462 = 4697
2a 200 x 25% = 50
2b 200 x 50% = 100
3 117 ÷ 9 = 13
4 5.3 x 2 = 10.6
4.2 x 2 = 8.4
2.5 x 4 = 10
3 x 4 = 12
10.6 + 8.4 + 10 + 12 = 41

Battle Sums

Level 1

1 50 + 50 + 50 + 50 = 200
2a leather + shield + weapon = 3
2b 6
3 $\frac{500}{1000} = \frac{1}{2}$
4 1285

Level 2

1 4 x 50 = 200 x 20 = 4000
2 200 + (200 – 6 = 194)
+ (200 + 5 = 205) = 599
3a 330 + 470 = 800
3b 60 + 340 = 400
3c $\frac{400}{800} = \frac{1}{2}$
4a 15 – 9 = 6
4b 6 x 60 = 360

Level 3

1 4 x 50 = 200 x 20 = 4000 x 4 = 16 000
2a 200 x 3 = 600 ÷ 10 = 60
2b 200 ÷ 4 = 50
2c 200 ÷ 4 = 50
2d 200 ÷ 5 = 40
3a 2200 + 1000 = 3200
3b 20 + 300 = 320
3c 3200 ÷ 320 = 10 = $\frac{1}{10}$
4a 1285 + 1939 = 3224
4b 3224 ÷ 100 = 32.24 = 32

Answers

Kingdom Calculations

Level 1

1 325
2a 2 x 4 = 8
2b 2 x 1 = 2
3 7 ÷ 2 = $3\frac{1}{2}$
4 150 + 75 = 225
5 17 + 17 = 34

Level 2

1 96 ÷ 2 = 48 ÷ 2 = 24
2 84 ÷ 4 = 21 ÷ 7 = 3
3 20 x 2 = 40
8 x 2 = 16
40 + 16 + 4 = 60
4 98 x 3 = 294
5 9 x 2 = 18
26 – 18 = 8

Level 3

1 3000
2 336 ÷ 4 = 84 ÷ 7 = 12
3a 220 + (50% x 220 = 110) = 330
3b 120 + (30% x 120 = 36) = 156
4 9 x 3.5 = 31.5 = 32
5 450 + 575 + 623 = 1648

Remarkable Ramesses

Level 1

1 1 + 4 + 1 + 1 + 1 + 1 = 9
2 X = B8 Y = D8 K = F8
M = H8 O = C5 P = G5
3 108 + 100 = 208
4 $\frac{60}{90} = \frac{6}{9} = \frac{2}{3}$

Level 2

1 $\frac{5}{9}$
2a 10 x 6 = 60 sq m
2b 4 x 4 =16
2c 6 x 2 = 12
2d 16 + 12 = 28
2e 8 x 2 = 16

Level 3

1a 300
1b 300 ÷ 9 = 33.3 = 33
1c 100 km
1d 900 x 4 = 3600

Answers

Theban Games

Level 1

1 14
2 14 ÷ 2 = 7
3 10 x 3 = 30
4 10
5 3 + 2 + 2 = 7

Level 2

1 14 ÷ 2 = 7
2 $\frac{2}{3}$
3a 7 x 22 = 154
3b 154 x 2 = 308
4 4 x 10 = 40 (pieces per day)
8 x 14 (pieces per set) = 112
(number of pieces needed)
112 ÷ 40 = 2.8 = 3

Level 3

1 14 ÷ 2 = 7
2 33.3
3a 7 x 124 = 868
3b 868 + 868 = 1736
4 4 x 10 = 40 (pieces per day)
36 x 14 (pieces per set) = 504
(number of pieces needed)
504 ÷ 40 = 12.6 = 13

King Tut

Level 1

1 1250
2 18 – 8 = 10
3a $\frac{6}{10}$
3b 6
3c 10 – 6 = 4
4 5 + 8 + 10 = 23

Level 2

1 1000 200 50 0
2 70 – 8 = 62
3a $\frac{6}{10}$
3b $\frac{4}{10}$
3c $\frac{6}{10} + \frac{4}{10} = 1$
4a 12 x 8 = 96
4b 12 x 10 = 120

Level 3

1 1327 + 1922 = 3249
2a 18 – 8 = 10 (Tut's reign)
2b 1184 – 1154 = 30 (Ramses' reign)
30 to 10 or 3 to 1
3 9 x 3 = 27 (working days per month)
27 x 9 = 243 (working days)
243 x 11 = 2673 (working hours)
4 5 + 8 + 10 = 23 (years) x 280 = 6440

Calendar Counting

Level 1

1 365
2 5 (360 + 5 = 365)
3 3 x 4 = 12
4 3 x 4 = 12 x 3 = 36

Level 2

1a 3 x 4 = 12 x 3 = 36 x 10 = 360
1b 5 (360 + 5 = 365)
2 360 ÷ 3 = 120
3 5 x 24 = 120
4 $2\frac{1}{3}$
(70 ÷ 30 = 2 remainder 10; $\frac{10}{30} = \frac{1}{3}$)

Level 3

1 3 x 4 = 12 x 3 = 36 x 10 = 360 + 5
= 365
2 365 x 9 = 3285
3 100 ÷ 4 = 25
4a 360 x 2 = 720 ÷ 3 = 240
4b $\frac{1}{3}$ = 33.3 = 33

CALENDAR, COLLECTS AND LECTIONARY

INTRODUCTION

The Calendar (The Christian Year)

The observance of the Christian calendar is an ancient feature of the Church's life. It enables us, in an ordered way, to hear the great story of salvation, celebrate God's mighty acts and be led into a deeper knowledge and love of Christ.

The calendar begins with Advent, a season of penitence and preparation. This leads to Christmas and Epiphany when we celebrate the Incarnation, God's supreme self-revelation. After a period of 'Ordinary Time' comes the preparatory season of Lent, a period of forty weekdays which reflect the forty days which Jesus spent in the desert. Passiontide begins on the fifth Sunday of Lent and culminates in the commemoration of the crucifixion on Good Friday. The great fifty days of Easter are a celebration of Christ's resurrection. Following the chronology in Acts, the Ascension is celebrated on the fortieth day and the coming of the Holy Spirit on the fiftieth, the Day of Pentecost. The following Sunday has developed into Trinity Sunday, after which we return to Ordinary Time until Advent begins again.

Liturgical colours are used in many churches to recognize and reflect the movement and moods of the Christian Year. A scheme in common use is: violet for preparation and penitence; white or gold for celebration and rejoicing; red for the blood of Christ and the fire of the Spirit; green for Ordinary Time. To help those who use colours in this way, guidance is included with the lectionary.

The Collects

The collect is one of the oldest models of Christian Prayer in the Western tradition. It gathers together (collects) the prayers of the congregation and is preceded by a moment for silent reflection. The collect usually forms part of the opening prayers but may also be said at other times.

The traditional form of the prayer is short with a definite structure. In the oldest prayers, which go back to at least the seventh century, the collect was usually a single sentence. Thomas Cranmer developed the collect form and, through **The Book of Common Prayer**, collects have become part of Methodist spirituality; for example, there are many echoes of them in Charles Wesley's hymns. The collects throughout this book bear witness both to this long history and to a modern renaissance, drawing, like the householder in the parable, from 'treasures new and old'.

The traditional structure of the collect in itself offers a paradigm of petitionary prayer. This structure is as follows:

(a) address to God (*Almighty God,*);

(b) a characteristic of God's nature (*to whom all hearts are open . . .*);

(c) a petition (*cleanse the thoughts of our hearts . . .*);

(d) the purpose of the petition (*that we may perfectly love you . . .*);

(e) conclusion (*through Christ our Lord*).

The simple ending may be filled out by a Trinitarian ascription of praise and glory (*who is alive and reigns with you, in the unity of the Holy Spirit, one God now and for ever*); and

(f) a final '**Amen**'.

At least two collects are offered here for each Sunday and some for other occasions. For certain days, when there may be a variety of services at different times, there is greater provision. The **NOTES** on page 523 indicate how the collects may be used.

The Lectionary

The lectionary for the Principal Service is derived from the ecumenical **Revised Common Lectionary** (**RCL**), which has won widespread acceptance in most English-speaking countries. **RCL** operates on a three-year cycle. Most of the Gospel readings in Year A are from Matthew, in Year B from Mark and in Year C from Luke. Readings from John occur in all three years. Much of the lectionary is offered in a semi-continuous form, following a particular book from Sunday to Sunday. During the greater part of Ordinary Time, **RCL** offers two sets of readings. In one, described below as 'continuous', the Old Testament reading forms part of a semi-continous series. In the other, described below as 'related', the Old Testament reading is linked with the Gospel.

The lectionary for a Second Service is derived from a lectionary authorised for use by the Church of England and designed to accompany **RCL**. Two readings are normally supplied in this lectionary, one from the Old Testament and one from the New Testament. If the New Testament reading is not from the Gospels, a third reading (from the Gospels) is provided, and this should always be read if the service is a celebration of ***Holy Communion***.

Readings are also supplied for special occasions, such as a Church Anniversary.

Finding the Collects and Readings

To find the appropriate readings for a given date, it is necessary first to identify the correct lectionary year by reference to the table on page 522. Then, if the date is between Advent Sunday and Epiphany (6 January), or between the Sunday before Lent and Trinity Sunday inclusive, the collect and readings for the Sunday or other day in the Church's calendar (for example, the Third Sunday of Easter) are used. For dates outside those periods, the collect and readings for the secular date (for example, the Sunday between 7 and 13 August) are used. Secular dates are stated inclusively.

MOVEABLE DATES TO THE YEAR 2025

YEAR	ADVENT SUNDAY	SUNDAY BEFORE LENT	ASH WEDNESDAY	EASTER	PENTECOST	TRINITY SUNDAY
A	29 November 1998	14 February 1999	17 February 1999	4 April 1999	23 May 1999	30 May 1999
B	28 November 1999	5 March 2000	8 March 2000	23 April 2000	11 June 2000	18 June 2000
C	3 December 2000	25 February 2001	28 February 2001	15 April 2001	3 June 2001	10 June 2001
A	2 December 2001	10 February 2002	13 February 2002	31 March 2002	19 May 2002	26 May 2002
B	1 December 2002	2 March 2003	5 March 2003	20 April 2003	8 June 2003	15 June 2003
C	30 November 2003	22 February 2004	25 February 2004	11 April 2004	30 May 2004	6 June 2004
A	28 November 2004	6 February 2005	9 February 2005	27 March 2005	15 May 2005	22 May 2005
B	27 November 2005	26 February 2006	1 March 2006	16 April 2006	4 June 2006	11 June 2006
C	3 December 2006	18 February 2007	21 February 2007	8 April 2007	27 May 2007	3 June 2007
A	2 December 2007	3 February 2008	6 February 2008	23 March 2008	11 May 2008	18 May 2008
B	30 November 2008	22 February 2009	25 February 2009	12 April 2009	31 May 2009	7 June 2009
C	29 November 2009	14 February 2010	17 February 2010	4 April 2010	23 May 2010	30 May 2010
A	28 November 2010	6 March 2011	9 March 2011	24 April 2011	12 June 2011	19 June 2011
B	27 November 2011	19 February 2012	22 February 2012	8 April 2012	27 May 2012	3 June 2012
C	2 December 2012	10 February 2013	13 February 2013	31 March 2013	19 May 2013	26 May 2013
A	1 December 2013	2 March 2014	5 March 2014	20 April 2014	8 June 2014	15 June 2014
B	30 November 2014	15 February 2015	18 February 2015	5 April 2015	24 May 2015	31 May 2015
C	29 November 2015	7 February 2016	10 February 2016	27 March 2016	15 May 2016	22 May 2016
A	27 November 2016	26 February 2017	1 March 2017	16 April 2017	4 June 2017	11 June 2017
B	3 December 2017	11 February 2018	14 February 2018	1 April 2018	20 May 2018	27 May 2018
C	2 December 2018	3 March 2019	6 March 2019	21 April 2019	9 June 2019	16 June 2019
A	1 December 2019	23 February 2020	26 February 2020	12 April 2020	31 May 2020	7 June 2020
B	29 November 2020	14 February 2021	17 February 2021	4 April 2021	23 May 2021	30 May 2021
C	28 November 2021	27 February 2022	2 March 2022	17 April 2022	5 June 2022	12 June 2022
A	27 November 2022	19 February 2023	22 February 2023	9 April 2023	28 May 2023	4 June 2023
B	3 December 2023	11 February 2024	14 February 2024	31 March 2024	19 May 2024	26 May 2024
C	1 December 2024	2 March 2025	5 March 2025	20 April 2025	8 June 2025	15 June 2025

THE COLLECTS

NOTES

1 One of the collects provided for each day should normally be included in the opening section of the Principal Service. Another collect may be said at a Second Service or, when appropriate, at a different point in the Principal Service.

2 In Lent and Advent, the seasonal collect may be said after one of the collects of the day.

First Sunday of Advent

The first collect, the collect of the Advent season, may be said on any day in Advent in addition to the collect of the day.

Almighty God,
give us grace to cast away the works of darkness
and to put on the armour of light,
now in the time of this mortal life,
in which your Son Jesus Christ
came to us in great humility:
that, on the last day,
when he shall come again in his glorious majesty
to judge the living and the dead,
we may rise to the life immortal;
through him who is alive and reigns with you,
in the unity of the Holy Spirit,
one God, now and for ever. **Amen.** 5*

Lord our God,
keep us your servants alert and watchful
as we await the return of Christ your Son,
so that when he comes and knocks at the door
he may find us vigilant in prayer,
with songs of praise on our lips.

We ask this through Jesus Christ our Lord,
who is alive and reigns with you,
in the unity of the Holy Spirit,
one God, now and for ever. **Amen.** 16

Second Sunday of Advent

God of all holiness,
your promises stand unshaken through all generations
and you lift up all who are burdened and brought low:
renew our hope in you,
as we wait for the coming in glory of Jesus Christ,
our Judge and our Saviour,
who is alive and reigns with you,
in the unity of the Holy Spirit,
one God, world without end. **Amen.** 27*

God of all time and space,
who are we, that you should come to us?
Yet you have visited your people
and redeemed us in your Son.
As we prepare to celebrate his birth,
make our hearts leap for joy at the sound of your word
and move us by your Spirit
to bless your wonderful works.
We ask this through him whose coming is certain,
whose day draws near,
even your Son, Jesus Christ our Saviour. **Amen.** 15*

The collect for Bible Sunday (page 561) may also be said.

Third Sunday of Advent

God for whom we wait and watch,
you sent your servant John the Baptist
to prepare your people for the coming of the Messiah.
Inspire the ministers and stewards of your truth
to turn our disobedient hearts to you;
that, when Christ shall come again in glory to be our judge,
we may stand with confidence before him,
who is alive and reigns with you,
in the unity of the Holy Spirit,
one God, world without end. **Amen.** 3*

God of mercy and power,
whose Son rules over all,
grant us so to live in obedience to your holy will,
that at his appearing
we may be raised to eternal life;
through Jesus Christ our Lord,
who is alive and reigns with you,
in the unity of the Holy Spirit,
one God, now and for ever. **Amen.**

Fourth Sunday of Advent

God our Redeemer,
you chose the Virgin Mary,
to be the mother of our Lord and Saviour.
Fill us with your grace
that in all things we may embrace your holy will
and with her rejoice in your salvation;
through Jesus Christ our Lord
who is alive and reigns with you,
in the unity of the Holy Spirit,
one God, now and for ever. **Amen.** 10*

All-powerful God,
let the splendour of your glory
rise in our hearts like the dawn,
that the darkness of the night may be scattered
and the coming of your only Son may reveal us
as children of the light.
We ask this through Jesus Christ our Lord,
who is alive and reigns with you,
in the unity of the Holy Spirit,
one God, now and for ever. **Amen.** 16

Christmas Eve

God, faithful and true,
make us eager in expectation,
as we look for the fulfilment of your promise
in Jesus Christ our Saviour. **Amen.** 21

Almighty God,
you make us glad with the yearly remembrance
of the birth of your Son Jesus Christ.
Grant that, as we joyfully receive him as our redeemer,
so we may with sure confidence behold him
when he shall come to be our judge;
who is alive and reigns with you,
in the unity of the Holy Spirit,
one God, now and for ever. **Amen.** 1*

Christmas Day (Midnight)

Eternal God, who made this most holy night to shine
with the brightness of your one true light:
bring us, who have known the revelation of that light on earth,
to see the radiance of your heavenly glory;
through Jesus Christ our Lord,
who is alive and reigns with you,
in the unity of the Holy Spirit,
one God, now and for ever. **Amen.** 12

God of light and hope,
of stars and surprises:
open our eyes to your glory
and our hearts to your presence,
that we may respond with joy to the angel song;
through Jesus Christ our Lord,
who is alive and reigns with you,
in the unity of the Holy Spirit,
one God, now and for ever. **Amen.** 22*

Christmas Day

Almighty God,
you have given us your only-begotten Son
to take our nature upon him
and as at this time to be born of a pure virgin.
Grant that we, who have been born again
and made your children by adoption and grace,
may daily be renewed by your Holy Spirit;

through Jesus Christ our Lord,
who is alive and reigns with you,
in the unity of the Holy Spirit,
one God, now and for ever. **Amen.** 5*

Ever-living God,
whose glory was revealed
in the Word made flesh:
may we, who have seen such splendour
in the coming of your Son,
be true witnesses to your self-giving love in the world;
through Jesus Christ our Lord,
who is alive and reigns with you,
in the unity of the Holy Spirit,
one God, now and for ever. **Amen.**

First Sunday of Christmas (26 to 31 December inclusive)

God of glory,
who wonderfully created us in your own image
and yet more wonderfully restored us
in your Son Jesus Christ:
grant that, as he came to share in our humanity,
so we may share in the life of his divinity;
who is alive and reigns with you,
in the unity of the Holy Spirit,
one God, now and for ever. **Amen.** 12*

Radiant God,
in Jesus Christ your light shines in our darkness,
giving joy in our sorrow
and revealing your presence in our loneliness.
Fill our hearts with your light
that in the darkness of this world
our lives may shine with your eternal splendour;
through Jesus Christ our Lord. **Amen.** 25*

Second Sunday of Christmas (1 to 5 January inclusive)

God of power and life,
the glory of all who believe in you;
fill the world with your splendour
and show the nations the light of your truth;
through Jesus Christ your Son our Lord,
who is alive and reigns with you,
in the unity of the Holy Spirit,
one God, now and for ever. **Amen.** 3*

God of beauty and light,
with the appearing of your Son
you have brought us into your new creation.
Renew in us your image and likeness
that our lives may reflect your glory;
through Jesus Christ our Lord,
who is alive and reigns with you,
in the unity of the Holy Spirit,
one God, now and for ever. **Amen.** 24*

The Epiphany (6 January) – or the preceding Sunday

Eternal God,
by a star you led wise men to the worship of your Son.
Guide by your light the nations of the earth,
that the whole world may see your glory;
through Jesus Christ our Lord,
who is alive and reigns with you,
in the unity of the Holy Spirit,
one God, now and for ever. **Amen.** 12*

Almighty God,
your Son our Saviour Jesus Christ
is the light of the world.
May your people
shine with the radiance of his glory,
that he may be known, worshipped and obeyed
to the ends of the earth;
who is alive and reigns with you,
in the unity of the Holy Spirit,
one God, now and for ever. **Amen.** 27*

Sunday between 7 and 13 January – Sunday after Epiphany and the First Sunday in Ordinary Time

God our Redeemer,
through Jesus Christ
you have assured your children of eternal life
and in Baptism have made us one in him.
Deliver us from the death of sin
and raise us to new life in Christ;
for he is alive and reigns with you,
in the unity of the Holy Spirit,
one God, now and for ever. **Amen.** 12

Eternal Father,
at the Baptism of Jesus
you revealed him to be your Son
and anointed him with the Holy Spirit.
Keep all who are born of water and the Spirit
faithful to their calling as your people;
through Jesus Christ our Lord. **Amen.** 4

Sunday between 14 and 20 January – Second Sunday in Ordinary Time

Living God,
in Christ you make all things new.
Transform the poverty of our nature
by the riches of your grace,
and in the renewal of our lives
make known your heavenly glory;
through Jesus Christ our Lord. **Amen.** 8

Almighty God,
by whose grace alone we are accepted
and called to your service,
strengthen us by your Spirit,
and make us worthy of our calling;
through Jesus Christ our Lord. **Amen.** 12

Sunday between 21 and 27 January – Third Sunday in Ordinary Time

Loving God,
through your Son you have called us to repent of our sin,
to believe the good news,
and to celebrate the coming of your kingdom.
Grant that we may hear the call to discipleship
and gladly proclaim the gospel to a waiting world;
through Jesus Christ our Lord. **Amen.**

Almighty God,
whose Son revealed in signs and miracles
the wonder of your saving love:
renew all your people with your heavenly grace,
and in all our weakness
sustain us by your mighty power;
through Jesus Christ our Lord. **Amen.** 12

Sunday between 28 January and 3 February – Fourth Sunday in Ordinary Time (unless it is the Sunday before Lent).

God of heaven and earth,
whose power is made fully known
in your pardoning mercy:
ever fill us with your grace,
that, entering more fully into your promises,
we may come to share in the good things of heaven;
through Jesus Christ our Lord. **Amen.**

Lord, you have taught us
that all our doings without love are worth nothing.
Send your Holy Spirit,
and pour into our hearts that most excellent gift of love,
the true bond of peace and of all virtues;
through Jesus Christ our Lord. **Amen.** 5*

Sunday between 4 and 10 February – Fifth Sunday in Ordinary Time (unless it is the Sunday before Lent or falls in Lent)

Loving God,
the light of the minds that know you,
the life of the souls that love you,
and the strength of the wills that serve you:
help us so to know you
that we may truly love you,
and so to love you
that we may truly serve you,
whom to serve is perfect freedom;
through Jesus Christ our Lord. **Amen.** 27*

God our Father,
whose Word has come among us:
may the light of faith, kindled in our hearts,
shine in our words and deeds;
through him who is Christ the Lord,
who is alive and reigns with you,
in the unity of the Holy Spirit,
one God, now and for ever. **Amen.** 3*

Sunday between 11 and 17 February – Sixth Sunday in Ordinary Time (unless it is the Sunday before Lent or falls in Lent)

O God,
forasmuch as without you we are not able to please you;
mercifully grant that your Holy Spirit
may in all things direct and rule our hearts;
through Jesus Christ our Lord. **Amen.** 5*

You alone, O God,
can satisfy our deepest hunger,
and protect us from the lure of wealth and power.
Teach us to seek your kingdom above all else,
that we may know the security and joy
of those who put their trust in you;
through Jesus Christ our Lord. **Amen.** 16*

Sunday between 18 and 24 February – Seventh Sunday in Ordinary Time (unless it is the Sunday before Lent or falls in Lent)

God of infinite mercy,
grant that we who know your pity
may rejoice in your forgiveness
and gladly forgive others,
for the sake of Jesus Christ our Saviour. **Amen.** 21

God of pardon and deliverance,
your forgiving love, revealed in Christ,
has brought to birth a new creation.
Raise us from our sins to walk in your ways,
that we may witness to your power
which makes all things new,
in Jesus Christ our Lord. **Amen.** 16

Sunday between 25 and 29 February – Eighth Sunday in Ordinary Time (unless it is the Sunday before Lent or falls in Lent)

Grant to us, Lord, we pray,
the spirit to think and do always those things that are right;
that we, who can do no good thing without you,
may by you be enabled to live according to your will;
through Jesus Christ our Lord. **Amen.** 5*

God of tenderness and compassion,
you led your people into the desert,
and embraced them there in love and faithfulness.
By word and sacrament
renew in us your covenant love,
that we may rejoice in your gift of new life;
through Jesus Christ our Lord. **Amen.** 16

Sunday before Lent

God of life and light,
your Son was revealed in majesty
before he suffered death on the cross.

Give us grace to perceive his glory,
that we may be strengthened to follow him
and be changed into his likeness, from glory to glory;
who is alive and reigns with you,
in the unity of the Holy Spirit,
one God, now and for ever. **Amen.** 7*

Lord God,
whose glory shines upon us
in the face of Jesus Christ,
and whose nature is made known to us
in the mystery of the cross:
number us, we pray,
among his faithful followers
for whom nothing matters
but the doing of your will;
through Jesus Christ our Lord. **Amen.** 26

Ash Wednesday

Almighty and everlasting God,
you hate nothing that you have made,
and forgive the sins of all those who are penitent.
Create and make in us new and contrite hearts,
that we, worthily lamenting our sins
and acknowledging our wretchedness,
may receive from you, the God of all mercy,
perfect remission and forgiveness;
through the merits of Jesus Christ,
our only mediator and advocate. **Amen.** 5*

OR

Almighty and merciful God,
you hate nothing that you have made,
and forgive the sins of all who are penitent.
Create in us new and contrite hearts,
so that when we turn to you and confess our sins
we may receive your full and perfect forgiveness;
through Jesus Christ our Lord. **Amen.** 21*

One of the above alternative versions of the collect for Lent may be said in addition to the collect of the day until the Fifth Sunday in Lent.

An additional collect for Ash Wednesday:

Remember, O Lord, what you have wrought in us,
and not what we deserve;
and as you have called us to your service,
make us worthy of our calling;
through Jesus Christ our Lord. **Amen.** 7*

First Sunday in Lent

Almighty God,
whose Son Jesus Christ
fasted forty days in the wilderness,
and was tempted as we are, yet without sin:
give us grace to discipline ourselves
in obedience to your Spirit;
and, as you know our weakness,
so may we know your power to save;
through Jesus Christ our Lord. **Amen.** 12

Gracious Father,
your blessèd Son Jesus Christ came from heaven
to be the true bread which gives life to the world.
Evermore give us this bread,
that he may live in us, and we in him;
through Jesus Christ our Lord. **Amen.** 3*

Second Sunday in Lent

Christ, Son of the living God,
who for a season laid aside the divine glory
and learned obedience through suffering:
teach us in all our afflictions
to raise our eyes to the place of your mercy
and to find in you our peace and deliverance.
We make our prayer in your name. **Amen.** 9*

Merciful Lord,
grant your people grace to withstand the temptations
of the world, the flesh and the devil,
and with pure hearts and minds to follow you,
the only God;
through Jesus Christ our Lord. **Amen.** 5*

Third Sunday in Lent

Almighty God,
whose most dear Son went not up to joy
but first he suffered pain,
and entered not into glory before he was crucified:
mercifully grant that we, walking in the way of the cross,
may find it none other than the way of life and peace;
through Jesus Christ our Lord. **Amen.** 2

Almighty God,
you see that we have no power of ourselves to help ourselves.
Keep us both outwardly in our bodies and inwardly in our souls,
that we may be defended from all adversities
which may happen to the body,
and from all evil thoughts
which may assault and hurt the soul;
through Jesus Christ our Lord. **Amen.** 5*

Fourth Sunday in Lent

Lord God,
whose blessèd Son our Saviour
gave his back to those who struck him
and did not hide his face from shame:
give us grace to endure
the sufferings of this present time
with sure confidence in the glory that shall be revealed;
through the same Jesus Christ our Lord. **Amen.** 6*

O God, rich in mercy,
you so loved the world
that, when we were dead in our sins,
you sent your only Son for our deliverance.
Lifted up from the earth,
he is light and life;
exalted upon the cross,
he is truth and salvation.
Raise us up with Christ
that we may walk as children of light.
We ask this through Christ,
who is alive and reigns with you
in the unity of the Holy Spirit,
holy and mighty God, for ever and for ever. **Amen.** 16*

Mothering Sunday

God of compassion,
whose Son Jesus Christ, the child of Mary,
shared the life of a home in Nazareth:
strengthen us each day,
that in joy and sorrow
we may know your presence;
through Jesus Christ our Lord. **Amen.** 23*

Fifth Sunday in Lent (First Sunday of the Passion)

Most merciful God,
who by the death and resurrection of your Son Jesus Christ
delivered and saved the world:
grant that by faith in him who suffered on the cross,
we may triumph in the power of his victory;
through Jesus Christ our Lord,
who is alive and reigns with you,
in the unity of the Holy Spirit,
one God, now and for ever. **Amen.** 12

Almighty God,
your Son came into the world
to free us all from sin and death.
Breathe upon us with the power of your Spirit,
that we may be raised to new life in Christ,
and serve you in holiness and righteousness all our days;
through the same Jesus Christ our Lord. **Amen.** 4

Sixth Sunday in Lent (Second Sunday of the Passion or Palm Sunday)

Eternal God,
in your tender love towards the human race
you sent your Son our Saviour Jesus Christ
to take our flesh and to suffer death upon a cross.
Grant that we may follow the example of his great humility,
and share in the glory of his resurrection;
through the same Jesus Christ our Lord. **Amen.** 5*

God of all-redeeming grace,
in your great love you gave your only Son
to die for the sins of the whole world.
Help us by your Holy Spirit
to worship you with reverence,
and to enter with joy
into the celebration of those mighty acts
whereby you bring us life and immortality;
through Jesus Christ our Lord. **Amen.** 4*

Maundy Thursday

God our Father,
you have invited us to share in the supper
which your Son gave to his Church.
Nourish us, we pray, by his presence,
and unite us in his love;
who is alive and reigns with you,
in the unity of the Holy Spirit,
one God, now and for ever. **Amen.** 17*

Gracious God,
we thank you for the gift of this sacrament
in which we remember Jesus Christ your Son.
May we who revere this sacred mystery
know and reveal in our lives
the fruits of his redemption;
who is alive and reigns with you,
in the unity of the Holy Spirit,
one God, now and for ever. **Amen.** 1*

Gracious God,
your Son Jesus Christ girded himself with a towel
and washed the feet of his disciples.
Give us the will to be the servants of others
as he was the servant of all,
who gave up his life and died for us,
yet lives and reigns with you and the Holy Spirit,
one God, now and for ever. **Amen.** 21

Good Friday

Gracious and eternal God,
look with mercy on this your family,
for which our Lord Jesus Christ
was content to be betrayed
and given up into the hands of sinners
and to suffer death upon the cross;
who is alive and glorified with you,
in the unity of the Holy Spirit,
one God, now and for ever. **Amen.** 5*

Almighty God,
your Son Jesus Christ
endured the cross for our sake.
Remove from us all coldness and cowardice of heart,
and give us courage
to take up our cross and follow him;
through the same Jesus Christ our Lord. **Amen.** 4

Almighty and everlasting God,
by your Spirit the whole body of the Church
is governed and sanctified.
Hear the prayers we offer for all your faithful people,
that in their vocation and ministry
each may serve you in holiness and truth,
to the glory of your name;
through Jesus Christ our Saviour. **Amen.** 1*

Eternal God,
bless all who look to Abraham
as the father of faith.
Set us free from prejudice, blindness,
and hardness of heart,
that in accordance with your will and guided by your truth
our life together may be for the glory of your name;
we ask this through Jesus Christ our Lord. **Amen.**

Holy Saturday

Grant, Lord,
that we who are baptized into the death
of your Son our Saviour Jesus Christ
may continually put to death our evil desires
and be buried with him;
that through the grave and gate of death
we may pass to our joyful resurrection;
through the merits of him
who died and was buried and rose again for us,
your Son Jesus Christ our Lord. **Amen.** 1*

Easter Day (Services after sunset until Easter Dawn)

God of glory,
you have filled this night with the radiance of Christ.
Renew in us our Baptism,
and bring us through the waters to the promised land;
through Jesus Christ our Redeemer,
who is alive and reigns with you,
in the unity of the Holy Spirit,
one God, now and for ever. **Amen.** 21*

Eternal God, giver of life and light,
you make this holy night shine
with the radiance of the risen Christ.
Renew your Church
with the joy and gladness of his presence,
that we may shine as lights in the world;
through Jesus Christ our Lord,
who is alive and reigns with you,
in the unity of the Holy Spirit,
one God, now and for ever. **Amen.** 4*

Easter Day (Services after dawn)

Lord of all life and power,
who through the mighty resurrection of your Son
overcame the old order of sin and death
to make all things new in him:
grant that we, being dead to sin
and alive to you in Jesus Christ,
may reign with him in glory;
to whom with you in the unity of the Holy Spirit
be praise and honour, glory and might,
now and in all eternity. **Amen.** 12

Most glorious God,
who on this day delivered us
by the mighty resurrection of your Son, Jesus Christ,
and made your whole creation new:
grant that we who celebrate with joy
his rising from the dead
may be raised from the death of sin
to the life of righteousness;
through him who is alive and reigns with you,
in the unity of the Holy Spirit,
one God, now and for ever. **Amen.** 21*

Second Sunday of Easter

Faithful God,
the strength of all who believe
and the hope of those who doubt;
may we, who have not seen, have faith
and receive the fullness of Christ's blessing;
who is alive and reigns with you,
in the unity of the Holy Spirit,
one God, now and for ever. **Amen.** 3

God of the prophets,
you fulfilled your promise
that Christ would suffer and rise to glory.
Open our minds to understand the scriptures
that we may be his witnesses to the ends of the earth.
We ask this through Jesus Christ our Lord,
who is alive and reigns with you,
in the unity of the Holy Spirit,
one God, world without end. **Amen.** 16

Third Sunday of Easter

God of life and love,
your Son made himself known to his disciples
in the breaking of the bread.
Open our eyes that we may see him
in his redeeming work;
who is alive and reigns with you,
in the unity of the Holy Spirit,
one God, now and for ever. **Amen.** 3*

Christ our friend,
you ask for our love
in spite of our betrayal.
Give us courage to embrace forgiveness,
know you again,
and trust ourselves in you;
we pray in your name. **Amen.** 20

Fourth Sunday of Easter

God of peace,
who brought again from the dead our Lord Jesus Christ,
that great Shepherd of the sheep,
with the blood of the eternal covenant:
make us perfect in every good work to do your will,
and work in us that which is well-pleasing in your sight;
through Jesus Christ our Lord,
who is alive and reigns with you,
in the unity of the Holy Spirit,
one God, now and for ever. **Amen.** 12*

Good Shepherd of the sheep,
by whom the lost are sought
and guided into the fold:
feed us and we shall be satisfied;
heal us and we shall be made whole;
and lead us, that we may be with you;
for you are alive and reign,
with the Father and the Holy Spirit,
one God, now and for ever. **Amen.** 21*

Fifth Sunday of Easter

Eternal God,
whose Son Jesus Christ
is the way, the truth and the life:
grant us to walk in his way,
to rejoice in his truth,
and to share his risen life;
who is alive and reigns with you,
in the unity of the Holy Spirit,
one God, now and for ever. **Amen.** 12*

Loving and eternal God,
through the resurrection of your Son,
help us to face the future
with courage and assurance,

knowing that nothing in life or death
can ever part us from your love for us
in Jesus Christ our Saviour;
who is alive and reigns with you,
in the unity of the Holy Spirit,
one God, now and for ever. **Amen.** 21*

Sixth Sunday of Easter

God of mercy,
as we rejoice in the resurrection of your Son,
the Bread of Life,
feed us with your plenty
and increase in us compassion for the hungry;
through Jesus Christ our Lord,
who is alive and reigns with you,
in the unity of the Holy Spirit,
one God, now and for ever. **Amen.**

Almighty and everlasting God,
you are always more ready to hear than we to pray,
and give more than either we desire or deserve.
Pour down upon us the abundance of your mercy,
forgiving us those things
of which our conscience is afraid
and giving us those good things
which we are not worthy to ask
save through the merits and mediation
of Jesus Christ your Son our Lord;
who is alive and reigns with you,
in the unity of the Holy Spirit,
one God, now and for ever. **Amen.** 12

Ascension Day

Eternal and gracious God,
grant that as we believe your Son,
our Saviour Jesus Christ,
to have ascended with triumph
into your kingdom in heaven,
so may we also in heart and mind ascend to where he is
and with him continually dwell;
who is alive and reigns with you,
in the unity of the Holy Spirit,
one God, now and for ever. **Amen.** 5*

Almighty and everlasting Father,
you raised our Lord Jesus Christ
to your right hand on high.
As we rejoice in his exaltation,
fill us with his Spirit,
that we may go into all the world
and faithfully proclaim the gospel.
This we ask through Jesus Christ our Lord,
who is alive and reigns with you,
in the unity of the Holy Spirit,
one God, for ever and ever. **Amen.** 27*

Seventh Sunday of Easter (Sunday in Ascensiontide)

Lord of Hosts,
purify our hearts
that the King of Glory may come in,
even your Son, Jesus our Redeemer;
for he is alive and reigns with you,
in the unity of the Holy Spirit,
one God, now and for ever. **Amen.** 9

Eternal God,
you have given all authority in heaven and on earth
to your Son, our Saviour Jesus Christ.
Grant that we may never lose
the vision of your kingdom
but serve you with hope and joy;

through him who lives and reigns with you,
in the unity of the Holy Spirit,
one God, now and for ever. **Amen.** 21*

or the collect for Ascension Day may be said.

Pentecost

God, who at this time
taught the hearts of your faithful people
by sending to them the light of your Holy Spirit:
grant us by the same Spirit
to have a right judgement in all things
and evermore to rejoice in his holy comfort;
through the merits of Christ Jesus our Saviour,
who is alive and reigns with you,
in the unity of the Holy Spirit,
one God, now and for ever. **Amen.** 12

Almighty God,
who on the day of Pentecost
sent your Holy Spirit on the disciples
with the wind from heaven and with tongues of flame,
filling them with joy and boldness to preach the gospel:
send us out in the power of the same Spirit
to witness to your truth
and to draw everyone to the fire of your love;
through Jesus Christ our Lord. **Amen.** 12*

Faithful God,
you fulfilled the promise of Easter
by sending your Holy Spirit
and opening the way of eternal life
to all the human race.
Keep us in the unity of your Spirit,
that every tongue may tell of your glory;
through Jesus Christ our Lord,
who is alive and reigns with you,
in the unity of the Holy Spirit,
one God, now and for ever. **Amen.** 3*

Trinity Sunday

Almighty and everlasting God,
you have given your servants grace,
by the confession of a true faith,
to acknowledge the glory of the eternal Trinity
and in the power of the divine majesty to worship the Unity.
Keep us steadfast in this faith,
that we may evermore be defended from all adversities;
through Jesus Christ our Lord,
who is alive and reigns with you,
in the unity of the Holy Spirit,
one God, now and for ever. **Amen.** 5*

Father God,
you have created all things
and through Christ revealed your salvation
in all the world.
Give us a vision of your glory
and by your Holy Spirit fill us with life and love
that we may praise and serve you
through Jesus Christ our Lord,
who is alive and reigns with you,
in the unity of the Holy Spirit,
one God, for ever and ever. **Amen.**

Sunday between 24 and 28 May
(if after Trinity Sunday) – Eighth Sunday in Ordinary Time

Grant to us, Lord, we pray,
the spirit to think and do always those things that are right;
that we, who can do no good thing without you,
may by you be enabled to live according to your will;
through Jesus Christ our Lord. **Amen.** 5*

God of tenderness and compassion,
you led your people into the desert,
and made them your own in love and faithfulness.
By word and sacrament
renew in us your covenant love,

that we may rejoice in your gift of new life;
through Jesus Christ our Lord. **Amen.** 16

Sunday between 29 May and 4 June inclusive
(if after Trinity Sunday) – Ninth Sunday in Ordinary Time

Almighty God,
you have built your Church
on the foundation of the apostles and prophets,
Jesus Christ himself being the chief cornerstone.
Join us together in unity of spirit by their teaching,
that we may become a holy temple, acceptable to you;
through Jesus Christ our Lord. **Amen.** 5*

Faithful God,
whose covenant love is new every morning:
open our eyes to your wisdom
and give us grace to keep faith with all your creation;
through Christ our Lord. **Amen.**

Sunday between 5 and 11 June inclusive
(if after Trinity Sunday) – Tenth Sunday in Ordinary Time

God, faithful and true,
you call every generation to make a pilgrim journey.
Guide our feet along the road of faith,
that we may put our whole trust in you;
through Jesus Christ our Lord. **Amen.**

Ever-loving God,
your Son Jesus Christ healed the sick
and restored them to wholeness of life.
Look with compassion on the anguish of the world,
and by your power make whole both people and nations;
through Jesus Christ our Lord. **Amen.** 12*

Sunday between 12 and 18 June inclusive
(if after Trinity Sunday) – Eleventh Sunday in Ordinary Time

Your glory, O God, fills heaven and earth
and all creation resounds with your praise.
As we rejoice in your presence,
may we know your power to save
and praise you for your faithfulness,
now and for ever;
through Jesus Christ our Lord. **Amen.**

Generous God,
you gather your people
and lavish your gifts upon us, day by day.
Grant that each experience of your pardon
may enlarge our own love,
until it meets the measure of your extravagant forgiveness,
through Jesus Christ our Lord. **Amen.** 16*

Sunday between 19 and 25 June inclusive
(if after Trinity Sunday) – Twelfth Sunday in Ordinary Time

Creator God,
in the beginning
your word subdued the chaos
and in the fullness of time
you sent Jesus, your Son,
to rebuke the forces of evil
and to make all things new.
By that same power
transform our fear into faith
that we may have courage to follow
in the way of your kingdom;
through the same Jesus Christ our Lord. **Amen.** 16*

God of all power and truth and grace,
you call your Church to love and praise.
Inspire us with zeal for your gospel,
and grant us boldness to proclaim your word,
that we and all the world may praise your name;
through Jesus Christ our Lord. **Amen.** 9*

Sunday between 26 June and 2 July inclusive – Thirteenth Sunday in Ordinary Time

Lord of heaven and earth,
you sent your Holy Spirit
to be the life and power of your Church.
Sow in our hearts the seeds of your grace
that we may bear the fruit of the Spirit,
in love and joy and peace;
through Jesus Christ our Lord. **Amen.** 12*

Merciful God,
out of the depths we cry to you
and you hear our prayer.
Make us attentive to the voice of your Son
that we may rise from the death of sin
and take our place in the new creation.
We make our prayer through Jesus Christ,
who lives and reigns with you,
in the unity of the Holy Spirit,
one God for ever and ever. **Amen.**

Sunday between 3 and 9 July inclusive – Fourteenth Sunday in Ordinary Time

Servant Lord,
grant us both the opportunity and the will
to serve you day by day.
May all that we do
and how we bear each other's burdens
be our offering of love and service
to the glory of your name. **Amen.** 21*

Boundless, O God, is your saving power;
your harvest reaches to the ends of the earth.
Set our hearts on fire for your kingdom
and put on our lips the good news of peace.
Grant us perseverance as heralds of your Gospel
and joy as disciples of your Son,
Jesus Christ our Lord;
who lives and reigns with you,
in the unity of the Holy Spirit,
one God for ever and ever. **Amen.** 16*

Sunday between 10 and 16 July inclusive – Fifteenth Sunday in Ordinary Time

Give us, we pray, gentle God,
a mind forgetful of past injury,
a will to seek the good of others
and a heart of love,
that we may learn to live
in the way of your Son, Jesus Christ,
through whom we pray. **Amen.** 21*

Eternal God, giver of love and peace,
you call your children to live together as one family.
Give us grace to learn your ways
and to do your will,
that we may bring justice and peace to all people,
in the name of Jesus Christ. **Amen.** 21

Sunday between 17 and 23 July inclusive – Sixteenth Sunday in Ordinary Time

Grant us, Lord,
not to be anxious about earthly things,
but to love things heavenly;
and even now,
while we are placed among things that are passing away,
to hold fast to those things which last for ever;
through Jesus Christ our Lord. **Amen.** 27*

Eternal God,
in Christ you make yourself our guest.
Amid all our cares and concerns
make us attentive to your voice
and alert to your presence,
that we may prize your word above all else;
through Jesus Christ our Lord. **Amen.** 16*

Sunday between 24 and 30 July inclusive – Seventeenth Sunday in Ordinary Time

Gracious God,
your Son Jesus Christ fed the hungry
with the bread of life
and the word of your kingdom.
Renew your people with your heavenly grace,
and in all our weakness
sustain us by your true and living bread,
even Jesus Christ our Lord. **Amen.** 3*

God, you have poured the Spirit of your Son into our hearts
so that we call you Father.
Give us grace to devote our freedom to your service
that we and all creation may be brought
into the glorious liberty of the children of God.
For the kingdom, the power, and the glory are yours,
now and for ever. **Amen.** 12*

Sunday between 31 July and 6 August inclusive – Eighteenth Sunday in Ordinary Time

Lord and giver of life,
you alone nourish and sustain your people,
through Christ, the bread of life.
Feed our hunger and quench our thirst,
that we may no longer work for what fails to satisfy,
but do what you require, in obedience and faith;
through Jesus Christ our Lord. **Amen.** 16*

Almighty God,
your Son has opened for us
a new and living way into your presence.
Give us new hearts and constant wills
to worship you in spirit and in truth;
through Jesus Christ our Lord. **Amen.** 12*

Sunday between 7 and 13 August inclusive – Nineteenth Sunday in Ordinary Time

Living God,
you have placed in the hearts of your children
a longing for your word and a hunger for your truth.
Grant that, believing in the One whom you have sent,
we may know him to be the true bread of heaven,
your Son, Jesus Christ our Lord. **Amen.** 27*

O God, the protector of all who trust in you,
without whom nothing is strong, nothing is holy:
increase and multiply upon us your mercy
that with you as our ruler and guide,
we may so pass through things temporal
that we finally lose not the things eternal;
grant this, heavenly Father,
for the sake of Jesus Christ our Lord. **Amen.** 5*

Sunday between 14 and 20 August inclusive – Twentieth Sunday in Ordinary Time

God of the nations,
to whose table all are invited
and in whose kingdom no one is a stranger:
hear the cries of the hungry
and mercifully extend to all the peoples on earth
the joy of your salvation;
through Jesus Christ our Lord. **Amen.** 16

To set the earth ablaze, O God,
your Son submitted to death on the cross,
and from his cup of suffering
you call the Church to drink.
When we are tempted
give us strength to run the race that lies before us,
and to keep our eyes fixed on Jesus;
who is alive and reigns with you,
in the unity of the Holy Spirit,
one God, now and for ever. **Amen.** 16

Sunday between 21 and 27 August inclusive – Twenty-first Sunday in Ordinary Time

Holy God,
you liberate the oppressed
and make a way of salvation.
Unite us with all who cry for justice,
and lead us together into freedom;
through our Lord and Liberator, Jesus Christ. **Amen.**

Merciful God,
grant that your Church,
being gathered by your Holy Spirit into one,
may reveal your glory among all peoples,
to the honour of your name;
through Jesus Christ our Lord. **Amen.** 4*

Sunday between 28 August and 3 September inclusive – Twenty-second Sunday in Ordinary Time

Redeemer God,
you heard the cry of your people
and sent Moses your servant
to lead them out of slavery.
Free us from the tyranny of sin and death
and, by the leading of your Spirit,
bring us to our promised land;
through Jesus Christ our Lord. **Amen.** 21*

God of all creation,
you call all peoples of the earth into your kingdom.
Grant that we, with young and old of all nations,
may boldly confess Jesus Christ as Lord;
to whom, with you and the Holy Spirit,
be all honour and praise, now and for ever. **Amen.** 27*

Sunday between 4 and 10 September inclusive – Twenty-third Sunday in Ordinary Time

O God, you bear your people ever on your heart and mind.
Watch over us in your protecting love,
that, strengthened by your grace
and led by your Spirit,
we may not miss your way for us
but enter into your glory,
made ready for all in Christ our Lord. **Amen.**

Go before us, Lord, in all that we do,
with your most gracious favour,
and guide us with your continual help,
that in all our works,
begun, continued and ended in you,
we may glorify your holy name,
and finally by your mercy obtain everlasting life;
through Jesus Christ our Lord. **Amen.** 5*

Sunday between 11 and 17 September inclusive – Twenty-fourth Sunday in Ordinary Time

God our Redeemer,
who called your Church to witness
that you were in Christ
reconciling the world to yourself:
help us so to proclaim the good news of your love
that all who hear it may be reconciled to you;
through Jesus Christ our Lord. **Amen.** 12*

Gracious God,
like a mother you give us new life,
and make us your children in Jesus Christ.
Look on us in your love,
and bring us to the inheritance which you promised.
Grant this through Jesus Christ, your Son. **Amen.** 27*

Sunday between 18 and 24 September inclusive – Twenty-fifth Sunday in Ordinary Time

Merciful God,
you have prepared for those who love you
such good things as pass our understanding.
Pour into our hearts such love towards you
that we, loving you above all things,
may obtain your promises,
which exceed all that we can desire;
through Jesus Christ our Lord. **Amen.** 12*

O God, surer than the breaking of the day,
in the morning, fill us with your love,
and in the evening, as the dew falls,
refresh us with your mercy,
that we may live according to your promises;
through Jesus Christ our Lord. **Amen.**

Sunday between 25 September and 1 October inclusive – Twenty-sixth Sunday in Ordinary Time

Gracious God,
you give the water of eternal life
through Jesus Christ your Son.
May we always turn to you,
the spring of life and source of goodness;
through the same Jesus Christ our Lord. **Amen.** 4*

Father of all,
you gave your only Son,
to take upon himself the form of a servant
and to be obedient even to death on a cross.
Give us the same mind that was in Christ Jesus
that, sharing in his humility,
we may come to be with him in his glory;
for he lives and reigns with you,
in the unity of the Holy Spirit,
one God, now and for ever. **Amen.** 12*

Sunday between 2 and 8 October inclusive – Twenty-seventh Sunday in Ordinary Time

Blessèd are you, O Lord,
and blessèd are those who observe and keep your law.
Help us to seek you with our whole heart,
to delight in your commandments
and to walk in the glorious liberty
given us by your Son, Jesus Christ,
in whose name we make our prayer. **Amen.** 9*

Almighty and everlasting God,
mercifully look upon our infirmities,
and in all our dangers and necessities
stretch out your hand to help and defend us;
through Jesus Christ our Lord. **Amen.** 5*

Sunday between 9 and 15 October inclusive – Twenty-eighth Sunday in Ordinary Time

Lord, in your goodness,
open our eyes to your light,
and so fill our hearts with your glory
that we may always acknowledge Jesus as Saviour,
and hold fast to his word in sincerity and truth.
We make our prayer through Jesus Christ our Lord. **Amen.**
13

God of all power and might,
the author and giver of all good things,
graft in our hearts the love of your name,
increase in us true religion,
nourish in us all goodness
and of your great mercy keep us in the same;
through Jesus Christ our Lord. **Amen.** 12*

Sunday between 16 and 22 October inclusive – Twenty-ninth Sunday in Ordinary Time

Lord Jesus Christ,
you have taught us
that what we do for the least of our brothers and sisters,
we do also for you.
Give us the will to be the servants of others
as you were the servant of all;
for you gave up your life and died for us,
but live and reign with the Father and the Holy Spirit,
one God, now and for ever. **Amen.** 12*

Almighty God,
you have created the heavens and the earth
and formed us in your own image.
Teach us to discern your hand in all your works,
and to serve you with reverence and thanksgiving;
through Jesus Christ our Lord,
who reigns, with you and the Holy Spirit,
supreme over all creation,
now and for ever. **Amen.** 12*

Sunday between 23 and 29 October inclusive – Thirtieth Sunday in Ordinary Time

Eternal God, giver of love and peace,
you call your children to live together as one family.
Give us grace to learn your ways
and to do your will,
that we may bring justice and peace to all people,
in the name of Jesus Christ. **Amen.** 21

Lord of creation,
you give new strength to our faith.
Grant that we may recognise your presence
in all life and history,
and face our trials with serenity and peace.
We ask this through our Lord Jesus Christ. **Amen.** 27*

All Saints (1 November) – or the Sunday between 30 October and 5 November inclusive

Almighty God,
you have knit together your chosen people
in one communion and fellowship
in the mystical body of your Son Christ our Lord.
Give us grace so to follow your blessèd saints
in all virtuous and godly living
that we may come to those inexpressible joys
which you have prepared for those who love you;
through Jesus Christ our Lord. **Amen.** 9*

Holy God,
you have called witnesses from every nation
and revealed your glory in their lives.
Grant to us the same faith and love
that, following their example,
we may be sustained by their fellowship
and rejoice in their triumph;
through Jesus Christ our Lord. **Amen.**

Sunday between 30 October and 5 November inclusive – Thirty-first Sunday in Ordinary Time

Merciful Lord,
you have taught us through your Son
that love is the fulfilling of the law.
Grant that we may love you with our whole heart
and our neighbours as ourselves;
through Jesus Christ our Lord. **Amen.** 12*

All-embracing God,
your care for us surpasses
even a mother's tender love.
Through your word and sacrament
renew our trust in your providence,
that we may abandon all anxiety
and seek first your kingdom.
We make our prayer through Jesus Christ our Lord. **Amen.**
16*

Sunday between 6 and 12 November inclusive – Thirty-second Sunday in Ordinary Time

Eternal God,
in whose perfect realm
no sword is drawn but the sword of justice,
and no strength known but the strength of love:
guide and inspire all who seek your kingdom,
that peoples and nations may find their security
in the love which casts out fear;
through Jesus Christ our Saviour. **Amen.** 9*

God of peace,
whose will is to restore all things
in your beloved Son, the King of all:
govern the hearts and minds of those in authority,
and bring the families of the nations,
divided and torn apart by the ravages of sin,
to be subject to his just and gentle rule;
who is alive and reigns with you,
in the unity of the Holy Spirit,
one God, now and for ever. **Amen.** 12*

Sunday between 13 and 19 November inclusive – Thirty-third Sunday in Ordinary Time

Eternal God,
from whom all thoughts of truth and peace proceed:
kindle, we pray, in every heart the true love of peace,
and guide with your pure and peaceable wisdom
those who take counsel for the nations of the earth;
that in justice and peace your kingdom may go forward,
till the earth is filled with the knowledge of your love;
through Jesus Christ our Lord. **Amen.** 7*

Almighty God,
you sent your Son Jesus Christ
to be the light of the world.
Free us from all that darkens and ensnares us,
and bring us to eternal light and joy;
through the power of him
who is alive and reigns with you,
in the unity of the Holy Spirit,
one God, now and for ever. **Amen.** 4

Sunday between 20 and 26 November inclusive – Sunday before Advent

Eternal Father,
whose Son Jesus Christ ascended to the throne of heaven
that he might rule over all things as Lord:
keep the Church in the unity of the Spirit
and in the bond of peace,
and bring the whole created order to worship at his feet;
who is alive and reigns with you and the Holy Spirit,
one God, now and for ever. **Amen.** 12

Stir up, O Lord,
the wills of your faithful people,
that they, bringing forth the fruit of good works,
may by you be richly rewarded;
through Jesus Christ our Lord. **Amen.** 5*

COLLECTS FOR SPECIAL DAYS PARTICULAR OCCASIONS OR CIRCUMSTANCES

Bible Sunday

Blessèd Lord,
who caused all holy scriptures to be written for our learning:
help us so to hear them,
read, mark, learn and inwardly digest them,
that through patience and the comfort of your holy word
we may embrace and ever hold fast
the hope of everlasting life,
which you have given us in our Saviour Jesus Christ. **Amen.**
5*

Christian Unity

Lord God, we thank you for calling us
into the company of those who trust in Christ
and seek to obey his will.
May your Spirit guide and strengthen us
in mission and service to your world;
for we are strangers no longer
but pilgrims together on the way to your kingdom;
through Jesus Christ our Lord. **Amen.** 11

God of all,
through the gift of your Spirit
you have united your people
in the confession of your name.
Lead us, by the same Spirit,
to show to the whole earth
one mind in faith
and one faith for justice;
through Jesus Christ our Lord. **Amen.** 4*

Church Anniversary

Almighty God,
to whose glory we celebrate the anniversary of this church:
we thank you for the fellowship
of those who have worshipped here,
and we pray that all who seek you here may find you,
and, being filled with the Holy Spirit,
may become a living temple,
a dwelling place for your life-giving presence in the world.
We ask it through Jesus Christ our Lord. **Amen.** 14*

Harvest Thanksgiving

Bountiful God,
you entrust your creation to our care.
Grant us grace so to order our common life
that we may use your gifts to your glory,
for the relief of those in need
and for our own well-being;
through Jesus Christ our Lord. **Amen.** 1*

John and Charles Wesley

Almighty God,
you raised up your servants, John and Charles Wesley,
to proclaim anew the gift of redemption
and the life of holiness.
Pour out your Spirit,
and revive your work among us;
that inspired by the same faith,
and upheld by the same grace in word and sacrament,
we and all your children may be made one
in the unity of your Church on earth,
even as in heaven we are made one in you;
through Jesus Christ our Lord. **Amen.** 19*

God of mercy,
who inspired John and Charles Wesley
with zeal for your gospel:
grant that all your people may boldly proclaim your word
and evermore rejoice in singing your praises;
through Jesus Christ our Lord. **Amen.** 9*

New Year: Watchnight

Lord of history,
to whom a thousand years are as a day:
renew us by your Holy Spirit,
that, while we have life and breath,
we may serve you with courage and hope;
through the grace of your Son,
our Saviour Jesus Christ. **Amen.**

Eternal God,
you sent your Son to be born among us
that we might be born again to newness of life.
Fill us with the gladness of your great redemption,
that as we begin this new year with your blessing,
we may continue it in your favour,
and live all our days as your children
in the name of Jesus Christ our Lord;
who is alive and reigns with you and the Holy Spirit,
one God, now and for ever. **Amen.** 4*

Remembrance Sunday

Eternal God,
in whose perfect realm
no sword is drawn but the sword of justice,
and no strength known but the strength of love:
guide and inspire all who seek your kingdom,
that peoples and nations may find their security
in the love which casts out fear;
through Jesus Christ our Saviour. **Amen.** 9*

THE LECTIONARY

NOTES

1 Verses are stated inclusively. The letter *a* indicates the first part of a verse, *b* the second and, occasionally, *c* the third part.

2 Parts of a passage shown in brackets may be omitted.

3 When a reading begins with a personal pronoun (for example, '*He*'), the reader should substitute the appropriate name (for example, '*Jesus*'). When a reading begins with a direct quotation (for example, when a gospel reading starts with the words of Jesus) the reader should begin, for example, '*Jesus said*'.

4 Bible references are to **The New Revised Standard Version (Anglicized Edition)**. Adaptations may be needed when other translations are used.

THE LECTIONARY

	Year A Beginning on the First Sunday of Advent in 1998, 2001, 2004, 2007, 2010, 2013, 2016, 2019, 2022, 2025, 2028	Year B Beginning on the First Sunday of Advent in 1999, 2002, 2005, 2008, 2011, 2014, 2017, 2020, 2023, 2026, 2029	Year C Beginning on the First Sunday of Advent in 2000, 2003, 2006, 2009, 2012, 2015, 2018, 2021, 2024, 2027, 2030
First Sunday of Advent (Violet)	**Principal Service** Isaiah 2:1-5 Psalm 122 Romans 13:11-14 Matthew 24:36-44	**Principal Service** Isaiah 64:1-9 Psalm 80:1-7, 17-19 1 Corinthians 1:3-9 Mark 13:24-37	**Principal Service** Jeremiah 33:14-16 Psalm 25:1-10 1 Thessalonians 3:9-13 Luke 21:25-36
	Second Service Isaiah 52:1-12 Psalm 9:1-8 (9-20) Matthew 24:15-28	**Second Service** Isaiah 1:1-20 Psalm 25:1-10 (11-22) Matthew 21:1-13	**Second Service** Joel 3:9-21 Psalm 9:1-8 (9-20) Revelation 14:13 - 15:4 John 3:1-17
Second Sunday of Advent (Violet)	**Principal Service** Isaiah 11:1-10 Psalm 72:1-7, 18-19 Romans 15:4-13 Matthew 3:1-12	**Principal Service** Isaiah 40:1-11 Psalm 85:1-2, 8-13 2 Peter 3:8-15*a* Mark 1:1-8	**Principal Service** Baruch 5:1-9 *or* Malachi 3:1-4 *Canticle:* Benedictus (Luke 1:68-79) Philippians 1:3-11 Luke 3:1-6
	Second Service 1 Kings 18:17-39 Psalm 11 John 1:19-28	**Second Service** 1 Kings 22:1-28 Psalm 40: (1-10) 11-17 Romans 15:4-13 Matthew 11:2-11	**Second Service** Isaiah 40:1-11 Psalm 75 Luke 1:1-25

Third Sunday of Advent (Violet)	**Principal Service** Isaiah 35:1-10 Psalm 146:5-10 *or Canticle:* Magnificat (Luke 1:46*b*-55) James 5:7-10 Matthew 11:2-11	**Principal Service** Isaiah 61:1-4, 8-11 Psalm 126 *or Canticle:* Magnificat (Luke 1:46*b*-55) 1 Thessalonians 5:16-24 John 1:6-8, 19-28	**Principal Service** Zephaniah 3:14-20 *Canticle:* Isaiah 12:2-6 Philippians 4:4-7 Luke 3:7-18
	Second Service Isaiah 5:8-30 Psalm 12 Acts 13:13-41 John 5:31-40	**Second Service** Malachi 3:1-4; 4:1-6 Psalm 68:1-8 (9-20) Philippians 4:4-7 Matthew 14:1-12	**Second Service** Isaiah 35:1-10 Psalm 50:1-6 Luke 1:57-66 (67-80)
Fourth Sunday of Advent (Violet)	**Principal Service** Isaiah 7:10-16 Psalm 80:1-7, 17-19 Romans 1:1-7 Matthew 1:18-25	**Principal Service** 2 Samuel 7:1-11, 16 *Canticle:* Magnificat (Luke 1:46*b*-55) *or* Psalm 89:1-4, 19-26 Romans 16:25-27 Luke 1:26-38	**Principal Service** Micah 5:2-5*a* *Canticle:* Magnificat (Luke 1:46*b*-55) *or* Psalm 80:1-7 Hebrews 10:5-10 Luke 1:39-45 (46-55)
	Second Service 1 Samuel 1:1-20 Psalm 113 Revelation 22:6-21 Luke 1:39-45	**Second Service** Zechariah 2:10-13 Psalm 113 Luke 1:39-55	**Second Service** Isaiah 10:33 - 11:10 Psalm 123 Matthew 1:18-25

Christmas Day
(White *or* Gold)

Any of the following sets of readings may be used on the evening of Christmas Eve and on Christmas Day. Set III should be used at some service during the celebration.

I Isaiah 9:2-7; Psalm 96; Titus 2:11-14; Luke 2:1-14 (15-20)
II Isaiah 62:6-12; Psalm 97; Titus 3:4-7; Luke 2:(1-7) 8-20
III Isaiah 52:7-10; Psalm 98; Hebrews 1:1-4 (5-12); John 1:1-14

	Year A	Year B	Year C
First Sunday of Christmas *(26 to 31 December inclusive)* (White *or* Gold)	**Principal Service** Isaiah 63:7-9 Psalm 148 Hebrews 2:10-18 Matthew 2:13-23	**Principal Service** Isaiah 61:10 - 62:3 Psalm 148 Galatians 4:4-7 Luke 2:22-40	**Principal Service** 1 Samuel 2:18-20, 26 Psalm 148 Colossians 3:12-17 Luke 2:41-52
	Second Service Isaiah 49:7-13 Psalm 132 Philippians 2:1-11 Luke 2:41-52	**Second Service** Isaiah 35:1-10 Psalm 132 Colossians 1:9-20 Luke 2:41-52	**Second Service** Isaiah 61:1-11 Psalm 132 Galatians 3:27 - 4:7 Luke 2:15-21

When Christmas Day falls on a Sunday, it is regarded as the First Sunday of the Christmas Season and the readings listed above are not required.

Second Sunday of Christmas *(1 to 5 January inclusive)* (White *or* Gold)	**Principal Service** Jeremiah 31:7-14 Psalm 147:12-20 Ephesians 1:3-14 John 1:(1-9) 10-18 *or* Sirach/Ecclesiasticus 24:1-12 *Canticle*: Wisdom of Solomon 10:15-21 Ephesians 1:3-14 John 1:(1-9) 10-18	**Principal Service** Jeremiah 31:7-14 Psalm 147:12-20 Ephesians 1:3-14 John 1:(1-9) 10-18 *or* Sirach/Ecclesiasticus 24:1-12 *Canticle*: Wisdom of Solomon 10:15-21 Ephesians 1:3-14 John 1:(1-9) 10-18	**Principal Service** Jeremiah 31:7-14 Psalm 147:12-20 Ephesians 1:3-14 John 1:(1-9) 10-18 *or* Sirach/Ecclesiasticus 24:1-12 *Canticle:* Wisdom of Solomon 10:15-21 Ephesians 1:3-14 John 1:(1-9) 10-18

	Second Service Isaiah 41:21 - 42:4 Psalm 135:1-14 (15-21) Colossians 1:1-14 Matthew 2:13-23	**Second Service** Isaiah 46:3-13 Psalm 135:1-14 (15-21) Romans 12:1-8 Matthew 2:13-23	**Second Service** 1 Samuel 1:20-28 Psalm 135:1-14 (15-21) 1 John 4:7-16 Matthew 2:13-23

The Epiphany *(6 January)*
(White *or* Gold)

Principal Service: Isaiah 60:1-6; Psalm 72:1-7, 10-14; Ephesians 3:1-12; Matthew 2:1-12

Second Service: Baruch 4:36 - 5:9 *or* Isaiah 60:1-9; Psalms 98; 100; John 2:1-11

When 6 January is a weekday, these readings may replace those of the preceding Sunday.

Sunday between 7 and 13 January *– Sunday after Epiphany and the First Sunday in Ordinary Time* (White *or* Gold)	**Principal Service** Isaiah 42:1-9 Psalm 29 Acts 10:34-43 Matthew 3:13-17	**Principal Service** Genesis 1:1-5 Psalm 29 Acts 19:1-7 Mark 1:4-11	**Principal Service** Isaiah 43:1-7 Psalm 29 Acts 8:14-17 Luke 3:15-17, 21-22
	Second Service Joshua 3:1-8, 14-17 Psalms 46 Hebrews 1:1-12 Luke 3:15-22	**Second Service** Isaiah 42:1-9 Psalms 46 Ephesians 2:1-10 Matthew 3:13-17	**Second Service** Isaiah 55:1-11 Psalms 46 Romans 6:1-11 Mark 1:4-11

	Year A	Year B	Year C
Sunday between 14 and 20 January – *Second Sunday in Ordinary Time* (Green)	**Principal Service** Isaiah 49:1-7 Psalm 40:1-11 1 Corinthians 1:1-9 John 1:29-42	**Principal Service** 1 Samuel 3:1-10 (11-20) Psalm 139:1-6, 13-18 1 Corinthians 6:12-20 John 1:43-51	**Principal Service** Isaiah 62:1-5 Psalm 36:5-10 1 Corinthians 12:1-11 John 2:1-11
	Second Service Ezekiel 2:1 - 3:4 Psalm 96 Galatians 1:11-24 John 1:43-51	**Second Service** Isaiah 60:9-22 Psalm 96 Hebrews 6:17 - 7:10 Matthew 8:5-13	**Second Service** 1 Samuel 3:1-20 Psalm 96 Ephesians 4:1-16 John 1:29-42
Sunday between 21 and 27 January – *Third Sunday in Ordinary Time* (Green)	**Principal Service** Isaiah 9:1-4 Psalm 27:1, 4-9 1 Corinthians 1:10-18 Matthew 4:12-23	**Principal Service** Jonah 3:1-5, 10 Psalm 62:5-12 1 Corinthians 7:29-31 Mark 1:14-20	**Principal Service** Nehemiah 8:1-3, 5-6, 8-10 Psalm 19 1 Corinthians 12:12-31*a* Luke 4:14-21
	Second Service Ecclesiastes 3:1-11 Psalm 33:1-12 (13-22) 1 Peter 1:3-12 Luke 4:14-21	**Second Service** Jeremiah 3:21 - 4:2 Psalm 33:1-12 (13-22) Titus 2:1-8, 11-14 Matthew 4:12-23	**Second Service** Numbers 9:15-23 Psalm 33:1-12 (13-22) 1 Corinthians 7:17-24 Mark 1:21-28

Sunday between 28 January and 3 February* – *Fourth Sunday in Ordinary Time* (Green)	**Principal Service** Micah 6:1-8 Psalm 15 1 Corinthians 1:18-31 Matthew 5:1-12	**Principal Service** Deuteronomy 18:15-20 Psalm 111 1 Corinthians 8:1-13 Mark 1:21-28	**Principal Service** Jeremiah 1:4-10 Psalm 71:1-6 1 Corinthians 13:1-13 Luke 4:21-30
	Second Service Genesis 28:10-22 Psalm 34:1-10 (11-22) Philemon 1-16 Mark 1:21-28	**Second Service** 1 Samuel 3:1-20 Psalm 34:1-10 (11-22) 1 Corinthians 14:12-20 Matthew 13:10-17	**Second Service** 1 Chronicles 29:6-19 Psalm 34:1-10 (11-22) Acts 7:44-50 John 4:19-29*a*
Sunday between 4 and 10 February* – *Fifth Sunday in Ordinary Time* (Green)	**Principal Service** Isaiah 58:1-9*a* (9*b*-12) Psalm 112:1-9 (10) 1 Corinthians 2:1-12 (13-16) Matthew 5:13-20	**Principal Service** Isaiah 40:21-31 Psalm 147:1-11, 20*c* 1 Corinthians 9:16-23 Mark 1:29-39	**Principal Service** Isaiah 6:1-8 (9-13) Psalm 138 1 Corinthians 15:1-11 Luke 5:1-11
	Second Service Amos 2:4-16 Psalm 4 Ephesians 4:17-32 Mark 1:29-39	**Second Service** Numbers 13:1-2, 27-33 Psalm 5 Philippians 2:12-28 Luke 5:1-11	**Second Service** Wisdom of Solomon 6:1-21 *or* Hosea 1:1-11 Psalm 2 Colossians 3:1-22 Matthew 5:13-20

* *Unless it is the Sunday before Lent or falls in Lent*

	Year A	Year B	Year C
Sunday between 11 and 17 February* *– Sixth Sunday in Ordinary Time* (Green)	**Principal Service** Deuteronomy 30:15-20 *or* Sirach/Ecclesiasticus 15:15-20 Psalm 119:1-8 1 Corinthians 3:1-9 Matthew 5:21-37	**Principal Service** 2 Kings 5:1-14 Psalm 30 1 Corinthians 9:24-27 Mark 1:40-45	**Principal Service** Jeremiah 17:5-10 Psalm 1 1 Corinthians 15:12-20 Luke 6:17-26
	Second Service Amos 3:1-8 Psalm 13 Ephesians 5:1-17 Mark 1:40-45	**Second Service** Numbers 20:2-13 Psalm 6 Philippians 3:7-21 Luke 6:17-26	**Second Service** Wisdom of Solomon 11:21 - 12:11 *or* Hosea 10:1-8, 12 Psalm 6 Galatians 4:8-20 Matthew 5:21-37
Sunday between 18 and 24 February* *– Seventh Sunday in Ordinary Time* (Green)	**Principal Service** Leviticus 19:1-2, 9-18 Psalm 119:33-40 1 Corinthians 3:10-11, 16-23 Matthew 5:38-48	**Principal Service** Isaiah 43:18-25 Psalm 41 2 Corinthians 1:18-22 Mark 2:1-12	**Principal Service** Genesis 45:3-11, 15 Psalm 37:1-11, 39-40 1 Corinthians 15:35-38, 42-50 Luke 6:27-38
	Second Service Amos 9:5-15 Psalm 18:1-19 *or* Psalm 18:20-29 Ephesians 6:1-20 Mark 2:1-12	**Second Service** Numbers 22:21 - 23:12 Psalm 10 Philippians 4:10-20 Luke 6:27-38	**Second Service** Hosea 14:1-9 Psalm 13 Galatians 5:2-10 Matthew 6:1-8

** Unless it is the Sunday before Lent or falls in Lent*

Sunday between 25 and 29 February* – *Eighth Sunday in Ordinary Time* (Green)	**Principal Service** Isaiah 49:8-16*a* Psalm 131 1 Corinthians 4:1-5 Matthew 6:24-34	**Principal Service** Hosea 2:14-20 Psalm 103:1-13, 22 2 Corinthians 3:1-6 Mark 2:13-22	**Principal Service** Sirach/Ecclesiasticus 27:4-7 *or* Isaiah 55:10-13 Psalm 92:1-4, 12-15 1 Corinthians 15:51-58 Luke 6:39-49
	Second Service Proverbs 8:1, 22-31 Psalm 148 Revelation 4:1-11 Luke 12:16-31	**Second Service** Genesis 2:4*b*-25 Psalm 65 Luke 8:22-35	**Second Service** Genesis 1:1 - 2:3 Psalm 147:(1-11) 12-20 Matthew 6:25-34
Sunday before Lent (Green)	**Principal Service** Exodus 24:12-18 Psalm 2 *or* Psalm 99 2 Peter 1:16-21 Matthew 17:1-9	**Principal Service** 2 Kings 2:1-12 Psalm 50:1-6 2 Corinthians 4:3-6 Mark 9:2-9	**Principal Service** Exodus 34:29-35 Psalm 99 2 Corinthians 3:12 - 4:2 Luke 9:28-36 (37-43)
	Second Service Sirach/Ecclesiasticus 48:1-10 *or* 2 Kings 2:1-12 Psalm 84 Matthew 17:(1-8) 9-23	**Second Service** 1 Kings 19:1-16 Psalm 2 2 Peter 1:16-21 Mark 9:(2-8) 9-13	**Second Service** Exodus 3:1-6 Psalm 89:(1-4) 5-12 (13-18) John 12:27-36*a*
Ash Wednesday (Violet)	Joel 2:1-2, 12-17 *or* Isaiah 58:1-12; Psalm 51:1-17; 2 Corinthians 5:20*b* - 6:10; Matthew 6:1-6, 16-21		

* *Unless it is the Sunday before Lent or falls in Lent*

	Year A	Year B	Year C
First Sunday in Lent (Violet)	**Principal Service** Genesis 2:15-17; 3:1-7 Psalm 32 Romans 5:12-19 Matthew 4:1-11	**Principal Service** Genesis 9:8-17 Psalm 25:1-10 1 Peter 3:18-22 Mark 1:9-15	**Principal Service** Deuteronomy 26:1-11 Psalm 91:1-2, 9-16 Romans 10:8*b*-13 Luke 4:1-13
	Second Service Deuteronomy 6:4-9, 16-25 Psalm 50:1-15 Luke 15:1-10	**Second Service** Genesis 2:15-17; 3:1-7 Psalm 119:17-32 Romans 5:12-19 Luke 13:31-35	**Second Service** Jonah 3:1-10 Psalm 119:73-88 Luke 18:9-14
Second Sunday in Lent (Violet)	**Principal Service** Genesis 12:1-4*a* Psalm 121 Romans 4:1-5, 13-17 John 3:1-17	**Principal Service** Genesis 17:1-7, 15-16 Psalm 22:23-31 Romans 4:13-25 Mark 8:31-38	**Principal Service** Genesis 15:1-12, 17-18 Psalm 27 Philippians 3:17 - 4:1 Luke 13:31-35
	Second Service Numbers 21:4-9 Psalm 135:1-14 (15-21) Luke 14:27-33	**Second Service** Genesis 12:1-9 Psalm 135:1-14 (15-21) Hebrews 11:1-3, 8-16	**Second Service** Jeremiah 22:1-9, 13-17 Psalm 135:1-14 (15-21) Luke 14:27-33
Third Sunday in Lent (Violet)	**Principal Service** Exodus 17:1-7 Psalm 95 Romans 5:1-11 John 4:5-42	**Principal Service** Exodus 20:1-17 Psalm 19 1 Corinthians 1:18-25 John 2:13-22	**Principal Service** Isaiah 55:1-9 Psalm 63:1-8 1 Corinthians 10:1-13 Luke 13:1-9

	Year A	Year B	Year C
	Second Service Joshua 1:1-9 Psalm 40 Ephesians 6:10-20 John 2:13-22	**Second Service** Exodus 5:1 - 6:1 Psalms 11; 12 Philippians 3:4*b*-14 Matthew 10:16-22	**Second Service** Genesis 28:10-19*a* Psalms 12; 13 John 1:35-51
Fourth Sunday in Lent (Violet)	**Principal Service** 1 Samuel 16:1-13 Psalm 23 Ephesians 5:8-14 John 9:1-41	**Principal Service** Numbers 21:4-9 Psalm 107:1-3, 17-22 Ephesians 2:1-10 John 3:14-21	**Principal Service** Joshua 5:9-12 Psalm 32 2 Corinthians 5:16-21 Luke 15:1-3, 11*b*-32
	Second Service Micah 7:1-20 *or* Prayer of Manasseh 1-15 Psalm 31:1-8 (9-16) James 5:1-20 John 3:14-21	**Second Service** Exodus 6:2-13 Psalms 13; 14 Romans 5:1-11 John 12:1-8	**Second Service** Prayer of Manasseh 1-15 *or* Isaiah 40:27 - 41:13 Psalm 30 2 Timothy 4:1-18 John 11:17-44
Or for **Mothering Sunday** (Violet)	Exodus 2:1-10 *or* 1 Samuel 1:20-28; Psalm 34:11-20 *or* Psalm 127:1-4; 2 Corinthians 1:3-7 *or* Colossians 3:12-17; Luke 2:33-35 *or* John 19:25-27		
Fifth Sunday in Lent *(First Sunday of the Passion)* (Violet)	**Principal Service** Ezekiel 37:1-14 Psalm 130 Romans 8:6-11 John 11:1-45	**Principal Service** Jeremiah 31:31-34 Psalm 51:1-12 *or* Psalm 119:9-16 Hebrews 5:5-10 John 12:20-33	**Principal Service** Isaiah 43:16-21 Psalm 126 Philippians 3:4*b*-14 John 12:1-8

	Year A	Year B	Year C
Fifth Sunday in Lent continued	**Second Service** Lamentations 3:19-33 Psalm 30 Matthew 20:17-34	**Second Service** Exodus 7:8-24 Psalm 34:1-10 (11-22) Romans 5:12-21 Luke 22:1-13	**Second Service** 2 Chronicles 35:1-6, 10-16 Psalm 35:1-9 (10-28) Luke 22:1-13
Sixth Sunday in Lent *(Second Sunday of the Passion or Palm Sunday)* (Violet *or* Red) **Entry into Jerusalem**	**Principal Service** Matthew 21:1-11 Psalm 118:1-2, 19-29	**Principal Service** Mark 11:1-11 *or* John 12:12-16 Psalm 118:1-2, 19-29	**Principal Service** Luke 19:28-40 Psalm 118:1-2, 19-29
The Passion	**Principal Service** Isaiah 50:4-9*a* Psalm 31:9-16 Philippians 2:5-11 Matthew 26:14 - 27:66 *or* Matthew 27:11-54	**Principal Service** Isaiah 50:4-9*a* Psalm 31:9-16 Philippians 2:5-11 Mark 14:1 - 15:47 *or* Mark 15:1-39 (40-47)	**Principal Service** Isaiah 50:4-9*a* Psalm 31:9-16 Philippians 2:5-11 Luke 22:14 - 23:56 *or* Luke 23:1-49
	Second Service Isaiah 5:1-7 Psalm 80 Matthew 21:33-46	**Second Service** Isaiah 5:1-7 Psalm 69:1-18 Mark 12:1-12	**Second Service** Isaiah 5:1-7 Psalm 69:1-18 Luke 20:9-19
Monday in Holy Week (Violet *or* Red)	Isaiah 42:1-9; Psalm 36:5-11; Hebrews 9:11-15; John 12:1-11		
Tuesday in Holy Week (Violet *or* Red)	Isaiah 49:1-7; Psalm 71:1-14; 1 Corinthians 1:18-31; John 12:20-36		

Wednesday in Holy Week
(Violet *or* Red)

Isaiah 50:4-9*a*; Psalm 70; Hebrews 12:1-3; John 13:21-32

Maundy Thursday
(White *or* Gold)

Exodus 12:1-4 (5-10) 11-14; Psalm 116:1-2, 12-19; 1 Corinthians 11:23-26; John 13:1-17, 31*b*-35

The readings for the Watch and the Vigil are given on pages 252 and 254.

Good Friday
(None *or* Red)

Isaiah 52:13 - 53:12; Psalm 22; Hebrews 10:16-25 *or* Hebrews 4:14-16; 5:7-9; John 18:1 - 19:42

Holy Saturday
(None)

Job 14:1-14 *or* Lamentations 3:1-9, 19-24; Psalm 31:1-4, 15-16; 1 Peter 4:1-8; Matthew 27:57-66 *or* John 19:38-42

The readings for the Easter Vigil are given in the text of the service which begins on page 265.

Easter Day
(White *or* Gold)

Principal Service
Acts 10:34-43
or Jeremiah 31:1-6
Psalm 118:1-2, 14-24
Colossians 3:1-4
or Acts 10:34-43
John 20:1-18
or Matthew 28:1-10

Second Service
Song of Solomon 3:2-5; 8:6-7
Psalms 114; 117
Revelation 1:12-18
John 20:11-18

Principal Service
Acts 10:34-43
or Isaiah 25:6-9
Psalm 118:1-2, 14-24
1 Corinthians 15:1-11
or Acts 10:34-43
John 20:1-18
or Mark 16:1-8

Second Service
Ezekiel 37:1-14
Psalms 114; 117
Luke 24:13-35

Principal Service
Acts 10:34-43
or Isaiah 65:17-25
Psalm 118:1-2, 14-24
1 Corinthians 15:19-26
or Acts 10:34-43
John 20:1-18
or Luke 24:1-12

Second Service
Isaiah 43:1-21
Psalms 66; 114; 117
1 Corinthians 15:1-11
John 20:19-23

	Year A	Year B	Year C
Second Sunday of Easter (White *or* Gold)	**Principal Service** Acts 2:14*a*, 22-32 Psalm 16 1 Peter 1:3-9 John 20:19-31	**Principal Service** Acts 4:32-35 Psalm 133 1 John 1:1 - 2:2 John 20:19-31	**Principal Service** Acts 5:27-32 Psalm 118:14-29 *or* Psalm 150 Revelation 1:4-8 John 20:19-31
	Second Service Daniel 6:(1-5) 6-23 Psalm 30:1-5 Mark 15:46 - 16:8	**Second Service** Isaiah 26:1-9, 19 Psalm 143:1-11 Luke 24:1-12	**Second Service** Isaiah (52:13-15) 53:1-6 (7-8) 9-12 Psalm 16 Luke 24:13-35
Third Sunday of Easter (White *or* Gold)	**Principal Service** Acts 2:14*a*, 36-41 Psalm 116:1-4, 12-19 1 Peter 1:17-23 Luke 24:13-35	**Principal Service** Acts 3:12-19 Psalm 4 1 John 3:1-7 Luke 24:36*b*-48	**Principal Service** Acts 9:1-6 (7-20) Psalm 30 Revelation 5:11-14 John 21:1-19
	Second Service Haggai 1:13 - 2:9 Psalm 48 1 Corinthians 3:10-17 John 2:13-22	**Second Service** Deuteronomy 7:7-13 Psalm 142 Revelation 2:1-11 Luke 16:19-31	**Second Service** Isaiah 38:9-20 Psalm 86 John 11:(17-26) 27-44
Fourth Sunday of Easter (White *or* Gold)	**Principal Service** Acts 2:42-47 Psalm 23 1 Peter 2:19-25 John 10:1-10	**Principal Service** Acts 4:5-12 Psalm 23 1 John 3:16-24 John 10:11-18	**Principal Service** Acts 9:36-43 Psalm 23 Revelation 7:9-17 John 10:22-30

	Second Service Ezra 3:1-13 Psalm 29:1-10 Ephesians 2:11-22 Luke 19:37-48	**Second Service** Exodus 16:4-15 Psalm 81:8-16 Revelation 2:12-17 John 6:30-40	**Second Service** Isaiah 63:7-14 Psalms 113; 114 Luke 24:36-49
Fifth Sunday of Easter (White *or* Gold)	**Principal Service** Acts 7:55-60 Psalm 31:1-5, 15-16 1 Peter 2:2-10 John 14:1-14	**Principal Service** Acts 8:26-40 Psalm 22:25-31 1 John 4:7-21 John 15:1-8	**Principal Service** Acts 11:1-18 Psalm 148 Revelation 21:1-6 John 13:31-35
	Second Service Zechariah 4:1-10 Psalm 147:1-11 Revelation 21:1-14 Luke 2:25-32 (33-38)	**Second Service** Isaiah 60:1-14 Psalm 96 Revelation 3:1-13 Mark 16:9-16	**Second Service** Daniel 6:(1-5) 6-23 Psalm 98 Mark 15:46 - 16:8
Sixth Sunday of Easter (White *or* Gold)	**Principal Service** Acts 17:22-31 Psalm 66:8-20 1 Peter 3:13-22 John 14:15-21	**Principal Service** Acts 10:44-48 Psalm 98 1 John 5:1-6 John 15:9-17	**Principal Service** Acts 16:9-15 Psalm 67 Revelation 21:10, 22 - 22:5 John 14:23-29 *or* John 5:1-9
	Second Service Zechariah 8:1-13 Psalms 36:5-10; 87 Revelation 21:22 - 22:5 John 21:1-14	**Second Service** Song of Solomon 4:16 - 5:2; 8:6-7 Psalm 45 Revelation 3:14-22 Luke 22:24-30	**Second Service** Zephaniah 3:14-20 Psalms 126; 127 Matthew 28:1-10, 16-20

	Year A	Year B	Year C
Ascension Day (White *or* Gold)	Acts 1:1-11; Psalm 47 *or* Psalm 93; Ephesians 1:15-23; Luke 24:44-53		
Seventh Sunday of Easter *(Sunday in Ascensiontide)* (White *or* Gold)	**Principal Service** Acts 1:6-14 Psalm 68:1-10, 32-35 1 Peter 4:12-14; 5:6-11 John 17:1-11	**Principal Service** Acts 1:15-17, 21-26 Psalm 1 1 John 5:9-13 John 17:6-19	**Principal Service** Acts 16:16-34 Psalm 97 Revelation 22:12-14, 16-17, 20-21 John 17:20-26
	Second Service 2 Samuel 23:1-5 Psalm 47 Ephesians 1:15-23 Mark 16:14-20	**Second Service** Isaiah 61:1-11 Psalm 147:1-11 Luke 4:14-21	**Second Service** Isaiah 44:1-8 Psalm 68:1-14 (15-18) 19-20 (21-35) Ephesians 4:7-16 Luke 24:44-53
Pentecost (Red)	**Principal Service** Acts 2:1-21 *or* Numbers 11:24-30 Psalm 104:24-34, 35*b* 1 Corinthians 12:3*b*-13 *or* Acts 2:1-21 John 20:19-23 *or* John 7:37-39	**Principal Service** Acts 2:1-21 *or* Ezekiel 37:1-14 Psalm 104:24-34, 35*b* Romans 8:22-27 *or* Acts 2:1-21 John 15:26-27; 16:4*b*-15	**Principal Service** Acts 2:1-21 *or* Genesis 11:1-9 Psalm 104:24-34, 35*b* Romans 8:14-17 *or* Acts 2:1-21 John 14:8-17 (25-27)

	Second Service Joel 2:21-32 Psalms 67; 133 Acts 2:14-21 (22-38) Luke 24:44-53	**Second Service** Ezekiel 36:22-28 Psalm 139:1-12 (13-18, 23-24) Acts 2:22-38 John 20:19-23	**Second Service** Exodus 33:7-20 Psalms 36:5-10; 150 2 Corinthians 3:4-18 John 16:4*b*-15
Trinity Sunday (White *or* Gold)	**Principal Service** Genesis 1:1 - 2:4*a* Psalm 8 2 Corinthians 13:11-13 Matthew 28:16-20	**Principal Service** Isaiah 6:1-8 Psalm 29 Romans 8:12-17 John 3:1-17	**Principal Service** Proverbs 8:1-4, 22-31 Psalm 8 Romans 5:1-5 John 16:12-15
	Second Service Isaiah 6:1-8 Psalms 93; 150 John 16:5-15	**Second Service** Ezekiel 1:4-10, 22-28*a* Psalm 104:1-9 Revelation 4:1-11 Mark 1:1-13	**Second Service** Exodus 3:1-15 Psalm 73:1-3, 16-28 John 3:1-17
Sunday between 24 and 28 May inclusive *(if after Trinity Sunday) – Eighth Sunday in Ordinary Time* (Green)	**Principal Service** Isaiah 49:8-16*a* Psalm 131 1 Corinthians 4:1-5 Matthew 6:24-34	**Principal Service** Hosea 2:14-20 Psalm 103:1-13, 22 2 Corinthians 3:1-6 Mark 2:13-22	**Principal Service** Sirach/Ecclesiasticus 27:4-7 *or* Isaiah 55:10-13 Psalm 92:1-4, 12-15 1 Corinthians 15:51-58 Luke 6:39-49
	Second Service Proverbs 8:1, 22-31 Psalm 148 Revelation 4:1-11 Luke 12:16-31	**Second Service** Genesis 2:4*b*-25 Psalm 65 Luke 8:22-35	**Second Service** Genesis 1:1 - 2:3 Psalm 147:(1-11) 12-20 Matthew 6:25-34

	Year A	Year B	Year C
Sunday between 29 May and 4 June inclusive *(if after Trinity Sunday) – Ninth Sunday in Ordinary Time* (Green)	**Principal Service** *Continuous* Genesis 6:9-22; 7:24; 8:14-19 Psalm 46 Romans 1:16-17; 3:22*b*-28 (29-31) Matthew 7:21-29 *Related* Deuteronomy 11:18-21, 26-28 Psalm 31:1-5, 19-24 Romans 1:16-17; 3:22*b*-28 (29-31) Matthew 7:21-29 **Second Service** Ruth 2:1-20*a* Psalm 33:(1-12) 13-22 Luke 8:4-15	**Principal Service** *Continuous* 1 Samuel 3:1-10 (11-20) Psalm 139:1-6, 13-18 2 Corinthians 4:5-12 Mark 2:23 - 3:6 *Related* Deuteronomy 5:12-15 Psalm 81:1-10 2 Corinthians 4:5-12 Mark 2:23 - 3:6 **Second Service** Jeremiah 5:1-19 Psalm 35:1-10 (11-28) Romans 7:7-25 Luke 7:1-10	**Principal Service** *Continuous* 1 Kings 18:20-21 (22-29) 30-39 Psalm 96 Galatians 1:1-12 Luke 7:1-10 *Related* 1 Kings 8:22-23, 41-43 Psalm 96:1-9 Galatians 1:1-12 Luke 7:1-10 **Second Service** Genesis 4:1-16 Psalm 39 Mark 3:7-19
Sunday between 5 and 11 June inclusive *(if after Trinity Sunday) – Tenth Sunday in Ordinary Time* (Green)	**Principal Service** *Continuous* Genesis 12:1-9 Psalm 33:1-12 Romans 4:13-25 Matthew 9:9-13, 18-26	**Principal Service** *Continuous* 1 Samuel 8:4-11 (12-15) 16-20 (11:14-15) Psalm 138 2 Corinthians 4:13 - 5:1 Mark 3:20-35	**Principal Service** *Continuous* 1 Kings 17:8-16 (17-24) Psalm 146 Galatians 1:11-24 Luke 7:11-17

	Related Hosea 5:15 - 6:6 Psalm 50:7-15 Romans 4:13-25 Matthew 9:9-13, 18-26	*Related* Genesis 3:8-15 Psalm 130 2 Corinthians 4:13 - 5:1 Mark 3:20-35	*Related* 1 Kings 17:17-24 Psalm 30 Galatians 1:11-24 Luke 7:11-17
	Second Service 1 Samuel 18:1-16 Psalm 41 Luke 8:41-56	**Second Service** Jeremiah 6:16-21 Psalm 37:1-11 (12-14) Romans 9:1-13 Luke 7:11-17	**Second Service** Genesis 8:15 - 9:17 Psalm 44:1-8 (9-26) Mark 4:1-20
Sunday between 12 and 18 June inclusive *(if after Trinity Sunday) – Eleventh Sunday in Ordinary Time* (Green)	**Principal Service** *Continuous* Genesis 18:1-15 (21:1-7) Psalm 116:1-2, 12-19 Romans 5:1-8 Matthew 9:35 - 10:8 (9-23)	**Principal Service** *Continuous* 1 Samuel 15:34 - 16:13 Psalm 20 2 Corinthians 5:6-10 (11-13) 14-17 Mark 4:26-34	**Principal Service** *Continuous* 1 Kings 21:1-10 (11-14) 15-21*a* Psalm 5:1-8 Galatians 2:15-21 Luke 7:36 - 8:3
	Related Exodus 19:2-8*a* Psalm 100 Romans 5:1-8 Matthew 9:35 - 10:8 (9-23)	*Related* Ezekiel 17:22-24 Psalm 92:1-4, 12-15 2 Corinthians 5:6-10 (11-13) 14-17 Mark 4:26-34	*Related* 2 Samuel 11:26 - 12:10, 13-15 Psalm 32 Galatians 2:15-21 Luke 7:36 - 8:3
	Second Service 1 Samuel 21:1-15 Psalm 43 Luke 11:14-28	**Second Service** Jeremiah 7:1-16 Psalm 39 Romans 9:14-26 Luke 7:36 - 8:3	**Second Service** Genesis 13:1-18 Psalm 52 Mark 4:21-41

	Year A	Year B	Year C
Sunday between 19 and 25 June inclusive *(if after Trinity Sunday)* *– Twelfth Sunday in Ordinary Time* (Green)	**Principal Service** *Continuous* Genesis 21:8-21 Psalm 86:1-10, 16-17 Romans 6:1*b*-11 Matthew 10:24-39	**Principal Service** *Continuous* 1 Samuel 17:(1*a*, 4-11, 19-23) 32-49 Psalm 9:9-20 *or* 1 Samuel 17:57 - 18:5, 10-16 Psalm 133 2 Corinthians 6:1-13 Mark 4:35-41	**Principal Service** *Continuous* 1 Kings 19:1-4 (5-7) 8-15*a* Psalms 42; 43 Galatians 3:23-29 Luke 8:26-39
	Related Jeremiah 20:7-13 Psalm 69:7-10 (11-15) 16-18 Romans 6:1*b*-11 Matthew 10:24-39	*Related* Job 38:1-11 Psalm 107:1-3, 23-32 2 Corinthians 6:1-13 Mark 4:35-41	*Related* Isaiah 65:1-9 Psalm 22:19-28 Galatians 3:23-29 Luke 8:26-39
	Second Service 1 Samuel 24:1-17 Psalm 46 Luke 14:12-24	**Second Service** Jeremiah 10:1-16 Psalm 49 Romans 11:25-36 Luke 8:26-39	**Second Service** Genesis 24:1-27 Psalm 57 Mark 5:21-43
Sunday between 26 June and 2 July inclusive *– Thirteenth Sunday in Ordinary Time* (Green)	**Principal Service** *Continuous* Genesis 22:1-14 Psalm 13 Romans 6:12-23 Matthew 10:40-42	**Principal Service** *Continuous* 2 Samuel 1:1, 17-27 Psalm 130 2 Corinthians 8:7-15 Mark 5:21-43	**Principal Service** *Continuous* 2 Kings 2:1-2, 6-14 Psalm 77:1-2, 11-20 Galatians 5:1, 13-25 Luke 9:51-62

	Related Jeremiah 28:5-9 Psalm 89:1-4, 15-18 Romans 6:12-23 Matthew 10:40-42	*Related* Wisdom of Solomon 1:13-15; 2:23-24 *or* Lamentations 3:23-33 Psalm 30 2 Corinthians 8:7-15 Mark 5:21-43	*Related* 1 Kings 19:15-16, 19-21 Psalm 16 Galatians 5:1, 13-25 Luke 9:51-62
	Second Service 1 Samuel 28:3-19 Psalm 50:1-15 (16-23) Luke 17:20-37	**Second Service** Jeremiah 11:1-14 Psalm 53 Romans 13:1-10 Luke 9:51-62	**Second Service** Genesis 27:1-40 Psalm 60 Mark 6:1-6
Sunday between 3 and 9 July inclusive *– Fourteenth Sunday in Ordinary Time* (Green)	**Principal Service** *Continuous* Genesis 24:34-38, 42-49, 58-67 Psalm 45:10-17 *or Canticle:* Song of Solomon 2:8-13 Romans 7:15-25*a* Matthew 11:16-19, 25-30	**Principal Service** *Continuous* 2 Samuel 5:1-5, 9-10 Psalm 48 2 Corinthians 12:2-10 Mark 6:1-13	**Principal Service** *Continuous* 2 Kings 5:1-14 Psalm 30 Galatians 6:(1-6) 7-16 Luke 10:1-11, 16-20
	Related Zechariah 9:9-12 Psalm 145:8-14 Romans 7:15-25*a* Matthew 11:16-19, 25-30	*Related* Ezekiel 2:1-5 Psalm 123 2 Corinthians 12:2-10 Mark 6:1-13	*Related* Isaiah 66:10-14 Psalm 66:1-9 Galatians 6:(1-6) 7-16 Luke 10:1-11, 16-20
	Second Service 2 Samuel 2:1-11; 3:1 Psalm 56 Luke 18:31 - 19:10	**Second Service** Jeremiah 20:1-11*a* Psalm 64 Romans 14:1-17 Luke 10:1-11, 16-20	**Second Service** Genesis 29:1-20 Psalm 65 Mark 6:7-29

	Year A	Year B	Year C
Sunday between 10 and 16 July inclusive *– Fifteenth Sunday in Ordinary Time* (Green)	**Principal Service** *Continuous* Genesis 25:19-34 Psalm 119:105-112 Romans 8:1-11 Matthew 13:1-9, 18-23 *Related* Isaiah 55:10-13 Psalm 65:(1-8) 9-13 Romans 8:1-11 Matthew 13:1-9, 18-23 **Second Service** 2 Samuel 7:18-29 Psalm 60 Luke 19:41 - 20:8	**Principal Service** *Continuous* 2 Samuel 6:1-5, 12*b*-19 Psalm 24 Ephesians 1:3-14 Mark 6:14-29 *Related* Amos 7:7-15 Psalm 85:8-13 Ephesians 1:3-14 Mark 6:14-29 **Second Service** Job 4:1; 5:6-27 *or* Sirach/Ecclesiasticus 4:11-31 Psalm 66:1-9 (10-20) Romans 15:14-29 Luke 10:25-37	**Principal Service** *Continuous* Amos 7:7-17 Psalm 82 Colossians 1:1-14 Luke 10:25-37 *Related* Deuteronomy 30:9-14 Psalm 25:1-10 Colossians 1:1-14 Luke 10:25-37 **Second Service** Genesis 32:9-30 Psalm 77:1-12 (13-20) Mark 7:1-23
Sunday between 17 and 23 July inclusive *– Sixteenth Sunday in Ordinary Time* (Green)	**Principal Service** *Continuous* Genesis 28:10-19*a* Psalm 139:1-12, 23-24 Romans 8:12-25 Matthew 13:24-30, 36-43	**Principal Service** *Continuous* 2 Samuel 7:1-14*a* Psalm 89:20-37 Ephesians 2:11-22 Mark 6:30-34, 53-56	**Principal Service** *Continuous* Amos 8:1-12 Psalm 52 Colossians 1:15-28 Luke 10:38-42

	Related Wisdom of Solomon 12:13, 16-19 *or* Isaiah 44:6-8 Psalm 86:11-17 Romans 8:12-25 Matthew 13:24-30, 36-43	*Related* Jeremiah 23:1-6 Psalm 23 Ephesians 2:11-22 Mark 6:30-34, 53-56	*Related* Genesis 18:1-10*a* Psalm 15 Colossians 1:15-28 Luke 10:38-42
	Second Service 1 Kings 2:10-12; 3:16-28 Psalm 67 Acts 4:1-22 Mark 6:30-34, 53-56	**Second Service** Job 13:13 - 14:6 *or* Sirach/Ecclesiasticus 18:1-14 Psalm 73:(1-20) 21-28 Hebrews 2:5-18 Luke 10:38-42	**Second Service** Genesis 41:1-16, 25-37 Psalm 81 1 Corinthians 4:8-13 John 4:31-35
Sunday between 24 and 30 July inclusive *– Seventeenth Sunday in Ordinary Time* (Green)	**Principal Service** *Continuous* Genesis 29:15-28 Psalm 105:1-11, 45*b* *or* Psalm 128 Romans 8:26-39 Matthew 13:31-33, 44-52	**Principal Service** *Continuous* 2 Samuel 11:1-15 Psalm 14 Ephesians 3:14-21 John 6:1-21	**Principal Service** *Continuous* Hosea 1:2-10 Psalm 85 Colossians 2:6-15 (16-19) Luke 11:1-13
	Related 1 Kings 3:5-12 Psalm 119:129-136 Romans 8:26-39 Matthew 13:31-33, 44-52	*Related* 2 Kings 4:42-44 Psalm 145:10-18 Ephesians 3:14-21 John 6:1-21	*Related* Genesis 18:20-32 Psalm 138 Colossians 2:6-15 (16-19) Luke 11:1-13

	Year A	Year B	Year C
Sunday between 24 and 30 July continued	**Second Service** 1 Kings 6:11-14, 23-38 Psalm 75 Acts 12:1-17 John 6:1-21	**Second Service** Job 19:1-27*a* *or* Sirach/Ecclesiasticus 38:24-34 Psalm 74:(1-11) 12-17 (18-23) Hebrews 8:1-13 Luke 11:1-13	**Second Service** Genesis 42:1-25 Psalm 88:1-9 (10-18) 1 Corinthians 10:1-24 Matthew 13:24-30 (31-43)
Sunday between 31 July and 6 August inclusive *– Eighteenth Sunday in Ordinary Time* (Green)	**Principal Service** *Continuous* Genesis 32:22-31 Psalm 17:1-7, 15 Romans 9:1-5 Matthew 14:13-21	**Principal Service** *Continuous* 2 Samuel 11:26 - 12:13*a* Psalm 51:1-12 Ephesians 4:1-16 John 6:24-35	**Principal Service** *Continuous* Hosea 11:1-11 Psalm 107:1-9, 43 Colossians 3:1-11 Luke 12:13-21
	Related Isaiah 55:1-5 Psalm 145:8-9, 14-21 Romans 9:1-5 Matthew 14:13-21	*Related* Exodus 16:2-4, 9-15 Psalm 78:23-29 Ephesians 4:1-16 John 6:24-35	*Related* Ecclesiastes 1:2, 12-14; 2:18-23 Psalm 49:1-12 Colossians 3:1-11 Luke 12:13-21
	Second Service 1 Kings 10:1-13 Psalm 80:1-7 (8-19) Acts 13:1-13 John 6:24-35	**Second Service** Job 28:1-28 *or* Sirach/Ecclesiasticus 42:15-25 Psalm 88:1-9 (10-18) Hebrews 11:17-31 Luke 12:13-21	**Second Service** Genesis 50:4-26 Psalm 107:1-12 (13-32) 1 Corinthians 14:1-19 Mark 6:45-52

Sunday between 7 and 13 August inclusive
– Nineteenth Sunday in Ordinary Time
(Green)

Principal Service
Continuous
Genesis 37:1-4, 12-28
Psalm 105:1-6, 16-22, 45*b*
Romans 10:5-15
Matthew 14:22-33

Related
1 Kings 19:9-18
Psalm 85:8-13
Romans 10:5-15
Matthew 14:22-33

Second Service
1 Kings 11:41 - 12:20
Psalm 86
Acts 14:8-20
John 6:35, 41-51

Principal Service
Continuous
2 Samuel 18:5-9, 15, 31-33
Psalm 130
Ephesians 4:25 - 5:2
John 6:35, 41-51

Related
1 Kings 19:4-8
Psalm 34:1-8
Ephesians 4:25 - 5:2
John 6:35, 41-51

Second Service
Job 39:1 - 40:4
or Sirach/Ecclesiasticus 43:13-33
Psalm 91:1-12 (13-16)
Hebrews 12:1-17
Luke 12:32-40

Principal Service
Continuous
Isaiah 1:1, 10-20
Psalm 50:1-8, 22-23
Hebrews 11:1-3, 8-16
Luke 12:32-40

Related
Genesis 15:1-6
Psalm 33:12-22
Hebrews 11:1-3, 8-16
Luke 12:32-40

Second Service
Isaiah 11:10 - 12:6
Psalm 108
2 Corinthians 1:1-22
Mark 7:24-30

Sunday between 14 and 20 August inclusive
– Twentieth Sunday in Ordinary Time
(Green)

Principal Service
Continuous
Genesis 45:1-15
Psalm 133
Romans 11:1-2*a*, 29-32
Matthew 15:(10-20) 21-28

Related
Isaiah 56:1, 6-8
Psalm 67
Romans 11:1-2*a*, 29-32
Matthew 15:(10-20) 21-28

Principal Service
Continuous
1 Kings 2:10-12; 3:3-14
Psalm 111
Ephesians 5:15-20
John 6:51-58

Related
Proverbs 9:1-6
Psalm 34:9-14
Ephesians 5:15-20
John 6:51-58

Principal Service
Continuous
Isaiah 5:1-7
Psalm 80:1-2, 8-19
Hebrews 11:29 - 12:2
Luke 12:49-56

Related
Jeremiah 23:23-29
Psalm 82
Hebrews 11:29 - 12:2
Luke 12:49-56

	Year A	Year B	Year C
Sunday between 14 and 20 August continued	**Second Service** 2 Kings 4:1-37 Psalm 90:1-12 (13-17) Acts 16:1-15 John 6:51-58	**Second Service** Exodus 2:23 - 3:10 Psalm 100 Hebrews 13:1-15 Luke 12:49-56	**Second Service** Isaiah 28:9-22 Psalm 119:17-24 (25-32) 2 Corinthians 8:1-9 Matthew 20:1-16
Sunday between 21 and 27 August inclusive *– Twenty-first Sunday in Ordinary Time* (Green)	**Principal Service** *Continuous* Exodus 1:8 - 2:10 Psalm 124 Romans 12:1-8 Matthew 16:13-20	**Principal Service** *Continuous* 1 Kings 8:(1, 6, 10-11) 22-30, 41-43 Psalm 84 Ephesians 6:10-20 John 6:56-69	**Principal Service** *Continuous* Jeremiah 1:4-10 Psalm 71:1-6 Hebrews 12:18-29 Luke 13:10-17
	Related Isaiah 51:1-6 Psalm 138 Romans 12:1-8 Matthew 16:13-20	*Related* Joshua 24:1-2*a*, 14-18 Psalm 34:15-22 Ephesians 6:10-20 John 6:56-69	*Related* Isaiah 58:9*b*-14 Psalm 103:1-8 Hebrews 12:18-29 Luke 13:10-17
	Second Service 2 Kings 6:8-23 Psalm 95 Acts 17:15-34 John 6:56-69	**Second Service** Exodus 4:27 - 5:1 Psalm 116:(1-11) 12-19 Hebrews 13:16-21 Luke 13:10-17	**Second Service** Isaiah 30:8-21 Psalm 119:49-56 (57-72) 2 Corinthians 9:1-15 Matthew 21:28-32

Sunday between 28 August and 3 September inclusive – *Twenty-second Sunday in Ordinary Time* (Green)	**Principal Service** *Continuous* Exodus 3:1-15 Psalm 105:1-6, 23-26, 45*c* Romans 12:9-21 Matthew 16:21-28 *Related* Jeremiah 15:15-21 Psalm 26:1-8 Romans 12:9-21 Matthew 16:21-28	**Principal Service** *Continuous* Song of Solomon 2:8-13 Psalm 45:1-2, 6-9 James 1:17-27 Mark 7:1-8, 14-15, 21-23 *Related* Deuteronomy 4:1-2, 6-9 Psalm 15 James 1:17-27 Mark 7:1-8, 14-15, 21-23	**Principal Service** *Continuous* Jeremiah 2:4-13 Psalm 81:1, 10-16 Hebrews 13:1-8, 15-16 Luke 14:1, 7-14 *Related* Sirach/Ecclesiasticus 10:12-18 *or* Proverbs 25:6-7 Psalm 112 Hebrews 13:1-8, 15-16 Luke 14:1, 7-14
	Second Service 2 Kings 6:24-25; 7:3-20 Psalm 105:1-15 Acts 18:1-16 Mark 7:1-8, 14-15, 21-23	**Second Service** Exodus 12:21-27 Psalm 119:(1-8) 9-16 Matthew 4:23 - 5:20	**Second Service** Isaiah 33:13-22 Psalm 119:81-88 (89-96) John 3:22-36
Sunday between 4 and 10 September inclusive – *Twenty-third Sunday in Ordinary Time* (Green)	**Principal Service** *Continuous* Exodus 12:1-14 Psalm 149 Romans 13:8-14 Matthew 18:15-20 *Related* Ezekiel 33:7-11 Psalm 119:33-40 Romans 13:8-14 Matthew 18:15-20	**Principal Service** *Continuous* Proverbs 22:1-2, 8-9, 22-23 Psalm 125 James 2:1-10 (11-13) 14-17 Mark 7:24-37 *Related* Isaiah 35:4-7*a* Psalm 146 James 2:1-10 (11-13) 14-17 Mark 7:24-37	**Principal Service** *Continuous* Jeremiah 18:1-11 Psalm 139:1-6, 13-18 Philemon 1-21 Luke 14:25-33 *Related* Deuteronomy 30:15-20 Psalm 1 Philemon 1-21 Luke 14:25-33

	Year A	Year B	Year C
Sunday between 4 and 10 September continued	**Second Service** Ezekiel 12:21 - 13:16 Psalm 108 Acts 19:1-20 Mark 7:24-37	**Second Service** Exodus 14:5-31 Psalm 119:(41-48) 49-56 Matthew 6:1-18	**Second Service** Isaiah 43:14 - 44:5 Psalm 121 John 5:30-47
Sunday between 11 and 17 September inclusive *– Twenty-fourth Sunday in Ordinary Time* (Green)	**Principal Service** *Continuous* Exodus 14:19-31 Psalm 114 *or Canticle:* Exodus 15:1*b*-11, 20-21 Romans 14:1-12 Matthew 18:21-35	**Principal Service** *Continuous* Proverbs 1:20-33 Psalm 19 *or Canticle:* Wisdom of Solomon 7:26 - 8:1 James 3:1-12 Mark 8:27-38	**Principal Service** *Continuous* Jeremiah 4:11-12, 22-28 Psalm 14 1 Timothy 1:12-17 Luke 15:1-10
	Related Genesis 50:15-21 Psalm 103:(1-7) 8-13 Romans 14:1-12 Matthew 18:21-35	*Related* Isaiah 50:4-9*a* Psalm 116:1-9 James 3:1-12 Mark 8:27-38	*Related* Exodus 32:7-14 Psalm 51:1-10 1 Timothy 1:12-17 Luke 15:1-10
	Second Service Ezekiel 20:1-8, 33-44 Psalm 119:41-48 (49-64) Acts 20:17-38 Mark 8:27-38	**Second Service** Exodus 18:13-26 Psalm 119:73-80 (81-88) Matthew 7:1-14	**Second Service** Isaiah 60:1-22 Psalms 124; 125 John 6:51-69

Sunday between 18 and 24 September inclusive – *Twenty-fifth Sunday in Ordinary Time* (Green)	**Principal Service** *Continuous* Exodus 16:2-15 Psalm 105:1-6, 37-45 Philippians 1:21-30 Matthew 20:1-16	**Principal Service** *Continuous* Proverbs 31:10-31 Psalm 1 James 3:13 - 4:3, 7-8*a* Mark 9:30-37	**Principal Service** *Continuous* Jeremiah 8:18 - 9:1 Psalm 79:1-9 1 Timothy 2:1-7 Luke 16:1-13
	Related Jonah 3:10 - 4:11 Psalm 145:1-8 Philippians 1:21-30 Matthew 20:1-16	*Related* Wisdom of Solomon 1:16 - 2:1, 12-22 *or* Jeremiah 11:18-20 Psalm 54 James 3:13 - 4:3, 7-8*a* Mark 9:30-37	*Related* Amos 8:4-7 Psalm 113 1 Timothy 2:1-7 Luke 16:1-13
	Second Service Ezekiel 33:23, 30 - 34:10 Psalm 119:(113-120) 121-128 (129-136) Acts 26:1, 9-25 Mark 9:30-37	**Second Service** Exodus 19:10-25 Psalm 119:137-144 (145-152) Matthew 8:23-34	**Second Service** Ezra 1:1-11 Psalm 129 John 7:14-36
Sunday between 25 September and 1 October inclusive – *Twenty-sixth Sunday in Ordinary Time* (Green)	**Principal Service** *Continuous* Exodus 17:1-7 Psalm 78:1-4, 12-16 Philippians 2:1-13 Matthew 21:23-32	**Principal Service** *Continuous* Esther 7:1-6, 9-10; 9:20-22 Psalm 124 James 5:13-20 Mark 9:38-50	**Principal Service** *Continuous* Jeremiah 32:1-3*a*, 6-15 Psalm 91:1-6, 14-16 1 Timothy 6:6-19 Luke 16:19-31

	Year A	Year B	Year C
Sunday between 25 September and 1 October continued	*Related* Ezekiel 18:1-4, 25-32 Psalm 25:1-9 Philippians 2:1-13 Matthew 21:23-32	*Related* Numbers 11:4-6, 10-16, 24-29 Psalm 19:7-14 James 5:13-20 Mark 9:38-50	*Related* Amos 6:1*a*, 4-7 Psalm 146 1 Timothy 6:6-19 Luke 16:19-31
	Second Service Ezekiel 37:15-28 Psalm 124 1 John 2:22-29 Mark 9:38-50	**Second Service** Exodus 24:1-18 Psalms 120; 121 Matthew 9:1-8	**Second Service** Nehemiah 2:1-20 Psalm 135:1-14 (15-21) John 8:31-38, 48-59
Sunday between 2 and 8 October inclusive *– Twenty-seventh Sunday in Ordinary Time* (Green)	**Principal Service** *Continuous* Exodus 20:1-4, 7-9, 12-20 Psalm 19 Philippians 3:4*b*-14 Matthew 21:33-46	**Principal Service** *Continuous* Job 1:1; 2:1-10 Psalm 26 Hebrews 1:1-4; 2:5-12 Mark 10:2-16	**Principal Service** *Continuous* Lamentations 1:1-6 *Canticle:* Lamentations 3:19-26 *or* Psalm 137 2 Timothy 1:1-14 Luke 17:5-10
	Related Isaiah 5:1-7 Psalm 80:7-15 Philippians 3:4*b*-14 Matthew 21:33-46	*Related* Genesis 2:18-24 Psalm 8 Hebrews 1:1-4; 2:5-12 Mark 10:2-16	*Related* Habakkuk 1:1-4; 2:1-4 Psalm 37:1-9 2 Timothy 1:1-14 Luke 17:5-10
	Second Service Proverbs 2:1-11 Psalm 136:1-9 (10-26) 1 John 2:1-17 Mark 10:2-16	**Second Service** Joshua 3:7-17 Psalms 125; 126 Matthew 10:1-22	**Second Service** Nehemiah 5:1-13 Psalm 142 John 9:1-41

Sunday between 9 and 15 October inclusive *– Twenty-eighth Sunday in Ordinary Time* (Green)	**Principal Service** *Continuous* Exodus 32:1-14 Psalm 106:1-6, 19-23 Philippians 4:1-9 Matthew 22:1-14 *Related* Isaiah 25:1-9 Psalm 23 Philippians 4:1-9 Matthew 22:1-14 **Second Service** Proverbs 3:1-18 Psalm 139:1-12 (13-18) 1 John 3:1-15 Mark 10:17-31	**Principal Service** *Continuous* Job 23:1-9, 16-17 Psalm 22:1-15 Hebrews 4:12-16 Mark 10:17-31 *Related* Amos 5:6-7, 10-15 Psalm 90:12-17 Hebrews 4:12-16 Mark 10:17-31 **Second Service** Joshua 5:13 - 6:20 Psalm 127 Matthew 11:20-30	**Principal Service** *Continuous* Jeremiah 29:1, 4-7 Psalm 66:1-12 2 Timothy 2:8-15 Luke 17:11-19 *Related* 2 Kings 5:1-3, 7-15*b* Psalm 111 2 Timothy 2:8-15 Luke 17:11-19 **Second Service** Nehemiah 6:1-16 Psalm 144 John 15:12-27
Sunday between 16 and 22 October inclusive *– Twenty-ninth Sunday in Ordinary Time* (Green)	**Principal Service** *Continuous* Exodus 33:12-23 Psalm 99 1 Thessalonians 1:1-10 Matthew 22:15-22 *Related* Isaiah 45:1-7 Psalm 96:1-9 (10-13) 1 Thessalonians 1:1-10 Matthew 22:15-22	**Principal Service** *Continuous* Job 38:1-7 (34-41) Psalm 104:1-9, 24, 35*c* Hebrews 5:1-10 Mark 10:35-45 *Related* Isaiah 53:4-12 Psalm 91:9-16 Hebrews 5:1-10 Mark 10:35-45	**Principal Service** *Continuous* Jeremiah 31:27-34 Psalm 119:97-104 2 Timothy 3:14 - 4:5 Luke 18:1-8 *Related* Genesis 32:22-31 Psalm 121 2 Timothy 3:14 - 4:5 Luke 18:1-8

	Year A	Year B	Year C
Sunday between 16 and 22 October continued	**Second Service** Proverbs 4:1-18 Psalm 142 1 John 3:16 - 4:6 Mark 10:35-45	**Second Service** Joshua 14:6-14 Psalm 141 Matthew 12:1-21	**Second Service** Nehemiah 8:9-18 Psalm 149 John 16:1-11
Sunday between 23 and 29 October inclusive *– Thirtieth Sunday in Ordinary Time* (Green)	**Principal Service** *Continuous* Deuteronomy 34:1-12 Psalm 90:1-6, 13-17 1 Thessalonians 2:1-8 Matthew 22:34-46 *Related* Leviticus 19:1-2, 15-18 Psalm 1 1 Thessalonians 2:1-8 Matthew 22:34-46	**Principal Service** *Continuous* Job 42:1-6, 10-17 Psalm 34:1-8 (19-22) Hebrews 7:23-28 Mark 10:46-52 *Related* Jeremiah 31:7-9 Psalm 126 Hebrews 7:23-28 Mark 10:46-52	**Principal Service** *Continuous* Joel 2:23-32 Psalm 65 2 Timothy 4:6-8, 16-18 Luke 18:9-14 *Related* Sirach/Ecclesiasticus 35:12-17 *or* Jeremiah 14:7-10, 19-22 Psalm 84:1-7 2 Timothy 4:6-8, 16-18 Luke 18:9-14
	Second Service Ecclesiastes 11:1 - 12:14 Psalm 119:89-104 2 Timothy 2:1-7 Mark 12:28-34	**Second Service** Ecclesiastes 11:1 - 12:14 Psalm 119:121-136 2 Timothy 2:1-7 Luke 18:9-14	**Second Service** Ecclesiastes 11:1 - 12:14 Psalm 119:1-16 2 Timothy 2:1-7 Matthew 22:34-46

All Saints **(1 November)** (White *or* Gold)	**Principal Service** Revelation 7:9-17 Psalm 34:1-10, 22 1 John 3:1-3 Matthew 5:1-12	**Principal Service** Wisdom of Solomon 3:1-9 *or* Isaiah 25:6-9 Psalm 24 Revelation 21:1-6*a* John 11:32-44	**Principal Service** Daniel 7:1-3, 15-18 Psalm 149 Ephesians 1:11-23 Luke 6:20-31
	Second Service Sirach/Ecclesiasticus 44:1-15 *or* Isaiah 40:27-31 Psalms 1; 5 Revelation 19:6-10 John 11:20-27	**Second Service** Isaiah 65:17-25 Psalms 148; 150 Hebrews 11:32 - 12:2 Mark 8:34 - 9:1	**Second Service** Isaiah 35:1-9 Psalms 15; 84 Luke 9:18-27

When 1 November is a weekday, these readings may replace those of the Sunday between 30 October and 5 November inclusive.

Sunday between 30 October and 5 November inclusive *– Thirty-first Sunday in Ordinary Time* (Green)	**Principal Service** *Continuous* Joshua 3:7-17 Psalm 107:1-7, 33-37 1 Thessalonians 2:9-13 Matthew 23:1-12	**Principal Service** *Continuous* Ruth 1:1-18 Psalm 146 Hebrews 9:11-14 Mark 12:28-34	**Principal Service** *Continuous* Habakkuk 1:1-4; 2:1-4 Psalm 119:137-144 2 Thessalonians 1:1-4, 11-12 Luke 19:1-10
	Related Micah 3:5-12 Psalm 43 1 Thessalonians 2:9-13 Matthew 23:1-12	*Related* Deuteronomy 6:1-9 Psalm 119:1-8 Hebrews 9:11-14 Mark 12:28-34	*Related* Isaiah 1:10-18 Psalm 32:1-7 2 Thessalonians 1:1-4, 11-12 Luke 19:1-10
	Second Service Daniel 7:1-18 Psalms 111; 117 Luke 6:17-31	**Second Service** Daniel 2:1-11 (12-24) 25-48 Psalm 145:1-9 (10-21) Revelation 7:9-17 Matthew 5:1-12	**Second Service** Lamentations 3:22-33 Psalm 145:1-9 (10-21) John 11:(1-31) 32-44

	Year A	Year B	Year C
Sunday between 6 and 12 November inclusive *– Thirty-second Sunday in Ordinary Time* (Green)	**Principal Service** *Continuous* Joshua 24:1-3*a*, 14-25 Psalm 78:1-7 1 Thessalonians 4:13-18 Matthew 25:1-13	**Principal Service** *Continuous* Ruth 3:1-5; 4:13-17 Psalm 127 Hebrews 9:24-28 Mark 12:38-44	**Principal Service** *Continuous* Haggai 1:15*b* - 2:9 Psalm 145:1-5, 17-21 *or* Psalm 98 2 Thessalonians 2:1-5, 13-17 Luke 20:27-38
	Related Wisdom of Solomon 6:12-16 *or* Amos 5:18-24 *Canticle:* Wisdom of Solomon 6:17-20 *or* Psalm 70 1 Thessalonians 4:13-18 Matthew 25:1-13	*Related* 1 Kings 17:8-16 Psalm 146 Hebrews 9:24-28 Mark 12:38-44	*Related* Job 19:23-27*a* Psalm 17:1-9 2 Thessalonians 2:1-5, 13-17 Luke 20:27-38
	Second Service Judges 7:2-22 Psalm 82 John 15:9-17	**Second Service** Isaiah 10:33 - 11:9 Psalm 46 John 14:(1-22) 23-29	**Second Service** 1 Kings 3:1-15 Psalm 40 Romans 8:31-39 Matthew 22:15-22
Sunday between 13 and 19 November inclusive *– Thirty-third Sunday in Ordinary Time* (Green)	**Principal Service** *Continuous* Judges 4:1-7 Psalm 123 1 Thessalonians 5:1-11 Matthew 25:14-30	**Principal Service** *Continuous* 1 Samuel 1:4-20 *Canticle:* 1 Samuel 2:1-10 Hebrews 10:11-14 (15-18) 19-25 Mark 13:1-8	**Principal Service** *Continuous* Isaiah 65:17-25 *Canticle:* Isaiah 12:1-6 2 Thessalonians 3:6-13 Luke 21:5-19

	Related Zephaniah 1:7, 12-18 Psalm 90:1-8 (9-11) 12 1 Thessalonians 5:1-11 Matthew 25:14-30	*Related* Daniel 12:1-3 Psalm 16 Hebrews 10:11-14 (15-18) 19-25 Mark 13:1-8	*Related* Malachi 4:1-2*a* Psalm 98 2 Thessalonians 3:6-13 Luke 21:5-19
	Second Service 1 Kings 1:(1-14) 15-40 Psalm 89:19-29 (30-37) Revelation 1:4-18 Luke 9:1-6	**Second Service** Daniel 3:(1-12) 13-30 Psalm 95 Matthew 13:24-30, 36-43	**Second Service** Daniel 6:1-28 Psalm 97 Matthew 13:1-9, 18-23
Sunday between 20 and 26 November inclusive *– Sunday before Advent* (White *or* Gold)	**Principal Service** *Continuous/Related* Ezekiel 34:11-16, 20-24 Psalm 95:1-7*a* *or* Psalm 100 Ephesians 1:15-23 Matthew 25:31-46	**Principal Service** *Continuous* 2 Samuel 23:1-7 Psalm 132:1-12 (13-18) Revelation 1:4*b*-8 John 18:33-37	**Principal Service** *Continuous/Related* Jeremiah 23:1-6 Psalm 46 *or Canticle:* Benedictus (Luke 1:68-79) Colossians 1:11-20 Luke 23:33-43
		Related Daniel 7:9-10, 13-14 Psalm 93 Revelation 1:4*b*-8 John 18:33-37	
	Second Service 2 Samuel 23:1-7 *or* 1 Maccabees 2:15-29 Psalm 93 Matthew 28:16-20	**Second Service** Daniel 5:1-31 Psalm 72:1-7 (8-20) John 6:1-15	**Second Service** 1 Samuel 8:4-20 Psalm 72:1-7 (8-20) John 18:33-37

Church Anniversary
(White *or* Gold)

Genesis 28:10-22 *or* 2 Chronicles 7:11-16; Psalm 84 *or* Psalm 122; Ephesians 2:19-22 *or* 1 Peter 2:1-5; Matthew 12:1-8 *or* John 4:19-26.

Covenant
(Red, *if in Ordinary Time*)

Exodus 24:3-11 *or* Deuteronomy 29:10-15; Jeremiah 31:31-34; Romans 12:1-2; John 15:1-10 *or* Mark 14:22-25. *Part of Psalm 51 is used in the service as a prayer.*

Harvest Thanksgiving
(Green)

Genesis 8:15-22 *or* Deuteronomy 26:1-11 *or* Ruth 2:1-23; Psalm 65; 1 Timothy 6:6-10 *or* Revelation 14:14-18; Matthew 6:25-33 *or* John 6:24-35.

John and Charles Wesley
(White *or* Gold)

Isaiah 12:1-6 *or* Isaiah 51:1-3,7-11; Psalm 130; Romans 5:1-11 *or* 2 Peter 1:1-11; Mark 12:28-37 *or* Luke 10:1-12, 17-20.

The readings are for use on Wesley Day (24 May), or on Aldersgate Sunday (24 May or the preceding Sunday), but should not normally be used at the Principal Service on Ascension Day, Pentecost, or Trinity Sunday.

New Year: Watchnight
(White *or* Gold)

Deuteronomy 8:1-20 *or* Ecclesiastes 3:1-15; Psalm 8 *or* Psalm 90; Revelation 21:1-6*a;* Matthew 25:31-46 *or* Luke 12:13-21 *or* Luke 12:35-50.

Remembrance Sunday
(Green)

Isaiah 25:1-9 *or* Isaiah 52:7-12 *or* Micah 4:1-8; Psalm 9:9-20 *or* Psalm 46; Romans 8:31-35, 37-39 *or* Revelation 22:1-5; Matthew 5:1-12 *or* Matthew 5:43-48 *or* John 15:9-17.

The related readings for the Sunday between 6 and 12 November may also be used; when Remembrance Sunday falls on 13 or 14 November, the related readings for the Sunday between 13 and 19 November may be used on the previous Sunday.

INDEX TO THE METHODIST LECTIONARY

as in *The Methodist Worship Book* 1999

prepared by Dudley Coates

The Principal Service Lectionary is derived from the ecumenical Revised Common Lectionary(RCL). Further information can be found in the introduction to the section 'Calendar, Collects and Lectionary' in *The Methodist Worship Book* (Methodist Publishing House, Peterborough, 1999). A full explanation of RCL can be found in *The Revised Common Lectionary* (Canterbury Press, Norwich, 1992). The Second Service Lectionary is derived from the Second Service Lectionary created by the Church of England on similar principles to those which underlie the Revised Common Lectionary and published in *The Christian Year: Calendar, Lectionary and Collects* (Church House Publishing, 1997).

The entries in the final column indicate P for 'Principal Service', *2nd* for 'Second Service'. Some of the Old Testament and Psalm readings for the Principal Service in Ordinary Time also indicate whether a reading is in the 'Continuous' set of readings (shown by C) or the 'Related' set of readings (shown by R). * indicates a reading used as a canticle in place of a Psalm. There is no entry in the final column for those weekdays and special occasions for which only one set of readings is provided.

Users of resource material from other traditions may find it helpful to know that some traditions (including the Church of England) use an alternative system for numbering Sundays. RCL provides both for the 'Ordinary Time' system used in *The Methodist Worship Book* and for an alternative system under which the first five Sundays of Ordinary Time are designated as Sundays after Epiphany and the remaining Sundays are given 'Proper' numbers. Under this system, the Sixth Sunday in Ordinary Time becomes 'Proper 1' and so on (with the 34th Sunday becoming 'Proper 29').

In this listing, all the references are simplified so that, for example, Easter 4 means the Fourth Sunday of Easter and Ordinary 11 the eleventh Sunday in Ordinary Time. Ordinary numbers are used for the Sundays in Ordinary Time, rather than the dates between which they fall. The subject listing has been created by the author of this index and does not form part of either RCL or the Church of England's Second Service lectionary. Whilst every effort has been made to ensure that this list is correct, in a task of this kind, it is impossible to ensure perfection. The author would be glad to receive notice (through the Methodist Publishing House) of any errors which users find.

READING	SUBJECT OF READING	Day	Year	Service
OLD TESTAMENT				
Genesis 1:1-5	The Spirit of God moves over the waters	Ordinary 1	B	P
Genesis 1:1 - 2:3	Creation	Ordinary 8	C	2nd
Genesis 1:1 - 2:4*a*	Creation	Easter Vigil	A/B/C	
		Trinity Sunday	A	P
Genesis 2:4*b*-25	The Garden of Eden	Ordinary 8	B	2nd
Genesis 2:15-17; 3:1-7	The fall	Lent 1	A	P
		Lent 1	B	2nd
Genesis 2:18-24	God institutes marriage	Ordinary 27	B	P-R
Genesis 3:8-15	The serpent is cursed	Ordinary 10	B	P-R
Genesis 4:1-16	Cain and Abel	Ordinary 9	C	2nd
Genesis 6:9-22; 7:24; 8:14-19	Noah's ark	Ordinary 9	A	P
Genesis 7:1-5, 11-18; 8:6-18; 9:8-13	The ark and the covenant	Easter Vigil	A/B/C	
Genesis 8:15-22	Seedtime and harvest shall not cease	Harvest	A/B/C	
Genesis 8:15 - 9:17	God makes a covenant with Noah	Ordinary 10	C	2nd
Genesis 9:8-17	God makes a covenant with Noah	Lent 1	B	P
Genesis 11:1-9	Disunity at Babel	Pentecost	C	P
Genesis 12:1-4*a*	God blesses Abram	Lent 2	A	P
Genesis 12:1-9	Abram comes to Canaan	Lent 2	B	2nd
		Ordinary 10	A	P-C
Genesis 13:1-18	Abram and Lot separate	Ordinary 11	C	2nd
Genesis 15:1-6	Abram's vision of descendants	Ordinary 19	C	P-R
Genesis 15:1-12, 17-18	God's covenant with Abram	Lent 2	C	P
Genesis 17:1-7, 15-16	Abraham and Sarai are blessed	Lent 2	B	P
Genesis 18:1-10*a*	Abraham and Sarah are promised a son	Ordinary 16	C	P-R
Genesis 18:1-15 (21:1-7)	Sarah laughs at the prospect of a son	Ordinary 11	A	P-C
Genesis 18:20-32	Abraham debates with God over Sodom	Ordinary 17	C	P-R
Genesis 21:8-21	Hagar and her son	Ordinary 12	A	P-C
Genesis 22:1-14	Abraham is ready to sacrifice Isaac	Ordinary 13	A	P-C
Genesis 22:1-18	Abraham is ready to sacrifice Isaac	Easter Vigil	A/B/C	
Genesis 24:1-27	Finding a wife for Isaac	Ordinary 12	C	2nd

Genesis 24:34-38, 42-49, 58-67	Rebekah becomes Isaac's wife	Ordinary 14	A	P-C
Genesis 25:19-34	Esau sells his birthright	Ordinary 15	A	P-C
Genesis 27:1-40	Esau and Jacob	Ordinary 13	C	2nd
Genesis 28:10-19*a*	God reveals himself to Jacob	Lent 3	C	2nd
		Ordinary 16	A	P-C
Genesis 28:10-22	God reveals himself to Jacob	Ordinary 4	A	2nd
		Anniversary	A/B/C	
Genesis 29:1-20	Jacob serves seven years for Rachel	Ordinary 14	C	2nd
Genesis 29:15-28	Jacob, Leah and Rachel	Ordinary 17	A	P-C
Genesis 32:9-30	Jacob wrestles with God	Ordinary 15	C	2nd
Genesis 32:22-31	Jacob wrestles with God	Ordinary 18	A	P-C
		Ordinary 29	C	P-R
Genesis 37:1-4, 12-28	Joseph is sold into slavery	Ordinary 19	A	P-C
Genesis 41:1-16, 25-37	Joseph interprets Pharaoh's dreams	Ordinary 16	C	2nd
Genesis 42:1-25	Jacob's sons come to Joseph in Egypt	Ordinary 17	C	2nd
Genesis 45:1-15	Joseph's brothers find him lord of Egypt	Ordinary 20	A	P-C
Genesis 45:3-11, 15	Joseph's brothers find him lord of Egypt	Ordinary 7	C	P
Genesis 50:4-26	Joseph buries his father	Ordinary 18	C	2nd
Genesis 50:15-21	Joseph forgives his brothers	Ordinary 24	A	P-R
Exodus 1:8 - 2:10	The birth of Moses amongst an enslaved people	Ordinary 21	A	P-C
Exodus 2:1-10	The birth and adoption of Moses	Mothering Sunday	A/B/C	
Exodus 2:23 - 3:10	Moses and the burning bush	Ordinary 20	B	2nd
Exodus 3:1-6	Moses and the burning bush	Sunday before Lent	C	2nd
Exodus 3:1-15	God commissions Moses and names Himself	Trinity Sunday	C	2nd
		Ordinary 22	A	P-C
Exodus 4:27 - 5:1	Moses asks Pharaoh to let the people go	Ordinary 21	B	2nd
Exodus 5:1 - 6:1	Pharaoh rejects Moses' plea	Lent 3	B	2nd
Exodus 6:2-13	God promises to release the slaves	Lent 4	B	2nd
Exodus 7:8-24	The first plagues	Lent 5 (Passion 1)	B	2nd
Exodus 12;1-4 (5-10) 11-14	The Passover instituted	Maundy Thursday	A/B/C	
Exodus 12:1-14	The Passover instituted	Ordinary 23	A	P-C
Exodus 12:21-27	Moses gives the Passover instructions	Ordinary 22	B	2nd

Exodus 14:5-31	Pharaoh chases the Israelites	Ordinary 23	B	2nd
Exodus 14:10-31; 15:20-21	The Israelites cross the sea	Easter Vigil	A/B/C	
Exodus 14:19-31	The Israelites cross the sea	Ordinary 24	A	P-C
Exodus 15:1*b*-11, 20-21	Song of triumph	Ordinary 24	A	P-C*
Exodus 15:1*b*-13, 17-18	Song of triumph	Easter Vigil	A/B/C	*
Exodus 16:2- 4, 9-15	The people are given manna in the desert	Ordinary 18	B	P-R
Exodus 16:2-15	The people are given manna in the desert	Ordinary 25	A	P-C
Exodus 16:4-15	The people are given manna in the desert	Easter 4	B	2nd
Exodus 17:1-7	The people are given water from the rock	Lent 3	A	P
		Ordinary 26	A	P-C
Exodus 18:13-26	Moses chooses judges	Ordinary 24	B	2nd
Exodus 19:2-8*a*	You shall be a holy nation	Ordinary 11	A	P-R
Exodus 19:10-25	The Lord speaks to Moses on Sinai	Ordinary 25	B	2nd
Exodus 20:1-4, 7-9, 12-20	The Ten Commandments	Ordinary 27	A	P-C
Exodus 20:1-17	The Ten Commandments	Lent 3	B	P
Exodus 24:1-18	Moses is given the tablets of stone	Ordinary 26	B	2nd
Exodus 24:3-11	The blood of the covenant	Covenant	A/B/C	
Exodus 24:12-18	Moses is given the tablets of stone	Sunday before Lent	A	P
Exodus 32:1-14	The golden calf	Ordinary 28	A	P-C
Exodus 32:7-14	The golden calf	Ordinary 24	C	P-R
Exodus 33:7-20	Moses experiences God’s glory	Pentecost	C	2nd
Exodus 33:12-23	Moses experiences God’s glory	Ordinary 29	A	P-C
Exodus 34:29-35	Moses face shines	Sunday before Lent	C	P
Leviticus 19:1-2, 9-18	Love your neighbour as yourself	Ordinary 7	A	P
Leviticus 19:1-2, 15-18	Love your neighbour as yourself	Ordinary 30	A	P-R
Numbers 9:15-23	The cloud and the fire in the desert	Ordinary 3	C	2nd
Numbers 11:4-6, 10-16, 24-29	Complaints in the desert	Ordinary 26	B	P-R
Numbers 11:24-30	Moses praises prophecy	Pentecost	A	P
Numbers 13:1-2, 27-33	The spies find a land of milk and honey	Ordinary 5	B	2nd
Numbers 20:2-13	The people are given water from the rock	Ordinary 6	B	2nd

Numbers 21:4-9	Moses and the serpents	Lent 2	A	2nd
		Lent 4	B	P
Numbers 22:21 - 23:12	Balaam and his donkey	Ordinary 7	B	2nd
Deuteronomy 4:1-2, 6-9	Moses commands obedience	Ordinary 22	B	P-R
Deuteronomy 5:12-15	Observe the Sabbath day	Ordinary 9	B	P-R
Deuteronomy 6:1-9	The great commandment	Ordinary 31	B	P-R
Deuteronomy 6:4-9, 16-25	The great commandment and its meaning	Lent 1	A	2nd
Deuteronomy 7:7-13	A chosen people	Easter 3	B	2nd
Deuteronomy 8:1-20	Do not forget the Lord your God	Watchnight	A/B/C	
Deuteronomy 11:18-21, 26-28	Put God's words in your heart	Ordinary 9	A	P-R
Deuteronomy 18:15-20	The promised prophet of God	Ordinary 4	B	P
Deuteronomy 26:1-11	Thanksgiving for God's loving care	Lent 1	C	P
		Harvest	A/B/C	
Deuteronomy 29:10-15	The covenant renewed	Covenant	A/B/C	
Deuteronomy 30:9-14	Obedience will be rewarded	Ordinary 15	C	P-R
Deuteronomy 30:15-20	The choice: life and death, good and evil	Ordinary 6	A	P
		Ordinary 23	C	P-R
Deuteronomy 34:1-12	Joshua succeeds Moses	Ordinary 30	A	P-C
Joshua 1:1-9	God's commission to Joshua	Lent 3	A	2nd
Joshua 3:1-8, 14-17	The Israelites cross the Jordan	Ordinary 1	A	2nd
Joshua 3:7-17	The Israelites cross the Jordan	Ordinary 27	B	2nd
		Ordinary 31	A	P-C
Joshua 5:9-12	Passover in the Promised Land	Lent 4	C	P
Joshua 5:13 - 6:20	Joshua captures Jericho	Ordinary 28	B	2nd
Joshua 14:6-14	Hebron promised to Caleb	Ordinary 29	B	2nd
Joshua 24:1-2*a*, 14-18	Joshua's final instructions to the people	Ordinary 21	B	P-R
Joshua 24:1-3*a*, 14-25	Joshua's final instructions to the people	Ordinary 32	A	P-C
Judges 4:1-7	Deborah promises victory at Tabor	Ordinary 33	A	P-C
Judges 7:2-22	Gideon defeats the Midianites	Ordinary 32	A	2nd

Ruth 2:1-20*a*	Ruth meets Boaz	Ordinary 9	A	2nd
Ruth 1:1-18	Ruth goes home with Naomi	Ordinary 31	B	P-C
Ruth 2:1-23	Ruth gleans the barley harvest	Harvest	A/B/C	
Ruth 3:1-5; 4:13-17	Ruth is married to Boaz	Ordinary 32	B	P-C
1 Samuel 1:1-20	Hannah conceives Samuel	Advent 4	A	2nd
1 Samuel 1:4-20	Hannah conceives Samuel	Ordinary 33	B	P-C
1 Samuel 1:20-28	Samuel is lent to the Lord	Christmas 2	C	2nd
		Mothering Sunday	A/B/C	
1 Samuel 2:1-10	Hannah's song of thanks	Ordinary 33	B	P-C*
1 Samuel 2:18-20, 26	The boy Samuel grows up	Christmas 1	C	P
1 Samuel 3:1-10 (11-20)	Speak, Lord, your servant hears	Ordinary 2	B	P
		Ordinary 9	B	P-C
1 Samuel 3:1-20	Speak, Lord, your servant hears	Ordinary 2	C	2nd
		Ordinary 4	B	2nd
1 Samuel 8:4-11 (12-15) 16-20; (11:14-15)	The people ask Samuel for a King	Ordinary 10	B	P-C
1 Samuel 8:4-20	The people ask Samuel for a King	Sunday before Advent	C	2nd
1 Samuel 15:34 - 16:13	Samuel anoints David for kingship	Ordinary 11	B	P-C
1 Samuel 16:1-13	Samuel anoints David for kingship	Lent 4	A	P
1 Samuel 17:(1*a*, 4-11, 19-23) 32-49	David and Goliath	Ordinary 12	B	P-C
1 Samuel 17:57 - 18:5, 10-16	David becomes an army commander	Ordinary 12	B	P-C
1 Samuel 18:1-16	Saul tries to kill David	Ordinary 10	A	2nd
1 Samuel 21:1-15	David takes the bread and flees to Gath	Ordinary 11	A	2nd
1 Samuel 24:1-17	David spares Saul's life	Ordinary 12	A	2nd
1 Samuel 28:3-19	Saul consults a medium	Ordinary 13	A	2nd
2 Samuel 1:1, 17-27	David mourns the death of Saul and Jonathan	Ordinary 13	B	P-C
2 Samuel 2:1-11; 3:1	David anointed King of Judah	Ordinary 14	A	2nd
2 Samuel 5:1-5, 9-10	David anointed King of all Israel	Ordinary 14	B	P-C
2 Samuel 6:1-5, 12*b*-19	David brings the ark to Jerusalem	Ordinary 15	B	P-C
2 Samuel 7:1-11, 16	God's covenant with David	Advent 4	B	P
2 Samuel 7:1-14*a*	God's covenant with David	Ordinary 16	B	P-C

2 Samuel 11:1-15	David commits adultery with Bathsheba	Ordinary 17	B	P-C
2 Samuel 7:18-29	David's prayer	Ordinary 15	A	2nd
2 Samuel 11:26 - 12:10, 13-15	David repents after Nathan's challenge	Ordinary 11	C	P-R
2 Samuel 11:26 - 12:13*a*	David repents after Nathan's challenge	Ordinary 18	B	P-C
2 Samuel 18:5-9, 15, 31-33	The rebellion and the death of Absalom	Ordinary 19	B	P-C
2 Samuel 23:1-5	David's last words	Easter 7	A	2nd
2 Samuel 23:1-7	David's last words	Sunday before Advent	B	P-C
		Sunday before Advent	A	2nd
1 Kings 1:(1-14) 15-40	The struggle for the succession to David	Ordinary 33	A	2nd
1 Kings 2:10-12; 3:3-14	Solomon succeeds to the throne	Ordinary 20	B	P-C
1 Kings 2:10-12; 3:16-28	The judgement of Solomon	Ordinary 16	A	2nd
1 Kings 3:1-15	Solomon's prayer for wisdom	Ordinary 32	C	2nd
1 Kings 3:5-12	Solomon seeks understanding for the kingship	Ordinary 17	A	P-R
1 Kings 6:11-14, 23-38	Instructions for building the temple	Ordinary 17	A	2nd
1 Kings 8:(1, 6, 10-11) 22-30, 41-43	Prayer at the dedication of the temple	Ordinary 21	B	P-C
1 Kings 8:22-23, 41-43	The prayer of Solomon	Ordinary 9	C	P-R
1 Kings 10:1-13	Visit of the Queen of Sheba	Ordinary 18	A	2nd
1 Kings 11:41 - 12:20	Rehoboam succeeds Solomon	Ordinary 19	A	2nd
1 Kings 17:8-16	The poor widow gives food to Elijah	Ordinary 32	B	P-R
1 Kings 17:8-16 (17-24)	The poor widow gives food to Elijah	Ordinary 10	C	P-C
1 Kings 17:17-24	Elijah raises the widow's son	Ordinary 10	C	P-R
1 Kings 18:17-39	Elijah's triumph over the priests of Baal	Advent 2	A	2nd
1 Kings 18:20-21 (22-29) 30-39	Elijah's triumph over the priests of Baal	Ordinary 9	C	P-C
1 Kings 19:1-4 (5-7) 8-15*a*	Elijah hears the still small voice	Ordinary 12	C	P-C
1 Kings 19:1-16	Elijah hears the still small voice	Sunday before Lent	B	2nd
1 Kings 19:4-8	Elijah flees to Horeb	Ordinary 19	B	P-R
1 Kings 19:9-18	Elijah hears the still small voice	Ordinary 19	A	P-R
1 Kings 19:15-16, 19-21	Elijah is told to call Elisha	Ordinary 13	C	P-R
1 Kings 21:1-10 (11-14) 15-21*a*	Naboth's vineyard	Ordinary 11	C	P-C
1 Kings 22:1-28	Israel and Judah campaign against Aram	Advent 2	B	2nd
2 Kings 2:1-2, 6-14	Elisha succeeds Elijah	Ordinary 13	C	P-C

2 Kings 2:1-12	Elisha watches Elijah's ascension	Sunday before Lent	B	P
		Sunday before Lent	A	2nd
2 Kings 4:1-37	Elisha and the widow's oil	Ordinary 20	A	2nd
2 Kings 4:42-44	Elisha feeds a crowd	Ordinary 17	B	P-R
2 Kings 5:1-3, 7-15*b*	Naaman is cured of leprosy	Ordinary 28	C	P-R
2 Kings 5:1-14	Naaman is cured of leprosy	Ordinary 6	B	P
		Ordinary 14	C	P-C
2 Kings 6:8-23	Elisha's role in the conflict with Samaria	Ordinary 21	A	2nd
2 Kings 6:24-25; 7:3-20	The Arameans flee	Ordinary 22	A	2nd
1 Chronicles 29:6-19	David gives thanks for the offerings	Ordinary 4	C	2nd
2 Chronicles 7:11-16	God speaks on the Temple's completion	Church Anniversary	A/B/C	
2 Chronicles 35:1-6, 10-16	Josiah celebrates the Passover	Lent 5 (Passion 1)	C	2nd
Ezra 1:1-11	Cyrus allows the exiles to return	Ordinary 25	C	2nd
Ezra 3:1-13	Worship restored at Jerusalem	Easter 4	A	2nd
Nehemiah 2:1-20	Nehemiah sent to Judah	Ordinary 26	C	2nd
Nehemiah 5:1-13	Nehemiah deals with oppression	Ordinary 27	C	2nd
Nehemiah 6:1-16	Intrigues of enemies foiled	Ordinary 28	C	2nd
Nehemiah 8:1-3, 5-6, 8-10	Ezra reads the law	Ordinary 3	C	P-C
Nehemiah 8:9-18	Ezra summons the people to obey the law	Ordinary 29	C	2nd
Esther 7:1-6, 9-10; 9:20-22	Haman's downfall	Ordinary 26	B	P-C
Job 1:1; 2:1-10	Job tempted to curse God	Ordinary 27	B	P-C
Job 4:1; 5:6-27	Job should submit to God's correction	Ordinary 15	B	2nd
Job 13:13 - 14:6	Part of Job's despondent prayer	Ordinary 16	B	2nd
Job 14:1-14	Part of Job's despondent prayer	Holy Saturday	A/B/C	
Job 19:1-27*a*	Job answers 'I know that my redeemer lives'	Ordinary 17	B	2nd
Job 19:23-27*a*	Job answers 'I know that my redeemer lives'	Ordinary 32	C	P-R
Job 23:1-9, 16-17	Job yearns for access to God	Ordinary 28	B	P-C

Job 38:1-7 (34-41)	The Lord answers Job	Ordinary 29	B	P-C
Job 28:1-28	Where is wisdom to be found?	Ordinary 18	B	2nd
Job 38:1-11	The Lord answers Job	Ordinary 12	B	P-R
Job 39:1 - 40:4	The Lord answers Job	Ordinary 19	B	2nd
Job 42:1-6, 10-17	Job is humbled and his fortunes are restored	Ordinary 30	B	P-C
Psalm 1	The Lord watches over the righteous	Ordinary 6	C	P
		Easter 7	B	P
		Ordinary 23	C	P-R
		Ordinary 25	B	P-C
		Ordinary 30	A	P-R
Psalms 1; 5	The Lord watches over the righteous	All Saints	A	2nd
Psalm 2	Why do the nations conspire?	Sunday before Lent	A	P
		Sunday before Lent	B	2nd
		Ordinary 5	C	2nd
Psalm 4	I will lie down in peace	Easter 3	B	P
		Ordinary 5	A	2nd
Psalm 5	Give ear to my words	Ordinary 5	B	2nd
Psalm 5:1-8	Give ear to my words	Ordinary 11	C	P-C
Psalm 6	Do not rebuke me in your anger	Ordinary 6	B/C	2nd
Psalm 8	How majestic is your name	Trinity Sunday	A/C	P
		Ordinary 27	B	P-R
		Watchnight	A/B/C	
Psalm 9:1-8 (9-20)	Give thanks with my whole heart	Advent 1	A/C	2nd
Psalm 9:9-20	A stronghold for the oppressed	Ordinary 12	B	P-C
		Remembrance	A/B/C	
Psalm 10	Why do you hide yourself?	Ordinary 7	B	2nd
Psalm 11	In the Lord I take refuge	Advent 2	A	2nd
Psalms 11; 12	In the Lord I take refuge	Lent 3	B	2nd
Psalm 12	The faithful have disappeared	Advent 3	A	2nd
Psalms 12; 13	The faithful have disappeared	Lent 3	C	2nd

Psalm 13	How long, O Lord	Ordinary 6	A	2nd
		Ordinary 7	C	2nd
		Ordinary 13	A	P-C
Psalms 13; 14	How long, O Lord	Lent 4	B	2nd
Psalm 14	Fools say in their hearts 'There is no God'	Ordinary 17	B	P-C
		Ordinary 24	C	P-C
Psalm 15	Who may abide?	Ordinary 4	A	P
		Ordinary 16	C	P-R
		Ordinary 22	B	P-R
Psalms 15; 84	Who may abide?	All Saints	C	2nd
Psalm 16	Protect me, O God	Easter 2	A	P
		Easter Vigil	A/B/C	
		Easter 2	C	2nd
		Ordinary 13	C	P-R
		Ordinary 33	B	P-R
Psalm 17:1-7, 15	Hear a just cause	Ordinary 18	A	P-C
Psalm 17:1-9	Hear a just cause	Ordinary 32	C	P-R
Psalm 18:1-19	The Lord is my rock	Ordinary 7	A	2nd
Psalm 18:20-29	God's way is perfect	Ordinary 7	A	2nd
Psalm 19	The heavens are telling	Easter Vigil	A/B/C	
		Ordinary 3	C	P
		Lent 3	B	P
		Ordinary 24	B	P-C
		Ordinary 27	A	P-C
Psalm 19:7-14	The law of the Lord is perfect	Ordinary 26	B	P-R
Psalm 20	The Lord answer you in the day of trouble	Ordinary 11	B	P-C
Psalm 22	Why have you forsaken me?	Good Friday	A/B/C	
Psalm 22:1-15	Why have you forsaken me?	Ordinary 28	B	P-C
Psalm 22:19-28	Come quickly to my aid	Ordinary 12	C	P-R
Psalm 22:23-31	Proclaim deliverance	Lent 2	B	P
Psalm 22:25-31	Proclaim deliverance	Easter 5	B	P

Psalm 23	The Lord is my shepherd	Lent 4	A	P
		Easter 4	A/B/C	P
		Ordinary 16	B	P-R
		Ordinary 28	A	P-R
Psalm 24	The earth is the Lord's	Ordinary 15	B	P-C
		All Saints	B	P
Psalm 25:1-9	My God, in you I trust	Ordinary 26	A	P-R
Psalm 25:1-10	My God, in you I trust	Advent 1	C	P
		Lent 1	B	P
		Ordinary 15	C	P-R
Psalm 25:1-10 (11-22)	My God, in you I trust	Advent 1	B	2nd
Psalm 26	Vindicate me, O Lord	Ordinary 27	B	P-C
Psalm 26:1-8	Vindicate me, O Lord	Ordinary 22	A	P-R
Psalm 27	The Lord is my light and my salvation	Lent 2	C	P
Psalm 27:1, 4-9	The Lord is my light and my salvation	Ordinary 3	A	P
Psalm 29	Ascribe glory to the Lord	Ordinary 1	A/B/C	P
		Trinity Sunday	B	P
Psalm 29:1-10	Ascribe glory to the Lord	Easter 4	A	2nd
Psalm 30	You turn mourning into dancing	Ordinary 6	B	P
		Lent 4	C	2nd
		Lent 5 (Passion 1)	A	2nd
		Easter 3	C	P
		Ordinary 10	C	P-R
		Ordinary 13	B	P-R
		Ordinary 14	C	P-C
Psalm 30:1-5	His favour is for a lifetime	Easter 2	A	2nd
Psalm 31:1-4, 15-16	In you, I seek refuge	Holy Saturday	A/B/C	
Psalm 31:1-8 (9-16)	In you, I seek refuge	Lent 4	A	2nd
Psalm 31:1-5, 15-16	In you, I seek refuge	Easter 5	A	P
Psalm 31:1-5, 19-24	In you, I seek refuge	Ordinary 9	A	P-R
Psalm 31:9-16	Let your face shine upon your servant	Lent 6 (Passion 2/Palm)	A/B/C	P

Psalm 32	Happy are those whose sin is covered	Lent 1	A	P
		Lent 4	C	P
		Ordinary 11	C	P-R
Psalm 32:1-7	Happy are those whose sin is covered	Ordinary 31	C	P-R
Psalm 33:1-12	Praise befits the upright	Ordinary 10	A	P-C
Psalm 33:1-12 (13-22)	Praise befits the upright	Ordinary 3	A/B/C	2nd
Psalm 33:(1-12) 13-22	The Lord sees all humankind	Ordinary 9	A	2nd
Psalm 33:12-22	Happy is the nation	Ordinary 19	C	P-R
Psalm 34 1-8	I will bless the Lord at all times	Ordinary 19	B	P-R
Psalm 34:1-8 (19-22)	I will bless the Lord at all times	Ordinary 30	B	P-C
Psalm 34:1-10 (11-22)	I will bless the Lord at all times	Lent 5 (Passion 1)	B	2nd
		Ordinary 4	A/B/C	2nd
Psalm 34:1-10, 22	I will bless the Lord at all times	All Saints	A	P
Psalm 34:9-14	Fear the Lord	Ordinary 20	B	P-R
Psalm 34:11-20	Come, listen to me	Mothering Sunday	A/B/C	
Psalm 34:15-22	The eyes of the Lord are on the righteous	Ordinary 21	B	P-R
Psalm 35:1-9 (10-28)	Fight against those who fight against me	Lent 5 (Passion 1)	C	2nd
Psalm 35:1-10 (11-28)	Fight against those who fight against me	Ordinary 9	B	2nd
Psalm 36:5-10	Steadfast love	Ordinary 2	C	P
Psalms 36:5-10; 87	Zion	Easter 6	A	2nd
Psalms 36:5-10; 150	Steadfast love	Pentecost	C	2nd
Psalm 36:5-11	Steadfast love	Monday in Holy Week	A/B/C	
Psalm 37:1-9	Do not envy wrongdoers	Ordinary 27	C	P-R
Psalm 37:1-11 (12-14)	Do not envy wrongdoers	Ordinary 10	B	2nd
Psalm 37:1-11, 39-40	Do not envy wrongdoers	Ordinary 7	C	P
Psalm 39	Let me know the measure of my days	Ordinary 9	C	2nd
		Ordinary 11	B	2nd
Psalm 40	I waited patiently for the Lord	Lent 3	A	2nd
		Ordinary 32	C	2nd
Psalm 40:1-11	I waited patiently for the Lord	Ordinary 2	A	P
Psalm 40:(1-10) 11-17	Do not withhold mercy	Advent 2	B	2nd
Psalm 41	Happy are those who consider the poor	Ordinary 7	B	P
		Ordinary 10	A	2nd

Psalms 42; 43	As a deer longs, so my soul longs	Easter Vigil	A/B/C	
		Ordinary 12	C	P
Psalm 43	Why are you cast down, my soul?	Ordinary 11	A	2nd
		Ordinary 31	A	P-R
Psalm 44:1-8 (9-26)	Redeem us for the sake of your steadfast love	Ordinary 10	C	2nd
Psalm 45	My heart overflows	Easter 6	B	2nd
Psalm 45:1-2, 6-9	My heart overflows	Ordinary 22	B	P-C
Psalm 45:10-17	The peoples will praise you	Ordinary 14	A	P-C
Psalm 46	God is our refuge and strength	Easter Vigil	A/B/C	
		Ordinary 9	A	P-C
		Ordinary 12	A	2nd
		Ordinary 32	B	2nd
		Sunday before Advent	C	P
		Remembrance	A/B/C	
Psalms 46; 47	God is our refuge and strength	Ordinary 1	A/B/C	2nd
Psalm 47	Clap your hands	Ascension Day	A/B/C	
		Easter 7	A	2nd
Psalm 48	Great is the Lord	Easter 3	A	2nd
		Ordinary 14	B	P-C
Psalm 49	Give ear, inhabitants of the world	Ordinary 12	B	2nd
Psalm 49:1-12	Give ear, inhabitants of the world	Ordinary 18	C	P-R
Psalm 50:1-6	From the rising of the sun to its setting	Advent 3	C	2nd
		Sunday before Lent	B	P
Psalm 50:1-8, 22-23	From the rising of the sun to its setting	Ordinary 19	C	P-C
Psalm 50:1-15	From the rising of the sun to its setting	Lent 1	A	2nd
Psalm 50:1-15 (16-23)	From the rising of the sun to its setting	Ordinary 13	A	2nd
Psalm 50:7-15	Call on me in the day of trouble	Ordinary 10	A	P-R
Psalm 51:1-10	Have mercy on me	Ordinary 24	C	P-R
Psalm 51:1-12	Have mercy on me	Lent 5 (Passion 1)	B	P
		Ordinary 18	B	P-C
Psalm 51:1-17	Have mercy on me	Ash Wednesday	A/B/C	
Psalm 52	Why do you boast?	Ordinary 11	C	2nd
		Ordinary 16	C	P-C

Psalm 53	Fools say in their hearts 'There is no God'	Ordinary 13	B	2nd
Psalm 54	Deliverance	Ordinary 25	B	P-R
Psalm 56	May I walk before God in the light of life	Ordinary 14	A	2nd
Psalm 57	In you my soul takes refuge	Ordinary 12	C	2nd
Psalm 60	With God we shall do valiantly	Ordinary 13	C	2nd
		Ordinary 15	A	2nd
Psalm 62:5-12	My rock and my salvation	Ordinary 3	B	P
Psalm 63:1-8	My soul thirsts for you	Lent 3	C	P
Psalm 64	Hear my voice in my complaint	Ordinary 14	B	2nd
Psalm 65	Praise is due to you in Zion	Ordinary 8	B	2nd
		Ordinary 14	C	2nd
		Ordinary 30	C	P
		Harvest	A/B/C	
Psalm 65:(1-8) 9-13	You enrich the earth	Ordinary 15	A	P-R
Psalms 66; 114; 117	Make a joyful noise	Easter Day	C	2nd
Psalm 66:1-9	Make a joyful noise	Ordinary 14	C	P-R
Psalm 66:1-9 (10-20)	Make a joyful noise	Ordinary 15	B	2nd
Psalm 66:1-12	Make a joyful noise	Ordinary 28	C	P-C
Psalm 66:8-20	Blessed be God for his steadfast love	Easter 6	A	P
Psalm 67	May God be gracious to us and bless us	Easter 6	C	P
		Ordinary 16	A	2nd
		Ordinary 20	A	P-R
Psalms 67; 133	May God be gracious to us and bless us	Pentecost	A	2nd
Psalm 68:1-14 (15-18) 19-20 (21-35)	Let God rise up	Easter 7	C	2nd
Psalm 68:1-8 (9-20)	Let God rise up	Advent 3	B	2nd
Psalm 68:1-10, 32-35	Let God rise up	Easter 7	A	P
Psalm 69:1-18	Save me, O God, for the waters	Lent 6 (Passion 2/Palm)	B/C	2nd
Psalm 69:7-10 (11-15) 16-18	Answer me	Ordinary 12	A	P-R
Psalm 70	Deliver me	Wednesday in Holy Wk	A/B/C	
		Ordinary 32	A	P-R
Psalm 71:1-6	Let me never be put to shame	Ordinary 4	C	P
		Ordinary 21	C	P
Psalm 71:1-14	Let me never be put to shame	Tuesday in Holy Week	A/B/C	

Psalm 72:1-7 (8-20)	Righteousness	Sunday before Advent	B/C	2nd
Psalm 72:1-7, 10-14	Deliverance	Epiphany	A/B/C	P
Psalm 72:1-7, 18-19	Righteousness	Advent 2	A	P
Psalm 73:1-3, 16-28	God is good to the upright	Trinity Sunday	C	2nd
Psalm 73:(1-20) 21-28	God is my portion for ever	Ordinary 16	B	2nd
Psalm 74:(1-11) 12-17 (18-23)	God is my King from of old	Ordinary 17	B	2nd
Psalm 75	People tell of your wondrous deeds	Ordinary 17	A	2nd
		Advent 2	C	2nd
Psalm 77:1-2,11-20	In trouble I seek the Lord	Ordinary 13	C	P-C
Psalm 77:1-12 (13-20)	In trouble I seek the Lord	Ordinary 15	C	2nd
Psalm 78:1-7	Give ear to my teaching	Ordinary 32	A	P-C
Psalm 78:1-4, 12-16	Give ear to my teaching	Ordinary 26	A	P-C
Psalm 78:23-29	He commanded the skies	Ordinary 18	B	P-R
Psalm 79:1-9	Help, deliver and forgive us	Ordinary 25	C	P-C
Psalm 80	Restore us	Lent 6 (Passion 2/Palm)	A	2nd
Psalm 80:1-2, 8-19	Restore us	Ordinary 20	C	P-C
Psalm 80:1-7	Restore us	Advent 4	C	P
Psalm 80:1-7 (8-19)	Restore us	Ordinary 18	A	2nd
Psalm 80:1-7, 17-19	Restore us	Advent 1	B	P
		Advent 4	A	P
Psalm 80:7-15	Restore us	Ordinary 27	A	P-R
Psalm 81	Sing aloud to God	Ordinary 16	C	2nd
Psalm 81:1-10	Sing aloud to God	Ordinary 9	B	P
Psalm 81:1, 10-16	Sing aloud to God	Ordinary 22	C	P-C
Psalm 81:8-16	Hear admonition	Easter 4	B	2nd
Psalm 82	Judge the earth	Ordinary 15	C	P-C
		Ordinary 20	C	P-R
		Ordinary 32	A	2nd
Psalm 84	How lovely is your dwelling place	Sunday before Lent	A	2nd
		Ordinary 21	B	P-C
		Anniversary	A/B/C	
Psalm 84:1-7	How lovely is your dwelling place	Ordinary 30	C	P-R
Psalm 85	Restoration	Ordinary 17	C	P-C

Psalm 85:1-2, 8-13	He will speak peace	Advent 2	B	P
Psalm 85:8-13	He will speak peace	Ordinary 15	B	P-R
		Ordinary 19	A	P-R
Psalm 86	Incline your ear and answer	Easter 3	C	2nd
		Ordinary 19	A	2nd
Psalm 86:1-10, 16-17	Incline your ear and answer	Ordinary 12	A	P-C
Psalm 86:11-17	Teach me your way	Ordinary 16	A	P-R
Psalm 88:1-9 (10-18)	Incline your ear to my cry	Ordinary 17	C	2nd
		Ordinary 18	B	2nd
Psalm 89:1-4, 15-18	Steadfast love	Ordinary 13	A	P-R
Psalm 89:1-4, 19-26	Steadfast love	Advent 4	B	P
Psalm 89:(1-4) 5-12 (13-18)	Steadfast love	Sunday before Lent	C	2nd
Psalm 89:19-29 (30-37)	Steadfast love	Ordinary 33	A	2nd
Psalm 89:20-37	Steadfast love	Ordinary 16	B	P-C
Psalm 90	You have been our dwelling place	Watchnight	A/B/C	
Psalm 90:1-6, 13-17	You have been our dwelling place	Ordinary 30	A	P-C
Psalm 90:1-8 (9-11) 12	You have been our dwelling place	Ordinary 33	A	P-R
Psalm 90:1-12 (13-17)	You have been our dwelling place	Ordinary 20	A	2nd
Psalm 90:12-17	Teach us to count our days	Ordinary 28	B	P-R
Psalm 91:1-2, 9-16	You who abide in the shadow of the Almighty	Lent 1	C	P
Psalm 91:1-6, 14-16	You who abide in the shadow of the Almighty	Ordinary 26	C	P-C
Psalm 91:1-12 (13-16)	You who abide in the shadow of the Almighty	Ordinary 19	B	2nd
Psalm 91:9-16	You have made the Lord your refuge	Ordinary 29	B	P-R
Psalm 92:1-4, 12-15	It is good to give thanks	Ordinary 8	C	P
		Ordinary 11	B	P-R
Psalm 93	The Lord is king	Ascension Day	A/B/C	
		Sunday before Advent	A	2nd
		Sunday before Advent	B	P-R
Psalms 93; 150	The Lord is king	Trinity Sunday	A	2nd
Psalm 95	Let us sing to the Lord	Lent 3	A	P
		Ordinary 21	A	2nd
		Ordinary 33	B	2nd
Psalm 95:1-7*a*	Let us sing to the Lord	Sunday before Advent	A	P-R

Psalm 96	Sing a new song to the Lord	Christmas Day I	A/B/C	
		Ordinary 2	A/B/C	2nd
		Easter 5	B	2nd
		Ordinary 9	C	P-C
Psalm 96:1-9 (10-13)	Sing a new song to the Lord	Ordinary 29	A	P-R
Psalm 96:1-9	Sing a new song to the Lord	Ordinary 9	C	P-R
Psalm 97	Earth rejoice, coastlands be glad	Christmas Day II	A/B/C	
		Easter 7	C	P
		Ordinary 33	C	2nd
Psalm 98	Sing a new song			
	for he has done marvellous things	Christmas Day III	A/B/C	
		Easter Vigil	A/B/C	
		Easter 5	C	2nd
		Easter 6	B	P
		Ordinary 32	C	P-C
		Ordinary 33	C	P-R
Psalms 98; 100	Sing a new song			
	for he has done marvellous things	Epiphany	A/B/C	2nd
Psalm 99	Extol the Lord our God	Sunday before Lent	A/C	P
		Ordinary 29	A	P-C
Psalm 100	Make a joyful noise	Ordinary 11	A	P-R
		Ordinary 20	B	2nd
		Sunday before Advent	A	P
Psalm 103:1-8	The Lord is slow to anger	Ordinary 21	C	P
Psalm 103:1-13, 22	The Lord has compassion, bless him	Ordinary 8	B	P
Psalm 103:(1-7) 8-13	The Lord is slow to anger	Ordinary 24	A	P-R
Psalm 104:1-9	You are clothed with honour and majesty	Trinity Sunday	B	2nd
Psalm 104:1-9, 24, 35*c*	You are clothed with honour and majesty	Ordinary 29	B	P-C
Psalm 104:24-34, 35*b*	How manifold are your works	Pentecost	A/B/C	P
Psalm 105:1-6, 16-22, 45*b*	Give thanks, call on his name	Ordinary 19	A	P-C
Psalm 105:1-6, 23-26, 45*c*	Give thanks, call on his name	Ordinary 22	A	P-C
Psalm 105:1-6, 37-45	Give thanks, call on his name	Ordinary 25	A	P-C
Psalm 105:1-11, 45*b*	Give thanks, call on his name	Ordinary 17	A	P-C

Psalm 105:1-15	Give thanks, call on his name	Ordinary 22	A	2nd
Psalm 106:1-6, 19-23	Give thanks for he is good	Ordinary 28	A	P-C
Psalm 107:1-3, 17-22	Give thanks for his steadfast love endures	Lent 4	B	P
Psalm 107:1-3, 23-32	Give thanks for his steadfast love endures	Ordinary 12	B	P-R
Psalm 107:1-7, 33-37	Give thanks for his steadfast love endures	Ordinary 31	A	P-C
Psalm 107:1-9, 43	Give thanks for his steadfast love endures	Ordinary 18	C	P-C
Psalm 107:1-12 (13-32)	Give thanks for his steadfast love endures	Ordinary 18	C	2nd
Psalm 108	My heart is steadfast	Ordinary 19	C	2nd
		Ordinary 23	A	2nd
Psalm 111	Give thanks in the congregation	Ordinary 4	B	P
		Ordinary 20	B	P-C
		Ordinary 28	C	P-R
Psalms 111; 117	Give thanks in the congregation	Ordinary 31	A	2nd
Psalm 112	Happy are those who fear the Lord	Ordinary 22	C	P-R
Psalm 112:1-9 (10)	Happy are those who fear the Lord	Ordinary 5	A	P
Psalm 113	From the rising of the sun, praise the Lord	Advent 4	A/B	2nd
		Ordinary 25	C	P-R
Psalms 113; 114	From the rising of the sun, praise the Lord	Easter 4	C	2nd
Psalm 114	When Israel went out from Egypt	Ordinary 24	A	P-C
Psalms 114, 117	When Israel went out from Egypt	Easter Day	A/B	2nd
Psalm 116:1-2, 12-19	What shall I return to the Lord	Maundy Thursday	A/B/C	
		Ordinary 11	A	P-C
Psalm 116:1-4, 12-19	What shall I return to the Lord	Easter 3	A	P
Psalm 116:1-9	I walk before the Lord	Ordinary 24	B	P-R
Psalm 116:(1-11) 12-19	What shall I return to the Lord	Ordinary 21	B	2nd
Psalm 118:1-2, 14-24	Give thanks, for he is good	Easter Day	A/B/C	P
Psalm 118:1-2, 19-29	Give thanks, for he is good	Lent 6 (Passion 2/Palm)	A/B/C	P
Psalm 118:14-29	Give thanks, for he is good	Easter 2	C	P
Psalm 119:1-8	Happy are those whose way is blameless	Ordinary 6	A	P
		Ordinary 31	B	P-R
Psalm 119:1-16	Happy are those whose way is blameless	Ordinary 30	C	2nd
Psalm 119:(1-8) 9-16	I will delight in your statutes	Ordinary 22	B	2nd
Psalm 119:9-16	I will delight in your statutes	Lent 5 (Passion 1)	B	P

Psalm 119:17-32	Deal bountifully that I may live	Lent 1	B	2nd
Psalm 119:17-24 (25-32)	Deal bountifully that I may live	Ordinary 20	C	2nd
Psalm 119:33-40	Teach me your statutes	Ordinary 7	A	P
		Ordinary 23	A	P-R
Psalm 119:41-48 (49-64)	Let your steadfast love come to me	Ordinary 24	A	2nd
Psalm 119:(41-48) 49-56	Remember your word	Ordinary 23	B	2nd
Psalm 119:49-56 (57-72)	Remember your word	Ordinary 21	C	2nd
Psalm 119:73-88	Your hands have made and fashioned me	Lent 1	C	2nd
Psalm 119:73-80 (81-88)	Your hands have made and fashioned me	Ordinary 24	B	2nd
Psalm 119:81-88 (89-96)	My soul languishes for your salvation	Ordinary 22	C	2nd
Psalm 119:89-104	Your word is firmly fixed in heaven	Ordinary 30	A	2nd
Psalm 119:97-104	How I love your law	Ordinary 29	C	P-C
Psalm 119:105-112	Your word is a lamp and a light	Ordinary 15	A	P-C
Psalm 119:(113-120) 121-128 (129-136)	Direct my steps	Ordinary 25	A	2nd
Psalm 119:121-136	Your decrees are wonderful	Ordinary 30	B	2nd
Psalm 119:129-136	Your decrees are wonderful	Ordinary 17	A	P-R
Psalm 119:137-144	Your judgements are right	Ordinary 31	C	P-C
Psalm 119:137-144 (145-152)	Your judgements are right	Ordinary 25	B	2nd
Psalms 120; 121	In distress I cry	Ordinary 26	B	2nd
Psalm 121	I lift my eyes to the hills	Lent 2	A	P
		Ordinary 23	C	2nd
		Ordinary 29	C	P-R
Psalm 122	I was glad when they said to me	Advent 1	A	P
		Anniversary	A/B/C	
Psalm 123	To you I lift up my eyes	Ordinary 14	B	P-R
		Ordinary 33	A	P
		Advent 4	C	2nd
Psalm 124	Our help is in the name of the Lord	Ordinary 21	A	P-C
		Ordinary 26	A	2nd
		Ordinary 26	B	P-C
Psalms 124; 125	Our help is in the name of the Lord	Ordinary 24	C	2nd
Psalm 125	Those who trust cannot be moved	Ordinary 23	B	P-C

Psalms 125; 126	Those who trust cannot be moved	Ordinary 27	B	2nd
Psalm 126	The Lord has done great things	Advent 3	B	P
		Lent 5 (Passion 1)	C	P
		Ordinary 30	B	P-R
Psalms 126; 127	The Lord has done great things	Easter 6	C	2nd
Psalm 127	Unless the Lord builds the house	Ordinary 28	B	2nd
		Ordinary 32	B	P-C
Psalm 127:1-4	Unless the Lord builds the house	Mothering Sunday	A/B/C	
Psalm 128	Happy is everyone who fears the Lord	Ordinary 17	A	P-C
Psalm 129	The Lord is righteous	Ordinary 25	C	2nd
Psalm 130	Out of the depths	Lent 5 (Passion 1)	A	P
		Ordinary 10	B	P-R
		Ordinary 13	B	P-C
		Ordinary 19	B	P-C
		Wesleys	A/B/C	
Psalm 131	Hope in the Lord	Ordinary 8	A	P
Psalm 132	Remember David	Christmas 1	A/B/C	2nd
Psalm 132:1-12 (13-18)	Remember David	Sunday before Advent	B	P-C
Psalm 133	Unity is good and pleasant	Easter 2	B	P
		Ordinary 12	B	P-C
		Ordinary 20	A	P-C
Psalm 135:1-14 (15-21)	Praise the Lord	Lent 2	A/B/C	2nd
		Christmas 2	A/B/C	2nd
		Ordinary 26	C	2nd
Psalm 136:1-9 (10-26)	Give thanks to the Lord who does [great] wonders	Ordinary 27	A	2nd
Psalm 136:1-9, 23-26	Give thanks to the Lord who rescued us	Easter Vigil	A/B/C	
Psalm 137	By the rivers of Babylon	Ordinary 27	C	P-C
Psalm 138	I called, you answered	Ordinary 5	C	P
		Ordinary 10	B	P-C
		Ordinary 17	C	P-R
		Ordinary 21	A	P-R

Psalm 139:1-6, 13-18	You have searched me and known me	Ordinary 2	B	P
		Ordinary 9	B	P-C
		Ordinary 23	C	P-C
Psalm 139:1-12 (13-18, 23-24)	You have searched me and known me	Pentecost	B	2nd
Psalm 139:1-12 (13-18)	You have searched me and known me	Ordinary 28	A	2nd
Psalm 139:1-12, 23-24	You have searched me and known me	Ordinary 16	A	P-C
Psalm 141	Give ear to my voice	Ordinary 29	B	2nd
Psalm 142	With my voice I cry	Easter 3	B	2nd
		Ordinary 27	C	2nd
		Ordinary 29	A	2nd
Psalm 143	Hear, answer, save	Easter Vigil	A/B/C	
Psalm 143:1-11	Hear, answer, save	Easter 2	B	2nd
Psalm 144	What are human beings that you regard them?	Ordinary 28	C	2nd
Psalm 145:1-9 (10-21)	I will extol you, my God and King	Ordinary 31	B/C	2nd
Psalm 145:1-5, 17-21	I will extol you, my God and King	Ordinary 32	C	P-C
Psalm 145:1-8	I will extol you, my God and King	Ordinary 25	A	P-R
Psalm 145:8-9, 14-21	The Lord is slow to anger	Ordinary 18	A	P-R
Psalm 145:8-14	The Lord is slow to anger	Ordinary 14	A	P-R
Psalm 145:10-18	All your works shall give thanks	Ordinary 17	B	P-R
Psalm 146	Do not put your trust in princes	Ordinary 10	C	P-C
		Ordinary 23	B	P-R
		Ordinary 26	C	P-R
		Ordinary 31	B	P-C
		Ordinary 32	B	P-R
Psalm 146:5-10	Happy are those whose hope is in the Lord	Advent 3	A	P
Psalm 147:1-11	A song of praise is fitting	Easter 5	A	2nd
		Easter 7	B	2nd
Psalm 147:1-11, 20*c*	A song of praise is fitting	Ordinary 5	B	P
Psalm 147:(1-11) 12-20	A song of praise is fitting	Ordinary 8	C	2nd
Psalm 147:12-20	Praise God for his blessings	Christmas 2	A/B/C	P
Psalm 148	Praise him in the heights	Christmas 1	A/B/C	P
		Easter 5	C	P
		Ordinary 8	A	2nd

Psalms 148; 150	Praise him in the heights	All Saints	B	2nd
Psalm 149	Sing a new song of praise	Ordinary 23	A	P-C
		Ordinary 29	C	2nd
		All Saints	C	P
Psalm 150	Let everything that breathes praise the Lord	Easter 2	C	P
Proverbs 1:20-33	Wisdom raises her voice	Ordinary 24	B	P-C
Proverbs 2:1-11	The Lord gives wisdom	Ordinary 27	A	2nd
Proverbs 3:1-18	Happy are those who find wisdom	Ordinary 28	A	2nd
Proverbs 4:1-18	Do not forsake my teaching	Ordinary 29	A	2nd
Proverbs 8:1, 22-31	Before the mountains, I was there	Ordinary 8	A	2nd
Proverbs 8:1-4, 22-31	The eternal divine wisdom	Trinity Sunday	C	P
Proverbs 8:1-8, 19-21; 9:4*b*-6	The words of my mouth are righteous	Easter Vigil	A/B/C	
Proverbs 9:1-6	Wisdom has built her house	Ordinary 20	B	P-R
Proverbs 22:1-2, 8-9, 22-23	True blessedness	Ordinary 23	B	P-C
Proverbs 25:6-7	Do not stand in the place of the great	Ordinary 22	C	P-R
Proverbs 31:10-31	A capable wife	Ordinary 25	B	P-C
Ecclesiastes 1:2, 12-14; 2:18-23	All is vanity	Ordinary 18	C	P-R
Ecclesiastes 3:1-11	Times and seasons	Ordinary 3	A	2nd
Ecclesiastes 3:1-15	There is a season	Watchnight	A/B/C	
Ecclesiastes 11:1-12:14	Youth and old age	Ordinary 30	A/B/C	2nd
Song of Solomon 2:8-13	The voice of my beloved	Ordinary 14	A	P-C*
Song of Solomon 2:8-13	The voice of my beloved	Ordinary 22	B	P-C
Song of Solomon 3:2-5; 8:6-7	Many waters cannot quench love	Easter Day	A	2nd
Song of Solomon 4:16 - 5:2, 8:6-7	Many waters cannot quench love	Easter 6	B	2nd
Isaiah 1:1, 10-20	True justice	Ordinary 19	C	P-C
Isaiah 1:10-18	True justice	Ordinary 31	C	P-R
Isaiah 1:1-20	True justice	Advent 1	B	2nd
Isaiah 2:1-5	God's Kingdom of peace	Advent 1	A	P

Isaiah 5:1-7	The vineyard of the Lord	Lent 6 (Passion 2/Palm)	A/B/C	2nd
		Ordinary 20	C	P-C
		Ordinary 27	A	P-R
Isaiah 5:8-30	Holiness challenges evil	Advent 3	A	2nd
Isaiah 6:1-8	Isaiah's vision of the holiness of God	Trinity Sunday	A	2nd
		Trinity Sunday	B	P
Isaiah 6:1-8 (9-13)	Isaiah's vision of the holiness of God	Ordinary 5	C	P
Isaiah 7:10-16	The promise of a Son	Advent 4	A	P
Isaiah 9:1-4	From darkness to light	Ordinary 3	A	P
Isaiah 9:2-7	Unto us a Son is given	Christmas Day I	A/B/C	
Isaiah 10:33 - 11:9	The character of the awaited Messiah	Ordinary 32	B	2nd
Isaiah 10:33 - 11:10	The character of the awaited Messiah	Advent 4	C	2nd
Isaiah 11:1-10	The character of the awaited Messiah	Advent 2	A	P
Isaiah 11:10 - 12:6	Give thanks to the Lord, make known his deeds	Ordinary 19	C	2nd
Isaiah 12:1-6	Surely God is my salvation	Wesleys	A/B/C	
Isaiah 12:1-6	Make known his deeds	Ordinary 33	C	P-C*
Isaiah 12:2-6	Make known his deeds	Advent 3	C	P*
		Easter Vigil	A/B/C	*
Isaiah 25:1-9	God will wipe away all tears	Ordinary 28	A	P-R
		Remembrance	A/B/C	
Isaiah 25:6-9	The salvation of God	Easter Day	B	P
		All Saints	B	P
Isaiah 26:1-9, 19	Judah's song of victory	Easter 2	B	2nd
Isaiah 28:9-22	Judgement on corruption	Ordinary 20	C	2nd
Isaiah 30:8-21	This is the way: walk in it	Ordinary 21	C	2nd
Isaiah 33:13-22	The Lord is judge and ruler	Ordinary 22	C	2nd
Isaiah 35:1-9	God is coming to save	All Saints	C	2nd
Isaiah 35:1-10	God is coming to save	Advent 3	A	P
		Advent 3	C	2nd
		Christmas 1	B	2nd
Isaiah 35:4-7*a*	God is coming to save	Ordinary 23	B	P
Isaiah 38:9-20	Hezekiah's writing after sickness	Easter 3	C	2nd

Isaiah 40:1-11	Preparing the way of the Lord	Advent 2	B	P
		Advent 2	C	2nd
Isaiah 40:21-31	Have you not known?	Ordinary 5	B	P-R
Isaiah 40:27-31	The Lord shall renew their strength	All Saints	A	2nd
Isaiah 40:27 - 41:13	The Lord shall renew their strength	Lent 4	C	2nd
Isaiah 41:21 - 42:4	Set forth your case	Christmas 2	A	2nd
Isaiah 42:1-9	The servant of the Lord	Monday in Holy Week	A/B/C	
		Ordinary 1	A	P
		Ordinary 1	B	2nd
Isaiah 43:1-7	I have called you by name	Ordinary 1	C	P
Isaiah 43:1-21	I have called you by name	Easter Day	C	2nd
Isaiah 43:14 - 44:5	God's blessing on Israel	Ordinary 23	C	2nd
Isaiah 43:16-21	The salvation of God's people	Lent 5 (Passion 1)	C	P
Isaiah 43:18-25	God forgives his people	Ordinary 7	B	P
Isaiah 44:1-8	Thus says the Lord	Easter 7	C	2nd
Isaiah 44:6-8	Thus says the Lord	Ordinary 16	A	P-R
Isaiah 45:1-7	Cyrus, God's instrument	Ordinary 29	A	P-R
Isaiah 46:3-13	I am God, there is no other	Christmas 2	B	2nd
Isaiah 49:1-7	The Lord's servant, a light to the nations	Ordinary 2	A	P
		Tuesday in Holy Week	A/B/C	
Isaiah 49:7-13	The Lord has comforted his people	Christmas 1	A	2nd
Isaiah 49:8-16*a*	I will not forget you	Ordinary 8	A	P
Isaiah 50:4-9*a*	The Lord's suffering servant	Lent 6 (Passion 2/Palm)	A/B/C	P
		Wednesday in Holy Wk	A/B/C	
		Ordinary 24	B	P-R
Isaiah 51:1-3, 7-11	The ransomed shall return	Wesleys	A/B/C	
Isaiah 51:1-6	Salvation is for ever	Ordinary 21	A	P-R
Isaiah 52:1-12	How beautiful on the mountains	Advent 1	A	2nd
Isaiah 52:7-10	Good tidings of salvation	Christmas Day III	A/B/C	
Isaiah 52:7-12	How beautiful on the mountains	Remembrance	A/B/C	
Isaiah 52:13 - 53:12	My servants shall be exalted and lifted up	Good Friday	A/B/C	
Isaiah (52:13-15) 53:1-6 (7-8) 9-12	He was despised and rejected	Easter 2	C	2nd
Isaiah 53:4-12	All we like sheep	Ordinary 29	B	P-R

Isaiah 55:1-5	Come to the waters	Ordinary 18	A	P
Isaiah 55:1-9	Come to the waters	Lent 3	C	P
Isaiah 55:1-11	Come to the waters	Easter Vigil	A/B/C	
		Ordinary 1	C	2nd
Isaiah 55:10-13	You shall go out in joy	Ordinary 8	C	P
		Ordinary 15	A	P-R
Isaiah 56:1, 6-8	The covenant extends to all who obey	Ordinary 20	A	P-R
Isaiah 58:1-9*a* (9*b*-12)	False and true worship	Ordinary 5	A	P
Isaiah 58:1-12	False and true worship	Ash Wednesday	A/B/C	
Isaiah 58:9*b*-14	False and true worship	Ordinary 21	C	P
Isaiah 60:1-6	The glory of the Lord	Epiphany	A/B/C	P
Isaiah 60:1-9	The glory of the Lord	Epiphany	A/B/C	2nd
Isaiah 60:1-14	The glory of the Lord	Easter 5	B	2nd
Isaiah 60:1-22	The glory of the Lord	Ordinary 24	C	2nd
Isaiah 60:9-22	The glory of the Lord	Ordinary 2	B	2nd
Isaiah 61:1-4, 8-11	Sent by the Spirit of the Lord	Advent 3	B	P
Isaiah 61:1-11	Sent by the Spirit of the Lord	Christmas 1	C	2nd
		Easter 7	B	2nd
Isaiah 61:10 - 62:3	The vindication and salvation of Zion	Christmas 1	B	P
Isaiah 62:1-5	The Lord delights in you	Ordinary 2	C	P
Isaiah 62:6-12	Salvation comes	Christmas Day II	A/B/C	
Isaiah 63:7-9	He has become our Saviour	Christmas 1	A	P
Isaiah 63:7-14	He has become our Saviour	Easter 4	C	2nd
Isaiah 64:1-9	You are our Father	Advent 1	B	P
Isaiah 65:1-9	My chosen shall inherit	Ordinary 12	C	P
Isaiah 65:17-25	God's new creation	Easter Day	C	P
		All Saints	B	2nd
		Ordinary 33	C	P-C
Isaiah 66:10-14	Rejoice with Jerusalem	Ordinary 14	C	P-R
Jeremiah 1:4-10	The call of Jeremiah	Ordinary 4	C	P
		Ordinary 21	C	P-C
Jeremiah 2:4-13	Jeremiah's instructions	Ordinary 22	C	P-C

Jeremiah 3:21 - 4:2	Israel's children have forgotten the Lord	Ordinary 3	B	2nd
Jeremiah 4:11-12, 22-28	My people are foolish	Ordinary 24	C	P-C
Jeremiah 5:1-19	Sorrow for a doomed nation	Ordinary 9	B	2nd
Jeremiah 6:16-21	A stubborn nation	Ordinary 10	B	2nd
Jeremiah 7:1-16	Amend your ways and your doings	Ordinary 11	B	2nd
Jeremiah 8:18 - 9:1	Mourning for the people	Ordinary 25	C	P-C
Jeremiah 10:1-16	The Lord is the true God	Ordinary 12	B	2nd
Jeremiah 11:1-14	My people have broken the covenant	Ordinary 13	B	2nd
Jeremiah 11:18-20	The lamb to the slaughter	Ordinary 25	B	P-R
Jeremiah 14:7-10, 19-22	Prayer in a drought	Ordinary 30	C	P-R
Jeremiah 15:15-21	I am with you, says the Lord	Ordinary 22	A	P-R
Jeremiah 17:5-10	Trust not in human nature but in the Lord	Ordinary 6	C	P
Jeremiah 18:1-11	The potter and the clay	Ordinary 23	C	P-C
Jeremiah 20:1-11*a*	Jeremiah denounces his persecutors	Ordinary 14	B	2nd
Jeremiah 20:7-13	Jeremiah unburdens his heart	Ordinary 12	A	P-R
Jeremiah 22:1-9, 13-17	Message to Judah	Lent 2	C	2nd
Jeremiah 23:1-6	He shall reign as King	Ordinary 16	B	P-R
		Sunday before Advent	C	P
Jeremiah 23:23-29	Is not my word like fire?	Ordinary 20	C	P-R
Jeremiah 28:5-9	True prophecy	Ordinary 13	A	P-R
Jeremiah 29:1, 4-7	Jeremiah writes to the exiles	Ordinary 28	C	P-C
Jeremiah 31:1-6	God's faithfulness	Easter Day	A	P
Jeremiah 31:7-9	God promises to bring his people home	Ordinary 30	B	P-R
Jeremiah 31:7-14	The redemption of God's people	Christmas 2	A/B/C	P
Jeremiah 31:27-34	Promise of a new covenant	Ordinary 29	C	P-C
Jeremiah 31:31-34	Promise of a new covenant	Lent 5 (Passion 1)	B	P
		Covenant	A/B/C	
Jeremiah 32:1-3*a*, 6-15	Jeremiah buys a field during the siege	Ordinary 26	C	P-C
Jeremiah 33:14-16	The Lord is our righteousness	Advent 1	C	P
Lamentations 1:1-6	The mourning of Zion	Ordinary 27	C	P-C
Lamentations 3:1-9, 19-24	God's steadfast love endures	Holy Saturday	A/B/C	
Lamentations 3:19-33	God's steadfast love endures	Lent 5 (Passion 1)	A	2nd

Lamentations 3:19-26	Steadfast love	Ordinary 27	C	P-C*
Lamentations 3:22-33	God's steadfast love endure	Ordinary 31	C	2nd
Lamentations 3:23-33	New every morning	Ordinary 13	B	P-R
Ezekiel 1:4-10, 22-28*a*	Visions of heaven	Trinity Sunday	B	2nd
Ezekiel 2:1-5	The call of Ezekiel	Ordinary 14	B	P-R
Ezekiel 2:1 - 3:4	The call of Ezekiel	Ordinary 2	A	2nd
Ezekiel 12:21 - 13:16	Judgement not postponed	Ordinary 23	A	2nd
Ezekiel 17:22-24	Trees shall know the Lord	Ordinary 11	B	P-R
Ezekiel 18:1-4, 25-32	I will judge you	Ordinary 26	A	P-R
Ezekiel 20:1-8, 33-44	God will restore Israel	Ordinary 24	A	2nd
Ezekiel 33:7-11	Ezekiel Israel's sentinel	Ordinary 23	A	P-R
Ezekiel 33:23, 30 - 34:10	Prophesy to the shepherds	Ordinary 25	A	2nd
Ezekiel 34:11-16, 20-24	The Lord finds and feeds his sheep	Sunday before Advent	A	P
Ezekiel 36:22-28	God will give a new heart and a new spirit	Pentecost	B	2nd
Ezekiel 36:24-28	God will give a new heart and a new spirit	Easter Vigil	A/B/C	
Ezekiel 37:1-14	The Spirit gives life	Lent 5 (Passion 1)	A	P
		Easter Vigil	A/B/C	
		Pentecost	B	P
		Easter Day	B	2nd
Ezekiel 37:15-28	An everlasting covenant of peace	Ordinary 26	A	2nd
Daniel 2:1-11 (12-24) 25-48	Daniel's interprets Nebuchadnezzar's dream	Ordinary 31	B	2nd
Daniel 3:(1-12) 13-30	The three are thrown into the fiery furnace	Ordinary 33	B	2nd
Daniel 5:1-31	Belshazzar's feast	Sunday before Advent	B	2nd
Daniel 6:(1-5) 6-23	Daniel and the lion's den	Easter 2	A	2nd
		Easter 5	C	2nd
Daniel 6:1-28	Daniel and the lion's den	Ordinary 33	C	2nd
Daniel 7:1-3, 15-18	Visions of the four beasts	All Saints	C	P
Daniel 7:1-18	Visions of the four beasts	Ordinary 31	A	2nd
Daniel 7:9-10, 13-14	Vision of kingship	Sunday before Advent	B	P
Daniel 12:1-3	Vision of the end times	Ordinary 33	B	P

Hosea 1:1-11	The call of Hosea	Ordinary 5	C	2nd
Hosea 1:2-10	The call of Hosea	Ordinary 17	C	P-C
Hosea 2:14-20	God's love for his people	Ordinary 8	B	P
Hosea 5:15 - 6:6	Let us return to the Lord	Ordinary 10	A	P-R
Hosea 10:1-8, 12	It is time to seek the Lord	Ordinary 6	C	2nd
Hosea 11:1-11	Out of Egypt I called my son	Ordinary 18	C	P-C
Hosea 14:1-9	Assurance of forgiveness	Ordinary 7	C	2nd
Joel 2:1-2, 12-17	Return to God and repent	Ash Wednesday	A/B/C	
Joel 2:21-32	God's Spirit poured out	Pentecost	A	2nd
Joel 2:23-32	God's Spirit poured out	Ordinary 30	C	P-C
Joel 3:9-21	Swords to ploughshares	Advent 1	C	2nd
Amos 2:4-16	Judgement on Israel	Ordinary 5	A	2nd
Amos 3:1-8	Judgement on a chosen people	Ordinary 6	A	2nd
Amos 5:6-7, 10-15	Seek good that you may live	Ordinary 28	B	P-C
Amos 5:18-24	Religious observance worthless without justice	Ordinary 32	A	P-R
Amos 6:1*a*, 4-7	Judgement on the secure	Ordinary 26	C	P-R
Amos 7:7-15	Prophecy on the plumb line	Ordinary 15	B	P-R
Amos 7:7-17	Prophecy on the plumb line	Ordinary 15	C	P-C
Amos 8:1-12	The basket of fruit	Ordinary 16	C	P-C
Amos 8:4-7	Do not cheat the poor	Ordinary 25	C	P-R
Amos 9:5-15	Restoration of David's kingdom	Ordinary 7	A	2nd
Jonah 3:1-5, 10	Nineveh repents at Jonah's preaching	Ordinary 3	B	P
Jonah 3:1-10	Nineveh repents at Jonah's preaching	Lent 1	C	2nd
Jonah 3:10 - 4:11	Jonah is reproved	Ordinary 25	A	P-R
Micah 3:5-12	Wicked rulers and prophets	Ordinary 31	A	P-R
Micah 4:1-8	Swords into ploughshares	Remembrance	A/B/C	
Micah 5:2-5*a*	A shepherd will come from Bethlehem	Advent 4	C	P
Micah 6:1-8	What does the Lord require?	Ordinary 4	A	P
Micah 7:1-20	Penitence and restoration	Lent 4	A	2nd

Habakkuk 1:1-4; 2:1-4	The righteous will live by his faithfulness	Ordinary 27	C	P-R
		Ordinary 31	C	P-C
Zephaniah 1:7, 12-18	The day of the Lord	Ordinary 33	A	P-R
Zephaniah 3:14-20	Rejoicing at God's restoration of his people	Advent 3	C	P
		Easter Vigil	A/B/C	
		Easter 6	C	2nd
Haggai 1:13 - 2:9	The future glory of the Temple	Easter 3	A	2nd
Haggai 1:15*b* - 2:9	The future glory of the Temple	Ordinary 32	C	P-C
Zechariah 2:10-13	I will come and dwell in your midst	Advent 4	B	2nd
Zechariah 4:1-10	Vision of a lampstand	Easter 5	A	2nd
Zechariah 8:1-13	Vision of a restored Jerusalem	Easter 6	A	2nd
Zechariah 9:9-12	Your king comes to you	Ordinary 14	A	P-R
Malachi 3:1-4	The Lord sends a messenger to prepare his way	Advent 2	C	P
Malachi 3:1-4; 4:1-6	A messenger foreshadows the Lord's day	Advent 3	B	2nd
Malachi 4:1-2*a*	The day of the Lord	Ordinary 33	C	P-R
APOCRYPHA				
Wisdom of Solomon 1:13-15; 2:23-24	God does not delight in death	Ordinary 13	B	P-R
Wisdom of Solomon 1:16 - 2:1, 12-22	Life as the ungodly see it	Ordinary 25	B	P-R
Wisdom of Solomon 3:1-9	Destiny of the righteous	All Saints	B	P
Wisdom of Solomon 6:1-21	Kings should seek wisdom	Ordinary 5	C	2nd
Wisdom of Solomon 6:12-16	Wisdom is radiant and unfading	Ordinary 32	A	P-R
Wisdom of Solomon 6:17-20	The beginning of wisdom	Ordinary 32	A	P-R*
Wisdom of Solomon 7:26 - 8:1	Wisdom reflects the working of God	Ordinary 24	B	P-C*
Wisdom of Solomon 10:15-21	Wisdom in the history of Israel	Christmas 2	A/B/C	P*
Wisdom of Solomon 11:21 - 12:11	God's power and mercy	Ordinary 6	C	2nd
Wisdom of Solomon 12:13, 16-19	God's sovereign power	Ordinary 16	A	P-R
Sirach/Ecclesiasticus 4:11-31	Wisdom teaches her children	Ordinary 15	B	2nd

Sirach/Ecclesiasticus 10:12-18	The sin of pride	Ordinary 22	C	P-R
Sirach/Ecclesiasticus 15:15-20	Keep the commandments and act faithfully	Ordinary 6	A	P
Sirach/Ecclesiasticus 18:1-14	The Lord is just and compassionate	Ordinary 16	B	2nd
Sirach/Ecclesiasticus 24:1-12	The wisdom of God comes to earth	Christmas 2	A/B/C	P
Sirach/Ecclesiasticus 27:4-7	The test of a man is in his words	Ordinary 8	C	P
Sirach/Ecclesiasticus 35:12-17	The Lord, the impartial judge	Ordinary 30	C	P-R
Sirach/Ecclesiasticus 38:24-34	Trades and crafts	Ordinary 17	B	2nd
Sirach/Ecclesiasticus 42:15-25	The marvellous works of the Lord	Ordinary 18	B	2nd
Sirach/Ecclesiasticus 43:13-33	The marvels of nature	Ordinary 19	B	2nd
Sirach/Ecclesiasticus 44:1-15	In honour of ancestors	All Saints	A	2nd
Sirach/Ecclesiasticus 48:1-10	Elijah	Sunday before Lent	A	2nd
Baruch 3:9-15, 32-4:4	Encouragement for Israel	Easter Vigil	A/B/C	
Baruch 4:36 - 5:9	Gathering of Israel	Epiphany	A/B/C	2nd
Baruch 5:1-9	Put on the beauty of the glory from the Lord	Advent 2	C	P
1 Maccabees 2:15-29	The leadership of Mattathias	Sunday before Advent	A	2nd
Prayer of Manasseh	Confession	Lent 4	A/C	2nd
NEW TESTAMENT				
Matthew 1:18-25	Jesus is born of Mary, betrothed to Joseph	Advent 4	A	P
		Advent 4	C	2nd
Matthew 2:1-12	The wise men come to worship Christ	Epiphany	A/B/C	P
Matthew 2:13-23	The escape into Egypt	Christmas 1	A	P
		Christmas 2	A/B/C	2nd
Matthew 3:1-12	John proclaims the coming Kingdom	Advent 2	A	P
Matthew 3:13-17	The baptism of Jesus	Ordinary 1	A	P
		Ordinary 1	B	2nd
Matthew 4:1-11	Jesus conquers temptation	Lent 1	A	P
Matthew 4:12-23	The hope of Isaiah is fulfilled	Ordinary 3	A	P
		Ordinary 3	B	2nd

Matthew 4:23 - 5:20	The opening of the Sermon on the Mount	Ordinary 22	B	2nd
Matthew 5:1-12	True blessedness	Ordinary 4	A	P
		All Saints	A	P
		Ordinary 31	B	2nd
		Remembrance	A/B/C	
Matthew 5:13-20	Salt, light and the kingdom of heaven	Ordinary 5	A	P
		Ordinary 5	C	2nd
Matthew 5:21-37	The fulfilment of the law	Ordinary 6	A	P
		Ordinary 6	C	2nd
Matthew 5:38-48	Be perfect	Ordinary 7	A	P
Matthew 5:43-48	Love your enemies	Remembrance	A/B/C	
Matthew 6:1-8	How to pray	Ordinary 7	C	2nd
Matthew 6:1-18	The Lord's Prayer	Ordinary 23	B	2nd
Matthew 6:1-6, 16-21	Give, pray and fast	Ash Wednesday	A/B/C	
Matthew 6:24-34	Do not worry	Ordinary 8	A	P
Matthew 6:25-33	Do not worry, consider the lilies	Harvest	A/B/C	
Matthew 6:25-34	Do not worry	Ordinary 8	C	2nd
Matthew 7:1-14	Do not judge; ask, search, knock	Ordinary 24	B	2nd
Matthew 7:21-29	Hearing the Lord's words and doing them	Ordinary 9	A	P
Matthew 8:5-13	The centurion's appeal to Jesus	Ordinary 2	B	2nd
Matthew 8:23-34	A storm stilled and demons enter a swineherd	Ordinary 25	B	2nd
Matthew 9:1-8	Healing a paralysed man	Ordinary 26	B	2nd
Matthew 9:9-13, 18-26	Matthew is called and two are healed	Ordinary 10	A	P
Matthew 9:35 - 10:8 (9-23)	The calling of the disciples	Ordinary 11	A	P
Matthew 10:1-22	Instructions to the disciples	Ordinary 27	B	2nd
Matthew 10:16-22	Coming persecution	Lent 3	B	2nd
Matthew 10:24-39	Fear not	Ordinary 12	A	P
Matthew 10:40-42	Christian discipleship	Ordinary 13	A	P
Matthew 11:2-11	Christ bears witness to John and to himself	Advent 3	A	P
		Advent 2	B	2nd
Matthew 11:16-19, 25-30	Come, I will give you rest	Ordinary 14	A	P
Matthew 11:20-30	Come, I will give you rest	Ordinary 28	B	2nd
Matthew 12:1-8	The son of man is Lord of the Sabbath	Anniversary	A/B/C	

Matthew 12:1-21	Lord of the Sabbath	Ordinary 29	B	2nd
Matthew 13:1-9, 18-23	The parable of the sower	Ordinary 15	A	P
		Ordinary 33	C	2nd
Matthew 13:10-17	Secrets of the kingdom	Ordinary 4	B	2nd
Matthew 13:24-30, 36-43	The parable of the weeds	Ordinary 16	A	P
		Ordinary 33	B	2nd
Matthew 13:24-30 (31-43)	The parable of the weeds	Ordinary 17	C	2nd
Matthew 13:31-33, 44-52	Parables of the kingdom	Ordinary 17	A	P
Matthew 14:1-12	The death of John the Baptist	Advent 3	B	2nd
Matthew 14:13-21	Jesus feeds the five thousand	Ordinary 18	A	P
Matthew 14:22-33	Lord, save me	Ordinary 19	A	P
Matthew 15:(10-20) 21-28	Great is your faith	Ordinary 20	A	P
Matthew 16:13-20	Peter confesses Jesus as the Christ	Ordinary 21	A	P
Matthew 16:21-28	The way of the cross	Ordinary 22	A	P
Matthew 17:1-9	The transfiguration	Sunday before Lent	A	P
Matthew 17:(1-8) 9-23	Teaching the disciples	Sunday before Lent	A	2nd
Matthew 18:15-20	Disputes among God's people	Ordinary 23	A	P
Matthew 18:21-35	The servant who would not forgive	Ordinary 24	A	P
Matthew 20:1-16	The parable of the labourers in the vineyard	Ordinary 20	C	2nd
		Ordinary 25	A	P
Matthew 20:17-34	Going up to Jerusalem	Lent 5 (Passion 1)	A	2nd
Matthew 21:1-11	Entry into Jerusalem	Lent 6 (Passion 2/Palm)	A	P
Matthew 21:1-13	Entry into Jerusalem	Advent 1	B	2nd
Matthew 21:23-32	Saying and doing	Ordinary 26	A	P
Matthew 21:28-32	Entering the kingdom	Ordinary 21	C	2nd
Matthew 21:33-46	The parable of the vineyard and the talents	Lent 6 (Passion 2/Palm)	A	2nd
		Ordinary 27	A	P
Matthew 22:1-14	The wedding feast	Ordinary 28	A	P
Matthew 22:15-22	Paying tax	Ordinary 29	A	P
		Ordinary 32	C	2nd
Matthew 22:34-46	The two great commandments	Ordinary 30	A	P
		Ordinary 30	C	2nd
Matthew 23:1-12	True greatness in being a servant	Ordinary 31	A	P

Matthew 24:15-28	False Messiahs and false prophets	Advent 1	A	2nd
Matthew 24:36-44	Be ready for the coming of the Lord	Advent 1	A	P
Matthew 25:1-13	The bridegroom is coming	Ordinary 32	A	P
Matthew 25:14-30	The parable of the talents	Ordinary 33	A	P
Matthew 25:31-36	Sheep and goats	Watchnight	A/B/C	
Matthew 25:31-46	The Son of man judges the nations	Sunday before Advent	A	P
Matthew 26:14 - 27 66	The Passion narrative	Lent 6 (Passion 2/Palm)	A	P
Matthew 26:30-75	Gethsemane, arrest and Peter's denial	Maundy Thursday	A	Watch
Matthew 26:30 - 27:61	The Passion narrative	Maundy Thursday	A	Vigil
Matthew 27:11-54	The trial before Pilate and crucifixion	Lent 6 (Passion 2/Palm)	A	P
Matthew 27:57-66	The burial	Holy Saturday	A/B/C	
Matthew 28:1-10	The first Easter Day	Easter Vigil	A	
		Easter Day	A	P
Matthew 28:1-10, 16-20	Resurrection and ascension	Easter 6	C	2nd
Matthew 28:16-20	The threefold name	Trinity Sunday	A	P
Matthew 28:16-20	The kingship of Christ	Sunday before Advent	A	2nd
Mark 1:1-8	John prepares the way of the Lord	Advent 2	B	P
Mark 1:1-13	Jesus is baptised by John and tempted	Trinity Sunday	B	2nd
Mark 1:4-11	John baptises Jesus	Ordinary 1	B	P
		Ordinary 1	C	2nd
Mark 1:9-15	The baptism and temptation of Jesus	Lent 1	B	P
Mark 1:14-20	Repent and believe the good news	Ordinary 3	B	P
Mark 1:21-28	A new teaching with authority	Ordinary 3	C	2nd
		Ordinary 4	B	P
		Ordinary 4	A	2nd
Mark 1:29-39	Christ the healer	Ordinary 5	B	P
		Ordinary 5	A	2nd
Mark 1:40-45	Jesus heals a leper	Ordinary 6	B	P
		Ordinary 6	A	2nd
Mark 2:1-12	The paralysed man is forgiven and cured	Ordinary 7	B	P
		Ordinary 7	A	2nd
Mark 2:13-22	Eating with sinners and tax collectors	Ordinary 8	B	P

Mark 2:23 - 3:6	The Lord of the Sabbath	Ordinary 9	B	P
Mark 3:7-19	Calling the disciples	Ordinary 9	C	2nd
Mark 3:20-35	Doing God's will	Ordinary 10	B	P
Mark 4:1-20	The parable of the sower	Ordinary 10	C	2nd
Mark 4:21-41	Parables told and a storm stilled	Ordinary 11	C	2nd
Mark 4:26-34	Parables of the seed	Ordinary 11	B	P
Mark 4:35-41	The stilling of the storm	Ordinary 12	B	P
Mark 5:21-43	The daughter of Jairus, a woman with haemorrhage	Ordinary 13	B	P
		Ordinary 12	C	2nd
Mark 6:1-6	Jesus rejected at Nazareth	Ordinary 13	C	2nd
Mark 6:1-13	Jesus rejected at Nazareth	Ordinary 14	B	P
Mark 6:7-29	The death of John the Baptist	Ordinary 14	C	2nd
Mark 6:14-29	The death of John the Baptist	Ordinary 15	B	P
Mark 6:30-34, 53-56	The compassion of Christ for unshepherded sheep	Ordinary 16	B	P
		Ordinary 16	A	2nd
Mark 6:45-52	Jesus stills the storm	Ordinary 18	C	2nd
Mark 7:1-8, 14-15, 21-23	What really makes people unclean	Ordinary 22	B	P
		Ordinary 22	A	2nd
Mark 7:1-23	What really makes people unclean	Ordinary 15	C	2nd
Mark 7:24-30	Jesus goes to Tyre	Ordinary 19	C	2nd
Mark 7:24-37	The deaf hear, the dumb speak	Ordinary 23	B	P
		Ordinary 23	A	2nd
Mark 8:27-38	The necessity of the cross	Ordinary 24	B	P
		Ordinary 24	A	2nd
Mark 8:31-38	The necessity of the cross	Lent 2	B	P
Mark 8:34 - 9:1	Saving and losing life for His sake	All Saints	B	2nd
Mark 9:2-9	The transfiguration	Sunday before Lent	B	P
Mark 9:(2-8) 9-13	Teaching after the transfiguration	Sunday before Lent	B	2nd
Mark 9:30-37	True greatness	Ordinary 25	B	P
		Ordinary 25	A	2nd

Mark 9:38-50	Whoever is not against us is for us	Ordinary 26	B	P
		Ordinary 26	A	2nd
Mark 10:2-16	God's pattern for family life	Ordinary 27	B	P
		Ordinary 27	A	2nd
Mark 10:17-31	The danger of riches	Ordinary 28	B	P
		Ordinary 28	A	2nd
Mark 10:35-45	James and John seek places of honour	Ordinary 29	B	P
		Ordinary 29	A	2nd
Mark 10:46-52	Jesus gives sight to Bartimaeus	Ordinary 30	B	P
Mark 11:1-11	Entry into Jerusalem	Lent 6 (Passion 2/Palm)	B	P
Mark 12:1-12	The parable of the vineyard	Lent 6 (Passion 2/Palm)	B	2nd
Mark 12:28-34	Jesus gives us two great commandments	Ordinary 31	B	P
		Ordinary 30	A	2nd
Mark 12:28-37	The great commandments	Wesleys	A/B/C	
Mark 12:38-44	The widow's offering in the Temple	Ordinary 32	B	P
Mark 13:1-8	Prophecy over the Temple	Ordinary 33	B	P
Mark 13:24-37	Watch, therefore	Advent 1	B	P
Mark 14:1 - 15:47	The Passion narrative	Lent 6 (Passion 2/Palm)	B	P
Mark 14:22-25	The blood of the covenant	Covenant	A/B/C	
Mark 14:26-72	Gethsemane, arrest and Peter's denial	Maundy Thursday	B	Watch
Mark 14:26 - 15:47	The Passion narrative	Maundy Thursday	B	Vigil
Mark 15:1-39 (40-47)	Trial before Pilate and crucifixion	Lent 6 (Passion 2/Palm)	B	P
Mark 15:46 - 16:8	The first Easter Day	Easter 2	A	2nd
		Easter 5	C	2nd
Mark 16:1-8	The first Easter Day	Easter Vigil	B	
		Easter Day	B	P
Mark 16:9-16	Resurrection appearances	Easter 5	B	2nd
Mark 16:14-20	Instructions to the disciples	Easter 7	A	2nd
Luke 1:1-25	Elizabeth and Zechariah	Advent 2	C	2nd
Luke 1:26-38	God calls Mary, and she obeys	Advent 4	B	P
Luke 1:39-45 (46-55)	Mary visits Elizabeth to their great joy	Advent 4	C	P
Luke 1:39-45	Mary visits Elizabeth to their great joy	Advent 4	A	2nd

Luke 1:39-55	Mary visits Elizabeth to their great joy	Advent 4	B	2nd
Luke 1:47*b*-55	Magnificat	Advent 3	A/B	P*
		Advent 4	B/C	P*
Luke 1:57-66 (67-80)	John is born and named	Advent 3	C	2nd
Luke 1:68-79	Benedictus	Advent 2	C	P*
		Sunday before Advent	C	P*
Luke 2:1-14 (15-20)	The Saviour is born	Christmas Day I	A/B/C	
Luke 2:(1-7) 8-20	The shepherds hear angels and come	Christmas Day II	A/B/C	
Luke 2:15-21	The shepherds come	Christmas 1	C	2nd
Luke 2:22-40	The presentation of Jesus in the Temple	Christmas 1	B	P
Luke 2:25-32 (33-38)	Simeon (and Anna) greet Jesus	Easter 5	A	2nd
Luke 2:33-35	Simeon greets Jesus	Mothering Sunday	A/B/C	
Luke 2:41-52	The boy Jesus found in the Temple	Christmas 1	A/B	2nd
		Christmas 1	C	P
Luke 3:1-6	The message of John the Baptist	Advent 2	C	P
Luke 3:7-18	The preaching of John the Baptist	Advent 3	C	P
Luke 3:15-17, 21-22	John baptises Jesus	Ordinary 1	C	P
Luke 3:15-22	John baptises Jesus	Ordinary 1	A	2nd
Luke 4:1-13	Jesus conquers temptation	Lent 1	C	P
Luke 4:14-21	Jesus in the synagogue at Nazareth	Ordinary 3	A	2nd
		Ordinary 3	C	P
		Easter 7	B	2nd
Luke 4:21-30	The rejection of Jesus at Nazareth	Ordinary 4	C	P
Luke 5:1-11	Jesus calls the fishermen	Ordinary 5	B	2nd
		Ordinary 5	C	P
Luke 6:17-26	Blessings and woes	Ordinary 6	B	2nd
		Ordinary 6	C	P
Luke 6:17-31	Do to others as you would have them do to you	Ordinary 31	A	2nd
Luke 6:20-31	Do to others as you would have them do to you	All Saints	C	P
Luke 6:27-38	Love, not friends only, but also enemies	Ordinary 7	B	2nd
		Ordinary 7	C	P
Luke 6:39-49	Hearing the Lord's words and doing them	Ordinary 8	C	P

Luke 7:1-10	The faith of the centurion	Ordinary 9	B	2nd
		Ordinary 9	C	P
Luke 7:11-17	Jesus raises the widow's son in Nain	Ordinary 10	B	2nd
		Ordinary 10	C	P
Luke 7:36 - 8:3	She loved much and was forgiven much	Ordinary 11	B	2nd
		Ordinary 11	C	P
Luke 8:4-15	The parable of the sower	Ordinary 9	A	2nd
Luke 8:22-35	A storm and a healing	Ordinary 8	B	2nd
Luke 8:26-39	Jesus heals the Gerasene Demoniac	Ordinary 12	B	2nd
		Ordinary 12	C	P
Luke 8:41-56	Jesus heals Jairus' daughter	Ordinary 10	A	2nd
Luke 9:1-6	The twelve sent out	Ordinary 33	A	2nd
Luke 9:18-27	Peter names the Christ	All Saints	C	2nd
Luke 9:28-36 (37-43)	The transfiguration	Sunday before Lent	C	P
Luke 9:51-62	The cost of discipleship	Ordinary 13	B	2nd
		Ordinary 13	C	P
Luke 10:1-11, 16-20	The Lord commissions the seventy	Ordinary 14	B	2nd
		Ordinary 14	C	P
Luke 10:1-12,17-20	Sending the seventy	Wesleys	A/B/C	
Luke 10:25-37	Who is my neighbour?	Ordinary 15	B	2nd
		Ordinary 15	C	P
Luke 10:38-42	Mary and Martha at Bethany	Ordinary 16	B	2nd
		Ordinary 16	C	P
Luke 11:1-13	Teach us to pray; ask, search, knock	Ordinary 17	B	2nd
		Ordinary 17	C	P
Luke 11:14-28	Casting out demons	Ordinary 11	A	2nd
Luke 12:13-21	The parable of the rich fool	Ordinary 18	B	2nd
		Ordinary 18	C	P
		Watchnight	A/B/C	
Luke 12:16-31	Do not worry	Ordinary 8	A	2nd
Luke 12:32-40	Be ready and watch	Ordinary 19	B	2nd
		Ordinary 19	C	P
Luke 12:35-50	Be dressed for action	Watchnight	A/B/C	

Luke 12:49-56	I came not to bring peace but division	Ordinary 20	B	2nd
		Ordinary 20	C	P
Luke 13:1-9	Repentance is our urgent need	Lent 3	C	P
Luke 13:10-17	Healing on the Sabbath	Ordinary 21	B	2nd
		Ordinary 21	C	P
Luke 13:31-35	The city that kills the prophets	Lent 1	B	2nd
		Lent 2	C	P
Luke 14:1, 7-14	Be ready to take the lowest place	Ordinary 22	C	P
Luke 14:12-24	The parable of the great dinner	Ordinary 12	A	2nd
Luke 14:25-33	Counting the cost of discipleship	Ordinary 23	C	P
Luke 14:27-33	Counting the cost of discipleship	Lent 2	A/C	2nd
Luke 15:1-3, 11*b*-32	The father and his two sons	Lent 4	C	P
Luke 15:1-10	The lost coin and the lost sheep	Lent 1	A	2nd
		Ordinary 24	C	P
Luke 16:1-13	Shrewd manager, unjust steward	Ordinary 25	C	P
Luke 16:19-31	The rich man and Lazarus	Easter 3	B	2nd
		Ordinary 26	C	P
Luke 17:5-10	Persevere in serving the Lord	Ordinary 27	C	P
Luke 17:11-19	Jesus cures ten lepers; one is thankful	Ordinary 28	C	P
Luke 17:20-37	The kingdom of God is among you	Ordinary 13	A	2nd
Luke 18:1-8	The parable of the unjust judge	Ordinary 29	C	P
Luke 18:9-14	The Pharisee and the tax collector			
		Lent 1	C	2nd
		Ordinary 30	B	2nd
		Ordinary 30	C	P
Luke 18:31 - 19:10	Jesus meets a blind man and Zacchaeus	Ordinary 14	A	2nd
Luke 19:1-10	Jesus and Zacchaeus	Ordinary 31	C	P
Luke 19:28-40	Entry into Jerusalem	Lent 6 (Passion 2/Palm)	C	P
Luke 19:37-48	Jesus enters the Temple	Easter 4	A	2nd
Luke 19:41 - 20:8	Entering the Temple, Jesus' authority			
	questioned	Ordinary 15	A	2nd
Luke 20:9-19	The parable of the vineyard	Lent 6 (Passion 2/Palm)	C	2nd
Luke 20:27-38	The God of the living	Ordinary 32	C	P

Luke 21:5-19	Endurance in the face of persecution	Ordinary 33	C	P
Luke 21:25-36	Your liberation is near	Advent 1	C	P
Luke 22:1-13	Preparing for the Passover	Lent 5 (Passion 1)	B/C	2nd
Luke 22:14 - 23:56	The Passion narrative	Lent 6 (Passion 2/Palm)	C	P
Luke 22:24-30	Disputes over leadership	Easter 6	B	2nd
Luke 22:24-23:56	The Passion narrative	Maundy Thursday	A	Vigil
Luke 22:39-65	Seized on the Mount of Olives	Maundy Thursday	A	Watch
Luke 23:1-49	The Passion narrative (part)	Lent 6 (Passion 2/Palm)	C	P
Luke 23:33-43	Crucifixion	Sunday before Advent	C	P
Luke 24:1-12	The first Easter Day	Easter Vigil	C	
		Easter Day	C	P
		Easter 2	B	2nd
Luke 24:13-35	On the road to Emmaus	Easter Day	B	2nd
		Easter 2	C	2nd
		Easter 3	A	P
Luke 24:36-49	The risen Christ makes himself known	Easter 4	C	2nd
Luke 24:36*b*-48	The risen Christ makes himself known	Easter 3	B	P
Luke 24:44-53	The promise of power from on high	Easter 7	C	2nd
		Ascension Day	A/B/C	
		Pentecost	A	2nd
John 1:1-14	The Word became flesh	Christmas Day III	A/B/C	
John 1:6-8, 19-28	The one who is to come stands among you	Advent 3	B	P
John 1:(1-9) 10-18	We have seen his glory	Christmas 2	A/B/C	P
John 1:19-28	The testimony of John	Advent 2	A	2nd
John 1:29-42	Behold, the lamb of God; John's disciples follow	Ordinary 2	A	P
		Ordinary 2	C	2nd
John 1:35-51	The first disciples of Jesus	Lent 3	C	2nd
John 1:43-51	Philip brings Nathanael to Jesus	Ordinary 2	B	P
		Ordinary 2	A	2nd
John 2:1-11	The wedding at Cana	Ordinary 2	C	P
		Epiphany	A/B/C	2nd

John 2:13-22	The cleansing of the temple	Lent 3	A	2nd
		Lent 3	B	P
		Easter 3	A	2nd
John 3:1-17	Nicodemus visits Jesus	Advent 1	C	2nd
		Lent 2	A	P
		Trinity Sunday	B	P
		Trinity Sunday	C	2nd
John 3:14-21	The Son is sent to save the world	Lent 4	A	2nd
		Lent 4	B	P
John 3:22-36	John answers questions	Ordinary 22	C	2nd
John 4:5-42	Christ, the water of life	Lent 3	A	P
John 4:19-26	Our ancestors worshipped on this mountain	Anniversary	A/B/C	
John 4:19-29*a*	Teaching about worship	Ordinary 4	C	2nd
John 4:31-35	Jesus speaks about food	Ordinary 16	C	2nd
John 5:1-9	A paralytic healed	Easter 6	C	P
John 5:30-47	Teaching about authority	Ordinary 23	C	2nd
John 5:31-40	Jesus' testimony	Advent 3	A	2nd
John 6:1-15	The feeding of the five thousand	Sunday before Advent	B	2nd
John 6:1-21	The feeding of the five thousand	Ordinary 17	A	2nd
		Ordinary 17	B	P
John 6:24-35	The bread of life	Ordinary 18	A	2nd
		Ordinary 18	B	P
		Harvest	A/B/C	
John 6:30-40	The bread of life	Easter 4	B	2nd
John 6:35, 41-51	The living bread from heaven	Ordinary 19	A	2nd
		Ordinary 19	B	P
John 6:51-58	My flesh is real food, my blood is real drink	Ordinary 20	A	2nd
		Ordinary 20	B	P
John 6:51-69	Words of eternal life	Ordinary 24	C	2nd
John 6:56-69	Jesus has the words of eternal life	Ordinary 21	A	2nd
		Ordinary 21	B	P
John 7:14-36	Jesus at the festival of Booths	Ordinary 25	C	2nd
John 7:37-39	Teaching on the Spirit	Pentecost	A	P

John 8:31-38, 48-59	Before Abraham was, I am	Ordinary 26	C	2nd
John 9:1-41	Christ gives sight to the man born blind	Lent 4	A	P
		Ordinary 27	C	2nd
John 10:1-10	The gate of the sheepfold	Easter 4	A	P
John 10:11-18	The Good Shepherd lays down his life	Easter 4	B	P
John 10:22-30	He gives his sheep eternal life	Easter 4	C	P
John 11:(1-31) 32-44	Jesus raises Lazarus	Ordinary 31	C	2nd
John 11:1-45	Christ the resurrection and the life	Lent 5 (Passion 1)	A	P
John 11:17-44	Jesus raises Lazarus	Lent 4	C	2nd
John 11:(17-26) 27-44	Jesus raises Lazarus	Easter 3	C	2nd
John 11:20-27	Christ the resurrection and the life	All Saints	A	2nd
John 11:32-44	Jesus raises Lazarus	All Saints	B	P
John 12:1-8	Mary anoints Jesus in Bethany	Lent 4	B	2nd
		Lent 5 (Passion 1)	C	P
John 12:1-11	Mary anoints Jesus in Bethany	Monday in Holy Week	A/B/C	
John 12:12-16	Entry into Jerusalem	Lent 6 (Passion 2/Palm)	B	P
John 12:20-33	Through death, a rich harvest	Lent 5 (Passion 1)	B	P
John 12:20-36	I will draw all people to me	Tuesday in Holy Week	A/B/C	
John 12:27-36*a*	Walk while you have the light	Sunday before Lent	C	2nd
John 13:1-17, 31*b*-35	Jesus washes his disciples feet and gives a new law	Maundy Thursday	A/B/C	
John 13:21-32	The betrayal of Jesus	Wednesday in Holy Wk	A/B/C	
John 13:31-35	The new commandment	Easter 5	C	P
John 14:(1-22) 23-29	Peace I leave with you	Ordinary 32	B	2nd
John 14:1-14	The way, the truth and the life	Easter 5	A	P
John 14:8-17 (25-27)	The Father will send the Spirit in my name	Pentecost	C	P
John 14:15-21	The promise of the Holy Spirit	Easter 6	A	P
John 14:23-29	I go to the Father who will send you the Spirit	Easter 6	C	P
John 15:1-8	He is the vine, we are the branches	Easter 5	B	P
John 15:1-10	He is the vine, we are the branches	Covenant	A/B/C	
John 15:9-17	You are my friends if you love one another	Easter 6	B	P
		Ordinary 32	A	2nd
		Remembrance	A/B/C	

John 15:12-27	Love one another	Ordinary 28	C	2nd
John 15:26-27; 16:4*b*-15	The Spirit will guide you into all truth	Pentecost	B	P
John 16:1-11	The work of the Spirit	Ordinary 29	C	2nd
John 16:4*b*-15	The Spirit will guide you into all truth	Pentecost	C	2nd
John 16:5-15	The Spirit will guide you into all truth	Trinity Sunday	A	2nd
John 16:12-15	Jesus speaks of the Father and of the Spirit	Trinity Sunday	C	P
John 17:1-11	The high-priestly prayer	Easter 7	A	P
John 17:6-19	Disciples do not belong to the world	Easter 7	B	P
John 17:20-26	May they be perfectly one	Easter 7	C	P
John 18:1 - 19:42	The passion narrative	Good Friday	A/B/C	
John 18:33-37	My kingship is not of this world	Sunday before Advent	B	P
		Sunday before Advent	C	2nd
John 19:25-27	Jesus speaks to his mother from the cross	Mothering Sunday	A/B/C	
John 19:38-42	Buried in Joseph's tomb	Holy Saturday	A/B/C	
John 20:1-18	The first Easter Day	Easter Day	A/B/C	P
John 20:11-18	Mary thinks she meets the gardener	Easter Day	A	2nd
John 20:19-23	Jesus appears to his disciples	Easter Day	C	2nd
John 20:19-23	The gift of the Spirit for mission	Pentecost	A	P
		Pentecost	B	2nd
John 20:19-31	The risen Christ with his disciples	Easter 2	A/B/C	P
John 21:1-14	Jesus meets his disciples by the lakeside	Easter 3	C	P
		Easter 6	A	2nd
Acts 1:1-11	The Ascension	Ascension Day	A/B/C	
Acts 1:6-14	They devoted themselves to prayer	Easter 7	A	P
Acts 1:15-17, 21-26	Matthias is chosen to replace Judas	Easter 7	B	P
Acts 2:1-21	The day of Pentecost	Pentecost	A/B/C	P
Acts 2:14*a*, 22-32	Peter proclaims the resurrection of Christ	Easter 2	A	P
Acts 2:14*a*, 36-41	Baptism in the name of the risen Christ	Easter 3	A	P
Acts 2:14-21 (22-38)	Peter foresees the last days	Pentecost	A	2nd
Acts 2:22-38	Peter proclaims the resurrection of Christ	Pentecost	B	2nd
Acts 2:42-47	The common life of the Jerusalem Christians	Easter 4	A	P
Acts 3:12-19	Peter preaches the risen Christ in the Temple	Easter 3	B	P

Acts 4:1-22	By his name we are saved	Ordinary 16	A	2nd
Acts 4:5-12	By his name we are saved	Easter 4	B	P
Acts 4:32-35	The apostles bear witness to the resurrection	Easter 2	B	P
Acts 5:27-32	Forgiveness given by the exalted Christ	Easter 2	C	P
Acts 7:44-50	God's dwelling place	Ordinary 4	C	2nd
Acts 7:55-60	Stephen sees a vision of Christ	Easter 5	A	P
Acts 8:14-17	Peter and John lay hands on baptised Samaritans	Ordinary 1	C	P
Acts 8:26-40	The conversion of the Ethiopian eunuch	Easter 5	B	P
Acts 9:1-6 (7-20)	The risen Christ appears to Saul	Easter 3	C	P
Acts 9:36-43	Peter heals Tabitha	Easter 4	C	P
Acts 10:34-43	Peter preaches the resurrection of Christ	Easter Day	A/B/C	P
		Ordinary 1	A	P
Acts 10:44-48	The Pentecost of the Gentiles	Easter 6	B	P
Acts 11:1-18	Peter tells of his vision of unclean things	Easter 5	C	P
Acts 12:1-17	Peter imprisoned, but escapes	Ordinary 17	A	2nd
Acts 13:1-13	Paul and Barnabas on Cyprus	Ordinary 18	A	2nd
Acts 13:13-41	Paul preaches in Antioch of Pisidia	Advent 3	A	2nd
Acts 14:8-20	Paul and Barnabas mistaken for gods	Ordinary 19	A	2nd
Acts 16:1-15	Crossing over to Macedonia	Ordinary 20	A	2nd
Acts 16:9-15	Crossing over to Macedonia	Easter 6	C	P
Acts 16:16-34	The ministry of Paul and Silas in prison	Easter 7	C	P
Acts 17:15-34	Paul preaches in Athens	Ordinary 21	A	2nd
Acts 17:22-31	Paul preaches in Athens	Easter 6	A	P
Acts 18:1-16	Paul in Corinth	Ordinary 22	A	2nd
Acts 19:1-7	Paul speaks about the baptism of John	Ordinary 1	B	P
Acts 19:1-20	Paul in Ephesus	Ordinary 23	A	2nd
Acts 20:17-38	A message to Christians in Ephesus	Ordinary 24	A	2nd
Acts 26:1, 9-25	Paul's defence before Agrippa	Ordinary 25	A	2nd
Romans 1:1-7	Jesus, Son of David, Son of God	Advent 4	A	P
Romans 1:16-17; 3:22*b*-28 (29-31)	All have sinned and fall short	Ordinary 9	A	P
Romans 4:1-5, 13-17	The example of Abraham	Lent 2	A	P

Romans 4:13-25	We receive God's promises by faith	Lent 2	B	P
		Ordinary 10	A	P
Romans 5:1-5	Peace and love given us by the Holy Trinity	Trinity Sunday	C	P
Romans 5:1-8	While we were still sinners, Christ dies for us	Ordinary 11	A	P
Romans 5:1-11	Salvation through God's love in Christ	Lent 3	A	P
		Lent 4	B	2nd
		Wesleys	A/B/C	
Romans 5:12-19	The obedience of Christ, the new Adam	Lent 1	A	P
		Lent 1	B	2nd
Romans 5:12-21	The obedience of Christ, the new Adam	Lent 5 (Passion 1)	B	2nd
Romans 6:1-11	Baptised into Christ's death and resurrection	Ordinary 1	C	2nd
Romans 6:1*b*-11	Baptised into Christ's death and resurrection	Ordinary 12	A	P
Romans 6:3-11	Baptised into Christ's death and resurrection	Easter Vigil	A/B/C	
Romans 6:12-23	Slaves of righteousness	Ordinary 13	A	P
Romans 7:7-25	The law and sin	Ordinary 9	B	2nd
Romans 7:15-25*a*	The struggle with fallen human nature	Ordinary 14	A	P
Romans 8:1-11	The flesh and the Spirit	Ordinary 15	A	P
Romans 8:6-11	The life-giving Spirit	Lent 5 (Passion 1)	A	P
Romans 8:12-17	Partakers of the divine nature	Trinity Sunday	B	P
Romans 8:12-25	Present suffering leads to future glory	Ordinary 16	A	P
Romans 8:14-17	Children of God by the Spirit	Pentecost	C	P
Romans 8:22-27	The Spirit prays within us	Pentecost	B	P
Romans 8:26-39	God works for good with those who love God	Ordinary 17	A	P
Romans 8:31-35, 37-39	Nothing can separate us from God's love	Remembrance	A/B/C	
Romans 8:31-39	Nothing can separate us from God's love	Ordinary 32	C	2nd
Romans 9:1-5	Paul protests his love for Israel	Ordinary 18	A	P
Romans 9:1-13	Paul protests his love for Israel	Ordinary 10	B	2nd
Romans 9:14-26	God's chosen people	Ordinary 11	B	2nd
Romans 10:5-15	How are they to believe?	Ordinary 19	A	P
Romans 10:8*b*-13	Salvation through Christ	Lent 1	C	P
Romans 11:1-2*a*, 29-32	God's mercy for all his people	Ordinary 20	A	P
Romans 11:25-36	All Israel will be saved	Ordinary 12	B	2nd
Romans 12:1-2	One body, many gifts	Covenant	A/B/C	

Romans 12:1-8	One body, many gifts	Christmas 2	B	2nd
		Ordinary 21	A	P
Romans 12:9-21	Overcome evil with good	Ordinary 22	A	P
Romans 13:1-10	Love is the fulfilling of the law	Ordinary 13	B	2nd
Romans 13:8-14	Salvation is nearer to us now	Ordinary 23	A	P
Romans 13:11-14	Put on the armour of light	Advent 1	A	P
Romans 14:1-12	We live to the Lord, not to ourselves	Ordinary 24	A	P
Romans 14:1-17	We live to the Lord, not to ourselves	Ordinary 14	B	2nd
Romans 15:4-13	Joy, peace and hope	Advent 2	A	P
		Advent 2	B	2nd
Romans 15:14-29	Paul's plan to visit Rome	Ordinary 15	B	2nd
Romans 16:25-27	God's mystery revealed in his Son	Advent 4	B	P
1 Corinthians 1:1-9	May God grant you grace and peace	Ordinary 2	A	P
1 Corinthians 1:3-9	God's grace and faithfulness	Advent 1	B	P
1 Corinthians 1:10-18	Agree among yourselves	Ordinary 3	A	P
1 Corinthians 1:18-25	Christ, the power and wisdom of God	Lent 3	B	P
1 Corinthians 1:18-31	Christ, the power and wisdom of God	Tuesday in Holy Week	A/B/C	
1 Corinthians 1:18-31	Christ, the power and wisdom of God	Ordinary 4	A	P
1 Corinthians 2:1-12 (13-16)	The proclamation of Christ crucified	Ordinary 5	A	P
1 Corinthians 3:1-9	God gives the growth	Ordinary 6	A	P
1 Corinthians 3:10-17	You are God's temple	Easter 3	A	2nd
1 Corinthians 3:10-11, 16-23	Belonging to Christ	Ordinary 7	A	P
1 Corinthians 4:1-5	The Lord judges his stewards	Ordinary 8	A	P
1 Corinthians 4:8-13	Fools for Christ	Ordinary 16	C	2nd
1 Corinthians 6:12-20	Your bodies are members of Christ	Ordinary 2	B	P
1 Corinthians 7:17-24	Lead the life to which God called you	Ordinary 3	C	2nd
1 Corinthians 7:29-31	We live in the last times	Ordinary 3	B	P
1 Corinthians 8:1-13	Food offered to idols and concern for others	Ordinary 4	B	P
1 Corinthians 9:16-23	The necessity of preaching the gospel	Ordinary 5	B	P
1 Corinthians 9:24-27	Running the race for an unfading wreath	Ordinary 6	B	P
1 Corinthians 10:1-13	Warnings from the history of Israel	Lent 3	C	P
1 Corinthians 10:1-24	Warnings about the Lord's table	Ordinary 17	C	2nd

1 Corinthians 11:23-26	The Last Supper	Maundy Thursday	A/B/C	
1 Corinthians 12:1-11	The gifts of the Spirit	Ordinary 2	C	P
1 Corinthians 12:3*b*-13	The Holy Spirit for each and all	Pentecost	A	P
1 Corinthians 12:12-31*a*	You are the body of Christ	Ordinary 3	C	P
1 Corinthians 13:1-13	Faith, hope and love	Ordinary 4	C	P
1 Corinthians 14:1-19	Speaking in tongues	Ordinary 18	C	2nd
1 Corinthians 14:12-20	Use spiritual gifts as adults	Ordinary 4	B	2nd
1 Corinthians 15:1-11	The gospel of the resurrection	Easter Day	B	P
		Easter Day	C	2nd
		Ordinary 5	C	P
1 Corinthians 15:12-20	Our hope is in the risen Christ	Ordinary 6	C	P
1 Corinthians 15:19-26	Christ conquers death	Easter Day	C	P
1 Corinthians 15:35-38, 42-50	The resurrection of the dead	Ordinary 7	C	P
1 Corinthians 15:51-58	Victory over death is ours through Christ	Ordinary 8	C	P
2 Corinthians 1:1-22	Paul's care for the Corinthians	Ordinary 19	C	2nd
2 Corinthians 1:3-7	Consolation in suffering	Mothering Sunday	A/B/C	
2 Corinthians 1:18-22	Jesus, the fulfilment of God's promise	Ordinary 7	B	P
2 Corinthians 3:1-6	Confidence through Christ	Ordinary 8	B	P
2 Corinthians 3:4-18	Seeing the glory of God	Pentecost	C	2nd
2 Corinthians 3:12 - 4:2	Freedom in the Spirit	Sunday before Lent	C	P
2 Corinthians 4:3-6	Jesus Christ is Lord	Sunday before Lent	B	P
2 Corinthians 4:5-12	The life of Jesus is to be seen in our life	Ordinary 9	B	P
2 Corinthians 4:13 - 5:1	Looking to the unseen things which are eternal	Ordinary 10	B	P
2 Corinthians 5:6-10 (11-13) 14-17	In Christ there is a new creation	Ordinary 11	B	P
2 Corinthians 5:16-21	Be reconciled to God	Lent 4	C	P
2 Corinthians 5:20*b*-6:10	Servants of God	Ash Wednesday	A/B/C	
2 Corinthians 6:1-13	Work together with God	Ordinary 12	B	P
2 Corinthians 8:1-9	He became poor that we might be rich	Ordinary 20	C	2nd
2 Corinthians 8:7-15	He became poor that we might be rich	Ordinary 13	B	P
2 Corinthians 9:1-15	Abundance and obedience	Ordinary 21	C	2nd
2 Corinthians 12:2-10	God's power made perfect in weakness	Ordinary 14	B	P
2 Corinthians 13:11-13	The love of the Holy Trinity	Trinity Sunday	A	P

Galatians 1:1-12	The gospel which Paul preached	Ordinary 9	C	P
Galatians 1:11-24	Paul's spiritual pilgrimage	Ordinary 2	A	2nd
		Ordinary 10	C	P
Galatians 2:15-21	Justified by faith in the Son of God	Ordinary 11	C	P
Galatians 3:23-29	All are one in Christ	Ordinary 12	C	P
Galatians 3:27 - 4:7	God adopts us as his children	Christmas 1	C	2nd
Galatians 4:4-7	God adopts us as his children	Christmas 1	B	P
Galatians 4:8-20	Paul is perplexed	Ordinary 6	C	2nd
Galatians 5:1, 13-25	Freedom in the Spirit, the fruit of the Spirit	Ordinary 13	C	P
Galatians 5:2-10	Faith working through love is all that counts	Ordinary 7	C	2nd
Galatians 6:(1-6) 7-16	The marks of the Lord Jesus	Ordinary 14	C	P
Ephesians 1:3-14	Chosen by God to be his children	Christmas 2	A/B/C	P
		Ordinary 15	B	P
Ephesians 1:11-23	God's power in Christ	All Saints	C	P
Ephesians 1:15-23	Christ, the head of his body, the church	Easter 7	A	2nd
		Ascension Day	A/B/C	P
		Sunday before Advent	A	P
Ephesians 2:1-10	The gift of salvation to those dead in sin	Lent 4	B	P
		Ordinary 1	B	2nd
Ephesians 2:11-22	Christ is our peace	Easter 4	A	2nd
		Ordinary 16	B	P
Ephesians 2:19-22	Christ the cornerstone	Anniversary	A/B/C	
Ephesians 3:1-12	The whole universe is to know God's purpose	Epiphany	A/B/C	
Ephesians 3:14-21	Paul's prayer for the Ephesians	Ordinary 17	B	P
Ephesians 4:1-16	One Lord, one faith, one baptism	Ordinary 2	C	2nd
		Ordinary 18	B	P
Ephesians 4:7-16	Gifts for maturity in love	Easter 7	C	2nd
Ephesians 4:17-32	Forgive, as God in Christ forgives	Ordinary 5	A	2nd
Ephesians 4:25 - 5:2	Walk in love, as Christ loved us	Ordinary 19	B	P
Ephesians 5:1-17	Walk in love, as Christ loved us	Ordinary 6	A	2nd
Ephesians 5:8-14	Walking in the light of Christ	Lent 4	A	P
Ephesians 5:15-20	Give thanks to God at all times	Ordinary 20	B	P

Ephesians 6:1-20	The whole armour of God	Ordinary 7	A	2nd
Ephesians 6:10-20	The whole armour of God	Lent 3	A	2nd
		Ordinary 21	B	P
Philippians 1:3-11	Prepare yourselves for the day of Christ	Advent 2	C	P
Philippians 1:21-30	Christ is to be honoured in every way	Ordinary 25	A	P
Philippians 2:1-11	The mind of Christ	Christmas 1	A	2nd
Philippians 2:1-13	The mind of Christ	Ordinary 26	A	P
Philippians 2:5-11	The obedience and exultation of Christ	Lent 6 (Passion 2/Palm)	A/B/C	P
Philippians 2:12-28	God is at work in you	Ordinary 5	B	2nd
Philippians 3:4*b*-14	I want only to know Christ	Lent 3	B	2nd
		Lent 5 (Passion 1)	C	P
		Ordinary 27	A	P
Philippians 3:7-21	Pressing on towards the goal	Ordinary 6	B	2nd
Philippians 3:17 - 4:1	Our transfiguration	Lent 2	C	P
Philippians 4:1-9	Rejoice in the Lord always	Ordinary 28	A	P
Philippians 4:4-7	Rejoice the Lord is near	Advent 3	B	2nd
		Advent 3	C	P
Philippians 4:10-20	God will satisfy every need	Ordinary 7	B	2nd
Colossians 1:1-14	Paul gives thanks for the faith of the Colossians	Christmas 2	A	2nd
		Ordinary 15	C	P
Colossians 1:9-20	The image of the invisible God	Christmas 1	B	2nd
Colossians 1:11-20	All things were created by him and for him	Sunday before Advent	C	P
Colossians 1:15-28	All things were created by him and for him	Ordinary 16	C	P
Colossians 2:6-15 (16-19)	Fullness of life through Christ in baptism	Ordinary 17	C	P
Colossians 3:1-4	Hidden with Christ in God	Easter Day	A	P
Colossians 3:1-11	Christ is all and in all	Ordinary 18	C	P
Colossians 3:1-22	Christ is all and in all	Ordinary 5	C	2nd
Colossians 3:12-17	Life in Christ	Christmas 1	C	P
		Mothering Sunday	A/B/C	
1 Thessalonians 1:1-10	Giving thanks for the Thessalonian church	Ordinary 29	A	P

1 Thessalonians 2:1-8	Paul's love for the Thessalonians	Ordinary 30	A	P
1 Thessalonians 2:9-13	Paul's joy over the Thessalonians	Ordinary 31	A	P
1 Thessalonians 3:9-13	Abounding in love to one another	Advent 1	C	P
1 Thessalonians 4:13-18	The dead in Christ will rise	Ordinary 32	A	P
1 Thessalonians 5:1-11	Be ready for the coming of the Lord	Ordinary 33	A	P
1 Thessalonians 5:16-24	May you be ready for the Lord's coming	Advent 3	B	P
2 Thessalonians 1:1-4, 11-12	May Jesus be glorified in you	Ordinary 31	C	P
2 Thessalonians 2:1-5, 13-17	Stand firm and wait for the coming of Christ	Ordinary 32	C	P
2 Thessalonians 3:6-13	A warning against being idle	Ordinary 33	C	P
1 Timothy 1:12-17	The mercy and salvation of Christ	Ordinary 24	C	P
1 Timothy 2:1-7	Salvation is for all	Ordinary 25	C	P
1 Timothy 6:6-10	Be content with food . . for the love of money	Harvest	A/B/C	
1 Timothy 6:6-19	Fight the good fight of faith	Ordinary 26	C	P
2 Timothy 1:1-14	Rekindle God's gift, guard the truth	Ordinary 27	C	P
2 Timothy 2:1-7	Be strong in grace	Ordinary 30	A/B/C	2nd
2 Timothy 2:8-15	Salvation in Christ Jesus	Ordinary 28	C	P
2 Timothy 3:14 - 4:5	The inspiration of scripture	Ordinary 29	C	P
2 Timothy 4:1-18	Paul's charge to Timothy	Lent 4	C	2nd
2 Timothy 4:6-8, 16-18	Paul's testimony to the Lord's faithfulness	Ordinary 30	C	P
Titus 2:1-8, 11-14	Teach sound doctrine	Ordinary 3	B	2nd
Titus 2:11-14	The grace of God has appeared	Christmas Day I	A/B/C	
Titus 3:4-7	We are saved by his love for us	Christmas Day II	A/B/C	
Philemon 1-16	Your runaway slave is your brother	Ordinary 4	A	2nd
Philemon 1-21	Your runaway slave is your brother	Ordinary 23	C	P
Hebrews 1:1-4 (5-12)	God now speaks to us through the Son	Christmas Day III	A/B/C	
Hebrews 1:1-4; 2:5-12	God now speaks to us through his Son	Ordinary 27	B	P
Hebrews 1:1-12	God now speaks to us through his Son	Ordinary 1	A	2nd

Hebrews 2:5-18	He has become with us in every respect	Ordinary 16	B	2nd
Hebrews 2:10-18	He has become with us in every respect	Christmas 1	A	P
Hebrews 4:12-16	The word of god is living and active	Ordinary 28	B	P
Hebrews 4:14-16; 5:7-9	The High Priest who has been tested	Good Friday	A/B/C	
Hebrews 5:1-10	Jesus the gentle High Priest	Ordinary 29	B	P
Hebrews 5:5-10	His obedience brings our salvation	Lent 5 (Passion 1)	B	P
Hebrews 6:17 - 7:10	A sure and steadfast hope	Ordinary 2	B	2nd
Hebrews 7:23-28	Jesus our eternal High Priest	Ordinary 30	B	P
Hebrews 8:1-13	Mediator of a better covenant	Ordinary 17	B	2nd
Hebrews 9:11-14	Christ our eternal sacrifice	Ordinary 31	B	P
Hebrews 9:11-15	Christ our eternal sacrifice	Monday in Holy Week	A/B/C	
Hebrews 9:24-28	Christ the sacrifice for sin	Ordinary 32	B	P
Hebrews 10:5-10	I am come to do your will	Advent 4	C	P
Hebrews 10:11-14 (15-18) 19-25	Christ's single offering for sin	Ordinary 33	B	P
Hebrews 10:16-25	Confidence in the new and living way	Good Friday	A/B/C	
Hebrews 11:1-3, 8-16	By faith, Abraham and Sarah obeyed	Lent 2	B	2nd
		Ordinary 19	C	P
Hebrews 11:17-31	The faith of the patriarchs	Ordinary 18	B	2nd
Hebrews 11:29 - 12:2	Looking to Jesus	Ordinary 20	C	P
Hebrews 11:32 - 12:2	Looking to Jesus	All Saints	B	2nd
Hebrews 12:1-3	Our eyes fixed on Jesus	Wednesday in Holy Wk	A/B/C	
Hebrews 12:1-17	Pursue peace and the grace of God	Ordinary 19	B	2nd
Hebrews 12:18-29	The city of the living God	Ordinary 21	C	P
Hebrews 13:1-8, 15-16	Continue in love to all	Ordinary 22	C	P
Hebrews 13:1-15	A continual sacrifice of praise to God	Ordinary 20	B	2nd
Hebrews 13:16-21	May the God of peace work among us	Ordinary 21	B	2nd
James 1:17-27	Be doers, not merely hearers	Ordinary 22	B	P
James 2:1-10 (11-13) 14-17	Can faith without works save you?	Ordinary 23	B	P
James 3:1-12	All make mistakes	Ordinary 24	B	P
James 3:13 - 4:3, 7-8*a*	Fruits of the wisdom from above	Ordinary 25	B	P
James 5:1-20	The Lord is at hand	Lent 4	A	2nd
James 5:7-10	Be patient until the coming of the Lord	Advent 3	A	P

James 5:13-20	The prayer of faith	Ordinary 26	B	P
1 Peter 1:3-9	We receive a new birth through his resurrection	Easter 2	A	P
1 Peter 1:3-12	We receive a new birth through his resurrection	Ordinary 3	A	2nd
1 Peter 1:17-23	You were ransomed to become holy	Easter 3	A	P
1 Peter 2:1-5	Come to him like living stones	Anniversary	A/B/C	
1 Peter 2:2-10	You are God's own people	Easter 5	A	P
1 Peter 2:19-25	The passion of the Good Shepherd	Easter 4	A	P
1 Peter 3:13-22	Christ died for us, once for all	Easter 6	A	P
1 Peter 3:18-22	Water, the symbol of baptism which saves us	Lent 1	B	P
1 Peter 4:1-8	Above all, maintain constant love	Holy Saturday	A/B/C	
1 Peter 4:12-14; 5:6-11	Sharing Christ's sufferings	Easter 7	A	P
2 Peter 1:1-11	Entry into the kingdom	Wesleys	A/B/C	
2 Peter 1:16-21	The voice from heaven	Sunday before Lent	A	P
		Sunday before Lent	B	2nd
2 Peter 3:8-15*a*	The day of the Lord will come, unexpectedly	Advent 2	B	P
1 John 1:1 - 2:2	Sin is conquered by the word of life	Easter 2	B	P
1 John 2:1-17	The love of God reached perfection in Christ	Ordinary 27	A	2nd
1 John 2:22-29	Warnings	Ordinary 26	A	2nd
1 John 3:1-3	We are God's children now	All Saints	A	P
1 John 3:1-7	We are the children of God	Easter 3	B	P
1 John 3:1-15	Children of god and children of the devil	Ordinary 28	A	2nd
1 John 3:16-24	Love one another and abide in him	Easter 4	B	P
1 John 3:16 - 4:6	Believe in his name	Ordinary 29	A	2nd
1 John 4:7-16	God loves us, we are to love one another	Christmas 2	C	2nd
1 John 4:7-21	God loves us, we are to love one another	Easter 5	B	P
1 John 5:1-6	To love God is to keep his commandments	Easter 6	B	P
1 John 5:9-13	The gift of eternal life	Easter 7	B	P
Revelation 1:4-8	Jesus Christ, the ruler of kings on earth	Easter 2	C	P
Revelation 1:4-18	John's vision of Christ	Ordinary 33	A	2nd
Revelation 1:4*b*-8	Jesus Christ, the ruler of kings on earth	Sunday before Advent	B	P

Revelation 1:12-18	I am alive for ever	Easter Day	A	2nd
Revelation 2:1-11	To the churches in Ephesus and Smyrna	Easter 3	B	2nd
Revelation 2:12-17	To the church in Pergamum	Easter 4	B	2nd
Revelation 3:1-13	To the churches in Sardis and Philadelphia	Easter 5	B	2nd
Revelation 3:14-22	To the church in Laodicea	Easter 6	B	2nd
Revelation 4:1-11	Holy and worthy is the Lord our God	Trinity Sunday	B	2nd
		Ordinary 8	A	2nd
Revelation 5:11-14	Worthy is the Lamb	Easter 3	C	P
Revelation 7:9-17	The Lamb is the shepherd	Easter 4	C	P
		All Saints	A	P
		Ordinary 31	B	2nd
Revelation 14:13 - 15:4	The harvest is ripe	Advent 1	C	2nd
Revelation 14:14-18	Angels reap the earth	Harvest	A/B/C	
Revelation 19:6-10	Blessed are those invited to the Lamb's supper	All Saints	A	2nd
Revelation 21:1-6*a*	God will wipe away all tears	All Saints	B	P
		Watchnight	A/B/C	
Revelation 21:1-6	God will wipe away all tears	Easter 5	C	P
Revelation 21:1-14	God will wipe away all tears	Easter 5	A	2nd
Revelation 21:10, 22 - 22:5	The holy city	Easter 6	C	P
Revelation 21:22 - 22:5	The holy city	Easter 6	A	2nd
Revelation 22:6-21	John's testimony	Advent 4	A	2nd
Revelation 22:1-5	The Lord God will be their light	Remembrance	A/B/C	
Revelation 22:12-14, 16-17, 20-21	Come, Lord Jesus	Easter 7	C	P

ACKNOWLEDGEMENTS

To enable the early availability in time for Advent Sunday 1998, it has not been possible to clear all copyright material prior to publication. All copyright owners have been approached but not all have had time to respond.

We would also want to stress as the compilers of the **Book of Common Order** of the Church of Scotland did, that:

> Many sources have contributed to the compilation of this book, and not all of them are now traceable. Individual members of the Committee prepared drafts, which were revised more or less drastically by the Committee, often resulting in final versions which looked little like the original drafts. Among the casualties of this sometimes protracted process was the identity of many of the sources; they could not be recalled, nor did there seem to be any way to track them down. The Panel wishes to record at once both its indebtedness to any who may recognise in this book rhythms and patterns, expressions and phrases, ideas and images which are their own, and its regret that it became impossible to ask permission or seek consent for their inclusion . . .
>
> If, through inadvertence, copyright material has been used without permission or acknowledgement, the publisher will be grateful to be informed and will be pleased to make the necessary correction in subsequent editions.

* denotes that a text has been altered.

The lectionary for the Principal Service is **The Revised Common Lectionary,** © 1992 The Consultation on Common Texts (CCT).

The lectionary for a Second Service is from **The Christian Year: Calendar, Lectionary and Collects,** © 1997 The Central Board of Finance of the Church of England.

The numbers shown against the collects on pages 523-563 refer to the following sources:

1 **The Alternative Service Book 1980**, © 1980 The Central Board of Finance of the Church of England

2 The American **Book of Common Prayer**, © 1928

3 **The Book of Alternative Services**, © 1985 The General Synod of the Anglican Church of Canada

4 **Book of Common Order** of the Church of Scotland, © 1994 Panel on Worship of the Church of Scotland

5 **The Book of Common Prayer** (1662) Crown ©

6 **The Book of Common Prayer** of the Episcopal Church of the United States of America, © 1979

7 **The Book of Common Prayer with the Additions and Deviations Proposed in 1928**, © Oxford University Press

8 **The Book of Common Worship** of the Church of South India, © 1963 Oxford University Press

9 **Celebrating Common Prayer**, © 1992 The European Province of the Society of Saint Francis

10 Frank Colquhoun, ed., **Parish Prayers** © 1964 Hodder and Stoughton

11 Council of Churches for Britain and Ireland

12 **The Daily Office Revised**, © 1978 The Joint Liturgical Group

13 **The Divine Office**, © 1974 Hierarchies of Australia, England and Wales

14 Neil Dixon, ed., **Companion to the Lectionary: Volume 3**, © 1983 Epworth Press

15 International Commission on English in the Liturgy, © 1973

16 International Commission on English in the Liturgy, © 1993-94: Proposed Revision of the **Sacramentary**

17 **Lent, Holy Week and Easter**, © 1984, 1986 The Central Board of Finance of the Church of England

18 C. L. MacDonnell, **After Communion**, © 1985 Mowbray

19 The Methodist Sacramental Fellowship

20 Janet Morley, **All Desires Known**, © 1988 Movement for the Ordination of Women / Women in Theology

21 **A New Zealand Prayer Book - He Karakia Mihinare o Aotearoa**, © 1989 The Provincial Secretary, the Church of the Province of New Zealand

22 Gordon Nodwell, **Worship for all Seasons 1**, United Church of Canada

23 Michael Perham and others, **Enriching the Christian Year**, © 1993 SPCK/Alcuin Club

24 Gail Ramshaw © 1988 : 7304 Boyer Street, Philadelphia PA19119

25 **Supplemental Liturgical Resources** © The Presbyterian Church (USA)

26 John V. Taylor, **Weep not for Me**, WCC Risk Books, 1986

27 **Uniting in Worship,** © 1998 The Uniting Church in Australia Assembly Commission on Liturgy